ngs gardens open for charity

CW00322317

The Yellow Book 2007

Photograph Clare Agnew

A GUIDE TO VISITING **THOUSANDS** OF GARDENS IN ENGLAND AND WALES

Garden Ulverscroft Close, Leicestershire Photograph Mr & Mrs M J Maddock

Photograph Ian Gowland

The National Gardens Scheme
A company limited by guarantee
Registered in England & Wales
Charity No. 1112664 Company No. 5631421
Registered & Head Office
Hatchlands Park East Clandon Guildford Surrey GU4 7RT
T 01483 211535 F 01483 211537 W www.ngs.org.uk
© The National Gardens Scheme 2007

Front cover 136 Avenue Road, London Photograph Nicola Stocken Tomkins

ngs gardens open for charity

THE**CONTENTS**

Photograph Ian Gowland

Garden Waystrode Manor, Kent Photograph Julie Maudlin

The Yellow Book 2007

© The National Gardens Scheme 2007

Published by The National Gardens Scheme, Hatchlands Park, East Clandon, Guildford, Surrey GU4 7RT

Production team: Caroline Anderson, Elna Broe, Valerie Caldwell, Julia Grant, Kali Masure, Elizabeth Milner, Wendy Morton, Janet Oldham, Valerie Piggott, Sue Reeve, Jane Sennett. With thanks to our NGS county volunteers who compile and check the information locally.

A catalogue record of this book is available from the British Library.

Typeset in the Helvetica Neue font family.

The paper for this book conforms to Environmental Management Standard SFS-EN ISO 14001 (ed 1996)

Design by James Pembroke Publishing, Bath, Somerset

Maps designed and produced by Mapworld, Henley-on-Thames

Data manipulation and image setting by utimestwo, Collingtree, Northamptonshire

Printing and binding by William Clowes Limited, Beccles, Suffolk

ISBN 978-1-905942-00-8 ISSN 1365-0572 EAN 9 781905 942008

Premier Cottages, get closer to Britain's beautiful gardens...

Discover Britain's beautiful gardens from our outstanding collection of independent and award winning 4 & 5 star holiday cottages. Book direct with the cottage owner.

Call for a brochure on 01271 336 050 or visit
www.premiercottages.net

GARDEN VISITING WITH THE YELLOW BOOK 2007

For 80 years The National Gardens Scheme has been providing garden visits for inspiration, relaxation or simply enjoying a delicious home-made tea in a delightful setting, and we know garden visitors await the arrival of the new Yellow Book in the same way as any herald of the spring. There is the excitement of discovering new gardens to visit, or seeing changes made by 'old friends'. What special events are happening this year? Which gardens have evening openings? Where can I take my children to learn more about wildflowers and wildlife?

Whatever your particular passion, you will find it in the 3,500 gardens in The Yellow Book 2007. New this year is the introduction of colour to the garden listings – new gardens are highlighted, maps are clearer and the diary pages easier to use.

On page 21 NGS President Zac Goldsmith writes about the community spirit that surrounds the garden openings. An opening day involves many volunteers, with friends and family drafted in to help with parking, ticket sales, baking cakes, serving teas and putting up signs. Even when the weather doesn't co-operate, garden owners, volunteer helpers and visitors find great enjoyment in this sense of community.

Throughout The Yellow Book you will also find gardens that open as a group. Sometimes this is a 'village opening', sometimes it's a street of gardens and sometimes just three or four gardens close to each other. Groups range in size from two gardens to as many as thirteen or fourteen and often with a whole range of different gardens within the group. Look out for the article in the book about two of these groups – Wroxham Gardens in Lancashire and Dorsington Gardens in Warwickshire. Your admission ticket will take you round all the gardens in a group. And don't forget that 'small is beautiful'. Read about Grenville Johnson and Alan Elms' stunning garden in Bristol.

Other special features in The Yellow Book 2007 include articles by Neil Lucas and Louise Adams on their 'labours of love', Chris Collins on why kids and gardens go together, Tim Rumball and John Thorp on the pleasure of growing and eating the 'fruits' of your hard work. Wildlife in gardens is an increasingly important topic and Cumbria Wildlife Trust explains how to get the maximum benefit for your garden, and to round things off, some topical tips from Kathy Brown on planting for high sun and low rainfall.

Garden 16 Glensford Gardens, Nottinghamshire Photograph Nicola Stocken Tomkins

Garden Coity Mawr, Powys Photograph Mr & Mrs Forwood

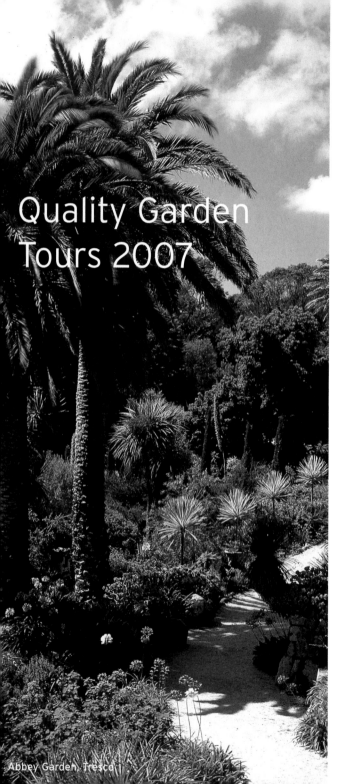

Quality Garden
Tours 2007

Abbey Garden, Tresco

brightwater
holidays

**Brightwater Holidays is
the UK's leading specialist
Garden Tour Operator.**

Our fully inclusive itineraries
combine the famous and grand
gardens with the small and private
gardens – most tours also visit
specialist nurseries. Travel by
coach, air, ferry and rail from
a variety of local pick up points
throughout the UK.

Tours include a full programme
of UK garden tours, continental
European holidays and exotic
far-away places. If you have your
own group and are looking for
a tailor made itinerary we are
happy to work to suit your
interest and budget.

Please contact us for a copy
of our comprehensive brochure
for 2007.

Brightwater Holidays Brochure out now call...
01334 657155

Brightwater Holidays Ltd
Eden Park House, Cupar, Fife KY15 4H'
T 01334 657155 F 01334 657144
info@brightwaterholidays.com
www.brightwaterholidays.com

Planning a visit?

Why not visit the NGS website www.ngs.org.uk before planning a visit? Look out for current news about the NGS, award-winning gardens, special events and useful features for gardener and garden visitor alike. At the heart of the website is GardenFinder. Here you can locate gardens to visit by date, by location or by specific garden feature. Use The Yellow Book and website to plan your visiting – not forgetting that many garden owners are happy to welcome visitors (individuals or groups) by prior appointment throughout the season. Many owners include photographs of their gardens, and some have their own web pages, to which we link. Owners also take the opportunity to write a fuller description of their garden.

The website also lists changes to opening dates and times. Although rare, weather in particular can wreak havoc with the best of plans.

Using The Yellow Book and www.ngs.org.uk together can really help you to get the most out of your garden visiting.

Royal gardens

By gracious permission of Her Majesty The Queen, the House and Grounds at Sandringham, Norfolk, will be open to the public during 2007. Sandringham has been part of The Yellow Book since 1927. For more information see the Norfolk gardens listings or visit www.sandringhamestate.co.uk

Also by gracious permission of Her Majesty The Queen, Frogmore House Garden, Windsor, will be open on Tuesday 17 May 2007 in aid of The National Gardens Scheme. For more information see the Berkshire gardens listing or visit www.royal.gov.uk

National Trust gardens

National Trust gardens preserve a very important part of our gardening heritage and over 100 of them are open in aid of the NGS on the days shown in The Yellow Book. Where the National Trust property has allocated an opening day to the NGS which is one of their normal opening days, National Trust members can still gain entry on production of their National Trust Membership Card. On such days donations to the NGS will be welcome. However where the day allocated is one on which the property would normally be closed, then collection of the NGS donation will be required.

Accommodation

Over 150 wonderful gardens with bed and breakfast, hotel or self-catering accommodation are listed in a county by county guide after the main garden directory.

National Plant Collections (NCCPG)

Over 120 of these important collections can be seen on NGS open days in 2007. A listing by plant name indicating which NGS garden holds the collection is to be found at the back of the book.

Garden Ednovean Farm, Cornwall Photograph C Taylor

Garden Wayford Manor, Somerset & Bristol Area Photograph Philip Smith

Bartlett Science.
We protect one of the most important growth investments you own.

Their beauty may be priceless, but the market value that trees add to your home is very tangible. Your investment in Bartlett tree care delivers one of the most reliable returns in your portfolio. Bartlett Science has been improving the landscape of tree care and growth investments since 1907.

For your nearest branch, call us at 0845 600 9000. Or visit us at www.bartlett.com.

**BARTLETT
TREE EXPERTS**
100TH ANNIVERSARY
1907 – 2007

Principal Offices

Bedford	Cirencester	Guildford	Radlett
Beaconsfield	Crawley Down	London	Sevenoaks
Bristol	Glossop	Macclesfield	York

ABOUT THE NGS

COMBINING A PASSION FOR GARDENING WITH THE DESIRE TO HELP PEOPLE IN NEED

What is it about the British and gardening? How is it that generation after generation perpetuates the nation's obsession with propagation, cultivation and rumination in the resulting piece of heaven?

Writers and observers have been trying to pin this down for years and have only succeeded by metaphor or example.

"Gardens are not made by sitting in the shade."
Rudyard Kipling, Author

"The love of gardening is a seed once sown that never dies." Gertrude Jekyll, Garden Designer

At the NGS we think that the thing which makes British gardens so special is a unique combination of private passion and generosity of spirit. The work in developing and maintaining the garden is seen as a personal responsibility, and it is the individual interpretation of different themes and fashions which produces such spectacular results. However, once the work is finished, our impulse is always to share both the result and the experience with others, in the hope that they will derive the same satisfaction from creating a garden of their own.

So, for most of us, the garden has a dual role. It is a retreat where we can work our frustrations into the soil and fulfil our ambitions without relying on anything, except perhaps the weather! Once finished, it becomes a place to celebrate and enjoy with friends and neighbours. The gardens in the NGS play a vital third role, to raise money for people who need care or support through chronic and life-threatening illnesses. We open 3,500 gardens each year and over the last 10 years we have raised over £15 million for charity.

We have a fascinating history, stretching over 80 years. Read more about this in our message from our Patron, HRH The Prince of Wales, or visit our website at www.ngs.org.uk.

Garden Pen-y-Bryn, Flintshire & Wrexham Photograph Nicola Stocken Tomkins

Garden Westcott Barton, Devon Photograph Howard Frank

"Flowers are restful to look at. They have neither emotions nor conflicts."

Sigmund Freud, Psychologist

BY APPOINTMENT TO
HER MAJESTY THE QUEEN
MANUFACTURERS OF CHOCOLATES
BENDICKS (MAYFAIR) LTD
WINCHESTER

BENDICKS

PROUD TO SUPPORT
THE NATIONAL GARDENS SCHEME

We are proud to be associated with the passion and dedication
that creates such beautiful gardens.

Using only the finest ingredients and traditional methods we invest time, care and
dedication into creating chocolates that are the best of their kind anywhere in the world.

Rensburg Sheppards Investment Management Limited
Quayside House Canal Wharf Leeds LS11 5PU
Telephone +44 (0)113 245 4488
Facsimile +44 (0)113 245 1188
Email info.leeds@rensburgsheppards.co.uk
Web www.rensburgsheppards.co.uk
DX 14088

Rensburg Sheppards

HAPPY 80TH BIRTHDAY

We are delighted to sponsor the National Gardens Scheme Yellow Book for the fourteenth consecutive year and we wish you very many happy returns on your 80th birthday. May you have many more.

The vision, patience and hard work which go into the gardens tended by your members have many parallels in the way in which we advise and manage the portfolios of the clients of Rensburg Sheppards.

We are proud to continue our support for both the Yellow Book and the website and look forward to doing so for many years to come.

M H Burns
Chief Executive

Member firm of the London Stock Exchange. Member of LIFFE. Authorised and regulated by the Financial Services Authority.
Rensburg Sheppards Investment Management Limited is registered in England. Registered No. 2122340.
Registered Office: Quayside House Canal Wharf Leeds LS11 5PU.
Offices at: Belfast Cheltenham Farnham Glasgow Leeds Liverpool London Manchester Reigate Sheffield.

CHAIRMAN'S MESSAGE

For over 80 years The National Gardens Scheme has been a rather well kept secret. In my case I came across it because, when I was fourteen, my great aunt let me take the money at the gate on her NGS garden open days. Louise Adams, who writes later in this book, took over a Sussex garden from her mother who first opened for us in 1996. Others get involved through village openings or through friends. Once engaged, people tend to get hooked! We regularly recognise gardens which have opened for over 50 years and our visitors come back to gardens again and again.

Photograph Mike Pritchard

In the 80 years since we were established, we have increased the number of gardens open from 609 to 3,500 and now we receive over half a million visitors each year. So how is it that many garden enthusiasts still don't know about us? One reason may be that, as a charity, our ethos has always been one of self-sufficiency. Even today we must rank among the national charities with the smallest staff, employing the equivalent of only nine full-time staff. We have chosen not to spend huge amounts on administration, preferring instead to distribute our money to the nursing, caring and gardening charities which we support. In 2006 we donated £1.75 million. You can read more about the charities we support on page 15 of this book.

I still find it remarkable that almost one third of our visitors come through personal recommendation, which is a great tribute to the quality and variety of the gardens which open for us. We are keen to retain that quality of intimacy and friendliness which characterises our open days, but we are also keen to ensure that other people don't miss out. So please tell your friends, your relations and all and sundry who love gardens about our afternoon and evening openings. We look forward to welcoming them into our gardens.

Chairman

In his introduction to the 1932 Yellow Book Christopher Hussey, then Editor of Country Life, conceived of "the whole kingdom...., when it was not occupied in sprawling towns, engaged in maintaining the garden". So much has changed since then and yet so little. Therefore, as The National Gardens Scheme celebrates eighty years of raising money for charity, it is perhaps an appropriate time to reflect on the role of the garden in promoting the nation's wellbeing.

In Christopher Hussey's time, many of the gardens which opened for The National Gardens Scheme were part of larger estates and reflected the traditions of the English landscape garden, enhanced and updated by Thomas Mawson, Gertrude Jekyll, Vita Sackville West and many other distinguished designers. Today the Scheme's gardens reflect the explosion in interest in gardening, be that in rural or urban areas, and of every type of space and shape.

The purpose of the garden openings is twofold: to share the pleasure and experience involved in developing the garden with other people and, of equal importance, to raise money for charities involved in nursing, caring and gardening.

This year, The National Gardens Scheme and Marie Curie Cancer Care, another charity of which I am patron, will celebrate ten years of partnership, during which the Scheme has helped fund nursing care for hundreds of people with a terminal illness. The record of partnership and support with the other beneficiary charities is equally impressive and I can only urge you to read about it in the book.

Many people choose to raise money for charity by running a marathon, organizing a jumble sale, or walking across a desert. For those of you who are unable or disinclined to take on such tasks, there is always the option of visiting a beautiful garden and enjoying a home-made tea, secure in the knowledge that you are contributing to the £1.75 million raised for charity each year.

I can only wish the volunteers, staff and garden owners of The National Gardens Scheme another happy and rewarding eighty years.

Like gardeners everywhere, we appreciate the importance of water…

At our family business we take the time and trouble to blend our tea to suit the water. Does that mean it's the best cup of tea in Britain?

To find more, please visit us at www.yorkshiretea.co.uk.

Yorkshire Tea. Try it. You'll see.

CHARITIESSUPPORTED

Macmillan Cancer Support
'improves the lives of people affected by cancer'
The charity does this by providing practical, medical, emotional and financial help. NGS has supported Macmillan's vital work by funding 127 Macmillan nurses to date. In 2006, the NGS has funded a skin cancer nurse in Taunton, and cancer information and support in Wandsworth, south-west London and Hartlepool.

Marie Curie Cancer Care
'provides home nursing to terminally ill people'
Over the last decade, the contribution from the NGS has funded Marie Curie Nurses in each of the NGS counties. Marie Curie Nurses deliver high quality nursing care, totally free, to give terminally ill people the choice of dying at home and provide support for their families.

Help the Hospices
'the national charity that supports the hospice movement'
Through their longstanding support of Help the Hospices, the NGS has supported the training of over 1,400 hospice nurses – helping them to gain new specialist skills and qualifications and so enabling them to give the best possible care for patients with terminal illness, along with their families and friends.

Crossroads – Caring for Carers
'gives care and support to carers'
The contribution from the NGS enables Crossroads to support local schemes throughout England and Wales to deliver practical quality services, enabling carers to receive a high quality service that is flexible, reliable and targeted to meet individual needs, giving them a break from caring responsibilities. Crossroads is committed to providing high quality services for carers and their families.

The Queen's
Nursing Institute

The Queen's Nursing Institute
'supports community nurses in finding innovative ways to provide patient care'
NGS funding has been central to the delivery of over 140 community nursing projects, making expert care available to a wide range of patients in England, Wales and Northern Ireland. NGS funds also provide a lifeline to community nurses who through age, illness or disability, are no longer able to work.

THE
ROYAL FUND FOR
GARDENERS'
CHILDREN

The Royal Fund For Gardeners' Children
'helps children in need'
The Scheme's funding enables ongoing support to orphaned and needy horticulturists' children, including regular allowances, bedding, clothing and the opportunity for a family holiday.

THE NATIONAL TRUST

NGS garden careerships (the National Trust)
'sponsors 12 trainee gardeners'
The NGS donation is vital in ensuring the long-term provision of professional skills and techniques, via the Garden Careership Training Scheme. The Trust recruits 12 gardeners per year into the Scheme. On graduation, after three years training, they are equipped for a wide range of gardening roles. Many careership graduates have continued their careers with the National Trust, eventually becoming Head Gardeners themselves.

PERENNIAL
GARDENERS' ROYAL BENEVOLENT SOCIETY
Helping Horticulturists In Need Since 1839

Perennial-Gardeners' Royal Benevolent Society
'helping horticulturists in need'
The NGS donation is vital and central to the work of this charity, going directly to horticulturists in need.

County Nursing Associations
'support retired and needy nurses'

Bonhams [1793]

The Garden Sale

Bonhams is delighted to announce their first sale dedicated to celebrating the glory of the garden.

The sale will include items of horticultural interest from a cross-section of disciplines, including pictures, prints, ceramics, glass, books, furniture, garden statuary, silver and objet d'art.

The sale will take place at Bonhams flagship London saleroom in New Bond Street on Wednesday 6 June 2007 and entries are invited until Wednesday 18 April 2007.

Illustrated: A fine French enamel plaque by Philippe Parpette, dated 1779
Sold for £26,400

For a free auction valuation, with a view to selling at Bonhams, please call:
Camilla Seymour
+44 (0) 20 7447 7425
camilla.seymour@bonhams.com
George Plumptre
+44 (0) 20 7468 8392
george.plumptre@bonhams.com

Bonhams
101 New Bond Street
London W1S 1SR
+44 (0) 20 7447 7447
+44 (0) 20 7447 7400 fax
www.bonhams.com

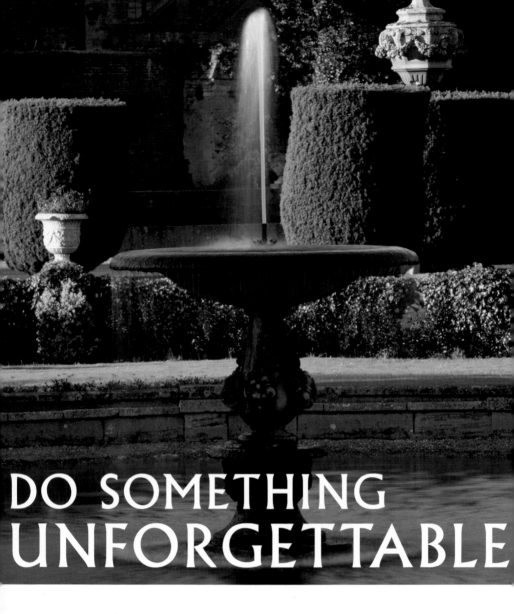

DO SOMETHING UNFORGETTABLE

Come and visit a beautiful place... explore secret corners, roam through parkland, stroll amongst the flowers and tuck into afternoon tea.

With hundreds of places to discover and enjoy, you're never more than an hour away from an amazing National Trust house or garden.

Call 0870 458 4000 to find one near you. **www.nationaltrust.org.uk/enjoy**

Registered Charity no. 205846   NT050008T

THE NATIONAL TRUST

LENDING A HAND

NGS FUNDING CONTINUES TO HELP
MARIE CURIE CANCER CARE

The NGS has now been supporting Marie Curie Cancer Care for a decade and has helped the charity to reach more patients throughout England and Wales. The funding from the NGS has enabled the charity to provide high quality nursing, totally free of charge to terminally ill people, giving them the choice of dying at home whilst supported by their families.

Research shows that 75 per cent of people would prefer to be cared for in their own home if they were terminally ill with cancer. In reality, most people die in a hospital – the last place they want to be. That's where Marie Curie Nurses can make an enormous difference.

Every year the presence of a Marie Curie Nurse enables thousands of cancer patients to receive hands-on care, so they can remain at home with their loved ones.

But for every family we help, there's another we can't. We want to reach these families – that's why we are working to make choice a reality for all.

Marie Curie Cancer Care is looking forward to marking the generosity of the 10th anniversary of the relationship with the NGS with a series of celebrations which are due to take place this year. The long-term support of the NGS is enormously appreciated.

CROSSROADS PROVIDES VITAL SERVICES
FOR MANY CARERS IN THE UK

Anyone can become a carer. Carers can be of any age, gender or background. Usually carers look after a relative or friend who cannot manage without their help because of illness, disability or frailty. There are six million carers in the UK, they are all unpaid.

At Crossroads we understand the impact that becoming a carer has on people's lives – looking after someone can be rewarding, but also stressful and costly. Many carers give up work or may lose their social life. We also know that carers say a break from their caring responsibilities is vital and can help them to continue to care.

Our work supports services for carers and the people they care for across the network of schemes in England and Wales. In 2005/6 Crossroads – Caring for Carers provided over 4.5 million hours of care and support to over 35,000 carers.

Providing services that carers trust and that help them to continue to care is Crossroads' aim.

"I have two special needs children and am a single mum. The service that Crossroads offers allows me much-needed time out to either go shopping – which is very difficult with the boys, or to catch up on sleep. The staff are very caring, fun to be around and are really good with the children."

Welcome to
BEAUTIFUL BRITAIN

"A wonderful magazine…"
A. Healey, Brixham, Devon

BEAUTIFUL BRITAIN

is the exciting new quarterly that brings you superb photographs and great articles on the whole of Britain for only £15* a year. Let us send you your first copy **FREE** when you take out a no-risk trial subscription. If you are not delighted, just cancel and receive a full refund – but please keep your first issue with our compliments. Complete the coupon today.

FREE FIRST COPY!
Risk-free subscription offer

Zac Goldsmith, NGS President

COMMUNITY
SPIRIT

VOLUNTEERS MAKE AN **INVALUABLE** CONTRIBUTION TO THE NGS

Photograph The Ecologist Magazine

One of the defining features of 'progress' in Britain has been the relentless decline of our communities. High streets have been usurped by out-of-town supermarkets. Playing fields have given way to building developments. The church no longer functions as a social network. Society has atomised and communities are no longer able to provide the services they have always provided.

But people need communities as a snail needs a shell, and around the country countless community-based organisations are working to reverse these trends. Schools are choosing to support their local farmers. Shoppers are choosing to buy their food from farmers' markets. But one of the most exciting examples of community action is The National Gardens Scheme.

Besides helping to cement and build upon local friendships and loyalties, the NGS provides a fantastic example of volunteers harnessing local talents and assets for the benefit of the local community. Unlike many other national charities, the NGS is still run by volunteers – over 300 of them – who organise garden events across the country throughout the spring and summer. The local knowledge and enterprise of the volunteers ensures that everyone has a chance to share their garden, large and small, formal or quirky, with the community.

Garden Minterne, Dorset Photograph Philip Smith

Garden The Old Manor, Dorsington Gardens Warwickshire

Everyone has fun but, at the end of the day, the money raised through admission fees is significant and makes a real difference to people's lives. In 2006 a community open day in Warwickshire raised £11,000 in one afternoon, and the total amount of money raised and distributed to charities at the end of 2005 exceeded £1.75 million.

As a result, the NGS has been able to fund the training of over 120 nurses to support people living with cancer, as well as many other valuable services including round-the-clock care for people who want to spend the end of their life at home, and respite care for people who look after members of their family.

Without the garden owners none of this would be possible, so we can take comfort from the fact that the NGS adds more than 500 new gardens to the Scheme each year. The NGS is therefore in good shape with rising contributions to charity, and because of the invaluable involvement of volunteers, without the overheads growing.

"The NGS has been able to fund the training of over 120 nurses to support people living with cancer"

Garden Little Larford, Worcestershire Photograph Suzanne Shacklock

Photograph Ian Gowland

Geographical Area Guide
Visit a garden near you

The areas shown on this map are specific to the
organisation of The National Gardens Scheme.
The Gardens of Wales, listed by area, follow the
Gardens of England.

Understanding this book

A simple guide for getting the most out of the listings section

Overview

The Yellow Book 2007 lists all gardens opening between January 2007 and early 2008. The listings pages include opening dates, admission prices and directions as well as a description of the main features of the garden. Garden entries are listed by county (see map on p.25) and are ordered alphabetically in each county. A map at the start of each county section shows the location of the gardens.

Green oval
A green oval indicates a garden within the county with a number that corresponds to the number in the listings.

Grey oval
A grey oval indicates gardens located in the neighbouring counties. Refer to the relevant county for details.

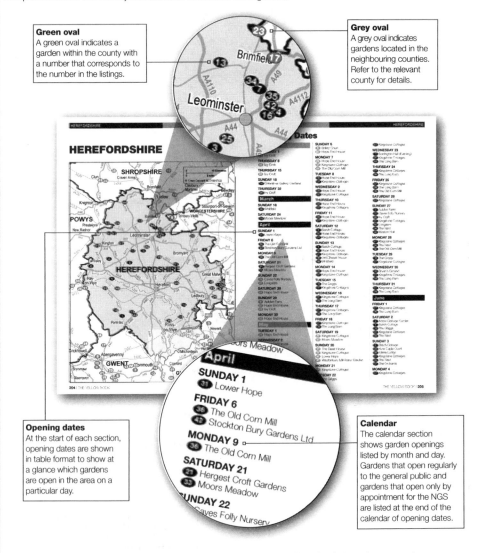

Opening dates
At the start of each section, opening dates are shown in table format to show at a glance which gardens are open in the area on a particular day.

Calendar
The calendar section shows garden openings listed by month and day. Gardens that open regularly to the general public and gardens that open only by appointment for the NGS are listed at the end of the calendar of opening dates.

All distances and sizes are approximate. **Coach parties** Only by appointment, please contact the garden direct to make arrangements. **Children** Must be accompanied by an adult. **Toilets** Not usually available at private gardens. **Updates** While every effort is made to ensure that entries are accurate, with so many gardens there will inevitably be last-minute changes. These will be publicised locally, and shown on the website.

County sections

Each county section includes a map (except London), a calendar of opening dates and then an alphabetical listing of each garden. Further information, including contact details for local volunteer teams, is at the end of each section.

Description
A short description of each garden covers the main landscape and planting features. This is written by garden owners and reviewed each year.

County name
The county name appears in the top corner of each page of the listings. Gardens in England are listed first, followed by gardens in Wales.

Index
To find a particular garden within a county please refer to the index at the back of the book.

Directions
A simple set of directions to each garden from the nearest major road is at the start of each section. Most gardens also list postcodes for use with computer or satellite navigation systems.

Admission price
The admission price applies to all visitors unless exceptions are noted eg, child free, concessions, etc.

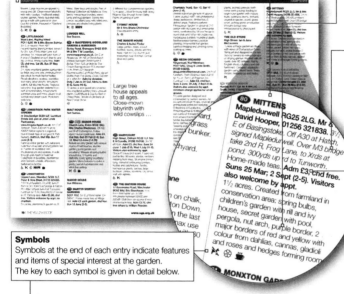

Symbols
Symbols at the end of each entry indicate features and items of special interest at the garden. The key to each symbol is given in detail below.

Website
Details of many NGS gardens and information about special events are on the NGS website
www.ngs.org.uk

Symbols, labels and notes explained

4 The number shown by each garden entry refers to that garden's position on the county map.

NEW Garden opening this year for the first time or reopening after a long break or under new ownership.

◆ This symbol denotes a garden that is open to the public on a regular basis. Gardens which carry this symbol contribute to The National Gardens Scheme either by opening on a specific day or days and/or by giving a guaranteed contribution to the Scheme. For opening information not given in the garden entry, please refer to the garden directly. Telephone numbers/website details, where available for gardens with this symbol, are given at the end of the garden text.

♿ Wheelchair access to at least the main features of the garden. Often

disabled parking is available close to, or in the owner's driveway.

🐕 No dogs except guide dogs. Where dogs are allowed they must be on leads.

🌱 Plants/produce usually for sale. Many garden owners propagate the unusual plants growing in their garden and offer them for sale. If proceeds go elsewhere this is shown at the garden opening.

NCCPG Garden that holds a NCCPG National Plant Collection.

🛏 This symbol indicates gardens that offer accommodation. For a detailed listing see the Accommodation Index beginning on page 557.

☕ Tea with biscuits and cake, normally available at a charge. If cream teas, homemade teas or light refreshments are available, this is

stated in the garden text. Wine is often available at Evening Openings. If proceeds go elsewhere this is shown at the garden opening.

OPEN BY APPOINTMENT
All gardens that open by appointment will be pleased to see visitors by prior arrangement. Some gardens can accommodate clubs and societies; some only small parties and some also have limited parking. All welcome visitors. Telephone direct or email to make an appointment.

PHOTOGRAPHS
Where taken at a garden opening, photographs must not be used for sale or reproduction without prior permission of the owner.

SHARE TO
If 'share to' is shown in a garden text, it indicates that a proportion of the money collected will be given to the nominated charity.

BEDFORDSHIRE

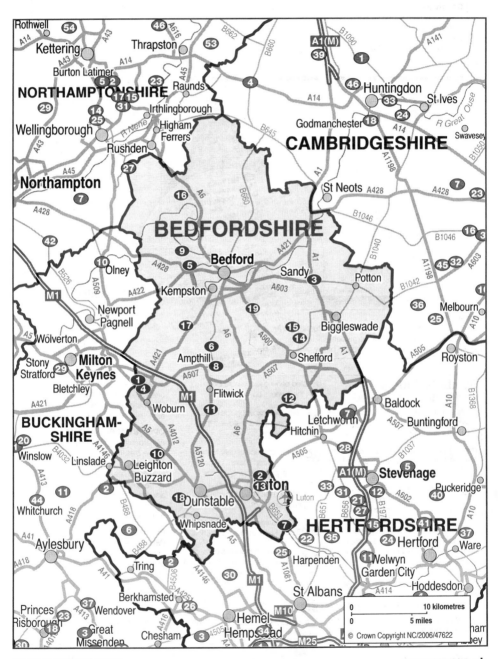

Opening Dates

April
SUNDAY 1
- 6 How End Cottage
- 11 The Old Vicarage

SUNDAY 8
- 8 King's Arms Path Garden

SUNDAY 22
- 5 59 Grange Lane

WEDNESDAY 25
- 15 Swiss Garden

May
THURSDAY 3
- 7 The Hyde Walled Garden

SUNDAY 6
- 3 The Firs

SUNDAY 20
- 18 Valley Forge

June
SUNDAY 3
- 11 The Old Vicarage
- 14 Southill Park

SATURDAY 9
- 12 Rosehill Cottage

SUNDAY 10
- 12 Rosehill Cottage

SATURDAY 23
- 7 The Hyde Walled Garden

SUNDAY 24
- 9 The Manor House
- 16 Tofte Manor Labyrinth & Garden

July
SUNDAY 1
- 6 How End Cottage
- 19 16 Wood Lane

SUNDAY 8
- 4 Flaxbourne Farm
- 17 Treize

August
SUNDAY 12
- 4 Flaxbourne Farm

September
SUNDAY 9
- 2 14 Fairford Avenue
- 13 Seal Point

Gardens open to the public
- 8 King's Arms Path Garden
- 9 The Manor House

By appointment only
- 1 Dawnedge Lodge
- 10 The Old Stables

The Gardens

ASCOTT
See Buckinghamshire.

CHEDDINGTON GARDENS
See Buckinghamshire.

COWPER & NEWTON MUSEUM GARDENS
See Buckinghamshire.

1 DAWNEDGE LODGE
Woburn Lane, Aspley Guise MK17 8JH. Phil & Lynne Wallace, 01908 582233, lynnewallace@hotmail.co.uk. 5m W of Ampthill. 3m from J13 M1. In Aspley Guise, turn L in centre of village at Moore Place Hotel. Home-made teas. Adm £2.50, chd free. Visitors welcome by appt May, June & July, also groups.
1-acre garden on top of a hill with great views to Woburn. Victorian walled garden, rescued 7yrs ago, with colour themed island beds, pergolas, terracotta pots on stone patio. Cutting garden, Alitex greenhouse and woodland garden (2003). Alliums and agapanthus good. Featured in 'Gardens Monthly'.

2 NEW 14 FAIRFORD AVENUE
Luton LU2 7ER. Brian & Ann Biddle, 01582 735669. 2m N of Luton town centre. Fairford Ave leads directly from Bradgers Hill Rd. Past Luton VI college situated off the Old Bedford Rd paralled to A6. Combined adm with **Seal Point** £3.50, chd free. Sun 9 Sept (2-6). Visitors also welcome by appt, throughout the year, adm £2.50, in early spring the hellebores and bulbs are in full bloom.
1/4-acre hillside garden, with many changes of level, twists and turns, disguising the long, narrow plot and giving some surprise views. Variety of shrubs, trees and herbaceous plants which will

tolerate poor, chalky soil give yr-round interest from snowdrops and hellebores to autumn flowering perennials.

3 THE FIRS
33 Bedford Road, Sandy SG19 1EP. Mr & Mrs D Sutton, 01767 691992, d.sutton7@ntlworld.com. 7m E of Bedford. On B1042 towards town centre. On rd parking. Home-made teas. Adm £2.50, chd free. Sun 6 May (2-5pm). Visitors also welcome by appt Apr to Aug.
1/4-acre town garden, featuring mixed flower beds, gravel garden, shady borders, wildlife and ornamental ponds. Sunken garden, courtyard, fruit and vegetable beds and hornbeam ave, spring flowers and tulip display. An example of what can be done in 6yrs. Gravel driveway and path.

4 FLAXBOURNE FARM
Salford Road, Aspley Guise MK17 8HZ. Geoff & Davina Barrett, 01908 585329. 5m W of Ampthill. 1m S of J13 of M1. Turn R in village centre, 1m over railway line. Home-made teas. Adm £3.50, chd free. Suns 8 July; 12 Aug (2-6pm). Visitors also welcome by appt mid June to end Aug, coaches permitted.
A beautiful and entertaining fun garden of 2 acres, lovingly developed with numerous water features, windmill, modern arches and bridges, small moated castle, lily pond, herbaceous borders. Shrubs and trees recently established, newly constructed Greek temple ruin, fernery and crow's nest. Bring the whole family and discover many more inspirational features Geoff was a finalist in the BBC 2005 Gardener of the Year competition. Woburn Sands Band play throughout openings.

5 59 GRANGE LANE
Bromham MK43 8PA. Mrs Mary Morris, 01234 822215, mary@gardenartist.freeserve.co.uk. 3m W of Bedford: A428 to Bromham, sign Oakley, into Village Rd. 3rd turning on L (Grange Lane), 59 is opp Springfield Drive on L. Home-made teas. Adm £2.50, chd free. Sun 22 Apr (11-5pm). Visitors also welcome

by appt June/July only. No coaches, groups up to 30.
An informal 150ft organic garden developed over 25yrs. Herbaceous border with colour groupings; mixed border; small woodland garden with camellias and many spring flowers and bulbs. Gravel areas. Some unusual plants; hardy geraniums; pulmonarias. Formal pond and white border. Vegetable garden using raised beds and companion planting.

6 **NEW** **HOW END COTTAGE**
How End Cottage, Houghton Conquest MK45 3JT. Jeremy & Gill Smith. *1m N of Ampthill. Turn R 1m from Ampthill off B530 towards Houghton Conquest. How End Rd 300yds on LH-side. Garden at end of rd, approx 1/2 m.* Home-made teas. **Adm £2.50, chd free, concessions £1.50.** **Suns 1 Apr; 1 July (2.30-5.30).** Approx 1 acre garden with 2 ponds, large vegetable garden, greenhouse and orchard. Large lawn gives an uninterrupted view of Houghton House. The garden contains mature trees and beds with many types of slow growing fir trees. Flower beds contain home grown bedding plants and roses. 3 acres of paddocks, wood and further mini paddock. Many spring bulbs.

7 **THE HYDE WALLED GARDEN**
East Hyde, Luton LU2 9PS. D J J Hambro Will Trust, 01892 871 240, ap@encompasssolutions.co.uk. *2m S of Luton. M1 exit J10/10a. A1081 S take 2nd L. At E Hyde turn R then immed L. Junction entrance on R. From A1 exit J4. Follow A3057 N to roundabout, 1st L to B653 Wheathamstead/Luton to E Hyde.* **Adm £2.50, chd free. Thur 3 May; Sat 23 June (2-5pm).** Walled garden adjoins the grounds of The Hyde (house not open). Extends to approx 1 acre and features rose garden, seasonal beds and herbaceous borders, imaginatively interspersed with hidden areas of formal lawn. An interesting group of Victorian greenhouses, coldframes and cucumber house are serviced from the potting shed in the adjoining vegetable garden. Bluebell walk in season. Gravel paths.

8 ♦ **KING'S ARMS PATH GARDEN**
Ampthill MK45 2PP. Ampthill Town Council, 01525 755648, bryden.k@ntlworld.com. *8m S of Bedford. Free parking in town centre. Entrance opp old Market Place, down King's Arms Yard.* **Adm £2, chd free. Suns 28 Jan, 25 Feb, 29 April, 27 May, Fri 22 June, Sat 28 July, Suns 26 August, 30 Sept, 28 Oct. For NGS: Sun 8 Apr (2.30-5pm).** Small woodland garden of about 1½ acres created by plantsman the late William Nourish. Trees, shrubs, bulbs and many interesting collections. Maintained since 1987 by 'The Friends of the Garden' on behalf of Ampthill Town Council.

Great swathes of roses and then late flowering clematis abound in this modern country garden . . .

LOUGHTON VILLAGE GARDENS
See Buckinghamshire.

9 ♦ **THE MANOR HOUSE**
Church Road, Stevington, nr Bedford MK43 7QB. Kathy Brown, 01234 822064, www.kathybrownsgarden.homestead.com. *5m NW of Bedford. Off A428 through Bromham.* **Adm £4, chd free. Sat 10, Sun 11 Feb 10.30-3; Suns 27 May; 29 July. For NGS: Sun 24 June (2-6pm).** Great swathes of roses and then late flowering clematis abound in this modern country garden designed and cared for by owners Simon and Kathy Brown. The French Garden with its jury scene, cottage garden, wild flower meadow, and several major container displays (most are long term), offer contrasting areas of interest with ornamental grass borders echoing world artists Hepworth and Hokusai: Mondrian and Rothko are also in evidence. Some gravel paths.

10 **THE OLD STABLES**
Hockliffe LU7 9NL. Mr & Mrs D X Victor, 01525 210633. *3m N of Dunstable. From A5 in Hockliffe, proceed W on A4012. Turn R after 1/4 m signed Goose Green leading to Church Lane, then L at church. Follow lane for 1/2 m & take tarmac drive on R.* **Adm £3, chd free. Visitors welcome by appt.** 2 acres, incl walled garden, with panoramic views of countryside. Large collection of plants incl peonies, hardy geraniums, clematis and tender bulbs, in formal and informal plantings.

11 **THE OLD VICARAGE**
Church Road, Westoning MK45 5JW. Ann & Colin Davies. *4m S of Ampthill. Off A5120, 2m N of M1 J12. 1/4 m up Church Rd, next to church.* **Adm £2.50, chd 50p. Suns 1 Apr; 3 June (2-6pm).** Traditional 2 acre vicarage garden with box and laurel hedges, large magnolia grandiflora, mature shrubs and trees; herbaceous beds, rose garden, pond and wild garden. Spring interest with hellebores and daffodils.

RAGGED HALL
See Hertfordshire.

12 **NEW** **ROSEHILL COTTAGE**
Rosehill Farm, Marquis Hill, Shillington SG5 3HE. Anne & Clare Simkins. *7m NW of Hitchin. Turn off A6 at roundabout at north end of Barton-le-Clay to Shillington. Follow signs to Stondon & Henlow, Rosehill Farm is at end of village by national speed limit sign. Also from A600 at Henlow Camp roundabout. Disabled parking in front of house.* Home-made teas. **Adm £3, chd free. Sat 9, Sun 10 June (11.30-5.30).** Wheelchair friendly 1-acre garden with mature trees, lawns and 4 island beds with mixed planting. Shrubs surround 2 fish ponds linked by a stream. Climbers on trellis enclosing raised vegetable beds. Croquet lawn will be in use. Shrub border.

⑬ SEAL POINT
7 Wendover Way, Luton LU2 7LS.
Mrs Danae Johnston, 01582 611567.
*2m from Luton town centre. In NE
Luton, turning N off Stockingstone Rd
A505 into Felstead Way then 2nd L
Wendover Way.* Home-made teas.
Combined adm with **14 Fairford
Avenue £3.50** , chd free. Sun 9 Sept
(2-6). Visitors also welcome by appt
May to Aug, up to 50 visitors,
coaches welcome one at a time.
A garden of delight, incls wildlife
spinney, lovely grasses, unusual trees
and shrubs; 3 water features and treetop balcony on which to enjoy
refreshments. Danae won Gardener of
the year E and SE 1999. We both love
visitors.
✕ ✿ ☕

⑭ SOUTHILL PARK
nr Biggleswade SG18 9LL. Mr & Mrs
Charles Whitbread. *3m W of
Biggleswade. In the village of Southill.
3m from A1.* Cream teas. **Adm £3.50,
chd free. Sun 3 June (2-5pm).**
Large garden, with mature trees and
flowering shrubs, herbaceous borders,
rose garden and wild garden. Large
conservatory with tropical plants. The
parkland was designed by Lancelot
'Capability' Brown in 1777.
♿ ✕ ✿ ☕

⑮ SWISS GARDEN
Old Warden Park SG18 9ER.
Shuttleworth Trust in Partnership
with Bedfordshire County Council,
01525 18453. *2m W of Biggleswade.
Signed from A1 & A600.* **Adm £5, chd
free, concessions £4** (share to
Friends of the Swiss Garden). **Wed
25 Apr (10-5pm).**
Designed in 1820s. 9-acre miniature
landscape garden with winding paths,
intertwining ponds, wrought iron
bridges, fernery grotto and tiny
buildings. Peacocks wander around
splendid trees and shrubs, with
daffodils, rhododendrons and roses in
season. Adjacent further acres of
native woodland.
♿ ✕ ✿ ☕

**⑯ TOFTE MANOR LABYRINTH
& GARDEN**
Souldrop Road, Sharnbrook
MK44 1HH. Mrs Suzy Castleman,
01234 781425,
www.toftelabyrinth.co.uk. *8m N of
Bedford. Off A6 between Bedford and
Rushden. Exit at roundabout signed
Sharnbrook, through village towards
Souldrop. At Y-Junction take R fork;
house is 400yds on L, through large
black wrought-iron gates.* Cream teas.
**Adm £3.50, chd free. Sun 24 June
(2-5pm).**
5 acres of mature and beautifully laid
out garden restored and modernised
to blend with C17 manor house.
Beautiful mature trees, colour themed
herbaceous borders. Sunken area with
central arbour and crystal ball like
water feature. Modern statued parterre
garden, unusual swings. Walks and
wild areas abound. Grass labyrinth in
the design of Chartres Cathedral,
France, incorporating crystals and
sacred geometry. Water which has
travelled the path of the labyrinth can
be drunk. This is an unusual spiritual
garden for those in search of
tranquillity.
✕ ✿ 🛏 ☕

Peacocks wander around splendid trees

⑰ TREIZE
Cranfield Road, Wootton Green
MK43 9EA. Roger & Anna Skipper.
*5m SW of Bedford. 10m NE of Milton
Keynes. C70 Kempston to Cranfield
rd, 1/2m SW of Wootton. Private Lane
on R opp Wootton Green Hamlet sign.
Bungalow 100yds along lane on R. Car
parking on open day in adjacent
meadow.* Home-made teas. **Adm
£2.50, chd free. Sun 8 July (2-6pm).**
1-acre plantsman's garden set out for
yr-round interest on heavy clay. Hidden
gardens and established herbaceous
borders; formal pond; rockery, gravel
beds. Many varieties of established
and younger trees, shrubs and vast

collection of perennials, incl over 150
varieties and species of penstemon.
♿ ✕ ✿ ☕

⑱ VALLEY FORGE
213 Castle Hill Road, Totternhoe
LU6 2DA. Pat & Mike Sutcliffe,
01525 221676,
sutcliffes@leylandman.co.uk. *2m W
of Dunstable. Turn R off B489 Aston
Clinton rd, 1/2m from Dunstable centre,
signed Totternhoe. Fronting main rd,
corner of Chapel Lane, 1m through
village. On rd parking.* Teas. **Adm £3,
chd free. Sun 20 May (2-5pm).
Visitors also welcome by appt April
& May, groups 6+.**
Garden to rear of C17 grade 2 listed
thatched cottage (not open). 1/2-acre
sloping site planted from scratch by
owners 15yrs ago. Imaginatively
landscaped, terraced on 4 levels, long
pergola, archways and steps
connecting to meandering pathways
that lead intriguingly through the
foliage. New small gravel garden,
ponds on 2 levels connected by small
cascade. Large range of shrubs,
perennials and trees compatible with
chalk, including the indiginous
Aylesbury Prune. The site also houses
The Mike Sutcliffe Collection of early
Leyland buses (1908-1934).
✕ ✿ ☕

⑲ NEW 16 WOOD LANE
Cotton End MK45 3AJ. Lesley
Bunker-Nixon & Eddie Wilkins.
*2m S of Bedford. A600 signed
Shefford from Bedford, 2nd L at
The Bell PH, into Wood Lane, past
Hall Way on RH-side.* Light
refreshments & teas. **Adm £2.50,
chd free. Sun 1 July (12-5).**
150ft garden consisting of cottage
style garden, containers and
bygones. Formal garden with large
koi pond with beautiful fish,
borders and lawns. Japanese
garden with bonsai trees, wooded
area with stream. Vegetable garden
based on an allotment. Wildlife
area with folly and chickens.
♿ ✕ ✿

Bedfordshire County Volunteers
County Organiser
Mike & Pat Sutcliffe, Valley Forge, 213 Castle Hill Road, Totternhoe, Dunstable LU6 2DA, 01525 221676
sutcliffes@leylandman.co.uk

County Treasurer
David Johnston, Seal Point, 7 Wendover Way, Luton LU2 7LS, 01582 611567

Publicity
Geoff & Davina Barrett, Flaxbourne Farm, Aspley Guise, Milton Keynes MK17 8HZ, 01908 585329, carole@boa.uk.com

BERKSHIRE

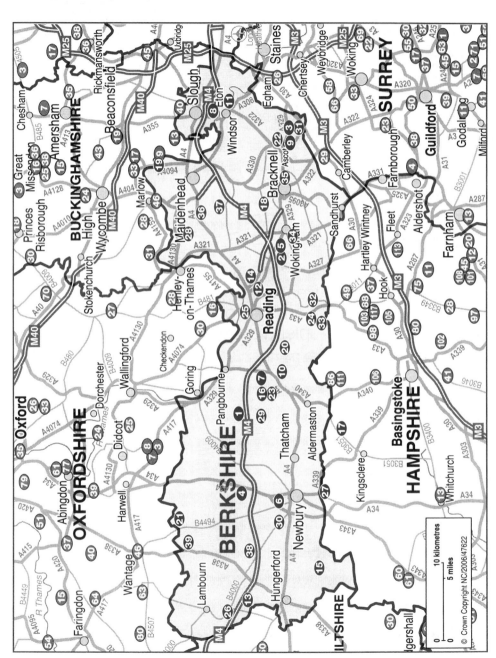

Opening Dates

April

SUNDAY 1
35 Two Bracknell Gardens

SUNDAY 15
12 The Harris Garden

SUNDAY 22
19 Odney Club
21 The Old Rectory Farnborough

WEDNESDAY 25
13 Inholmes
26 Rooksnest

May

WEDNESDAY 2
37 Waltham Place Gardens

SUNDAY 6
18 Moor Close Gardens

MONDAY 7
18 Moor Close Gardens

WEDNESDAY 9
18 Moor Close Gardens
37 Waltham Place Gardens

SUNDAY 13
21 The Old Rectory Farnborough
29 Stanford Dingley Gardens

TUESDAY 15
11 Frogmore House Garden

WEDNESDAY 16
18 Moor Close Gardens
37 Waltham Place Gardens

SUNDAY 20
2 Bearwood College

WEDNESDAY 23
18 Moor Close Gardens
37 Waltham Place Gardens

SUNDAY 27
18 Moor Close Gardens

MONDAY 28
18 Moor Close Gardens
31 Sunningdale Park

WEDNESDAY 30
18 Moor Close Gardens
37 Waltham Place Gardens

June

SUNDAY 3
10 Folly Farm

WEDNESDAY 6
18 Moor Close Gardens
37 Waltham Place Gardens

SATURDAY 9
25 The RISC Roof Garden, Reading

SUNDAY 10
15 Kirby House

25 The RISC Roof Garden, Reading
30 Stockcross House

WEDNESDAY 13
18 Moor Close Gardens
37 Waltham Place Gardens

SATURDAY 16
8 Eton College Gardens

SUNDAY 17
16 Mariners
18 Moor Close Gardens
39 Woolley Park

WEDNESDAY 20
18 Moor Close Gardens
37 Waltham Place Gardens

SUNDAY 24
21 The Old Rectory Farnborough
24 The Priory
27 Sandleford Place

TUESDAY 26
38 Welford Park

WEDNESDAY 27
13 Inholmes
18 Moor Close Gardens
26 Rooksnest
37 Waltham Place Gardens

July

SUNDAY 1
4 Chieveley Manor
35 Two Bracknell Gardens

WEDNESDAY 4
18 Moor Close Gardens
37 Waltham Place Gardens

SATURDAY 7
25 The RISC Roof Garden, Reading

SUNDAY 8
18 Moor Close Gardens
25 The RISC Roof Garden, Reading
32 Swallowfield Horticultural Society

WEDNESDAY 11
18 Moor Close Gardens
37 Waltham Place Gardens

SUNDAY 15
33 Thrive's Trunkwell Garden Project

WEDNESDAY 18
18 Moor Close Gardens
37 Waltham Place Gardens

THURSDAY 19
6 Donnington Castle House

SUNDAY 22
3 Boxwood House

WEDNESDAY 25
18 Moor Close Gardens
37 Waltham Place Gardens

August

WEDNESDAY 1
37 Waltham Place Gardens

SUNDAY 5
9 Fairacre
20 The Old Rectory Burghfield

WEDNESDAY 8
37 Waltham Place Gardens

SATURDAY 11
25 The RISC Roof Garden, Reading

SUNDAY 12
25 The RISC Roof Garden, Reading
34 Timberlea

WEDNESDAY 15
37 Waltham Place Gardens

WEDNESDAY 22
37 Waltham Place Gardens

SUNDAY 26
1 Ashampstead Common Gardens
18 Moor Close Gardens
22 Old Waterfield

MONDAY 27
18 Moor Close Gardens

WEDNESDAY 29
37 Waltham Place Gardens

September

WEDNESDAY 5
37 Waltham Place Gardens

SATURDAY 8
25 The RISC Roof Garden, Reading

SUNDAY 9
12 The Harris Garden
25 The RISC Roof Garden, Reading

WEDNESDAY 12
37 Waltham Place Gardens

WEDNESDAY 19
37 Waltham Place Gardens

WEDNESDAY 26
37 Waltham Place Gardens

Gardens open to the public

7 Englefield House
37 Waltham Place Gardens
38 Welford Park

By appointment only

5 6 Crecy Close
14 Ivydene
17 Meadow House
23 Potash
28 Scotlands
36 Two Littlewick Green Gardens

The Gardens

❶ NEW ASHAMPSTEAD COMMON GARDENS
RG8 8QS. *2m E of Yattendon along Yattendon Lane. L into Sucks Lane for car parking.* Home-made teas at Baggage Chute. **Combined adm £3, chd free. Sun 26 Aug (2-5.30).**
Gardens beyond the village and beside the pretty Ashampstead Garden.

NEW BAGGAGE CHUTE
Colin & Caroline Butler
Lower terraced garden with colourful mix of shrubs and perennials leading to large informal pond. Vegetable and cutting garden. Hillside slopes feature prairie style mix of flowers and grasses with long views over surrounding countryside.

NEW FARRIERS COTTAGE
Jackie Lomas
Small immaculate cottage garden designed and planted by owner. Formal front garden in woodland setting leading to colourful mix of shrubs and herbaceous planting at the back

❷ BEARWOOD COLLEGE
Winnersh RG41 5BG, 0118 978 7645, secondmaster@bearwood college.co.uk. *5m SE of Reading. Off B3030, 1m S of A329/ B3030 intersection at Winnersh, midway between Reading and Wokingham. Look for Bearwood Rd & Bearwood College sign.* Cream teas. **Adm £3, chd free. Sun 20 May (2-5). Visitors also welcome by appt.**
Late C19 mansion and parkland now an independent school. Walks through mature woodland, pinetum, rhododendrons and grassland. Lake and natural margins. Pulham water garden under restoration. Some mansion rooms open.

❸ BOXWOOD HOUSE
Heathfield Avenue, Sunninghill SL5 0AL. Mr J P H Morrow & Mr R E G Beard. *6m S of Windsor. From A30 at Sunningdale, take Broomhall Lane, after ¹/₂m follow signs to car park. From A329 turn into Silwood Rd and R*

to Larch Ave. Home-made teas. **Adm £2.50, chd free. Sun 22 July (1-6).**
³/₄-acre designer's, plantsman's and flower arrangers garden in woodland setting with emphasis to plant and colour association. Large range of herbaceous perennials, large leaved hostas, acers, grasses, topiary, climbers, interesting foliage plants with pergola, woodland garden, natural style pond and many tender plant combinations in pots.

❹ CHIEVELEY MANOR
RG20 8UT. Mr & Mrs C J Spence. *5m N of Newbury. Take A34 N, pass under M4, then L to Chieveley. After ¹/₂m L up Manor Lane.* Home-made teas. **Adm £3, chd free. Sun 1 July (2-5.30).**
Large garden with fine views over stud farm. Walled garden containing borders, shrubs and rose garden. Listed house (not open). Newly planted bed.

CLIVEDEN
See Buckinghamshire.

❺ 6 CRECY CLOSE
RG41 3UZ. John & Anne Massey, 0188 9019099, www.acorngardenservices.co.uk. *Take A329 towards Reading. 1m after town centre, L at Woosehill roundabout, end of dual carriageway turn R, take 1st L and 5th on L.* **Adm £2.50, chd free. Visitors welcome by appt, May to Sept, groups 10+.**
Professional garden designers; the garden offers many design ideas for the small garden together with interesting and unusual plants.

DIPLEY MILL
See Hampshire.

❻ DONNINGTON CASTLE HOUSE
Castle Lane RG14 2LE. Mr & Mrs B Stewart-Brown. *1m N of Newbury. Follow signs to Donnington Castle. Entrance on R towards top of main castle entrance. Car park through wooden gates.* Cream teas. **Adm £3.50, chd free. Thur 19 July (10-5).**
Large mature garden with many parts planted during last 5yrs. Herbaceous borders, roses, mixed borders, fine mature trees, lawns. Newly planted woodland and garden walks.

> Hillside slopes feature a prairie style mix of flowers and grasses, with long views . . .

❼ ◆ ENGLEFIELD HOUSE
RG7 5EN. Sir William & Lady Benyon, 01189 302221, www.englefield.co.uk. *6m W of Reading. 1¹/₂m from J12 M4. 1m from Theale. Entrance on A340 3m S of Pangbourne.* **Adm £3, chd free. Mon all yr. Mon to Thurs incl from 1 Apr to 1 Oct (10-6).**
9-acre woodland garden with interesting variety of trees and shrubs, stream, water garden descending to formal terraces with stone balustrades making background for deep borders. Small enclosed gardens of differing character incl children's garden with joke fountains. All enclosed by deer park with lake.

❽ ETON COLLEGE GARDENS
SL4 6DB. Eton College. *¹/₂m N of Windsor. Parking off B3022 Slough to Eton rd, signed to R, S of junction with Datchet Rd (Pocock's Lane), walk across playing fields to entry. Or continue S on B3022 through T-lights in Eton, then signed 50yds on L (called Barnes Pool and suitable for wheelchairs). 100yds walk to entry.* **Adm £2.50, chd 75p. Sat 16 June (2-6).**
Gardens incl Provost's Garden, Fellows' Garden, Headmaster's Garden and Luxmoore's garden (an island in the Thames, created by a housemaster about 1880 and reached across an attractive bridge). Gardens adjoin ancient buildings. Gravel paths, mown grass to Luxmoore's.

9 FAIRACRE
Ravensdale Road, South Ascot
SL5 9HJ. David & Mary Nichols. *6m
E of Bracknell. On A330 1/2m S of
Ascot Racecourse, turn R into
Coronation Rd, 2nd R to Woodlands
Ride, Ravensdale Rd 150yds on R. No
cars except disabled in unmade
Ravensdale Rd.* Home-made teas.
**Adm £2.50, chd free. Sun 5 Aug
(2-5).**
1 1/2 acres. Banks of large
rhododendrons and azaleas, sunken
garden with mix of annuals and
perennials, beds of flowering shrubs,
herbaceous borders, collection of
conifers, kitchen garden. Some 'tree
ring' paths & gravel entrance.
&. ✗ ⊕ ☕

10 FOLLY FARM
Sulhamstead RG7 4DF. Sir
Desmond & Lady Pitcher. *7m SW of
Reading. From A4 between Reading
and Newbury (2m W of M4 J12) take
rd marked Sulhamstead at Spring Inn.*
Teas. **Adm £3, chd free. Sun 3 June
(2-6).**
One of the few remaining gardens
where Lutyens architecture remains
intact. Garden, laid out by Gertrude
Jekyll, has been planted to owners'
taste bearing in mind Jekyll and
Lutyens original design. Raised white
garden, sunken rose garden, spring
bulbs, herbaceous borders, ilex walk,
avenues of limes, yew hedges, formal
pools. Tropical greenhouses and
organic vegetable garden. House not
open.
✗ ☕

**11 FROGMORE HOUSE
GARDEN**
Windsor SL4 2HT. Her Majesty The
Queen, www.royal.gov.uk. *1m SE of
Windsor. Entrance via Park St gate into
Long Walk (follow AA signs). Visitors
are requested kindly to keep on the
route to the garden & not stray into the
Home Park. Stn & bus stop: Windsor
(20 mins walk from gardens); Green
Line bus no 701, from London. Limited
parking for cars only (free). Coaches by
appointment only.* Light refreshments &
teas. **Adm £4.50 to garden, chd free.
House Adm £4.50 Adult, £2.50
Child, £3.50 Concessions. Tue 15
May (10-5.30 last adm 4pm).**
30 acres of landscaped gardens rich in
history and beauty. Large lake, fine
trees, lawns, flowers and flowering
shrubs. The Royal Mausoleum, within
the grounds, will also be open to those
visiting the gardens. Gravel paths. For

tickets apply to NGS, Hatchlands Park,
East Clandon, Guildford, Surrey GU4
7RT, Tel 01483 211535,
www.ngs.org.uk.
&. ✗ ☕

GRANGE DRIVE WOOBURN
See Buckinghamshire.

12 THE HARRIS GARDEN
Whiteknights RG6 6AS. The
University of Reading, School of
Biological Sciences, www.
friendsoftheharrisgarden.org.uk. *1 1/2
m S of Reading town centre. Off A327,
Shinfield Rd. Turn R just inside Pepper
Lane entrance to campus.* Home-
made teas. **Adm £3, chd free. Suns
15 Apr; 9 Sept (2-6).**
12-acre research and teaching garden.
Rose gardens, herbaceous borders,
winter garden, herb garden, jungle
garden. Extensive glasshouses. Many
plants labelled. Gravel & grass paths.
&. ✗ ⊕ ☕

Cutting and vegetable gardens, specimen trees leading to bluebell walk . . .

HECKFIELD PLACE
See Hampshire.

13 INHOLMES
Woodlands St Mary RG17 7SY. Lady
Williams. *3m SE Lambourn. From
A338 take B4000 towards Lambourn,
Inholmes signed.* Teas. **Adm £3.50, £5
combined with Rooksnest, chd
free. Weds 25 Apr; 27 June (11-4).**
Newly re-established, incl large walled
garden, colour co-ordinated
herbaceous border, cutting and
vegetable garden, tulip display, formal
gardens, parkland walk with specimen
trees leading to bluebell wood. Mainly
gravel paths.
&. ✗ ⊕ ☕

14 IVYDENE
283 Loddon Bridge Road, Woodley
RG5 4BE. Janet & Bill Bonney, 0118
969 7591, janbonney2003@aol.com.
*3 1/2m W of Reading. A4 from Reading
towards Maidenhead. Woodley lies
midway between. Loddon Bridge Rd is
the main rd through the small town.
Garden about 100yds S of the 'Just
Tiles' roundabout. Parking is in adjacent
rd.* **Adm £2, chd free. Visitors
welcome by appt for groups, 5-15.**
Small urban gardener's garden approx
120ft x 30ft, specialising in ornamental
grasses with over 50 varieties
integrated into both front and back
gardens. Autumn viewing shows
grasses to best advantage. New
seaside garden and stained glass
features. Featured in 'Amateur
Gardening' Oct 2006.

15 KIRBY HOUSE
Inkpen RG17 9DE. Mr & Mrs R
Astor. *3 1/2m SE of Hungerford. A4 to
Kintbury. L at Xrds in Kintbury (by
Corner Stores) towards Coombe. 2m
out of Kintbury turn L immed beyond
Crown & Garter PH, turn L at junction,
house & garden at bottom of hill on R.*
**Adm £3.50, chd £1. Sun 10 June
(2-5).**
6 acres in beautiful setting with views
of S Berkshire Downs across lawn and
parkland. C18 Queen Anne House (not
open). Formal rose borders, double
herbaceous border in kitchen garden,
colour themed border between yew
buttress hedges. Lily pond garden,
reflecting pond with fountain, lake.
✗

LITTLE COOPERS
See Hampshire.

16 MARINERS
Mariners Lane, Bradfield RG7 6HU.
Anthony & Fenja Anderson, 0118
974 5226. *10m W of Reading. M4 J12
take A4 direction Newbury 1m. At
roundabout exit A340 direction
Pangbourne. 400yds turn L direction
Bradfield. After 1m, turn L direction
Southend Bradfield. After 1m opp
signpost direction Tutts Clump turn R
into Mariners Lane.* **Adm £3, chd free.
Sun 17 June (2-6). Visitors also
welcome by appt 18th June-15 July.**
1 1/2-acre sloping site with creative
feature made of slopes. Rich mixture of
herbaceous planting incl unusual
plants and grasses arranged in colour
themes with emphasis on plant form
and texture. Garden of old varieties of
shrub roses, species and climbing
roses. Streamside walk, orchard,

sundial garden and 1-acre wild flower meadow. Some steep slopes & some (fine) gravel areas.

 ♿ ✈ Ⓢ

⑰ MEADOW HOUSE
Ashford Hill RG19 8BN. Mr & Mrs G A Jones, 0118 981 6005, harriet@rosejones.freeserve.co.uk. *8m SE of Newbury. On B3051. Take turning at SW end of village signed Wolverton Common & Wheathold. House on R approx 350yds down unmade track.* **Adm £2.50, chd free. Visitors welcome by appt.**
Approx 1³/₄-acre plantsman's garden in beautiful rural surroundings. Designed by owners to create a feeling of tranquillity and space. Pond with waterside planting, mixed shrub, rose and herbaceous borders. Trellis with wisteria, roses and clematis.

♿ ✈

⑱ MOOR CLOSE GARDENS
Popeswood Road, Binfield RG42 4AN. Newbold College. *2m W of Bracknell. Off B3408. From Bracknell turn R at Binfield T-lights, from A329(M) take B3408, turn L at Binfield T-lights. Follow signs.* **Adm £2, chd free. Sun 6, Mon 7, Weds 9, 16, 23, Sun 27, Mon 28, Wed 30 May; Weds 6, 13, Sun 17, Weds 20, 27 June; Wed 4, Sun 8, Weds 11, 18, 25 July; Sun 26, Mon 27 Aug (2-5).**
Grade II listed garden designed 1911-13 by Oliver Hill, following Lutyens and Jekyll. The famous architect's first commission and a rare example of his early work. Series of linked courts and gardens incl herb garden, water parterre, Italianate garden with partitions, pergola and pools. Now in the course of restoration.

✈ Ⓢ

⑲ ODNEY CLUB
Odney Lane, Cookham SL6 9SR. John Lewis Partnership. *3m N of Maidenhead. Off A4094 S of Cookham Bridge. Car park in grounds.* **Cream teas. Adm £3, chd free (share to Thames Valley Adventure Playground). Sun 22 Apr (2-6).**
This 120-acre site beside the Thames is continuously developing and takes a full afternoon to visit. A favourite with Stanley Spencer who featured our magnolia in his work. Magnificent wisteria, specimen trees, herbaceous borders, side gardens, spring bedding and ornamental lake.

♿ ☕

An explosion of rare and interesting plants beautifully combined for colour and texture, stunning views . . .

OLD MEADOWS
See Hampshire.

THE OLD MILL
See Wiltshire.

⑳ THE OLD RECTORY BURGHFIELD
RG30 3TH. Mr A R Merton, 0118 983 3141, neilcollins53@gmail.com. *5m SW of Reading. Turn S off A4 to Burghfield village, R after Hatch Gate Inn, entrance on R.* **Teas. Adm £3, chd free. Sun 5 Aug (12-4). Visitors also welcome by appt anytime, for groups 10+, incl coaches.**
4¹/₂-acre plantsman's garden. Snowdrops, hellebores, old roses, shrub borders, woodland area, ponds, orchard, kitchen garden, terrace pots and late summer flowering double herbaceous borders. Georgian house (not open).

✈ Ⓢ ☕

㉑ THE OLD RECTORY FARNBOROUGH
Wantage OX12 8NX. Mr & Mrs Michael Todhunter. *4m SE of Wantage. Take B4494 Wantage-Newbury Rd, after 4m turn E at sign for Farnborough.* **Light refreshments & home-made teas. Adm £3.50, chd free (share to Farnborough PCC). Suns 22 Apr; 13 May; 24 June (2-5.30).**
In a series of immaculately tended garden rooms, incl herbaceous borders, arboretum, boules, rose, pool and vegetable gardens, there is an explosion of rare and interesting plants, beautifully combined for colour and texture. With stunning views across the countryside, it is the perfect setting for the C1749 rectory (not open), once home of John Betjeman, in memory of whom John Piper created a window in the local church.

✈ Ⓢ ☕

OLD THATCH
See Buckinghamshire.

㉒ OLD WATERFIELD
Winkfield Road, Ascot SL5 7LJ. Hugh & Catherine Stevenson. *6m SW of Windsor. On A330 (Winkfield Rd) midway between A329 and A332 to E of Ascot Racecourse. Parking on Practice Ground (by kind permission of Royal Ascot Golf Club) adjacent to house.* **Home-made teas. Adm £3, chd free (share to The Sick Children's Trust). Sun 26 Aug (2-5).**
4-acres. The original cottage garden, incl a large and productive kitchen garden, was extended by 3-acres of specimen trees and orchard planted in 2003.

♿ ✈ Ⓢ ☕

㉓ POTASH
Mariners Lane, Southend Bradfield RG7 6HU. Mr & Mrs J W C Mooney, 0118 9744264, john@potash.plus.com. *10m W of Reading. From M4 J12 take A4 W 1m. At roundabout exit A340 direction Pangbourne, turn L after 400yds direction Bradfield. After 1m turn L direction Southend Bradfield. 1m opposite Southend Bradfield sign turn R. Potash is 400yds on L by Beech Hedge.* **Teas. Adm £3, chd free. Visitors welcome by appt, incl coaches.**
5-acre garden. Wide range of plants, many unusual specimens and interest throughout the yr from snowdrops to autumn colour. Daffodils a feature, shrubs, tea roses, herbaceous borders, bog garden feeding a clay-lined pond, young woodland and space to sit and contemplate the view. Dogs very welcome. Featured in 'GGG 2006'.

♿ ☕

THE PRIORS FARM
See Hampshire.

㉔ THE PRIORY
Beech Hill RG7 2BJ. Mr & Mrs C
Carter, 01189 833146,
tita@betcarter.org. *5m S of Reading.
M4 J11. Follow signs to A33, then L at
roundabout signed Swallowfield. After
1¼ m, R by Murco garage to Beech
Hill. When in village turn opp church
into Wood Lane, then R down Priory
Dr - house at end of drive.* Home-
made teas. **Adm £2.50, chd free. Sun
24 June (2-5.30). Visitors also
welcome by appt.**
Extensive gardens in grounds of former
C12 Benedictine Priory (not open),
rebuilt 1648. Beside the R Loddon, the
mature gardens are being restored and
re-developed. Large formal walled
garden with espalier fruit trees, lawns,
extensive mixed and recently replanted
herbaceous borders, vegetables and
roses. Woodland, lake and new Italian
style water garden in progress. Fine
trees.

**㉕ THE RISC ROOF GARDEN,
READING**
35-39 London Street RG1 4PS.
Reading International Solidarity
Centre, 0118 958 6692,
www.risc.org.uk/garden. *5 mins walk
from Oracle shopping centre.* Teas.
**Adm £2.50, chd free (share to
WEB/RISC). Sats & Suns 9, 10 June;
7, 8 July; 11, 12 Aug; 8, 9 Sept (12-
4). Visitors also welcome by appt for
groups 10-15.**
Small town centre roof garden
developed to demonstrate
sustainability and our dependance on
plants. All plants in the garden have an
economic use for food, clothing,
medicine etc. The garden can
accommodate a maximum of 20
people at a time so book a tour if you
are not prepared to wait. Roof garden
accessible by external staircase. Water
harvesting system and drip irrigation
powered by renewable energy.
Featured on Gardener's World, BBC2
Sept 2006.

㉖ ROOKSNEST
Ermine Street, Lambourn
Woodlands RG17 7SB. Dr & Mrs M
D Sackler, 07939 495736/01488
72991, kathrynkidby@tiscali .co.uk.
*2m S of Lambourn. From A338
Wantage rd, along B4000. Nearest
village, Lambourn. Rooksnest signed
on B4000.* Home-made teas. **Adm £3,**

£5 combined with **Inholmes,** chd
free. **Weds 25 Apr; 27 June (11-4).
Visitors also welcome by appt.**
Approx 10-acre exceptionally fine
traditional English garden. Sunken
garden recently restored with help from
Arabella Lennox-Boyd. Terraces, rose
garden, lilies, pond, herbaceous
border, herb garden, organic vegetable
garden. Many specimen trees and fine
shrubs.

㉗ SANDLEFORD PLACE
Newtown RG20 9AY. Mr & Mrs Alan
Gatward, 01635 40726,
melgatward@bigfoot.com. *1½ m S of
Newbury. On A339. House is at W
side of Swan roundabout.* Home-made
teas. **Adm £3, chd free. Sun 24 June
(2-6). Visitors also welcome by appt.**
4-acre grounds around a former old
mill and granary. Many varied shrub
and herbaceous borders crammed
with plants for naturalistic effect. Walled
garden with a wide range of plants
arranged for yr-round interest, flowers,
foliage and scent. Kitchen garden and
herb bed. Wild flowers in meadow and
along river. Unusual plants for sale,
some seen in the garden. Weeping
tree water feature.

㉘ SCOTLANDS
Cockpole Green, Wargrave
RG10 8QP. Mr Michael Payne &
family, 01628 822648. *6m W of
Maidenhead, 4m E of Henley. In centre
of triangle formed by A4130, A321 to
Wargrave & A4 at Knowl Hill - midway
between Warren Row Village &
Cockpole Green.* **Adm £3, chd free.
Visitors welcome by appt.**
4-acre garden surrounding C17
farmhouse (not open). Clipped yews,
shrub borders, grass paths through
trees to woodland and pond-gardens
with Repton design rustic summer
house. Rocks with waterfall and
gazebo. Featured in 'GGG 2007', with
star.

SHERFIELD SCHOOL
See Hampshire.

**㉙ STANFORD DINGLEY
GARDENS**
RG7 6LS. *5m SW of Pangbourne.
From A4 take A340 (Pangbourne Rd),
1st L to Bradfield, after Bradfield, L at
Xrds , 2½ m, L into village.* Teas.
**Combined adm £4, chd £1. Sun 13
May (2-5.30).**

One of Berkshire's most beautiful
villages set within the valley of the R
Pang.

BRADFIELD FARM
Mrs Anna Newton, 01189
744113. *Pink house in centre of
village.* **Visitors also welcome by
appt.**
½-acre plantsman's garden with
wide variety of plants. Driveway
behind with rare and interesting
trees leading (across fields) to
6-acre wild garden beside R Pang.
Long undisturbed ground and
mown walks, enjoy native flora and
fauna. Home of Brian Davis
Garden School. Gravel paths, slight
slopes.

**BRIDGE COTTAGE
Mr B White & Mrs A
Featherstone.** *Between Bull PH
and R Pang, same side as The Bull*
Cottage style 'room' garden
planted mainly to shrubs and small
borders, gravel garden, vegetable
and fruit areas, benches and chairs
afford places to relax. Gravel &
narrow paths.

**NEW INGLE SPRING
David & Indra Townsend**
A long and relatively narrow
2½-acre garden beside and
overlooking the R Ingle, with a
range of different plantings.
Restored by present owners over
the past 5yrs. Partial wheelchair
access. Narrow bridge without
handrails over R Ingle.

**THE SPRING
Mr & Mrs Mark Hawkesworth.**
Opp The Old Boot PH
Cottage garden with spring-fed
pond and stream, mature tree
specimens, fruit trees and
vegetable area, herbaceous
borders, views over water
meadow.

㉚ STOCKCROSS HOUSE
Church Road RG20 8LP. Susan &
Edward Vandyk. *3m W of Newbury.
1m W of A4/A34 (Newbury bypass)
junction on B4000. From M4, J14,
take B4000 to Stockcross.* Home-
made teas. **Adm £2.50, chd free. Sun
10 June (2-5.30).**
1½-acre garden developed over past
10yrs with an emphasis on plant
partnerships and colour combinations.
Herbaceous borders, shrubs, roses,

pergola and pond, vegetable and cutting gardens, all maintained to a high standard. Access to most of garden.

STOKE POGES MEMORIAL GARDENS
See Buckinghamshire.

Kitchen garden with raised beds, fruit cages and greenhouses. Other interests in hidden corners . . .

③① SUNNINGDALE PARK
Larch Avenue, Ascot SL5 0QE. National School of Government/Verve Venues. *6m S of Windsor. On A30 at Sunningdale take Broomhall Lane. After 1/2m turn R into Larch Ave. Or from A329 turn into Silwood Rd towards Sunningdale.* Home-made teas. **Adm £4, chd free. Mon 28 May (2-5).**
Over 20 acres of beautifully landscaped gardens reputedly designed after Capability Brown. Terrace garden and Victorian rockery designed by Pulham incl cave and water features. Lake area with paved walks, extensive lawns with specimen trees and flower beds, impressive massed rhododendrons. Beautiful 1m woodland walk. Grade II listed building (not open). Free garden history tour.

③② SWALLOWFIELD HORTICULTURAL SOCIETY
RG7 1QX. *5m S of Reading. M4 J11 & A33/B3349, signed Swallowfield. Tickets and maps at Village Hall in centre.* Lunch, light refreshments & teas. **Combined adm £4, chd free, concessions £2. Sun 8 July (11-5).**
Min 8 gardens, varying in size from 3 acres to small village gardens. 3 gardens detailed.

GREENWINGS
Liz & Ray Jones
Approx 1 1/2 acres designed and planted by owners over past 30yrs. Features incl pond, tree ferns, shrubs and mixed flower border. Greenhouse with orchids.

WESSEX HOUSE
Val Payne
Mature 1/2-acre garden, shrubs, rose beds, raised vegetable beds, large greenhouse and 5in gauge model railway.

NEW WHEELERS FARM HOUSE
Sue Middlemist
Large garden in development, a flock of Coridale sheep and splendid views across the Blackwater.

③③ THRIVE'S TRUNKWELL GARDEN PROJECT
Beech Hill, Reading RG7 2AT. *Thrive, www.thrive.org.uk. 7m S of Reading. M4 J11, follow signs to A33, L at roundabout signed Swallowfield. After 1 1/4m, R by Murco garage to Beech Hill. From S keep through Swallowfield on B3349, after Mill House restaurant turn L, bear R, then L at Xrds to Beech Hill. Signs in village.* Teas. **Adm £2.50, chd £1 (share to Thrive). Sun 15 July (2-4.30).**
3-acre site with Victorian walled garden run by Thrive, a national charity which uses gardening to support and inspire disabled people. Formal and informal interest, nature trail, pond, butterfly garden, trained fruit and cut flower areas, potager, glasshouse, sensory and cottage gardens.

③④ TIMBERLEA
17 Oaklands Drive, Wokingham RG41 2SA. Mr & Mrs F Preston, 0118 978 4629, nina.fred@tinyonline.co.uk. *1m SW of Wokingham. M4 J10 or M3 J3. From Wokingham take A321 under 2 railway bridges, Tesco store is between. Immed turn R at mini roundabout, Molly Millars Lane. 3rd rd on L is Oaklands Drive. After 100yds, R into cul-de-sac.* Light refreshments & teas. **Adm £2, chd free. Sun 12 Aug (2-6). Visitors also welcome by appt for groups up to 30 during May to Sept. Groups or individuals most welcome.**
Something of interest at every turn! Triangular plot lends itself to hidden corners. Different levels, arches and

pergolas lead to new vistas, well established borders of perennial planting, kitchen garden with raised beds, fruit cages and greenhouses. Front garden includes waterfall, stream and pond with private decked seating area. New area developed during winter 06. Wheelchairs limited by woodchip & shallow steps. 1st Prize Wokingham Best All Year Round Garden 2006.

③⑤ NEW TWO BRACKNELL GARDENS
RG12 9BH. *1m S of Bracknell town centre. From M4 take A329(M) to Bracknell and follow each garden directions.* Cream teas at Shaftesbury Close. **Combined adm £3, chd free. Suns 1 Apr; 1 July (2-5).**

DEVONIA
Broad Lane RG12 9BH. Andrew Radgick, 01344 450914, aradgick@aol.com. *At 3rd roundabout take 2nd exit into Broad Lane. 3rd house on L after railway bridge. From M3 take A322 towards Bracknell. At Horse & Groom roundabout take 4th exit into Broad Lane.* **Adm £2, chd free. Visitors also welcome by appt.**
1/3-acre plantaholic's garden designed for all seasons and planted to require minimal watering. Divided into several areas to provide appropriate conditions for over 1000 different shrubs, perennials, bulbs and alpines, incl many rare and unusual. Hot and dry front garden, shady and sheltered corners to the rear.

10 SHAFTESBURY CLOSE
Harmanswater RG12 9PX. Gill Cheetham, 01344 423440, gillcheetham@btopenworld. com. *At sports centre roundabout take exit to Harmanswater. Turn L on 2 mini roundabouts into Nightingale Crescent. Shaftesbury Close is 2nd turning on R.* **Adm £2.50, chd free. Visitors also welcome by appt.**
Woodland garden, at its best during winter and spring. Many different ericaceous shrubs and plants. Walled garden, scree and alpine beds. Beds planted to reflect climatic changes.

Exuberant cottage garden . . . an old chalk pit with plants, mostly scented, for dry chalky soil . . .

36 TWO LITTLEWICK GREEN GARDENS
Littlewick Green SL6 3QU, 01628 825718, lynnpenfold@waitrose.com. *2m W of Maidenhead on A4. Turn S into Jubilee Rd. Park as directed. The Thatch is next to cricket pitch. Pass Thatch for Rosemary Cottage, 200yds further on, off Coronation Rd.* Light refreshments & teas. **Combined adm £3.50, chd £1. Visitors welcome by appt, end Apr to mid-July.** Small village of houses around the green.

ROSEMARY COTTAGE
Lynne Emmerson
Small garden, limited access, around old gothic-style cottage (not open) with over 50 different clematis. Patio with seasonal colour. Secret gravel garden featuring spring bulbs and cottage favourites incl geraniums, campanulas, pinks and aquilegias, late summer phlox, rustic seating and water feature.

THE THATCH
Lynn & David Penfold. Visitors also welcome by appt, end April to mid-July.
³/₄-acre exuberant cottage garden complements thatched cottage (not open) on village green. Waterfall, pool, bog garden and terraced beds in old chalkpit. Plants, mostly scented, planted for dry, chalky soil. Herbaceous beds, shrubs, mature trees, tiny woodland garden. June is high-point of yr, for old roses especially, but garden is fresh and colourful in spring. Narrow bridge, one steep slope.

THE VYNE
See Hampshire.

37 ♦ WALTHAM PLACE GARDENS
Church Hill, White Waltham SL6 3JH. Mr & Mrs N Oppenheimer, 01628 825517, www.walthamplace.com. *3¹/₂ m S of Maidenhead. From M4 J8/9 take A404. Follow signs for White Waltham. Pass airfield on RH-side. Take L turn signed Windsor/Paley St. Pass the church, follow signs for parking. From Bracknell/Wokingham A3095 to A330 direction Maidenhead. Turn L at Paley St B3024 to White Waltham. Follow parking signs.* **Adm £3.50, chd £1. Fridays, May -Sept. A walk with the gardener at 11 & 2, other days by appointment. For NGS: Weds, 2 May to 26 Sept (10-4).**
New style naturalistic gardens (Henk Gerritsen) where weeds meet garden plants in an ancient framework of wonderful specimen trees. With organic kitchen garden and farm, several walled gardens, grasspath maze, lake and woodland with bluebells, camellias and rhododendrons. Explore the boundaries between nature and garden in our 170-acre nature inspired paradise. Featured in 'The English Garden' Oct 2006.

38 ♦ WELFORD PARK
Newbury RG20 8HU. Mrs J H Puxley, 01488 608203, www.welfordpark.co.uk. *6m NW of Newbury. On Lambourn Valley Rd. Entrance on Newbury-Lambourn rd. Please use clearly marked car park.* **House and Garden Adm £8.00 (by prior arrangement), Garden only Adm £3.50, chd free. 30 Jan-4 Mar Tues to Suns (not Fri) (11-5). 1-30 Jun, closed Suns. For NGS: Tue 26 June (2-6).**
Formal garden with herbaceous and rose pergolas. Spacious parkland and wonderful trees. Woodland walk by R Lambourn.

WEST SILCHESTER HALL
See Hampshire.

39 WOOLLEY PARK
Wantage OX12 8NJ. Mrs P Wroughton. *5m S of Wantage. A338. Turn L at sign to Woolley.* Home-made teas. **Adm £2.50, chd free. Sun 17 June (2-6).**
Large park, fine trees and views. Two linked walled gardens sensitively planted with a wide variety of interesting plants. Gravel paths.

Berkshire County Volunteers

County Organiser
Jeremy Bayliss, Loddon Lower Farm, Lambs Lane, Swallowfield, Reading RG7 1JE, 0118 988 3218, jeremy@baylissnet.com

County Treasurer
Hugh Priestley, Jennets Hill House, Stanford Dingley, Reading RG7 6JP, 01189 744349/0207 730 664, hughpriestley1@aol.com

Press & Publicity Officer
Fenja Anderson, Mariners, Mariners Lane, Southend, Reading RG7 6HU, 0118 974 5226, fenjaanderson@aol.com

Assistant County Organiser
Anthony Jones, Meadow House, Ashford Hill, Thatcham RG19 8BN, 0118 981 6005
Nina Preston, Timberlea, 17 Oaklands Drive, Wokingham RG41 2SA, 0118 978 4629, nina.fred@tinyonline.co.uk
Christopher Verity, Boundary House, Brimpton Common, Reading RG7 4RT, 0118 9814849

BUCKINGHAMSHIRE

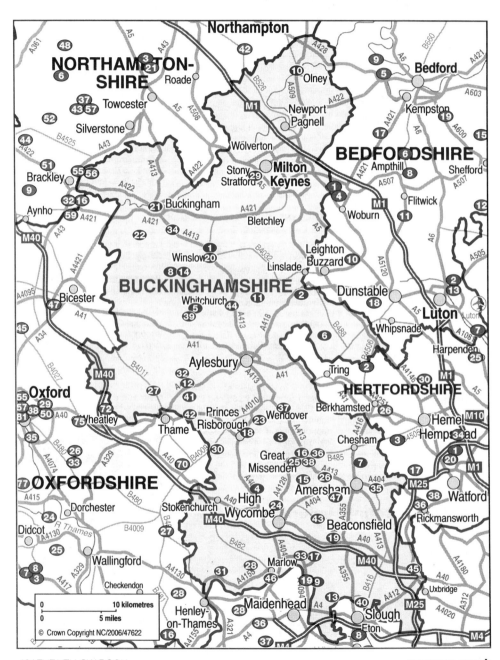

Opening Dates

February

SUNDAY 25
39 Quainton Gardens

March

SUNDAY 4
44 Whitchurch Gardens

SATURDAY 24
40 Stoke Poges Memorial Gardens

SUNDAY 25
5 Capricorner

April

SUNDAY 1
7 Chesham Bois House

SUNDAY 8
35 Overstroud Cottage

THURSDAY 12
16 Gipsy House
37 The Plant Specialist

SUNDAY 15
27 Long Crendon Gardens

SATURDAY 21
34 The Old Vicarage

SUNDAY 22
9 Cliveden
34 The Old Vicarage
39 Stoke Poges Memorial Gardens
46 Whitewalls

SUNDAY 29
5 Capricorner
35 6 Oldfield Close
44 Whitchurch Gardens

May

SUNDAY 6
40 The Manor House, Bledlow

MONDAY 7
2 Ascott
41 Turn End

THURSDAY 10
16 Gipsy House
37 The Plant Specialist

SUNDAY 13
7 Chesham Bois House
15 Fressingwood

WEDNESDAY 16
13 Dorneywood Garden
39 Stoke Poges Memorial Gardens

SUNDAY 20
36 Overstroud Cottage
45 The White House

SATURDAY 26
33 Old Thatch

SUNDAY 27
5 Capricorner
25 The Lee Gardens at Swan Bottom

MONDAY 28
14 East Claydon and Verney Junction Gardens

WEDNESDAY 30
13 Dorneywood Garden

June

THURSDAY 7
16 Gipsy House
38 The Plant Specialist

SATURDAY 9
10 Cowper & Newton Museum Gardens

SUNDAY 10
10 Cowper & Newton Museum Gardens
11 Cublington Gardens
26 Little Missenden Gardens
27 Long Crendon Gardens

THURSDAY 14
23 Homelands

SUNDAY 17
4 Bradenham Manor
24 Hughenden Manor
31 The Manor House, Hambleden
32 Nether Winchendon House
30 The Manor House, Bledlow
42 Tythrop Park

THURSDAY 21
28 Lords Wood

SATURDAY 23
37 11 The Paddocks

SUNDAY 24
5 Capricorner
12 Cuddington Gardens
17 Grange Drive Wooburn
22 Hillesden House
36 11 The Paddocks

WEDNESDAY 27
18 Greenways

THURSDAY 28
18 Greenways

FRIDAY 29
37 11 The Paddocks (Evening)
47 Woodrow Farm (Evening)

July

SUNDAY 1
6 Cheddington Gardens
29 Loughton Village Gardens
47 Woodrow Farm

WEDNESDAY 4
13 Dorneywood Garden

SUNDAY 8
7 Chesham Bois House

THURSDAY 12
16 Gipsy House
38 The Plant Specialist

FRIDAY 13
23 Homelands (Evening)

SUNDAY 15
45 The White House
46 Whitewalls

SATURDAY 28
13 Dorneywood Garden

SUNDAY 29
5 Capricorner

August

THURSDAY 9
23 Homelands

SUNDAY 26
5 Capricorner

MONDAY 27
2 Ascott

September

WEDNESDAY 5
9 Cliveden

SUNDAY 9
8 Claydon House
46 Whitewalls

SUNDAY 30
5 Capricorner

Gardens open to the public

2 Ascott
8 Claydon House
9 Cliveden
10 Cowper & Newton Museum Gardens
24 Hughenden Manor
31 Nether Winchendon House
33 Old Thatch
38 The Plant Specialist
39 Stoke Poges Memorial Gardens

By appointment only

1 Abbotts House
3 Blossoms
19 Hall Barn
20 19 Highfield Road
21 Hill House
43 Watercroft

The Gardens

① ABBOTTS HOUSE
10 Church Street, Winslow
MK18 3AN. Mrs Jane Rennie, 01296
712326. *9m N of Aylesbury. On A413
into Winslow. From town centre take
Horn St & R into Church St.* Adm
£2.50, chd free. Visitors welcome by
appt, groups max 20, best June-
July, refreshments if booked.
Garden on different levels divided into
4. Courtyard near house with white
wisteria arbour, woodland garden
(planted 2yrs ago) with rose arbour,
swimming pool garden with grasses.
Walled Victorian kitchen garden with
glass houses, potager, fruit pergola,
wall trained fruit and many
mediterranean plants. Featured in
'Gardening Which' June 2006.
🎍 ✿ ☕

② ◆ ASCOTT
Wing LU7 0PS. Sir Evelyn de
Rothschild, The National Trust,
01296 688242,
www.ascottestate.co.uk. *2m SW of
Leighton Buzzard, 8m NE of Aylesbury.*
Adm £4, chd £2. For NGS: Mons 7
May; 27 Aug (2 - last entry 5).
Combining Victorian formality with early
C20 natural style and recent plantings
to lead it into the C21, with a recently
completed garden designed by
Jacques and Peter Wirtz who
designed the gardens at Alnwick
Castle , and also a Richard Long
Sculpture. Terraced lawns with
specimen and ornamental trees,
panoramic views to the Chilterns.
Naturalised bulbs, mirror-image
herbaceous borders, impressive
topiary incl box and yew sundial.
🎍 ❁

③ BLOSSOMS
Cobblers Hill HP16 9PW. Dr & Mrs F
Hytten, 01494 863140. *2½m NW of
Great Missenden. By Rignall Rd,
signed Butler's Cross, to Kings Lane
1½m on R, then to top of Cobblers
Hill. Turn R at yellow stone marker &
after 50yds turn R again at stone,
marked Blossoms.* Adm £2.50, chd
free. Visitors welcome by appt, all yr,
no coach access, max 20 for home
made teas but no limit on visitor
numbers.
4 acres began as hill-top fields, plus 1-
acre beechwood. Lawns, old apple
orchard, small lake, water, troughs,
scree and patio gardens. Large areas
of bluebells, wild daffodils and other
spring bulbs. Large climbing roses,

flowering cherries and many other
interesting trees incl acers, eucalyptus
and willows. Foliage effects throughout
yr. Featured in 'Garden News' Apr &
'Gardening Which' Jun 2006.
🎍 ☕

④ NEW BRADENHAM MANOR
HP14 4HF. The National Trust,
07989 390940,
len.bernamont@national
trust.org.uk. *2½m NW of High
Wycombe, 5m S of Princes
Risborough. On A4010, turn by
Red Lion Pub, car park signed.*
Adm £3, chd £1. Sun 17 June
(1-5).
Unique opportunity to see the ongoing restoration of the C17
gardens, with views of the village
and countryside. Reinstated
Victorian summer border, yew
hedges, parterre and wilderness at
various stages of restoration.
Garden plan & interpretation,
guided tour at 2pm.
🎍

⑤ CAPRICORNER
Church Street HP22 4AP. Mrs G
Davis. *7m NW of Aylesbury, 7m SW of
Winslow. Off A41.* Adm £1, chd free.
Suns, 25 Mar; 29 Apr; 27 May; 24
June; 29 July; 26 Aug; 30 Sept (1-5).
Also open with Quainton Gardens.
Small garden planted for yr-round
interest with many scented plants,
winter flowering shrubs and bulbs,
small woodland glade.
🎍

⑥ CHEDDINGTON GARDENS
LU7 0RQ. *11m E of Aylesbury, 7m S
of Leighton Buzzard. Turn off B489 at
Pitstone. Turn off B488 at Cheddington
stn, turn off Cheddington/Long
Marston rd.* Home-made teas at
Methodist Chapel on the green.
Combined adm £4, chd free (15%
share to Chapel and St Giles
Church). Sun 1 July (2-6).
Long village with green. Maps for
visitors.
☕

BRIDGE COTTAGE
Mr & Mrs J Maddocks-Born
Informal garden of about 1 acre,
newly planted, with herbaceous
and shrub borders, wildlife and
ornamental pond, on the site of a
'ridge & furrow' field/fruit orchard.
❁

GENERALS YARD
Trefor Hamer
Formerly stables to the manor
house and home to a horse called
General. The gardens which were
landscaped from sloping fields
provide an eclectic mix of
herbaceous borders, quiet
corners and cameos of the
English countryside with stunning
views.

THE OLD POST OFFICE
Alan & Wendy Tipple
Cottage-style garden, softly
planted with lavender, roses,
clematis, herbaceous borders,
shaded area and a small pond.
Interesting low maintenance gravel
garden to front.

ROSE COTTAGE
Mrs Margery Jones
½-acre cottage garden filled with
small rooms with max use of
space. A balance of evergreens
and deciduous resulting in a
garden for all seasons, incl a late
border with herbs, vegetable
parterre and wildlife pond.
❁

21 STATION ROAD
Mr & Mrs P Jay
½-acre informal garden with wild
flower and wildlife conservation
area, herbaceous and shrub
borders, trees, herbs and kitchen
garden.
✿

WOODSTOCK COTTAGE
Mr & Mrs D Bradford
Front garden laid to gravel with
assorted shrubs. Back courtyard
and patio with small fountain at
base of ancient elder tree.
❁

⑦ CHESHAM BOIS HOUSE
85 Bois Lane, Chesham Bois
HP6 6DF. Julia Plaistowe, 01494
726476,
www.cheshamboishouse.co.uk. *1m
N of Amersham-on-the-Hill. From
Amersham-on-the-Hill follow
Sycamore Rd, over double mini
roundabout, which turns into Bois
Lane. Past village shops, house is ½m
on L. Parking in road or on R at school
& at scout hut.* Home-made teas. Adm
£3, chd free. Suns 1 Apr; 13 May
(2-5.30); 8 July (2-6). Visitors also
welcome by appt.
Up a drive of mostly old lime trees, a
late Georgian house (not open)
surrounded by 3-acre garden of yr-

round interest. Walled garden, small ornamental canal and rill with gazebo, herbaceous borders with tender and unusual plants, clipped trees and lawns with winding paths through old orchard. Primroses, daffodils and hellebores in spring. C13 and C14 excavations possibly continuing. Channel 4 filmed a Time Team dig in the garden, to be shown Jan, Feb or Mar 2007. Gravel drive.

    ⅄ 🛝 ♨

8 NEW ◆ CLAYDON HOUSE
Middle Claydon MK18 2EX. Sir Edmund & Lady Verney, 01296 738061, daphneverney@tiscali.co.uk. *4m S of Buckingham. Signed, nr village, adjacent to church.* **Adm £3.50, chd free. Sat-Wed, 24 Mar-31 Oct (1-5). For NGS: Sun 9 Sept (2-5).**
Large country house garden under gradual redevelopment and redesign. Herbaceous borders, mixed plantings, shrubs, annuals and tender perennials. 2-acre Victorian kitchen garden planted with vegetables and flowers and adjacent walled flower garden with large pond, borders, and a restored Victorian Glasshouse. Chemically free vegetables. Attractions around National Trust house.

    ⅄ 🛝 ♨

9 ◆ CLIVEDEN
Taplow SL6 0JA. The National Trust. *2m N of Taplow. Leave M4 at J7 or M40 at J4 & follow brown tourism signs.* **Adm £7.50, chd £3.70. For NGS: Sun 22 Apr; Wed 5 Sept (2-6).**
Separate gardens within extensive grounds 1st laid out in C18. Water garden, secret garden, topiary, herbaceous borders, woodland walks and views of R Thames. Timber steps lead down yew tree walk to river.

    ⅄ 🛝

10 ◆ COWPER & NEWTON MUSEUM GARDENS
Olney MK46 4AJ. Mrs E Knight, 01234 711516/713719, www. cowperandnewtonmuseum.org.uk. *5m N of Newport Pagnell. 12m S of Wellingborough. On A509. Please park on Market Place, Cattle Market Car Park or in High Street.* **Adm £2, chd free. Tues to Sat, Mar to Dec (10.30-4.30). For NGS: Sat 9, Sun 10 June (10.30-4.30).**
Restored walled flower garden with

plants pre 1800, many mentioned by C18 poet, William Cowper, who said of himself 'Gardening was, of all employments, that in which I succeeded best'. Summerhouse garden in Victorian kitchen style with organic, new and old vegetables. Herb and medicinal plant borders in memory of the garden's original use by an apothecary. Biblical planting in commemoration of Rev. John Newton's bi-centenary. Featured in 'Gardening Which' 2006.

    ⅄ 🛝 ♨

Herb and medicinal plant borders in memory of the garden's original use . . .

11 CUBLINGTON GARDENS
LU7 0LQ. *5m SE of Winslow, 5m NE of Aylesbury. From Aylesbury take A413 Buckingham Rd. After 4m, at Whitchurch, turn R to Cublington.* Home-made teas at The Old Rectory & The Old Stables. **Combined adm £4, chd free. Sun 10 June (2-6).**
♨

LARKSPUR HOUSE
Wing Road.
Mr & Mrs S I Jenkins
S-facing family garden planted in 1996 to create a mix of moods and style, eclectic planting suggests a Mediterranean patio, moving to a tropical shade garden then to a cottage garden. Small kitchen garden.

THE OLD RECTORY
High Street. Mr & Mrs J Naylor
2-acre country garden with herbaceous border, rose beds, shrubs and mature trees, vegetables, ponds and climbing plants.

    🛝

THE OLD STABLES
Reads Lane. Mr & Mrs George
Varied established gardens surround C18 house (not open).

Borders, trees, water features, lawns, pots, vegetables. Restored walls enclose unusual walled garden. Maze, putting green, small orchard, tree house, rose garden and revolving summer-house. Some gravel paths.

    🛝

12 CUDDINGTON GARDENS
nr Thame HP18 0AP. *3½m NE Thame, 5m SW Aylesbury. Off A418. Parking signed in village. Wheelchair visitor parking phone 01844 290129.* Home-made teas at Tyringham Hall. **Combined adm £4, chd free. Sun 24 June (2-6).**
Very picturesque village. Cottage garden plantings provide colour throughout and complement the pretty village greens. C13 church with attractive churchyard and wild-flower reserve. Romantic dell with waterfall in Tibbys Lane adjoining Tyringham Hall. Plants at The Bernard Hall. Art gallery at Dadbrook House. Winners of Thames & Chiltern in Bloom, 2nd in Best Kept Village Awards, 2006.

DADBROOK HOUSE
Gerald & Clico Kingsbury, 01844 290129, www.dadbrookgallery.co.uk.
Visitors also welcome by appt in Jun & July.
Imaginatively laid out to incl formal area with knot garden, ha ha flanked by mixed borders, topiary, small lake, gravel courtyard, walled kitchen garden, fine trees, willow and wooden statues. Wheelchair users phone for special entrance.

    ⅄ 🛝

THE OLD STABLES
Mr & Mrs R Bates
Walled, flower arranger's garden providing peaceful setting with wide variety of plants in mixed beds and containers. Arched walkway planted with roses, wisteria and other climbers. Well-stocked conservatory.

    ⅄

TYRINGHAM HALL
Mrs Sherry Scott
Medieval house that will be partly open. Flower filled patios, large lawns, herbaceous borders. Mature trees, bog area featuring water garden with tufted ducks. Raised beds with organic vegetables.

    ♨

⑬ DORNEYWOOD GARDEN
Burnham SL1 8PY. The National Trust, 01628 665361, secretary. dorneywood@btopenworld.com. *1m E of Taplow, 5m S of Beaconsfield. From Burnham village take Dropmore Rd, at end of 30mph limit take R fork into Dorneywood Rd. Entrance is 1m on R. From M40 J2, take A355 to Slough then 1st R to Burnham, 2m then 2nd L after Jolly Woodman, signed Dorneywood Rd. Dorneywood is about 1m on L.* Adm £4, chd 5+ £3, NT members £3. Weds 16, 30 May; 4 July, Sat 28 July (2-5). **All adm by e-mail or written application (to The Secretary) at least 2 weeks before open day.** Visitors also welcome by appt. By written application, April-July, groups 15-50.
6-acre country house garden on several levels with herbaceous borders, greenhouses, rose, cottage and kitchen gardens, lily pond and conservatory. Gravel paths.
&. ✕ ⊛ ☕

⑭ EAST CLAYDON AND VERNEY JUNCTION GARDENS
MK18 2NA. *2½m SW Winslow.* Home-made teas at Village Hall. **Combined adm £4, chd free. Mon 28 May (2-6).**
Attractive village with beautiful C13 church.
☕

1 EMERALD CLOSE
Mr & Mrs L Woodhouse
Small garden with collection of deciduous and coniferous bonsai.

INGLENOOKS
St Mary's Road MK18 2NA.
Mr & Mrs D Polhill
Cottage garden surrounding C17 thatched cottage (not open). Some gravel paths.
&.

3 JUBILEE COTTAGES
Mr & Mrs R O'Connell
Established narrow mid-terrace garden with separate 'rooms' linked by a boardwalk. Vegetable garden and fruit trees.
✕ ⊛

LITTLEWORTH FARM
Verney Junction MK18 2LA.
Mrs Elspeth O'Halloran. *From E Claydon, take Sandhill Rd, 1m, 1st R*
½ acre with walled herbaceous and formal kitchen gardens.

THE OLD VICARAGE
Church Way MK18 2ND. Mr & Mrs Nigel Turnbull, 01296 712127, turnbullesther@hotmail.com. Visitors also welcome by appt during June.
1½-acre on clay, started in 1991 and aimed at yr-round interest. Shrubs, herbaceous and secret dell garden, a wall of ceanothus. Natural clay-lined pond. Planting to encourage wildlife. Access via gravel drive.
&. ✕ ⊛

THE PUMP HOUSE
St Mary's Road MK18 2NA. Mr & Mrs P M Piddington
¾ acre garden with mature trees, shrubs, borders and fishponds.
&.

ETON COLLEGE GARDENS
See Berkshire.

EVENLEY WOOD GARDEN
See Northamptonshire.

⑮ FRESSINGWOOD
Hare Lane, Little Kingshill HP16 0EF. Mr & Mrs J & M Bateson. *1m S of Gt Missenden, 4m W of Amersham. From A413 Amersham to Aylesbury rd, turn L at Chiltern Hospital, signed Gt & Little Kingshill. Take 1st L into Nags Head Lane. Turn R under railway bridge & 1st L into New Rd. Continue to top, turn into Hare Lane, 1st house on R.* Home-made teas. **Adm £2.50, chd free. Sun 13 May (2-6).**
½ acre garden with yr-round colour. Shrubbery, small formal garden, herb garden, pergolas with wisteria, roses and clematis, topiary. Landscaped terrace. Formal lily pond and bonsai collection. Many interesting features.
&. ✕ ⊛ ☕

⑯ GIPSY HOUSE
Whitefield Lane, Gt Missenden HP16 0BP. Mrs Felicity Dahl, 01494 890465. *5m NW Amersham. Take A413 to Gt Missenden. From High St turn into Whitefield Lane, continue under railway bridge. Small Georgian house on R. Park in field opp house.* Home-made teas. **Adm £4, combined with The Plant Specialist, chd free. Thurs 12 Apr; 10 May; 7 June; 12 July (2-5).**
Home of the late Roald Dahl. York stone terrace, pleached lime walk to writing hut bordered with hosta, hellebore and allium. Sunken garden

with water feature, sundial garden with topiary oaks, borders planted with herbaceous perennials and assorted roses in themed colours. Small walled vegetable garden with terraced beds, espalier fruits, herbs and greenhouse with vine, peaches and nectarines. Wild-flower meadow. Maze, Gipsy Caravan and Willy Wonka's Truck.
✕ ☕

⑰ GRANGE DRIVE WOOBURN
Wooburn Green HP10 0QD. *On A4094, 2m SW of A40, between Bourne End & Wooburn. From the church, heading to Maidenhead, Grange Drive is on the L.* Home-made teas at Magnolia House. **Combined adm £3, chd free. Sun 24 June (2-5).**
Private tree-lined drive which forms the entrance to a country house.
☕

MAGNOLIA HOUSE
Alan & Elaine Ford
½ acre containing 24 mature trees incl magnificent copper beech and magnolia reaching the rooftop. Small cactus bed, ferns, stream leading to pond overlooked by acers, small vegetable garden and greenhouses.
✕ ⊛

THE SHADES
Pauline & Maurice Kirkpatrick
Drive approached through mature trees, area of shade-loving plants, beds of shrubs, roses and herbaceous plants. Rear garden with working well surrounded by shrubs, conifers and acers. Original green slate water features and scree garden with alpine plants.
✕ ⊛

⑱ NEW GREENWAYS
Whiteleaf HP27 0LY. Mr & Mrs K Muras. *3m E Princes Risborough. 4m NW Gt Missenden. From A4010 take Gt Missenden turn, 1st R into Upper Icknield Way, ½m 1st L, follow signs.* Cream teas. **Adm £2.50, chd free. Wed 27, Thur 28 June (2-6).**
Pretty cottage garden on thin chalk surrounding a C16 thatched cottage with climbing roses, delphiniums and lavender hedges. Stunning views across the Chilterns in an area of outstanding natural beauty.
✕ ⊛ ☕

⑲ HALL BARN
Windsor End, Beaconsfield
HP9 2SG. The Hon Mrs Farncombe.
1/2 m S of Beaconsfield. Lodge gate
300yds S of St Mary and All Saints'
Church in Old Town centre. Adm £3,
chd free. Visitors welcome by appt,
apply in writing to the owner as
above.
Historical landscaped garden laid out
between 1680-1730 for the poet
Edmund Waller and his descendants.
Features 300-yr-old 'cloud formation'
yew hedges, formal lake and vistas
ending with classical buildings and
statues. Wooded walks around the
grove offer respite from the heat on
sunny days. One of the original
gardens opening in 1927. Gravel
paths.
&

Slate herb
garden, sundial
table and hosta
hotel, young
and old alike
love the quirky
features . . .

⑳ 19 HIGHFIELD ROAD
Winslow MK18 3DU. Mrs Gwladys
Tonge, 18002 01296 713489 (text
direct/type talk),
mail@gwladystonge.co.uk. 5m SE of
Buckingham, 9m N of Aylesbury. On
A413 Winslow to Buckingham, take
last turning L, 200yds after garage,
50yds before turning to Great
Horwood. Adm £4 inc tea & cake,
chd free. Visitors welcome by appt,
individuals or groups up to 18.
Very small garden with extensive range
of attractive hardy plants providing
beauty and excitement for each
season. Trees, shrubs, rose pergola,
clematis and other climbers, bulbs, incl
interesting snowdrop collection, ferns,
grasses, evergreen and herbaceous
perennials demonstrate ingenious use
of space and grow happily together.
✖ ⊛ ☕

㉑ HILL HOUSE
Castle Street MK18 1BS. Mr & Mrs P
Thorogood, 07860 714758,
llt@pjt.powernet.co.uk. Buckingham
centre. On L of vehicle entrance to
Parish Church (spire very visible).
Castle St clearly marked as you face

Old Town Hall at central town
roundabout. Home-made teas. Adm
£2.50, chd free. Visitors welcome by
appt, from the end of May-Nov, any
size group.
Peaceful 1/3-acre town garden on old
castle walls, whose aim is ease of
maintenance, yr-round interest and
colour in relatively small space. 2
shallow steps may require help.
& ✖ ⊨ ☕

㉒ HILLESDEN HOUSE
Church End, Hillesden MK18 4DB.
Mr & Mrs R M Faccenda. 3m S of
Buckingham. Next to church in
Hillesden. Home-made teas. Adm
£3.50, chd free. Sun 24 June (2-5).
By superb perpendicular church
'Cathedral in the Fields'. Lawns,
shrubberies, rose, alpine and foliage
gardens. Clipped hedges,
conservatory. Surrounded by park with
red deer. Large lakes with ornamental
duck and carp. Large wild flower
areas. Views over countryside and
wonderful walks. Many birds and other
wildlife. More new lakes and large area
planted with trees and shrubs.
& ✖ ⊛ ☕

㉓ HOMELANDS
Springs Lane, Ellesborough
HP17 0XD. Jean & Tony Young,
01296 622306. 6m SE of Aylesbury,
4m NE of Princes Risborough. On
B4010, 1 1/2 m W of Wendover. Springs
Lane is between the Village Hall at
Butlers Cross and St. Peter and St.
Paul's Church. Narrow lane, uneven
surface. Home-made teas. Adm
£2.50, chd free. Thurs 14 June; 9
Aug (2-5). Evening Opening wine,
Fri 13 July (6-8.30). Visitors also
welcome by appt Jun to Sept.
3/4-acre garden on chalk with adjoining
wild flower meadow. Wildlife pond,
rockery, bog garden, water features.
Gazebo and pergola walk, wide range
of mixed shrub and herbaceous
borders. Hidden corners, sitting out
areas, gravel bed and vegetable plot.
& ☕

㉔ ♦ HUGHENDEN MANOR
High Wycombe HP14 4LA. The
National Trust, 01494 755573,
www.nationaltrust.org.uk. 1 1/2 m N of
High Wycombe. On W side of Great
Missenden Rd A4128, past church,
into NT woodland car-park. House
and Garden Adm £6.40, chd £3.20,
family £16, Garden only Adm £2.60,
chd £1.90. 3 Mar to 28 Oct, Wed to
Sun. For NGS: Sun 17 June (11-5).

Mary Anne Disraeli's colour schemes
inspire spring and summer bedding in
formal parterre. Unusual conifers,
planted from photographs taken at
time of Disraeli's death. Old English
apple orchard with picnic area. Beech
woodland walks. Mediterranean
border. The walled garden under redevelopment will be open too.
Interpretation talks & guides - Meet the
Gardener - Hughenden, 60yrs in trust.
Disabled parking next to walled
garden. Arboretum requires strong
helper, some gravel too.
& ✖ ⊛ ☕

**㉕ THE LEE GARDENS AT
SWAN BOTTOM**
Gt Missenden HP16 9NU. 3m N of
Great Missenden, 3m SE of Wendover.
Follow A413 Gt Missenden to
Wendover. Turn 3rd R up Rocky Lane.
After 2m turn L at 1st Xrds. 200yds
turn R down drive. Home-made teas at
Kingswood House. Combined adm
£4.50, chd free. Sun 27 May (2-5).
Swan Bottom is a hamlet less that 1m
N of the secluded and picturesque
village of The Lee, at the centre of
which is the green created by Arthur
Liberty who founded Libertys of
Regent Street. C13 church with fine
wall paintings.
☕

2 KINGSWOOD COTTAGES
Mr & Mrs J Swain, 01494
837752, swaino@talk21.com.
Visitors also welcome by appt
in May & Jun, groups 20+.
2-acre garden and woodland
surrounded by meadows. Winding
paths lead to hidden surprises
and sculptures. Slate herb garden,
secluded sundial table, specimen
trees, wildlife pond, hosta hotel.
Young and old alike love the
quirky features. Featured in
'Amateur Gardening' May 2006.
Gravel drive, some narrow paths.
& ✖

KINGSWOOD HOUSE
Mr & Mrs T Hart, 01494 837328,
judy.hart@virgin.net. Visitors
also welcome by appt in May &
June, groups 20+.
4-acre mature family garden in an
'Area of Outstanding Natural
Beauty'. Features incl a white
garden surrounding a formal pond
with fountain, wildlife pond, hot
colour borders, sundial garden,
fruit and vegetable areas. Some
gravel paths.
& ✖ ⊛

26 NEW LITTLE MISSENDEN GARDENS

HP7 0RD. 2½m NW of Old Amersham. On A413. Home-made teas at Mill End Cottages. **Combined adm £4, chd free. Sun 10 June (2-6).** Attractive Chiltern village in an area of outstanding natural beauty. Anglo-saxon church built 975. Village used several times as a 'set' for film and TV.

NEW HOLLYDYKE HOUSE
Bob and Sandra Wetherall
3-acre garden, herbaceous borders, shrubs and trees. White garden, old fashioned roses, koi and lily ponds. Small stumpery.

NEW THE MANOR HOUSE
Mr & Mrs T A Cuff
9-acres, in a glorious setting. Gravel paths. Woodland path not circular.

1 MILL END COTTAGES
Philip & Eileen Sharman
1-acre semi-formal topiary garden. Open views, glasshouse and vegetable area. Rose pergolas, architectural and sculptural features. Initial gravel access.

NEW MISSENDEN HOUSE
Wilf Stevenson
A mixture of traditional and modern. Herbaceous and lawns together with a Christopher Bradley Hole zen garden and bamboo playground.

27 LONG CRENDON GARDENS

HP18 9EF. 2m N of Thame. On Thame/Bicester rd B4011. Teas at Church House (Apr & Jun), at Croft House (Jun). **Combined adm £3 Apr; £4 June, chd free (10% share to Crendon Day Centre). Suns 15 Apr; 10 June (2-6).** Attractive large village with many old/listed buildings. Maps available for all visitors.

BAKER'S CLOSE
Mr & Mrs Peter Vaines. Not open 10 Jun.
2 acres on SW slope. Partly walled with courtyard, terraced lawns, rockery with pond, roses, shrubs, herbaceous plantings and wild area.

BARRY'S CLOSE
Mr & Mrs Richard Salmon. Not open 10 Jun.
2-acre sloping garden with interesting collection of trees and shrubs. Herbaceous border, spring-fed pools and water garden.
&

BRADDENS YARD
Mr & Mrs P Simpson. Not open 15 Apr.
½-acre walled garden largely created over past 15yrs. Collection of roses, herbaceous and climbing plants. Arched walk with clematis, honeysuckle and roses, pond and small bothy garden.

CROFT HOUSE
Cdr & Mrs Peter Everett. Not open 15 Apr.
½ acre walled garden with a variety of plants and shrubs, some unusual and of interest to flower arrangers. Water feature, greenhouse and conservatory.
✕

NEW KETCHMORE HOUSE
Mr & Mrs C Plumb. Not open 15 Apr.
Very attractive wildlife friendly cottage garden laid out in 3 sections; courtyard with raised pond, entertaining area with bog garden and lawn and vegetable area. Great variety of plants and shrubs.
& ✕

MANOR HOUSE
Mr & Mrs N West
6-acre garden, lawns sweep down to 2 ornamental lakes, each with small island, walk along lower lake with many varieties of willow. New herbaceous borders, fine views towards Chilterns. Fairly steep slopes to lakes.
& ✕

MULBERRY HOUSE
Mr & Mrs C Weston. Not open 15 Apr.
1-acre, old vicarage garden, recently restored. Set amongst mature trees, now incl formal knot garden, woodland walk, pond, vegetable garden, numerous beds and lawns, a notable monkey puzzle tree and a mulberry tree.
✕

THE OLD CROWN
Mr & Mrs R H Bradbury
1¼ acre on SW slope. More than 250 assorted roses, colourful annual and perennial plants in numerous beds, incl 50-60 clematis, flowering shrubs, assorted colourful pots and containers, statues, 2 sizeable vegetable plots. Great variety and very many spring bulbs.
& ✿

THORNTON COTTAGE
Charlotte Duncan,
www.lotteduncan.com. Not open 15 April.
Typical country cottage garden with a beautiful outlook. Feature of flowering shrubs in unspoilt setting with herbaceous beds and borders. Many roses - bushes, ramblers and climbers. Herb and vegetable garden. New sunken patio and courtyard with borders.
✕

Old fashioned roses, lily ponds . . .

28 NEW LORDS WOOD

Frieth Road SL7 2QS. Mr & Mrs Messum. 1½m NW Marlow. Off A4155, turn at Platts Garage into Oxford Rd, towards Frieth, 1½m. Garden is 100yds past Marlow Common turn, on L. Teas. **Adm £4, chd free. Thu 21 June (11-5).** 5-acre garden plus orchard, woodland and meadow with superb views over the Chilterns. Kitchen, cut flower and herb gardens, herbaceous and mixed borders with varied planting styles, water garden and rockery, summer garden and 'native species' garden. Many pots and planters with summer bedding. Much developed over the last 8 yrs, with many recent planting schemes. Gravel, steep slopes.
& ✕ ☕

29 LOUGHTON VILLAGE GARDENS

MK8 9ER. Mr R Blackburn. 1m W of Central Milton Keynes. Between Watling Street (V4) and Portway roundabout (A5). Off Portway (H5) then

follow signs. Car park in paddock - signed. Light refreshments & teas at All Saints' Church Room. **Combined adm £4, chd free (share to All Saints' Parish Church). Sun 1 July (11.30-5.30).** A village at the heart of the new town of Milton Keynes. Maps for all visitors. Flower Festival in church, display & demonstration stalls.

BEECH COTTAGE
3 School Lane. **Mrs C Rose** This listed cottage and barn are situated in the picturesque setting of Loughton's Conservation Area. Colourful garden contains an ancient copper beech and walnut tree with patios, containers and hanging baskets. Featured in 'Garden Answers' 2006.

GARDENERS COTTAGE
5 School Lane. **Sally & Don Reid** Georgian Cottage adjacent to All Saints Church. Following several years under cover, the garden was newly created in 2001. York stone patio steps down to mixed beds. Informal cottage style planting with herb and vegetable beds.

NEW 82 LINCESLADE GROVE
Peter & Rosemary Scott, 01908 236737, rosemary.scott@tesco.net. **Visitors also welcome by appt, Apr to Aug, groups 10 max.** Professionally landscaped modern garden planted and developed by owners over past 4yrs. Pebbled-bordered pond, variety of grasses, shrubs, climbers, fruits, vegetables and herbaceous plants to provide yr-round interest with low maintenance.

2 LUCY LANE
Mr & Mrs P Wason Landscaped garden wrapped around a modern bungalow. Natural slope and increasingly dry climate have influenced the design of rockery and gravel beds, patio, pond and mixed borders.

MANOR COTTAGE
Gillian O'Reilly
2³/₄ acres on the edge of Loughton Brook, created from a wilderness 22yrs ago. Now a beautiful cottage garden, mixed herbaceous borders, fruit trees, water feature, ancient poplar tree.

NORDBERIE
John & Rozi Rowcroft James Surprisingly mature garden, 33x45ft, constructed by the present owners in 2001/2. Combines traditional and modern ideas including herb garden, walled patio, fish pond, grasses, climbers and shrubs surrounding a central lawn.

30 THE MANOR HOUSE, BLEDLOW
Bledlow HP27 9PB. **The Lord & Lady Carrington,** 020 7585 4243 or 32a Ovington Street, London SW3 1LR. *9m NW of High Wycombe, 3m SW of Princes Risborough. 1/2 m off B4009 in middle of Bledlow village.* Teas (May), Home-made teas (Jun). **Adm £5, chd free. Suns 6 May; 17 June (2-6). Visitors also welcome by appt.** Paved garden, parterres, shrub borders, old roses and walled kitchen garden. Water garden with paths, bridges and walkways, fed by 14 chalk springs. Also 2 acres with sculptures and landscaped planting. No wheelchair access to Lyde Garden.

31 THE MANOR HOUSE, HAMBLEDEN
Hambleden RG9 6SG. **Maria Carmela, Viscountess Hambleden.** *3¹/₂ m NE Henley-on-Thames, 8m SW High Wycombe. 1m N of A4155.* Teas at Hambleden Church Hall. **Adm £3.50, chd free. Sun 17 June (2-6).** Informal garden, sweeping lawns, mature trees and an exceptional rose garden designed by Peter Beales with a profusion of old fashioned scented roses. Large terrace on the S side of the house takes you to a magnificent conservatory with stunning plants climbing 30ft.

32 ◆ NETHER WINCHENDON HOUSE
Nether Winchendon HP18 0DY. **Mr Robert Spencer Bernard.** *6m SW of Aylesbury, 6m from Thame.* Teas, weather permitting. **Adm £3, chd free. For NGS: Sun 17 June (2-5).** 5 acres; fine and rare trees and shrubs, variety of hedges, herbaceous borders and naturalised spring bulbs. Recent changes. Medieval and Tudor manor house (not open) in picturesque village with beautiful church.

ODNEY CLUB
See Berkshire.

33 ◆ OLD THATCH
Coldmoorholme Lane, Well End SL8 5PS. **Jacky Hawthorne,** 01628 527518, info@jackyhawthorne.co.uk. *3m E Marlow, 1m NW Bourne End. Off A4155. Thatched house on L just before the Spade Oak PH. Car park 100yds on, towards the R Thames.* **Adm £3, chd £1. Sun 27 May, Sats & Suns, Jun to Aug, Aug Bank Hol (11-5). For NGS: Sat 26 May (11-5).** Listed thatched cottage (not open), famous home of Enid Blyton and source of many of her stories. 2 acres, derelict in 1990, now contain beautiful palettes of colour, stunning ornamental grasses and wonderful design features. Cottage garden, lavender terrace, rose arbour, formal garden, water circle. Teas in room claimed by EB to be Dick Turpin's stable, containing secret treasures.

34 THE OLD VICARAGE
Thornborough Road, Padbury MK18 2AH. **Mr & Mrs H Morley-Fletcher,** 01280 813045, belindamf@freenet.co.uk. *2m S of Buckingham, 4m NW of Winslow. On A413, signed in village.* Home-made teas. **Adm £3, chd free. Sat 21, Sun 22 Apr (2-6). Visitors also welcome by appt.** 2¹/₂ acres on 3 levels, flowering shrubs and trees. Vegetable garden, pond and sunken garden, parterre and millennium arch. Magnolias and trilliums. Sunken garden can be viewed from above by wheelchair users.

35 6 OLDFIELD CLOSE
Little Chalfont HP6 6SU. **Jolyon & Phyllis Lea,** 01494 762384. *3m E of Amersham. Take A404 E through Little Chalfont, 1st R after railway bridge, R again into Oakington Ave.* Home-made teas. **Adm £2, chd free. Sun 29 Apr (2-5). Visitors also welcome by appt.** Mature ¹/₆ acre garden of shrub borders, peat beds, rock plants, troughs and alpine house. Over 2,000 species and varieties of rare and interesting plants, incl spring bulbs, cyclamen and dwarf rhododendrons. Wide range of plants.

36 OVERSTROUD COTTAGE
The Dell, Frith Hill, Gt Missenden
HP16 9QE. Mr & Mrs Jonathan
Brooke, 01494 862701,
susie@jandsbrooke.co.uk. *1/2m E Gt
Missenden. Turn E off A413 at Gt
Missenden onto B485 Frith Hill to
Chesham rd. White Gothic cottage set
back in lay-by 100yds up hill on L.
Parking on R at church.* Cream teas at
Parish Church. **Adm £2.50, chd 50p.
Suns 8 Apr; 20 May (2-6).** Visitors
also welcome by appt, Mar to Jun,
groups 15+.
Artistic chalk garden on 2 levels.
Collection of C17/C18 plants. Potager.
Snowdrops, narcissi, hellebores,
succulents, primulas, pulmonarias,
geraniums, species roses and lily
pond. Garden studio with painting
exhibition.

Space used to create illusion of size . . .

37 11 THE PADDOCKS
Wendover HP22 6HE. Mr & Mrs E
Rye. *5m from Aylesbury, on A413. At
Wendover after approx 1/2m, turn L at
mini-roundabout into Wharf Rd.
Entrance is 2nd on L. From Gt
Missenden, turn L at Clock Tower, then
R at next mini-roundabout.* **Adm £2,
chd free. Sat 23, Sun 24 June (2-6).
Evening Opening £2, wine, Fri 29
June (6-8.30).**
Small peaceful garden with mixed
borders of colourful herbaceous
perennials and a special show of David
Austin roses and delphiniums. Cool
hosta walk and tremendous variety of
plants in a small area. White garden
with peaceful arbour 'The Magic of
Moonlight'. Many unusual plants.

PATCHWORK
See Hertfordshire.

38 ◆ THE PLANT SPECIALIST
Whitefield Lane, Gt Missenden
HP16 0BH. Sean Walter, 01494
866650. *5m NW Amersham. A413 to
Gt Missenden. Whitefield Lane opp*

---

*Missenden Abbey. Under railway
bridge on the L.* **Adm £4, combined
with Gypsy House, chd free.** Thur,
Fri, Sat (10-6) Apr to Oct. For NGS:
Thurs 12 Apr; 10 May; 7 June; 12
July (2-5).
Nursery with herbaceous perennials
and grasses, many planted in display
gardens.

39 QUAINTON GARDENS
HP22 4BW. *7m NW of Aylesbury, 7m
SW of Winslow. Nr Waddesdon turn
off A41. Light refreshments & teas at
Thorngumbald.* **Combined adm £2,
chd free. Sun 25 Feb (12-4).**
Charming village with green and
windmill.

CAPRICORNER
Mrs Davis
(See separate entry).

THORNGUMBALD
13 Station Road. Jane Lydall
Small heavily planted cottage
garden designed for yr-round
interest and to please all the
senses. Drifts of snowdrops,
hellebores and crocus form carpet
under clipped evergreens and
shrubs. Partial wheelchair access.

RAGGED HALL
See Hertfordshire.

**40 ◆ STOKE POGES MEMORIAL
GARDENS**
Church Lane SL2 4NZ. South Bucks
District Council, 01753 537619,
graham.pattison@southbucks.gov.
uk. *1m N of Slough, 1m S of Stoke
Poges. From Stoke Poges take B416
towards Slough, turn R at crossroads
with Church Lane. From Slough take
Stoke Poges Lane which leads into
Church Lane. Next to St Giles Church.*
Adm £3.50, chd free. Open all yr,
dawn to dusk. For NGS: **Sat 24 Mar;
Sun 22 Apr; Wed 16 May (2-5).**
Unique 20-acre Grade II registered
garden constructed 1934-9. Rock and
water gardens, sunken colonnade,
rose garden incl 500 individual gated
gardens. Spring garden, bulbs,
wisteria, rhododendrons. Recently
completed £1m renovation. First
flowering of recently replanted main
avenue - 7000 bulbs, narcissus 'Mount
Hood' and tulip 'Purissima'. Guided
tours on the hour 2, 3, 4pm.

---

41 TURN END
Townside, Haddenham HP17 8BG.
Peter Aldington. *3m NE of Thame,
5m SW of Aylesbury. Turn off A418 to
Haddenham. Turn at Rising Sun to
Townside. Please park at a distance
with consideration for neighbours.*
Teas. **Adm £3, chd £1 (share to Turn
End Charitable Trust). Mon 7 May (2-
5.30).**
Architect's own post-war listed house
(not open). Garden less than 1 acre,
space used to create illusion of size.
Series of enclosed gardens, sunken or
raised, sunny or shady, each different
yet harmonious, contrast with lawns,
borders and glades. Spring bulbs,
irises, old roses and climbers.
Courtyard with fish pool. Wheelchairs
need help through special entrance,
gravel paths.

Black Hamburgh and Muscat Hamburgh vines from Hampton Court, 150 years ago . . .

VERSIONS FARM
See Northamptonshire.

TURWESTON MILL
See Northamptonshire.

42 TYTHROP PARK
Kingsey HP17 8LT. Jonathan &
Medina Marks, www.tythrop.com.
*2m E of Thame, 4m NW of Princes
Risborough. Via A4129, lodge gates
just outside Kingsey.* Cream teas. **Adm
£4.50, chd free (share to NCH Action
for Children). Sun 17 June (2-6).**
7 acres. Formal gardens with many fine
trees and shrubs. Intricate dwarf box
parterre with fountains. Large walled
garden with wide variety of fruit trees,
soft fruits and vegetables, divided by
rows of roses and flowers. Magnificent
greenhouse containing Black
Hamburgh and Muscat Hamburgh
vines propagated from vine at
Hampton Court 150yrs ago. Secluded
water garden with attractive walks and
old roses. Nut grove, wilderness area,
arboretum.

43 WATERCROFT
Church Road, Penn HP10 8NX. Mr &
Mrs Paul Hunnings, 01494 816535,
mary@maryberry.co.uk. *3m NW of
Beaconsfield, 3m W of Amersham. On
B474, 600yds on L past Holy Trinity
Church.* Home-made teas. **Adm
£3.50, chd free. Visitors welcome by
appt, mid-June to mid-July, groups
20-40, also *Evening visits*, wine.**
Mature 3-acre chalk and clay garden.
Unusual spring bulbs and hellebores.
Large weeping ash. Rose walk with
350 roses. Courtyard with summer
pots and box topiary. Large natural old
pond with diving ducks, newly
extended and replanted. Italianate
garden with 13-yr-old yew hedges and
fine view. Wild flower meadow with
wild roses. Formal herb garden with
culinary herbs, small vegetable garden
with hebe hedge. Glasshouse with
unusual pelargoniums.

44 WHITCHURCH GARDENS
HP22 4JS. *4m N of Aylesbury, 4m S
of Winslow. On A413.* Home-made
teas at Priory Court (Mar). **Combined
adm £3 Mar, £3.50 Apr, chd free.
Sun 4 Mar (1-5); Sun 29 Apr (2-6).**
Large village with many thatched

cottages in the quieter older parts,
down small lanes. 1 garden in Oving,
1m W. Maps provided.

FIELDING HOUSE
Mrs A Fraser
Designed and planted by the
present owner over the last 11yrs,
this long narrow free draining
partly sloping garden is exposed
to the full force of SW winds and
is dominated by a large old walnut
tree. Gravel beds, mixed shrub
and herbaceous borders, with a
large collection of hellebores,
burgeoning collection of
snowdrops, erythronium and
species tulips. Far reaching views
over the vale.

THE OLD SCHOOL
Oving HP22 4HL. Mr & Mrs M
Ryan. Not open 29 Apr.
Playground now a walled lawn
backed by herbaceous borders.
Fine views from old orchard
planted with roses and spring
bulbs, encl patio with collection of
scented-leaf geraniums, hellebore
collection.

PARK HOUSE BARN
John & Mary Amos. Not open
4 Mar.
Very small walled garden, gravel
area, raised beds with herbaceous
plants, roses and clematis. Many
pots and containers.

PRIORY COURT
52 High Street HP22 4JS. Mr &
Mrs Ian Durrell, 01296 641563.
Visitors also welcome by appt,
groups 10+, incl coaches.
Approx 2/3-acre, split-level, all-
season walled garden with bulbs,
rose beds, shrubbery, herb bed,
fruit cage and herbaceous
borders. Water feature, decking
and summer house. Gravel path
to garden.

QUENINGTON HOUSE
7 High Street HP22 4JU. Mr &
Mrs David Ryder Richardson.
Not open 29 Apr.
1-acre of cultivated garden with
views over the Vale of Aylesbury.
Secluded shrubbery, children's
play area and unusual water
feature.

Did you find the 'cloud formation yew hedges . . . or Willy Wonka's truck? . . .

THATCHINGS
Mr & Mrs S Cole. Not open 4 Mar. Traditional cottage garden with informal flower beds, vegetable garden, pond area and meadow with fruit trees.

45 THE WHITE HOUSE
Village Road, Denham Village UB9 5BE. Mr & Mrs P G Courtenay-Luck. *3m NW of Uxbridge, 7m E of Beaconsfield. Signed from A40 or A412. Parking in village rd. The White House is in centre of village.* Cream teas. **Adm £4, chd free. Suns 20 May; 15 July (2-5).** Well established 6-acre, formal garden in picturesque setting. Mature trees and hedges, with R Misbourne meandering through lawns. Shrubberies, flower beds, rockery, rose garden and orchard. Large walled garden with Italian garden and developing laburnum walk. Herb garden, vegetable plot and Victorian greenhouses.
占 ❀ ☕

46 WHITEWALLS
Quarry Wood Road, Marlow SL7 1RE. Mr W H Williams, 01628 482573. *1/2 m S Marlow. From Marlow cross over bridge. 1st L, 3rd house on L, white garden wall.* **Adm £2.50, chd free. Suns 22 Apr; 15 July; 9 Sept (2-5). Visitors also welcome by appt.**

Thames-side garden approx 1/2 acre with spectacular view of weir. Large lily pond, interesting planting of trees, shrubs, herbaceous perennials and bedding, large conservatory.
占

WOODCHIPPINGS
See Northamptonshire.

47 NEW WOODROW FARM
Woodrow HP7 0RP. Mrs Francesca Murray, 01494 434846, francesca.murray@dsl.pipex.com. *2m S Amersham. Take A404 from Amersham, 2m past Crematorium, turn R to Woodrow. 100yds, turn down track on R, 3rd on L.* Light refreshments & teas. **Adm £2.50, chd free. Evening Opening** wine, Fri 29 June (6-9) Sun 1 July (2-6). Visitors also welcome by appt, May to Sept. Former working farm. 2 1/2-acre garden has been developed over last 3yrs to incl herbaceous border, raised vegetable patch, ponds, patio/courtyard, orchard and water features. Mature planting and lawns enclose this tranquil Chiltern setting.
❀ ☕

Buckinghamshire County Volunteers

County Organiser
Maggie Bateson, Fressingwood, Hare Lane, Little Kingshill HP16 0EF, 01494 866265, jmbateson@btopenworld.com

County Treasurer
Trish Swain, 2 Kingswood Cottages, Swan Lane, The Lee, Great Missenden HP16 9NU, 01494 837752, swaino@talk21.com

Press & Publicity Officer
Sandra Wetherall, Holydyke House, Little Missenden, Amersham HP7 0RD, 01494 862264, sandra@robertjamespartnership.com

Assistant County Organiser
Rosemary Brown, 2 Spencer Road, Aylesbury HP21 7LR, 01296 429605, grahama.brown@virgin.net
Judy Hart, Kingswood House, The Lee, Great Missenden HP16 9NU, 01494 837328, judy.hart@virgin.net
Mhairi Sharpley, The Old Sun House, Pednor, Chesham HP5 2SZ, 01494 782870, mhairisharpley@btinternet.com

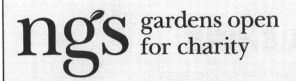

Frogmore House Garden

Windsor Home Park

By gracious permission of Her Majesty The Queen Frogmore House Garden will be open to the public on Tuesday 15 May 2007

Visitors to the gardens may also visit the Royal Mausoleum without charge

Opening times:
From 10am to 5.30pm (last admission 4pm)

Admission: £4.00
(accompanied children 16 and under – free)

For more details or to book a ticket please telephone The National Gardens Scheme on 01483 211535 or e-mail: orders@ngs.org.uk. Alternatively write to The National Gardens Scheme, Hatchlands Park, East Clandon, Guildford, Surrey GU4 7RT, stating the number of tickets required and enclosing a sterling cheque made payable to: The National Gardens Scheme

All major credit/debit cards accepted

CAMBRIDGESHIRE

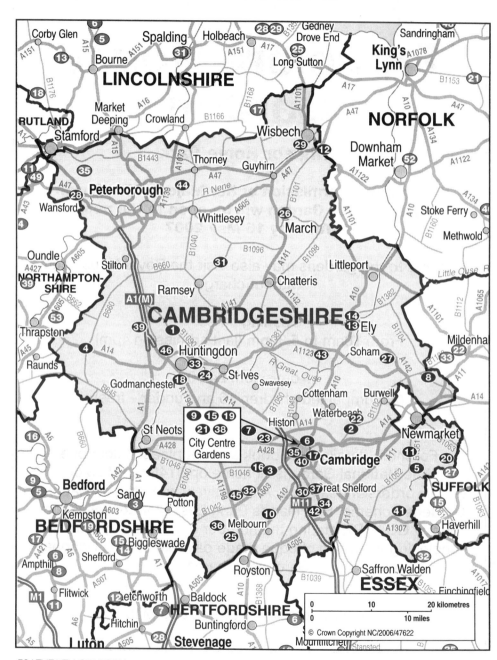

Opening Dates

March

SUNDAY 25
44 Willow Holt

April

SUNDAY 1
3 Barton Gardens
8 Chippenham Park
20 Kirtling Tower
27 Netherhall Manor

SUNDAY 15
38 Trinity College, Fellows' Garden

SUNDAY 22
20 Kirtling Tower

SUNDAY 29
44 Willow Holt

May

SUNDAY 6
27 Netherhall Manor
40 Upwater Lodge

MONDAY 7
13 Ely Gardens 1
40 Upwater Lodge

THURSDAY 10
16 Greystones

SUNDAY 13
3 Barton Gardens
21 Leckhampton

SUNDAY 20
1 Abbots Ripton Hall
10 Docwra's Manor
28 The Old Pump House
44 Willow Holt

SUNDAY 27
12 Elm & Fridaybridge Gardens
18 Island Hall

THURSDAY 31
16 Greystones

June

SUNDAY 3
6 Chesterton Gardens
14 Ely Gardens II
30 Priesthouse
37 Stapleford Gardens

SATURDAY 9
43 Wilburton Gardens

SUNDAY 10
4 Catworth, Molesworth & Brington Gardens
22 Lode Gardens
43 Wilburton Gardens

THURSDAY 14
35 4 Selwyn Gardens (Evening)

SUNDAY 17
8 Chippenham Park
23 Madingley Hall
33 River View
39 Upton Gardens
42 Whittlesford Gardens

WEDNESDAY 20
29 Peckover House

THURSDAY 21
16 Greystones

SUNDAY 24
2 Anglesey Abbey, Gardens & Lode Mill
31 Ramsey Forty Foot
32 Rectory Farm House
44 Willow Holt
46 Wytchwood

July

SUNDAY 1
12 Elm & Fridaybridge Gardens
15 Emmanuel College Garden & Fellows' Garden
34 Sawston Gardens

SUNDAY 8
9 Clare College Fellows' Garden
19 King's College Fellows' Garden
22 Lode Gardens

THURSDAY 12
16 Greystones

SUNDAY 15
22 Lode Gardens

THURSDAY 19
45 Wimpole Hall

SUNDAY 29
44 Willow Holt

August

SUNDAY 5
27 Netherhall Manor

SUNDAY 12
27 Netherhall Manor

SUNDAY 19
17 Highsett Town Gardens
44 Willow Holt

SUNDAY 26
17 Highsett Town Gardens

September

SUNDAY 9
2 Anglesey Abbey, Gardens & Lode Mill

SUNDAY 30
44 Willow Holt

October

SUNDAY 7
8 Chippenham Park

SUNDAY 28
44 Willow Holt

Gardens open to the public

2 Anglesey Abbey, Gardens & Lode Mill
10 Docwra's Manor
24 The Manor
29 Peckover House
45 Wimpole Hall

By appointment only

5 Cherryoaks
7 Childerley Hall
11 Dullingham House
25 Mill House
26 Mosspaul
36 South Farm & Brook Cottage
41 Weaver's Cottage

The Gardens

1 **ABBOTS RIPTON HALL**
Abbots Ripton PE17 2PQ. The Lord & Lady De Ramsey. *2m N of Huntingdon. On B1090.* Light refreshments & teas. **Adm £3, chd free (share to Ramsey Abbey Walled Kitchen Garden Trust). Sun 20 May (2-5).**
Laning Roper, Humphrey Waterfield and Jim Russell helped design the garden. Extensive herbaceous borders; rose circle with both old and modern roses. Many follies and lake. Some gravel paths, stream.
&. ⌘ ⊗

2 ♦ **ANGLESEY ABBEY, GARDENS & LODE MILL**
Cambridge CB5 9EJ. The National Trust, 01223 810080, www.nationaltrust.org.uk/angleseyabbey. *6m NE of Cambridge. From A14 turn N on to B1102 through Stow-cum-Quy.* **House and Garden adm £8.40, chd £4.20, Garden only adm £4.75, chd £2.40. For opening dates & times, please tel or see website. For NGS: Sun 24 June; Sun 9 Sept (1-5).**
100 acres surrounding an Elizabethan manor created from the remains of a priory founded in reign of Henry I. Garden created during last 80yrs;

avenues of beautiful trees; groups of statuary; hedges enclosing small intimate gardens; snowdrops and hyacinths; herbaceous border (June); wild flower meadows, dahlia beds (July-October); winter garden.

③ BARTON GARDENS
Cambridge CB3 7AY. *3¹/₂m SW of Cambridge. M11 J12. Take A603 towards Sandy, in village turn R for Comberton Rd.* Home-made teas at village hall. **Combined adm £3, chd free. Suns 1 Apr; 13 May (2-5).** Delightful group of gardens of wide appeal and expertise.

NEW DORMERS
4 Comberton Road. **Nigel & Jean Hobday.** *Adjacent to village pond.* **Not open 1 Apr.** Large lawn with mature trees and herbaceous borders.

FARM COTTAGE
18 High Street. **Dr R M Belbin, 01223 263058, meredith@belbin.com. Visitors also welcome by appt, small groups only March to July.** A landscaped feel in a cottage garden with woodland walk and walled herbaceous beds. Courtyard garden.

GLEBE HOUSE
1 High Street. **David & Sue Rapley.** *Top of High St* 1-acre mature, partly wooded and walled garden with large (unfenced) duck pond and timber decking, formal fruit/herb garden. Italiante style courtyard garden. Landscaped secret garden with gazebo.

114 HIGH STREET
Mr & Mrs Greenfield. *On High St next to White Horse PH* Cottage garden, unusual slope with spring flowers and shrubs. Tarmac to gravel drive.

31 NEW ROAD
Dr & Mrs D Macdonald Cottage garden with good show of spring flowers, mature shrubs and trees. Kitchen garden. Featured in 'Garden News'.

Our haven which we enjoy sharing with garden visitors . . .

THE SIX HOUSES
33-45 Comberton Road. **Perennial (GRBS).** *Last property on LH-side going to Comberton* Renovated garden, incl winter and dry gardens. Many new plants and trees. Lovely spring bulbs and small wood. NGS award for being open 20yrs.

NEW 247 WIMPOLE ROAD
Ray & Nikki Scrivens Established country garden and small paddock with room for animals and birds, wild, domestic and ornamental.

NEW WINDY CORNER
245 Wimpole Road. **Mike & Jules Webber** Contemporay cottage style garden of perennials and shrubs with a jungle overtone.

④ CATWORTH, MOLESWORTH & BRINGTON GARDENS
nr Huntingdon PE28 0PF. *10m W of Huntingdon.* For Catworth & Brington turn off A14 onto B660 (Catworth S bound) approx 7m W of A14 junction with A1. Village is on the N side of A14 flyover. Molesworth is on the A14, 8m W of the A1. Home-made teas at Molesworth House & Yew Tree Cottage. **Combined adm £3, chd free. Sun 10 June (2-6).**

32 HIGH STREET
Catworth. **Colin Small** Long narrow garden approx ¹/₄-acre. Large informal patio, pergola with herbaceous borders and containers of unusual foliage plants; lawn with herbaceous borders either side, native woodland area. Many rare plants, collection of salvias and ferns.

MOLESWORTH HOUSE
Molesworth. **John Prentis.** *Next to the church in Molesworth* Classic Victorian rectory garden of approx 2¹/₂ acres. Bit of everything; old-fashioned and proud of it. Also rather groovy new tropical house.

THE POPLARS
Molesworth. **Nick Frost.** *By willow tree, opp Barnsby footpath* Garden on hillside set in terraces, wonderful ponds and waterfall surrounded by excellent planting. Created over the last 3yrs. Long low steps to pond areas.

YEW TREE COTTAGE
Brington. **Mr & Mrs D G Eggleston.** *After village sign continue past school, up hill, Yew Tree Cottage is thatched cottage on L* Informal garden, approx 1 acre, complements the C17 building (not open) and comprises flower beds, lawns, vegetable patch, boggy area, copses and orchard. Plants in pots and hanging baskets. Gravel drive.

⑤ CHERRYOAKS
Bradley Road, Burrough Green CB8 9NH. **Sylvia & Ron Allworthy, 01638 507479.** *6m S of Newmarket. From A11 Northbound take A1304 Newmarket, turn R at Xrds in Six Mile Bottom to Brinkley. Turn L at T-junction B1052, then R B1061 Newmarket to Haverhill rd. As you enter Burrough Green house 1st on L next to 40 limit sign. Parking both sides of rd on verges.* **Adm £3, chd free. Visitors welcome by appt Apr to Aug, teas provided and coaches permitted.** Approx 2-acre garden, established and maintained by ourselves over 7yrs. Planted for foliage effect, flower and plant interest all yr-round. Large pond and waterfall with bog garden. Patio with water feature, overflowing with containers of acid lovers as soil is clay. Posts, ropes and structure full of clematis, roses, wisteria etc. Aboretum, soft fruit, vegetables and compost area. Our haven which we enjoy sharing with garden visitors. Gravel drive, grass paths.

6 🆕 **CHESTERTON GARDENS**
CB4 1BT. *N on Elizabeth Way A1134 at roundabout take 3rd exit into High St, then 3rd R into Chapel St, 1st L Church St. St Andrews Rd is a continuation of Chapel St.* **Combined adm £2, chd free. Sun 3 June (10-2).**

🆕 **30 CHURCH STREET**
Suzanne Sanders
In this very small urban front and back garden, now 3yrs old, my aim was to provide some privacy and a crowded but not too chaotic planting of trees and shrubs.

🆕 **57 ST ANDREWS ROAD**
Jan & Tim Clay
Small townhouse garden built on three levels and planted with a variety of trees, shrubs, roses, clematis and perennials. Nearly 3yrs old, it was designed to be an informal and relaxing haven for the owners.

7 **CHILDERLEY HALL**
Dry Drayton CB3 8BB. **Mr & Mrs John Jenkins, 01954 210271.** *6m W of Cambridge. On A428 opp Caldecote turn.* **Adm £2.50. Visitors welcome by appt.**
Romantic 4-acre garden (grade II historic garden) surrounds part Tudor house (not open). Winding paths lead through herbaceous borders to secret areas. Large collection shrub roses and good variety of plants and trees.
🌿

8 **CHIPPENHAM PARK**
Chippenham, nr Newmarket CB7 5PT. **Mr & Mrs Eustace Crawley, 01638 720221/fax 01638 721991.** *5m NE of Newmarket. 1m off A11.* **Light refreshments & teas. Adm £4, chd free. Suns 1 Apr; 17 June; 7 Oct (11-5). Visitors also welcome by appt.**
The house (not open), gardens, lake, canals and 350-acre park enclosed by wall 3¹/₂m long, built after Admiral Lord Russell petitioned William III in 1696 for permission to make a park. Gardens have been extended and restocked by Anne Crawley, descendant of John Tharp who bought the estate in 1791. Superb display of narcissus and early flowering shrubs followed by extensive summer borders and dramatic autumn colours. Many plants stalls.
♿ 🌿 ♻ ☕

9 **CLARE COLLEGE FELLOWS' GARDEN**
Trinity Lane, Cambridge CB2 1TL. The Master & Fellows, **www.clare.cam.ac.uk.** *Central to city. From Queens Rd or city centre via Senate House Passage, Old Court & Clare Bridge.* **Adm £2.50, chd free. Sun 8 July (2-6).**
2 acres. One of the most famous gardens on the Cambridge Backs. Herbaceous borders; sunken pond garden and fine specimen trees.
♿ 🌿

New paddock borders start bold and exotic, leading to greens and creams, mauves, red and blues . . .

10 ♦ **DOCWRA'S MANOR**
Meldreth Road, Shepreth SG8 6PS. Mrs John Raven, 01763 260677, **www.docwrasmanorgarden.co.uk.** *8m S of Cambridge. ¹/₂m W of A10. Cambridge-Royston bus stops at gate opp the War Memorial in Shepreth. King's Cross-Cambridge train stop 5 min walk.* **Adm £4, chd free. All yr Weds, Fris (10-4.30), 1st Sun in month Apr to Oct (2-4). For NGS: Sun 20 May (2-5.30).**
2¹/₂ acres of choice plants in series of enclosed gardens. VAQAS award.
♿ 🌿 ♻

11 **DULLINGHAM HOUSE**
nr Newmarket CB8 9UP. Sir Martin & Lady Nourse, 01638 508186, **lavinia.nourse@btinternet.com.** *4m S of Newmarket. Off A1034.* **Adm £3, chd free. Visitors welcome by appt, June & July.**
The grounds were landscaped by Humphrey Repton in 1799 and the view remains virtually intact today. To the rear there is a substantial walled garden with magnificent long shrub/herbaceous borders. The garden encompasses a fine claire voie and historic bowling green.
♿ 🌿

12 **ELM & FRIDAYBRIDGE GARDENS**
Elm/Wisbech PE14 0HU. *Turn off A47 towards Downham Mk. 1st turning L on bend almost opp Blacksmiths Arms.* Home-made teas at Florence House (July only). **Combined adm £3, chd free. Suns 27 May; 1 July (10-4). Not open Florence House 27 May.**
☕

22 ELMFIELD DRIVE
Vivien & Andrew Steed. *(Access to rear garden only available from no 24)*
Front garden with perennials, clematis and grasses. Rear garden with herbaceous border, nature pond and wide variety of interesting plants incl many hostas and bamboo.
🌿 ♻

24 ELMFIELD DRIVE
Kathleen & Tony Price. *Off A47 towards Downham Market, 1st turning L on bend opp Blacksmith's Arms PH*
Approx ¹/₃ acre containing a variety of herbaceous plants, spring, summer and autumn bulbs together with flowering shrubs, incl over 70 clematis. Plus small arid garden and fish pond. Wheelchair access: most of garden on grass - no concrete paths. Wheelchair access to most of garden on grass only.
♿ 🌿

FLORENCE HOUSE
Back Road, Fridaybridge. Mr & Mrs Stevenson, 01945 860268, roddy.stevenson@btconnect.com. *On B1101. In Fridaybridge centre turn R in front of Chequers PH on to Back Rd.* **Not open 27 May. Visitors also welcome by appt anytime.**
Large sweeping borders in this 25yr-old 1¹/₂-acre garden, growing a modern mix of trees, shrubs, perennials and over 30 varieties of rose. The new paddock borders start bold and exotic, leading to greens and creams, mauves, red and blues finishing with a woodland area underplanted with bulbs, ferns, hellebores. WC. Picnic area. Car parking on compacted gravel, help given if necessary.
♿ 🌿 ♻

⓭ ELY GARDENS 1
14m N of Cambridge. Follow signs to cathedral, from A10. and yellow signs to Barton Rd. Map given at first garden visited. **Combined £2, chd free. Mon 7 May (2-5).**
Historic city with famous cathedral. Three delightful gardens all within easy walking distance of the cathedral. Teas at The Old Fire Engine House.

THE BISHOP'S HOUSE
The Rt Reverend the Bishop of Ely & Mrs Russell
Walled garden, former cloisters of monastery. Rose garden in June; box hedging. Mixed herbaceous and kitchen garden. Gravel paths, but wheelchairs can use lawn area.
&

HAZELDENE
36 Barton Road. Mike & Juliette Tuplin. *Nr Barton Rd car park*
Organic garden reflecting an interest in wildlife. Interesting planting and structures incl kitchen garden with raised beds, living roofs, courtyard garden.

THE OLD FIRE ENGINE HOUSE
St Mary's Street. Mr & Mrs M R Jarman
Delightful walled country garden within the shadow of Ely cathedral. Cottage garden plants in beds and borders around old fruit trees. Described by those who see it as 'an oasis of peace'.
☒

Meadow being developed to encourage wildlife and wild flowers, with area of cornfield planting . . .

⓮ ELY GARDENS II
CB7 4TX. *14m N of Cambridge. Approaching Ely from A10 follow signs to the cathedral, or yellow signs in Prickwillow Rd. Maps given at first garden visited.* Teas at Old Palace and Roswell House. **Combined adm £3, chd free. Sun 3 June (2-6).**
Historic city with famous cathedral and river frontage. Delightful group of gardens with wide appeal and expertise.

ALTON HOUSE
46 Prickwillow Road. Judy & Tim Graven
Enclosed town garden, mature trees, good selection of shade tolerant shrubs. Alpine and grass areas. Domed aviary.
&

BELMONT HOUSE
Mr & Mrs P J Stanning, t.stanning@virgin.net. Visitors also welcome by appt May/June.
Designed 1/2-acre garden with interesting and unusual plants.
& ☒ ⊗

THE BISHOP'S HOUSE
The Gallery. The Rt Reverend the Bishop of Ely & Mrs Russell (see Ely 1 Gardens entry).
& ☒

12 CHAPEL STREET
Ken & Linda Ellis, 01353 664219, ken.ellis1@ntlworld.com. Visitors also welcome by appt May to Oct.
Small town garden with lots of interesting corners. The plants reflect the eclectic outlook of the gardeners towards plants. Themes from alpine to herbaceous border. All linked by a railway! At least, that's the excuse...
& ☒ ⊗

THE OLD PALACE
Sue Ryder Care
1 1/2 acres with duck pond in fine setting next to cathedral. Interesting mixed borders, superb trees incl possibly the oldest and largest London plane tree in the country. Recreation of a Chelsea Flower Show Bronze Medal courtyard garden.
& ☒ ⊗

ROSEWELL HOUSE
60 Prickwillow Road. Mr & Mrs A Bullivant, 01353 667355. Visitors also welcome by appt June only.
Herbaceous borders with old roses and shrubs. Pond and kitchen garden. Secluded 'sitting areas'. Splendid views of Ely cathedral and surrounding fenland. Meadow being developed to encourage wildlife and wild flowers, with area of cornfield planting. Wheelchair access through sidegate.
& ☒ ⊗

⓯ EMMANUEL COLLEGE GARDEN & FELLOWS' GARDEN
Cambridge CB2 3AP. *Car parks at Parker's Piece & Lion Yard, within 5 mins walk.* **Adm £2, chd free. Sun 1 July (2-5).**
One of the most beautiful gardens in Cambridge. Buildings of C17 to C20 surrounding 3 large gardens with pools, herb garden, herbaceous borders, fine trees incl dawn redwood. Access allowed to Fellows' Garden (NGS day only) with magnificent oriental plane and more herbaceous borders.
& ☒ ⊗

⓰ GREYSTONES
Swaynes Lane, Comberton CB3 7EF. Dr & Mrs L Davies, 01223 262686, alison@ldassoc.demon.co.uk. *5m SW of Cambridge. M11 J12. At Comberton village Xrds turn into South Street towards church. Then 1st L into Swaynes Lane.* **Adm £2.50, chd free. Thurs 10, 31 May; 21 June; 12 July (2-5). Visitors also welcome by appt.**
Artistically designed plantswoman's garden of 1/2 acre. Planted for year round interest. Thursday visits for Peony in May, Roses in June and the vibrant hot border in July.
& ☒ ⊗ ☕

⓱ NEW HIGHSETT TOWN GARDENS
CB2 1NZ. *Cambridge City centre. From Cambridge stn, 1st R from Station Rd into Tenison Rd, take 2nd L into Tenison Ave, access to Highsett immed ahead. No parking permitted within Highsett Estate.* Light refreshments & teas. **Donations welcome, chd free. Suns 19, 26 Aug (2.30-5.30).**
Two small town gardens set in attractive communal grounds.

NEW 70 HIGHSETT
Gilli Haarhoff
Small town garden with stone patio, raised beds, planting in a theme of green, grey, purple and white, grey trellis and 2 mirrors with a stainless steel water feature gives the garden a modern stream line effect.

NEW 84 HIGHSETT
Sharon Carpenter & Simon Nesbit
Winding path leads you through small exotic jungle, featuring bananas, ensetes, gingers, tree ferns and bamboo.

HOLLY TREE FARM
See Lincolnshire.

18 ISLAND HALL
Godmanchester PE29 2BA. Mr Christopher & Lady Linda Vane Percy. *1m S of Huntingdon (A1). 15m NW of Cambridge (A14). In centre of Godmanchester next to free car park.* Teas. **Adm £3, chd free. Sun 27 May (12-5).**
3-acre grounds. Mid C18 mansion (not open). Tranquil riverside setting with mature trees. Chinese bridge over Saxon mill race to an embowered island with wild flowers. Garden restored in 1983 to mid C18 formal design, with box hedging, clipped hornbeams, parterres, topiary and good vistas over borrowed landscape, punctuated with C18 wrought iron and stone urns.

19 KING'S COLLEGE FELLOWS' GARDEN
Queens Road, Cambridge CB2 1ST. Provost & Scholars of King's College, domus.bursar@kings.cam.ac.uk. *In Cambridge, the Backs. Entry by gate at junction of Queens Rd & West Rd. Parking at Lion Yard 10mins walk, or some pay & display places in West Rd.* Cream teas. **Adm £3, chd free. Sun 8 July (2-5.30).**
Fine example of a Victorian garden with rare specimen trees.

20 KIRTLING TOWER
Newmarket Road, Kirtling CB8 9PA. The Lord & Lady Fairhaven. *6m SE of Newmarket. From Newmarket head towards Saxon Street village, through village to Kirtling, turn L at war*

memorial, entrance is signed on L. Light refreshments & teas. **Adm £4, chd free (share to All Saints Church, Kirtling). Suns 1, 22 Apr (11-4).**
Kirtling Tower is surrounded on 3 sides by a moat. The garden of 5 acres was started by the present owners 6yrs ago. Main features are the spring garden, secret, walled and cutting gardens. Original Tudor walk. The spring garden is planted with 70,000 bulbs - daffodils, narcissus and camassias in memory of The Hon Rupert Broughton (1970-2000).

Winding path leads you through small exotic jungle, featuring bananas, ensetes, gingers, tree ferns and bamboo . . .

21 LECKHAMPTON
37 Grange Road, Cambridge CB2 1RH. Corpus Christi College. *Runs N to S between Madingley Rd (A1303) & A603. Drive entrance opp Selwyn College. No parking available on site.* Home-made teas. **Adm £3, chd free. Sun 13 May (2-6).**
10 acres comprising formal lawns and extensive wild gardens, featuring walkways and tree-lined avenues, fine specimen trees under-planted with spring bulbs, cowslips, anemones, fritillaries and a large area of lupins. Grass and gravel paths.

22 LODE GARDENS
CB5 9ER. *10m NE of Cambridge. Take B1102 from Stow-cum-Quy roundabout, NE of Cambridge at junction with A14, Lode is 2m from roundabout.* Teas at 21 Lode Road. **Combined adm £3, chd free. Suns 10 June; 8, 15 July (11-5).**
Picturesque village to the E of Anglesey Abbey Garden.

NEW CARPENTERS END
10 High Street. Mr & Mrs Paul Webb
³/₄ acre recently developed garden. Shrubs, trees with fine lawn, next to church yard. Some gravel paths.

21 LODE ROAD
Mr Richard P Ayres, 01223 811873. *Visitors also welcome by appt.*
Small garden, designed by the owner (retired head gardener at Anglesey Abbey NT) adjoining C15 thatched cottage (not open). Planted with bold groups of herbaceous plants complementing a fine lawn and creating an element of mystery and delight.

WILD ROSE COTTAGE
Church Walk. Joy Martin, 01223 812990, www.wildrosegarden.co.uk. *Visitors also welcome by appt.*
An overflowing cottage garden, with laburnum/rose tunnel, wildlife pond, circular vegetable garden edged with lavender and sage, wild flower spiral all entered through arches of roses and clematis.

23 MADINGLEY HALL
nr Cambridge CB3 8AQ. University of Cambridge, www.cont-ed.cam.ac.uk. *4m W of Cambridge. 1m from M11 Exit 13.* Cream teas. **Adm £3, chd free (share to Madingley Church Restoration Fund). Sun 17 June (2.30-5.30).**
C16 Hall (not open) set in 8 acres of attractive grounds. Features incl landscaped walled garden with hazel walk, alpine bed, medicinal border and rose pergola. Meadow, topiary, mature trees and wide variety of hardy plants. Gravel paths in meadow and walled garden, slopes.

24 ◆ THE MANOR
Hemingford Grey PE28 9BN. Mrs D S Boston, 01480 463134, www.greenknowe.co.uk. *4m E of Huntingdon. Off A14. Entrance to garden by small gate off river towpath. No parking at house except for disabled by arrangement with owner. Park in village.* **Adm £2, chd free.**

Open daily (11-5) (dusk in winter) . Garden designed and planted by author Lucy Boston, surrounds C12 manor house on which Green Knowe books were based (house open only by appt). 4 acres with topiary; over 200 old roses, bearded iris collection and large herbaceous borders with mainly scented plants. Enclosed by river, moat and wilderness.

& ⊗

㉕ MILL HOUSE
22 Fen Road, North End, Bassingbourn SG8 5PQ. Mr & Mrs A Jackson, 01763 243491, millhouseval@btinternet.com. *2m N of Royston. On the NW outskirts of Bassingbourn. 1m from Church, on the rd to Shingay. Take North End at the war memorial in the centre of Bassingbourn which is just W of the A1198 (do not take Mill Lane).* **Adm £3.50, chd free. Visitors welcome by appt, garden clubs and groups specially welcomed May to Sept and Snowdrop time.**
Garden created over many years by retired garden designer owners and divided up into interesting enclosures, providing unusual formal and informal settings for many rare trees, shrubs, herbaceous plants, clematis and topiary whiich provide yr round interest. Wonderful elevated view over countryside and garden. New winter garden.

⋊ ⊗

㉖ MOSSPAUL
6 Orchard Road, March PE15 9DD. Dinah Lilley, 01354 653396. *18m E of Peterborough. A605/A141. Nr Town Centre. Take 3rd turning on L off Elwyn Rd, straight down, 4th house on R.* **Adm £2, chd free. Visitors welcome by appt May to Aug.**
Large secluded garden with variety of mature shrubs, ornamental trees and specimen conifers. Lawns and mixed borders, Ponds. Fruit garden with cordon trees and soft fruit.

&

㉗ NETHERHALL MANOR
Soham CB7 5AB. Timothy Clark. *6m Ely, 6m Newmarket. Enter Soham from Newmarket, Tanners Lane is 2nd R 100yds after cemetery. Enter Soham from Ely, Tanners Lane is 2nd L after War Memorial.* Home-made teas. **Adm £2, chd 50p. Suns 1 Apr; 6 May; 5, 12 Aug (2-5).**
1-acre walled garden incl courtyard. April - crown imperials, Victorian

hyacinths and old primroses. May - florist's ranunculus (picotee and bizarre), and tulips (rose, bizarre, bybloemen), also varieties of lily of the valley. Aug - formal beds of Victorian pelargoniums, calceolarias, fuchsia, lobelias and heliotropes, an organic seasonal kitchen garden. Internationally known collection of historic garden plants. Featured in 'Cambridge Daily News', & Country Life.

⋊ ⚏

Wonderful elevated view over countryside and garden . . .

㉘ NEW THE OLD PUMP HOUSE
Old Leicester Road, Wansford PE8 6NQ. Mrs J Johnson, 01780 782174, pawsandclaws@hotmail.com. *Take A47 towards Leicester from A1/A47 junction. ¼m turn L towards Kings Cliffe garden 200yds.* **Adm £2.50, chd free. Sun 20 May (1-5).**
Paws and Claws is a functional Boarding Cattery in 2 acres. The garden has grown over the years and comprises herbaceous beds, surrounded by walnut, lime, field maple and hawthorne hedges. Divided into 'rooms' with interesting features, sculptures, plants and statuary. On a slope, majority of garden is accessible.

& ⊗

㉙ ♦ PECKOVER HOUSE
North Brink, Wisbech PE13 1JR. National Trust, 01945 583463. *centre of Wisbech on N banks of R Nene. Within easy walking distance of town bus stn. Nearest car park in Chapel Rd - no parking on property. Disabled blue badge parking outside property.* **House and Garden adm £5, chd £2.50, Garden only adm £3, chd £1.50. For opening dates & times please tel. For NGS: Wed 20 June (12-5).**
Said to be one of the best examples of a Victorian town house garden, Peckover is a 2-acre site offering many

areas of interest. These incl herbaceous borders, bedding, roses, trees, ponds, lawns cut flower border, ferns, summerhouses and orangery with 3 very old fruiting orange trees and colourful display of pot plants throughout the season. Guided walk (roses) by gardeners in charge 2pm £1.

& ⋊ ⊗ ⚏

㉚ PRIESTHOUSE
33 Church Street, Little Shelford CB2 5HG. Mr & Mrs J Lury. *4m S of Cambridge. On R of village church.* **Adm £2, chd free. Sun 3 June (2-5.30).**
1-acre garden of lawns, shingle paths and drives, clipped trees and shrubs, long borders designed to offset a listed neo-gothic rectory (not open). Separate rose, herb, kitchen and courtyard gardens and orchard. Exhibition of C19 oil paintings (Cambridge Fine Art) open in The Coach House.

& ⋊ ⚏

㉛ RAMSEY FORTY FOOT
nr Ramsey PE26 2YA. *3m N of Ramsey. From Ramsey (B1096) travel through Ramsey Forty Foot, just before bridge over drain, turn R, First Cottage 300yds on R, next door to The Elms.* Home-made teas at First Cottage & The Willows. **Combined adm £2, chd free. Sun 24 June (2-6).**
⚏

THE ELMS
Mrs J Shotbolt & Mr R Shotbolt, www.shotbolt.com
1½-acre water garden around C19 clay pit backed by massive elms. beautifully landscaped with shrubs, perennials, ferns and large collection of bog and aquatic plants. 3 lakes full of wildlife.

FIRST COTTAGE
Hollow Road. Mr & Mrs R Fort
150ft x 40ft garden with herbaceous borders, shrub beds; ornamental pond and rockery. Miniature steam railway.
⊗

THE WILLOWS
Jane & Andrew Sills. *Turn L down private rd opp George PH. Park in Hollow Rd*
⅓-acre cottage garden with riverside location. Old roses, herbaceous beds; shrubs, ferns; pond; vegetable and herb garden.
⊗

㉜ NEW RECTORY FARM HOUSE
Orwell SG8 5RB. Mr & Mrs Pinnington. *8m W of Cambridge. On & north of A603, towards Wimpole from Cambridge.* Cream teas. **Adm £3, chd free (share to local Church). Sun 24 June (11-5).**
2 acre garden on exposed site developed from a field 9yrs ago. Enclosed spaces filled with roses, lavender and herbaceous plants, surrounded by box and hornbeam hedges. Garden designed and planted by Peter Reynolds. Adjoining field saved from cultivation for potential wild flower meadow. Some gravel paths.
ᵅ ⅍ ☕

㉝ NEW RIVER VIEW
Wyton PE28 2AA. John Meeks. *2m E of Huntingdon. Opp Hartford Marina.* **Adm £3, chd free, concessions £2. Sun 17 June (2-6).**
4-acre garden. Unusual trees and shrubs, water features, ponds, topiary and much more.
ᵅ ⅍

㉞ SAWSTON GARDENS
CB2 4LA. *5m SE of Cambridge. 3m from M11 J10. A505 follow signs to Sawston.* Home-made teas at St Mary's Church. **Combined adm £3, chd 50p. Sun 1 July (2-6).**
Large village with several Grade II listed buildings.
☕

NEW 1A CHURCH LANE
Mr & Mrs M Carpenter
Bungalow with garden on 4 sides, with selection of roses, trellis arches, pond, annual and perennial plants. Opp church where teas are available.

30 CHURCHFIELD AVENUE
Mr & Mrs I Butler
Ex-council property with medium-sized garden. Circular lawns surrounded by shrubs, annual and perennial plants. Decking area covered by a grapevined pergola. Small pond with waterfall, secluded mirror to give effect of another garden, mixture of shrubs climbers, annual and perennial plants. Partial wheelchair access.

DRIFT HOUSE
19a Babraham Road. Mr & Mrs A Osborne
1960's architect designed house (not open) set in $1/3$ acre. Mixture of shrubs, trees, climbers, bulbs and annuals. Vegetable garden and fruit trees, pond and lawns.
ᵅ ✿

54 HIGH STREET
Dr & Mrs Maunder
C16/18 farmhouse (not open) with lawns and flowerbeds, kitchen garden with chickens, rose garden and paved area where once the goats were housed.
ᵅ

NEW 27 SUNDERLANDS AVENUE
Mr Brett O' Hagan
Mixture of contemporary and new materials used incl water feature, oak sleepers, natural stone and stainless steel. Planting incls bamboo's, grasses and herbs in blues, pinks and green. Winner. Construction of show gardens at Gardeners World NEC (Silver Gilt) & Chelsea Flower Show (Silver).

VINE COTTAGE
Dr & Mrs T Wreghitt
C17 house (not open) surrounded by mature garden. Contemporary garden featuring Japanese courtyard adjacent to recent extension.
ᵅ

㉟ NEW 4 SELWYN GARDENS
CB3 9AX. Mrs Louise Swarbrick. *Grange Rd runs N to S between Madingley Rd (A1303) & Barton Rd (A603).* **Evening Opening £2.50, chd free, wine, Thur 14 June (5-7).**
Family garden. Walled so no vista. Attempted to create space and interest through dense planting and areas within the garden itself. Lots of traditional cottage plants with a splash of exotic colour to catch the eye.
⅍

㊱ SOUTH FARM & BROOK COTTAGE
Shingay-cum-Wendy SG8 0HR. Philip Paxman, 01223 207581, www.south-farm.co.uk. *12m W of*

Cambridge. Off A603. 5m N of Royston off A1198. **Adm £3, chd free. Visitors welcome by appt groups of 10+ May to Sept.**
Garden established over 30yrs on farmland site. 8 acres ring fenced by hardwood planting. Eco-garden with reed bed, wild flowers, ponds. Extensive vegetable garden. Restored listed barnyard (open). Also Private Nature Reserve with lake, otters, beautiful dragon flies and native crayfish, wild flowers. Neighbouring Brook Cottage (Mr & Mrs Charvile) Countryman's cottage garden. Abundant yr-long mixed colour, spilling over boundary stream, intermixed with traditional vegetables and poultry.
ᵅ ⅍ ⌂

Lake with otters, dragon flies and native crayfish . . .

㊲ NEW STAPLEFORD GARDENS
CB2 5SY. *4m S of Cambridge City Centre.* Light refreshments & teas. **Combined adm £3, chd free (share to East Anglia Childrens Hospice). Sun 3 June (11-5).**
☕

NEW 57 LONDON ROAD
Mrs M Spriggs. *on A1301 next to Church St*
Garden intergrated with that of 59 - 61, access to 5 Priams Way forming a series of garden rooms.
⅍

NEW 59 - 61 LONDON ROAD
Dr & Mrs S Jones. *On A1301 next to Church St*
Medium sized garden arranged in 'rooms'. Gravel garden, herbaceous beds, kitchen garden, fruit cage, alpine, pit and summer houses. Access to 5 Priams Way.
⅍

NEW 5 PRIAMS WAY
Mr Anthony Smith. *Off London Rd, easiest access via 59 - 61 London Rd*
Small garden with herbaceous beds and pergola.
⅍

NEW THE STONE HOUSE
40 Mingle Lane. Sir James &
Lady Mirrlees. *5 mins fron
Shelford Stn*
Lawns, trees and shrubs.
&. ✗

**38 TRINITY COLLEGE,
FELLOWS' GARDEN**
Queen's Road, Cambridge
CB2 1TQ. Trinity College. *City centre.*
Adm £2, chd free. Sun 15 Apr (2-5).
Garden of 8 acres, originally laid out in
the 1870s by W B Thomas. Lawns
with mixed borders, shrubs and
specimen trees. Drifts of spring bulbs.
Recent extension of landscaped area
among new college buildings to W of
main garden. Gravel paths.
&. ✗

39 UPTON GARDENS
PE28 5YF. *8m NW of Huntingdon.
From A1(M) from N, & A14 from
Cambridge, take B1043 (The
Alconburys) & follow signs to Upton.
From A1 from S take B1043 then as
above.* Light refreshments & teas.
Combined adm £3, chd free. Sun 17
June (1-5).
Small attractive village surrounded by
fields. At the heart stands an ancient
and beautiful church which will be
decorated with flowers on the day.
Many of our best gardens can be
viewed from the road, incl those on
Upton Park. This private residential
park welcomes visitors during the open
day.
☕

GRANARY COTTAGE
David & Jill Oakley
Family garden; mixture of lawn,
trees and vegetables.

OLD SCHOOL HOUSE
Lynn Gibson
Country garden with arbours,
retreats and glasshouses. Mixture
of cottage garden species such as
hardy geraniums, delphiniums and
foxglove with more specialised
tender, scented and climbing
plants. These incl hibiscus,
gingers, jasmine, hostas and
oleanders. Partial wheelchair
access.
&. ✗

NEW SPINNEY CLOSE
R Bates, 07971 337581. *Bottom
of hill in the spinney*
Natural woodland covering 70%

with the remainder given over to
lawn, pots and wild flowers. The
aim of the garden started in May
06 is a return to a more natural
enviroment for wildlife. Flat gravel
drive.
&.

UPTON HOUSE COTTAGE
Main Street. Barry Freeman
Very large beautifully maincured
lawn with mature shrubs and
summer flowers. Windmill and koi
carp pond.
✗

1 UPTON PARK
Doris Mary Dove
Cottage gardens, mixed borders.
&. ✗ ⊛

THE WARREN
Green Lane. David & Melanie
Tudor
English garden with
Mediterranean twist. Comprising
water features, play area, outside
dining/entertaining area with spa.
&. ✗ ⊛

WOODEND
Main Street. Roger & Dorothy
Holt
Medium garden, divided into
indentifiable areas. Selection of
grass, cannas and variety of
mature plants in raised beds.
Arbour.
&.

40 NEW UPWATER LODGE
23 Chaucer Road, Cambridge
CB2 2EB. George & Jane
Pearson. *1m S of Cambridge. Off
Trumpington Rd (A1309), nr
Brooklands Ave junction.* Light
refreshments & teas. Adm £3,
chd free. Sun 6, Mon 7 May
(2-5).
6 acres broadly flat, mature
English-style gardens, fine lawns
lead to dyke, bridge and water
meadow abutting R Granta. Criss-
crossed with mown paths. Fen
land area is home to small flock of
rare breed sheep. Four 100yr old
wisteria clad Edwardian house
facade. Borders planted for yr
round interest. Also poultry, pond
and bluebell walk. Some gravel,
small slope.
&. ✗ ☕

Fen land area is home to small flock of rare breed sheep . . .

WALCOT HALL
See Lincolnshire.

41 WEAVER'S COTTAGE
35 Streetly End, West Wickham
CB1 6RP. Miss Sylvia Norton, 01223
892399. *8m NW of Haverhill. On
A1307 between Linton & Haverhill turn
N at Horseheath towards W Wickham.
Weaver's Cottage is 9th on R after 40
sign.* Adm £2, chd 50p. Visitors
welcome by appt April - spring
bulbs, lathyrus, May - July - roses
and lathyrus.
1/2-acre garden exuberantly planted for
fragrance with spring bulbs; shrubs;
herbaceous; climbers; old roses. Scree
garden. NCCPG National Collection of
Lathyrus.
✗ **NCCPG**

42 WHITTLESFORD GARDENS
CB2 4NR. *7m S of Cambridge. 1m NE
of J10 M11 & A505.* Home-made teas.
Combined adm £3, chd free (share
to Parish Church). Sun 17 June
(2-6).
Flowers in Parish Church C11. Maps.
Parking nr church.
☕

THE GUILDHALL
Professors P & M Spufford
Knot garden.
&.

23 NEWTON ROAD
Mr F Winter
Cottage garden, herbaceous
plants, shrubs, fish pond.
Allotment consisting of
vegetables, fruit, flowers and bird
aviary.
&. ⊛

14 NORTH ROAD
Mr & Mrs R Adderley
Shady secluded garden with
rockery and pond.
&. ✗

5 PARSONAGE COURT
Mrs L Button. *Please park on rd*
Trees, shrubs and large pond.

RAYNERS FARM
North RoadMr & Mrs C Morton
Medieval-style herb beds in walled
garden of C15 timber-framed
farmhouse (not open). Restored
barns, large pond and free-range
poultry.

RYECROFT
1 Middlemoor Road. Mr & Mrs P
A Goodman
Paddock; shrubs and compost
making.

11 SCOTTS GARDENS
Mr & Mrs M Walker
Shady walled garden with shrub
borders; pond and waterfall.

43 WILBURTON GARDENS
CB6 3PU. *4m SW of Ely. Wilburton a
small rural fenland village on the A1123
& B1049 (Twenty Pence Rd).* Teas at 3
Millfield Lane (Sat), cold drinks at
Redlands (Sun). **Combined adm £3,
chd free. Sat 9, Sun 10 June (2-5).**

LONG BALLAND
21 Twenty Pence Road. Susan
Everitt. *B1049, opp garden
centre*
1-acre garden with with open
lawns, herbaceous borders, old-
fashioned roses and pergola
covered in clematis, honeysuckle
and rambling roses. Orchard with
a large variety of fruit trees.

3 MILLFIELD LANE
Brian & Ruth Everitt. *On A1123
to village take 2nd L Millfield Lane,
bungalow 2nd on L*

Plenty of seats and shade. Haven for wildlife . . .

³/₄-acre garden with herbaceous
borders, shrubs and roses. 96ft
pergola with clematis, roses,
honeysuckle and wisteria. Island
beds, two small ponds, and
summerhouse with patio. Small
coppice of silver birch
underplanted with spring bulbs.

REDLANDS
Twenty Pence Road. Wendy
Francis-Wood & Derek Wood,
01353 740073. Visitors also
welcome by appt, for large
groups May and June.
2-acre garden designed informally
where plants (especially the 300
roses) ramble and scramble at
will. Paths meander through the
many different trees and shrubs.
Pools and meadow areas
encourage wildlife. Scent and
colour predominate.

44 WILLOW HOLT
Willow Hall Lane, Thorney PE6 0QN.
Angie & Jonathan Jones, 01733
222367, janda.salix@virgin.net. *4m E
of Peterborough. From A47, between
Eye & Thorney turn S into Willow Hall
Lane. 2m on R. NOT in Thorney
Village.* Teas. **Adm £2, chd free. Suns
25 Mar; 29 Apr; 20 May; 24 June; 29
July; 19 Aug; 30 Sept; 28 Oct (11-5).**
Visitors also welcome by appt, any
number, no parking for coaches.

Different, quirky, uncivilised; we gauge
as a compliment those visitors'
comments from 2006. There's plenty
to delight plant lovers here, but it will
take more than a dozen years to make
a conventional garden from 2 acres
comprising former gravel diggings,
local rubbish tip and agricultural field
corner.

45 ◆ WIMPOLE HALL
Arrington SG8 0BW. The National
Trust, 01223 206000,
www.wimpole.org. *5m N of Royston.
Signed off A603 to Sandy 7m from
Cambridge or off A1198.* **Adm £3.20,
chd £1.75. Open daily except Thurs
& Fris. For NGS: Thur 19 July (10.30-
5).**
Part of 350-acre park. Restored Dutch
garden and Victorian parterres on N
lawns. Fine trees, marked walks in
park. National Collection of walnuts.
Walled vegetable garden. Chance to
see the recreated Sir John Soane
glasshouse financed with the help of
the National Gardens Scheme.

46 WYTCHWOOD
7 Owl End, Great Stukeley
PE28 4AQ. Mr David Cox, 01480
454835. *2m N of Huntingdon. On
B1043. Parking at village hall, Owl End.*
Home-made teas. **Adm £3, chd free.
Sun 24 June (1.30-5.30).** Visitors
also welcome by appt, April, May,
June & early July.
2-acre garden. Brightly planted
borders of perennials, annuals and
shrubs, lawns and ponds. Dry garden
planted 2001. 1 acre of wild plants,
grasses set among rowan, maple and
birch trees leading to spinney. Planted
with native trees, ferns, hostas and
foxgloves. Plenty of seats and shade.
Haven for wildlife. Gravel drive.

Cambridgeshire County Volunteers

County Organiser
George Stevenson, 1a The Village, Orton Longueville, Peterborough PE2 7DN, 01733 391506, ChrisGeorge1a@aol.com

County Treasurer
Lyndon Davies, 19 Swaynes Lane, Comberton, Cambridge CB3 7EF, 01223 262 686, lyndon@ldassoc.demon.co.uk

Leaflet Coordinator
Alison Gould, The Grange, Church Road, Easton, Nr Huntingdon, PE18 0TU, 01480 89043

Assistant County Organisers
John Drake, Hardwicke House, Fen Ditton CB5 8TF, 01223 292246
Patsy Glazebrook, 15 Bentley Road, Cambridge CB2 8AW, 01223 301302, glazebrc@doctors.net.uk
Christine Stevenson, 1a The Village, Orton Longueville, Peterborough PE2 7DN, 01733 391506, ChrisGeorge1a@aol.com
Pam Bullivant, Rosewell House, 60 Prickwillow Road, Ely CB7 4TX, 01353 667355, pam.bullivant@talk21.com

CHESHIRE

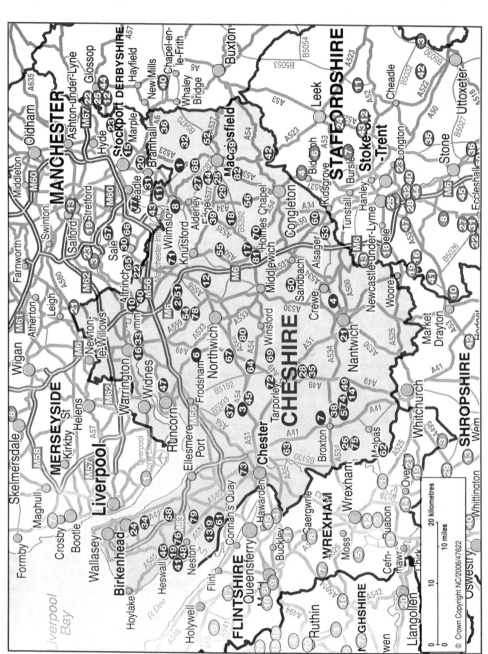

Opening Dates

April

SUNDAY 1
- 54 Parm Place
- 63 Saighton Grange

SUNDAY 15
- 17 Dane Mount
- 81 Woodcroft

WEDNESDAY 18
- 72 Tirley Garth

SUNDAY 22
- 9 Briarfield
- 58 Poulton Hall
- 72 Tirley Garth

SATURDAY 28
- 5 Bank House
- 6 Bluebell Cottage Gardens
- 56 Pikelow Farm

SUNDAY 29
- 5 Bank House
- 22 Dunham Massey
- 35 Long Acre
- 46 Newton House
- 53 Orchard House

May

SUNDAY 6
- 28 Haughton Hall

MONDAY 7
- 41 Maylands
- 76 69 Well Lane

WEDNESDAY 9
- 71 Tatton Park

SATURDAY 12
- 8 9 Bourne Street

SUNDAY 13
- 7 Bolesworth Castle
- 8 9 Bourne Street
- 27 Hare Hill Gardens
- 29 Henbury Hall
- 40 Mayfield
- 70 Swettenham Village

SATURDAY 19
- 55 Peover Hall Gardens

SUNDAY 20
- 21 Dorfold Hall
- 55 Peover Hall Gardens
- 59 Ridgehill
- 79 Willaston Village Gardens

MONDAY 21
- 50 The Old Hough (Evening)

WEDNESDAY 23
- 14 Cholmondeley Castle Garden

SUNDAY 27
- 4 Badgerswood Gardens
- 25 Far Hills

- 37 Manley Knoll
- 44 The Mount
- 45 Mount Pleasant

MONDAY 28
- 4 Badgerswood Gardens
- 45 Mount Pleasant

June

SATURDAY 2
- 5 Bank House
- 47 Norton Priory Museum & Gardens
- 51 The Old Parsonage

SUNDAY 3
- 5 Bank House
- 51 The Old Parsonage

FRIDAY 8
- 24 Fairview Cottage (Evening)

SUNDAY 10
- 1 Adlington Hall
- 10 15 Brook Road
- 12 Bucklow Farm
- 31 73 Hill Top Avenue
- 67 Stonyford Cottage
- 77 West Drive Gardens

MONDAY 11
- 50 The Old Hough (Evening)

WEDNESDAY 13
- 71 Tatton Park

FRIDAY 15
- 78 Westage Farm (Evening)

SATURDAY 16
- 38 Manor Farm
- 74 The Valve House
- 78 Westage Farm

SUNDAY 17
- 10 15 Brook Road
- 19 29 Dee Park Road
- 26 Grafton Lodge
- 38 Manor Farm
- 66 199 Stockport Road
- 74 The Valve House
- 78 Westage Farm

MONDAY 18
- 50 The Old Hough (Evening)

FRIDAY 22
- 26 Grafton Lodge (Evening)

SATURDAY 23
- 15 2 Claremont Avenue
- 42 Millpool

SUNDAY 24
- 13 Burton Village Gardens
- 15 2 Claremont Avenue
- 18 Deans Rough Farm
- 32 Hillside Cottage
- 35 Long Acre
- 42 Millpool

SATURDAY 30
- 52 One House Nursery

July

SUNDAY 1
- 22 Dunham Massey
- 52 One House Nursery
- 64 Sandymere
- 68 Summerdown
- 80 Wood End Cottage

SATURDAY 7
- 57 17 Poplar Grove

SUNDAY 8
- 23 Edith Terrace Gardens
- 54 Parm Place
- 57 17 Poplar Grove
- 75 The Well House

SATURDAY 14
- 16 68 Cranborne Avenue
- 40 Mayfield

SUNDAY 15
- 3 Ashton House
- 16 68 Cranborne Avenue
- 39 The Manor House
- 40 Mayfield
- 56 Pikelow Farm
- 69 Sunnyside Farm
- 73 80 Upton Park

SATURDAY 21
- 62 The Rowans

SUNDAY 22
- 11 Brooke Cottage
- 34 King's Lane Dawson Allotments
- 58 Poulton Hall
- 62 The Rowans

WEDNESDAY 25
- 80 Wood End Cottage

SATURDAY 28
- 65 The School House

SUNDAY 29
- 20 19 Dorchester Road
- 43 31 Moss Lane
- 65 The School House

August

SATURDAY 4
- 2 Arley Hall & Gardens

SUNDAY 5
- 6 Bluebell Cottage Gardens
- 31 73 Hill Top Avenue
- 66 199 Stockport Road

SUNDAY 12
- 48 The Old Farm

SUNDAY 19
- 30 35 Heyes Lane
- 69 Sunnyside Farm

WEDNESDAY 22
30 35 Heyes Lane

September
FRIDAY 7
49 The Old Hall (Evening)

SATURDAY 8
49 The Old Hall
82 3 Woodhouse Lane

SUNDAY 9
36 Lyme Park
39 The Manor House
70 Swettenham Village
82 3 Woodhouse Lane

SATURDAY 29
45 Mount Pleasant

SUNDAY 30
45 Mount Pleasant

October
SUNDAY 7
22 Dunham Massey

Gardens open to the public
1 Adlington Hall
2 Arley Hall & Gardens
14 Cholmondeley Castle Garden
22 Dunham Massey
27 Hare Hill Gardens
36 Lyme Park
45 Mount Pleasant
47 Norton Priory Museum & Gardens
55 Peover Hall Gardens
60 Rode Hall
67 Stonyford Cottage
69 Sunnyside Farm
71 Tatton Park

By appointment only
33 62 Irwell Road
61 Rosewood

The Gardens

1 ♦ **ADLINGTON HALL**
Macclesfield SK10 4LF. Mrs Camilla Legh, 01625 829206, www.adlingtonhall.com. *4m N of Macclesfield. Well signed off A523 at Adlington.* House and Garden adm £6, Garden only adm £4, chd £2. Aug Weds to Suns (not 19 Aug). For NGS: Sun 10 June (2-5).
6 acres of formal gardens with herbaceous borders, rose garden; rockeries; yew maze; water garden. Lawns with open views across ha-ha. 32-acre wilderness with mature plantings, various follies incl a 'Temple

to Diana'; woodland walk. Yew and ancient lime walks. Fower parterre. Limited wheelchair access.
   丙 ☕

Children's garden with vegetables, herbs, living willow maze and tunnels . . .

2 ♦ **ARLEY HALL & GARDENS**
Northwich CW9 6NA. The Viscount Ashbrook, 01565 777353, www.arleyhallandgardens.com. *4m W of Knutsford. Well signed from M6 J19 & 20, & M56 J9 & 10.* Adm £5, chd £2, concessions £4.50. Tues to Suns & Bank Hols 31 Mar to 30 Sept (Hall open Tues & Suns only). For NGS: Sat 4 Aug (11-5) (hall not open).
One of Britain's finest gardens, Arley has been lovingly created by the same family over 250yrs and is famous for its yew buttressed herbaceous border, avenue of ilex columns, walled garden, pleached lime avenue and Victorian Rootree. A garden of great atmosphere, interest and vitality throughout the seasons. Specialist nursery adjacent.
   ♿ ❀ ☕

3 **NEW** **ASHTON HOUSE**
Church Road, Ashton Hayes CH3 8AB. Mr & Mrs K Sheppard, 01829 752761, kevin@sheppard61.fsnet.co.uk. *7m E of Chester. Off A54, take B5393 to Ashton. 200yds past Golden Lion, R into Pentre Lane. 1st gateway on L into field.* Home-made teas. Adm £3, chd free (share to Hospice of the Good Shepherd, Backford). Sun 15 July (1-5). Visitors also welcome by appt, June & July only.
Country garden with stream, natural pond and interesting trees, incl old monkey puzzle. Children's garden with vegetables, herbs, living willow maze and tunnels, woodland area.
   ♿ 丙 ☕

4 **BADGERSWOOD GARDENS**
100 Church Lane, Wistaston CW2 8EQ. Karen White & Mary Sadler. *2m SW of Crewe. Midway between Crewe & Nantwich off A534, take Church Lane approx 1/2m to No. 100.* Car park 3 mins walk from garden. Home-made teas. Adm £3, chd free. Sun 27, Mon 28 May (1.30-5).
2 individual gardens set in approx 2/3 acre. Diverse planting with mature trees incl a wide range of shade and sun-loving plants. Several colourful herbaceous borders and interesting island beds featuring varied shrubs and perennials. Also a productive kitchen garden, fruit trees, wildlife pond and restful seating areas. Tarporley Band playing 27 May.
   ♿ 丙 ❀ ☕

5 **BANK HOUSE**
Goldford Lane, Bickerton SY 14 8LL. Dr & Mrs M A Voisey. *4m NE of Malpas. 11m S of Chester on A41 turn L at Broxton roundabout to Nantwich on A534. Take 5th R (13/4m) to Bickerton. Take 2nd R into Goldford Lane. Bank House is nearly 1m on L. Field parking.* Home-made teas. Adm £3, chd free. Sats, Suns 28, 29 Apr; 2, 3 June (2-6).
13/4-acre garden at the foot of Bickerton Hill, in area of outstanding beauty, with extensive views to Derbyshire and the Marches. Sheltered, terraced borders stocked with a wide range of shrubs, trees and herbaceous plants; established wild garden, Millennium garden with water features and productive vegetable garden. Unfenced swimming pool and ponds. Gravel paths, fairly steep slopes.
   ♿ ❀ ☕

BIDDULPH GRANGE GARDEN
See Staffordshire & part of West Midlands

6 **BLUEBELL COTTAGE GARDENS**
Lodge Lane, Dutton WA4 4HP. Sue and Dave Beesley, www.bluebellcottagegardens.co.uk. *5m W of Northwich. From M56 (J10) take A49 (Whitchurch) turn R at T-lights towards Runcorn. Then 1st turning L.* Light refreshments & teas. Adm £4, chd free. Sat 28 Apr; Sun 5 Aug (12-5).
Cottage garden featuring herbaceous borders stocked with unusual perennials. Large pond; scree; bog

area. 'Grasses Garden' in 1½-acre garden, situated within picturesque, environmentally friendly scenery; meadow and woodland. Adjacent nursery. Sue Beesley has won the BBC's 2006 Gardener of the Year Award.

 ♿ ⚘ ☕

❼ BOLESWORTH CASTLE
Tattenhall CH3 9HQ. Mr & Mrs A G Barbour. *8m S of Chester. Enter by lodge on A41.* Home-made teas. **Adm £4, chd free (share to Burwardsley Church). Sun 13 May (2-5).**
Landscape with rhododendrons, shrubs and borders. Woodland walk replanted 1993-2006. Partial wheelchair access. Dogs on leads.

♿ ☕

Delightful setting for afternoon tea on the terrace . . .

❽ 9 BOURNE STREET
Wilmslow SK9 5HD. Lucille Sumner & Melanie & Keith Harris, www.wilmslowgarden.co.uk. *¼m W of central Wilmslow. Take A538 from Wilmslow towards Manchester Airport. Bourne St 2nd on L after fire stn. Or from M56 (J6), take A538 to Wilmslow. Bourne St on R.* **Adm £2.50, chd free. Sat 12, Sun 13 May (11-5).**
¼-acre organic garden, evolved over three generations of one family. Mature trees incl ginkgo biloba, azaleas, rhododendrons and exotic foliage. Fish pond; greenhouse; water features and hens. Peaceful and secret garden with a surprise around every corner.

♿ ⚘ ☕

❾ BRIARFIELD
The Rake, Burton, Neston CH64 5TL. Liz Carter, 0151 336 2304, carter.burton@virgin.net. *9m NW of Chester. Turn off A540 at Willaston-Burton Xrds T-lights & follow rd for 1m to Burton village centre.* Home-made teas. **Adm £3, chd free. Sun 22 Apr (2-5). Opening with Burton Village Gardens Sun 24 June. Visitors also welcome by appt anytime of yr, coaches permitted.**
Sheltered S facing sandy slope, home

to many specialist plants, some available in plant sale. Colourful shrubs, bulbs, alpines and several water features compete for your attention as you wander through the four distinctly different gardens. Always something new, this year a major revamp of the main home garden. Featured on BBC's North West Tonight.

♿ ⚘ ☕

❿ 15 BROOK ROAD
Lymm WA13 9AH. Zoe & Simon Chaddock. *6m E of Warrington. From M6 J20 take B5158 (Cherry Lane) to Lymm for 1.7m. At A56 (Church Rd) turn R then 1st L into Brookfield Rd, over xrds then L into Whitbarrow Rd. Concealed 1st R into Brook Rd (cul-de-sac).* Home-made teas. **Adm £2.50, chd free. Suns 10, 17 June (1-6).**
Compact heavily planted sloping garden with a great variety of features. The upper lawn has a wildlife pond and busy borders whilst the lower section incls a raised fruit bed, vintage water feature and secluded area under a pergola.

♿ ⚘ ☕

⓫ BROOKE COTTAGE
Church Road, Handforth SK9 3LT. Barry & Melanie Davy. *1m N of Wilmslow. In the centre of Handforth Village, behind the Health Centre and Library. Turn off Wilmslow Rd next to St Chads Parish Church and follow Church Rd round to R. Garden last on L.* Home-made teas. **Adm £2.50, chd free. Sun 22 July (12-5).**
Small garden separated into 3 areas. Woodland garden, tree ferns, hydrangeas, hellebores, hostas and astrantias. Patio featuring many large leaved plants incl banana, canna, ligularia, bamboo, dahlias, hemerocallis and small pond. Long mixed border and island beds with grasses and late flowering perennials.

♿ ☕

⓬ BUCKLOW FARM
Pinfold Lane, Plumley WA16 9RP. Dawn & Peter Freeman. *2m S of Knutsford. M6 J19, head to Chester A556. L at 2nd set of T-lights by Smoker PH. In 1¼m L at concealed Xrds, 1st R. From Knutsford A5033, L at Sudlow Lane. Follow rd, becomes Pinfold Lane.* Home-made teas. **Adm £3, chd free (share to Knutsford Methodist Church). Sun 10 June (2-5).**
Country garden with shrubs, perennial

borders, rambling roses, herb garden, vegetable patch, wildlife pond/water feature and alpines. Landscaped and planted over the last 18yrs with recorded changes. Free range hens. Wheelchair access, cobbles in the yard and entrance but reasonably flat in the garden area.

♿ ♿ ⚘ ☕

⓭ BURTON VILLAGE GARDENS
Wirral CH64 5SJ. *9m NW of Chester. Turn off A540 at Willaston-Burton Xrds T-lights & follow rd for 1m to Burton.* Home-made teas. **Combined adm £4, chd free (share to Claire House Children's Hospice). Sun 24 June (2-6).**
Gardens in centre of village, maps given to all visitors. Teas on Burton Manor terrace, glorious view across gardens to Cheshire countryside.

☕

BRIARFIELD
The Rake, Burton. Liz Carter
(See separate entry).

♿ ⚘

BURTON MANOR
Burton. College Principal, Keith Chandler
Three geometric gardens on E, S and N sides of house, essentially as designed by Thomas Mawson in 1906, with mature trees; sunken parterre; yew hedges; formal flower beds and deep lily ponds. Delightful setting for afternoon tea on the terrace.

♿ ⚘

⓮ ◆ CHOLMONDELEY CASTLE GARDEN
Malpas SY14 8AH. The Marchioness of Cholmondeley, 01829 720383, penny@cholmondeleycastle.co.uk. *4m NE of Malpas. Off A41 Chester-Whitchurch rd & A49 Whitchurch-Tarporley rd.* **Garden adm £4, chd £1.50. Weds, Thurs, Suns & Bank Hols Apr to Sept; Suns 7, 21 Oct autumn tints. For NGS: Wed 23 May (11.30-5).**
Romantically landscaped gardens. Azaleas, rhododendrons, flowering shrubs, rare trees, herbaceous borders and water gardens. Lakeside picnic area; rare breeds of farm animals and aviary breeds, incl llamas. Private chapel in the park. Newly developed water garden and garden mosaic by Maggie Howarth. In memory of the 6th Marquess of Cholmondeley.

♿ ⚘

⓯ 2 CLAREMONT AVENUE
Marple SK6 6JE. Eric & Maggie
Britten. *4m SE of Stockport. Turn L off
Stockport Rd at Marple Hall Drive,
Claremont Ave 1st on L.* Home-made
teas at 35 Claremont Ave (just across
the rd). **Adm £2.50, chd free. Sat 23,
Sun 24 June (1-7).**
Artist and plantswoman's small garden,
densely planted with a huge variety of
plants, many unusual. With hand-built
pottery and other imaginative features,
there is a surprise round every corner.
Small wildlife pond and waterfall, bog
garden, secret woodland garden,
raised beds, living willow 'den'. This is
a relaxed, fun garden, where plants
take precedence. Worth exploring at
any time of yr. Exhibition of paintings -
most for sale. Opportunity to make
handpainted silk scarf in 1/2 hr - adults
and children, also (possibly) for children
- Ian and his exploding custard!.
🌾 ⊗ 🍵

CLOUD COTTAGE
See Derbyshire.

COURTWOOD HOUSE
See Staffordshire & part of West
Midlands.

A relaxed, fun
garden, where
plants take
precedence.
Worth
exploring at
any time of
year . . .

⓰ 68 CRANBORNE AVENUE
Warrington WA4 6DE. Mr & Mrs J
Carter. *1m S of Warrington Centre.
From Stockton Heath N on A49 over
swing bridge. L at 2nd set of T-lights
into Gainsborough Rd, 4th L into
Cranbone Ave.* **Adm £2.50, chd free.
Sat 14, Sun 15 July (11-6).**
Luxuriant planting makes this a secret
place. An oasis of calm from life's busy
pace. Colour and scent enhance and
grace with water and glass expanding
the space.
🌾 ⊗

⓱ ❚NEW❚ DANE MOUNT
Middlewich Road, Holmes
Chapel CW4 7EB. Mr & Mrs D
Monks. *4m E of Middlewich.
Approx 1m E of M6 J18.* Home-
made teas. **Combined adm with
Woodcroft £4, chd free. Sun 15
Apr (1-5).**
1/4-acre garden full of colourful
spring bulbs, camellias and early
flowering clematis. Interesting
layout with features incl pottery and
garden sculptures. Exhibition of
paintings in summer house.
🚻 🌾 ⊗ 🍵

⓲ DEANS ROUGH FARM
Lower Withington SK11 9DF. Mr &
Mrs Brian Chesworth. *3m S of
Chelford. 5m N of Holmes Chapel.
A535 nr Jodrell Bank turn into
Catchpenny Lane. 11/2m turn R into no
through rd (opp bungalow), 400yds
turn L into Deans Rough Farm.* Home-
made teas. **Adm £3, chd free. Sun 24
June (2-6).**
Area of 11/2 acres; informal cottage
garden around house. Herbaceous
and mixed borders and old roses.
Potager; large natural pond with wild
flowers. Woodland area with bog
garden.
🚻 🌾 ⊗ 🍵

⓳ 29 DEE PARK ROAD
Gayton CH60 3RG. E Lewis, 0151
342 5893. *7m S of Birkenhead. SE of
Heswall. From Devon Doorway/Glegg
Arms roundabout at Heswall, travel SE
in Chester direction on A540 for
approx 1/4m. Turn R into Gayton Lane,
5th L into Dee Park Rd. Garden on L
after 1/4m.* Home-made teas. **Adm
£2.50, chd free. Sun 17 June
(2-5.30). Visitors also welcome by
appt.**
Mature trees and shrubs, climbing
roses, clematis, mixed shrub,
herbaceous borders and island beds
provide yr-round interest. Set around
gravel areas with thymes and alpines.
Secret garden and lovely patio with
colourful shrubs.
🚻 🌾 ⊗ 🍵

⓴ 19 DORCHESTER ROAD
Hazel Grove SK7 5JR. John &
Sandra Shatwell, 0161 440 8574. *4m
S of Stockport. On A5143 at junction
of Dorchester Rd and Jacksons Lane.
From Stockport take A6 S for approx
1m, R on A5102 for 2m, L at
roundabout on A5143. Garden on L
after mini-roundabout. Parking at*

*shops or school (further up Jacksons
Lane).* Home-made teas. **Adm £2.50,
chd free. Sun 29 July (1-5).** Visitors
also welcome by appt.
Suburban garden redesigned and
planted in 2003. 150sq yd front garden
with David Austin and hybrid tea roses
around a central gazebo. 400sq yd
back garden with pond and waterfall,
pergola, lawn. Colour-themed borders
with perennials, annuals and small
trees set against a background of
beech trees. Featured on BBC
Northwest.
🚻 🌾 ⊗ 🍵

㉑ DORFOLD HALL
Nantwich CW5 8LD. Mr & Mrs
Richard Roundell. *1m W of Nantwich.
On A534 between Nantwich & Acton.*
**Adm £5, chd £2.50. Sun 20 May (2-
5.30).**
18-acre garden surrounding C17
house (not open) with formal approach;
lawns and herbaceous borders;
spectacular spring woodland garden
with rhododendrons, azaleas,
magnolias and bulbs.
🌾 ⊗ 🍵

㉒ ♦ DUNHAM MASSEY
Altrincham WA14 4SJ. The National
Trust, 0161 941 1025,
dunhammassey@nationaltrust.
org.uk. *3m SW of Altrincham. Off A56.
Well signed.* **House and Garden adm
£7.50, chd £3.75, Garden only adm
£5, chd £2.50. Daily 17 Mar to 28
Oct. For NGS: Suns 29 Apr; 1 July;
7 Oct (11-5.30).**
Great plantsman's garden. Magnificent
trees reflected in moat; richly planted
borders vibrant with colour and subtle
textures. The Orangery, Mount and
Bark House give a sense of the
garden's long history. Sweeping lawns,
lush borders, shady woodland, a
formal parterre set the stage while
collections of shade-, moisture- and
acid-loving plants such as blue
poppies, Chinese lilies and hydrangeas
contribute to an ever-changing scene.
🚻 🌾 ⊗ 🍵

㉓ EDITH TERRACE GARDENS
Compstall, nr Marple SK6 5JF. The
Edith Terrace Group. *6m E of
Stockport. Take Bredbury junction off
M60. Follow Romiley-Marple Bridge
sign on B6104. Turn into Compstall at
Etherow Country Park sign. Take 1st R,
situated at end of Montagu St. Parking
in village public car parks - short walk
to Edith Terrace.* Home-made teas.
Adm £4, chd free. Sun 8 July (1-5).

Series of gardens in mixed style from cottage to formal, situated to front and rear of Victorian terrace; described by BBC 'Gardeners' World' magazine as 'a colourful and beautiful living space'. Mixed herbaceous perennials, ornamental backyards and back alleyway. In lakeside setting in the conserved mill village of Compstall, adjacent to Etherow Country Park.

Watering can collection and replica Somerset and Dorset Railway signal box . . .

24 NEW FAIRVIEW COTTAGE
15 Fairview Road, Oxton, Wirral CH43 5SD. Ian & Christine Wray. *1m SW of Birkenhead. From M53 J3, east on A552, L onto B5151 & immed 1st R into Fairview Rd.* **Evening Opening £3, chd free, wine, Fri 8 June (6.30-9.30).** Architects walled garden in conservation area. Small but with creative use of space - subdivision, terraces, steps, views. Pond, woodland, shade loving plants and interesting herbaceous border. Frames 1830s sandstone cottage. Watering can collection and replica Somerset and Dorset Railway signal box.

25 FAR HILLS
Andertons Lane, Henbury SK11 9PB. Mr & Mrs Ian Warburton, 01625 431800. *2m W of Macclesfield. Along A537 opp Blacksmiths Arms. At Henbury go up Pepper St. Turn L into Church Lane then Andertons Lane in 100yds.* Home-made teas at The Mount. **Combined adm with The Mount £4.50, chd free. Sun 27 May (2-5.30). Visitors also welcome by appt.**
Mixed 1/2-acre garden; planted for yr-round interest with regard to wildlife. Trees; shrubs; herbaceous perennials; small pond; fruit and vegetable area; native copse.

10 FERN DENE
See Staffordshire & part of West Midlands.

FIELD HOUSE FARM
See Staffordshire & part of West Midlands.

GAMESLEY FOLD COTTAGE
See Derbyshire.

26 GRAFTON LODGE
Tilston SY14 7JE. Simon Carter & Derren Gilhooley, 01829 250670, simoncar@aol.com. *12m S of Chester. A41 S from Chester turning towards Wrexham on A534 at Broxton roundabout. Past Carden Park Hotel & turn at Cock-a-Barton PH towards Stretton & Tilston. Through Stretton, garden on R before reaching Tilston.* Home-made teas. **Adm £4, chd free. Sun 17 June (1-6). Evening Opening wine, Fri 22 June (5-8). Visitors also welcome by appt.**
Colourful garden of 2 acres with lawns, natural and formal ponds, specimen trees, many mature shrubs and several garden rooms incl herb garden, standard rose circle, large pergola with varied climbers, herbaceous beds, perfumed gazebo, orchard, roof terrace with far reaching views over garden and countryside. Garden of interest throughout the yr. Category Winner - Chester in Bloom. Gravel drive.

27 ◆ HARE HILL GARDENS
Over Alderley SK10 4QB. The National Trust, 01625 828836. *2m E of Alderley Edge. Between Alderley Edge & Prestbury. Turn off N at B5087 at Greyhound Rd.* **Adm £3.20, chd £1.50. For NGS: Sun 13 May (10-5).**
Attractive spring garden featuring a fine display of rhododendrons and azaleas; good collection of hollies and other specimen trees and shrubs. 10-acre garden incl a walled garden which hosts many wall shrubs incl clematis and vines; borders are planted with agapanthus and geraniums. Partially suitable for wheelchairs.

28 HAUGHTON HALL
Bunbury CW6 9RH. Mrs R J Posnett. *5m NW of Nantwich. Off A534 Nantwich to Wrexham rd, 6m SE of Tarporley via A49.* Home-made teas. **Adm £3.50, chd £1. Sun 6 May (2-6).**
Medium-sized garden; species rhododendrons, azaleas, shrubs, rock garden; lake with temple; waterfall. Collection of ornamental trees.

29 HENBURY HALL
nr Macclesfield SK11 9PJ. Sebastian de Ferranti Esq. *2m W of Macclesfield. On A537. Turn down School Lane Henbury at Blacksmiths Arms. East Lodge on R.* Home-made teas. **Adm £5, chd £1. Sun 13 May (2-5).**
Large garden with lake, beautifully landscaped and full of variety. Azaleas, rhododendrons, flowering shrubs; rare trees; herbaceous borders.

30 35 HEYES LANE
Timperley, Altrincham WA15 6EF. Mr & Mrs David Eastwood. *1 1/2 m NE of Altrincham. Heyes Lane, a turning off Park Rd (B5165) 1m from junction with A56 Altrincham-Manchester rd. Or from A560 turn W in Timperley Village for 1/4 m. Newsagents shop on corner.* **Adm £2.50, chd free. Sun 19, Wed 22 Aug (2-5).**
Small mature suburban garden 30ft x 90ft on sandy soil, maintained by a keen plantswoman member of the Organic Movement (HDRA). Improved accessibility with several changes to this yr-round garden; trees; small pond; greenhouses; many kinds of fruit with a good collection of interesting and unusual plants. Due for some rejuvenation after 'middle aged' spread.

31 73 HILL TOP AVENUE
Cheadle Hulme SK8 7HZ. Mr & Mrs Martin Land, 0161 486 0055. *4m S of Stockport. Turn off A34 (new bypass) at roundabout signed Cheadle Hulme (B5094). Take 2nd turn L into Gillbent Rd, signed Cheadle Hulme Sports Centre. Go to end, small roundabout, turn R into Church Rd. 2nd rd on L is Hill Top Ave. From Stockport or Bramhall turn R or L into Church Rd by The Church Inn. Hill Top Ave is 1st rd on R.* Home-made teas. **Adm £3, chd free (share to Arthritis Research Campaign). Suns 10 June; 5 Aug (2-6). Visitors also welcome by appt, for groups of 4+.**
1/6-acre plantswoman's garden. Well stocked with a wide range of sun-loving herbaceous plants, shrub and

climbing roses, many clematis varieties, pond and damp area, shade-loving woodland plants and small unusual trees, in an originally designed, long narrow garden.

🏵 ⊛ ☕

㉜ HILLSIDE COTTAGE
Shrigley Road, Pott Shrigley
SK10 5SG. Anne & Phil Geoghegan. *6m N of Macclesfield. On A523. At Legh Arms T-lights turn into Brookledge Lane signed Pott Shrigley. After 1¹/₂m signed Shrigley Hall turn L signed Higher Poynton. After 1m turn R at Methodist Chapel. Field parking with short walk to garden.* Home-made teas. **Adm £3, chd free (share to Great Dane Adoption Society). Sun 24 June (1-5).**
Approx ¹/₄-acre on the edge of the Peak District National Park. North facing slope with superb views of the Cheshire plain. Planting on several levels has provided different areas of interest and character within the natural landscape; using a variety of shrubs, small trees, roses and herbaceous planting. Featured on BBC Northwest.

🏵 ☕

㉝ 62 IRWELL ROAD
Warrington WA4 6BB. Mr & Mrs D Griffiths, 01925 244267, digriffiths62@hotmail.com. *1m S of Warrington town centre. From Stockton Heath N on A49 over swing bridge. L at 2nd set of T-lights into Gainsborough Rd, 2nd R into Irwell Rd. No 62 approx halfway down on R.* Home-made teas/wine. **Visitors welcome by appt. Evenings July only, adm £3, chd free, minimum group of 6, max 15.**
Award-winning secret garden with a magical atmosphere. Prepare to be 'spellbound' when you visit this tiny, but inspirational garden and enjoy an evening visit enhanced by fragrance and candle-light. Described by visitors as ... 'A hidden retreat from the real world'! 'A wonderland'! 'Great ideas ... much to inspire!'. Featured in 'Garden Answers' July (reader Garden of the Month).

🏵 ☕

㉞ KING'S LANE DAWSON ALLOTMENTS
Bebington, Wirral CH63 8NZ. *2¹/₂m S of Birkenhead Centre. From J4 M53 exit B5151 (Mount Rd) for Birkenhead. In approx 1.7m turn R into Broadway, at roundabout, exit*

straight ahead into King's Lane. Entrance on R, opp Conville Boulevard. Parking on adjacent rds; limited disabled parking within allotment site. Disabled access will be available to main path, but not necessarily to the individual allotments. Home-made teas. **Adm £3, chd free. Sun 22 July (2-5).**
Dawson Allotments consist of 68 plots Rented from from Wirral MBC and run as a society; they vary from novice to expert plots. Many plot-holders will be on hand to answer questions on their different approaches and crops. The opening is at the peak of the picking and showing season. A great opportunity for children and their families to see how fruit and vegetables are grown. There will be information on availability and management of allotments. Produce for sale. Featured in 'Cheshire Life'.

♿ 🏵 ⊛ ☕

A great opportunity for children and their families to see how fruit and vegetables are grown . . .

㉟ LONG ACRE
Wyche Lane, Bunbury CW6 9PS. Mr & Mrs M Bourne, 01829 260944, mike@thebournes249.wanadoo. co.uk. *3¹/₂m SE of Tarporley. On A49. Turn 2nd L after Wild Boar Hotel to Bunbury. L at 1st rd junction then 1st R by Nags Head PH 400yds on L. From A51 turn to Bunbury until Nags Head. Turn into Wyche Lane before PH car park. 400yds to garden. Disabled parking in lane adjacent to garden.* Home-made teas. **Adm £3.50, chd free (share to (29 Apr) Horses & Ponies Protection Assoc & (24 June) St Boniface Church, Bunbury). Suns 29 Apr; 24 June (2-5). Visitors also welcome by appt for groups of 10+.**

Plantswoman's garden of approx 1 acre with unusual plants and trees. Roses, pool gardens, small vineyard. Exotic conservatory; herbaceous; specialise in proteas, S African bulbs, clivia and streptocarpus. Spring garden with camellias, magnolias, bulbs. Newly planted area with rare trees. Partial wheelchair access.

♿ 🏵 ⊛ ☕

㊱ ♦ LYME PARK
Disley SK12 2NX. The National Trust, 01663 762023, lymepark@nationaltrust.org.uk. *6m SE of Stockport. Just W of Disley on A6.* **House and Garden adm £7, chd £3.50, Garden only £3.80, chd £2.20. Sats, Suns March, Nov & Dec 12-3 (gardens). Daily Apr to end Oct. For NGS: Sun 9 Sept (11-4.30).**
17-acre garden retaining many original features from Tudor and Jacobean times. High Victorian style bedding, Dutch garden, Gertrude Jekyll style herbaceous border, Edwardian rose garden, Wyatt orangery and many other features. Also rare trees, lake, ravine garden, lawns, mixed borders and rare Wyatt garden.

♿ 🏵 ☕

㊲ MANLEY KNOLL
Manley Road, Manley WA6 9DX. Mr & Mrs R Fildes. *3m N of Tarvin. On B5393, via Ashton & Mouldsworth. 3m S of Frodsham, via Alvanley.* Home-made teas. **Adm £3.50, chd free. Sun 27 May (2-5).**
Terraced garden with rhododendrons, azaleas etc. Quarry garden.

🏵 ☕

㊳ NEW MANOR FARM
Egerton Green SY14 8AW. Tim & Jan Dilworth. *4m NE of Malpas. From Chester take A41 S, at Broxton roundabout turn L onto A534, 1st R after Coppermine PH (to Bickerton). Fork L at Bickerton School. Garden 2nd on R. On A49 turn opp Cholmondeley Arms to Cholmondeley Castle. Garden 3m on L.* Home-made teas. **Combined adm with The Valve House £4, chd free. Sat 16, Sun 17 June (2-5.30).**
Formal country garden of elegant proportions featuring Hidcote-style summer house and formal lily canals. Nepeta walk and rose garden with views to Bickerton Hills.

♿ ⊛ ⊨ ☕

39 THE MANOR HOUSE
Chelford SK11 9AH. Lynne Murphy.
6m W of Macclesfield. 5m E of
Knutsford, on A537 Knutsford to
Macclesfield rd. At roundabout in
Chelford (Shell Garage) follow signs for
car parking. (Macclesfield Rd). **Adm
£3.50, chd free. Suns 15 July; 9 Sept
(2-5).**
The Manor House: garden of 12 acres,
undergoing redevelopment. Variety and
many interesting features. Formal
pond, lake, stream and water features.
Walled garden, conservatory,
herbaceous and elegant planting. Bold
and unusual sculptures. Prairie garden
leading down to lake. Always
something new. Featured in 'The Daily
Telegraph' & GGG.
🎗 ✿ ☕

3rd L into Latchford Rd. Garden on L.
Park on rd or at 69 Well Lane. Home-
made teas at 69 Well Lane. **Combined
adm £4 with 69 Well Lane, chd free.
Mon 7 May (1-5).** Visitors also
welcome by appt.
Approx ½ acre with maturing plantings
against background of mature oaks.
Range of growing conditions and long
season. Incl rhododendrons, wisteria,
magnolia, pond, rockery, herbaceous
borders. Continually evolving planting.
🚻 🎗 ✿ ☕

42 MILLPOOL
Smithy Lane, Bosley SK11 0NZ. Joe
& Barbara Fray. 5m S of Macclesfield.
Just off A523 at Bosley. Turn L 1m S of
A54 T-lights. From Leek, turn R, 2½m
N of The Royal Oak PH at Rushton.

44 THE MOUNT
Andertons Lane, Whirley, Henbury,
nr Macclesfield SK11 9PB. Mr & Mrs
Nicholas Payne, 01625 422920,
ngs@themount1.freeserve.co.uk. 2m
due W of Macclesfield. Along A537
opp Blacksmiths Arms. At Henbury go
up Pepper St. Turn L into Church Lane
then Andertons Lane in 100yds.
Home-made teas. **Combined adm
with Far Hills £4.50, chd free. Sun
27 May (2-5.30).** Visitors also
welcome by appt.
Approx 2 acres with interesting trees
incl Eucryphia x nymansensis, fern
leaved beech and Sciadopitys.
Shrubberies; herbaceous border and
short vista of Irish yews. Water features
and landscaped swimming pool. Far
views to Wales.
🚻 🎗 ✿ ☕

45 ◆ MOUNT PLEASANT
Yeld Lane, Kelsall CW6 0TB. Dave
Darlington & Louise Worthington,
01829 751592/07971 086239,
www.mountpleasantgardens.co.uk.
8m E of Chester. Off A54 at T-lights
into Kelsall. Turn into Yeld Lane opp
Farmers Arms PH, 200yds on L. **Adm
£3, chd free. Sats, Suns, Weds May
to Sept. For NGS: Sun 27, Mon 28
May; Sat 29, Sun 30 Sept (12-5).**
10 acres of landscaped garden and
woodland started in 1994 with
impressive views over the Cheshire
countryside. Steeply terraced in
places. Specimen trees,
rhododendrons, azaleas, conifers,
mixed and herbaceous borders; 4
ponds, formal and wildlife. Vegetable
garden and stumpery with tree ferns,
sculptures. New wild flower meadow
for 2006 and Japanese garden 2007.
Sculptor at work.
🎗 ✿ ☕

Designer's evolving garden balancing enthusiasm with the need for low maintenance . . .

40 NEW MAYFIELD
The Peppers, Lymm WA13 0JA.
Janet Bashforth & Barrie
Renshaw, 01925 756107,
janet@bashforth.fslife.co.uk. 3m
NE J20 M6, 4m W J7 M56 follow
signs for Lymm. Home-made teas.
**Adm £2.50, chd free. Sun 13
May; Sat 14, Sun 15 July (12-5).**
Visitors also welcome by appt.
Constantly evolving plantswoman's
garden, approx ⅓ acre with mature
trees, mixed borders containing
herbaceous perennials, shrubs and
bulbs, dry shaded border. The S-
facing garden has a large number
of grasses. Interesting structures
and features throughout, designed
to give maximum seasonal interest.
🚻 🎗 ✿ ☕

41 MAYLANDS
Latchford Road, Gayton CH60 3RN.
John & Ann Hinde, 0151 342 8557,
john.hinde@maylands.com. 7m S of
Birkenhead. From
Devon Doorway/Glegg Arms
roundabout at Heswall travel SE in
Chester direction on A540 approx
¼m. Turn R into Gayton Lane, take

Please follow direction to parking
areas. No parking at garden. Home-
made teas. **Adm £3, chd free. Sat 23,
Sun 24 June (1-5).**
Garden designed to extend the
seasons with colour, texture and scent.
Lush herbaceous borders and areas of
deep shade. Small stream, pond and
bog garden. Gravel plantings;
containers and a fine collection of
bonsai trees. Come and sit awhile and
share our pleasure. Discovery sheet for
children.
✿ ☕

43 31 MOSS LANE
Styal SK9 4LF. Anne & Stephen
Beswick. 2m N of Wilmslow. From
M56 J5 towards Airport Terminal 1
then Cheadle, continue to T-junction.
Turn R at T-lights then next R to Moss
Lane. No 31 is 200yds on L. **Adm £3,
chd free. Sun 29 July (1-5).**
Designer's evolving garden balancing
enthusiasm with the need for low
maintenance. Ground cover, mixed
borders, wild flower area, wildlife pond,
secret garden and fruit arch. N-facing
front garden specialising in shady
planting and ferns.
🚻 🎗 ✿ ☕

46 NEWTON HOUSE
18 Well Lane, Heswall CH60 8NF.
John & Eileen Harsant. 7m S of
Birkenhead. SE of Heswall. From
Devon Doorway/Glegg Arms
roundabout on A540, take E exit
directly opp Devon Doorway into Well
Lane. This forks L from Dawstone Rd
in ¼m. Garden is approx 50yds on R
down Well Lane after fork.There is no
parking at garden. Park in Dawstone
Rd or Well Lane before the fork,
avoiding driveways. Home-made teas.
**Adm £3, chd free. Sun 29 Apr
(2-5.30).**
Wide range of rhododendrons - hybrid
species, unusual and tender varieties,
Japanese and deciduous azaleas,

magnolias. Growing collection of unusual camellias together with spectacular old favourites. Closely planted borders around sweeping lawns on light acid soil, will interest the general visitor and specialist plantsman. Productive vegetable area, which incl extensive fruit plantings. Caution needed if wet, as route mainly lawn.

 ♿ ☕

47 ♦ NORTON PRIORY MUSEUM & GARDENS
Runcorn WA7 1SX. Norton Priory Museum Trust, 01928 569895. *2m SW of Runcorn. From M56 J11 turn for Warrington & follow signs. From Warrington take A56 for Runcorn & follow signs.* **Museum & Garden adm £4.95, chd/concessions £3.50. Museum open 12-5 & Walled Garden 12-4 Apr to Oct 1.30-4.30, weekends & Bank Hols 12-6. Nov to Mar 12-4. For NGS: Sat 2 June (1.30-4.30).**
16 acres of gardens. Georgian summerhouses, rock garden and stream glade, 3-acre walled garden of similar date (1760s) recently restored. Rosewalk, colour borders, herb and cottage gardens. Priory ruins also open with medieval herb garden and sensory planters.

♿ ⌜ ❀

48 THE OLD FARM
Gayton Farm Road, Gayton CH60 8NN. A Gamon. *7m S of Birkenhead. SE of Heswall. From Devon Doorway roundabout on A540, take the exit directly opp the Devon Doorway into Well Lane. Parking on Well Lane in approx 1/2m. Garden entrance is up cobbled rd which is L as the main rd takes a R.* Home-made teas. **Adm £2.50, chd free. Sun 12 Aug (2-5.30).**
1/3-acre, in 3rd generation ownership, set on slopes of Dee estuary, against mid C18 farm building (not open). Main garden has 3 tiers, created from old sloping, cobbled farmyard with pond, roses, vegetables, soft fruit and bedding. Rose parterre completes the garden.

☕

49 NEW THE OLD HALL
Cholmondeley, Malpas SY14 8HB. Didi & James Clegg. *7m N of Whitchurch. 7m S of Tarporley on A49. Turn into Cholmondeley Park through*

Sandstone Lodge, entrance on A49 - 1m N of Cholmondeley Arms or 11/2m S of A534 junction. After 1/2m fork L. Park in field before chapel, disabled parking available. Home-made teas. **Adm £4, chd free. Evening Opening wine & light refreshments, Fri 7 Sept (5.30-8); Sat 8 Sept (2-5.30).**
21/2 acre garden, in parkland setting, created over the last 15yrs by the Cleggs, divided by beech hedges into areas of different interest incl secret garden and small arboretum. Some gravel.

♿ ⌜ ☕

2-acre garden in attractive and secretive rural setting in secluded part of Arley Estate . . .

50 THE OLD HOUGH
Forge Mill Lane, Warmingham CW10 0HQ. Mr & Mrs D S Varey. *3m from Middlewich. 4m from Sandbach. From Middlewich take A530 to Nantwich. At Wimboldsley School turn L to Warmingham L again at T-junction. Garden 1/2 m on R. From Sandbach take A533 to Middlewich, 1/2 m after Fox Inn on L turn into Mill Lane. At T-junction on canal bridge turn R. Stay on this rd. Garden 2m on. Ample parking.* **Adm £4, chd free (share to Warmingham Church Roof Fund). Evening Openings wine, Mons 21 May; 11, 18 June (6-9).**
2 acres enclosing period house. Borders, interesting trees, well-clothed walls. Lawns with wildlife pond, woodland border, backdrop of mature oakwood. Front lawns with yew

---

hedges, box feature, fish pond. High beech hedge separates Victorian courtyard from which rill flows down stone steps under hedge arch into pond. From top of rill a long vista through garden. Reclaimed materials used extensively. Wheelchair access: tour incls one area of setts, small amount of gravel and involves retracing route. WCs.

♿ ⌜

51 THE OLD PARSONAGE
Arley Green, via Arley Hall & Gardens CW9 6LZ. The Viscount & Viscountess Ashbrook. *5m NNE of Northwich. 3m Great Budworth. M6 J19 & 20 & M56 J10. Follow signs to Arley Hall & Gardens. From Arley Hall notices to Old Parsonage which lies across park at Arley Green.* Home-made teas. **Adm £4, chd free (share to Save The Children Fund). Sat 2, Sun 3 June (2-5.30 last entry).**
2-acre garden in attractive and secretive rural setting in secluded part of Arley Estate, with ancient yew hedges, herbaceous and mixed borders, shrub roses, climbers, leading to woodland garden and unfenced pond with gunnera and water plants. Rhododendrons, azaleas, meconopsis, cardiocrinums, some interesting and unusual trees. Wheelchair access over mown grass - few paths.

♿ ❀ ☕

52 ONE HOUSE NURSERY
Rainow SK11 0AD. Louise Baylis. *21/2m NE of Macclesfield. On A537 Macclesfield to Buxton rd. 21/2m from Macclesfield stn.* Home-made teas. **Adm £3, chd free. Sat 30 June; Sun 1 July (10-5).**
1/2-acre plantswoman's garden featuring hostas, rare and unusual woodland and sun-loving perennials, rockery, gravel garden, sculptures and hornbeam arbour. Stunning views over Cheshire Plain. A short walk away is an atmospheric 1/3-acre historic early C18 walled kitchen garden, hidden for 60yrs and recently restored. Heritage vegetables, gardening and farming bygones, orchard with rare-breed pigs. Featured on BBC Northwest Tonight.

⌜ ❀ ☕

53 ORCHARD HOUSE
72 Audley Road, Alsager ST7 2QN. Mr & Mrs J Trinder, 01270 874833. *6m S of Congleton. 3m W of Kidsgrove. At T-lights in Alsager town centre turn L towards Audley, house is 300yds on R beyond level Xing. Or M6*

J16 to North Stoke on A500, 1st L to Alsager, 2m, just beyond Manor House Hotel on L. Home-made teas. **Adm £2.50, chd free. Sun 29 Apr (11-5). Visitors also welcome by appt.** Fascinated by plants from an early age, we have an unusual collection of diverse plants. Our long narrow garden is organised to accomodate shrubs, herbaceous plants, alpines, grasses, ferns and specialising in bulbs and irises. Featured in 'Sunday Sentinel'.

54 PARM PLACE
High Street, Great Budworth CW9 6HF. Peter & Jane Fairclough, 01606 891131, pfair@btinternet.com. *3m N of Northwich. Great Budworth on E side of A559 between Northwich & Warrington, 4m from J10 M56, also 4m from J19 M6. Parm Place is W of village on S side of High Street.* Home-made teas. **Adm £3, chd free (share to Great Ormond Street Hospital). Suns 1 Apr; 8 July (1-5). Visitors also welcome by appt.**
Well-stocked ½-acre garden with stunning views towards S Cheshire. Curving lawns, shrubs, colourful herbaceous borders, roses, water features, rockery, gravel bed with grasses. Fruit and vegetable plots. In spring large collection of bulbs and flowers, camellias, hellebores and blossom. Featured in 'Swedish Homes & Gardens'.

55 ◆ PEOVER HALL GARDENS
Knutsford WA16 6SW. Randle Brooks Esq, 01565 830395, richard.massey@mellerbraggins.co m. *4m S of Knutsford. Turn off A50 at Whipping Stocks Inn, down Stocks Lane. Follow signs to Peover Hall & Church. Entrance off Goostrey Lane clearly signed.* **Adm £3, chd £2. Mons, Thurs except Bank Hols Apr to Oct. For NGS: Sat 19, Sun 20 May (2-5).**
15 acres. 5 walled gardens; C19 dell, rhododendrons, pleached limes, topiary. Grade II Carolean Stables and C18 park.

56 PIKELOW FARM
School Lane, Marton SK11 9HD. David & Ann Taylor. *3m N of Congleton. In Marton Village take rd signed Marton Heath Trout Pools; ³/₄m down School Lane on R.* Light refreshments & teas. **Adm £3, chd**

free. **Sat 28 Apr; Sun 15 July (2-5).** Peace and tranquillity of a private Nature Reserve with 3 beautifully landscaped lakes bordered by wild flowers; native trees and plants. Small garden with pools - daffodils, pansies and wallflowers in spring and amazing colourful begonias in July. Guided tours of lakes.

57 17 POPLAR GROVE
Sale M33 3AX. Mr Gordon Cooke. *3m N of Altrincham. From the A6144 at Brooklands stn turn into Hope Rd. Poplar Grove 3rd on R.* Home-made teas. **Adm £3, chd free. Sat 7, Sun 8 July (2-5).**
This garden is 'deceptively spacious', being two gardens joined together. The owner is a ceramic artist/landscape designer. Features incl sculpture garden; pebble mosaic 'cave', scented area and living roof. Many tender and borderline plants thrive in this city microclimate such as *Acacia dealbata; lochroma australis* and Rhododendron 'Fragrantissima'. Ceramic Exhibition. Featured in 'Daily Telegraph. Winner - The Times 'Best Back Gardens Competition'.

58 POULTON HALL
Poulton Lancelyn, Bebington CH63 9LN. The Lancelyn Green Family. *2m S of Bebington. From M53, J4 towards Bebington; at T-lights R along Poulton Rd; house 1m on R.* Home-made teas. **Adm £3.50, chd free. Suns 22 Apr; 22 July (2-5.30). Visitors also welcome by appt, on dates nr NGS days.**
3 acres; front lawns with view of the house, wild flower meadow, shrubbery and walled gardens. Features incl Alice in Wonderland Walk and wood sculptures by Jim Heath - the Jabberwock, the Storyteller's Chair and Robin Hood (these relate to the books of Roger Lancelyn Green). Sundial garden for the visually impaired,

sponsored by Bebington Rotary Club. Herb garden parterre and witch's garden. As a powerful memorial to Richard Lancelyn Green a new monumental metal sculpture of enigmatic contemporay form has been created by Sue Sharples, who designed the bronze Viking head. Songs by the Wirral Singers and School Botanical painting display. Gravel paths.

59 RIDGEHILL
Sutton SK11 0LU. Mr & Mrs Martin McMillan, 01260 252353. *2m SE of Macclesfield. From Macclesfield take A523 to Leek after Silk Rd look for t-lights signed Langley, Wincle & Sutton turn L into Byron's Lane, under canal bridge 1st L to Langley at junction Church House PH. Ridgehill Rd is opp turn up Ridgehill Rd, garden on R.* Cream teas. **Adm £4.50, chd free. Sun 20 May (10-4). Visitors also welcome by appt.**
Country garden set in 4 acres overlooking the Cheshire plain. Ponds and water features, shrubbery with rhododendrons, azaleas, camellias etc. Herbaceous borders, blue and winter gardens, topiary areas.

60 ◆ RODE HALL
Church Lane, Scholar Green ST7 3QP. Sir Richard & Lady Baker Wilbraham, 01270 882961, www.rodehall.co.uk. *5m SW of Congleton. Between Scholar Green (A34) & Rode Heath (A50).* **House and Garden adm £5, concessions/chd over 12 £4, Garden only adm £3, concessions/chd over 12 £2.50. Snowdrops Feb daily (except Mons) (12-4). Tues, Weds, Thurs & Bank Hols 1 April to 30 Sept (2-5).**
Nesfield's terrace and rose garden with view over Humphry Repton's landscape is a feature of Rode gardens, as is the woodland garden with terraced rock garden and grotto. Other attractions incl the walk to the

Beautifully landscaped lakes bordered by wild flowers; native trees and plants . . .

lake, restored ice house, working walled kitchen garden and new Italian garden. Fine display of snowdrops in February. Featured in 'Cheshire Life'.

❀ ☕

⑥ ROSEWOOD
Puddington CH64 5SS. Mr & Mrs C E J Brabin, 0151 353 1193, angela.brabin@tesco.net. *6m N of Chester. Turn L (W) off Chester to Hoylake A540 to Puddington. Park by village green. Walk to Old Hall Lane, 30yds away then through archway on L to garden. Owner will meet you at green by appt.* **Adm £3, chd free. Visitors welcome by appt.**
1-acre garden incl small wood, approx 100 rhododendron species and 50 camellias, both spring and autumn flowering, mature flowering dogwoods incl Cornus kousa, kousa chinensis and capitata. Very rare *Michelia yunnanensis* growing and flowering outside. Most of the above raised from seed by owner, some of which are available for sale. A wide range of other species, most of flowering size, in garden. Featured in 'Amateur Gardening'.

♿ ❀

⑥ NEW THE ROWANS
Oldcastle Lane, Threapwood SY14 7AY. Paul Philpotts & Alan Bourne. *3m SW of Malpas. Leave Malpas by B5069 for Wrexham, pass church on R, continue for 3m, take 1st L after Threapwood PO. 1st L into Oldcastle Lane, garden 1st bungalow on R. Light refreshments & teas.* **Adm £3.50, chd free. Sat 21, Sun 22 July (2-5.30).**
Garden restored after many years of neglect, it has been redesigned with an Italian theme, with new borders and beds with roses, perennials and numerous magnolias, rhododendrons and feature trees. Woodland dell, secret garden, formal ponds and many

seating areas to sit and enjoy the garden. Winner - Chester in Bloom - Best Large Garden.

🍴 ❀ ☕

⑥ SAIGHTON GRANGE
(Abbey Gate College), Saighton CH3 6EN. The Governors of Abbey Gate College. *4m SE of Chester. Take A41 towards Waverton turn R to Saighton. Grange is at the end of village. Home-made teas.* **Adm £3, chd free (share to Garden Gate Fund). Sun 1 Apr (12-4).**
The gardens at Abbey Gate College are a little masterpiece of garden design. From the symmetrical vista through the clipped yews hedges, which are undergoing restoration, to the Japanese garden, which is beginning to blossom, all provide a tantalising glimpse of what has been and what is yet to come. This garden is still in the process of restoration.

🍴 ☕

⑥ SANDYMERE
Cotebrook CW6 9EH. John & Alex Timpson. *5m N of Tarporley. On A54 about 300yds W of T-lights at Xrds of A49/A54. Home-made teas.* **Adm £4, chd free. Sun 1 July (2-5.30).**
16 landscaped acres of beautiful Cheshire countryside with terraces, walled garden and amazing new hosta garden. Long views, native wildlife and tranquillity of 3 lakes. Elegant planting schemes, shady seats and sun-splashed borders, mature pine woods and rolling lawns accented by graceful wooden structures. Different every year: witness the evolution.

♿ 🍴 ❀ ☕

⑥ NEW THE SCHOOL HOUSE
School Lane, Dunham Massey WA14 4SE. Andrew Bushell & Peter White. *1½m SW of Altringham. From M56 J4 follow*

signs for Dunham Massey Hall (NT). Turn into Woodhouse Lane becoming School Lane 100yds after Axe Cleaver PH. Home-made teas. **Adm £3, chd free. Sat 28, Sun 29 July (1-5).**
Cottage garden divided into rooms. In picturesque setting attached to village hall and beside the Bridgewater canal. Incl herbaceous borders, rose and bog garden.

♿ 🍴 ❀ ☕

SMITHY COTTAGE
See Staffordshire & part of West Midlands.

⑥ 199 STOCKPORT ROAD
Timperley WA15 7SF. Eric & Shirley Robinson. *1½m NE of Altrincham. Take A560 out of Altrincham, in 1m take B5165 towards Timperley. B5165 is Stockport rd. Home-made teas.* **Adm £2.50, chd free. Suns 17 June; 5 Aug (1-5).**
Overstuffed, cottage-style garden owned by 2 plantaholics, one an enthusiastic gardener, the other a very keen flower arranger. The garden is full of colourful herbaceous perennials, shrubs and hostas, and has a small brick-built pond complete with small koi and goldfish. You will not believe how many plants there are in such a small garden. Newly designed front garden with water feature.

🍴 ☕

⑥ ◆ STONYFORD COTTAGE
Stonyford Lane, Oakmere CW8 2TF. Janet & Tony Overland, 01606 888128, tony-overland@yahoo.co.uk. *5m SW of Northwich. Turn R off A556 (Northwich to Chester). At Xrds ¾m past A49 junction (signpost Norley-Kingsley NB not Cuddington signs). Entrance ½m on L.* **Adm £3, chd free. Tues - Suns & Bank Hol Mons April - Sept 12-5. For NGS: Sun 10 June (1.30-5.30).**
This informal natural garden has been developed around a 'Monet' style pool with bridges to an island, woodland walk and damp garden. Unusual waterside plants, iris and primulas. Adjacent specialist plant nursery.

♿ 🍴 ❀ ☕

⑥ SUMMERDOWN
27 Castle Hill, Prestbury SK10 4AS. Kate & Paul Boutinot, 01625 422920. *3m NW of Macclesfield. From Prestbury take A538 towards Wilmslow. Garden 3 drives on L after*

Woodland dell, secret garden, formal ponds and many seating areas to sit and enjoy the garden . . .

2nd turning to Castlegate. Please park considerately in Castlegate or car parks in village (12min walk). No parking on property except for disabled by prior tel arrangement. Home-made teas. **Adm £3.50, chd free. Sun 1 July (11-5.30). Visitors also welcome by appt.**
Landscaped in 2004 this 1¼ acre garden has established boundaries with mature trees and distant views. Stream, pond, fountain, temple and parterre garden are complemented by already well established plantings of David Austin roses, grasses, hostas, catalpas, tree ferns, gunneras and much more! Glasshouse and raised vegetable area. Gravel paths and slopes.

69 ♦ SUNNYSIDE FARM
Shop Lane, Little Budworth CW6 9HA. Mike & Joan Smeethe, 01829 760618. *3m NE of Tarporley. The signed field parking for NGS days is reached directly off A54 approx 1m E of T-lights at A54/A49 Xrds by taking track opp. Longstone Lane 250yds W of Shrewsbury Arms (limited parking for disabled only, at house, please tel). Parking non NGS days Shop Lane opp Shrewsbury Arms. Teas (NGS days only).* **Adm £3.50, chd free. Fris July & Aug 10-4. For NGS: Suns 15 July; 19 Aug (1-5).**
5 acres of woodland, wild flower meadow and country garden bursting with colour and interest spring to autumn. Cottage garden with traditional and contemporay plantings, tranquil pool garden, long border with late flowering bold perennials and dramatic grasses, decorative potager and fruit garden. Orchard with beehives and much, much more. A wealth of unusual plants and interesting colour schemes. For 2007 newly planted acer glade and woodland walks.

70 SWETTENHAM VILLAGE
CW12 2LD. *5m NW of Congleton. Turn off A54 N 2m W of Congleton or turn E off A535 at Twemlow Green, NE of Holmes Chapel. Follow signs to Swettenham. Parking at Swettenham Arms PH. Entrance at side of PH.* Home-made teas at Dane Edge. **Combined adm £5, chd free. Suns 13 May; 9 Sept (12-4).**

DANE EDGE
Mr & Mrs J Cunningham
Steep riverside garden of 10½ acres leading down to a beautiful and partially wooded wildlife haven with pleasant walks by R Dane. Peacocks roaming the garden.

♦ THE QUINTA ARBORETUM
Swettenham. Tatton Garden Society, www.tattongardensociety.co.uk. **Daily (not Christmas Day) 9 to dusk.**
Arboretum on a 28-acre site established since 1948 with over 4,000 species of trees incl collections of birch, pine, oak and flowering shrubs. Bluebell bank and snowdrops. 40 camellias and 64 rhododendrons planted 2004. Collection of 120 hebes. Lake.

71 ♦ TATTON PARK
Knutsford WA16 6QN. **The National Trust, leased to Cheshire County Council, 01625 534400, www.tattonpark.org.uk/attractions.** *2½m N of Knutsford. Well signed on M56 J7 & from M6 J19.* **House and Garden adm £5, chd £3, park entry £4.20, Garden only adm £3.50, chd £2. Tues - Suns high season 10-6 last entry 5; low season 11-4 last entry 3. For NGS: Weds 9 May; 13 June (10-6 last entry 5).**
Features include orangery by Wyatt, fernery by Paxton, restored Japanese garden, Italian and rose gardens. Greek monument and African hut. Hybrid azaleas and rhododendrons; swamp cypresses, tree ferns, tall redwoods, bamboos and pines. Fully restored productive walled gardens. Pinery/vinery opened 2006.

72 TIRLEY GARTH
Utkinton CW6 0LZ. *2m N of Tarporley. 2m S of Kelsall. Entrance 500yds from village of Utkinton. At N of Tarporley take Utkinton rd.* Home-made teas. **Adm £4, chd free. Wed 18, Sun 22 Apr (1-5).**
40-acre garden, terraced and landscaped. Designed by Thomas Mawson, it is the only Grade II* Arts & Crafts garden in Cheshire and is considered an exceptionally important example of an early C20 garden laid out in both formal and informal styles, which remain complete and in excellent condition. Wollemi pine planted 2007. Partial wheelchair access.

73 80 UPTON PARK
Upton by Chester CH2 1DQ. Lynne & Phil Pearn, 01244 390326, lynnepearn@hotmail.com. *1½m NE of Chester. From A41 ring rd NE of*

Courtyard area with ancient espalier pear tree, numerous pots, a well and Victorian conservatory with vine and bougainvillea . . .

Chester turn towards Chester at Shell garage T-lights at Upton Heath. Proceed ½m down Heath Rd (traffic calming) to mini roundabout, turn L. After ¼m car park is on R beside library. Follow signs to walk 200yds across playing field. Disabled parking available, directions from marshall in car park. Home-made teas. **Adm £3, chd free. Sun 15 July (11-5). Visitors also welcome by appt.**
Plantswoman's garden of ¼ acre designed for yr-round interest and constantly changing. Featuring mixed beds where interesting iron and willow work features mingle with the flowers, colourful banked herbaceous bed, small vegetable plot, greenhouses, ferns and pond. Courtyard area with ancient espalier pear tree, numerous pots, a well and Victorian conservatory with vine and bougainvillea. Artist/sculptor working in garden. Prize-winner 'Chester in Bloom'.

74 **NEW** **THE VALVE HOUSE**
Egerton Green, nr Malpas
SY14 8AW. Dr Nicola Reynolds.
*4m NE of Malpas. From Chester
take A41 S, at Broxton roundabout
turn L onto A534, 1st R after
Coppermine PH (to Bickerton).
Fork L at Bickerton School. Garden
2nd on R. On A49 turn opp
Cholmondeley Arms to
Cholmondeley Castle. Garden opp
Manor Farm.* Home-made teas at
Manor Farm. **Combined adm with
Manor Farm £4, chd free (share
to Bickerton Village Hall). Sat 16,
Sun 17 June (2-5.30).**
Medium sized plantswomen's
garden with many interesting
features, well stocked herbaceous
borders with an abundance of
unusual plants. Wildlife pond with
Monet-style bridge, productive
vegetable and fruit gardens and
rare breed chickens.
🏃 ❀ ☕

and ragged robin. Wild flower
meadow. Antique shop and Victorian
parlour. Category Winner - Chester in
Bloom.
🏃 ☕

76 **69 WELL LANE**
Gayton CH60 8NH. Angus & Sally
Clark, 0151 342 3321,
aandsclark@aol.com. *7m S of
Birkenhead. SE of Heswall. From the
Devon Doorway/Glegg Arms
roundabout at Heswall, travel SE in the
direction of Chester for approx 1/4m.
Turn R into Gayton Lane for about 1/2m
then L into Well Lane. Garden approx
200yds on L. Park on rd or at
Maylands.* Home-made teas.
**Combined adm with Maylands £4,
chd free. Mon 7 May (1-5). Visitors
also welcome by appt.**
This undulating and established 3/4-
acre garden, surrounded by a
woodland backdrop, has sandy acid
soil and contains interesting shrubs,
many spring flowering (rhododendrons,

mature trees and incl woodland walk,
wildlife pond, unusual containers and
ceramics, these gardens are a
plantperson's delight. Fantastic plant
stall as usual. New developments in all
gardens incl revamped herbaceous
border at no.6.
🏃 ❀ ☕

78 **WESTAGE FARM**
Westage Lane, Great Budworth
CW9 6HJ. Jean & Peter Davies,
01606 892383,
pj@budworth94.fsnet.co.uk. *3m N
of Northwich. 4m W of Knutsford. Gt
Budworth is on E side of A559
between Northwich & Warrington,
4m from J10 M 56, and 4m from J19
M6. Garden is 400yds to E of village.
Follow Gt Budworth signs.* Home-
made teas. **Adm £3.50, chd free.
Evening Opening wine, Fri 15
June (7-9); Sat 16, Sun 17 June
(1-5). Visitors also welcome by
appt, April to July, groups of 10+,
coaches welcome.**
Family 2 acre garden with herbaceous
and mixed borders. Colour-themed
plots, raised vegetable and soft fruit
beds, orchards with many old fruit
varieties. Greenhouses, cutting garden
and pebble area. Many interesting and
light hearted features. Vineyard planted
1996 from which wine is made.
Woodland garden with wild flowers
and plenty of seats to sit and relax. 2
acre paddock with donkeys, free range
hens and ducks with pond area. Tours
and talks by owners. Ice Cream Farm
(300yds). Historic village of Gt
Budworth church open. Featured in
'Cheshire Life'.
♿ 🏃 ❀ 🛏 ☕

Here are three hidden gems in a suburban setting, each with its individual character . . .

WEEPING ASH
See Lancashire, Merseyside &
Greater Manchester.

75 **THE WELL HOUSE**
Tilston SY14 7DP. Mrs S H French-
Greenslade, 01829 250332. *3m NW
of Malpas. On A41, 1st turn R after
Broxton roundabout, L on Malpas Rd
through Tilston. House & antique shop
on L.* Cream teas. **Adm £3.50, chd
free (share to Cystic Fibrosis Trust).
Sun 8 July (1.30-5.30). Visitors also
welcome by appt, March - July incl,
coaches permitted.**
1-acre cottage garden, bridge over
natural stream, spring bulbs,
perennials, herbs and shrubs. New
triple pond and waterfall feature.
Adjoining 3/4-acre field being made
into wild flower meadow; first seeding
late 2003. Large bog area of kingcups

azaleas, magnolias etc). Old restored
farm outbuildings. Partial wheelchair
access.
♿ 🏃 ❀ ☕

77 **WEST DRIVE GARDENS**
4, 6, 9 West Drive, Gatley SK8 4JJ.
Mr & Mrs D J Gane, Mrs T Bishop,
Mr & Mrs K L Marsden & Mr J
Needham. *4m N of Wilmslow. On
B5166. From J5 (M56) drive past
airport to B5166 (Styal Rd). L towards
Gatley. Pass over T-lights at Heald
Green. West Drive is last turn on R
before Gatley Village. Cul-de-sac,
please do not park beyond the notice.*
Home-made teas. **Combined adm
£5, chd free (share to St Anns
Hospice, Heald Green). Sun 10 June
(10.30-4.30).**
Here are three hidden gems in a
suburban setting, each with its
individual character. Surrounded by

79 **WILLASTON VILLAGE
GARDENS**
Willaston CH64 1TE. *8m N of
Chester. Take A540 Chester to West
Kirby rd; turn R on B5151 to Willaston;
at village centre turn R into Hooton Rd.
Change Lane is 3/4m on R opp garage.
All 3 gardens are entered from Change
Hey garden. Parking available in field at
bottom of Change Lane on RH-side.
15 mins walk from Hooton stn along
B5133 in direction of Willaston.
Change Lane on LH-side opp garage.
Leave M53 J5. Join A41, travel in
direction of Queensferry, N Wales.
1/4m at T- lights turn R B5133. Along
Hooton Rd, after 3/4m Hooton Stn on
L. Then as from Hooton Stn.* Home-
made teas. **Combined adm £4, chd
free. Sun 20 May (2-5).**
☕

CHANGE HEY
Change Lane CH64 1TE. Mr &
Mrs Keith Butcher
2-acre garden with mature trees,
developing woodland area
underplanted with rhododendrons
and azaleas.

THE DUTCH HOUSE
Joan & Michael Ring
1/3-acre cottage-style garden with
some formality. The rear garden
vista, terminating with a 1920
Boulton & Paul revolving
summerhouse, is surrounded on
2 sides by mature beech, oak
and pine trees. Some gravel
paths.

SILVERBURN
Prof M P & Dr A M Escudier
Just under 1/2-acre garden
designed by garden owners. A
plantsman's garden with
interesting herbaceous beds and
mixed borders, species and old-
fashioned roses, rhododendrons,
azaleas, attractive trees, vegetable
garden and small orchard.

⑧⓪ WOOD END COTTAGE
Grange Lane, Whitegate CW8 2BQ.
Mr & Mrs M R Everett, 01606
888236. *4m SW of Northwich. Turn S
off A556 (Northwich bypass) at
Sandiway PO T-lights; after 1³/₄m, turn
L to Whitegate village; opp school
follow Grange Lane for 300yds.* Home-
made teas. **Adm £3.50, chd free
(share to The Macular Disease
Society). Sun 1, Wed 25 July (2-5).
Visitors also welcome by appt, May,
June & July only.**

Plantsman's traditional country garden
of 1/2 acre in attractive setting, gently
sloping to a natural stream. Shade and
moisture-loving plants. Well-stocked
herbaceous borders with many
unusual plants particularly featuring
delphiniums (1 July) and many varieties
of phlox (25 July). Red border, roses
and clematis. Background of mature
trees.

⑧① 𝗡𝗘𝗪 WOODCROFT
1 Oakfield Rise, Holmes Chapel
CW4 7DY. Mr & Mrs R Spencer,
01477 533482. *4m E of
Middlewich. In Holmes Chapel at
roundabout take A54 to
Middlewich. Parking available at
County Primary School, 1/2m on L,
turn L into Brookfield Dr, next R.
Limited parking at 1 Oakfield Rise.*
Home-made teas at Dane Mount.
**Combined adm with Dane
Mount £4, chd free. Sun 15 Apr
(1-5). Visitors also welcome by
appt.**
Medium sized garden incorporates
maturing spring flowering shrubs,
conifers and heathers with an array

of different bulbs. A large raised
bed is a feature in the back garden
which also contains fruit trees,
vegetable patch, rose bed and
herbaceous planting. Winner
'Holmes Chapel Best Front
Garden' award.

**⑧② 𝗡𝗘𝗪 3 WOODHOUSE
LANE**
Gawsworth SK11 9QQ. Shirley
Campbell & John Helm. *3m SW
of Macclesfield. Take A536 from
Macclesfield, after approx 3m turn
L at Xrds into Church Lane (signed
Gawsworth Hall). Take 1st L into
Woodhouse Lane garden on L.*
Home-made teas. **Adm £3, chd
free. Sat 8, Sun 9 Sept (2-5).**
Gently sloping 1/3 acre garden in
the pretty village of Gawsworth,
designed for yr-round interest.
Perennials, annuals, dahlias and
cannas provide plenty of late
summer colour. Pond,
greenhouses, small vegetable
garden.

Gently sloping 1/3 acre garden in the pretty village of Gawsworth

CORNWALL

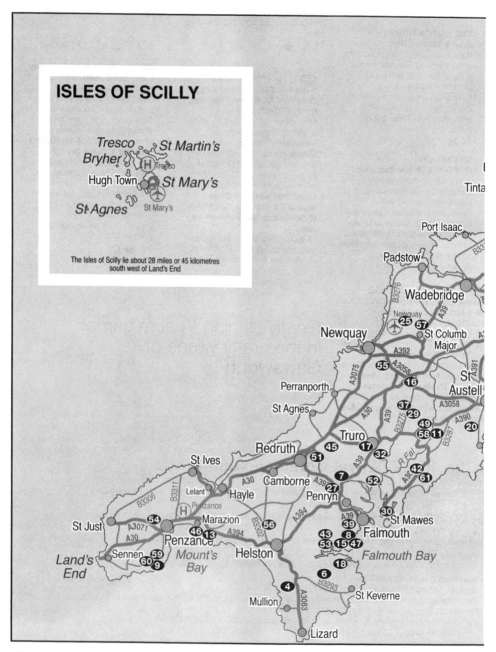

ISLES OF SCILLY

Tresco
Bryher
St Martin's
Hugh Town
St Mary's
St Agnes

The Isles of Scilly lie about 28 miles or 45 kilometres
south west of Land's End

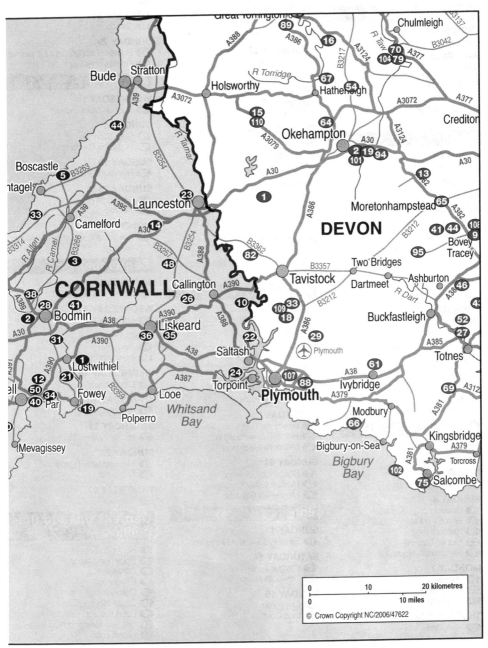

© Crown Copyright NC/2006/47622

Opening Dates

February

SUNDAY 18
54 Trengwainton

March

SUNDAY 11
24 Ince Castle

SATURDAY 17
52 Trelissick

SUNDAY 18
44 Poundstock Gardens

SATURDAY 24
15 Glendurgan

April

SUNDAY 1
50 Tregrehan

SUNDAY 8
24 Ince Castle

THURSDAY 12
10 Cotehele

SUNDAY 15
7 Carclew Gardens
30 Lamorran House
61 Trist House

TUESDAY 17
55 Trerice

THURSDAY 19
38 Pencarrow

SUNDAY 22
39 Penjerrick Garden

SUNDAY 29
11 Creed House
29 Ladock House

MONDAY 30
46 St Michael's Mount

May

THURSDAY 3
19 Headland

FRIDAY 4
34 Marsh Villa Gardens

SUNDAY 6
1 Boconnoc
4 Bonython Manor
18 Hallowarren
23 Higher Truscott
37 Nansawsan House

MONDAY 7
18 Hallowarren
36 Moyclare
51 Tregullow

THURSDAY 10
19 Headland

SUNDAY 13
2 Bodwannick
3 Bolts Quarry Farm
24 Ince Castle
57 Trewan Hall

WEDNESDAY 16
31 Lanhydrock

THURSDAY 17
19 Headland

SATURDAY 19
41 Pinsla Garden & Nursery

SUNDAY 20
41 Pinsla Garden & Nursery

THURSDAY 24
19 Headland

SATURDAY 26
9 Chygurno

SUNDAY 27
9 Chygurno
18 Hallowarren
32 Little Park Farm
33 Long Hay

MONDAY 28
18 Hallowarren
25 The Japanese Garden & Bonsai Nursery

June

SUNDAY 3
23 Higher Truscott
48 Trebartha

SUNDAY 17
6 Caervallack
28 Kingberry
33 Long Hay
42 Poppy Cottage Garden
53 Trenarth (Evening)

SATURDAY 23
5 Boscastle Gardens
21 Hidden Valley Gardens
35 Menheniot Gardens

SUNDAY 24
5 Boscastle Gardens
21 Hidden Valley Gardens
35 Menheniot Gardens

July

SUNDAY 1
14 Ellis Gardens and Nurseries

SATURDAY 14
9 Chygurno
59 Trewoofe House

SUNDAY 15
9 Chygurno
24 Ince Castle

SUNDAY 22
13 Ednovean Farm
16 Goenrounsen
27 Kennall House

TUESDAY 24
55 Trerice

SUNDAY 29
43 Potager Garden (Day & Evening)
45 Roseland House

August

WEDNESDAY 1
44 Poundstock Gardens

SUNDAY 5
17 Grey Stones
22 Highcroft Gardens

SUNDAY 19
22 Highcroft Gardens

SUNDAY 26
45 Roseland House
53 Trenarth

MONDAY 27
25 The Japanese Garden & Bonsai Nursery

September

SATURDAY 1
34 Marsh Villa Gardens

WEDNESDAY 12
10 Cotehele

SUNDAY 16
49 Tregoose
54 Trengwainton

WEDNESDAY 19
31 Lanhydrock

THURSDAY 20
15 Glendurgan

SATURDAY 22
21 Hidden Valley Gardens

SUNDAY 23
21 Hidden Valley Gardens
48 Trebartha

THURSDAY 27
52 Trelissick

Gardens open to the public

1 Boconnoc
4 Bonython Manor
8 Carwinion
9 Chygurno
10 Cotehele
11 Creed House
12 Eden Project
14 Ellis Gardens and Nurseries
15 Glendurgan

19 Headland
20 The Lost Gardens of Heligan
21 Hidden Valley Gardens
25 The Japanese Garden & Bonsai Nursery
26 Ken Caro
30 Lamorran House
31 Lanhydrock
34 Marsh Villa Gardens
38 Pencarrow
39 Penjerrick Garden
40 Pine Lodge Gardens & Nursery
41 Pinsla Garden & Nursery
42 Poppy Cottage Garden
43 Potager Garden
45 Roseland House
46 St Michael's Mount
47 Trebah
50 Tregrehan
52 Trelissick
54 Trengwainton
55 Trerice
56 Trevarno Gardens and the National Museum of Gardening
58 Trewithen
59 Trewoofe House
60 Trewoofe Orchard
61 Trist House

The Gardens

ALDER
See Devon.

1 ◆ BOCONNOC
Lostwithiel PL22 0RG. Mr Anthony Fortescue, 01208 872507, adgfortescue@btinternet.com. *4m E of Lostwithiel. 2m E of A390. Turn off A390 at Middle Taphouse.* **Garden only adm £4.50, chd free, house £3, chd free. Suns 15, 22, 29 Apr; 13, 20, 27 May (2-5.30). For NGS: Sun 6 May (2-5.30).**
Gardens covering some 20 acres, surrounded by parkland and woods. Magnificent trees, flowering shrubs and views. Set in C18 picturesque landscape which surrounds the church and Boconnoc House (both open). Teas in the stable yard designed by Sir John Soane. Model railway exhibition. Featured in 'Daily Telegraph'.
& 💮

2 BODWANNICK
Nanstallon PL30 5LN. Mr P M & Mrs W M Appleton, 01208 831427. *2½ m W of Bodmin. A389 turn at Pottery signed Nanstallon, L at Xrds signed Hoopers Bridge then sharp R.* **Adm £2.50, chd free (share to FLEET). Sun 13 May (2-5). Visitors also welcome by appt.**
Approx 1-acre compact garden incl water garden, herbaceous, granite Cornish cross, roses, shade garden and shrubs. Over 50 varieties of daffodils and narcissi. Large stone circle. Plantsman's garden.
💮

3 BOLTS QUARRY FARM
Penvorder Lane, St Breward PL30 4NY. George & Jackie Greengrass, 01208 851592. *8m NE of Bodmin. From village shop, drive down hill through village to grass triangle & bus shelter. 1st L into Penvorder Lane & drive up hill. Garden last property on L.* Light refreshments. **Adm £3, chd free. Sun 13 May (2-6). Visitors also welcome by appt May & June only.**
'Mowhay' granite garden with rhododendron walk. Many different plants and shrubs. Bluebell trail through property to 2-acre young broadleaf tree plantation and quarry garden covered in bluebells during May. Wonderful views. Natural pond garden. Recital by St Breward Silver Band. Bluebell Trail.
💮 ☕

Circle garden, constructed in colour concrete with Mediterranean planting . . .

4 ◆ BONYTHON MANOR
Cury Cross Lanes TR12 7BA. Mr & Mrs Richard Nathan, 01326 240234, sue@bonythonmanor.co.uk. *5m S of Helston. On main A3083 Helston to Lizard Rd. Turn L at Cury Cross Lanes (Wheel Inn). Entrance 300yds on R.* **Adm £5, chd £2. Tues to Fri incl 3 Apr to 28 Sept (closed Good Fri & Public Holidays) (10-4.30). For NGS: Sun 6 May (2-5).**
Magnificent 20-acre colour garden incl sweeping hydrangea drive to Georgian manor (not open). Herbaceous walled garden, potager with vegetables and picking flowers; 3 lakes in valley planted with ornamental grasses, perennials and South African flowers. A 'must see' for all seasons colour.
& ☕ 💮 ╠═╣ ☕

5 BOSCASTLE GARDENS
PL35 0BJ. *5m N of Camelford. Park in doctor's surgery car park at top of village (clearly signed). Limited parking for disabled at both gardens. Maps provided.* Home-made teas at Half Acre. **Combined adm £3, chd free. Sat 23, Sun 24 June (1.30-6).**
Boscastle Harbour is well-known to visitors. Both gardens are in older part of village, overlooking cliff, land and sea. Both gardens featured in Cornwall Gardens Guide.
☕

HALF ACRE
Carole Vincent
Sculpture in an acre of 3 gardens: cottage; small wood; the Blue Circle garden, constructed in colour concrete with Mediterranean planting. Studio open, painting exhibition.
╳ 💮

WILDWOOD
Alex & Ian Stewart
Garden of magic deception. Front traditional, rear - lawns leading to wood with pond, tree ferns and shade-loving shrubs.
╳

6 CAERVALLACK
St Martin in Meneague TR12 6DF. Mr M Robinson & Ms L McClary, 01326 221339, mat@carvallack.f9.co.uk, www.build-art.co.uk. *5m SE of Helston. Go through Mawgan village, over 2 bridges, past Gear Farm shop; garden next farmhouse on LH-side.* Cream teas. **Adm £3.50, chd free (share to Shelter Box Trust). Sun 17 June (2-5). Visitors also welcome by appt.**
An 'English' garden arranged into rooms. Flowing herbaceous borders with many varieties of roses. Contemporary architecture incl new cob walls, water features and unique 54ft timber and wire covered bridge. Walled orchard, vegetable garden and wild 2-acre field.
╳ 💮 ☕

❼ CARCLEW GARDENS
Perran-ar-Worthal TR3 7PB. The Chope Family. *5m SW of Truro. From A39 turn E at Perran-ar-Worthal. Bus: alight Perran-ar-Worthal 1m.* Home-made teas. **Adm £3.50, chd free. Sun 15 Apr (2-6).**
One of the original NGS gardens first opened in 1927 and home to the 'Sir Charles Lemon' rhododendron. 200 years of history are reflected in this large private garden with rare and mature specimen trees and shrubs, 'listed' walls, fine terraces and ornamental water.
🎭 ☕

Above Mounts Bay with sweeping sea views, a garden of contrasts . . .

❽ ♦ CARWINION
Mawnan Smith TR11 5JA. Anthony & Jane Rogers, 01326 250258, www.carwinion.com. *3m W of Falmouth. 500yds from centre of Mawnan Smith.* **Adm £4, chd free, concessions £3.50. Daily (10-5.30).**
Luxuriant, traditional, 14-acre Cornish valley garden with delightful walk running down to R Helford. Home of UK's premier collection of bamboos. Hardy fern nursery. Ferns and wild flowers abound. A garden of yesterday and tomorrow. Some steep slopes and steps.
♿ ❀ 🍴 ☕

❾ ♦ CHYGURNO
Lamorna TR19 6XH. Dr & Mrs Robert Moule, 01736 732153. *4m S of Penzance. Off B3315. Follow signs for The Cove Restaurant. Garden is at top of hill, past Hotel on LH side.* **Adm £3, chd free. Weds only Apr, May June; Weds & Suns July, Aug (2-5). For NGS: Sats, Suns 26, 27 May (2-5); 14, 15 July (11-5).**
Beautiful, unique, 3-acre cliffside garden overlooking Lamorna Cove.

Planting started in 1998, mainly S-hemisphere shrubs and exotics with hydrangeas, camellias and rhododendrons. Woodland area with tree ferns set against large granite outcrops. Garden terraced with steep steps and paths. Plenty of benches so you can take a rest and enjoy the wonderful views. Well worth the effort. Featured in Sunday Times and Garden News.

THE CIDER HOUSE
See Devon.

❿ ♦ COTEHELE
Saltash PL12 6TA. The National Trust, 01579 351346, www.nationaltrust.org.uk. *2m E of St Dominick. 4m from Gunnislake. (Turn at St Ann's Chapel); 8m SW of Tavistock; 14m from Plymouth via Tamar Bridge.* **House and garden adm £8.40, chd £4.20, garden only adm £5.20, chd £2.60. Garden open daily (11-dusk), house 17 Mar to 31 Oct (11-4). For NGS: Thur 12 Apr; Wed 12 Sept (11-dusk).**
Formal garden, orchard and meadow. Terrace garden falling to sheltered valley with ponds, stream and unusual shrubs. Fine medieval house (one of the least altered in the country); armour, tapestries, furniture. Some steep slopes, gravel paths.
♿ 🎭 ❀ ☕

⓫ ♦ CREED HOUSE
Creed TR2 4SL. Mr & Mrs W R Croggon, 01872 530372. *6m SW of St Austell. From the centre of Grampound on A390, take rd signed to Creed. After 1m turn L opp Creed Church & garden is on L.* Teas on NGS day. **Adm £3, chd free. Open daily Feb to Oct (10-5). For NGS: Sun 29 Apr (11-5.30).**
5-acre landscaped Georgian rectory garden; tranquil rural setting; spacious lawns. Tree collection; rhododendrons; sunken cobbled yard and formal walled herbaceous garden. Trickle stream to ponds and bog. Natural woodland walk. Restoration began 1974 - continues and incl recent planting. Featured in the Good Gardens Guide.
❀ 🍴 ☕

⓬ ♦ EDEN PROJECT
Bodelva PL24 2SG. The Eden Trust, 01726 811911, www.edenproject.com. *4m E of St Austell. Brown signs from A30 & A390.* **Adm £14, chd £5, senior citizens £10. April to Oct (10-6, last adm**

4.30); Nov to Mar (10-4.30, last adm 3). See website for full details.
The world's largest greenhouses nestle in a giant 50-metre deep crater the size of 30 football pitches, the centrepiece of a spectacular global garden. Eden is a gateway to the fascinating world of plants and people and a vibrant reminder of how we need each other for our mutual survival.
♿ 🎭 ❀ ☕

⓭ EDNOVEAN FARM
Perranuthnoe TR20 9LZ. Christine & Charles Taylor, 01736 711883, www.ednoveanfarm.co.uk/gardens. *3m E of Penzance. From A394 ½m E of Marazion, turn seawards at Perran Xrds beside Dynasty Restaurant. Continue towards Perranuthnoe, parking in field beside Perranuthnoe sign. Up hill to garden.* Cream teas. **Adm £3, chd free. Sun 22 July (1-5). Visitors also welcome by appt July/Aug for groups of 10+.**
Above Mounts Bay with sweeping sea views incl St Michael's Mount. A garden of contrasts. Formal parterres and courtyards around a converted barn, opening to flowing lawns, finishing with Italian and gravel gardens. Box, date palms, olive trees and figs in the courtyards, grasses, phormiums, cordalines beyond. Featured in 'Gardening News'.
❀ 🍴 ☕

⓮ NEW ♦ ELLIS GARDENS AND NURSERIES
Medrow, Polyphant, Launceston PL15 7PS. Tim & Sue Ellis, 01566 86641, timellis@ellisnurseries.wanadoo.co.uk. *6m W of Launceston. From A30 take turning to Blackhill Quarry. Proceed up hill to village green. L at bottom of green and keep to L round bend. Garden 4th on R.* Cream teas from midday, NGS day only. **Adm £2, chd free. Easter to Sept (9-5). For NGS: Sun 1 July (10-5).**
Newly-created and developing ¾ acre perennial flower garden with willow tunnel, wildlife pond and new white garden. Large collection of euphorbias planted throughout. Full of colour from May to Sept. Large collection of plants for sale. Silver gilt medal winner and best Novice entry, Royal Cornwall Show. Some compacted gravel paths. Deep, unfenced pond.
♿ ❀ ☕

THE GARDEN HOUSE
See Devon.

⑮ ◆ GLENDURGAN
Mawnan Smith TR11 5JZ. The
National Trust, 01326 250906,
www.nationaltrust.org.uk. *5m SW of
Falmouth. Take rd to Helford Passage.
Follow NT signs.* **Adm £5.20, chd
£2.60. Tues to Sat 10 Feb to 27 Oct,
also Bank Hol Mons (closed Good
Friday). For NGS: Sat 24 Mar; Thur
20 Sept (10.30-5.30).**
Valley garden running down to Durgan
village on R Helford. In spring large
displays of rhododendrons, camellias
and magnolias with drifts of primroses,
bluebells and aquilegia below. Many
specimen trees, laurel maze dating
from 1833 and giant's stride. Steep
slopes with gravel and steps. Limited
wheelchair access only.
🖚 ⊕ 👜

⑯ GOENROUNSEN
Carnego Lane, Summercourt
TR8 5BQ. Andrew & Angela Bailey,
01872 510604,
goenrounsen@yahoo.co.uk. *10 m
NE of Truro. Exit A30 for Summercourt.
At centre of village T-lights with 'corner
shop'. Take the lane down beside shop
(Carnego Lane). Garden ¹/₂ m on L. No
access for coaches.* Home-made teas.
**Adm £3, chd free. Sun 22 July (2-5).
Visitors also welcome by appt May
to Oct, groups of 8+.**
Formal garden with mature acid-loving
shrubs and specimen trees
surrounded by wild flower meadow,
young arboretum, orchard and large
wildlife pond. Old Cornish lane leads to
copse of ancient oaks underplanted
with young tree ferns. Hydrangea
garden with 750 shrubs. Beautiful and
tranquil setting of 13 acres.
🖚 👜

⑰ GREY STONES
15 Trethowan Heights, off
Penwethers Lane, Truro TR1 3QQ.
Roddy & Rachel Macpherson-Rait,
01872 261140. *¹/₄ m W of County Hall
Truro. On A390 Truro to Redruth rd.
1st L after County Arms PH, down
Penwethers Lane.* Cream teas. **Adm
£3, chd free. Sun 5 Aug (1-5).
Visitors also welcome by appt
July/Aug only.**
¹/₂-acre plant-lovers' garden created
over last 6yrs. Winding paths lead to 2
ponds and adjoining rill. Herbaceous
borders, rockery, box beds, green and
white tranquil garden; bamboo/restio
area complements large number of
grasses, lilies and exotics. Well-

stocked, colourful summer garden.
Partial wheelchair access, gravel paths.
🔥 🖚 ⊕ 👜

⑱ HALLOWARREN
Carne, Manaccan TR12 6HD. Mrs
Mark Osman, 01326 231224. *10m E
of Helston. 1m out of the centre of
Manaccan village. Downhill past inn on
R, follow sign to Carne. House on R.*
Home-made teas. **Adm £2.50, chd
free. Suns, Mons 6, 7, 27, 28 May (2-
6). Visitors also welcome by appt.**
2-acre garden and orchard leading to a
beautiful wooded valley and bordering
stream. Mixture of the natural and
cultivated, bog and cottage garden
with primulas, lilies and kitchen herbs,
unusual shrubs and trees. Walk along
valley through old woodland full of
native bluebells. The ethos of this
garden is harmony with nature and it is
run on organic lines. Ducks, geese and
chickens.
🖚 ⊕ 🚶 👜

HARTLAND ABBEY
See Devon.

⑲ ◆ HEADLAND
Polruan PL23 1PW. Jean Hill, 01726
870243,
www.headlandgarden.co.uk. *¹/₂ m SE
of Fowey. Passenger ferry from Fowey,
10 min walk along West St & up
Battery Lane. Or follow signs to
Polruan (on E of Fowey Estuary).
Ignore first car park, turn L for second
car park (overlooking harbour), turn L
(on foot) down St Saviour's Hill.* **Adm
£2.50, chd £1. Thurs only 31 May to
30 Aug (2-6). For NGS: Thurs only 3
to 24 May (2-6).**
1¹/₄-acre cliff garden with magnificent
sea, coastal and estuary views on 3
sides. Planted to withstand salty gales
yet incls subtropical plants with
intimate places to sit and savour the
views. Paths wind through the garden
past rocky outcrops down to a
secluded swimming cove.
🖚 👜

**⑳ ◆ THE LOST GARDENS OF
HELIGAN**
Pentewan PL26 6EN. Heligan
Gardens Ltd, 01726 845100,
www.heligan.com. *5m S of St Austell.
From St Austell take B3273 signed
Mevagissey, follow signs.* **Adm £8.50,
chd £5, concessions £7.50, family
£23.50. Daily all year except 24, 25
Dec (10-6; 10-5 in winter; last adm
1¹/₂ hrs before close).**
'The Nation's Favourite Garden' offers

200 acres for exploration, which
include productive gardens, pleasure
grounds, a lush 22-acre subtropical
jungle, and walks through sustainably
managed ancient woodlands,
wetlands and farmland.
🔥 🖚 ⊕ 👜

Prairie planting
containing 2,500
plants of
herbaceous and
grasses . . .

**㉑ ◆ HIDDEN VALLEY
GARDENS**
Treesmill, Par PL24 2TU. Tricia
Howard, 01208 873225,
www.hiddenvalleygardens.co.uk.
*2m SW of Lostwithiel. From St Austell,
take A390 towards Lostwithiel. After
6m turn R on to B3269 signed Fowey,
after 200yds turn R signed Treesmill.
After 1m turn L, signed to the gardens
(¹/₂ m). At end of lane after Colwith
Farm.* Cream teas on NGS days only.
**Adm £2, chd free. Daily 20 Mar to 31
Oct. For NGS: Sats, Suns 23, 24
June; 22, 23 Sept (10-6).**
4-acre colourful garden in secluded
valley with specialist plant nursery.
Mediterranean area with gazebo and
country views. Courtyard garden with
raised beds, wildlife pond and bog.
Many other herbaceous beds in
cottage-style planting incl hot colour
border. Irises flowering at June
opening. Featured in 'Cornwall Today'.
⊕ 🚶 👜

㉒ HIGHCROFT GARDENS
Cargreen PL12 6PA. Mr & Mrs B J
Richards, 01752 842219. *5m NW of
Saltash. 5m from Callington on A388
take Landulph Cargreen turning. 2m
on, turn L at Landulph Xrds. Parking by
Methodist Church.* Cream teas. **Adm
£3, chd free. Suns 5, 19 Aug (1.30-
5.30). Visitors also welcome by appt
Aug & early Sept only for groups of
10+.**
3-acre garden in beautiful Tamar Valley.
Japanese-style garden, hot border,
pastel border, grasses, arboretum with
hemerocallis and new blue borders.
Prairie planting containing 2,500 plants
of herbaceous and grasses. Buddleia
and shrub rose bank. Pond. All at their
best in Aug and Sept.
🖚 ⊕ 👜

㉓ HIGHER TRUSCOTT
St Stephens, Launceston PL15 8LA.
Mr & Mrs J C Mann. *3m NW of
Launceston. From Launceston B3254
turn W at St Stephens toward
Egloskerry. Signed.* Home-made teas.
**Adm £3, chd free. Suns 6 May; 3
June (2-5).**
1-acre plantsman's garden. Elevated
position with fine views. Trees and
shrubs with interesting underplanting.
Yr-round interest with climbers,
herbaceous, alpines and troughs.
✗ ❀ ☕

㉔ INCE CASTLE
Saltash PL12 4RA. Lord and Lady
Boyd. *3m SW of Saltash. From A38 at
Stoketon Cross take turn signed
Trematon, then Elmgate. No large
coaches.* Home-made teas. **Adm
£3.00, chd free. Suns 11 Mar; 8 Apr;
13 May; 15 July (2-5).**
5-acre garden, woodlands, borders,
orchard, bulbs, shell house and lovely
views of R Lynher.
♿ ☕

**㉕ ◆ THE JAPANESE GARDEN
& BONSAI NURSERY**
St Mawgan TR8 4ET. Mr & Mrs Hore,
01637 860116,
www.thebonsainursery.com. *6m E of
Newquay. 1¹/₂m from N coast. Signs
from A3059 & B3276.* **Adm £3.50,
chd £1.50, groups 10+ £3. Open
daily (closed Xmas day to New
Year's day) (10-6/5.30 winter). For
NGS: Mons 28 May; 27 Aug (10-6).**
Authentic Japanese garden set in
1¹/₂ acres, water garden with Koi pond,
stroll and Zen gardens, bamboo grove.
Japanese maples, azaleas and
ornamental grasses in abundance.
Entrance free to adjacent specialist
Bonsai and Japanese garden
nurseries. Featured prominently in
exhibition at Embassy of Japan,
London. Gravel paths.
♿ ✗ ❀

㉖ ◆ KEN CARO
Bicton, nr Liskeard PL14 5RF.
Mr K R Willcock & Mrs Willcock,
01579 362446. *5m NE of Liskeard.
From A390 to Callington turn off N at
St Ive. Take Pensilva Rd, follow brown
tourist signs, approx 1m off main rd.*
**Adm £4.50, chd £2. Gps of 12+ £4.
Daily 25 Feb to 30 Sept (10-6).**
5-acre connoisseur's garden.
Panoramic views, full of unusual plants
and shrubs with yr-round colour. Lily
ponds, garden sculptures. Iris beds,
shrub roses, hydrangeas, camellias,

magnolias, good collection of hollies.
Plenty of seating to watch the wild bird
life. New picnic area, meadow and
woodland walk. Featured in 'Cornwall
Today'.
❀ ☕

㉗ KENNALL HOUSE
Ponsanooth TR3 7HJ. Mr & Mrs N
Wilson-Holt, 01872 870557. *4m NW
of Falmouth. A393 Falmouth to
Redruth, L at Ponsanooth PO for
0.3m. Garden on L.* **Teas. Adm £3,
chd free. Sun 22 July (2-5.30).
Visitors also welcome by appt.**
6-acre garden in extended grounds in
valley setting. Incl mixture of typical
British species and exotics. Wide
variety of trees, shrubs and
herbaceous plants. Bisected by fast-
flowing stream with ponds and walled
garden.
☕

㉘ KINGBERRY
Rhind Street, Bodmin PL31 2EL. Dr
& Mrs M S Stead. *N side of town,
100yds uphill from Westberry Hotel.
Limited parking on hill, otherwise car
parks in town centre.* Cream teas.
Adm £3, chd free. Sun 17 June (2-5).
Surprising haven in centre of this
county town. ²/₃-acre formal town
garden with abundantly planted
herbaceous borders, original stone
walls covered in climbers, ornamental
pond, gravel terrace, conservatory filled
with tender specimens and more
informal orchard. Garden sculptures
and unusual plants. Featured in
'Cornwall Gardens Guide' by D Pett.
✗ ❀ ☕

㉙ LADOCK HOUSE
Ladock TR2 4PL. G J & Lady Mary
Holborow, 01726 882274. *7m NE of
Truro. Just off B3275.* Car park &
entrance by church. Cream teas in
church. **Adm £3, chd free. Sun 29
Apr (2-5). Visitors also welcome by
appt for groups of 10+.**
Georgian Old Rectory with 4 acres of
lawns, rhododendrons, camellias and
azaleas with many woodland glades,
all planted during last 30 yrs. Bluebell
walk.
♿ ☕

㉚ ◆ LAMORRAN HOUSE
Upper Castle Road, St Mawes, Truro
TR2 5BZ. Robert Dudley-Cooke,
01326 270800,
www.lamorrangardens.co.uk.
*A3078, L past garage at entrance to St
Mawes. ³/₄m on L. ¹/₄m from castle if*

using passenger ferry service. **Adm
£5.50, chd free. Weds, Fris, Apr to
end Sept (10-5). For NGS: Sun 15
Apr (10-5).**
4-acre subtropical garden overlooking
Falmouth bay. Designed by the owner
in an Italianate/Cote d'Azur style.
Extensive collection of Mediterranean
and subtropical plants reflects both
design and remarkable micro-climate.
Beautiful collection of Japanese
azaleas and tender rhododendrons.
Featured on BBC Gardeners World.
Many steps.
✗

㉛ ◆ LANHYDROCK
Bodmin PL30 5AD. The National
Trust, 01208 265950,
www.nationaltrust.org.uk. *2¹/₂m SE
of Bodmin. 2¹/₂m on B3268. Stn:
Bodmin Parkway 1³/₄m.* **House and
garden adm £9.40, chd £4.70,
garden only adm £5.30, chd £2.65.
Gardens open all yr (10 - 6), house
open mid-Mar to end Oct, Tues to
Suns and Bank Hol Mons (11 - 5.30).
For NGS: Weds 16 May; 19 Sept
(10-6).**
Large formal garden laid out 1857;
shrub garden with good specimens of
rhododendrons and magnolias and fine
views. Partial wheelchair access, gravel
paths and slopes to higher woodland
garden.
♿ ✗ ❀ ☕

㉜ NEW LITTLE PARK FARM
Malpas TR1 1SX. Mr & Mrs W
Roberts. *1¹/₂m S of Truro.
A39/A390 roundabout at Truro
Police Station, take exit to Malpas.
Follow river on R, passing park and
cricket ground, then 1st L up lane
marked Park Farm. Little Park Farm
1st on R.* Cream teas. **Adm £3,
chd free. Sun 27 May (2-5.30).**
New garden created over last 5 yrs
from farm land. Formal area,
newly-planted plum/apple orchard,
large pond, lavender/santolina
banks, vegetables, small wooded
glade. Lovely S-facing views to
river.
✗ ☕

㉝ LONG HAY
Treligga, Delabole PL33 9EE. Bett &
Mick Hartley. *10m N of Wadebridge.
Take B3314 Pendoggett to Delabole
Rd. Turn L at Westdowns from
Pendoggett, R fom Delabole. Signed*

Treligga (N). Turn L after entering hamlet. Long Hay on L, after 30yds white gate. Parking past gate, turn L into farmyard. Cream teas. **Adm £2.50, chd free. Suns 27 May; 17 June (2-5).**
$^2/_3$-acre abundant cottage garden with beautiful vistas of the N coast and sea. Herbaceous beds, shrubs, pond, greenhouse and lawns. Meadow overlooking sea with paths leading to copse, vegetable plots, orchard and greenhouse. Cornish coastal garden in beautiful but harsh environment.

34 ◆ MARSH VILLA GARDENS
St Andrew's Road, Par PL24 2LU. Judith Stephens, 01726 815920, marshvillagarden@onetel.com. *5m E of St Austell. Leave A390 at St Blazey T-lights, by church. 1st L, garden 600yds on L.* **Adm £3.50, chd free. Sun to Wed Apr to Oct (11-6).** For NGS: **Fri 4 May; Sat 1 Sept (11-6).**
Approx 3-acre garden featuring large pond, streams, bog garden. Extensive herbaceous beds, mixed borders, woodland and marshland walks in former estuary. New features incl alpine bed and substantial rose and clematis pergola. Hard gravel paths and grass.

35 MENHENIOT GARDENS
Menheniot Village PL14 3QU. *4m SE of Liskeard. Take A38 from Liskeard to Plymouth. Turn L at Menheniot turning. 1m to centre of village. Maps and entrance stickers from The Old School opp Parish Church.* Light lunches (12-2) at The Old School; Cream teas (2-5.30) at Bodway Farm. **Adm £3.50, chd free. Sat 23, Sun 24 June (12-5.30).**
Wherever you garden you are sure to find inspiration from these interesting and varied village gardens; large, sloping, formal, cottage, even small patio and a natural wood, with many spectacular views. The allotments and several others new to NGS. East Down Barn featured in 'Creative Gardeners' and 'The Cornwall Gardens Guide' both by D E Pett.

36 MOYCLARE
Lodge Hill, Liskeard PL14 4EH. Elizabeth & Philip Henslowe. $^1/_2 m$ S *of Liskeard centre. Approx 300yds S of Liskeard railway stn on St Keyne-Duloe rd (B3254).* **Adm £3, chd free. Mon 7 May (2-5).**
Mrs Louis (Moira) Reid began planting

unusual trees, shrubs and plants (many variegated) in 1927. Now being revived and rejuvenated by her niece, the 1-acre garden continues to be a plant-lover's delight. Camellia 'Moira Reid', Brachyglottis 'Moira Reid', Astrantia 'Moira Reid' and Cytisus 'Moyclare Pink' are amongst those discovered there.

Find inspiration from these interesting and varied village gardens . . .

37 NANSAWSAN HOUSE
Ladock, Truro TR2 4PW. Michael & Maureen Cole, 01726 882392. *7m NE of Truro. On B3275, follow yellow signs. Use Falmouth Arms and Community Hall car parks.* Cream teas. **Adm £2.50, chd free. Sun 6 May (2-5).** Visitors also welcome by appt April, May only for groups of 15+.
$1^1/_2$-acre garden, once part of Victorian estate garden. From house, paths meander through rhododendrons, camellias, azaleas and perennial borders taking in secret corners, fishpond, greenhouse, summerhouse and gazebo with wider vistas. Unusual trees, shrubs and climbers. Gravel paths.

38 ◆ PENCARROW
Washaway, Bodmin PL30 3AG. Molesworth-St Aubyn family, 01208 841369, info@pencarrow.co.uk. *4m NW of Bodmin. Signed off A389 & B3266.* **House and garden adm £8, chd £4, garden only adm £4, chd £1. Daily 1 Mar to 31 Oct (9.30-5.30), house Sun to Thur incl (11-5).** For NGS: **Thur 19 Apr (11-5).**
A surprise around every corner. Family-owned grade 2* listed garden. Find an Iron Age fort, Victorian rockery, Italian gardens, ice house, lakeside and woodland walks for dogs off leads! You can also visit the fine Georgian house with its superb collection of paintings, furniture, porcelain and some antique dolls. Featured on DVD 'The Heart of a Garden' & ITV Great Country Houses. Leaflets available from house entrance for those with mobility difficulties, explaining routes alternative to steps.

39 ◆ PENJERRICK GARDEN
Budock, nr Falmouth TR11 5ED. Mrs Rachel Morin, 01872 870105, www.penjerrickgarden.co.uk. *3m SW of Falmouth. Between Budock-Mawnan Smith, opp. Penmorvah Manor Hotel. Room for one coach outside gate.* **Adm £2.50, chd £1. Please phone or see website for opening dates and times.** For NGS: **Sun 22 Apr (1.30-4.30).**
15-acre subtropical garden, home to important rhododendron hybrids and the C19 Quaker Fox family. The upper garden with sea view contains rhododendrons, camellias, magnolias, bamboos, tree ferns and magnificent trees. Across a bridge a luxuriant valley features ponds in a wild primeval setting. Suitable for adventurous fit people wearing gumboots. Featured on BBC4 Tales From The Jungle.

40 ◆ PINE LODGE GARDENS & NURSERY
Holmbush, St Austell PL25 3RQ. Mr & Mrs R H J Clemo, 01726 73500, garden@pine-lodge.co.uk. *1m E of St Austell. On A390 between Holmbush & St Blazey at junction of A391.* **Adm £5.50, chd £3, concessions £5. Open daily except 24, 25, 26 Dec (10-5).**
30-acre estate comprises gardens within a garden. Some 6,000 plants, all labelled, have been thoughtfully laid out using original designs and colour combinations to provide maximum interest. Rhododendrons, magnolias, camellias, herbaceous borders with many rare and tender plants, marsh gardens, tranquil fish ponds, lake with black swans within the park, pinetum. Japanese garden and arboretum. Holder of National Collection of Grevilleas. 3-acre winter garden under construction. Featured in 'Cornwall Today' & 'Cornwall'. **NCCPG**

41 ◆ PINSLA GARDEN & NURSERY
Cardinham PL30 4AY. Mark & Claire Woodbine, 01208 821339, www.pinslagarden.net. *3^1/_2 m E of Bodmin. From A30 roundabout take A38 towards Plymouth, 1st L to Cardinham & Fletchers Bridge, 2m on R.* **Adm £2.50, chd free. Daily 1 Mar to 31 Oct.** For NGS: **Sat 19, Sun 20 May (10-6).**
Romantic $1^1/_2$ acres of inspirational planting and design surrounded by woodland. Herbaceous and shrub

borders, jungle, ponds, cottage garden, orchard, alpines on scree; stone circle in meadow; tree tunnel. Paths lined with granite boulders and set with slate, stone and incised abstract patterns. Some gravel paths.

 ♿ ✿ ☕

㊷ NEW ◆ POPPY COTTAGE GARDEN

Ruan High Lanes, Truro TR2 5JR. Tina Pritchard & David Primmer, 01872 501411. *1m NW of Veryan. On the Roseland Peninsula, 4m from Tregony on A3078 rd to St Mawes.* Adm £2.50, chd free. Weds, Thurs, Fris and alt Suns, May to Sept (2-5.30). **For NGS: Sun 17 June (2-5.30).**
An inspirational plantsman's garden combining colour, form and texture, approx 1 acre, divided into many rooms. From established cottage garden, extra land acquired in 2003 enabled the creation of different gardens filled with many beautiful and unusual shrubs, trees, bulbs, herbaceous and exotics, all colour-themed. Wildlife pond with stream and bridge. Small orchard with duck pond, many ornamental ducks and chickens.

♿ ✿ ☕

PORTINGTON
See Devon.

㊸ ◆ POTAGER GARDEN

High Cross, Constantine TR11 5RE. Peter Skerrett & Dan Thomas, 01326 341258, www.potagergardennursery.co.uk. *7m SW of Falmouth. Towards Constantine. In High Cross turn L at grass triangle with white signpost to Port Navas. Garden 100yds on R.* Adm £2.50, chd free. Please phone for opening times. **For NGS: Sun 29 July (2-8).**
New organic garden emerging from old nursery near Helford Estuary. Garden provides relaxed environment with informal mix of herbaceous planting accentuated with vegetables and fruit. Home-made cooking in the Glasshouse Café, hammocks, games and sculpture make Potager a friendly and peaceful retreat. Featured in 'The Times'.

♿ ✿ ☕

㊹ POUNDSTOCK GARDENS

Poundstock EX23 0AU. *5m S of Bude, off A39.* Lunches and light refreshments at Southfield. Cream teas at The Barn House. **Combined adm £3, chd free (share to Poundstock Church). Sun 18 Mar; Wed 1 Aug (11-5).**
Direction maps given to visitors. Both gardens featured in 'The Cornwall Gardens Guide' by D E Pett.

☕

THE BARN HOUSE
Penhalt. Tim & Sandy Dingle. *From A39 take Widemouth, Bude (coastal route). L at Widemouth Manor Hotel towards Millook for 1/2 m*
Come and see what can be done in an exposed coastal situation. Begun in 1996. Herbaceous and shrub borders, pond and kitchen garden. Wildlife walk through 10 acres of field and scrub. Partial wheelchair access.

♿ ✿ ☕

SOUTHFIELD
Vicarage Lane. Mr P R & Mrs J A Marfleet, 01288 361233. *Off A39 at Bangor Xrds (chapel on corner). Turn into Vicarage Lane, signed Poundstock Church. Approx 200yds on L.* **Visitors also welcome by appt.**
3 acres of wildlife woodland and garden. Woodland walks with daffodils, rhododendrons and hydrangeas. Mainly broadleaf trees planted 1994. Garden with borders of mixed shrubs, trees and perennial plants giving yr-round interest. Kitchen garden. Beautiful views. Many wild birds. Partial wheelchair access. Very steep grass paths in woodland.

♿ ✿ ☕

㊺ ◆ ROSELAND HOUSE

Chacewater TR4 8QB. Mr & Mrs Pridham, 01872 560451, www.roselandhouse.co.uk. *4m W of Truro. At Truro end of main st. Parking in village car park (100yds) or surrounding rds.* Adm £3, chd free. Tues, Weds (1-6) Apr to Sept. **For NGS: Suns 29 July; 26 Aug (2-5).**
1-acre garden subdivided by walls and trellises hosting a wide range of climbers. Mixed borders of unusual plants, Victorian conservatory and greenhouse extend the gardening yr. Holders of National Collection of Clematis *viticella cvs*. Some slopes.

♿ ✿ NCCPG ☕

㊻ ◆ ST MICHAEL'S MOUNT

Marazion TR17 0HT. James & Mary St Aubyn, 01736 710507, clare@manor-office.co.uk. *2 1/2 m E of Penzance. 1/2 m from shore at Marazion by Causeway; otherwise by motor boat.* **Castle & garden adm £9.40, chd £3.20, garden only £3, chd free.** Gardens Mon-Fri, 30 Apr to 30 Jun; Thurs, Fris 1 Jul to 31 Oct. Castle Sun-Fri, 1 Apr to 31 Oct. (10.30-5.30, last adm 4.45 on the island). **For NGS: Mon 30 Apr (10.30-5.30).**
Flowering shrubs; rock plants, spectacular castle; fine sea views. Steep climb to castle, uneven cobbled surfaces, sensible shoes advised.

🐾 ✿ ☕

An inspirational plantsman's garden . . .

㊼ ◆ TREBAH

Mawnan Smith TR11 5JZ. Trebah Garden Trust, 01326 252200, www.trebah-garden.co.uk. *4m from Falmouth. Follow tourist signs from Hillhead roundabout on A39 approach to Falmouth or Treliever Cross roundabout on junction of A39-A394. Parking for coaches.* **Adm: 1 Mar to 31 Oct, £6.50, chd £2, concessions £6; 1Nov to 28 Feb, £3, chd £1, concessions £2.50. Daily all yr (10.30-5/dusk if earlier).**
26-acre S-facing ravine garden, planted in 1830s. Extensive collection rare/mature trees/shrubs incl glades; huge tree ferns 100yrs old, subtropical exotics. Hydrangea collection covers 2 1/2 acres. Water garden, waterfalls, rock pool stocked with mature koi carp. Enchanted garden for plantsman/artist/family. Play area/trails for children. Use of private beach. Gravel paths and some steep slopes. Buggies available.

♿ ✿ ☕

48 TREBARTHA
nr Launceston PL15 7PD. The
Latham Family. *6m SW of
Launceston. North Hill, SW of
Launceston nr junction of B3254 &
B3257.* Cream teas. **Adm £3, chd
free. Suns 3 June; 23 Sept (2-5).**
Wooded area with lake surrounded by
walks of flowering shrubs; woodland
trail through fine woods with cascades
and waterfalls; American glade with
fine trees. No coaches. Featured on
Radio Cornwall.

49 TREGOOSE
Grampound TR2 4DB. Mr & Mrs
Anthony O'Connor,
www.tregoose.co.uk. *7m E of Truro,
1m W of Grampound. Off A390. Lane
entrance is 100yds W of New Stables
Xrds & 1/2 m E of Trewithen
roundabout.* Cream teas.
**Adm £3, chd free, concessions
£2.50. Sun 16 Sept (1-5).**
2-acre garden. Woodland area with
early spring shrubs underplanted with
snowdrops, erythroniums, hellebores
and small narcissus cultivars. Summer
and autumn flowering areas incl walled
garden overtopped by Acacia
baileyana purpurea, scarlet blue and
yellow border and potager full of herbs
and cutting beds with arches covered
with gourds, roses and honeysuckle.

50 TREGREHAN
Par PL24 2SJ. Mr T Hudson, 01726
814389, www.tregrehan.org. *1m W
of St Blazey. Entrance on A390 opp
Britannia Inn.* **Adm £4.50, chd free.
Weds, Suns, Bank Hol Mons 15 Mar
to 31 May (10.30-5); Weds only 6
June to 29 Aug (2-5). For NGS: Sun
1 Apr (10.30-5).**
Garden largely created since early
C19. Woodland of 20 acres containing
fine trees, award winning camellias
raised by late owner and many
interesting plants forming a temperate
rainforest. Show greenhouses built
1846, a feature containing softer
species. Partial wheelchair access.

51 TREGULLOW
Scorrier TR16 5AY. Mr & Mrs James
Williams. *2m E of Redruth. Leave A30
at Scorrier. Follow signs to St Day &
Carharrack on B3298. 1m out of
Scorrier turn R at Tolgullow Village sign.
Go through white gates by lodge.*
Cream teas. **Adm £3.50, chd £1. Mon
7 May (1-5).**
An idyllic Cornish spring garden a mere
3m from the Atlantic. Tregullow is
blessed with unfolding vistas of intense
colour as you explore your way around
its 15 acres. First planted by the
Williams family in C19, the gardens
have been carefully restored and
replanted since the 1970s. Mostly
accessible to wheelchairs but 2 flights
of granite steps need to be bypassed.

52 ◆ TRELISSICK
Feock TR3 6QL. The National Trust,
01872 862090,
www.nationaltrust.org.uk. *4m S of
Truro. Nr King Harry Ferry. On B3289.*
**Adm £5.80, chd £2.90. Daily 11 Feb
to 31 Oct (10.30-5.30); 1 Nov to 10
Feb (11-4). Closed Xmas & New Yr.
For NGS: Sat 17 Mar; Thur 27 Sept
(10.30-5.30).**
Planted with tender shrubs; magnolias,
camellias and rhododendrons with
many named species characteristic of
Cornish gardens. National Collection of
Photinias and Azaras. Fine woodlands
encircle the gardens through which a
varied circular walk can be enjoyed.
Superb view over Falmouth harbour.
Georgian house, not open. Now
accessible by foot ferry from Truro,
Falmouth and St Mawes, Apr-Sept.

53 TRENARTH
High Cross, Constantine TR11 5JN.
Mrs L M Nottingham, 01326 340444,
lmnottingham@tiscali.co.uk. *6m SW
of Falmouth. Nearest main rds A39-
A394 Truro to Helston-Falmouth: follow
signs for Constantine. At High Cross
garage, 1 1/2 m before Constantine, turn
L signed Mawnan, then R after 30yds
down dead end lane. Garden at end of
lane.* Home-made teas. **Adm £2.50,
chd free. Sun 26 Aug (2-5). Evening
Opening £3.50, wine, Sun 17 June
(6-8).** Visitors also welcome by appt.
4-acre garden surrounding C17
farmhouse in lovely pastoral setting -
not a road in sight or sound. Yr-round
interest. Emphasis on unusual plants,
structure and form, with a hint of
quirkiness - not all is what it seems!
Courtyard, C18 garden walls, yew
rooms, prize-winning vegetable
garden, traditional potting shed,
'puddled' pond, orchard, green lane
walk down to R Helford.

54 ◆ TRENGWAINTON
Madron, nr Penzance TR20 8RZ.
The National Trust, 01736 363148,
www@nationaltrust.org.uk. *2m NW
of Penzance. 1/2 m W of Heamoor. On
Penzance-Morvah rd (B3312), 1/2 m off
St Just rd (A3071).* **Adm £5.20, chd
£2.60. Suns to Thurs, 11 Feb to 28
Oct. For NGS: Suns 18 Feb; 16 Sept
(10-5).**
Sheltered garden with an abundance
of exotic trees and shrubs. Picturesque
stream running through valley and
stunning views of Mounts Bay from
terrace. Mysterious walled gardens,
reputedly built to the dimensions of
Noah's Ark. Early flowering camellias
and rhododendrons. Dogs on leads
welcome except in Tearoom Garden.
Featured on BBC Gardeners' World.
3/4 garden accessible to wheelchair
users. Gravel paths, steady incline.

55 ◆ TRERICE
nr Newquay PL30 4DE. The National
Trust, 01637 875404,
www.nationaltrust.org.uk. *3m SE of
Newquay. From Newquay via A392 &
A3058; turn R at Kestle Mill (NT signs).*
**House & garden adm £6.40, chd
£3.20, concessions £5.60, garden
only adm £2.20, chd £1.10,
concessions £2. Daily except Sats,
18 Mar to 28 Oct. For NGS: Tues 17
Apr; 24 July (10.30-5).**
Summer/autumn-flowering garden
unusual in content and layout and for
neutral alkaline soil varieties. Orchard
planted with old varieties of fruit trees.
Small museum traces history of lawn
mower.

**56 ◆ TREVARNO GARDENS
AND THE NATIONAL MUSEUM OF
GARDENING**
Helston TR13 0RU. Messrs M Sagin
& N Helsby, 01326 574274,
www.trevarno.co.uk. *3m NW of
Helston. Signed from Crowntown on
B3303.* **Museum and Garden adm
£5.75, chd £2.10, concessions
£4.45. Open daily except Xmas Day
& Boxing Day (10.30-5).**
Unforgettable gardening experience
combining Victorian garden with
fountain garden conservatory, unique
range of craft workshops and National
Museum of Gardening, Britain's largest
and most comprehensive collection of
antique tools, implements, memorabilia
and ephemera. Vintage soap and
nostalgic toy museum (small additional
charge). New woodland adventure play
area and estate walk. Featured in 'The
Telegraph'.

57 TREWAN HALL
St Columb TR9 6DB. Mrs P M Hill. *6m E of Newquay. N of St Columb Major, off A39 to Wadebridge. 1st turning on L signed to St Eval & Talskiddy. Entrance ³/₄m on L in woodland.* Home-made teas. **Adm £3, chd free. Sun 13 May (2-5.30).**
Set in 36 acres of fields and bluebell woodland, with gardens round the house. Mixed beds, roses and specimen trees. Driveway bordered by rhododendrons and hydrangeas. Lovely views over the Lanherne Valley. Trewan Hall (not open) built in 1633 is a fine centrepiece for garden. Families welcome.

58 ◆ TREWITHEN
Truro TR2 4DD. Mr & Mrs Michael Galsworthy, 01726 883647, www.trewithengardens.co.uk. *¹/₂m E of Probus. Entrance on A390 Truro-St Austell rd. Signed.* **Adm prices and opening times vary according to season; please phone or visit website for details**
Internationally renowned and historic garden of 30 acres laid out between 1912 and 1960 with much of original seed and plant material collected by Ward and Forrest. Famed for towering magnolias and rhododendrons and a very large collection of camellias. Flattish ground amidst original woodland park and magnificent landscaped lawn vistas.

A hint of quirkiness – not all is what it seems!

59 ◆ TREWOOFE HOUSE
Lamorna TR19 6PA. Mrs H M Pigott, 01736 810269. *4m SW of Penzance. Take B3315 from Penzance via Newlyn towards Lamorna. At top of hill take sharp turn signed Trewoofe.* Light refreshments and teas on NGS day in Village Hall. **Adm £2.50, chd free. Suns & Weds May, June, July (2-5). Group visits welcome by prior arrangement. For NGS: Sat 14 July (11-5).**
2-acre garden at top of Lamorna Valley with ancient mill leat. Bog garden planted with a variety of primulas, many kinds of iris, astilbes and arums. Shrub and perennial beds planted for all-yr interest. Small fruit garden with espalier and cordon-trained apple and pear trees. Conservatory with semi-tender climbers and vine. Featured in 'Cornwall Gardens Guide' by D Pett, 'Cornwall Today' and GGG.

60 NEW ◆ TREWOOFE ORCHARD
Lamorna TR19 6BW. Dick & Barbara Waterson, 01736 810214, dickwaterson@onetel.com. *4m SW of Penzance. on B3315, Signed from Lamorna Cove turning.* Cream teas/light refreshments by arrangement for groups of 10+. **Adm £2.50, chd free. Most days (10-dusk). Please tel to confirm before travelling any distance.**
4-acre valley garden, secluded and tranquil. 2 acres of woodland; more formal planting around the house. Stunning waterfall, stream, still pond and rills. Spring bulbs, camellias, arums, hostas and new tree ferns. Plenty of seats and well-defined paths. Magical setting. Water everywhere to delight the senses. Full of butterflies, bird song and busy bees. Partial wheelchair access, some steps and steep slopes.

61 ◆ TRIST HOUSE
Veryan TR2 5QA. Mr & Mrs Graham Salmon, 01872 501422, www.tristhouse.co.uk. *6m SE of Truro. Centre of Veryan on Portloe rd just past Roseland stores. Disabled parking by house.* **Adm £3.50, chd free. Suns, Tues & Bank Hols, 1 April to 18 Sept (2-5.30) and by arrangement. For NGS: Sun 15 Apr (2-5.30).**
5 acres. Romantic, intimate garden in flower throughout spring and summer with lovely display of tulips, roses and herbaceous plants. Large rockeries built in the 1830s. Featured in 'Gardeners' World'. Some steep ramps. No access to woodland/rockery areas.

WHIBBLE HILL HOUSE
See Devon.

WILDSIDE
See Devon.

Cornwall County Volunteers

County Organiser
William Croggon, Creed House, Creed, Grampound, Truro TR2 4SL, 01872 530372

County Treasurer
Nigel Rimmer, 11 Melvill Road, Falmouth TR11 4AS, 01326 313429

Leaflets
Peter Stanley, Mazey Cottage, Tangies, Gunwalloe, Helston TR12 7PU, 01326 565868, peterestanley@btinternet.com

Publicity
Hugh Tapper, Trethewey Barns, Ruan Lanihorne, Tregony, Truro TR2 5TH, 01872 530567 h@truro.tv

Assistant County Organisers
Ginnie Clotworthy, Trethew, Lanlivery, Bodmin PL30 5BZ, 01208 872612, gilesclotworthy@btopenworld.com
Lally Croggon, Creed House, Creed, Grampound, Truro TR2 4SL, 01872 530372
Caroline Latham, Stonaford Manor, North Hill, Launceston PL15 7PE, 01566 782970
Alison O'Connor, Tregoose, Grampound, Truro TR2 4DB, 01726 882460
Marion Stanley, Mazey Cottage, Tangies, Gunwalloe, Helston TR12 7PU, 01326 565868
Virginia Vyvyan-Robinson, Mellingey Mill House, St Issey, Wadebridge, PL27 7QU, 01841 540511

ngs gardens open for charity

We had a mallard sitting on eggs in our hanging basket. Many visitors were concerned about how the ducklings would get out – they managed it successfully …

Rectory Cottage, Worcestershire

CUMBRIA

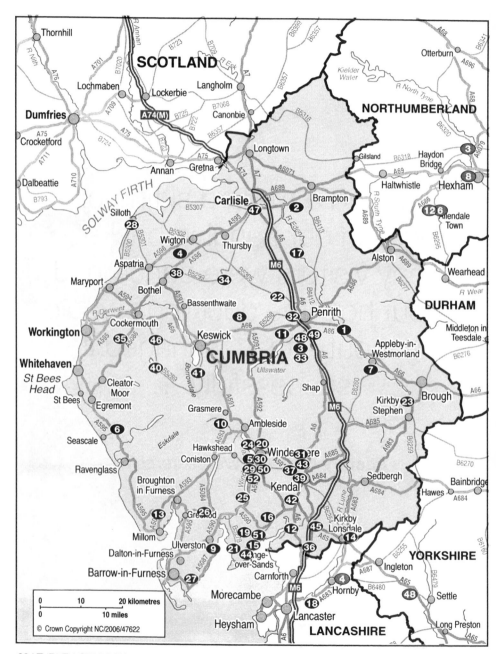

0   10   20 kilometres
0   10 miles
© Crown Copyright NC/2006/47622

Opening Dates

March

FRIDAY 30
10 Copt Howe

April

FRIDAY 6
10 Copt Howe

SATURDAY 7
10 Copt Howe

SUNDAY 8
10 Copt Howe
45 Summerdale House

WEDNESDAY 11
10 Copt Howe

WEDNESDAY 18
10 Copt Howe

WEDNESDAY 25
10 Copt Howe

SATURDAY 28
10 Copt Howe

SUNDAY 29
11 Dalemain

May

WEDNESDAY 2
10 Copt Howe

FRIDAY 4
8 Chapelside

SATURDAY 5
8 Chapelside
37 Plumgarths

SUNDAY 6
5 Brackenrigg Lodge
9 Conishead Priory
12 Dallam Tower
45 Summerdale House
50 Windy Hall

WEDNESDAY 9
10 Copt Howe

THURSDAY 10
15 Graythwaite Manor Hotel

SATURDAY 12
1 Acorn Bank
10 Copt Howe

SUNDAY 13
10 Copt Howe

WEDNESDAY 16
10 Copt Howe
24 The Lake District Visitor Centre at Brockhole
25 Lakeside Hotel

FRIDAY 18
8 Chapelside

SATURDAY 19
6 Buckbarrow House
8 Chapelside
29 Lindeth Fell Country House Hotel

SUNDAY 20
6 Buckbarrow House
14 Fell Yeat
28 Lilac Cottage Gardens
30 Matson Ground

FRIDAY 25
10 Copt Howe

SATURDAY 26
10 Copt Howe

SUNDAY 27
10 Copt Howe
16 Halecat
18 Heywood House
33 The Nook

MONDAY 28
10 Copt Howe

TUESDAY 29
41 Scarthwaite

WEDNESDAY 30
10 Copt Howe

June

FRIDAY 1
8 Chapelside

SATURDAY 2
8 Chapelside
10 Copt Howe

SUNDAY 3
19 High Beckside Farm
51 Yewbarrow House

WEDNESDAY 6
10 Copt Howe
32 Newton Rigg Campus Gardens (Evening)

SATURDAY 9
1 Acorn Bank
37 Plumgarths

SUNDAY 10
3 Askham Hall
5 Brackenrigg Lodge
38 Quarry Hill House
49 Winderwath
50 Windy Hall

WEDNESDAY 13
10 Copt Howe

FRIDAY 15
8 Chapelside
10 Copt Howe

SATURDAY 16
8 Chapelside

SUNDAY 17
4 Beech House
7 Castle Bank
16 Halecat
17 Hazel Cottage
39 1 Queens Place

WEDNESDAY 20
10 Copt Howe

FRIDAY 22
10 Copt Howe

SATURDAY 23
40 Rannerdale Cottage

SUNDAY 24
34 The Old Rectory
39 1 Queens Place
40 Rannerdale Cottage
43 Sprint Mill
52 Yews

TUESDAY 26
41 Scarthwaite
44 Stone Edge (Day & Evening)

WEDNESDAY 27
10 Copt Howe
36 Pear Tree Cottage (Evening)

FRIDAY 29
8 Chapelside

SATURDAY 30
8 Chapelside
10 Copt Howe
47 Tullie House

July

SUNDAY 1
18 Heywood House
27 Leece Village Gardens
47 Tullie House
51 Yewbarrow House

FRIDAY 6
8 Chapelside
10 Copt Howe

SATURDAY 7
1 Acorn Bank
8 Chapelside

SUNDAY 8
22 Hutton-in-the-Forest
48 Whitbysteads

WEDNESDAY 11
10 Copt Howe
21 Holker Hall Gardens

FRIDAY 13
8 Chapelside

SATURDAY 14
8 Chapelside

SUNDAY 15
36 Pear Tree Cottage

WEDNESDAY 18
10 Copt Howe

FRIDAY 20
10 Copt Howe

SUNDAY 22
2 The Acres
16 Halecat
23 Kirkby Stephen Gardens
31 Meadow House

TUESDAY 24
41 Scarthwaite

THURSDAY 26
15 Graythwaite Manor Hotel
20 Holehird Gardens

SATURDAY 28
13 Dunningwell Hall

SUNDAY 29
13 Dunningwell Hall
31 Meadow House
43 Sprint Mill

MONDAY 30
46 Swinside End Farm

August

SATURDAY 4
42 Sizergh Castle

SUNDAY 5
45 Summerdale House
51 Yewbarrow House

WEDNESDAY 15
24 The Lake District Visitor Centre at Brockhole

SUNDAY 19
22 Hutton-in-the-Forest

September

SUNDAY 2
11 Dalemain
51 Yewbarrow House

WEDNESDAY 5
25 Lakeside Hotel

THURSDAY 6
15 Graythwaite Manor Hotel

SUNDAY 9
36 Pear Tree Cottage

SUNDAY 16
7 Castle Bank

WEDNESDAY 26
32 Newton Rigg Campus Gardens (Evening)

Gardens open to the public

1 Acorn Bank
9 Conishead Priory
10 Copt Howe
11 Dalemain
15 Graythwaite Manor Hotel

20 Holehird Gardens
21 Holker Hall Gardens
22 Hutton-in-the-Forest
24 The Lake District Visitor Centre at Brockhole
42 Sizergh Castle
47 Tullie House
49 Winderwath

By appointment only

26 Langholme Mill
35 The Old Rectory

The Gardens

1 ◆ **ACORN BANK**
Temple Sowerby CA10 1SP. The National Trust, 017683 61893, www.nationaltrust.org.uk. 6m E of Penrith. On A66; 1/2m N of Temple Sowerby. Bus: Penrith-Appleby at Carlisle-Darlington; alight Culgaith Rd end. Adm £3.40, chd £1.70. Wed to Sun & Bank Hol Mons 24 Mar to 28 Oct. For NGS: Sats 12 May; 9 June; 7 July (10-5).
Medium-sized walled garden; fine herb garden; orchard and mixed borders; wild garden with woodland/riverside walk leading to a partly restored watermill open to the public. Dogs on leads only in woodland walk.
  ♿ ⛪ ☕

Design features using reclaimed materials . . .

2 **THE ACRES**
How Mill CA8 9JL. Lynda Fraser. 7m E of Carlisle. Turn off A69 at T-lights in Corby Hill towards Heads Nook, take 1st L signed Hayton & Castle Carrock. Proceed 2¾m to White Cottage on R as rd forks. Home-made teas. Adm £2, chd 50p. Sun 22 July (11-4.30).
1/3-acre organic flower arranger's garden specialising in foliage. Herbaceous, wildlife and pond areas. Design features using reclaimed materials. Featured in 'Flora International'.
 ♿ ⛪ ☕

3 **ASKHAM HALL**
Penrith CA10 2PF. Countess of Lonsdale. 5m S of Penrith. Turn off A6 for Lowther & Askham. Home-made teas. Adm £3, chd free (share to Askham & Lowther Churches). Sun 10 June (2-5).
Askham Hall is a pele tower (not open), incorporating C14, C16 and early C18 elements in courtyard plan. Splendid formal outlines of garden with terraces of herbaceous borders and original topiary, probably from late C17. Herb garden and recently created meadow area with trees and pond. Kitchen garden, basically organic. Featured on Radio Cumbria.
 ⛪ ☕

4 **NEW** **BEECH HOUSE**
Woodrow CA7 0AT. Mr & Mrs L B J McDonnell. 3m W of Wigton. On A595 take turning signed Waverton. At first xrds take turning signed Wigton. First house 250yds in L. Home-made teas. Adm £3, chd free. Sun 17 June (2-5).
Approx 3/4 acre of informal garden with lawns, mixed shrub/herbaceous borders, stream and ponds.
 ♿ ⛪ ☕

5 **NEW** **BRACKENRIGG LODGE**
Windy Hall Road, Bowness-on-Windermere LA23 3HY. Lynne Bush. 1m S of Bowness. Just off B5284 on Windy Hall Rd, opp Linthwaite Country House Hotel entrance. Home-made teas at Windy Hall. Adm £3, chd free. Combined with **Windy Hall** £5. Suns 6 May; 10 June (10-5).
3 acres of wildlife garden run on organic lines with a combination of native and cultivated plants, shrubs and trees. Water features created from a diverted culvert giving streams, waterfall and pond. Woodland area, bog garden, wild flower meadows. Haphazard pruning and netted plants due to regular deer visitations. Stout footwear.
 ⛪ ♻ ☕

6 **BUCKBARROW HOUSE**
Denton Park Court, Gosforth CA20 1BN. John Maddison, 019467 25431, JohnMaddGosf@aol.com. 13m S of Whitehaven. Turn off A595. Through centre of Gosforth Village. At 'Y' junction take L fork towards

Wasdale. After 150yds turn L (before church) into Denton Park. Keep bearing R. House is last on R in Denton Park Court. Light refreshments & teas. **Adm £2.50, chd free. Sat 19, Sun 20 May (12-4).** Visitors also welcome by appt, max groups 12 or less.
Small densely planted garden approx 23yds x 49yds. Numerous compartments incl wildlife pond, Japanese gravel garden, shrub area, cottage garden borders and natural stream. Decking area. Decorative stone front garden. Over 30 acers, mostly Japanese palmatum.

7 CASTLE BANK
Appleby-in-Westmorland CA16 6SN. Mrs T Jones. *¾m SW of Appleby. On B6260 Appleby to Orton: 12m from J38 M6. On A66 Appleby is approx 38m NW of Scotch Corner. Parking very limited at garden, please park in Appleby.* **Adm £2.50, chd free. Suns 17 June; 16 Sept (2-5).**
The 3-acre garden lay derelict for 30yrs. The R Eden's weir sounds throughout the long walk under yews and across the lawns now set with beds of perennials and grasses. The walled garden with climbing roses, borders and shrubbery is home to many small birds.

8 CHAPELSIDE
Mungrisdale, Penrith CA11 0XR. Tricia & Robin Acland, 01768 779672. *12m W of Penrith. On A66 take unclassified rd N, signed Mungrisdale Village. House is far end of scattered village on L immed after tiny church on R. Use parish church room parking at foot of our short drive.* **Adm £2, chd free (share to Mungrisdale Parish Church). Fris, Sats 4, 5, 18, 19 May; 1, 2, 15, 16, 29, 30 June; 6, 7, 13, 14 July (11-5).** Visitors also welcome by appt at other times, please ring.
1-acre informal garden at foot of fell; run on organic lines to encourage wildlife. Yr-round texture and colour with a wide range of plants. Tiny stream and large pond. Art constructions in and out, local stone used creatively. Fine views, so unkind winds.

CLEARBECK HOUSE
See Lancashire, Merseyside & Greater Manchester.

9 ♦ CONISHEAD PRIORY
LA12 9QQ. Manjushri Kadampa Meditation Centre, 01229 584029, www.manjushri.org. *2m S of Ulverston on coast rd. 30 mins from M6 J36, follow A590 to Ulverston then L onto coastal rd. Car parking free.* **Adm £3, chd free. Open weekends & Bank Hols Easter to end Oct (except festival times 19 May to 3 June & 14 July to 12 Aug incl). For NGS: Sun 6 May (2-5).**
40 acres of gardens and woodland surrounding historic mansion. Temple garden an oasis of peace, restored greenhouse, lake and wildlife garden, arboretum, cottage gardens. Woodland walks to Morecombe Bay. Gift shop. Guided tours approx 1hr adm £1.50 with garden ticket.

10 ♦ COPT HOWE
Chapel Stile, Great Langdale LA22 9JR. Professor R N Haszeldine, Open additional days Apr to Aug, tel 015394 37685 for recorded message. *5m W of Ambleside. ¼m past Chapel Stile.* **Adm £3, chd free. For NGS: Fri 30 Mar; Fri 6, Sat 7, Sun 8, Weds 11, 18, 25, Sat 28 Apr; Weds 2, 9, 16, 30 Sat 12, Sun 13 May; Fri 25 to Mon 28 May; Sat 2, 30, Weds, 6 13, 20, 27, Fris 15, 22 June; Fris 6, 20, Weds 11, 18 July (12-5).**
2-acre plantsman's mountain paradise garden. Superb views Langdale Pikes. Extensive collections of acers, camellias, azaleas, rhododendrons, oaks, beeches, rare shrubs, trees, unusual perennials; herbaceous and bulbous species; alpines, trough gardens; rare conifers; expedition plants from worldwide mountainous regions. Outstanding spring and autumn colour. Wildlife sanctuary, red squirrels, badgers, slow-worms, hotel for wild birds. Major new garden extensions. Featured in many papers, magazines, radio and TV programmes.

11 ♦ DALEMAIN
Penrith CA11 0HB. Mr & Mrs R B Hasell-McCosh, 017684 86450, www.dalemain.com. *3m SW of Penrith. On A592 Penrith to Ullswater, 3m from M6 J40.* **House and Garden adm £6.50, Garden only adm £4.50, chd free. Sun to Thur 4 Feb to 29 Mar (gdns only 11-4) 1 Apr to 28 Oct (house 11-4) (gdns 10.30-5).** Tearoom. **For NGS: Suns 29 Apr; 2 Sept (10.30-5).**

Delightful 5-acre plantsman's gardens, set against the grandeur of the Lakeland Fells and parkland. Herbaceous borders; rose walk with old-fashioned roses and named ancient apple trees; *Abies Cephalonica* fir; tulip tree and Tudor knot garden. Wild garden with blue Himalayan poppies. Woodland walks.

12 DALLAM TOWER
Milnthorpe LA7 7AG. Mr & Mrs R T Villiers-Smith. *7m S of Kendal. 7m N of Carnforth. Nr junction of A6 & B5282. Stn: Arnside, 4m; Lancaster, 15m.* Cream teas. **Adm £2.50, chd free. Sun 6 May (2-5).**
Large garden; natural rock garden, water garden; wood walks, lawns, shrubs. C19 cast iron orangery.

Ruins of a dovecote/ summerhouse available for viewing . . .

13 NEW DUNNINGWELL HALL
The Green LA18 5JT. Mrs Susan Brown. *3m N of Millom. Between A595 & A5903. From west coast heading S towards Silecroft on A595 signed M6. After approx 3m turn R at Dunningwell sign then L at T-junction, entrance on L. From North East leave A595 and take A5903 near 'The Green' toward Millom after 400yds turn R at Dunningwell sign entrance 400yds.* Cream teas. **Adm £2.50, chd free. Sat 28, Sun 29 July (11-5).**
Victorian formal gardens and woodlands, 2 Victorian ponds, another believed to be of Queen Anne origin. Ruins of a dovecote/summerhouse available for viewing. Pet cemetery (24 graves). Statuary in abundance Oriental, African, abstract, traditional - some for sale. Display of border plants, pampas, bamboo fearnery and hopefully a bog garden. (Limited access of 5 acres). Some uneven and steep paths, visible tree roots.

Planting of disused railway siding providing home to wildlife . . .

⑭ FELL YEAT
Casterton, nr Kirkby Lonsdale
LA6 2JW. Mr & Mrs O S Benson. *1m
E of Casterton Village. On the rd to Bull
Pot. Leave A65 at Devils Bridge, follow
A683 for 1m, take the R fork to High
Casterton at golf course, straight
across at two sets of Xrds, the house
is immed on the L, 1/4m from no-
through-rd sign.* Cream teas. **Adm £3,
chd free. Sun 20 May (1-5).**
1-acre informal country garden with
many unusual plants. Divided into
garden 'rooms'. 2 small ponds,
herbaceous borders, old roses, ferns
and small developing woodland
garden. National Collection of *Ligularia*.
Featured on TV Look Northwest.
🏃 ✿ **NCCPG** ☕

**⑮ NEW ◆ GRAYTHWAITE
MANOR HOTEL**
Fernhill Road, Grange-over-
Sands LA11 7JE. Mr J Duncan.
*Follow B5277 through Grange-
over-Sands, almost opp fire stn
turn up Fernhill Rd, then 1st L up
hill. Well signed.* **Adm £3, chd
free. Visit garden when hotel
open 9 to dusk. For NGS: Thurs
10 May; 26 July; 6 Sept (10-5).**
First laid out in 1899 by a German
gardener. Garden is 6 acres and
features quarry garden, water
garden and rockery using natural
stone. Unusual stone arch and
large pergola. Topiary. Bright
summer bedding and views over
Morecambe Bay. Cumbria in
Bloom Jackie Sanderson Trophy
'Best Hotel in Cumbria', South
Lakeland Trophy 'Best Commercial
Premises in Borough and Gold
Award Grange in Bloom.
♿ 🏃 ☕

⑯ HALECAT
Witherslack LA11 6RU. Mrs Michael
Stanley, 015395 52536,
matthewbardgett@hotmail.com.
*10m SW of Kendal. From A590 turn
into Witherslack following the Halecat*

brown signs. L in township at another
brown sign & L again, signpost
'Cartmel Fell'; gates on L & Halecat
Nursery. Map on Halecat website.
Light refreshments & teas at Nursery.
**Adm £2, chd free. Suns 27 May; 17
June; 22 July (10-5). Visitors also
welcome by appt.**
Medium-sized garden; mixed shrub
and herbaceous borders, terrace,
sunken garden; gazebo; daffodils and
cherries in spring; wild flower meadow;
beautiful view over Kent estuary to
Arnside. Adjacent nursery.
♿ ✿ ☕

⑰ HAZEL COTTAGE
Armathwaite CA4 9PG. Mr D Ryland
& Mr J Thexton. *8m SE of Carlisle.
Turn off A6 just S of High Hesket
signed Armathwaite, after 2m house
facing you at T-junction.* Home-made
teas. **Adm £3, chd free. Sun 17 June
(12-5).**
Developing flower arrangers and
plantsmans garden. Extending to
approx 5 acres. Incls herbaceous
borders, pergola, ponds and 2yr-old
planting of disused railway siding
providing home to wildlife. Many
variegated and unusual plants.
🏃 ✿ ☕

⑱ HEYWOOD HOUSE
Heywood House, Brookhouse
LA2 9PW. Mike & Lorraine Cave,
01524 770977. *4m E of Lancaster.
From J34 M6, follow A683 to
Caton/Kirkby Lonsdale. At mini island
turn R to Brookhouse. At Black Bull PH
turn R, garden 3/4m on LH-side.*
Home-made teas. **Adm £3, chd free.
Sun 27 May; Sun 1 July (11-5).
Visitors also welcome by appt in
June, groups 10+.**
Secluded 2-acre garden with many
unusual trees and shrubs, sweeping
lawns with beautiful herbaceous
borders leading to large natural wildlife
pond, gravel garden, pergolas with an
abundance of roses and climbers, folly,
woodland garden with natural stream.
An alternative view can be enjoyed
from the garden railway.
🏃 ✿ ☕

⑲ HIGH BECKSIDE FARM
Beckside, Cartmel LA11 7SW. Mr &
Mrs P J McCabe, 015395 36528.
*11/4m N of Cartmel. Take Haverthwaite
rd, R at the village shop in square pass
alongside race course & drive for
11/4m to car park in nearby field.* **Adm
£2.50, chd free. Sun 3 June (1-5).
Visitors also welcome by appt.**
Semi-wild garden, conservation area
with ponds, waterfowl. Large variety of
plants and shrubs. Approx 3 acres of
mixed woodland, 11 acres of wild
flowers on hillside with views over
valley and bay. Small house garden.
5 mins walk to ponds. Stout shoes.
🏃 ☕

⑳ ◆ HOLEHIRD GARDENS
Windermere LA23 1NP. Lakeland
Horticultural Society, 015394 46008,
www.holehirdgardens.org.uk. *2m N
of Windermere. Off A592 Patterdale
Rd.* Garden signed on R. **Adm £3, by
donation, chd free. Open daily see
website for details. For NGS: Thur
26 July (10-5).**
The garden is run by volunteers
with the aim of promoting knowledge
of the cultivation of alpine and
herbaceous plants, shrubs and trees,
especially those suited to Lakeland
conditions. One of the best labelled
gardens in the UK. National
Collections of *Astilbe, Hydrangea*
and *Polystichum* (ferns). Set on the
fellside with stunning views over
Windermere the walled garden gives
protection to mixed borders whilst
alpine houses protect an always
colourful array of tiny gems.
Consistently voted among the top
gardens in Britain and Europe.
Featured in national & local press,
specialist publications. Scientific
Status for Hydrangea Collection.
♿ 🏃 ✿ **NCCPG**

㉑ ◆ HOLKER HALL GARDENS
Cark-in-Cartmel LA11 7PL. Lord &
Lady Cavendish, 015395 58328,
www.holker-hall.co.uk. *4m W of
Grange-over-Sands. 12m W of M6
(J36).* **House and Garden adm £9.25,
chd £5, concessions £8.50, Garden
only adm £5.95, chd £5,
concessions £5.25. Gardens 1 Apr
to 28 Oct Sun to Fri. For Hall see
website. For NGS: Wed 11 July
(10.30-5.30).**
A garden for all seasons within the
Gulf Stream, benefiting plants
from throughout the world incl
exotic planting. Woodland garden
with extensive collection of

rhododendrons flowering Jan to late summer. National Collection of *Styracaceae*. Ancient oaks, magnolias, camellias and largest common lime in UK. Guided walks in garden 11.30am & 3pm starting from kiosk (donations to NGS).

&. ⅍ ⊕ **NCCPG** ☕

㉒ ◆ HUTTON-IN-THE-FOREST
Penrith CA11 9TH. Lord Inglewood, 017684 84449, www.hutton-in-the-forest.co.uk. *6m NW of Penrith. On B5305, 3m from exit 41 of M6 towards Wigton.* **House and Garden adm £5.50, chd £2.50, Garden only adm £3.50, chd £1. Sun - Fri Apr to Oct (gdns only); House Weds, Thurs, Suns & Bank Hol Mons 4 to 15 Apr, 2 May to 30 Sept 12.30-4. For NGS: Suns 8 July; 19 Aug (11-5).**
Magnificent grounds with C18 walled flower garden, terraces and lake. C19 low garden, specimen trees and topiary; woodland walk and dovecote. Medieval house with C17, C18 and C19 additions.

&. ☕

㉓ NEW KIRKBY STEPHEN GARDENS
CA17 4PG. *2m N of Kirkby Stephen. North on A685 just N of Kirkby Stephen, turn L signed Gt Musgrave/Warcop (B6259) after approx 1m turn L as signed.* Home-made teas at Winton Park. **Combined adm £4.50, chd free. Sun 22 July (11-5).**
A paired opening providing a contrast in style between creative use of space in a modest-sized town garden and large country garden.

☕

NEW WESTVIEW
Fletcher Hill. Reg & Irene Metcalfe. *Kirkby Stephen town centre, T-lights opp Pine Design*
Medium sized secret town-centre walled cottage-type garden with perennials, shrubs, large hosta bed (many varieties), cental lawn, wildlife pond and adjoining prairie style nursery beds.

⅍ ⊕

NEW WINTON PARK
Mr Anthony Kilvington
2 acre country garden with many fine conifers, acers and rhododendrons, herbaceous

borders, hostas, ferns, grasses and over 700 roses. Two formal ponds, plus secret wildlife pond with koi and other fish. Stunning views.

&. ⅍

㉔ ◆ THE LAKE DISTRICT VISITOR CENTRE AT BROCKHOLE
Windermere LA23 1LJ. Lake District National Park Authority, 015394 40271, www.lake-district.gov.uk. *2m NW of Windermere. On A591 between Windermere & Ambleside.* Light refreshments & teas. **Adm free (pay and display parking). Open 10 to dusk all-yr-round. For NGS: Weds 16 May; 15 Aug (10-4).**
Grade II listed arts and crafts garden designed by Thomas Mawson. 30 acres of formal and informal gardens with many unusual shrubs suited to acid soil and mild aspect. Adventure playground and access to shores of Windermere. Garden currently under redevelopment with plans for a full scale restoration. May opening is for plantaholics, August opening is aimed at families with gardening activities for children. Electric mobility vehicles available at Visitor Centre.

&. ⊕ ☕

Woodland garden surrounding mill race stream with bridges . . .

㉕ LAKESIDE HOTEL
Lake Windermere, Newby Bridge LA12 8AT. Mr N R Talbot, 015395 30001, sales@lakesidehotel.co.uk. *1m N of Newby Bridge. On S shore of Lake Windermere. From A590 at Newby Bridge, cross the bridge which leads onto the Hawkshead rd. Follow this rd for 1m, hotel on the R.* Complimentary parking available. Light refreshments & teas. **Adm £2.50, chd free. Weds 16 May; 5 Sept (11-5). Visitors also welcome by appt.**
Magnificent lake shore setting overlooking Gummers How. Gardens planted with a spectacular range of interesting trees, shrubs and

perennials. Aromatherapy, scented and subtropical themed gardens. Winter border. Huge rooftop garden with espalier apples. A wealth of seasonal bedding utilising uncommon and rare varieties. Lakeview conservatory filled with scented pelargoniums.

⅍ ⊕ ⊫ ☕

㉖ NEW LANGHOLME MILL
Woodgate, Lowick Green LA12 8ES. Judith & Graham Sanderson, 01229 885215, info@langholmemill.co.uk. *7m NW of Ulverston. Take A5092 at Greenodd towards Boughton for 3¾m on L ½m after school.* **Adm £3, chd free. Visitors welcome by appt, groups also welcome all year.**
Approx 1 acre of woodland garden surrounding mill race stream with bridges, hosting well established rhododendrons, hostas and acers.

⊫

㉗ LEECE VILLAGE GARDENS
LA12 0QP. *2m E of Barrow-in-Furness. 6m SW of Ulverston. J36 M6 onto A590 to Ulverston. A5087 coast rd to Barrow. Approx 8m turn R for Leece Village (signed, look for concrete sea wall on L). Village parking for gardens.* Light refreshments & teas. **Combined adm £3, chd free. Sun 1 July (11-5).**
Small village clustered around tarn. Maps given to all visitors.

☕

4 DALE GARTH
S J & G W Shaw
Mid terrace property. Front garden with intensively planted mixed borders, lawn, bench and small pond. Enclosed back garden - wild hedge, plant covered walls and fences. Grass, glasshouse, pear tree and layered borders.

&. ⅍ ⊕

RAISING HOUSE
Vivien & Neil Hudson, 01229 431539, mikehuddy@aol.com. **Visitors also welcome by appt.**
Plant lovers garden on SW slope. Developed (with still more to do) over last 5yrs with emphasis on flowering plants, incl many unusual shrubs, grasses, herbaceous perennials and climbers. Alpine scree and troughs. Access by steps. Featured in 'NW Evening Mail'.

⅍ ⊕

WINANDER
Mrs Enid Cockshott
1-acre, eco-friendly garden amid mature trees on an E-facing slope. Patio area with wildlife pond; large organic vegetable and fruit area. Alpines, mixed borders, quiet seating areas with views across Leece Tarn and out to Morecambe Bay.

WOOD GARTH
Harry & Rita Butcher
Sheltered village garden. Formal area with traditionally planted containers and herbaceous border. Trees and native flora to attract wildlife. Lawned area with differential mowing. Access by steps.

28 NEW LILAC COTTAGE GARDENS
Blitterlees CA7 4JJ. Lynn & Jeff Downham, 016973 32171, lilaccottage@tiscali.co.uk. *1m S of Silloth. On B5300 the Maryport to Silloth rd.* Home-made teas. **Adm £2.50, chd free. Sun 20 May (11-5).**
Approx 1-acre garden set in compartments in a coastal setting. Featuring raised and woodland gardens, herbaceous borders, large lawned areas and sandstone gazebo. Each garden has an individual theme, well stocked with plants, shrubs and trees providing colour and interest all-yr round. Magnolia trees are a particular feature of the garden, which should be on show in May.

29 LINDETH FELL COUNTRY HOUSE HOTEL
Lyth Valley Road, Bowness-on-Windermere LA23 3JP. Air Cdr & Mrs P A Kennedy, 015394 43286, www.lindethfell.co.uk. *1m S of Bowness. On A5074. From centre of Bowness opp St Martins church turn L, signed Kendal A5074. 200yds on L after Xrds at Ferry View.* Home-made teas. **Adm £3, chd free. Sat 19 May (2-5).** Visitors also welcome by appt in May, June & July, coaches permitted - short wheel base only.
6 acres of lawns and landscaped grounds on the hills above Lake Windermere, designed by Mawson around 1909; conifers and specimen

trees best in spring and early summer with a colourful display of rhododendrons, azaleas and Japanese maples; grounds offer splendid views to Coniston mountains. Partial wheelchair access: To terrace in front of house looking over garden and view.

30 MATSON GROUND
Windermere LA23 2NH. Matson Ground Estate Co Ltd. *²/₃m E of Bowness. From Kendal turn R off B5284 signed Heathwaite, 100yds after Windermere Golf Club. Garden on L after ¹/₃m. From Bowness turn L onto B5284 from A5074. After ¹/₂m turn L at Xrds. Garden on L ¹/₂m along lane.* **Adm £2.50, chd free. Sun 20 May (2-5).**
Stream flows through ornamental garden to large pond in the wild garden of spring bulbs, later wild flowers. Azaleas, rhododendrons, large mixed shrub/herbaceous borders, topiary work, white garden, spring/summer border, camomile lawn on terrace. ¹/₂-acre walled kitchen garden and greenhouses. 2-acre woodland.

31 MEADOW HOUSE
Garnett Bridge Road, Burneside LA8 9AY. Paul & Anne-Marie Burrill. *4m N of Kendal. Leave A591 2m N of Kendal signed R towards Burneside. Continue to village centre past Premier Store. After ¹/₂m turn L towards Longsleddale (opp Burneside Hall). After ³/₄m turn L signed Meadow House. Go immed R over cattle grid. Park as directed, majority of parking in field.* Home-made teas. **Adm £3, chd free (share to The Christie Hospital Appeal). Suns 22, 29 July (1-5).**
Developing 1¹/₂-acre rural garden with superb S-facing countryside views. Of special interest are water features with ponds and streams; large vegetable and fruit garden with glasshouses and polytunnel. The garden blends ornamental beauty with food production, home to ducks, chickens

and our own honey bees. All this and donkeys too. Featured in 'Westmorland Gazette', & on BBC2 Open Gardens.

32 NEWTON RIGG CAMPUS GARDENS
Newton Rigg, Penrith CA11 0AH. *1m W of Penrith. 3m W from J40 & J41 off M6. ¹/₂m off the B5288 W of Penrith.* **Adm £2.50, chd free. Evening Openings Weds 6 June; 26 Sept (6.30-8.30).**
The gardens and campus grounds have much of horticultural interest incl herbaceous borders, ponds, organic garden with fruit cage and display of composting techniques, woodland walk, summer scented garden, 2 arboretums, tropical display house, annual meadows, pleached hornbeam walkway and extensive range of ornamental trees and shrubs. Guided tour of gardens 6.30 to 7.15, also of the campus trees at 7.15 to 8.30. Tours lead by Horticultural lecturer Shelagh Todd and head gardener Con Maguire. Featured in 'Cumbria Life'.

The garden blends ornamental beauty, home to ducks, chickens and our own honey bees . . .

33 THE NOOK
Helton CA10 2QA. Brenda & Philip Freedman. *6m S of Penrith. A6 S from Penrith. After Eamont Bridge turn R to Pooley Bridge. Fork L to Askham. Through Askham 1m to Helton. Follow signs.* Home-made teas. **Adm £2.50, chd free. Sun 27 May (11-4.30).**
¹/₃-acre with outstanding views of Lowther valley and fells beyond. Plantsmans' garden, with many unusual plants. Garden divided into 3 areas: front cottage flower garden, side fruit and vegetable garden, main garden with species rhododrums, rockeries, scree garden, stone troughs, herbs, conifers, pond and water garden. Steps but can provide a ramp, also fairly steep slope.

34 **NEW** **THE OLD RECTORY**
Caldbeck CA7 8DP. Mrs Anne
Cartmell, 016974 78484.
*Caldbeck village centre, between
shop & church over cattlegrid.*
**Adm £3, chd free. Sun 24 June
(11-4).**
Established garden surrounding
Georgian house (not open). Mature
trees and shrubs, formal and
herbaceous area. Large walled
vegetable garden.
&. &

35 **THE OLD RECTORY**
Dean, Workington CA14 4TH. Mr F
H & Mrs J S Wheeler, 01946 861840.
*5m SW of Cockermouth. Last house in
Dean on rd to Workington, on L
beyond church.* **Adm £2, chd free.**
**Visitors welcome by appt
throughout the year, individuals &
groups welcome.**
Over 1 acre. with interest throughout
the year from aconites and spring
bulbs to autumn colours. Informal
rooms with wide range of trees,
shrubs and herbaceous perennials,
many relatively rare and tender, various
shrub and climbing roses. Mixed
shrubberies, woodland and damp
areas, scree garden and rockeries.
Featured in 'Cumbria Life', 'Gardens
Monthly' and 'Gardens of the Lake
District'.
&

36 **PEAR TREE COTTAGE**
Dalton, Burton-in-Kendal LA6 1NN.
Linda & Alec Greening, 01524
781624,
www.peartreecottagecumbria.co.uk.
*4m W of Kirkby Lonsdale. 10m S of
Kendal. From village of Burton-in-
Kendal (A6070), follow Vicarage Lane
for 1m. Parking at farm, 50yds before
garden (signed).* Home-made teas.
**Adm £3.00, chd free. Sun 15 July
(11-5); Sun 9 Sept (11-4). Evening
Opening £4.00, wine, Wed 27 June
(6-9). Visitors also welcome by appt
for groups of 10 or more.**
1/3-acre cottage garden. A peaceful
and relaxing garden, harmonising with
its rural setting. Diverse planting areas,
including packed herbaceous borders,
rambling roses, wildlife pond and bog
garden, fernery and gravel garden.
Intensively planted, incl much to
interest the plantsman and general
garden visitor alike. Increasing
collections of ferns, hardy geraniums
and clematis. Prizewinner 'The English
Garden' photo competition (country

garden section). 1st Prizewinner
Gardens Monthly photo competition.
& & &

37 **NEW** **PLUMGARTHS**
Crook Road LA8 8LX. Cumbria
Wildlife Trust,
www.cumbriawildlifetrust.org.uk.
*2m NW of Kendal. At N Kendal
roundabout, take exit signed
Crook. Parking 120 metres on L,
entrance to garden is opp.* Home-
made teas. **Adm £2.50, chd free.
Sats 5 May; 9 June (11-4).**
Developing 2¹/₂ acre organic wildlife
garden with pond, small woodland
with composting area and log
piles, flowering tulip tree, native
wild flower bed, flame flower
growing through yew hedges.
Mixture of formal and informal,
herbaceous borders, beech
hedges. Mini nature reserve. Gravel
paths, disabled wc.
& & &

38 **QUARRY HILL HOUSE**
Mealsgate CA7 3AE. Mr & Mrs
Charles Woodhouse, 016973 71225,
charles.woodhouse@ukgateway.net.
*1m E of Mealsgate. 1/2m W of
Boltongate(8m SSW of Wigton). At
Mealsgate, on A595 Cockermouth to
Carlisle rd, turn E onto B5299 for
Boltongate, Ireby & Caldbeck. Approx
1m along rd, entrance gates to Quarry
Hill House on L.* Home-made teas.
**Adm £3, chd free (share to Hospice
at Home Carlisle & N Lakeland). Sun
10 June (1.30-5). Visitors also
welcome by appt.**
Parkland setting with views of
Skiddaw, northern fells and Solway
Firth. 3-acre traditional gardens,
created over many years by the late
Rosemary Shaw and her gardener the
late Terry Hodgson. Herbaceous
borders, shrubs, trees and large
vegetable garden. Also wild flowers
and many specimen trees in 25-acre
park and woodland shrubbery. Dyke
kest created in 2001 by Peter Whiles.
Re-creation for wildlife of ponds and

wetlands in former shooting woods.
Featured in 'Lake District Life' & BBC
Radio Cumbria.
& & &

39 **1 QUEENS PLACE**
Queens Road, Kendal LA9 4PJ. Mr
& Mrs T Hunte, 01539 730786. *From
Windermere A591 to Plumgarths
roundabout. A5284 Kendal for 1m,
turn R into Queens Rd, 500yds on L.*
**Adm £2.50, chd free. Suns 17, 24
June (11-4). Visitors also welcome
by appt, small groups only.**
High on a hillside overlooking Kendal
and the fells beyond, a spectacular
town garden with a touch of the
tropics, gently sloping with cleverly
designed limestone terraces and
pathways. Packed with very interesting
plantings incl tree ferns, trachycarpus,
phormiums, grasses, herbaceous
perennials, and small alpine garden.
Award winner Kendal in Bloom.
&

A peaceful and relaxing garden, harmonising with its rural setting . . .

40 **RANNERDALE COTTAGE**
Buttermere CA13 9UY. The McElney
Family. *8m S of Cockermouth. 10m W
of Keswick. B5289 on Crummock
Water, in the Buttermere Valley.* Light
refreshments & teas. **Adm £2.50, chd
free. Sat 23, Sun 24 June (11-5).**
1/2-acre cottage garden with beck and
woodland walk overlooking Crummock
Water, splendid mountain views.
Herbaceous, shrubs, roses, perennial
geraniums, tree peonies, pond with
fish.
& &

41 **SCARTHWAITE**
Grange-in-Borrowdale CA12 5UQ.
Mr & Mrs E C Hicks, 017687 77233.
*5m S of Keswick. From Keswick take
B5289 to Grange. Cross rd bridge, into
village, house 1/4m on L. Bridge NOT
suitable for coaches but mini buses
may cross. (1/4m walk from far side of
bridge for coach parties). The
Keswick/Seatoller bus & Stagecoach
Honister Rambler bus stop at Grange*

Organic garden (a typical NGS!) combining the wild and natural . . .

Bridge. **Adm £2, chd free. Tues 29 May; 26 June; 24 July (1-5).** Visitors also welcome by appt on weekdays ONLY, not weekends or Bank Hols. This ¹/₃-acre garden gives the impression of woodland; focusing on naturalistic planting of ferns, hostas and bulbs, many varieties of hardy geraniums, clematis and other plants growing in the profusion of a cottage garden.

🏃

㊷ ◆ SIZERGH CASTLE
nr Kendal LA8 8AE. The National Trust, 015395 60951, www.nationaltrust.org.uk. *3m S of Kendal. Approach rd leaves A590 close to & S of A590/A591 interchange.* **Adm £4, chd £2. Sun to Thur 1 Apr to 28 Oct. For NGS: Sat 4 Aug (11-5).**
²/₃-acre limestone rock garden, largest owned by National Trust; collection of Japanese maples, dwarf conifers, hardy ferns, primulas, gentians, perennials and bulbs; water garden, aquatic plants; on castle walls shrubs and climbers, many half-hardy; south garden with specimen roses, lilies, shrubs and ground cover. Wild flower areas, herbaceous borders, crab apple orchard with spring bulbs, 'Dutch' garden. Terraced garden and lake; kitchen garden, vegetables, herbs, flowers; fruit orchard with spring bulbs. Guided walk by Head Gardener 3pm.
♿ 🏃 ⊕ **NCCPG** ☕

㊸ NEW SPRINT MILL
Burneside LA8 9AQ. Edward & Romola Acland. *2m N of Kendal. From Burneside follow signs to Skelsmergh for ¹/₂m then L to Sprint Mill.* Light refreshments & teas. **Adm £2, chd free. Suns 24 June; 29 July (11-5).**
Unorthodox 5-acre organic garden (atypical NGS!) combining the wild and natural alongside provision of owners' wood, fruit and vegetables. Path beside river, strategic hand-crafted seats, old water mill building to be explored. Large vegetable and soft fruit area, following no-dig and permaculture principles. Hand-tools prevail, scythe and fork rather than mower. Unconventional art and crafts display, green-wood craft demonstration and slide show presentation of garden development. Featured on BBC2 Open Gardens.
🏃 ☕

㊹ STONE EDGE
Jack Hill, Allithwaite LA11 7QB. Ian & Julie Chambers, 015395 33895. *2m W of Grange-over-Sands. On B5277. Jack Hill is on L just before Allithwaite Village. Parking available in The Pheasent Inn car park at bottom of Jack Hill approx 100 metres. Ltd parking for the not so fit near house.* Home-made teas. **Adm £3, chd free** (share to St Mary's Hospice, Ulverston). **Day & Evening Opening** wine, Tue 26 June (10-8.30). Visitors also welcome by appt.
A garden in harmony with nature; incl formal lavender garden; border with shrubs, climbers and perennials; herbs grown for use in the kitchen. Spectacular specimens form a Mediterranean garden; woodland garden meanders down to a pond. Steep slope in woodland garden. Pots abound. Fantasic views over Morecambe Bay. Garden room and new potting garden shed. Featured in 'Cumbria Life' & on Radio Cumbria.
🏃 ☕

㊺ SUMMERDALE HOUSE
Nook, nr Lupton LA6 1PE. David & Gail Sheals, 015395 67210, sheals@btinternet.com. *7m S of Kendal. 6m W of Kirkby Lonsdale. From J36 M6 take A65 to Kirkby Lonsdale, at Nook take R turn Farleton.* Home-made soup & bread, teas 8 Apr, Home-made teas (May & Aug). **Adm £3, chd free. Suns 8 Apr; 6 May; 5 Aug (11-5).** Visitors also welcome by appt, groups of 10+.
1¹/₂-acre part-walled country garden restored and developed over last 10yrs by owners. Beautiful setting with fine views across to Farleton Fell. Herbaceous borders, formal and informal ponds, woodland planting, old orchard and new meadow planting. Interesting range of herbaceous perennials, many of which are propagated by owners. Featured in 'Lake District Life', on North West Tonight & Radio Cumbria.
🏃 ⊕ ☕

㊻ NEW SWINSIDE END FARM
Scales, High Lorton CA13 9UA. Mrs Karen Nicholson, 01900 85134. *5m S of Cockermouth. From Keswick A66 take B5292 to Braithwaite. Climb Whinlatter pass, 1¹/₂m after visitor centre signed Hopebeck fork L. Bear R at next fork to Lorton. Farm on L at next L fork. From Lorton follow C2C cycle signs.* **Adm £2.50, chd free. Mon 30 July (11-4.30).** Visitors also welcome by appt.
Evolving large garden of well-stocked herbaceous borders with superb view of Lorton Vale. Informal borders of perennials, shrubs and grasses in colour-themed area. Planted old agricultural equipent and pergolas. Traditional planted stone walls, wishing well and small pond. Summerhouse.
🏃 ▭

㊼ NEW ◆ TULLIE HOUSE
Castle Street, Carlisle CA3 8TP. Carlisle City Council, www.tulliehouse.co.uk. *City Centre. Signed as Museum on brown signs, see website for map.* **Adm by donation. All year. For NGS: Sat 30 June; Sun 1 July (10-5).**
Beds in front of Jacobean house are planted to reflect C17. Mature Arbutus unedo and Cornus kousa grow alongside a host of new planting incl *Fatsia japonica variegata: Eucryphia glutinosa.* Roman style planting incl fig, vines, myrtle, acanthus and variety of herbs. Meet the gardener with Ian Corri. The Roman Link with curator of archaeology, and the garden from the wildlife prospective with our natural sciences curator.
♿ ⊕ ☕

New Mediterranean style garden on 4¹/₂-acre elevated site with magnificent views over Morecambe Bay . . .

51 YEWBARROW HOUSE
Hampsfell Road, Grange-over-Sands LA11 6BE. Jonathan & Margaret Denby, 015395 32469, www.yewbarrowhouse.co.uk. ¹/₄m from town centre. Follow signs in centre of Grange. Turn R at HSBC Bank into Pig Lane, 1st L into Hampsfell Rd. Garden 200yds on L. Cream teas. **Adm £3, chd free. Suns 3 June; 1 July; 5 Aug; 2 Sept (11-4). Visitors also welcome by appt.**
New Mediterranean style garden on 4¹/₂-acre elevated site with magnificent views over Morecambe Bay. The garden features a restored walled Victorian kitchen garden; Italianate terrace garden; exotic gravel garden; fern garden, Japanese Hot Spring pool. Dahlia trial beds and orangery. Featured in 'Sunday Telegraph'.

48 WHITBYSTEADS
Askham CA10 2PG. Mr Thomas Lowther. 6m S of Penrith. Turn R at Eamont Bridge. Turn L at Y fork after railway bridge signed Askham. Turn R at Queen's Head up hill, ignore Dead End sign, garden ³/₄m from village. Home-made teas. **Adm £3, chd free (share to Lowther Church). Sun 8 July (2-5).**
1-acre garden on several levels surrounding farmhouse (not open) on edge of fells, (850ft) wide. Variety of shrub roses, unusual herbaceous plants and geraniums. Magnificent views over Eden Valley.

49 ◆ WINDERWATH
Temple Sowerby CA10 2AG. Miss Jane Pollock, 01768 88250. 5m E of Penrith. On A66. **Adm £3, chd free. Mon to Fri 31 Mar to 31 Oct 10-4, Sats 10-12. For NGS: Sun 10 June (1-4).**
Mature gardens with interesting and rare trees, herbaceous, Himalayan and alpine plants. Vegetable garden, pond area with picnic benches. Second-hand garden tools for sale. Partial wheelchair access.

50 WINDY HALL
Crook Road, Windermere LA23 3JA. Diane & David Kinsman, 015394 46238, dhewitt-kinsman@fba.org.uk. 1m S of Bowness-on-Windermere. On B5284 up Linthwaite Country House Hotel driveway. Home-made teas. **Adm £3, chd free. Combined with Brackenrigg Lodge £5. Suns 6 May; 10 June (10-5). Visitors also welcome by appt.**
4-acre owner designed and maintained garden. Woodland underplanted with species rhododendrons, camellias, magnolias and hydrangeas; Japanese influenced quarry garden; alpine area with gunnera; wild flower meadow; kitchen, 'privy' and 'Best' gardens. Waterfowl garden with many stewartias. Redesigned pond garden with plants raised from seed collected by David in China. NCCPG Collections of Aruncus and Filipendula; Naturlised moss gardens and paths in woodland bluebells and foxgloves in abundance, wide variety of native birds, many nest in gardens. Black, multi-horned hebridean sheep and lambs. Rare breed of pheasants from China and Nepal, exotic ducks and geese. Featured in many newspaper and magazine articles.

52 YEWS
Bowness-on-Windermere LA23 3JR. Sir Oliver & Lady Scott. 1m S of Bowness-on-Windermere. A5074. Middle Entrance Drive, 50yds. Home-made teas. **Adm £3, chd free (share to Macmillan Nurses). Sun 24 June (2-5.30).**
Medium-sized formal Edwardian garden; fine trees, ha-ha, herbaceous borders; greenhouse. Bog area being developed, bamboo, primula, hosta. Young yew maze and vegetable garden.

DERBYSHIRE

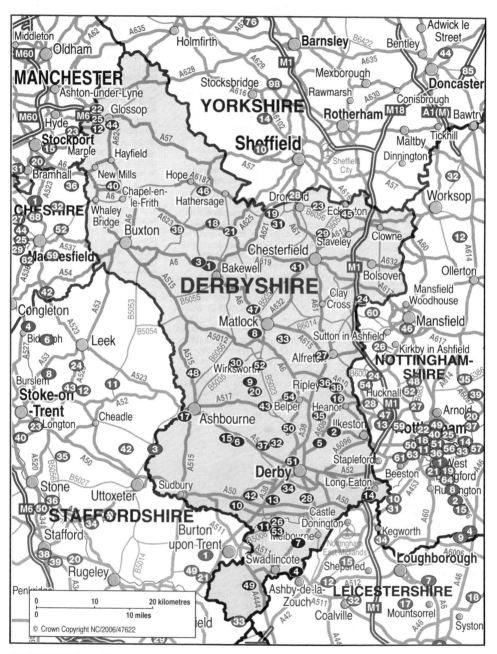

Opening Dates

February

SATURDAY 17
10 Cherry Tree Cottage

SUNDAY 18
10 Cherry Tree Cottage

April

SUNDAY 1
17 Dove Cottage

MONDAY 2
15 Dam Farm House

TUESDAY 3
15 Dam Farm House

FRIDAY 6
15 Dam Farm House

SATURDAY 7
10 Cherry Tree Cottage

SUNDAY 8
10 Cherry Tree Cottage
37 Meynell Langley Trials Garden

TUESDAY 10
15 Dam Farm House

FRIDAY 13
15 Dam Farm House

MONDAY 16
15 Dam Farm House

TUESDAY 17
15 Dam Farm House

WEDNESDAY 18
4 Bluebell Arboretum
8 Cascades

FRIDAY 20
15 Dam Farm House

SUNDAY 22
4 Bluebell Arboretum
26 37 High Street
52 Windward

MONDAY 23
15 Dam Farm House

TUESDAY 24
15 Dam Farm House

FRIDAY 27
15 Dam Farm House

MONDAY 30
15 Dam Farm House

May

TUESDAY 1
15 Dam Farm House

FRIDAY 4
15 Dam Farm House

SUNDAY 6
18 Eyam Hall
54 35 Wyver Lane

MONDAY 7
6 The Burrows Gardens
54 35 Wyver Lane

TUESDAY 8
15 Dam Farm House

FRIDAY 11
15 Dam Farm House

SUNDAY 13
5 Broomfield Hall
10 Cherry Tree Cottage
12 Cloud Cottage
21 Fir Croft
37 Meynell Langley Trials Garden

MONDAY 14
15 Dam Farm House

TUESDAY 15
15 Dam Farm House

FRIDAY 18
15 Dam Farm House

SATURDAY 19
31 Horsleygate Hall
52 Windward

SUNDAY 20
12 Cloud Cottage
31 Horsleygate Hall
52 Windward

MONDAY 21
15 Dam Farm House

TUESDAY 22
15 Dam Farm House

WEDNESDAY 23
4 Bluebell Arboretum
8 Cascades

FRIDAY 25
15 Dam Farm House

SUNDAY 27
4 Bluebell Arboretum
11 10 Chestnut Way
12 Cloud Cottage
17 Dove Cottage
39 Monksway
44 Quarryside
53 Woodend Cottage

MONDAY 28
6 The Burrows Gardens
11 10 Chestnut Way
46 Shatton Hall Farm

TUESDAY 29
15 Dam Farm House

WEDNESDAY 30
32 Kedleston Hall

June

FRIDAY 1
15 Dam Farm House

SUNDAY 3
21 Fir Croft
22 Gamesley Fold Cottage
27 Highfield House
29 Hillside
34 Littleover Lane Allotments
39 Monksway

MONDAY 4
15 Dam Farm House

TUESDAY 5
15 Dam Farm House

WEDNESDAY 6
22 Gamesley Fold Cottage

FRIDAY 8
15 Dam Farm House

SATURDAY 9
2 334 Belper Road

SUNDAY 10
2 334 Belper Road
10 Cherry Tree Cottage
18 Eyam Hall
22 Gamesley Fold Cottage
26 37 High Street
35 9 Main Street
37 Meynell Langley Trials Garden
39 Monksway
41 Park Hall
43 Postern House
54 35 Wyver Lane

MONDAY 11
15 Dam Farm House

TUESDAY 12
15 Dam Farm House

WEDNESDAY 13
4 Bluebell Arboretum

FRIDAY 15
15 Dam Farm House

SUNDAY 17
4 Bluebell Arboretum
9 Cashel
19 Fanshawe Gate Hall
21 Fir Croft
39 Monksway

MONDAY 18
6 The Burrows Gardens
15 Dam Farm House

TUESDAY 19
15 Dam Farm House

WEDNESDAY 20
8 Cascades
22 Gamesley Fold Cottage

FRIDAY 22
- **15** Dam Farm House

SUNDAY 24
- **1** Ashford Hall
- **17** Dove Cottage
- **19** Fanshawe Gate Hall
- **25** High Roost
- **27** Highfield House
- **39** Monksway
- **40** Otterbrook
- **50** Wharfedale

MONDAY 25
- **15** Dam Farm House

TUESDAY 26
- **15** Dam Farm House

FRIDAY 29
- **13** Clovermead (Evening)
- **15** Dam Farm House

July

SUNDAY 1
- **1** Ashford Hall
- **19** Fanshawe Gate Hall
- **20** Field Farm
- **39** Monksway
- **41** Park Hall
- **44** Quarryside

MONDAY 2
- **6** The Burrows Gardens
- **15** Dam Farm House

TUESDAY 3
- **15** Dam Farm House

FRIDAY 6
- **15** Dam Farm House

SUNDAY 8
- **13** Clovermead
- **19** Fanshawe Gate Hall
- **37** Meynell Langley Trials Garden

MONDAY 9
- **15** Dam Farm House

TUESDAY 10
- **15** Dam Farm House

FRIDAY 13
- **15** Dam Farm House

SUNDAY 15
- **8** Cascades
- **11** 10 Chestnut Way
- **20** Field Farm
- **24** Hardwick Hall
- **36** 2 Manvers Street
- **43** Postern House
- **53** Woodend Cottage

MONDAY 16
- **15** Dam Farm House

TUESDAY 17
- **15** Dam Farm House

WEDNESDAY 18
- **4** Bluebell Arboretum
- **7** Calke Abbey

FRIDAY 20
- **15** Dam Farm House

SATURDAY 21
- **28** 11 Highgrove Drive

SUNDAY 22
- **4** Bluebell Arboretum
- **28** 11 Highgrove Drive
- **50** Wharfedale

MONDAY 23
- **15** Dam Farm House

TUESDAY 24
- **15** Dam Farm House

FRIDAY 27
- **15** Dam Farm House

SUNDAY 29
- **13** Clovermead
- **14** The Cottage
- **17** Dove Cottage
- **46** Shatton Hall Farm

MONDAY 30
- **15** Dam Farm House

TUESDAY 31
- **15** Dam Farm House

August

WEDNESDAY 1
- **8** Cascades

FRIDAY 3
- **15** Dam Farm House

SUNDAY 5
- **16** 62A Denby Lane
- **35** 9 Main Street

MONDAY 6
- **6** The Burrows Gardens
- **15** Dam Farm House

TUESDAY 7
- **15** Dam Farm House

FRIDAY 10
- **15** Dam Farm House

SUNDAY 12
- **38** 23 Mill Lane
- **49** 7 Warren Drive
- **53** Woodend Cottage

MONDAY 13
- **15** Dam Farm House

TUESDAY 14
- **15** Dam Farm House

WEDNESDAY 15
- **4** Bluebell Arboretum

FRIDAY 17
- **15** Dam Farm House

SUNDAY 19
- **4** Bluebell Arboretum
- **37** Meynell Langley Trials Garden

MONDAY 20
- **15** Dam Farm House

TUESDAY 21
- **15** Dam Farm House

FRIDAY 24
- **15** Dam Farm House

SATURDAY 25
- **42** 19 Portland Street

SUNDAY 26
- **42** 19 Portland Street
- **50** Wharfedale

MONDAY 27
- **6** The Burrows Gardens
- **48** Tissington Hall

TUESDAY 28
- **15** Dam Farm House

FRIDAY 31
- **15** Dam Farm House

September

SUNDAY 2
- **34** Littleover Lane Allotments

MONDAY 3
- **15** Dam Farm House

TUESDAY 4
- **15** Dam Farm House

FRIDAY 7
- **15** Dam Farm House

SUNDAY 9
- **37** Meynell Langley Trials Garden
- **52** Windward

MONDAY 10
- **6** The Burrows Gardens
- **15** Dam Farm House

TUESDAY 11
- **15** Dam Farm House

FRIDAY 14
- **15** Dam Farm House

MONDAY 17
- **15** Dam Farm House

TUESDAY 18
- **15** Dam Farm House

WEDNESDAY 19
- **4** Bluebell Arboretum

FRIDAY 21
- **15** Dam Farm House

SUNDAY 23
- **4** Bluebell Arboretum

MONDAY 24
- **15** Dam Farm House

TUESDAY 25
- **15** Dam Farm House

FRIDAY 28
- **15** Dam Farm House

October

MONDAY 1
15 Dam Farm House

TUESDAY 2
15 Dam Farm House

FRIDAY 5
15 Dam Farm House

MONDAY 8
15 Dam Farm House

TUESDAY 9
15 Dam Farm House

FRIDAY 12
15 Dam Farm House

MONDAY 15
15 Dam Farm House

TUESDAY 16
15 Dam Farm House

FRIDAY 19
15 Dam Farm House

MONDAY 22
15 Dam Farm House

TUESDAY 23
15 Dam Farm House

FRIDAY 26
15 Dam Farm House

SUNDAY 28
4 Bluebell Arboretum

MONDAY 29
15 Dam Farm House

TUESDAY 30
15 Dam Farm House

February 2008

SATURDAY 16
10 Cherry Tree Cottage

SUNDAY 17
10 Cherry Tree Cottage

Gardens open to the public

4 Bluebell Arboretum
6 The Burrows Gardens
7 Calke Abbey
8 Cascades
18 Eyam Hall
24 Hardwick Hall
30 Hopton Hall Gardens
32 Kedleston Hall
33 Lea Gardens
37 Meynell Langley Trials Garden
43 Postern House
45 Renishaw Hall
48 Tissington Hall

By appointment only

3 Birchfield

23 The Gardens at Dobholme Fishery
47 Spindlewood
51 26 Wheeldon Avenue

The Gardens

1 ASHFORD HALL
Ashford-in-the-Water DE45 1QA. Mr & Mrs Jasper Olivier, 01629 814798. *2m NW of Bakewell. On A6 turn onto A6020 towards Chesterfield, after 300yds turn R up drive immed after cricket field.* Home-made teas. Adm £3, chd free. Suns 24 June; 1 July (2-5). Visitors also welcome by appt for groups 12+, 15 Jun - 15 Jul only. Large landscape garden with beautiful views beside R Wye. Magnificent old yew hedges, river walk, rose garden and walled kitchen garden. Featured in 'The English Garden', 'Derbyshire Life and Countryside', 2006.

BANKCROFT FARM
See Staffordshire & part of West Midlands.

THE BEECHES
See Staffordshire & part of West Midlands.

2 334 BELPER ROAD
Stanley Common DE7 6FY. Gill & Colin Hancock, 0115 930 1061. *7m N of Derby. 3m W of Ilkeston. On A609, 3/4m from Rose & Crown Xrds (A608). Please park in field up farm drive or Working Men's Club rear car park if wet.* Home-made teas. Adm £2.50, chd free. Sat 9 (2-5), Sun 10 June (12-5). Visitors also welcome by appt, all yr (spring for snowdrops & hellebores). Predominantly shrubs and perennials in a 3/4-acre maturing garden with many seating areas. Large kitchen garden and greenhouses. Replanted pond area with bog plants, ferns and a renovated D.C.C workmans hut, now a summerhouse. 1/2 m walk around a 6yr old wood and 1/2-acre lake. Highly recommended home-made cakes.

3 BIRCHFIELD
Dukes Drive, Ashford in the Water DE45 1QQ, www.birchfieldgarden.com. *2m NW of Bakewell. On A6 to Buxton.* Adm £2, chd free (share to Thornhill Memorial Trust). Visitors welcome by appt Apr - Sept incl for

individuals, any size groups and coaches. Beautifully situated terraced garden of approx 3/4 acre. Designed for yr-round colour, it contains wide variety of shrubs and perennials, bulbs and water gardens. Dry garden with grasses and bamboos recently constructed. Arboretum with wild flowers has been developed on a further 11/4 acres.
🎏 ☕

Magnificent old yew hedges, river walk, rose garden and walled kitchen garden . . .

4 ♦ BLUEBELL ARBORETUM
Smisby LE65 2TA. Robert & Suzette Vernon, 01530 413700, sales@bluebellnursery.com. *1m N of Ashby-de-la-Zouch. Arboretum is clearly signed in Annwell Lane, 1/4m S, through village of Smisby which is off B5006, between Ticknall & Ashby-de-la-Zouch.* Adm £2.50, chd free. Open daily throughout yr (10.30-4.30) Closed Suns Nov-Feb, Easter Sun & 24 Dec to 4 Jan. For NGS: Wed 18, Sun 22 Apr; Wed 23, Sun 27 May; Wed 13, Sun 17 June; Wed 18, Sun 22 July; Wed 15, Sun 19 Aug; Wed 19, Sun 23 Sept; Sun 28 Oct (10.30-4.30).
5-acre arboretum planted in last 15yrs incl many specimens of rare trees and shrubs. Bring wellingtons in wet weather. Please be aware this is not a wood full of bluebells, despite the name. Adjacent specialist nursery.
♿ 🎏

5 BROOMFIELD HALL
Morley DE7 6DN. Derby College, 01332 836610, jean.beacock@derby-college.ac.uk. *4m N of Derby. 6m S of Heanor On A608.* Light refreshments & teas. Adm £2.50, chd free. Sun 13 May (12-4). Visitors also welcome by appt.

Landscaped garden of 25 acres. Shrubs, trees, rose collection, herbaceous borders; glasshouses; walled garden; garden tour guides. Themed gardens, plant centre. National Collection of old roses. Large Gold Medal Winners Derbyshire County Show & Bakewell Show, 2006.
  👌 🐾 ⊕ NCCPG ☕

Stunning butterfly bed and wild flower meadow . . .

6 ◆ THE BURROWS GARDENS
Burrows Lane, Brailsford, Ashbourne DE6 3BU. Mr B C Dalton, 01335 360745, www.burrowsgardens.com. *5m SE of Ashbourne; 5m NW of Derby. From Ashbourne: A52 towards Derby 5m to Brailsford. Turn R after Rose & Crown PH, then 1st L. Continue 1/2 m, garden on R. From Derby: leave Derby on A52 towards Ashbourne, after Kirk Langley stay on A52 for 1 1/2 m. Turn L signed Dalbury. 1/2 m R at grass triangle, garden in front of you. Follow AA signs.* Adm £3.50, chd free. 6, 20, 27 May; 3, 10, 17, 24 June; 1, 8, 22, 29 July; 5, 12, 26 Aug; 2, 9, 16, Sept. Other times by appt. Coaches welcome. For NGS: Mons 7, 28 May; 18 June; 2 July; 6, 27 Aug; 10 Sept (10.30-4.30).
Loved by visitors in my first year of opening. Parkland leads to a wide variety of classical themes running throughout the 5 acres of beautiful garden. Statuary, water features and exquisite ironwork enhance glorious plantings. Featured in 'English Garden' & 'Derbyshire Life' magazines 2006.
👌 🐾 ☕

7 ◆ CALKE ABBEY
Ticknall DE73 1LE. The National Trust, 01332 863822, www.nationaltrust.org.uk. *10m S of Derby. On A514 at Ticknall between Swadlincote & Melbourne.* Adm £5, chd £2.50. Please phone or visit website for other opening times. For NGS: Wed 18 July (11-5).

Extensive early C18 walled gardens. Flower garden with summer bedding and famous auricula theatre. Impressive collection of glasshouses and garden buildings. Vegetable garden growing heirloom varieties of fruit and vegetables, on sale to visitors. Auriculas from April to May (flowering dates may vary). Gravel paths and some steep slopes. Volunteer driven buggy available for use.
👌 🐾 ⊕ ☕

8 ◆ CASCADES
Clatterway, Bonsall DE4 2AH. Alan & Elizabeth Clements, 01629 822813, enquiries@cascadesgardens.com. *5m SW of Matlock. From Cromford A6 T-lights turn towards Wirksworth. Turn R along Via Gellia, signed Buxton & Bonsall. After 1m turn R up hill towards Bonsall village. Cascades on R at top of hill.* Adm £3, chd free. Weds & Suns 1 April to 30 Sept. Anyday by appt - groups welcome. For NGS: Weds 18 Apr; 23 May; 20 June; Sun 15 July; Wed 1 Aug (10-5).
Fascinating 4-acre garden in spectacularly natural surroundings with woodland, high cliffs, stream, ponds, a ruined corn mill and old lead mine. Secluded areas provide peaceful views of the extensive collection of plants, shrubs and trees. The nursery has a wide range of unusual herbaceous perennial plants.
👌 ⊕ 🛏 ☕

9 ◆ CASHEL
Kirk Ireton DE6 3JX. Anita & Jeremy Butt, 01335 370495. *2m S of Wirksworth. Turn off B5023 (Duffield-Wirksworth rd). Follow rd to Kirk Ireton, take sharp R turn at church corner. Follow lane for 200yds. Garden on RH-side. Parking on LH-side 80yds beyond house.* Adm £2.50, chd free. Sun 17 June (2-5). Visitors also welcome by appt.
3-acre garden situated on sloping site, featuring terraced ravine and several wood sculptures by local artists. Open views of surrounding countryside. Many interesting trees, shrubs and plants.
⊕ ☕

10 ◆ CHERRY TREE COTTAGE
Sutton Lane, Hilton DE65 5FB. Mrs A Hamblin, 01283 733778. *7m W of Derby. Turn off A516 opp the Old Talbot Inn in village centre.* Adm £2, chd free. Sat 17, Sun 18 Feb (Snowdrops); Sat 7, Sun 8 Apr; Suns

13 May; 10 June; Sat 16, Sun 17 Feb 2008 (2-5). Visitors also welcome by appt Feb, Apr, May & June only, for groups of 10+.
Plant lover's C18 cottage garden. Approx 1/3 acre with herbaceous borders, herb and scree garden, gravel garden with small water feature. Many unusual and interesting plants. Species aquilegias, geraniums, iris, campanula, pulmonaria etc. Gravel drive and shallow steps - help available.
👌 ⊕ ☕

11 10 CHESTNUT WAY
Repton DE65 6FQ. Robert & Pauline Little, 01283 702267, www.littlegarden.org.uk. *6m S of Derby. From A38, S of Derby, follow signs to Willington, then Repton. In Repton turn R at roundabout. Chestnut Way is 1/4 m up hill, on L.* Home-made teas. Adm £2.50, chd free. Sun 27, Mon 28 May; Sun 15 July (1-5). Visitors also welcome by appt, groups of 10+.
Meander through an acre of natural borders, mature trees, and intimate woodland to a stunning butterfly bed and wild flower meadow. Behind the natural look, a pair of passionate, practical, organic gardeners gently manage the vast range of plants, incl hundreds of shrubs, herbaceous perennials and clematis. Enjoy.
👌 ⊕ ☕

59 CHURCH LANE
See Nottinghamshire.

12 CLOUD COTTAGE
Simmondley SK13 6JN. Mr & Mrs R G Lomas, 01457 862033. *1m SW of Glossop. On High Lane between Simmondley & Charlesworth. From M67 take A57, turn R at Mottram (1st T-lights) through Broadbottom & Charlesworth. In Charlesworth up Town Lane by the side of Grey Mare. Cloud Cottage is 1/2 m on R. From Glossop, A57 towards Manchester, turn L at 2nd of two mini roundabouts up Simmondley Lane, Cloud Cottage is on L after passing Hare & Hounds.* Adm £3, chd free. Suns 13, 20, 27 May (2-5). Visitors also welcome by appt during May.
1 1/4-acre arboretum/rhododendron garden. Altitude 750ft on side of hill in Peak District National Park. Collections of conifers, most over 40yrs old. Species and hybrid rhododendron; wide variety of shrubs; Japanese-inspired garden with 3 ponds.
👌

⓭ CLOVERMEAD
Commonpiece Lane, Findern, Derby
DE65 6AF. David & Rosemary
Noblet, 01283 702237. *4m S of
Derby. From Findern village green, turn
R at church into Lower Green, R turn
into Commonpiece Lane, approx
500yds on R.* Home-made teas. **Adm
£2, chd free. Suns 8, 29 July (2-6).
Evening Opening £3, wine, Fri 29
June (6.30-9.30).** Visitors also
welcome by appt.
Cottage garden set in approx ³/₄ acre.
Garden rooms full of perennial flowers.
Honeysuckle, roses, jasmine and
sweet peas scent the air. Pergolas and
archways with clematis, fishponds and
bandstand with seating. Greenhouses,
vegetable plot and wildlife orchard.

⚔ ⊛ ☕

⓮ THE COTTAGE
25 Plant Lane, Old Sawley, Long
Eaton NG10 3BJ. Ernie & Averil
Carver, 0115 9728659. *2m SW of
Long Eaton. From Long Eaton green
take sign for town centre. Onto B6540
through to Old Sawley, take R at Nags
Head PH into Wiln Rd. 400yds take R
turn into Plant Lane at the Railway Inn.
Garden 200yds on R.* Light
refreshments & teas. **Adm £2, chd
free. Sun 29 July (2-6).** Visitors also
welcome by appt in July for groups
10+.
Cottage garden full of colour, steeped
in herbaceous borders. Annual plants
raised from the greenhouse. Number
of surprising features. Summerhouse in
a walled sheltered garden, providing a
charming environment. Winners
Erewash in Bloom. 1st Prize Best Front
Garden 2006. 1st Prize Best Rear
Garden Med-Lge 2006.

♿ ⊛ ☕

⓯ DAM FARM HOUSE
Yeldersley Lane, Ednaston
DE6 3BA. Mrs J M Player, 01335
360291. *5m SE of Ashbourne. On
A52, opp Ednaston village turn, gate
on R 500yds.* Refreshments by
request. **Adm £3.50, chd free. Mons,
Tues, Fris, 2 Apr to 30 Oct (9-4).** Not
open Bank Hol Mons 9 Apr; 7 May;
28 May; 27 Aug. Visitors also
welcome by appt, also coach
parties.
3 acres incl a stunning young
arboretum, beautifully situated.
Contains mixed borders, scree.
Unusual plants have been collected.
From spring to autumn it is full of
colour with interesting rare trees and
plants, many of which are propagated

for sale in the nursery. Partial
wheelchair access.

⚔ ⊛ ☕

⓰ 62A DENBY LANE
Loscoe DE75 7RX. Mrs J
Charlesworth. *12m NW of
Nottingham. Between Codnor &
Heanor, on A6007. Follow Denby sign.*
Light refreshments & teas. **Adm £1.50,
chd free. Sun 5 Aug (2-5).**
All-year round garden with hostas,
ferns, grasses, perennials, dahlias,
shrubs, conifers and vegetable plot.
Small pond with waterfall and stream.
Japanese features, pergola with
seating area and summer house. W.C.

⚔ ⊛ ☕

⓱ DOVE COTTAGE
Clifton, Ashbourne DE6 2JQ.
Stephen & Anne Liverman, 01335
343545,
astrantiamajor@hotmail.co.uk. *1¹/₂m
SW of Ashbourne. Enter Clifton village.
Turn R at Xrds by church. Travel
100yds turn L, Dove Cottage 1st
house on L. Always well signed on
open days.* **Adm £3, chd free (share
to British Heart Foundation,
Ashbourne). Suns 1 Apr; 27 May; 24
June; 29 July (1-5).** Visitors also
welcome by appt.
³/₄-acre garden by R Dove, extensively
replanted winter 2003 - 2004.
Emphasis on establishing collections of
hardy plants and shrubs incl
alchemillas, alliums, berberis,
geraniums, euphorbias, hostas, lilies,
variegated and silver foliage plants inc
astrantias. Plantsman's garden. Area
growing new heucheras and other
purple flowering plants and foliage.
Woodland area planted with daffodils
and shade loving plants.

⚔ ⊛

EDITH TERRACE GARDENS
See Cheshire & Wirral.

⓲ ◆ EYAM HALL
Eyam S32 5QW. Mr & Mrs R H V
Wright, 01433 631976,
www.eyamhall.com. *6m N of
Bakewell. Follow A623 through Stoney
Middleton, turn R to Eyam, follow signs
to Eyam Hall.* House and garden adm
£6.25, chd £4, concessions £5.75,
garden only adm £2, chd £1. **Wed,
Thur, Sun, Bank Hol Mon, 1 July - 30
Aug. Easter Sun & Mon, 8, 9 April;
Spring BH 27, 28 May (12-4).** For
NGS: **Suns 6 May; 10 June (1-5).**
C17 seat of the Wright family, the
traditional walled garden has four

distinct areas; the knot garden, the
potager, the bowling green and the
pleasure lawn with glorious rose walk
and herbaceous border. A formal
gravelled walk is edged with lavender
and espaliered fruit trees and planted
with exotic specimens. The restoration
is ongoing and the garden continues to
develop. Separate entrance for
wheelchair users.

♿ ☕

Honeysuckle, roses, jasmine and sweet peas scent the air . . .

⓳ FANSHAWE GATE HALL
Holmesfield S18 7WA. Mr & Mrs
John Ramsden, 0114 289 0391,
www.fgh.org.uk. *2m W of Dronfield.
Situated on the edge of the Peak
National Park. Follow B6054 towards
Owler Bar. 1st R turn after church
signed Fanshawe Gate Lane.* Light
refreshments. **Adm £2, chd free
(share to Oesophageal Patients
Assoc). Suns 17, 24 June; Suns 1, 8
July (11-5).** Visitors also welcome by
appt June & July only, groups of
10+, small coaches.
C13 seat of the Fanshawe family. Old-
fashioned cottage-style garden. Many
stone features, fine C16 dovecote.
Upper walled garden with herbaceous,
variegated and fern plantings, water
features, terracing and lawns. Lower
courtyard with knot garden and herb
border. Restored terraced orchard
representing a medieval tilt yard;
wildlife pond. Garden continues to
develop. Featured in 'The English
Garden', Look North Y.T.V, East
Midlands Today and GGG 2007.

♿ ⚔ ⊛ ☕

FELLEY PRIORY
See Nottinghamshire.

⓴ FIELD FARM
Kirk Ireton, Ashbourne DE6 3JU.
Graham & Irene Dougan, 01335
370958, www.fieldfarmgarden.info.
*2m S of Wirksworth. At top of Main St,
Kirk Ireton turn L signed Blackwall, on
sharp RH-bend find Field Lane
(unmade rd), Field Farm 400yds.
Parking in adjacent field.*

Home-made teas. **Adm £3, chd free. Suns 1, 15 July (2-5).** Visitors also welcome by appt 1 April to 30 Sept. Garden for plant lovers in beautiful setting with glorious views. 2 acres overflowing with rare trees and shrubs, mixed herbaceous beds, borders; arches; pergolas; water features; alpines; fuchsias and herbs. Shrub and climbing roses planted imaginatively throughout the garden. Gravelled courtyard with raised beds, troughs, planters, summer baskets and pots. Spring bulbs and new foliage, summer fragrance and autumn colour. An idyllic garden planted for all seasons. Garden Tour and talk with the owners plus wine & nibbles for evening 'by appt' visits. Coaches must disembark in village. Some gravel paths & undulating lawns.

21 FIR CROFT
Froggatt Road, Calver S32 3ZD. Dr S B Furness,
www.alpineplantcentre.co.uk. *4m N of Bakewell. At junction of B6001 with A625 (formerly B6054), adjacent to Power Garage.* **Adm by donation. Suns 13 May; 3, 17 June (2-5).** Massive scree with many rarities. Plantsman's garden; rockeries; water garden and nursery; extensive collection (over 3000 varieties) of alpines; conifers; over 800 sempervivums, 500 saxifrages and 350 primulas. Tufa and scree beds. Featured on BBC 'Gardeners' World ', 2006.

22 GAMESLEY FOLD COTTAGE
Glossop SK13 6JJ. Mrs G Carr, 01457 867856,
www.gamesleyfold.co.uk. *2m W of Glossop. Off A626 Glossop to Marple rd, nr Charlesworth. Turn down lane directly opp St Margaret's School. White cottage at bottom.* Home-made teas. **Adm £2, chd free. Suns 3, 10 June (1-5) Weds 6, 20 June (1-4).** Visitors also welcome by appt for groups of 10+ June & July. Coaches permitted.
Old-fashioned cottage garden. Spring garden with herbaceous borders, shrubs and rhododendrons, wild flowers and herbs in profusion to attract butterflies and wildlife. Adjacent cottage garden plant nursery with a good selection of herbs and wild flower plants for sale.

23 THE GARDENS AT DOBHOLME FISHERY
Troway, nr Coal Aston S43 2ES. Paul & Pauline Calvert, 01246 451337. *3m NE of Dronfield. Halfway along B6056, Dronfield to Eckington rd, 2¹/₂m from each. Coming from Dronfield turn L at Blackamoor Head Inn for Troway. Follow signs in village.* **Adm £3 incl tea/coffee. Visitors welcome by appt for groups of 15+ from May to July.**
Situated in beautiful conservation area of Moss Valley. Developed on sloping site of approx 3 acres around fishing ponds. Designed to encourage wildlife; planted in a wild, natural look. Heavy clay with many springs; stone quarried from the site is widely used to pave the pond sides. Sloping uneven terrain. Potager vegetable garden and herb garden.

GORENE
See Nottinghamshire.

GRAFTON COTTAGE
See Staffordshire & part of West Midlands.

24 ♦ HARDWICK HALL
Doe Lea, Chesterfield S44 5QJ. The National Trust, 01246 850430, www.nationaltrust.org.uk. *8m SE of Chesterfield. S of A617. Signed from J29 M1.* **House and garden adm £9, chd £4.50, garden only adm £4.50, chd £2.25. Apr to Oct Weds, Thurs, Sats, Suns, BH Mons & Good Fri. Gardens (11-5.30), Hall (12-4.30).** For NGS: **Sun 15 July (11-5.30).**
Grass walks between yew and hornbeam hedges; cedar trees; herb garden; herbaceous and rose borders. Finest example of Elizabethan house in the country. Gravel paths, some steps. Manual wheelchairs available to loan.

THE HAYLOFT
See Nottinghamshire.

25 HIGH ROOST
27 Storthmeadow Road, Simmondley, Glossop SK13 6UZ. Peter & Christina Harris, 01457 863888,
peter@pharris54.fsnet.co.uk. *³/₄m SW of Glossop. From M67 take A57, turn R at Mottram (1st T-lights), through Broadbottom and Charlesworth. In Charlesworth turn R up Town Lane by side of Grey Mare PH, continue up High Lane, past Hare & Hounds PH, Storthmeadow Rd is 2nd turn on L. From Glossop, A57 towards Manchester, L at 2nd mini roundabout, up Simmondley Lane, turn R into Storthmeadow Rd, nr top, no 27 last house on L. On road parking nearby, please take care not to block drives.* Light refreshments & teas. **Adm £2, chd free. Sun 24 June (1-5). Visitors also welcome by appt Jun - Aug for groups 10+, no coaches.**
Youngish suburban garden with interesting layout on terraced slopes with views over fields and hills. Winding paths, archways and steps explore different garden 'rooms' planted for yr-round interest. Much of planting designed to attract wildlife. Several small water features, pots, troughs, planters and innovative surprises tucked away in hidden corners will reward the curious visitor. Tiered alpine bed. Craft stalls. Winner 'Glossop in Bloom' (large gardens) 2006.

An idyllic garden planted for all seasons . . .

26 37 HIGH STREET
Repton DE65 6GD. David & Jan Roberts. *6m S of Derby. From A38, A50 junction S of Derby follow signs to Willington, then Repton. In Repton continue past island and shops. Garden is on LH-side.* Home-made teas. **Adm £2, chd free. Suns 22 Apr; 10 June (2-5.30).**
1-acre garden for all seasons divided by Repton Brook with formal and wildlife ponds. Mixed borders of shrubs and herbaceous perennials, rhododendrons and woodland. Grasses, bamboos and roses. Container planting for spring and summer colour and alpine troughs - something for everyone. Wheelchair access to top part of garden only.

27 NEW HIGHFIELD HOUSE
Wingfield Road, Oakerthorpe,
Alfreton DE55 7AP. Paul & Ruth
Peat & Janet Costall, 01773
521342. *Approx 1m from Alfreton
town centre on A615 Alfreton-
Matlock Rd. From Matlock: A615
to Alfreton. Turn R into Alfreton Golf
Club. From Derby: A38 to Alfreton.
A615 to Matlock. After houses on
L-hand side of Wingfield Rd, turn L
into Alfreton Golf Club.* Home-
made & cream teas. **Adm £2.50,
chd free. Suns 3, 24 June (1-5).
Visitors also welcome by appt
June only. Groups 10+. Garden
not accessible by coach.**
Delightful family garden of ³/₄ of an
acre, laid out by current owners
from an abandoned vegetable
garden and field. Individual areas
include a shady garden, small area
of woodland, tree house, laburnum
arch, orchard, lawns and
herbaceous borders. Pleasant level
walk to Derbyshire Wildlife Trust
Nature reserve, where there is a
damned brook, pond and
boardwalk. Beautiful spotted
orchids in natural environment.
Garden on different levels; steps,
board walk and some gravel areas.
& ✕ ✿ ☕

Beautiful snowdrops set in 5 acres of natural woodland . . .

28 11 HIGHGROVE DRIVE
Chellaston, Derby DE73 5XA. Ms
Sarah Bacon. *2m SE of city centre.
Leave Derby ring rd at Allenton (steel
footbridge) on rd to Melbourne via
Chellaston. 1m on R (A514). Leave
A50 at J3, head to Derby via
Chellaston. 1¹/₂m on L (A514). Rd is
on hill top into 'new estate' on SE side
Derby. Limited street parking in cul-de-
sac. Disabled parking on drive.* **Adm
£2, chd free. Sat 21 (2-6), Sun 22
July (11-5).**
Small suburban garden. Lawn, paved
areas, pond with waterfall, water

feature, Japanese corner,
Mediterranean yard, small patio with
topiary. Grape, kiwi, greenhouse and
garden shed in enclosed area. Pots,
hanging baskets, automatic watering,
lights and pond fountain. A big garden
in a small space. Front garden highly
recommended 'Derby in Bloom' 2006.
Featured on front page 'Evening
Telegraph' supplement.
& ✕ ☕

29 HILLSIDE
286 Handley Road, New Whittington
S43 2ET. E J Lee, 01246 454960. *3m
N of Chesterfield. From A6135, take
B6052 through Eckington & Marsh
Lane 3m. Turn L at Xrds signed
Whittington, then 1m. From Coal Aston
(Sheffield), take B6056 towards
Chesterfield to give way sign, then 1m.
From Chesterfield, take B6052.* **Adm
£2, chd free. Sun 3 June (2-5).
Visitors also welcome by appt all yr.**
¹/₃-acre sloping site. Herbaceous
borders, rock garden, alpines, streams,
pools, bog gardens, alpine house.
Acers, bamboos, collection of approx
150 varieties of ferns, eucalypts,
euphorbias, grasses, conifers,
Himalayan bed. 1500 plants
permanently labelled. Year-round
interest. Mini Plant Fair with stands
from Golden Cottage Plants, Friends of
the Botanical Gardens, Sheffield &
South Pennine Hardy Plant Society.
✿ ☕

30 ◆ HOPTON HALL GARDENS
Hopton Village DE4 4DF. Mr & Mrs
W Brogden, 01629 540878. *6m NE of
Ashbourne. From B5035 (Ashbourne
to Matlock rd) turn into villages of
Carsington & Hopton. Continue
through village, Hall & gardens clearly
signed. Follow signs to car park.* **Adm
£3.50, chd free. Sat 3 Feb to Sun 11
Mar incl. (10.30-4).**
Beautiful snowdrops set in 5 acres of
natural woodland plus 4 acres of
formal gardens incl an historic walled
garden, rose walk and formal lawns. 8
acres of informal garden incl 2 ponds,
small wildlife lake and 2 small
arboretums. Mainly firm paths.
✕ ✿ ☕

31 HORSLEYGATE HALL
Horsleygate Lane, Holmesfield S18
7WD. Robert & Margaret Ford, 0114
289 0333. *6m NE of Chesterfield.
Follow B6051 from Owler Bar (A621)
towards Chesterfield; after 1m take
1st L onto Horsleygate Lane. Park
in field on R.* Home-made teas.

**Adm £3, chd free. Sat 19, Sun 20
May (1-5). Visitors also welcome by
appt.**
2-acre plantsman's garden. Sloping
site incl woodland garden; hot sun
terrace; rockeries; pools; fern area;
jungle garden; mixed borders and
ornamental kitchen garden. An overall
theme of informality with walls,
terraces, paths and quirky statuary,
gazebo and breeze house thatched in
heather.
✿ ☕

32 ◆ KEDLESTON HALL
Kedleston DE22 5JH. The National
Trust, 01332 844053,
bhensher@nationaltrust.org.uk. *5m
NW of Derby. Signed from junction of
A38-A52.* **House and garden adm
£8, chd £4, family £20, garden only
adm £3.60, chd £1.80, family £9.** For
NGS: **Wed 30 May (10-6).**
12 acres. A broad open lawn, bounded
by a ha-ha, marks the C18 informal
garden. Formal layout to the W was
introduced early this century when
summerhouse and orangery, both
designed by George Richardson in late
C18, were moved to their present
position. Gardens at their best during
May and June when the azaleas and
rhododendrons are one mass of
colour. The Long Walk, a woodland
walk of some 3m, is bright with spring
flowers.
& ✕

33 ◆ LEA GARDENS
Lea, Nr Matlock DE4 5GH. Mr & Mrs
J Tye, 01629 534380,
www.leagarden.co.uk. *5m SE of
Matlock. Lea. Off A6. Also off A615.*
**Adm £3.50, chd 50p. Daily 20 Mar to
30 June (10-5).**
Rare collection of rhododendrons,
azaleas, kalmias, alpines and conifers
in delightful woodland setting. Gardens
are sited on remains of medieval quarry
and cover about 4 acres. Specialised
plant nursery of rhododendrons and
azaleas on site. Teashop offering light
lunches and home-made cakes open
daily. Music Day Sun 10 June (12-5).
Persons in wheelchairs admitted free.
Some slopes & gravel paths.
& ✿ ☕

**34 LITTLEOVER LANE
ALLOTMENTS**
19 Littleover Lane, Derby DE23 6JH.
Littleover Lane Allotments Assoc,
01332 770096,
davidkenyon@tinyworld.co.uk. *3m
SW of Derby. Off Derby ring rd A5111*

into Stenson Rd. R into Littleover Lane.
Garden on L. On street parking opp
Foremark Ave. Light refreshments &
teas. **Adm £3, chd free, concessions
£2. Suns 3 June; 2 Sept (11-5).
Visitors also welcome by appt, April
to Oct.**
Allotment site with plots cultivated in a
variety of styles. A Schools' Centre incl
greenhouses and walled garden and
museum collection of heritage
gardening equipment. A range of
heritage vegetable varieties grown.
Wildlife area under development. Plant
sale June, Produce sale Sept. Best site
'Derby in Bloom' 2006. Paths stoned,
some slopes. W.C with disabled
access.

♿ ⨀ ☕

Allotment site with plots cultivated in a variety of styles . . .

35 9 MAIN STREET
Horsley Woodhouse DE7 6AU.
Alison Napier, 01332 881629. *3m SW
of Heanor. 6m N of Derby. Turn off
A608 Derby to Heanor rd at Smalley,
towards Belper, (A609). Garden on
A609, 1m from Smalley turning.*
Home-made teas. **Adm £2, chd free.
Suns 10 June; 5 Aug (2-5). Visitors
also welcome by appt.**
1/3-acre hilltop garden overlooking
lovely farmland view. Terracing,
borders, lawns and pergola create
space for an informal layout with
planting for colour effect. Features incl
large wildlife pond with water lilies, bog
garden and small formal pool.
Emphasis on carefully selected
herbaceous perennials mixed with
shrubs and old-fashioned roses.
Wheelchair-adapted WC.

♿ ⨀ ☕

36 2 MANVERS STREET
Ripley DE5 3EQ. Mrs D Wood & Mr
D Hawkins, 01773 743962. *Ripley
Town centre to Derby rd turn L opp
Leisure Centre onto Heath Rd. 1st turn
R onto Meadow Rd, 1st L onto
Manvers St.* Home-made teas. **Adm
£2, chd free. Sun 15 July (2-6).
Visitors also welcome by appt, July
only.**
S-facing secluded colourful garden
with patio, lawn, mixed borders, incl

perennials, annuals and shrubs. Fish
pond, water features; pergola
supporting Virginia creeper and
clematis. Arbour with seating and
several summer hanging baskets and
planters.

✓ ⨀ ☕

**37 NEW ♦ MEYNELL
LANGLEY TRIALS GARDEN**
Lodge Lane (off Flagshaw Lane),
Derby DE6 4NT. Robert & Karen
Walker, 01332 824358,
enquiries@meynell-langley-
gardens.co.uk. *4m W of Derby, nr
Kedleston Hall. Head W out of
Derby on A52. At Kirk Langley turn
R onto Flagshaw Lane (signed to
Kedleston Hall) then R onto Lodge
Lane. Follw Meynell Langley Gdns
sign for 1¹/₂m.* **Adm £2, chd free.
Open daily Easter Sun to 7 Oct.
For NGS: Suns 8 Apr; 13 May;
10 June; 8 July; 19 Aug; 9 Sept
(10-4).**
Formal ³/₄-acre Victorian-style
garden established 14 yrs,
displaying and trialling new and
existing varieties of bedding plants,
herbaceous perennials and
vegetable plants grown at the
adjacent nursery. Over 100
hanging baskets and floral
displays. 50 varieties of apple, pear
and other fruit. Summer fruit tree
pruning demonstrations 19 Aug.
Adm includes comprehensive plant
listings & fruit varieties.

♿ ✓ ⨀

38 23 MILL LANE
Codnor DE5 9QF. Mrs S Jackson,
01773 745707. *12m NW of
Nottingham. 10m N of Derby. Mill Lane
situated opp Codnor Market Place
(Clock Tower) on A610. 2 car parks
nearby.* Tea & cream cakes. **Adm
£1.50, chd free. Sun 12 Aug (1-6).
Visitors also welcome by appt.**
Lawn, herbaceous borders, pond,
waterfall; clematis and Mediterranean
garden. Raffle & plant stall. 1st Prize
Codnor Parish Council 'Best Kept
Garden' Comp 2006.

✓ ⨀ ☕

39 MONKSWAY
Summer Cross, Tideswell, nr Buxton
SK17 8HU. Mr & Mrs R Porter,
01298 871687,
www.monkswaygarden.co.uk. *9m
NE of Buxton. On the B6049. Turn up
Parke Rd, opp Nat West Bank, off
Queen St. Take L turn at top & then 1st*

R onto Summer Cross. Monksway is
4th semi-detached house on L.
Limited parking. **Adm £2, chd free.
Suns 27 May; 3, 10, 17, 24 June; 1
July (11-4). Visitors also welcome by
appt for groups of 10+.**
Gently sloping garden 1000ft above
sea level. Gravel/paved paths and
archways meander through well-
stocked beds and borders of
perennials, shrubs and climbers.
Garden planted for all-yr interest. An
aviary and water features complete the
scene.

**THE OLD RECTORY, CLIFTON
CAMPVILLE**
See Staffordshire & part of West
Midlands.

ONE HOUSE NURSERY
See Cheshire & Wirral.

40 OTTERBROOK
Alders Lane, Chinley, High Peak
SK23 6DP. Mary & Dennis Sharp,
01663 750335. *3m W of Whaley
Bridge. Otterbrook is reached by
300yd walk up Alders Lane on
outskirts of village off Buxton Rd
(B6062) between Chinley & Chapel-en-
le-Frith. Parking is very limited at house
so please park on Buxton Rd.* Home-
made teas. **Adm £2.50, chd free. Sun
24 June (2-5). Visitors also welcome
by appt.**
Wander in this 1-acre garden between
colour-themed beds and borders,
along paths to focal points and views
of the surrounding hills. Trees, shrubs
and plants, many moisture-loving,
provide contrasting form and texture
and complement the ponds and bog
garden. Pergolas and structures give
cohesion. A small potager is included.

✓ ⨀ ☕

20 THE PADDOCKS
See Nottinghamshire.

41 PARK HALL
Walton Back Lane, Walton,
Chesterfield S42 7LT. Kim &
Margaret Staniforth, 01246 567412,
kim.staniforth@virgin.net. *2m SW of
Chesterfield. From Chesterfield take
A632 for Matlock. After start of 40mph
section take 1st R into Acorn Ridge
and then L into Walton Back Lane.
300yds on R, at end of high stone wall.
Park on field side of Walton Back Lane
only.* Home-made teas. **Adm £3, chd
50p. Suns 10 June; 1 July (2-5.30).
Visitors also welcome by appt for
parties of 10+.**
2-acre plantsman's garden in a

beautiful setting surrounding C17 house, not open. Four main 'rooms' - terraced garden, park area with forest trees, croquet lawn and new millennium garden now fully mature. Within these are a woodland walk, fernery, yew hedges and topiary, water features, pergolas, arbours, herbaceous borders, rhododendrons, camellias, azaleas, hydrangeas, 150 roses and a circular pleached hedge. New feature for 2007, a small auricula theatre. Children's Garden Trail & Prize.

⑫ 19 PORTLAND STREET
Etwall DE65 6JF. **Paul & Fran Harvey, 01283 734360.** *6m W of Derby. In centre of Etwall Village, at Spread Eagle PH turn into Willington Rd then immed R into Portland St (behind PH car park).* **Home-made teas. Adm £2.50, chd free. Sat 25, Sun 26 Aug (11-5). Visitors also welcome by appt.**
Our tranquil garden is packed with plants for yr-round interest. This ¹/₃ acre has been developed since 1992 with significant changes every year. Many rare and unusual shrubs and perennials, fabulous colour and tremendous scent; pond, small stream; oriental garden; pergola; exhibition dahlias; collections incl picea, agapanthus and crocosmia, but no lawn. New planting in front garden for 2007.

ᕫ ⚬ ☕

⑬ ♦ POSTERN HOUSE
Turnditch DE56 2LX. **Liz & Nick Ruby, 01773 550732, www.postern.co.uk.** *3m W of Belper. Off A517 Belper to Ashbourne rd, entering Turnditch from Belper direction 50yds past bridge over river; turn L into unmarked lane (just before 30mph sign). 3rd house on R.* **Adm £2.50, chd free. Suns 1 Jul, 5 Aug (2-5.30). Open to groups of 10+ by appt May to Aug. For NGS: Suns 10 June; 15 July (2-5.30).**
¹/₃-acre plant lovers' garden set in beautiful rolling countryside. Large borders full of spring and summer flowering herbaceous plants and shrubs incl an ever increasing collection of hostas and hardy geraniums. Climbers ramble over walls, trees and a large gazebo. Pots, troughs and baskets add colourful seasonal interest. Large fruit and vegetable areas make this a garden for everyone. Uneven paths, wheelchair access on lawns.

ᕫ ⚬ ☕

⑭ NEW QUARRYSIDE
1 King Charles Court, Glossop SK13 8NJ. **Sue & Ron Astles, 01457 857015.** *1m S of Glossop town centre. From Glossop centre take A624 towards Hayfield & Chapel-en-le-Frith. About ³/₄ m along turn L into Whitfield Ave. At top turn R into Hague St & 1st L into King Charles Court. Light refreshments & teas.* **Adm £2, chd free (share to Beechwood Cancer Care Centre, Stockport). Suns 27 May; 1 July (2-5). Visitors also welcome by appt June to July, groups 10 & under.**
Small peaceful garden in quarry setting with exposed rock strata and interesting nooks and crannies on two terraces, with an emphasis on texture and colour. All yr-round natural planting with two water features to attract wildlife. Display of contemporary garden ceramics by Jim Robinson of Holmfirth incl his unusual slab-built vases and plate forms for garden settings.

✂ ⚬ ☕

⑮ ♦ RENISHAW HALL
Renishaw, nr Sheffield S21 3WB. **Sir Reresby & Lady Sitwell, 01246 432310, www.sitwell.co.uk.** *4m W of Sheffield. From J30 M1 take A6135 towards Sheffield. Renishaw Hall is 3m from motorway.* **Adm £5, chd under 10 free, concessions £4.20. Thurs to Suns, Bank Hol Mons 29 Mar to 30 Sept (10.30-4.30).**
Home of Sir Reresby and Lady Sitwell. Romantic, formal 2 Italianate gardens divided into rooms by yew hedges. Bluebell woods, magnolias and rhododendrons in spring woodland gardens. Over a thousand roses in June with peonies and clematis. Deep herbaceous borders with collections of unusual plants. National Collection of Yuccas and sculpture walk. Arts & Crafts, Food & Farming events, Plant Fairs, Open Air Theatre, Galleries & Museums. Featured on BBC 'Gardeners' World', 'Curious House Guest' and BBC Radio Sheffield, 2006.

ᕫ ⚬ NCCPG ☕

⑯ SHATTON HALL FARM
Bamford S33 0BG. **Mr & Mrs J Kellie, 01433 620635, www.peakfarmholidays.co.uk.** *3m W of Hathersage. Take A6187 from Hathersage, turn L to Shatton, after 2m (opp High Peak Garden Centre). After ¹/₂ m turn R through ford, drive*

¹/₂ m & house is on L over cattle grids. **Home-made teas. Adm £3, chd free. Mon 28 May; Sun 29 July (1.30-5). Visitors also welcome by appt.**
Original walled garden of C16. Farmhouse now spills out to water gardens and sheltered slopes, planted informally and merging into the picturesque landscape. Among the great variety of unusual plants and shrubs, sculpture and willow features add interest to this maturing and still expanding garden. An increasing variety of live willow structures have been planted. Labelled walks in woodland and streamside.

⚬ ⊨ ☕

⑰ SPINDLEWOOD
Strathallan Close, Darley Dale DE4 2HJ. **Mr & Mrs J G Ball, 01629 735701.** *3m N of Matlock. After The Grouse Inn, turn R up Whitworth Rd. Park on L by railings, on Whitworth Rd. Elderly/disabled may continue to private parking areas down the Close and within entrance to garden. Teas/lunches by arrangement at local hall.* **Adm £3, chd free (share to Darley Dale Methodist Church). Visitors welcome by appt June & July, afternoons preferred. Coaches accommodated in Whitworth Road.**
A central stream cascades down a gentle slope and divides the ³/₄-acre lawn. Pond is bridged alongside a bog garden. Herbaceous and shrubby beds extend around the whole area. Other sections incl herbs, wild area and semi-tropical plants in pots on large patio.

ᕫ ⚬ ☕

STONEHILL QUARRY GARDEN
See Staffordshire & part of West Midlands

TEVERSAL MANOR GARDENS
See Nottinghamshire.

⑱ ♦ TISSINGTON HALL
nr Ashbourne DE6 1RA. **Sir Richard & Lady FitzHerbert.** *4m N of Ashbourne. E of A515 on Ashbourne to Buxton rd.* **House and garden adm £6.50, chd £3.50, concessions £5, garden only adm £3, chd £1. 9-13 Apr, 28 May, 1 Jun, Tues-Fri 24 Jul - 24 Aug. For NGS: Mon 27 Aug (1.30-4).**
Large garden; roses, herbaceous borders.

✂ ⚬ ☕

49 7 WARREN DRIVE
Linton DE12 6QP. Keith & Phyl
Hutchinson, 01283 761088, keith-
phyl@hutch7warren.freeserve.co.uk.
*6m SE of Burton-on-Trent. Take A444
out of Burton for 5m. After Toons
Warehouse on R, take 3rd exit at
roundabout. Take 1st R & continue for
1m uphill past The Square & Compass
PH on R. After 200yds turn L into
Warren Drive.* Home-made teas. **Adm
£2, chd free. Sun 12 Aug (2-5.30).
Visitors also welcome by appt.**
This cottage-style garden on 2 levels,
overlooking countryside is a plantperson's delight. Many unusual plants
in an eclectic mix which fill colour-
themed borders, pergolas, gazebo,
stream, pond and pots galore. Quirky
shapes incl a 'Heligan' head, vegetables
in raised beds and a new front garden
planned for drought-tolerance add
further interest. Winding paths and
various seating areas present new and
unexpected views. Photograhed for
'Garden News' Aug 2006.
🌿 ❀ ☕

50 WHARFEDALE
34 Broadway, Duffield, Belper
DE56 4BU. Roger & Sue Roberts,
01332 841905. *4m N of Derby. Turn
onto B5023 Wirksworth rd (Broadway)
off A6 midway between Belper &
Derby.* Home-made teas. **Adm £2.50,
chd free. Suns 24 June; 22 July; 26
Aug (11-5). Visitors also welcome by
appt, for groups of 15+ from 16 Apr
to 12 Oct, evenings and weekends
only.**
Plant enthusiasts' garden with over
800 varieties of choice and unusual
shrubs, trees, perennials and bulbs.
Themed borders incl Mediterranean,
late summer tropical and single colour
schemes. Cottage garden to front.
12yrs old with Italianate walled scented
garden and woodland pond with raised
walkway. Eclectic and unusual garden
providing lots of ideas. New Japanese
tea garden with stream and pavilion.
& 🌿 ❀ ☕

51 26 WHEELDON AVENUE
Derby DE22 1HN. Ian Griffiths,
01332 342204. *1m N of Derby. 1m
from city centre & approached directly
off the Kedleston Rd or from A6
Duffield Rd via West Bank Ave.* Limited
on-street parking. **Visitors welcome by
appt, May, June & July, groups of 6+.**
Tiny Victorian walled garden near to
city centre. Lawn and herbaceous
borders with old roses, lupins,
delphiniums and foxgloves. Small
terrace with topiary and herb garden.
Featured in 'Period Living' 2006, also
featured on BBC TV, becoming known
as one of the smallest gardens open to
the public.
& ❀

Many unusual plants in an eclectic mix . . .

52 WINDWARD
62 Summer Lane, Wirksworth
DE4 4EB. Audrey & Andrew Winkler,
01629 822681,
audrey.winkler@w3z.co.uk. *5m S of
Matlock. 1/2m from Wirksworth town
centre off B5023 Wirksworth to
Duffield rd. After approx 300yds, turn R
at mini island onto Summer Lane.*
Windward is approx 500yds on R,
rockery at roadside. Home-made teas.
**Adm £2.50, chd free (share to
Ruddington Framework Knitters
Museum). Sat 19 May (2-5); Suns 22
Apr; 20 May; 9 Sept (11-5). Visitors
also welcome by appt Apr to Sept,
groups of 15+.**
Lush, green garden of about 1 acre,
wildlife-friendly and almost organic.
Romantic ambiance with mature trees
and shrubs and interesting nooks and
crannies. Ponds, hostas, gravel
garden, rockery, grasses, roses,
rhododendrons, Leylandii crinkle-
crankle hedge, woodland paths and

bulbs, mixed borders and small
meadow area. A garden for relaxation
with several seating areas. Artists are
invited to paint in the garden and
demonstrate their work.
🌿 ☕

53 WOODEND COTTAGE
134 Main Street, Repton DE65 6FB.
Wendy & Stephen Longden, 01283
703259. *6m S of Derby. From A38, S
of Derby, follow signs to Willington,
then Repton. In Repton, straight on at
roundabout through village. Woodend
Cottage is 1m on R before Woodend
Children's Nursery.* Home-made teas.
**Adm £2, chd free. Suns 27 May; 15
July; 12 Aug (1-5). Visitors also
welcome by appt.**
Plant lover's garden with glorious views
on sloping site. 2½ acres developed
organically over last 5yrs for yr-round
interest. On lower levels, hardy
perennials, grasses, shrubs and shade-
loving plants are arranged informally
and connected via lawns, thyme bed,
pond and pergolas. Grassed meadows
beyond lead naturally into wildlife area,
mixed woodland and fruit, vegetable
and herb potager. Esp colourful in July
& Aug. Some gravel paths, steps and
steep slopes.
🌿 ❀ ☕

54 35 WYVER LANE
Belper DE56 2UB. Jim & Brenda
Stannering, 01773 824280. *8m N of
Derby. Take A6 from Derby through
Belper to T-lights at triangle. Turn L for
A517 to Ashbourne, over river bridge,
1st R onto Wyver Lane. Parking in
River Gardens, entrance on A6.* Home-
made teas. **Adm £1.50, chd free. Sun
6, Mon 7 May; Sun 10 June (1-5).
Visitors also welcome by appt, until
end of July.**
Cottage garden of approx 500sq yds
on side of R Derwent opp Belper River
Gardens. Full of hardy perennial plants
with pergola, troughs, greenhouse,
small pond.
❀ ☕

Derbyshire Volunteer Team

County Organiser
Irene Dougan, Field Farm, Field Lane, Kirk Ireton, Ashbourne DE6 3JU, 01335 370958, dougan@lineone.net

County Treasurer; Leaflet Coordinator
Graham Dougan, Field Farm, Field Lane, Kirk Ireton, Ashbourne DE6 3JU, 01335 370958, dougan@lineone.net

Publicity
Christine Morris, 9 Langdale Avenue, Ravenshead NG15 9EA, 01623 793827, christine@ravenshead.demon.co.uk

Assistant County Organisers
Gill and Colin Hancock, 334 Belper Road, Stanley Common, nr Ilkeston DE7 6FY, 01159 301061
Kate & Peter Spencer, The Riddings Farm, Kirk Ireton, Ashbourne DE6 3LB, 01335 370331

Cottage-style front garden.
Rear garden with patios,
rockery and pond, decking and
pergola. Unusual gazebo
inspired by half-remembered
Indonesian holiday. Lush
planting with bananas, ferns,
bamboos, gunnera.
Assortment of pots.
Penguin …

24 Chestnut Road, London

DEVON

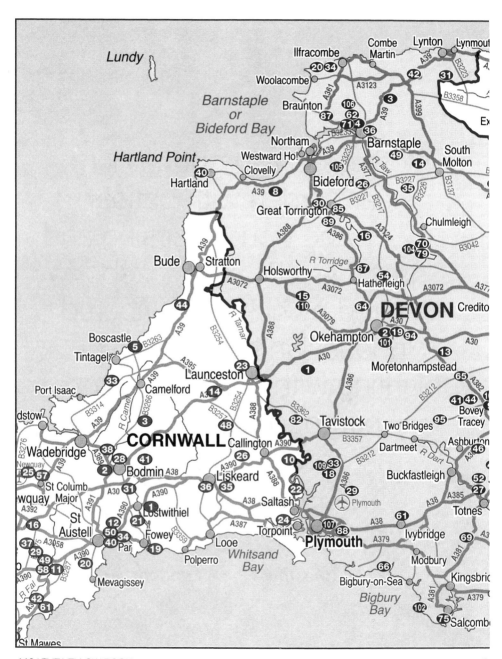

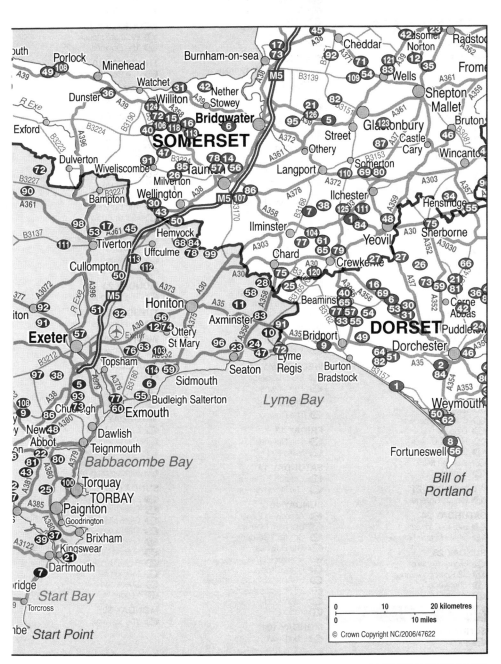

Opening Dates

January

EVERY SUNDAY
- **91** Sherwood

February

SUNDAY 4
- **57** Little Cumbre
- **91** Sherwood

SUNDAY 11
- **57** Little Cumbre
- **91** Sherwood

SUNDAY 18
- **57** Little Cumbre
- **91** Sherwood

SUNDAY 25
- **57** Little Cumbre
- **91** Sherwood

March

SATURDAY 3
- **68** Newton Farm

SUNDAY 4
- **29** Dippers
- **68** Newton Farm
- **91** Sherwood

WEDNESDAY 7
- **6** Bicton College

SATURDAY 10
- **68** Newton Farm

SUNDAY 11
- **29** Dippers
- **68** Newton Farm
- **77** 38 Phillipps Avenue
- **91** Sherwood
- **114** Yonder Hill

SUNDAY 18
- **23** Colyford Gardens
- **29** Dippers
- **44** Higher Knowle
- **91** Sherwood
- **97** Sowton Mill
- **114** Yonder Hill

WEDNESDAY 21
- **6** Bicton College

SATURDAY 24
- **6** Bicton College
- **15** Chapel Farm House

SUNDAY 25
- **44** Higher Knowle
- **77** 38 Phillipps Avenue
- **91** Sherwood
- **114** Yonder Hill

April

SUNDAY 1
- **1** Alder

- **41** Heathercombe
- **44** Higher Knowle
- **77** 38 Phillipps Avenue
- **86** Rock House Garden
- **91** Sherwood
- **112** Wood Barton
- **114** Yonder Hill

THURSDAY 5
- **8** Bocombe Mill Cottage

FRIDAY 6
- **30** The Downes
- **114** Yonder Hill

SATURDAY 7
- **30** The Downes

SUNDAY 8
- **30** The Downes
- **44** Higher Knowle
- **45** Holbrook Garden
- **50** Kia-Ora Farm & Gardens
- **60** Littleham House Cottage
- **77** 38 Phillipps Avenue
- **91** Sherwood
- **112** Wood Barton
- **114** Yonder Hill

MONDAY 9
- **30** The Downes
- **44** Higher Knowle
- **45** Holbrook Garden
- **50** Kia-Ora Farm & Gardens
- **51** Killerton Garden
- **114** Yonder Hill

TUESDAY 10
- **30** The Downes

WEDNESDAY 11
- **6** Bicton College
- **30** The Downes

THURSDAY 12
- **30** The Downes

FRIDAY 13
- **30** The Downes
- **62** Marwood Hill

SATURDAY 14
- **21** Coleton Fishacre
- **30** The Downes

SUNDAY 15
- **2** Andrew's Corner
- **5** Bickham House
- **23** Colyford Gardens
- **30** The Downes
- **36** Gorwell House
- **44** Higher Knowle
- **60** Littleham House Cottage
- **77** 38 Phillipps Avenue
- **91** Sherwood
- **114** Yonder Hill

MONDAY 16
- **30** The Downes

TUESDAY 17
- **5** Bickham House
- **30** The Downes
- **74** Otter Nurseries

WEDNESDAY 18
- **5** Bickham House
- **30** The Downes

THURSDAY 19
- **30** The Downes

FRIDAY 20
- **30** The Downes

SATURDAY 21
- **15** Chapel Farm House
- **30** The Downes
- **92** Shobrooke Park Gardens

SUNDAY 22
- **14** Castle Hill
- **29** Dippers
- **30** The Downes
- **44** Higher Knowle
- **50** Kia-Ora Farm & Gardens
- **86** Rock House Garden
- **87** St Merryn
- **91** Sherwood
- **114** Yonder Hill

MONDAY 23
- **30** The Downes

TUESDAY 24
- **30** The Downes

WEDNESDAY 25
- **30** The Downes

THURSDAY 26
- **30** The Downes

FRIDAY 27
- **30** The Downes

SATURDAY 28
- **19** Cleave House
- **30** The Downes
- **37** Greenway Garden
- **38** Haldon Grange
- **63** Metcombe Brake

SUNDAY 29
- **6** Bicton College
- **17** Chevithorne Barton
- **19** Cleave House
- **30** The Downes
- **37** Greenway Garden
- **38** Haldon Grange
- **44** Higher Knowle
- **63** Metcombe Brake
- **91** Sherwood
- **114** Yonder Hill

MONDAY 30
- **30** The Downes

May

TUESDAY 1
- 30 The Downes
- 74 Otter Nurseries

WEDNESDAY 2
- 6 Bicton College
- 30 The Downes
- 42 Heddon Hall
- 81 Pleasant View

THURSDAY 3
- 8 Bocombe Mill Cottage
- 30 The Downes

FRIDAY 4
- 30 The Downes
- 88 Saltram House

SATURDAY 5
- 28 Dicot
- 30 The Downes
- 38 Haldon Grange
- 66 Mothecombe House
- 78 Pikes Cottage
- 92 Shobrooke Park Gardens

SUNDAY 6
- 2 Andrew's Corner
- 28 Dicot
- 30 The Downes
- 35 Glebe Cottage
- 38 Haldon Grange
- 44 Higher Knowle
- 45 Holbrook Garden
- 50 Kia-Ora Farm & Gardens
- 53 Knightshayes Court Garden
- 63 Metcombe Brake
- 66 Mothecombe House
- 69 North Boreston Farm
- 75 Overbeck's
- 78 Pikes Cottage
- 91 Sherwood
- 101 Taikoo
- 106 Westcott Barton
- 73 Whitstone Farm
- 114 Yonder Hill

MONDAY 7
- 30 The Downes
- 38 Haldon Grange
- 44 Higher Knowle
- 45 Holbrook Garden
- 50 Kia-Ora Farm & Gardens
- 63 Metcombe Brake
- 69 North Boreston Farm
- 106 Westcott Barton
- 114 Yonder Hill

TUESDAY 8
- 30 The Downes

WEDNESDAY 9
- 30 The Downes
- 38 Haldon Grange
- 81 Pleasant View

THURSDAY 10
- 30 The Downes
- 109 Wildside

FRIDAY 11
- 30 The Downes

SATURDAY 12
- 13 Castle Drogo
- 30 The Downes
- 104 The Water Garden
- 111 Withleigh Farm
- 113 Woody Park

SUNDAY 13
- 5 Bickham House
- 17 Chevithorne Barton
- 21 Coleton Fishacre
- 30 The Downes
- 44 Higher Knowle
- 77 38 Phillipps Avenue
- 91 Sherwood
- 95 Southcombe Gardens
- 98 Spillifords Wildlife Garden
- 104 The Water Garden
- 111 Withleigh Farm
- 113 Woody Park
- 114 Yonder Hill

MONDAY 14
- 30 The Downes

TUESDAY 15
- 5 Bickham House
- 30 The Downes
- 74 Otter Nurseries

WEDNESDAY 16
- 5 Bickham House
- 18 The Cider House
- 30 The Downes
- 38 Haldon Grange
- 51 Killerton Garden
- 81 Pleasant View

THURSDAY 17
- 2 Andrew's Corner (Evening)
- 30 The Downes

FRIDAY 18
- 30 The Downes
- 72 The Old Vicarage

SATURDAY 19
- 15 Chapel Farm House
- 30 The Downes
- 70 The Old Glebe
- 72 The Old Vicarage
- 78 Pikes Cottage
- 99 Springdale
- 104 The Water Garden
- 113 Woody Park

SUNDAY 20
- 1 Alder
- 6 Bicton College
- 14 Castle Hill
- 30 The Downes
- 36 Gorwell House
- 41 Heathercombe
- 44 Higher Knowle
- 47 Hortus
- 50 Kia-Ora Farm & Gardens
- 52 Kingston House
- 70 The Old Glebe

- 72 The Old Vicarage
- 78 Pikes Cottage
- 81 Pleasant View
- 86 Rock House Garden
- 87 St Merryn
- 91 Sherwood
- 99 Springdale
- 104 The Water Garden
- 113 Woody Park
- 114 Yonder Hill

MONDAY 21
- 30 The Downes
- 99 Springdale

TUESDAY 22
- 30 The Downes

WEDNESDAY 23
- 30 The Downes
- 38 Haldon Grange
- 81 Pleasant View

THURSDAY 24
- 30 The Downes

FRIDAY 25
- 30 The Downes
- 88 Saltram House

SATURDAY 26
- 19 Cleave House
- 30 The Downes
- 38 Haldon Grange
- 41 Heathercombe
- 65 Moretonhampstead Gardens
- 68 Newton Farm
- 78 Pikes Cottage
- 104 The Water Garden

SUNDAY 27
- 2 Andrew's Corner
- 19 Cleave House
- 29 Dippers
- 30 The Downes
- 31 Durcombe Water
- 38 Haldon Grange
- 41 Heathercombe
- 44 Higher Knowle
- 45 Holbrook Garden
- 50 Kia-Ora Farm & Gardens
- 65 Moretonhampstead Gardens
- 68 Newton Farm
- 70 The Old Glebe
- 77 38 Phillipps Avenue
- 78 Pikes Cottage
- 91 Sherwood
- 95 Southcombe Gardens
- 104 The Water Garden
- 106 Westcott Barton
- 114 Yonder Hill

MONDAY 28
- 12 Cadhay
- 29 Dippers
- 30 The Downes
- 31 Durcombe Water
- 44 Higher Knowle
- 45 Holbrook Garden
- 50 Kia-Ora Farm & Gardens

65 Moretonhampstead Gardens
70 The Old Glebe
78 Pikes Cottage
95 Southcombe Gardens
104 The Water Garden
106 Westcott Barton
114 Yonder Hill

TUESDAY 29
30 The Downes

WEDNESDAY 30
30 The Downes
81 Pleasant View

THURSDAY 31
30 The Downes

June

FRIDAY 1
30 The Downes

SATURDAY 2
9 Bovey Tracey Gardens
30 The Downes
65 Moretonhampstead Gardens
68 Newton Farm
96 Southleigh Gardens
104 The Water Garden

SUNDAY 3
2 Andrew's Corner
4 Barleycott
9 Bovey Tracey Gardens
16 Cherubeer Gardens
30 The Downes
65 Moretonhampstead Gardens
68 Newton Farm
77 38 Phillipps Avenue
91 Sherwood
95 Southcombe Gardens
96 Southleigh Gardens
104 The Water Garden
114 Yonder Hill

MONDAY 4
30 The Downes

TUESDAY 5
30 The Downes

WEDNESDAY 6
30 The Downes
68 Newton Farm

THURSDAY 7
8 Bocombe Mill Cottage
30 The Downes

FRIDAY 8
8 Bocombe Mill Cottage
30 The Downes

SATURDAY 9
8 Bocombe Mill Cottage
30 The Downes
68 Newton Farm
76 Owls Barn
83 Prospect House
94 South Tawton Gardens

104 The Water Garden

SUNDAY 10
5 Bickham House
27 Dartington Hall Gardens
30 The Downes
36 Gorwell House
48 Ideford Gardens
50 Kia-Ora Farm & Gardens
64 Milland Farm
68 Newton Farm
71 The Old Rectory
76 Owls Barn
82 Portington
83 Prospect House
84 Regency House
91 Sherwood
94 South Tawton Gardens
95 Southcombe Gardens
98 Spillifords Wildlife Garden
104 The Water Garden
114 Yonder Hill

TUESDAY 12
5 Bickham House

WEDNESDAY 13
5 Bickham House
6 Bicton College

THURSDAY 14
25 Compton Castle
98 Spillifords Wildlife Garden

FRIDAY 15
12 Cadhay

SATURDAY 16
73 The Orangery
92 Shobrooke Park Gardens
104 The Water Garden
105 Webbery Gardens
107 Whibble Hill House

SUNDAY 17
18 The Cider House
26 The Croft
47 Hortus
48 Ideford Gardens
52 Kingston House
73 The Orangery
77 38 Phillipps Avenue
82 Portington
87 St Merryn
91 Sherwood
95 Southcombe Gardens
104 The Water Garden
105 Webbery Gardens
107 Whibble Hill House
114 Yonder Hill

WEDNESDAY 20
22 Collepardo

THURSDAY 21
22 Collepardo

FRIDAY 22
22 Collepardo

SATURDAY 23
15 Chapel Farm House

22 Collepardo
24 Combpyne Manor
28 Dicot
68 Newton Farm
94 South Tawton Gardens
104 The Water Garden

SUNDAY 24
2 Andrew's Corner
22 Collepardo
24 Combpyne Manor
28 Dicot
32 Feebers Gardens
49 Kerscott House
50 Kia-Ora Farm & Gardens
52 Kingston House (Evening)
56 Little Ash Farm
59 Littlecourt Cottages
68 Newton Farm
84 Regency House
86 Rock House Garden
91 Sherwood
93 South Kenwood
94 South Tawton Gardens
101 Taikoo
103 1 Tipton Lodge
104 The Water Garden
106 Westcott Barton
110 Winsford Walled Garden
114 Yonder Hill

MONDAY 25
103 1 Tipton Lodge
106 Westcott Barton

WEDNESDAY 27
68 Newton Farm
75 Overbeck's

THURSDAY 28
18 The Cider House
109 Wildside

FRIDAY 29
24 Combpyne Manor

SATURDAY 30
3 Arlington Court
6 Bicton College
10 Bramble Hayes
24 Combpyne Manor
68 Newton Farm
78 Pikes Cottage
99 Springdale

July

SUNDAY 1
10 Bramble Hayes
24 Combpyne Manor
68 Newton Farm
71 The Old Rectory
78 Pikes Cottage
89 School House
91 Sherwood
93 South Kenwood
98 Spillifords Wildlife Garden
99 Springdale
114 Yonder Hill

MONDAY 2
- (10) Bramble Hayes
- (99) Springdale

TUESDAY 3
- (10) Bramble Hayes

WEDNESDAY 4
- (22) Collepardo

THURSDAY 5
- (8) Bocombe Mill Cottage
- (22) Collepardo

FRIDAY 6
- (8) Bocombe Mill Cottage
- (22) Collepardo
- (72) The Old Vicarage

SATURDAY 7
- (8) Bocombe Mill Cottage
- (22) Collepardo
- (24) Combpyne Manor
- (72) The Old Vicarage

SUNDAY 8
- (5) Bickham House
- (6) Bicton College
- (16) Cherubeer Gardens
- (22) Collepardo
- (24) Combpyne Manor
- (50) Kia-Ora Farm & Gardens
- (59) Littlecourt Cottages
- (64) Milland Farm
- (72) The Old Vicarage
- (77) 38 Phillipps Avenue
- (91) Sherwood
- (114) Yonder Hill

TUESDAY 10
- (5) Bickham House

WEDNESDAY 11
- (5) Bickham House
- (68) Newton Farm

FRIDAY 13
- (12) Cadhay

SATURDAY 14
- (68) Newton Farm
- (90) Shapcott Barton Estate

SUNDAY 15
- (2) Andrew's Corner
- (26) The Croft
- (47) Hortus
- (52) Kingston House
- (68) Newton Farm
- (90) Shapcott Barton Estate
- (91) Sherwood
- (114) Yonder Hill

TUESDAY 17
- (102) Tamarisks

WEDNESDAY 18
- (68) Newton Farm
- (102) Tamarisks

THURSDAY 19
- (90) Shapcott Barton Estate

SATURDAY 21
- (15) Chapel Farm House
- (78) Pikes Cottage

SUNDAY 22
- (4) Barleycott
- (17) Chevithorne Barton
- (32) Feebers Gardens
- (36) Gorwell House
- (50) Kia-Ora Farm & Gardens
- (56) Little Ash Farm
- (59) Littlecourt Cottages
- (67) Nethercott House
- (78) Pikes Cottage
- (86) Rock House Garden
- (91) Sherwood
- (110) Winsford Walled Garden
- (114) Yonder Hill

WEDNESDAY 25
- (4) Barleycott (Evening)
- (6) Bicton College
- (90) Shapcott Barton Estate

SATURDAY 28
- (19) Cleave House
- (28) Dicot
- (68) Newton Farm
- (79) Pine Cottage
- (101) Taikoo

SUNDAY 29
- (19) Cleave House
- (28) Dicot
- (35) Glebe Cottage
- (42) Heddon Hall
- (49) Kerscott House
- (54) Lakesland
- (68) Newton Farm
- (77) 38 Phillipps Avenue
- (79) Pine Cottage
- (91) Sherwood
- (114) Yonder Hill

MONDAY 30
- (79) Pine Cottage

August

WEDNESDAY 1
- (90) Shapcott Barton Estate

THURSDAY 2
- (2) Andrew's Corner (Evening)
- (8) Bocombe Mill Cottage

SATURDAY 4
- (68) Newton Farm
- (83) Prospect House
- (100) Squirrels

SUNDAY 5
- (50) Kia-Ora Farm & Gardens
- (64) Milland Farm
- (68) Newton Farm
- (71) The Old Rectory
- (83) Prospect House
- (91) Sherwood
- (100) Squirrels
- (114) Yonder Hill

WEDNESDAY 8
- (6) Bicton College
- (68) Newton Farm
- (90) Shapcott Barton Estate

THURSDAY 9
- (90) Shapcott Barton Estate

SATURDAY 11
- (10) Bramble Hayes
- (56) Little Ash Farm
- (68) Newton Farm
- (100) Squirrels

SUNDAY 12
- (5) Bickham House
- (10) Bramble Hayes
- (50) Kia-Ora Farm & Gardens
- (56) Little Ash Farm
- (68) Newton Farm
- (91) Sherwood
- (114) Yonder Hill

MONDAY 13
- (10) Bramble Hayes

TUESDAY 14
- (5) Bickham House
- (10) Bramble Hayes

WEDNESDAY 15
- (5) Bickham House
- (68) Newton Farm

SATURDAY 18
- (6) Bicton College
- (15) Chapel Farm House

SUNDAY 19
- (26) The Croft
- (46) Hole Farm
- (47) Hortus
- (69) North Boreston Farm
- (91) Sherwood
- (114) Yonder Hill

MONDAY 20
- (69) North Boreston Farm

SATURDAY 25
- (78) Pikes Cottage

SUNDAY 26
- (32) Feebers Gardens
- (50) Kia-Ora Farm & Gardens
- (54) Lakesland
- (77) 38 Phillipps Avenue
- (78) Pikes Cottage
- (91) Sherwood
- (106) Westcott Barton
- (110) Winsford Walled Garden
- (114) Yonder Hill

MONDAY 27
- (50) Kia-Ora Farm & Gardens
- (54) Lakesland
- (78) Pikes Cottage
- (106) Westcott Barton
- (114) Yonder Hill

September

SUNDAY 2
- (5) Bickham House

18 The Cider House
36 Gorwell House
77 38 Phillipps Avenue
86 Rock House Garden
91 Sherwood
114 Yonder Hill

TUESDAY 4
5 Bickham House

WEDNESDAY 5
5 Bickham House
6 Bicton College

THURSDAY 6
8 Bocombe Mill Cottage

FRIDAY 7
62 Marwood Hill

SATURDAY 8
13 Castle Drogo

SUNDAY 9
35 Glebe Cottage
43 High Barn
50 Kia-Ora Farm & Gardens
58 Little Winsors
71 The Old Rectory
91 Sherwood
97 Sowton Mill
114 Yonder Hill

WEDNESDAY 12
58 Little Winsors

SUNDAY 16
43 High Barn
47 Hortus
53 Knightshayes Court Garden
86 Rock House Garden
91 Sherwood
73 Whitstone Farm
114 Yonder Hill

TUESDAY 18
45 Holbrook Garden
74 Otter Nurseries

WEDNESDAY 19
45 Holbrook Garden

SATURDAY 22
15 Chapel Farm House
68 Newton Farm

SUNDAY 23
6 Bicton College
58 Little Winsors
68 Newton Farm
86 Rock House Garden
91 Sherwood
110 Winsford Walled Garden
114 Yonder Hill

WEDNESDAY 26
58 Little Winsors

SATURDAY 29
68 Newton Farm
78 Pikes Cottage

SUNDAY 30
68 Newton Farm

78 Pikes Cottage
91 Sherwood
114 Yonder Hill

October

SUNDAY 7
36 Gorwell House
86 Rock House Garden
91 Sherwood
114 Yonder Hill

SUNDAY 14
6 Bicton College
91 Sherwood
114 Yonder Hill

SUNDAY 21
2 Andrew's Corner
91 Sherwood
114 Yonder Hill

WEDNESDAY 24
6 Bicton College

SUNDAY 28
91 Sherwood
114 Yonder Hill

November

EVERY SUNDAY
91 Sherwood

December

EVERY SUNDAY
91 Sherwood

January 2008

EVERY SUNDAY
91 Sherwood

February 2008

SUNDAY 3
16 Cherubeer Gardens
57 Little Cumbre
91 Sherwood

SUNDAY 10
16 Cherubeer Gardens
57 Little Cumbre
91 Sherwood

SUNDAY 17
57 Little Cumbre
91 Sherwood

SUNDAY 24
57 Little Cumbre
91 Sherwood

Private gardens opening regularly for the NGS

20 Cliffe
30 The Downes
34 The Gate House
68 Newton Farm

Gardens open to the public

3 Arlington Court
6 Bicton College
7 Blackpool Gardens
11 Burrow Farm Gardens
13 Castle Drogo
14 Castle Hill
21 Coleton Fishacre
25 Compton Castle
27 Dartington Hall Gardens
33 The Garden House
35 Glebe Cottage
37 Greenway Garden
40 Hartland Abbey
42 Heddon Hall
45 Holbrook Garden
51 Killerton Garden
53 Knightshayes Court Garden
61 Lukesland
62 Marwood Hill
74 Otter Nurseries
75 Overbeck's
80 Plant World
85 RHS Garden Rosemoor
86 Rock House Garden
88 Saltram House
90 Shapcott Barton Estate
109 Wildside
110 Winsford Walled Garden

By appointment only

39 Hamblyn's Coombe
55 Lee Ford

The Gardens

ABBOTSBURY GARDENS
See Dorset.

① ALDER
Lewdown EX20 4PJ. Bob & Anne Westlake, 01566 783909. *8m W of Okehampton, 8m E of Launceston. On old A30 (W Devon Drive).* Cream teas. **Adm £2.50, chd free. Suns 1 Apr; 20 May (2-6). Visitors also welcome by appt.**
Large garden created over last 21yrs with shrubs and herbaceous areas and views over landscaped valley. Woodland walks with 4-acre lake in former quarry. Bluebell wood in spring. New rill and water feature.
   ⛔ ⊛ ☕

② ANDREW'S CORNER
Belstone EX20 1RD. Robin & Edwina Hill, 01837 840332, edwinarobin_hill@yahoo.co.uk. *3m E of Okehampton. In village signed Skaigh. Parking restricted but cars may be left on nearby common.* Cream teas. **Adm £2.50, chd free. Suns 15 Apr; 6, 27 May; 3, 24 June; 15 July; 21 Oct (2.30-5.30). Evening Openings £3.50, wine, Thurs 17 May; 2 Aug (7-10). Visitors also welcome by appt.**
Well-established, wildlife-friendly, well-labelled plantsman's garden in stunning high moorland setting. Variety of garden habitats incl woodland areas, bog garden, pond; wide range of unusual trees, shrubs, herbaceous plants for yr-round effect incl alpines, rhododendrons, bulbs and maples; spectacular autumn colour. New organic kitchen garden, greenhouse and traditional breed chickens. Wheelchair access difficult in wet conditions.
   ⛔ ✂ ⊛ ☕

③ ARLINGTON COURT
Arlington, Barnstaple EX31 4LP. The National Trust, 01271 850296, www.nationaltrust.org.uk. *7m NE of Barnstaple. On A39. From E use A399.* **House and garden adm £7.40, chd £3.70, garden only adm £5.20, chd £2.60. Suns to Fris, 18 Mar to 28 Oct (10.30-5), house (11-5). For NGS: Sat 30 June (10.30-5).**
Rolling parkland and woods with lake. Rhododendrons and azaleas; fine specimen trees; small terraced Victorian garden with herbaceous borders and conservatory. Walled garden in process of being restored.

Regency house containing fascinating collections. Carriage collection in the stables, carriage rides. Guided walks with Head Gardener at 11 and 2, focusing on recently-restored walled kitchen garden. All those donating to NGS on the day can take away a sample of garden produce. Mainly gravel paths, sloping formal and walled gardens.
   ⛔ ⊛ ☕

④ BARLEYCOTT
Blakewell EX31 4ES. Les & Barbara Shapland, 01271 375002, lb.shapland@onetel.net. *2m N of Barnstaple. ½m past hospital off B3230 to Ilfracombe at Blakewell Fisheries. Follow signs to Barleycott.* Home-made teas 3 June/22 July. **Adm £2.50, chd free. Suns 3 June; 22 July (11-5). Evening Opening £3.50, wine, Wed 25 July (5-8). Visitors also welcome by appt.**
3-acre, S-sloping garden started in 1989 set in beautiful countryside. Unusual trees, conifers and shrubs. Lavender walk, vegetable plot, orchard and pond. Lime tree avenue leading to folly and secret Japanese-style garden. Lower garden, rockpool, with large waterfall.
   ✂ ☕

Lime tree avenue leading to folly and secret Japanese-style garden . . .

⑤ BICKHAM HOUSE
Kenn EX6 7XL. John & Julia Tremlett, 01392 832671, jandjtremlett@hotmail.com. *6m S of Exeter. 1m off A38. Leave A38 at Kennford Services, follow signs to Kenn. 1st R in village, follow lane for ¾m to end of no-through rd.* Cream teas. **Adm £3, chd free. Suns, Tues, Weds (2-5) 15, 17, 18 Apr; 13, 15, 16 May; 10, 12, 13 June; 8, 10, 11 July; 12, 14, 15 August; 2, 4, 5 September. Visitors also welcome by appt incl coaches.**
7 acres in secluded wooded valley; lawns, mature trees and shrubs, naturalised bulbs, mixed borders with

unusual perennials, wild flower banks for butterflies. Edwardian conservatory, small formal parterre with lily pond; 1-acre walled kitchen garden with profusion of vegetables, fruit and flowers, palm tree avenue leading to Millennium summerhouse. Lakeside walk. Featured in 'The English Garden', 'Country Life', 'Devon Country Gardener' and on BBC TV Spotlight.
   ⛔ ✂ ⊛ ☕

⑥ ◆ BICTON COLLEGE
East Budleigh EX9 7BY, 01395 562353, pechampion@bicton.ac.uk. *3m N of Budleigh Salterton. Use Sidmouth Lodge entrance on B3178 and follow NGS signs.* **Adm £2, chd free. Open daily 1 Mar to 31 Oct; 1 Nov to 28 Feb Mon to Fri, except Good Fri/Easter Sun. Closed Xmas week. (10-4). For NGS: Weds 5, 21, Sat 24 Mar; Wed 11, Sun 29 Apr; Wed 2, Sun 20 May; Wed 13, Sat 30 June; Sun 8, Wed 25 July; Wed 8, Sat 18 Aug; Wed 5, Sun 23 Sept; Sun 14, Wed 24 Oct.**
Renowned monkey puzzle avenue; walled garden. Rich variety of plants in beds and borders, many rare, laid out for teaching and effect. National Collection of pittosporum; arboretum with magnolias, cherries and camellias. Many magnificent mature trees (some are 'Champion Trees'). Stunning spring and autumn colour. All set in English Heritage Grade 1 listed landscape. Guided tours with Paul Champion, garden manager, £3 (incl adm) Weds 21 Mar, 24 Oct 2pm (meet at plant centre). Featured on BBC2 Springwatch. Some paths in arboretum not accessible by wheelchair.
   ⛔ ⊛ NCCPG ☕

⑦ ◆ BLACKPOOL GARDENS
Dartmouth TQ6 0RG. Sir Geoffrey Newman, 01803 770606, www.blackpoolsands.co.uk. *3m SW of Dartmouth. From Dartmouth follow brown signs to Blackpool Sands on A379. Entrance to gardens via Blackpool Sands car park.* **Adm £2.50, chd free. Daily April to Oct (10-4).**
Tenderly restored C19 subtropical plantsman's garden with collection of mature and newly-planted tender and unusual trees, shrubs and carpet of spring flowers. Paths and steps lead gradually uphill to the Captain's seat and spectacular coastal views. Recent plantings follow the S hemisphere theme with callistemons, pittosporums, acacias and buddlejas.
   ✂ ☕

8 BOCOMBE MILL COTTAGE

Bocombe EX39 5PH. Mr Chris
Butler & Mr David Burrows, 01237
451293, www.bocombe.co.uk. 6m E
of Clovelly, 9m SW of Bideford. From
A39 just outside Horns Cross village,
turn to Foxdown. At Xrds take lane
signed Bocombe. At T-junction turn R.
100yds on R. Limited parking. **Adm
£2.50, chd £1. Thurs 5 Apr; 3 May;
Thur, Fri, Sat 7, 8, 9 June; 5, 6, 7
July; Thurs 2 Aug; 6 Sept (11-4).
Visitors also welcome by appt Mar
to Sept.**
5 acres of gardens and wild meadow
in small wooded valley, a wildlife
haven. Many flower gardens,
3 newly-developed. Streams, bog
gardens and small lakes. Kitchen
garden, orchard, soft fruit garden,
shrubbery. All grown organically. Goats
on hillside. Plan and tree guide.
Circular walk (boots or wellies needed)
of just under 1m.

 ❀

BOSCASTLE GARDENS

See Cornwall.

9 BOVEY TRACEY GARDENS

TQ13 9NA. 6m N of Newton Abbot.
Gateway to Dartmoor. Take A382 to
Bovey Tracey. Car parking available at
Mary St & Station Rd car parks. Home-
made teas. **Combined adm £3, chd
free. Sat 2, Sun 3 June (2-6).**
☕

ASHWELL

East Street. Bill & Diane Riddell
1-acre Victorian walled garden
presently undergoing restoration.
On a steep slope with glorious
views. Vineyard, orchard and
mature trees incl impressive
arbutus.

 🏠

2 DEVON HOUSE DRIVE

Mrs P Miskin. Near entrance to
Coombe Cross Hotel
Interesting variety of roses.
Herbaceous borders with
contrasting colours and shapes.
Organic and companion planting.
Fruit trees, herbs and vegetable
areas.

NEW DOWN PARK

Shewte Cross. Susan
Macready. 1m from Fire Station
roundabout on Manaton Rd.
Parking available
Well-maintained, colourful, mature
garden. Great variety of
rhododendrons, azaleas,

camellias and unusual shrubs.
Formal pond and alpine garden.

NEW HILARY HOUSE

Ashburton Road TQ13 9BZ.
Alison & Stephen Arnold. Past
Brimley PO
Mature garden presently
undergoing a makeover. Incl
modest kitchen garden, new
orchard, herbaceous borders and
natural woodland fronting onto
small lake with pocket areas to
enjoy different vistas at all times of
day. Gravel paths, sloping lawn,
unfenced lake.

NEW OLD WHITSTONE

Jinny & Richard Aldridge.
Limited parking at top of
Whitstone Lane
Come and see our old farmhouse
garden undergoing renovation and
enjoy the views to Haytor. Steps
and gates divide different areas
which incl herbaceous borders
and small, steep wood.

PARKE VIEW

Fore Street TQ13 9AD. Peter &
Judy Hall. Next to The Old
Cottage tea shop
1-acre garden developed over 12
yrs, shape largely dictated by old
stone walls and outbuildings.
Wide selection of roses, shrubs
and flowers.

YONDER

Whitstone Lane,
Moretonhampstead Rd
TQ13 9LZ. Mr & Mrs John
Awcock
Mature cottage garden.
Restoration in progress. Many
varieties of acer and clematis.
Interesting new plantings.

10 BRAMBLE HAYES

Yawl Hill Lane, Uplyme DT7 3RP.
Martin & Celia Young, 01297
443084, www.sittingspiritually.co.uk.
3m E of Axminster. From E A35,
100metres E of Devon sign, L into Red
Lane, over 2 Xrds into Yawl Hill Lane,
garden 0.8m on R. From W A35
through Raymonds Hill, R into Red
Lane then as above. From Lyme Regis,
B3165 through Uplyme/Yawl to Yawl
Hill Lane. Home-made teas. **Adm £3,
chd free. Daily Sat 30 June to Tue 3
July; Sat 11 Aug to Tue 14 Aug (11-
6). Visitors also welcome by appt.**

1/3 acre. Sensory garden with
meandering paths. Seats for enjoying
the vistas and plant combinations.
Herbaceous perennials balance Feng
Shui colour, texture and form. The
seaside/spiritual feel within the garden
and wooded backdrop provide perfect
setting for sitting and contemplating.
Wonderful lawn. Art display in
summerhouse. Owner is swing seat
maker. Featured on BBC2 Open
Gardens.

11 ◆ BURROW FARM GARDENS

Dalwood EX13 7ET. Mary & John
Benger, 01404 831285,
www.burrowfarmgardens.co.uk.
3¹/₂m W of Axminster. From A35 turn
N at Taunton Xrds then follow brown
signs. **Adm £4, chd 50p. Daily 1 Apr
to 30 Sept (10-7).**
Secluded 10-acre garden of informal
design with many unusual shrubs and
herbaceous plants. Pergola walk with
shrub roses. Woodland with
rhododendrons and azaleas, ponds
and large bog garden. Terraced
courtyard featuring later flowering
plants. Rill garden with water feature;
traditional stone summerhouse and
informal planting all with wonderful
views. Prince of Wales Award of
Honour for training students in rural
skills.

12 CADHAY

Ottery St Mary EX11 1QT. Rupert
Thistlethwayte, www.cadhay.org.uk.
1m NW of Ottery St Mary. On B3176.
**Adm £2, chd free. Mon 28 May; Fri
15 June; 13 July (2-4.30).**
Tranquil 2-acre garden in lovely setting
between the Elizabethan Manor house
(open) and ancient stew ponds.
Carefully planned double herbaceous
borders particularly colourful in
summer. Small part-walled water
garden, roses, lilies and clematis.
Finalist Country Life 'Best Manor
House'. Uneven paths.

13 ◆ CASTLE DROGO

Drewsteignton EX6 6PB. The
National Trust, 01647 433306. 12m
W of Exeter. 5m S of A30. Follow
brown signs. **House and garden adm
£7.40 & chd £3.70, garden only adm
£4.75, chd £2.60. Daily 17 Mar to 28
Oct except Tues. For NGS: Sats 12
May; 8 Sept (10.30-5.30).**
Medium-sized Grade II* listed garden
with formal structures designed by
George Dillistone during the late

1920s. These consist of formal rose beds, herbaceous borders and circular croquet lawn surrounded by mature yew hedges. Rhododendron garden overlooks spectacular views of Teign Valley Gorge and Dartmoor. Ongoing work in summerhouse area with new woodland plantings gradually being introduced.

⑭ ♦ CASTLE HILL
Filleigh EX32 0RQ. **The Earl & Countess of Arran, 01598 760336 ext 4.** *4m W of South Molton. From A361 Tiverton to Barnstaple leave at roundabout on B3226 signed Filleigh.* Teas Suns/Bank Hols May to Aug. **Adm £4, chd free. Daily except Sats 1 Feb to 30 Sept and every Sun throughout yr (11-5). For NGS: Suns 22 Apr; 20 May (11-5).** Palladian house in extensive C18 Grade I landscape park and garden. Arboretum and woodlands with camellias, rhododendrons, magnolias, azaleas and other shrubs and rare trees in abundance. Summer millenium garden designed by Xa Tollemache with topiary water sculpture by Giles Rayner. Many C18 follies and a 1730 castle on the hill with magnificent views to Exmoor, Dartmoor and Lundy Island.

⑮ CHAPEL FARM HOUSE
Halwill Junction EX21 5UF. **Robin & Toshie Hull, 01409 221594.** *12m NW of Okehampton. On A3079. At W end of village.* **Adm £2, chd free. Sats 24 Mar; 21 Apr; 19 May; 23 June; 21 July; 18 Aug; 22 Sept (11-5). Visitors also welcome by appt.** Approx ¹/₂-acre garden started in 1992 by present owners, landscaped with shrub borders, heathers, rhododendrons and azaleas. Alpine bed. Kitchen garden. 2 small greenhouses for mixed use. Small bonsai collection. 3 acres of mixed young woodland added in 1995 with wildlife and flowers.

⑯ CHERUBEER GARDENS
Dolton EX19 8PP. *8m SE of Great Torrington. 2m E of Dolton. From A3124 turn S towards Stafford Moor Fisheries, take 1st R, gardens 500m on L.* Home-made teas at Higher Cherubeer. **Combined adm £3, chd free. Suns 3 June; 8 July (2-6); 3, 10 Feb 2008 (1-5).**

CHERUBEER
Janet Brown
Cottage garden set around a C15 thatched house (not open). Garden divided into compartments with ponds, paths, and steps filled with colourful perennials and herbs set off by mature shrubs and trees.

HIGHER CHERUBEER
Jo & Tom Hynes
1-acre country garden with gravelled courtyard, raised beds and alpine house, lawns, large herbaceous border, shady woodland beds, large kitchen garden, greenhouse, colourful collection of basketry willows. Winter opening for hardy cyclamen, snowdrop varieties and hellebores. Featured on BBC2 Open Gardens and in 'Devon Life'. Partial wheelchair access if accompanied. Gravel paths, slopes and steps.

MIDDLE CHERUBEER
Dr & Mrs Barty & Heather Hynes
Colourful small garden. Three separate areas with bog garden, pond and massed herbaceous perennials interlinked with paths.

⑰ NEW CHEVITHORNE BARTON
Tiverton EX16 7QB. **Michael & Arabella Heathcoat Amory.** *3m NE of Tiverton. M5 J27, A373 towards Tiverton. Immed past golf course, R then R at next T-junction. Over bridge, L through Craze Lowman, carry on through lanes to T-junction, R then 1st L.* Home-made teas. **Adm £3, chd free. Suns 29 Apr; 13 May; 22 July (2-5.30).** Terraced walled garden, summer borders and romantic woodland of rare trees and shrubs. In spring, garden features large collection of magnolias, camellias, rhododendrons and azaleas. Also incl one of only two NCCPG oak collections situated in 12 hectares of parkland and comprising over 200 different species. Limited disability access.
NCCPG

CHIDEOCK MANOR
See Dorset.

⑱ THE CIDER HOUSE
Buckland Abbey, Yelverton PL20 6EZ. **Mr & Mrs M J Stone, 01822 853285,** www.cider-house.co.uk. *8m N of Plymouth. From A386 Plymouth to Tavistock rd, follow NT signs to Buckland Abbey. At Xrds before Abbey entrance turn N signed Buckland Monachorum. Drive 200yds on L, or short walk for visitors to Abbey.* Light refreshments & teas 28 June, cream teas other days. **Adm £3, chd free. Wed 16 May; Sun 17 Jun (2-6), Thur 28 June (11-5); Sun 2 Sept (2-6). Visitors also welcome by appt.** 3 acres in peaceful surroundings looking down to Tavy valley. Terrace gardens complement the medieval house (not open), herb garden, woodland and herbaceous borders, wild garden with rhododendrons, camellias and other shrubs. Former walled kitchen garden productively maintained to give abundance of fruit, vegetables and flowers.

⑲ CLEAVE HOUSE
Sticklepath EX20 2NL. **Ann & Roger Bowden, 01837 840481,** bowdens2@eclipse.co.uk. *3¹/₂m E of Okehampton. On old A30 towards Exeter. Cleave House on L in village, on main rd just past R turn for Skaigh.* **Adm £2, chd free (share to NCCPG). Sats, Suns 28, 29 Apr; 26, 27 May; 28, 29 July. Visitors also welcome by appt.** ¹/₂-acre garden with mixed planting for all season interest. National Collection of hostas with 1000 varieties.
NCCPG

Summer borders and romantic woodland of rare trees . . .

20 CLIFFE

Lee, Ilfracombe EX34 8LR. Dr & Mrs Humphreys. *3m W of Ilfracombe. Garden is past sea front at Lee, 150yds up coast rd, through wrought iron gates on L. Lee Bay car park 260yds (no parking on approach rd).* Adm £2, chd free. Daily Apr to Sept incl (9-5). Cliffside garden with spectacular coastal scenery. Mixture of planting incl shade and woodland. Camellias, daffodils and azaleas in spring. National Collection of Heucheras and schizostylis. Always something to see. Mixed herbaceous borders.

 NCCPG

21 ♦ COLETON FISHACRE

nr Kingswear TQ6 0EQ. The National Trust, 01803 752466, coletonfishacre@nationaltrust.org.uk. *3m E of Dartmouth. Lower Ferry Rd. Follow brown signs. Lane leading to Coleton Fishacre is narrow and can be busy on fine days. Use of passing places and reversing may be necessary. Coach parties must book.* House and Garden Adm £6.40 chd £3.20, Garden only Adm £5.90, chd £3. Weds to Suns and Bank Hol Mons 17 Mar to 28 Oct (10.30-5), house (11-4.30, last entry 4). For NGS: Sat 14 Apr; Sun 13 May (10.30-5). 24-acre garden created by Rupert and Lady Dorothy D'Oyly Carte between 1925 and 1948. Re-established and developed by NT since 1983. Wide range of tender and uncommon trees and shrubs in spectacular coastal setting. Advisory wheelchair route map available.

&. ℀ ✿ ☕

22 COLLEPARDO

3 Keyberry Park, Newton Abbot TQ12 1BZ. Betty & Don Frampton. *Take A380 for Newton Abbot. From Penn Inn roundabout follow sign for town centre. Take 1st L, 1st R, 2nd L.* Home-made/cream teas. Adm £2.50, chd free. Daily Wed 20 to Sun 24 June; Wed 4 to Sun 8 July (11-5). ⅓-acre lawn-free garden laid out in series of interlinked colour-themed smaller areas. Incl 400 metres of meandering gravel pathways, circular rockery of 20 metres, herbaceous borders, pond, walkway, gazebo and over 1,500 different varieties of plants, shrubs and trees. Featured in 'Guardian' and 'Devon Life'.

℀ ✿ ☕

Exotic Japanese garden with tea house, koi carp pond and cascading stream . . .

23 COLYFORD GARDENS

Midway between Sidmouth & Lyme Regis off A3052. at Paddocks. Combined adm £3, chd free. Suns 18 Mar; 15 Apr (1-5). Ancient borough renowned for Michaelmas Goose Fayre that dates from 1208.

PADDOCKS

Stafford Lane EX24 6HQ. Alan & Wendy Davis, 01297 552472, wendyandalan@yahoo.co.uk. *W end of Colyford. Park in Colyton Grammar School.* Visitors also welcome by appt.
A first spring opening for Paddocks provides a welcome opportunity to view the spring-flowering bulbs, trees and shrubs in the borders of this 2-acre garden.

&. ℀ ✿

THE VINYARD

Seaton Road EX24 6QW. Mollie & Michael Pickup. *At Colyford PO turn off A3052 into Seaton Rd, 5th house on L*
Flower arranger's 1¼-acre garden with extensive sea and Axe valley views. Many spring-flowering bulbs, shrubs and perennials, woodland area, small orchard, soft fruit, vegetables, ponds and scree bed. This being our 1st spring, rather than summer, opening, we look forward to sharing the early beauty of the garden with all visitors. Delightful, tranquil setting within natural Devon banks.

&. ✿

24 COMBPYNE MANOR

EX13 8SX. Nicky & Donald Campbell. *4m W of Lyme Regis. From Rousdon (A3052) follow sign to Combpyne.* Home-made/cream teas. Adm £2.50, chd free. Sat 23, Sun 24, Fri 29, Sat 30 Jun; Sun 1, Sat 7, Sun 8 July (11-5). 3½ acres of mature gardens geared to conservation and wildlife. Unusual planting within medieval walls for yr-round interest. Large organic vegetable plot. 'Wild' garden with contoured paths managed to reduce fertility and create spectacular flower-rich slopes. Native woodland area. Wonderful views.

℀ ☕

25 ♦ COMPTON CASTLE

Marldon, Paignton TQ3 1TA. The National Trust, 01803 842382, greenway@nationaltrust.org.uk. *3m W of Torquay. 1½m N of Marldon. From Newton Abbot - Totnes rd A381 turn L at Ipplepen Xrds & W off Torbay Ring Rd via Marldon.* Adm £3.90, chd £1.95. Mons, Weds, Thurs, 4 Apr to 25 Oct (10-1, 2-5). For NGS: Thur 14 June (10-1, 2-5). Small formal courtyard gardens, rose garden. Newly established knot garden. Access to the usually private fruit and vegetable garden. Incl access to fortified Manor House with restored medieval great hall.

℀ ☕

COTHAY MANOR GARDENS

See Somerset & Bristol Area.

26 THE CROFT

Yarnscombe EX31 3LW. Sam & Margaret Jewell, 01769 560535, margandsam@herdsgardens.fsnet. co.uk. *4m NE of Torrington, 8m S of Barnstaple. From A377, turn W opp Chapelton railway stn. After 3m drive on L at village sign. From B3232, ¼m N of Hunshaw TV mast Xrds, turn E for 2m. Parking in village hall car park nearby.* Adm £3, chd free (share to N Devon Animal Ambulance). Suns 17 June; 15 July; 19 Aug (2-6). Visitors also welcome by appt.
1-acre plantswoman's garden featuring exotic Japanese garden with tea house, koi carp pond and cascading stream, tropical garden with exotic shrubs and perennials. Herbaceous borders with unusual plants and shrubs. Bog garden with collection of irises, astilbes and moisture-loving plants, duck pond. Featured in 'Devon Life'.

&. ✿

LIFE ON THE WILD SIDE

GO ORGANIC... AND DISCOVER A HAVEN FOR WILDLIFE

There are roughly 667,000 acres of gardens in the UK – more than the area of all our National Nature Reserves put together. Although individually these gardens are small, they make up an important and continuous patchwork of habitats for all sorts of wildlife.

Cumbria Wildlife Trust's organic garden, Kendal, is treated with as much love and care as its 40 nature reserves. At only 2.5 acres it is surprising how many different areas there are for wildlife here. The small woodland provides the main height in the garden, giving homes to birds, bats and insects. Water boatmen and dragonflies have already set up home in the freshly dug pond – ready for children's pond dipping in the spring – and we are also hoping to attract some frogs and newts. Blackbirds nest in the extensive yew and beech hedgerows, and robins, tits and finches make the most of our bird feeding station, all year round.

Our native wildflower bed provides a home for old hay meadow species that are rarely seen in our fields anymore. With 150 species, the bed is packed full of a rainbow of colours, from the tall and graceful melancholy thistle to the more delicate devil's-bit scabious. The flowers provide food for bees, butterflies and other insects and the teasels produce seeds that are picked out by gold finches. Modern cultivated flowers often don't produce pollen or nectar at all. Our wildflower bed is buzzing in the spring compared to some of our formal flower borders.

The composting area and log piles provide shelter for insects and small mammals. Insects love the rotting wood caused by fungi that are working to return nutrients from the wood to the ground. Leaves also provide good cover and we make sure that we don't tidy up leaf-fall or cut the grass short in the autumn and winter. Just leaving a small patch of your garden to grow wild will provide winter homes and food. Why not leave that out-of-sight patch behind the shed to do its own thing?

Cumbria Wildlife Trust is opening its garden for NGS for the first time this year. Do come and enjoy our garden and perhaps glean a few ideas for your own.

Garden Plumgarths House & Wood, Cumbria
Photographs Cumbria Wildlife Trust

Chris Collins, BBC TV's Blue Peter Gardener, TV Presenter

GET THE KIDS GARDENING!

IT'S TIME FOR HORTICULTURE TO ATTRACT
A YOUNGER FOLLOWING

There has been a definite wind of change in gardening over the last year. A subject that quite rightly has its roots among the tranquil surroundings of lawns, flowers and cream teas is looking to new horizons. It's time, and rightly so, for horticulture to shed its image of belonging to the more senior members of society and embrace our younger generation.

Working with children and in schools as I do, I can promise that every child I engage with, out in the air and touching the soil, automatically responds to working with plants and gardens. I feel this is genetic, or even if you like, spiritual. I believe there is a switch inside us all that is turned on once we engage with anything that is related to the natural world. What better way than to achieve this than through gardening.

There is much more to gardening than knowing the Latin names of plants; much more than striped lawns and striking hanging baskets. These things belong to those of us with experience of this pastime. Let us think about the other contributions that gardening can make, especially to the young mind.

Firstly, if a child is to create an outdoor space, get them to sit down, let their

Garden Fernbank, Congresbury Gardens, Somerset & Photograph Rowan Isaacs

Garden 67 & 69 Shepherds Lane, Surrey Photograph Kali Masure

imagination run and ask them to draw how they see the garden. We have now stirred up the artist in them.

Now get them to measure out an area in the garden (or balcony!) – maths now enters the equation. Next comes the physical effort of bringing the idea to life, and physical exercise as we know is an important issue to our young people. We can work as a family, let's get them away from that television. These are all important life skills but most important is nurturing the creation, the caring of plants. This, as every gardener knows, is so satisfying once the bug is caught. It is with you for life and is going to be, outside all of life's complications, an endless source of comfort.

I say these words with conviction and feel no shame in their sentimental leanings. It is important to pass on the gift of gardening to our kids. What a head start we have! With organisations such as The National Gardens Scheme and countless other organisations and societies that make up the horticultural culture of this island, may we keep this fine art moving for centuries to come.

Garden Little Larford, Worcestershire Photograph Suzanne Shacklock

Garden Holywell Hall, Lincolnshire Photograph Rowan Isaacs

Garden Driftwood, Northamptonshire Photograph Brian & Nina Chapple

"There's much more to gardening than knowing the Latin names of plants"

FOOD FOR THOUGHT

MODEST AMBITION IS **THE KEY TO SUCCESSFUL VEGETABLE GROWING,** SAYS TIM RUMBALL FROM AMATEUR GARDENING

For gardeners, growing plants is the ultimate satisfaction, but eating good food comes close second. It's no surprise, then, that ordinary gardeners are discovering that it's easy to grow their own fruit and vegetable crops, and that they don't need a big garden, either. The key is to have modest ambitions – start with a few things that are easy and trouble-free.

Herbs, like coriander, basil and chives, are easy to raise in small pots of multi-purpose compost on any bright windowsill. For the price of a couple of packets of seeds you can have fresh, home-grown herbs throughout spring, summer and autumn.

Climbing French beans and runner beans are very successful in large pots on the patio. Three or four seeds in a ten litre pot, with a tripod of canes for support, will provide pickings for several weeks in summer.

For winter harvest, try a big container with two or three plants of rainbow chard. The plants look fabulous and the generous leaf is a good substitute for spinach.

Tomatoes are widely grown, but why not complete the salad bowl with a standard-sized seed tray filled with multi-purpose compost and sown with cut-and-come-again mixed salad leaves, and another with three rows of radishes?

And, for desert, a few pots of perpetual strawberries will go down a treat. All they need is water and a regular dose of fertiliser.

All these are easy if you sow containers in spring/summer and set the pots in a sunny spot in the garden, on a patio or even a veranda.

A veg patch in the garden will enable you to try some slightly more challenging crops – like carrots, leeks, courgettes, onions and sweetcorn. They do need a bit more space, but are not difficult to grow. And if you get bitten by the bug and want even more planting space, why not put your name down for an allotment and really get growing!

"For the price of a couple of packets of seeds you can have fresh, home-grown herbs"

Photographs Amateur Gardening

GARDEN GOURMET

CHEF JOHN THORP RECOMMENDS SOME DELICIOUS DISHES FOR AL FRESCO DINING

John Thorp is a professional chef with a long track record of cooking fine food in the hotel and catering industry and on television. He opens his garden, Fuchsia View, Carlton (near Nottingham) for the NGS. We asked him for some ideas for food to enjoy in the garden and he has come up with these simple, but mouth-watering, suggestions.

Carrot and Potato Bake

8oz onions
8oz carrots
8oz potatoes
1 crushed clove of garlic
1 oz butter, plus some for greasing
Salt and pepper

Preheat oven to 170C / 352F / Gas mark 3. Cut the vegetables into thin matchsticks and mix together. Melt the butter in a saucepan and cook the crushed garlic for about 30 seconds, so the flavour of the garlic is incorporated in the butter. Add the vegetables to the butter, season and mix well, remove from heat and really mix together to blend with the butter and garlic. Put in a seven inch buttered cake tin, pressing down well to flatten into a round cake. Bake for about one hour or until the vegetables are crisp at the edges and tender in the middle.

Potato and Mushroom Medley

Prep time: 5 minutes
Cooking time: 25 minutes
1lb/700g fresh new potatoes
2oz/50g butter
Chopped parsley
1oz/25g chopped sage
6oz/150g button mushrooms
12 shallots
8fl oz red wine
6fl oz vegetable stock

Cut the potatoes in half and fry in a large saucepan with the butter and shallots for about five minutes, add the wine and stock, season, bring to the boil and simmer for 30 minutes. Stir in the halved button mushrooms and sage, cook for a further five minutes until the potatoes are just cooked. Serve in a hot dish, sprinkle with chopped parsley.

Gazpacho

Prep time:
20 minutes
2lb/900g plum
  tomatoes
  skinned and
  de-seeded
1 medium
  cucumber peeled
  and de-seeded
1 small chopped onion
3 cloves garlic, crushed
6 red peppers, seeded
  and chopped
4fl oz sherry vinegar

Liquidise all of the ingredients, pass through a fine conical strainer and season, add a little Tabasco to taste. Gazpacho is delicious on its own or served with croutons but can also be served with prawns or vegetable mousse served in the centre. Serve this soup cold.

Fresh Green Beans Wrapped in Bacon

Prep time: 15 minutes
Cooking time: 20 minutes
1lb/450g thin green beans
6 rashers of back bacon
Pint of vegetable stock

Wash, top and tail the beans, cook in boiling salted water for about seven to eight minutes until nearly cooked, drain and refresh under cold water. Place in six bundles on a board, wrap a rasher of bacon around each bundle. Butter an ovenproof dish, place the bundles in the dish, pour in the stock, cover with foil and bake in an oven for about 15 minutes. Remove the foil and cook for a further four minutes to allow the bacon to crisp a little.

Garden Lower House, Powys Photograph Nicky & Pete Daw

Garden White Barn, Hampshire Photograph Barrie Knight

YOUR OWN
PERSONAL
TOUR GUIDE

WHAT BETTER WAY TO VISIT A GARDEN THAN
BY APPOINTMENT!

Why not organise a day out with friends or for your local horticultural group by calling one of the NGS's many 'by appointment' gardens.

The NGS has around 600 gardens which welcome visitors throughout the year 'by appointment', and garden owners are delighted to share their wonderful gardens.

Gardens that open 'by appointment' enjoy welcoming individuals, small groups or larger horticultural groups. Many gardens welcome coaches (see the individual garden entry in The Yellow Book or on the website, www.ngs.org.uk.)

Some gardens would not be able to manage the large number of visitors on a normal open day, perhaps due to parking restrictions or size of the garden, so they only open 'by appointment' – but the gardens are all of the same high standard. A list of 'by appointment only' gardens can be found after the diary section for each county in The Yellow Book.

Garden South Newington House, Oxfordshire Photograph John Ainley

Garden Hamblyn's Coombe, Devon Photograph

Garden Rosewood, Cheshire Photograph Mr & Mrs C E J Brabin

Garden 18 Queens Gate, Somerset & Bristol Area

Other garden owners who give the NGS specific open days are also more than happy to share their garden with visitors 'by appointment' throughout the year.

The NGS's generous garden owners are very accommodating! You can enjoy the peace and quiet of a private visit, wander around the garden at your own pace and gain a more intimate experience of a garden. Feel free to ask the garden owner questions; it's a fantastic opportunity to learn the secret of their growing success.

"Enjoy the peace and quiet of a private visit, wander around the garden at your own pace and gain a more intimate experience of a garden"

Garden Timbers, Kent Photograph Sue Robinson

Grenville Johnson and Alan Elms, Garden Owners

SMALL IS BEAUTIFUL

A SMALL BUT PERFECTLY FORMED TOWN HOUSE GARDEN WITH **THE 'WOW FACTOR'**

Our garden is unique in that it must be one of the smallest gardens in The National Gardens Scheme as it measures 20 feet by 16 feet (6.1m x 5.5m) and is situated at the rear of a Victorian town house approximately 2.5 miles from Bristol city centre.

In the autumn of 2004, a mature Magnolia began to lean over the whole plot. We decided to clear the entire site, and moved seven tons of waste and rubble which filled six large skips, we then set about redesigning the whole garden.

The new garden was designed as two outdoor 'rooms' on two decked levels with the lower area leading directly from the house. The upper deck also serves as a dining area in warm weather. We commissioned a company specialising in faux rockwork to install a rocky outcrop, a pond and water cascade and a temple ruin folly. Much of the garden is container-grown and this provides flexibility and space as well as giving all year interest. The emphasis has been placed on pattern, colour, texture and form with large planters and containers filled with luscious exotic plants. The garden is very sheltered although it extends over a north-south axis. The statuary and other architectural details were utilised from the former garden scheme. The high fence panels were constructed to our design.

We hope our garden has what we call the 'wow factor', with elements of surprise and wit as well as being a place of tranquillity and beauty. The garden is surprisingly quiet considering it is surrounded by other Victorian terraced houses, and is not far from one of the major commuter roads to Bristol city centre.

Garden 28 Kensington Road, Somerset & Bristol Area
Photograph Alan Elms

27 ◆ DARTINGTON HALL GARDENS
Dartington TQ9 6EL. Dartington Hall Trust, 01803 862367, www.dartingtonhall.org.uk. *1¹/₂m NW of Totnes. From Totnes take A384, turn R at Dartington Parish Church. Proceed up hill for 1m. Hall & gardens on R. Car parking on L.* Adm £3, chd free. For NGS: Sun 10 June (10-6). 28-acre modern garden, created since 1925 around C14 medieval hall (not open). Courtyard and tournament ground. Recent additions incl dry landscape Japanese garden. Extensive wild flower meadows and new mixed shrub and herbaceous border. Peter Randall-Page sculpture. 60th consecutive yr opening for NGS. Guided tour of hall and gardens at 2.30pm.
& ⚔ ⊨ ☕

28 DICOT
Chardstock EX13 7DF. Mr & Mrs F Clarkson. *5m N of Axminster. Axminster to Chard A358 at Tytherleigh to Chardstock. R at George Inn, L fork to Hook, R to Burridge, 2nd house on L.* Home-made teas. Adm £2.50, chd £1. Sats, Suns 5, 6 May; 23, 24 June; 28, 29 July (2-5.30).
3-acre enthusiasts' garden; trees, unusual shrubs and conifers, bog orchids in June. Stream, mixed borders, fish pool, Japanese garden, and other surprises.
⚔ ☕

29 DIPPERS
Shaugh Prior PL7 5HA. Mr R J Hubble & Mrs S M Tracey. *8m NE of Plymouth. Garden 100yds down lane opp church near top of village. Park in village or at Whitethorn PH. No parking in lane but dropping off point for disabled.* Adm £2.50, chd free. Suns, 4, 11, 18 Mar; 22 Apr; Sun 27, Mon 28 May (1-5).
³/₄-acre eco-friendly plantsman's garden containing around 2500 different plants. Emphasis on foliage contrast and all-yr interest. Large colour range of hellebores, extensive collection of dwarf bulbs and alpines in raised beds, troughs, tufa and alpine house. Unusual trees and shrubs. National Collection of dianthus species (pinks). Developing small nature reserve adjacent to garden with wildflower meadow, stream and bluebell wood. Kingcups, yellow flag iris, cowslips, ragged robin, vetches and many other native species abound. 16 bird nest boxes.
⚔ ⊛ NCCPG

30 THE DOWNES
Bideford EX39 5LB. Mr & Mrs R C Stanley-Baker, 01805 622244. *3m NW of Great Torrington. On A386 between Bideford & Torrington. Drive leads off A386 4¹/₂m from Bideford, 2¹/₂m from Torrington. Do not go to Monkleigh.* Adm £2.50, chd 50p. Daily Fri 6 Apr to Sun 10 June. Visitors also welcome by appt, no coaches.
15 acres with landscaped lawns; fine views overlooking fields and woodlands in Torridge Valley; many unusual trees and shrubs; small arboretum; woodland walks, bluebells.
⚔ ⊛

Eco-friendly plantsman's garden containing around 2500 different plants . . .

31 DURCOMBE WATER
Furzehill, Barbrook, Lynton EX35 6LN. Pam & David Sydenham, 01598 753658. *3m S of Lynton. From Barnstaple take A39 towards Lynton. On entering Barbrook go past Total garage (do not turn to Lynton) take the next turn R (about 100yds). Follow this single track rd for 2m, gates on L.* Home-made teas. Adm £2.50, chd free. Sun 27, Mon 28 May (11-5). Visitors also welcome by appt.
Set in Exmoor National Park beside open moorland with superb views, delightfully secluded steeply-terraced garden providing profusion of yr-round colour. Includes conifers, heathers, many old-fashioned annuals and perennials together with trees and shrubs. The garden offers peace and tranquillity enhanced by spring-fed streams and ponds, and waterfalls dropping 40ft via 8 tiered ponds. Fruit and vegetable garden and many unusual features. Large extension in progress (2¹/₂ acres total garden) with ponds, waterfalls, landscaping and small woodland.
☕

32 FEEBERS GARDENS
nr Broadclyst EX5 3DQ. *8m NE of Exeter. From B3181 Exeter to Taunton bear E at Dog Village to Whimple. After 1¹/₂m fork L for Westwood.* Cream teas. Combined adm £3, chd free. Suns 24 June; 22 July; 26 Aug (2-6). 3 cottage gardens in a Devon hamlet.
☕

1 FEEBERS COTTAGE
Mr & Mrs M J Squires, 01404 822118. Visitors also welcome by appt.
Evolving cottage garden of 1 acre - a maze of pathways, herbaceous, shrubs and trees. In spring, 60 different snowdrops; in autumn, colchicums and cyclamen. Caution, paths can be slippery.
& ⚔ ⊛

2 FEEBERS COTTAGE
Bob & Ena Williams
Delightful, colourful urban garden in the middle of two cottage gardens.
&

3 FEEBERS COTTAGE
Richard & Karen Burrell
Contemporary cottage garden with formal vegetable area, established fruit trees, flower beds and rose arbour. Some quirky features incl BBQ house. Numerous places to sit and enjoy a cream tea.
& ⚔ ⊛

FERNHILL
See Somerset & Bristol Area.

FORDE ABBEY GARDENS
See Dorset.

33 ◆ THE GARDEN HOUSE
Buckland Monachorum, Yelverton PL20 7LQ. The Fortescue Garden Trust, 01822 854769, www.thegardenhouse.org.uk. *10m N of Plymouth. Signed off A386 at Yelverton.* Adm £5, chd £2, groups of 10+ £4.50. Pre-booked Christmas lunches and snowdrop walks in winter. Open daily 1 Mar to 31 Oct (10.30-5).
8 acres, incl romantic walled garden surrounding ruins of medieval vicarage. Other areas in pioneering 'new naturalism' style, inspired by great natural landscapes. South African garden, quarry garden, cottage garden, acer glade. Stunning views and more than 6,000 plant varieties. Famous for spring bulb meadow,

rhododendrons, camellias, innovative planting and yr-round colour and interest. 'Where Carol Klein goes for inspiration' ('The Guardian'). Featured on BBC Gardeners' World. Limited wheelchair access.

③④ THE GATE HOUSE
Lee EX34 8LR. Mr & Mrs D Booker, 01271 862409, bookerlee@btopenworld.com. *3m W of Ilfracombe. Park in village car park. Take lane alongside The Grampus public house. Garden is approx 30 metres past inn buildings.* Adm by donation. Open most days May through July but wise to check by phone/email.
2¼ acres, where no chemicals are used, only few minutes walk from the sea and dramatic coastal scenery. Peaceful streamside garden with range of habitats; bog garden, National Collection of Rodgersia, at their best June/July, woodland, herbaceous borders, patio gardens with semi-hardy 'exotics'. Gravel paths.
  NCCPG

③⑤ ◆ GLEBE COTTAGE
Warkleigh EX37 9DH. Carol Klein, 01769 540554, www.glebecottageplants.co.uk. *5m SW of South Molton. On the road between Chittlehamholt and Chittlehampton - 1m from Chittlehamholt.* Adm £3, chd free. Garden & nursery open Weds, Thurs, Fris (10-1, 2-5). For NGS: Suns 6 May; 29 July; 9 Sept (2-5).
1-acre S-facing garden with variety of situations. In spring small woodland garden with stumpery, hellebores and pulmonarias is interesting. Terraced beds and 'brick' garden with many newly-planted areas, including hot summer and autumn flowers and foliage. Home of BBC Gardeners' World presenter; BBC Features 'Grow Your Own Vegetables' and Gardeners' World 'Scent Special' and 'Colour Special'.

③⑥ GORWELL HOUSE
Barnstaple EX32 7JP. Dr J A Marston. *1m E of Barnstaple centre on Bratton Fleming rd. Drive entrance between two lodges on L.* Cream teas May to Sept. Adm £3, chd free. Suns 15 Apr; 20 May; 10 June; 22 July; 2 Sept; 7 Oct (2-6).
Created mostly since 1979, this 4-acre garden overlooking the Taw estuary

has a benign microclimate which allows many rare and tender plants to grow and thrive, both in the open and in the walled garden. Several strategically-placed follies complementing the enclosures and vistas within the garden. Some gravel paths and steep slopes.

GREENCOMBE
See Somerset & Bristol Area.

③⑦ ◆ GREENWAY GARDEN
Galampton nr Brixham TQ5 0ES. The National Trust, 01803 661905, www.nationaltrust.org.uk. *1½m SE of Galmpton. A3022 towards Brixham. R turn signed Galmpton, follow brown signs for Greenway Quay. Entrance 1½m on L. For ferry service from Dartmouth or Dittisham ring 01803 844010.* Adm £5.20, chd £2.60, green transport users £4.40, chd £2.20. Wed to Sat incl, 1 Mar to 6 Oct, (10.30-5). For NGS: Sat 28, Sun 29 Apr (10.30-5).
Renowned for rare half-hardy plants underplanted with native wild flowers. Greenway has an atmosphere of wildness and timelessness, a true secret garden of peace and tranquillity with wonderful views of R Dart.

An atmosphere of wildness and timelessness, a true secret garden of peace and tranquillity . . .

③⑧ HALDON GRANGE
Dunchideock EX6 7YE. Ted Phythian, 01392 832349. *5m SW of Exeter. From A30 at Exeter pass through Ide village to Dunchideock 5m. In centre of village turn L to Lord*

Haldon Hotel, Haldon Grange just past hotel drive. From A38 (S) turn L on top of Haldon Hill follow Dunchideock signs, R at village centre (at thatched house) to Lord Haldon Hotel. Light refreshments & teas. Adm £3, chd free. Apr - Sat 28, Sun 29; May - Sat 5 to Mon 7, Weds 9, 16, 23, Sat 26, Sun 27. Visitors also welcome by appt May to end July, groups of 5+. No coaches.
12-acre well-established garden with camellias, magnolias, azaleas and rhododendrons; rare and mature trees; small lake and ponds with river and water cascades as a feature.

③⑨ HAMBLYN'S COOMBE
Dittisham TQ6 0HE. Bridget McCrum, 01803 722228. *3m N of Dartmouth. From Red Lion Inn follow The Level until it forks & go straight up steep private rd and through 'River Farm' gate. Continue straight on to end of farm track as signed.* Adm £3, chd free. Visitors welcome by appt all yr except July & Aug for groups, max 15. No coaches.
7-acre garden with stunning views across the river to Greenway House and sloping steeply to R Dart at bottom of garden. Extensive planting of trees and shrubs with unusual design features accompanying Bridget McCrum's stone carvings and bronzes. Wild flower meadow and woods. Good rhododendrons and camellias, ferns and bamboos, acers and hydrangeas. Exceptional autumn colour.

HANGERIDGE FARM
See Somerset & Bristol Area.

④⓪ ◆ HARTLAND ABBEY
Hartland, nr Bideford EX39 6DT. Sir Hugh & Lady Stucley, 01884 860225/01237 441234, www.hartlandabbey.com. *15m W of Bideford, 15m N of Bude. Turn off A39 W of Clovelly Cross to Hartland. Abbey between Hartland & Hartland Quay.* House and Garden Adm £8, chd over 9 £2.50, Garden only Adm £4.50, chd £1. House & garden: Weds, Thurs, Suns & BH 1 Apr - 26 May; Suns - Thurs incl 27 May - 30 Sept. Gardens only: Daily except Sats 1 Apr - 30 Sept.
From camellias and bulbs of spring to the deep blue hydrangeas of late summer, this is a magical house and garden full of surprises. Wend your way along paths to the bog garden and fernery designed by Jekyll, lost

since 1914. C18 walled gardens and glasshouses thrive again growing tender and rare plants incl huge Echium pininana. Walk to the beach through carpets of bluebells. Peacocks, black sheep, donkeys. Featured in 'Country Life', 'The Lady' & 'Devon Life'. Limited wheelchair access, steep paths and steps.

41 HEATHERCOMBE
Manaton TQ13 9XE. Claude & Margaret Pike Woodlands Trust, 01647 221222/221350, www.heathercombe.com. *7m NW of Bovey Tracey. From Bovey Tracey take rd to Becky Falls and Manaton. Continue on same rd for 2m beyond village. At Heatree Cross follow sign straight ahead to Heathercombe. At top of hill continue straight ahead to Heathercombe. (From Widecombe take rd past Natsworthy).* Cream teas. **Adm £3, chd free. Sun 1 Apr (2-5.30); Sun 20 May (11-5.30), Sat 26 May (2-5.30), Sun 27 May (11-5.30). Visitors also welcome by appt.**
Tranquil wooded valley 1,000 feet up on Dartmoor provides setting for variety of developing garden areas extending over 30 acres, providing yr-round interest; woodland walks beside streams, ponds and lake amongst snowdrops, daffodils and bluebells; well-labelled 'parkland' plantings incl over 100 varieties of rhododendrons and 400 specimen trees, many providing autumn colour; medieval longhouse summer garden with varied rooms of herbaceous plantings and recently-established wild flower meadow in orchard of West Country fruit trees; sandy paths. Featured in Dartmoor 'Country Magazine'.

42 ◆ HEDDON HALL
Parracombe EX31 4QL. Mr & Mrs de Falbe, 01598 763541, www.heddonhallgardens.co.uk. *10m NE of Barnstaple. Follow A39 towards Lynton around Parracombe (avoiding village centre), then turn L down towards the village; entrance 200 yds on L.* **Adm £4, chd free. Suns Feb (12-4); Weds, Suns, May to July (2-5.30). For NGS: Wed 2 May; Sun 29 July (2-5.30).**
Stunning walled garden laid out by Penelope Hobhouse with clipped box and cordoned apple trees, herbaceous secret garden and natural rockery leading to a bog garden and 3 stew ponds. Very much a gardeners' garden, beautifully maintained, with

many rare species, ferns, mature shrubs and trees all thriving in 4 acres of this sheltered Exmoor valley. Gravel paths and some steep slopes. Wheelchair users please call prior to visit.

43 HIGH BARN
Torbryan TQ12 5UW. John & Ann Holl, 01803 812339, john-ann@ambrook.fsnet.co.uk. *4m S of Newton Abbot. From A381 at Causeway Cross, turn into Ipplepen. Take Broadhempston Rd. Turn L at Poole Cross signed to Totnes. Garden 400yds on L.* Cream teas. **Adm £3, chd free (share to Totnes Parochial Church Council). Suns 9, 16 Sept (2-6). Visitors also welcome by appt.**
1-acre garden started in 1992 from cider orchard. Formal areas near house with rill and exuberant planting. Herbaceous borders; use of grasses for textural contrast; island beds with species roses, unusual shrubs and trees blending into countryside with planting to encourage wildlife. Full of autumn colour with berries and perennials. Featured on BBC Spotlight. Grass and gravel paths.

HIGHCROFT GARDENS
See Cornwall.

44 HIGHER KNOWLE
Lustleigh TQ13 9SP. Mr & Mrs D R A Quicke, 01647 277275, quicke@connectfree.co.uk. *3m NW of Bovey Tracey. Take A382 towards Moretonhampstead. In 2½m turn L for Lustleigh; in ¼m L then R; in ¼m steep drive L.* **Adm £2.50, chd free. Suns & Bank Hol Mons 18 Mar to 28 May inclusive (11-6). Visitors also welcome by appt Mar to May incl.**
3-acre woodland garden around 1914 house (not open) with Lutyens-style features. Spectacular views to Dartmoor, sheltered hillside garden usually avoids late frosts. Old oak wood with primroses and bluebells among giant boulders, mature Asiatic magnolias in late March, camellias, new hybrid magnolias, rhododendrons, azaleas and embothriums.

HIGHER TRUSCOTT
See Cornwall.

45 ◆ HOLBROOK GARDEN
Sampford Shrubs, Sampford Peverell EX16 7EN. Martin Hughes-Jones & Susan Proud, 01884 821164, www.holbrookgarden.com.

1m NW from M5 J27. From J27 follow brown signs to 'Minnows' camping site then continue 300 metres up Holbrook Hill (on Holcombe Rogus Rd). **Adm £3, chd free. Tues to Sats, Apr to Oct (9-5). For NGS: Suns, Mons 8, 9 Apr; 6, 7, 27, 28 May; Tue 18, Wed 19 Sept (9-5).**
2-acre S-facing garden with innovative plantings inspired by natural plant populations; vibrant Mediterranean colours; the garden continually evolves - many experimental plantings - wet garden, stone garden. Perfumes, songbirds and nests everywhere. Large crocosmia and pulmonaria collections, National Collection of Heleniums, organic vegetable garden.

46 HOLE FARM
nr Bickington TQ12 6PE. Rev Ian Graham-Orlebar, 01626 821298, ianorlebar@aol.com. *5m NE of Ashburton. From A383 Ashburton to Newton Abbot rd, 3m NE of Ashburton signed Gale, Burne, Woodland. Follow signs to Farlacombe, after 2m, at top of hill, lane on R to Hole Farm.* Home-made teas. **Adm £3, chd £1. Sun 19 Aug (2-5). Visitors also welcome by appt, no access for coaches.**
2½-acre valley garden with woodland, wild garden, 2 ponds, 3 herbaceous borders, bog areas and wildlife plantation. Old farm and buildings, not open.

HOOPER'S HOLDING
See Somerset & Bristol Area.

47 HORTUS
Shrubbery Bungalow, School Lane, Rousdon DT7 3XW. Mark & Marie-Elaine Houghton, 01297 444019, www.hortusnursery.com. *3m E of Seaton. On A3052 midway between Seaton & Lyme Regis, next to Rousdon garage. Look for roadside signs & red phone box.* Home-made teas. **Adm £2.50, chd free. Suns 20 May; 17 June; 15 July; 19 Aug; 16 Sept (11-5). Visitors also welcome by appt.**
Imaginatively-designed garden featuring over 1,000 different plant types. Colour-themed borders planted in naturalistic style for interest through summer and autumn. Pebble beach with seaside plants; gravel terrace with over 100 grasses; scented walk; Mediterranean patio with tender plants in pots. New Jurassic border. Adjacent nursery. Tomato tasting (up to

30 different varieties) Aug and Sept. Educational feature describing plants from the Jurassic period. Featured in 'Easy Gardening', 'Amateur Gardening', 'Devon Life' & 'Sunday Mirror'. Gravel paths.

 ᵴ ⋇ ⊕ ☕

48 NEW IDEFORD GARDENS
4m NNE of Newton Abbot. Between Ideford and Kingsteignton E off A380 (Newton Abbot to Exeter rd). Home-made teas at Coombe Farm. **Combined adm £3, chd free. Suns 10, 17 June (11-5).**
Both gardens are in small hamlets consisting of only a handful of houses, just 2m apart.
☕

NEW COOMBE FARM
Ideford Combe TQ12 3GS. Lyn and Nigel Edwards. *From Exeter S on A380, exit at Eagle Farm (signed B3195 Ideford Combe and Kingsteignton). 150yds L down 'no through rd', 1st on L. From S A380 exit at Eagle Farm (signed Kingsteignton & Ideford Combe B3195). Follow signs to Ideford Combe*
Approx 1 acre, developed over past 8 yrs. Surrounded by mature trees and paddocks with views across valley. Divided into 7 distinct areas with a surprise around each corner. Herbaceous perennials, mixed beds, hedges and trees. Of special interest - many heavily-scented roses and productive kitchen garden.
⋇ ⊕

NEW WELL COTTAGE
Olchard TQ12 3GX. Joe & Wendy Taylor. *S on A380, sharp L exit signed Olchard. Downhill, R opp postbox on pole, garden on L. N from Newton Abbot on A380, exit at Wapperwell. R under dual carriageway to T-junction. L then almost immed R into lane signed Olchard. 1/2m, L opp post box, garden on L*
1/2-acre of lawn/mixed borders on different levels. Beautifully planted with emphasis on creating a cottage garden.
⋇

49 KERSCOTT HOUSE
Swimbridge EX32 0QA. Jessica & Peter Duncan, www.kerscottgarden.co.uk. *6m E of Barnstaple. On Barnstaple-*

Swimbridge-South Molton rd (not A361), 1m E of Swimbridge turn R at top of hill, immed fork L, 100yds on L, 1st gate past house. Home-made teas. **Adm £2.50, chd free. Suns 24 June; 29 July (2-6).**
6 acres surrounding C16 farmhouse (not open) in peaceful rural setting. Garden evolved from scratch since 1985, owner designed/maintained. Naturalistic site-generated planting flowing through vistas combining dry gravel, shady and boggy areas. Atmospheric and harmonious, with living willow constructions, woodland, ponds, wildlife meadow. Unusual plants, Mediterranean garden within roofless barn.
ᵴ ⊕ ☕

Atmospheric and harmonious, with living willow constructions, woodland, ponds, wildlife meadow . . .

50 KIA-ORA FARM & GARDENS
Knowle Lane, Cullompton EX15 1PZ. Mrs M B Disney, 01884 32347, rosie@kiaorafarm.co.uk. *6m SE of Tiverton. J28 of M5. Straight through Cullompton town centre to roundabout, take 3rd exit into Swallow Way, follow rd through houses up to sharp R-hand bend. On bend turn L into Knowle Lane, garden beside Rugby Club.* Cream teas. **Adm £2.50, chd free. Suns, Bank Hol Mons 8, 9, 22 Apr; 6, 7, 20, 27, 28 May; 10, 24 June; 8, 22 July; 5, 12, 26, 27 Aug; 9 Sept (2-6).** Visitors also welcome by appt, coach access & parking, afternoon or evening, home-made cream teas or BBQ.
10 acres of extensively planted gardens and lakes. Charming, peaceful garden with lawns, large lakes, ponds, bog garden and various water features incl ducks and wildlife. Many areas with individual character, mature trees and shrubs, rhododendrons, azaleas, heathers, roses, herbaceous borders

and rockeries. Several new features incl nursery avenue, wisteria walk, novelty crazy golf and many more! Surprises everywhere! Come and see what's new for 2007. Gravel entrance but mostly grass.
ᵴ ⋇ ⊕ ☕

51 ♦ KILLERTON GARDEN
Broadclyst EX5 3LE. The National Trust, 01392 881345, www.nationaltrust.org.uk. *8m N of Exeter. Take B3181 Exeter to Cullompton rd, after 7m fork left & follow NT signs.* **Adm £5.60, chd £2.80. Daily all year (10.30-dusk). For NGS: Mon 9 Apr; Wed 16 May (11-6).**
20 acres of spectacular hillside gardens with naturalised bulbs, sweeping down to large open lawns. Delightful walks through fine collection of rare trees and shrubs; herbaceous borders.
ᵴ ⋇ ⊕ ☕

52 KINGSTON HOUSE
Staverton TQ9 6AR. Mr & Mrs M R Corfield, 01803 762235, www.kingston-estate.co.uk. *4m NE of Totnes. A384 Totnes to Buckfastleigh, from Staverton, 1m due N of Sea Trout Inn, follow signs to Kingston.* Cream teas. **Adm £3.50, chd 50p (share to Animals in Distress). Suns 20 May; 17 June; 15 July (2-6). Evening Opening** £4.50, wine, Sun 24 June (6-8). Visitors also welcome by appt, no coaches.
George II 1735 house grade II (not open). Gardens restored in keeping with the period. Walled garden, rose garden, pleached limes and hornbeams, vegetable garden. Unusual formal garden with santolinas, lavender and camomile. Large new formal parterre. 6000 tulips in bloom mid-May. Gravel paths.
ᵴ ⋇ ⊫ ☕

53 ♦ KNIGHTSHAYES COURT GARDEN
Tiverton EX16 7RQ. The National Trust, 01884 254665, www.nationaltrust.org.uk. *2m N of Tiverton. Via A396 Tiverton to Bampton rd; turn E in Bolham, signed Knightshayes; entrance 1/2m on L.* **House and Garden Adm £7.40, chd £3.70, Garden only Adm £5.90, chd £3. For NGS: Suns 6 May; 16 Sept (11-5).**
Large 'Garden in the Wood', 50 acres of landscaped gardens with pleasant walks and views over Exe valley.

Choice collections of unusual plants, incl acers, birches, rhododendrons, azaleas, camellias, magnolias, roses, spring bulbs, alpines and herbaceous borders; formal gardens; walled kitchen garden.

 ♿ ✱ ☉ ☕

KNOWLE FARM
See Dorset.

54 NEW LAKESLAND
Splatt, Broadwoodkelly, Winkleigh EX19 8EQ. Diana & Bruce Tigwell, 01837 83707. *From B3124 Winkleigh to N Tawton, through Broadwoodkelly 1m SW.* Cream teas. **Adm £3, chd free. Sun 29 July; Sun 26, Mon 27 Aug (2-6). Visitors also welcome by appt.** 4$\frac{1}{2}$-acre garden, winding through hay meadows, developed over last 3 yrs, with a further 4 acres of ancient bluebell and orchid wood. Walled potager with citrus house. Large variety of fruit. 2 large ponds with planted wildlife islands, water lilies and spring-fed spa. Organic and wildlife-friendly. Featured on BBC2 Open Gardens.

✱ ☉ ☕

55 LEE FORD
Budleigh Salterton EX9 7AJ. Mr & Mrs N Lindsay-Fynn, 01395 445894, crescent@leeford.co.uk. *3$\frac{1}{2}$m E of Exmouth. In Knowle village.* **Adm £4 & £1 guided tour. Minimum charge per group £64, chd free. Visitors welcome by appt Mon to Thur (10-4), Apr to Sept, other times by special arrangement.**
Extensive, formal and woodland garden, largely developed in the 1950s, but recently much extended with mass displays of camellias, rhododendrons and azaleas, incl many rare varieties. Traditional walled garden filled with fruit and vegetables, herb garden, bog garden, rose garden, hydrangea collection, greenhouses. Ornamental conservatory and Adam pavilion.

♿

LIFT THE LATCH
See Somerset & Bristol Area.

56 LITTLE ASH FARM
Fenny Bridges, Honiton EX14 3BL. Sadie & Robert Reid, 01404 850271. *3m W of Honiton. Leave A30 at Iron Bridge from Honiton 1m, Patteson's Cross from Exeter $\frac{1}{2}$m, & follow NGS*

signs. Home-made teas. **Adm £3, chd free. Suns 24 June; 22 July; Sat 11, Sun 12 Aug (2-6). Visitors also welcome by appt max 20 people.** Peaceful garden within 1 acre with adjoining farmland and extensive views. Immaculate lawns, new and established trees and shrubs. Three linked ponds and delightful rill through the garden. Fruit and vegetable garden and 'grape' house. Golf putting course. Furniture workshop and showroom. Entry across cobbled yard or gravel drive.

♿ ✱ ⎰ ☕

57 LITTLE CUMBRE
145 Pennsylvania Road, Exeter EX4 6DZ. Dr Margaret Lloyd, 01392 258315. *1m due N of city centre. From town centre take Longbrook St, continue N up hill approx 1m. Near top of hill.* **Adm £3, chd free. Suns 4, 11, 18, 25 Feb; Suns 3, 10, 17, 24 Feb 2008 (12-3.30). Visitors also welcome by appt for groups Feb to June.**
1-acre garden and woodland with extensive views to Dartmoor and Exe Estuary. Many linked areas of garden on sloping site with scented winter shrubs. Wonderful display of snowdrops, about 30 varieties, and colourful hellebores. Camellias and late spring colour. Limited wheelchair access.

♿ ✱ ☉

58 NEW LITTLE WINSORS
Membury EX13 7TG. Janet Andrew. *3$\frac{1}{2}$m NW of Axminster. From A30, follow signs to Ferne Animal Sanctuary and on towards Axminster. R at Star Cross to Membury, then signed. From A35 take B3261. $\frac{3}{4}$m W of Axminster, turn to Membury. L at Star Cross then follow signs. Narrow lanes with passing places.* **Adm £2.50, chd free. Sun 9, Sun 12, Sun 23, Wed 26 Sept (11-5).**
Gerald's Garden. Exposed hillside country garden of 1 acre with distant views, created from a field 7 yrs ago. Thoughtful, flowing design with borders of shrubs, hardy perennials and grasses. Planted for yr-round flower, foliage/bark interest. 2 large ponds and newly-planted bog garden. Ongoing development. Featured on BBC2 Open Gardens. Sloping site, uneven grass.

♿ ✱ ☕

59 NEW LITTLECOURT COTTAGES
EX10 8HF. Geoffrey Ward & Selwyn Kissman. *1m N of Sidmouth seafront. From N take B3176 to Sidmouth seafront/Bedford Car Park. Take Station Rd, past Manor Rd and immed up Seafield Rd. Garden 100yds on R. Regret no parking at garden, car parks nearby.* Home-made teas. **Adm £2.50, chd free. Suns 24 June; 8, 22 July (11-5).**
Oasis of calm in middle of Sidmouth. A series of rooms for the plantaholic. Courtyard gardens behind house; in front, main lawn and water feature. Rare and tender plants everywhere. Exceptional basket colour. Best 'Britain in Bloom' medium garden category.
☕

60 LITTLEHAM HOUSE COTTAGE
11 Douglas Avenue, Exmouth EX8 2EY. Pat & Phil Attard, 01395 266750. *$\frac{1}{4}$m from Exmouth seafront. Go E along seafront, turn L into Maer Rd by Fortes Kiosk, L again. Public car park on R. Short 250yd walk to garden. A little unrestricted parking in Douglas Ave.* Home-made teas. **Adm £2, chd free. Suns 8, 15 Apr (2-5.30). Visitors also welcome by appt.**
This secret garden is full of colour, foliage and flair. Winding paths lead you to horticultural surprises round every corner; spring bulbs, camellias and other treasures abound in this cottage garden. Organically-grown vegetables, herbs and a variety of fruit trees - something for everyone. Featured on BBC2 Open Gardens. Gravel paths.

♿ ☉ ☕

61 ◆ LUKESLAND
Harford, Ivybridge PL21 0JF. Mrs R Howell & Mr & Mrs J Howell, 01752 691749/893390, www.lukesland.co.uk. *10m E of Plymouth. Turn off A38 at Ivybridge. 1$\frac{1}{2}$m N on Harford rd, E side of Erme valley.* **Adm £4 spring, £3.50 autumn, chd free. Suns, Weds & Bank Hols, 1 Apr to 17 June (2-6); 14 Oct to 11 Nov (11-4). Also all Sats in May. Otherwise by appt.**
24 acres of flowering shrubs, wild flowers and rare trees with pinetum in Dartmoor National Park. Beautiful setting of small valley around Addicombe Brook with lakes,

numerous waterfalls and pools. Extensive and unusual collection of rhododendrons, a champion *Magnolia campbelli* and a huge *Davidia involucrata*. Superb spring and autumn colour. Children's Trail - different for spring and autumn each yr.

62 ◆ MARWOOD HILL
Marwood EX31 4EB. Dr J A Snowdon, 01271 342528, www.marwoodhillgarden.co.uk. *4m N of Barnstaple. Signed from A361 & B3230. Outside Guineaford village, opp Marwood church. See website for map.* Adm £4.50, chd free, £4 for groups. Open every day except Christmas Day. For NGS: Fri 13 Apr; Fri 7 Sept (9.30-5.30).
20 acres with 3 small lakes. Extensive collection of camellias under glass and in open; daffodils, rhododendrons, rare flowering shrubs, rock and alpine scree; waterside planting; bog garden; many clematis; Australian native plants and many eucalyptus. National Collections of astilbe, *Iris ensata*, tulbaghia. Dogs on leads welcome. Featured on BBC Gardeners' World and in 'The English Garden'.
&. ⊗ NCCPG 🍵

MELPLASH COURT
See Dorset.

Cyclamen, snowdrops and daffodils and spectacular display of bluebells . . .

63 METCOMBE BRAKE
Higher Metcombe EX11 1SR. Mike & Kate Peirce, 01404 811499, kate@metcombe.plus.com. *2¹/₂ m SW of Ottery St Mary. From A30 (E of Exeter) Daisymount turnoff. Take B3180 S, past 2 L turns to West Hill. Turn L at Tipton Cross & travel 0.7m towards Tipton St John; or from A3052 turn N on B3180 at Halfway Inn. Travel 1.6m & turn R at Tipton Cross etc.* Cream teas. Adm £3, chd free. Sat 28, Sun 29 Apr; Sun 6, Mon 7 May (2-6). Visitors also welcome by appt 15 Mar - 31 May.
Delightful woodland garden with much original 1930s planting, yet in constant

state of evolution. Stunning examples of scented loderi rhododendrons along with many others. Lots of azaleas and old camellias. New acer feature, cyclamen, snowdrops and daffodils in season and spectacular display of bluebells. 6 acres. Garden will not open if very windy. Wheelchair access to most parts of garden.
&. ⊗ 🍵

64 MILLAND FARM
nr Northlew EX20 3BX. Julia & John Barton, 01837 810313, milland.farm@btopenworld.com. *5m NW of Okehampton. Leave A30 at Sowton Cross Services. W end of Okehampton bypass A386 towards Bideford & Torrington. Approx 3m at Hilltown Cross turn L towards Northlew. 3m turn R at bottom of steep hill towards Inwardleigh. Garden is 2nd entrance on L.* Home-made teas. Adm £2, chd free. Suns 10 June; 8 July; 5 Aug (11-6). Visitors also welcome by appt.
1-acre garden surrounded by fields and river in sheltered valley location. Garden features colour-themed herbaceous borders, S-facing gravel garden and aromatic herb garden. The 1¹/₂-acre meadow provides a wonderful habitat for many species of wild flowers as well as many different butterflies.
🐾 ⊗ 🍵

65 MORETONHAMPSTEAD GARDENS
TQ13 8PW. *12m W of Exeter & N of Newton Abbot. On E slopes of Dartmoor National Park. Parking at both gardens.* Cream teas. Combined adm £3.50, chd free. Sat 26, Sun 27, Mon 28 May; Sat 2, Sun 3 June (2-6).
Two complementary gardens of differing character in the geographical centre of Devon, close to the edge of Dartmoor. Superb walking country. Dogs on leads welcome.
🍵

MARDON
Graham & Mary Wilson. *From centre of village, head towards church, turn L into Lime St. Bottom of hill on R*
Spacious and well-maintained 4-acre garden surrounding Edwardian house (not open) in small Dartmoor coombe. Formal terraces leading from rose garden to large lawn with long herbaceous border and lower wildlife meadow bordering

extensive rhododendron planting. Woodland walk along stream leading to fernery and pond with thatched boathouse, in richly-planted setting. Productive vegetable garden.
&.

SUTTON MEAD
Edward & Miranda Allhusen, 01647 440296, miranda@allhusen.co.uk. *¹/₂ m N of village on A382. R at de-restriction sign.* Visitors also welcome by appt.
3¹/₂-acre garden of contrasts on gently-sloping hillside. Woodland of mature and recent plantings, hornbeam tunnel and rill fed round pond. Potager vegetable garden with unusual concrete greenhouse. Granite walls mingling with imaginative planting of trees and shrubs. Croquet lawn, rhododendrons and azaleas. Spring-fed ponds with granite seat at water's edge. Bog garden and new orchard. Fine views of Dartmoor from all corners of garden.
&. ⊗

66 MOTHECOMBE HOUSE
Holbeton PL8 1LA. Mr & Mrs A Mildmay-White. *From A379 between Yealmpton & Modbury turn S for Holbeton. Continue 2m to Mothecombe.* Cream teas. Adm £3.50, chd free. Sat 5, Sun 6 May (2-5).
Walled gardens, herbaceous borders. Orchard with spring bulbs; camellia walk and flowering shrubs. Bog garden; streams and pond; bluebell woods leading to private beach. Queen Anne house, not open. Gravel paths, some slopes.
&. 🐾 ⊗ 🍵

67 NETHERCOTT HOUSE
Iddesleigh, nr Winkleigh EX19 8BG. Farms for City Children. *3m NE of Hatherleigh. 5m from Winkleigh. From Hatherleigh follow signs to Iddesleigh. After approx 3m turn L at Week Cross. 2nd entrance on L. Parking in adjacent field.* Cream teas. Adm £2, chd free. Sun 22 July (2-5.30).
Working Victorian walled garden. This garden is used to grow a variety of vegetables for visiting children. As part of the children's week they help with planting and sowing. Vegetables are used in the kitchen for the children's meals. Gravel paths.
&. 🐾 ⊗ 🍵

68 NEWTON FARM
Hemyock EX15 3QS. Mr & Mrs J F J
M Ward, 01823 680410. ½ m S of
Hemyock. On Old Dunkeswell Abbey
Rd, from Wellington take Monument
Hemyock Rd in centre of Hemyock,
turn L by pump. From Honiton take
Taunton rd top of hill L to Dunkeswell
Cross aerodrome, turn R at first major
Xrds, follow signs. Home-made teas.
Adm £2.50, chd free. Sats, Suns,
Weds 3, 4, 10, 11 Mar; 26, 27 May;
2, 3, 6, 9, 10, 23, 24, 27, 30 June;
1, 11, 14, 15, 18, 28, 29 July;
4, 5, 8, 11, 12, 15 Aug; 22, 23, 29,
30 Sept. Weekends (10-6); Weds
(2-6) Visitors also welcome by appt.
5 acres in Blackdown Hills with views
over Culm Valley. S-facing garden: 8
large herbaceous borders, young
maze, hornbeam walk, iris and
hemerocallis garden. N garden: dwarf
rhododendrons, dwarf conifers and
pines. National Collections Gentianas
and Rhodohypoxis, bog. Woodland
garden, many rare and unusual trees.
Planting and development continue.
New 1½ acres open grown Iris ensata
and hemerocallis for the visitor to walk
through. Wild flower meadow approx
3 acres. Deep lake, 2 ponds.
   NCCPG 💮

**69 NEW NORTH BORESTON
FARM**
TQ9 7LD. Rob & Jan Wagstaff,
01548 821320. 5m S of Totnes.
From A381 Totnes to Kingsbridge
rd, at Halwell take rd to Moreleigh.
From edge of Moreleigh village,
follow yellow NGS signs. Home-
made teas. Adm £3, chd free.
Suns, Mons 6, 7 May; 19, 20 Aug
(2-5). Visitors also welcome by
appt Apr to Sept.
C17 farmhouse with steeply-
sloping 3-acre garden of very
different areas, plus 2-acre bluebell
wood. Rhododendrons and
camellias, over 100 varieties of
each. Good range of hydrangeas.
Herbaceous, fuchsias and acers.
Large spring-fed ponds, stream.
Collection of unusual crocosmias
and hemerocallis. Bridge to exotic
garden with palms, bamboos,
bananas, tropical bulbs and many
rare and unusual plants. Orchard.
Featured in 'Devon Life' and 'The
English Garden'. Some steep
slopes and unfenced ponds.
☒ ⊛ ⊨ 💮

Exotic
garden with
palms,
bamboos,
bananas
and tropical
bulbs . . .

70 THE OLD GLEBE
Eggesford EX18 7QU. Mr & Mrs
Nigel Wright. 20m NW of Exeter. Turn
S off A377 at Eggesford stn (halfway
between Exeter & Barnstaple), cross
railway & River Taw, drive straight uphill
(signed Brushford) for ¾ m; turn R into
bridleway. Home-made teas. Adm
£2.50, chd £1 (share to Chulmleigh
& District Abbeyfield). Sat 19, Suns
20, 27, Mon 28 May (2-5).
7-acre garden of former Georgian
rectory (not open) with mature trees
and several lawns, courtyard, walled
herbaceous borders, bog garden and
small lake; emphasis on species and
hybrid rhododendrons and azaleas,
750 varieties. Adjacent rhododendron
nursery open by appt.
& ☒ ⊛ ☕

71 NEW THE OLD RECTORY
Ashford EX31 4BY. Mrs Ann
Burnham, 01271 377408. 3m W of
Barnstaple. A361 to Braunton. At
end of dual carriageway, R to
Ashford. Approx 1m, follow rd
round to L, 1st house on L. Adm
£2.50, chd free. Suns 10 June; 1
July; 5 Aug; 9 Sept (11-6).
Visitors also welcome by appt.
Recently-created garden of approx
1½ acres. Open, S-facing with
superb views of Taw Estuary. Top
garden has been redesigned with
new and interesting planting.
Lower garden, previously a
paddock, now included in flower
garden.
& ⊛ ⊨

**THE OLD RECTORY,
NETHERBURY**
See Dorset.

72 THE OLD VICARAGE
West Anstey EX36 3PE. Mr & Mrs
Moss. 9m E of South Molton. From
South Molton 9m E on B3227 to
Jubilee Inn. Sign to West Anstey. Turn
L for ¼ m then dog-leg L then R
following signs. Through Yeomill to T-
junction. R following sign for ½ m.
Garden 1st house on L. Cream teas.
Adm £2, chd free. Fri 18 May to Sun
20 May; Fri 6 July to Sun 8 July (2-
5.30).
Croquet lawn leads to multi-level
garden overlooking three large ponds
with winding paths and overviews.
Brook with waterfall flows through
garden past fascinating thatched
summerhouse. Benched deck
overhangs first pond. Features mixed
rhododendrons in spring and large
collection of Japanese iris in summer.
💮

73 NEW THE ORANGERY
Mamhead EX6 8HE. Sir Malcolm
& Lady Field. 8m S of Exeter.
From Exeter: A380, up steep hill,
1st L before bridge at top, L at end
of slip road. From W: A380, L to
Mamhead, 1st R in woods, over
Xrds, down hill, 1st L at tiny Xrds. L
down drive at black & white
Dawlish Lodge. From Starcross:
Up hill to A380. 2½ m, L to
Mamhead House. Cream teas.
Adm £3.50, chd free. Sat 16, Sun
17 June (12-5).
Robert Adam C18 orangery (not
open) surrounded by 7 acres of
Capability Brown landscaping, incl
original cedar trees. Garden being
restored and redesigned with help
of national designer Georgia
Langton. Stunning views down to
Exe Estuary. New planting of
rhododendrons, camellias, azaleas
and hydrangeas. Romantic hidden
lake among trees. Ice house and
steep woodland walks. Local
produce.
⊛ ☕

**74 NEW ♦ OTTER
NURSERIES**
Gosford Road, Ottery St Mary
EX11 1LZ. Malcolm & Marilyn
White, 01404 815815 ext 241,
helen@otternurseries.co.uk.
Follow brown tourist signs on A30
Honiton to Exeter rd. Adm £4 incl
tea/coffee, chd free. For NGS:
Tues 17 Apr; 1, 15 May; 18 Sept
(10 onwards - please pre-book
with Helen Wagstaffe).

Not a garden but a fascinating 'behind the scenes' tour of Devon's favourite garden centre. Owner Marilyn White guides you around nursery growing areas. Spring tours look at young plants raised to bring gardens to glorious summer colour. Autumn tour reveals the secrets of perfect poinsettias, colourful cyclamen, autumn and winter plants.

⑦⑤ ◆ OVERBECK'S
Sharpitor, Salcombe TQ8 8LW. The National Trust, 01548 842893, www.nationaltrust.org.uk. 1½m SW of Salcombe. Follow NT signs. Adm £5.80, chd £2.90, family (1 adult) £8.70. For NGS: Sun 6 May; Wed 27 June (11-6).
7-acre exotic coastal garden, Grade II* listed, with rare plants and shrubs; spectacular views over Salcombe estuary. Garden tour 1.30.

⑦⑥ NEW OWLS BARN
The Chestnuts, Aylesbeare EX5 2BY. Pauline & Ray Mulligan. 3m E of Exeter airport. A3052 Exeter to Sidmouth, turn L at Halfway Inn. ½m, park in Village Way. Garden on R past school. From Ottery St Mary, go through West Hill, L onto B3180, R at Tipton X. At Aylesbeare, L through village, garden signed on L. Home-made teas. Adm £2.50, chd free. Sat 9, Sun 10 June (2-5.30).
Peaceful ¾-acre village garden - a haven for wildlife. Small woodland, natural bog with pond, gravel areas and Mediterranean bed made on N-facing slope of heavy clay. Contrasting foliage with plenty of unusual perennials, grasses, billowing roses, clematis, fruit and vegetables. Imaginatively-designed with surprises round every corner. Featured on BBC2 Open Gardens. Wheelchair access to most areas.

⑦⑦ 38 PHILLIPPS AVENUE
Exmouth EX8 3HZ. Roger & Brenda Stuckey, 01395 273636, stuckeysalpines@aol.com. From Exeter, turn L just before 1st set of T-lights in Exmouth into Hulham Rd then 1st L. Adm £1.50, chd free. Suns 11, 25 May; 1, 8, 15 Apr; 13, 27 May; 3, 17 June; 8, 29 July; 26 Aug; 2 Sept (2-5). Visitors also welcome by appt.

Small highly-specialised suburban garden with extensive collection of alpine and rock garden plants in scree beds, rock gardens, troughs and tufa bed. Many rare and unusual specimens. Small nursery attached to garden. Featured in RHS 'The Garden', 'Devon Life' and BBC 'Gardeners' World'.

⑦⑧ PIKES COTTAGE
Madford, Hemyock EX15 3QZ. Christine Carver, 01823 680345, bridget.carver@btinternet.com. 7m N of Honiton. Off A30 to Wolford Chapel & through Dunkeswell towards Hemyock, then follow signs from Gypsy Cross. Or 7m S of Wellington off M5 J26 to Hemyock, then follow signs. Turn in at gates opp Madford Farm & up farm track. Cream teas. Adm £2.50, chd free. Sats, Suns, Bank Hol Mons 5, 6, 19, 20, 26, 27, 28 May; 30 June; 1, 21, 22 July; 25, 26, 27 Aug; 29, 30 Sept (2-6). Visitors also welcome by appt Mar to Oct. Coaches must stop at Hemyock, minibuses can be hired from Redwoods Coaches.
Set in 19 acres of bluebell woods (hilly access). 6 acres of cultivated garden incl herb area, scree, shrubs, Antipodean and sensory gardens. 1½-acre lawn slopes to large pond. Steps up to arboretum. Seating. Wisteria tunnel. Model village and nature trail for children.

Surprises round every corner . . .

⑦⑨ PINE COTTAGE
No 1 Fourways, Eggesford EX18 7QZ. Dick & Lorna Fulcher. 4m SW of Chulmleigh. Turn S off A377 at Eggesford stn (halfway between Exeter & Barnstaple). 1m uphill beside war memorial cross. Parking in field beside Tarka Trail. Adm £1.50, chd free (share to Friends of Eggesford All Saints Trust). Sat 28, Sun 29, Mon 30 July (2-5).
Small plantsman's garden with a variety of hardy and tender perennials incl meconopsis, primulas, crocosmia and hedychiums etc. Many different plants propagated on site in nursery. National Collection of agapanthus, at their best in July and August.
⊛ NCCPG

⑧⓪ ◆ PLANT WORLD
St Marychurch Road, Newton Abbot TQ12 4SE. Ray Brown, 01803 872939, www.plant-world-seeds.com. 1½m from Penn Inn roundabout. Follow brown tourist signs at the end of the A380 dual carriageway from Exeter. Adm £3, chd free. 31 Mar to 14 Oct incl (9-5).
The 4 acres of landscape gardens with fabulous views have been called Devon's 'Little Outdoor Eden'. Representing each of the five continents, they offer an extensive collection of rare and exotic plants from around the world. National Collection of Primula (sect Cortusoides). Superb mature cottage garden and Mediterranean garden will delight the visitor. Choice plants seen in garden are sold in our plantsman's nursery. Featured in 'The Telegraph' and on BBC TV.
⊛ NCCPG ☕

⑧① PLEASANT VIEW
Newton Abbot TQ12 6DG. Mr & Mrs B D Yeo. 2m from Newton Abbot. Two Mile Oak, nr Denbury. On A381 to Totnes. R at Two Mile Oak PH signed Denbury. ¾m on L. Adm £2.50, chd free. Weds 2, 9, 16 May; Sun 20 May; Weds 23, 30 May (2-5).
2-acre plantsman's garden surrounded by open countryside with far reaching views. S-facing over limestone with a wide range of choice and uncommon shrubs in island beds. Many collections of different plants incl berberis, viburnum, olearia, shrubby lonicera, abelia, philadelphus, salvias and many other semi-hardy plants, giving colour all season. Additional 2-acre field planted as a meadow with individual specimen shrubs. Buddleia and other features to encourage wildlife. Adjacent nursery.

⑧② PORTINGTON
nr Lamerton PL19 8QY. Mr & Mrs I A Dingle. 3m NW of Tavistock. From Tavistock B3362 to Launceston. ¼m beyond Blacksmiths Arms, Lamerton, fork L (signed Chipshop). Over Xrds (signed Horsebridge) first L then L again (signed Portington). From Launceston turn R at Carrs Garage and R again (signed Horsebridge), then as above. Home-made teas. Adm £2, chd free (share to Plymouth Samaritans). Suns 10, 17 June (2-5.30).
Garden in peaceful rural setting with fine views over surrounding

countryside. Mixed planting with shrubs and borders. Walk through woodland and fields to small lake.

✿ ☕

POUNDSTOCK GARDENS
See Cornwall.

83 PROSPECT HOUSE
Lyme Road, Axminster EX13 5BH. Peter Wadeley, 01297 631210, wadeley@onetel.com. *From Axminster town centre (Trinity Square) proceed uphill past George Hotel into Lyme St & Lyme Rd. Garden approx 1/2 m up rd on R, just before petrol stn.* Home-made teas. **Adm £2.50, chd free. Sats, Suns 9, 10 June; 4, 5 Aug (1.30-5.30). Visitors also welcome by appt.**
1-acre plantsman's garden hidden behind high stone walls and with Axe valley views. Well-stocked borders with rare shrubs and colourful perennials, many reckoned to be borderline tender. 140 varieties of salvia, some for sale. A gem, not to be missed.

⋊ ✿ ☕

84 REGENCY HOUSE
Hemyock EX15 3RQ. Mrs Jenny Parsons, 01823 680238. *8m N of Honiton. M5 J26. From Hemyock take Dunkeswell-Honiton rd. Entrance 1/2 m on R from Catherine Wheel PH & church.* Disabled parking (only) at house. Cream teas. **Adm £3.50, chd £1.75. Suns 10, 24 June (11-6). Visitors also welcome by appt, no coaches.**
5-acre plantsman's garden, approached across a private ford. Walled vegetable and fruit garden, lake, ponds, bog plantings and sweeping lawns. The shelter afforded by S slope allows many unusual and slightly tender plants. Visitors provided with comprehensive plant list and map. Gravel and grass, sloping paths.

♿ ⋊ ✿ ▱ ☕

85 ◆ RHS GARDEN ROSEMOOR
Great Torrington EX38 8PH. The Royal Horticultural Society, 01805 624067, www.rhs.org.uk/rosemoor. *1m SE of Great Torrington. On A3124 to Exeter.* **Adm £6, chd £2, under 6 free. Every day except Christmas Day (see website for details).**
65-acre plantsman's garden plus woodlands; rhododendrons (species and hybrids), ornamental trees and shrubs, woodland garden, species and old-fashioned roses, scree and raised beds with alpine plants, arboretum.

2000 roses in 200 varieties, two colour-theme gardens, herb garden, potager, 220yds of herbaceous border, large stream and bog garden, cottage garden, foliage and fruit and vegetable garden.

♿ ⋊ ✿ ☕

86 ◆ ROCK HOUSE GARDEN
Station Hill, Chudleigh TQ13 0EE. Mrs D B & B Boulton, 01626 852134, www.therockgardens.co.uk. *8m SW of Exeter. A38 Exeter to Plymouth signed Chudleigh. S edge of town. Entrance at Rock Nursery.* **Adm £3, chd £1.50. For NGS: Suns 1, 22 Apr; 20 May; 24 June; 22 July; 2, 16, 23 Sept; 7 Oct (9-5).**
Garden in ancient bishop's palace quarry with massive limestone rock. Delights for all seasons. Rare and unusual trees and shrubs. Massed bulbs in spring. Autumn brings one of the finest displays of cyclamen. Cave and ponds with koi and orfe. Walk with spectacular views of Dartmoor and access to Chudleigh rock, glen and waterfall.

✿ ☕

87 ST MERRYN
Higher Park Road, Braunton EX33 2LG. Dr W & Mrs Ros Bradford, 01271 813805, www.st-merryn.co.uk. *5m W of Barnstaple. In centre of Braunton turn R at T-lights round Nat West Bank. At top of Heanton St turn L and immed R into Lower Park Rd. Continue until you see Tyspane Nursing Home on L then turn L into unmarked lane & R at top. Pink house 200yds on R. Parking where available.* Home-made teas. **Adm £2.50, chd free. Suns 22 Apr; 20 May; 17 June (12-5). Visitors also welcome by appt.**
Sheltered 2/3-acre cottage-style garden with emphasis on scent and colour and planned for all-yr interest. Small fish ponds, thatched summerhouse, rockery. New areas of scented rhododendrons, azaleas and camellias; shrub and herbaceous borders with seating and winding paths set off by lawns and mature trees.

♿ ⋊ ✿ ▱ ☕

88 ◆ SALTRAM HOUSE
Plympton PL7 1UH. The National Trust, 01752 336500 Ms P Hammond, www.nationaltrust.org.uk. *3m E of Plymouth. S of A38, 2m W of Plympton.* **Adm £4, chd £2. All yr, Sat to Thur. Mar to Oct (11-5); Nov to**

Feb (11-4). For NGS: Fri 4, 25 May (11-5).
20 acres with fine specimen trees; spring garden; rhododendrons and azaleas. C18 orangery and octagonal garden house. (George II mansion with magnificent plasterwork and decorations, incl 2 rooms designed by Robert Adam). Good variety of evergreens, incl many tender and unusual shrubs, esp from the southern hemisphere. Long grass areas with bulbs and wild flowers, new developments. Gallery with arts and crafts for sale. Garden tours available, trails for all ages.

♿ ⋊ ✿ ☕

89 SCHOOL HOUSE
Little Torrington, Torrington EX38 8PS. Mr & Mrs M Sampson, 01805 623445, mjsampsonlt@btopenworld.com. *2m S Torrington on A386. Village of Little Torrington signed, follow signs to village green, park here, walk 50yds along bridle path to School House.* Home-made teas at Village Hall. **Adm £2.50, chd free. Sun 1 July (2-5.30). Visitors also welcome by appt June/July only.**
2/3-acre informally planted cottage garden. Wildlife pond with adjacent 'natural' planting under old apple tree. 2 ornamental pools. Arbour and pergola with a variety of climbers. Trees, shrubs, herbaceous and annual planting with some colour-themed areas. Small raised bed for alpines. Model railway operating.

⋊ ✿ ☕

90 ◆ SHAPCOTT BARTON ESTATE
(East Knowstone Manor), East Knowstone, South Molton EX36 4EE. Anita Allen, 01398 341664. *13m NW of Tiverton. J27 M5 take Tiverton exit. 61/2 m to roundabout, take exit South Molton 10m, on A361. Turn R signed Knowstone (picnic area). Leave A361 at this point, travel 11/4 m to Roachhill, through hamlet, turn L at Wiston Cross, entrance on L 1/4 m.* **Adm £2.50, chd free. Open by appt non-NGS days. For NGS: Sat 14, Sun 15, Thur 19, Wed 25 July; Wed 1, 8, Thur 9 Aug (11-4.30).**
Very large garden of 200-acre estate. Restored old fish ponds and woodland garden around Culm Measures; stream and peat bog areas. National Collection of Shasta Daisies (*Leucanthemum superbum*) (over 70 cultivars). Orchard planted with

Clearings blaze with wild flowers and survivor garden flowers . . . benches to sit and stare . . .

unusual fruit trees, a 'Jardin paysan' with naturalistic planting to encourage wildlife. Over 70 different cultivars of the butterfly bush Buddleia davidii, grown to encourage native butterflies. The rare swallowtail butterfly was found here and photographed in 2006. Picnics welcome, many seats and tables. Featured in 'Devon Country Gardener'. Local press and radio coverage. Some parts difficult to access by the less able-bodied.
 NCCPG

91 SHERWOOD
Newton St Cyres, Exeter EX5 5BT. John & Prue Quicke, 01392 851216. *2m SE of Crediton. Off A377 Exeter to Barnstaple rd, ³/₄m Crediton side of Newton St Cyres, signed Sherwood, entrance to drive in 1³/₄m.* **Adm £3, chd free (share to Newton St Cyres Parish Church). Every Sun, 7 Jan 2007 to 24 Feb 2008 (2-5). Visitors also welcome by appt, access for coaches reasonable with care.**
15 acres comprising 2 steep valleys. Mature trees, wild daffodils, primroses, bluebells and other wild flowers; extensive collections of magnolias, camellias, rhododendrons, azaleas (mainly deciduous), heathers, acers, cotoneasters, hostas, hydrangeas, buddleias, berberis and other ornamental trees and shrubs. National Collections of magnolias, Knap Hill azaleas and berberis. New woodland area being planted with shade-loving perennials, incl epimedium. Featured in RHS 'The Garden'. Steep slopes, ponds.
NCCPG

92 SHOBROOKE PARK GARDENS
Crediton EX17 1DG. Dr & Mrs J R Shelley, 01363 775153, jack@shobrookepark.com. *1m NE of Crediton. On A3072.* **Cream teas. Adm £3, chd free. Sats 21 Apr; 5 May; 16 June (2-5). Visitors also welcome by appt April to June for groups of 15+.**
15-acre woodland garden laid out in mid-C19 incl extensive Portland Stone terraces with views over 200-acre park with ponds. In process of being

restored with extensive new planting amongst old rhododendrons incl reconstructed Victorian rose garden.

93 SOUTH KENWOOD
Oxton, nr Kenton EX6 8EX. Sir John & Lady Jennings. *6m S of Exeter. From A380 (Exeter to Newton Abbot-Torquay rd) turn L signed Mamhead & Starcross. After 2m turn L for Oxton. Take next L for Oxton. In 1m turn L to South Kenwood. From coast rd turn R at Starcross into New Road. After ¹/₄m turn R for Mamhead. In 2m turn R for Oxton, then as above.* **Cream teas. Adm £2.50, chd free. Suns 24 June; 1 July (2-5).**
10-acre garden in wooded valley nestling under the Haldon hills. Streams running through, well-planted ponds, bog gardens and small lake with wildfowl. Colour-themed borders, lawns, terrace, pergola walk, rose garden and conservatory. Masses of interesting planting, shrubs and mature trees.

94 SOUTH TAWTON GARDENS
EX20 2LP. *6m E of Okehampton. Park in village square, walk through churchyard.* **Cream teas at Glebe House. Combined adm £3, chd free. Sat 9, Sun 10, Sat 23, Sun 24 June (2-6).**
Small village built around Parish Church. Historic church rooms recently restored open to public. Art exhibition in church house (small exhibition of paintings by garden owner).

BLACKHALL MANOR
Roger & Jacqueline Yeates
Small cottage garden around C16 thatched listed house (not open) on N edge of Dartmoor. Planted with trees, shrubs and herbaceous perennials to give interest throughout the year. Cobbled paths and pond.

GLEBE HOUSE
John & Welmoed Perrin. *Turning next to Seven Stars. Glebe House*

facing at end of rd
Space with backdrop of hills, moor and meadow. A ha-ha conceals a young vineyard; mature trees frame two ponds and living arches. Rockeries support well stocked borders; an original courtyard creates a small orangerie.

95 NEW SOUTHCOMBE GARDENS
Dartmoor, Widecombe-in-the-Moor TQ13 7TU. *6m W of Bovey Tracey. Take B3387 from Bovey Tracey. After village church take rd SW for 200yds then sharp R, signed Southcombe, up steep hill. After 200yds, pass C17 farmhouse & park on L. Alternatively park in public car park in village and walk.* **Cream teas 27/28 May only at Southcombe Barn. Combined adm £3.50, chd free. Suns 13, 27, Mon 28 May; Suns 3, 10, 17 June (2-5).**
Village famous for its Fair, Uncle Tom Cobley and its C14 church - the 'Cathedral of the Moor'. Featured on BBC TV Spotlight.

NEW SOUTHCOMBE BARN
Amanda Sabin & Stephen Hobson
3-acre woodland garden with exotic and native trees between long lawn and rocky stream. Clearings blaze with wild flowers and survivor garden flowers. Benches to sit and stare.

SOUTHCOMBE HOUSE
Widecombe-in-the-Moor. Dr & Mrs JR Seale, 01364 621365. Visitors also welcome by appt, no coaches.
5 acres, SE-facing garden, arboretum and wild flower meadow with bulbs in spring and four orchid species (Early Purple, Southern Marsh, Common Spotted and Greater Butterfly). On steep slope at 900ft above sea level with fine views to nearby tors.

96 SOUTHLEIGH GARDENS
EX24 6JB. *2m W of Colyton. Signs from Hangmans Cross on A3052 or from Hare & Hounds, Putt's Corner on Honiton-Sidmouth rd, then 2nd turning on L past Farway Wildlife Park, via 2m lane. Parking at village hall or considerably in rd below.* Cream teas

in Village Hall opp Popes Cottage. **Combined adm £3, chd free. Sat 2, Sun 3 June (2-5.30).**

POPES COTTAGE
Irene & Eric Daniels, 01404 871210. *Next to church.* **Visitors also welcome by appt mid-May to Aug.**
²/₃-acre country garden blending into spectacular valley view. Mixed borders of shrubs, perennials and alpines, some unusual. Small fruit and vegetable section with bulging greenhouse. Artificial stream through small ponds. Emphasis on wildlife.

NEW SOUTH BANK
Jo Connor, 01404 871251. *Nr church.* **Visitors also welcome by appt mid-May to Aug.**
³/₄ acre. Mixed beds, pond, patio garden, orchard, small vegetable plot, shrubberies. Lovely views. Beautiful in spring/early summer. Pergola with swing seat.

97 SOWTON MILL
Dunsford EX6 7JN. A Cooke & S Newton, 01647 252347/252263, sonianewton@sowtonmill.eclipse.co .uk. *7m W of Exeter. From Dunsford take B3193 S for ¹/₂ m. Entrance straight ahead off sharp R bend by bridge. From A38 N along Teign Valley for 8m. Sharp R after humpback bridge.* Home-made teas. **Adm £2.70, chd free (share to Cygnet Training Theatre). Suns 18 Mar (2-5); 9 Sept (2-6). Visitors also welcome by appt.**
4 acres laid out around former mill (not open), leat and river. Part woodland with multitudes of wild flowers in spring, ornamental trees and shrubs, mixed borders and scree. Yr-round interest.

98 SPILLIFORDS WILDLIFE GARDEN
Lower Washfield, Tiverton EX16 9PE. Dr Gavin Haig. *3m N of Tiverton. Take A396 Tiverton to Bampton rd, turn L over iron bridge signed Stoodleigh. Turn L again after crossing bridge marked Washfield, & L again on hill following Washfield sign. Bridge is approx 2m from link rd roundabout. Spillifords is 1st house on L after Hatswell - some 400 metres onwards. Parking in top field through*

double five barred gate. Home-made teas. **Adm £3, chd free. Sun 13 May; Sun 10, Thur 14 June; Sun 1 July (3-5.30).**
Specialist wildlife garden leading down to R Exe. Banks and islands of mixed wild flowers and herbs. Many nesting birds, including flycatchers and warblers, and breeding butterflies. Ponds and marsh areas. Riverside tree house, about 50 nestboxes. Annually 30 different butterflies - including rare Marsh Fritillary. Picnic areas. About 4 acres. Kingfisher, dipper and otter frequent visitors. Please telephone 01884 252422 if weather doubtful. Featured regularly in 'Devon Life'. Some steep slopes.

99 NEW SPRINGDALE
Smeatharpe, Honiton EX14 9RF. Graham & Ann Salmon. *8m N of Honiton. Park at Village Hall, N end of Smeatharpe. Garden approx 5 mins walk, follow signs down bridleway.* Home-made teas. **Adm £3, chd free (share to The Blackdown Support Group). Sat 19, Sun 20, Mon 21 May; Sat 30 June; Sun 1, Mon 2 July (2-6).**
Developing 2-acre plantsman's garden set amidst 18 acres of SSSI in magnificent Blackdown Hills. Extensive planting of choice trees, shrubs and perennials enhances this varied habitat. Waterside and alpine beds, complemented by cacti and auricula collections. Damp, acid garden designed for plants, wildlife and people to enjoy. Public bridleway through adjoining SSSI. Water-resistant footwear advised.

Town garden landscaped with small ponds and 7ft waterfall . . .

100 NEW SQUIRRELS
98 Barton Road, Torquay TQ2 7NS. Graham & Carol Starkie. *From Newton Abbot take A380 to Torquay. After Focus DIY on L, turn L at T-lights up Old Woods Hill. 1st L into Barton Rd, bungalow 200yds on L.* **Adm £2, chd free. Sat 4, Sun 5, Sat 11 Aug (2-5).**
Plantsman's small town garden landscaped with small ponds and 7ft waterfall. Interlinked areas incl Japanese, Italianate, Tropical. Specialising in fruit incl peaches, figs, kiwi. Tender plants incl bananas, tree fern, brugmansia, lantanas, oleanders, abutilons, bougainvilleas. Colourful pergolas and lawn area. Environmentally friendly water feature. Winner of Environmentally Friendly Garden section of Bay Blooms Competition Torbay.

STOWLEYS
See Somerset & Bristol Area.

101 TAIKOO
Belstone EX20 1QZ. Richard & Rosamund Bernays, 01837 840217, richard@bernays.net. *3m SE of Okehampton. Fork L at stocks in middle of village. 300yds on R. Park in field.* Cream teas. **Adm £3, chd free. Suns 6 May; 24 June; Sat 28 July (2-5). Visitors also welcome by appt.**
3-acre hillside moorland garden, restored over past 8yrs. Interesting collections of rhododendrons, fuchsias, hydrangeas, magnolias, camellias, roses and other shrubs and trees. Herb garden and water features. Magnificent views over Dartmoor. Featured on Radio Devon.

102 TAMARISKS
Inner Hope Cove TQ7 3HH. Barbara Anderson, 01548 561745, barbara@tamarisks.fsnet.co.uk. *6m SW of Kingsbridge. Turn off A381 at Malborough between Kingsbridge & Salcombe. 2m further, on entering Hope Cove, turn L at sign to Inner Hope. After ¹/₄ m, turn R into lane beneath Sun Bay Hotel. Tamarisks is next house. Park opp hotel or in lane (larger car park in Outer Hope, follow path leading to Inner Hope into lane).* Home-made teas. **Adm £2.50, chd free (share to Butterfly Conservation & BTO Birdwatch). Tue 17, Wed 18**

July (11-6). Visitors also welcome by appt.

Sloping 1/3 acre directly above sea with magnificent view. Garden is exciting with rustic steps, extensive stonework, ponds, rockeries, feature corners, patios, 'wild' terrace overlooking sea. Very colourful. Demonstrates what can flourish at seaside - notably hydrangeas, mallows, crocosmia, achillea, sea holly, convolvulus, lavender, sedum, roses, grasses, ferns, fruit trees. Bird and butterfly haven. Butterfly Conservation table with representatives and pamphlets. Roman chequerboard herb garden. Featured on Radio Devon.

103 1 TIPTON LODGE

Tipton St John, Sidmouth EX10 0AW. Angela Avis & Robin Pickering, 01404 813371. *3m N of Sidmouth. From Exeter take A3052 towards Sidmouth. L on B3176 at Bowd Inn toward Ottery St Mary. After 1 1/2 m turn into Tipton St John. After village sign, 1 Tipton Lodge is the second driveway on R about 100yds before Golden Lion PH. Parking for disabled only, other parking in village.* Home-made teas. **Adm £2, chd free. Sun 24, Mon 25 June (10-6). Visitors also welcome by appt.**
3/4 acre designed to reflect mid-Victorian house. Formal grass walks between double herbaceous borders and avenue of white weeping roses. Old shrub roses, small woodland area incl tree ferns, potager-style vegetable garden. All organic. Exuberant romantic planting.

TREBARTHA

See Cornwall.

104 THE WATER GARDEN

Wembworthy EX18 7SG. Mr J M Smith. *10m NE of Okehampton. From A377 at Eggesford station follow signs to Wembworthy (2m W). From Winkleigh take Wembworthy to Eggesford rd (2m E). Turn at Xrd sign at Lymington Arms.* Home-made teas. **Adm £2.50, chd free. Sats, Suns, 12 May to 24 June; Mon 28 May (2-6).**
Naturalistic William Robinson-style 1-acre garden with 'wilderness' planting, incorporating exotics and native species around clay pond/swamp area with 60-metre board walk of distressed oak, allowing close inspection of plants and wildlife. Many other water features displayed among irises, ferns, trees, shrubs, clematis and unusual plants.

Some hot, dry, stony slopes. Conservatory. Potager garden. Featured in RHS 'The Garden'.

WAYFORD MANOR

See Somerset & Bristol Area.

105 WEBBERY GARDENS

Alverdiscott EX39 4PS. *2 1/2 m E of Bideford. Either from Bideford (East the Water) along Alverdiscott Rd, or from Barnstaple to Torrington on B3232, take rd to Bideford at Alverdiscott and pass through Stoney Cross.* Home-made teas. **Combined adm £3, chd 50p. Sat 16, Sun 17 June (2-6).**

LITTLE WEBBERY

EX39 4PS. Mr & Mrs J A Yewdall, 01271 858206, jayewdall@surfree.co.uk. Visitors also welcome by appt. Approx 3 acres in valley setting with pond, lake, mature trees and 2 ha-has. Walled kitchen garden with yew and box hedging; greenhouse; rose garden; trellises; shrubs and climbing plants. 3 mature borders. Some gravel paths.

LITTLE WEBBERY COTTAGE

EX39 4PU. Mr & Mrs J A Yewdall
Self-contained cottage garden with wide selection of flowering plants and shrubs incl pergolas with roses, clematis and jasmine.

106 WESTCOTT BARTON

Marwood, Barnstaple EX31 4EF. Howard Frank, 01271 812842, www.westcottbarton.co.uk. *From Barnstaple 4m N to Guineaford, continue N for 1m. Turn L, signed Middle Marwood and Patsford, 2nd L at Westcott Barton sign.* Cream teas. **Adm £3, chd free. Suns, Mons 6, 7, 27, 28 May; 24, 25 June; 26, 27 May (2-6). Visitors also welcome by appt (no large coaches).**
2-acre developing valley garden with stream, bridge and several ponds. Wide variety of planting: rhododendrons, camellias, clematis, hydrangeas, gunnera, rose garden. Masses of interest. Garden surrounds C12 farmhouse (not open) with cobbled courtyard, range of outbuildings and water wheel.

107 WHIBBLE HILL HOUSE

9 Priory Road, Plymouth PL3 5EN. Dr Imogen Montague. *1 1/4 m from centre of Plymouth. Via Mutley Plain & Mannamead Rd. Turn R at Emmanuel Church T-lights into Compton Park Rd. Follow rd downhill until L-hand fork into Priory Rd. House 30yds on L, street parking.* Home-made teas. **Adm £2, chd free. Sat 16, Sun 17 June (11-5). Visitors also welcome by appt.**
Small Georgian walled garden planted in 2003, crammed with extensive collection of bamboos, acers and other exotic and architectural plants mixed with herbaceous perennials. Central formal beds, others more 'jungly'. Wildlife pond, bog garden, tree fern grove and Edwardian conservatory. Sloping garden with many steps.

108 WHITSTONE FARM

Whitstone Lane, Bovey Tracey TQ13 9NA. Katie & Alan Bunn, 01626 832258, katie@whitstonefarm.co.uk. *1/2 m N of Bovey Tracey. From A382 turn toward hospital (signed hospital opp golf range) after 1/3 m turn L at swinging sign 'Private road leading to Whitstone'. Follow lane uphill & bend to L. Whitstone Farm on R at end of long barn. Limited parking.* Tea & cakes. **Adm £3, chd free. Suns 6 May; 16 Sept (2-5).**
Over 3 acres of steep hillside garden with stunning views of Haytor and Dartmoor. An aboretum planted 36yrs ago of over 250 trees from all over the world, including magnolias, camellias, acers, alders, betula and sorbus. Water feature. Garden constantly being updated.

109 NEW ♦ WILDSIDE

Green Lane, Buckland Monachorum PL20 7NP. Mr K & Mrs R Wiley, 01822 855755, www.wildsideplants.com. *1/4 m W of Buckland Monachorum. Follow brown signs to Garden House from A386. Past Garden House, continue str on for 0.7m. Garden 300yds past village on L.* **Adm £3, chd free. Thurs only mid-Mar to end Sept. For NGS: Thurs 10 May; 28 June (10-5).**
Created from field in just 3 yrs by ex Head Gardener of The Garden House. Wide range of habitats and different plant varieties are grown in

a naturalistic style, giving displays of colour throughout the season. Adjacent nursery. Featured in 'The Daily Telegraph'.

110 ◆ WINSFORD WALLED GARDEN
Halwill Junction EX21 5XT. Aileen Birks & Mike Gilmore, 01409 221477, www.winsfordwalledgarden.co.uk. *12m NW of Okehampton. On A3079 follow brown tourism signs from centre of Halwill Junction.* Adm £4.50, chd under 14 free. Daily 1 May to 31 Oct. For NGS: Suns 24 June; 22 July; 26 Aug; 23 Sept (9-5). Walled summer flower garden since 1883. Latest evolution began 1999. The achievement since will amaze and inspire. Summer interest packed with features past and present. Heading towards 4000 varieties. Well-labelled. Original teak greenhouses, huge new alpine house. Highly informative exhibition. Guided tours. Electric mobility vehicles. Gravel paths.

111 WITHLEIGH FARM
Withleigh Village EX16 8JG. T Matheson, 01884 253853. *3m W of Tiverton. On B3137, 10yds W of 1st small 30mph sign on L, entrance to drive by white gate.* Cream teas. Adm £3, chd free (share to Arthritis Research & Cancer Research). Sat 12, Sun 13 May (2-5). Visitors also welcome by appt.

Peaceful undisturbed rural setting with valley garden, 23yrs in making; stream, pond and waterside plantings; bluebell walk under canopy of mature oak and beech; wild flower meadow, primroses and daffodils in spring: wild orchids in June. Dogs on leads.

WOLVERHOLLOW
See Dorset.

112 WOOD BARTON
Kentisbeare EX15 2AT. Mr & Mrs Richard Horton, 01884 266285. *8m SE of Tiverton, 3m E of Cullompton. 3m from M5 J28. Take A373 Cullompton to Honiton rd. After 2m turn L signed Bradfield & Willand on Horn Rd for 1m, turn R at Xrds. Farm drive ½m on L. Bull on sign.* Home-made teas. Adm £3, chd free, concessions £2. Suns 1, 8 Apr (2-5). Visitors also welcome by appt. 2-acre arboretum planted 57yrs ago with species trees on S-facing slope. Magnolias, two davidia, azaleas, camellias, rhododendrons, acers; several ponds and water feature. Autumn colour.

113 NEW WOODY PARK
Bradfield, Cullompton EX15 2RB. Colin & Enid Folds. *½ m E of Willand. M5 J28 towards Honiton. 1st L to Bradfield, follow signs. M5 J27 towards Wellington. R at 1st roundabout to Willand. Follow signs.* Home-made teas.

Adm £3, chd free. Sats, Suns 12, 13, 19, 20 May (2-5). 35-acre water garden with landscaped lakes and ponds created by the owners from a maize field over last 15 yrs. Lakes and islands landscaped with trees, shrubs and marginals. Woodland with bluebells, large collection of hybrid rhododendrons and azaleas. Around house, lawns, beds and koi pond.

114 YONDER HILL
Shepherds Lane, Colaton Raleigh EX10 0LP. Judy McKay & Eddie Stevenson, 01395 567075. *3m N of Budleigh Salterton. On B3178 between Newton Poppleford and Colaton Raleigh, take turning signed to Dotton, then immed R into small lane. ¼m, 1st house on R. Ample parking.* Adm £2.50, chd £1. Every Sun 11 Mar to 28 Oct incl; Fri 6 Apr; Bank Hol Mons 9 Apr; 7, 28 May; 27 Aug (1-5). Visitors also welcome by appt weekdays (11-4). Please tel at 10am to confirm. Peaceful 3¼-acre inspirational paradise. Relax, forget your troubles for a while. Unconventional planting, lots of surprises. Trees, shrubs, herbaceous, ferns, shady walks, sunny glades, young woods, orchard, vegetables. Several collections. Wildlife friendly. Must see to appreciate. Tea/coffee and biscuits in rest room, make it yourself as you like it. Picnics welcome. Wheelchair available.

Devon County Volunteers

County Organisers
Edward & Miranda Allhusen, Sutton Mead, Moretonhampstead, Newton Abbot TQ13 8PW, 01647 440296, miranda@allhusen.co.uk

County Treasurer
Julia Tremlett, Bickham House, Kenn, Nr Exeter EX6 7XL, 01392 832671, jandjtremlett@hotmail.com

Publicity
Alan Davis, Paddocks, Stafford Lane, Colyford EX24 6HQ, 01297 552472, alan.davis@theiet.org

Assistant County Organisers
Central Miranda Allhusen (address as above)
Torbay Jo Gibson, Arcadia, Ashcombe Road, Dawlish EX7 0QW, 01626 862102, hecate105@yahoo.co.uk
North Jo Hynes, Higher Cherubeer, Dolton, Winkleigh EX19 8PP, 01805 804265, hynesjo@gmail.com
Exeter Margaret Lloyd, Little Cumbre, 145 Pennsylvania Road, Exeter EX4 6OZ, 01392 258315,
East Kate Peirce, Metcombe Brake, Higher Metcombe, Ottery St. Mary EX11 1SR, 01404 811499, kate@metcombe.plus.com
North East Diane Rowe, Little Southey, Northcott, Cullompton EX15 3LT, 01884 840545, diane@little-southey.demon.co.uk
South Jo Smith, 2 Homefield Cottage, Sherford, Kingsbridge TQ7 2AT, 01548 531618, jofrancis5@btopenworld.com
South West Michael & Sarah Stone, The Cider House, Buckland Abbey, Yelverton PL20 6EZ, 01822 853285, michael.stone@cider-house.co.uk

DORSET

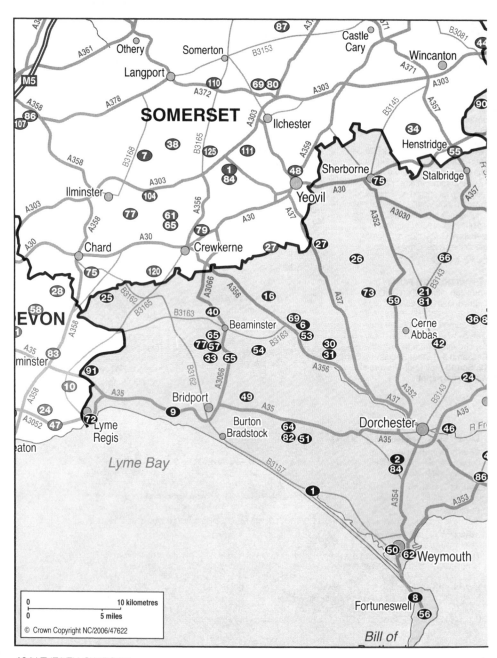

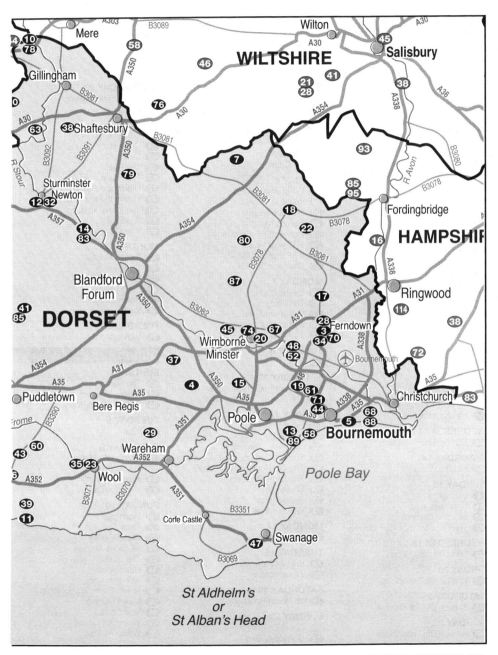

Opening Dates

February

SUNDAY 18
56 Mews Cottage
87 Welcome Thatch

March

SUNDAY 11
27 Frankham Farm
87 Welcome Thatch

SUNDAY 18
76 Shute Farm
78 Snape Cottage Plantsman's Garden

SUNDAY 25
10 Chiffchaffs
35 Herons Mead

April

SUNDAY 1
87 Welcome Thatch

WEDNESDAY 4
18 Cranborne Manor Garden
22 Edmondsham House

FRIDAY 6
19 44 Daws Avenue

SATURDAY 7
49 Knowle Farm

SUNDAY 8
3 Beech Mead
20 Deans Court
35 Herons Mead

MONDAY 9
3 Beech Mead
20 Deans Court
22 Edmondsham House
27 Frankham Farm
42 Ivy House Garden
56 Mews Cottage

WEDNESDAY 11
22 Edmondsham House

SATURDAY 14
60 Moreton Gardens

SUNDAY 15
4 Bexington
21 Domineys Yard
60 Moreton Gardens
64 The Old Rectory, Litton Cheney

WEDNESDAY 18
22 Edmondsham House

FRIDAY 20
47 Knitson Old Farmhouse

SATURDAY 21
47 Knitson Old Farmhouse

SUNDAY 22
47 Knitson Old Farmhouse

71 46 Roslin Road South
88 Wentworth College

WEDNESDAY 25
9 Chideock Manor
22 Edmondsham House
40 Horn Park

SUNDAY 29
6 Broomhill
9 Chideock Manor
15 Corfe Barn
28 The Glade
33 Hatchlands
53 Manor Farm, Higher Wraxall
57 The Mill House

May

THURSDAY 3
41 Ivy Cottage

SUNDAY 6
16 Corscombe House
19 44 Daws Avenue
20 Deans Court
35 Herons Mead
39 Holworth Farmhouse
58 10 Milner Road
68 54 Parkwood Road
87 Welcome Thatch

MONDAY 7
20 Deans Court
23 The Ferns
27 Frankham Farm
42 Ivy House Garden
58 10 Milner Road

TUESDAY 8
62 'Ola'

SATURDAY 12
68 54 Parkwood Road (Evening)
73 The Secret Garden

SUNDAY 13
4 Bexington
28 The Glade
43 Japanese Gardens
64 The Old Rectory, Litton Cheney
65 The Old Rectory, Netherbury
73 The Secret Garden
76 Shute Farm
77 Slape Manor
91 Wolverhollow

MONDAY 14
79 Springhead

TUESDAY 15
49 Knowle Farm
91 Wolverhollow

SATURDAY 19
71 46 Roslin Road South

SUNDAY 20
8 Chesil Gallery
21 Domineys Yard

24 4 Flower Cottage
27 Frankham Farm
37 Highwood Garden
52 Manor Farm, Hampreston
55 Melplash Court
67 Park Homer Drive Gardens
69 Rampisham Manor
71 46 Roslin Road South

TUESDAY 22
62 'Ola'

WEDNESDAY 23
69 Rampisham Manor

SUNDAY 27
12 Coach House
14 Coombe Cottage
15 Corfe Barn
20 Deans Court
28 The Glade
32 Ham Gate
37 Highwood Garden
39 Holworth Farmhouse
43 Japanese Gardens
83 Toad Hall
85 Vine Cottage

MONDAY 28
12 Coach House
15 Corfe Barn
20 Deans Court
23 The Ferns
35 Herons Mead
91 Wolverhollow

TUESDAY 29
91 Wolverhollow

June

SUNDAY 3
23 The Ferns
36 Higher Melcombe
68 54 Parkwood Road

TUESDAY 5
62 'Ola'

SATURDAY 9
18 Cranborne Manor Garden
34 Hazelwood
45 Kingston Lacy

SUNDAY 10
4 Bexington
7 Chalk Cottage
8 Chesil Gallery
19 44 Daws Avenue
28 The Glade
34 Hazelwood
45 Kingston Lacy
52 Manor Farm, Hampreston
56 Mews Cottage
85 Vine Cottage
86 Warmwell House
87 Welcome Thatch

MONDAY 11
79 Springhead

TUESDAY 12
64 The Old Rectory, Litton Cheney

WEDNESDAY 13
7 Chalk Cottage

FRIDAY 15
72 St Michael's House

SATURDAY 16
7 Chalk Cottage (Evening)
44 74 Keith Road
71 46 Roslin Road South
72 St Michael's House (Evening)

SUNDAY 17
7 Chalk Cottage
20 Deans Court
27 Frankham Farm
29 Greenacres
35 Herons Mead
39 Holworth Farmhouse
44 74 Keith Road
63 The Old Rectory, Fifehead Magdalen
71 46 Roslin Road South
78 Snape Cottage Plantsman's Garden
81 Sticky Wicket

TUESDAY 19
7 Chalk Cottage (Evening)

WEDNESDAY 20
2 Ashton Farm
5 Boscombe Beechwood Centre

THURSDAY 21
11 Cliff House (Evening)

SUNDAY 24
2 Ashton Farm
8 Chesil Gallery
11 Cliff House
15 Corfe Barn
30 Greenings
31 Grovestall Farm
50 102 Lanehouse Rocks Road
56 Mews Cottage
82 Tithe Barn House
89 24a Western Avenue

MONDAY 25
30 Greenings
31 Grovestall Farm

WEDNESDAY 27
5 Boscombe Beechwood Centre
9 Chideock Manor
35 Herons Mead
55 Melplash Court
67 Park Homer Drive Gardens

July

SUNDAY 1
9 Chideock Manor
23 The Ferns
33 Hatchlands
57 The Mill House

61 4 Noel Road

MONDAY 2
49 Knowle Farm (Evening)

WEDNESDAY 4
5 Boscombe Beechwood Centre
40 Horn Park
80 Stanbridge Mill

THURSDAY 5
41 Ivy Cottage

SATURDAY 7
44 74 Keith Road
71 46 Roslin Road South
72 St Michael's House (Evening)

SUNDAY 8
4 Bexington
6 Broomhill
8 Chesil Gallery
39 Holworth Farmhouse
44 74 Keith Road
50 102 Lanehouse Rocks Road
56 Mews Cottage
69 Rampisham Manor
71 46 Roslin Road South
72 St Michael's House
87 Welcome Thatch

WEDNESDAY 11
5 Boscombe Beechwood Centre
53 Manor Farm, Higher Wraxall
69 Rampisham Manor

SUNDAY 15
16 Corscombe House
17 Cottesmore Farm
29 Greenacres
36 Higher Melcombe
50 102 Lanehouse Rocks Road
61 4 Noel Road
70 357 Ringwood Road

SUNDAY 22
8 Chesil Gallery
17 Cottesmore Farm
38 Hilltop
50 102 Lanehouse Rocks Road
56 Mews Cottage
86 Warmwell House

THURSDAY 26
38 Hilltop

SUNDAY 29
38 Hilltop
39 Holworth Farmhouse
74 The Secret Garden at Serles House
89 24a Western Avenue

August

WEDNESDAY 1
66 The Old Rectory, Pulham
70 357 Ringwood Road

THURSDAY 2
38 Hilltop

FRIDAY 3
68 54 Parkwood Road (Evening)

SATURDAY 4
47 Knitson Old Farmhouse

SUNDAY 5
8 Chesil Gallery
38 Hilltop
47 Knitson Old Farmhouse
50 102 Lanehouse Rocks Road
66 The Old Rectory, Pulham

MONDAY 6
47 Knitson Old Farmhouse

TUESDAY 7
47 Knitson Old Farmhouse

WEDNESDAY 8
47 Knitson Old Farmhouse

THURSDAY 9
38 Hilltop
47 Knitson Old Farmhouse

FRIDAY 10
47 Knitson Old Farmhouse

SATURDAY 11
47 Knitson Old Farmhouse

SUNDAY 12
4 Bexington
8 Chesil Gallery
21 Domineys Yard
38 Hilltop
47 Knitson Old Farmhouse
56 Mews Cottage
70 357 Ringwood Road
74 The Secret Garden at Serles House

WEDNESDAY 15
6 Broomhill

SUNDAY 19
29 Greenacres
81 Sticky Wicket

SATURDAY 25
74 The Secret Garden at Serles House (Evening)

SUNDAY 26
10 Chiffchaffs
14 Coombe Cottage
17 Cottesmore Farm
20 Deans Court
74 The Secret Garden at Serles House
83 Toad Hall

MONDAY 27
20 Deans Court
74 The Secret Garden at Serles House

September

SUNDAY 2
19 44 Daws Avenue

THURSDAY 6
41 Ivy Cottage

SATURDAY 8
74 The Secret Garden at Serles House (Evening)

SUNDAY 9
4 Bexington
20 Deans Court
24 4 Flower Cottage
52 Manor Farm, Hampreston
53 Manor Farm, Higher Wraxall
74 The Secret Garden at Serles House

SUNDAY 16
74 The Secret Garden at Serles House
88 Wentworth College

SUNDAY 23
49 Knowle Farm
87 Welcome Thatch

October

WEDNESDAY 3
22 Edmondsham House

WEDNESDAY 10
22 Edmondsham House

SUNDAY 14
56 Mews Cottage

WEDNESDAY 17
22 Edmondsham House

SUNDAY 21
21 Domineys Yard

WEDNESDAY 24
22 Edmondsham House

December

SATURDAY 1
68 54 Parkwood Road (Evening)

SATURDAY 8
74 The Secret Garden at Serles House (Evening)

Private gardens opening regularly for the NGS

38 Hilltop

Gardens open to the public

1 Abbotsbury Gardens
10 Chiffchaffs
13 Compton Acres Gardens
18 Cranborne Manor Garden
22 Edmondsham House
25 Forde Abbey Gardens
38 Hilltop
39 Holworth Farmhouse
40 Horn Park
41 Ivy Cottage
45 Kingston Lacy
46 Kingston Maurward Gardens
48 Knoll Gardens and Nursery

54 Mapperton Gardens
59 Minterne
60 Moreton Gardens
75 Sherborne Castle
78 Snape Cottage Plantsman's Garden
79 Springhead
81 Sticky Wicket
83 Toad Hall
84 Upwey Wishing Well

By appointment only

26 Frampton Farm
51 Langebride House
90 Weston House

The Gardens

1 ◆ **ABBOTSBURY GARDENS**
nr Weymouth DT3 4LA. Ilchester Estates, 01305 871412, www.abbotsbury-tourism.co.uk/gardens. *8m W of Weymouth. From B3157 Weymouth-Bridport, 200yds W of Abbotsbury village.* **Adm £7.50, chd 5-15 £4.50, OAP £7. Mar to Oct (10-6) Nov to Feb (10-4).**
20 acres, started in 1760 and considerably extended in C19. Much recent replanting, very fine collection of rhododendrons, camellias, azaleas. Unique maritime micro-climate enables a flourishing Mediterranean bank and southern hemisphere garden to grow rare and tender plants. In summer there are palm trees, bananas, cannas; ponds and streamside plantings. Children's play area, sculpture trail, plant sales, shop, aviaries and Colonial tea-house. Major display garden at Chelsea Flower Show on theme of Jurassic Coast 2006.
♿ ❀ ☕

Visitors are enticed into the walled garden or led along secret paths . . .

APPLE COURT
See Hampshire.

2 NEW **ASHTON FARM**
Martinstown DT2 9HA. James & Jenny Shanahan. *3m SW of Dorchester. From A35 take A354 towards Weymouth, after ³/₄ m L to Winterborne Monkton, through gated rd for 1¹/₂m. After sharp R-hand bend, L into drive to car park.* Home-made teas. **Adm £3, chd free. Wed 20, Sun 24 June (2-5.30).**
Nestling below Maiden Castle this exuberant garden, surrounded by meadow and woodland, is largely informal with an emphasis on attracting wildlife. Overflowing with old-fashioned roses, flowering shrubs and herbaceous borders, visitors are enticed into the walled garden or led along secret paths, some steep, onto pastoral views. Working artist's studio open.
➚ ❀ ☕

3 **BEECH MEAD**
13 St Mary's Road, Ferndown BH22 9HB. Susan & Peter Clarkson, 01202 874224. *From town centre take Church Rd, turn R into St Mary's Rd. 2mins walk from nearby free Tesco car park.* Light refreshments & teas. **Adm £2, chd free. Sun 8 Apr (11-5), Mon 9 Apr (1-5). Visitors also welcome by appt for groups of 10+.**
Planned and designed by owners since Autumn 2002. Colourful garden containing large, unusual, collection of perennials, flowering climbers, acers, camellias, grasses, phormiums and many bulbs. Circular lawn surrounded by slate and gravel beds, bog garden, stream and small wildlife pond. Gazebo and arbours, a garden that explodes with colour and interest. A must for plantaholics. Prize Winner Ferndown in Bloom. Featured in 'House Beautiful' and 'Amateur Gardening'. Some gravel.
♿ ➚ ❀ ☕

4 **BEXINGTON**
Lime Kiln Road, Lytchett Matravers BH16 6EL. Mr & Mrs Robin Crumpler, 01202 622068. *5m SW of Wimborne Minster. Opp old school at W end of village.* Cream teas. **Adm £2, chd free. Suns 15 Apr; 13 May; 10 June; 8 July; 12 Aug; 9 Sept (2-5.30). Visitors also welcome by appt.**
Colourful garden of ¹/₂ acre maintained by owners, with mixed borders of many interesting and unusual plants, shrubs and trees. Bog garden of primulas, hostas etc. Rockery,

collection of grasses and ferns, with walkways over bog area connecting two lawns, making a garden of interest from spring bulbs to autumn colour. Featured in 'Amateur Gardening'.

    க்

5 NEW BOSCOMBE BEECHWOOD CENTRE

2A Owls Rd, Boscombe BH5 1AA. Mary Cooper & Emma Hilliard, 01202 309745, margaret.parker@bournemouth. gov.uk. ½m N of Boscombe Pier. Off Christchurch Rd, at corner of St Johns & Owls Rd. Parking for disabled on site, otherwise in adj rds or car parks in Hawkwood Rd or Sea Rd. Light refreshments & teas. **Adm £2 incl cup of tea, chd free. Weds 20, 27 June; 4, 11 July (11-3). Visitors also welcome by appt June/July only.**
A day resource centre for disabled adults with sight/hearing problems or mental health needs. Narrow, meandering garden full of variety. Closely planted with water feature, incorporating herbs, roses, secret shady areas and hot spots. Tended by clients and staff. Enjoy a drink and biscuit. Adm to centre on request.

BRAEMOOR
See Hampshire.

BRAMBLE HAYES
See Devon.

6 BROOMHILL

Rampisham DT2 0PU. Mr & Mrs D Parry, 01935 83266. 11m NW of Dorchester. From Yeovil take A37 towards Dorchester, 7m turn R signed Evershot. From Dorchester take A37 to Yeovil, 4m turn L A356 signed Crewkerne; at start of wireless masts R to Rampisham. Follow signs. Home-made teas Apr & Aug. **Adm £3, chd free. Suns 29 Apr; 8 July; Wed 15 Aug (2-6). Also open Manor Farm, Higher Wraxall 29 Apr, Rampisham Manor 8 July. Visitors also welcome by appt.**
Delightful 1-acre garden, which incorporates a disused farmyard and paddock. Pretty trellised entrance leads to an abundance of exciting plantings in mixed borders and island beds. Lawns slope gently down to

large wildlife pond and bog garden. Mown paths take you around the pond to a less formal area of mixed trees and shrubs. Plenty to see from April to September.

BUCKLAND STEAD
See Hampshire.

7 CHALK COTTAGE

Deanland, Sixpenny Handley SP5 5PD. Tim & Christine Reynolds, 01725 552995. 11m NE of Blandford. From Xrds in Handley Village, follow Dean Lane towards Bowerchalke. Outside village, take L turn to Deanland. Parking ¾m on L on all-weather riding arena; garden 250yds on R. Home-made teas. **Adm £2.50, chd free (share to Salisbury Hospice). Sun 10, Wed 13, Sun 17 June (2-6pm). Evening Openings £4.50, wine, Sat 16, Tue 19 June (6-9pm). Visitors also welcome by appt.**
Colourful ⅓-acre SW-sloping old-fashioned cottage garden overlooking field and woods. Abundance of annuals, perennials, shrubs and clematis framed by trees covered with scented ramblers. Designed around four flat lawns connected by inclines or steps. Wild flower area. Quiet places to sit. Selling plants a speciality, including unusual varieties. Also tawny owls to see.

8 CHESIL GALLERY

Pebble Lane, Chiswell DT5 1AW. Mrs Margaret Somerville, 01305 822738, www.chiswellcommunity.org. 3m N of Portland Bill. S of Weymouth. Follow signs to Portland; from Victoria Square turn R into Chiswell & immed R into Pebble Lane. Park in car park by Bluefish Restaurant. **Adm £2.50, chd free (share to Chiswell Community Trust). Suns 20 May; 10, 24 June; 8, 22 July; 5, 12 Aug (2-5). Also open Mews Cottage 10, 24 June; 8, 22 July; 12 Aug. Visitors also welcome by appt.**
Small and delightful shingle garden in the lee of the Chesil Bank. 2 courtyard gardens provide a domestic adjunct to artists' studio. On upper level flowering plants of coastal regions (some rare) have been naturalised. Information on the Chesil Beach and its ecology available and also on Chiswell Walled Garden (also open), a community project nearby. Teas provided at Chiswell Walled

Garden by local community members. Please phone beforehand if wheelchair user.

க்

9 CHIDEOCK MANOR

Chideock, nr Bridport DT6 6LF. Mr & Mrs Howard Coates. 2m W of Bridport on A35. In centre of village turn N at church. The Manor is ¼m along this rd on R. Home-made teas. **Adm £3.50, chd free. Weds, Suns 25, 29 Apr; 27 June; 1 July (2-5.30).** Large formal and informal gardens, some in process of development. Bog garden beside stream. Woodland and lakeside walks. Walled vegetable garden and orchard. Yew hedges and many mature trees. Lime walk. Herbaceous borders. Rose and clematis arches. Fine views. Adjoining Romanesque Catholic Church is open and well worth a visit.

க் பூ

An abundance of exciting plantings, plenty to see from April to September . . .

10 ◆ CHIFFCHAFFS

Chaffeymoor, Bourton SP8 5BY. Mr & Mrs K R Potts, 01747 840841. 3m E of Wincanton. W end of Bourton. N of A303. **Adm £3, chd £1. Weds, Thurs mid-Mar to mid-Oct; Suns 22 Apr; 6, 20, 27 May; 10, 24 June; 15 July; 8, 23 Sept (2-5). For NGS: Suns 25 Mar; 26 Aug (2-5).**
A garden for all seasons with many interesting plants, bulbs, shrubs, herbaceous border, shrub roses. Attractive walk to woodland garden with far-reaching views across Blackmore Vale.

பூ

Luxuriant tropical planting, an acre of considerable interest . . .

⑪ CLIFF HOUSE

Holworth DT2 8NJ. Paul & Kristine Ross Skinner. *8m SE of Dorchester. Take A352 to Warmwell Cross roundabout. 3rd L to Weymouth A353. After Poxwell turn sharp L to Ringstead. Continue on this rd, ignoring R turn to Ringstead, park in NT car park. Follow gravel track through gate on far side. Continue down hill through 2 more gateways. Follow signs to Cliff House. Walk approx 15mins.* **Adm £3, chd free. Sun 24 June (2-6). Evening Opening** Thur 21 June (6-9). Steep 2-acre clifftop garden, begun in 1998 and still evolving. Emphasis on wind and drought-resistant plants with healing, aromatic and tactile properties. Extensive drifts of Mediterranean plants, in particular lavender, set against sculpted shapes of clipped rosemary, hedging and statuesque pines. Spectacular views. Many steps - not for the faint-hearted.
�

⑫ NEW COACH HOUSE

Church Street, Sturminster Newton DT10 1DB. Ann & Hugh Hay. *Bottom of Church St.* Home-made teas at Ham Gate. **Adm £2, chd free. Sun 27, Mon 28 May (2-6). Also open Ham Gate Sun 27 May.** Small town garden. Following 24 yrs at Sweetwell, Fiddleford, the Hays are making a new garden. 18 months on, the former coach house and yard are transforming into a relaxed, informal garden with vista across river meadows. Partial wheelchair access.

COKER WOOD COTTAGE

See Somerset & Bristol Area.

COMBPYNE MANOR

See Devon.

⑬ ◆ COMPTON ACRES GARDENS

Poole BH13 7ES, 01202 700778, events@comptonacres.co.uk. *2m E of Poole. Signed from Bournemouth & Poole. Wilts & Dorset Buses 150, 151. Yellow Bus 12 stops at entrance.* **Adm £6.95, chd £3.95, concessions £6.45, family (2 adults, 3 chd) £16. Daily (not open Xmas Day/Boxing Day), summer (9-6), winter (10-4).** 10 acres of themed gardens, rare and specie plants, events and exhibitions, spectacular views over Poole Harbour and Purbeck Hills. Discover peace and tranquillity, and draw ideas and inspiration from the large Japanese and Italian gardens. Enjoy the Rock and Water garden and its large collection of Koi Carp and Terrapins.
♿ ✕ ⊛ ☕

⑭ COOMBE COTTAGE

Shillingstone DT11 0SF. Mike & Jennie Adams, 01258 860220. *5m NW of Blandford. On A357 next to PO Stores on main rd. Parking advised in Gunn Lane.* **Adm £2, chd free. Suns 27 May; 26 Aug (2-6pm). Visitors also welcome by appt.** 1/3-acre plantsman's mixed garden, delineated by walls, hedges and arbours, with a long season of herbaceous and woody perennials, climbers, bulbs and self-seeding annuals (many unusual and subtropical, combining flower-power with bold foliage), densely packed broad borders, pots and large plant house.
⊛

⑮ CORFE BARN

Corfe Lodge Road, Broadstone BH18 9NQ. Mr & Mrs John McDavid. *1m W of Broadstone centre. From main roundabout in Broadstone, W along Clarendon Rd 3/4 m, N into Roman Rd, after 50yds W into Corfe Lodge Rd.* Home-made teas. **Adm £2, chd free. Suns 29 Apr; 27 May; Mon 28 May; Sun 24 June (2-5).** 2/3 acre on three levels on site of C19 lavender farm. Informal country garden with much to interest both gardeners and flower arrangers. Parts of the original farm have been incorporated in the design. A particular feature of the garden is the use of old walls.
✕ ⊛ ☕

⑯ CORSCOMBE HOUSE

Corscombe DT2 0NU. Jim Bartos. *3 1/2 m N of Beaminster. From Dorchester A356 to Crewkerne, take 1st turn to Corscombe, R signed Church. Or A37 Yeovil to Dorchester, turn W signed Sutton Bingham/ Halstock/ Corscombe. Straight past Fox Inn, up hill, L signed Church.* Cream teas 6 May only in Rectory garden/Village Hall. **Adm £3, chd free. Suns 6 May; 15 July (2-6).** Garden established since 1995 in grounds of former rectory with view of Church. Garden rooms with colour-themed cool and hot borders, sunny and shady beds, parterre, reflecting pool, part-walled vegetable garden and orchard and meadow with obelisk. Tulips, narcissi and other bulbs for spring opening.
⊛ ☕

⑰ COTTESMORE FARM

Newmans Lane BH22 0LW. Paul & Valerie Guppy, 01202 871939. *1m N of West Moors. Off B3072 Bournemouth to Verwood rd. Car parking in owner's field.* Home-made teas. **Adm £3, chd free (share to Cats Protection). Suns 15, 22 July; 26 Aug (2-4.30). Visitors also welcome by appt** July, Aug & Sept, individuals or small groups. Luxuriant tropical planting; bananas, bamboos, gunneras and over 100 palms. Many rare plants incl beds dedicated to Australian and S American species. Large herbaceous borders, grass beds and wild flower area. Fancy fowl and rare breed sheep making an acre of considerable interest.
♿ ✕ ☕

⑱ ◆ CRANBORNE MANOR GARDEN

Cranborne BH21 5PP. Viscount Cranborne, 01725 517248, www.cranborne.co.uk. *10m N of Wimborne on B3078.* **Adm £4, chd 50p, concessions £3.50. Weds Mar-Sept. For NGS: Wed 4 Apr; Sat 9 June (9-5, last entry 4).** Beautiful and historic garden laid out in C17 by John Tradescant and enlarged in C20, featuring several gardens surrounded by walls and yew hedges; white garden, herb and mount gardens, water and wild garden. Many interesting plants, with fine trees and avenues.
♿ ✕ ⊛ ☕

THE DAIRY HOUSE
See Somerset & Bristol Area.

⑲ 44 DAWS AVENUE
Wallisdown BH11 8SD. Carol & John Farrance. *3m W of Bournemouth. Going N from Wallisdown roundabout take 1st L into Canford Ave then 1st R into Daws Ave.* Home-made teas. Adm £2, chd free. Fri 6 Apr; Suns 6 May; 10 June; 2 Sept (2-5). Small town garden offering yr-round interest with emphasis in spring on camellias and magnolias, underplanted with daphnes, hellebores, erythroniums and trilliums. Roses provide summer colour and in autumn rare hydrangeas, hibiscus and eucryphias are in bloom. Small courtyard leads to main area, where stream can be appreciated from summerhouse.

A garden to enjoy every day come rain or shine . . .

⑳ DEANS COURT
Deans Court Lane, Wimborne Minster BH21 1EE. Sir Michael & Lady Hanham. *1/4m SE of Minster. Just off B3073 in centre of Wimborne. Entry from Deans Court Lane - continuation of High St at junction with East St & King St over pavement & past bollard.* Free parking. Cream teas. Adm £3.50, chd free, senior citizens £2.50. Suns, Mons 8, 9 Apr; 6, 7, 27, 28 May; 17 June; 26, 27 Aug; 9 Sept. 13 acres on R Allen; partly wild, with historic specimen trees. House originally the Deanery to the Minster. Herb garden, rose garden. Long serpentine wall. The house will be open by prior written appointment. Some gravel paths.

DICOT
See Devon.

㉑ DOMINEYS YARD
Buckland Newton DT2 7BS. Mr & Mrs W Gueterbock, 01300 345295, www.domineys.com. *11m N of Dorchester, 11m S of Sherborne. 2m E A352 or take B3143. Take 'no through rd' between Church & Gaggle of Geese. Entrance 100metres on L. Park & picnic in arboretum on R, 10metres before garden entrance.* Cream teas. Adm £3.50, chd free (share to Arthritis Research Campaign). Suns 15 Apr; 20 May; 12 Aug; 21 Oct (2-6). Visitors also welcome by appt. Attractive, comprehensive all-seasons garden of 2 1/2 acres, where change continues after 46 yrs. Small, separate, 12 yr-old arboretum full of interest - trees, shrubs and bulbs. Views and vistas, pots and patios, fruit and vegetables. A garden to enjoy every day come rain or shine. Each month brings highlights and variation and interest for all. Partial wheelchair access. Slight slopes, gravel/grass paths.

㉒ ◆ EDMONDSHAM HOUSE
nr Cranborne BH21 5RE. Mrs Julia Smith, 01725 517207. *9m NE of Wimborne. 9m W of Ringwood. Between Cranborne & Verwood. Edmondsham off B3081.* Home-made teas Weds in April & Oct only. **House and Garden Adm £4, chd £1, under 5 free, Garden only Adm £2, chd 50p, under 5 free. Suns, Weds, 1 Apr to 31 Oct (2-5), house also open Weds, Apr & Oct only. For NGS: Wed 4, Mon 9 Apr; Weds only: 11 Apr to 25 Apr; 3 Oct to 24 Oct.** An historic 6-acre garden of C16 house. Interesting mature specimen trees and shrubs. Spring bulbs and blossom, autumn cyclamen. Early church, Victorian dairy and stable block, medieval grass cock pit. Walled garden with vegetables, fruit and traditional herbaceous borders planted to sustain long period of interest. Managed organically. Featured in 'Dorset' magazine & 'Gardening Which'. Gravel paths. No disabled toilet facilities.

㉓ THE FERNS
BH20 6HE. John & Jill Redfern. *Approaching Wool from Wareham, turn R just before level crossing into East Burton Rd. Garden on R, just under a mile down this rd.* Home-made teas. Adm £1.50, chd free.

Mons 7, 28 May; Suns 3 June; 1 July (2-5). Also open **Herons Mead** 28 May. Profusely planted with varied herbaceous borders and shrubs. Interesting use of hard landscaping. Fruit and vegetable garden leads to small woodland garden and a scene from Dorset clay-mining history. 'A lovely, secret garden' (Dorset Life).

㉔ 4 FLOWER COTTAGE
Lower Waterston DT2 7SR. Mrs A J Penniston, 01305 848694. *5m NE of Dorchester. From Puddletown: On B3142 take rd from bypass for Piddlehinton & Piddletrenthide. 2m on R. From Dorchester: B3143, 1st R.* Home-made teas. Adm £1.50, chd free. Suns 20 May; 9 Sept (2-6). Visitors also welcome by appt. Colourful, 1/3-acre cottage garden, packed with plants. Herbaceous borders, scree, fernery and vegetables within a design of several small gardens.

㉕ ◆ FORDE ABBEY GARDENS
Chard TA20 4LU. Mr Mark Roper, 01460 221290, www.fordeabbey.co.uk. *4m SE of Chard. Signed off A30 Chard-Crewkerne & A358 Chard-Axminster. Also from Broadwindsor.* Please phone 01460 221290 for adm prices. Gardens open daily throughout the yr (10 - last adm 4.30). 30 acres, fine shrubs, magnificent specimen trees, ponds, herbaceous borders, rockery, bog garden containing superb collection of Asiatic primulas, Ionic temple, working kitchen garden supplying the restaurant. Centenary fountain, England's highest powered fountain. Gravel paths, some steep slopes.

FOREST LODGE
See Somerset & Bristol Area.

㉖ FRAMPTON FARM
Chetnole Road, Leigh, Sherborne DT9 6HJ. Judy & John Tuke, 01935 872269. *6m SW of Sherborne. A352 from Sherborne to Dorchester. Turn at Longburton towards Leigh. Drive 4 1/2m & fork L in Leigh at Village Cross. House is 1/2m on R. Or A37 from Yeovil to Dorchester. Turn at Melbury House towards Leigh via Chetnole. House 1m on L from Chetnole Inn.* Adm £2, chd free. Visitors welcome by appt.

Garden created from former working farmyards into series of garden rooms; cottage garden, golden garden, white garden and old-fashioned roses; small arboretum and wild flower meadow. Some gravel paths.

2-acre informal, wildlife-friendly garden beside the River Stour . . .

㉗ FRANKHAM FARM
Ryme Intrinseca DT9 6JT. Richard & Jo Earle, 01935 872304. *3m S of Yeovil. A37 Yeovil-Dorchester; turn E; drive ¼m on L.* Home-made teas. **Adm £2.50, chd free. Sun 11 Mar; Mon 9 Apr; Mon 7, Sun 20 May; Sun 17 June (2-5.30).** Visitors also welcome by appt, individuals or groups, coaches permitted.
3½-acre garden, begun in 1960s by owners for yr-round interest. Perennials and roses round house and stone farm buildings. Extensive wall plantings incl roses and clematis, herbaceous borders, productive vegetable and fruit garden. Many unusual shrubs and trees, particularly hardwoods, shelter belts of trees forming woodland walks, under-planted with camellias, rhododendrons, hydrangeas and spring bulbs. Plenty to see from February onwards.

GANTS MILL & GARDEN
See Somerset & Bristol Area.

㉘ THE GLADE
Woodland Walk, Ferndown BH22 9LP. Mary & Roger Angus. *¾m NE of Ferndown centre. N off Wimborne Rd East, nr Tricketts Cross roundabout, Woodland Walk is a metalled but single carriageway lane with no parking bays; please park on main rd and access on foot (5 mins/330yds).* Home-made teas. **Adm £2.50, chd free. Suns 29 Apr; 13, 27**

May; 10 June (2-5.30).
1¾-acre landscaped garden in sylvan setting. Mature trees and shrubbery incl stewartia, taxodium, camellia, azalea, rhododendron, kalmia. Younger plantings incl prunus, malus, pieris, solanum, amalanchier, rambling roses. Woodland walks with wild anemones, primroses, bluebells. Stream and large wildlife pond with primulas, marginals and waterlilies. Bog garden, wet meadow, spring bulbs, herbaceous and mixed borders. 'Best Garden Open for Charity' Ferndown in Bloom.

㉙ GREENACRES
Bere Road, Coldharbour, Wareham BH20 7PA. John & Pat Jacobs, 01929 553821. *2½m NW of Wareham. From roundabout adjacent to stn take Wareham-Bere Regis rd. House ½m past Silent Woman Inn.* Cream teas. **Adm £2.50, chd free. Suns 17 June; 15 July; 19 Aug (2-6).** Visitors also welcome by appt.
2⅓-acre plantswoman's garden nestling in Wareham Forest. Lawns punctuated by colourful island beds designed for summer interest. Unusual perennials, shrubs and specimen trees, incl a flowering-size liriodendron. Stone water feature with 2 small ponds connected by tumbling water. Rare breed poultry.

㉚ GREENINGS
Chilfrome DT2 0HA. Mr & Mrs David Philp. *Please see Grovestall Farm for dirns. E end of village, next to church.* Teas at Grovestall Farm. **Adm £2.50, chd free. Sun 24, Mon 25 June (2-6).** Also open **Grovestall Farm.**
Plantsman's cottage garden. Well-established herbaceous borders, pond with solar-powered fountain, greenhouses. 95% organic.

㉛ GROVESTALL FARM
Chilfrome DT2 0HA. Mr & Mrs David Orr. *10m NW of Dorchester. From Yeovil take A37 to Dorchester. 10½m turn R into Maiden Newton, R at T-junction and 1st R to Chilfrome. From Dorchester take A37 to Yeovil. 7m turn L into Maiden Newton, then as above.* Follow signs. *Caution on narrow final lane.* Home-made teas. **Adm £2.50, chd free. Sun 24, Mon 25 June (2-6).** Also open **Greenings.**
2-acre, 5-7 yr-old garden created around old farm buildings. Densely planted former yard, walled kitchen

garden and 2 small, formal gardens linked by iris and lavender walk. The very rural setting includes a 6-acre 6 yr-old broadleaf wood with mown rides.

㉜ HAM GATE
Penny Street, Sturminster Newton DT10 1DF. Mr & Mrs H E M Barnes. *7½m W of Blandford. 11m E of Sherborne. Off A357. Take turn opp Nat West Bank. Park in car park or down Penny St. Ham Gate at bottom of Penny St.* Home-made teas. **Adm £2.50, chd free. Sun 27 May (2-6).** Also open **Coach House.**
2-acre informal, wildlife-friendly garden with mature trees, mixed borders and rolling lawns. Tranquil setting beside the R Stour and with distant views over the water meadows. Slopes steeply down to river bank.

㉝ HATCHLANDS
Netherbury DT6 5NA. Dr & Mrs John Freeman. *2m SW of Beaminster. Turn R off A3066 Beaminster to Bridport Rd, signed Netherbury. Car park at Xrds at bottom of hill. 200yds up bridle path.* Home-made teas July only. **Adm £3 Apr, £3.50 July, chd free. Suns 29 Apr; 1 July (2-6).** Also open **The Mill House.**
Country hillside garden set within 3 acres. Tall yew hedges, rose garden, herbaceous and fuchsia beds, lavender and pelargoniums, all below an old redbrick wall. Lawns, croquet court and mature broadleaf trees.

㉞ HAZELWOOD
19 Hazel Drive, Ferndown BH22 9SP. Keith & Christine Wilcox. *1m N of Ferndown. Wimborne Rd E, N into Queens Rd at T-lights then L into Beaufoys Ave & immed R into Willow Way. Bottom of hill turn R into Hazel Drive.* Home-made/cream teas. **Adm £2, chd free. Sat 9, Sun 10 June (11-5).**
Plantsman's garden 114ft × 60ft with much to investigate. Varied areas with intense planting of exotics, climbers and perennial families, many being rarely-seen, unusual plants. Foliage is important and water creates different habitats. Enhanced by the backdrop of a nature reserve, supporting prolific wildlife. A calm atmosphere for the visitor. Photograph display, linking garden with wildlife.

HEDDON HALL
See Devon.

HENSTRIDGE GARDENS
See Somerset & Bristol Area.

35 HERONS MEAD
East Burton Road, East Burton,
Wool BH20 6HF. Ron & Angela
Millington, 01929 463872. *6m W of
Wareham on A352. Approaching Wool
from Wareham, turn R just before level
crossing into East Burton Rd. Herons
Mead 3/4m on L.* Home-made teas.
Adm £2.50, chd free. Suns 25 Mar; 8
Apr; Sun 6, Mon 28 May; Sun 17,
Wed 27 June (2-5). Also open **The
Ferns** 28 May. Visitors also
welcome by appt for groups of 10+.
Long 1/2-acre garden winding through
plant-filled borders, island beds, tiny
orchard, kitchen/herb garden,
exuberant cottage garden with old
roses, finally circling a woodland
garden. Spring bulbs, hellebores,
epimediums, pulmonarias, foxgloves,
roses tumbling through trees in
summer. Cactus collection. Newly-
created wildlife pond. Teas served
around brightly painted 'chattelhouse'.

36 HIGHER MELCOMBE
Melcombe Bingham DT2 7PB. Mr M
C Woodhouse. *11m NE of
Dorchester. Puddletown exit on A35.
Follow signs for Cheselbourne then
Melcombe Bingham.* Teas. Adm £3,
chd free. Suns 3 June; 15 July (12-4).
Approached through a lime avenue up
private rd, the 2-acre garden is set in
quiet valley surrounded by downland.
Traditional English garden around C16
manor house and chapel with
herbaceous beds, roses and
magnificent copper beech and
wonderful woodland views.

37 HIGHWOOD GARDEN
Charborough Park, Wareham
BH20 7EW. H W Drax Esq,
www.charborough.co.uk. *6m E of
Bere Regis. Behind long wall on A31
between Wimborne & Bere Regis.
Enter park by Almer lodge if travelling
from W, or Blandford or Lion Lodges if
travelling from E. Follow signpost to
Estate Office, then Highwood Garden.*
Home-made teas. Adm £4, chd £2
(share to Morden PCC). Suns 20, 27
May (2.30-6).
Large woodland garden with
rhododendrons and azaleas.

38 ◆ HILLTOP
Woodville, Stour Provost SP8 5LY.
Josse & Brian Emerson, 01747
838512, www.hilltopgarden.co.uk.
*5m N of Sturminster Newton. On
B3092 turn R at Stour Provost Xrds,
signed Woodville. After 1 1/4m thatched
cottage on R.* Adm £2, chd free.
Group visits by arrangement. For
NGS: Sun 22 July, Thur 26, Sun 29
July; Thurs 2, 9, Suns 5, 12 Aug
(2-6).
Well-established garden overflowing
with a wealth of different and
interesting perennials. Bold yet
complementary plant combinations in
curved and sweeping borders give a
colourful and truly inspirational display.
Relax, take a seat in this peaceful
country garden and absorb the
tranquillity of the Blackmore Vale.
Nursery open Thurs, Mar-Sept.
Regrettably unsuitable for wheelchairs.

Plants grown specially to encourage birds, bees and butterflies . . . garage roof garden . . .

39 ◆ HOLWORTH FARMHOUSE
Holworth, nr Owermoigne DT2 8NH.
Anthony & Philippa Bush, 01305
852242, www.inarcadia-
gardendesign.co.uk. *7m E of
Dorchester. 1m S of A352. Follow
signs to Holworth.* Adm £2.50, chd
free. Weds 2 May to 29 Aug incl. For
NGS: Suns 6, 27 May; 17 June; 8, 29
July (2-6).
Over past 26yrs this unique setting has
been transformed into a garden with a
range of styles and wide variety of
features. Here you have the formal and
informal, light and shade, running and
still water, places to explore and places
for peaceful contemplation. Planted
with a wide range of mature and
unusual trees, shrubs and perennials
and surrounded by stunning views. We
are also experimenting with
hydroponics, with emphasis on water
conservation. Partial wheelchair
access.

40 ◆ HORN PARK
Beaminster DT8 3HB. Mr & Mrs
David Ashcroft, 01308 862212.
*1 1/2m N of Beaminster. On A3066
from Beaminster, L before tunnel (see
signs).* Home-made teas on NGS
days, otherwise by arrangement. Adm
£3.50, chd free. Tues to Thurs, Apr
to Oct (9.30-5.30) by appt, incl
groups. For NGS: Weds 25 Apr; 4
July (2-5).
Large garden with magnificent view to
sea. Plantsman's garden, many rare
plants and shrubs in terraced,
herbaceous, rock and water gardens.
Woodland garden and walks in bluebell
woods. Good autumn colouring. Wild
flower meadow with 164 varieties incl
orchids. Partial wheelchair access.

HORTUS
See Devon.

41 ◆ IVY COTTAGE
Aller Lane, Ansty DT2 7PX. Anne &
Alan Stevens, 01258 880053. *12m N
of Dorchester. Ansty is 6m N of
Puddletown & 4m W of Milton Abbas.
Aller Lane is a turning near the Fox Inn
& Ansty Post Office.* Adm £3, chd
free. Every Thur May to Sept incl.
For NGS: Thurs 3 May; 5 July; 6
Sept (11-5).
Sparkling little stream runs through this
charming cottage garden of 1 3/4 acres.
Plantsman's garden specialising in
unusual perennials, moisture-loving
plants; specimen trees and shrubs.
Many of the plants grown specially to
encourage birds, bees and butterflies
to the garden. Well laid out kitchen
garden with mixture of vegetables, fruit
and flowers. Garage roof garden can
be viewed from nearby high path. You
are welcome to picnic in the garden.

42 IVY HOUSE GARDEN
Piddletrenthide DT2 7QF. Bridget
Bowen, 01300 348255,
biddybowen@aol.com. *9m N of
Dorchester. On B3143. In middle of
Piddletrenthide village, opp PO/village
stores near Piddle Inn.* Home-made
teas. Adm £3, chd free. Mons 9 Apr;
7 May (2-5). Visitors also welcome
by appt May/June, up to 20 people.
Unusual and challenging 1/2-acre
plantsman's garden set on steep
hillside, with fine views. Themed areas
and mixed borders, wildlife ponds,
propagating garden, greenhouses and
polytunnel with nearby allotment.
Daffodils, tulips, violets and hellebores

in quantity for spring openings. Come prepared for steep terrain and a warm welcome. Planted as a wildlife-friendly garden. Wheelchair access to courtyard only.

  ♿ ✕ ✿ 🍵

43 JAPANESE GARDENS
38 Bingham's Road, Crossways DT2 8BW. Mr & Mrs Geoffrey Northcote, 01305 854538. *6m E of Dorchester. Off Dick O th' Banks Rd, & the B3390. Parking in village.* **Adm £2.50, chd free. Suns 13, 27 May (1-5). Visitors also welcome by appt Apr to Sept, max 16 persons.**
Two unusual small gardens, designed by owner. Front garden features a green 'Turtle' island, pebble sea and contrasting yellow/blue borders. 'Sansui' and 'Moon Gate' mural paintings. Rear garden 26ft x 36ft symbolises 'River of Life' with 'Moon Waves' bridge, Torre gateway, railed decking, hand-carved red granite features amid contrasting red/green foliage and flower forms.

  ✕

44 74 KEITH ROAD
Talbot Woods BH3 7DX. Mr J Dustan. *1m NW Bournemouth centre. W of N end of Glenferness Ave.* **Adm £2, chd free. Sats, Suns 16, 17 June; 7, 8 July (2-5). Also open 46 Roslin Road South.**
Suburban cottage-style garden of ¼ acre, consisting of mixed borders of annuals, perennials, shrubs and fruit. Features incl pond, arches, summerhouse and productive greenhouse. Many climbing plants and gazebo.

  ♿ ✿

45 ◆ KINGSTON LACY
Wimborne Minster BH21 4EA. The National Trust, 01202 883402, kingstonlacy@nationaltrust.org.uk. *1½m W of Wimborne Minster. On the Wimborne-Blandford rd B3082.* **House and Garden Adm £10, chd £5, Garden only Adm £5, chd £2.50. Opening dates and times vary according to season. Please phone or visit website for details. For NGS: Sat 9, Sun 10 June (10.30-6).**
32-acre garden, 9 acres of lawn, lime avenue, rhododendrons, azaleas and National Collection of convallarias. Parterre is planted in summer with salmon-pink Begonia semperflorens and Heliotropium 'Marine'. Victorian fernery with 25 different types of fern and National Collection of Anemone

nemorosa. Roses incl 'Bonica', 'Cardinal Hume', 'Nozomi' and 'Amber Queen'. Newly-restored Japanese garden in accordance with Henrietta Bankes' creation of 1910.

  ♿ ✕ ✿ NCCPG 🍵

46 ◆ KINGSTON MAURWARD GARDENS
Dorchester DT2 8PY, 01305 215003, www.kmc.ac.uk/gardens. *1m E of Dorchester. Off A35. Follow brown Tourist Information signs.* **Adm £5, chd £3, concessions £4.50. Open daily 3 Jan to 21 Dec (10-5.30 or dusk if earlier).**
National Collections of penstemons and salvias. Classic Georgian mansion (not open) set in 35 acres of gardens laid out in C18 and C20 with 5-acre lake. Terraces and gardens divided by hedges and stone balustrades. Stone features and interesting plants. Elizabethan walled garden laid out as demonstration. Nature and tree trails. Animal park. Partial wheelchair access. Gravel paths, steps and steep slope.

  ♿ ✕ ✿ NCCPG 🍵

Tranquil setting with many restful seating areas . . .

47 KNITSON OLD FARMHOUSE
nr Swanage BH20 5JB. Rachel & Mark Helfer, 01929 421681, rachel@knitson.co.uk. *1m NW of Swanage. 3m E of Corfe Castle. Signed L off A351 Knitson. Ample parking in yard or in adjacent field.* **Cream teas. Adm £2.50, chd 50p, concessions £2. Daily Fri 20 Apr to Sun 22 Apr; Sat 4 Aug to Sun 12 Aug (1-5). Visitors also welcome by appt (no large coaches).**
Mature cottage garden. Herbaceous borders, rockeries, climbers, shrubs - 40 hostas. Large organic kitchen garden for self-sufficiency in fruit and vegetables incl kiwis! Many Roman and medieval Purbeck stone artefacts used in garden design, with ancient stone cottage and new moon-arch as backdrops. Some slopes. Grass and flagstone paths. 80% wheelchair access.

  ♿ ✕ ✿ 🍵

48 ◆ KNOLL GARDENS AND NURSERY
Hampreston BH21 7ND. Mr Neil Lucas, 01202 873931, www.knollgardens.co.uk. *2½m W of Ferndown. ETB brown signs from A31. Large car park.* **Adm £4.50, chd £3, concessions £4. Weds to Suns 1 Feb to 16 Dec, Tues also May to Oct (10-5 or dusk if earlier).**
Exciting collection of grasses and perennials thrives within an informal setting of mature and unusual trees, shrubs and pools, creating a relaxed and intimate atmosphere. Mediterranean-style gravel garden, eye-catching Dragon Garden and new Decennium border planted in the naturalistic style. Nationally acclaimed nursery specialising in grasses and perennials. National Collections of pennisetum, deciduous ceanothus and phygelius.

  ♿ ✕ ✿ NCCPG 🍵

49 KNOWLE FARM
Uploders, nr Bridport DT6 4NS. Alison & John Halliday, 01308 485492, www.knowlefarmbandb.com. *1½m E of Bridport. Leave A35 signed to Uploders about 2m E of Bridport. Turn back under A35 to reach Uploders. Turn L at T-junction (Crown Inn on L). Knowle Farm is 200yds on R, opp chapel. Careful roadside parking unless using Crown Inn (lunches served).* **Home-made teas. Adm £3, chd free. Sat 7 Apr; Tue 15 May; Sun 23 Sept (1-6). Evening Opening, wine, light refreshments, Mon 2 July (5-9). Visitors also welcome by appt.**
1-acre informal valley garden on 3 levels with slopes and steps bordered by R Asker in conservation area. Tranquil setting with many restful seating areas. Wide variety of interesting and unusual plants. Extensive planting around old trees and mature shrubs. Bog garden, rose walk, small orchard meadow, riverside walk, kitchen garden, hens. Plantaholic's greenhouse. Partial wheelchair access.

  ♿ ✿ 🛏 🍵

50 102 LANEHOUSE ROCKS ROAD
Weymouth DT4 9DJ. Julie & Paul Smith, 01305 774892, juliepaul@lanehouserocks.freeserve.co.uk. *Lanehouse Rocks Rd is off Chickerell Rd on W side of Weymouth, N of Wyke Regis. No 102 is on R nr petrol station.* **Home-made TEAS.**

Adm £2, chd free. Suns 24 June; 8, 15, 22 July; 5 Aug (2-6). Visitors also welcome by appt July only, coaches or groups of 10+.
Small town garden with patio area enclosed by specimen palms and agaves. Honeysuckle archway leads to gravelled pond area and waterfall, full of large Koi carp. Borders of geraniums, phormiums and fatsias give an exotic feel, while baskets and containers add a riot of colour.
🖐 ❀ ☕

⑤① LANGEBRIDE HOUSE
Long Bredy DT2 9HU. Mrs J Greener, 01308 482257. *8m W of Dorchester. S off A35, well signed.* Adm £3, chd free. Visitors welcome by appt Feb to June incl.
Substantial old rectory garden with many designs for easier management. 200-yr-old beech trees, pleached limes, yew hedges, extensive collections of spring bulbs, herbaceous plants, flowering trees and shrubs. Some steep slopes.
🚻 🖐

Sunken parterre planted with old roses and climbers . . .

LIFT THE LATCH
See Somerset & Bristol Area.

THE LITTLE COTTAGE
See Hampshire.

MACPENNYS WOODLAND GARDEN & NURSERIES
See Hampshire.

⑤② MANOR FARM, HAMPRESTON
BH21 7LX. Guy & Anne Trehane. *2¹/₂m E of Wimborne, 2¹/₂m W of Ferndown. From Canford Bottom roundabout on A31, take exit B3073 Ham Lane. ¹/₂m turn R at Hampreston Xrds. House at bottom of village.* Home-made teas. Adm £3, chd free. Suns 20 May; 10 June; 9 Sept (2-5).
Traditional farmhouse garden designed

and cared for by 3 generations of the Trehane family who have farmed here for over 90yrs. Garden now being restored and thoughtfully replanted with herbaceous borders and rose beds within box and yew hedges. Mature shrubbery, water and bog garden.
🚻 🖐 ☕

⑤③ MANOR FARM, HIGHER WRAXALL
DT2 0HR. Vianna Dene, 01935 83638, rusty@denewear.co.uk. *10m NW of Dorchester. From Yeovil take A37 towards Dorchester. 7m turn R signed Evershot. Turn L in Rampisham, 1m turn R - see signs.* Cream teas 9 Sept. Adm £2.50, chd free. Sun 29 Apr; Wed 11 July; Sun 9 Sept (2-6).
Also open **Broomhill** 29 Apr & **Rampisham Manor** 11 July. Visitors also welcome by appt.
²/₃-acre young garden. Well laid out with exciting colour and plant combinations in different areas. Sunken parterre planted with old roses and climbers. Wildlife pond has a stunning view across W Dorset valley. Vegetable garden.
🚻 🖐 ❀ ☕

⑤④ ♦ MAPPERTON GARDENS
nr Beaminster DT8 3NR. The Earl & Countess of Sandwich, 01308 862645, www.mapperton.com. *6m N of Bridport. Off A35/A3066. 2m SE of Beaminster off B3163.* House and Garden Adm £8, chd £4, Garden only Adm £4, chd £2. Sun-Fri Mar to Oct (11-5).
Terraced valley gardens surrounding Tudor/Jacobean manor house. On upper levels, walled croquet lawn, orangery and Italianate formal garden with fountains, topiary, grottoes, ponds and herbaceous borders. Below, C17 summerhouse, fishponds, topiary and borders. Lower garden with specimen shrubs and rare trees, leading to woodland and spring gardens. Partial wheelchair access. Plant Fair Sun 22 Apr. Featured in 'Country Life'.
🚻 🖐 ❀ ☕

⑤⑤ MELPLASH COURT
Melplash DT6 3UH. Mrs Timothy Lewis. *4m N of Bridport. On A3066, just N of Melplash. Turn W & enter between field gates next to big gates & long ave of chestnut trees.* Home-made teas. Adm £4, chd free. Sun 20 May; Wed 27 June (2-6).
Gardens, originally designed by Lady Diana Tiarks, continue to evolve and

consist of park planting, bog garden, croquet lawn and adjacent borders. Formal kitchen garden and herb garden, ponds, streams and lake; new borders and areas of interest are added and opened up each yr.
❀ ☕

⑤⑥ MEWS COTTAGE
34 Easton Street, Portland DT5 1BT. Peter & Jill Pitman, 01305 820377, penstemon@waitrose.com. *3m S of Weymouth. Situated on top of the Island, 50yds past Punchbowl Inn, small lane on L. Park in main street & follow signs.* Cream teas 9 Apr only, home-made teas other days. Adm £1.50, chd free. £2.50 9 Apr only. Sun 18 Feb; Mon 9 Apr; Suns 10, 24 June; 8, 22 July; 12 Aug; 14 Oct (2-5). Also open **Chesil Gallery** Suns 10, 24 June; 8, 22 July; 12 Aug. Visitors also welcome by appt.
Spring sees hellebores, snowdrops and other bulbs. Summer, over 90 named agapanthus grow amongst National Collection of penstemon. Fernery with fossil collection. Autumn colour is crowned by *Nerine bowdenii*, plus pond with arum lilies and herbaceous planting, all in ¹/₄ acre. Extra attraction for 2007, ceramics by Tiffany. Featured in 'Gardening Which' and on Solent Radio. Partial wheelchair access. 2 steps to WC.
🚻 🖐 ❀ **NCCPG** ☕

⑤⑦ THE MILL HOUSE
Crook Hill, Netherbury DT6 5LX. Michael & Giustina Ryan, 01308 488267, themillhouse@dial.pipex.com. *1m S of Beaminster. Turn R off A3066 Beaminster to Bridport rd at signpost to Netherbury. Car park at Xrds at bottom of hill.* Cream teas. Adm £3, chd free. Suns 29 Apr; 1 July (2-6).
Also open **Hatchlands.** Visitors also welcome by appt Apr to Sept for groups of 10+, coaches permitted.
Several small gardens arranged round the Mill, its stream and pond, incl formal walled garden, terraced flower garden and mill stream garden. Emphasis on scented flowers, hardy geraniums, lilies, spring bulbs, clematis and water irises. The remaining 4 acres of grounds are planted with a wide variety of trees: magnolias, acers, oaks, eucalyptus, birches, liriodendrons, nothofagus, willows, alders and conifers. Partial wheelchair access. Featured in 'Dorset Country Gardener'.
🚻 ❀ ☕

58 10 MILNER ROAD

Westbourne BH4 8AD. Mr & Mrs Colin Harding. 1¹/₂m W of Bournemouth. E of Westbourne on Poole Rd. S at T-lights into Clarendon Rd. Cross over Westcliff Rd into Westovercliff Dr. 1st R, then 1st L and 1st R into Milner Rd. Home-made teas. **Adm £3, chd free. Sun 6, Mon 7 May (11-5).**
This modern clifftop garden was designed and constructed by Colin Harding in 1986 in a natural style with key formal accents. Natural driftwood sculptures incl driftwood conservatory and other structures. Wide range of maturing trees and shrubs incl magnolias and camellias within mature holly and rhododendron hedges. Range of hellebore and late spring bulbs. Handwoven textiles using natural dyes from garden plants.
& ✗ ☕

Lovingly restored from neglected overgrown 'jungle' . . .

59 ◆ MINTERNE

Minterne Magna DT2 7AU. The Hon Mr & Mrs Henry Digby, 01300 341370, www.minterne.co.uk. 2m N of Cerne Abbas. On A352 Dorchester-Sherborne rd. **Adm £4, chd free. Open daily Mar to Oct (10-6).**
Minterne valley, landscaped in C18, home of the Churchill and Digby families for 350yrs. Wild woodland gardens are laid out in a horseshoe below Minterne House, with over 1m of walks, providing a new vista at each turn. Rhododendrons and magnolias tower over small lakes, streams, and cascades. Maples and many rare trees provide spectacular autumn colouring.

60 ◆ MORETON GARDENS

nr Dorchester DT2 8RH. The Penny Family, 01929 405084. 7m E of Dorchester. 3m W of Wool. Signed from B3390 & 1m E of Moreton stn.

Next to Lawrence of Arabia's grave in village of Moreton. **Adm £3.50, chd free. Daily Apr to Oct (10-5); Weds to Suns, Nov to Mar (10-4). For NGS: Sat 14, Sun 15 Apr (10-5).**
A garden recreated in an old setting in the picturesque village of Moreton. 3 acres of lawns, mixed borders, woodland, stream and ponds, bog garden, pergola; summerhouse and fountain. Spring flowers and much more. Enjoy a picnic in the garden. Featured on UKTV's Gardens. Firm gravel paths.
& ✗ ⊛ ☕

MULBERRY HOUSE
See Hampshire.

61 4 NOEL ROAD

Wallisdown BH10 4DP. Lesley & Ivor Pond. 4m NE of Poole. From Wallisdown Xrds enter Kinson Rd. Take 5th rd on R, Kingsbere Ave. Noel Rd is first on R. Home-made teas. **Adm £2, chd free. Suns 1, 15 July (2-5).**
Small garden, 100ft × 30ft, with big ideas. On sloping ground there are many Roman features incl water features and temple. Most planting is in containers. 'I also like a big element of surprise and you do not get more surprising than a Roman Temple at the end of a suburban garden' (Amateur Gardening magazine). Several new features. Come and give us your opinion 'Is this garden over the top?'. Featured in 'Bournemouth Daily Echo' and on Solent Radio.
✗ ☕

OAKDENE
See Hampshire.

62 'OLA'

47 Old Castle Road, Weymouth DT4 8QE. Jane Uff & Elaine Smith. Rodwell, Weymouth. 1m from Weymouth centre. Follow signs to Portland. Off Buxton Rd, proceed to lower end of Old Castle Rd. Bungalow just past Sandsfoot Castle ruins/gardens. Easy access by foot off Rodwell Trail at Sandsfoot Castle. Home-made teas. **Adm £2, chd free. Tues 8, 22 May; 5 June (2-5).**
Seaside garden with stunning views overlooking Portland Harbour. 1930s-designed garden, once part of Sandfoot Castle estate. Mixed herbaceous borders, shrubs and roses. Rockeries, fish pond, vegetables, orchard and '7 dwarfs' bank. Circular sunken stone walled area with box bushes and statuary.

Lovingly restored from neglected overgrown 'jungle'.
✗ ☕

63 THE OLD RECTORY, FIFEHEAD MAGDALEN

SP8 5RT. Mrs Patricia Lidsey, 01258 820293. 5m S of Gillingham. Just S of A30, signed from the A30. Cream teas. **Adm £2, chd free. Sun 17 June (2-6pm). Visitors also welcome by appt.**
Medium-sized garden with interesting shrubs and perennials; pond; grandchildren's garden.
& ⊛ ☕

64 THE OLD RECTORY, LITTON CHENEY

Dorchester DT2 9AH. Mr & Mrs Hugh Lindsay, 01308 482383, hugh_lindsay@talk21.com. 9m W of Dorchester. 1m S of A35, 6m E of Bridport. Small village in the beautiful Bride Valley. Park in village and follow signs. Home-made teas. **Adm £3, chd free. Suns 15 Apr; 13 May; Tue 12 June (2-5.30).** Visitors also welcome by appt Mar to June.
Steep paths lead to 4 acres of natural woodland with many springs, streams and 2 small lakes; mostly native plants and many primulas (stout shoes recommended). Cloud-pruned boxes. Small walled garden, partly paved, formal layout with informal planting and prolific quince tree. Kitchen garden, orchard and wild flower lawn. Partial wheelchair access. Steep paths, 2 small lakes.
& ⊛ ☕

65 THE OLD RECTORY, NETHERBURY

DT6 5NB. Amanda & Simon Mehigan, 01308 488757. 2m SW of Beaminster. Turn off A3066 Beaminster/Bridport rd & go over river Brit, into centre of village & up hill. The Old Rectory on L opp church. Home-made teas. **Adm £3, chd free. Sun 13 May (2-6). Also opening Slape Manor 13 May.** Visitors also welcome by appt May/June only.
Garden of approx 5 acres, developed over last 12yrs, incl formal courtyard, bog garden with stream and pond, vegetable garden, wild flower areas and orchards featuring spring bulbs, hellebores, bog primulas and irises. Many mature broadleaved trees incl massive ginkgo. Featured in 'Elle Decoration' and 'Gardens in Perspective' by Jenny Harpur.

66 THE OLD RECTORY, PULHAM
DT2 7EA. Mr & Mrs N Elliott, 01258 817595. *13m N of Dorchester. 8m SE of Sherborne. On B3143 turn E at Xrds in Pulham. Signed Cannings Court.* Adm £3, chd free. Wed 1, Sun 5 Aug (2-6). Visitors also welcome by appt. 4 acres of formal and informal gardens surround C18 rectory (not open) with superb views. Yew hedges enclose circular herbaceous borders with late summer colour. Mature trees. Restored pond and waterfall. Exuberantly-planted terrace and purple and white terrace beds. Box parterres. Fernery. Pleached hornbeam circle. Ha-ha. Shrubbery and two 5-acre woods with mown rides.

67 NEW PARK HOMER DRIVE GARDENS
Colehill BH21 2SR. *1m NE of Wimborne. From Canford Bottom roundabout where A31 meets B3073, exit N marked Colehill for 1m. Turn L into Park Homer Rd, leading to Park Homer Dr.* Home-made teas at 28 Park Homer Dr. Combined adm £3, chd free. Sun 20 May; Wed 27 June (2-6). 5 very different gardens - 3 sloping and 2 level - showing a variety of plantings in a valley setting.

NEW 4 PARK HOMER DRIVE
Barbara & Geoff Burge
Steep woodland garden with views to Bournemouth. Small lawns with well-planted borders and pond. Unsuitable for the less mobile, steep steps.

NEW 7 PARK HOMER DRIVE
Pauline Weaver
Steep woodland garden filled with shade-loving plants. Steps lead to a quiet sitting area. Unsuitable for the less mobile.

NEW 15 PARK HOMER DRIVE
Bill & Glenda Dunn
Suburban garden with small pond and waterfall, arches, rockery and gravel area. Planted extravagantly and colourfully. Partial wheelchair access.

NEW 18 PARK HOMER DRIVE
Carolyn & Alan Nash
Small, colourful garden. Densely-planted beds surround immaculate lawn and pond.

NEW 28 PARK HOMER DRIVE
Kay & Mike Jeffrey
Large sloping lawn, patio and decking area where teas will be served. Partial wheelchair access.

68 54 PARKWOOD ROAD
Bournemouth BH5 2BL. Mr & Mrs Andrew Rickett. *3m E of Bournemouth. Turn S off Christchurch Rd between Boscombe and Pokesdown Stn.* Home-made/cream teas 6 May, 3 June. Adm £2.50, chd free. Suns 6 May; 3 June (2-5). Evening Openings £3, wine, Sat 12 May; Fri 3 Aug (7.30-9.30); Sat 1 Dec (7-9). Small town garden, approx 30ft x 120 ft, planted out 5yrs ago by enthusiastic first time gardeners. Herbaceous perennials and shrubs with mature trees, small pond and lawn give the garden a natural, relaxed atmosphere. Contrasting areas of moisture, shade and dryness. Live music for evening openings, mulled wine Dec.

A garden that is loved and it shows . . .

PROSPECT HOUSE
See Devon.

69 RAMPISHAM MANOR
Rampisham DT2 0PT. Mr & Mrs Boileau, 01935 83612, harriet@cubbins.co.uk. *11m NW of Dorchester. From Yeovil take A37 towards Dorchester, 7m turn R signed Evershot. From Dorchester take A37 to Yeovil, 4m turn L A356 signed Crewkerne; at start of wireless masts R to Rampisham. Follow signs.* Home-made teas 20/23 May, cream teas 8,

11 July. Adm £3.50, chd free. Sun 20, Wed 23 May (2-5); Sun 8, Wed 11 July (2-5.30). Also open Broomhill 8 July & Manor Farm, Higher Wraxall 11 July. Visitors also welcome by appt May to July incl, groups of 10+, coaches permitted. 3-acre stylish garden in lovely rural setting. Wide variety of planting incl late spring bulbs and new spectacular iris bed (hopefully) for May openings. Mature shrubs, rose beds. Spacious lawns and woodland walk. Upper garden with oriental inspired area and hidden vegetable garden. River and lake nature walk.

70 357 RINGWOOD ROAD
Ferndown BH22 9AE. Lyn & Malcolm Ovens, 01202 896071, www.mgovens.freeserve.co.uk. *3/4m S of Ferndown. On A348 towards Longham. Parking in Glenmoor Rd.* Home-made teas. Adm £2, chd free. Sun 15 July; Wed 1 Aug; Sun 12 Aug; Suns (11-5), Wed (1-4). Visitors also welcome by appt late June to early Sept only, garden groups & wheelchair users welcome. 100ft × 30ft his and hers garden. Front in cottage style with a varied composition of perennials, lilies and 105 different clematis. Chosen to give a riot of colour into autumn. At rear, walk through a Moorish doorway into an exotic garden where brugmansia, cannas, oleander, banana etc come together in an eclectic design. Conservatory with bougainvillea. A garden that is loved and it shows. Shortlisted BBC Gardener of the Year.

71 46 ROSLIN ROAD SOUTH
Talbot Woods BH3 7EG. Mrs Penny Slade, 01202 510243. *1m NW of Bournemouth. W of N end of Glenferness Ave in Talbot Woods area of Bournemouth.* Home-made teas. Adm £2, chd free. Sun 22 Apr; Sats, Suns 19, 20 May; 16, 17 June; 7, 8 July (2-5). Also open 74 Keith Road June/July. Visitors also welcome by appt Apr to Jul, coaches permitted. Plantswoman's 1/3-acre walled town garden planted with many unusual and rare plants. Sunken gravel garden with collection of grasses, surrounded by colourful mixed borders. Features incl many well planted containers, raised octagonal alpine bed, pergola leading to enclosed patio, cutting beds and fruit cage, greenhouses and frames.

⑫ NEW ST MICHAEL'S HOUSE
Pound Street, Lyme Regis DT7 3HY. Penny Keiner Ross, 01297 442503, pennykeiner@rediffmail.com.
From town centre, proceed up Broad St, L into Pound St (A3052 to Exeter). 100yds on L. Street parking opp or in Holmbush car park further up on L. Home-made teas. **Adm £2.50, chd free. Fri 15 June; Sun 8 July (12-6). Evening Openings £4, wine, Sats 16 June; 7 July (6-10). Visitors also welcome by appt.**
Formal enclosed town garden. Courtyard, planted 2 yrs ago on site of former hotel dining room, reflects owner's passion for India. Persian-style gazebo leads into jasmine and rose-scented garden with glimpses of Lyme Bay. 1st prize Lyme Regis in Bloom 2006.
🎋 ☕

SANDLE COTTAGE
See Hampshire.

⑬ THE SECRET GARDEN
The Friary, Hilfield DT2 7BE. The Society of St Francis, 01300 341345, Brother Vincent. *10m N of Dorchester. On A352. 1st L after village, 1st turning on R signed The Friary. From Yeovil turn off A37 signed Batcombe, 3rd turning on L.* Teas. **Adm £3, chd free. Sat 12, Sun 13 May (2-5). Visitors also welcome by appt.**
Small woodland garden begun in 1950s then neglected. Reclamation began in 1984. New plantings added in 1998-1999, bamboo in 2004, further plantings of rhododendrons and bamboo in 2006. Mature trees, rhododendrons, azaleas, magnolias, camellias (some camellias grown from seed collected in China), other choice shrubs with a stream on all sides crossed by bridges. Stout shoes recommended.
🎋 ☕

⑭ THE SECRET GARDEN AT SERLES HOUSE
47 Victoria Road, Wimborne BH21 1EN. Ian Willis, 01202 880430. *Centre of Wimborne. On B3082 W of town, very near hospital, Westfield car park 300yds. Off-road parking close by.* **Adm £2, chd free (share to Wimborne Civic Society). Suns 29 July; 12 Aug; Sun 26, Mon 27 Aug;**

Suns 9, 16 Sept (2.30-5.30). **Evening Openings £3, wine, Sats 25 Aug, 8 Sept (8-10); 8 Dec (6-9). Visitors also welcome by appt.**
Described as extraordinary in 'Dorset Country Gardener', this garden is for people of all ages. The plantings fit in with over 60 relics rescued from oblivion by Ian Willis. The Anglo-Indian conservatory, plant-pot man, tree-house and cannons from the Solent are highlights of this remarkable experience. Piano music during evening openings. Special winter opening 8 Dec with Christmas music, Father Christmas, wine & mince pies. Featured in 'Dorset Country Gardener' and in 'Great British Eccentrics' (Best Garden Open to the Public).
🎋

The plantings fit in with over 60 relics rescued from oblivion . . .

⑮ ◆ SHERBORNE CASTLE
New Rd, Sherborne DT9 3PY. Mr J K Wingfield Digby, 01935 813182/812072, www.sherbornecastle.com. *1/2 m E of Sherborne. On New Road B3145. Follow brown signs to 'Sherborne Castles' from A30 & A352.* **Castle and garden adm £8.50, chd free, senior citizens £8, garden only adm £4, chd free. Open daily except Mons and Fris, Apr to Oct (11-4.30 (last entry)). Castle interior opens later at 2pm Sats.**
30+ acres. A Capability Brown garden with magnificent vistas across the surrounding landscape, incl lake and fine ruined castle. Herbaceous planting, notable trees, a mixture of ornamental planting and managed

wilderness are all linked together with lawn and pathways providing colour and interest throughout the seasons. New 'Dry Grounds Walk' opened 2005. Special events through season - see website for details. Featured on Channel 5's Treasure Houses. Gravel/grass paths and some steep slopes, please phone for further details.
♿ ☕

⑯ SHUTE FARM
Donhead St Mary SP7 9DG. Mr & Mrs J Douglas. *5m E of Shaftesbury. Take A350 towards Warminster from Shaftesbury. Turn R at 1st turning out of Shaftesbury, signed Wincombe & Donhead St Mary. At Donhead St Mary, turn R at T-junction. 1st house on L opp tel box.* Home-made teas. **Adm £3, chd free. Suns 18 Mar; 13 May (11-4).**
Cottage garden around thatched house. Plenty to see and explore, incl stream, pond, kitchen garden and wild flower garden. Neat and tidy garden by house, getting wilder as it meets the fields. Alpacas, rare breed chickens, ducks and bees. Magnificent views over the Donheads.
🎋 ❀ ☕

⑰ SLAPE MANOR
Netherbury DT6 5LH. Mr & Mrs Antony Hichens. *1m SW of Beaminster. Turn W off A3066 to village of Netherbury. House 1/3 m S of Netherbury on back rd to Bridport.* Home-made teas. **Adm £4, chd under 12 free. Sun 13 May (2-5.30). Also open The Old Rectory, Netherbury.**
River valley garden, extensive lawns, streams and lake. Azaleas, magnolias, rhododendrons, large clump *Phyllostachys nigra* 'Boryana' and specimen trees. Lakeside walks. Some gravel paths, flat grass lawns. Unfenced water features.
♿ ❀ ☕

⑱ ◆ SNAPE COTTAGE PLANTSMAN'S GARDEN
Chaffeymoor, Bourton, Gillingham SP8 5BZ. Ian & Angela Whinfield, 01747 840330 (evenings), www.snapestakes.com. *5m NW of Gillingham. At W end of Bourton, N of A303. Opp Chiffchaffs.* **Adm £2.50, chd free. Last 2 Suns in each month Feb to Aug incl; every Thur May to Aug incl, groups by prior arrangement (10.30-5). For NGS: Suns 18 Mar; 17 June.**

Country garden containing exceptional collection of hardy plants and bulbs, artistically arranged in informal cottage garden style, organically managed and clearly labelled. Main interests are plant history and nature conservation. Specialities incl snowdrops, hellebores, primula vulgaris cvrs, 'old' daffodils, pulmonarias, auriculas, dianthus, herbs, irises and geraniums. Wildlife pond, beautiful views, tranquil atmosphere. Featured in 'Gardening Which' and on BBC Gardeners' World.

79 ◆ SPRINGHEAD
Fontmell Magna SP7 0NU. *The Springhead Trust, 01747 811853, www.springheadtrust.co.uk. 4m S of Shaftesbury. From Shaftesbury or Blandford take A350 to Fontmell Magna. In centre of village, turn E up Mill St, opp PH. Follow stream up twisty, narrow lane to Springhead on sharp bend. Large, white thatched house attached to mill. Light refreshments & teas.* **Adm £3.50, chd free. Mon 9 Apr (10-4), Fris 31 Aug (10-3); 12 Oct (10-4). For NGS: Mons 14 May; 11 June (10-3).**
Lakeside garden above mill. Icy spring water bubbles from beneath the chalk. Walks with prospects punctuated by peaceful resting places: noble trees, Venetian rotunda, terraced landscaping reflecting Iron Age Lynchets above. Bog garden, wild areas, themed planting of herbaceous beds, old roses and unusual shrubs. Some gravel paths, steep slope, wooden bridge with rails.

80 STANBRIDGE MILL
nr Gussage All Saints BH21 5EP. *Mr James Fairfax, 01258 841067. 7m N of Wimborne. On B3078 to Cranborne 150yds from Horton Inn on Shaftesbury rd.* **Adm £4.50, chd free. Wed 4 July (10.30-5.30). Visitors also welcome by appt July/Aug/Sept, guided tours for groups of 10-35.**
Hidden garden created in 1990s around C18 water mill (not open) on R Allen. Series of linked formal gardens featuring herbaceous and iris borders, pleached limes, white walk and wisteria-clad pergola. 20-acre nature reserve with reed beds and established shelter belts. Grazing meadows with wild flowers and flock of Dorset Horn sheep.

81 ◆ STICKY WICKET
Buckland Newton DT2 7BY. *Mrs P Lewis, 01300 345476, www.stickywicketgarden.co.uk. 11m N of Dorchester. 9m S of Sherborne. 3m E of A352 or take B3143 from Sturminster Newton. T-junction midway church, school & 300yds from Gaggle of Geese PH. Home-made teas on NGS days only.* **Adm £3.50, chd £1.50. Thurs, Fris 1 June to 28 Sept (10.30-8). For NGS: Suns 17 June; 19 Aug (2-6).**
Created since 1986, the garden is designed and planted as a haven for wildlife. Wandering through the 3 acres of gardens and meadows is a delightful experience and opportunity for both naturalist and plantsman to enjoy the colour-blended mingling of ornamental plants with wild flowers and grasses; a centre of information about naturalistic and wildlife gardening. 17 June Meadows Day, 19 Aug Butterfly Day (with Butterfly Conservation). Narrow gravel paths.

20-acre nature reserve with reed beds and established shelter belts . . .

STOURHEAD GARDEN
See Wiltshire.

82 TITHE BARN HOUSE
Chalk Pit Lane, Litton Cheney DT2 9AN. *Letizia & Antony Longland, 01308 482219. 10m W of Dorchester. 1m S of A35. Small village in beautiful Bride Valley. Follow signs in centre of village. Park on verge.* **Adm £3, chd free. Sun 24 June (2-5.30). Visitors also welcome by appt**

June/July only for groups of 10+. Just over an acre plus paddock. Wonderful views of almost the entire Bride Valley. Pergolas, lawns, mature trees, olives, shrubs, incl good roses, climbers and herbaceous plants, many pots, reflecting pool.

83 ◆ TOAD HALL
The Cross, Shillingstone DT11 0SP. *Elizabeth Arden & Norman Rogerson, 01258 861941, www.toadhalluk.co.uk. 5m NW of Blandford. On A357. Drive is opp Old Village Cross on highest point of village. Parking in village.* **Adm £2.50, chd 50p. Thurs June-Aug (2-5). For NGS: Suns 27 May; 26 Aug.**
Plantsman's country garden still developing. 1 acre on S-facing slope with wonderful views. Several different styled areas and growing habitats. Gardens incl Italian, decking, water, rockery, vegetable and wild. Relatively new area experimenting with different types of annual meadow and grass beds. Wheelchair access to decking overlooking gardens.

84 ◆ UPWEY WISHING WELL
161 Church Street, Upwey DT3 5QE. *Pauline, John & Julia Waring, 01305 814470. 3m N of Weymouth. On B3159 & just off Dorchester to Weymouth rd (A354). Home-made lunches.* **Entrance through café, adm free, but donations welcomed for NGS charities. Open daily (10-5), closed 2 weeks over Christmas & New Year.**
A tranquil, well-stocked water garden. Large natural spring, which is the source of the R Wey, is known as the Wishing Well and is an ancient monument. A fine show of bog primulas in May/June. Huge gunneras and unusual foliage plants provide a unique and exotic setting.

85 VINE COTTAGE
Melcombe Bingham DT2 7PE. *Wendy & Robert Jackson. 11m NE of Dorchester. Melcombe Bingham is 5m N of Puddletown and 5m W of Milton Abbas. Vine Cottage is in centre of village and just 1/4m past Fox Inn. Home-made teas.* **Adm £2.50, chd free. Suns 27 May; 10 June (11-5).**
Compact, well-stocked cottage garden with a wealth of interesting and unusual perennials and numerous containers. Specific areas incl patios,

pergola, arch trelliswork that host many roses and clematis, plus alpine-planted sink gardens. Emphasis on imaginative use of colour. Partial wheelchair access.

86 WARMWELL HOUSE

Warmwell DT2 8HQ. **Mr & Mrs H J C Ross Skinner.** *7m SE of Dorchester. Warmwell is signed off A352 between Dorchester & Wool. House is in centre of village.* **Adm £2.50, chd free. Suns 10 June; 22 July (2-6).**
An old garden with a Jacobean house (not open) set on ancient site of Domesday building. The 1617 front with Dutch gabelling has informal gardens. Square Dutch garden and maze on hill behind house. Mature topiary box plants for sale. Slopes, possibly slippery on damp/wet days, suitable only for strong wheelchair attendant.

WATERDALE HOUSE
See Wiltshire.

WAYFORD MANOR
See Somerset & Bristol Area.

87 WELCOME THATCH

Witchampton BH21 5AR. **Mrs Diana Guy, 01258 840894, diana.welcomethatch@btopenworld .com.** *3¹/₂m N of Wimborne. B3078 L to Witchampton, through village past church & club to last but one house on R. Parking available in club car park, otherwise on road beyond the cottage.* Home-made teas. **Adm £2.50, chd free. Suns 18 Feb; 11 Mar (1-4.30). 1 Apr; 6 May; 10 June; 8 July; 23 Sept (2-5).** Visitors also welcome by appt, coaches permitted.
Large cottage garden in idyllic village setting. Traditional borders lushly planted with unusual plants for long season of interest. Hanging baskets, containers, wildlife ponds and stream, productive greenhouse and vegetable gardens, dry gardens, prairie-style borders, oriental garden and tropical border. Thatched summerhouse, garden room with tender plants. Ample

seating, tranquil views. Partial wheelchair access, some steps.

88 WENTWORTH COLLEGE

College Road, Boscombe, Bournemouth BH5 2DY. **The Bursar.** *3m E of Bournemouth. Turn N from Boscombe Overcliff Drive into Woodland Ave. Then 1st R into College Rd.* Home-made teas. **Adm £2.50, chd free. Suns 22 Apr; 16 Sept (2-4.30).**
Originally the seaside estate of Lord Portman, Wentworth Lodge was built in 1872. The main Victorian house has gradually been extended to accommodate the needs of Wentworth College. Formal gardens have been restored to reflect their origins. The grounds also incl woodland with mature specimen trees and rhododendrons in approx 3 acres.

A dream of tropical planting ...
like coming into a different
world . . .

TARRANT VALLEY NEAR BLANDFORD

Peaceful, rural cottage Bed & Breakfast
Part of working farm -
locally sourced breakfast
Excellent pub within easy
walking distance

01258 830528
www.ramblerscottage.co.uk

89 24A WESTERN AVENUE
Branksome Park, Poole BH13 7AN.
Mr & Mrs Peter Jackson, 01202
708388,
peter@branpark.wanadoo.co.uk. *3m
W of Bournemouth. 1/2 m inland from
Branksome Chine beach. From S end
Wessex Way (A338) take The Avenue.
At T-lights turn R into Western Rd. At
church turn R into Western Ave.
Home-made teas.* **Adm £3, chd free.
Suns 24 June; 29 July (2-6). Visitors
also welcome by appt 17 June to 30
July for groups of 10+.**
'This secluded and magical 1-acre
garden captures the spirit of warmer
climes and begs for repeated visits'
('Gardening Which'); 'A dream of
tropical planting ... like coming into a
different world' ('Amateur Gardening').
June sees the rose garden at its best
whilst herbaceous beds shine in July.
Italian courtyard, wall and woodland
gardens, topiary and driftwood
sculptures.

90 WESTON HOUSE
Buckhorn Weston SP8 5HG. Mr &
Mrs E A W Bullock, 01963 371005.
*4m W of Gillingham, 3m SE of
Wincanton. From A30 turn N to
Kington Magna, continue towards
Buckhorn Weston & after railway
bridge take L turn towards Wincanton.
2nd on L is Weston House. Home-
made teas by arrangement.* **Adm
£2.50, chd free. Visitors welcome by
appt Apr to July incl.**
1-acre garden. Old walls host clematis
and roses. Mixed borders incl about 90
varieties old and modern roses, shrubs
and perennials. Small woodland of
ferns and shade-loving plants leads to
old orchard with ornamental grasses
and unusual trees, wildlife and flower
meadow areas, natural pond. Lawns
frame views of Blackmore Vale.

WHITE BARN
See Hampshire.

Shady valley with babbling brook . . .

91 WOLVERHOLLOW
Elsdons Lane, Monkton Wyld
DT6 6DA. Mr & Mrs D Wiscombe.
*4m N of Lyme Regis. 4m NW of
Charmouth. Monkton Wyld is signed
from A35 approx 4m NW of
Charmouth off dual carriageway.
Wolverhollow is next to the church.
Home-made teas.* **Adm £2.50, chd
free. Sun 13, Tue 15, Mon 28, Tue 29
May (11-5).**
Over 1 acre of informal garden. Lawns,
with unusual summerhouse, lead past
borders and rockeries to shady valley
with babbling brook. Numerous paths
pass wide variety of colourful and
uncommon plants. This year an area of
field sympathetically extends the
garden with streamside planting and
meadow.

Dorset County Volunteers

County Organiser
Harriet Boileau, Rampisham Manor, Dorchester DT2 0PT, 01935 83612, Harriet@Cubbins.co.uk

County Treasurer
Michael Gallagher, 6 West Street, Chickerell, Weymouth DT3 4DY, 01305 772557, michael.gallagher1@virgin.net

Publicity & Leaflets
Howard Ffitch, Brook House, Purse Caundle, Sherborne, DT9 5DY, 01963 250120, howard@ffwriter.fsnet.co.uk

Events
Carol Lindsay, The Old Rectory, Litton Cheney, Dorchester, DT2 9AH, 01308 482383, hugh_lindsay@talk21.com

Assistant County Organisers
West Central Harriet Boileau (contact details as above)
South Philippa & Anthony Bush, Holworth Farmhouse, Holworth, Dorchester DT2 8NH, 01305 852242, bushinarcadia@yahoo.co.uk
West Alison Halliday, Knowle Farm, Uploders, Bridport DT6 4NS, 01308 485492, alison@knowle-farm.fsnet.co.uk
Central Wendy Jackson, Vine Cottage, Melcombe Bingham, Dorchester DT2 7PE, 01258 880720, wendy@vinecott.fsnet.co.uk
North Caroline Renner, Croft Farm, Fontmell Magna, Shaftesbury SP7 0NR, 01747 811140, jamesrenner@talktalk.net
East, Bournmouth & Poole Penny Slade, 46 Roslin Road South, Bournemouth BH3 7EG, 01202 510243

DURHAM

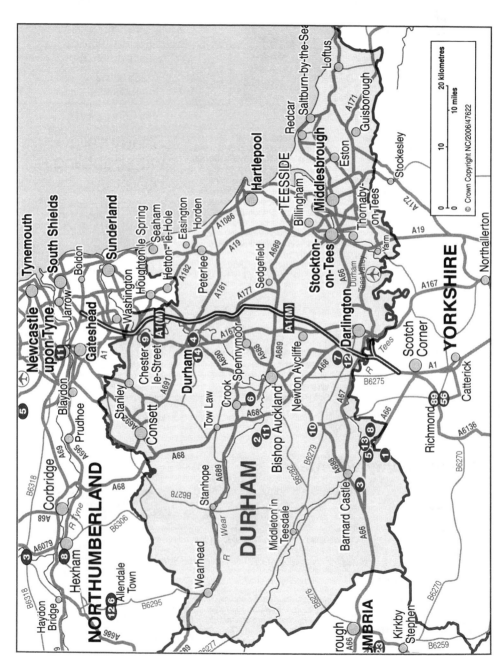

Opening Dates

April

SUNDAY 22
⑧ The Old Vicarage, Hutton Magna

June

SUNDAY 10
① Barningham Village Gardens
② Bedburn Hall

SUNDAY 17
⑤ Gardens in the Square
⑨ Park Road South Gardens

SUNDAY 24
⑫ Thornton Hall

SATURDAY 30
④ Crook Hall & Gardens

July

SUNDAY 1
③ Browside

SUNDAY 8
⑬ Thorpe Gardens

SUNDAY 15
⑦ Low Walworth Hall

SUNDAY 22
⑪ Ravensford Farm

SUNDAY 29
⑭ West Farm Court Gardens

Gardens open to the public

④ Crook Hall & Gardens
⑩ Raby Castle

By appointment only

⑥ 10 Low Row

The Gardens

① BARNINGHAM VILLAGE GARDENS
DL11 7DW. *6m SE of Barnard Castle. 9m W of Scotch Corner turn S off A66 at Greta Bridge, or from A66 motel via Newsham.* Home-made teas in village hall. **Adm £3, chd free. Sun 10 June (1-5).**
Quaint moorland village in conservation area. Approx 8 gardens open incl preview of 'Plantsman's Corner', a rare plant nursery opening 2010. Demonstrations throughout afternoon of various propagation techniques in 'Plantsmans Corner'. Partial wheelchair access.
♿ ✿ ☕

② BEDBURN HALL
Hamsterley DL13 3NN. I G Bonas, 01388 488231. *9m NW of Bishop Auckland. From A68 at Witton-le-Wear, turn off W to Hamsterley; turn N from Hamsterley to Bedburn, 1m. From Wolsingham on B6293 turn SE for 3m.* Home-made teas. **Adm £3, chd free. Sun 10 June (2-6). Visitors also welcome by appt June, July & Aug.**
Medium-sized S-facing terraced garden with large conservatory and greenhouse, lake, streams, woodland, lawns. Fuchsia collection and lavender bed, herbaceous border, fruit cage and rose garden. Gardener on hand to advise. Staindrop silver band will be playing. Enter by main gate, not field entrance.
♿ ✕ ✿ ☕

③ BROWSIDE
Boldron, Barnard Castle DL12 9RQ. Mr & Mrs R D Kearton. *3m S of Barnard Castle. On A66 3m W of Greta Bridge, turn R to Boldron, then proceed 1/2m, entrance opp junction. From Barnard Castle take A67 to Bowes, after 2m turn L to Boldron.* Home-made teas. **Adm £2.50, chd free. Sun 1 July (1-5.30).**
1 1/4 acres with unusual water features and large collection of conifers, wide range of plants and imaginative stone objects.
♿ ✿ ☕

④ ♦ CROOK HALL & GARDENS
Sidegate, Durham City DH1 5SZ. Maggie Bell, 0191 384 8028, www.crookhallgardens.co.uk. *Crook Hall is short walk from Durham's Market Place. Follow the tourist info signs. Parking available at entrance.* House and Garden adm £4.50, chd /concessions £4. 5 - 10 April incl; Suns & Bank Hols in May & Sept; daily (except Mon & Tue) 27 May to 9 Sept. For NGS: Sat 30 June (11-5).
Described in Country Life as having 'history, romance and beauty'. Intriguing medieval manor house surrounded by 4 acres of fine gardens. Visitors can enjoy magnificent cathedral views from the 2 walled gardens. Other garden 'rooms' incl the silver and white garden, orchard, moat, pool and maze. Featured on BBC Gardeners World.
✕ ☕

⑤ GARDENS IN THE SQUARE
The Square, Greta Bridge DL12 9SD. The Lady Gilbertson Settlement Trust & Mr & Mrs Peter Gilbertson. *3 1/2m SE of Barnard Castle. A66 W from Scotch Corner, after 8 1/2m L to Greta Bridge. 300yds from junction on L.* Home-made teas. **Adm £2.50, chd free. Sun 17 June (2-6).**
Collection of small gardens adjoining original coaching inn (not open) on the R Greta. One with a selection of unusual plants, old roses, herbs and pottager. Walk on river bank to woodland with banks of bluebells, foxgloves and ancient yew trees. Designated SSSI. Location the subject of many of John Sell Cotman's paintings.
♿ ✕ ✿ 🛏 ☕

⑥ NEW 10 LOW ROW
North Bitchburn, Crook DL15 8AJ. Mrs Ann Pickering, 01388 766345. *3m NW of Bishop Auckland. A689 N to Howden Le Wear, R up the bank before petrol stn. 1st R in village at 30mph sign.* **Adm £2, chd free. Visitors welcome by appt all year (not Tues), small groups only.**
Quirky original garden with 90% grown from seeds and cuttings. Extensive views over the Wear valley. An amazing garden created without commercially bought plants or expense. Totally organic and environmentally friendly. A haven for wildlife.
✕ ✿

⑦ LOW WALWORTH HALL
Darlington DL2 2NA. Mr & Mrs Worrall, 01325 468004, vanessaworrall@hotmail.com. *3 1/2m NW of Darlington. On B6279 Staindrop rd (1/2m drive).* Home-made teas. **Adm £3, chd free. Sun 15 July (2-5). Visitors also welcome by appt.**
Old walled garden; herbaceous borders, shrubs, roses; formal and wildlife ponds. Japanese and Zen gardens. Millennium fantasy garden and secret garden. Fruit and vegetable gardens. Tree walk. African theme garden. Some gravel paths.
♿ ✿ ☕

8 THE OLD VICARAGE, HUTTON MAGNA
nr Richmond, N Yorkshire DL11 7HJ. Mr & Mrs D M Raw. *8m SE of Barnard Castle. 6m W of Scotch Corner on A66, Penrith direction. Signed Hutton Magna R. Continue to, and through, village. Garden 200yds past village on L, on corner of T-junction.* Home-made teas. **Adm £3, chd free. Sun 22 Apr (2-5.30).**
S-facing garden, elevation 450ft. Plantings, since 1978, now maturing within original design contemporary to 1887 house (not open). Cut and topiary hedging, old orchard; rose and herbaceous borders featuring hellebores in profusion, with tulips and primulas.
⋇ ⊛ ☕

9 NEW PARK ROAD SOUTH GARDENS
Chester Le Street DH3 3LS. *4m N of Durham. A167 N towards Chester Le Street. L at roundabout (Durham Rd) to town centre. 1st R for parking and rear access to gardens only. S from A1 - 3rd roundabout then R as above.* Home-made teas. **Combined adm £2.50, chd free (share to St Cuthberts Hospice). Sun 17 June (2-5).**
Two plantswomens' gardens showing all yr round interest with colour, texture and foliage. One with a green courtyard garden and one with roses. Well-stocked herbacous borders. Solar dome. Craft Stall.
☕

NEW 25 PARK ROAD SOUTH
Mrs Allwyn Middleton, 0191 388 3225. *Visitors also welcome by appt . Easter to Sept, groups under 10.*
⋇ ⊛

NEW 26 PARK ROAD SOUTH
Mrs P Palmer.
⋇ ⊛

10 ◆ RABY CASTLE
Staindrop DL2 3AH. Lord Barnard, 01833 660202, www.rabycastle.com. *12m NW of Darlington, 1m N of Staindrop. On A688 8m NE of Barnard Castle.* **House and Garden adm £9, chd £4, concessions £8, Garden only adm £4, chd £2.50, concessions £3.50. Easter Sat to Mon, Bank Hols Sats; Sun to Wed May, June & Sept; daily except Sats July, Aug (gdn 11-5.30, castle 1-5).**
C18 walled gardens set within the grounds of Raby Castle. Designers such as Thomas White and James Paine have worked to establish the gardens, which now extend to 5 acres, display herbaceous borders, old yew hedges, formal rose gardens and informal heather and conifer gardens.
&. ⋇ ⊛

11 RAVENSFORD FARM
Hamsterley DL13 3NH. Mr & Mrs J Peacock, 01388 488305, peacock@ravensford.eclipse.co.uk. *7m W of Bishop Auckland. From A68 at Witton-le-Wear turn off W to Hamsterley. Go through village & turn L just before tennis courts.* Home-made teas. **Adm £3, chd 50p. Sun 22 July (2.30-5). Visitors also welcome by appt, no coaches please.**
2½-acre garden created since 1986 to blend with surrounding countryside and provide yr-round colour. Small wood progressively underplanted, 2 ponds, sunken garden, rhododendron walk and mixed borders containing flowering shrubs, many roses and herbaceous perennials - and a few surprises. New ornamental vegetable cages. Wheelchair access only with assistance.
&. ⋇ ⊛ ☕

12 THORNTON HALL
Staindrop Road, Darlington DL2 2NB. Mr & Mrs M P Manners, 01325 374260, mannersfarmsltd@msn.com. *On B6279 Staindrop Rd. 3m W of Darlington.* **Adm £4, chd free. Sun 24 June (2-5). Visitors also welcome by appt.**

C16 Grade I listed hall (not open). 2-acre walled gardens, recently planted. Plantsman's garden with emphasis on colour-themed borders, plant associations, form and foliage. Unusual perennials, interspersed with interesting trees and shrubs in mixed herbaceous borders, incl large collection of 200 hostas and 100 interesting roses. 2 ponds, one with designer waterfall.
&. ⋇ ⊛

13 THORPE GARDENS
DL12 9TU. *5m SE of Barnard Castle. 9m from Scotch Corner W on A66. Turn R at Peel House Farm Shop signed Wycliffe and Whorlton, 1m from A66.* Home-made teas. **Adm £3, chd free. Sun 8 July (2-5).**
Charming hamlet, 3 cottage gardens, one approx ¼ acre with some unusual plants. This year incl Thorpe Hall, a large interesting garden in the course of development by a professional designer.
&. ⋇ ⊛ ☕

14 NEW WEST FARM COURT GARDENS
Broompark DH7 7RN. Mrs Ann Millmore. *3m W of Durham. From Durham A690 to Crook, turn R at Stonebridge roundabout signed Broompark. Turn L 40yds after Loves PH. Park on main rd in layby just beyond PH.* Home-made teas. **Adm £3, chd free (share to St Cuthbert's Hospice). Sun 29 July (1.30-5.30).**
5 varied suburban gardens with assorted features. Good selection of perennials. One miniature garden with summerhouse, one newly landscaped with terracing. Some gardens have water features. Inspirational for smaller gardens. Plant Sale.
⊛ ☕

Durham County Volunteers

County Organiser
Shanah Smailes, The Stables, Chapman's Court, Catterick Village DL10 7UE, 01748 812887, shanah@smailes.go-plus.net

Assistant County Organiser
Elizabeth Carrick, Green House, Stone Man Lane, Gayles, nr Richmond DL11 7JB, 01833 621199, elizabeth@ecarrick.fsnet.co.uk

Grass runway, aviators welcome. Designer Thomas Heatherwick's hairy sitooterie provides an additional surprise. 1920s bicycle shop and motor museum . . .

Barnard's Farm, Essex

ESSEX

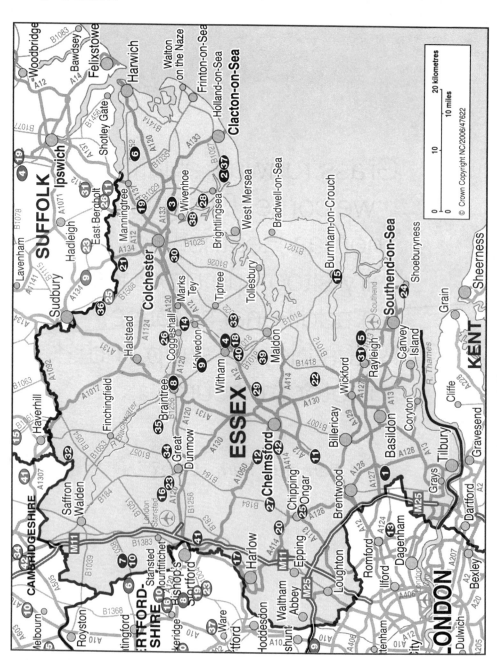

Opening Dates

March

SUNDAY 25
- 19 Green Island
- 42 Writtle College

April

THURSDAY 5
- 1 Barnards Farm
- 14 Feeringbury Manor

FRIDAY 6
- 14 Feeringbury Manor
- 18 Glen Chantry

SUNDAY 8
- 38 Tudor Roost

MONDAY 9
- 4 Braxted Place
- 38 Tudor Roost

THURSDAY 12
- 1 Barnards Farm
- 14 Feeringbury Manor

FRIDAY 13
- 14 Feeringbury Manor

SATURDAY 14
- 34 St Helens

SUNDAY 15
- 33 The Rookery

WEDNESDAY 18
- 12 Dragons

THURSDAY 19
- 1 Barnards Farm
- 14 Feeringbury Manor

FRIDAY 20
- 14 Feeringbury Manor

SATURDAY 21
- 38 Tudor Roost

SUNDAY 22
- 4 Braxted Place
- 20 Hobbans Farm
- 38 Tudor Roost

THURSDAY 26
- 1 Barnards Farm
- 14 Feeringbury Manor

FRIDAY 27
- 14 Feeringbury Manor
- 40 Wickham Place Farm

SUNDAY 29
- 39 Ulting Wick

May

WEDNESDAY 2
- 35 Saling Hall

THURSDAY 3
- 1 Barnards Farm

- 14 Feeringbury Manor

FRIDAY 4
- 14 Feeringbury Manor
- 18 Glen Chantry
- 40 Wickham Place Farm

SUNDAY 6
- 4 Braxted Place
- 20 Hobbans Farm

MONDAY 7
- 4 Braxted Place

WEDNESDAY 9
- 35 Saling Hall

THURSDAY 10
- 1 Barnards Farm
- 14 Feeringbury Manor

FRIDAY 11
- 14 Feeringbury Manor
- 40 Wickham Place Farm

SATURDAY 12
- 2 Barnfield

SUNDAY 13
- 2 Barnfield
- 27 The Mill House

WEDNESDAY 16
- 12 Dragons
- 35 Saling Hall

THURSDAY 17
- 1 Barnards Farm
- 14 Feeringbury Manor

FRIDAY 18
- 14 Feeringbury Manor
- 40 Wickham Place Farm

SATURDAY 19
- 6 Chippins

SUNDAY 20
- 20 Hobbans Farm

WEDNESDAY 23
- 35 Saling Hall

THURSDAY 24
- 1 Barnards Farm
- 14 Feeringbury Manor

FRIDAY 25
- 14 Feeringbury Manor
- 40 Wickham Place Farm

SUNDAY 27
- 4 Braxted Place
- 27 The Mill House
- 38 Tudor Roost

MONDAY 28
- 4 Braxted Place
- 23 Little Easton Gardens
- 38 Tudor Roost

WEDNESDAY 30
- 35 Saling Hall

THURSDAY 31
- 1 Barnards Farm
- 14 Feeringbury Manor

June

FRIDAY 1
- 14 Feeringbury Manor
- 18 Glen Chantry
- 40 Wickham Place Farm

SUNDAY 3
- 4 Braxted Place
- 11 23 Docklands Avenue
- 20 Hobbans Farm
- 28 Moverons
- 29 The Old Rectory

TUESDAY 5
- 38 Tudor Roost

WEDNESDAY 6
- 35 Saling Hall

THURSDAY 7
- 1 Barnards Farm
- 14 Feeringbury Manor

FRIDAY 8
- 14 Feeringbury Manor
- 40 Wickham Place Farm

SUNDAY 10
- 13 Edelweiss
- 41 Woolards Ash

TUESDAY 12
- 38 Tudor Roost

WEDNESDAY 13
- 35 Saling Hall

THURSDAY 14
- 1 Barnards Farm
- 14 Feeringbury Manor

FRIDAY 15
- 14 Feeringbury Manor
- 40 Wickham Place Farm

SATURDAY 16
- 34 St Helens

SUNDAY 17
- 7 Clavering Gardens
- 10 Deers
- 20 Hobbans Farm
- 31 Orchard Cottage

TUESDAY 19
- 38 Tudor Roost

WEDNESDAY 20
- 12 Dragons
- 35 Saling Hall

THURSDAY 21
- 1 Barnards Farm
- 14 Feeringbury Manor

FRIDAY 22
- 14 Feeringbury Manor

Feeringbury Manor

15 4 Fernlea Road
40 Wickham Place Farm

SUNDAY 24
1 Barnards Farm
32 Parsonage House
38 Tudor Roost

TUESDAY 26
38 Tudor Roost

WEDNESDAY 27
35 Saling Hall

THURSDAY 28
1 Barnards Farm
14 Feeringbury Manor

FRIDAY 29
14 Feeringbury Manor
40 Wickham Place Farm

July

SUNDAY 1
8 352 Coggeshall Road
11 23 Docklands Avenue
20 Hobbans Farm
25 Little Myles

WEDNESDAY 4
35 Saling Hall

THURSDAY 5
1 Barnards Farm
14 Feeringbury Manor

FRIDAY 6
14 Feeringbury Manor
15 4 Fernlea Road
18 Glen Chantry
40 Wickham Place Farm

SUNDAY 8
19 Green Island
33 The Rookery

WEDNESDAY 11
35 Saling Hall

THURSDAY 12
1 Barnards Farm
14 Feeringbury Manor

FRIDAY 13
14 Feeringbury Manor
40 Wickham Place Farm

SATURDAY 14
2 Barnfield
6 Chippins

SUNDAY 15
2 Barnfield
20 Hobbans Farm
42 Writtle College

WEDNESDAY 18
12 Dragons
35 Saling Hall

THURSDAY 19
1 Barnards Farm
14 Feeringbury Manor

FRIDAY 20
14 Feeringbury Manor
40 Wickham Place Farm

SATURDAY 21
38 Tudor Roost

SUNDAY 22
31 Orchard Cottage
38 Tudor Roost

WEDNESDAY 25
35 Saling Hall

THURSDAY 26
1 Barnards Farm
14 Feeringbury Manor

FRIDAY 27
14 Feeringbury Manor
40 Wickham Place Farm

SUNDAY 29
13 Edelweiss

August

FRIDAY 3
18 Glen Chantry

SATURDAY 4
38 Tudor Roost

SUNDAY 5
38 Tudor Roost

WEDNESDAY 15
12 Dragons

SATURDAY 18
24 Little Foxes

SUNDAY 19
24 Little Foxes

SUNDAY 26
10 Deers
13 Edelweiss
38 Tudor Roost

MONDAY 27
13 Edelweiss
38 Tudor Roost

September

SUNDAY 2
1 Barnards Farm
20 Hobbans Farm
33 The Rookery

THURSDAY 6
14 Feeringbury Manor

FRIDAY 7
14 Feeringbury Manor

SUNDAY 9
28 Moverons

THURSDAY 13
14 Feeringbury Manor

FRIDAY 14
14 Feeringbury Manor
34 St Helens

SUNDAY 16
20 Hobbans Farm

WEDNESDAY 19
12 Dragons

THURSDAY 20
14 Feeringbury Manor

FRIDAY 21
14 Feeringbury Manor

THURSDAY 27
14 Feeringbury Manor

FRIDAY 28
14 Feeringbury Manor

October

SUNDAY 7
19 Green Island

November

SUNDAY 11
19 Green Island

February 2008

SUNDAY 17
19 Green Island

Private gardens opening regularly for the NGS

14 Feeringbury Manor
38 Tudor Roost

Gardens open to the public

3 Beth Chatto Gardens
9 Cressing Temple
16 The Gardens of Easton Lodge
17 The Gibberd Garden
18 Glen Chantry
19 Green Island
22 RHS Garden Hyde Hall
26 Marks Hall Gardens & Arboretum

By appointment only

5 Canonteign
21 Horkesley Hall
30 Olivers
36 Shrubs Farm
37 Springvale

The Gardens

① BARNARDS FARM

Brentwood Road, West Horndon CM13 3LX. Bernard & Sylvia Holmes & The Christabella Charitable Trust, 01277 811262, www.barnardsfarm.org. *5m S of Brentwood. On A128, 1½m S of A127. Halfway House flyover. From the junction continue on A128 under the railway bridge. Garden on R just past bridge.* Teas (Suns), Light lunches (Thurs). **Adm £4, chd free (share to St Francis Church, West Horndon). Thurs, 5 Apr to 26 July (11-4.30); Suns 24 June; 2 Sept (2-5.30). Visitors also welcome by appt, for groups of 30+, special needs 10+.** Significant sculpture collection, is elegantly displayed throughout 17 hectares of landscaped garden, woodland and ponds. Panoramic views from rose-covered belvedere, Japanese, vegetable and bog gardens, parterre, herbaceous borders. National Collection malus. Grass runway, aviators welcome. Designer Thomas Heatherwick's hairy sitooterie provide an additional surprise. 1920s bicycle shop and motor museum, plant sales (Suns only). Thurrock Youth Jazz Orchestra (Suns). Featured in House & Garden.

  ♿ ✕ ⌘ NCCPG ☕

② BARNFIELD

35 Point Clear Road, St Osyth CO16 8EP. Christine & Paul Harman, 01255 820215, christine.harman@essexcc.gov.uk. *4m W of Clacton on Sea. W of Xrds in village, towards Point Clear, across the dam approx 300yds up hill on L.* Light refreshments & teas. **Adm £2, chd free. Sats, Suns 12, 13 May; 14, 15 July (10-5). Visitors also welcome by appt.** Wander through a collection of native trees, 2 rare black poplar, katsura, sweet gum maple, honey locust, Chinese elm and ginkgo. Greenhouses with collections of cacti and succulents, dry garden, ornamental pond, 2 fern gardens and new bog garden with giant gunnera by natural stream. See our working model railway layout. Plenty of seats to rest on. Gravel side alley, gradual slope to stream bridge.

  ♿ ⌘ ☕

③ ♦ BETH CHATTO GARDENS

Elmstead Market CO7 7DB. Mrs Beth Chatto, 01206 822007, www.bethchatto.co.uk. *¼m E of Elmstead Market. On A133.* Light refreshments & teas. **Adm £4.50, chd free, for groups 25+ £4. Mons to Sats, Mar to Oct (9-5); Mons to Fris Nov to Feb (9-4). Closed on Suns.** 5 acres of attractively landscaped garden with many unusual plants, shown in wide range of conditions from hot and dry to water garden. Famous gravel garden and woodland garden. Disabled wc and parking.

  ♿ ✕ ⌘ ☕

④ BRAXTED PLACE

Kelvedon Road, Little Braxted CM8 3LD. Mr & Mrs J Booker, 01621 891502. *2m S of Witham. J22 A12 follow signs to Little Braxted along narrow winding lane past mill & church. 1m on, the lane joins Kelvedon Rd. Straight on for 400yds keep L at village green. House ahead with Green Man PH on R. Turn L into small parking area opp chapel.* Home-made teas. **Adm £2.50, chd free. Mons, Suns 9, 22 Apr; 6, 7, 27, 28 May, 3 June (11-5). Visitors also welcome by appt.** Mature organic garden of approx 1 acre surrounding Georgian former rectory (not open), with attached Victorian chapel (open with garden). Walled kitchen and herb garden, conservatory, gravel garden. Informal lawns, borders, wild areas and mature trees give a romantic feel especially in spring.

  ✕ ⌘ ☕

⑤ CANONTEIGN

47 Hill Lane, Hawkwell SS5 4HW. Margaret Taylor, 01702 206387, brian.brianhockley@hockley34.freeserve.co.uk. *4m NE of Rayleigh. Leave A127 at Rayleigh Weir, take A129 to Rayleigh through town. Then B1013 to Hockley-Hawkwell 4m. Train: 10 mins walk from Hockley stn. Bus: no 8 Rayleigh-Southend White Hart Garage stop, 2 min walk.* **Adm £3.50 incl refreshments, chd free. Visitors welcome by appt.** Exciting colourful garden, approx 76ft x 70ft, many different scenes. Tender plants and varied perennials, unusual plants in containers, water features, aviary, fish, arches and pergolas. Topiarised conifers. Conservatory with bougainvillea and other varieties of plants.

  ✕ ☕

⑥ NEW CHIPPINS

Heath Road, Bradfield CO11 2UZ. Kit & Ceri Leese, 01255 870730, ceri.leese1@tiscali.co.uk. *3m E of Manningtree. On B1352, take main rd through village. Bungalow is directly opp primary school.* Home-made teas. **Adm £2, chd free. Sats 19 May; 14 July (11-5). Visitors also welcome by appt.** Plantaholics paradise packed with interest all yr. Mixed borders with decorative trees, shrubs and perennials. 30ft stream and ponds, densely planted with hostas, tree ferns and some tropical marginals. Irises, tree peony and alliums in spring. Explosion of colour in summer with unusual hemercallis and abundance of tubs and hanging baskets.

  ♿ ✕ ☕

⑦ CLAVERING GARDENS

CB11 4PX. *7m N of Bishops Stortford. On B1038. Turn W off B1383 at Newport.* Home-made teas at April Cottage. **Combined adm £3.50, chd free. Sun 17 June (2-5).** Popular village with many C16 & 17 timber-framed dwellings, beautiful C14 church.

  ☕

APRIL COTTAGE

Mr & Mrs Harris
Charming thatched cottage with small, very colourful garden packed with many unusual plants, old fashioned roses, bog garden and raised pond.

Explosion of colour in summer with unusual hemercallis and abundance of tubs and hanging baskets . . .

DEERS
Mr & Mrs S H Cooke
(See separate entry).
🅰

PIERCEWEBBS
Mr & Mrs B R William-Powlett
Old walled garden, shrubs, lawns, ha-ha, yew with topiary and stilt hedges, pond and trellised rose garden. Extensive views.
&

Sau Lin arrived from Hong Kong to become entralled with English gardening 'This is my little heaven' she says of her garden . . .

⑧ NEW 352 COGGESHALL ROAD
Braintree CM7 9EH. Sau Lin Goss, 01376 329753, richiegoss@hotmail.com. *15m W of Colchester. 10m N of Chelmsford. From M11 J8 take A120 Colchester. Follow A120 to Braintree roundabout (McDonalds). 1st exit into xxxx Rd follow to T-lights. R into Coggeshall Rd. 500yds on R opp bus company.* Light refreshments & teas. **Adm £2.50, chd free. Sun 1 July (11-5). Visitors also welcome by appt, Suns June, July & Aug. Groups of up to 25, 3 weeks notice required.**
Sau Lin arrived from Hong Kong to become entralled with English gardening 'This is my little heaven' she says of her garden which has various themed areas. perennials.

⑨ NEW ◆ CRESSING TEMPLE
Witham Road, Cressing CM77 8PD. Essex County Council, 01376 584903. *Misway between Braintree & Witham on B1018. Follow brown tourist signs.* **Adm £3.50, chd free, concessions £2.50. Daily (not Sat) 1 March to 31 Oct 10-5, Mon to Fri 1 Nov to 28 Feb 10-4.**
Tudor (originial) walled garden in tranquil setting, featuring reconstructed Elizabethen knot garden, forecourt, nosegay garden, medicinal border and fountain centrepiece. Inspired by 'A Midsummer Night's Dream', only plants, trees and foliage available to the Tudor gardener are found here. Guided tours are available on request. Recently-planted Cullen garden is lawn with curving borders enclosed by herbaceous plants and shrubs. Two 800 yr-old timber framed barns built by the Knights Templar form a beautiful backdrop to the walled garden. Visitors can wander the 7 acres of this ancient moated site. Featured on BBC Cash in the Attic & How We Built Britain.
🅰 ⊕ ☕

⑩ DEERS
Clavering CB11 4PX. Mr & Mrs S H Cooke. *7m N of Bishops Stortford. On B1038. Turn W off B1383 (old A11) at Newport.* Home-made teas. **Adm £3.50, chd free. Sun 26 Aug (2-5). Open with Clavering Gardens Sun 17 June.**
9 acres. Judged by visitors to be a very romantic garden. Shrub and herbaceous borders; ponds with water lilies; old roses in formal garden; pool garden; walled vegetable garden; field and woodland walks.
& 🅰 ☕

⑪ 23 DOCKLANDS AVENUE
Ingatestone CM4 9DS. Paul & Doreen Crowder. *6m SW of Chelmsford. Take A414 to Margaretting, then B1002 to Ingatestone (6m). Docklands Ave 1st L at village sign (opp playing field).* Tea & cakes. **Adm £2.50, chd free. Suns 3 June; 1 July (11-5).**
True plant enthusiast's mature-acre garden, with many surprises. Gravelled area of poppies and eremurus, copse of tree ferns, arisagma, huge delphiniums, 'pale and interesting'

border, pond edged with iris and primula, 90+ clematis, orchid house and much more.
& 🅰 ⊕ ☕

⑫ DRAGONS
Boyton Cross, Chelmsford CM1 4LS. Mrs Margot Grice, 01245 248651. *5m W of Chelmsford. On A1060. 1/2m west of The Hare PH.* **Adm £2, chd free. Weds 18 Apr; 16 May; 20 June; 18 July; 15 Aug; 19 Sept (10-5). Visitors also welcome by appt.**
Plantsman's garden of 2/3 acre. Front garden, mature dwarf conifers and grasses, 2 ponds, patios, scree garden and colour-themed borders. Summerhouse overlooking stream and farmland.
🅰 ⊕ ☕

⑬ EDELWEISS
20 Hartland Road, Hornchurch RM12 4AD. Joan H Hogg & Pat F Lowery, 01708 454610. *6m SW of Brentwood. From Romford E along the A124 past Tesco on L, turn R into Albany Rd opp church on corner of Park Lane on the L. Go to the bottom of Albany Rd, humps all the way, turn L at the end into Hartland Rd.* Home-made teas. **Adm £1.50, chd free. Suns 10 June; 29 July; 26, Mon 27 Aug (3-6). Visitors also welcome by appt, June & July.**
Small town garden 200ft x 25ft. Laid out to maximise small narrow plot and featuring many containers, baskets, seasonal bedding and mixed borders. Narrow access and steps not suitable for push-chairs or wheelchairs. Vegetable plot, poultry, dovecote and tiny prize-winning front garden. 'Secret Garden' with Pets' Remembrance Corner. Prize-winner 'Havering in Bloom'.
⊕ ☕

⑭ FEERINGBURY MANOR
Coggeshall Road, Feering CO5 9RB. Mr & Mrs Giles Coode-Adams, 01376 561946, sonia@coode-adams.demon.co.uk. *12m SW of Colchester. Between Coggeshall & Feering on Coggeshall Rd, 1m from Feering.* **Adm £3, chd free (share to Firstsite). Thurs, Fris, 5 Apr to 27 July; 6 Sept to 28 Sept (8-4). Visitors also welcome by appt.**
Flower beds and arboretum expand as we collect more interesting plants. We have gone wild in the pursuit of continual colour. Gardener, Ellen Fairbanks, propagates energetically by

seed and cuttings. The ex-rose bed, now pink and purple, is newly backed by a fantastic sculptured steel trellis, 50 metres long by Ben Coode-Adams. Featured in 'The English Garden'. Some steep slopes.

&. ✗ ⊛

⑮ NEW 4 FERNLEA ROAD
Burnham-on-Crouch CM0 8EJ.
Frances & Andrew Franklin,
franklins@2s.com. *Take B1010 to Burnham-on-Crouch. Then cross the railway bridge take 4th turn on R, Hillside Rd. Fernlea Rd 2nd L, no.4 nr end of cul de sac on L.* Home-made teas. **Adm £2.50, chd free. Fris 22 June; 6 July (1-6). Visitors also welcome by appt, June & July only.**
Small Mediterranean style garden on edge of riverside park. The planting, which is informal and exuberant, features several unusual varieties. Several seating areas, large covered pergola, mosaics, sculptures, water features and loads of pots - also a number of innovative solutions for dealing with drought. Garden will contain sculptures as part of the Burnham Art Trail. The 'trail' has many sites in this lovely small riverside town.

&. ☕

Several seating areas, mosaics, sculptures, water features and loads of pots . . .

⑯ ◆ THE GARDENS OF EASTON LODGE
Great Dunmow CM6 2BB. Mr & Mrs B Creasey, 01371 876979, www.eastonlodge.co.uk. *1½ m N of Dunmow. Brown heritage signs from A120, W of Dunmow.* **Adm £4.20, chd £1.70, concessions £3.80. Feb - Mar Snowdrops daily Noon til Dusk. Fris, Sats, Suns & Bank Hols 6 Apr to 28 Oct (11-6).**

Home of 'Darling Daisy', Countess of Warwick, who in 1903 commissioned Harold Peto to lay out Italian and Japanese gardens. Abandoned 1950; major restoration since 1993 incl brick and cobble courtyard, ponds, C17 dovecote, conservatory and pavilion. Work started on sunken Italian garden. Living millennium sundial and Shakespeare border. History Exhibition. Wheelchair access except snowdrops. Subject to heavy rainfall in winter.

&. ⊛ ☕

⑰ ◆ THE GIBBERD GARDEN
Marsh Lane, Harlow CM17 0NA. The Gibberd Garden Trust, 01279 442112, www.thegibberdgarden.co.uk. *3m E of Harlow. Marsh Lane is a narrow turning off B183 (to Hatfield Heath), approx 2m E of junction with A414. Look for 'Gibberd Garden' brown signs on A414 & on R opp garden entrance on B183.* **Adm £4, chd free, concessions £2.50. Sats, Suns, Weds, Bank Hols Mar to Sept 2-6.**
7-acre C20 garden designed by Sir Frederick Gibberd, on side of small valley. Terraces, wild garden, landscaped vistas, pools and streams, 'Roman Temple', moated log 'castle', gazebo, tree house and large collection of modern sculpture. Featured in 'Grand Designs'.

&. ☕

⑱ ◆ GLEN CHANTRY
Wickham Bishops CM8 3LG. Mr & Mrs W G Staines, 01621 891342, www.glenchantry.demon.co.uk. *1½ m SE of Witham. Take Maldon Rd, 1st L to Wickham Bishops. Cross narrow bridge over R Blackwater. Turn immed L up Ishams Chase by side of Blue Mills.* **Adm £3.50, chd 50p. Fris, Sats 6 Apr to 1 Sept (10-4). For NGS: Fris 6 Apr; 4 May; 1 June; 6 July; 3 Aug (10-4).**
3-acre garden, emphasis on mixed borders, unusual perennials and shrub roses. Limestone rock gardens, ponds, formal specialist white garden, foliage beds with grasses and hostas. Famous adjacent Specialist Perennial Nursery.

✗ ⊛ ☕

⑲ ◆ GREEN ISLAND
Park Road, Ardleigh CO7 7SP. Fiona Edmond, 01206 230455, www.greenislandgardens.co.uk. *3m NE of Colchester. From Ardleigh village centre, take B1029 towards Great Bromley. Park Rd is 2nd on R after*

level Xing. Garden is last on L. **Adm £3, chd £1. Suns, Weds, Thurs, Bank Hol Mons, 1 March to 12 Oct. For NGS: Suns 25 Mar; 8 July; 7 Oct; 11 Nov (10-5); 2008 17 Feb.**
'A garden in the making', professionally designed by Fiona Edmond, beautifully situated in 19 acres of woodland. Huge variety of unusual plants with lots of interest all yr with emphasis on scent and autumn colour. Mixed borders, water garden, woodland walks, seaside garden, tree house and gravel garden. Garden design exhibition, contemporary sculptures. Large area of woodland redevelopment. Snowdrops and bluebells not to be missed.

&. ✗ ⊛ ☕

24 HILLS ROAD
See London.

⑳ HOBBANS FARM
Bobbingworth CM5 0LZ. John & Ann Webster, 01277 890245. *10m W of Chelmsford. N of A414 between Ongar Four Wantz roundabout & N Weald 'Talbot' roundabout just past Blake Hall Gardens. 1st farm entrance on R after St Germain's Church.* Home-made teas. **Adm £2.50, chd free. Suns 22 Apr; 6, 20 May; 3, 17 June; 1, 15 July; 2, 16 Sept (2-5). Visitors also welcome by appt.**
Romantic, tranquil gardens surrounding C16 farmhouse (not open) and barns. Herbaceous treasures jostle with shrubs and old roses. Honeysuckle, roses, clematis clamber through trees, up walls and over arches. Crab apples underplanted with narcissi, unusual trees. Walk through meadows past willow and young birch to wild garden, wood and pond with bridge to ancient oak. Take tea in pot yard amidst grasses, bamboos and ferns. Featured on Sky TV 'Britains Favourite Blooms - Honeysuckle'.

&. ✗ ⊛ ☕

㉑ HORKESLEY HALL
Little Horkesley, Colchester CO6 4DB. Mr & Mrs Johnny Eddis, 01206 271371, pollyeddis@hotmail.com. *3m N of Colchester. W of A134. Access is via church car park.* **Visitors welcome by appt. Teas by arrangement, guided tour if required.**
7-8 acres of romantic garden surrounding classical house (not open) with appeal for all ages. Stream feeds 2 lakes, many wonderful trees some very rare. The largest ginkgo tree

Restored late C18 watermill. The only working turbine powered mill in East Anglia . . .

outside Kew. Walled garden, pear ave, acer walk, fruit, cutflowers and vegetables, blossom, bulbs, rhododendrons, herbaceous, autumn colour and many spring bulbs and blossom. Rare hens and black swans. Visitors looked after by owners with tea indoors or on the lawn. Gravel paths and slopes.

㉒ ◆ RHS GARDEN HYDE HALL
Buckhatch Lane, Rettendon CM3 8ET. Royal Horticultural Society, 01245 400256, www.rhs.org.uk. *7m SE of Chelmsford, 6m NE of Wickford. Signed from A130, at Rettendon.* Adm £5, chd £1. Open all yr except Christmas Day, for opening times see website or tel.
28-acre mixed garden. Many flowering trees, shrubs, perennials and colour themed borders, spring and summer bulbs. Large ponds with water lilies and marginal plants, woodland and alpine plantings. Extensive rose gardens. National Collection of viburnum. Highly acclaimed 'Dry Garden' of drought tolerant plants, and Australian/New Zealand border.

㉓ LITTLE EASTON GARDENS
CM6 2HZ. *1/2 m N of Great Dunmow. 1st turning L, on the B184 to Thaxted.* Home-made teas in Elmbridge Mill. Combined adm £3.50, chd free (share to Macmillan Cancer Support). Mon 28 May (2-5).
Small village with lovely church and lakes.

CHURCH LODGE
Vivienne Crossland
A fun garden. Infused with vibrance and peace which will both surprise and delight! Many quirky corners and interesting features - look for the surprising stag.

ELMBRIDGE MILL
Dr & Mrs Grahame Swan
Mill house (not open) with mill stream one side flowing under the house, R Chelmer on other. Approx 1 acre of trees, flowers and shrubs; roses climbing through orchard trees; walk up to mill pool with the addition of a new bridge across the mill race. Romantic garden full of interesting plants.

㉔ LITTLE FOXES
Marcus Gardens, Thorpe Bay SS1 3LF. Mrs Dorothy Goode. *2 1/2 m E of Southend. From Thorpe Bay stn (S-side) proceed E, take 4th on R into Marcus Ave then 2nd L into Marcus Gdns.* Adm £2, chd 50p. Sat 18, Sun 19 Aug (2-5).
This award-winning garden, close to the sea, has been described as an oasis of foliage and flowers. Secluded by trees, the 1/3 acre features island beds and long borders set in lawns and planted with an interesting variety of colourful hardy perennials, grasses, flowering shrubs and beautiful foliage. Many planted containers. Colour-themed areas and pretty water feature. Collection of special hostas. Tranquil garden for plant lovers. Seaside walks and views close by. Featured on BBC Essex Radio.

㉕ LITTLE MYLES
Ongar Road, Stondon Massey CM15 0LD. Judy & Adrian Cowan. *1 1/2 m SE of Chipping Ongar. Turn off A128 at Stag PH, Marden Ash, (Ongar) towards Stondon Massey. Over bridge, 1st house on R after S bend. (400yds the Ongar side of Stondon Massey Church).* Home-made teas. Adm £3, chd £1. Sun 1 July (11-4).
Romantic garden surrounded by wild flowers and grasses, set in 3 acres. Full borders, hidden features, meandering paths, pond, hornbeam pergola and stream. Herb garden, full of nectar-rich and scented herbs, used for

handmade herbal cosmetics. New Asian garden with pots, statues and bamboo.

㉖ ◆ MARKS HALL GARDENS & ARBORETUM
Coggeshall CO6 1TG. Thomas Phillips Price Trust, 01376 563796, www.markshall.org. *1 1/2 m N of Coggeshall. Follow brown & white tourism signs from A120 Coggeshall by pass.* Adm £3, chd £1, groups £2 per head. Tues to Sun Apr to Oct (10.30-5), Fri to Sun Nov to Mar 10.30 - dusk.
The walled garden at Marks Hall is a unique blend of traditional long borders within C17 walls and 5 contemporary gardens. These combine inventive landscaping, grass sculpture and stunningly colourful mass plantings. On the opp lake bank is a millennium walk designed for winter shape, scent and colour surrounded by over 100 acres of arboretum, incl species from all continents.

㉗ THE MILL HOUSE
Queen Street, Fyfield CM5 0RZ. Mr & Mrs D Baker. *From Ongar. From A414 take B184 (N) at Four Wantz roundabout. Turn R in centre of village, 150 metres ahead, by river.* Adm £3, chd free. Sun 13, 27 May (11-5).
1 1/2-acre garden, ponds and borders by R Roding. Restored late C18 watermill. The only working turbine powered mill in East Anglia. Opening 13th May will be to co-incide with National Mills Weekend. Water permitting, there will be regular demonstrations of the mill working. The windmill at Aythorp Roding (4m) will also be open. Some areas not accessible for wheelchairs in wet weather, access to ground floor only of mill.

㉘ MOVERONS
Brightlingsea CO7 0SB. Lesley Orrock, 01206 305498, lesley@moverons.com. *7m SE of Colchester. B1027. Turn R in Thorrington onto B1029 signed Brightlingsea. At old church turn R signed Moverons Farm, follow lane & garden signs for approx 1m.* Home-made teas. Adm £2.50, chd free. Suns 3 June; 9 Sept (11-5). Visitors also welcome by appt, groups of 10+, coaches welcome.
Maturing 4 1/2-acre garden designed by

owner. Wide variety of planting incl walled garden, bog and poolside, hot colours, drought beds and range of mixed beds for sun and shade filled with shrubs and perennials. 2 large ponds with landscaped vistas, mature trees and stunning estuary views. Featured in 'Essex Life' & 'Garden News'.

♟ ✿ ☕

29 THE OLD RECTORY
Boreham CM3 3EP. Sir Jeffery & Lady Bowman, 01245 467233, bowmansuzy@aol.com. *4m NE of Chelmsford. Take B1137 Boreham Village, turn into Church Rd at Red Lion PH.* 1/2 m along on R opp church. Home-made teas. **Adm £2.50, chd free. Sun 3 June (2-5). Visitors also welcome by appt May & June.**
2 1/2 acre garden surrounding C15 house (not open). Ponds, stream, with bridges and primulas, small meadow and wood with interesting trees and shrubs, herbaceous borders and vegetable garden. Constantly being improved. Partial wheelchair access: soft ground by stream, gravel drive, chairs can go over lawn.
♿ ♟ ✿ ☕

30 OLIVERS
Olivers Lane, Colchester CO2 0HJ. Mr & Mrs D Edwards, gay.edwards@virgin.net. *3m SW of Colchester. Between B1022 & B1026. From zoo continue 1m towards Colchester. Turn R at roundabout (Cunobelin Way) & R into Olivers Lane. From Colchester via Maldon Rd turn L at roundabout, R into Olivers Lane.* Light refreshments & teas. **Adm £3, chd free. Visitors welcome by appt any time of year, any number.** Parking for 2 coaches. Tour of garden and refreshments included in admission.
Peaceful wooded garden overlooking Roman river valley. Dramatic bedding, yew backed borders closely planted with wide variety of plants. Refreshments on terrace of C18 redbrick house (not open) overlooking lakes, lawns and meadow. Woodland with fine trees, underplanted with shrubs and carpeted with a mass of spring bulbs and bluebells. Featured in 'The English Garden'.
♿ ♟ ☕

31 ORCHARD COTTAGE
219 Hockley Road, Rayleigh SS6 8BH. Heather & Harry Brickwood, 01268 743838,

henry.brickwood@homecall.co.uk. *1m NE from town centre. Leave A127 at Rayleigh and take B1013 to Hockley. Garden opp the white & blue sign for Hockley. Park opp on grass.* Home-made teas. **Adm £2.50, chd free. Suns 17 June; 22 July (11-5). Visitors also welcome by appt May to Aug, groups of 4+.**
The garden, about 3/4-acres, has had several trees and conifers removed to enlarge and allow more light to borders. For the June opening the main feature will be the aquilegias, 100's of them, these will be backed up by roses, lilies and numerous other herbaceous perennials, the July feature will be hemerocallis, more lillies, agapanthus plus colour themed beds. There is a pond, stream and many flowering shrubs. Featured on BBC Essex. Entrance is on a hill, gravel drive.
♿ ♟ ✿ ☕

32 PARSONAGE HOUSE
Helions Bumpstead CB9 7AD. The Hon & Mrs Nigel Turner. *3m S of Haverhill. 8m NE of Saffron Walden. From Xrds in village centre turn up Church Hill, follow rd for 1m. Park in field opp.* Home-made teas. **Adm £3.50, chd free. Sun 24 June (2-5).**
C15 house (not open) surrounded by 3 acres of formal gardens with mixed borders, topiary, pond, potager and greenhouse. Further 3-acre wild flower meadow with rare trees and further 3 acres of newly-planted orchard of old East Anglian apple varieties.
♿ ♟ ✿ ☕

33 NEW THE ROOKERY
Rookery Lane, Gt Totham, Maldon CM9 8DF. Ted & Linda Walker. *2m S of Tiptree. Situated in Gt Totham N, Rookery Lane is off B1022 Maldon to Colchester rd.* **Adm £2.50, chd free. Suns 15 Apr (12-4); 8 July; 2 Sept (1-5).**
Surprising garden with plant collections of roses, hemerocallis, clematis, rhododendrons and, in spring, many bulbs. In the distance a wooded glen with stream,

waterside plants and amazing swathe of intensely blue hydrangeas. Ponds with koi carp and small waterfall.
♟

34 NEW ST HELENS
High Street, Stebbing CM6 3SE. Stephen & Joan Bazlington, 01371 856495, revbaz@care4free.net. *3m E of Great Dunmow. Leave Gt Dunmow on B1256. Take 1st L to Stebbing, at T-junction turn L into High St, garden 2nd house on R.* Teas. **Adm £2.50, chd free. Sats 14 Apr; 16 June; Fri 14 Sept (11-5).**
1-acre garden, created out of a damp bat willow plantation from 1987. Sloping S-wards with springs flowing into a hidden pond crossed by 'Monet' bridge. Mature hedges create vistas of surprise as gentle paths weave through shrubs and plants blending to achieve peace and purpose in this rural idyll.
♟ ☕

35 SALING HALL
Great Saling, Braintree CM7 5DT. Mr & Mrs Hugh Johnson. *6m NW of Braintree. Turn N off B1256 (old A120) between Gt Dunmow & Braintree signed Great Saling & the Bardfields. Saling Hall is at end of village on L.* **Adm £3, chd free (share to St James Church, Gt Saling). Weds 2 May to 25 July (2-5). Visitors also welcome by appt weekdays only, by written application, see above.**
12-acre garden of many moods created since 1960s, around a C17 House (not open). Old walled flower gardens; landscape with many rare trees and shrubs; moat, ponds, groves and glades. Temple of Pisces. Hugh Johnson has published his gardening diary monthly since 1975, as 'Tradescant' and now in 'Garden Illustrated'.
♿ ♟

In the distance a wooded glen with stream and amazing swathe of intensely blue hydrangeas . . .

Densely planted subtropical area with architectural and exotic plants – cannas, bananas, palms . . .

36 SHRUBS FARM

Lamarsh CO8 5EA. Mr & Mrs Robert Erith, 01787 227520, www.shrubsfarm.co.uk. 1¼m from Bures. On rd to Lamarsh, the drive is signed to Shrubs Farm. Refreshments by arrangement. Adm £4, chd free. Visitors welcome by appt, guided tours for individuals, small or large parties welcome. Ample parking for cars and coaches.

2 acres of mature and developing gardens with shrub borders, lawns, roses and trees. For walkers there are 50 acres of parkland and meadow with wild flower paths and woodland trails. Dogs on lead in this area. Much new hedgerow and tree planting incl over 50 species of oak has taken place over the past 25yrs. Superb 10m views to N and E over the Stour valley. Ancient coppice and pollard trees in the woods incl the largest goat pussy willow (Salix caprea) in England. A rare orchid, Bee orchid variety bicolour was found in June 2005, with 27 plants it is the largest colony yet discovered in the British Isles. Large C18 barn available if wet. Featured in 'Essex Life' magazine. Wheelchair access in parts of park and woodland could be difficult in wet weather.

37 SPRINGVALE

Beach Road, St Osyth CO16 8SB. Mr & Mrs M A Roberts, 01255 822310, roberts.stosyth@tesco.net. 4m W of Clacton-on-Sea. 500yds S of Xrds in village, towards Seawick, just

---

across the brook. Adm £2.50, chd free. Visitors welcome by appt, 12+ May to July, combined £4 (share to Friends of the Church) with guided tour of beautiful Tudor church. 1-acre garden full of surprises, from miniature knot garden to the 'Roman' temple housing garden memorabilia. Designed in rooms, with a wide variety of shrubs, perennials, roses, clematis and grasses. Wildlife areas, pond and stream. Gravel paths and steep slopes off main route.

38 TUDOR ROOST

18 Frere Way, Fingringhoe CO5 7BP. Chris & Linda Pegden, 01206 729831, c.pegden@virgin.net. 5m S of Colchester. In centre of village by Whalebone PH. Follow sign to Ballast Quay, after ½m turn R into Brook Hall Rd, then 1st L into Frere Way. Home-made teas. Adm £2.50, chd free. Suns, Mons, Sat 8, 9, 21, 22 Apr; 27, 28 May; Tues, 5 June to 26 June; Sun 24 June; Sats, Suns 21, 22 July; 4, 5, 26 Aug, Mon 27 Aug (2-5.30). Visitors also welcome by appt.

An unexpected hidden colourful ¼-acre garden. Well manicured grassy paths wind round island beds and ponds. Densely planted subtropical area with architectural and exotic plants - cannas, bananas, palms, agapanthus, agaves and tree ferns surround a colourful gazebo. Garden planted to provide yr-round colour and encourage wildlife. Many peaceful seating areas. Within 1m of local Nature reserve. Featured in 'Garden News'.

39 ULTING WICK

Ulting CM9 6QX. Mr & Mrs B Burrough, 01245 380216, philippa.burrough@btinternet.com. 3m NW of Maldon. Take turning to Ulting (Ulting Lane) off B1019 at Langford, after 2.2m at T-junction, garden is opp. Home-made teas. Adm £3, chd free. Sun 29 Apr (2-5). Visitors also welcome by appt. Parking space for 2 coaches. 4-acre garden set around C16 farmhouse and barns (C17 barn open) still undergoing major changes with emphasis on colour. Herbaceous borders, spring, striking pink, white and cutting gardens provide yr-round interest. Natural pond and stream bordered by mature willows and beds containing moisture and shade loving plants. Vegetable garden with Victorian style glasshouse, 3 acre woodland

---

planted in 2004. Walk to peaceful All Saints Ulting Church by R Chelmer, signed from garden. Church will be open for talk on its history.

WALTHAM FOREST REGISTER OFFICE
See London.

40 WICKHAM PLACE FARM

Station Road, Wickham Bishops CM8 3JB. Mrs J Wilson, 01621 891282, www.wickhamplacefarm.co.uk. 2½m SE of Witham. Take B1018 from Witham to Maldon. After going under A12 take 3rd L (Station Rd). 1st house on L. Home-made teas. Adm £2.50, chd free (share to Farleigh Hospice). Fris, 27 Apr to 27 July; 7 Sept to 28 Sept (11-4). Visitors also welcome by appt, groups and coaches 10+ anytime by appt.

2-acre walled garden with huge climbers and roses filled by shrubs, perennials and bulbs. Renowned for stunning wisterias in May/June, one over 250ft long. 12 acres of mixed woodland, superb in Sept, incl rabbit-resistant plants and bulbs, features lovely walks. Yr-round colour; knot garden.

41 WOOLARDS ASH

Hatfield Broad Oak CM22 7JY. Mr & Mrs Michael Herbert, 01279 718284. 5m SE of Bishops Stortford. From Hatfield Broad Oak follow B183 N (towards Takeley). After ¾m take 1st R (signed to Taverners Green & Broomshawbury), then 2nd R to Woolards Ash. From Takeley, B183 S (towards Hatfield Broad Oak). After ¾m 1st L (signed Canfield & High Roding), then 2nd L to Woolards Ash. Home-made teas. Adm £3.50, chd free. Sun 10 June (2-5). Visitors also welcome by appt May to July only, groups of 12+, coaches permitted.

Peacocks, guinea fowl and bantams roam this beautiful 3-acre garden, divided into 5 areas by beech and yew hedges, all set in a pastoral landscape. The main area has 2 large subtly planted borders of old roses, shrubs, herbaceous plants and ha-ha with distant views. The walled pool garden provides a tranquil setting for mature borders with further shrub borders, mature trees and wild areas planted with bulbs and old roses, small vegetable garden.

42 WRITTLE COLLEGE
Writtle CM1 3RR, 01245 424200,
www.writtle.ac.uk. *4m W of
Chelmsford. On A414, nr Writtle
village, clearly signed.* **Adm £3, chd
free, concessions £2.** Suns 25 Mar;
15 July (10-4).
Approx 15 acres; informal lawns with
naturalised bulbs in spring and wild
flowers in summer, large tree
collection, mixed shrub and
herbaceous borders, heathers and
alpines. Landscaped gardens
designed and built by students
including 'Centenary' garden and subtropical 'Hot 'n' Spicy' garden.
Development of new 13-acre parkland
area. Orchard meadows, recently
started on the site of an old apple
orchard. Landscaped glasshouses.
Featured in local press.

Essex County Volunteers

County Organiser
Jill Cowley, Park Farm, Chatham Hall Lane, Great Waltham CM3 1BZ, 01245 360 871, jill@jillcowley.wanadoo.co.uk

County Treasurer
Linda Holdaway, Woodpeckers, Mangapp Chase, Burnham-on-Crouch CM0 8QQ, 01621 782137, linda@ahmpi.co.uk

Assistant County Organisers
Derek Bracey, Park Farm, Chatham Hall Lane, Great Waltham, Chelmsford CM3 1BZ, 01245 360871
Susan & Doug Copeland, Wickets, Langley Upper Green, Saffron Walden CB11 4RY, 01799 550553
    susan.copeland2@btinternet.com

Publicity
Arliss Porter, 16 Anglesea Road, Wivenhoe CO7 9JR, 01206 828227, email aporter211@yahoo.co.uk

GLOUCESTERSHIRE

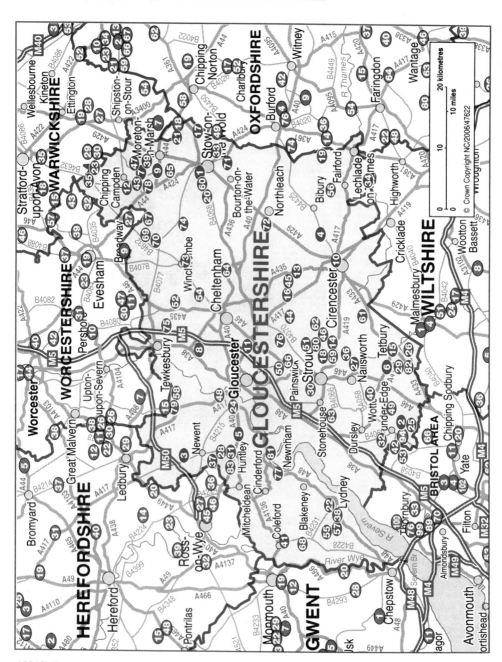

Opening Dates

January

SUNDAY 28
28 Home Farm

February

SUNDAY 11
28 Home Farm
76 Trench Hill

SUNDAY 18
75 Tinpenny Farm
76 Trench Hill

SUNDAY 25
34 Kempsford Manor

March

SATURDAY 3
59 Redwood

SUNDAY 4
22 Green Cottage
34 Kempsford Manor
59 Redwood

SUNDAY 11
22 Green Cottage
34 Kempsford Manor

SUNDAY 18
34 Kempsford Manor
66 Sheephouse
75 Tinpenny Farm
76 Trench Hill

SUNDAY 25
28 Home Farm

April

SUNDAY 1
1 Abbotswood
24 Highnam Court
44 Misarden Park
70 Stanway Fountain & Water Garden

FRIDAY 6
43 Mill Dene Garden

SUNDAY 8
6 Beverston Castle
36 Lammas Park
76 Trench Hill

MONDAY 9
3 Baldwins
6 Beverston Castle
34 Kempsford Manor
76 Trench Hill

SUNDAY 15
28 Home Farm
39 Malvern Mill
47 The Old Chequer

WEDNESDAY 18
38 Lydney Park Spring Garden

SUNDAY 22
41 Meadow Cottage
43 Mill Dene Garden
61 Rodmarton Manor
63 Rosemary Cottage
75 Tinpenny Farm

MONDAY 23
35 Kiftsgate Court

SUNDAY 29
1 Abbotswood
16 Cotswold Farm
28 Home Farm
34 Kempsford Manor

May

SUNDAY 6
18 Eastcombe, Bussage and Brownshill Gardens
22 Green Cottage
24 Highnam Court
30 Humphreys End House
57 Ramblers
58 The Red House
78 Upton Wold
83 Willow Lodge

MONDAY 7
18 Eastcombe, Bussage and Brownshill Gardens
19 Eastleach House
83 Willow Lodge

FRIDAY 11
26 Hodges Barn

SUNDAY 13
13 Cerney House Gardens
22 Green Cottage
26 Hodges Barn
48 The Old Vicarage
54 Pigeon House
55 Priors Mesne
75 Tinpenny Farm

MONDAY 14
26 Hodges Barn

SATURDAY 19
38 Lydney Park Spring Garden

SUNDAY 20
3 Baldwins
22 Green Cottage
41 Meadow Cottage
55 Priors Mesne
58 The Red House
70 Stanway Fountain & Water Garden
72 Stowell Park
79 Vine Farm

THURSDAY 24
4 Barnsley House

SATURDAY 26
29 Hookhouse Pottery

SUNDAY 27
8 Boddington Manor
22 Green Cottage
29 Hookhouse Pottery
34 Kempsford Manor
40 The Matara Garden
82 Westonbirt School Gardens
83 Willow Lodge

MONDAY 28
3 Baldwins
29 Hookhouse Pottery
34 Kempsford Manor
37 Lower Farm House
82 Westonbirt School Gardens
83 Willow Lodge

TUESDAY 29
29 Hookhouse Pottery

WEDNESDAY 30
29 Hookhouse Pottery

THURSDAY 31
9 Bourton House Garden
29 Hookhouse Pottery

June

FRIDAY 1
29 Hookhouse Pottery

SATURDAY 2
20 Eyford Gardens
29 Hookhouse Pottery
46 The Old Chapel
57 Ramblers (Evening)

SUNDAY 3
22 Green Cottage
24 Highnam Court
27 Holcombe Glen Cottage
29 Hookhouse Pottery
36 Lammas Park
46 The Old Chapel
48 The Old Vicarage
54 Pigeon House

MONDAY 4
46 The Old Chapel

TUESDAY 5
46 The Old Chapel

WEDNESDAY 6
12 Campden House
22 Green Cottage
46 The Old Chapel
76 Trench Hill

THURSDAY 7
46 The Old Chapel

FRIDAY 8
26 Hodges Barn
46 The Old Chapel

SATURDAY 9
46 The Old Chapel

SUNDAY 10
(3) Baldwins
(7) Blockley Gardens
(11) Brockworth Court
(22) Green Cottage
(26) Hodges Barn
(32) Hunts Court
(34) Kempsford Manor
(39) Malvern Mill
(46) The Old Chapel
(47) The Old Chequer
(57) Ramblers
(64) Sandywell Gardens

MONDAY 11
(26) Hodges Barn
(46) The Old Chapel

TUESDAY 12
(21) Grange Farm
(46) The Old Chapel

WEDNESDAY 13
(12) Campden House
(22) Green Cottage
(46) The Old Chapel
(60) Rockcliffe
(76) Trench Hill

THURSDAY 14
(46) The Old Chapel

FRIDAY 15
(46) The Old Chapel

SATURDAY 16
(14) Chalford Gardens
(46) The Old Chapel

SUNDAY 17
(14) Chalford Gardens
(22) Green Cottage
(25) Hillesley House
(30) Humphreys End House
(32) Hunts Court
(46) The Old Chapel
(51) Paulmead
(58) The Red House
(69) Stanton Gardens
(75) Tinpenny Farm
(79) Vine Farm
(80) Wells Cottage

TUESDAY 19
(21) Grange Farm

WEDNESDAY 20
(17) Daylesford House
(22) Green Cottage
(60) Rockcliffe
(76) Trench Hill

SUNDAY 24
(10) 25 Bowling Green Road
(22) Green Cottage
(32) Hunts Court
(33) Icomb Place
(44) Misarden Park
(56) Quenington Gardens
(62) Rookwoods
(64) Sandywell Gardens
(72) Stowell Park
(78) Upton Wold

MONDAY 25
(10) 25 Bowling Green Road

WEDNESDAY 27
(67) Snowshill Manor
(76) Trench Hill

THURSDAY 28
(9) Bourton House Garden
(30) Humphreys End House (Evening)

SATURDAY 30
(5) Berrys Place Farm

July

SUNDAY 1
(3) Baldwins
(5) Berrys Place Farm
(10) 25 Bowling Green Road
(24) Highnam Court
(43) Mill Dene Garden
(45) Moor Wood
(68) South Lodge
(71) Stone House

MONDAY 2
(10) 25 Bowling Green Road

WEDNESDAY 4
(29) Hookhouse Pottery

SUNDAY 8
(10) 25 Bowling Green Road
(41) Meadow Cottage
(74) Temple Guiting Manor

MONDAY 9
(10) 25 Bowling Green Road

WEDNESDAY 11
(20) Eyford Gardens

SUNDAY 15
(11) Brockworth Court
(49) Ozleworth Park
(63) Rosemary Cottage
(65) Sezincote
(75) Tinpenny Farm
(76) Trench Hill

THURSDAY 19
(4) Barnsley House

SUNDAY 22
(10) 25 Bowling Green Road
(34) Kempsford Manor

MONDAY 23
(10) 25 Bowling Green Road

THURSDAY 26
(9) Bourton House Garden

SUNDAY 29
(40) The Matara Garden

August

SUNDAY 5
(24) Highnam Court

SUNDAY 12
(7) Blockley Gardens
(34) Kempsford Manor
(83) Willow Lodge

MONDAY 13
(35) Kiftsgate Court
(83) Willow Lodge

SUNDAY 19
(34) Kempsford Manor

SUNDAY 26
(34) Kempsford Manor
(41) Meadow Cottage
(42) Merline House
(76) Trench Hill

MONDAY 27
(34) Kempsford Manor
(42) Merline House

THURSDAY 30
(9) Bourton House Garden

September

SUNDAY 2
(16) Cotswold Farm
(24) Highnam Court
(32) Hunts Court

THURSDAY 6
(4) Barnsley House

SUNDAY 9
(32) Hunts Court
(34) Kempsford Manor
(73) Sudeley Castle Gardens & Exhibitions
(76) Trench Hill
(81) Westbury Court Garden

SUNDAY 16
(23) Hidcote Manor Garden
(34) Kempsford Manor
(75) Tinpenny Farm

THURSDAY 27
(9) Bourton House Garden

SUNDAY 30
(40) The Matara Garden

October

SUNDAY 14
(75) Tinpenny Farm

THURSDAY 25
(9) Bourton House Garden

February 2008

SUNDAY 10
(76) Trench Hill

SUNDAY 17
(76) Trench Hill

Private gardens opening regularly for the NGS

- **22** Green Cottage
- **75** Tinpenny Farm
- **76** Trench Hill
- **83** Willow Lodge

Gardens open to the public

- **9** Bourton House Garden
- **13** Cerney House Gardens
- **19** Eastleach House
- **23** Hidcote Manor Garden
- **32** Hunts Court
- **34** Kempsford Manor
- **35** Kiftsgate Court
- **38** Lydney Park Spring Garden
- **40** The Matara Garden
- **43** Mill Dene Garden
- **44** Misarden Park
- **50** Painswick Rococo Garden
- **61** Rodmarton Manor
- **65** Sezincote
- **67** Snowshill Manor
- **70** Stanway Fountain & Water Garden
- **71** Stone House
- **73** Sudeley Castle Gardens & Exhibitions
- **81** Westbury Court Garden
- **82** Westonbirt School Gardens

By appointment only

- **2** Alderley Grange
- **15** The Chipping Croft
- **31** Huntley Manor
- **52** Pear Tree Cottage
- **53** Pemberley Lodge
- **77** Upper Merton House

The Gardens

ABBEY HOUSE GARDENS
See Wiltshire.

1 ABBOTSWOOD
Stow-on-the-Wold GL54 1EN. Mr R Scully. *1m W of Stow-on-the-Wold. On B4068 nr Lower Swell or B4077 nr Upper Swell.* Home-made teas. **Adm £3, chd free. Suns 1, 29 Apr (1.30-6).**

Massed plantings of spring bulbs, heathers, flowering shrubs and rhododendrons in dramatic, landscaped hillside stream gardens; fine herbaceous planting in elegant formal gardens with lily pond, terraced lawn and fountain created by Sir Edwin Lutyens. Partial wheelchair access only, some gravel paths, steep slopes and steps.

2 ALDERLEY GRANGE
Alderley GL12 7QT. Mr Guy & the Hon Mrs Acloque, 01453 842161. *2m S of Wotton-under-Edge. Turn NW off A46 Bath to Stroud rd, at Dunkirk.* **Adm £3.50, chd free. Visitors welcome by appt June only.**
Walled garden with fine trees, roses; herb gardens and aromatic plants.

ASTHALL MANOR
See Oxfordshire.

3 BALDWINS
Birches Lane, nr Newent GL18 1DN. Mrs Sue Clive, 01531 821640/020 7834 8233. *1½m N of Newent. Off B4215, half-way between Newent & Dymock, signed Botloes Green & Pool Hill. Baldwins, formerly The Bungalow, is first on L on edge of Three Choirs Vineyard.* Home-made teas, tea only 9 Apr. **Adm £2.50, chd free (share to Downs Syndrome Assoc). Mon 9 Apr; Sun 20, Mon 28 May; Suns 10 June; 1 July (1.30-5). Visitors also welcome by appt May, June & July.**
With the Malvern Hills and Three Choirs Vineyard as a backdrop this ½-acre garden takes an individual approach. Herbaceous, cottage and wild flowers, hard and soft fruits, unusual custom-built water and architectural features and terraced vegetable beds are brought together with artistic intent.

4 BARNSLEY HOUSE
nr Cirencester GL7 5EE. Mr Tim Haigh & Mr Rupert Pendered, reception@barnsleyhouse.com. *4m NE of Cirencester. On B4425.* Light refreshments & teas; also available at The Village Pub. **Adm £5, chd £2.50. Thurs 24 May; 19 July; 6 Sept (11-5). Visitors also welcome by appt.**
Mature family garden, created by the late Rosemary Verey, with interesting collection of shrubs and trees; ground cover; herbaceous borders; pond garden; laburnum walk; knot and herb gardens; potager; C18 summerhouses. C17 house (not open). Garden open to the public on only seven days during the year.

5 BERRYS PLACE FARM
Churcham GL2 8AS. Anne Thomas. *6m W of Gloucester. A40 towards Ross. Turning R into Bulley Lane at Birdwood.* Home-made & cream teas. **Adm £3, chd free (share to The Forge). Sat 30 June; Sun 1 July (11-6).**
Country garden, approx 1 acre, surrounded by farmland and old orcharding. Lawns and mixed herbaceous borders with some old roses. Formal kitchen garden leading to lake and summerhouse with a variety of water lilies and carp. All shared with peacocks and ducks. Featured in Glos Echo Weekend Magazine.

6 BEVERSTON CASTLE
nr Tetbury GL8 8TU. Mrs A L Rook. *2m W of Tetbury. On A4135 rd to Dursley between Tetbury & Calcot Xrds.* Home-made teas. **Adm £3.50, chd under 14 free, concessions £2.50 (OAP & 14-18) (share to Tetbury British Legion). Sun 8, Mon 9 Apr (2-5.30).**
Overlooked by romantic C12-C17 castle ruin (not open), overflowingly planted paved terrace leads from C18 house (not open) across moat to sloping lawn with spring bulbs in abundance, and full herbaceous and shrub borders. Large walled kitchen garden and greenhouses, orchids. Terrace slippery if wet.

7 BLOCKLEY GARDENS
GL56 9HT. *3m NW of Moreton-in-Marsh. Take A44 Moreton to Broadway rd; turning E.* Teas at St George's Hall 10 June; home-made teas at Box Cottage 12 Aug. **Combined adm £5 (10 June); £4 (12 Aug) chd free. Suns 10 June; 12 Aug (2-6).**
Popular Cotswold hillside village with

Massed plantings of spring bulbs, heathers, flowering shrubs and rhododendrons . . .

great variety of high quality gardens; some walking necessary and some gardens not safe for small children. Bus provided 10 Jun only.

BOX COTTAGE
Patricia Milligan-Baldwin
New garden with a range of garden rooms, terraces and ponds.

3 THE DELL
Ms E Powell. Not open Sun 12 Aug.
Very small garden situated on the side of Blockley Brook. Restricted entry.

New planting of acers, birches, liquidambars in meadow setting . . .

4 THE DELL
Viola & Bernard Stubbs. Not open Sun 12 Aug.
Fairly small garden, sloping down to Blockley Brook.

GRANGE COTTAGE
Mill Lane GL56 9HT. Alison & Guy Heitmann, www.garden-designer.biz. Not open Sun 10 June.
New owners have redesigned this multi-layered garden, with interest from May to Oct. Mixture of traditional and contemporary, from lush perennial plantings to cool green spaces.

HOLLYROSE HOUSE
3 The Clementines. Mr & Mrs Peter Saunders. Not open Sun 12 Aug.
Small terraced garden.

MALVERN MILL
Mr & Mrs J Bourne. Not open Sun 12 Aug.
(See separate entry).

THE MANOR HOUSE
George & Zoe Thompson
Top garden with lawn, roses, lavender and pergola. Lower garden beneath listed wall terraced with borders, box hedging and lawn leading to brook. Separate vegetable and herb garden with espaliered and cordoned fruits.

MILL DENE GARDEN
School Lane. Mr & Mrs B S Dare,
www.milldenegarden.co.uk
(See separate entry). Partial wheelchair access.

THE OLD CHEQUER
Mr & Mrs Linley, 01386 700647, g.f.linley@tesco.net. Not open Sun 12 Aug. Visitors also welcome by appt Apr to July.
(See separate entry).

THE OLD SILK MILL
Mr & Mrs A Goodrick-Clarke.
Not open Sun 12 Aug.
Old mill garden divided by brook to form picturesque millpond and race. Herbaceous walk, water garden and formal herb garden.

PEAR TREES
Mrs J Beckwith. Not open Sun 12 Aug.
Charming long narrow garden with entrance at rear and sunny gravel front garden.

PORCH HOUSE
Mr & Mrs C Johnson. Not open Sun 12 Aug.
Centrally located village garden with countryside views. Pear tree walk, knot garden and mixed borders.

4 THE CLEMENTINES
Kathy Illingworth. Not open Sun 12 Aug.
Hillside garden on several levels with views over Cotswold countryside. Features a range of herbaceous perennials and shrubs, pond and stream, deck, lawned area and meadow with wild flowers.

8 BODDINGTON MANOR
Boddington GL51 0TJ. Robert Hitchins Ltd. *3m W of Cheltenham. Off A4019 Cheltenham to Tewkesbury rd. After crossing M5, take first turning L, signed to Boddington.* Light refreshments & teas. **Adm £2.50, chd free. Sun 27 May (11-5).**
Old garden sympathetically restored since 1985 incl wild flower woodland walk, mature specimen trees, extensive lawns and lakes; established pinetum and bog garden. New planting of acers, birches, liquidambars in meadow setting. Neo-gothic manor house (not open). Country Garden Market.

9 ♦ BOURTON HOUSE GARDEN
Bourton-on-the-Hill GL56 9AE. Mr & Mrs R Paice, 01386 700754, www.bourtonhouse.com. *2m W of Moreton-in-Marsh. On A44.* **Adm £5.50, chd free, concessions £5. Weds to Fris 23 May to 31 Aug; Thurs & Fris, Sept to end Oct; Bank Hols Sun, Mon end May & end Aug (10-5).** For NGS: **Thurs 31 May; 28 June; 26 July; 30 Aug; 27 Sept; 25 Oct (10-5).**
Surrounding a delightful C18 Cotswold manor house (not open) and C16 tithe barn, this exciting 3-acre garden positively fizzes with ideas. Featuring flamboyant borders, imaginative topiary, profusions of herbaceous borders and exotic plants and, not least, a myriad of magically planted pots; a plantsman's paradise. Some gravel paths.

10 25 BOWLING GREEN ROAD
Cirencester GL7 2HD. Fr John & Susan Beck, 01285 653778, sjb@beck-hems.org.uk. *On NW edge of Cirencester. Take A435 to Spitalgate/Whiteway T-lights, turn into The Whiteway, then 1st L into Bowling Green Rd to No 25 on R of rd bend. Please respect neighbours' driveways, no pavement parking.* **Adm £2.50, chd free. Sun 24, Mon 25 June; Suns, Mons 1, 2, 8, 9, 22, 23 July. Suns (2-5); Mons (11-4). Visitors also welcome by appt mid June to end July, also groups.**
Mount an expedition to meander amidst pergolas, pots, pools and paths and muse on myriads (400+!) of daring, different and delightful daylilies, vying for space with priceless perennials, countless curvaceous

clematis, romantic roses, graceful grasses, hopeful hostas, friendly frogs and sylph-like lawns celebrating the British Hosta & Hemerocallis Society's Silver Jubilee.

✤

⑪ NEW BROCKWORTH COURT
Brockworth GL3 4QU. Mr & Mrs Tim Wiltshire. *6m E of Gloucester; 6m W of Cheltenham. From A46 Stroud/ Cheltenham off A417 turn into Mill Lane. At T-junction turn R, L, R. Garden next to St George's Church.* Light refreshments & teas. **Adm £3.50, chd free. Suns 10 June; 15 July (2-6).** Small manor house (not open) which once belonged to Llanthony Priory and the Guise family. Restored C13 tithe barn (open). Garden approx 1½ acres, has recently undergone much restoration work. Dew pond with Monet bridge, carp and water lilies. Many unusual plants and mostly in farmhouse style. Interesting former monastic kitchen garden, organic. Some craft displays. Norman church next door, open.

♿ ✤ ☕

BROUGHTON POGGS & FILKINS GARDENS
See Oxfordshire.

⑫ CAMPDEN HOUSE
Chipping Campden GL55 6UP. The Hon Philip & Mrs Smith. *½m SW of Chipping Campden. Entrance on Chipping Campden to Weston Subedge rd, approx ¼m SW of Campden, 1¼m drive.* Teas. **Adm £3, chd free. Weds 6, 13 June (2-6).** 2 acres featuring mixed borders of plant and colour interest around house and C17 tithe barn (neither open). Set in fine parkland in hidden valley with lakes and ponds. Woodland walk, vegetable garden. Some steps and slopes.

♿ ☕

⑬ ◆ CERNEY HOUSE GARDENS
North Cerney GL7 7BX. Sir Michael & Lady Angus, 01285 831205, barbara@cerneygardens.com. *4m NW of Cirencester. On A435 Cheltenham rd. Turn L opp Bathurst Arms, past church up hill, pillared gates on R.*

Adm £4, chd £1. Tues, Weds, Fris, Suns, Easter to end July (10-5). For NGS: Sun 13 May (10-5). Romantic walled garden filled with old-fashioned roses and herbaceous borders. Working kitchen garden, scented garden, well-labelled herb garden, Who's Who beds and genera borders. Spring bulbs in abundance all around the wooded grounds. Bothy pottery. Tulip Festival. Gravel paths and some slopes.

♿ ⚔ ✤

⑭ CHALFORD GARDENS
Chalford Vale GL6 8PN. *4m E of Stroud; 9m from Cirencester. On A419 to Cirencester. Gardens are high above Chalford Vale & reached on foot by steep climb from car park on main rd or from High St.* **Combined adm £4, chd free. Sat 16, Sun 17 June (2-5).** Hillside village with many quaint lanes, S-facing.

MARLE HILL HOUSE
Mike & Leslie Doyle-Davidson
1-acre Victorian woodland garden, containing a number of interlinked secret, formal and natural areas on steep terraced hillside with ponds, folly, nut tunnel, moongate and ship treehouse.

⚔

THE OLD CHAPEL
Marle Hill. F J & F Owen
(See separate entry).

⚔

THANET HOUSE
High Street. Jennifer & Roger Tann. *On Chalford Vale High St nr PO* Streamside multi-level garden with Italian flavour; a ruin, pond, packhorse bridge and (former) textile industry connections.

CHASTLETON GARDENS
See Oxfordshire.

⑮ THE CHIPPING CROFT
26 The Chipping, Tetbury GL8 8EY. Dr & Mrs P W Taylor, 01666 503178. *10m W of Cirencester. At bottom of Chipping Hill approached downhill from The Chipping market place. Up private drive after black door in wall. Free long-term car park 250yds: entrance nr Royal Oak PH.* **Adm £3.50, chd free. Visitors welcome by appt.** 2-acre, secluded, walled town garden on three levels, with mature trees, shrubs, herbaceous borders, rose beds and unusual plants; spring

blossom and bulbs; mid and late summer colourful planting. Series of formal gardens, incl fruit and vegetable/flower potager all informally planted; also water garden. C17 Cotswold house (not open). Good garden to 'twin' with visit to nearby Highgrove. Partial wheelchair access.

♿ ✤

Dew pond with Monet bridge, carp and water lilies . . .

⑯ COTSWOLD FARM
nr Duntisbourne Abbots, Cirencester GL7 7JS. Mrs Mark Birchall, 01285 821857. *5m NW of Cirencester. Off the old A417. From Cirencester turn L signed Duntisbourne Abbots Services, then immed R & R again into underpass. Private drive straight ahead. From Gloucester turn L signed Duntisbourne Abbots Services. Pass services; private drive on L.* Home-made teas. **Adm £4, chd free (share to A Rocha). Suns 29 Apr; 2 Sept (2-6). Visitors also welcome by appt, snowdrops in Feb.** Cotswold garden in lovely position overlooking quiet valley on different levels with terrace designed by Norman Jewson in 1938; shrubs and trees, mixed borders, snowdrops, alpine border, shrub roses and newly replanted 'bog garden'. Croquet and toys for children on lawn. Walled kitchen garden.

✤ ☕

DAUNTSEY GARDENS
See Wiltshire.

⑰ DAYLESFORD HOUSE
Daylesford GL56 0YQ. Sir Anthony & Lady Bamford. *5m W of Chipping Norton. Off A436. Between Stow-on-the-Wold & Chipping Norton. Teas at Daylesford Farm Shop.* **Adm £4, chd free. Wed 20 June (2-5).** Magnificent C18 landscape grounds created 1790 for Warren Hastings, greatly restored and enhanced by

present owners. Lakeside and woodland walks within natural wild flower meadows. Large walled garden planted formally, centred around orchid, peach and working glasshouses. Trellised rose garden. Collection of citrus within period orangery. Newly created Secret Garden with pavilion and formal pools. Very large garden with substantial distances to be walked. Disabled access possible but many gravel paths and steep slopes.

♿ ⚑ ⊕ ☕

⑱ EASTCOMBE, BUSSAGE AND BROWNSHILL GARDENS
GL6 8DD. *3m E of Stroud. 2m N of A419 Stroud to Cirencester rd on turning signed to Bisley & Eastcombe.* Home-made teas at Eastcombe Village Hall. **Combined adm £4, chd free (share to Cotswold Care Hospice, Cobalt Unit & Victim Support Glos). Sun 6, Mon 7 May (2-6).**
A group of gardens, large and small, set in a picturesque hilltop location. Some approachable only by foot. (Exhibitions may be on view in village hall). Please park considerately in villages.
☕

BEECHCROFT
Beech Lane, Brownshill.
Mr & Mrs R H Salt
Traditional garden surrounding an Edwardian house (not open) with a cottage garden feel. Mature trees, shrubs, herbaceous borders, wild area, herb garden, conservatory, potting shed, vegetable garden and greenhouse. Some gravel paths.
♿ ⌂

BREWERS COTTAGE
Eastcombe. Mr & Mrs N Carter
Easily managed hillside garden with laburnum-covered pergola. Shady and sunny borders and a small hidden courtyard with fountain. Vegetable garden. All-yr colour.

HAMPTON VIEW
The Ridge, Bussage. Geraldine M Carter
Garden recently re-designed and planted extensively. Archway from path invites you up steps to raised lawn with fresh water pond and private sitting area. Path leads through fruit tree pergola to summerhouse and greenhouse.

A group of gardens, large and small, set in a picturesque hilltop location . . .

HOLT END
The Ridge, Bussage.
Jackie & Maurice Rutter
Sloping, woodland edge, informal.
⊕

LITTLE DORMERS
64 Lypiatt View, Bussage.
Bernadette Scahill
Small terraced garden with a mixture of unusual acid-loving plants and waterfall feature.
♿ ⚑

ROSE COTTAGE
The Street, Eastcombe.
Mrs J Shipman
Old-fashioned walled cottage garden, terraced to take advantage of hillside site and beautiful views. Large level lawn but steep, uneven steps up terraces.
⚑

1 THE LAURELS
The Street, Eastcombe.
Andrew & Ruth Fraser
Terraced garden on several levels joined by flights of steps with herbaceous borders, shrubs, small pond and terraced vegetable garden, largely reconstructed by present owners. Parking in The Street, Eastcombe very difficult.
⚑

VATCH RISE
Eastcombe. Peggy Abbott
Well-stocked garden with wide variety of bulbs, colour co-ordinated herbaceous borders and small vegetable garden. Outstanding views of Toadsmoor Valley.
♿ ⊕

NEW WOODLANDS HOUSE
Cowswell Lane, Bussage. Amy Cleary
Small sloping garden with steps leading down to sunken area. Also small Japanese garden and deck with views over Toadsmoor Valley. Vegetable and soft fruit section.
⚑

NEW WOODVIEW
Wells Road, Eastcombe. Julian & Eileen Horn-Smith
Recently terraced and replanted with pretty views over the Toadsmoor Valley. Covering a hillside, this garden is unsuitable for those with walking difficulties.

⑲ ♦ EASTLEACH HOUSE
Eastleach Martin GL7 3NW. Mrs David Richards,
www.eastleachhouse.com. *5m NE of Fairford. From Fairford on A417, signed to Eastleach on L. 4m to village, turn R down hill towards bridge. Entrance to garden by church gates. No access for coaches - drop visitors at gate and park outside village, or off A361 bet Burford & Lechlade.* **Adm £5, chd under 16 free. Fris June & July (2-5) Groups all yr by appt. For NGS: Mon 7 May (2-5).**
Large traditional all-yr-round garden. Wooded hilltop position with long views S and W. New parkland, lime avenue and arboretum. Wild flower walk, wildlife pond, lawns, walled and rill gardens, with modern herbaceous borders, yew and box hedges, iris and paeony borders, lily ponds, formal herb, topiary and knot gardens. Rambling roses into trees. Gravel paths and some steep slopes. Limited parking at house for disabled.
♿ ⚑ ⊕

⑳ EYFORD GARDENS
Upper Slaughter GL54 2JN. *3m W of Stow on the Wold. On the B4068 (formerly A436), between Lower Swell & Naunton.* Home-made & cream teas. **Combined adm £5, chd free. Sat 2 June; Wed 11 July (11-4).**
2 gardens near to each other, just outside village.
☕

EYFORD HOUSE
Mrs C A Heber Percy. *Stone Lodge on R, with white iron gates & cattle grid*
1½-acre sloping N garden, ornamental shrubs and trees. Laid out originally by Graham Stuart

Thomas, 1976. West garden and terrace, red border, walled kitchen garden, two lakes with pleasant walks and views (boots needed). Holy well.

EYFORD KNOLL
Mrs S Prest. *At Xrds turn R for Cotswold Farm Park, entrance 400yds on R*
Cottage garden, with C18 fountain from Faringdon House, gardens redesigned 9yrs ago by Lady Aird.

GADFIELD ELM HOUSE
See Worcestershire.

㉑ GRANGE FARM
Evenlode, nr Moreton-in-Marsh GL56 0NT. Lady Aird, 01608 650607, meaird@aol.com. *3m N of Stow-on-the-Wold. E of A429 Fosseway & 1½m from Broadwell.* Light refreshments & teas. **Adm £2.50, chd free. Tues 12, 19 June (10.30-5). Visitors also welcome by appt May, June, July.**
From the rose covered house, past the lawn and herbaceous borders to the water garden and ancient apple trees spreading over spring bulbs in May this garden is full of yr-round interest. Vegetable garden, sunken garden and yew circle and shady tranquil places to sit. Featured in 'English Garden' March 2006.
♿ 🍽 ☕

㉒ GREEN COTTAGE
Lydney GL15 6BS. Mr & Mrs F Baber, www.peony.ukgardeners.com. *¼m SW of Lydney. Approaching Lydney from Gloucester, keep to A48 through Lydney. Leaving Lydney turn R into narrow lane at de-limit sign. Garden 1st R. Shady parking.* Home-made teas (Suns May & June). **Adm £2.50, chd free. Suns 4, 11 Mar (1-4); Suns, 6, 13, 20, 27 May; Suns, 3, 10, 17, 24 June; Weds, 6,13, 20 June (2-5).**
1½-acre country garden planted for seasonal interest and wildlife. Mature trees, stream, duckpond and bog garden. Developing woodland area planted with ferns, hellebores, daphnes and other shade lovers. Cottage garden. Wide range of herbaceous peonies, incl National Collection of rare Victorian and Edwardian lactiflora cultivars (best in June), early peonies May. Featured in 'The English Garden Magazine' 2006.
♿ ⊕ ☕

HELLENS
See Herefordshire.

㉓ ◆ HIDCOTE MANOR GARDEN
Hidcote Bartrim, Chipping Campden, nr Mickleton GL55 6LR. The National Trust, 01386 438333, www.nationaltrust.org.uk. *4m NE of Chipping Campden. Off B4081, close to the village of Mickleton.* **Adm £7.30, chd £3.65. Phone or see website for other opening times. For NGS: Sun 16 Sept (10-5).**
One of England's great gardens, 10½-acre 'Arts and Crafts' masterpiece created by Major Lawrence Johnston. Series of outdoor rooms, each with a different character and separated by walls and hedges of many different species. Many rare trees and shrubs, outstanding herbaceous borders and unusual plant species from all over the world.
🍽 ⊕ ☕

Developing woodland area planted with ferns, hellebores, daphnes and other shade lovers . . .

㉔ HIGHNAM COURT
Highnam GL2 8DP. Roger Head. *2m W of Gloucester. Leave Gloucester on A40 towards Ross on Wye. DO NOT take Newent turning, but proceed to next big Highnam roundabout. Take R exit for Highnam Court entrance directly off roundabout.* Light refreshments. **Adm £4, chd free (share to Highnam Church). Suns 1 Apr; 6 May; 3 June; 1 July; 5 Aug; 2 Sept (11-5).**
40 acres of Victorian landscaped gardens surrounding magnificent Grade I house (not open), set out by the artist Thomas Gambier Parry. Lakes, shrubberies and listed Pulhamite water gardens with grottos and fernery. Exciting ornamental lakes, and woodland areas. New extensive 1-acre rose garden and many new features. Gravel paths and steps.
♿ ☕

㉕ HILLESLEY HOUSE
Hillesley, nr Wotton-under-Edge GL12 7RD. Fiona & Jeremy Walsh, 07971 854260 Stewart (Head Gardener). *3m from Wotton-under-Edge. On rd to Hawkesbury Upton & A46 from Wotton-under-Edge.* Teas. **Adm £3, chd free. Sun 17 June (2-6). Visitors also welcome by appt, call for details/times throughout the yr.**
Extensive revamping and planting of 4 acres of walled, secret and open garden, plus vegetable garden and arboretum. Unusual topiary. Rose beds and borders. Plenty of exciting ideas are being continued this yr.
⊕ ☕

㉖ HODGES BARN
Shipton Moyne GL8 8PR. Mrs C N Hornby. *3m S of Tetbury. On Malmesbury side of village.* **Adm £5, chd free. Fri 11, Sun 13, Mon 14 May; Fri 8, Sun 10, Mon 11 June (2-6).**
Very unusual C15 dovecote converted into family home (not open). Cotswold stone walls act as host to climbing and rambling roses, clematis, vines, hydrangeas, and together with yew, rose and tapestry hedges create formality around house. Mixed shrub and herbaceous borders, shrub roses; water garden; woodland garden planted with cherries, magnolias and spring bulbs. Also open for NGS, adjoining garden of Hodges Farmhouse by kind permission of Mrs Clive Lamb. 8th Best Spring Garden in Independent Magazine 2006.
♿

㉗ HOLCOMBE GLEN COTTAGE
Minchinhampton GL6 9AJ. Christine & Terry Sharpe. *1m E of Nailsworth. From Nailsworth take Avening Rd B4014. Turn L at Weighbridge Inn. Turn L 100yds into Holcombe Glen. 1st house on L. From Minchinhampton 1¼m via Well Hill or New Rd.* Light refreshments & teas. **Adm £3, chd free (share to Cotswold Care Hospice). Sun 3 June (12-5).**
3 acres incl springs and ponds. Small waterfalls feed river and stream, giving bog and meadow areas full of wildlife and wild flowers. Above these, terraced walled garden for vegetables and herbaceous plants.
⊕ ☕

㉘ HOME FARM
Huntley GL19 3HQ. Mrs T Freeman, 01452 830209, torill@ukgateway.net. *4m S of Newent. On B4216 ½m off*

A40 in Huntley travelling towards Newent. **Adm £2.50, chd free. Suns 28 Jan; 11 Feb; 25 Mar; 15, 29 Apr (2-5). Visitors also welcome by appt, Feb, Mar & Apr.** Set in elevated position with exceptional views. 1m walk through woods and fields to show carpets of spring flowers. Enclosed garden with fern border, sundial and heather bed. White and mixed shrub borders. Stout footwear advisable in winter.

29 NEW **HOOKHOUSE POTTERY**
Hookhouse Lane, Tetbury GL8 8TZ. **Lise & Christopher White, 01666 880297, white@hookhouse.freeserve.co. uk.** *2½m WSW of Tetbury. From Tetbury take A4135 towards Dursley, then take 2nd L signed Leighterton. Hookhouse pottery is 1½m on R. Home-made & cream teas.* **Adm £2.50, chd free. Daily Sat 26 May to Sun 3 June; Wed 4 July (10-6). Visitors also welcome by appt.** Interesting layout with alternation of open perspectives and intimate corners. Borders, shrubs, woodland glade, water garden with flowform cascades, vegetable garden with raised beds, orchard. Handthrown pots made on premises, sculptural pieces, garden games. Run on organic principles. Art & craft exhibition incl garden exhibits 26 May to 3 June only. Pottery showroom incl garden pots (all dates). Two unfenced ponds.
 ⅏ ⊛ ☕

30 **HUMPHREYS END HOUSE**
Randwick, nr Stroud GL6 6EW. **Pat & Jim Hutton, 01453 765401, pat.hutton1@googlemail.com.** *2m NW of Stroud. M5 J13, follow signs to Cashes Green & Randwick. At Townsend, turn R. Parking, look for signs. Cream teas.* **Adm £2.50, chd free. Suns 6 May; 17 June (2-6). Evening Opening £3.50, wine, Thur 28 June (6-9). Visitors also welcome by appt, May, Jun & Jul.** Different areas of contrasting mood and interesting planting surrounding listed C16 farmhouse (not open). A wildlife friendly garden. New pond area, old roses, grasses and organic vegetables.
⊛ ☕

31 **HUNTLEY MANOR**
Huntley GL19 3HQ. **Prof Tim Congdon & Mrs Dorianne Congdon.** *4m S of Newent. On B4216 1/2m off A40 in Huntley travelling towards Newent. Please bring picnics.* **Adm £5, chd free. Visitors welcome by appt, groups of 10+, small coaches welcome. Send cheques to County Treasurer. Apply in writing to Mrs D Congdon, Huntley Manor, Huntley, Glos GL19 3HQ.** Park-like grounds surround the gothic 'French Château' style house (open by arrangement) built in 1862 by S S Teulon. Informal beds of mature shrubbery and rare specimen trees (tulip tree reputed to be tallest in the country after Kew), intersperse with sweeping lawns down to lake. Woodland walk with giant redwoods; exotic waterfowl and peacocks roam the grounds. Excellent for club outings and AGMs.
 ⅏

32 ♦ **HUNTS COURT**
North Nibley GL11 6DZ. **Mr & Mrs T K Marshall, 01453 547440.** *2m NW of Wotton-under-Edge. From Wotton B4060 Dursley rd turn R in North Nibley at Black Horse; fork L after 1/4m.* **Adm £3, chd free. Tues to Sats all yr (9-12.30 & 1.45-5) except Good Fri & Aug. For NGS: Suns, 10, 17, 24 June; 2, 9 Sept (2-6).** A plant lover's garden with unusual shrubs, 450 varieties old roses, large collection of penstemons and hardy geraniums in peaceful 2½-acre garden set against tree-clad hills and Tyndale monument. Recently planted mini-arboretum. House (not open) possible birthplace of William Tyndale. Picnic area.
 ⅏ ⊛ ☕

33 **ICOMB PLACE**
nr Stow-on-the-Wold GL54 1JD. **T L F Royle.** *2m S of Stow. After 2m on A424 Burford Rd turn L to Icomb village. Cream teas.* **Adm £3, chd £2 (share to St Mary's Church, Icomb). Sun 24 June (2-6).** Gardens were laid down in first decade of C20 and consist of ponds, water garden and arboretum with a potager

added by the present owners. One of the first gardens opened under the NGS. Plant sale in aid of Glos Gardens & Landscape Trust. 2nd prize Open Garden Comp, Moreton Show. Unfenced ponds & steep paths.
 & ⅏ ⊛ ☕

34 ♦ **KEMPSFORD MANOR**
High Street, Kempsford GL7 4EQ. **Mrs Z I Williamson, ipek@kempsfordmanor.co.uk.** *3m S of Fairford. Take A419 from Cirencester or Swindon. Kempsford is signed 10m (approx) from each. The Manor is in the centre of village.* **House and garden adm £5, garden only adm £3, chd free. For NGS: Sun 25 Feb; Suns 4, 11, 18 Mar; Mon 9, Sun 29 Apr; Sun 27, Mon 28 May; Sun 10 June; Sun 22 July; Suns 12, 19, 26, Mon 27 Aug; Suns 9, 16 Sept (2-5).** Early spring garden with variety of bulbs incl snowdrop walk along old canal. Peaceful, expansive summer garden for relaxation, adjacent to cricket field, croquet and outdoor games for children. Tea is served by log fire in early spring. Talks: 18 Mar Snowdrops (11.30-5); 10 June Summer gardens (11.30-5); 12 Aug Gardening Questions (11.30-6). Light lunch available, please book, £7.
 & ⅏ ⊨ ☕

KENCOT GARDENS
See Oxfordshire.

35 ♦ **KIFTSGATE COURT**
nr Chipping Campden GL55 6LN. **Mr & Mrs J G Chambers, 01386 438777, kiftsgate@aol.com.** *4m NE of Chipping Campden. Adjacent to Hidcote National Trust Garden. 1m E of B4632 & B4081.* **Adm £5.50, chd £1.50. Daily except Thur & Fri May, June & July (12-6); Sun, Mon, Wed, Apr, Aug & Sept (2-6). For NGS: Mons 23 Apr; 13 Aug (2-6).** Magnificent situation and views; many unusual plants and shrubs; tree peonies, hydrangeas, abutilons, species and old-fashioned roses, incl largest rose in England, *Rosa filipes* 'Kiftsgate'.
⅏ ⊛ ☕

Set in elevated position with exceptional views . . .

KINGSTONE COTTAGES
See Herefordshire.

36 LAMMAS PARK
Cuckoo Row, Minchinhampton
GL6 9HA. Mr P Grover, 01453
886471. *4m SE of Stroud. From
Market Sq down High St for 100yds,
turn R at Xrds. After 300yds turn L,
Lammas Park 100yds on L.* **Adm £3,
chd free. Suns 8 Apr; 3 June (12-5).
Visitors also welcome by appt.**
2½ acres around Cotswold 'Arts and
Crafts' style house (not open).
Herbaceous borders, pleached lime
allée, wild garden, alpines, restored
C17 'hanging gardens' with tunnel.
Superb views.

THE LONG BARN
See Herefordshire.

37 LOWER FARM HOUSE
Cliffords Mesne GL18 1JT. Gareth &
Sarah Williams. *2m S of Newent.
From Newent follow signs to Cliffords
Mesne & Birds of Prey Centre (1½m).
Approx ½ m beyond 'centre', turn
L at Xrds. Signed Kents Green.
Garden 150yds down hill on bend.
Car park (limited if wet).* Home-made
teas. **Adm £3, chd free. Mon 28 May
(1-6).**
2-acre garden, incl woodland, stream
and large natural lily pond with rockery
and bog garden. Herbaceous borders,
pergola walk, terrace with ornamental
fishpond, kitchen and herb garden;
many interesting and unusual trees and
shrubs. Gravel paths.

**38 ◆ LYDNEY PARK SPRING
GARDEN**
Lydney GL15 6BU. The Viscount
Bledisloe, 01594 842844/842922,
tracey_lydneype@btconnect.com.
*½m SW of Lydney. On A48
Gloucester to Chepstow rd between
Lydney & Aylburton. Drive is directly off
A48.* **Adm £3 18 Apr, £4 19 May, chd
50p. Suns, Weds & Bank Hol Mons
1 Apr to 6 May; also daily 6 May - 3
June. For NGS: Wed 18 Apr; Sat 19
May (10-5).**
Spring garden in 8-acre woodland
valley with lakes, profusion of
rhododendrons, azaleas and other
flowering shrubs. Formal garden;
magnolias and daffodils (April). Picnics
in deer park which has fine trees.
Important Roman Temple site and
museum. Teas in family dining room
(otherwise house not open).

39 MALVERN MILL
High Street, Blockley GL56 9HA. Mr
& Mrs J Bourne. *3m NW of Moreton-
in-Marsh. Take A44 Moreton to
Broadway Rd; turning N of Bourton-
on-the-Hill B4479, follow signs in
village.* **Adm £2.50, (£3.50 if incl Old
Chequer garden). Sun 15 Apr (12-5);
Sun 10 June (2-6). Also opening with
Blockley Gardens 10 June.**
Old water mill with pond and brook;
kitchen garden and orchard; cottage
flower garden; wild flower meadow,
rare breed sheep.

A plantaholic craftworker's creation with shrubs, perennials, spring bulbs . . .

40 ◆ THE MATARA GARDEN
Kingscote GL8 8YA. Herons Mead
Ltd, 01453 861050,
www.matara.co.uk. *5½m NW of
Tetbury. On A4135 towards Dursley. At
the Hunters Hall Inn turn R into
Kingscote village. Enter Park at 1st
gate on R.* Tea & cakes NGS days only.
**Adm £4, chd free, concessions £3.
Tues & Thurs 1 May to 30 Sept (1-5).
For NGS: Suns 27 May; 29 July; 30
Sept (1-5).**
A unique meditative garden alive with
inspiration from around the world.
Labyrinths, medicine wheel, ponds,
sculptures and walled ornamental
vegetable garden. We are developing
an Eastern woodland walk and wild
flower meadow. Matara is a spiritual
garden dedicated to the full expression
of the human spirit. All set within a 28-
acre parkland.

41 MEADOW COTTAGE
59 Coalway Road, Coalway, nr
Coleford GL16 7HL. Mrs Pamela
Buckland, 01594 833444. *1m SE of
Coleford. From Coleford take Lydney &
Chepstow Rd at T-lights in town. Turn
L after police stn, signed Coalway &
Parkend. Garden on L ½m up hill opp
layby.* Home-made teas. **Adm £2.50,
chd free. Suns 22 Apr; 20 May; 8
July; 26 Aug (2-6). Visitors also
welcome by appt April to Sept.**
⅓-acre cottage garden, a plantaholic
craftworker's creation with shrubs,
perennials, spring bulbs in colourful
borders and interlinking garden rooms.
Lawned area. Gravel paths leading to
small pond with waterfall and bog
garden. Vegetable garden in raised
beds. Gravel garden with grasses,
bamboos and pots and containers in
abundance.

42 NEW MERLINE HOUSE
1a Horsford Road, Charfield
GL12 8SU. Mrs Pauline Scull,
01453 844021. *2½m from J14 of
M5. B4058; in Charfield turn into
Station Rd (opp Texaco garage)
then 2nd L.* Home-made teas.
**Adm £2.50, chd free (share to
Cotswold Care Hospice). Sun
26, Mon 27 Aug (2-5). Visitors
also welcome by appt for small
groups & individuals.**
Small garden formerly consisting of
swimming pool, tarmac, concrete
and conifers. Four yrs on is
transformed to area packed with
herbaceous perennials, shrubs,
roses and clematis, some growing
in very little soil, round central
pond. No grass.

43 ◆ MILL DENE GARDEN
School Lane, Blockley GL56 9HU.
Mr & Mrs B S Dare, 01386 700457,
www.milldenegarden.co.uk. *3m NW
of Moreton-in-Marsh. From A44, follow
brown signs from Bourton-on-the-Hill,
to Blockley. 1⅓m down hill turn L
behind village gates. Parking for 8 cars.*
**Adm £4.50, chd £1, concessions £4.
Tues to Fris 3 Apr to 31 Oct (10-5).
Closed 24-27 Jul incl. For NGS: Fri
6, Sun 22 Apr; Sun 1 July (2-5).**
This garden surrounds a Cotswold
stone water-mill, set in a tiny steep
sided valley. It seems to have evolved
naturally in English 'country garden'
style. A millpond, stream, grotto,

potager and trompe l'oeil all contribute to the owner's design for surprise, concealment, scent, colour and, above all, fun. New - 'scratch & sniff' herb garden. Partial wheelchair access.

🏃 🏵 🛏 ☕

44 ◆ MISARDEN PARK
Miserden GL6 7JA. Major M T N H Wills, 01285 821303, estate.office@misardenestate.co.uk. *6m NW of Cirencester. Follow signs off A417 or B4070 from Stroud.* Adm £4, chd free. Tues, Weds,Thurs 3 Apr to 27 Sept (9.30-5). For NGS: Suns 1 Apr; 24 June (2-6).
Essentially formal, dating from C17, magnificent position overlooking the Golden Valley. Walled garden with long herbaceous borders (undergoing restoration), yew walk leading to a lower lawn with rill and summerhouse. Aboretum with spring bulbs en masse. Climbing roses and newly planted rose walk linking parterre. Silver and grey border, blue border and scented border. New blue gold walkway below house. Gentle slope down.

🏃 🏃 🏵 ☕

45 MOOR WOOD
Woodmancote GL7 7EB. Mr & Mrs Henry Robinson, 01285 831397, henry@moorwood.fslife.co.uk. *3¹/₂m NW of Cirencester. Turn L off A435 to Cheltenham at North Cerney, signed Woodmancote 1¹/₄m; entrance in village on L beside lodge with white gates.* Adm £3, chd free (share to Cobalt Unit, Cheltenham). Sun 1 July (2-6). Visitors also welcome by appt 20 June to 3 July only. Coaches permitted. Groups of 10+ can get conducted tour.
2 acres of shrub, orchard and wild flower gardens in isolated valley setting. Holder of the National Collection of rambler roses.

🏃 NCCPG ☕

46 THE OLD CHAPEL
Marle Hill, Chalford Vale GL6 8PN. F J & F Owen. *4m E of Stroud. On A419 to Cirencester. Above Chalford Vale, steep climb from car park on main rd, up Marle Hill.* Adm £3, chd free. Daily Sat 2 June to Sun 17 June (10-5). Also opening with **Chalford Gardens** 16, 17 June (2-5).
1-acre Victorian chapel garden on precipitous hillside. A tiered tapestry of herbaceous borders, formal potager, small orchard, pond and summerhouse, old roses. Gothic pergola and rose tunnel, all laid out on

terraced S-facing Marle Cliff. Annual studio art exhibition. See website: www.johnandfionaowen.com.

47 THE OLD CHEQUER
Draycott, nr Blockley GL56 9LB. Mr & Mrs H Linley, 01386 700647. *2m NE of Moreton-in-Marsh. Nr Blockley.* Home-made teas. Adm £2.50 (£3.50 if incl Malvern Mill), chd free. Sun 15 Apr (11-4); Sun 10 June (2-6). Also opening with **Malvern Mill** 15 Apr **Blockley Gardens** 10 June. Visitors also welcome by appt, Apr to July only.
Peaceful country garden, created by owner, set in 2 acres of old orchard with original ridge and furrow. Emphasis on spring planting but still maintaining yr-round interest. Kitchen garden/soft fruit, herbaceous and shrubs in island beds. Croquet lawn, unusual plants, alpines and dry gravel borders.

🏃 🏃 🏵 ☕

THE OLD CORN MILL
See Herefordshire.

A tiered tapestry of herbaceous borders . . .

48 THE OLD VICARAGE
Maisemore GL2 8HU. Mr & Mrs George Hayter. *1¹/₂m NW of Gloucester. Take the A417 to Ledbury. Cross the R Severn in Maisemore. 1st R beside White Hart PH called The Rudge. ¹/₂m from PH car park on L.* Light refreshments, wine & cream teas. Adm £3, chd free. Suns 13 May; 3 June (11-6).
Flower arranger's garden of approx 2 acres. Delightful rose garden edged with lavender. Richly planted herbaceous borders with many unusual plants interspersed with shrubs. Potager with flowers for cutting, fruit and vegetables. Knot garden, which leads to large rock garden. Beside rock garden is 'Pooh Corner' where within an old ash tree is

a wonderful tree house and play-ship. Easy access & parking. Some gravel & narrow paths.

🏃 🏃 🏵 ☕

49 OZLEWORTH PARK
Wotton-under-Edge GL12 7QA. Mr & Mrs M J C Stone. *5m S of Dursley. Approach from A4135 Tetbury to Dursley rd. At junction with B4058, turn S on single track lane signed Ozleworth. Follow signs for approx 2m until reaching gates with eagles on gateposts. Follow signs down drive.* Light refreshments & teas. Adm £4, chd free. Sun 15 July (2-5).
Renovated over past 12yrs. Approx 10 acres with rose garden, Victorian bath house, lily ponds, small lake; also glasshouses, orchard and vegetable area. Some areas not accessible via wheelchair.

🏃 🏃 ☕

50 ◆ PAINSWICK ROCOCO GARDEN
Painswick GL6 6TH. Painswick Rococo Garden Trust, 01452 813204, www.rococogarden.org.uk. *¹/₄m N of Painswick. ¹/₂m outside village on B4073.* Adm £5, chd £2.50, concessions £4. Daily 10 Jan to 31 Oct (11-5).
Unique C18 garden from the brief Rococo period, combining contemporary buildings, vistas, ponds, kitchen garden and winding woodland walks. Anniversary maze.

🏵

PARK FARM
See Somerset & Bristol Area.

51 PAULMEAD
Bisley GL6 7AG. Judy & Philip Howard. *5m E of Stroud. On S edge of Bisley at head of Toadsmoor Valley on top of Cotswolds. Garden & car park well signed in Bisley village. Disabled can be dropped off at garden prior to parking car.* Adm £3, or £4 for 2 gardens, chd free. Sun 17 June (2-6). Combined with **Wells Cottage, Bisley.**
Approx 1-acre landscaped garden constructed in stages over last 17yrs. Terraced in three main levels: natural stream garden; formal herbaceous and shrub borders; yew and beech hedges; formal vegetable garden; lawns; summerhouse with exterior wooden decking by pond and thatched roof over well head. New unusual tree house.

🏃 🏃

Small beautiful riverside garden – old-fashioned roses a feature . . .

52 PEAR TREE COTTAGE
58 Malleson Road, Gotherington
GL52 9EX. Mr & Mrs E Manders-
Trett, 01242 674592,
edandmary@tiscali.co.uk. *4m N of
Cheltenham. From A435 turn R into
Gotherington 1m after end of Bishop's
Cleeve bypass. Garden is on L approx
100yds past Shutter Inn.* **Visitors
welcome by appt, Feb - Jun garden
at its best, other dates considered.**
Mainly informal country garden approx
1/2-acre with pond and gravel garden,
grasses and herbaceous borders,
trees and shrubs surrounding lawns.
Wild garden and orchard lead to
greenhouses, herb and vegetable
gardens. Spring bulbs and early
summer perennials and shrubs
particularly colourful. Featured in
'Amateur Gardening' & 'Glos Echo'
2006.

53 PEMBERLEY LODGE
Churchend Lane, Old Charfield
GL12 8LJ. Rob & Yvette
Andrewartha, 01454 260885. *31/2 m
SW of Wotton-under-Edge. Off B4058
from Wotton-under Edge through
Charfield Village. At top of Charfield
Hill, turn L. 2m from M5 J14, at Xrds
on B4509 go straight across into
Churchend Lane.* **Visitors welcome
by appt.**
Small private garden designed and
planted in 2002 by Lesley Rosser.
Densely planted for all-yr-round
interest, maturing well. Incorporates
trees, shrubs, perennials, grasses,
water, gravel and hard landscaping to
give an informal peaceful feel. New roof
garden added in 2006.

54 PIGEON HOUSE
Southam Lane, Southam GL52 3NY.
Mr & Mrs Julian Taylor, 01242
529342, julian.taylor@zen.co.uk. *3m
NE of Cheltenham. Off B4632 toward
Winchcombe. Parking available
adjacent to Southam Tithe Barn.* **Adm
£3, chd free. Suns 13 May; 3 June
(2-5). Visitors also welcome by appt
May-Sept, groups of 10+.**
2-acre garden surrounding Cotswold
stone manor (not open) of medieval

origin. Small lake with island and
separate water garden with linked
pools featuring water margin and bog
plants. Extensive lawns on several
levels; wide range of flowering shrubs
and borders designed to create a
multitude of vistas; woodland area with
shade-loving plants and many spring
bulbs.

THE POUND HOUSE
See Wiltshire.

55 PRIORS MESNE
Aylburton, nr Lydney GL15 6DX. Mr
& Mrs Brian Thornton. *3m NW of
Lydney. At the George PH in Aylburton
take St Briavels rd off A48. Go up hill
for 2m to T-junction. Turn sharp L, go
down hill for approx 200 metres. Turn
R into entrance marked Priors Mesne
private rd. Go to end of drive some
300 metres. Home-made teas.* **Adm
£3, chd free (share to Rainbow Trust
Children's Charity). Suns 13, 20 May
(11-5).**
Approached down an avenue of
mature lime trees, this large terraced
garden enjoys distant views over deer
park to Severn Estuary and Cotswolds
beyond. Collection of rhododendrons,
azaleas, magnolias and acers set
amongst three magnificent copper
beeches, water feature and woodland
walk through bluebells. Featured in
'The Forester' & 'Glos Citizen' 2006.

56 QUENINGTON GARDENS
nr Fairford GL7 5BW. *8m NE of
Cirencester. Teas at The Old Rectory.*
**Combined adm £4, chd free. Sun 24
June (2-6).**
A rarely visited Coln Valley village
delighting its infrequent visitors with
C12 Norman church and C17 stone
cottages (not open). An opportunity to
discover the horticultural treasures
behind those Cotswold stone walls
and visit 4 very different but charming
gardens incorporating everything from
the exotic and the organic to the
simple cottage garden; a range of
vistas from riverside to seclusion.

BANK VIEW
Mrs J A Moulden
Terraced garden with wonderful
views over the R Coln.

THE OLD RECTORY
Mr & Mrs D Abel Smith, 01285
750358,
lucy@realityandbeyond.co.uk.
Visitors also welcome by appt.
On the banks of the mill race and
the R Coln, this is an organic
garden of variety. Mature trees
and new plantings, large
vegetable garden, herbaceous,
shade, pool and bog gardens.
Home of the 10th biennial
sculpture show 'Fresh Air 2007'. A
charity set up by the Abel Smiths
to promote contemporary
sculpture. This is a selling
exhibition with the work of over
100 artists set in this interesting
and diverse garden, 17 June to 8
July.

POOL HAY
Mrs E A Morris
Small beautiful riverside garden -
old-fashioned roses a feature.

YEW TREE COTTAGES
Mr J Lindon
Quintessential cottage garden.

57 RAMBLERS
Lower Common, Aylburton, nr
Lydney GL15 6DS. Jane & Leslie
Hale. *11/2 m W of Lydney. Off A48
Gloucester to Chepstow Rd. From
Lydney through Aylburton, out of de-
limit turn R signed Aylburton Common,
3/4 m along lane. Home-made teas.*
**Adm £2.50, chd free. Suns 6 May;
10 June (2-6). Evening Opening
£3.50, wine, Sat 2 June (6-9).**
Peaceful medium-sized country garden
with informal cottage planting,
herbaceous borders and small pond
looking through hedge 'windows' onto
wild flower meadow. Front woodland
garden with shade-loving plants and
topiary. Large productive vegetable
garden. Recently planted apple
orchard.

58 THE RED HOUSE
Pillows Green, Staunton, nr
Gloucester GL19 3NU. Mr & Mrs W
K Turner, 01452 840505,
keith@redhouse.ip.uk.com. *8m NW
of Gloucester. On A417 from Staunton
Xrds, 1/2 m off B4208.*

Adm £2.50, £4 for 2 gardens, chd free. Suns 6, 20 May; 17 June (2-6). Combined with **Vine Farm** 20 May & 17 June. Visitors also welcome by appt.
Split-level 2-acre organic and wildlife garden with herbaceous borders, containing many native wild plants, ponds; gravel garden and terrace with containers; parterre; also flower meadow. C17 house open by appt. Garden designed and maintained by owners. New 'Victorian' greenhouse.

59 REDWOOD
Bussage GL6 8AZ. David & Rita Collins. *3m E of Stroud. 2m N of A419 Stroud to Cirencester on turning signed to Bisley & Eastcombe. Please park with consideration.* Adm £2.50, chd free (share to Cotswold Care Hospice). Sat 3, Sun 4 Mar (1-4).
Terraced hillside garden with a variety of hard landscaping, lawns, pond and pergolas. Borders and rockery contain many unusual trees, shrubs and plants, especially single and double hellebores and other early flowering varieties. Many flowering hellebores for sale.
⊛

60 ROCKCLIFFE
nr Lower Swell GL54 2JW. Mr & Mrs Simon Keswick. *2m SW of Stow-on-the-Wold. On B4068. From Stow-on-the-Wold to Cheltenham go through Lower Swell. Climb hill staying on B4068. Converted barn on L. Round corner & start dropping down hill. Rockcliffe halfway down on R.* Home-made teas. Adm £3.50, chd free. Weds 13, 20 June (12-5).
Large traditional English garden 7 acres incl pink, white and blue gardens, herbaceous border, rose terrace; walled kitchen garden and orchard; greenhouses and new stone dovecot with pathway of topiary birds leading up through orchard to it. Featured in 'English Garden' Magazine 2007.
⚘ ⊛ ☕

Split-level 2-acre organic and wildlife garden with herbaceous borders . . .

61 ♦ RODMARTON MANOR
Cirencester GL7 6PF. Mr & Mrs Simon Biddulph, 01285 841253, www.rodmarton-manor.co.uk. *5m NE of Tetbury. Off A433. Between Cirencester & Tetbury.* House and garden adm £7, chd £3.50 (5-15yrs), garden only adm £4, chd £1 (5-15yrs). Please phone or visit website for other opening times. For NGS: Sun 22 Apr (2-5).
The 8-acre garden of this fine 'Arts and Crafts' house is a series of 'outdoor rooms' each with its own distinctive character. Leisure garden, winter garden, troughery, topiary, hedges, lawns, rockery, containers, wild garden, kitchen garden, magnificent herbaceous borders. Snowdrop collection.
⚘ ⚘ ☕

62 ROOKWOODS
Waterlane, nr Bisley GL6 7PN. Mr & Mrs Des Althorp. *5m E of Stroud. Between Sapperton & Bisley. Turn down No Through Rd in Waterlane then follow signs.* Home-made teas. Adm £3, chd free. Sun 24 June (2-6).
3-acre, well structured garden with herbaceous borders to colour themes. Pleached whitebeam around pool area. Wide variety of old-fashioned and modern climbing and shrub roses (mostly labelled), water gardens and outstanding views.
⊛ ☕

63 ROSEMARY COTTAGE
8 Peter Street, Frocester GL10 3TQ. Eric & Madeline Sadler, 01453 827607. *4m SW of Stroud. J13 M5. A419 towards Stroud, turn R at 1st roundabout to Eastington. Next roundabout turn L to Frocester. At Xrds turn R down beside The George PH. Park in field 200yds on L. Cottage further 200yds on R.* Home-made teas. Adm £3, chd free (share to WSPA). Suns 22 Apr; 15 July (2-6). Visitors also welcome by appt, Apr-Jul.
1/2-acre on gentle S-facing slope. Plantsman's garden. Lots of mixed

borders with cottage garden-style planting. Sorry no room for a lawn. National Collection of *Rosmarinus officinalis* best viewed in April. New National Collection of Erigeron cultivars, best viewed in July.
⚘ ⚘ ⊛ NCCPG ☕

SALFORD GARDENS
See Oxfordshire.

64 SANDYWELL GARDENS
nr Whittington, Cheltenham GL54 4HF. *5m E of Cheltenham. On A40 between Whittington & Andoversford.* Home-made teas at Barn House. Combined adm £4, chd free. Suns 10, 24 June (11-5).
Two complementary walled gardens, totalling 3 acres, within the former kitchen garden of Sandywell Park. Set within open Cotswold landscape, the gardens have been created over 20yrs utilising original features alongside new. Gardens incl mature trees, varied borders, secret corners, lawns, water features, walkways and avenues.
☕

BARN HOUSE
Shirley & Gordon Sills, 01242 820606, shirley.sills@tesco.net. Adm £2.50. Visitors also welcome by appt 10 June to 10 July only, groups 10+. Coaches permitted.
Plantaholic designer's own 2 1/2-acre walled garden, divided by hedges and pergolas into several heavily-planted 'rooms', both formal and informal incl scented, yellow and rose gardens. Wildlife stream with pond and formal water features.
⚘ ⊛

GARDEN COTTAGE
Charles Fogg & Gilly Bogdiukiewicz, shirley.sills@tesco.net. Visitors also welcome by appt 10 June to 10 July only. Groups 10+.
Peaceful, 1/2-acre, cottage garden with four interconnecting walled areas, of different character and separate levels, incl; borders, lawns, gravel areas and patios. Also stone, marble and wooden features, urns, tubs, baskets and greenhouse.
⚘

65 ◆ SEZINCOTE
nr Moreton-in-Marsh GL56 9AW. Mr & Mrs D Peake, 01386 700444, www.sezincote.co.uk. *3m SW of Moreton-in-Marsh. From Moreton-in-Marsh turn W along A44 towards Evesham; after 1½m (just before Bourton-on-the-Hill) take turn L, by stone lodge with white gate.* **Adm £4, chd £1.50. Please phone or visit website for other opening times. For NGS: Sun 15 July (2-6).**
Exotic oriental water garden by Repton and Daniell with lake, pools and meandering stream, banked with massed perennials. Large semi-circular orangery, formal Indian garden, fountain, temple and unusual trees of vast size in lawn and wooded park setting. House in Indian manner designed by Samuel Pepys Cockerell. Cover story 'Cotswold Life'. Gravel paths & steep slopes.

  ♿ ☕

One of the most picturesque and unspoilt C17 Cotswold villages with many gardens to explore . . .

66 SHEEPHOUSE
Stepping Stone Lane, Painswick GL6 6RX. Lawrence & Lindsay Gardiner. *¼m E of Painswick. From A46 through Painswick take Stamages Lane (below car park) & follow signs. Parking in Painswick will assist parking at house & provide lovely partly steep 1m walk.* **Adm £3, chd free (share to The MARAH Trust Ltd). Sun 18 Mar (2-5).**
1¼-acre garden surrounding C15, C17 and C19 country house (not open). Extensively re-designed and developed. Formal holly and clipped yew drive; water feature with weir; knot garden; formal potager designed by Robert Bryant. 40,000 spring bulbs; hellebores; beautiful mature trees. Unfenced water.

♿ ☕

67 ◆ SNOWSHILL MANOR
nr Broadway WR12 7JU. The National Trust, 01386 852410, www.nationaltrust.org.uk. *2½m S of Broadway. Off A44 bypass into Broadway village.* **House and garden adm £7.70, chd £3.90, family £19.60, garden only adm £4.20, chd £2.10, family £10.60. Open 24 Mar to 28 Oct, Weds to Suns & Bank Hols, garden (11-5.30), house (12-5). For NGS: Wed 27 June (11-5.30).**
An Arts & Crafts inspired terraced garden in which organic and natural methods only are used. Highlights incl tranquil ponds, old roses, old-fashioned flowers and herbaceous borders rich in plants of special interest. Working kitchen garden.

☕ ❀

68 NEW SOUTH LODGE
Church Road, Clearwell, Coleford GL16 8LG. Andrew & Jane Macbean. *2m S of Coleford. Off B4228. Follow signs to Clearwell. Garden on L of castle driveway. Park at Castle Farm.* **Home-made teas. Adm £2.50, chd free. Sun 1 July (11-5).**
Set in the peaceful, rural village of Clearwell, this 2-acre, organic garden is on a sloping site which used to be a part of the grounds of Clearwell Castle. A developing garden which includes large area of trees and shrubs, with some unusual specimens; good selection of fruit trees; wild flower meadow and wildlife pond; colourful borders; vegetable garden and small formal pond.

☕ ❀ ☕

69 STANTON GARDENS
nr Broadway WR12 7NE. Mr K J Ryland. *3m SW of Broadway. Off B4632, between Broadway (3m) & Winchcombe (6m).* **Home-made teas. Adm £4.50, chd free (share to Stanton Church & Church Hall). Sun 17 June (2-6).**
One of the most picturesque and unspoilt C17 Cotswold villages with many gardens to explore (22 open in 2006) ranging from charming cottage to large formal gardens of appeal to visitors of all tastes. Cannot guarantee wheelchair access to all gardens. Disabled WC.

♿ ❀ ☕

70 ◆ STANWAY FOUNTAIN & WATER GARDEN
nr Winchcombe GL54 5PQ. Lord Neidpath, 01386 584528, www.stanwayfountain.co.uk. *9m NE of Cheltenham. 1m E of B4632 Cheltenham to Broadway rd or B4077 Toddington to Stow-on-the-Wold rd.* **House and garden adm £6, chd £1.50, concessions £4.50, garden only adm £4, chd £1, concessions £3. Please phone or visit website for other opening times. For NGS: Suns 1 Apr; 20 May (2-5).**
20 acres of planted landscape in early C18 formal setting. Recent restoration of canal, upper pond and 165ft high fountain have re-created one of the most interesting baroque water gardens in Britain. Striking C16 manor with gatehouse, tithe barn and church. Britain's highest fountain, the world's highest gravity fountain.

☕

71 ◆ STONE HOUSE
Wyck Rissington GL54 2PN. Mr & Mrs Andrew Lukas, 01451 810337, www.stonehousegarden.co.uk. *3m S of Stow-on-the-Wold. Off A429 between Bourton-on-the-Water & Stow-on-the-Wold. Last house in village behind high bank on R.* **Home-made teas in village hall. Adm £4, chd free. For NGS: Sun 1 July (2-6).**
2 acres full of unusual bulbs, shrubs and herbaceous plants. Crab apple walk, rose borders, herb and water garden, meadow walk. Plantswoman's garden with yr-round interest. Rare plant sales, 9 Mar, 28 May, 18 Sept, contact for info. Some paths may be slippery.

♿ ❀ ☕

72 STOWELL PARK
Northleach GL54 3LE. The Lord & Lady Vestey, 01285 720610 Neil, Head Gardener. *8m NE of Cirencester. Off Fosseway A429 2m SW of Northleach.* **Home-made teas. Adm £4, chd free. Suns 20 May; 24 June (2-5). Visitors also welcome by appt for groups of 10+.**
Magnificent lawned terraces with stunning views over Coln Valley. Fine collection of old-fashioned roses and herbaceous plants, with pleached lime approach to C14 house (not open). Two large walled gardens containing vegetables, fruit, cut flowers and range of greenhouses. Long rose pergola and wide, plant-filled borders divided into colour sections. Plant Sale - 20 May only.

❀ ☕

73 ◆ SUDELEY CASTLE GARDENS & EXHIBITIONS
Winchcombe GL54 5JD. Lord & Lady Ashcombe & Henry & Mollie Dent Brocklehurst, 01242 602308, www.sudeleycastle.co.uk. *8m NE of Cheltenham. On B4632 (A46) or 10m from J9 M5. Bus service operates bet Winchcombe & Cheltenham or Broadway.* Exhibitions & gardens adm £7.20, chd £4.20, concessions £6.20. Open daily 31 Mar to 28 Oct. Please phone or check website, as details subject to change. For NGS: Sun 9 Sept (10.30-5).
Magnificent gardens work themselves seamlessly around castle buildings. Individual gardens incl Queen's Garden with old-fashioned roses, perennials, herbs; Tudor knot garden with water feature; Heritage Seed Library garden. Also formal pools, spring bulbs and fine trees in extensive grounds. Adjacent plant centre. Limited wheelchair access; gravel paths & steep slope nr church.
& ♣ ❀ ☕

75 TINPENNY FARM
Fiddington, nr Tewkesbury GL20 7BJ. E S Horton, 01684 292668. *2½m SE of Tewkesbury. From M5 J9 take A46 exit towards Evesham. Just after T-lights turn R to Fiddington. After 1½m turn R to Walton Cardiff. Entrance 1st on R.* Adm £2.50, chd free. Tues to Thurs all yr. Suns 18 Feb; 18 Mar; 22 Apr; 13 May; 17 June; 15 July; 16 Sept; 14 Oct (12-5). Visitors also welcome by appt.
Amazing collection of plants incl hellebores, iris, hemerocallis, hostas. Do not expect a weed-free zone! But to see what can be achieved with a wind-swept site on impenetrable clay, please do visit. Some gravel.
& ♣ ❀

76 TRENCH HILL
Sheepscombe GL6 6TZ. Celia & Dave Hargrave, 01452 814306, celia.hargrave@btconnect.com. *1½m E of Painswick. On A46 to Cheltenham after Painswick, turn R to*

77 NEW UPPER MERTON HOUSE
High Street, Newnham-on-Severn GL14 1AD. Roger Grounds & Diana Grenfell, 01594 517146, diana@uppermerton.co.uk. *Halfway bet Chepstow & Gloucester on A48. On service rd parallel to High St bet Victoria Hotel & Dean Rd.* Teas at Cottonwood, High Street. Adm £2.50, chd 50p. Visitors welcome by appt Weds (2-5) June, July, Aug. Coaches permitted. Groups 10+.
Small, recently created, formal but exuberantly planted, town garden. Collection of hostas, day lilies, ornamental grasses, ferns, palms and many unusual plants displayed to benefit from different levels, incl stone steps, courtyards and terrace. National Collection of miniature hosta. Parking available in village carpark. Access to garden only via flight of stone steps.
♣ NCCPG ☕

78 UPTON WOLD
nr Moreton-in-Marsh GL56 9TR. Mr & Mrs I R S Bond, 01386 700666, admin@northwickestate.co.uk. *3½m W of Moreton-in-Marsh. On A44 1m past A424 junction at Troopers Lodge Garage.* Adm £5, chd free. Suns 6 May; 24 June (10-6). Visitors also welcome by appt May to July.
Ever-developing and changing garden, architecturally and imaginatively laid out around C17 house (not open) with commanding views. Yew hedges; herbaceous walk; some unusual plants and trees; vegetables; pond and woodland gardens. National Collection of Juglans.
♣ ❀ NCCPG

Plantings of spring bulbs with thousands of snowdrops and hellebores . . .

79 VINE FARM
Malvern Road, Staunton GL19 3NZ. Alex & Jane Morton, 01452 840171, oaks@vinefarm.ip.uk.com. *7m NE of Newent. Staunton ½ way between Ledbury & Gloucester on A417. In village, from mini roundabout, take B4208 to Malvern. Approx ½m on L is Vine Farm.* Home-made teas. Adm £2.50, £4 two gardens, chd free. Suns 20 May; 17 June (2-6). Combined with **The Red House** 20 May & 17 June. Visitors also welcome by appt, end of May, June & July.

74 TEMPLE GUITING MANOR
Temple Guiting, nr Stow on the Wold GL54 5RP. Mr S Collins. *7m from Stow on the Wold. From Stow on the Wold take B4077 towards Tewkesbury. On descending hill bear L to village (signed) ½m. Garden in centre of village on R.* Adm £3, chd free. Sun 8 July (2-6).
First and second stages complete of newly designed formal contemporary gardens (by Jinny Blom) to Grade I listed historic manor house (not open) in Windrush Valley. Dry Stone Wall Assoc of GB Pinnacle Award 2006, presented by HRH, Prince Charles to Gilbert Sterling-Lee (Walls), Jinny Blom (Garden Design) & Ptolemy Dean (Consultant Architect).
♣ ☕

Sheepscombe. Approx 1½ m (before reaching village) turn L by telegraph poles, Trench Hill at top of lane. Home-made teas. Adm £2.50, chd free. Suns 11, 18 Feb (11-4); Sun 18 Mar; Sun 8, Mon 9 Apr; Weds, 6, 13, 20, 27 June; Suns 15 July; 26 Aug; 9 Sept (11-6); 10, 17 Feb 2008 (11-4). Visitors also welcome by appt.
Approx 3 acres set in small woodland with panoramic views. Variety of herbaceous and mixed borders, rose garden, extensive vegetable plots, wild flower areas, plantings of spring bulbs with thousands of snowdrops and hellebores, woodland walk, 2 small ponds, waterfall and larger conservation pond. Interesting wooden sculptures. Run on organic principles. Featured in 'Cotswold Life' 2006.
& ♣ ❀ ☕

Newly opened up garden which is currently being developed. Herbaceous borders, roses, honeysuckles and clematis. Also large productive vegetable garden with pergola, orchard and ponds. Mature trees surround the property of several acres, and the aim is a peaceful blend of countryside and garden.

🏃 ☕

Rambling roses on rope pergola . . .

80 WELLS COTTAGE
Wells Road, Bisley GL6 7AG. Mr & Mrs Michael Flint. *5m E of Stroud. Garden & car park well signed in Bisley village. Garden lies on S edge of village at head of Toadsmoor Valley, above A419.* Adm £3 (£4 for 2 gardens). No children under 16. Sun 17 June (2-6). Combined with **Paulmead.** Just under an acre. Terraced on several levels with beautiful views

over valley. Much informal planting of trees and shrubs to give colour and texture. Lawns and herbaceous borders. Collection of grasses. Formal pond area. Rambling roses on rope pergola. Vegetable garden with raised beds. Limited wheelchair access, steep slope and steps to top garden.

🛏

81 ◆ WESTBURY COURT GARDEN
Westbury-on-Severn GL14 1PD. The National Trust, www.nationaltrust.org.uk. *9m SW of Gloucester. On A48.* Adm £4.25, chd £2.15. For NGS: Sun 9 Sept (10-4). Formal Dutch-style water garden, earliest remaining in England; canals, summerhouse, over 100 species of plants grown in England, and recreated vegetable plots, growing crops all from before 1700.

🚻 🏃

WESTON MEWS
See Herefordshire.

82 ◆ WESTONBIRT SCHOOL GARDENS
Westonbirt GL8 8QG. Westonbirt School, 01666 881338, www.westonbirt.gloucs.sch.uk. *3m SW of Tetbury. Opp Westonbirt Arboretum, on the A433 (follow brown tourist information signs).* Adm £3.50, chd £2. 24 Mar to 22 April; 15 July to 9 Sept; 28 Oct to 4 Nov. For NGS: Sun 27, Mon 28 May (1-4.30). 22 acres. Former private garden of Robert Holford, founder of Westonbirt Arboretum. Formal Victorian gardens

incl walled Italian garden, terraced pleasure garden, rustic walks, lake, statuary and grotto. Rare, exotic trees and shrubs. Beautiful views of Westonbirt House, now Westonbirt School, not open. Gravel paths & steep slopes.

🚻 ☕

WESTWELL MANOR
See Oxfordshire.

WHITEHILL FARM
See Oxfordshire.

83 WILLOW LODGE
nr Longhope GL17 0RA. John & Sheila Wood, 01452 831211, www.willowgardens.fsnet.co.uk. *10m W of Gloucester, 6m E of Ross-on-Wye. On A40 between Huntley & Lea.* Home-made teas. Adm £3, chd free. Sun 6, Mon 7, Sun 27, Mon 28 May; Sun 12, Mon 13 Aug (1-5). Visitors also welcome by appt Apr to Aug, coaches welcome. Plantsman's garden with unusual and rare plants, herbaceous borders, shrubs and alpine garden. Many woodland plants incl trilliums, erythroniums, hellebores etc. Large bog garden with marginals and Asiatic primulas. Fish pond and stream. Exceptional arboretum containing approx 400 different trees and shrubs, from all over the temperate world. Areas of wild flowers in 4-acre grounds. Plants labelled. Conducted tours of the garden and arboretum by arrangement. Featured in RHS 'Garden Finder', 2006.

🚻 🏃 🐕 ☕

Gloucestershire County Volunteers

County Organiser; Leaflet Coordinator
Stella Martin, Dundry Lodge, France Lynch, Stroud, Gloucestershire GL6 8LP, 01453 883419, martin@franlyn.fsnet.co.uk

County Treasurer
Graham Baber, 11 Corinium Gate, Cirencester, Gloucestershire GL7 2PX, 01285 650961, grayanjen@onetel.com

Publicity
Madeline Sadler, Rosemary Cottage, 8 Peter Street, Frocester, Stonehouse, Gloucestershire GL10 3TQ, 01453 827607
  rosemarycottage@supanet.com

Assistant County Organisers
Barbara Adams, Warners Court, Charfield, Wotton under Edge, Gloucestershire GL12 8TG, 01454 261078
Meryl King, Springfield, Lower Chedworth, Cheltenham, Gloucestershire GL54 4AN, 01285 720278, MerylKing@compuserve.com
Tony Marlow, Greenedge, 32 Dr Browns Road, , Minchinhampton, Gloucestershire GL6 9BT, 01453 883531
Anne Palmer, 10 Vineyard Street, Winchcombe, Gloucestershire GL54 5LP, 01242 603761
Julian Taylor, Pigeon House, Southam Lane, Southam, Cheltenham, Gloucestershire GL52 3NY, 01242 529342,
  julian.taylor@zen.co.uk
Sally Whittal, Waterside, Church Lane, Churcham, Gloucester, Gloucestershire GL2 8AF, 01452 750753
  sallyatwaterside@waitrose.com

HAMPSHIRE

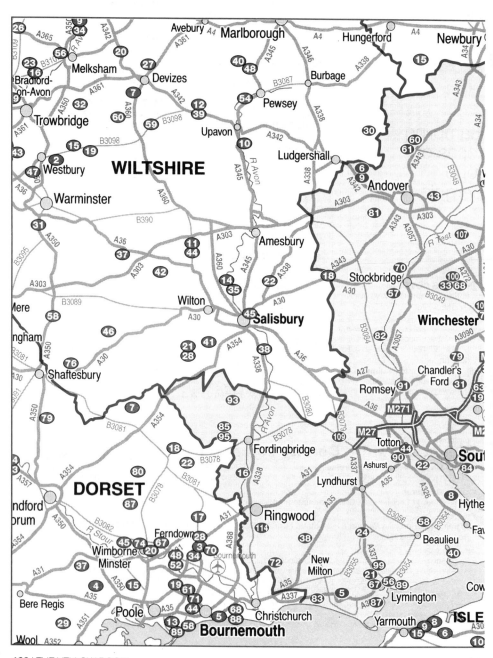

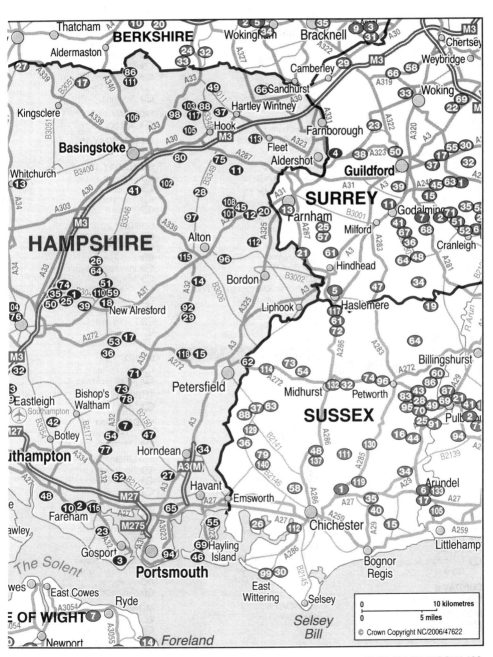

Opening Dates

February

SATURDAY 10
18 Brandy Mount House

SUNDAY 11
68 Little Court

SUNDAY 18
17 Bramdean House
68 Little Court

MONDAY 19
68 Little Court

TUESDAY 20
68 Little Court

SUNDAY 25
73 Manor House

March

SUNDAY 4
18 Brandy Mount House
48 Heathlands

SUNDAY 11
49 Heckfield Place

SUNDAY 18
6 Appleshaw Manor

SUNDAY 25
8 Atheling Villas
47 Hambledon House
50 Highfield
80 Mittens
98 Sherfield School

WEDNESDAY 28
11 Beechenwood Farm

April

SUNDAY 1
33 Crawley Gardens
39 East Lane
42 Flintstones
47 Hambledon House
48 Heathlands
115 The White Cottage

MONDAY 2
33 Crawley Gardens
115 The White Cottage

WEDNESDAY 4
11 Beechenwood Farm

FRIDAY 6
11 Beechenwood Farm
50 Highfield
82 Mottisfont Abbey & Garden

SUNDAY 8
38 Durmast House

MONDAY 9
68 Little Court

WEDNESDAY 11
11 Beechenwood Farm

SUNDAY 15
17 Bramdean House
110 Weir House

WEDNESDAY 18
11 Beechenwood Farm

SATURDAY 21
96 'Selborne'

SUNDAY 22
20 Broadhatch House
47 Hambledon House
53 Hinton Ampner
57 Houghton Lodge Garden
93 St Christopher's
96 'Selborne'

MONDAY 23
53 Hinton Ampner

WEDNESDAY 25
11 Beechenwood Farm

SATURDAY 28
73 Walbury

SUNDAY 29
2 80 Abbey Road
13 Bere Mill
14 Berry Cottage
56 Hordle Walhampton School
65 60 Lealand Road
73 Walbury

MONDAY 30
13 Bere Mill

May

TUESDAY 1
68 Little Court

WEDNESDAY 2
11 Beechenwood Farm

SUNDAY 6
1 Abbey Cottage
8 Atheling Villas
15 Bluebell Cottage
27 Closewood House
31 The Cottage
46 Garden Cottage
66 Little Coopers
89 Pylewell Park
92 Rotherfield Park
105 Valentine Cottage

MONDAY 7
1 Abbey Cottage
15 Bluebell Cottage
27 Closewood House
31 The Cottage

TUESDAY 8
107 Wades House

WEDNESDAY 9
11 Beechenwood Farm

SATURDAY 12
87 Pennington House

SUNDAY 13
17 Bramdean House
46 Garden Cottage
58 The House in the Wood
63 53 Ladywood
87 Pennington House
89 Pylewell Park
101 Treetops

MONDAY 14
63 53 Ladywood

WEDNESDAY 16
11 Beechenwood Farm

SATURDAY 19
19 6 Breamore Close
96 'Selborne'
110 Weir House
116 Wisteria Cottage

SUNDAY 20
19 6 Breamore Close
31 The Cottage
34 Crookley Pool
47 Hambledon House
54 Holywell
62 Kimpton House
64 Lake House
96 'Selborne'
103 Tylney Hall Hotel
110 Weir House
116 Wisteria Cottage

MONDAY 21
31 The Cottage
34 Crookley Pool

TUESDAY 22
64 Lake House

WEDNESDAY 23
4 23 Anglesey Road
11 Beechenwood Farm

SATURDAY 26
14 Berry Cottage
45 Froyle Gardens
69 Littlewood

SUNDAY 27
14 Berry Cottage
25 Chilland House
45 Froyle Gardens
69 Littlewood
81 Monxton Gardens
91 Romsey Gardens
109 Waldrons
111 West Silchester Hall

MONDAY 28
25 Chilland House
81 Monxton Gardens
91 Romsey Gardens

109 Waldrons
111 West Silchester Hall

WEDNESDAY 30
11 Beechenwood Farm
24 21 Chestnut Road (Day & Evening)

THURSDAY 31
24 21 Chestnut Road (Day & Evening)
60 Ibthorpe House

June

FRIDAY 1
68 Little Court

SUNDAY 3
42 Flintstones
60 Ibthorpe House
77 Meon Orchard
106 The Vyne

MONDAY 4
42 Flintstones

WEDNESDAY 6
8 Atheling Villas
11 Beechenwood Farm
21 Buckland Stead

FRIDAY 8
55 The Homestead (Evening)

SATURDAY 9
12 Bentley Village Gardens
24 21 Chestnut Road

SUNDAY 10
9 Barncroft Gardens
12 Bentley Village Gardens
14 Berry Cottage
17 Bramdean House
22 Bury Farm
24 21 Chestnut Road
27 Closewood House
30 Conholt Park
35 Cygnet House
55 The Homestead
65 60 Lealand Road
73 Manor House
74 Martyr Worthy Gardens
76 The Mathom House
82 Mottisfont Abbey & Garden
105 Valentine Cottage

MONDAY 11
1 Abbey Cottage
9 Barncroft Gardens
35 Cygnet House

TUESDAY 12
42 Flintstones (Evening)

WEDNESDAY 13
7 Appletree House
11 Beechenwood Farm
50 Highfield
73 Manor House

FRIDAY 15
50 Highfield
96 'Selborne' (Evening)

SATURDAY 16
44 The Fountains
76 The Mathom House
90 27 Reynolds Dale
96 'Selborne'

SUNDAY 17
8 Atheling Villas
26 71 Church Close
27 Closewood House
32 Cranbury Park
41 Farleigh House
44 The Fountains
70 Longstock Park Water Garden
78 Meonstoke Gardens
85 Oakdene
86 Old Meadows
90 27 Reynolds Dale
93 St Christopher's
96 'Selborne'
103 Tylney Hall Hotel

MONDAY 18
26 71 Church Close

WEDNESDAY 20
11 Beechenwood Farm
21 Buckland Stead
36 Dean House
67 The Little Cottage

THURSDAY 21
33 Crawley Gardens

FRIDAY 22
16 Braemoor

SUNDAY 24
10 19 Barnwood Road
16 Braemoor
29 Colemore House Gardens
30 Conholt Park
33 Crawley Gardens
37 Dipley Mill
49 Heckfield Place
63 53 Ladywood
75 Marycourt
85 Oakdene
110 Weir House

MONDAY 25
10 19 Barnwood Road (Evening)
29 Colemore House Gardens
63 53 Ladywood

TUESDAY 26
83 Mulberry House

WEDNESDAY 27
57 Houghton Lodge Garden

SATURDAY 30
23 2 Carisbrooke Road

July

SUNDAY 1
23 2 Carisbrooke Road
36 Dean House
38 Durmast House
75 Marycourt
83 Mulberry House

111 West Silchester Hall
113 Whispers

WEDNESDAY 4
7 Appletree House
21 Buckland Stead
57 Houghton Lodge Garden
67 The Little Cottage
75 Marycourt

FRIDAY 6
16 Braemoor
28 The Coach House (Evening)

SATURDAY 7
84 49 Newtown Road with 26 & 29 Weston Allotments

SUNDAY 8
16 Braemoor
28 The Coach House
53 Hinton Ampner
54 Holywell
62 Kimpton House
84 49 Newtown Road with 26 & 29 Weston Allotments
117 1 Wogsbarne Cottages
118 Wrens Farm

MONDAY 9
53 Hinton Ampner

FRIDAY 13
2 80 Abbey Road (Evening)

SATURDAY 14
104 Ulvik

SUNDAY 15
17 Bramdean House
41 Farleigh House
47 Hambledon House
79 Merdon Manor
88 The Priors Farm
95 Sandle Cottage
103 Tylney Hall Hotel
104 Ulvik
105 Valentine Cottage
118 Wrens Farm

MONDAY 16
47 Hambledon House
104 Ulvik

TUESDAY 17
104 Ulvik

WEDNESDAY 18
21 Buckland Stead
67 The Little Cottage

THURSDAY 19
100 Tanglefoot

FRIDAY 20
116 Wisteria Cottage (Evening)

SATURDAY 21
14 Berry Cottage

SUNDAY 22
14 Berry Cottage
94 28 St Ronan's Avenue
95 Sandle Cottage

97 Shalden Park House
100 Tanglefoot

WEDNESDAY 25
106 The Vyne (Evening)

FRIDAY 27
16 Braemoor

SUNDAY 29
16 Braemoor
77 Meon Orchard
95 Sandle Cottage
111 West Silchester Hall

August

SATURDAY 4
94 28 St Ronan's Avenue
(Evening)
96 'Selborne'

SUNDAY 5
51 Hill House
96 'Selborne'

MONDAY 6
96 'Selborne'

TUESDAY 7
51 Hill House

SATURDAY 11
14 Berry Cottage
104 Ulvik

SUNDAY 12
14 Berry Cottage
17 Bramdean House
59 The Hyde
104 Ulvik
115 The White Cottage

MONDAY 13
104 Ulvik
115 The White Cottage

TUESDAY 14
59 The Hyde
104 Ulvik

WEDNESDAY 15
21 Buckland Stead
67 The Little Cottage

SATURDAY 18
112 Wheatley House

SUNDAY 19
65 60 Lealand Road
112 Wheatley House

FRIDAY 24
16 Braemoor

SUNDAY 26
1 Abbey Cottage
16 Braemoor
48 Heathlands
94 28 St Ronan's Avenue

MONDAY 27
1 Abbey Cottage
47 Hambledon House

September

SUNDAY 2
14 Berry Cottage
77 Meon Orchard
80 Mittens
107 Wades House

MONDAY 3
107 Wades House

WEDNESDAY 5
21 Buckland Stead
67 The Little Cottage

SATURDAY 8
53 Hinton Ampner

SUNDAY 9
17 Bramdean House
53 Hinton Ampner
59 The Hyde
61 Ibthorpe Tower
68 Little Court

WEDNESDAY 12
61 Ibthorpe Tower

SUNDAY 16
28 The Coach House
47 Hambledon House
52 2 Hillside Cottages
92 Rotherfield Park
110 Weir House

WEDNESDAY 19
7 Appletree House

SUNDAY 23
20 Broadhatch House

WEDNESDAY 26
4 23 Anglesey Road

October

SUNDAY 14
49 Heckfield Place

February 2008

SUNDAY 17
17 Bramdean House
68 Little Court

TUESDAY 19
68 Little Court

SUNDAY 24
68 Little Court

TUESDAY 26
68 Little Court

Private gardens opening regularly for the NGS

11 Beechenwood Farm
68 Little Court
114 White Barn

Gardens open to the public

3 Alverstoke Crescent Garden
5 Apple Court
17 Bramdean House
40 Exbury Gardens & Steam Railway
53 Hinton Ampner
57 Houghton Lodge Garden
72 Macpennys Woodland Garden & Nurseries
82 Mottisfont Abbey & Garden
99 Spinners
106 The Vyne

By appointment only

43 Forest Edge
71 Longthatch
102 Tunworth Old Rectory
114 White Barn

The Gardens

1 ABBEY COTTAGE
Itchen Abbas SO21 1BN. Patrick Daniell, 01962 779575, www.abbeycottage.net. 2½m W of Alresford. On B3047 between Kingworthy and Alresford, ½m E of the Trout Inn at Itchen Abbas. Home-made teas (not 11 June). **Adm £3, chd free. Sun 6, Mon 7 May; Mon 11 June; Sun 26, Mon 27 Aug (12-5). Also open 11 June Cygnet House. Visitors also welcome by appt.** This organic garden, on alkaline soil, is a fine garden by any standards. Inside the C18 walls of an old kitchen garden there are enclosures, on different levels, which together create an inspirational garden. The adjoining meadow contains specimen trees, an orchard, spring bulbs, summer wild flowers and a plantation of native trees.

2 80 ABBEY ROAD
Fareham PO15 5HW. Brian & Vivienne Garford, 01329 843939, vgarford@aol.com. 1m W of Farnham. From M27 J9 take A27 towards Fareham. At top of hill past Titchfield gyratory, turn L at T-lights past Highland Rd. Turn 4th R into Blackbrook Rd. Abbey Rd 4th turning on L. Home-made teas. **Adm £2, chd free. Sun 29 Apr (11-5). Evening Opening £3, wine, Fri 13 July (6-9). Visitors also welcome by appt.** Small garden with extensive collection of herbs and unusual plants of botanical and historical interest, many of which are for sale. Formal box

edging provides structure for the more relaxed planting. Interesting use of containers, and other ideas for small gardens. Two small ponds and tiny meadow area attract wide range of butterflies and other wildlife. Garden trails for children. Living willow seat, new planting for 2007.

🏃 ✿ ☕

❸ ◆ ALVERSTOKE CRESCENT GARDEN
Crescent Road, Gosport PO12 2DH. Gosport Borough Council, 02392 586403. *1m S of Gosport. From A32 & Gosport follow signs for Stokes Bay. Continue alongside bay to small roundabout, turn L into Anglesey Rd. Crescent Garden signed 50yds on R.* **Adm by donation. Open daily all yr.** Restored Regency ornamental garden, designed to enhance fine Crescent (Owen, 1826). Trees, walks and flowers lovingly maintained by community/Council partnership. Garden's considerable local historic interest now highlighted by impressive restoration and creative planting of adjacent St Mark's churchyard. Worth seeing together - heritage, history and horticulture: a fascinating package. Winner Green Flag award 2006/7. English Heritage sponsored Green Heritage Site award, shared with church. Gravel paths, limited wheelchair access to churchyard.

♿

❹ 23 ANGLESEY ROAD
Aldershot GU12 4RF. Adrian & Elizabeth Whiteley, 01252 677623. *On E edge of Aldershot. From A331 take A323 towards Aldershot. Keep in R-hand lane, turn R at T-lights into North Lane, then immed L into Lower Newport Rd. Round bend turn immed R into Newport Rd, 1st R into Wilson Rd. Round L-hand bend turn immed R into Roberts Rd, Anglesey Rd 1st on L. Please park considerately in local rds.* **Adm £2, chd free. Weds 23 May; 26 Sept (1-5). Visitors also welcome by appt.** Botanist's untypical suburban garden, 48ft x 28ft (combined front and back), now in its 9th yr. An eclectic mix of rare, unfamiliar and everyday plants gives yr-round interest. Unusually-shaped plot echoed in strongly geometric, densely-planted beds. Small pond, greenhouse, fern border and seating areas complete the picture.

🏃 ✿ ☕

Winding paths, large pond and rockery, summerhouse, gravel garden, secret sitting places . . .

❺ ◆ APPLE COURT
Hordle, Lymington SO41 0HU. Charles & Angela Meads, 01590 642130, www.applecourt.com. *4m W of Lymington. From A337 between Lymington & New Milton, turn into Hordle Lane at Royal Oak at Downton Xrds.* **Adm £3, chd free. Fris, Sats, Suns & Bank Hol Mons 2 Mar to 28 Oct (10-5).** 1½-acre formally designed and exuberantly planted sheltered walled garden. Theatrical white garden, extensive ornamental grass plantings, subtropical borders. 70 metre hosta walk. International display gardens of day lilies, fern walk, Japanese-style garden with koi pond. Featured in 'Amateur Gardening', 'Daily Telegraph' & 'Hampshire Life'.

♿ 🏃 ✿ ⬛ ☕

❻ APPLESHAW MANOR
nr Andover SP11 9BH. Mr & Mrs Patrick Walker. *5m NW of Andover. Take A342 Andover to Marlborough rd. Turn to Appleshaw 1m W of Weyhill. Fork L at playing field, on R after ½m, nr church. Disabled parking by house.* Home-made teas. **Adm £2.80, chd free. Sun 18 Mar (2-5).** 7-acre walled mature gardens, incl wide lawns, wood garden, arboretum, kitchen garden and pond. Carpets of spring bulbs and notable yew and beech hedges.

♿ ✿ ☕

❼ APPLETREE HOUSE
Station Road, Soberton SO32 3QU. Mrs J Dover, 01489 877333. *10m N of Fareham. A32 N to Droxford, at Xrds turn R B2150. Turn R under bridge into Station Rd, garden 1m. Parking in lay-by 300yds or in rd.* Home-made teas, light lunches 19 Sept. **Adm £2.50, chd free. Weds 13 June; 4 July (1.30-5); 19 Sept (12-3.30). Visitors also welcome by appt, individuals or groups of up to 30.** Romantic, small woodland-style country garden 40yds x 14yds with richly-planted island beds set in a meandering lawn. Trees, rare shrubs, unusual roses and clematis join with bulbs, grasses and herbaceous perennials in variety to give yr-round

interest. Also hosta corner, small fernery and a Mediterranean sitting area. Changes in progress.

🏃 ✿ ☕

❽ ATHELING VILLAS
16 Atheling Road, Hythe, Southampton SO45 6BR. Mary & Peter York, 02380 849349, peterandmaryyork@tiscali.co.uk. *7m E of Lyndhurst. Leave M27 J2, follow A326 signed Hythe and Fawley. Go across all roundabouts until Dibden roundabout (½m after Marchwood Priory Hospital). Turn L towards Hythe. After Shell garage, Atheling Road is 2nd L.* Home-made teas. **Adm £2.50, chd free. Suns 25 Mar; 6 May; Wed 6, Sun 17 June (2-5pm). Visitors also welcome by appt, groups of 10+. Refreshments by arrangement.** Formal front garden and informal rear garden of mid-Victorian villa, planted for all-yr interest. ⅓ acre; wide range of less usual trees and shrubs, also herbaceous. Ericaceous planting and species bulbs provide rich spring interest. Trained fruit on original garden wall; several seating areas. Self-guide leaflet highlights plants of current interest. Addition of gravel garden for drought-resistant plants.

🏃 ✿ ☕

❾ BARNCROFT GARDENS
Appleshaw SP11 9BU. *5m NW of Andover. Take A342 Andover to Marlborough rd to Appleshaw 1m W of Weyhill. After ½m park on R in field.* Home-made teas at Haleakala. **Combined adm £3, chd free. Sun 10, Mon 11 June (2-5.30).** Small pretty village, population approx 500. Lovely church, pub and village green.

☕

HALEAKALA
Jenny & Roger Bateman
Half-acre 6yr-old shrub and herbaceous garden, designed by owners for yr-round colour and interest. Winding paths, large pond and rockery, summerhouse, gravel garden, secret sitting places, unusual plants.

🏃

THE YELLOW BOOK I **187**

THE JAYS
Judith & Alec Clarke
Half-acre garden redesigned and restored in past 6yrs. Various fruit and flowering trees, mixed borders, rockeries, fish pond and bog garden.

Step through the gate to an enchanting garden designed for peace . . .

⑩ 19 BARNWOOD ROAD
Fareham PO15 5LA. Jill & Michael Hill, thegarden19@btinternet.com. *1m W of Fareham. From M27 J9 take A27 towards Fareham. At top of hill past Titchfield Mill PH turn L at T-lights into Highlands Rd. Take 4th turning R into Blackbrook Rd, Meadow Bank 4th turning on R. Barnwood Rd is off Meadow Bank.* Home-made teas. **Adm £2.50, chd free. Sun 24 June (11-5). Evening Opening Mon 25 June (7-9).** Visitors also welcome by appt, for groups of 10+. Please write or email.
Step through the gate to an enchanting garden designed for peace with an abundance of floral colour and delightful features. Greek-style courtyard leads to natural pond with bridge and bog garden, complemented by a thatched summerhouse and jetty, designed and built by owners. Secret pathways, mosaic seating area and hexagonal greenhouse.

⑪ BEECHENWOOD FARM
Odiham RG29 1JA. Mr & Mrs M Heber-Percy, 01256 702300, beechenwood@totalise.co.uk. *5m SE of Hook. Turn S into King St from Odiham High St. Turn L after cricket ground for Hillside. Take 2nd turn R after 1½m, modern house ½m.* Home-made teas. **Adm £3, chd free. Every Wed 28 Mar to 20 June; Fri 6 Apr (2-5).** Visitors also welcome by appt, no coaches.
2-acre garden of many parts; woodland garden with spring bulbs,

walled herb garden, rose garden, pergola, containers, orchard and rock garden with grasses and ferns. Belvedere with spectacular views. 8-acre copse of native species (planted 1992) with grassed rides and paths. Featured in 'Hampshire Life'. Gravel drive.

⑫ BENTLEY VILLAGE GARDENS
GU10 5JA. *4m NE of Alton off A31 (Bentley bypass). Turn off A31 into village. At Xrds, Main Road, 2 gardens at E end of village, one at W end. Follow signs.* Home-made teas at Bay Tree Cottage. **Combined adm £3, chd free. Sat 9, Sun 10 June (2-6).**
Three small gardens, each very different, in Bentley village. Maps given to all visitors. Art work at Avenue Cottage.

AVENUE COTTAGE
David & Rosie Darrah, 01420 23225. *At Main Rd turn E, ½m on R.* Visitors also welcome by appt.
Very pretty cottage garden with formal herb garden and potager. Gravel path.

BAY TREE COTTAGE
Andrew & Mary Thomson. *At Main Road turn E, approx ¼m on R. Opp playing field*
Cottage garden of approx ¼ acre. Incl herbaceous, shrubbery, herb garden, vegetables and soft fruit.

THE KILNS
Mascha & Richard Tyrrell, 01420 520377. *L at Xrds, 200yds on R is lane marked Bentley Garden Farm. Last house down lane on R.* Visitors also welcome by appt.
Garden reclaimed from a concrete wasteland. Unusual plants in mixed herbaceous borders; courtyard and lawns.

⑬ BERE MILL
London Road, Whitchurch RG28 7NH. Rupert & Elizabeth Nabarro, 01256 892210, rnabarro@aol.com. *9m E of Andover, 12m N of Winchester. In centre of Whitchurch, take London Rd at roundabout. Up hill 1m, turn R 50yds beyond The Gables on R.* **Adm £3, chd free. Sun 29, Mon 30 Apr (2-6).**

Visitors also welcome by appt throughout season.
Garden created since 1993 around the 1712 mill (not open) where Portals first made bank notepaper. Set by the R Test and carrier streams, a large lozenge-shaped site, loosely fashioned on a Japanese scroll garden. Herbaceous and Mediterranean beds; replanted walled orchard and vegetable garden; wisteria garden and lake with Japanese tea-house. Extensively planted with bulbs; irises a speciality. Unfenced and unguarded rivers and streams. Featured in 'Country Homes & Interiors'. Drop-off point for disabled at garden.

⑭ NEW BERRY COTTAGE
Church Road, Farringdon, nr Alton GU34 3EG. Mrs P Watts, 01420 588318. *3m S of Alton off A32. Turn L at Xrds, Ist L into Church Rd. Follow rd past Masseys Folley, 2nd house on R opp church.* Cream teas. **Adm £2, chd free. Sun 29 Apr; Sat 26, Sun 27 May; Sun 10 June; Sat 21, Sun 22 July; Sat 11, Sun 12 Aug; Sun 2 Sept (2.30-6).** Visitors also welcome by appt in June & July.
Small organic cottage garden with all-yr interest. Spring bulbs, roses, clematis and herbaceous borders. Pond and bog garden. Shrubbery and small kitchen garden.

⑮ BLUEBELL COTTAGE
Broadway, Froxfield, Petersfield GU32 1DT. Mr & Mrs T Clarke. *3½m NW of Petersfield. Between top of Stoner Hill & Froxfield Green, or take sign to Froxfield off A272 opp Bordean House & follow yellow signs.* **Adm £2, chd free. Sun 6, Mon 7 May (2-6).**
One-acre, owner-maintained garden incl a small bluebell wood, mature trees, lawns, mixed borders, arbour overlooking the pond, summerhouse, bridge over dry ditch, conservatory, kitchen garden with raised beds, fruit garden and greenhouse.

⑯ BRAEMOOR
Bleak Hill, Harbridge, Fordingbridge BH24 3PX. Tracy & John Netherway & Judy Spratt, 01425 652983, jnetherway@btinternet.com. *2½m S of Fordingbridge. Turn off A338 at*

Spiral yew maze. Mystery passage leads to octagonal plunge pool with sun pavilion . . .

Ibsley. Go through Harbridge village to T-junction at top of hill, turn R for ¹/₄m. Cream teas. **Adm £2.50, chd free. Fris, Suns: 22, 24 June; 6, 8, 27, 29 July; 24, 26 Aug (2-5.30). Visitors also welcome by appt.**
³/₄-acre garden of mixed cottage-style herbaceous borders and shrubs. Roses and unusual plants. Small stream and pond. Patio areas with pots and containers. Grasses in gravel scree. Two greenhouses with cacti and carnivorous plants. Vegetable and fruit garden. Small flock of fancy bantams. Small adjacent nursery.

⑰ ◆ BRAMDEAN HOUSE
Bramdean SO24 0JU. Mr & Mrs H Wakefield, 01962 771214. *4m S of Alresford. In centre of village on A272.* **Adm £3.50, chd free. For NGS: Suns 18 Feb; 15 Apr; 13 May; 10 June; 15 July; 12 Aug; 9 Sept (2-5). Sun 17 Feb 2008.**
Traditional 6-acre garden on chalk, famous for mirror-image herbaceous borders. Carpets of bulbs, especially snowdrops, in the spring. Very many unusual plants incl collection of old-fashioned sweet peas. 1-acre kitchen garden featuring prizewinning vegetables, fruit and flowers. Group visits by arrangement, not weekends. Featured on BBC2 The Gardener's Year and first of 10 Best Gardens to Visit in 'The Independent'.

⑱ BRANDY MOUNT HOUSE
Alresford SO24 9EG. Caryl & Michael Baron, www.brandymount.co.uk. *nr Alresford centre. From centre, 1st R in East St before Sun Lane. Please leave cars in Broad St or stn car park.* Home-made teas. **Adm £2, chd free. Sat 10 Feb (11-4); Sun 4 Mar (2-5).**
1-acre, informal plantsman's garden. Spring bulbs, hellebores, species geraniums. National Collections of snowdrops and daphnes. European primulas, expanding collection of dwarf narcissi, herbaceous and woodland plants. Clarence Elliott Memorial Award

for article in Alpine Garden Soc Bulletin. Limited wheelchair access: no unsupervised wheelchairs or mobility cars allowed.

⑲ 6 BREAMORE CLOSE
Eastleigh SO50 4QB. Mr & Mrs R Trenchard. *1m N of Eastleigh. M3 J12, follow signs to Eastleigh. Turn R at roundabout into Woodside Ave, then 1st L into Broadlands Ave (park here).* Breamore Close 3rd on L. Home-made teas. **Adm £2, chd free. Sat 19, Sun 20 May (1-5.30).**
Delightful ¹/₂-acre garden with distinctive planting themes in different areas. Shrubs, trees and herbaceous plants give good spring and early summer colour, with magnificent wisteria display (flowers 3ft-4ft long) intermingled with clematis and roses over pergola. Featured on BBC TV The Gardener's Year.

⑳ BROADHATCH HOUSE
Bentley, Farnham GU10 5JJ. Bruce & Lizzie Powell, 01420 23185, lizzie.powell@btconnect.com. *4m NE of Alton. Turn off A31 (Bentley bypass), through village up School Lane. R to Perrylands, after 300yds drive on R.* Home-made teas. **Adm £3, chd free (share to Treloar Trust). Suns 22 Apr; 23 Sept (2-5.30). Visitors also welcome by appt in June & July only, coaches permitted.**
3¹/₂ acres with yew hedges separating different gardens. Formal pools and large borders, climber-covered walls, and potager. Very wide range of interesting and rare plants.

㉑ BUCKLAND STEAD
Sway Road, nr Lymington SO41 8NN. Valerie & John Woolcott, 01590 673465, valwoolcott@ukonline.co.uk. *1m N of Lymington town centre. Off A337. Pass Toll House Inn, 1st L into Sway Rd. After 300yds, at sharp R-hand bend, turn L into Buckland Granaries*

entrance. Follow signs to garden. **Adm £2, chd free. Weds 6, 20 June; 4, 18 July; 15 Aug; 5 Sept (11-1 & 2-5). Also open The Little Cottage (not 6 June). Visitors also welcome by appt, small groups.**
¹/₄-acre garden designed and developed by owners with a glimpse of the IOW over farmland. Formally planted with many beautiful roses and lavender edging. Shady walk to back garden contains ferns, grasses and hostas, to well-stocked less formal area with colour themes, pergola, arches and water features.

㉒ BURY FARM
Marchwood SO40 4UD. Mr & Mrs Barker-Mill. *6m W of Southampton. Off A326 between Totton & Marchwood. Follow yellow signs.* Home-made teas. **Adm £2.50, chd free. Sun 10 June (11-5).**
Contemporary organic garden of large sculpture and shrubs, started in 1983. Walled circular kitchen garden in potager style with 4-colour garden and well-head pool at centre. Spiral yew maze. Mystery passage leads to octagonal plunge pool with sun pavilion.

㉓ 2 CARISBROOKE ROAD
Gosport PO13 0HQ. Chris & Norma Matthews. *3m S of Fareham. Exit M27 J11 signed Fareham Central. Follow A32, Gosport. Take fork at Newgate Lane signed Lee-on-Solent. At 3rd roundabout 1st exit B3334 signed Rowner. L at T-lights, 1st house on R.* Home-made teas. **Adm £2.50, chd free. Sat 30 June; Sun 1 July (10-4).**
¹/₃-acre cottage-style garden developed by owners over 16yrs. Shrubs, herbaceous perennials, gravel and alpine gardens give yr-round interest. Raised organic kitchen garden. Interesting colourful baskets and containers with plants propagated by owners. Wildlife areas, newly refurbished pond and stream.

CHALK COTTAGE
See Dorset.

㉔ 21 CHESTNUT ROAD
Brockenhurst SO42 7RF. Iain & Mary Hayter. *4m S of Lyndhurst. S on A337 to Brockenhurst, take R fork B3055, Grigg Lane, opp Careys Manor Hotel. Garden 500yds from junction via 2nd L*

Chestnut Rd and 2nd L again for no 21. Parking limited; please use village car park nearby. Home-made teas. **Adm £2.50, chd free. Wed 30, Thur 31 May (also 6-9, see below); Sat 9, Sun 10 June (11-5). Evening Opening, £3, wine Thur 31 May (6-9).** Once grass tennis courts, the garden has colour from perennials, shrubs and roses, divided by hedges with wild flower and vegetable area and fruit cage. Featuring American irises and scented old English roses, this 1/3 acre has a pond, raised deck, summerhouse, pergolas, arches and water features.

Azaleas, bog garden, camellias, dogwoods, erythroniums, free-range bantams . . .

25 CHILLAND HOUSE
Martyr Worthy SO21 1EB. Mr & Mrs Andrew Impey. *7m NE of Winchester. On B3047 between Martyr Worthy & Itchen Abbas, signed Chilland.* **Adm £2.50, chd free. Sun 27, Mon 28 May (2-5).**
4 acres with stream overlooking R Itchen and watermeadows, woods and farmland beyond. Large collection of mature shrubs planned for yr-round colour effects. Many fine trees and shrubs incl huge plane and ancient mulberry, nutwalk, spring bulbs, clematis, herbaceous borders and flowering shrubs.

26 71 CHURCH CLOSE
Northington SO24 9TH. Mr & Mrs Swithinbank, 01962 733623, sharonswithinbank@yahoo.co.uk. *4m N of Alresford. Follow B3046 N from Alresford to Northington. From Basingstoke or Winchester take A33, turning at dual carriageway to Northington. Park in church car park.* Home-made teas. **Adm £2.50, chd**

free. **Sun 17, Mon 18 June (11-5). Visitors also welcome by appt.**
There is a peaceful view across the Candover Valley from this mature cottage garden. The garden is on chalk and falls away from a terraced cottage on a 1/3-acre sloping site. The garden will inspire you with its planting, use of colour and delightful features such as a circular potager, old apple trees and hazel arches supporting clematis, honeysuckle, sweet peas, climbing roses and hydrangea. Featured on BBC TV The Gardener's Year.

27 CLOSEWOOD HOUSE
Newlands Lane, Denmead PO7 6TP. Mrs P Clowes. *1m W of Waterlooville. Take Closewood Rd to W of B2150 between Waterlooville & Denmead. Turn L at T-junction after 1/2 m. Signs to car park after 330yds.* Home-made teas. **Adm £3.50, chd free. Sun 6, Mon 7 May; Suns 10, 17 June (2-5).**
4 1/2 acres. Collection of scented roses incl large climbers and shrubs with good vistas between sections. 200 different specimen trees and grass walk. Box parterre, fishpond and large abstract sculpture. Picnics welcome by stream.

28 THE COACH HOUSE
South Warnborough RG29 1RR. John & Sarah Taylor, 01256 862782, johntaylormw@hotmail.com. *5m N of Alton on B3349. In the middle of village opp village shop/post office. Car parking in lay-by opp.* Home-made teas Suns only. **Adm £2.50, chd free. Suns 8 July; 16 Sept (2-6). Evening Opening £4, wine, Fri 6 July (5-9). Visitors also welcome by appt.**
3/4-acre of semi-walled garden almost entirely given over to plantings of perennials and grasses in a naturalistic and informal style. Gravel planting and deep generous beds with an emphasis on height and proximity to plants. Featured in 'The English Garden', Woman's Weekly' & 'Hampshire Life' and on BBC TV The Gardener's Year. Gravel paths.

29 COLEMORE HOUSE GARDENS
Colemore, Alton GU34 3RX. Mr & Mrs Simon de Zoete. *5m S of Alton. Take turning to Colemore (Shell Lane) off A32, just S of E Tisted.* Home-made teas. **Adm £3, chd free. Sun 24, Mon 25 June (2-6).**

Situated in beautiful unspoilt country, 2 1/2 acres with wide variety of unusual plants. Yew and box hedges, mixed herbaceous and shrub borders, yellow and blue garden, rose walk (featured on front cover of the 2006 Yellow Book) and excellent lawns. Garden is being constantly developed and incl spectacular water rill, swimming pool garden and the creation of a wild flower, tree and shrub area. Many different roses, salvias, penstemons and tender plants and bulbs.

30 CONHOLT PARK
Chute SP11 9HA. Professor Caroline Tisdall. *7m N of Andover. Turn N off A342 Andover to Devizes rd at Weyhill Church. Go 5m N through Clanville & Tangley Bottom. Turn L at Conholt 1/2 m on R, just off Chute causeway. A343 to Hurstbourne Tarrant, turn to and go through Vernham Dean, next turn L signed Conholt.* Home-made teas. **Adm £3, chd free. Suns 10, 24 June (2-5).**
10 acres surrounding Regency house (not open), rose, 'Calor', Shakespeare, winter and secret gardens. Restored 1 1/2-acre walled garden with potager, berry wall, rare fruit orchard, white border, mahonia, hardy geraniums and allium collections. All completely organic. Romantic Edwardian Ladies' Walk and possibly longest maze in Britain. Ornate copper rose fountain. On farm unusual animals incl bison, wild boar and a shire horse.

31 THE COTTAGE
16 Lakewood Road, Chandler's Ford SO53 1ES. Hugh & Barbara Sykes, 02380 254521. *2m NW of Eastleigh. Leave M3 at J12, follow signs to Chandler's Ford. At King Rufus on Winchester Rd, turn R into Merdon Ave, then 3rd rd on L.* Home-made teas. **Adm £2.50, chd free. Suns, Mons 6, 7, 20, 21 May (2-6). Visitors also welcome by appt in Apr & May.**
3/4 acre. Azaleas, bog garden, camellias, dogwoods, erythroniums, free-range bantams, greenhouse grapes, honey from our bees, irises, jasmines, kitchen garden, landscaping began in 1950, maintained by owners, new planting, osmunda, ponds, quiz for children, rhododendrons, smilacina, trilliums, unusual plants, viscum, wildlife areas, eXuberant foliage, yr-round interest, zantedeschia.

32 CRANBURY PARK

Otterbourne SO21 2HL. Mr & Mrs Chamberlayne-Macdonald. *3m NW of Eastleigh. Main entrance on old A33 between Winchester and Southampton, by bus stop at top of Otterbourne Hill. Entrances also in Hocombe Rd, Chandler's Ford and next to church in Otterbourne.* Home-made teas. Adm £5, chd free (share to St Denys Church, Chilworth). Sun 17 June (2-6).

Extensive pleasure grounds laid out in late C18 and early C19 by Papworth; fountains, rose garden, specimen trees and pinetum, lakeside walk and fern walk. Family carriages and collection of prams will be on view, also photos of King George VI, Eisenhower and Montgomery reviewing Canadian troops at Cranbury before D-Day.

& ✿ ☕

33 CRAWLEY GARDENS

nr Winchester SO21 2PU. *5m NW of Winchester. Off A272 or A3049 Winchester to Stockbridge rd. Parking at top of village nr church or in Littleton Rd.* Home-made teas at Village Hall, or Little Court, weather permitting. Combined adm: Apr £3.50, June £4, chd free. Sun 1, Mon 2 Apr; Thur 21, Sun 24 June (2-5.30).

Exceptionally pretty small village with thatched houses, C14 church and village pond. Many other good front gardens visible from the road.

☕

BARN COTTAGE
Mr & Mrs K Wren. Not open 1, 2 April.
Garden created in 2003, originally part of Manor Lodge. Collection of coppiced birch with magnificent Cerise Bouquet rose leading to trellised courtyard garden that incl a variety of roses, clematis and ground covering plants behind clipped box. Short gravel drive, single negotiable steps.

& ✗

LITTLE COURT
Prof & Mrs A R Elkington
(See separate entry).

& ✗ ✿

PAIGE COTTAGE
Mr & Mrs T W Parker
1 acre of traditional English country garden incl grass tennis court (not open) and walled Italian-style swimming pool (not open); roses climbing into apple trees. Spring garden with large variety of bulbs and wild flowers.

& ✗

TANGLEFOOT
Mr & Mrs F J Fratter. Not open 1, 2 Apr.
(See separate entry).

& ✗ ✿

34 CROOKLEY POOL

Blendworth Lane, Horndean PO8 0NB. Mr & Mrs Simon Privett, 02392 592662. *5m S of Petersfield. 2m E of Waterlooville, off A3. From Horndean village go up Blendworth Lane between bakery and hairdresser. Entrance 200yds before church on L with white railings, behind Gales Brewery.* Home-made teas. Adm £3.50, chd free. Sun 20, Mon 21 May (2-5). Visitors also welcome by appt.

English country garden built in the Edwardian period around a swimming pool and walled kitchen garden. Well-stocked greenhouses full of tender perennials and climbers. Wisteria-covered walls and terraces give a Mediterranean feel to the garden.

& ✗ ✿ ☕

35 CYGNET HOUSE

Martyr Worthy SO21 1DZ. Mr & Mrs Shane Chichester, 01962 779315. *5m E of Winchester. On B3047, 1st house on R after war memorial.* Adm £2, chd free. Sun 10 June (2-6), Mon 11 June (11-5). Opening with **Martyr Worthy Gardens** 10 June. Also open 11 June **Abbey Cottage**. Visitors also welcome by appt.

This attractively laid out terraced garden, with stunning views over the Itchen Valley, has been developed by the owners, both keen gardeners since 1980. The emphasis has been on colour and design as well as incorporating interesting and unusual plants. A large number of old-

fashioned roses. Unfenced swimming pool. Gravel paths, some steep slopes.

& ✿

36 DEAN HOUSE

Kilmeston SO24 0NL. Mr P H R Gwyn. *5m S of Alresford. Via village of Cheriton or off A272 signed at Cheriton Xrds.* Cream teas. Adm £3, chd free. Wed 20 June (10-4); Sun 1 July (12-5).

7 acres; orchard, paddock, with small formal pond, spacious lawns, mixed and herbaceous borders surrounding symmetrical rose garden, planted tunnel, working walled kitchen garden and generously stocked glasshouses. Wheelchair access to main part of garden, many gravel paths.

& ☕

37 DIPLEY MILL

Dipley RG27 8JP. Mr J P McMonigall. *2m NE of Hook. Turn E off B3349 at Mattingley (1½m N of Hook) signed Hartley Wintney, West Green and Dipley. Dipley Mill ½m on L just over bridge.* Home-made teas. Adm £3, chd free (share to St Michael's Hospice). Sun 24 June (2-6).

Mentioned in Domesday Book, Mill House (not open) sits on an island site beside the R Whitewater in remarkably picturesque setting. Large garden where herbaceous borders surround millpond. Tree ferns, fuchsia garden, pleached hornbeams, roses, hothouse with subtropical plants. Wild flower meadow.

✗ ☕

38 DURMAST HOUSE

Burley BH24 4AT. Mr & Mrs P E G Daubeney, 01425 403527, philip@daubeney.co.uk. *5m SE of Ringwood. Off Burley to Lyndhurst rd, nr White Buck Hotel.* Cream teas. Adm £2.50, chd free (share to Delhi Commonwealth Womens Assn Clinic). Suns 8 Apr; 1 July (2-5). Visitors also welcome by appt.

4 acres designed by Gertrude Jekyll in 1907, in process of being restored from original plans. Formal rose garden edged with lavender, 130yr-old Monterey pine, mimosa tree, Victorian rockery, coach house. Lutyens-style summerhouse on original site and Jekyll herbaceous borders. Restored azalea walk. Listed in Hampshire register of historic gardens. To be featured on BBC TV Gardeners' World 2007. Gravel and grass paths.

& ✿ ☕

Exceptionally pretty small village with thatched houses, 14th Century church and village pond . . .

39 EAST LANE
Ovington SO24 0RA. Sir Peter & Lady Ramsbotham. *1m W of Alresford, off A31. From A31, Winchester to Alresford, immed after roundabout 1m W of Alresford, small sign to Ovington. Turn sharp L up incline, down small country rd to Ovington. East Lane is only house on L, 500yds down hill towards Bush Inn.* **Adm £2.50, chd free. Sun 1 Apr (2.30-5.30).**
Charming 5-acre woodland garden. Large lawn leading up to white gazebo and arboretum with fine views. Collection of mature shrubs interspersed with an acre of spring bulbs. Herbaceous borders. Walled rose garden. Large terraced water garden overlooking water meadows with stream flowing through.

Large terraced water garden overlooking water meadows with stream flowing through . . .

40 ◆ EXBURY GARDENS & STEAM RAILWAY
Southampton SO45 1AZ. Edmund de Rothschild, 02380 891203, www.exbury.co.uk. *16m S of Southampton. 4m Beaulieu. Exbury 20mins M27 J2.* **Open daily 17 Mar to 4 Nov. Opening times and prices vary according to season. Please phone or visit website for details.**
Created by Lionel de Rothschild in the 1920s, the gardens are a stunning vision of his inspiration offering 200 acres of natural beauty and horticultural variety. Woodland garden with world-famous displays of rhododendrons, azaleas, camellias and magnolias. Rock garden, exotic garden, herbaceous gardens, ponds, cascades, river walk and seasonal trails. Steam railway (wheelchair accessible) and Summer Lane Garden are popular favourites. Buggy Tours available for the less mobile.

41 FARLEIGH HOUSE
Farleigh Wallop, nr Basingstoke RG25 2HT. The Earl & Countess of Portsmouth. *3m SE of Basingstoke. Off B3046 Basingstoke to Preston Candover rd.* Cream teas. **Adm £3.50, chd free. Suns 17 June; 15 July (2-5).**
Contemporary garden of great tranquillity designed by Georgia Langton, surrounded by wonderful views. 3-acre walled garden in three sections: ornamental potager, formal rose garden and wild rose garden. Greenhouse full of exotics, serpentine yew walk, contemplative pond garden and lake with planting for wildlife. Approx 10 acres and 1 hour to walk around.

42 FLINTSTONES
Sciviers Lane, Durley SO32 2AG. June & Bill Butler, 01489 860880. *5m E of Eastleigh. From M3 J11 follow signs for Marwell Zoo. From B2177 turn R opp Woodman PH. From M27 J7 follow signs for Fair Oak then Durley, turn L at Robin Hood PH.* Teas Apr, home-made teas June. **Adm £2.50, chd free** (share to Camphill Village Trust & Durley Church). **Sun 1 Apr (2-5); Sun 3, Mon 4 June (2-6). Evening Opening £4, wine, Tue 12 June (6-8.30).** Visitors also welcome by appt in Apr, May & June only, for 30 max, no coaches.
3/4 acre designed and developed entirely by owners. Plantswoman's garden densely planted on clay, with many unusual and interesting plants, providing a pleasing tapestry effect of texture and colour, for all-yr interest.

43 FOREST EDGE
Andover Down SP11 6LJ. Annette & David Beeson, 01264 364526, www.forest-edge.co.uk. *2m E of Andover. On B3400 to Whitchurch. Watch for B&B sign. Please avoid parking on brow of hill.* **Adm £2.50, chd free. Visitors welcome by appt June 3-10 for spring and early summer meadow; July 22-29 for summer meadow and butterflies.** Coaches permitted.
1-acre eco-friendly garden adjacent to Harewood Forest. Succession of wild daffodils, cowslips, meadow saxifrages and buttercups in spring meadow. Summer meadow rich in native species incl orchids. Wild pond and hedges. Wild flower herbaceous bed. Shrub borders with exotic and British

herbaceous plants. Dwarf conifers in gravel areas. Unfenced pond. Gravel patio and drive to cross. Beware mole hills!

44 NEW THE FOUNTAINS
34 Frampton Way, Totton SO40 9AE. Mrs J Abel. *5m W of Southampton. M271 J3 onto A35 Totton bypass for Im to roundabout. Circle roundabout and return up A35. Immed L into Rushington Ave, then follow signs. Home-made teas.* **Adm £2.50, chd free. Sat 16, Sun 17 June (2-5.30). Also open nearby 27 Reynolds Dale.**
Unusually shaped 1/4-acre garden bordered by hedges and filled with a variety of fruit trees, soft fruit cordons and espaliers. Trellis covered in rambling roses and clematis. Plantswoman's garden designed for continual interest with wildlife ponds and chickens. 'Cottage garden meets the Good Life'.

45 FROYLE GARDENS
GU34 4JH. *5m NE of Alton. Access to Lower Froyle from A31 between Alton & Farnham, at Bentley. Follow signs from Lower Froyle to Upper Froyle.* Home-made teas at Lower Froyle Village Hall. **Combined adm £4, chd free. Sat 26, Sun 27 May (2-6).**
'The Village of Saints'. Maps given to all visitors. Display of rare vestments at St Mary's Church, Upper Froyle.

BRAMLINS
Lower Froyle. Mrs A Blunt
Informally planted to harmonise with surrounding countryside and to provide variety of material for nationally-known flower arranger. Wild flowers in small orchard. Conservatory with unusual plants.

BROCAS FARM
Lower Froyle. Mr & Mrs J Dundas
Grade II listed house (not open) covered in roses, wisteria and clematis. 2 acres of well-established mature gardens divided by yew and beech hedges. Herbaceous borders, interesting small arboretum, orchard and

charming box hedged kitchen garden. Gravel path, main features accessible on grass.

 ♿ ✂

THE COTTAGE
Lower Froyle. **Mr & Mrs Carr**
Not only plants but a collection of animals frequently associated with a true cottage garden.

✂ ♿

THE OLD SCHOOL
Upper Froyle. **Nigel & Linda Bulpitt**
Mature garden, mainly perennials with climbing roses and shrubs. Small wild area making a foil between garden and countryside.

♿ ✂

TREETOPS
Upper Froyle. **Mr & Mrs J Cresswell**
(See separate entry).

✂ ♿

WALBURY
Lower Froyle. **Mr & Mrs Milam**
(See separate entry).

♿ ♿

WARREN COTTAGE
Lower Froyle. **Mrs A A Robertson**
Garden surrounds C18 cottage (not open). Many interesting plants and lovely views.

✂ ♿

46 GARDEN COTTAGE
3 St Helens Road, Hayling Island PO11 0BT. **Mr & Mrs Norman Vaughan.** *6m S of Havant. From Beachlands on seafront, turn R, then 3rd on R into Staunton Ave, then 1st L. Parking in drive. Police dispensation for rd parking.* Light refreshments & teas. **Adm by donation. Suns 6, 13 May (11-2).**
Ongoing refurbishment to reduce labour-intensive maintenance, but retaining main features of interesting trees, shrubs and roses, set off by fine lawn. Thatched summerhouse.

♿ ✂ ♿ ☕

47 HAMBLEDON HOUSE
Hambledon PO7 4RU. **Capt & Mrs David Hart Dyke,** 02392 632380. *8m SW of Petersfield, 5m NW of Waterlooville. In village centre.* Home-made teas. **Adm £3, chd free. Suns 25 Mar; 1, 22 Apr; 20 May; Sun 15, Mon 16 July; Mon 27 Aug: Sun 16 Sept (2-5).** Visitors also welcome by

appt Apr to Sept for groups.
2 acres partly walled plantsman's garden for all seasons. Large borders filled with wide variety of unusual shrubs and imaginative plant combinations. Large collection of salvias, hardy geraniums and ornamental grasses. Hidden, secluded areas reveal surprise views of garden and village rooftops.

✂ ♿ ☕

48 HEATHLANDS
47 Locks Road, Locks Heath, nr Fareham SO31 6NS. **Dr & Mrs John Burwell.** *5m W of Fareham. From M27 J9, go W on A27 towards Southampton. After 1m in Parkgate turn L into Locks Rd after pelican crossing. 47 is 1m down on R.* Home-made teas. **Adm £3, chd free. Suns 4 Mar; 1 Apr; 26 Aug (2-5.30).**
1-acre plantsman's garden designed and developed by owner since 1967. Yr-round interest against background of evergreens and mature trees. Spring bulbs, rhododendrons, paulownias, cyclamen, ferns and many unusual plants. Topiary peacock, small herbaceous border, scree and secret garden. National Collection of Japanese anemones. Featured on BBC Gardeners' World.

♿ ♿ **NCCPG** ☕

49 NEW HECKFIELD PLACE
Heckfield RG27 0LD. **Pomegranet.** *9m S of Reading. 4½ NW of Hartley Wintney on B3011.* Cream teas. **Adm £5, chd free. Suns 11 Mar; 24 June; 14 Oct (10-4.30).**
75 acres of Georgian/Victorian pinetum/arboretum with lakes, walled garden and herbacous borders, in the process of very extensive restoration. Some trees are notable for their size and age and are documented. Historic garden demonstration.

✂ ♿ ☕

50 HIGHFIELD
Malthouse Close, Easton SO21 1ES. **Mr & Mrs Geoff Dee,** 01962 779426. *3m E of Winchester. From B3047 (Winchester to Alresford) take turn signed Easton. Pass Cricketers Inn on L, and immed turn R up hill. In 200yds turn R into Malthouse Close, Highfield at end.* **Adm £2, chd free. Sun 25 Mar (1.30-4.30); Fri 6 Apr; Wed 13, Fri 15 June (2-5).**

Visitors also welcome by appt.
This ½-acre garden started in 1967 when a local farmer rotavated it for us. Now we have a pond, many herbaceous borders, vegetable garden, terrace and conservatory, together yielding colour most of the year, from spring bulbs and hellebores, summer borders, agapanthus, Michaelmas daisies, sedums and nerine lilies.

♿ ♿

Not only plants but a collection of animals frequently associated with a true cottage garden . . .

51 HILL HOUSE
Old Alresford SO24 9DY. **Mrs W F Richardson.** *1m W of Alresford. From Alresford 1m along B3046 towards Basingstoke, then R by church.* Home-made teas. **Adm £2.50, chd free. Sun 5, Tue 7 Aug (1.30-5).**
2 acres with large old-fashioned herbaceous border, established in 1938, and shrub beds set around large lawn; large kitchen garden. Dried flowers. Dexter cows and bantams.

♿ ♿ ☕

52 2 HILLSIDE COTTAGES
Trampers Lane, North Boarhunt PO17 6DA. **John & Lynsey Pink,** 01329 832786, lynsey@lynsey14.fsnet.co.uk. *5m N of Fareham. 3m E of Wickham. From A32 at Wickham take B2177 E. Trampers Lane 2nd on L (approx 2m). Hillside Cottages approx ½m on L.* Home-made teas. **Adm £2.50, chd free. Sun 16 Sept (2-6). Visitors also welcome by appt.**
An acre of plantsman's garden with sweeping mixed borders. Island bed annually planted with exotic plants and salvias dominates the view from the house. Holders of the National Collection of salvia sp. which are planted throughout the garden along with many unusual shrubs and herbaceous plants. No steps but sloping grass.

♿ ♿ **NCCPG** ☕

53 ◆ HINTON AMPNER

Alresford SO24 0LA. The National Trust, 01962 771305, www.nationaltrust.org.uk. 3¹/₂m S of Alresford. S on A272 Petersfield to Winchester rd. **Garden adm £5.50, chd £2.75. House & garden £6.50, chd £3.25. Opening days & times vary according to season; please phone or visit website for details.** For NGS: Suns, Mons 22, 23 Apr; 8, 9 July; Sat 8, Sun 9 Sept (11-5). 12 acres; C20 shrub garden designed by Ralph Dutton. Strong architectural elements using yew and box topiary; spectacular views. Bold effects using simple plants, restrained and dramatic bedding. Orchard with spring wild flowers and bulbs within formal box hedges; magnolia and philadelphus walks. Dell garden made from chalk pit. Shrub rose border dating from 1950s. Walled garden under restoration. Map available to show wheelchair-accessible areas.

54 HOLYWELL

Swanmore SO32 2QE. Earl & Countess of Clarendon. 12m SE of Winchester. On A32 between Droxford and Wickham. Light refreshments & teas. **Adm £3.50, chd free. Suns 20 May; 8 July (2-6).** Large garden in rural woodland and lakeside setting. Colourful organic kitchen garden, greenhouse, borders, roses, trees and shrubs. Pergola walk. Mature woodland garden with many acid-loving specimens. Featured in 'Daily Echo'.

55 THE HOMESTEAD

Northney Road, Hayling Island PO11 0NF. Stan & Mary Pike, 02392 464888. 3m S of Havant. From A27 Havant/Hayling Island roundabout, travel S over Langstone Bridge & turn immed L into Northney Rd. 1st house on R after Langstone Hotel. Home-made teas. **Adm £2.50, chd free. Sun 10 June (2-5.30) Evening Opening, wine & light refreshments, Fri 8 June (6-9). Visitors also welcome by appt.** One-acre garden developed and maintained by owners. Features incl pleached lime walk, pergola, arbour and ponds. Lawn surrounded by herbaceous beds and shrub borders with additional alpine beds and interesting trees. Small walled garden contains trained fruit trees, formal herb garden and vegetables.

56 HORDLE WALHAMPTON SCHOOL

Beaulieu Road, Lymington SO41 5ZG. Hordle Walhampton School Trust Ltd. 1m E of Lymington. From Lymington follow signs to Beaulieu (B3054) for 1m & turn R into main entrance at 1st school sign 200yds after reaching top of hill. Home-made teas. **Adm £3, chd 50p (share to St John's Church). Sun 29 Apr (2-6).** 97-acre grounds of C18/19 manor (not open). Landscape: naturalistic derived from C18 formal and English styles and influence of Capability Brown. Garden styles/origins: late C19/early C20 Italianate revival with influence of Harold Peto; early C20 Arts and Crafts with designs by Thomas Mawson; early C19 picturesque/Gothic. Features: lakes, canal, mount, banana house, shell grotto, C19 trees, mature shrubs, terraces, vistas and views of IOW. Guided tours. Gravel paths, some steps/steep slopes. Unfenced ponds.

57 ◆ HOUGHTON LODGE GARDEN

nr Stockbridge SO20 6LQ. Captain M W Busk, 01264 810502, www.houghtonlodge.co.uk. 1¹/₂m S of Stockbridge. From A30 on minor rd towards Houghton village. **Adm £5, chd free. Daily (not Weds) Mar to Sept. For NGS: Sun 22 Apr; Weds 27 June; 4 July (10-5).** Tranquil setting of spacious lawns and fine trees frames an enchanting C18 Cottage Orné overlooking the unspoilt beauty of R Test, fringed with wild flowers. Mown meadow walks. Traditional kitchen garden. Formal and informal planting. New displays of spring bulbs, greenhouses with orchids. Children's quiz and drawing materials. Snorting topiary 'dragon'. Lots of seats.

58 THE HOUSE IN THE WOOD

Beaulieu SO42 7YN. Victoria Roberts. 8m NE of Lymington. Leaving the entrance to Beaulieu motor museum on R (B3056) take the next R turn signed Ipley Cross. Take 2nd gravel drive on RH-bend, approx ¹/₂m. Cream teas. **Adm £3, chd free. Sun 13 May (2-6pm).** Charming woodland garden set in 12 acres specialising in rhododendrons and azaleas. Large lawn, views and walk down to a lake at the bottom.

The area was used during the war to train the Special Operations Executive.

Quintessentially English garden much visited by Jane Austen. Also Dora Carrington, the painter, lived here . . .

59 THE HYDE

Old Alresford SO24 9DH. Sue Alexander, 01962 732043. 1m W of Alresford. From Alresford 1m along B3046 towards Basingstoke. House in centre of village, opp village green. Home-made teas. **Adm £3, chd free. Sun 12, Tue 14 Aug; Sun 9 Sept (1.30-5). Visitors also welcome by appt 1 Aug to 9 Sept.** Tucked away behind an old field hedge, a delightful ³/₄-acre garden created by the owner to attract wildlife and reflect her flower arranging passion for colour and texture. Flowing borders contain an abundant mixture of perennials, half-hardies, annuals, grasses and shrubs. Interesting new planting for shady and dry areas. Featured in BBC The Gardener's Year. Short gravel drive at entrance.

60 NEW IBTHORPE HOUSE

Ibthorpe SP11 0BY. Colonel & Mrs Robert ffrench Blake. 6m N of Andover. Off A343 at bottom of hill in Hurstbourne Tarrant turn L, signed Upton and Ibthorpe. ¹/₂m on R. Home-made teas. **Adm £3, chd free. Thur 31 May; Sun 3 June (2-6).** Quintessentially English garden much visited by Jane Austen. Also Dora Carrington, the painter, lived here in her youth. This historic house is surrounded by a walled garden with mixed borders, double paeony beds and traditional kitchen garden. Teas served in old thatched grainstore overlooking secret garden.

61 IBTHORPE TOWER
Windmill Hill, Hurtsbourne Tarrant SP11 0DQ. Mr & Mrs P Gregory. *5m N of Andover. Off A343 at top of Hurstbourne Hill, signed The Chutes and Tangley. 1st turning on R.* Cream teas. **Adm £3, chd free. Sun 9, Wed 12 Sept (11-5).**
3½ acres of garden planted in contemporary style, focusing on colour and texture, in tranquil spot, elevated and with glorious views. Large wildlife pond, woodland garden, potager and long banks and large borders planted with hardy perennials in imaginative drifts.

❀ ☕

KENT HOUSE
See Sussex.

62 KIMPTON HOUSE
Lower Durford Wood, nr Petersfield GU31 5AS. Mr & Mrs Christopher Napier, 01730 892151. *1½m NE of Petersfield. B2070 N of Petersfield towards Rake. Pass A272 junction to Midhurst. ½m further on turn R into white gates marked 'Durford Wood, Lower Wood only'. Kimpton House ½m on R.* **Adm £3, chd free. Suns 20 May; 8 July (2-6). Visitors also welcome by appt, groups of 10+. No coaches.**
10 acres of gardens with panoramic views of S Downs. Large traditional herbaceous and shrub borders with topiary in a formal setting. Contemporary tropical garden where temperatures regularly reach 110°F. Formal French garden of pleaching and topiary. Herb garden. Woodland areas. Water features and wild flower butterfly meadow.

⅋ ⊀

KIRBY HOUSE
See Berkshire.

63 53 LADYWOOD
Eastleigh SO50 4RW. Mr & Mrs D Ward, 02380 615389. *1m N of Eastleigh. Leave M3 J12. Follow signs to Eastleigh. Turn R at roundabout into Woodside Ave, then 2nd R into Bosville. Ladywood 5th on R. Park in Bosville.* Home-made teas Suns only. **Adm £3, chd free. Suns (11-5), Mons (2-5) 13, 14 May; 24, 25 June. Visitors also welcome by appt Apr to July for groups of 10+.**
45ft x 45ft with dozens of ideas for small gardens. Over 1800 different plants labelled. Trellis fences provide vertical space for many clematis and

unusual climbers to wander. Many special interest foliage plants from pulmonarias in spring, through brunneras, heucheras and miniature hostas to a wonderful display of phlox paniculata and grasses in July. All carefully designed to create peace and harmony in a delightful town garden. Featured on BBC TV The Gardener's Year'.

⊀ ❀ ☕

Each room is hidden from the next and contrasts sharply in style and colour . . .

64 LAKE HOUSE
Northington SO24 9TG. Lord Ashburton. *4m N of Alresford. Off B3046. Follow English Heritage signs to The Grange, then directions.* Home-made teas. **Adm £4, chd free. Sun 20, Tue 22 May (1.30-5.30). Visitors also welcome by appt, please apply in writing. Access unsuitable for coaches.**
2 large lakes in Candover Valley set off by mature woodland with waterfalls, abundant bird life, long landscaped vistas and folly. 1½-acre walled garden, mixed borders, long herbaceous border, rose pergola leading to moon gate. Formal kitchen garden, flowering pots, conservatory and greenhouses. Picnicking by lakes.

⅋ ❀ ☕

65 60 LEALAND ROAD
Drayton, Portsmouth PO6 1LZ. Mr F G Jacob, 02392 370030, jacob60lea@tiscali.co.uk. *2m E of Cosham. Old A27 (Havant Rd) between Cosham & Bedhampton.* Home-made teas. **Adm £2, chd free. Suns 29 Apr; 10 June; 19 Aug (1-5). Visitors also welcome by appt.**
Prizewinning garden with a difference, created by the owner since 1969. Plants from around the world incl palms, yuccas, echiums and cannas. Designed for maximum effect with lily ponds and rockery. Incl collection of bamboos and grasses, also cacti and other exotics in greenhouse.

⅋ ⊀ ❀ ☕

66 LITTLE COOPERS
Coopers Hill, Eversley RG27 0QA. Mr & Mrs J K Oldale. *4m N of Fleet. On B3016, signed from A30 (W of Blackbushe Airport) and from B3272 (E of Eversley cricket ground). Signed car parking at Westfield Farm, 100yds from garden.* Home-made teas. **Adm £3, chd free. Sun 6 May (2-5.30).**
10 acres. A walk will take you through woodland carpeted with bluebells. Rhododendrons, azaleas, many unusual shrubs. Water and bog gardens; extensive lawn with conifers; heathers; Mediterranean, rose, small Japanese and dry gardens. Water garden not accessible to wheelchairs, but can be viewed from lawn.

⅋ ❀ ☕

67 THE LITTLE COTTAGE
Southampton Road (A337), Lymington SO41 9GZ. Peter & Lyn Prior, 01590 679395. *1m N of Lymington town centre. On A337 opp Toll House Inn.* **Adm £2. Weds 20 June; 4, 18 July; 1 Aug; 5 Sept (11-1 & 2-5). Also open Buckland Stead. Visitors also welcome by appt 20 June to 5 Sept only.**
Garden of unique and artistic design using unusual and interesting plants arranged to form pictures with arches, arbours and urns in secret rooms. Each room is hidden from the next and contrasts sharply in style and colour to stimulate, calm, excite or amaze, incl an outrageous black and white garden. Regret unsuitable for children. Featured in 'Hampshire Life', 'Sunday Mirror' & GGG.

⊀

68 LITTLE COURT
Crawley, nr Winchester SO21 2PU. Prof & Mrs A R Elkington, 01962 776365, elkslc@tiscali.co.uk. *5m NW of Winchester. Off A272 or B3049, in Crawley village; 300yds from either village pond or church.* Home-made teas (Suns & Bank Hols only) at Village Hall or Little Court, weather permitting. **Adm £3, chd free. Suns 11, 18, Mon 19, Tue 20 Feb; Easter Mon 9 Apr; Tue 1 May; Fri 1 June; Sun 9 Sept (2-5.30). Suns 17, 24, Tues 19, 26 Feb 2008. Opening with Crawley Gardens Sun, Mon 1, 2 Apr; Thur, Sun 21, 24 June. Visitors also welcome by appt.**
3 acres on gently rising ground, in 7 distinct sections each with rustic seats and vistas. Prolific naturalised spring bulbs, climbing roses, diverse perennials. Woodland walk with wild

flowers. Large tree house appeals to young and old. Close-mown labyrinth with wild cowslips. Traditional walled kitchen garden. Newly acquired field, giving a walk with panoramic view. Quiz for children. Featured in 'Gardens Illustrated'.

 ⟨symbols⟩

⑥⑨ LITTLEWOOD
West Lane, Hayling Island PO11 0JW. Mr & Mrs Steven Schrier. *3m S of Havant. From A27 Havant/Hayling Island junction, travel S for 2m, turn R into West Lane and continue 1m. House set back from rd in wood. Disabled should drive to very top of drive.* Home-made teas. **Adm £3, chd free. Sat 26, Sun 27 May (11-5).**
2¹/₂-acre woodland garden surrounded by fields and near sea, protected from sea winds by multi-barrier hedge. Rhododendrons, azaleas, camellias and many other shrubs. Woodland walk to full-size tree house. Features incl pond, bog garden watered from roof of conservatory, house plants, summerhouse and many places to sit outside and under cover. Picnickers welcome.

 ⟨symbols⟩

⑦⓪ LONGSTOCK PARK WATER GARDEN
nr Stockbridge SO20 6JF. Leckford Estate Ltd, part of John Lewis Partnership, www.longstockpark.co.uk. *4m S of Andover. From A30 turn N on to A3057; follow signs to Longstock.* Home-made teas at Longstock Park Nursery. **Adm £4, chd 50p. Sun 17 June (2-5).**
Famous water garden with extensive collection of aquatic and bog plants set in 7 acres of woodland with rhododendrons and azaleas. A walk through park leads to National Collections of *Buddleia*, penstemon and *Clematis viticella*, arboretum, herbaceous border.

 ⟨symbols⟩ NCCPG ⟨symbol⟩

⑦① LONGTHATCH
Lippen Lane, Warnford SO32 3LE. Peter & Vera Short, 01730 829285. *12m N of Fareham. On A32, turn R from N or L from S at George & Falcon PH. After 100yds turn R at T-junction, continue for ¹/₄m; thatched C17 house on R. Parking opp.* **Adm £2.50, chd free. Visitors welcome by appt, no coaches.**
3¹/₂ acres, plantsman's garden on R

Meon. Rare trees and shrubs. Part of National Collection of *Helleborus*. Fine lawns, herbaceous borders, island beds and bog gardens. Spring-fed ponds, woodland area with hellebores, primulas and shade-loving plants.

⟨symbols⟩ NCCPG

LOWDER MILL
See Sussex.

⑦② ◆ MACPENNYS WOODLAND GARDEN & NURSERIES
Burley Road, Bransgore BH23 8DB. Mr & Mrs T M Lowndes, www.macpennys.co.uk. *6m S of Ringwood, 5m NE of Christchurch. Midway between Christchurch & Burley. From A35, at Xrds by The Crown Bransgore turn R & proceed ¹/₄m. From A31 (towards Bournemouth) L at Picket Post, signed Burley, then R at Burley Cross. Garden on L after 2m.* **Adm by donation. Daily 2 Jan to 24 Dec, Mons to Sats (9-5), Suns (10-5).**
12 acres; 4-acre gravel pit converted into woodland garden; many unusual plants. Gold Medal & Cup for Best in Class (Trees, Shrubs & Climbers) at New Forest Show.

⟨symbol⟩

MALT HOUSE
See Sussex.

⑦③ NEW MANOR HOUSE
Church Lane, Exton SO32 3NU. Mrs Charles Blackmore. *Off A32 just N of Corhampton. Follow signs.* Home-made teas. **Adm £3, chd free. Sun 25 Feb (2-4); Sun 10, Wed 13 June (2-5.30).**
Mature country garden with various rooms of herbaceous, kitchen garden, pond garden and woodland. Masses of spring bulbs: snowdrops, crocuses and daffodils; lovely spring woodland garden. Many features to make a pretty peaceful environment and attractive setting.

⟨symbols⟩

MANOR HOUSE
See Wiltshire.

⑦④ MARTYR WORTHY GARDENS
SO21 1DZ. *5m E of Winchester. On B3047.* Home-made teas at Village Hall. **Adm £2 each garden, chd free. Sun 10 June (2-6).**

2 different but complementary gardens ¹/₄m apart. Joined by lovely walk along Pilgrims Way through Itchen Valley. Plenty of parking at both.

⟨symbol⟩

CYGNET HOUSE
Mr & Mrs Shane Chichester (See separate entry).

 ⟨symbols⟩

THE MANOR HOUSE
Charles & Isobel Pinder
Large garden, roses, mixed borders, lawns, shrubs and fine trees, next to C12 church and footbridge over R Itchen. Gravel drive and paths.

 ⟨symbol⟩

Large tree
house appeals
to all ages.
Close-mown
labyrinth
with wild
cowslips . . .

⑦⑤ MARYCOURT
High Street, Odiham RG29 1LF. Mrs E A Conville, 01256 702100. *3m SE of Hook.* **Adm £3, chd free. Suns 24 June; 1 July (2-6), Wed 4 July (11-6). Visitors also welcome by appt.**
Grade II* house (not open). 1 acre with paddocks; old roses, shrubs, ramblers dripping from trees. Silver/pink border; long, colourful herbaceous borders; hostas and delphiniums. Tender, herbaceous plants, cannas, large fuchsias, dahlias, abutilons. Dry stone wall with alpines.

 ⟨symbols⟩

⑦⑥ THE MATHOM HOUSE
17 Bereweeke Road, Winchester SO22 6AJ. Eric Eisenhauer. *¹/₃m from Winchester stn. In NW Winchester between B3420 and B3049. Walk from stn approx 8 mins.* Home-made teas. **Adm £2.75, chd free (share to William Rowden Charitable Trust). Sun 10, Sat 16 June (1-6).**

Diverse suburban gardens of approx 1 acre, started 1997 with professional design assistance, divided into 6 distinct areas. Features parterre 'Pleasuance Garden' in classical C17 design with old roses and ornamental herbs, overlooked by 9ft box hedge in cloud style and 100yr-old Judas tree. Herbaceous borders, woodland glade, Mediterranean-themed poolside planting, ornamental fruit garden, bamboo hedging and climbing roses snaking up trees.

77 MEON ORCHARD
Kingsmead, N of Wickham PO17 5AU. Doug & Linda Smith, 01329 833253, doug.smith@btinternet.com. *5m N of Fareham. From Wickham take A32 N for 1¹/₂m. Turn L at Roebuck Inn. Continue ¹/₂m.* Adm £3, chd free. Suns 3 June; 29 July; 2 Sept (2-6). Visitors also welcome by appt, minimum charge applies for small groups.
1¹/₂-acre garden designed and constructed by current owners. An exceptional range of rare, unusual and architectural plants incl National Collections of Eucalyptus, Podocarpaceae & Araliaceae. Much use made of dramatic foliage plants from around the world, both hardy and tender, big bananas, huge taros, tree ferns, cannas, hedychiums and palms. Streams and ponds, combined with an extensive range of planters, complete the display. Owners available to answer questions. Plant sale of the exotic and rare Sun 2 Sept. Featured in 'Hampshire Life'.

78 MEONSTOKE GARDENS
SO32 3NF. *12m SE of Winchester. Just off A32 between Corhampton & Droxford. Parking in field on R in Rectory Lane, opp Barton House.* Cream teas at Barton House. Combined adm £3, chd free. Sun 17 June (2-6).
Small pretty village on Meon River with village pub and beautiful C13 church.

BARTON HOUSE
Rectory Lane. Peter Neill & Alison Munro
4-acre village garden on chalk adjoining church. Traditional flint and cob walled garden with peonies, roses, herbaceous plants; arched gateway (with horse teeth paving) leading to

large outer garden with mature trees, extensive lawns, orchard, vegetable garden, pond, grass court, putting green and bunker. Wooden bridge over Winterbourne to churchyard.

THE OLD STORE
High Street. Ian & Jane McCormick
¹/₃-acre cottage garden on chalk, with views of Corhampton Down. Terraced and designed in the last 9yrs by owners to make max use of sloping garden. Planted with 80 roses, over 50 varieties, mainly English shrub, climbers and old-fashioned. Compact vegetable garden using raised beds. Trees, shrubs, herbaceous and herbs.

79 MERDON MANOR
Hursley. Mr & Mrs J C Smith, 01962 775215/281, vronk@bluebottle.com. *5m SW of Winchester. From A3090 Winchester to Romsey rd, turn R at Standon to Slackstead; proceed 1¹/₂m.* Home-made teas. Adm £3, chd free. Sun 15 July (2-6). Visitors also welcome by appt, any number at any time by arrangement.
5 acres with panoramic views; herbaceous border, water lilies, large wisteria; selection of roses; fruit-bearing lemon trees and small secret walled water garden. Ha-ha and black Hebridean (St Kilda) sheep.

Mixed thyme patch and kitchen garden with developed compost and leaf mould systems . . .

80 MITTENS
Mapledurwell RG25 2LG. Mr & Mrs David Hooper, 01256 321838. *3¹/₂m E of Basingstoke. Off A30 at Hatch, signed Mapledurwell. Over M3 bridge take 2nd R, Frog Lane, to Xrds at pond. 300yds up rd to Tunworth.* Home-made teas. Adm £3, chd free. Suns 25 Mar; 2 Sept (2-5). Visitors also welcome by appt.
1¹/₂ acres. Created from farmland in conservation area; spring bulbs, children's garden with rill and ivy house, secret garden with pool, pergola, nut arch, purple border, 2 major borders of red and yellow with colour from dahlias, cannas, gladioli and roses and hedges forming rooms.

HUTCHENS COTTAGE
Mr & Mrs R A Crick
³/₄-acre cottage garden with interesting scented plants: old roses, clematis, shrubs incl daphnes, mature trees, small orchard; mixed thyme patch and kitchen garden with developed compost and leaf mould systems.

WHITE GABLES
Mr & Mrs D Eaglesham
Cottage-style garden of ¹/₃ acre, leading down to Pill Hill Brook. Interesting trees and shrubs, old roses and herbaceous plants.

81 MONXTON GARDENS
SP11 8AS. *3m W of Andover. Between A303 & A343; parking in field on L in Chalkpit Lane.* Cream teas at village hall. Combined adm £3, chd free. Sun 27, Mon 28 May (2-5.30). Festival of Flowers in neighbouring village of Amport, 1m.

82 ◆ MOTTISFONT ABBEY & GARDEN
Romsey SO51 0LP. The National Trust, 01794 340757, www.nationaltrust.org.uk. *4¹/₂m NW of Romsey. From A3057 Romsey to Stockbridge turn W at sign to Mottisfont. Wheelchairs & battery car service available at garden.* House & garden £8.50, chd £4.20. Garden only £7.50, chd £3.80. Family tickets available. Opening days & times vary according to season; please phone or visit website for details. For NGS: Fri 6 Apr (11-5); Sun 10 June (11-7.30).
Built C12 as Augustinian priory, now

house of some note. 30-acre landscaped garden incl spring or 'font', from which house derives its name, magnificent ancient trees and walled gardens with National Collection of over 300 varieties of old roses. Tranquil walks in grounds, along the R Test and in the glorious countryside of the estate.

  ♿ NCCPG ☕

83 MULBERRY HOUSE
7 Moorland Avenue, Barton-on-Sea BH25 7DB. Rosemary & John Owen, 01425 612066, rojowen@btinternet.com. *6m W of Lymington. From the A337 (S of New Milton), going W, take L turn into Barton Court Ave and 4th R into Moorland Ave.* Home-made teas. **Adm £2.50, chd free (share to Oakhaven Hospice). Tues 26 June; Sun 1 July (2-5). Visitors also welcome by appt.** Pretty family garden of 1/4 acre with old-fashioned and modern roses; a scramble of clematis; traditional fruit trees incl medlar, mulberry and quince, plus hazel and cob nuts; good selection of hardy geraniums, and herb and vegetable areas. Late summer colour with a number of viticella clematis, salvias and penstemons. Relaxed, organic garden with much native planting to attract insect and bird life. Mason bee nests. Some narrow paths.

  ♿ ☕

84 49 NEWTOWN ROAD WITH 26 & 29 WESTON ALLOTMENTS
Woolston SO19 9HX. Mrs Belinda Hayes, 02380 396524. *3m E of Southampton City Centre. Leave M27 J8, follow signs for Hamble-le-Rice. At Windhover roundabout, take 2nd exit past Tesco into Hamble Lane B3397. R into Portsmouth Rd, 1m L at 2nd mini roundabout into Upper Weston Lane, 2nd L into Newtown Rd. Disabled parking only at allotments, other parking on public rd. 9 houses between garden and allotments.* Home-made teas. **Adm £2.50, chd free. Sat 7, Sun 8 July (2-5). Visitors also welcome by appt, July only.** Long narrow garden with patio, pool, unusual perennials, lawn, climbers, many containers and hanging baskets with bedding plants. Allotments packed with vegetables, fruit and flowers for floral art. Winner Best Garden Southampton in Bloom & 2nd Best Allotment, Hampshire Federation of Horticultural Societies.

♿ ☕

85 OAKDENE
Sandleheath, Fordingbridge SP6 1TD. Shirley & Chris Stanford, 01425 652133. *11/2m W of Fordingbridge. Adjacent to St Aldhelm's Church.* Cream teas. **Adm £3, chd free. Suns 17, 24 June (2-5.30). Visitors also welcome by appt in June & July only.** 2-acre garden for rose lovers with more than 400 in formal beds and mixed borders, on long pergolas and climbing through fruit trees. 30 varieties of apple grow in the orchard and on arches in the walled organic kitchen garden, along with pears, plums and an abundance of flowers, fruit and vegetables. Greenhouses, dovecotes with resident doves. Free-range hens. New planting and features always in progress. Featured on ITV Village Voices.

  ♿ ☕

86 OLD MEADOWS
Bramley Road, Silchester RG7 2LL. Dr & Mrs J M Fowler, 01256 881450. *7m N of Basingstoke. 7m S of Reading. Off A340 between Reading & Basingstoke, on rd to Bramley.* Home-made teas. **Adm £3, chd free. Sun 17 June (2-6). Visitors also welcome by appt at any time of the yr, coaches permitted.** 5 acres incl maze in the meadow, a blue tree and hundreds of wild orchids on lawn April and September. Walled garden with diverse plants and vegetables, beautiful rose garden and carpets of old-fashioned spring bulbs. Hand-made living willow/hazel seats and arches. Rare geese, peacocks and hens. Recently restored C17 barn. Children very welcome.

  ♿ ☕

87 PENNINGTON HOUSE
Ridgeway Lane, Lymington SO41 8AA. Sue Stowell & John Leach, 01590 675855, suestowell@greenclose.co.uk. *11/2m S of Lymington. S on A337 from Lymington approx 1/3m to Pennington roundabout. Turn L & immed fork L into Ridgeway Lane. Continue for 1/3m until Chequers PH. Turn R immed by post box into private drive.* Home-made teas (weather permitting). **Adm £3, chd £2 (share to Arthritis Research Campaign). Sat 12, Sun 13 May (2-5). Visitors also welcome by appt.** 7 acre garden created around 1910 and entirely organic for the last 14yrs. Substantial rockery of mature acers. Stream and pond. Italian sunken garden, rose garden, organic 1/2-acre

walled Victorian kitchen garden in full use. Magnificent wisteria on the house. Featured in 'Southampton Echo' and on BBC Radio Solent.

  ♿ ☕

88 THE PRIORS FARM
Reading Road, Mattingley RG27 8JU. Mr Miles Hudson. *11/2m N of Hook. On B3349 Reading Rd. Parking on green just N of Leather Bottle PH. Entrance by gate on green parking area.* Home-made teas. **Adm £3, chd free. Sun 15 July (2-5).** 31/2-acre mixed border garden, rose garden and orchard area with cedar and other trees. Bog garden area and swimming pool area. C15 granary and goatery. Herb bed. Statuary.

  ☕

Allotments packed with vegetables, fruit and flowers . . .

89 PYLEWELL PARK
Lymington SO41 5SJ. Lord Teynham. *2m E of Lymington. Beyond IOW car ferry.* **Adm £3, chd free. Suns 6, 13 May (2-5).** Very large garden of botanical interest, dating from 1900. Fine trees, flowering shrubs, rhododendrons, with walk beside the lakes and seashore.

90 NEW 27 REYNOLDS DALE
Ashurst, Southampton SO40 7PS. Ms F Barnes, 02380 860046, http://homepages.enterprise.net/fbarnes/garden. *6m W of Southampton. From M27, J2 take A326 to Fawley. At 4th roundabout L into Cocklydown Lane. At mini roundabout L into Ibbotson Way. 1st L into Reynolds Dale and follow signs.* **Adm £2, chd free. Sat 16, Sun 17 June (2.30-5.30). Also open nearby The Fountains. Visitors also welcome by appt.** Small 5yr-old garden with a chambered nautilus theme (Oliver Wendell Holmes), designed to be shared with 3 lively Springer Spaniels. No lawn, so lots of space for plants. Hard landscaping incl pond you can sit beside.

91 ROMSEY GARDENS
SO51 8EU. *All within walking distance of Romsey Abbey, clearly signed.* Home-made teas at King John's House. **Combined adm £4, chd free. Sun 27, Mon 28 May (11-5.30).** Small attractive market town with notable Norman C12 Abbey.

KING JOHN'S GARDEN
Church Street. Friends of King John's Garden & Test Valley Borough Council
Listed C13 house (not open). Historic garden planted with material available up to 1700. Award-winning Victorian garden and North Courtyard with water features.

4 MILL LANE
4 Mill Lane. Miss J Flindall, 01794 513926. Visitors also welcome by appt, garden clubs welcome.
Small, long, floriferous town garden. S-facing. Backdrop Romsey Abbey; original sculpture and attractive hard landscaping.

92 ROTHERFIELD PARK
East Tisted, Alton GU34 3QE. Sir James & Lady Scott, 01420 588207. *4m S of Alton on A32.* Home-made teas. **Adm £2.50, chd free. Suns 6 May; 16 Sept (2-5).** Visitors also welcome by appt in May & Sept only.
Take some ancient ingredients: ice house, ha-ha, lime avenue; add a walled garden, fruit and vegetables, trees and hedges; set this 12-acre plot in an early C19 park (picnic here from noon) and mix to coin clichés about. Mix in a bluebell wood in May and apple-picking in September. Garden used for filming Agatha Christie's *After the Funeral* with David Suchet as Hercule Poirot. Reasonable wheelchair access to walled garden.

93 ST CHRISTOPHER'S
Whitsbury SP6 3PZ. Christine Southey & David Mussell, 01725 518404. *3¹/₂m NW of Fordingbridge. In village centre, 200yds down from Cartwheel PH.* Cream teas in village hall or garden, weather permitting. **Adm £2.50, chd free. Suns 22 Apr; 17 June (2-6).** Visitors also welcome by appt, Apr to Aug preferred, but always something to see.

Tranquil ³/₄-acre long, sloping garden with superb views. Alpines in S-facing scree bed with unusual bulbs, incl dwarf iris, tulips and narcissi, and alpine troughs. In spring, wild banks of bluebells and primroses; in summer, 25ft rambling roses, beds of delphiniums, perennial geraniums, eremurus and many herbaceous treasures. Pond and bog garden. Conservatory with unusual plants; fruit and vegetable garden and several secret seating areas. Breathtaking bluebell walk (approx 1m) on public footpaths adjacent to garden.

94 28 ST RONAN'S AVENUE
Southsea PO4 0QE. Mr I Craig, 02392 787331, www.28stronansavenue.co.uk. *Turn into St Ronan's Rd from Albert Rd at junction opp Trinity Methodist Church. St Ronan's Ave is a cul-de-sac off St Ronan's Rd. Alternatively, follow signs to seafront and then follow yellow NGS signs from canoe lake and Eastern Parade. Park at Craneswater School.* Home-made teas. **Adm £2, chd free. Suns 22 July; 26 Aug (2-6). Evening Opening £3.50, wine, Sat 4 Aug (5-8).** Visitors also welcome by appt.
145ft x 25ft town garden. Created from derelict land and newly planted in 1999. Bold planting incl ferns, cannas, bananas, wild flower area, herbaceous borders, bog garden, vegetable beds and dry garden. Sculpture made by owner from recycled materials.

SANDHILL FARM HOUSE
See Sussex.

95 SANDLE COTTAGE
Sandleheath, Fordingbridge SP6 1PY. Peter & Yo Beech, 01425 654638, www.sandlecottage.com. *2m W of Fordingbridge. Turn R at Sandleheath Xrds. Entrance 50yds on L. Ample field parking.* Home-made teas. **Adm £2.50, chd free (share to Fordingbridge URC). Suns 15, 22, 29 July (1.30-5.30).**
3-acre garden designed and maintained by the owners with displays of dahlias (best on 22 and 29 July), annuals, sweet peas (best on 15 July) and exotics. Features incl traditional walled kitchen garden with many varieties of vegetables; pretty sunken garden; formal lawn with sharp edges; two greenhouses; small lake with cascading waterfall; circular summerhouse in own cottage garden and new woodland walk. Plenty of

seating and shade. Featured on BBC Radio Solent.

SANDLEFORD PLACE
See Berkshire.

Meandering paths provide changing vistas and views ... teas in the dappled shade of the orchard, comfortable on warm summer days ...

96 'SELBORNE'
Caker Lane, East Worldham, Alton GU34 3AE. Brian & Mary Jones, 01420 83389, mary.trigwell-jones@virgin.net. *2m SE of Alton. On B3004 at Alton end of East Worldham opp The Three Horseshoes PH (please note, NOT in the village of Selborne). Parking signed.* Home-made teas. **Adm £2, chd free (share to St Mary's Church June, Tafara Mission Zimbabwe Aug). Sats, Suns: 21, 22 Apr; 19, 20 May; 16, 17 June; Sat, Sun, Mon 4, 5, 6 Aug (2-6). Evening Opening, wine, Fri 15 June (6-9).** Visitors also welcome by appt May to early Aug, individuals and groups welcome.
¹/₂-acre mature garden with old established orchard of named varieties. Meandering paths provide changing vistas and views across farmland. Mixed borders feature a large collection of hardy geraniums with alliums, euphorbias and other herbaceous plants and shrubs designed for yr-round effect. Shrubbery and soft fruit garden with greenhouse feature, metal and stone sculptures, containers, summerhouses and small conservatory. Teas in the dappled shade of the orchard, comfortable on warm summer days. Book stall. Some narrow paths may be slippery when wet.

97 SHALDEN PARK HOUSE

Shalden GU34 4DS. Michael D C C Campbell. 4^1/$_2$m NW of Alton. B3349 from Alton or J5 M3. Turn W at Golden Pot PH marked Herriard, Lasham, Shalden. Entrance ^{1}/$_4$m on L. Light refreshments & teas. **Adm £3, chd free. Sun 22 July (2-5).** 4-acre garden surrounded by woodland, redesigned in 2005/6 by Georgia Langton. Extensive views. Herbaceous borders. Walled kitchen garden and glasshouses. Early stage arboretum. Lunchtime picnics welcome.

98 SHERFIELD SCHOOL

Reading Road, Sherfield-on-Loddon RG27 0HT, www.sherfieldschool.co.uk. 5m N of Basingstoke. On A33 near Sherfield-on-Loddon. **Adm £3, chd free. Sun 25 Mar (11-4).** 74 acres of formal gardens. Carpets of daffodils along the drive, ornamental lawns, topiary hedges, woodlands and lake walks set around the impressive C19 mansion house.

99 ♦ SPINNERS

Spinners, School Lane, Boldre SO41 5QE. Peter Chappell, 01590 673347. 1^1/$_2$m N of Lymington. Signed off A337 Brockenhurst to Lymington rd (do not follow sign to Boldre Church). **Adm £2.50, chd under 6 free. Tues to Sats 3 Apr to 14 Sept (10-5).** Azaleas, rhododendrons, hydrangeas, maples and other rare shrubs interplanted with huge range of plants and woodland bulbs, especially erythroniums and trilliums. New plantings of Teller lace-cap hydrangeas and a range of the newer magnolias. Visited by people from all over the temperate world. Featured on Meridian TV Village Voice.

SWALLOWFIELD HORTICULTURAL SOCIETY

See Berkshire.

100 TANGLEFOOT

Crawley, nr Winchester SO21 2QB. Mr & Mrs F J Fratter, 01962 776243, fred@tanglefoot-house.demon.co.uk. 5m NW of Winchester. Private lane beside entrance to Crawley Court (Arqiva). Drop-off & disabled parking only at house, other parking on public rd 400m or in field 50m. Cold drinks.

Sinuous shapes with many nooks and crannies . . . wooded areas for shade-loving plants . . .

Adm £2.50, chd free. Thur 19, Sun 22 July (2-5.30). Opening with Crawley Gardens 21, 24 June. Visitors also welcome by appt, summer only. Approx ^{1}/$_2$ acre on chalk, designed and developed by owners, with mature shrubs, colour-themed herbaceous and mixed borders, raised lily pond, herb wheel and developing wild flower area. Divided into areas by the planting, and bounded on one side by a magnificent Victorian wall, covered with trained top fruit, protecting a compact productive kitchen garden and greenhouse.

101 TREETOPS

Upper Froyle GU34 4JH. Mr & Mrs J Cresswell. 3m NE of Alton on A31. On lane to Upper Froyle, just behind Hen & Chicken Inn. Home-made teas. **Adm £1.50, chd free. Sun 13 May (2-5). Opening with Froyle Gardens 26, 27 May.** Medium-sized garden, richly planted with many unusual plants, herbaceous borders, shrubs and newly-refurbished pond.

102 TUNWORTH OLD RECTORY

Tunworth, nr Basingstoke RG25 2NB. The Hon Mrs Julian Berry, 01256 471436. 4m SE of Basingstoke. Turn S off A30 at sign to Tunworth. **Adm £3, chd free. Visitors welcome by appt in May, July & Aug.** Laid out with yew hedges, enclosing different aspects. Double mixed border; ruby wedding garden; pleached hornbeam walk; lime avenue; ornamental pond; interesting trees incl beech-lined walk to church. Decorative pots. Walks in park. Some slopes, mostly grass; wheelchair helper advisable.

103 TYLNEY HALL HOTEL

Ridge Lane, Rotherwick RG27 9AZ. The Manager, www.tylneyhall.com. 3m NW of Hook. From M3 J5 via A287 & Newnham, M4 J11 via B3349 & Rotherwick. Cream teas. **Adm £3, chd free. Suns 20 May; 17 June; 15 July (10-5).** Large garden of 66 acres with extensive woodlands and fine vistas being restored with new planting. Fine avenues of wellingtonias; rhododendrons and azaleas; Italian garden; lakes, large water and rock garden, dry stone walls originally designed with assistance of Gertrude Jekyll.

104 ULVIK

114 Harestock Road, Winchester SO22 6NY. Mr & Mrs G G Way, 01962 852361. 1m N of Winchester. 5th house on L in Harestock Rd off A3049 (old A272). Soft drinks. **Adm £2, chd free. Sat 14 to Tues 17 July incl: Sat 11 to Tues 14 Aug incl (2-6). Visitors also welcome by appt June and July only.** Completely enclosed hedged garden of ^{1}/$_2$ acre designed to create interesting and unfolding views and sinuous shapes with many nooks and crannies. Fairly naturalistic planting of mixed herbaceous borders, large variety of shrubs, many ornamental grasses, prairie-style border, small vegetable area, pond, wooded areas for shade-loving plants and features to encourage wildlife. Fun sculptures and children's discovery quiz.

UPPARK

See Sussex.

105 VALENTINE COTTAGE

Newnham Road, Newnham, nr Basingstoke RG27 9AE. Mr & Mrs P Brown, 01256 762049, gillbrown@pccs.org.uk. 2m NW of Hook. From Hook A30 towards Basingstoke. After approx 1m turn R at Dorchester Arms into Old School Rd, signed Newnham. At end of Old School Rd turn L into Newnham Rd. Home-made teas. **Adm £3, chd free. Suns 6 May; 10 June; 15 July (2-5.30). Visitors also welcome by appt May, June & July.** Exuberant cottage garden of ^{2}/$_3$ acre, specialising in clematis; laid out into individual smaller gardens.

106 ◆ THE VYNE
Sherborne St John RG24 9HL. The
National Trust, 01256 883858,
www.nationaltrust.org.uk. *4m N of
Basingstoke. Between Sherborne St
John & Bramley. From A340 turn E at
NT signs.* House & garden £8, chd
£4; garden only £5, chd £2.50.
Opening dates and times vary
according to season. Please phone
or visit website for details. For NGS:
Sun 3 June (11-5). **Evening Picnic**
£5, chd £2.50 Wed 25 July (5-9).
13 acres with extensive lawns, lake,
fine trees, herbaceous border and
Edwardian-style summerhouse garden.
Extensive woodland and parkland
walks. Evening picnic.
&. ⅍ ⊕ ☕

107 WADES HOUSE
Barton Stacey SO21 3RJ. Mr & Mrs
A Briscoe, 01962 760516,
jenny.roo@btinternet.com. *Midway
between A303 & A30 nr Andover.
Approached from S entrance to village.*
Home-made teas. **Adm** £3, chd free.
Tue 8 May; Sun 2, Mon 3 Sept (2.30-
5.30). **Visitors also welcome by
appt.**
2 acres on shallow chalky soil of formal
herbaceous borders, rose garden of
old-fashioned roses and pergola,
landscaping, orchard, woodland walk
and kitchen garden. Spectacular
seasonal planting in tubs.
Greenhouses and enviable lawns.
&. ⊕ ⊨ ☕

108 WALBURY
Lower Froyle, Alton GU34 4LJ. Mr &
Mrs E Milam, 01420 22216,
walbury@mwclub.net. *5m NE of
Alton. Access to Lower Froyle from
A31 between Alton and Farnham at
Bentley. Walbury nr village hall where
parking available.* Home-made teas.
Adm £1.50, chd free. Sat 28, Sun 29
Apr (2-5). Opening with **Froyle
Gardens** 26, 27 May. **Visitors also
welcome by appt.**
Cottage garden atmosphere with small
pond. Lower area is a small, formal,
colour-themed garden, informally
planted with many unusual plants.
Many spring bulbs and new alpine
house.
&. ⊕ ☕

109 WALDRONS
Brook SO43 7HE. Major & Mrs J
Robinson. *4m N of Lyndhurst. On
B3079 1m W from J1 M27. 1st house
L past Green Dragon PH & directly opp
Bell PH.* Home-made teas.

Adm £2.50, chd free. Sun 27, Mon
28 May (2-5).
Secluded 1-acre garden on the edge
of the New Forest containing shrubs,
herbaceous and rose beds, and a
raised gravel garden. A variety of
cottage plants cover the arbour, trellis
and arches. Small kitchen and herb
garden with Victorian-style
greenhouse. Conservatory open for
teas and ample seating in the garden
to relax and enjoy the atmosphere and
views.
&. ⅍ ⊕ ☕

110 WEIR HOUSE
Abbotstone Road, Alresford
SO24 9DG. Mr & Mrs G Hollingbery,
01962 736493, george@gmeh.com.
*½ m N of Alresford. From Alresford
down Broad St (B3046) past Globe
PH. Take 1st L, signed Abbotstone.
Park in signed field.* Light refreshments
& teas (not 15 Apr or 16 Sept). **Adm**
£3, chd free. Sun 15 Apr; Sat 19,
Sun 20 May; Suns 24 June; 16 Sept
(2-5). **Visitors also welcome by appt.**
Spectacular riverside garden.
Contemporary vegetable and cut
flower garden incorporating over 100
different crops, surprising uses for
scaffolding and painters' ladders and
sculpture by Mark Merer. Children will
enjoy the animals and can also use the
playground at their own risk. Rose
garden and pool area may be under
reconstruction. Featured in 'The
English Garden'. Garden mostly
accessible but some small obstacles
for wheelchair users. Much open
water, children must be supervised at
all times.
&. ⊕ ☕

111 WEST SILCHESTER HALL
Silchester RG7 2LX. Mrs Jenny
Jowett, 0118 970 0278. *7m N of
Basingstoke. 7m S of Reading, off
A340 (signed from centre of village).*
Home-made teas. **Adm** £3, chd free.
Sun 27, Mon 28 May; Suns 1, 29
July (2-5.30). **Visitors also welcome
by appt, groups only, coaches
permitted.**
1½ acres, plantsman artist's garden
with interest over a long period. Good
herbaceous borders, rose and shrub
borders, rhododendrons and many
acid-loving plants. Pond and bog
garden, kitchen garden, interesting
display of half hardies. Studio open
with exhibition of paintings and cards
by owners.
&. ⅍ ⊕ ☕

112 WHEATLEY HOUSE
between Binsted and Kingsley
GU35 9PA. Mr & Mrs Michael
Adlington, 01420 23113,
mikeadlington36@tiscali.co.uk. *4m E
of Alton, 5m SW of Farnham. From
Alton follow signs to Holybourne &
Binsted. At end of Binsted turn R
signed Wheatley. ¾ m down lane on L.
From Farnham/Bordon on A325 take
turn signed Binsted at Buckshorn Oak.
1½ m turn L signed Wheatley.* Home-
made teas. **Sat 18, Sun 19 Aug (1.30-5.30). Visitors
also welcome by appt.**
Magnificent setting with panoramic
views over fields and forests. Sweeping
mixed borders, shrubberies, roses and
grasses. 1½ acres, designed by artist-
owner. The colours are spectacular!
Craft stalls and specialist nursery in
and around old barn.
&. ⅍ ⊕ ☕

Environmental issues tackled head on with infectious enthusiasm, mulching master class given . . .

113 WHISPERS
Chatter Alley, Dogmersfield
RG27 8SS. Mr & Mrs John Selfe. *3m
W of Fleet. Turn N to Dogmersfield off
A287 Odiham to Farnham rd. Turn L
by Queen's Head PH.* Home-made
teas. **Adm** £3, chd free (share to
Samantha Dickson Research Trust).
Sun 1 July (12-5).
Two-acre garden of wide sweeping
lawns interspersed with large floating
borders of vibrant colour, texture and
form for all-yr display. Wide variety of
plants and trees incl many from the S
hemisphere. Spectacular waterfall
cascading over large slabs of rock
magically disappears below terrace.
Environmental issues tackled head on
with infectious enthusiasm, mulching
master class given. Other features incl
gazebo, bamboo tea house, rockstone
seat, kitchen garden and greenhouse.
⅍ ⊕ ☕

Summerhouse on stilts surrounded by dry garden shaped as the African continent . . .

114 WHITE BARN
Woodend Road, Crow Hill,
Ringwood BH24 3DG. Marilyn &
Barrie Knight, 01425 473527,
bandmknight@btinternet.com. *2m
SE of Ringwood. From Ringwood take
B3347 towards Winkton & Sopley.
After 1m turn L immed after petrol stn
into Moortown Lane, proceed 1m,
Woodend Rd on L.* **Adm £3, chd free.**
Visitors welcome by appt,
individuals and groups are very
welcome. To arrange a visit in May,
June & July, please email or phone
at any time.
Beautiful, well-planned ³/₄-acre garden,
with a large variety of unusual plants,
roses and clematis, is complemented
by lovely views to create a serene
atmosphere. Bird life abounds and you
will not be disappointed.
♿ ⚥ ☕

115 THE WHITE COTTAGE
35 Wellhouse Road, Beech, Alton
GU34 4AQ. Mr & Mrs P Conyers,
01420 89355. *2m N of Alton. Leave
Alton on Basingstoke Rd A339. After*

*approx 1m turn L to Medstead &
Beech. Wellhouse Rd is 2nd on R.
Parking at village hall at bottom of rd,
limited parking at house.* **Adm £2, chd
free. Suns, Mons 1, 2 Apr; 12, 13
Aug (2-5). Visitors also welcome by
appt.**
1-acre chalk garden with wide range of
shrubs and plants; colourful
herbaceous borders and large
collection of hellebores and bulbs.
Greenhouses, conservatory with
exotics and scree bed. Pond now filled
and replaced with pebble area and
fountain for display of sun-loving
plants. Steep drive but access by car
possible. Grass paths.
♿ ⚥ ☕

WILDHAM
See Sussex.

116 WISTERIA COTTAGE
15 Gudge Heath Lane, Fareham
PO15 5AB. Gill & Colin Gittins,
01329 319544. *1m W of Fareham
town centre. From Fareham take A27
direction Southampton. At T-lights
immed after railway stn bridge, turn R
into Gudge Heath Lane. No 15 is
approx 100yds on RH-side (parking for
disabled badge holders only).
Suggested parking, railway stn, 4 mins
walk. Home-made teas.* **Adm £2.50,
chd free. Sat 19, Sun 20 May (10.30-
5). Evening Opening with music
£3.50, wine, Fri 20 Jul (6.30-10).
Visitors also welcome by appt 19
May to 30 Sept for groups of 10+.**
¹/₂-acre garden with decking area
which leads through the wisteria walk
to sun terrace, beach garden and
Japanesque area. Across the Monet-
style bridge are the lower garden and
woodland walk which meanders up

through high pines to a viewing point.
Summerhouse on stilts surrounded by
dry garden shaped as the African
continent. Stream water feature
planned for 2007. Music at Evening
Opening with Solent Sounds Singers
(ladies 4-part harmony singers).
⚥ ☕

117 1 WOGSBARNE COTTAGES
Rotherwick RG27 9BL. Mr R & Miss
S Whistler. *2¹/₂m N of Hook. M3 J5,
M4 J11, A30 or A33 via B3349.* **Adm
£2.50, chd free. Sun 8 July (2-5.30).**
True cottage garden with flowers,
vegetables, ornamental pond and
alpine garden. Vintage motorcycle
display (weather permitting). Some
gravel paths.
♿ ⚥ ⚥ ☕

118 NEW WRENS FARM
Lower Bordean GU32 1ER.
Major & Mrs R A Wilson, 01730
263983. *4m W of Petersfield, 3m E
of W Meon Hut. From A3 take
A272 towards Winchester. After
3m turn R at small Xrds with
bicycle symbol on sign, then
immed R again. Teas & wine.* **Adm
£2.50, chd free. Suns 8, 15 July
(2-6). Visitors also welcome by
appt.**
Plantsman's garden in former
farmyard setting. Mixed and
herbaceous borders. Gravel beds
focus on plants for hot, dry
conditions. Mediterranean-type
terrace with vine-covered pergola
and sun-loving plants. Wine
tasting.
♿ ⚥ ⚥ ☕

Hampshire County Volunteers

County Organiser
and Central West area Patricia Elkington, Little Court, Crawley, Winchester SO21 2PU, 01962 776365, elkslc@tiscali.co.uk

County Treasurer
Fred Fratter, Tanglefoot, Crawley, Winchester SO21 2QB, 01962 776243, fred@tanglefoot-house.demon.co.uk

Assistant County Organisers
Central East Jane Chichester, Cygnet House, Martyr Worthy, Winchester, SO21 1DZ, 01962 779315
    janechichester@hotmail.co.uk
East Sally Macpherson, Stedham House, Droxford, Southampton SO32 3PB, 01489 877006, sally@macp.clara.co.uk
North Cynthia Oldale, Little Coopers, Coopers Hill, Eversley RG27 0QA, 01252 872229
North East Elizabeth Powell, Broadhatch House, Bentley, nr Farnham GU10 5JJ, 01420 23185,
    lizzie.powell@btconnect.com
North West Carol Pratt, Field House, Monxton, Andover SP11 8AS, 01264 710 305, carolacap@yahoo.co.uk
West Christopher Stanford, Oakdene, Sandleheath, Fordingbridge SP6 1TD, 01425 652133
South Barbara Sykes, The Cottage, 16 Lakewood Road, Chandler's Ford SO53 1ES, 02380 254521, barandhugh@aol.com
South West Sybil Warner, Birchwood House, Cadnam, Southampton SO40 2NR, 02380 813400,
    sybilwarnerhome@aol.com

Garden Tours 2007

London & South East

Exclusive visits to private gardens including guided tours by owners during the weeks of Chelsea & Hampton Court Flower Shows

All gardens open for charity
11th successful year

Wednesday 23rd May – South West London gardens

Thursday 24th May – Surrey gardens

Friday 25th May – North London gardens

Tuesday 3rd July – Outer & South London gardens

Wednesday 4th July – Berkshire/Oxfordshire gardens

£75 per person

Tours normally commence between 9.30am and 10.00am and finish late afternoon. Price includes all visits, transport, lunch, wine, tea, coffee and VAT. Full details will be sent on confirmation of booking.

For more details or to book a tour please telephone Penny Snell on 01932 864532 or e-mail: pennysnellflowers@btinternet.com. Alternatively write to Penny Snell (NGS), Moleshill House, The Fairmile, Cobham KT11 1BG, stating the date and tour required and enclosing a sterling cheque made payable to: The National Gardens Scheme. A refund will only be made if the place can be resold. A friend may come in your place.

HEREFORDSHIRE

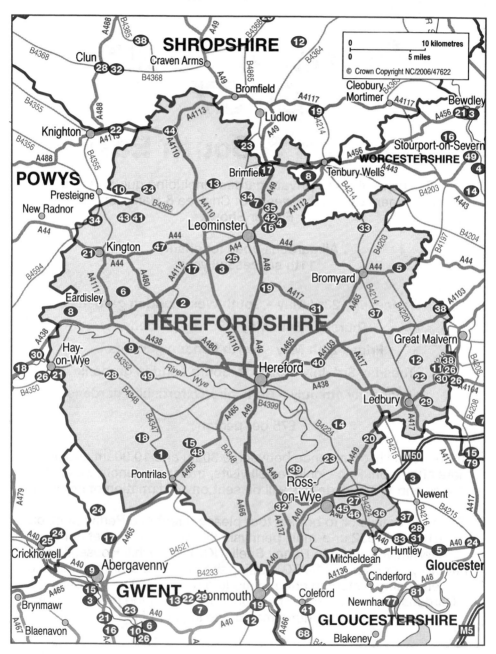

Opening Dates

February
THURSDAY 1
㉕ Ivy Croft

THURSDAY 8
㉕ Ivy Croft

THURSDAY 15
㉕ Ivy Croft

SUNDAY 18
⑮ Galanthus Gallery Gardens

THURSDAY 22
㉕ Ivy Croft

March
SUNDAY 18
㊽ Whitfield

SATURDAY 24
㉝ Moors Meadow

April
SUNDAY 1
㉛ Lower Hope

FRIDAY 6
㊱ The Old Corn Mill
㊷ Stockton Bury Gardens Ltd

MONDAY 9
㊱ The Old Corn Mill

SATURDAY 21
㉑ Hergest Croft Gardens
㉝ Moors Meadow

SUNDAY 22
⑪ Caves Folly Nursery
㉚ Longacre

SATURDAY 28
㉒ Hope End House

SUNDAY 29
③ Aulden Farm
㉒ Hope End House
㉕ Ivy Croft

MONDAY 30
㉒ Hope End House

May
TUESDAY 1
㉒ Hope End House

WEDNESDAY 2
㉒ Hope End House

THURSDAY 3
㉒ Hope End House

FRIDAY 4
② Arrow Cottage Garden
㉒ Hope End House

SATURDAY 5
㉒ Hope End House

SUNDAY 6
⑧ Brilley Court
㉒ Hope End House

MONDAY 7
㉒ Hope End House
㉗ Kingstone Cottages
㊱ The Old Corn Mill

TUESDAY 8
㉒ Hope End House
㉗ Kingstone Cottages

WEDNESDAY 9
㉒ Hope End House
㉗ Kingstone Cottages

THURSDAY 10
㉒ Hope End House
㉗ Kingstone Cottages

FRIDAY 11
㉒ Hope End House
㉗ Kingstone Cottages

SATURDAY 12
⑥ Batch Cottage
㉒ Hope End House
㉗ Kingstone Cottages

SUNDAY 13
⑥ Batch Cottage
㉒ Hope End House
㉗ Kingstone Cottages
㉟ Old Chapel House
㊽ Whitfield

MONDAY 14
㉒ Hope End House
㉗ Kingstone Cottages

TUESDAY 15
⑱ The Griggs
㉗ Kingstone Cottages

WEDNESDAY 16
㉗ Kingstone Cottages
㉙ The Long Barn

THURSDAY 17
㉗ Kingstone Cottages
㉙ The Long Barn

FRIDAY 18
㉗ Kingstone Cottages
㉙ The Long Barn

SATURDAY 19
㉗ Kingstone Cottages
㉝ Moors Meadow

SUNDAY 20
⑰ The Great House
㉗ Kingstone Cottages
㉛ Lower Hope
㊼ Westonbury Mill Water Garden

MONDAY 21
㉗ Kingstone Cottages

TUESDAY 22
⑱ The Griggs

SUNDAY 6
㉗ Kingstone Cottages

WEDNESDAY 23
⑦ Berrington Hall (Evening)
㉗ Kingstone Cottages
㉙ The Long Barn

THURSDAY 24
㉗ Kingstone Cottages
㉙ The Long Barn

FRIDAY 25
㉗ Kingstone Cottages
㉙ The Long Barn
㊱ The Old Corn Mill

SATURDAY 26
㉗ Kingstone Cottages

SUNDAY 27
③ Aulden Farm
⑪ Caves Folly Nursery
㉕ Ivy Croft
㉗ Kingstone Cottages
㉚ Longacre
㉞ The Nest
㊺ Weston Hall

MONDAY 28
㉗ Kingstone Cottages
㉞ The Nest
㊱ The Old Corn Mill

TUESDAY 29
⑱ The Griggs
㉗ Kingstone Cottages

WEDNESDAY 30
⑩ Bryan's Ground
㉗ Kingstone Cottages
㉙ The Long Barn

THURSDAY 31
㉗ Kingstone Cottages
㉙ The Long Barn

June
FRIDAY 1
㉗ Kingstone Cottages
㉙ The Long Barn

SATURDAY 2
② Arrow Cottage Garden
⑥ Batch Cottage
⑱ The Griggs
㉗ Kingstone Cottages
㉞ The Nest

SUNDAY 3
⑥ Batch Cottage
㉓ How Caple Court
㉖ Kilima Lodge
㉗ Kingstone Cottages
㉞ The Nest
㊲ The Orchards

MONDAY 4
㉗ Kingstone Cottages

TUESDAY 5
⑱ The Griggs
㉗ Kingstone Cottages

WEDNESDAY 6
⑲ Hampton Court
㉗ Kingstone Cottages
㉙ The Long Barn

THURSDAY 7
㉗ Kingstone Cottages
㉙ The Long Barn

FRIDAY 8
㉗ Kingstone Cottages
㉙ The Long Barn

SATURDAY 9
㉗ Kingstone Cottages

SUNDAY 10
⑤ The Bannut
㉗ Kingstone Cottages
㉟ Old Chapel House
㊵ Shucknall Court

MONDAY 11
㉗ Kingstone Cottages

TUESDAY 12
⑱ The Griggs
㉗ Kingstone Cottages

WEDNESDAY 13
㉗ Kingstone Cottages
㉙ The Long Barn

THURSDAY 14
㉗ Kingstone Cottages
㉙ The Long Barn

FRIDAY 15
⑬ Croft Castle
㉗ Kingstone Cottages
㉙ The Long Barn

SATURDAY 16
㉗ Kingstone Cottages
㉜ Michaelchurch Court
㊴ Shieldbrook

SUNDAY 17
⑮ Galanthus Gallery Gardens
㉔ Ivy Cottage
㉗ Kingstone Cottages
㉜ Michaelchurch Court
㊲ The Orchards
㊴ Shieldbrook
㊸ Upper Tan House

MONDAY 18
㉔ Ivy Cottage
㉗ Kingstone Cottages

TUESDAY 19
⑱ The Griggs
㉗ Kingstone Cottages

WEDNESDAY 20
㉗ Kingstone Cottages
㉙ The Long Barn

THURSDAY 21
㉗ Kingstone Cottages
㉙ The Long Barn

FRIDAY 22
⑳ Hellens
㉗ Kingstone Cottages
㉙ The Long Barn

SATURDAY 23
⑳ Hellens
㉗ Kingstone Cottages
㉝ Moors Meadow

SUNDAY 24
④ Bachefield House
⑪ Caves Folly Nursery
⑫ Coddington Vineyard
⑭ Croose Farm
㉗ Kingstone Cottages
㉚ Longacre

MONDAY 25
㉗ Kingstone Cottages

TUESDAY 26
⑱ The Griggs
㉗ Kingstone Cottages

WEDNESDAY 27
㉗ Kingstone Cottages
㉙ The Long Barn

THURSDAY 28
㉗ Kingstone Cottages
㉙ The Long Barn

FRIDAY 29
㉗ Kingstone Cottages
㉙ The Long Barn

SATURDAY 30
㉗ Kingstone Cottages

July

SUNDAY 1
③ Aulden Farm
⑭ Croose Farm
㉕ Ivy Croft
㉗ Kingstone Cottages
㊲ The Orchards
㊶ Staunton Park

MONDAY 2
㉗ Kingstone Cottages

TUESDAY 3
⑱ The Griggs
㉗ Kingstone Cottages

WEDNESDAY 4
㉗ Kingstone Cottages
㉙ The Long Barn

THURSDAY 5
㉗ Kingstone Cottages
㉙ The Long Barn

FRIDAY 6
㉗ Kingstone Cottages
㉙ The Long Barn

SATURDAY 7
⑱ The Griggs

SUNDAY 8
⑨ Brobury House Gardens
㉛ Lower Hope

TUESDAY 10
⑱ The Griggs

WEDNESDAY 11
㉙ The Long Barn

THURSDAY 12
㉙ The Long Barn

FRIDAY 13
㉙ The Long Barn

SUNDAY 15
⑤ The Bannut
⑮ Galanthus Gallery Gardens
㊲ The Orchards
㊹ Walford Gardens

TUESDAY 17
⑱ The Griggs

WEDNESDAY 18
㉙ The Long Barn

THURSDAY 19
㉙ The Long Barn

FRIDAY 20
㉙ The Long Barn

SUNDAY 22
㊾ The Wiggly Garden

TUESDAY 24
⑱ The Griggs

WEDNESDAY 25
㉙ The Long Barn

THURSDAY 26
㉙ The Long Barn

FRIDAY 27
㉙ The Long Barn

SATURDAY 28
㉝ Moors Meadow

SUNDAY 29
㊲ The Orchards
㊾ The Wiggly Garden

TUESDAY 31
⑱ The Griggs

August

WEDNESDAY 1
㉙ The Long Barn
㊳ The Picton Garden

THURSDAY 2
㉙ The Long Barn
㊳ The Picton Garden

FRIDAY 3
㉙ The Long Barn
㊳ The Picton Garden

SATURDAY 4
㊳ The Picton Garden

SUNDAY 5
⑪ Caves Folly Nursery

30 Longacre
38 The Picton Garden

WEDNESDAY 8
29 The Long Barn
38 The Picton Garden

THURSDAY 9
29 The Long Barn
38 The Picton Garden

FRIDAY 10
29 The Long Barn
38 The Picton Garden

SATURDAY 11
38 The Picton Garden

SUNDAY 12
4 Bachefield House
37 The Orchards
38 The Picton Garden

WEDNESDAY 15
29 The Long Barn
38 The Picton Garden

THURSDAY 16
29 The Long Barn
38 The Picton Garden

FRIDAY 17
29 The Long Barn
38 The Picton Garden

SATURDAY 18
33 Moors Meadow
38 The Picton Garden

SUNDAY 19
5 The Bannut
38 The Picton Garden

WEDNESDAY 22
29 The Long Barn
38 The Picton Garden

THURSDAY 23
29 The Long Barn
38 The Picton Garden

FRIDAY 24
29 The Long Barn
38 The Picton Garden

SATURDAY 25
38 The Picton Garden

SUNDAY 26
3 Aulden Farm
25 Ivy Croft
37 The Orchards
38 The Picton Garden

MONDAY 27
38 The Picton Garden

TUESDAY 28
38 The Picton Garden

WEDNESDAY 29
29 The Long Barn
38 The Picton Garden

THURSDAY 30
29 The Long Barn

38 The Picton Garden

FRIDAY 31
29 The Long Barn
38 The Picton Garden

September

SATURDAY 1
38 The Picton Garden

SUNDAY 2
38 The Picton Garden

MONDAY 3
38 The Picton Garden

TUESDAY 4
38 The Picton Garden

WEDNESDAY 5
29 The Long Barn
38 The Picton Garden

THURSDAY 6
29 The Long Barn
38 The Picton Garden

FRIDAY 7
29 The Long Barn
38 The Picton Garden

SATURDAY 8
38 The Picton Garden

SUNDAY 9
38 The Picton Garden

MONDAY 10
38 The Picton Garden

TUESDAY 11
38 The Picton Garden

WEDNESDAY 12
29 The Long Barn
38 The Picton Garden

THURSDAY 13
29 The Long Barn
38 The Picton Garden

FRIDAY 14
29 The Long Barn
38 The Picton Garden
42 Stockton Bury Gardens Ltd

SATURDAY 15
21 Hergest Croft Gardens
38 The Picton Garden

SUNDAY 16
25 Ivy Croft
38 The Picton Garden

MONDAY 17
38 The Picton Garden

TUESDAY 18
38 The Picton Garden

WEDNESDAY 19
38 The Picton Garden

THURSDAY 20
38 The Picton Garden

FRIDAY 21
38 The Picton Garden

SATURDAY 22
38 The Picton Garden

SUNDAY 23
38 The Picton Garden

MONDAY 24
38 The Picton Garden

TUESDAY 25
38 The Picton Garden

WEDNESDAY 26
38 The Picton Garden

THURSDAY 27
38 The Picton Garden

FRIDAY 28
38 The Picton Garden

SATURDAY 29
38 The Picton Garden

SUNDAY 30
31 Lower Hope
38 The Picton Garden

October

MONDAY 1
38 The Picton Garden

TUESDAY 2
38 The Picton Garden

WEDNESDAY 3
38 The Picton Garden

THURSDAY 4
38 The Picton Garden

FRIDAY 5
38 The Picton Garden

SATURDAY 6
38 The Picton Garden

SUNDAY 7
9 Brobury House Gardens
38 The Picton Garden

MONDAY 8
38 The Picton Garden

TUESDAY 9
38 The Picton Garden

WEDNESDAY 10
38 The Picton Garden

THURSDAY 11
38 The Picton Garden

FRIDAY 12
38 The Picton Garden

SATURDAY 13
38 The Picton Garden

SUNDAY 14
38 The Picton Garden

SUNDAY 21
30 Longacre

February 2008

THURSDAY 7
㉕ Ivy Croft

THURSDAY 14
㉕ Ivy Croft

THURSDAY 21
㉕ Ivy Croft

THURSDAY 28
㉕ Ivy Croft

Private gardens opening regularly for the NGS

㉗ Kingstone Cottages
㉙ The Long Barn
㊳ The Picton Garden

Gardens open to the public

❶ Abbey Dore Court Garden
❸ Aulden Farm
❺ The Bannut
❼ Berrington Hall
❾ Brobury House Gardens
❿ Bryan's Ground
⓭ Croft Castle
⓯ Galanthus Gallery Gardens
⓳ Hampton Court
⓴ Hellens
㉑ Hergest Croft Gardens
㉓ How Caple Court
㉕ Ivy Croft
㉝ Moors Meadow
㊸ Staunton Park
㊷ Stockton Bury Gardens Ltd
㊸ Westonbury Mill Water Garden
㊹ The Wiggly Garden

By appointment only

⓰ Grantsfield
㉘ Little Llanavon
㊻ Weston Mews

The Gardens

❶ ♦ ABBEY DORE COURT GARDEN
Abbey Dore HR2 0AD. Mrs Charis Ward, 01981 240419, www.abbeydorecourt.co.uk. *11m SW of Hereford. From A465 midway Hereford-Abergavenny turn W, signed Abbey Dore, then 2½m.* **Adm £3.50, chd £1. Tues, Thurs, Sats, Suns & Bank Hol Mons 31 Mar to 30 Sept 11-5.30.**
Peaceful 6-acre garden comprising 6 widely differing areas. A field, now a garden, with trees, shrubs, borders and gazebo. The long purple, gold and

silver borders leading to the riverside walk and wild garden. A bridge across the R Dore into the meadow with interesting trees. Cottage type garden round the house and walled garden with formal arches, paths and borders, all full of interesting shrubs and herbaceous perennials, especially hellebores, peonies, astrantia and clematis.
    ᕷ ✕ ⊛

❷ ARROW COTTAGE GARDEN
Ledgemoor, nr Weobley HR4 8RN. David & Janet Martin, 01344 622181, www.arrowcottagegarden.co.uk. *8m SE of Kington. From Weobley take unclassified rd direction Wormsley (Kings Pyon-Canon Pyon), after 1m, turn L signed Ledgemoor. 2nd R (no through rd). 1st house on L. Park in field before the cottage.* **Adm £3.50, chd £1. Fri 4 May (11-4); Sat 2 June (1-4).**
Set amidst an idyllic landscape in rural countryside, this romantic 2-acre garden combines formal design, follies, water features and topiary with exuberant and imaginative planting. The 23 separate rooms each stand alone, whilst combining to make a truly fascinating, cohesive garden.
    ✕ ⊛ ⊨ ☕

❸ ♦ AULDEN FARM
Aulden, Leominster HR6 0JT. Alun & Jill Whitehead, 01568 720129, www.auldenfarm.co.uk. *4m SW of Leominster. From Leominster take Ivington/Upper Hill Rd. ³⁄₄m after Ivington Church, turn R (signed Aulden), garden 1m on R. From A4110 signed Ivington, take 2nd R (approx ³⁄₄m), garden ³⁄₄m on L.* Teas at Ivy Croft on NGS days only. **Adm £2.50, chd free. Tues & Thurs Apr to Aug, Thurs Mar & Sept (10-5). For NGS: Suns 29 Apr; 27 May. Combined with Ivy Croft adm £4, chd free, 1 Jul, 26 Aug (2-5.30).**
Informally planted country garden and nursery surrounding old farmhouse. Many different aspects to enjoy, all in a garden of 2 acres. Numerous iris incl ditch containing ensatas and natural pond surrounded by sibiricas. Hemerocallis also strongly represented. Garden started from scratch in 1997 and still evolving. Home-made ice-cream NGS days only.
    ᕷ ✕ ⊛ ☕

Stumpery, woodland walk and wooden sculptures . . .

❹ NEW BACHEFIELD HOUSE
Kimbolton HR6 0EP. Jim & Rowena Gale. *3m E of Leominster. Take A4112 off A49 (signed Leysters), after 10yds 1st R (signed Stretford/Hammish). 1st L to Grantsfield over Xrds (signed Bache), continue for approx 1m garden on R past rd to Gorsty Hill.* Home-made teas. **Adm £3, chd free. Suns 24 June; 12 Aug (2-5.30).**
Charming traditional ²⁄₃-acre cottage garden on hill slope, designed for yr-round interest. Pond, summerhouse with fine views, mixed borders, emphasis on old roses, hemerocallis, hardy geraniums, cyclamens and range of unusual plants. Collection of old-fashioned pinks.
    ✕ ⊛ ☕

BALDWINS
See Gloucestershire North & Central.

❺ ♦ THE BANNUT
Bringsty WR6 5TA. Daphne & Maurice Everett, 01885 482206, www.bannut.co.uk. *2½m E of Bromyard. On A44 Worcester Rd, ½m E of entrance to National Trust, Brockhampton.* Light lunches & teas from 12.30. **Adm £3, chd £1.50. Weds, Sats, Suns, Bank Hols 6 Apr to 30 Sept. For NGS: Suns 10 June; 15 July; 19 Aug (12.30-5).**
2½ acres of formal and informal gardens, with much to enjoy throughout the seasons and lovely views to the Malvern Hills. Manicured hedges divide colourful garden rooms, which incl a yellow and white garden, romantic arbour garden, secret garden and unusual knot garden. Spectacular heather gardens, woodland garden, many unusual and interesting trees and shrubs.
    ᕷ ⊛ ☕

❻ BATCH COTTAGE
Almeley HR3 6PT. Jeremy & Elizabeth Russell, 01544 327469. *16m NW of Hereford. 2m off A438-A4111 to Kington, turn R at Eardisley.* Cream teas. **Adm £3, chd free. Sats, Suns 12, 13 May; 2, 3 June (2-5.30). Visitors also welcome by appt.**

Maturing conservation-oriented garden of some 2½ acres with streams and large pond, set in a natural valley, surrounded by woodland and orchard. Over 360 labelled trees and shrubs, mixed borders, fern and bog beds, wild flower bank, stumpery, woodland walk and wooden sculptures. Steep slope (optional), unfenced pond.

 ♿ ⚓ ✿ ☕

7 ◆ **BERRINGTON HALL**
Leominster HR8 2HB. The National Trust, 01568 615721, berrington.hall@nationaltrust.org.uk. 3m N of Leominster. On A49, signed. Buses: Midland Red (W) 92, 292 alight Luston 2m. **Adm £4.20, chd £2.10.** Open 3 to 16 Mar (weekends only); Sats to Weds 17 Mar to 1 Nov (house 1-5 last adm 4.30) (gdn 11-5). For NGS: **Evening Opening** Wed 23 May (7-9).
Extensive views over Capability Brown park; formal garden; wall plants, unusual trees, camellia collection, herbaceous plants, wisteria. Woodland walk, rhododendrons, walled garden with historic apple collection. Gravel paths.

♿ ⚓ ✿ ☕

3-acre country garden, set in middle of lovely Woolhope dome . . .

BIRTSMORTON COURT
See Worcestershire.

8 ◆ **BRILLEY COURT**
Whitney-on-Wye HR3 6JF. Mr & Mrs David Bulmer, 01497 831467. 6m NE of Hay-on-Wye. 5m SW of Kington. 1½m off A438 Hereford to Brecon rd signed to Brilley. Cream teas. **Adm £3, chd free, concessions £2.50.** Sun 6 May (2-6). Visitors also welcome by appt, coaches permitted & groups.
3 acre garden, walled, ornamental kitchen garden. Tulip collection, herbaceous borders. 7 acre wild valley stream garden.

♿ ☕

9 ◆ **BROBURY HOUSE GARDENS**
Brobury by Bredwardine HR3 6BS. Keith & Pru Cartwright, 01981 500229, www.broburyhouse.co.uk. 10m W of Hereford. S off A438 signed Bredwardine & Brobury. Garden 1m L before bridge. **Adm £3, chd £1.** Open throughout the yr 10 til dusk. For NGS: Suns 8 July; 7 Oct (10-5).
5 acres of gardens, set on the banks of an exquisitely beautiful section of the R Wye, offer the visitor a delightful combination of Victorian terraces with mature specimen trees, inspiring water features, architectural planting and woodland areas. Redesign and development is ongoing. Bring a picnic, your paint brushes, binoculars and linger awhile. Wheelchair users, strong able bodied assistant advisable.

♿ ⊨ ☕

10 ◆ **BRYAN'S GROUND**
Letchmoor Lane, nr Stapleton, Presteigne LD8 2LP. David Wheeler & Simon Dorrell, 01544 260001, www.bryansground.co.uk. 12m NW of Leominster. Between Kinsham & Stapleton. At Mortimers Cross take B4362 signed Presteigne. At Combe, follow signs. **Adm £5, chd £1, concessions £4.** Suns, Mons 6 May to 9 July. For NGS: Wed 30 May (2-5).
Romantic Edwardian Arts and Crafts 8-acre garden. Yew and box topiary, parterres, sunk garden, formal herb garden, partly-walled kitchen garden. Colour-themed flower and shrub borders with 'Sulking House'. Heritage apple orchard, formal pools, belvedere, lighthouse, dovecote and Edwardian greenhouse. Arboretum. Home of Hortus, The International Garden Journal. Featured in 'Country Life' & 'The Oldie'.

♿ ⚓ ✿ ☕

11 ◆ **CAVES FOLLY NURSERY**
Evendine Lane, Colwall WR13 6DY. Wil Leaper & Bridget Evans, 01684 540631, www.cavesfolly.com. 1¼m NE of Ledbury. B4218. Between Malvern & Ledbury. Evendine Lane, off Colwall Green. Car parking at Caves Folly. Home-made teas. Combined adm with **Longacre** £3, chd free. Suns 22 Apr; 27 May; 24 June; 5 Aug (2-5). Visitors also welcome by appt, June to Aug only, up to 50, coaches welcome. Organic teas, lunches etc available for parties and talks on organic gardening.
Organic nursery established 21yrs

specialising in alpines, herbaceous perennials and grasses, some unusual. All plants grown peat-free and organically. Herbaceous borders, solar powered water features and display gardens. Meadow walk with pond, ducks and 'willow dome'. Grass and gravel paths.

♿ ⚓ ✿ ☕

12 **CODDINGTON VINEYARD**
Coddington HR8 1JJ. Denis & Ann Savage. 4m NE of Ledbury. From Ledbury to Malvern rd A449, follow brown signs to Coddington Vineyard. Home-made teas. **Adm £3, chd free.** Sun 24 June (2-6).
5 acres incl 2-acre vineyard, listed farmhouse, threshing barn and cider mill. Garden with terraces,wild flower meadow, woodland with tree ferns, pond and stream. Unusual perennials, trees and shrubs. Winery on view. Wine tasting incl.

♿ ✿ ☕

13 ◆ **CROFT CASTLE**
Leominster HR6 9PW. The National Trust, 01568 780246, croftcastle@nationaltrust.org.uk. 5m NW of Leominster. On B4362 (off B4361, Leominster to Ludlow rd). **Adm £4, chd £2.** Weds to Suns 1 Apr to 30 Sept. For NGS: Fri 15 June (12-5).
Large garden; borders; walled garden; landscaped park and walks in Fishpool Valley; fine old avenues.

♿ ⚓ ✿ ☕

14 **CROOSE FARM**
Woolhope HR1 4RD. Mr & Mrs R Malim. 5m N of Ross-on-Wye. Woolhope is E of the B4224 halfway between Ross-on-Wye & Hereford. From centre of village take rd opp church signed Sollars Hope & The Hyde. Garden is ¾m on L. Home-made teas. **Adm £3, chd free.** Suns 24 June; 1 July (1-6).
3-acre country garden, set in middle of lovely Woolhope dome, created from original farmyard in 1987. Stocked with a great variety of shrubs, trees, herbaceous and roses and wild flower meadow.

♿ ✿ ☕

15 ◆ **GALANTHUS GALLERY GARDENS**
Wormbridge HR2 9DH. Mr & Mrs D Kellett, 01981 570506, www.galanthusgallery.com. 8m SW of Hereford. On the A465 towards Abergavenny. Galanthus Gallery signed

Wild flower meadows, wildlife pond and large productive kitchen garden. A garden to lose oneself in . . .

immed off rd in centre of Wormbridge. **Adm £3, chd free. For NGS: Suns 18 Feb; 17 June; 15 July (10.30-4.30).** 2½-acre garden with wonderful views to the Black Mountains, next to contemporary art gallery. Walled garden with magnolia, acers and herbaceous borders, leading to sloped garden with rill. Thousands of snowdrops in drifts are a particular feature in early spring. Duck pond, magnificent copper beeches and swamp cypresses. Cafe with sunny courtyard provides home-made light lunches, teas and irresistible cakes (closed Weds).

❀ ☕

⑯ GRANTSFIELD
nr Kimbolton HR6 0ET. Colonel & Mrs J G T Polley, 01568 613338. *3m NE of Leominster. A49 N from Leominster, A4112 turn R & follow signs. No parking for coaches - drop & collect visitors in village; (minibus acceptable). A44 W to Leominster. Turn R at Drum Xrds (notice up).* **Adm £3, chd free. Visitors welcome by appt, 1 Apr to 30 Sept, anytime.** Contrasting styles in gardens of old stone farmhouse; wide variety of unusual plants, trees and shrubs, old roses, climbers, herbaceous borders, superb views. 1½-acre orchard and kitchen garden with flowering and specimen trees and shrubs. Spring bulbs.

 ❀

⑰ THE GREAT HOUSE
Dilwyn HR4 8HX. Tom & Jane Hawksley, 01544 318007, www.thegreathouse-dilwyn.co.uk. *7m W of Leominster. A44 from Leominster joining A4112 (signed Brecon). Turn L into Dilwyn village. House on RH-side opp village green.* Home-made teas. **Adm £3, chd free. Sun 20 May (2-5). Visitors also welcome by appt.** 1½-acre all-yr garden, designed and created by owners over the last 9yrs. Spring bulbs, traditional rose gardens, yew and beech hedging, raised knot garden, decorative stone and brickwork. 40ft reflecting pool and pleached hornbeams lining the drive all add interest to this country garden which is fronted by wonderful C18 wrought iron gates.

🍴 ❀ ⊫ ☕

⑱ THE GRIGGS
Newton St Margarets HR2 0QY. John & Bridget Biggs, 01981 510629, www.artaura.co.uk/thegriggs. *14m SW of Hereford. Take B4348 to Vowchurch, turn L, signed Michaelchurch Escley, continue for 2½m, then follow NGS signs. Signs will be posted locally for those approaching from Longtown & Ewyas Harold.* Home-made teas. **Adm £3, chd free (share to Community Action, Nepal). Tues 15 May to 31 July (2-5); Sats 2 June; 7 July (2-6). Visitors also welcome by appt.** Located in a remote scenic setting between the Golden Valley and the Black Mountains, a floriferous country garden of 1½ acres, managed organically and incl extensive mixed borders, wild flower meadows, wildlife pond and large productive kitchen garden. A garden to lose oneself in. Some gravel paths.

& 🍴 ☕

⑲ ◆ HAMPTON COURT
Hope-under-Dinmore HR6 0PN, 01568 797777, office@hamptoncourt.org.uk. *5m S of Leominster. On A417, 500yds from junction with A49.* **Adm £5, chd £3, concessions £4.50. Tues to Thurs, weekends & Bank Hols 6 Apr to 28 Oct. For NGS: Wed 6 June (11-5).** Exciting mix of new and old gardens within the grounds of C15 castle. Work started to rebuild gardens in 1996. Newly restored formal walled garden, herbaceous borders, Dutch garden, sunken garden with waterfall and thatched hermitage and organic kitchen garden. Featured in 'House & Garden'.

& 🍴 ❀ ☕

⑳ ◆ HELLENS
Much Marcle HR8 2LY. Pennington Mellor Munthe Charity Trust, 01531 660504, www.hellensmanor.com. *6m from Ross-on-Wye. 4m SW of Ledbury, off A449.* **Adm £2.50, chd free. For NGS: Fri 22 (2-5), Sat 23 June (2-7.30). Wine on terrace 6pm.** Interesting manor house (ground floor open). Gardens are being gently redeveloped to reflect the C17 ambience of the house. They incorporate a rare octagonal dovecote, two knot gardens and young yew labyrinth. Lawns, herb and kitchen gardens; short woodland and pond walk.

& ❀ ☕

㉑ ◆ HERGEST CROFT GARDENS
Kington HR5 3EG. Mr W L Banks, 01544 230160, www.hergest.co.uk. *½m W of Kington. ½m off A44 on Welsh side of Kington. Turn L at Rhayader end of bypass; then 1st R; gardens ¼m on L.* **Adm £5.50, chd free. Weekends in Mar; daily 1 Apr to 28 Oct. For NGS: Sats 21 Apr; 15 Sept (12-5.30).** 4 gardens for all seasons, from spring bulbs to spectacular autumn colour, incl spring and summer borders, roses, brilliant azaleas and old-fashioned kitchen garden growing unusual vegetables. Brightly coloured rhododendrons 30ft high grow in Park Wood. Over 60 champion trees in one of the finest collections of trees and shrubs in the British Isles. Some areas not accessible to wheelchairs.

& ❀ **NCCPG** ☕

㉒ HOPE END HOUSE
Raycombe Lane, Hope End HR8 1JQ. Mrs P J Maiden, 01531 635890. *2m NE of Ledbury. From Ledbury, take Bromyard rd N. ⅓m from stn turn R signed Wellington Heath & Hope End, uphill for 1½m to T-junction, turn R. Continue for ½m. Turn into Raycombe Lane, entrance from this lane on R. Signed after 1m. Parking in woodland & lane.* **Adm £2.50, chd free. Daily Sat 28 Apr to Mon 14 May (10-4). Visitors also welcome by appt, May & June.** Woodland walk through 30 acres parkland (not garden), Oyster Hill originally laid out in the early C19. 6-acre bluebell walk through Cockshute, steep slopes in woodland. Perfect for picnics.

⊫

㉓ ◆ HOW CAPLE COURT
How Caple HR1 4SX. Mr & Mrs
Roger Lee, 01989 740626,
www.howcaplecourt.com. *5m N of
Ross-on-Wye. 10m S of Hereford. On
B4224; turn R at How Caple Xrds,
garden 400yds on L.* **Adm £3, chd
free. Daily Mon 12 Mar to Sun 14
Oct. For NGS: Sun 3 June (10-5).**
11 acres; Edwardian gardens set high
above R Wye. These important Arts
and Crafts gardens, in their heyday
immaculately formal, have with the
passing of time relaxed, into an
intensely romantic semi-wilderness,
redolant of a lost 'Golden Afternoon'.
A magnificently atmospheric Italianate
water garden can be discovered
almost hidden in surrounding
woodland. Medieval church in
grounds.

㉔ IVY COTTAGE
Kinsham LD8 2HN. Jane & Richard
Barton, 01544 267154,
jane@barton3.freeserve.co.uk. *12m
NW of Leominster. From Mortimers
Cross take B4362 towards Presteigne.
Turn R at Combe towards Lingen for
1m.* Easy parking. Teas. **Adm £2.50,
chd free. Sun 17, Mon 18 June (2-6).
Visitors also welcome by appt June
& July only, coaches permitted,
groups 6+.**
Cottage garden developed over 12yrs.
Mixed borders planted for colour, scent
and all-yr interest. Shrub roses,
clematis and wide range of perennials,
some unusual, incl many hardy
geraniums, astrantias, campanulas and
asters. Shade areas, pergolas,
vegetable garden and fruit trees in
1/2-acre setting.

㉕ ◆ IVY CROFT
Ivington Green, Leominster
HR6 0JN. Sue & Roger Norman,
01568 720344,
www.ivycroft.freeserve.co.uk. *3m
SW of Leominster. From Leominster
take Ryelands Rd to Ivington. Turn R at
church, garden 3/4m on R. From
A4110 signed Ivington, garden 13/4m
on L.* **Adm £2.50, chd free. Thurs Apr
to Sept. For NGS: Thurs 1 Feb to 22
Feb (9-4); Sun 16 Sept (2-5.30).
Combined adm £4, chd free with
Aulden Farm Suns 29 Apr; 27 May;
1 July; 26 Aug; (2-5.30). 2008 Thurs
7 Feb to 28 Feb (9-4).**
Garden created since 1997 surrounds
C17 cottage in 4 acres of rich
grassland. Plant lovers' garden

designed for all-yr interest. Raised
beds, mixed herbaceous borders,
trees, alpines, troughs, formal
vegetable garden framed by trained
fruit trees; collections of ferns, willows
and snowdrops.

Meandering paths among shrubs in shady spring garden . . .

㉖ KILIMA LODGE
Evendine Lane, Colwall WR13 6DT.
Mr & Mrs W B Stallard. *Halfway
between Malvern & Ledbury. On A449
Malvern - Ledbury rd, take B4218 to
Colwall. Nr Yew Tree PH take rd signed
Evendine.* Home-made teas. **Adm
£2.50, chd free. Sun 3 June (2-5).**
2-acre garden, which has evolved to
lead the eye to the surrounding views
of the Malverns hills, planted with trees,
shrubs and many unusual plants.
Water feature and interesting paved
area. Facilities for children incl quad
bike and fish feeding. Combines well
with a walk on the Malvern hills.

㉗ KINGSTONE COTTAGES
Weston under Penyard, nr Ross-on-
Wye HR9 7PH. Mr & Mrs M Hughes,
www.hoohouse.plus.com. *2m E of
Ross-on-Wye. A40 Ross to
Gloucester, turn off at Weston Cross
PH to Linton, then 2nd L to Rudhall.*
**Adm £2, chd free. Daily Mon 7 May
to Fri 6 July (10-5).**
Informal 11/2-acre cottage garden
containing National Collection of old
pinks and carnations and other
unusual plants. Terraced beds, ponds,
grotto, summerhouse, lovely views.
Separate parterre garden containing
the collection. Much of the garden
replanted 2004 and being extended
into new areas. Featured in various
press articles & on Gardeners World.

㉘ LITTLE LLANAVON
Dorstone HR3 6AT. John & Jenny
Chippindale, 01981 550984,
john.chippindale@virgin.net. *2m N of
Peterchurch. In the Golden Valley, 15m
W of Hereford on B4348, 1/2m towards
Peterchurch from Dorstone.* **Adm
£2.50, chd free. Visitors welcome by
appt, May to Sept.**
1/2-acre S-facing cottage-style walled
garden in lovely rural location.
Meandering paths among shrubs in
shady spring garden. Hot gravel area
and herbaceous borders closely
planted with select perennials and
grasses, many unusual. Good late
colour. Featured in 'Homes &
Gardens'.

LLOWES COURT
See Powys.

㉙ THE LONG BARN
Eastnor HR8 1EL. Fay & Roger
Oates, www.rogeroates.com. *2m E
of Ledbury. On A438 Ledbury to
Tewkesbury rd. From Ledbury take
Malvern rd & turn R after 11/4m
towards Eastnor-Tewkesbury. Roger
Oates Studio 3/4m along rd, on LH-
side. Situated behind the design studio
of Roger Oates Design Co. Parking in
car park.* **Adm £2.50, chd free (share
to The Gloucester MS Information
Therapy Centre). Every Weds to
Fris, 16 May to 14 Sept (11-5).**
New garden planted over last 10yrs,
made for owners' pleasure. Strong
design structure with mixed, natural
crowded plantings of perennials and
herbaceous plants, selected for
fragrance and texture. Sitting in the
landscape, garden is small, less than
1/3 acre, and enclosed, set by edge of
3-acre orchard. Featured in 'Gardens
Illustrated'.

㉚ LONGACRE
Evendine Lane, Colwall Green
WR13 6DT. Mr D M Pudsey, 01684
540377, davidpudsey@onetel.com.
*3m S of Malvern. Off Colwall Green.
Off B4218. Car parking at Caves Folly
Nursery.* Home-made teas at Caves
Folly (not Oct). **Adm Combined £3,
chd free.** Combined adm £3, chd
free with **Caves Folly Nursery** Suns
22 Apr; 27 May; 24 June; 5 Aug;
Longacre adm £2, chd free only
**Sun 21 Oct (2-5). Visitors also
welcome by appt.**
3-acre garden-cum-arboretum
developed since 1970. Island beds of

trees and shrubs, some underplanted with bulbs and herbaceous perennials, present a sequence of contrasting pictures and views through the seasons. There are no 'rooms' - rather long vistas lead the eye and feet, while the feeling of spaciousness is enhanced by glimpses caught between trunks and through gaps in the planting. Over 50 types of conifer provide the background to maples, rhododendrons, azaleas, dogwoods, eucryphias etc.

 ⟨⟩ ✕ ☕

There are no 'rooms' – rather long vistas lead the eye and feet . . .

㉛ LOWER HOPE
Ullingswick HR1 3JF. Mr & Mrs Clive Richards. 5m S of Bromyard. From Hereford take A465 N to Bromyard. After 6m turn L at Burley Gate on A417 signed Leominster. Approx 2m take 3rd turning on R signed Lower Hope & Pencombe, 1/2m on LH-side. Tea & Cake. Adm £3, chd £1 (share to Hydrosense Appeal). Suns 1 Apr; 20 May; 8 July; 30 Sept (2-5).
5-acre garden facing S and W. Herbaceous borders, rose walks and gardens, laburnum tunnel, Mediterranean garden, bog gardens. Lime tree walk, lake landscaped with wild flowers; streams, ponds. Conservatories and large glasshouse with exotic species orchids, bougainvilleas. Prizewinning herd of pedigree Hereford cattle, flock of pedigree Suffolk sheep.

✕ ⊛ ☕

LOWER HOUSE
See Powys.

㉜ MICHAELCHURCH COURT
St Owens Cross HR2 8LD. Dr & Mrs D J L Smith. 7m N of Ross-on-Wye. From Ross-on-Wye take A49, turn L onto B4521 signed Abergavenny; turn R at Xrds. After 1/4m turn L at 1st opportunity into narrow rd to Michaelchurch Court. From Hereford approx 12m S on A49; approx 1/4m after Harewood End turn R signed Orcop, 1st minor Xrds turn L. At next minor Xrds turn L. Teas. Adm £2.50, chd free. Sat 16, Sun 17 June (2.30-5.30).
C17 farmhouse (not open), in open countryside near Norman church. Approx 3 acres incl large pond, stream with flower border. Old-fashioned roses and herbaceous borders set amongst lawns, one long border backed by high wall covered with climbing roses, honeysuckle. Long pergola covered with roses, honeysuckle, clematis and wisteria leads to sunken garden with

water feature and seating area. Climbing roses and hydrangeas over 20ft high cover house. Arboretum and wild flower meadow planted 2001. Featured in many magazines.

✕ ☕

㉝ ◆ MOORS MEADOW
Collington HR7 4LZ. Ros Bissell, 01885 410318, www.moorsmeadow.co.uk. 4m N of Bromyard. On B4214 turn L up lane, over two cattle grids turn R. Adm £4, chd £1. Fri to Tue Mar to end Sept. For NGS: Sats 24 Mar; 21 Apr; 19 May; 23 June; 28 July; 18 Aug (11-5).
Intriguing 7-acre organic hillside garden overlooking Kyre Valley. Hundreds of varieties of trees and shrubs from around the world, countless spring bulbs, brimming herbaceous beds, grass garden, fernery, water features, herb and kitchen gardens. Many unusual seats, sculptures and abundant wildlife. All plants in the nursery are propagated from the garden. Working blacksmith on site. Featured on BBC TV Midlands Today.

✕ ⊛

㉞ THE NEST
Moreton, Eye HR6 0DP. Sue Evans & Guy Poulton. 3m N of Leominster. A49. L in Ashton. 1m on L signed The Nest Cottage Garden. Home-made teas. Adm £3, chd free. Sun 27, Mon 28 May; Sat 2, Sun 3 June (2-5).
Drive entrance between Stourport-Leominster canal remnant and 3-acre wild flower meadow. 1530s yeoman's timber-framed house (not open). Potager, soft and hard fruits. Rockeries, scree and gravel gardens. Shrubberies and summer garden with water feature. Wet area with primulas. Ferns, 60 varieties. Pond, waterfall and Mediterranean area. Very wildlife friendly. Crafts demonstration 27, 28 May.

 ⟨⟩ ✕ ⊛ ☕

㉟ OLD CHAPEL HOUSE
Kimbolton, Leominster HR6 0HF. Stephen & Penny Usher & Audrey Brown. 2m NE of Leominster. A49 N from Leominster. A4112 into Kimbolton. Garden on R at bottom of hill. From Tenbury Wells S A4112 6m Kimbolton. Park in village hall car park 5mins walk, please follow signs. Disabled parking at garden. Home-made teas. Adm £3, chd free. Suns 13 May; 10 June (2-5).
S-facing 1-acre garden with mill stream and mill race developed into a wildlife garden. Potager and cutting garden for flower arranger. Formal box parterre with old roses and lavender walk. Croquet lawn with gazebo and herbaceous borders. Gravel paths.

 ⟨⟩ ✕ ⊛ ☕

㊱ THE OLD CORN MILL
Aston Crews HR9 7LW. Mrs Jill Hunter, 01989 750059. 5m E of Ross-on-Wye. A40 Ross to Gloucester. Turn L at T-lights at Lea Xrds onto B4222 signed Newent. Garden 1/2m on L. Parking for disabled down drive. Adm £2.50, chd free. Fris, Mons 6 Apr; 7, 25, 28 May (11-5). Visitors also welcome by appt all yr for individuals & small groups, photographers & artists most welcome.
Tranquil garden in wooded valley. Native trees, streams, meadow areas and small orchard, informal flower and shrub beds providing yr-round interest. Picnics welcome. Featured in 'Daily Telegraph' & on BBC Hereford & Worcester.

✕ ⊛ ☕

㊲ THE ORCHARDS
Golden Valley, Bishops Frome, nr Bromyard WR6 5BN. Mr & Mrs Robert Humphries, 01885 490273. 14m E of Hereford. A4103 turn L at bottom of Fromes Hill, through village of Bishops Frome on B4214. Turn R immed after de-regulation signs along narrow track for 250yds. Park in field by garden. Adm £2.50, chd free. Suns 3, 17 June; 1, 15, 29 July; 12, 26 Aug (2-6).
1-acre garden designed in areas on various levels. 15 water features incl Japanese water garden and tea house, Mediterranean area, rose garden with rill, also aviary. Large rose, clematis, fuchsia and dahlia collections. Seating areas on all levels. New projects every yr.

✕ ⊛ ☕

PEN-Y-MAES
See Powys.

38 THE PICTON GARDEN
Old Court Nurseries, Colwall
WR13 6QE. Mr & Mrs Paul Picton,
01684 540416,
www.autumnasters.co.uk. *3m W of
Malvern. On B4218 (Walwyn Rd) N of
Colwall Stone. Turn off A449 from
Ledbury or Malvern.* **Adm £3, chd
free. Weds to Suns 1 Aug to 26 Aug;
Daily Mon 27 Aug to Sun 14 Oct (11-
5). Visitors also welcome by appt,
15 to 28 Oct.**
1½ acres W of Malvern Hills. A myriad
of late summer perennials in Aug. In
Sept and Oct huge, colourful borders
display the NCCPG National Collection
of Michaelmas daisies; backed by
autumn colouring trees and shrubs.
Many unusual plants to be seen.
Featured in 'Daily Telegraph', 'Country
Life', 'Worcestershire Life' & on BBC
Gardeners World & BBC Hereford &
Worcester.
✂ ⊛ NCCPG

THE RED HOUSE
See Gloucestershire North &
Central.

39 SHIELDBROOK
Kings Caple HR1 4UB. Sue & Oliver
Sharp. *7m S of Hereford. Take A49
from Hereford or Ross. Take 1st rd
signed to Hoarwithy (there are 3). Go
past New Harp PH on R, then next R
over R Wye. Up the hill take 2nd R into
Kings Caple, down hill over Xrds then
Shieldbrook ½ m on L.* Home-made
teas. **Adm £3, chd free. Sat 16, Sun
17 June (2-6). Visitors also welcome
by appt.**
1-acre country garden planted for yr-
round interest featuring grasses,
shrubs and perennials. Rose garden
and orchard, healing garden with pond
and rockery. Sculpture garden of local
sculptor's work is of special interest.
Stream runs through the garden and
there are many secret corners. Garden
managed organically. Sculpture
demonstration by local sculptor
Andrew Dodwell. Featured in 'Hereford
Times'. Some gravel.
& ✂ ⚘ ☕

40 SHUCKNALL COURT
Hereford HR1 4BH. Mr & Mrs Henry
Moore, 01432 850230,
cessa.moore@btconnect.com. *5m E
of Hereford. On A4103, signed
(southerly) Weston Beggard.* Cream
teas. **Adm £3, chd free. Sun 10 June
(11-5). Visitors also welcome by**

appt May, depending on the season.
Large collection of species, old-
fashioned and shrub roses. Mixed
borders in old walled farmhouse
garden. Wild garden, small stream
garden, vegetables and fruit. Tree
peonies in late Apr/May by appt only.
Featured in 'Hereford Times'. Gravel
path - help for wheelchairs available.
& ✂ ⚘ ☕

It keeps us busy but badgers and rabbits do not always help . . .

SHUTTIFIELD COTTAGE
See Worcestershire.

41 ♦ STAUNTON PARK
Staunton Green HR6 9LE. Susan
Fode, 01544 388556. *3m N of
Pembridge. From Pembridge (on A44)
take rd signed Presteigne, Shobdon.
After 3m look out for red phone box on
R. Staunton Park is 150yds on L. Do
not go to Staunton-on-Arrow.* **Adm £3,
chd free. Every Thurs 17 May to 30
Aug 11-5.** For NGS: **Sun 1 July (2-
5.30).**
10-acre garden and grounds incl drive
with stately wellingtonias, rose garden,
separate kitchen garden, herbaceous
borders and Victorian rock garden,
lake and lakeside walk. Specimen trees
incl mature monkey puzzle, gigantic
liriodendron, *Davidia involucrata*,
Ginkgo bilobas and several ancient
oaksl. Talk on propagation by Stephen
Lloyd.
& ✂ ⚘ ☕

**42 ♦ STOCKTON BURY
GARDENS LTD**
Kimbolton HR6 0HB. Raymond G
Treasure Esq, 01568 613432. *2m NE
of Leominster. On A49 turn R onto
A4112 Kimbolton rd. Gardens are
300yds on R.* **Adm £4. Weds to
Suns1 Apr to begining Oct.** For
NGS: **Fris 6 Apr; 14 Sept (12-5).**
Superb, sheltered 4-acre garden with a
very long growing season giving colour
and interest all yr. Extensive collection
of plants, many rare and unusual set

amongst medieval buildings, a real
kitchen garden. Pigeon house; tithe
barn; grotto; cider press; pools; ruined
chapel and rill, all surrounded by
unspoilt countryside. Unsuitable for
children. (This is no ordinary garden).
Restaurant (lunches & teas).
& ✂ ⚘ ☕

TAWRYN
See Powys.

43 UPPER TAN HOUSE
Stansbatch HR6 9LJ. Mr & Mrs
James Weymouth, 01544 260574,
www.uppertanhouse.com. *12m W of
Leominster. From Pembridge take A44
to Rhayader. In middle of Pembridge
turn R signed Shobdon & Presteigne.
Stansbatch is 4m on this rd.* Teas.
**Adm £3, chd free. Sun 17 June (2-5).
Visitors also welcome by appt.**
1½-acre, S-facing, informal garden in
beautiful setting. Deep borders sloping
down to lawn and brook. Interesting
collection of herbaceous plants and
shrubs; good late summer colour.
Pond and bog garden. Formal
vegetable garden. Natural wild flower
meadow incl orchids in June. Reed
beds.
✂ ⚘ ☕

**44 NEW WALFORD
GARDENS**
*1m W of Leintwardine. On A4113,
Knighton Rd.* Home-made teas at
Walford House. **Combined adm
£3.50, chd free. Sun 15 July (2-
5.30).**
Walford - small Hamlet, 1m W of
the Roman Settlement of
Bravonium - Leintwardine. With
Brampton Bryan a very pretty
village 1m along A4113.

NEW WALFORD GRANGE
Mr & Mrs G MacFarquhar
4-acre garden a mixture of formal and informal areas - ponds visited by kingfishers and otters, mini arboretum, kitchen garden, orchard and nuttery. Planting designed to please flower arrangers.

NEW WALFORD HOUSE
Mr & Mrs V Richards
1-acre garden with old fruit trees, shrubs, small vegetable plot, secluded sitting area and new formal rose bed. It keeps us busy but badgers and rabbits do not always help.

This year we will be having a series of short informal talks on bees, bugs, worms, composting and a lot more . . .

THE WALLED GARDEN
See Powys.

45 NEW WESTON HALL
Weston-under-Penyard
HR9 7NS. Mr P & Miss L Aldrich-Blake. *1m E of Ross-on-Wye. On A40 towards Gloucester. Parking in field with entrance off lane 1/4m before house.* **Adm £3.50, chd free. Sun 27 May (2-6).**
6 acres surrounding Elizabethan house (not open). Large walled garden with herbaceous borders, vegetables and fruit, overlooked by Millennium folly. Lawns with both mature and recently planted trees, shrubs with many unusual varieties. Ornamental ponds and small lake. Traditional country house garden, but evolving after 4 generations in the family.

46 WESTON MEWS
Weston-under-Penyard HR97NZ.
Ann Rothwell & John Hercock,
01989 563823. *2m E of Ross-on-Wye. Going towards Gloucester on A40, continue approx 100yds past the Weston Cross PH and turn R into grey brick-paved courtyard.* **Adm £3, chd free (share to St Michael's Hospice). Visitors welcome by appt, 26 May to 22 July 11-8. Evening visits welcome. Refreshments available.**
Walled ex-kitchen garden divided by yew and box hedges. Traditional in style and planting with large herbaceous beds and borders at different levels. Broad range of plants incl roses. Enclosed garden with sundial. Large vine house.

47 ♦ WESTONBURY MILL WATER GARDEN
Pembridge HR6 9HZ. Richard Pim,
01544 388650, www.
westonburymillwatergardens.com.
8m W of Leominster. On A44
11/2m W of village of Pembridge, L into signed drive. **Adm £3.50, chd £1. Daily 1 Apr to 30 Sept. For NGS: Sun 20 May (11-5).**
2-acre water mill garden situated amid fields and orchards. Colourful waterside plantings of bog and moisture-loving plants around a tangle of streams and ponds, together with a natural bog garden in the area of the Old Mill pond. Unusual water features incl stone tower with water wheel.

48 WHITFIELD
Wormbridge HR2 9BA. Mr & Mrs Edward Clive, 01981 570202, tboyd@globalnet.co.uk. *8m SW of Hereford. On A465 Hereford to Abergavenny rd.* Home-made teas. **Adm £3, chd free. Suns 18 Mar; 13 May (2-6). Visitors also welcome by appt.**
Parkland, wild flowers, ponds, walled garden, many flowering magnolias (species and hybrids), 1780 ginkgo tree, 11/2m woodland walk with 1851 redwood grove. Picnic parties welcome.

49 ♦ THE WIGGLY GARDEN
Wiggly Wigglers, Blakemere
HR2 9PX. Duchy of Cornwall, 01981 500391, www.wigglywigglers.co.uk. *9m W of Hereford. On B4352, halfway between Hereford and Hay-on-Wye.* **Adm £2.50, chd free. Garden open by prior arrangement 8-5. For NGS: Suns 22, 29 July (2-5).**
The Wiggly Garden: Bringing nature home: Our walled garden is an oasis for wildlife, full of wild flowers, perennials, trees and hedges to attract wildlife. This year we will be having a series of short informal talks on bees, bugs, worms, composting and a lot more.

Herefordshire County Volunteers

County Organiser
Mrs Rosemary Verity, Crowards Mill, Eyton, Leominster HR6 OAD, 01568 615200, crowards@tiscali.co.uk

County Treasurer
Mr Michael Robins, Newsholme, 77 Bridge Street, Ledbury HR8 2AN, 01531 632232

Publicity
Mrs Sue Evans, The Nest, Moreton, Eye, nr Leominster HR6 0DP, 01568 614501, sue@thenest99.freeserve.co.uk

Assistant County Organisers
Lady Curtis, South Parade House, Ledbury HR8 2HB
Dr J A F Evans, 7 St Margaret's Road, Hereford HR1 1TS, 01432 273000, anthonyelizabeth@stmargarets7.fsnet.co.uk
Mrs Nicola Harper, Kymmin Cottage, Hopley's Green, Almeley, Hereford HR3 6QX, 01544 340680
Mrs Gill Mullin, The White House, Lea, Ross-on-Wye HR9 7LQ, 01989 750593, gill@longorchard.plus.com
Mr Graham Spencer, 4 Nightingale Way, Hereford HR1 2NQ, 01432 267744, gramy.spencer@virgin.net

ngs gardens open for charity

While form and foliage
take precedence over
flowers, fruit and football
are important too ...

64a Kings Road, London

HERTFORDSHIRE

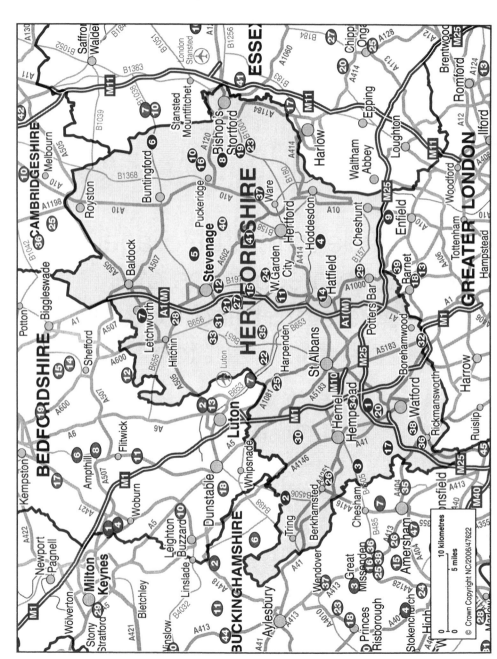

Opening Dates

March

SATURDAY 3
🟡9 Capel Manor Gardens

SUNDAY 4
🟡9 Capel Manor Gardens

April

SUNDAY 1
🟡6 Brent Pelham Gardens

SUNDAY 22
🟡32 St Mary's Croft
🟡33 St Paul's Walden Bury

SUNDAY 29
🟡25 20 Park Avenue South

May

SUNDAY 6
🟡1 The Abbots House
🟡26 Patchwork
🟡30 Ragged Hall

MONDAY 7
🟡20 Hunton Park

SUNDAY 13
🟡6 Brent Pelham Gardens
🟡39 West Lodge Park

SUNDAY 20
🟡10 Cockhamsted
🟡32 St Mary's Croft

SUNDAY 27
🟡17 Great Sarratt Hall
🟡23 Moor Place
🟡29 Queenswood School
🟡40 The White House

MONDAY 28
🟡29 Queenswood School

June

FRIDAY 1
🟡15 The End House (Evening)

SUNDAY 3
🟡2 Ashridge
🟡8 Bromley Hall
🟡15 The End House

FRIDAY 8
🟡37 Thundridge Hill House (Evening)

SATURDAY 9
🟡35 Shaw's Corner (Evening)

SUNDAY 10
🟡4 Bayford House
🟡18 13 Greenhill Park
🟡27 Plummers Farm

SUNDAY 17
🟡12 Ducklings
🟡24 106 Orchard Road
🟡34 Serge Hill Gardens

🟡41 Woodhall Park

WEDNESDAY 20
🟡24 106 Orchard Road

FRIDAY 22
🟡24 106 Orchard Road (Evening)

SUNDAY 24
🟡1 The Abbots House
🟡5 Benington Lordship
🟡13 207 East Barnet Road
🟡22 Mackerye End Gardens

TUESDAY 26
🟡32 St Mary's Croft (Evening)

July

SUNDAY 1
🟡25 20 Park Avenue South
🟡30 Ragged Hall
🟡38 Waterdell House

THURSDAY 5
🟡14 East Garden at Hatfield House

SUNDAY 15
🟡3 The Barn

SUNDAY 22
🟡11 35 Digswell Road
🟡28 The Priory
🟡31 Rustling End Cottage

WEDNESDAY 25
🟡31 Rustling End Cottage

FRIDAY 27
🟡31 Rustling End Cottage (Evening)

SATURDAY 28
🟡16 The Fuchsia Garden

SUNDAY 29
🟡16 The Fuchsia Garden

August

SATURDAY 4
🟡16 The Fuchsia Garden

SUNDAY 5
🟡16 The Fuchsia Garden

FRIDAY 10
🟡7 44 Broadwater Avenue (Evening)

SUNDAY 12
🟡7 44 Broadwater Avenue

SUNDAY 19
🟡26 Patchwork

SUNDAY 26
🟡1 The Abbots House

September

THURSDAY 6
🟡21 Knebworth House Gardens

October

SATURDAY 6
🟡9 Capel Manor Gardens

SUNDAY 7
🟡9 Capel Manor Gardens

SUNDAY 28
🟡39 West Lodge Park

Gardens open to the public

🟡5 Benington Lordship
🟡9 Capel Manor Gardens
🟡14 East Garden at Hatfield House
🟡19 Hopleys
🟡20 Hunton Park
🟡21 Knebworth House Gardens
🟡33 St Paul's Walden Bury
🟡35 Shaw's Corner

By appointment only

🟡36 Stresa

The Gardens

🟡1 **THE ABBOTS HOUSE**
10 High Street, Abbots Langley
WD5 0AR. Peter & Sue Tomson,
01923 264946,
peter.tomson@btinternet.com. *5m
NW of Watford. Exit J20 on M25. Take
A4251 signed Kings Langley. R at 1st
roundabout (Home Park Industrial
Estate). R at T-junction. Follow rd,
under railway bridge and the yellow
signs will become apparent. Free
parking in village car park.* Home-made
teas. **Adm £3.50, chd free (share to
Friends of St Lawrence Church).
Suns 6 May; 24 June; 26 Aug (2-5).
Visitors also welcome by appt, also
groups.**
1³/₄-acre garden with interesting trees,
shrubs, mixed borders, sunken
garden, pond, wild flower meadow,
conservatory. Exotic garden. A garden
of 'rooms' with different styles and
moods. Many half-hardy plants. Plants
propagated from the garden. Some
gravel paths.
 ♿ ✕ ❀ ☕ ☕

Island surrounded
by C14 moat.
Remote, romantic
with extensive
views . . .

2 ASHRIDGE

Berkhamsted HP4 1NS. (Ashridge (Bonar Law Memorial) Trust), www.ashridge.com. 3m N of Berkhamsted. A4251, 1m S of Little Gaddesden. Cream teas. **Adm £3.50, chd /concessions £2. Sun 3 June (2-6).**
The gardens at Ashridge cover 190 acres and form part of the Grade II* Registered Landscape of Ashridge Park. Based on designs by Humphry Repton in 1813 which were modified by Jeffry Wyatville, the gardens are made up of a number of small gardens, as well as a large lawn area leading to avenues of trees affording views out to the old parkland. House not open. Paths lead to many features within the formal gardens, areas of parkland not accessible.

3 THE BARN

Stoney Lane, Bovingdon HP3 0LY. Richard Daynes. 3m SW of Hemel Hempstead. At lower end of Bovingdon High St turn into Church St, Bull PH on corner, car park 60yds on L, short walk to garden. Home-made teas. **Adm £2.50, chd free (share to St Lawrence Church). Sun 15 July (2-6).**
Medium-sized garden around converted agricultural building in 16 acres. Garden divided into rooms; roses along with clematis, honeysuckle, topiary, water features and woodland. Wild flower meadow and pond along with small orchard.

4 BAYFORD HOUSE

Bayford SG13 8PX. Mr & Mrs Robert Wilson Stephens. 3m S of Hertford. Off B158 between Hatfield & Hertford. S end of Bayford Village. Home-made teas. **Adm £4, chd free. Sun 10 June (2-5.30).**
4 acre garden surrounding C18 brick house (not open). Mature and young specimen trees. Mixed shrub and herbaceous borders, variety of roses. 1 acre walled garden with flowers, fruit and vegetables. Gravel paths.

5 ◆ BENINGTON LORDSHIP

nr Stevenage SG2 7BS. Mr & Mrs R R A Bott, 01438 869668, www.beningtonlordship.co.uk. 5m E of Stevenage. In Benington Village, signs off A602. Next to church. **Adm £3.50, chd free. For other dates and times please tel or see website. For NGS: Sun 24 June (2-5).**
7-acre garden incl historic buildings, kitchen garden, lakes, roses. Spectacular borders, unspoilt panoramic views. Children's trail. Bennington Floral Festival.

6 BRENT PELHAM GARDENS

SG9 0HH. 8 m NW of Bishops Stortford. On B1038 by the church and on E side of village. Home-made teas at Pelham House. **Combined adm £4, chd free. Suns 1 Apr; 13 May (2-5).**

CHURCH COTTAGE

Mr & Mrs G D Clark
Semi-woodland garden with mature trees. Extensive planting around large natural pond, many unusual plants.

PELHAM HOUSE

Mr & Mrs D K Haselgrove, 01279 777473. Visitors also welcome by appt.
3½-acre informal garden on alkaline clay started by present owner in 1986. Plenty of interest to the plantsman. Wide variety of trees and shrubs especially birches and oaks. Bulb frames, raised beds with alpines and acid-loving plants and small formal area with ponds. Many daffodils and tulips.

7 44 BROADWATER AVENUE

Letchworth Garden City SG6 3HJ. Karen & Ian Smith. ½ m SW Letchworth town centre. A1(M) J9 signed Letchworth. Straight on at 1st three roundabouts, 4th roundabout take 4th exit then R into Braodwater Ave. Home-made teas. **Adm £2, chd free. Sun 12 Aug (1-5). Evening Opening wine, Fri 10 Aug (6-9).**
Town garden in the Letchworth Garden City conservation area that successfully combines a family garden with a plantswoman's garden. Out of the ordinary, unusual herbaceous plants and shrubs. Rare pelargoniums in pots. Attractive front garden designed for yr-round interest.

8 BROMLEY HALL

Standon, Ware SG11 1NY. Julian & Edwina Robarts, 01279 842422, edwina.robarts@btinternet.com. 6m W of Bishop's Stortford. On Standon to Much Hadham rd. **Adm £4, chd free. Sun 3 June (2-5.30). Visitors also welcome by appt for groups of 10+.**
Mature 4½-acre garden surrounding C16 farmhouse (not open). It is both an architectural and a plantsman's garden with an immaculate kitchen garden. Good use has been made of walls and hedges to shelter borders filled with a mixture of shrubs, foliage plants and unusual perennials. Mown paths through rough grass reveal glimpses of countryside beyond. Petanque court. Access over gravel.

9 ◆ CAPEL MANOR GARDENS

Bullsmoor Lane, Enfield, Middlesex EN1 4RQ. Capel Manor Charitable Corporation, 020 8366 4442, www.capel.ac.uk. 2m from Cheshunt. 3 mins from junction M25/A10. **Adm £5, chd £2, concessions £4. For other dates please tel or see website. For NGS: Sats, Suns 3, 4 Mar; 6, 7 Oct (10-5).**
30 acres of historical and modern theme gardens, Japanese garden, large Italian style maze, rock and water features. Walled garden with rose collection and woodland walks. Also trial and demonstration gardens run by 'Gardening Which?' together with small model gardens, incl new front gardens designed to inspire and provide ideas. National Collection of Sarcococca. Chrysanthemum Show (Oct).

Mown paths through rough grass reveal glimpses of countryside beyond . . .

CLAVERING GARDENS
See Essex.

10 COCKHAMSTED
Braughing SG11 2NT. **David & Jan Marques.** *7m N of Ware. W of Bishops Stortford. 2m E of village towards Braughing Friars. 1st turn L in Friars Rd.* Home-made teas. **Adm £3, chd free. Sun 20 May (2-6).**
Lovely country garden surrounded by open fields. 2 acres of informal planting. Alliums, grasses, tree paeonies, early roses. Island surrounded by C14 moat. Remote and romantic with extensive views.
  🚾 ♿ 🐕 ⊕ ☕

11 NEW 35 DIGSWELL ROAD
Welwyn Garden City AL8 7PB. **Adrian & Clare de Baat.** *1/2m N of Welwyn Garden City centre. From the Campus roundabout in centre of City take N exit just past public library into Digswell Rd. Over the White Bridge, 200yds on L.* Home-made teas. **Adm £2.50, chd free. Sun 22 July (2-5.30).**
Large mature trees and hedges surround town garden of approx 1/3 acre. Wide Oudolf-inspired herbaceous borders packed with perennial plants and ornamental grasses surround lawn. Beyond, grass paths link island beds and lead to exotic garden with unusual less hardy plants. Grass paths, gentle slopes.
  ♿ 🐕 ⊕ ☕

12 DUCKLINGS
12 Burghley Close, Stevenage SG2 8SX. **Sue & Alan Batchelor.** *1m S of Stevenage. On B197. Turn L at Roebuck Travel Lodge. Straight over mini roundabout, 1st L into Burghley Close. Street parking available.* Home-made teas at 11 Burghley Close (next door). **Adm £2.50, chd free. Sun 17 June (12-5).**
Charming small town garden. Intensely planted. Full of interest throughout the seasons. An attractive example of gardening without lawns.
🐕 ⊕ ☕

13 207 EAST BARNET ROAD
New Barnet EN4 8QS. **Margaret Chadwick, 020 8440 0377, magg1ee@hotmail.com.** *M25 J24 then A111 to Cockfosters. Underground stations High Barnet or*

Cockfosters. On bus route 184, 307 & 326. Home-made teas. **Adm £2, chd free. Sun 24 June (2-5). Visitors also welcome by appt.**
Delightful example of minute courtyard garden 25ft x 30ft. High fences are covered with clematis, honeysuckle and passion flowers, roses and vines scramble over an arch above a seat. Small pond with goldfish and water plants. Many interesting and unusual plants, mainly in pots. Featured in 'Garden News'.
🐕 ⊕ ☕

Designer bantams and Moroccan treehouse. Interesting and inspirational . . .

14 NEW ♦ EAST GARDEN AT HATFIELD HOUSE
AL9 5NQ. **The Marquess of Salisbury, 01707 287010, www.hatfield-house.co.uk.** *Opp Hatfield Stn, 21m N of London, M25 J23. 7m A1(M) J4 signed off A414 & A1000.* **Adm £8.50, chd free. Daily West Garden and Park, Thurs East Garden only, House Wed to Sun. For NGS: (East Garden) Thur 5 July (11-5.30).**
Dating from C17, the gardens at Hatfield House have evolved into a gardeners' paradise. The East garden, which was laid out by the 5th Marquess of Salisbury, stretches down to the lake and is formally planted with an elegant parterre, box topiary, glorious herbaceous borders, orchards and vegetable garden.
♿ 🐕 ☕

15 NEW THE END HOUSE
15 Hangmans Lane, Welwyn AL6 0TJ. **Sarah & John Marsh.** *2m NE of Welwyn. A1 J6 over 2 roundabouts turn L at next turning B197 for approx 11/2m towards Knebworth. Turn L into Cannonfield Rd after 1m car park on L. Short woodland walk to garden. Disabled parking only at garden.* Home-made teas. **Adm £3, chd free. Sun 3 June (12-6). Afternoon & Evening Opening** wine, **Fri 1 June (4-9).**
Plantswoman's peaceful 1/2 acre woodland garden which incls jungle walk, tropical planting, bog and dell garden, pond and various water features. Archway to secret garden. Designer bantams and Moroccan treehouse. Interesting and inspirational.
🐕 ⊕ ☕

16 NEW THE FUCHSIA GARDEN
Stortford Lane, Braughing SG11 2PS. **Ray & Christine Ayres.** *2m E of Puckeridge. 4m W of Bishops Stortford. On A120 between Little Hadham & Standon. Turn into Lane signed Braughing at Howe Fencing.* **Adm £3, chd free (share to Bal Vikas Orphanage, Orissa). Sats, Suns 28, 29 July; 4, 5 Aug (12-6).**
Over 200 varieties of fuchsias are, displayed at eye level view in raised beds together with fragrant lilies. Mature hostas, ferns, grasses and many unusual plants complement the whole garden. Featured in 'Hertfordshire Life'. Some unlevel walkways.
♿ 🐕 ⊕

17 GREAT SARRATT HALL
Sarratt, Rickmansworth WD3 4PD. **Mr H M Neal.** *5m N of Rickmansworth. From Watford N via A41 (or M1 J5) to Kings Langley; left (W) to Sarratt; garden is 1st on R after village sign.* Home-made teas. **Adm £4, chd free (under 12) (share to The Courtauld Institute of Art). Sun 27 May (2-6).**
4 acres. Herbaceous and mixed shrub borders; pond, moisture-loving plants and trees; walled kitchen garden; rhododendrons, magnolias, camellias; new planting of specialist conifers and rare trees.
♿ 🐕 ⊕ ☕

18 **13 GREENHILL PARK**
Barnet EN5 1HQ. Sally & Andy Fry.
*1m S of High Barnet. 1/2m S of High
Barnet tube stn. Take 1st L after
Odeon Cinema, Weaver PH on corner.
Buses: 34, 234, 263, 326, 84.* Home-
made teas. **Adm £2, chd free. Sun 10
June (2-5).**
An oasis in suburbia. Approx 1/4-acre.
Entrance via living willow and clematis
arbour. Colourful herbaceous borders,
wildlife pond, summer house, mature
trees, shady fern garden. Series of
rustic arches link main garden to path
through wildlife-friendly secret garden,
incorporating tree fern collection,
acers, stumpery and architectural
plants.
💢 ⊕ ☕

19 ◆ **HOPLEYS**
High Street, Much Hadham
SG10 6BU. Mr Aubrey Barker, 01279
842509, www.hopleys.co.uk. *5m W
of Bishop's Stortford. On B1004. M11
(J8) 7m or A10 (Puckeridge) 5m via
A120. 50yds N of Bull PH in centre of
Much Hadham.* **Adm £2, chd free.
Open every Mon, Wed to Sat (9-5),
Sun (2-5) Mar to Oct.**
31/2 acres of constantly developing
garden; trees, shrubs, herbaceous and
alpines; island beds with mixed
planting in parkland setting; pond
recently refurbished.
🔥 💢 ⊕ ☕

20 ◆ **HUNTON PARK**
Hunton Bridge WD4 8PN. Verve
Venues, 01923 261511,
hunton@verve-venues.com. *3m N of
Watford. 1m S of J20 off M25. Exit J20
follow signs to Watford A41, turn L at
T-lights after 1/2m signed Abbots
Langley. Follow Bridge Rd 1/2m up hill,
Hunton Park on RH-side.* **Adm £3,
chd free. For NGS: Mon 7 May
(10-4).**
The 22-acre grounds incl terraced
lawns, woodland and woodland
plantings, small pond, herbaceous
border, heather garden. Rose beds,
mature trees and plants of seasonal

interest. Partial wheelchair access,
steep slopes.
🔥 💢

THE HYDE WALLED GARDEN
See Bedfordshire.

21 ◆ **KNEBWORTH HOUSE
GARDENS**
Knebworth SG3 6PY. The Hon Henry
Lytton Cobbold, 01438 812661,
www.knebworthhouse.com. *28m N
of London. Direct access from A1(M)
J7 at Stevenage. Stn & bus stop:
Stevenage 3m.* **Adm £5,
chd/concessions £2. See website
for details. For NGS: Thur 6 Sept
(11-4).**
Historic home of Bulwer Lytton,
Victorian novelist and statesman.
Knebworth's magnificent gardens were
laid out by Lutyens in 1910. Lutyens'
pollarded lime avenues, Gertrude
Jekyll's herb garden, the newly
restored maze, yew hedges, roses and
herbaceous borders are key features of
the formal gardens with peaceful
woodland walks beyond. Gold garden,
green garden, brick garden, walled
vegetable and herb garden.
🔥 💢 ⊕ ☕

22 **MACKERYE END GARDENS**
Harpenden AL5 5DR. *1m E of
Harpenden. A1 J4, follow signs
Wheathampstead then Luton. Gardens
on R. M1 J10 follow Lower Luton Rd
(B653) to Cherry Tree Restaurant. Turn
L follow signs to Mackerye End.* Teas
at Mackerye End House. **Combined
adm £4, chd free. Sun 24 June (2-5).**
Small hamlet between Batford and
Porters End.
☕

EIGHTACRE
Mr & Mrs S Cutmore
2-acre garden incl shrub and
herbaceous beds, wildlife pond,
raised vegetable beds,
greenhouse and orchards.
💢

HOLLYBUSH COTTAGE
Mr & Mrs Prosser
Well established cottage garden
around this listed house (not
open).
💢

MACKERYE END FARM
Mr & Mrs A Clark
3-acre garden in grounds of
restored, listed C16 farmhouse
(not open) with extensive new
mixed borders, yew hedge and
large pond, rose garden and
fountain. Rear borders lead to old
mulberry tree, small arboretum,
laurels, orchard with various fruit
trees and well-house.
💢

MACKERYE END HOUSE
Mr & Mrs G Penn
1550 Grade 1 manor house (not
open) set in 11 acres of gardens
and park. Front garden set in
framework of formal yew hedges
with long border and fine C17 tulip
tree. Victorian walled garden now
divided into smaller sections; path
maze; cutting garden; quiet
garden. W garden enclosed by
pergola walk of old English roses
and vines.
💢

23 **MOOR PLACE**
Much Hadham SG10 6AA. Mr & Mrs
B M Norman. *5m W of Bishop's
Stortford. Entrance either at war
memorial or at Hadham Cross.* Home-
made teas. **Adm £4, chd free. Sun 27
May (2-5.30).**
2 C18 walled gardens. Herbaceous
borders. Large area of shrubbery,
lawns, hedges and trees. 2 ponds.
Approx 10 acres.
🔥 💢 ⊕ ☕

24 **106 ORCHARD ROAD**
Tewin AL6 0LZ. Linda Adams, 01438
798147, alannio@btinternet.com. *3m
N of Welwyn Garden City. Take B1000
between Hertford & Welwyn Garden
City signed Tewin. In village stay on L
past the Rose & Crown PH on to
Upper Green Road towards Burnham
Green. Pass Plume of Feathers PH.
Tewin Orchard 200yds on L. Park in
field opp.* Home-made teas. **Adm £3,
chd free. Sun 17 (2-6), Wed 20 June
(10.30-1). Evening Opening** wine,
Fri 22 June (6.30-9). Visitors also
welcome by appt March to end
Sept.
Spacious garden behind listed modern
movement house (not open). Elements

An oasis in suburbia . . .
entrance via living willow and
clematis arbour

Topiary animals and quirky features enhance a profusion of small trees, grasses and perennials . . .

of 1935 garden - lawns, lily pond, colourful beds and borders. Productive fruit and vegetable area. Small orchard part of the Hertfordshire Millennium orchard initiative. Unusual trees and shrubs. Peaceful country setting and beautiful views. Front garden features rabbit-resistant plants.

  ᬗ ❀ ⨌ 👟

25 20 PARK AVENUE SOUTH
Harpenden AL5 2EA. Miss Isobel M Leek. 6m N of St Albans. Off A1081 turn W by The Cock Inn & War Memorial up Rothamsted Ave Hill; 3rd on L. Adm £3, chd free. Suns 29 Apr; 1 July (2-5).
Topiary animals and quirky features enhance a profusion of small trees, grasses and perennials. Tulips, gold and brown leaved shrubs, primulas and pulmonarias delight in spring. Yr-round interest from perennials, colourful vegetables in small raised beds, experimental, drought-combating, gravel garden. Greenhouse, conservatory, aviary. Many seats.

  ⋊ ❀ 👟

26 PATCHWORK
22 Hall Park Gate, Berkhamsted HP4 2NJ. Jean & Peter Block, 01442 864731. 3m W of Hemel Hempstead. Entering E side of Berkhamsted on A4251, turn L 200yds after 40mph sign. Home-made teas. Adm £2.50, chd free. Suns 6 May; 19 Aug (2-5). Visitors also welcome by appt, March to Oct.
1/4-acre garden with lots of yr-round colour, interest and perfume; a riot of colour on opening days. Sloping site with background of colourful trees, rockeries, two small ponds, patios, shrubs and trees, spring bulbs, herbaceous border, roses, bedding, fuchsias, sweet peas, dahlias, patio pots and tubs galore and hanging baskets. Featured in 'Gardens Monthly'.

  ❀ 👟

27 PLUMMERS FARM
nr Welwyn AL6 9UE. Mrs Helena Hodgins. 1m N of Welwyn. On B656 turn R signed Rabley Heath & Potters Heath follow lane for 1m. Turn L into Sally Deards Lane, Plummers Farm on R approx 1/4m. Adm £3, chd free. Sun 10 June (2-6).
Large country garden, beautifully maintained with open sunny borders, planted in the contemporary style, aromatic garden, large mixed borders. Oak pergola planted with wisteria and late flowering clematis. Small wild flower meadow establishing. Firm gravel paths.

  ᬗ ⋊

28 THE PRIORY
Little Wymondley SG4 7HD. John & Ann Hope. 1m W of Stevenage. Travelling N A1(M) J8, 2nd exit to Little Wymondley, then 1st R Priory Lane. Garden approx 1/2m on R. Light refreshments & teas. Adm £3.50, chd free. Sun 22 July (11-5).
Garden occupies an area of 6 acres approx 2 acres of which are within the moat which formed the boundary of the former ecclesiastical buildings. The garden has been developed in the last 5yrs.

  ᬗ ⋊ 👟

29 QUEENSWOOD SCHOOL
Shepherds Way, Brookmans Park, Hatfield AL9 6NS. 3m N of Potters Bar. From S: M25 J24 signed Potters Bar. In 1/2m at lights turn R onto A1000 signed Hatfield. In 2m turn R onto B157. School is 1/2m on R. From N: A1000 from Hatfield. In 5m turn L onto B157. Light refreshments & teas. Adm £2.50, chd/concessions £1.50. Sun 27, Mon 28 May (11-6).
120 acres of informal gardens and woodlands. Rhododendrons, fine specimen trees, shrubs and herbaceous borders. Glasshouses. Fine views to Chiltern Hills. Picnic area. Some gravel paths.

  ᬗ ⋊ ❀ 👟

30 RAGGED HALL
Gaddesden Row, nr Hemel Hempstead HP2 6HJ. Mr & Mrs Anthony Vincent, 01442 255680. 4m N of Hemel Hempstead. Take A4146 to Water End. Turn R up hill for 2m, turn R at T-junction. House is 3rd L past Chequers PH. Home-made teas. Adm £3, chd free. Suns 6 May; 1 July (2-5.30).
Garden of 1 1/2 acres. Some new landscaping and late summer border. Mixed borders. Some unusual plants. Pond garden and cutting garden. Potager with vegetables and flowers. Brass Band will play.

  ᬗ ⋊ ❀ 👟

31 RUSTLING END COTTAGE
Rustling End, nr Codicote SG4 8TD. Julie & Tim Wise, 01438 821509, www.rustlingend.com. 1m N of Codicote. From B656 turn L into '3 Houses Lane' then R to Rustling End. House is 2nd on L. Adm £3, chd free. Sun 22, Wed 25 July (11-5). Afternoon & Evening Opening £3, wine, Fri 27 July (4-9).
Attractive C18 cottage (not open) surrounded by fields and woodland. 1/2-acre plantswoman's garden, continually evolving. Walk through the meadow to a cottage garden with contemporary planting incl a sunny gravel terrace with drought tolerant planting. N-facing shady borders, topiary, wildlife pond with bog planting, late flowering deep perennial borders and small kitchen garden.

  ⋊ ❀

32 ST MARY'S CROFT
Fortune Lane, Elstree WD6 3RY. Hilde & Lionel Wainstein, 020 8953 3022, hildewainstein@hotmail.co.uk. 2m SW of Borehamwood. Off A411 Barnet Lane. Leave M25 at J23, then take A1 London. R at first roundabout, L at next roundabout onto Barnet Lane, Fortune Lane is on L in Elstree Village. Careful parking on Barnet Lane and in Fortune Lane (L only). Light refreshments & teas. Adm £3, chd free (share to Herts & Beds NCCPG). Suns 22 Apr (1-5); 20 May (11-6). Evening Opening wine, Tue 26 June (5.30-9.30). Visitors also welcome by appt.
1-acre designer/plantswoman's garden. Grass, shrub and perennial plantings, wild flower meadow, large wildlife pond, bog garden, herbs, rock garden, delightful spring woodland, summerhouse. National collection of Akebias flowering April. Continuing

interest throughout the season. Wide range of unusual plants for sale, most propagated from garden. Access over shingle.

♿ ☹ **NCCPG**

㉝ ♦ ST PAUL'S WALDEN BURY
Hitchin SG4 8BP. Simon & Caroline Bowes Lyon, 01438 871218, spw@boweslyon.demon.co.uk. *5m S of Hitchin. On B651; 1/2m N of Whitwell.* **Adm £3.50, chd 50p, concessions £2. Suns 13 May; 3 June. For NGS: Sun 22 Apr (2-7).** Formal woodland garden, covering 60 acres, laid out 1730. Grade 1 listed. Long rides lined with clipped beech hedges lead to temples, statues, lake, ponds, and outdoor theatre. Seasonal displays of snowdrops, daffodils, irises, magnolias, rhododendrons, woodland paeonies and lilies. Wild flower areas. Childhood home of the late Queen Mother.

♿

Historical garden, belonging to George Bernard Shaw from 1906 until his death in 1950 . . .

㉞ SERGE HILL GARDENS
WD5 0RY. *1/2m E of Bedmond. Past White Hart PH, in Bedmond, then 1/2m on, down Serge Hill Lane.* Home-made teas at Serge Hill. **Combined adm £5, chd free. Sun 17 June (2-5).**

🍵

THE BARN
Tom Stuart-Smith & family
1-acre garden. Small sheltered courtyard planted with unusual shrubs and perennials, contrasts with more open garden with views over wild flower meadow.

🐈 ☹

SERGE HILL
Sir Murray & Lady Stuart-Smith
Regency house (not open) in parkland setting with fine kitchen garden of 1/2 acre. A range of unusual wall plants, mixed border, 100yds long.

🐈

㉟ ♦ SHAW'S CORNER
Ayot St Lawrence AL6 9BX. The National Trust, 01438 820307, www.nationaltrust.org.uk. *2m NE of Wheathampstead. At SW end of village, approx 2m on B653 (A1 J4 - M1 J10). Signed from B653 (Shaw's Corner/The Ayots).* **House and Garden adm £4.50, chd £2.25. Weds to Suns & Bank Hols Mons 17 Mar to 28 Oct, (house 1pm, gardens 12 - 5.30 last adm 4.30). For NGS: Evening Opening £3.50, chd £1.50, wine, Sat 9 June (6-9).**

Approx 4 acres with richly planted borders, orchard, small meadow, wooded areas and views over the Hertfordshire countryside. Historical garden, belonging to George Bernard Shaw from 1906 until his death in 1950. Hidden among the trees is the revolving summerhouse where Shaw retreated to write. Music provided by the Ionian Singers, choir specialising in English music. Featured in Hertfordshire 'Life Magazine' & on BBC Three Counties Radio.

♿ 🐈 ☹

㊱ STRESA
126 The Drive, Rickmansworth WD3 4DP. Roger & Patt Trigg, 01923 774293, roger.trigg@tiscali.co.uk. *1m NW of Rickmansworth. From M25 J18 take A404 towards Rickmansworth for 200yds, turn R into The Clump, then 1st L into The Drive. From Rickmansworth take A404 toward Amersham for approx 1/3m, L into Valley Road, 1st L into The Drive.* **Adm £2.50, chd free. Visitors welcome by appt, groups of 12-30 with garden tour if required. Home-made teas available on request.**
Approx 1/2 acre plantsman's garden. The front garden is a sunny part-gravel area of alpines, Mediterranean plants, borderline-hardiness plants, dogwoods and collection of grasses. Small woodland area leads to rear garden which features continually evolving borders of perennials and shrubs incl hostas, heucheras, euphorbias, rhododendrons and other shade-loving plants. Astilbes and phlox highlight the summer display; conservatory features sub-tropical plants. (Plant-identifying map and list is available for visitors). Featured in 'Hertfordshire Life'.

🐈 ☹ 🍵

㊲ THUNDRIDGE HILL HOUSE
Cold Christmas Lane, Ware SG12 0UE. Mr & Mrs Christopher Melluish, 01920 462500, c.melluish@btopenworld.com. *2m NE of Ware. 3/4m from The Sow & Pigs PH off the A10 down Cold Christmas Lane, crossing new bypass.* **Adm £3, chd free. Evening Opening wine, Fri 8 June (6-8). Visitors also welcome by appt, coaches permitted.**
Well-established garden of approx 21/2 acres; good variety of plants, shrubs and roses, attractive hedges. Several delightful places to sit. Wonderful views in and out of the garden with fine views down to the Rib Valley. 'A most popular garden to visit'. Plant stall.

🐈 ☹

㊳ WATERDELL HOUSE
Little Green Lane, Croxley Green WD3 3JH. Mr & Mrs Peter Ward, 01923 772775, pmjward@btinternet.com. *11/2m NE of Rickmansworth. M25, J18, direction Rickmansworth up into A412 towards Watford. From A412 turn L signed Sarratt, along Croxley Green, fork R past Coach & Horses, cross Baldwins Lane into Little Green Lane, then L at top.* Cream teas. **Adm £4, chd free, concessions £3. Sun 1 July (2-5.30). Visitors also welcome by appt.**
11/2-acre walled garden systematically developed over more than 50yrs by present owner/gardener: mature and young trees, topiary holly hedge, herbaceous borders, modern island beds of shrubs, old-fashioned roses, pelargoniums, grasses and pond gardens.

🐈 🐈 ☹ 🍵

Grassland park full of mature trees incl ancient oak and hornbeam, traversed by river and lake. Visitors welcome to walk and picnic in the park.

---

39 WEST LODGE PARK
Cockfosters Road, Hadley Wood EN4 0PY. Beales Hotels. *2m S of Potters Bar. On A111. J24 from M25 signed Cockfosters*. Home-made teas. **Adm £3, chd free. Suns 13 May (2-5); 28 Oct (1-4).**
10-acre Beale Arboretum consists of over 700 varieties of trees and shrubs, incl National Collections of hornbeam cultivars, with a good selection of conifers, oaks, maples and mountain ash. A network of paths has been laid out, and most specimens are labelled. 2 rare Wollemi pines. Partial wheelchair access, gravel paths.
♿ 👂 ❀ NCCPG 🛌 ☕

40 NEW THE WHITE HOUSE
Munden Road, Dane End, Ware SG12 0LP. Jonathan & Sally Pool, 01920 438733, jonathanpool@tiscali.co.uk. *5m N of Hertford. Off A602 turn N to Dane End. 2m W of Watton at Stone*. Cream teas. **Adm £3.50, chd free. Sun 27 May (2-5.30). Visitors also welcome by appt.**
23 yr-old 1½ acre country garden, designed by owner surrounding 1830s Dower House (not open) to incl vegetables, orchard, hedges, shrubs and herbaceous plants.
♿ 👂 ❀ ☕

41 WOODHALL PARK
Watton-at-Stone SG14 3NF. Mr & Mrs Ralph Abel Smith. *4m N of Hertford. 6m S of Stevenage, 4m NW of Ware. Main lodge entrance to Woodhall Park is on A119, Hertford to Stevenage, between villages of Stapleford & Watton-at-Stone*. Home-made teas. **Adm £4, chd free. Sun 17 June (12-5.30).**
Mature 4-acre garden created out of surrounding parkland in 1957 when C18 stable block was converted (not open). Special features: courtyard, climbing and shrub roses, herbaceous and mixed borders, kitchen garden, plants propagated from garden, mature trees, gravel paths and areas to sit with unspoilt views. Grassland park full of mature trees incl ancient oak and hornbeam, traversed by river and lake. Visitors welcome to walk and picnic in the park. Featured in 'Hertfordshire Mercury'. Gravel paths.
♿ 👂 ❀ ☕

Hertfordshire County Volunteers

County Organiser
Edwina Robarts, Bromley Hall, Standon, Ware, SG11 1NY, 01279 842422, edwina.robarts@btinternet.com

County Treasurer
Virginia Newton, South Barn, Kettle Green, Much Hadham, SG10 6AE, 01279 843232, vnewton@moatfarmhouse.co.uk

Assistant County Organisers
Michael Belderbos, 6 High Elms, Hatching Green, Harpenden AL5 2JU, 01582 712612
Marigold Harvey, Upwick Hall, Little Hadham, Ware SG11 2JY, 01279 771769, marigold@upwick.com
Rösli Lancaster, Manor Cottage, Aspenden, Buntingford SG9 9PB, 01763 271711
Jan Marques, Cockhamsted, Braughing, Ware SG11 2NT, 01279 771312, cockhamsted@freeuk.com
Christopher Melluish, Thundridge Hill House, Cold Christmas Lane, Ware SG12 0UF, 01920 462500, c.melluish@btinternet.com
Karen Smith, 44 Broadwater Avenue, Letchworth Garden City SG6 3HU, 01462 673133, 1.smith@laingorourke.com
Julie Wise, Rustling End Cottage, Rustling End, nr Codicote SG4 8TD, 01438 821509, juliewise@f2s.com

ISLE OF WIGHT

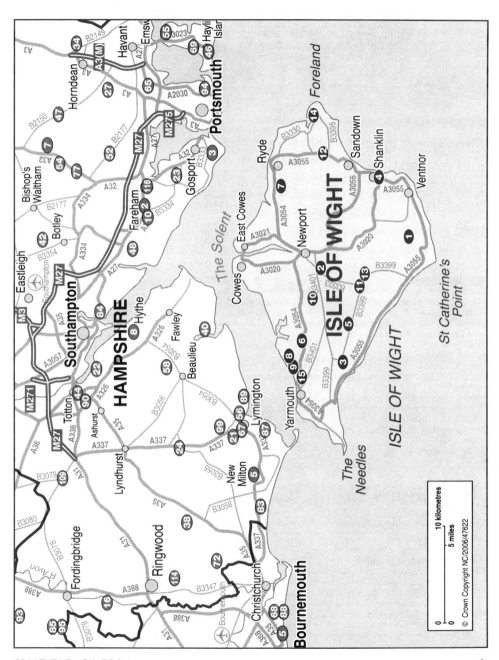

Opening Dates

April

THURSDAY 5
⓮ Pitt House

May

SUNDAY 6
❸ Brook House

SUNDAY 20
❷ Badminton

June

SUNDAY 3
⓾ Meadowsweet

SUNDAY 10
⓬ Nunwell House

SATURDAY 16
❽ Hamstead Grange (Evening)

SUNDAY 17
⓭ The Old Rectory

THURSDAY 28
⓮ Pitt House

SATURDAY 30
❶ Ashknowle House

July

SUNDAY 1
❶ Ashknowle House
⓯ Thorley Manor

SATURDAY 7
❹ Chine House

SUNDAY 8
❹ Chine House

THURSDAY 26
⓮ Pitt House

August

SUNDAY 19
❺ Coombe Farm
❻ Crab Cottage

THURSDAY 23
⓮ Pitt House

By appointment only

❼ 4 Greenway
❾ Highwood
⓫ Northcourt Gardens

The Gardens

❶ ASHKNOWLE HOUSE
Whitwell PO38 2PP. Mr & Mrs K
Fradgley. *4m W of Ventnor. From
Ventnor rd turn for Ashknowle Lane
next to Old Rectory. Lane is unmade.
Car parking in village but field parking
available, except when wet.* **Adm
£2.50, chd free. Sat 30 June; Sun 1
July (2-5).**
A variety of features to explore in the
grounds of this Victorian house. Mature
and young woodlands, borders, wildlife
pond and other water features. The
well-maintained kitchen garden is
highly productive and boasts a wide
range of fruit and vegetables grown in
cages, tunnels, glasshouses and
raised beds.

⚒ ❀ ☕

❷ BADMINTON
Clatterford Shute, Carisbrooke
PO30 1PD. Mr & Mrs G S Montrose.
*1½ m SW of Newport. Free parking in
Carisbrooke Castle car park. Public
footpath to Millers Lane in corner of car
park leads down to garden, approx
200yds. Parking for disabled can be
arranged; please telephone prior to
opening. Home-made teas.* **Adm
£2.50, chd free. Sun 20 May (2-5).**
One-acre garden on sheltered S- and
W-facing site with good vistas. Planted
for all-yr interest with many different
shrubs, trees and perennials to give
variety, structure and colour. Natural
stream and pond being developed
alongside kitchen garden.

❀ ☕

❸ BROOK HOUSE
Brook PO30 4EJ. Mr & Mrs G
Walters. *3m E of Freshwater. From the
Military Rd, turn into and continue
through Brook village and up hill.
Entrance to house on L immed before
T-junction at top of hill. For car park,
turn L at T-junction, L again opp
church into signed field.* Home-made
teas. **Adm £2.50, chd free. Sun 6
May (2-5).**
Established garden of approx 3 acres
with several different areas, incl some
classic English country borders and
beds around the lawns; orchard,
vegetable garden and, as a key
feature, an old sunken rose walk.

⚒ 🛏 ☕

❹ CHINE HOUSE
Chine Avenue, Shanklin Old Village
PO37 6AQ. *In
centre of village opp Vernon Meadow
car park. Georgian white house.* **Adm
£2.50, chd free. Sat 7, Sun 8 July
(2-5).**
Traditional front garden and tropical
rear garden, with many rare and
unusual plants. A number of water
features incl rill and pond with
waterfalls. Bridge and Victorian
gazebo, ¾ acre.

❺ COOMBE FARM
Combe Lane, Brighstone PO30 4AY.
Mr & Mrs James Dawes, 01983
740402. *¼ m W of Brighstone. From
Calbourne follow rd to Brighstone.
Pass Brighstone sign. 100yds turn L at
Chalk Barn. Parking in field.* **Adm
£2.50, chd free. Sun 19 Aug (2.30-5).
Visitors also welcome by appt, no
coaches or groups.**
Garden started from scratch in 1997
around C18 farmhouse (not open).
Organic vegetable garden. Gravel
garden and extensive mixed plantings
designed by owners. Limited
wheelchair access.

⚒ ❀ ☕

We welcome visitors all year to
our unforgiving clay garden
(boots necessary in inclement
weather!) . . .

6 CRAB COTTAGE
Mill Road, Shalfleet PO30 4NE. Mr & Mrs Peter Scott, 01983 531319, mencia@btinternet.com. *3½ m E of Yarmouth. Turn past New Inn into Mill Rd. Please park before going through NT gates. Entrance is first on L, less than 5 mins walk.* Home-made teas. **Adm £2.50, chd free. Sun 19 Aug (11-5). Visitors also welcome by appt.**
Lovely views over Newtown Creek and Solent. 1¼ acres of gravelly soil exposed to the Westerlies. Walled garden with herbaceous borders leading to terraced sunken garden with ornamental pond and pavilion planted with exotics, tender shrubs and herbaceous perennials. Mixed rose borders. Croquet lawn leading to grass path through wild flower meadow and flowering shrubs to waterlily pond and woodland walk. Gravel paths, slopes.

7 4 GREENWAY
Binstead PO33 3SD. Mr & Mrs G Riddell, 01983 565406. *2m W of Ryde. From A3054 turn into Newnham Rd at the top of Binstead Hill. Take 1st L into Kings Rd, 1st R into Parkway, 1st R into The Mall and 1st L into Greenway.* Home-made teas. **Adm £2, chd free. Visitors welcome by appt June, July & Aug, for groups of 10+.**
Inspirational award-winning small garden. Huge variety of plants for all-yr colour and interest. Hot border, pergolas, wildlife ponds, with several places to sit and enjoy the garden. Constantly evolving and very colourful during summer months.

8 HAMSTEAD GRANGE
Yarmouth PO41 0YE. Mr & Mrs Tom Young. *3m E of Yarmouth. Entrance to 1½ m private drive on A3054.* Light refreshments. **Evening Opening £2.50, wine, Sat 16 June (5-8).**
3 acres with rose garden, shrubs, lawns, trees and water garden. New

lavender hedge planted to complement the spectacular view of the Solent.

9 HIGHWOOD
Cranmore PO41 0XS. Mr & Mrs Cooper, 01983 760550, ross.cooper@virgin.net. *2m E of Yarmouth on A3054. 2m from Yarmouth, turning on LH-side, opp bus shelter, unmade rd.* **Adm £2.50, chd free. Visitors welcome by appt all yr, please phone first.**
We welcome visitors all yr to our unforgiving clay garden (boots necessary in inclement weather!). Approx 2½ acres of garden on a 10-acre S-facing slope, incl pond, borders of shrubs and perennials and oak copse full of interesting 'woodlanders'.

10 MEADOWSWEET
5 Great Park Cottages, off Betty-Haunt Lane, Carisbrooke PO30 4HR. Gunda Cross, 01983 529930. *4m SW of Newport. From A3054 Newport to Yarmouth rd turn L at crossroads Porchfield-Calbourne into Betty-Haunt Lane, over bridge and into lane on R. Parking along L side on grass verge, past Meadowsweet.* Home-made teas. **Adm £2.50, chd free. Sun 3 June (11-4). Visitors also welcome by appt May to Aug for groups of 10+.**
From windswept barren 2-acre cattle field to developing tranquil country garden. Natural, mainly native, planting and wild flowers. Cottagey front garden, herb garden, orchard, fruit cage and large pond. The good life and haven for wildlife!

11 NORTHCOURT GARDENS
Shorwell PO30 3JG. Mrs C D Harrison, Mr & Mrs J Harrison, 01983 740415, www.northcourt.info. *4m SW of Newport. On entering Shorwell from Carisbrooke, entrance on R, immed after rustic footbridge.*

Teas by arrangement. **Adm £3, chd free. Visitors welcome by appt, groups only.**
15 acres incl bathhouse, walled kitchen garden, stream. Terraced Mediterranean and sunken subtropical garden. Many shrubs and tender plants. Jacobean manor house (part open). Green Island award, Gold Medal. Limited wheelchair access.

12 NUNWELL HOUSE
Coach Lane, Brading PO36 0JQ. Colonel & Mrs J A Aylmer. *3m S of Ryde. Signed off A3055 in Brading into Coach Lane.* Home-made teas. **Adm £2.50, chd free. Sun 10 June (2-5).**
5-acres of beautifully set formal and shrub gardens with *Cornus kousa* and old-fashioned shrub roses prominent. Exceptional Solent views from the terraces. Small arboretum laid out by Vernon Russell Smith and replanned walled garden with herbaceous borders. House (not open) developed over 5 centuries and full of architectural interest.

13 NEW THE OLD RECTORY
Kingston Road, Kingston, Ventnor PO38 2JZ. Derek & Louise Ness. *8m S of Newport. On entering Shorwell from Carisbrooke, take L turn at mini roundabout towards Chale (B3399). Follow rd until you see Kingston sign, house 2nd on L after this. Park in adjacent field.* Home-made teas. **Adm £2.50, chd free. Sun 17 June (2-5).**
Country garden with formal structure developing, containing rambling planting incl a growing collection of old and English roses. Also of interest are the ornamental walled kitchen garden and recently-planted orchard. Look out for the newly-uncovered stone well in the conservatory garden.

14 PITT HOUSE
Love Lane, Bembridge PO35 5NF. Mr L J Martin, 01983 872243. *Enter Bembridge village, pass museum & take 1st L into Love Lane. Continue down lane (5 min walk) as far as bend; Pitt House is on L. Enter tall wrought iron gates. By car enter Ducie Ave 1st L before museum. Pitt House at bottom on R. Parking in Ducie Ave.*

> From windswept barren 2-acre cattle field to developing tranquil country garden . . . the good life and haven for wildlife!

Home-made teas. **Adm £2.50, chd free. Thurs 5 Apr; 28 June; 26 July; 23 Aug (1-5). Visitors also welcome by appt.**
Approx 4 acres with varied aspects and beautiful sea views. A number of sculptures dotted around garden; also Victorian greenhouse, mini waterfall and 4 ponds. Summer bedding display and hanging baskets.

  ♿ ✕ ☕

⑮ THORLEY MANOR
Yarmouth PO41 0SJ. **Mr & Mrs Anthony Blest.** *1m E of Yarmouth. From Bouldnor take Wilmingham Lane. House ½ m on L.* Home-made teas. **Adm £2.50, chd free. Sun 1 July (2.30-5).**
Delightful informal gardens of over 3 acres surrounding Manor House (not open). The long-neglected water garden has been fully restored. Charming walled garden for tea. Eccentric head gardener.

✕ ⊛ ☕

Approx 4 acres with varied aspects and beautiful sea views. A number of sculptures dotted around garden . . .

Isle of Wight County Volunteers

County Organiser
Bunny Cove, The Old Rectory, St James Street, Yarmouth PO41 0NU, 01983 760555, bryony@bcove.wanadoo.co.uk

County Treasurer
Belinda Walters, Brook House, Brook, Newport PO30 4EJ, 01983 740535, belindawalters@hotmail.co.uk

Assistant County Organisers
Jenny Fradgley, Ashknowle House, Ashknowle Lane, Whitwell, Ventnor PO38 2PP, 01983 730805
Sukie Hillyard, The Coach House, Duver Road, St Helens, Ryde PO33 1XY, 01983 875163
Helen Peplow, Dog Kennel Cottage, Broad Lane, Thorley PO41 0UH, 01983 756712
Jane Wolley Dod, Bakers Farmhouse, Gate Lane, Freshwater Bay PO40 9QD, 01983 752040, wolleydod@hotmail.com

KENT

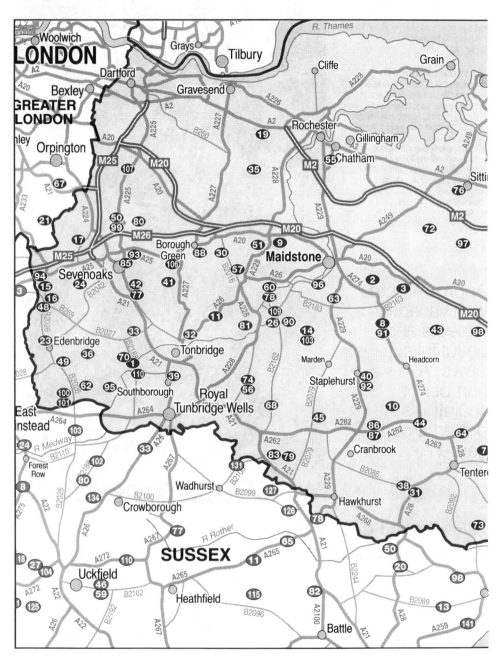

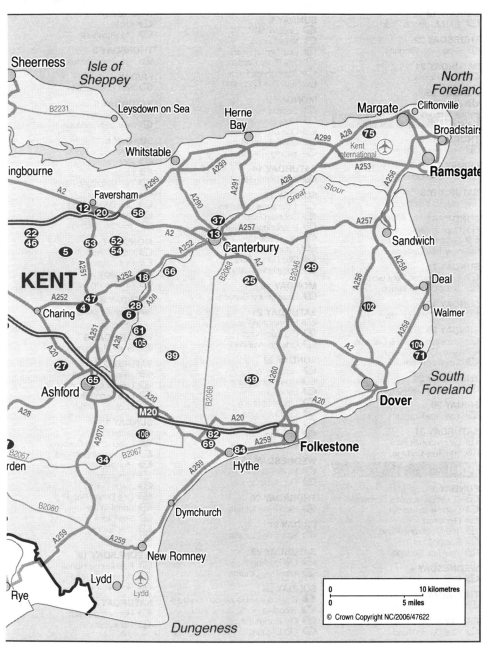

Opening Dates

February

SATURDAY 17
90 Southover

SUNDAY 18
55 190 Maidstone Road

THURSDAY 22
11 Broadview Gardens

SATURDAY 24
57 Mere House

SUNDAY 25
57 Mere House

March

THURSDAY 1
110 Yew Tree Cottage

FRIDAY 2
110 Yew Tree Cottage

SATURDAY 3
110 Yew Tree Cottage

SUNDAY 4
20 Copton Ash
30 Great Comp Garden
110 Yew Tree Cottage

SUNDAY 11
29 Goodnestone Park Gardens
30 Great Comp Garden

SUNDAY 18
30 Great Comp Garden

SUNDAY 25
27 Godinton House & Gardens
30 Great Comp Garden
95 Stonewall Park

THURSDAY 29
110 Yew Tree Cottage

FRIDAY 30
110 Yew Tree Cottage

SATURDAY 31
47 Laurenden Forstal
110 Yew Tree Cottage

April

SUNDAY 1
27 Godinton House & Gardens
28 Godmersham Park
37 Highlands
55 190 Maidstone Road
92 Spilsill Court
110 Yew Tree Cottage

WEDNESDAY 4
42 Knole

THURSDAY 5
110 Yew Tree Cottage

FRIDAY 6
65 One Dering Road

110 Yew Tree Cottage

SATURDAY 7
65 One Dering Road
110 Yew Tree Cottage

SUNDAY 8
20 Copton Ash
57 Mere House
65 One Dering Road
71 The Pines Garden
87 Sissinghurst Place
110 Yew Tree Cottage

MONDAY 9
20 Copton Ash
57 Mere House
65 One Dering Road
87 Sissinghurst Place
109 Yalding Gardens

SATURDAY 14
65 One Dering Road

SUNDAY 15
10 1 Brickwall Cottages
19 Cobham Hall
23 Edenbridge House
38 Hole Park
54 Luton House
65 One Dering Road
88 Sotts Hole Cottage

MONDAY 16
86 Sissinghurst Garden

SATURDAY 21
39 Honnington Farm
62 Old Buckhurst
65 One Dering Road

SUNDAY 22
7 Boldshaves
39 Honnington Farm
52 Longacre
58 Mount Ephraim
62 Old Buckhurst
65 One Dering Road
87 Sissinghurst Place
105 Withersdane Hall

WEDNESDAY 25
56 Marle Place
62 Old Buckhurst

THURSDAY 26
110 Yew Tree Cottage

FRIDAY 27
110 Yew Tree Cottage

SATURDAY 28
62 Old Buckhurst
110 Yew Tree Cottage

SUNDAY 29
9 Bradbourne House and Gardens
12 Brogdale Horticultural Trust
62 Old Buckhurst
63 Old Orchard

81 St Michael's Gardens
110 Yew Tree Cottage

May

WEDNESDAY 2
42 Knole
62 Old Buckhurst

THURSDAY 3
110 Yew Tree Cottage

FRIDAY 4
110 Yew Tree Cottage

SATURDAY 5
65 One Dering Road
110 Yew Tree Cottage

SUNDAY 6
23 Edenbridge House
25 Flint Cottage
52 Longacre
55 190 Maidstone Road
62 Old Buckhurst
65 One Dering Road
95 Stonewall Park
110 Yew Tree Cottage

MONDAY 7
20 Copton Ash
25 Flint Cottage
52 Longacre
65 One Dering Road

TUESDAY 8
77 Riverhill House Gardens

WEDNESDAY 9
31 Great Maytham Hall

SATURDAY 12
10 1 Brickwall Cottages
24 Emmetts Garden
65 One Dering Road
83 Scotney Castle

SUNDAY 13
3 Battel Hall
4 Beech Court Gardens
10 1 Brickwall Cottages
37 Highlands
52 Longacre
54 Luton House
65 One Dering Road
82 Sandling Park
84 Sea Close
93 The Spinney
97 Torry Hill

WEDNESDAY 16
23 Edenbridge House
70 Penshurst Place
78 Rock Farm

SATURDAY 19
39 Honnington Farm
78 Rock Farm

SUNDAY 20
- **6** Bilting House
- **15** Charts Edge
- **38** Hole Park
- **39** Honnington Farm
- **45** Ladham House
- **52** Longacre
- **62** Old Buckhurst
- **74** Puxted House
- **98** Tram Hatch
- **101** Waystrode Manor

TUESDAY 22
- **77** Riverhill House Gardens

THURSDAY 24
- **110** Yew Tree Cottage

FRIDAY 25
- **44** Kypp Cottage
- **110** Yew Tree Cottage

SATURDAY 26
- **40** Iden Croft Herb Gardens
- **44** Kypp Cottage
- **65** One Dering Road
- **79** Rogers Rough
- **110** Yew Tree Cottage

SUNDAY 27
- **7** Boldshaves
- **40** Iden Croft Herb Gardens
- **44** Kypp Cottage
- **52** Longacre
- **61** Olantigh
- **62** Old Buckhurst
- **63** Old Orchard
- **65** One Dering Road
- **71** The Pines Garden
- **72** Placketts Hole (Evening)
- **79** Rogers Rough
- **81** St Michael's Gardens
- **103** Whitehurst
- **106** Woodhay
- **110** Yew Tree Cottage

MONDAY 28
- **8** Boyton Court
- **20** Copton Ash
- **44** Kypp Cottage
- **52** Longacre
- **65** One Dering Road
- **103** Whitehurst

TUESDAY 29
- **44** Kypp Cottage
- **103** Whitehurst

WEDNESDAY 30
- **44** Kypp Cottage
- **103** Whitehurst

THURSDAY 31
- **110** Yew Tree Cottage

June

FRIDAY 1
- **44** Kypp Cottage
- **110** Yew Tree Cottage

SATURDAY 2
- **13** Canterbury Cathedral Gardens
- **44** Kypp Cottage
- **65** One Dering Road
- **110** Yew Tree Cottage

SUNDAY 3
- **13** Canterbury Cathedral Gardens
- **14** Chainhurst Cottage Gardens
- **21** Cottage Farm
- **59** Mounts Court Farmhouse
- **60** Nettlestead Place
- **62** Old Buckhurst
- **65** One Dering Road
- **88** Sotts Hole Cottage
- **110** Yew Tree Cottage

MONDAY 4
- **44** Kypp Cottage
- **86** Sissinghurst Garden

TUESDAY 5
- **44** Kypp Cottage

WEDNESDAY 6
- **14** Chainhurst Cottage Gardens (Evening)
- **42** Knole
- **44** Kypp Cottage
- **62** Old Buckhurst

THURSDAY 7
- **44** Kypp Cottage

FRIDAY 8
- **44** Kypp Cottage

SATURDAY 9
- **44** Kypp Cottage
- **65** One Dering Road
- **68** Orchard End
- **73** Primrose Cottage

SUNDAY 10
- **6** Bilting House
- **21** Cottage Farm
- **35** Haydown
- **46** Larch Cottage
- **48** Lewins
- **55** 190 Maidstone Road
- **62** Old Buckhurst
- **65** One Dering Road
- **68** Orchard End
- **73** Primrose Cottage
- **80** St Clere
- **81** St Michael's Gardens
- **97** Torry Hill

MONDAY 11
- **44** Kypp Cottage
- **73** Primrose Cottage

TUESDAY 12
- **44** Kypp Cottage

WEDNESDAY 13
- **31** Great Maytham Hall
- **38** Hole Park (Evening)
- **44** Kypp Cottage
- **48** Lewins
- **56** Marle Place
- **70** Penshurst Place

- **78** Rock Farm
- **100** Upper Pryors (Day & Evening)
- **101** Waystrode Manor
- **73** Wyckhurst

THURSDAY 14
- **41** Ightham Mote
- **44** Kypp Cottage

FRIDAY 15
- **21** Cottage Farm (Evening)
- **44** Kypp Cottage

SATURDAY 16
- **44** Kypp Cottage
- **65** One Dering Road
- **78** Rock Farm
- **79** Rogers Rough
- **73** Wyckhurst

SUNDAY 17
- **15** Charts Edge
- **17** Chevening
- **21** Cottage Farm
- **23** Edenbridge House
- **47** Laurenden Forstal
- **65** One Dering Road
- **74** Puxted House
- **79** Rogers Rough
- **73** Wyckhurst

MONDAY 18
- **44** Kypp Cottage

TUESDAY 19
- **44** Kypp Cottage

WEDNESDAY 20
- **23** Edenbridge House (Evening)
- **37** Highlands
- **44** Kypp Cottage
- **48** Lewins (Evening)
- **78** Rock Farm
- **97** Torry Hill (Evening)

THURSDAY 21
- **26** Garden Organic Yalding
- **44** Kypp Cottage

FRIDAY 22
- **44** Kypp Cottage

SATURDAY 23
- **34** Hannafore
- **43** Knowle Hill Farm (Evening)
- **44** Kypp Cottage
- **65** One Dering Road
- **78** Rock Farm

SUNDAY 24
- **7** Boldshaves
- **21** Cottage Farm
- **22** Doddington Place
- **33** Hall Place
- **38** Hole Park
- **51** Little Went
- **62** Old Buckhurst
- **65** One Dering Road
- **66** The Orangery
- **75** Quex House Gardens
- **85** Sevenoaks Allotments
- **92** Spilsill Court

98 Tram Hatch
101 Waystrode Manor
104 Windy Ridge

MONDAY 25
44 Kypp Cottage

TUESDAY 26
5 Belmont
44 Kypp Cottage

WEDNESDAY 27
44 Kypp Cottage
78 Rock Farm

THURSDAY 28
44 Kypp Cottage
110 Yew Tree Cottage

FRIDAY 29
44 Kypp Cottage
110 Yew Tree Cottage

SATURDAY 30
40 Iden Croft Herb Gardens
44 Kypp Cottage
78 Rock Farm
110 Yew Tree Cottage

July

SUNDAY 1
23 Edenbridge House
32 115 Hadlow Road
40 Iden Croft Herb Gardens
53 Lords
62 Old Buckhurst
81 St Michael's Gardens
84 Sea Close
110 Yew Tree Cottage

TUESDAY 3
73 Primrose Cottage

WEDNESDAY 4
16 Chartwell
42 Knole
62 Old Buckhurst
73 Primrose Cottage
78 Rock Farm

THURSDAY 5
110 Yew Tree Cottage

FRIDAY 6
110 Yew Tree Cottage

SATURDAY 7
2 Ashley
65 One Dering Road
78 Rock Farm
110 Yew Tree Cottage

SUNDAY 8
2 Ashley
8 Boyton Court (Evening)
33 Hall Place
65 One Dering Road
94 Squerryes Court
110 Yew Tree Cottage

WEDNESDAY 11
78 Rock Farm

SATURDAY 14
62 Old Buckhurst
65 One Dering Road
68 Orchard End

SUNDAY 15
15 Charts Edge
19 Cobham Hall
22 Doddington Place
46 Larch Cottage
65 One Dering Road
68 Orchard End
91 Sparks Hall
98 Tram Hatch
107 The World Garden at Lullingstone Castle

SATURDAY 21
65 One Dering Road

SUNDAY 22
37 Highlands
59 Mounts Court Farmhouse
65 One Dering Road
67 Orchard Cottage
104 Windy Ridge

THURSDAY 26
44 Kypp Cottage
110 Yew Tree Cottage

FRIDAY 27
44 Kypp Cottage
110 Yew Tree Cottage

SATURDAY 28
44 Kypp Cottage
110 Yew Tree Cottage

SUNDAY 29
32 115 Hadlow Road
44 Kypp Cottage
62 Old Buckhurst
66 The Orangery
88 Sotts Hole Cottage
110 Yew Tree Cottage

August

WEDNESDAY 1
42 Knole

THURSDAY 2
110 Yew Tree Cottage

FRIDAY 3
44 Kypp Cottage
110 Yew Tree Cottage

SATURDAY 4
44 Kypp Cottage
65 One Dering Road
110 Yew Tree Cottage

SUNDAY 5
4 Beech Court Gardens
44 Kypp Cottage
49 Leydens
62 Old Buckhurst
65 One Dering Road
76 Riddles Road Allotments
110 Yew Tree Cottage

WEDNESDAY 8
56 Marle Place

FRIDAY 10
44 Kypp Cottage

SATURDAY 11
44 Kypp Cottage
65 One Dering Road

SUNDAY 12
44 Kypp Cottage
65 One Dering Road

MONDAY 13
86 Sissinghurst Garden

WEDNESDAY 15
75 Quex House Gardens (Evening)
84 Sea Close

THURSDAY 16
26 Garden Organic Yalding

FRIDAY 17
44 Kypp Cottage

SATURDAY 18
44 Kypp Cottage

SUNDAY 19
44 Kypp Cottage
47 Laurenden Forstal
102 West Studdal Farm

FRIDAY 24
44 Kypp Cottage
71 The Pines Garden

SATURDAY 25
18 Chilham Castle
44 Kypp Cottage
65 One Dering Road

SUNDAY 26
32 115 Hadlow Road
44 Kypp Cottage
52 Longacre
65 One Dering Road
105 Withersdane Hall

MONDAY 27
44 Kypp Cottage
52 Longacre
65 One Dering Road

TUESDAY 28
44 Kypp Cottage

WEDNESDAY 29
44 Kypp Cottage

THURSDAY 30
44 Kypp Cottage
110 Yew Tree Cottage

FRIDAY 31
44 Kypp Cottage
110 Yew Tree Cottage

September

SATURDAY 1
62 Old Buckhurst
65 One Dering Road
110 Yew Tree Cottage

SUNDAY 2
- ⑪ Broadview Gardens
- ㉒ Old Buckhurst
- ㉕ One Dering Road
- ㉙ Squerryes Court
- ⑩ Yew Tree Cottage

WEDNESDAY 5
- ㉒ Old Buckhurst

THURSDAY 6
- ⑩ Yew Tree Cottage

FRIDAY 7
- ⑩ Yew Tree Cottage

SATURDAY 8
- ㉒ Old Buckhurst
- ⑩ Yew Tree Cottage

SUNDAY 9
- ㉒ Doddington Place
- ㉓ Edenbridge House
- ㉙ Goodnestone Park Gardens
- ㊸ Knowle Hill Farm
- ㊾ Little Oast
- ㉒ Old Buckhurst
- ㊷ Rock Farm
- ㊼ Sotts Hole Cottage
- ⑩ Yew Tree Cottage

WEDNESDAY 12
- ㉓ Edenbridge House

SATURDAY 15
- ㊽ Orchard End

SUNDAY 16
- ㊿ Nettlestead Place
- ㊽ Orchard End
- ⑩ Windy Ridge

SUNDAY 23
- ㊾ Mount Ephraim
- ㋑ Placketts Hole (Evening)
- ㊴ Sea Close

THURSDAY 27
- ⑩ Yew Tree Cottage

FRIDAY 28
- ⑩ Yew Tree Cottage

SATURDAY 29
- ⑩ Yew Tree Cottage

SUNDAY 30
- ⑩ Yew Tree Cottage

October

MONDAY 8
- ㊻ Sissinghurst Garden

SUNDAY 14
- ㊳ Hole Park
- ㊲ Mere House

SATURDAY 20
- ⑱ Chilham Castle

SUNDAY 28
- ⑫ Brogdale Horticultural Trust

November

SUNDAY 4
- ㉚ Great Comp Garden

SUNDAY 11
- ④ Beech Court Gardens

Private gardens opening regularly for the NGS
- ㊹ Kypp Cottage
- ㉕ One Dering Road
- ㊲ Rock Farm
- ⑩ Yew Tree Cottage

Gardens open to the public
- ④ Beech Court Gardens
- ⑤ Belmont
- ⑪ Broadview Gardens
- ⑫ Brogdale Horticultural Trust
- ⑮ Charts Edge
- ⑯ Chartwell
- ⑱ Chilham Castle
- ⑲ Cobham Hall
- ㉒ Doddington Place
- ㉓ Edenbridge House
- ㉔ Emmetts Garden
- ㉖ Garden Organic Yalding
- ㉗ Godinton House & Gardens
- ㉙ Goodnestone Park Gardens
- ㉚ Great Comp Garden
- ㊱ Hever Castle & Gardens
- ㊳ Hole Park
- ㊵ Iden Croft Herb Gardens
- ㊶ Ightham Mote
- ㊷ Knole
- ㊼ Marle Place
- ㊾ Mount Ephraim
- ㉒ Old Buckhurst
- ㊹ Penshurst Place
- ㊸ The Pines Garden
- ㊻ Quex House Gardens
- ㊼ Riverhill House Gardens
- ㊸ Scotney Castle
- ㊻ Sissinghurst Garden
- ㉙ Squerryes Court
- ⑩ The World Garden at Lullingstone Castle

By appointment only
- ① Abbotsmerry Barn
- ㊽ Old Place Farm
- ㊽ Pedlinge Court
- ㊾ South Hill Farm
- ㊻ Timbers
- ㊾ Troutbeck

The Gardens

① ABBOTSMERRY BARN
Salmans Lane, Penshurst TN11 8DJ.
Margaret & Keith Wallis, 01892
870900, www.abbotsmerry.co.uk.
*5m W of Tonbridge. Off B2176 in
direction Leigh: 200yds N of Penshurst
turn L, 1m down lane with speed
ramps.* **Adm £4, chd free. Visitors
welcome by appt.**
Garden developed over 22yrs on a
7½-acre undulating S-facing slope to
take advantage of existing features and
differing planting conditions.
Herbaceous plants and roses are
complemented by bulbs, shrubs and
trees to provide a cheerful variety of
flowers and foliage.
✗ ⊛

ARDEN LODGE
See Surrey.

② ASHLEY
White Horse Lane, Otham,
Maidstone ME15 8RQ. Susan &
Roger Chartier. *4m SE of Maidstone.
From A20 or A274 follow signs for
Otham or Stoneacre; located between
White Horse PH and Simmonds Lane.*
**Adm £2, chd free (share to Kent
Autistic Trust). Sat 7, Sun 8 July
(2-6).**
Originally part of Otham's Kent
cobnut orchard, ⅓-acre garden
has been developed since 1993.
Many unusual perennials, pond with
bridge, and productive kitchen
garden. Raised bed displaying
collection of over 30 scented-leaf
pelargoniums.
♿ ✗ ⊛

BATEMAN'S
See Sussex.

③ BATTEL HALL
Burberry Lane, Leeds, Maidstone
ME17 1RH. Mr John D Money. *5m E
of Maidstone. From A20 Hollingbourne
roundabout take B2163 S (signed
Leeds Castle). At top of hill take
Burberry Lane, house 100yds on R.*
Home-made teas. **Adm £2, chd (over
7) £1. Sun 13 May (2-5.30).**
Garden of approx 1 acre created since
1954 around medieval house (not
open); very ancient wisteria, mixed
planting of bulbs, shrubs, roses and
herbaceous plants.
♿ ✗ ☕

4 ◆ **BEECH COURT GARDENS**
Challock TN25 4DJ. Mr & Mrs
Vyvyan Harmsworth, 01233 740735,
www.beechcourtgardens.co.uk. 5m
N of Ashford. W of Xrds A251/A252,
off the Lees. Adm £4.50, chd £1,
concessions £3.80. Apr to Sept (not
Fris). Weekends in Oct, Nov by
arrangement. For NGS: Suns 13
May; 5 Aug; Remembrance Sunday
11 Nov (12-dusk).
Informal woodland garden surrounding
medieval farmhouse (not open). Spring
bulbs, rhododendrons, azaleas and
viburnums give superb spring colour;
climbing roses, summer borders and
hydrangeas follow; fine collection of
trees incl acers give autumn colour;
plus extensive lawns, meandering
paths and surprising vistas. Picnic
area.
♿ ⚑ ⊛ ☕

A natural spring
has been
harnessed to
create ponds . . .

5 ◆ **BELMONT**
Belmont Park, Throwley, Faversham
ME13 0HH. Harris (Belmont) Charity,
01795 890202, www.belmont-
house.org. 4¹/₂ m SW of Faversham.
A251 Faversham-Ashford. At
Badlesmere, brown tourist signs to
Belmont. Adm £3, chd £1. From Mar
31 open daily all yr (10-6, or dusk if
earlier). For NGS: Tue 26 June
(10-6).
House surrounded by large formal
lawns dotted with fine specimen trees,
woodland area, pinetum and small
walled garden, the latter containing
long borders, wisteria and large rose
border. Large walled kitchen garden,
recently restored (designed by Arabella
Lennox Boyd), features mix of lawns,
fruit, vegetables and flowers. Also
formal beds, nuttery and wild grass.
♿ ⊛ ☕

6 **BILTING HOUSE**
nr Ashford TN25 4HA. Mr John Erle-
Drax. 5m NE of Ashford. A28, 9m
from Canterbury. Wye 1¹/₂ m. Home-
made teas. Adm £2.50, chd £1.25.
Suns 20 May; 10 June (2-6).
6-acre garden with ha-ha set in
beautiful part of Stour Valley. Wide

variety of rhododendrons, azaleas and
ornamental shrubs. Woodland walk
with spring bulbs. Mature arboretum
with new planting of specimen trees.
Rose garden and herbaceous borders.
Conservatory.
♿ ⚑ ☕

7 **NEW** **BOLDSHAVES**
Woodchurch, nr Ashford
TN26 3RA. Mr & Mrs Peregrine
Massey, 01233 860302. Between
Woodchurch & High Halden. From
A28 towards Ashford, turn R at
village green in High Halden. 2nd
R, Redbrook St, towards
Woodchurch, before R on
unmarked lane. After ¹/₂ m R
through brick entrance. Ignore oast
house on L, follow signs to car
park. Cream teas. Adm £4, chd
free (share to Kent Minds). Suns
22 Apr; 27 May; 24 June (2-6).
Visitors also welcome by appt
last Sun of month (not Apr, May,
June) for groups of 8+,
minibuses but no coaches
please. £5 per person.
7-acre garden with a number of
new features being developed.
Partly terraced, S-facing, with
ornamental trees and shrubs,
walled garden, herbaceous
borders, bluebell walks, woodland
and ponds. Paintings & home-
made produce for sale. Grass
paths.
♿ ⚑ ⊛ ☕

8 **BOYTON COURT**
Sutton Valence ME17 3BY. Richard
& Patricia Stileman, 01622 844065,
richstileman@aol.com. 5m SE of
Maidstone. ¹/₂ m E of centre of Sutton
Valence, turn R at 1st Xrds on rd from
Sutton Valence to E Sutton, Boyton
Court 200yds on L. Home-made teas.
Adm £3.50, chd free. Mon 28 May
(11-5). Evening Opening, wine &
light refreshments, Sun 8 July (6-10).
Visitors also welcome by appt,
groups of 10+.
3-acre garden on S edge of greensand
ridge affording spectacular views over
the Weald. Garden falls in series of
slopes and terraces through which
water from a natural spring has been
harnessed to create ponds and other
water features. Large mixed borders
and several intimate areas featuring
yew, box, Austin roses, irises, lavender,
perennial geraniums, sedums etc.
⚑ ⇋ ☕

9 **BRADBOURNE HOUSE AND**
GARDENS
East Malling ME19 6DZ. East
Malling Trust for Horticultural
Research. 4m NW of Maidstone.
Entrance is E of New Rd, which runs
from Larkfield on A20 S to E Malling.
Home-made teas. Adm £3, chd free.
Sun 29 Apr (2-5) with music by
local classical quartet.
The Hatton Fruit Garden consists of
demonstration fruit gardens of
particular interest to amateurs, in
walled former kitchen garden and incl
intensive forms of apples and pears.
Members of staff will be available for
questions. Children's quiz, musical
entertainment and viewing of
Bradbourne House also provided.
Exhibits by scientists from local
Horticultural Research Centre.
Featured in 'Kent Messenger'. Gravel
paths. Disabled access to ground floor
of House.
♿ ⚑ ⊛ ☕

10 ◆ **1 BRICKWALL COTTAGES**
Frittenden TN17 2DH. Mrs Sue
Martin, 01580 852425. 6m NW of
Tenterden. E of A229 between
Cranbrook & Staplehurst & W of A274
between Biddenden & Headcorn. Park
in village & walk along footpath opp
school. Home-made teas. Adm £2,
chd free. Sun 15 Apr; Sat 12, Sun 13
May (2-5.30). Visitors also welcome
by appt.
Small cottage garden in centre of
village which incl borders full of unusual
hardy perennials. Some alterations are
planned: the lavender walk will be
replaced by a pergola and formal
pond; more beds will be dug to
accommodate the National Collection
of geums (provisional status). Shade
areas with woodland plants. Specialist
nursery.
♿ ⊛ **NCCPG** ☕

11 ◆ **BROADVIEW GARDENS**
Hadlow College, Hadlow TN11 0AL.
Hadlow College, 01732 853211,
www.hadlow.ac.uk. 1m NE of
Tonbridge. On A26 9m SW of
Maidstone. Adm £2, chd free.
Gardens open all yr 10-5, Suns 10-4.
For NGS: Thur 22 Feb (10-5); Sun 2
Sept (10-4).
8 acres of ornamental planting in
attractive landscape setting; 100 meter
double long border, island beds with
mixed plantings, lake and water
gardens; series of demonstration
gardens incl Italian, oriental and

cottage gardens. National Collections of *Anemone japonica* and hellebores.

12 ◆ BROGDALE HORTICULTURAL TRUST
Faversham ME13 8XZ. Brogdale Horticultural Trust, 01795 535286, www.brogdale.org.uk. *1/2 m S of Faversham. M2 J6, turn L towards Faversham, follow brown tourist signs. From stn make for A2, turn R then L into Brogdale Rd (3/4 m aprox).* **Adm £5, chd £4.50, concessions £3 (incl guided tour). Daily Apr to early Nov.** For NGS: Suns 29 Apr; 28 Oct (10-5).
The National Fruit Collections. 60 acres of orchards with 4,000 old and new varieties of apples, pears, plums and cherries. Guided walks through fruit collections and expert advice. Fruit tastings and sales in Oct. Miniature railway. Featured on BBC TV Gardeners' World & in 'The Times'.

13 CANTERBURY CATHEDRAL GARDENS
CT1 2EP, www.canterbury-cathedral.org. *Canterbury Cathedral Precincts. Enter Precincts by main Christchurch gate. No access for cars: please use park & ride and public car parks.* Gardens will be signed within Precincts. **Combined Cathedral and NGS gardens ticket £8, concessions £7. Precinct pass holders £3. Sat 2 June (11-5.30), Sun 3 June (2-5.30).**
Five gardens all set against the magnificent background of Canterbury Cathedral. This year we are holding the official opening of our new Medicinal Herb Garden on the first day of our Open Weekend. Not a formal garden, nor a 'traditional' one, this is more a collection of herbs, most of which are to be found growing wild in the countryside and which nowadays are called weeds or wild flowers! The majority of plants found here would have found a place in the remedies of the 'infirmerer', as for today's modern herbalists. We are hoping to have herbalists on hand over our Open Days to give talks, demonstrations and answer questions. Some wheelchair limitation.

ARCHDEACONRY 29 THE PRECINCTS
3/4 acre of medieval walled garden with mixed planting of roses, shrubs, grasses and very old mulberry tree.

THE DEANERY
The Dean
Large garden of over 1 acre with small orchard and 'wild' area, lawns, herbaceous border and vegetable garden.

15 THE PRECINCTS
Canon & Mrs E Condry
Large walled garden bounded on one side by the City Wall. Large herbaceous bank. A little more formal, in keeping with this historical house.

19 THE PRECINCTS
Small enclosed garden with a view dominated by the Cathedral.

22 THE PRECINCTS
Canon Clare Edwards
Front garden planted to attract birds and insects. Back garden a very small walled 'secret' garden.

New rainbow borders and rill, fine views over North Downs . . .

14 CHAINHURST COTTAGE GARDENS
Chainhurst, Marden TN12 9SU. *6m S of Maidstone, 3m N of Marden. From Marden proceed along Pattenden Lane; at T-junction turn L, follow signs to Chainhurst. In Chainhurst take 2nd turning on L. From Maidstone take A229. At Stile Bridge Inn fork R, then 1st R until NGS signs appear.* Home-made teas. **Combined adm £3.50, chd free. Sun 3 June (2-6). Evening Opening, £4, wine, Wed 6 June (6-9).**
Rural hamlet surrounded by arable farmland.

1 CHAINHURST COTTAGES
Audrey & John Beeching
Informal cottage garden, gravel area with mixed grasses and water feature alongside a blue and yellow border. Meadow with hedge of native species. Summerhouse, paved terrace, lily pond, vegetable and cutting garden.

3 CHAINHURST COTTAGES
Heather & Richard Scott
Cottage garden of more formal design with clipped box hedging and Mediterranean planting. Double herbaceous borders with burgundy and silver plants. Greenhouse, vegetable beds and pergola leading to lower gravelled area with vine-covered wall.

15 ◆ CHARTS EDGE
Westerham TN16 1PL.
Mr & Mrs J Bigwood, 01732 504556, www.chartsedgegardens.co.uk. *1/2 m S of Westerham, 4m N of Edenbridge. On B2026 towards Chartwell.* **Adm £3.50, chd free. Suns & Fris mid Apr to mid Sept.** For NGS: Suns 20 May; 17 June; 15 July (2-5).
7-acre hillside garden being restored by present owners; large collection of rhododendrons, azaleas and magnolias; specimen trees and newly-planted mixed borders; many rare plants; majority of plants labelled; Victorian folly; walled fruit garden; rock garden. Water gardens and cascade. New rainbow borders and rill. Fine views over N Downs.

16 ◆ CHARTWELL
nr Westerham TN16 1PS. The National Trust, 01732 868381, www.nationaltrust.org.uk. *4m N of Edenbridge. 2m S of Westerham. Fork L off B2026 after 11/2 m.* **House & garden £10.80, chd £5.40. Garden only £5.40, chd £2.70. Weds to Suns 17 Mar to 1 July & 5 Sept to 28 Oct. Tues to Suns 3 July to 2 Sept (11-5).** For NGS: Wed 4 July (11-5).
12-acre informal gardens on hillside with glorious views over Weald of Kent. Water garden and lakes together with red-brick wall built by Sir Winston Churchill, former owner of Chartwell. Avenue of golden roses given by Sir Winston's children on his golden wedding anniversary runs down the centre of a productive kitchen garden, re-established in 2004.

17 CHEVENING
nr Sevenoaks TN14 6HG. The Board of Trustees of the Chevening Estate. *4m NW of Sevenoaks. Turn N off A25 at Sundridge T-lights on to B2211; at Chevening Xrds 11/2 m turn L.* Home-made teas. **Adm £3.50, chd free. Sun 17 June (2-5.30).**

27 acres with lawns and woodland garden, lake, maze, formal rides, parterre. Gravel paths, unfenced lake.

 ♿ ⊕ ☕

18 ◆ **CHILHAM CASTLE**
Chilham CT4 8DB. Mr & Mrs Wheeler, tessawheeler@chilham-castle.co.uk. *6m SW of Canterbury. No access to Castle grounds from Chilham Square. Follow yellow signs for car park and gardens entrance from A252, 1/2m from Chilham village towards Charing, signed on L Village Hall/Chilham Park. Car park & entrance at top of hill.* **Adm £4, chd under 5 free, concessions £3. Open second Tuesday of month, Apr to Sept (10-3). For NGS: Sats 25 Aug; 20 Oct (2-5.30).**
Garden surrounding Jacobean mansion (not open) leads onto C17 terraces with herbaceous borders comprehensively restored and designed by Lady Mary Keen and Pip Morrison. Topiary frames the magnificent views with lake walk below. Extensive kitchen and cutting garden beyond spring bulb filled Quiet Garden. Established trees and ha-ha leads onto park.

🍴 ☕

19 ◆ **COBHAM HALL**
Cobham DA12 3BL. Mr N G Powell, 01474 823371, www.cobhamhall.com. *5m W of Rochester. 8m E of M25 J2. Take A2 to exit signed Cobham, Shorne, Higham. Driveway entrance within 100yds on S side of A2.* **House & garden £4.50, chd/concessions £3.50. Garden only £2.50. Suns & Weds 28 Mar to 18 Apr, 11 July to 2 Sept, also Good Fri & Easter Mon. For NGS: Suns 15 Apr; 15 July (2-5).**
Beautiful Elizabethan mansion in 142 acres, landscaped by Humphry Repton at end C18. Herbaceous borders, formal parterres, C17 and C18 garden walls, yew hedges, lime avenue. Park with fine mature trees (cedars, oaks, ginkgos) and acres of naturalised daffodils, snowdrops and bluebells. Scheme to restore the grounds and garden buildings, incl Darnley Mausoleum, phase 1 due for completion spring 2007. Restoration of old pump house, aviary, bastion and Repton's seat in progress. Clearance of Pleasure Grounds to return to parkland of 1850 plan. Venue for filming BBC TV *Bleak House.*

♿ ☕

COLUMCILLE
See London.

20 **COPTON ASH**
105 Ashford Road, Faversham ME13 8XW. Drs Tim & Gillian Ingram, 01795 535919. *1/2m S of Faversham. On A251 Faversham to Ashford rd, opp E-bound J6 with M2.* Home-made teas. **Adm £2, chd free. Sun 4 Mar (12-4); Sun 8, Mon 9 Apr; Mons 7, 28 May (2-6). Visitors also welcome by appt.**
Garden grown out of a love and fascination with plants from an early age. Contains very wide collection incl many rarities and newly introduced species raised from wild seed. Special interest in woodland flowers, snowdrops and hellebores with flowering trees and shrubs of spring. Wide range of drought-tolerant plants. Gravel entrance, grass paths.

♿ 🍴 ⊕ ☕

21 ◆ **COTTAGE FARM**
Cackets Lane, Cudham TN14 7QG. Phil & Karen Baxter, 01959 532506. *5m NW of Sevenoaks, 4m SW of Orpington. Sign for Cudham from Green-Street-Green roundabout on A21. 3m into village, turn L past garage. 2nd block cottages on R. Entrance through working farmyard.* Cream teas. **Adm £4, chd free (share to Harris HospisCare). Suns 3, 10, 17, 24 June (1.30-5.30), (Sun 17 followed by BBQ, extra £3.50). Evening Opening £6, cheese & wine, Fri 15 June (7-9.30). Visitors also welcome by appt June only, coaches permitted.**
Cottage garden. No lawns! Intimate and individual style. Approx 1 acre. Self-sufficient vegetable and fruit gardens, with raised beds growing vegetables for exhibition. Tropical garden, fernery, greenhouses with tender and tropical fruits and flowers; rose-covered pergolas and wildlife ponds. Created and maintained by owner. New 2007 cutting garden. Featured in 'Kitchen Garden' & on Life TV Secret Gardens. Many gravel and bark paths, wheelchair user will need strong pusher.

♿ ⊕ 🛏 ☕

22 ◆ **DODDINGTON PLACE**
nr Sittingbourne ME9 0BB. Mr & Mrs Richard Oldfield, 01795 886385, www.doddington-place-gardens.co.uk. *6m SE of Sittingbourne. From A20 turn N opp Lenham or from A2 turn S at Teynham or Ospringe (Faversham), all 4m.* **Adm**

£4, chd £1. Suns & Bank Hol Mons Easter to end June (2-5). For NGS: Suns 24 June; 15 July; 9 Sept (2-5).
10-acre garden, landscaped with wide views; trees and yew hedges; woodland garden with azaleas and rhododendrons; Edwardian rock garden in midst of restoration (not wheelchair accessible); formal garden with mixed borders. Gothic folly.

♿ ⊕ ☕

Garden grown out of a love and fascination with plants . . .

23 ◆ **EDENBRIDGE HOUSE**
Edenbridge TN8 6SJ. Mrs M T Lloyd, 01732 862122, Ddgloyd@aol.com. *1 1/2m N of Edenbridge. Nr Marlpit Hill, on B2026.* Teas on NGS days. **Adm £3, chd free. Tues, Weds & Thurs, Apr to Sept (2-5). For NGS: Suns, Weds: 15 Apr; 6, 16 May; 17 June; 1 July; 9, 12 Sept (Suns 2-6, Weds 1-5). Evening Opening, £4, wine, 20 June (6-9).**
House part C16 (not open). 5-acre garden laid out in 1930s as a series of rooms, with herbaceous and mixed borders, old-fashioned and shrub roses, alpines, ornamental trees and shrubs, water and gravel gardens, orchard and wildlife pond, kitchen garden and greenhouses; many unusual plants. Group visits by arrangement.

♿ ⊕ ☕

24 ◆ **EMMETTS GARDEN**
Ide Hill TN14 6AY. The National Trust, 01732 868381, www.nationaltrust.org.uk. *5m SW of Sevenoaks. 1 1/2m S of A25 on Sundridge-Ide Hill Rd. 1 1/2m N of Ide Hill off B2042.* **Adm £5.50, chd £1. Tues to Suns 17 Mar to 3 Jun. Weds to Suns 6 June to 1 July. Weds, Sats & Suns 4 July to 28 Oct (11-5). For NGS: Sat 12 May (11-5 last adm 4.15).**
5-acre hillside garden, with the highest tree top in Kent, noted for its fine collection of rare trees and flowering shrubs. The garden is particularly fine in spring, while a rose garden, rock garden and extensive planting of acers for autumn colour extend the interest throughout the season.

♿ ⊕ ☕

㉕ FLINT COTTAGE
Bishopsbourne CT4 5BJ. Mr & Mrs
P J Sinnock, 01227 830691,
lesley@stew-pot.fsnet.co.uk. *4m SE
of Canterbury. Turn off A2 to Bridge,
through village, turn W at church,
follow garden signs.* Home-made teas.
Adm £2.50. Sun 6, Mon 7 May (2-
5.30). Visitors also welcome by appt
Apr to June only, for groups of 8+.
Small garden: the entrance to the
garden has large Scots pine
underplanted with trees and shrubs
and wildlife pond. Main garden: 3
ponds and 2 water features; bog
areas; mixed borders; alpines in sink
gardens; herb garden; vegetables in
raised beds. Bonsai display. Oil &
watercolour paintings on show, some
for sale. Regret not suitable for children
owing to ponds.

🎋 ❀ 🏠 ☕

**㉖ ◆ GARDEN ORGANIC
YALDING**
Benover Road, nr Maidstone
ME18 6EX. Garden Organic, 024
7630 3517,
www.gardenorganic.org.uk. *6m SW
of Maidstone, 1/2m S of Yalding, on
B2162. Yalding served by buses from
Maidstone & Tonbridge, railway stn
11/2m.* Adm £4, chd £1, concessions
£3.50. Weds to Suns & Bank Hols 31
Mar to 28 Oct. For NGS: Thurs 21
June; 16 Aug (10-5).
5 acres of stunning gardens tracing the
history of gardening from medieval
times to the present day. Children's
garden. Home cooking a speciality.

♿ 🎋 ❀ ☕

**㉗ ◆ GODINTON HOUSE &
GARDENS**
Godinton Lane, Ashford TN23 3BP.
Godinton House Preservation Trust,
01233 620773, www.godinton-
house-gardens.co.uk. *11/2m W of
Ashford. M20 J9 to Ashford. Take A20
towards Charing and Lenham, then
follow brown tourist signs.* House &
garden £6, chd free (incl guided
tour). Garden only £3, chd free.
Gardens Thurs to Mons 25 Mar to
28 Oct. House Fris to Suns 6 Apr to
9 Oct. For NGS: Suns 25 Mar; 1 Apr
(2-5.30).
Formal area designed c1900 by
Reginald Blomfield. Famous for its vast
yew hedge, cut to reflect the distinctive
gables, topiary, formal and informal
ponds. In spring the wild garden is a
mass of daffodils with fritillaries and
other spring flowers. Walled garden
contains the Delphinium Society's

border, greenhouse and cutting
garden. The intimate Italian garden has
Mediterranean-style planting. Rose
garden. Wonderful setting for the
Jacobean house. Featured in 'Daily
Telegraph'.

♿ 🎋 ❀ ☕

Rose beds, herbaceous borders and superb daffodils in restored wilderness . . .

㉘ GODMERSHAM PARK
Godmersham CT4 7DT. Mr John B
Sunley. *5m NE of Ashford. Off A28,
midway between Canterbury &
Ashford.* Home-made teas. Adm £3,
chd free. Sun 1 Apr (1-5).
Associations with Jane Austen. Early
Georgian mansion (not open) in
beautiful downland setting, 24 acres of
formal and landscaped gardens,
topiary, rose beds, herbaceous borders
and superb daffodils in restored
wilderness.

❀ ☕

**㉙ ◆ GOODNESTONE PARK
GARDENS**
Wingham CT3 1PL. Margaret, Lady
FitzWalter, 01304 840107, www.
goodnestoneparkgardens.co.uk. *6m
SE of Canterbury. Village lies S of
B2046 from A2 to Wingham. Brown
tourist signs off B2046.* Adm £4.50,
chd (6-16) £1, concessions £4. Suns
only 18 Feb to 21 Mar. 21 Mar to 5
Oct, Weds to Sats (11-5), Suns (12-
5). For NGS: Suns 11 Mar; 9 Sep
(12-5).
10-12 acres; good trees; woodland
garden, snowdrops, spring bulbs,
walled garden with old-fashioned
roses. Connections with Jane Austen
who stayed here. 2 arboretums
planted 1984 & 2001, gravel garden
established 2003. Picnics allowed.

♿ 🎋 ❀ ☕

㉚ ◆ GREAT COMP GARDEN
Platt TN15 8QS. Great Comp
Charitable Trust, 01732 886154,
www.greatcomp.co.uk. *7m E of
Sevenoaks. A20 at Wrotham Heath,
take Seven Mile Lane, B2016; at 1st
Xrds turn R; garden on L 1/2m.*

Adm £4.50, chd £1. Daily 1 Apr to 31
Oct. For NGS: Suns 4, 11, 18, 25
Mar; 4 Nov (11-5).
Skilfully designed 7-acre garden of
exceptional beauty. Spacious setting of
well-maintained lawns and paths lead
visitors through plantsman's collection
of trees, shrubs, heathers and
herbaceous plants. Good autumn
colour. Early C17 house (not open).
Magnolias, hellebores and snowflakes
are great feature in spring. A great
variety of perennials in summer incl
salvias, dahlias and crocosmias.
Featured in 'Daily Mail'.

♿ 🎋 ❀ ☕

㉛ GREAT MAYTHAM HALL
Maytham Road, Rolvenden
TN17 4NE. The Sunley Group, 01580
241346. *3m from Tenterden. Maytham
Rd off A28 at Rolvenden Church, 1/2m
from village on R.* Adm £4, chd free.
Wed 9 May; Wed 13 June (11-5).
Visitors also welcome by appt from
Apr to Oct, max 10, no coaches.
Lutyens-designed gardens famous for
having inspired Frances Hodgson
Burnett to write 'The Secret Garden'
(pre-Lutyens). Parkland, woodland with
bluebells. Walled garden with
herbaceous beds and rose pergola.
Pond garden with mixed shrubbery
and herbaceous borders. Interesting
specimen trees. Large lawned area
with far-reaching views. Featured on
Grand Designs.

🎋

㉜ 115 HADLOW ROAD
Tonbridge TN9 1QE. Mr & Mrs
Richard Esdale, 01732 353738.
*11/2m N of Tonbridge stn. Take A26
from N end of High St signed
Maidstone, house 1m on L in service
rd.* Home-made teas. Adm £2.50, chd
free. Suns 1, 29 July; 26 Aug (2-6).
Visitors also welcome by appt,
groups & individuals, coaches
permitted.
1/3-acre unusual terraced garden with
large collection of modern roses, island
herbaceous border, many clematis,
hardy fuchsias, heathers, grasses,
hostas, phormiums, and ferns, shrub
borders, alpines, annuals, kitchen
garden and pond; well labelled.

🎋 ☕

㉝ HALL PLACE
Leigh TN11 8HH. The Lady
Hollenden. *4m W of Tonbridge. From
A21 Sevenoaks to Tonbridge, B245 to
Hildenborough, then R onto B2027
through Leigh & on R.* Home-made

teas. **Adm £5, chd £2. Suns 24 June; 8 July (2-6).**
Large outstanding garden with 11-acre lake, lakeside walk crossing over picturesque bridges. Many rare and interesting trees and shrubs. Rolls-Royce Enthusiasts' Club 24 June. 30-40 Rolls-Royces & Bentleys usually attend.

 ♿ ☕

34 NEW HANNAFORE
Ruckinge TN26 2PB. Mrs Susan Causton. *4m S of Ashford. M20 J10, take A2070 signed Lydd. Take turning to Lydd/Ham Street. At Xrds in village, L to Ruckinge on B2067. Through Ruckinge, past church and Blue Anchor PH, Hannafore last house on R. Parking at Blue Anchor or village hall, except disabled at house. Coffee & cakes morning in church from 10-12.* **Adm £2.50, chd free (share to Ruckinge Church). Sat 23 June (12-5).**
Country garden set on edge of Romney Marsh leading to lovely views. Large mixed borders with unusual perennials, roses and shrubs. Young orchard incl apricot, quince and gages. Many climbers round the house and terrace crammed full with very large selection of pots full of colour.

 ♿ ✂

Massed bluebells, orchids in flower meadow and glorious autumn colours make this a garden for all seasons . . .

35 HAYDOWN
Great Buckland, Luddesdown DA13 0XF. Dr & Mrs I D Edeleanu, 01474 814329. *6m W of Rochester. 4m S of A2. Take turning for Cobham, at war memorial straight ahead down hill, under railway bridge to T-junction. Turn R, after 200yds take L fork, follow narrow lane for 1½m. Entrance on L after riding stables.* Home-made teas & wine. **Adm £3, chd free (share to**

Rotary Club of Northfleet). **Sun 10 June (2-5).** Visitors also welcome by appt May to July.
North Downs 9-acre hillside garden incl woodland with indigenous and unusual trees and meadowland with many varieties of wild orchids; orchard; ponds, vineyard (wine available) and other features. Conducted garden tours.

✂ ☸ ☕

36 ◆ HEVER CASTLE & GARDENS
nr Edenbridge TN8 7NG. Broadland Properties Ltd, 01732 865224, www.hevercastle.co.uk. *3m SE of Edenbridge. Between Sevenoaks & East Grinstead off B2026. Signed from J5 & J6 of M25, A21, A264.* **For adm prices please phone or visit website. Daily 1 Mar to 30 Nov, gardens from 11, castle from 12 (last exit 6pm).**
Romantic double moated castle, the childhood home of Anne Boleyn, in award-winning gardens. 110 metre-long herbaceous border planted in Edwardian style, colours from white through blues, pinks and hot colours. Formal Italian gardens with statuary, sculpture and fountains; large lake; 'splashing' water maze; rose garden, Tudor herb and knot garden, topiary, maze. Spring Garden Week 19-25 Mar; Rose Week 15-21 Jun. No dogs in grounds.

 ♿ ✂ ☸ ☕

37 HIGHLANDS
Hackington Close, St Stephen's, Canterbury CT2 7BB. Dr & Mrs B T Grayson. *1m N of Canterbury. At the foot of St Stephen's Hill, 200yds N of Archbishops School, on rd to Tyler Hill & Chestfield. Car parking on St Stephen's Hill Rd or Downs Rd, opp Hackington Close or nearby side sts.* Home-made teas. **Adm £3, chd free. Suns 1 Apr; Sun 13 May (2-5); Wed 20 June; Sun 22 July (11-5).**
2-acre peaceful garden, set in S-facing bowl, with sweeps of narcissus in spring and island beds of herbaceous perennials, roses, azaleas, acers, hydrangeas, hebes and other shrubs. Many conifer and broad-leafed trees, incl plantation of ornamental trees. Two ponds, small alpine bed and hanging gardens feature.

 ♿ ✂ ☸ ☕

38 ◆ HOLE PARK
Rolvenden, Cranbrook TN17 4JB. Mr & Mrs E G Barham, 01580 241344, www.holepark.com. *4m SW*

of Tenterden. Midway between Rolvenden & Beneden on B2086. **Adm £4, chd 50p. Suns & Bank Hol Mons 1 Apr to 1 July incl; Suns 30 Sept; 7, 14, 21 Oct. Weds & Thurs Apr to end Oct. For NGS: Suns 15 Apr; 20 May; 24 June; 14 Oct (2-6). Evening Opening,** wine, **Wed 13 June (5-8).**
First opened in 1927. 15-acre garden surrounded by parkland with beautiful views, yew hedges, large lawns and specimen trees. Walled gardens, pools and mixed borders combine with bulbs, rhododendrons and azaleas. Massed bluebells in woodland walk, standard wisterias, orchids in flower meadow and glorious autumn colours make this a garden for all seasons.

 ♿ ✂ ☸ ☕

39 HONNINGTON FARM
Vauxhall Lane, Southborough, Tunbridge Wells TN4 0XD. Mrs Ann Tyler, 07780 800790, sianburgess@gmail.com. *Between Tonbridge and Tunbridge Wells, E of A26 signed Honnington Equestrian Centre.* Cream teas. **Adm £3.50, chd free. Sats, Suns 21, 22 Apr; 19, 20 May (11-4).** Visitors also welcome by appt Apr to Sept for groups of 5+.
6-acre garden developed over several yrs by present owner. Heavy clay soil is enriched yearly and produces a wide range of habitats, incl water and bog gardens, primrose and bluebell walks. Wildlife promotion a priority. New natural swimming pool in newly planted wild flower meadow. Resident sculptor exhibiting. Now selling climbing roses.

✂ ☸ ☕

40 ◆ IDEN CROFT HERB GARDENS
Frittenden Road, Staplehurst TN12 0DH. Mr Philip Haynes, 01580 891432, www.herbs-uk.com. *9m S of Maidstone. Brown tourist signs on A229 just S of Staplehurst.* **Adm £4, chd free, concessions £3. Mons to Sats (9-5), Suns & Bank Hols (11-5). For NGS: Sat 26, Sun 27 May; Sat 30 June; Sun 1 July (11-5).**
Created over the past 34yrs. Threaded with winding paths, which lead to Tudor walled garden. Unique atmosphere, with massed rosemary, wall plants and herbaceous borders. Themed gardens incl culinary, medicinal, pot-pourri and sensory. National Plant Collections of mentha, nepeta and origanum and large collections of lavenders and thyme.

 ♿ ☸ **NCCPG** ☕

41 ◆ **IGHTHAM MOTE**
Ivy Hatch TN15 0NT. **The National Trust, 01732 811371, www.nationaltrust.org.uk.** *6m E of Sevenoaks. Off A25, 2¹/₂m S of Ightham. Buses from rail stns Sevenoaks or Borough Green to Ivy Hatch, ¹/₂m walk to Ightham Mote.* **Adm £9.50, chd £4.75. Daily 4 Mar to 28 Oct. For NGS: Thur 14 June (10-5.30 last adm 5).**
14-acre garden and moated medieval manor c1330. Mixed borders with many unusual plants; lawns; courtyard; orchard of Kent apples; water features incl small lake, leading to woodland walk with trees, rhododendrons and other shrubs.
&. ✕ ❀ ☕

42 ◆ **KNOLE**
Sevenoaks TN15 0RP. **The Lord Sackville & The National Trust, 01732 462100, www.nationaltrust.org.uk.** *1m SE of Sevenoaks, well signed. Stn: Sevenoaks.* **House & garden £10.50, chd £5.25. Garden only £2, chd £1. Weds 17 Mar to 28 Oct (11-4, last adm 3.30). For NGS: Weds 4 Apr; 2 May; 6 June; 4 July; 1 Aug (11-4 last adm 3.30).**
Pleasance, deer park, landscape garden, herb garden.
&. ✕ ☕

43 **KNOWLE HILL FARM**
Ulcombe ME17 1ES. **The Hon Andrew & Mrs Cairns, 01622 850240.** *7m SE of Maidstone. From M20 J8 follow A20 towards Lenham for approx 2m. Turn R to Ulcombe. After 1¹/₂m, 1st L, ¹/₂m 1st R. Past Pepper Box PH, 1m 1st L.* Home-made teas on Sun. **Adm £3, chd free. Sun 9 Sept (2-6). Evening Opening, wine, Sat 23 June (5-8). Visitors also welcome by appt May to Sept.**
1¹/₂-acre garden created over last 21yrs on S-facing slope of the Downs with spectacular views. Mixed borders contain Mediterranean and tender plants, roses and grasses. Pool and rill is enclosed within small walled garden planted mainly with white flowers. Easy-care planting around entrance. New layout and planting incl mini vegetable and herb garden. Steep slopes.
&. ✕ ❀ ☕

44 **KYPP COTTAGE**
Woolpack Corner, Biddenden TN27 8BU. **Mrs Zena Grant, 01580 291480.** *5m N of Tenterden. 1m S of*
Biddenden on A262 at junction with Benenden Rd. Home-made teas. **Adm £2, chd free (share to All Saints Church, Biddenden). Fri 25 to Wed 30 May incl. All June (not Suns). Thur 26 to Sun 29 July incl. Every Fri, Sat & Sun in Aug, also Mon 27 Aug to Fri 31 Aug incl. (May/June all dates 11-5.30; July/Aug Mons to Sats 11-5.30, Suns 2-5.30). Visitors also welcome by appt in June & Aug for groups of 10+, coaches permitted.**
Not for the tidy minded! ¹/₂-acre romantic foliage enfolding garden where shrubs, 200 different roses, mainly scented, and 60 clematis ramble and entwine. Thick tapestry of ground cover, predominantly geraniums, ferns and shade lovers in semi-woodland. Summerhouse. Garden created from builder's yard, planted and maintained by owner. Small collection hydrangeas and Euphorbia Nymans.
✕ ☕

Living willow shelter with earth seat overlooking pond . . .

45 **LADHAM HOUSE**
Goudhurst TN17 1DB. **Mr Guy Johnson.** *8m E of Tunbridge Wells. On NE of village, off A262. Through village towards Cranbrook, turn L at The Chequers PH. 2nd R into Ladham Rd, main gates approx 500yds on L.* Home-made teas. **Adm £3.50, chd 50p. Sun 20 May (2-5).**
10 acres with rolling lawns, fine specimen trees, rhododendrons, camellias, azaleas, shrubs and magnolias. Arboretum. Spectacular twin mixed borders; ha-ha; fountain and bog gardens. Fine view. Edwardian rockery reopened but inaccessible to wheelchairs.
&. ✕ ☕

46 **LARCH COTTAGE**
Seed Road, nr Doddington ME9 0NN. **Mr & Mrs J Howell, www.larchcottagegarden.co.uk.** *2¹/₂m S of Doddington, 9m S of Sittingbourne. From A2 nr Ospringe to Newnham turn L by church, 2¹/₂m S*
along Seed Rd. From A20 nr Lenham proceed to Warren St. At Harrow turn N, follow signs for Newnham along Slade Rd, approx 1¹/₂m. From Doddington village follow signs up Hopes Hill (opp butcher). **Adm £3, chd free. Suns 10 June; 15 July (11-5).**
3-acre garden on N Downs developed and maintained by owners over the past 28yrs. Contrasting areas incl knot garden, woodland and rhododendrons, colour-themed mixed borders, ponds and secret garden.
✕ ❀ ☕

47 **LAURENDEN FORSTAL**
Blind Lane, Challock TN25 4AU. **Mrs M Cottrell.** *6m N of Ashford. Close to junction of A251 & A252, access from both. All parking in field off village hall car park behind house.* Home-made teas. **Adm £2.50, chd under 12 free. Sat 31 Mar; Suns 17 June; 19 Aug (2-6).**
2-acre garden with woodland and rhododendrons, around part C14 house (not open). Rose walk and extensive yew hedging framing lawns and borders. Partly walled rose garden overlooking large wildlife pond; courtyard white garden. Vegetable garden with raised beds, living willow shelter with earth seat overlooking pond. Featured in GGG. Gravel drive, some uneven paths.
&. ❀ ☕

48 **NEW** **LEWINS**
Main Road, Crockham Hill, Edenbridge TN8 6RB. **Derek & Valerie Roberts.** *3m N of Edenbridge, 2¹/₂m S of Westerham. M25, J6, then A25. After 4m turn R, Crockham Hill on B269 (Kent Hatch Rd). Entering Westerham from E take B2026 towards Edenbridge, through Crockham Hill, Lewins last house on L at 40mph sign.* **Adm £2.50, chd free. Sun 10, Wed 13 June (11-5.30). Evening Opening £3.50, wine, Wed 20 June (6-9).**
Large Victorian house (not open) with 4-acre garden on S-facing slope at 400ft with superb panoramic views. 3 ponds, one with fountain, raised beds and selection of interesting trees and shrubs. Over 600 roses incl 200yd rose hedge. Small vineyard. Gravel paths, some gentle slopes. No wheelchair access to natural pond area.
&. ☕

49 LEYDENS
Edenbridge TN8 5NH. Mr Roger
Platts. *1m S of Edenbridge. On B2026
towards Hartfield (use Nursery
entrance & car park).* Adm £3.50, chd
free. Sun 5 Aug (12-5). Also open
Old Buckhurst.
Private garden of garden designer,
nursery owner and author who created
the NGS Garden at Chelsea in 2002,
winning Gold and Best in Show.
Garden at Leydens started in
1999/2000 and under constant
development, featuring a wide range of
shrubs and perennials and a newly-
laid-out front garden/drive area. Plenty
of planting ideas, several water
features, plants clearly labelled and fact
sheet available. Wild flower meadow
and adjacent nursery, display and
propagation beds. New area of garden
for 2007.

50 LITTLE OAST
High Street, Otford TN14 5PH. Mrs
Pam Hadrill, 01959 523637. *3m N of
Sevenoaks. At W end of village, just
past Horns PH, turn R into private
drive. (Please park in public car park
opp Bull PH or in Catholic Church car
park 80yds past Little Oast).* Home-
made teas. Adm £2.50, chd free. Sun
9 Sept (2-5). Visitors also welcome
by appt, groups of 10+.
This tranquil and peaceful garden has
taken over 50yrs to become what it is
today, full of mature trees, plants, ferns,
grasses and shrubs, 3 summerhouses
and a pond, with seats in secluded
corners where you can enjoy your tea
and cakes.

51 LITTLE WENT
106 High Street, West Malling
ME19 6NE. Anne Baring, 01732
843388. *5m W of Maidstone. In middle
of West Malling opp car park; entry
through gates marked.* Home-made
teas. Adm £3, chd free (share to St
Mary's Church). Sun 24 June (12-6).
Visitors also welcome by appt.
Long narrow secret garden, fish
ponds, aviary with lovebirds,
conservatory, gravel garden. Exhibition
of paintings for sale. Market Day in
High St (8-1).

52 LONGACRE
Selling ME13 9SE. Dr & Mrs G
Thomas, 01227 752254. *5m SE of
Faversham. From A2 (M2) or A251
follow signs for Selling, passing White*

*Lion on L. 2nd R & immed L, continue
for ¼ m. From A252 at Chilham, take
turning signed Selling at Badgers Hill
Garden Centre. L at 2nd Xrds, next R,
L & then R.* Home-made teas. Adm
£2.50, chd free. Sun 22 Apr; Suns,
Bank Hol Mons 6, 7, 13, 20, 27, 28
May; Sun 26, Mon 27 Aug (2-5).
Visitors also welcome by appt.
Plantsman's garden with wide variety
of interesting plants, gravel garden and
raised vegetable beds. We aim to have
colour and interest throughout spring
and summer using bulbs, annuals and
many containers with cannas,
eucomis, *Arundo donax*, etc.
Conservatory displays range of tender
plants.

Plenty of planting ideas, several water features, plants clearly labelled . . .

53 LORDS
Ashford Road, Sheldwich,
Faversham ME13 0NJ. Jane Wade.
*4m S of Faversham. From A2 or M2
take A251. ½ m S of Sheldwich church
find entrance lane on R side adjacent
to wood.* Adm £3, chd free. Sun 1
July (2-6).
C18 walled garden with organic
vegetables, Mediterranean herb
terrace, rose walk and flowery mead
under fruit trees. Old specimen trees
incl 100ft tulip tree, yew hedges,
lawns, cherry orchard, ponds and
woodland walk.

54 LUTON HOUSE
Selling ME13 9RQ. Sir John & Lady
Swire, 01227 752234. *4m SE of
Faversham. From A2 (M2) or A251
make for White Lion, entrance 30yds E
on same side of rd.* Adm £3, chd free.
Suns 15 Apr; 13 May (2-6). Visitors
also welcome by appt in early
summer for 10+, no coaches.
6 acres; C19 landscaped garden;
ornamental ponds; trees underplanted
with azaleas, camellias, woodland
plants. Hellebores, spring bulbs,
magnolias, cherries, daphnes, halesias,
maples, Judas trees and cyclamen.
Featured in local press and radio.

55 190 MAIDSTONE ROAD
Chatham ME4 6EW. Dr M K
Douglas, 01634 842216. *1m S of
Chatham on A230.* Home-made teas
(not 18 Feb). Adm £1.50, chd free.
Suns 18 Feb; 1 Apr; 6 May; 10 June
(2-5). Visitors also welcome by appt.
Informal ¼-acre garden; herbaceous
borders on either side of former tennis
court; scree garden and pool; many
snowdrops and other spring bulbs.
Doll's house (¹/₁₂ scale model of house)
may also be viewed. Featured in 'Kent
Life' & 'Amateur Gardening'.

56 ◆ MARLE PLACE
Brenchley TN12 7HS. Mr & Mrs
Gerald Williams, 01892 722304,
www.marleplace.co.uk. *8m SE of
Tonbridge. From A21 Kippings Cross
roundabout take B2160 to Matfield, R
to Brenchley, then follow brown tourist
signs. From A21 Forstal Farm
roundabout take B2162 Horsmonden
rd and follow signs.* Adm £4.50, chd
£1, concessions £4. Fris to Mons 1
Apr to 30 Sept. For NGS: Weds 25
Apr; 13 June; 8 Aug (10-6).
Victorian gazebo, plantsman's shrub
borders, walled scented garden,
Edwardian rockery, herbaceous
borders, bog and kitchen gardens.
Woodland walks, mosaic terrace,
artists' studios, gallery. Autumn colour.
Restored Victorian 40ft greenhouse
with orchid collection. C17 listed house
(not open). Collection of interesting
chickens. Gardening for Wildlife Gold
Award.

57 MERE HOUSE
Mereworth ME18 5NB. Mr & Mrs
Andrew Wells, www.mere-
house.co.uk. *7m E of Tonbridge.
From A26 turn N on to B2016 & then
into Mereworth village. 3¹/₂ m S of
M20/M26 J, take A20, then B2016 to
Mereworth.* Home-made teas (also
light lunches 24, 25 Feb). Adm £2.50,
chd free. Sat 24, Sun 25 Feb (11-
3.30); Sun 8, Mon 9 Apr; Sun 14 Oct
(2-5).
6-acre garden with C18 lake. Daffodils,
lawns, herbaceous borders,
ornamental shrubs and trees with
foliage contrast and striking autumn
colour. Kentish cobnut plat, woodland
walk and major new tree planting and
landscaping. Featured in 'NFU
Countryside'.

58 ◆ **MOUNT EPHRAIM**
Hernhill, Faversham ME13 9TX. Mrs
M N Dawes, Mr & Mrs E S Dawes,
01227 751496,
www.mountephraimgardens.co.uk.
*3m E of Faversham. From end of M2,
then A299 take slip rd 1st L to Hernhill,
signed to gardens.* **Adm £4, chd £1,
groups £3.50. Weds, Thurs, Sats,
Suns, Easter to end Sept (1-5), Bank
Hols (11-5).** For NGS: Suns 22 Apr;
23 Sept (1-5).
Herbaceous border; topiary; daffodils
and rhododendrons; rose terraces
leading to small lake. Rock garden with
pools; water garden; young arboretum;
new grass maze. Rose garden with
arches and pergola planted to
celebrate the millennium. Magnificent
trees. Superb views over fruit farms to
Swale estuary. New grass maze.
Featured in RHS 'The Garden'. Limited
wheelchair access, steep slopes &
steps.

&. ⊛ ☕

59 **MOUNTS COURT
FARMHOUSE**
Acrise, nr Folkestone CT18 8LQ.
Graham & Geraldine Fish, 01303
840598,
graham.s.fish@btinternet.com. *6m
NW of Folkestone. From A260
Folkestone to Canterbury rd, turn L at
Swingfield (Densole) opp Black Horse
Inn, 1¹/₂m towards Elham & Lyminge,
on N side.* Home-made teas. **Adm
£2.50, chd free. Suns 3 June; Sun 22
July (2-5). Visitors also welcome by
appt, groups of 10+, coaches
permitted.**
1¹/₂ acres surrounded by open
farmland; variety of trees, shrubs,
grasses and herbaceous plants; pond
and bog garden. 20,000 gallon
rainwater reservoir waters garden and
keeps pond topped up; compost
heated to 170° for fast turnover.

&. ⊛ ☕

60 **NETTLESTEAD PLACE**
Nettlestead ME18 5HA. Mr & Mrs
Roy Tucker, 01622 812205,
www.nettlesteadplace.co.uk. *6m
W/SW of Maidstone. Turn S off A26
onto B2015 then 1m on L, next to
Nettlestead Church.* Home-made teas.
**Adm £4, chd free. Suns 3 June; 16
Sept (2-5.30). Visitors also welcome
by appt.**
C13 manor house in 10-acre
plantsman's garden. Large formal rose
garden. Large herbaceous garden of
island beds with rose and clematis
walkway leading to garden of China

roses. Fine collection of trees and
shrubs; sunken pond garden, terraces,
bamboos, glen garden, acer lawn.
Young pinetum adjacent to garden.
Wonderful open country views. Church
adjacent to garden with fine early C15
windows. Starred garden in GGG.
Sunken pond garden not wheelchair
accessible at water level.

&. ☕

19 OAKHILL ROAD
Orpington. See London.

61 **OLANTIGH**
Olantigh Road, Wye TN25 5EW. Mr
& Mrs J R H Loudon. *10m SW of
Canterbury, 6m NE of Ashford. Turn off
A28 to Wye. 1m from Wye on Olantigh
rd towards Godmersham.* **Adm £3,
chd free. Sun 27 May (2-5).**
Edwardian garden in beautiful 20-acre
setting; wide variety of trees; river
garden; rockery; shrubbery;
herbaceous border; extensive lawns;
tree sculpture and woodland walks.
Sorry, no teas, but please feel free to
bring your own.

62 ◆ **OLD BUCKHURST**
Markbeech, nr Edenbridge
TN8 5PH. Mr & Mrs J Gladstone,
01342 850825,
www.oldbuckhurst.co.uk. *4m SE of
Edenbridge. B2026, at Queens Arms
PH turn E to Markbeech. In approx
1¹/₂m, 1st house on R after leaving
Markbeech.* **Adm £3, chd free. Every
Wed & 1st & last Sats, May to July.**
For NGS: Weds, Sats, Suns 21, 22,
25, 28, 29 Apr; 2, 6, 20, 27 May; 3, 6,
10, 24 June; 1, 4, 14, 29 July; 5 Aug;
1, 2, 5, 8, 9 Sept (11-5.30). Also
open 5 Aug **Leydens**.
1-acre partly-walled cottage garden
around C15 listed farmhouse with
catslip roof (not open). Shrubs, clematis,
climbing and shrub roses, anemones,
astilbes, campanulas, eryngiums, day
lilies in July/Aug, hardy geraniums,
grasses, iris, jasmine, lilies, peonies,
poppies, penstemons, wisteria. Yr-
round interest using structure, texture,
scent and colour. WC. Group visits by
arrangement. Featured in 'Country Life'
& on UK Style TV.

 ⊛

63 **OLD ORCHARD**
56 Valley Drive, Loose, Maidstone
ME15 9TL. Mike & Hazel Brett,
01622 746941. *2¹/₂m S of Maidstone.
On A229, turn R towards Loose village,
parking on hill; at top of hill take
footpath to Valley Drive. On-site*

parking for disabled, please phone for
directions. Home-made teas. **Adm
£2.50, chd free (share to Talking
Newspapers). Suns 29 Apr; 27 May
(2-6). Visitors also welcome by appt,
individuals & groups.**
Plantlovers' S-facing acre garden
adjoining Loose Valley Conservation
Area. Meandering grass paths around
informal island beds containing many
unusual trees, shrubs and perennials.
Extensive rockeries, screes and alpine
troughs. Small arboretum for foliage
form and colour. Featured in 'Amateur
Gardening'.

&. ⊛ ☕

64 **OLD PLACE FARM**
High Halden TN26 3JG. Mr & Mrs
Jeffrey Eker, 01233 850202,
jeffreyeker@tiscali.co.uk. *10m SW of
Ashford. From A28, centre of village,
take Woodchurch Rd (opp Chequers
PH) for ¹/₂m.* Home-made teas by prior
arrangement. **Adm £3.50, chd free.
Visitors welcome by appt, individuals
& groups, guided tours £5.**
4-acre garden, mainly designed by
Anthony du Gard Pasley, surrounding
period farmhouse (not open) and
buildings, with paved herb garden and
parterres, small lake, ponds, lawns,
mixed borders, cutting garden and
potager, old shrub roses, foliage plants
and specimen trees. 2 bridges leading
to woodland and fields. New woodland
topiary garden. Tulips a special feature.
A whimsical creation. Featured in
'Homes & Gardens' & 'Garden Design
Journal'. Starred garden in GGG.

&. ☕

65 **ONE DERING ROAD**
Ashford TN24 8DB. Mrs
Claire de Sousa Barry,
07979 816104,
nazgulnota-bene@ntlworld.com.
*Town centre. Just off Hythe Rd nr
Henwood roundabout. Short walk from
pay and display car park located just
past fire stn in Henwood Rd. Please do
not park in Dering Rd.* Home-made
teas, Bank Hol weekends & private
visits only. **Adm £2.50, regret children
not admitted. Fri 6 to Mon 9 Apr
incl, Sats, Suns in Apr (not 1, 28, 29);
Sats, Suns & Bank Hol Mons in May
(not 19, 20); Sats, Suns in June (not
30); Sats, Suns in July (not 1, 28, 29);
Sats, Suns & Bank Hol Mon in Aug
(not 18, 19); Sat 1, Sun 2 Sept (2-5).
Visitors also welcome by appt May
to Aug, teas by arrangement.
No coaches.**
Plantsperson's romantic town garden
with optimum use of space.

Successional planting for yr-round interest. Pittosporum, robinia, crinodendron, cardiocrinum. Cascading roses, clematis, jasmine, honeysuckle, delphiniums, arisaemas, trilliums, uvularias, camellias and rhododendrons. A host of other unusual plants. Visitors say 'inspiring, exceptional, really lovely. Surprises round every corner, I'll be back!' Featured in 'Country Homes & Interiors' & on Radio Kent.

✕ ⊛ ☕

66 THE ORANGERY
Mystole CT4 7DB. Rex Stickland & Anne Prasse. *5m SW of Canterbury. Turn off A28 through Shalmsford Street. After 1¹/₂ m at Xrds turn R down hill. Keep straight on, ignoring rds on L (Pennypot Lane) & R. Ignore drive on L signed 'Mystole House only' & at sharp bend in 600yds turn L into private drive signed Mystole Farm.* Home-made teas. **Adm £2.50, chd free. Suns 24 June; 29 July (1-7).**
1¹/₂-acre gardens around C18 orangery, now a house (not open). Front gardens, established well-stocked herbaceous border and large walled garden with a wide variety of shrubs and mixed borders. Splendid views from terraces over ha-ha and paddocks to the lovely Chartham Downs. Water features and very interesting collection of modern sculptures set in natural surroundings.

& ☕

Medicinal and culinary herbs with a backdrop of trees and shrubs . . .

67 ORCHARD COTTAGE
3 Woodlands Road, Bickley BR1 2AD. Mrs J M Wall, 020 8467 4190. *1¹/₂ m E of Bromley. About 400yds from the A222. From Bickley Park Rd turn into Pines Rd, then 1st R into Woodlands Rd, No 3 is 1st house on L.* Home-made teas. **Adm £2.50, chd free (share to Diabetes UK). Sun 22 July (2-5). Visitors also welcome by appt Feb/Mar for snowdrops, hellebores & camellias.**
Attractive, colourful and varied ¹/₃-acre garden, compartmentalised and themed, with many interesting and unusual herbaceous plants and

shrubs. Incl areas of scree beds, troughs and pots with alpines and other specialist plants. Unusual plants & local honey for sale.

& ✕ ⊛ ☕

68 ORCHARD END
Cock Lane, Spelmonden Road, Horsmonden TN12 8EQ. Mr & Mrs Hugh Nye, 01892 723118. *8m E of Tunbridge Wells. From A21 going S turn L at roundabout towards Horsmonden on B2162. After 2m turn R into Spelmonden Rd, ¹/₂ m to top of hill, R into Cock Lane. Garden 50yds on R.* Light refreshments & teas. **Adm £3, chd free. Sats, Suns 9, 10 June; 14, 15 July; 15, 16 Sept (11-5.30). Visitors also welcome by appt.**
Classically English garden on 1¹/₂-acre sloping site, landscaped 12yrs ago by owners' garden designer son. Divided into rooms with linking vistas. Incl hot borders, cottage and white gardens, exotics with pergola, raised summerhouse overlooking lawns and drive planting. Formal fish pond with bog garden. Ornamental vegetable and fruit areas. Wildlife orchard. Display & sale of pictures by local artists. Featured in 'Kent Life'. Unfenced ponds, unsuitable for small children.

✕ ⊛ ☕

69 PEDLINGE COURT
Pedlinge, Saltwood CT21 4JJ. Mr & Mrs J P Scrivens, 01303 269959. *¹/₂ m W of Hythe. Top of hill, on A261 from Hythe up hill signed M20 & Ashford opp sign 'Pedlinge'. From Newingreen 1m opp sign 'Hythe twinned with....'.* **Adm £3 (share to Cats Protection). Visitors welcome by appt mid May to mid July, for small groups.**
1¹/₂-acre garden with a profusion of interesting plants around C14 farmhouse (not open), birthplace of the orchid foxglove 'Saltwood Summer'. Wide variety of cottage garden plants, ferns, old shrub roses, medicinal and culinary herbs with a backdrop of trees and shrubs incl topiary. Featured in 'The English Garden' & 'Kent Life'.

✕ ⊛

70 ◆ PENSHURST PLACE
Penshurst TN11 8DG. Viscount De L'Isle, 01892 870307, www.penshurstplace.com. *6m NW of Tunbridge Wells. SW of Tonbridge on B2176, signed from A26 N of Tunbridge Wells.* **House & garden £7.50, chd £5, concessions £7. Garden only £6, chd £4.50,**

concessions £5.50. Apr to Oct, gardens 10.30-6, house 12-4. For NGS: Weds 16 May; 13 June (10.30-6, last entry 5).
10 acres of garden dating back to C14; garden divided into series of rooms by over a mile of clipped yew hedge; profusion of spring bulbs: herbaceous borders; formal rose garden; famous peony border. Toy museum. All-yr interest.

& ✕ ☕

71 ◆ THE PINES GARDEN
St Margaret's Bay CT15 6DZ. St Margaret's Bay Trust, 01304 851737, www.baytrust.org.uk. *4¹/₂ m NE of Dover. Approach village of St Margaret's-at-Cliffe off A258 Dover/Deal rd. Continue through village centre & down Bay Hill. Signed just before beach.* **Adm £3, chd 50p, concessions £2.50. For NGS: Suns 8 Apr; 27 May; Fri 24 Aug (10-5).**
Adjacent to cliff walks and beach, this mature garden offers a mixture of open undulating parkland, trees, shrubs and secluded areas. Lake, waterfall, grass labyrinth, roundhouse shelter, famous Oscar Nemon statue of Winston Churchill. Chalk-constructed conference centre with grass-covered roof. Garden open all yr (10-5), not Christmas Day. Museum (2-5) & tearoom (12-5): Easter, Bank Hol Mons & from end of May to early Sept, Weds to Suns. Access for disabled, ample seating, picnics.

& ☕

72 PLACKETTS HOLE
Bicknor, nr Sittingbourne ME9 8BA. Mr & Mrs D P Wainman, 01622 884258, aj@aj-wainman.demon. co.uk. *5m S of Sittingbourne. W of B2163. Signed from Hollingbourne Hill & from A249 at Stockbury Valley.* Light refreshments. **Evening Openings, wine, Sun 27 May (5.30-8). Sun 23 Sept (4.30-7). Visitors also welcome by appt May to July only, for groups of 10+, no coaches.**
3-acre garden in Kent's North Downs AONB. In May early-flowering wild hybrid and Scottish roses are at their best along with a large variety of shrubs, perennials, specimen trees, clematis and irises. In late Sept Japanese anemones, sedums, verbena and cyclamen abound. Newly-planted formal herb garden, informal pond, and small walled kitchen garden. Some gravel paths and short steep slopes.

& ✕ ⊛ ☕

73 PRIMROSE COTTAGE
Rose Hill, Wittersham, Tenterden
TN30 7HE. Jenny & Michael Clarke,
01797 270820,
j.m.g.clarke@btinternet.com. *6m S of
Tenterden. Signed off B2082 1m E of
centre of Wittersham at highest point
of Isle of Oxney.* Sorry, no teas, but you
are welcome to picnic in our field. **Adm
£2.50, chd free. Sat 9, Sun 10, Mon
11 June; Tue 3, Wed 4 July (2-5).
Visitors also welcome by appt in
June & July for groups of 10+.**
Joyful jumble of cottage garden plants,
many unusual. Rose pergola walk, well
and water feature. Vegetable garden in
blocks for easy maintenance.
Spectacular views to N Downs. A
peaceful garden maintained by
owners.
& ☒ ⊕

74 PUXTED HOUSE
Brenchley Road, Brenchley
TN12 7PB. Mr P J Oliver-Smith,
01892 722057, pjospux@aol.com.
*6m SE of Tonbridge. From A21, 1m S
of Pembury turn N onto B2160, turn R
at Xrds in Matfield signed Brenchley.
1/4m from Xrds stop at 30mph sign at
village entrance.* Cream teas. **Adm £3,
chd free. Suns 20 May; 17 June
(2-6). Visitors also welcome by appt.**
1 1/2 acres, planted with scented and
coloured foliage shrubs selected to
ensure yr-long changing effects.
Meandering gravel paths lead from the
alpine garden via herbaceous borders
and croquet lawn with its thyme
terrace to formal rose garden and
thereafter swing amongst oriental
woodland plants and bamboos about
a lily pond. Large glasshouse protects
many Australasian shrubs and cacti.
Gravel paths.
& ☒ ⊕ ☕

75 ◆ QUEX HOUSE GARDENS
Quex Park, Birchington CT7 0BH.
The Powell-Cotton Museum Trust,
01843 842168,
pcmuseum@btconnect.com. *3m W
of Margate. 10m NE of Canterbury.
A28 towards Margate, then rd to Acol
to Quex Park. Follow signs for Powell-
Cotton Museum, Quex Park.* House &
garden £5, chd (5-16) & concessions
£4. Garden only £1.50, chd free,
concessions £1. 18 Mar to 29 Oct,
Suns to Thurs & Bank Hols (11-5).
For NGS: Sun 24 June (11-5).
**Evening Opening with music,
wine & plant stalls, Wed 15 Aug
(6-9).**
15 acres of woodland and gardens

with fine specimen trees unusual on
Thanet, spring bulbs, wisteria, shrub
borders, old figs and mulberries,
herbaceous borders. Victorian walled
garden with cucumber house, long
glasshouses, cactus house, fruiting
trees. Peacocks, dovecote, woodland
walk, wildlife pond, children's maze,
croquet lawn, picnic grove, lawns and
fountains.
& ☒ ⊕ ☕

**76 RIDDLES ROAD
ALLOTMENTS**
Sittingbourne ME10 1LF.
Sittingbourne Allotment and
Gardeners' Society. *1/2m S of
Sittingbourne. At A2/A249 junction turn
E off roundabout towards
Sittingbourne. After approx 1m turn R
into Borden Lane, just after Coniston
Hotel. Riddles Rd 2nd L after approx
1/2m.* **Adm £2, chd free, OAP £1.
Sun 5 Aug (11-4).**
This is a standard allotment site: a
number of plots will be demonstrated
showing a variety of horticultural
techniques for growing fruit and
vegetables and some flowers.
☒

**77 ◆ RIVERHILL HOUSE
GARDENS**
Sevenoaks TN15 0RR. The Rogers
Family, 01732 458802. *2m S of
Sevenoaks on A225.* **Adm £3, chd
50p. Suns & Bank Hol weekends, 1
Apr to 17 June. For NGS: Tues 8, 22
May (11-5).**
Mature hillside garden with extensive
views; specimen trees, sheltered
terraces with roses and rare shrubs;
bluebell wood with rhododendrons and
azaleas; picnics allowed. Personal
welcome from members of the family.
Unsuitable for wheelchairs but users
may have free access to the tea
terrace - on the level and with views
across the garden.
☒ ⊕ ☕

78 ROCK FARM
Gibbs Hill, Nettlestead ME18 5HT.
Mrs S E Corfe, 01622 812244. *6m W
of Maidstone. Turn S off A26 onto
B2015, then 1m S of Wateringbury
turn R up Gibbs Hill.* **Adm £4, chd free
(share to St Mary the Virgin). Wed,
Sat 16, 19 May; every Wed & Sat 13
June to 11 July (11-5); Sun 9 Sept
(2-6). Visitors also welcome by appt.**
2-acre garden set around old Kentish
farmhouse (not open) in beautiful
setting; created with emphasis on all-yr
interest and ease of maintenance.

Plantsman's collection of shrubs, trees
and perennials for alkaline soil;
extensive herbaceous border,
vegetable area, bog garden and
plantings around two large natural
ponds. Featured in 'The English
Garden'.
☒ ⌂

Joyful jumble of cottage garden plants, many unusual. Rose pergola walk, well and water feature . . .

79 ROGERS ROUGH
Kilndown TN17 2RP. Richard &
Hilary Bird, 01892 890554,
richardbird@rogersrough.demon.co.
uk. *10m SE of Tonbridge. From A21
2m S of Lamberhurst turn E into
Kilndown; take 1st R down Chick's
Lane until rd divides.* Home-made
teas. **Adm £3, chd free. Sats, Suns
26, 27 May; 16, 17 June (11-5.30).
Visitors also welcome by appt mid-
May to July only.**
Garden writer's 1 1/2-acre garden,
divided into many smaller gardens
containing herbaceous borders, rock
gardens, shrubs, small wood and
pond. Very wide range of plants, incl
some unusual ones. Extensive views.
& ☒ ⊕ ☕

80 ST CLERE
Kemsing TN15 6NL. Mr & Mrs
Ronnie Norman. *6m NE of
Sevenoaks. Take A25 from Sevenoaks
toward Maidstone; 1m past Seal turn L
signed Heaverham & Kemsing. In
Heaverham take rd to R signed
Wrotham & W Kingsdown; in 75yds
straight ahead marked private rd; 1st L
& follow rd to house.* Home-made
teas. **Adm £3, chd 50p. Sun 10 June
(2-5.30).**
4-acre garden, full of interest. Formal
terraces surrounding C17 mansion (not
open), with beautiful views of the Kent
countryside. Herbaceous and shrub
borders, productive kitchen and herb
gardens, lawns and rare trees.
☒ ☕

81 ST MICHAEL'S GARDENS

East Peckham TN12 5NH, 01622 813687. peterstmichaels@aol.com. *5m NE of Tonbridge, 5m SW of Maidstone. On A26 at Mereworth roundabout take S exit (A228 Paddock Wood). After 1¹/₂m turn L into Roydon Hall Rd. Gardens ¹/₂m up hill on L. From Paddock Wood A228 towards West Malling. 1m after roundabout with Wheelbarrow turn R into Roydon Hall Rd.* Home-made teas. **Combined adm £3.50, chd free (share to Friends of St Michael's Church). Suns 29 Apr; 27 May; 10 June; 1 July (2-5). Visitors also welcome by appt to all 3 gardens.**
Victorian house, cottage garden and cottage yard.

CUCKOO COTTAGE
Mr Gavin Walter & Miss Emma Gaspar
Born from a desire to add life and colour to a derelict and shady yard, a slate scree base is used with pots and containers.

&

ST MICHAEL'S HOUSE
Brig & Mrs W Magan
Grey stone old vicarage with yew topiary hedges surrounding flower beds planned in coordinated colours. Lovely display of tulips followed by splendid irises, then a mass of roses from red-hot to old soft colours. Wonderful views from the meadow.

& ⊛

ST MICHAEL'S COTTAGE
Mr Peter & Mrs Pauline Fox
Garden designed so it cannot be seen all at once. Formal garden, woodland, pond, collection of ornamental grasses and herb garden. Traditional cottage garden with collection of lavenders, hostas, clematis, shrubs, ferns, heathers and wildlife area.

⊛

82 SANDLING PARK

Hythe CT21 4HN. The Hardy Family. *1¹/₂m NW of Hythe. Entrance off A20 only. From M20 J11 turn E onto A20. Entrance ¹/₄m.* **Adm £4, chd £1 (share to Saltwood Church). Sun 13 May (10-5).**
25-acre woodland garden with an extensive collection of trees and shrubs with rhododendrons, azaleas, magnolias and other interesting plants that also relish acid soil. Limited wheelchair access.

⚲ ☕

83 ◆ SCOTNEY CASTLE

Lamberhurst TN3 8JN. The National Trust, 01892 893868, www.nationaltrust.org.uk. *6m SE of Tunbridge Wells. On A21 London-Hastings, brown tourist signs. Bus: (Mon to Sat) Tunbridge Wells-Wadhurst, alight Lamberhurst Green.* **Garden only adm £5.70, chd £2.90. Opening dates & times vary according to season. Please phone or visit website for details. For NGS: Sat 12 May (11-5).**
Picturesque landscape garden, created by the Hussey family in the 1840s surrounding moated C14 Castle. Picnic area in car park.

& ⚲ ⊛

84 SEA CLOSE

Cannongate Road, Hythe CT21 5PX. Major & Mrs R H Blizard, 01303 266093. *¹/₂m from Hythe towards Folkestone (A259), on L. Signed.* Light refreshments. **Adm £2.50, chd free (share to Royal Signals Benevolent Fund, Venetian Fête 15 Aug). Suns 13 May; 1 July (2-5); Wed 15 Aug (11-4); Sun 23 Sept (2-4). Visitors also welcome by appt at any time.**
29th yr of opening by 85yr-old and his wife, totally unaided from concept to present day. Discover what will grow with TLC in a steep, dry, SE, coastal, all-yr-round garden - sophora, carpenteria, fascicularia, agapanthus, amaryllis, plus many other unusual plants and shrubs. Mini collections of iris, crocosmia and Michaelmas daisy. Planted for maximum effect. Gorgeous sea view. Hythe Venetian Fête 15 August, starts 4pm.

⚲ ⊛ ☕

85 SEVENOAKS ALLOTMENTS

Allotment Lane, off Quaker Hall Lane, Sevenoaks TN13 3TX. Sevenoaks Allotment Holders Assn. *Quaker Hall Lane is off A225, St John's Hill. Site directly behind St John's Church.* Home-made teas. **Adm £2.50, chd free. Sun 24 June (10-5).**
The Association self-manages 11¹/₂ acres of productive allotment gardens situated in the heart of the town. A wide cross-section of allotment owners grow a massive variety of flowers, fruit and vegetables using a number of different techniques. Gardeners cite healthy produce, exercise and relaxation in a beautiful open space as reasons to rent a plot. Featured on Radio Kent. Steep slopes.

& ⊛ ☕

86 ◆ SISSINGHURST GARDEN

Sissinghurst TN172AB. The National Trust, 01580 710700, www.nationaltrust.org.uk. *16m E of Tunbridge Wells. On A262 1m E of village. Bus: Arriva Maidstone-Hastings, alight Sissinghurst 1¹/₄m. Direct bus Tue, Fri & Sun 25 Mar to 30 Sept. Stn: Staplehurst.* **Adm £8.60, chd £4. 17 Mar to 28 Oct: Mons, Tues, Fris (11-6.30); Sats, Suns, Bank Hols (10-6.30). For NGS: Mons 16 Apr; 4 June; 13 Aug; 8 Oct (11-6.30).**
Garden created by the late Vita Sackville-West and Sir Harold Nicolson. Spring garden, herb garden, cottage garden, white garden, rose garden. Tudor building and tower, partly open to public. Moat. Exhibition on history of the garden and property in the oast buildings.

& ⚲ ⊛ ☕

87 SISSINGHURST PLACE

Sissinghurst TN17 2JP. Mr & Mrs Simon macLachlan. *10m E of Tunbridge Wells. E of Sissinghurst village, ¹/₂m from Sissinghurst NT garden on A262.* **Adm £3, chd free (share to Kent Community Foundation). Sun, Mon 8, 9, Sun 22 Apr (12-4).**
Large garden, established yew hedges and lime walk, herbaceous beds, topiary, climbers and flower beds in ruin of old house. Orchard and woodland garden with hellebores, daffodils and spring bulbs. Fine trees and views. Featured in 'The English Garden'.

& ⚲

88 SOTTS HOLE COTTAGE

Crouch Lane, Borough Green TN15 8QL. Mr & Mrs Jim Vinson. *7m E of Sevenoaks. Crouch Lane runs SE from A25 between Esso garage & Black Horse PH, garden at bottom of 2nd hill, approx ³/₄m.* Home-made teas. **Adm £2.50, chd free. Suns 15 Apr; 3 June; 29 July; 9 Sept (11-6).**
6 acres of landscaped cottage garden relying entirely on the threat of visitors to motivate the owners to maintain it. We look forward to seeing you.

⚲ ☕

89 SOUTH HILL FARM

Hastingleigh TN25 5HL. Sir Charles Jessel, 01233 750325. *4¹/₂m E of Ashford. Turn off A28 to Wye, go through village & ascend Wye Downs. In 2m turn R at Xrds marked Brabourne & South Hill, then 1st L. Or*

from Stone St (B2068) turn W opp Stelling Minnis, follow signs to Hastingleigh. Continue towards Wye & turn L at Xrds marked Brabourne & South Hill, then 1st L. **Adm £3.50, incl tea & biscuits, chd free. Visitors welcome by appt mid to end June preferred, for groups of 4 to 50. Coaches permitted.**
2 acres high up on N Downs, C17/18 house (not open); old walls; ha-ha; formal water garden; old and new roses; unusual shrubs, perennials and foliage plants.

90 SOUTHOVER
Grove Lane, Hunton ME15 0SE. David & Anke Way, tel/fax 01622 820876. 6m S of Maidstone. Turn W from A229 to B2163. At Xrds past Coxheath turn L down Hunton Hill past church to school, then R into Grove Lane. Or from Yalding war memorial follow Vicarage Rd into Hunton to school, then L into Grove Lane. **Adm £3, chd free (share to Hunton C of E Primary School). Sat 17 Feb (10.30-3.30). Visitors also welcome by appt at any time of yr for groups of 15+, coaches permitted.**
1½-acre enthusiasts' garden developed over 27yrs to accommodate ever-expanding plant collection. Many new and unusual perennials. Formal and informal areas and selected viewing points; strong on internal and external vistas. Rapidly expanding collection of snowdrop species and cultivars. New emphasis on spring borders for early bulbs. Attractive rural location amidst farmland. Gold award, Gardening for Wildlife. Deep, steep-sided pond near entrance.

91 SPARKS HALL
Forsham Lane, Sutton Valence ME17 3EW. Charles Day & Virginia Routh, 01622 843248, virginia.routh@gmail.com. 6m SE of Maidstone. From Maidstone take A274 towards Headcorn. At bottom of Sutton Valence hill turn R into Forsham Lane. Sparks Hall 1/3 m on L next to oast house. Home-made teas. **Adm £3, chd free. Sun 15 July (2-6). Visitors also welcome by appt.**
Kentish hall house dating from C16 in idyllic setting, surrounded by sheep and orchards with far-reaching views. The 1½-acre garden was created 15yrs ago. Formal Elizabethan garden with rill and fountain surrounded by yew hedges; rose garden; collection of old-fashioned apples grown as step-

over; natural pond and several herbaceous borders.

92 SPILSILL COURT
Frittenden Road, Staplehurst TN12 0DJ. Mrs Doonie Marshall. 8m S of Maidstone. To Staplehurst on A229 (Maidstone to Hastings). From S enter village, turn R immed after garage on R & just before 30mph sign, into Frittenden Rd; garden 1/2 m on L. From N go through village to 40mph sign, immed turn L into Frittenden Rd. April tea/coffee all day. June tea /coffee 11-1, cream teas 2.30-4.30. **Adm £2, chd 50p. Suns 1 Apr; 24 June (11-5).**
Approx 4 acres of garden, orchard and paddock; series of gardens incl blue, white and silver; roses; lawns; shrubs, trees and ponds. Small private chapel. Jacob sheep and unusual poultry.

93 THE SPINNEY
38 Wildernesse Mount, Sevenoaks TN13 3SQ. Patricia McAlister, 01732 461434. 1½ m N of Sevenoaks. 3m from M25 J5, follow A25 towards Maidstone to Seal Hollow Rd. Turn R at T-lights; 400yds, turn R at Hillingdon Avenue & 1st L into Wildernesse Mount. Proceed to turning circle (1/4 m). No 38 on L. Light refreshments & teas. **Adm £3, chd free, concessions £2.50. Sun 13 May (12-6). Visitors also welcome by appt.**
Garden set in 2/3 acre surrounding house (not open). Mainly spring garden - camellias, magnolias, rhododendrons, azaleas and pieris. Good collection of trees - rowans (hybrids), liriodendron (variegated), eucalyptus, cercidiphyllum, robinia, birch, amelanchier, various acers, pine, Atlantic cedar, various conifers. Interesting water feature. Lawns/garden on 3 levels incl terrace garden.

94 ◆ SQUERRYES COURT
Westerham TN16 1SJ. Mrs John Warde, 01959 562345, www.squerryes.co.uk. 1/2 m W of Westerham. Signed from A25. **House & garden £6.50, chd £3.50, concessions £6. Garden £4, chd £2, concessions £3.50. Weds, Thurs, Suns & Bank Hol Mons, 1 Apr to 30 Sept. For NGS: Suns 8 July; 2 Sept (11.30-5).**
15 acres of well-documented historic garden, C18 landscape. Part of the formal garden has been restored by

the family using C18 plan. Lake, spring bulbs, azaleas, herbaceous borders, C18 dovecote, cenotaph commemorating Gen Wolfe; woodland walks. Children's Garden Trail by Kent Gardens Trust.

95 STONEWALL PARK
Chiddingstone Hoath TN8 7DG. Mr & Mrs Valentine Fleming. 4m SE of Edenbridge. Via B2026. Halfway between Markbeech & Penshurst. Home-made teas. **Adm £3, chd free (share to Sarah Matheson Trust & St Mary's Church). Suns 25 Mar; 6 May (1.30-5).**
Large walled garden with herbaceous borders and vegetable garden backed by 100yr-old espalier pear trees. A sea of wild daffodils in March. 12 acres of woodland garden in romantic setting featuring species rhododendrons, magnolias, azaleas, range of interesting trees and shrubs, wandering paths and lakes.

Expanding collection of snowdrop species and cultivars . . .

96 TIMBERS
Dean Street, East Farleigh, nr Maidstone ME15 0HS. Mrs Sue Robinson, 01622 729568, sue@suerobinson.wanadoo.co.uk. 2m S of Maidstone. From Maidstone take B2010 to East Farleigh. Opp The Bull turn into Vicarage Lane, then L into Forge Lane and L into Dean St. Garden 50yds on R, park through gates in front of house. Home-made teas. **Adm £3, chd free. Visitors welcome by appt Apr to end July and Sept for groups of 8+, coaches permitted. Guided visits.**
5-acre garden, well stocked with unusual hardy plants, annuals and shrubs designed with flower arranger's eye. Formal areas comprising parterre, pergola, herbaceous, vegetables, fruit, lawns and mature specimen trees surrounded by 100yr-old Kentish cobnut plat, wild flower meadow and woodland. Aviaries stocked with foreign birds. WC. Limited wheelchair access, gravel and steep, uneven slopes.

TITSEY PLACE GARDENS
See Surrey.

97 TORRY HILL
Frinsted/Milstead ME9 0SP. The Lord & Lady Kingsdown, 01795 830258, lady.kingsdown@btinternet.com. *5m S of Sittingbourne. From M20 J8 take A20 (Lenham), roundabout by Ramada Inn turn L for Hollingbourne & Frinsted (B2163). From M2 J5 take A249 towards Maidstone, then L through Bredgar/Milstead. Parking available for disabled on request.* Home-made teas. **Adm £3, chd free** (share to St Dunstan's Church). **Suns 13 May; 10 June** (2-5.30). **Evening Opening Wed 20 June** (6.30-9.00). **Visitors also welcome by appt.**
8 acres; large lawns, specimen trees, flowering cherries, rhododendrons, azaleas and naturalised daffodils; walled gardens with lawns, shrubs, herbaceous borders, rose garden incl shrub roses, wild flower areas and vegetables. Extensive views to Medway and Thames estuaries. Very uneven surface in rose garden due to ancient crazy paving.
&. ✗ ⊛ ☕

98 TRAM HATCH
Charing Heath TN27 0BN. Mrs P Scrivens, 01233 713373. *10m NW of Ashford. A20 turn towards Charing railway stn. Continue on Pluckley Rd over motorway, 1st R signed Barnfield to end. Turn L, follow lane past Barnfield, Tram Hatch on L.* Home-made teas. **Adm £3, chd free. Suns 20 May; 24 June; 15 July** (1-5.30). **Visitors also welcome by appt, groups of 15+, coaches permitted.**
C14 manor house with tithe barn (not open) set in 3 acres of formal garden with the Great River Stour edging its boundary. Vegetable and fruit garden, orchard, rose garden, bog garden and 2 large ponds, one with ornamental wildfowl. Large variety of plants and trees.
&. ✗ ⊛ ☕

99 TROUTBECK
Otford TN14 5PH. Dr & Mrs Huw Alban Davies, 01959 525439, box@river-garden.co.uk. *3m N of Sevenoaks. At W end of village.* Light refreshments, wine & teas. **Adm £3, chd free. Visitors welcome by appt June, July & Sept only, for individuals & groups.**
3-acre garden surrounded by branches of R Darent. Developed over 16yrs combining the informal landscape of

the river, a central pond and small wild meadow with structural planting using box and yew. Knots and topiary shapes are displayed. Topiary demonstration for groups by arrangement. Featured in 'Country Homes & Interiors'.
⊛ ☕

100 UPPER PRYORS
Cowden TN8 7HB. Mr & Mrs S G Smith. *4¹/₂m SE of Edenbridge. From B2026 Edenbridge-Hartfield, turn R at Cowden Xrds & take 1st drive on R.* Home-made teas. **Adm £3, chd free. Day £3 (1-6) & Evening Opening £4, wine, Wed 13 June** (6-9).
10 acres of country garden surrounding C16 house with herbaceous colour, magnificent lawns, water gardens and wooded/field areas.
✗ ☕

Very uneven surface in rose garden due to ancient crazy paving . . .

101 WAYSTRODE MANOR
Spode Lane, Cowden TN8 7HW. Mrs Jill Wright. *4¹/₂m SE of Edenbridge. From B2026 Edenbridge to Hartfield, turn off at Cowden Pound.* Home-made teas. **Adm £3, chd 50p. Sun 20 May; Wed 13, Sun 24 June.**
House C15 (not open). 8 acres; sweeping lawns, borders, ponds, bulbs, shrub roses, clematis and many tender plants. Orangery. All trees and shrubs labelled.
&. ✗ ⊛ ☕

102 WEST STUDDAL FARM
West Studdal, nr Dover CT15 5BJ. Mr & Mrs Peter Lumsden. *4m SW of Deal. 6m N of Dover halfway between Eastry & Whitfield. Take A256 from A2. At 1st roundabout turn S signed Studdal. At top of hill turn R, entrance ¹/₄m by yellow cottage.* Home-made teas in dodecagonal folly. **Adm £2.50, chd free. Sun 19 Aug** (2-6).
Medium-sized garden around old farmhouse (not open) set by itself in small valley; herbaceous borders, roses and fine lawns protected by old walls and beech hedges.
&. ⊛ ☕

103 WHITEHURST
Chainhurst TN12 9SU. John & Lyn Mercy. *6m S of Maidstone, 3m N of Marden. From Marden stn turn R into Pattenden Lane & under railway bridge; at T-junction turn L; at next fork bear R to Chainhurst, then 2nd turning on L.* Home-made teas. **Adm £3, chd £1. Sun 27 May to Wed 30 May incl** (2-5).
1¹/₂ acres of romantic, rather wild garden with many delightful and unexpected features. Victorian spiral staircase leads to a treetop walk; water tumbles down stone steps to a rill and on to several ponds; tunnels of yew and dogwood; walled rose garden; courtyards and lawns. Exhibition of root dwellings. Craft demonstration of miniature porcelain.
✗ ☕

104 WINDY RIDGE
Victory Road, St Margarets-at-Cliffe CT15 6HF. Mr & Mrs D Ryder, 01304 853225, www.gardenplants-nursery.co.uk. *4¹/₂m NE of Dover. From Duke of York roundabout on A2 N of Dover follow A258 signed Deal. Take 3rd rd on R (Station Rd), then 3rd rd on L (Collingwood Rd). Continue onto unmade track & follow signs (approx ¹/₂ m). Telephone for map.* Light refreshments & home-made teas. **Adm £2.50, chd free. Suns 24 June; 22 July; 16 Sept** (2-6).
Plantsman's garden on top of chalk hill, with extensive views over open country and sea. Island beds of shrubs and perennials (many rare). Large collection of penstemon and salvia. Wildlife pond. Gravel seating area and viewpoint. Additional ²/₃-acre extension to garden. Small specialist nursery.
⊛ ☕

105 WITHERSDANE HALL
Wye TN25 5AH. Imperial College Wye Campus. *3m NE of Ashford. A28 take fork signed Wye. Bus from Ashford to Canterbury via Wye. Pass Imperial College Wye Campus & continue up Scotton St.* Home-made teas. **Adm £2.50, chd 50p. Suns 22 Apr; 26 Aug** (2-5).
Well-labelled garden of educational and botanical interest. Much of garden laid out in 1950s on formal lines within the old walled kitchen garden, creating series of small gardens surrounded by yew hedges. Incl culinary herb, pool, rose, sundial and wild flower gardens, herbaceous borders. Magnificent mulberry tree, *Sequoiadendron giganteum* and unusual plants incl

toothache tree *Zanthoxylum americanum* and *Photinia beauverdiana*. Gravel paths. Ramp for wheelchairs.

106 WOODHAY
Copt Hall Road, Ightham Common TN15 9DU. **John & Rosemary Bickley.** *3m E of Sevenoaks. From Borough Green W on A25 for 1¹/₂m, L into Common Rd. ¹/₄m, park before Harrow PH. At Xrds R into Copt Hall Rd, 2nd house on A25 for 1³/₄m. After Crown Point PH, R into Coach Rd and park in rd. Copt Hall Rd 1st L, walk down hill ¹/₄m, garden on R.* **Home-made teas. Adm £2.50, chd free. Sun 27 May (11-4.30).**
1¹/₄-acre sloping informal garden privately orchestrated by owners, incorporating specimen trees, shrubs and many varied herbaceous plants. Pond and small stream - a delight not to be missed.

107 ◆ THE WORLD GARDEN AT LULLINGSTONE CASTLE
Eynsford DA4 0JA. **Guy Hart Dyke, 01322 862114,** www.lullingstonecastle.co.uk. *1m from Eynsford. M25 J3, signs to Brands Hatch then Eynsford. In Eynsford turn R at church over ford bridge. Follow lane under viaduct, with Lullingstone Roman Villa on R, to private rd sign, follow signs for World Garden.* **Adm £6, chd £3, concessions £5.50. April to Sept, Fris & Sats 12-5, Suns & Bank Hol Mons (2-6). For NGS: Sun 15 July (2-6).**
Interactive world map of plants laid out as a map of the world within a walled

garden. The oceans are your pathways as you navigate the world in 1 acre. You can stroll around Mt Everest, sip water from an Asian waterfall, see Ayers Rock and walk alongside the Andes whilst reading intrepid tales of plant hunters. Discover the origins of plants - you'll be amazed where they come from! Featured on BBC TV.

108 WYCKHURST
Mill Road, Aldington TN25 7AJ. **Mr & Mrs C Older, 01233 720395.** *4m SE of Ashford. Leave M20 at J10, on A20 travel 2m to Aldington turning; turn R at Xrds; proceed 1¹/₂m to Aldington village hall. Turn R and immed L by Walnut Tree. Take rd down Forge Hill signed to Dymchurch, after ¹/₄m turn R into Mill Rd.* **Home-made teas & wine. Adm £3, chd free. Wed 13, Sat 16, Sun 17 June (11-dusk). Visitors also welcome by appt.**
C16 cottage (not open). 1-acre cottage garden in romantic setting with unusual topiary; extensive views across Romney Marsh; continually developing garden.

109 YALDING GARDENS
ME18 6EU. *6m SW of Maidstone. 2 gardens S & W of village. Ploughman's lunches & home-made teas at Parsonage Oasts.* **Combined adm £3, chd free. Mon 9 Apr (12.30-5.30).**

CONGELOW HOUSE
Mrs M B Cooper. *From village centre take rd signed Collier Street, garden 500yds on R*
4-acre garden created from an orchard in 1973; backbone of

interesting ornamental trees planted about 1850, with a variety of recent plantings. Pleasure gardens incl daffodils, rhododendrons, irises, roses and shrub roses.

PARSONAGE OASTS
Edward & Jennifer Raikes. *Between Yalding village & stn, turn off at Anchor PH over canal bridge, continue 100yds up lane* ³/₄-acre riverside garden with walls, shrubs, daffodils, spectacular magnolia. Featured in 'Period Living'.

110 YEW TREE COTTAGE
Penshurst TN11 8AD. **Mrs Pam Tuppen, 01892 870689.** *4m SW of Tonbridge. From A26 Tonbridge to Tunbridge Wells, join B2176 Bidborough to Penshurst rd. 2m W of Bidborough, 1m before Penshurst. Utterly unsuitable for coaches. Please phone if needing advice for directions.* **Adm £2, chd free. Thurs, Fris, Sats & Suns, first & last week of month, Mar to Sept incl (11-5). Please see diary section for exact dates. Visitors also welcome by appt at any time.**
Small hillside cottage garden with lots of seats and secret corners, full of unusual plants - hellebores, spring bulbs, old roses, perennials. Autumn colour; something to see in all seasons. Created and maintained by owner. Please visit throughout long opening period to ease pressure on small garden.

Kent County Volunteers

County Organiser
Felicity Ward, Hookwood House, Shipbourne TN11 9RJ, 01732 810525, hookwood1@yahoo.co.uk

County Treasurer
Simon Toynbee, Old Tong Farm, Brenchley TN12 7HT, 020 7566 5551, stoynbee@pro-asset.com

Publicity
Ingrid Morgan Hitchcock, 6 Brookhurst Gardens, Southborough, Tunbridge Wells TN4 0NA, 01892 528341
ingrid@morganhitchcock.co.uk

Radio
Jane Streatfeild, Hoath House, Chiddingstone Hoath, Edenbridge TN8 7DB, 01342 850362,
janestreatfeild@hoath-house.freeserve.co.uk

Assistant County Organisers
Marylyn Bacon, Ramsden Farm, Stone-cum-Ebony, Tenterden TN30 7JB, 01797 270300, streakybacon@kent.uk.net
Clare Barham, Hole Park, Rolvenden, Cranbrook TN17 4JB, 01580 241386, clarebarham@holepark.com
Virginia Latham, Stowting Hill House, Ashford TN25 6BE, 01303 862881, vjlatham@hotmail.com
Caroline Loder-Symonds, Denne Hill Farm, Womenswold, Canterbury CT4 6HD, 01227 831203, cloder_symonds@hotmail.com
Elspeth Napier, 53 High Street, East Malling ME19 6AJ, 01732 522146, elspeth@cherryvilla.demon.co.uk

LANCASHIRE
Greater Manchester & surrounding areas

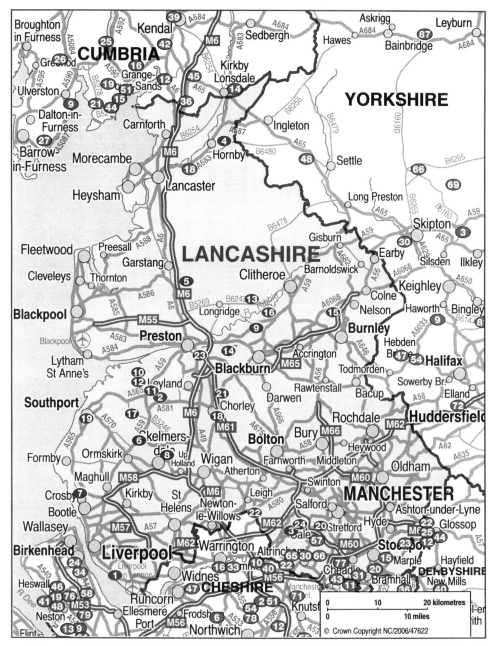

Opening Dates

February
SUNDAY 18
22 Weeping Ash
SUNDAY 25
22 Weeping Ash

May
SUNDAY 6
18 The Ridges
SUNDAY 20
7 Crosby Hall
11 Hazelwood & Hazel Cottage
22 Weeping Ash
SATURDAY 26
3 Brookfield
4 Clearbeck House
SUNDAY 27
17 Perennial Paradise

June
SATURDAY 2
15 Montford Cottage
SUNDAY 3
1 480 Aigburth Road
11 Hazelwood & Hazel Cottage
13 Huntingdon Hall
15 Montford Cottage
SUNDAY 10
6 Crabtree Lane Gardens
14 Mill Barn & Primrose Cottage
SUNDAY 17
6 Crabtree Lane Gardens
11 Hazelwood & Hazel Cottage
FRIDAY 22
23 Willow House (Evening)
SUNDAY 24
4 Clearbeck House
12 Hesketh Bank Village Gardens
14 Mill Barn & Primrose Cottage
23 Willow House
SATURDAY 30
13 Huntingdon Hall

July
SUNDAY 1
2 Bretherton Gardens
4 Clearbeck House
8 Cypress House
10 Hawthornes Nursery Garden
19 14 Saxon Road
24 Wroxham Gardens
SATURDAY 7
20 Southlands
21 The Stones & Roses Garden
SUNDAY 8
17 Perennial Paradise

19 14 Saxon Road
20 Southlands
21 The Stones & Roses Garden
FRIDAY 13
16 The Old Zoo Garden
SATURDAY 14
3 Brookfield
SUNDAY 15
16 The Old Zoo Garden
22 Weeping Ash
SUNDAY 29
10 Hawthornes Nursery Garden
17 Perennial Paradise

August
SUNDAY 5
11 Hazelwood & Hazel Cottage
SUNDAY 12
17 Perennial Paradise
SUNDAY 26
9 Greenacre
18 The Ridges
MONDAY 27
9 Greenacre

September
SUNDAY 16
22 Weeping Ash

October
SUNDAY 7
14 Mill Barn & Primrose Cottage
SUNDAY 14
14 Mill Barn & Primrose Cottage

Gardens open to the public
5 Cobble Hey Farm & Gardens
18 The Ridges

The Gardens

1 **480 AIGBURTH ROAD**
Liverpool L19 3QE. Mrs Bridget Spiegl, 0151 427 2344. *4m S of Liverpool town centre. On main rd (A561) between city & Runcorn bridge. Just past Liverpool Cricket Club, on LH-side of rd going towards the city.* Adm £1.50, chd free (share to Mpala Mobile Clinic). Sun 3 June (2-5). Visitors also welcome by appt. Plantswoman's small town garden. Mixed herbaceous and shrubs. Some interesting and unusual plants.

2 **BRETHERTON GARDENS**
PR26 9AN. *8m SW of Preston. Between Southport & Preston, from A59, take B5247 towards Chorley for 1m. Gardens off North Rd (B5248) & South Rd (B5247).* Home-made teas. **Combined adm £3.50, chd free. Sun 1 July (12-5).** Maps available at each garden.

HAZEL COTTAGE
6 South View, Bamfords Fold. John & Kris Jolley
(See separate entry for Hazelwood & Hazel Cottage).

HAZELWOOD
North Road. Jacqueline Iddon & Thompson Dagnall
(See separate entry for Hazelwood & Hazel Cottage).

MAGNOLIA COTTAGE
South Road. Mikki Boston, 01772 600895. Visitors also welcome by appt, June to Aug,

Shade-loving plants, mostly green and white, give the garden an air of peace and tranquillity . . .

groups up to 25, no coaches. Small shady garden architecturally designed creating 3 rooms each with their own individual features; shade-loving plants, mostly green and white, give the garden an air of peace and tranquillity.

 ♿ ✝

Late summer wow factor with dahlias, begonias, perennials . . . emphasis on colour . . .

❸ BROOKFIELD
11 Irlam Road, Flixton M41 6JR. Bob & Beryl Wheeler. *2¹/₂m SW of Urmston. From J10 on M60 go S through 2 roundabouts to T-lights, turn R into Moorside Rd. At next roundabout take 2nd rd signed Lymm, after next T-lights take 5th rd on R Irlam Rd.* Home-made teas. **Adm £2, chd free. Sats 26 May; 14 July (1-5).**
¹/₃-acre town garden on triangular plot divided into sections with several pathways. Herbaceous beds and borders with mature trees and shrubs planned for yr-round effect; rockery, pond and water feature; shade areas; patio with troughs and containers. Greenhouse.

♿ ✝ ❊ ☕

❹ CLEARBECK HOUSE
Mewith Lane, Higher Tatham LA2 8PJ. Peter & Bronwen Osborne, 015242 61029, clearbeckarts@yahoo.co.uk. *13m NE of Lancaster. Signed from Wray (M6 J34, A683, B6480) & Low Bentham.* Light refreshments & teas. **Adm £2.50, chd free. Sat 26 May; Suns 24 June; 1 July (11-5). Visitors also welcome by appt, coaches permitted.**
'A surprise round every corner' is the most common response as visitors encounter fountains, streams, ponds, sculptures, boathouses and follies: (Rapunzel's tower, temple, turf maze, walk-through pyramid). 2-acre wildlife lake attracts many species of insects and birds. Planting incl herbaceous borders, grasses, bog plants and many roses. Featured in GGG.

♿ ❊ ☕

❺ ◆ COBBLE HEY FARM & GARDENS
Claughton-on-Brock PR3 0QN. Mr & Mrs D Miller, 01995 602643, www.cobblehey.co.uk. *4m S of Garstang. Leave M6 at J32 or 33. Take brown sign from A6 nr Bilsborough. Claughton is 2m E, up Butt Hill Lane, 2nd farm rd on L.* **Adm £3, chd £1.50, concessions £2.50. Open Thurs to Mons from Feb 1 10.30-4.30.**
2-acre hillside garden on working farm. Mature beds of hardy herbaceous

perennials; over 200 species of phlox, primulas and hellebores; natural streams with stone banks. Woodland and colour-themed garden, prairie and potterage under development. Featured in 'Lancashire Life', 'Daily Telegraph'. Double award winner Lancashire & Blackpool TB - small visitor attraction & rural business.

♿ ✝ ❊ ☕

❻ CRABTREE LANE GARDENS
Burscough L40 0RW. *3m NE of Ormskirk. Follow A59 Preston - Liverpool rd to Burscough. From N before 1st bridge turn R into Redcat Lane - brown sign Martin Mere. From S pass through village over 2nd bridge, then L into Redcat Lane, after ³/₄m turn L into Crabtree Lane. Gardens by level Xing.* Home-made teas. **Combined adm £3, chd free. Suns 10, 17 June (1-5).**
Featured in Lancashire Gardener, & on Radio Lancashire.

☕

79 CRABTREE LANE
Sandra & Peter Curl, 01704 893713, peter.curl@aimiafoods.com. Visitors also welcome by appt.
¹/₂ acre comprising different areas. Patio with hostas and grasses; herbaceous area surrounded by beech hedge, island beds with conifers and shrubs. Rose garden and 2 ponds; pergola for relaxing surrounded by climbers and wisteria.

♿ ✝ ❊

81 CRABTREE LANE
Prue & Barry Cooper, 01704 893239. Visitors also welcome by appt.
Small plantswoman's enclosed garden, 6ft old brick wall, pond and water features. Old-fashioned rockery; vine-covered pergola, trompe l'oeil. Beds comprising shrubs but mostly herbaceous plants. Arches with clematis and climbing roses.

♿ ✝

❼ NEW CROSBY HALL
Back Lane, Little Crosby, Liverpool L23 4UA. Mark Blundell. *8m N of Liverpool. From church in Little Crosby take Back Lane. Entrance ¹/₄m on R.* **Adm £3, chd free. Sun 20 May (2-5).**
4-acre garden, originally designed by John Webb circa 1815, set in parkland of 120-acre estate. Many fine trees, rhododendrons and azaleas. Special features in this developing garden incl Victorian stone archway, decorative walled garden, espalier pears and wisteria, new orchard and Zen garden. Gravel paths throughout.

♿ ✝ ☕

❽ NEW CYPRESS HOUSE
Higher Lane, Dalton, nr Wigan WN8 7RP. David & Coleta Houghton, 01257 463822, www.cypresshousegarden.com. *5m E of Ormskirk. M6 J27. Follow A5209 in direction of Ormskirk. Proceed to 1st mini-roundabout E of Newburgh, turn L onto Higher Lane. Garden 1m on R.* Light refreshments & teas. **Adm £2.50, chd free. Sun 1 July (1-6). Visitors also welcome by appt.**
³/₄-acre garden, exposed and overlooking the West Lancashire plain. Mixed informal plantings which incl shrubs and trees, conifers, acers, hostas, heucheras and herbaceous. Many rare and unusual plants. Large rockery and water feature. Newly established alpine and vine house. ¹/₄-acre newly planted arboretum with rare and unusual trees.

✝ ☕

❾ GREENACRE
157 Ribchester Road, Clayton-le-Dale BB1 9EE. Dorothy & Andrew Richards, 01254 249694. *3¹/₂m N of Blackburn. Leave M6 J31. Take A59 towards Clitheroe. In 7m at T-lights turn R towards Blackburn along B6245. Garden ¹/₂m on RH-side. Park nearby or at Salesbury Memorial Hall,*

500yds on RH-side. Disabled parking nearby. Adm £2.50, chd free (share to Vitalise). Sun 26, Mon 27 Aug (1.30-5). Visitors also welcome by appt, May, July to Sept, groups of 15+.
Peaceful 1-acre garden on edge of Ribble Valley. Broad sweep of lawn with mixed beds, colour phased throughout the yr. Late summer wow factor with dahlias, begonias, perennials. Emphasis on colour, shapes, textures and contrasts, raised deck for viewing. Visitor information for flowerbeds. Interesting use of hedging, vegetables, compost system and orchard. Featured in 'Lancashire Evening Telegraph'.

⑩ HAWTHORNES NURSERY GARDEN
Marsh Road, Hesketh Bank PR4 6XT. Mr & Mrs R Hodson, 01772 812379, www.hawthornes-nursery.co.uk. *10m SW of Preston. From Preston take A59 towards Liverpool. Turn R at T-lights at Tarleton. Through Tarleton Village into Hesketh Bank. Large car park at Station Rd/Shore Rd. WC.* Home-made teas. Adm £2.50, chd free. Suns 1, 29 July (1-5). Visitors also welcome by appt, June to Sept. Groups of 10+, coaches permitted.
1-acre plant lover's garden. Intensively planted borders and beds with 150 old-fashioned shrub and climbing roses, over 200 clematis. (Rare and unusual herbaceous and viticella clematis. National Collection of viticellas). Interplanted with dramatic collection of hardy geraniums, phlox, aconitums, lythrums and heleniums for later colour. Adjoining nursery. Featured in 'Lancashire Magazine', Lancashire Gardener, GGG & on Radio Lancashire.

Herbaceous borders and large stream-fed pond with woodland walk . . .

⑪ HAZELWOOD & HAZEL COTTAGE
Bretherton PR26 9AH. *8m SW of Preston. Between Southport & Preston, from A59 take B5247 towards Chorley for 1m. Gardens off North Rd B5248 & South Rd B5247.* Home-made teas. Combined adm £3, chd free. Suns 20 May; 3, 17 June; 5 Aug (12-5). Also open with **Bretherton Gardens** 1 July.
Maps available at both gardens.

HAZEL COTTAGE
6 South View, Bamford Fold. John & Kris Jolley, 01772 600896. *(off South Rd).* Visitors also welcome by appt.
Victorian cottager's plot divided into rooms to filter the wind and disguise the shape. Emphasis on foliage and form with many seed-raised perennials. Mixed borders; kitchen garden; ponds; orchard. Lancashire and Yorkshire themed borders.

HAZELWOOD
North Road. Jacqueline Iddon & Thompson Dagnall
1¹/₂-acre garden and hardy plant nursery, originally orchard, now has gravel garden with silver and variegated foliage plants; shrubs; herbaceous borders and large stream-fed pond with woodland walk, sculpture and Victorian fern house. New for 2007 brick-built summerhouse. Featured in Flora, international magazine.

⑫ HESKETH BANK VILLAGE GARDENS
PR4 6RQ. *10m SW of Preston. From Preston take A59 towards Liverpool, then turn R at T-lights for Tarleton village. Straight through Tarleton to Hesketh Bank.* Teas. Combined adm £3, chd free. Sun 24 June (11-5). Free vintage bus between gardens. Maps available at each garden. Featured in 'Lancashire Magazine'.

31 BECCONSALL LANE
Mr & Mrs J Baxter, 01772 813018. Visitors also welcome by appt.
Cottage-style garden with pond, white and green beds and semi-woodland walk. Organic garden. Hot bed.

74 CHAPEL ROAD
Mr & Mrs T Iddon, 01772 813172. Visitors also welcome by appt, June & July only.
Compact colourful garden. Wide variety of plants. Pond, arbour and gazebo.

11 DOUGLAS AVENUE
Mr & Mrs J Cook
Large established garden with lawns, mature trees, mixed herbaceous borders and naturalised areas, with pond.

155 STATION ROAD
Mr & Mrs G Hale
Large garden with lawns; cottage-style herbaceous borders. Summerhouse and pond.

WEDGWOOD
Shore Road. Mr & Mrs D Watson, 01772 816509, heskethbank@aol.com. Visitors also welcome by appt, June & July only.
An old garden which is being developed into diverse planting areas. These incl gravel, woodland, herbaceous, formal pond, lawns, large glasshouse, orchard with meadow and colour-themed parterre rainbow-garden.

⑬ HUNTINGDON HALL
Huntingdon Hall Lane, Dutton PR3 2ZT. Mr & Mrs J E Ashcroft. *6m NE of Preston. Leave M6 J31. Take A59 towards Clitheroe, turn L at 1st T-lights to Ribchester along B6245. After bridge over R Ribble take next R up Gallows Lane. T-junction turn L. Next R into Huntingdon Hall Lane.* Home-made teas & wine. Adm £2.50, chd free. Sun 3, Sat 30 June (11-5).
C17 house (not open) in glorious countryside. Garden features incl: formal layout with pleached limes, developing herbaceous beds, woodland walk, terraced pond, many unusual plants.

⑭ MILL BARN & PRIMROSE COTTAGE
Goosefoot Close, Samlesbury PR5 0SS. Chris Mortimer & Susan Childs, 01254 853300, chris@millbarn.net. *6m E of Preston. From M6 J31 2¹/₂m on A59/A677 B/burn. Turn S. Nabs Head Lane, then Goosefoot Lane.* Light refreshments &

teas (June), Teas (Oct). **Adm £2.50, chd free.** Suns 10, 24 June (11-4.30); 7, 14 Oct (2-5). Visitors also welcome by appt.
Tranquil terraced garden along the banks of R Darwen. A garden to stimulate the imagination, ranging from the semi-formal to the bucolic. Primrose Bank (adjacent garden), now maturing follows the contours of the hillside. Featured in 'The Independent' 10 best summer gardens. Partial wheelchair access.

& ⊗ ⊨ ☕

Ponds; scree; dell; ha-ha, and old Lancashire pit, situated within picturesque enviromentally friendly scenery . . .

⑮ MONTFORD COTTAGE
Cuckstool Lane, Fence, nr Burnley BB12 9NZ. Craig Bullock & Tony Morris, www.montford.p3online.net. *4m N of Burnley. From J13 M65, take A6068 (signs for Fence) & in 2m turn L onto B6248 (signs for Brierfield). Proceed down hill for 1/2 m (past Forest PH). Entrance to garden on L, with limited car park further down hill.* Cream teas. **Adm £3, chd 50p.** Sat 2, Sun 3 June (2-6).
1-acre walled garden, established over the last 23yrs. 2007 new projects synthesize with mature plantings to enhance this plantsman's collection. Artist/photographer/floral designer create a garden with individual identity. Many seats and shelters provide the opportunity to relax and soak up the atmosphere.

& ⊗ ☕

⑯ THE OLD ZOO GARDEN
Cherry Drive, Brockhall Village BB6 8AY. Gerald & Linda Hitman, 01254 244811. *5m N Blackburn. Leave M6 J31, take A59 Clitheroe approx 10m. Follow signs for Old Langho & Brockhall Village. Just prior to Blackburn roundabout (junction A666) follow signs to The Old Zoo. Partial access for wheelchairs & prams.* Light refreshments & teas. **Adm £5, chd free.** Fri 13, Sun 15 July (11-4). Visitors also welcome by appt. Guided tours of garden and use of leisure facilities of The Avenue Hotel are availabe to parties 20+. For details www.theavenuehotel.co.uk.
15 acres. The Old Zoo garden is constructed with pleasure in mind; it encloses figurative sculpture, 16 varieties of Lancashire apples, water courses, unusual planting and very unusual earth workings. The size and speed with which The Old Zoo has been constructed has made it one of the North's premier gardens, with its acclaim growing by the week.

⊨ ☕

⑰ PERENNIAL PARADISE
Boundary House Farm, Holmeswood L40 1UA. Graham & Linda Birchall, www.holmeswoodplants.co.uk. *10m NW of Ormskirk. From A59 at Rufford take B5246 W 3m to Boundary House Farm signed. From A565 Southport to Preston turn R at roundabout towards Martin Mere. B 5246.* Cream teas. **Adm £2.50, chd free.** Suns 27 May; 8, 29 July; 12 Aug (11-5).
Large cottage garden featuring island and herbaceous borders well-stocked and incl many unusual perennials. Ponds; scree; dell; ha-ha, and old Lancashire pit, situated within picturesque enviromentally friendly scenery. New area being developed to incl colour-themed borders with yr-round interest. Embothrium magnificent in May.

& ✗ ⊗ ☕

⑱ ◆ THE RIDGES
Weavers Brow, Cowling Road, Chorley PR6 9EB. Mr & Mrs J M Barlow, 01257 279981, barbara@barlowridges.co.uk. *2m SE of Chorley. J27 M6 or J8 M61 approaching Chorley on A6, follow signs for town centre, then signs for Cowling & Rivington. From A6 S turn R at 1st roundabout, R at Morrison's. Up Brooke St, take Cowling Brow, approx 1/4 m garden on RH-side.* **Adm £2.50,**

chd free. Bank Hols Suns, Mons 7, 27, 28 May; 27 Aug; Weds in June, July (11-7). For NGS: Suns 6 May; 26 Aug (11-5).
2 1/2 acres. Incl old walled kitchen garden, cottage-style; herbaceous borders; new natural garden with stream, ponds. Laburnum arch leads to large formal lawn, surrounded by natural woodland. Shrub borders and trees with contrasting foliage. New walled area planted with scented roses and herbs. Paved area with dovecote. New wall feature with Italian influence. Featured in 'Lancashire Gardener' & 'Lancashire Design & Living'.

& ⊗ ⊨ ☕

⑲ 14 SAXON ROAD
Birkdale PR8 2AX. Margaret & Geoff Fletcher, 01704 567742. *1m S of Southport. Off A565 Southport to Liverpool rd. 4th rd on L after roundabout opp St James Church.* Home-made teas. **Adm £2, chd free (share to Cancer Research UK).** Suns 1, 8 July (10.30-4.30). Visitors also welcome by appt, groups 10+.
1/4-acre walled garden containing long border, informal beds, raised areas, winding gravel and bark paths. Greenhouse, conservatory gazebo, 2 ponds, 2 water features; fruit and vegetable beds. Mature trees and shrubs, climbing roses, clematis and many hardy plants.

& ✗ ⊗ ☕ ☕

⑳ SOUTHLANDS
12 Sandy Lane, Stretford M32 9DA. Maureen Sawyer & Duncan Watmough, 0161 283 9425, www.southlands12.com. *3m S of Manchester. Sandy Lane (B5213) is situated off A5181 (A56) 1/4 m from M60 J7.* Home-made teas. **Adm £2.50, chd free (share to Christie Hospital).** Sat 7, Sun 8 July (1-6). Visitors also welcome by appt June to end of Aug. Guided tour for groups of 10+.
Artist's 1/4-acre town garden making full use of structures and living screens to create a number of intimate gardens each with its own theme incl courtyard, Mediterranean, ornamental, woodland and organic kitchen gardens with large glasshouse. Many exotics and unusual herbaceous perennials, 2 ponds and water feature. New moss garden. Live jazz twice daily (weather permitting). Exhibition of art work derived from garden. Featured in 'All Things Bright & Beautiful'.

& ✗ ⊗ ☕

㉑ THE STONES & ROSES GARDEN
White Coppice Farm, White Coppice PR6 9DF. Raymond & Linda Smith,
www.stonesandroses.org. *3m NE of Chorley. J8 M61. A674 to Blackburn. 3rd R to Heapey & White Coppice. Parking next to garden. Quiet time between 4-5.* Home-made teas. **Adm £2.50, chd free. Sat 7, Sun 8 July (2-5).**
Still developing 3-acre garden where the cows used to live. Sunken garden, 500 roses, fountains, waterfalls, stonework, rockery, herbaceous. New this yr, fruit tree walk to millpond with wild flower planting. Set in lovely hamlet. Featured on BBC Northwest. Gravel paths.
&. ⚒ ⊛ ☕

Raised decking area with hosta borders and passiflora arch; children's play area with Wendy house . . .

㉒ WEEPING ASH
Bents Garden Centre, Warrington Road, Glazebury WA3 5NS. John Bent, 01942 266300, www.bents.co.uk. *15m W of Manchester. Located next to Bents Garden Centre, just off the East Lancs rd A580 at Greyhound roundabout nr Leigh. Follow brown 'Garden Centre' signs.* Light refreshments & teas at Bents Garden Centre. **Adm £2.50, chd free** (share to local charity). **Suns 18, 25 Feb; 20 May; 15 July; 16 Sept (11-4.30).** Visitors also welcome by appt, groups of 10+.

2-acre garden of all-yr interest. Broad sweep of lawn with mixed borders of shrubs and herbaceous perennials leads to secret areas where pools, rose beds and island beds create scenes of clarity and perfection. Hot Mediterranean planting leads to further extensive lawn and impressive herbaceous border. Adjacent to 2006 award winning Bents Garden Centre. Featured on BBC Look North.
&. ⚒ ⊛ ☕

㉓ WILLOW HOUSE
106 Higher Walton Road, Walton-le-Dale PR5 4HR. Sue & Michael Coupe, 01772 257042, francescoupe@hotmail.com. *3m SW of Preston. Exit 29 M6. M65 exit 1, M61 exit Bamber Bridge/Chorley. Bungalow on A675 (nr to Inside Out Restaurant).* Cream teas. **Adm £2, chd 50p (share to RPH Renal Unit). Sun 24 June (1-4). Evening Opening £4, chd £1, wine, Fri 22 June (6-9).** Visitors also welcome by appt June only.
Approx 1/3 acre, overlooking fields to ancient woodland. Herbaceous borders, small box parterre. Pond with koi; rockery and summerhouse. Grasses and alpine troughs. Thyme path. Many unusual ideas. French garden bric a brac for sale. Music on Evening Opening. Featured in 'Lancashire Gardens' & on TV Granada Reports. Gravel paths, some steps.
&. ⚒ ⊛ ☕

㉔ WROXHAM GARDENS
Davyhulme M41 5TE. *1m SW of Urmston. From J10 on M60 follow Urmston signs, to 2nd roundabout, take 3rd exit and immediate 1st R into Davyhulme Rd. Gardens short walk behind St Mary's Church.* **Combined adm £2.50, chd free. Sun 1 July (1-5).**
☕

12 BOWERS AVENUE
Mel & Phil Gibbs. *Access via Wroxham Gdns*
Small town garden, with many

cottage style plants, incl roses and clematis, pots, shrubs and patio for all-round interest.
⚒ ⊛

1 WROXHAM AVENUE
Liz & Emile Auld
Town garden with shaped lawn; borders with shrubs and perennials; patio area. Raised decking area with hosta borders and passiflora arch; children's play area with Wendy house. Pebble water feature.
&. ⚒ ⊛

2 WROXHAM AVENUE
Margaret & Bren Kinnucane
Town garden with raised edge beds containing mature shrubs and herbaceous perennials; wildlife pond with seating area and raised patio with troughs, containers and water feature.
⊛

9 WROXHAM AVENUE
Jonathan & Katrina Myers
Triangular SE-facing formal garden comprising stone patio, an irregularly-shaped lawn, shrubs, conifers and heather. To the E corner there is a terracotta pot water feature, whilst in the opp corner a traditional two-tier fountain. Slightly raised area bordered by grasses and phormium.
&. ⚒ ⊛

11 WROXHAM AVENUE
Alan Slack
Unusual triangular-shaped plot with lots going on. Decking; patio areas; pergola with climbers; vegetable plot, herb garden; alpine sinks; pond with waterfall; rockery; lawn area. Well-stocked mature borders, much 'architectural'. Conservatory; greenhouse; shed and kennel.
&. ⊛

Lancashire County Volunteers
County Organiser
Ray & Brenda Doldon, 2 Gorse Way, Formby, Merseyside L37 1PB, 01704 834253, ray@doldon.plus.com
County Treasurer
Ray Doldon, 2 Gorse Way, Formby, Merseyside L37 1PB, ray@doldon.plus.com
Assistant County Organisers
Margaret & Geoff Fletcher, 14 Saxon Road, Birkdale, Southport, Merseyside PR8 2AX, 01704 567742,
    geoffwfletcher@hotmail.co.uk

LEICESTERSHIRE & RUTLAND

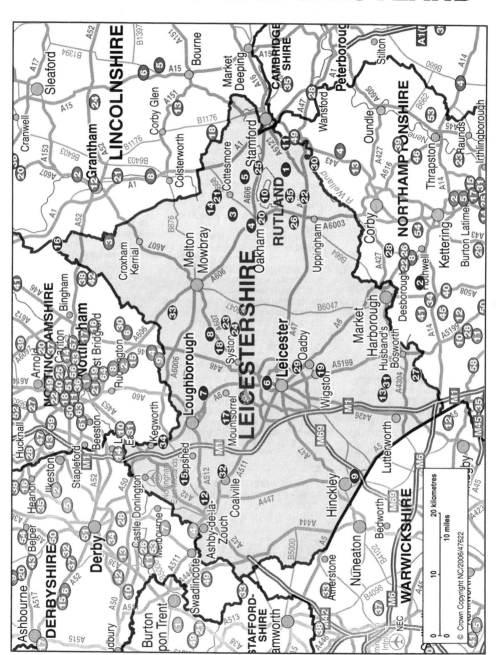

Opening Dates

February

SUNDAY 25
33 Wartnaby Gardens

March

SUNDAY 4
18 1700 Melton Road

SUNDAY 11
16 The Homestead

SUNDAY 25
5 Barnsdale Gardens
23 Parkside

April

SUNDAY 8
17 Long Close

SUNDAY 29
21 The Old Hall
33 Wartnaby Gardens

May

SATURDAY 5
17 Long Close (Evening)

SUNDAY 6
4 Barleythorpe Gardens
23 Parkside

MONDAY 7
9 Burbage Gardens

SUNDAY 13
6 Belgrave Hall Museum & Gardens
19 Mill House
34 Whatton Gardens

SUNDAY 20
3 Ashwell Gardens
32 Warren Hills Cottage

SUNDAY 27
10 Chestnuts
17 Long Close

WEDNESDAY 30
2 Arthingworth Manor Gardens

June

SUNDAY 3
12 The Dairy
25 Prebendal House
31 Walton Gardens

WEDNESDAY 6
2 Arthingworth Manor Gardens
28 Stoke Albany House

SUNDAY 10
9 Burbage Gardens
27 South Kilworth Gardens

WEDNESDAY 13
2 Arthingworth Manor Gardens

28 Stoke Albany House

SUNDAY 17
7 Beveridge Street Gardens
26 Ridlington Gardens
33 Wartnaby Gardens

WEDNESDAY 20
2 Arthingworth Manor Gardens
28 Stoke Albany House
30 Wakerley Manor (Evening)

SATURDAY 23
2 Arthingworth Manor with village gardens

SUNDAY 24
2 Arthingworth Manor with village gardens
8 Brooksby Melton College
13 Gilmorton Gardens
22 The Park House
27 South Kilworth Gardens
32 Warren Hills Cottage

WEDNESDAY 27
2 Arthingworth Manor Gardens
11 The Court House (Evening)
13 Gilmorton Gardens (Day & Evening)
28 Stoke Albany House

July

SUNDAY 1
34 Whatton Gardens
35 Wing Gardens

WEDNESDAY 4
2 Arthingworth Manor Gardens
28 Stoke Albany House

FRIDAY 6
12 The Dairy (Evening)

SUNDAY 8
15 Hill Park Farm

WEDNESDAY 11
2 Arthingworth Manor Gardens
28 Stoke Albany House

SUNDAY 15
1 Acre End
31 Walton Gardens (Day & Evening)

WEDNESDAY 18
2 Arthingworth Manor Gardens
28 Stoke Albany House

SUNDAY 22
19 Mill House

WEDNESDAY 25
2 Arthingworth Manor Gardens

SUNDAY 29
29 University of Leicester 'Harold Martin' Botanic Garden
32 Warren Hills Cottage

August

SUNDAY 26
20 Mirwood

September

SUNDAY 9
6 Belgrave Hall Museum & Gardens

October

SUNDAY 7
18 1700 Melton Road

SUNDAY 21
5 Barnsdale Gardens

Private gardens opening regularly for the NGS

2 Arthingworth Manor Gardens
17 Long Close
28 Stoke Albany House

Gardens open to the public

5 Barnsdale Gardens
18 1700 Melton Road
34 Whatton Gardens

By appointment only

14 Hill House
24 Pine House

The Gardens

1 ACRE END
The Jetties, North Luffenham
LE15 8JX. Jim & Mima Bolton,
01780 720906. *7m SE of Oakham. Via Manton & Edith Weston, 7m SW of Stamford via Ketton. 2m off A47 through Morcott village.* Light refreshments & teas at North Luffenham Community Centre. **Adm £3, chd free. Sun 15 July (11-5).** Visitors also welcome by appt, mid Jun to mid Aug, groups welcome.

All organically managed to encourage wildlife . . .

1-acre garden, imaginatively designed and intensively planted, incl knot garden, oriental courtyard garden, mixed borders, circular lawn with island beds, herb and wild flower garden. Working fruit and vegetable garden, long herbaceous border and woodland garden. Many unusual trees, shrubs, herbaceous perennials and tender exotics in containers. All organically managed to encourage wildlife. Studio Art Exhibition (share to NGS). Challenging Quiz. Mainly grass paths & lawns, some gravel.

& ✕ ⊕ ☕

❷ ARTHINGWORTH MANOR GARDENS

Arthingworth, Market Harborough LE16 8JT. W L S Guinness. *5m S of Market Harborough. Via A508 at 4m L to Arthingworth; from Northampton via A508. At Kelmarsh turn R at bottom of hill. In village follow road round, keep church on L, farm on R, parking on L.* Teas (Weds) light refreshments 23, 24 June in village hall. **Adm £1.75, chd free (share to village hall & church). Weds 30 May; 6 June to 25 July (2-5); Sat 23, Sun 24 June (12-5) Adm £3 incl village gardens.**
White garden; delphiniums; herbaceous and mixed borders; vegetables and fruit. 3-acre arboretum. 23, 24 June village gardens open. Home-made teas, plant stall. Gravel paths, steep slopes, some steps.

& ☕

❸ ASHWELL GARDENS

LE15 7LW. *3m N of Oakham. Via B668 towards Cottesmore, turn L for Ashwell.* Light refreshments, teas & lunches. **Combined adm £3, chd free (share to VC Grave Restoration Fund at Ashwell Church). Sun 20 May (11.45-6).**
☕

NEW ASHWELL COTTAGE
Church Close. Mrs P Menzies-Gow
Country garden of approx ³/₄ acre surrounding a thatched cottage. Informal lawns and flower beds are surrounded by mature trees and shrubs. Gravel drive.

ASHWELL HOUSE
Mr & Mrs S D Pettifer, 01572 722833. Visitors also welcome by appt in summer months. Refreshments.
Celebrates the 20th year of

Flowering shrubs, large weeping trees . . .

opening this 1¹/₂-acre walled vicarage garden, 1812. Against background of ancient trees; front lawns are bordered by interesting shrubs and plants with classical summer pavilion. The formal swimming pool garden leads to traditional planting of vegetables and fruit. Willow work will be demonstrated by John Shone.

❹ BARLEYTHORPE GARDENS

LE15 7EQ. *1m from Oakham on A6006 towards Melton Mowbray. Car park in Pasture Lane 1st turn L in Barleythorpe by phone box. Please park in field on L not on lane.* Teas at Dairy Cottage. **Combined adm £3, chd free. Sun 6 May (2-5).**
☕

BARLEYTHORPE HOUSE
8 Manor Lane. Mr R Turner & Mr & Mrs J Turner
Flowering shrubs, large weeping trees, small lake and woodland walk. (Children only acc by adult). Grass paths & gravel around lake, slopes can be slippery if wet.
&

DAIRY COTTAGE
Pasture Lane. Mr & Mrs W Smith
Cottage-style garden at rear with interesting shrubs and spring bulbs. Paved/walled garden to front (with pond) and lime hedge. Separate semi-formal orchard. Gravel access to main garden.
& ⊕

❺ ◆ BARNSDALE GARDENS

The Avenue, Exton, nr Oakham LE15 8AH. Nick & Sue Hamilton, 01572 813200, office@barnsdalegardens.co.uk. *3m E of Oakham. Turn off A606 at Barnsdale Lodge Hotel then 1m on L.* **Adm £6, chd £2, concessions £5. Open daily Mar to May, Sept, Oct (9-5); June to Aug (9-7); Nov to Feb (10-4). For NGS: Suns 25 Mar; 21 Oct (9-5).**
8 acres of individual gardens used by

the late Geoff Hamilton for BBC TV 'Gardeners' World'. Wide variety of ideas and garden designs for all-yr interest. Enjoyed by gardeners and non-gardeners alike. Gold at 'Gardeners' World Live' 2006; Silver Gilt medal winner at Chelsea Flower Show 2006.

& ✕ ⊕ ☕

BAXTER FARM
See Nottinghamshire.

❻ BELGRAVE HALL MUSEUM & GARDENS

Church Road off Thurcaston Road, Belgrave, Leicester LE4 5PE. Leicester City Council, 0116 2666 590, www.leicester.gov.uk/museums - for other open dates. *1¹/₂m N of Leicester. From A6/A563 junction at Redhill roundabout take A6030 Loughborough Rd towards city, signed Outdoor Pursuits Centre. Turn R at 1st T-lights and L at Talbot PH.* **Adm £2, chd free. Suns 13 May; 9 Sept (1-4.30). Visitors also welcome by appt for groups.**
Historic Grade II listed garden. House and walled garden date from 1709. Includes formal garden, herbaceous garden, rose walks, Victorian evergreen garden, rock and water garden, botanic beds, herb border, woodland garden. Alpine, temperate and tropical glasshouses with wide collection of plants incl banana and citrus.
& ✕

BELVOIR CASTLE
See Lincolnshire.

Herbaceous garden, rose walks, Victorian evergreen garden . . .

❼ NEW BEVERIDGE STREET GARDENS

Barrow on Soar LE12 8PL. *2m S of Loughborough.* Home-made teas at 4 Beveridge St. **Combined adm £2, chd free. Sun 17 June (11-4).**
An old Leicestershire village with pleasant walks along banks of River Soar. Plant sales.
☕

NEW APRICOT COTTAGE
11 Beveridge Street. Jane
Atkinson. *Follow signs to village
centre, High St, then 1st R to
church, 1st R*
Small garden of intrigue and
serenity with architectural plants,
lights and water.

**NEW THE OLD WALLED
GARDEN**
49 Beveridge Street, Barrow on
Soar. Roger & Jo Chappell
Very old walled garden with mainly
cottage-style herbaceous plants in
a variety of settings incl lawns and
borders, ponds, hot and shady
areas, rockery and herb garden.
Many plants take advantage of the
walls incl clematis, climbing roses,
vines and fruit trees.

BISHOPS COTTAGE
See Nottinghamshire.

**8 BROOKSBY MELTON
COLLEGE**
Brooksby, nr Melton Mowbray
LE14 2LJ. Chief Executive. *6m SW
of Melton Mowbray. From A607 (9m
from Leicester or 6m from Melton
Mowbray) turn at Brooksby; entrance
100yds. Bus: Leicester-Melton
Mowbray; alight Brooksby turn,
100yds.* Cream teas. **Adm £2, chd
free. Sun 24 June (12-4).**
Extensive lawns, lake, stream,
specimen trees, shrub borders,
herbaceous beds, rose garden,
topiary, wild flower meadows, rock
gardens, pergola. National Collections
of *Liriope* and *Ophiopogon.* Church
built 1220.
NCCPG

9 BURBAGE GARDENS
LE10 2LR. *1m S of Hinckley. From
M69 J1, take B4109 signed Hinckley.
1st L after 2nd roundabout into
Sketchley Manor Estate then 1st R, 1st
L. All gardens within walking distance.*
Home-made teas. **Combined adm
£3, chd free. Mon 7 May; Sun 10
June (1-5).**
A pleasant West Leicestershire village.

6 DENIS ROAD
Mr & Mrs D A Dawkins.
Sketchley Manor Est
Small garden designed to
appear much larger with wide
range of plants incl hardy
geraniums, ferns, hostas, foliage
plants, species clematis,

hellebores and spring bulbs.
Alpines in sinks. Large collection
of snowdrops.

7 HALL ROAD
Don & Mary Baker. *Sketchley
Manor Est*
Medium-sized garden; mixed
borders; foliage plants; good
mixture of shrubs. Hellebores and
spring bulbs, collection of
snowdrops. Hostas, hardy
geraniums and unusual perennials;
pond. Late summer colour.

13 HALL ROAD
Mr & Mrs G A & A J Kierton.
Sketchley Manor Est
Decorative medium-sized flower
garden, incoporating pool and
waterfall, herbaceous borders,
central lawn, scree garden, 2
patios, pergola, summer house;
greenhouse and small fountain.
Abundance of summer colour.

18 HALL ROAD
Mrs M A Clamp. *Sketchley
Manor Est*
Small garden, newly redesigned
incl herbaceous borders. Shrubs.
Pergola and gravel area.

CHESTNUT COTTAGE
See Nottinghamshire.

10 CHESTNUTS
Hambleton LE15 8TJ. Mr & Mrs A
Tibbert. *3½m E of Oakham. Turn R at
church. 70yds down hill. Turn L at
village hall on to a track, 3rd house on
R. Only gravel drive.* Home-made
cakes & cream teas. **Adm £2, chd
free. Sun 27 May (10-6).**
Sloping S-facing garden of approx
1½ acres overlooking Rutland Water.
Various borders of shrubs and
perennials lead down to rose arbour
and then to natural pond hidden by
willow trees at the bottom of garden. A
sloping garden, help can be given for
wheelchairs.

59 CHURCH LANE
See Nottinghamshire.

THE COTTAGE
See Derbyshire.

COTTAGE FARM
See Nottinghamshire.

11 THE COURT HOUSE
Geeston, Ketton PE9 3RH. Bas &
Jane Clarke. *3m W of Stamford. On
the A43 in middle of Collyweston take
rd to Ketton (1½m). Turn into Geeston
Rd the Court House 200yds on R.*
Home-made teas. **Adm £2, chd free.
Evening Opening** Wed 27 June
(5-9).
2½-acre garden incl formal garden
(designed by Bunny Guinness), walled
vegetable garden, immaculate lawns,
wild flower meadow, woodland and
river. Sloping paths and some steps.

Herbaceous borders containing many unusual and architectural plants . . .

12 THE DAIRY
Moor Lane, Coleorton LE67 8FQ. Mr
& Mrs J B Moseley, 01530 834539.
*2m E of Ashby De La Zouch. Off A512
200yds W of Peggs Green
roundabout.* Light refreshments. **Adm
£2, chd free. Sun 3 June (1.30-5).
Evening Opening** wine £3, Fri 6
July (7-9). Visitors also welcome by
appt May, June & July only, groups
of 10+, coaches permitted.
Approx ½-acre of mature trees, shrubs
and herbaceous borders containing
many unusual and architectural plants.
Herb garden, fragrant roses, pergola,
Japanese garden and newly created
dry area with grasses and agaves. The
separate 'rooms' of the garden create
surprises around every corner. Large
selection of plants for sale.

13 GILMORTON GARDENS
Nr Lutterworth LE17 5LY. *12m S of
Leicester. 4m from J20 of M1.
Proceed through Lutterworth town
centre. Turn R at police stn. Follow
signs to Gilmorton. From Leicester
follow A426 towards Lutterworth. At
Dunton Bassett turn L signed to
Gilmorton. Also A50
Leicester/Northampton Rd via
Bruntingthorpe signed Gilmorton.* Light

refreshments & teas in village hall. Combined adm £3, chd free. **Sun 24 June (11-6). Day & Evening Opening** £3, Wed 27 June (2-9). Sun 24 June combined with **South Kilworth Gardens** optional combined adm £5 to cover all gardens open in both villages. Very old village with interesting Victorian Church which will be open. Excellent Kempe stained glass windows.

'AL MANZEL'
Main Street. David & Janet Grundy, 01455 556586. *Nr Crown PH end of Main St opp Porlock Drive.* **Visitors also welcome by appt any time after our opening in June.**
Average-size plant lovers' garden constructed from an old walled farmyard, with many interesting plants, structures and features. Ponds and running water, rockery, gravel garden, greenhouse, formal garden. Extensive use of small trees, clematis and plants in pots.
&

TUDOR COTTAGE
Main Street. Mr & Mrs Dolby. *Opp 'Al Manzel'.* **Visitors also welcome by appt, will open with other 2 gardens if convenient.**
Cottage garden with 'quirky' features. Hard landscaping with stream and water features. Parterre.
&

ULVERSCROFT CLOSE
Ashby Road. Mr & Mrs M J Maddock, 01455 553226, www.maddock-garden.co.uk. **Visitors also welcome by appt.**
1/2-acre garden on two levels. Upper level features conservatory, courtyard, tree-lined paved walkway. Lower level has pond, bog garden and stream situated in colourful herbaceous and shrub borders hosting over 120 clematis. Formal kitchen garden. Featured in 'Amateur Gardening', May 2006.

HALL FARM COTTAGE
See Nottinghamshire.

THE HAYLOFT
See Nottinghamshire.

⑭ HILL HOUSE
18 Teigh Road, Market Overton LE15 7PW. Brian & Judith Taylor, 01572 767337. *6m N of Oakham. Beyond Cottesmore, 5m from A1 via Thistleton, 10m E from Melton Mowbray via Wymondham.* Home-made teas. **Adm £2, chd free. Visitors welcome by appt July to Sept, groups of 10+, coaches permitted.**
Owner-maintained plant enthusiasts' garden consisting mainly of mixed beds designed to provide colour and interest from mid-June to the end of Sept. The emphasis is on architectural plants and unusual hardy and tender perennials. Ornamental pond.

⑮ NEW HILL PARK FARM
Dodgeford Lane, Belton, Loughborough LE12 9TE. John & Jean Adkin. *6m W of Loughborough. Dodgeford Lane off B5324 bet Belton & Osgathorpe.* Home-made teas. **Adm £2, chd free. Sun 8 July (11-5).**
Medium-sized garden to a working farm with wonderful views over Charnwood Forest. Herbaceous borders, rock garden; many planted stone troughs and new pergola with clematis and roses.

HOLYWELL HALL
See Lincolnshire.

Winter, spring, summer and autumn colour, a garden for all seasons . . .

⑯ THE HOMESTEAD
Normanton-by-Bottesford NG13 0EP. Mr & Mrs J E Palmer, 01949 842745. *8m W of Grantham. On A52. In Bottesford turn N, signed Normanton; last house on R before disused airfield.* Home-made teas. **Adm £1.50, chd free. Sun 11 Mar (2-6). Visitors also welcome by appt.**

3/4-acre informal plant lover's garden. Vegetable garden, small orchard, woodland area, many hellebores, snowdrops and single peonies. Collections of hostas and sempervivums. National Collection of heliotropes.
❀ NCCPG

LITTLE PONTON HALL
See Lincolnshire.

⑰ LONG CLOSE
Main St, Woodhouse Eaves LE12 8RZ. John Oakland & Pene Johnson, 01509 890616 (business hours), www.longclose.org.uk. *4m S of Loughborough. Nr M1 J23. From A6, W in Quorn.* Home-made teas Sun 8 April, Sun 27 May. **Adm £3.50, chd 50p. Daily Tues to Sats & Bank Hol Mons Mar to July; Sept & Oct (9.30-5.30).** Tickets Pene Crafts Gift Shop opp. Tea/coffee facilities for daily visits. **Suns 8 Apr, Specialist Plant Fair (1-5); 27 May (2-6). Evening Opening** £5, wine, Sat 5 May (6-8). **Group visits welcome, catering by arrangement.**
5-acres spring bulbs, rhododendrons, azaleas, camellias, magnolias, many rare shrubs, mature trees, lily ponds; terraced lawns, herbaceous borders, potager in walled kitchen garden, penstemon collection, wild flower meadow walk. New contemplation quiet area. Winter, spring, summer and autumn colour, a garden for all seasons. Featured in 'Garden News Magazine', 2006. Large selection of plants for sale.

THE MALTINGS
See Northamptonshire.

MANOR FARM HOUSE
See Nottinghamshire.

⑱ ♦ 1700 MELTON ROAD
Rearsby LE7 4YR. Mrs Hazel Kaye. *6m NE of Leicester. On A607.* Refreshments. **Adm £2, chd free. For NGS: Suns 4 Mar; 7 Oct (2-5).**
In March hellebores, early flowering shrubs and daffodils feature; in October Michaelmas daisies, colchicum and shrubs with colourful berries and foliage. 1 1/2 acres with wide range of interesting plants. National Collection of *Tradescantia* (Andersoniana Group). Grass paths.
& NCCPG

⑲ MILL HOUSE
118 Welford Road, Wigston, Leicester LE18 3SN. Mr & Mrs P Measures, 01162 885409. *4m S of Leicester. 1m S of Wigston, on main old A50.* Light refreshments & teas. **Adm £1.40, chd free. Suns 13 May; 22 July (11-5).** Visitors also welcome by appt May to Aug. Walled town garden; large amount of plant variety. Unusual and interesting design features.

 ♿ 🐾 ⊛ ☕

Serpentine yew hedge, mature trees, medieval ha-ha and fish ponds . . .

⑳ MIRWOOD
69a Brooke Road, Oakham LE15 6HG. Kevin & Kate O'Brien, 01572 755535. *200yds from town centre. Turn into Mill St at roundabout opp library at X-roads/T-lights. Parking available in Brooke Rd car park (free on Sun). Garden 200yds on RH-side.* Home-made teas. **Adm £2, chd free** (share to Melton & Rutland MS Society). **Sun 26 Aug (1-6).** Visitors also welcome by appt for groups throughout yr.
³/₄-acre garden containing large collection of rare and unusual shrubs and trees. Seasonal formal beds, recently built folly, vegetable garden, yr-round interest particularly with spring bulbs.

 ♿ ⊛ ☕

NEWBRAY HOUSE
See Nottinghamshire.

㉑ THE OLD HALL
Main Street, Market Overton LE15 7PL. Mr & Mrs Timothy Hart, 01572 767145, stefa@hambleton.co.uk. *6m N of Oakham. Beyond Cottesmore; 5m from A1 via Thistleton. 10m E from Melton Mowbray via Wymondham.* Home-made teas in village hall. **Adm £3, chd free. Sun 29 Apr (2-6).** Visitors also welcome by appt Apr to Sept, Mon-Fri.

Garden is set on a southerly ridge overlooking Catmose Vale. Garden now on four levels with stone walls and yew hedges dividing the garden up in to enclosed areas with herbaceous borders, shrubs, and young and mature trees. In 2006 the lower part of garden was planted with new shrubs to create a walk with mown paths. There are plans to tackle the ponds at the bottom of the garden and to design a small vegetable garden adjacent to the swimming pool. Gravel paths & sloping grass paths. Unfenced water. Children to be accompanied at all times.

 ♿ 🐾 ☕

THE OLD RECTORY, CLIFTON CAMPVILLE
See Staffordshire & part of West Midlands.

㉒ NEW THE PARK HOUSE
Glaston Park, Spring Lane, Glaston LE15 9BW. Sheila & Stuart Makings. *6m S of Oakham on A47. 2m E of A6003 Uppingham roundabout travelling on A47 towards Peterborough.* Home-made teas in village hall. **Adm £2.50, chd free. Sun 24 June (2-6).**
4 acres approx of historic parkland, formerly part of grounds of Glaston Hall. Informal walks incl extensive lime arbour. Serpentine yew hedge, mature trees, medieval ha-ha and fish ponds. Herbaceous borders, traditional rose garden. Rural views, wildlife friendly. Ancient trees, some of which probably the oldest of their type in country, eg 800yr+ Holm oak. Children's play area. Ornamental wildfowl. Gravel paths. Unfenced water, children welcome but must be supervised at all times by accompanying adult.

 ♿ ⊛ ☕

㉓ NEW PARKSIDE
6 Park Hill, Gaddesby LE7 4WH. Mr & Mrs D Wyrko. *8m NE of Leicester. A607 Rearsby bypass turn off for Gaddesby. L at Cheney Arms. Garden 400yds on R.* **Adm £2, chd free. Suns 25 Mar; 6 May (11-5).**
1¼-acre garden and woodland in process of re-development from original planting. Mature trees and shrubs, together with informal mixed borders, planted to encourage wildlife and provide a

family friendly environment. Newly created vegetable and fruit area together with garden pond. Many spring bulbs and hellebores in a woodland setting.

 🐾 ⊛ ☕

㉔ PINE HOUSE
Gaddesby LE7 4XE. Mr & Mrs T Milward, 01664 840213. *8m NE of Leicester. From A607, turn off for Gaddesby.* Home-made teas. **Adm £3, chd free.** Visitors welcome by appt, coaches permitted and groups of 10 +.
2-acre garden with fine mature trees, woodland walk, and water garden. Herb and potager garden and wisteria archway to Victorian vinery. Pleached lime trees, mixed borders with rare and unusual plants and rock garden; new gravel garden and terracotta pot garden. Interesting topiary hedges and box trees. 1 Star Status GGG 2006.

 🐾 ⊛ ☕

㉕ PREBENDAL HOUSE
Empingham LE15 8PW. Mr & Mrs J Partridge. *5m E of Oakham. 5m W of Stamford. On A606.* Home-made teas. **Adm £3, chd free. Sun 3 June (2-5.30).**
House (not open) built in 1688; summer palace for the Bishop of Lincoln. 4-acre garden incl herbaceous borders, water garden, topiary and kitchen gardens.

 ⊛ ☕

㉖ RIDLINGTON GARDENS
2¹/₂m N of Uppingham. *Turn off A47 to Ayston from Uppington roundabout.* Light refreshments & home-made teas at village hall. **Combined adm £3, chd free (share to Ridlington Church). Sun 17 June (2-5).** Village map available to all visitors.

 ☕

CHRISTMAS COTTAGE
2 West Lane. Mr & Mrs D Batten Medium-sized garden with orchard, vegetable plot, chicken run and terrace with Mediterranean influence.

HILLSIDE FARMHOUSE
Richard & Debra Thatcher Informal cottage garden with pond, shady area, small herb garden, vegetable terrace, orchard and steep gradient to bog garden and newly planted meadow area.

9 MAIN STREET
Ian & Yvonne MacDonald
Small cottage garden, mainly roses, lavender hedges, box hedging and rockeries. Many unusual variegated plants and tubs. Well stocked vegetable garden. Sloping garden, main top path uneven, but amazing views. Gravel paths.

RIDLINGTON HOUSE
Mr & Mrs Moubray
1¹/₂ acres; roses; herbaceous border; flowering shrubs; vegetables; orchard.

ROSEBRIAR
See Northamptonshire.

27 NEW SOUTH KILWORTH GARDENS
Nr Lutterworth LE17 6DX. *15m S of Leicester. From M1 J20, take A4304 towards Market Harborough. At Walcote turn R, signed South Kilworth.* Home-made teas at Croft Acre. **Combined adm £3, chd free** (share to Rainbow Trust). Suns 10 June (11-5), 24 June (11-6). **Combined with Gilmorton Gardens** Sun 24 June (4m from S Kilworth). Optional combined adm £5 to cover all gardens open in both villages.
Small village tucked away in SW corner of Leicestershire, with excellent views over Avon valley and Hemplow hills.

CROFT ACRE
The Belt, South Kilworth LE17 6DX. **Colin & Verena Olle, 01858 575791, colin.olle@tiscali.co.uk.** *15m S of Leicester. At White Hart PH take rd signed North Kilworth. The Belt is a bridleway 250yds on R. Parking on North Rd.* Home-made teas. Visitors also welcome by appt 16 May to 4 July.
1-acre garden with mixed herbaceous borders and island beds containing wide selection of shrubs and perennials. Pergolas with clematis and roses. Ponds and small stream. Rose garden with water feature. Vegetable garden. Summerhouse and garden 'room' seating areas.

NEW OAK TREE HOUSE
North Road, South Kilworth LE17 6DU. Pam & Martin Shave. *From centre of village take rd to N Kilworth. 300yds down North Rd on RH-side (just after bridleway, The Belt)*
Newly created garden of ²/₃ acre. Formal layout with greenhouse, ornamental vegetable plot, pond and herbaceous borders. Patio with numerous pots and hanging baskets. Arched pergola with roses and clematis, leading to gravel patio. Access to pond & greenhouse via steps.

28 STOKE ALBANY HOUSE
Stoke Albany LE16 8PT. Mr & Mrs A M Vinton, 01858 535227. *4m E of Market Harborough. Via A427 to Corby; turn to Stoke Albany; R at the White Horse (B669); garden ¹/₂m on L.* **Adm £3, chd free** (share to Marie Curie Cancer Care). Weds, 6 June to 18 July (2-4.30). Visitors also welcome by appt June to July, Tues & Weds only for groups of 10+.
4-acre country-house garden; fine trees and shrubs with wide herbaceous borders and sweeping striped lawn. Good display of bulbs in spring, roses June and July. Walled grey garden; nepeta walk arched with roses, parterre with box and roses. Mediterranean garden. Heated greenhouse, potager with topiary, water feature garden and sculptures.

Nepeta walk arched with roses . . .

29 UNIVERSITY OF LEICESTER 'HAROLD MARTIN' BOTANIC GARDEN
'The Knoll', Glebe Road, Oadby LE2 2NA. University of Leicester. *1¹/₂m SE of Leicester. On outskirts of city opp race course.* **Adm £2, chd free.** Sun 29 July (11-4).
16-acre garden incl grounds of Beaumont Hall, The Knoll, Southmeade and Hastings House. Wide variety of ornamental features

Emphasis on wildlife friendly flowers . . .

and glasshouses laid out for educational purposes incl National Collections of aubrieta, Lawson cypress, hardy fuchsia and skimmia.

30 WAKERLEY MANOR
Wakerley, nr Uppingham LE15 8PA. Mr A D A W Forbes. *5m E of Uppingham. R off A47 Uppingham to Peterborough rd through Barrowden, or from A43 Stamford to Corby rd between Duddington & Bulwick.* **Evening Opening £3, chd free** (Share to St Mary the Virgin Church, South Luffenham), wine, Wed 20 June (5-8.30).
4 acres lawns, shrubs, herbaceous; kitchen garden; 3 greenhouses. Sloping lawns.

31 WALTON GARDENS
LE17 5RP. *4m NE of Lutterworth. M1 exit 20 and, via Lutterworth follow signs for Kimcote and Walton, or from Leicester take A5199. After Shearsby turn R signed Bruntingthorpe. Follow signs.* Home-made teas at Orchards. **Combined adm £2.50, chd free. Sun 3 June (11-5); Day & evening opening** Sun 15 July (11-5) & (6.30-8.30) Adm £3.50 in evening, wine.
Small village in South Leicestershire. Village maps given to all visitors.

THE MEADOWS
Mowsley Lane. Mr & Mrs Falkner
Plantsman's garden, with emphasis on wildlife friendly flowers. Two ponds, conservatory with unusual plants and many plants in containers.

NEW THE OLD HALL
Hall Lane, Walton. Mr & Mrs Field
1¹/₂-acre garden with interesting trees and large natural pond. Play area for children.

ORCHARDS
Hall Lane. Mr & Mrs G Cousins.
1¼-acre green leaf garden with colour from flowers not foliage. Extensive use of grasses. Views of the countryside. Featured in 'Amateur Gardening', June 2006.

SANDYLAND
Hall Lane. Martin & Linda Goddard
Gently sloping cottage garden with attractive rural views. Herbaceous plants, shrubs, containers, terraced garden, pond and kitchen garden.

32 WARREN HILLS COTTAGE
Warren Hills Road, Coalville LE67 4UX. Mr Graham Waters, 01530 812350, www.warrenhills.co.uk. 5m NW of Leicester. Approx 4m NW of M1 J22 on B587 Copt Oak to Whitwick Rd, between Bulls Head and Forest Rock PH. Cream teas. Adm £2, chd 50p. Suns 20 May; 24 June; 29 July (12-5). Visitors also welcome by appt for group visits Apr to Sept day or evening, teas/refreshments as req. Established 2-acre cottage-style garden filled with hardy and unusual perennials incl display area for National Collection of astrantias. Features incl large well-stocked pond, stream, raised beds, pergola and alpine area. Colour and interest changing through the season from spring to autumn. Some gravel paths & grass slopes may make wheelchair access difficult.

NCCPG

33 WARTNABY GARDENS
Wartnaby, Nr Melton Mowbray LE14 3HY. Lady King, 01664 822549, www.wartnabygardenlabels.co.uk. 4m NW of Melton Mowbray. From A606 turn W in Ab Kettleby, from A46 at Six Hills Hotel turn E on A676. Home-made teas & light refreshments. Adm £2.50 (Feb), £3 (Apr & June), chd free (share to Wartnaby Church). Suns 25 Feb; 29 Apr; 17 June (11-4). Visitors also welcome by appt.
Large garden. Shrubs, herbaceous borders, rose garden with a good collection of old-fashioned roses and others; formal vegetable garden, series of ponds, spring garden and woodland walks.

Colour and interest changing through the season from spring to autumn . . .

34 ◆ WHATTON GARDENS
nr Loughborough LE12 5BG. Lord & Lady Crawshaw, www.whattongardens.co.uk. 4m NE of Loughborough. On A6 between Hathern & Kegworth; 2½m SE of J24 on M1. Teas on Suns. Adm £3, chd free. Suns to Fris Mar to end Oct (11-5). For NGS: Suns 13 May; 1 July (11-5).
Dating from the 1800, 15 acres of formal and informal garden incl many interesting and unusual features: carpets of bulbs in spring, followed by many flowering shrubs, old-fashioned herbaceous border and formal rose garden. Magnificent ancient trees, extensive lawns, woodland garden and ponds. A garden to relax in for an afternoon.

35 WING GARDENS
nr Oakham LE15 8SE. 2m S of Rutland Water. Off A6003 between Oakham & Uppingham. Home-made teas at village hall. Combined adm £3, chd free. Sun 1 July (2-5.30).
Pretty stone village with medieval church and turf maze. C17 country inn. Garden location map given to all visitors.

AUTUMN HOUSE
Top Street. Jane & Jeremy Wood
½-acre garden comprising mixed borders, patio areas, a variety of trees, orchard and newly planted rose parterre.

TOWNSEND HOUSE
David & Jeffy Wood. Opp village hall
Cottage garden with mixed borders, roses and clematis. Walled gravel garden with swimming pool, vegetable garden. Children to be accompanied at all times.

WINGWELL
5 Top Street. John & Rose Dejardin
Evolving garden with emphasis on bold use of plants, particularly herbaceous, and interesting use of stone and paving with water. Featuring an exhibition of contemporary sculpture throughout the summer.

Leicestershire & Rutland County Volunteers

County Organiser, County Treasurer and Leaflet Coordinator – Leicestershire
John Oakland, Long Close, Woodhouse Eaves, Loughborough LE12 8RZ, 01509 890376

County Organiser, Leaflet Coordinator – Rutland
Jennifer Wood, Townsend House, Morcott Road, Wing, Nr Oakham, Rutland LE15 8SA, 01572 737465

County Treasurer – Rutland
David Wood, Townsend House, Morcott Road, Wing, nr Oakham, Rutland LE15 8SA, 01572 737465, rdavidwood@easynet.co.uk

Publicity – Rutland
Michael Peck, Parsons Orchard, Post Office Lane, Lyndon, Nr Oakham LE15 8TX, 01572 737248

Assistant County Organiser – Rutland
Rose Dejardin, 5 Top Street, Wing, Nr Oakham LE15 8SE, 01572 737557

LINCOLNSHIRE

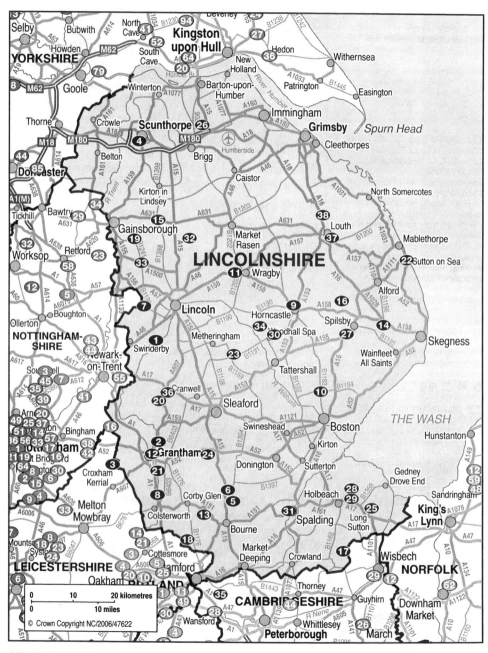

Opening Dates

February

SATURDAY 17
5 21 Chapel Street

SUNDAY 18
5 21 Chapel Street

March

THURSDAY 1
5 21 Chapel Street

SUNDAY 11
7 Doddington Hall Gardens

SATURDAY 24
2 Belton House

April

MONDAY 9
5 21 Chapel Street

SUNDAY 15
38 Woodlands

SUNDAY 22
13 Grimsthorpe Castle
27 The Old Rectory

WEDNESDAY 25
17 Holly Tree Farm

THURSDAY 26
17 Holly Tree Farm

SUNDAY 29
11 Goltho House

May

THURSDAY 3
5 21 Chapel Street

SUNDAY 6
21 Little Ponton Hall

SUNDAY 13
22 Marigold Cottage
25 Monmouth House

WEDNESDAY 16
7 Doddington Hall Gardens

THURSDAY 17
24 The Moat

SUNDAY 20
6 Dalton

SUNDAY 27
27 The Old Rectory
34 2 School House
38 Woodlands

MONDAY 28
34 2 School House

WEDNESDAY 30
17 Holly Tree Farm

THURSDAY 31
17 Holly Tree Farm

June

SUNDAY 3
10 Fishtoft Drove Gardens
19 Kexby House
23 Martin Gardens

WEDNESDAY 6
8 Easton Walled Gardens

THURSDAY 7
5 21 Chapel Street

SATURDAY 9
31 68 Pennygate

SUNDAY 10
17 Holly Tree Farm
31 68 Pennygate
35 Walcot Hall

THURSDAY 14
13 Grimsthorpe Castle

SUNDAY 17
12 Grantham House
20 Les All√©es
38 Woodlands

FRIDAY 22
18 Holywell Hall

SUNDAY 24
14 Gunby Hall
28 The Old Vicarage
29 Old White House

WEDNESDAY 27
17 Holly Tree Farm

THURSDAY 28
17 Holly Tree Farm

July

SUNDAY 1
30 Orchard House

THURSDAY 5
5 21 Chapel Street

SATURDAY 7
2 Belton House

SUNDAY 8
11 Goltho House
26 Old Quarry Lodge
33 73 Saxilby Road

WEDNESDAY 11
31 68 Pennygate
37 68 Watts Lane

SATURDAY 14
31 68 Pennygate

SUNDAY 15
31 68 Pennygate
34 2 School House

WEDNESDAY 25
17 Holly Tree Farm

THURSDAY 26
17 Holly Tree Farm

August

WEDNESDAY 1
3 Belvoir Castle

THURSDAY 2
3 Belvoir Castle
5 21 Chapel Street

SATURDAY 4
3 Belvoir Castle

SUNDAY 5
3 Belvoir Castle
16 Harrington Hall

TUESDAY 7
3 Belvoir Castle

WEDNESDAY 8
3 Belvoir Castle

THURSDAY 9
3 Belvoir Castle

SATURDAY 11
3 Belvoir Castle
31 68 Pennygate

SUNDAY 12
3 Belvoir Castle
31 68 Pennygate
37 68 Watts Lane

TUESDAY 14
3 Belvoir Castle

WEDNESDAY 15
3 Belvoir Castle

THURSDAY 16
3 Belvoir Castle

SATURDAY 18
3 Belvoir Castle

SUNDAY 19
3 Belvoir Castle
12 Grantham House
26 Old Quarry Lodge
38 Woodlands

TUESDAY 21
3 Belvoir Castle

WEDNESDAY 22
3 Belvoir Castle

THURSDAY 23
3 Belvoir Castle

SATURDAY 25
3 Belvoir Castle

SUNDAY 26
3 Belvoir Castle

TUESDAY 28
3 Belvoir Castle

WEDNESDAY 29
③ Belvoir Castle
⑰ Holly Tree Farm

THURSDAY 30
③ Belvoir Castle
⑰ Holly Tree Farm

September

SUNDAY 2
① Aubourn Hall
⑮ Hall Farm

THURSDAY 6
⑤ 21 Chapel Street

SATURDAY 8
② Belton House

SUNDAY 9
㉜ Saxby Village Gardens

SATURDAY 15
④ 56 Burringham Road

SUNDAY 16
④ 56 Burringham Road

October

SUNDAY 7
⑤ 21 Chapel Street

February 2008

SATURDAY 9
㉑ Little Ponton Hall

SUNDAY 10
㉑ Little Ponton Hall

SATURDAY 23
⑤ 21 Chapel Street

SUNDAY 24
⑤ 21 Chapel Street

Plantsman's
garden full
of rare and
exotic
treasures,
featuring
plants from
all regions
of the
world . . .

Gardens open to the public

② Belton House
③ Belvoir Castle
⑧ Easton Walled Gardens
⑫ Grantham House
⑬ Grimsthorpe Castle
⑭ Gunby Hall
⑮ Hall Farm
㉝ 73 Saxilby Road

By appointment only

⑨ 15 Elmhirst Road
㊱ Washdyke Farm

The Gardens

① AUBOURN HALL
Harmston Road, Aubourn, nr
Lincoln LN5 9DZ. Lady Nevile. *7m
SW of Lincoln. Signed off A607 at
Harmston & off A46 at Thorpe.* **Adm
£2.50, chd free. Sun 2 Sept (2-5).**
Approx 5 acres. Lawns, mature trees,
shrubs, roses, mixed borders, new wild
garden and topiary, spring bulbs and
ponds. C11 church adjoining. Some
gravel paths.
  ሁ   ✕   ✿   ☕

THE BEECHES
See Nottinghamshire.

② ♦ BELTON HOUSE
Grantham NG32 2LS. **The National
Trust, www.nationaltrust.org.uk.** *3m
NE of Grantham. On A607 Grantham
to Lincoln rd. Easily reached & signed
from A1 (Grantham N junction).* **Adm
garden only £7, chd £4.50. For NGS:
Sats 24 Mar; 7 July; 8 Sept (11-5.30).**
Belton House gardens include formal
Italian and Dutch areas with informal
gardens that will satisfy even the
keenest horticulturalist. These 35 acres
to the north of the house are a popular
attraction in their own right. Five main
areas each have their own unique
planting scheme. Orangery by Sir
Jeffrey Wyatville.
  ሁ   ✕   ☕

③ ♦ BELVOIR CASTLE
Grantham NG32 4DQ. **The Duke &
Duchess of Rutland, 01476 871004,
mary@belvoircastle.com.** *9m from
Grantham. Follow brown heritage signs
for Belvoir Castle on A52, A1, A607.*
**House and garden adm £10,
concessions £9, chd £5. Garden
only adm £5, chd free, concessions
£5. For NGS: Tues, Weds, Thurs, 1**

Aug to 30 Aug; Sats, Suns, 4 Aug to
26 Aug (11-5).
English Heritage Grade 2 garden.
Secluded in steep woodland ½ m from
castle. A haven of tranquillity created
around original moss house. Magical
hillside setting in natural amphitheatre
with fresh water springs. Many mature
specimen trees and shrubs ensure all-
yr colour. Rhododendrons, azaleas,
naturalised daffodils, primroses and
bluebells. Tallest bird cherry (90ft) and
yew tree (93ft) in British Isles. Flat
shoes essential. Rose garden with
sculpture exhibition. Wheelchair access
only to Rose Garden. Some steep
slopes & grassy paths esp to Spring
Gardens.
  ሁ   ✕   ☕

④ 56 BURRINGHAM ROAD
Ashby, Scunthorpe DN17 2DE. **Mr &
Mrs Foster, 01724 334480,
kevin56foster@yahoo.co.uk.** *½ m S
of Scunthorpe, in district of Ashby.
Approaching Scunthorpe A159 from S
turn L on B1450 (Burringham Rd).
Garden 200yds on L. Park in Monks
Rd. Parking also outside garden, no
restrictions but busy road.* Light
refreshments & teas. **Adm £2, chd
free** (share to Lindsey Lodge
Hospice, Scunthorpe). **Sat 15, Sun
16 Sept (10-5).** Visitors also
welcome by appt June onwards.
Please give 7 days notice.
⅓-acre plantsman's garden full of rare
and exotic treasures, featuring plants
from all regions of the world. Species
include cactus, succulents, gingers,
cannas, dahlias, echiums, unusual
salvias, various bananas, proteas,
leucodendrons, restios, grasses and
several varieties of tree ferns.
September is the best month to see
garden in its full maturity. Large koi and
wildlife pond. Free seed collection.
Please bring suitable containers. Short
gravel drive, wheelchair helper
required.
  ሁ   ✕   ✿   ☕

⑤ 21 CHAPEL STREET
Hacconby, Bourne PE10 0UL. **Cliff &
Joan Curtis, 01778 570314.** *3m N of
Bourne. A15, turn E at Xrds into
Hacconby.* Home-made teas. **Adm
£1.50, chd free. Sat 17 Feb, Sun 18
Feb; Thur 1 Mar; Mon 9 Apr; Thurs 3
May; 7 June; 5 July; 2 Aug; 6 Sept;
Sun 7 Oct; Sat 23, Sun 24 Feb 2008
Adm £2. Sats, Suns, Mons (11-5)
Thurs (2-6).** Visitors also welcome
by appt anytime.
Cottage garden overflowing with
plants for yr-round interest; special

interest alpines, bulbs, herbaceous. Early opening for hellebores and snowdrop collection. Asters for late opening.

⑥ DALTON
10 Wendover Close, Rippingale PE10 0TQ. Chris & Tim Bladon. *5½m N of Bourne. Rippingale is signed on the A15. On entering village at the Rippengale / Kirby Underwood Xrd, Wendover Close is 1st turning on L. Garden at end of the close.* Home-made teas. **Adm £2, chd free. Sun 20 May (11-5).** Peaceful village garden of approx ½ an acre containing usual and unusual herbaceous plants, shrubs and trees of general and specialist interest in a secluded situation. Shingle drive of 30 metres access to garden.

⑦ [NEW] DODDINGTON HALL GARDENS
Lincoln LN6 4RU. Claire & James Birch. *5m W of Lincoln. Signed clearly from A46 Lincoln bypass & A57, 3m.* **Adm £3.90, chd £1.95 (11 Mar) £5.60, chd £2.80 (16 May). Sun 11 Mar (1-5); Wed 16 May (12-5).** 5 acres of romantic walled and wild gardens. Pageant of naturalised spring bulbs and scented shrubs from Feb to May. Spectacular iris display late May/early June in box-edged parterres of West Garden. Sumptuous herbaceous borders throughout summer; extraordinary ancient chestnut trees; turf maze; temple of the winds. Newly resurrected walled Kitchen Garden opening Apr 2007. Very much a family-owned and run garden. 'BBC Homes & Antiques'; 'Sunday Times', both June 2007. 'BBC Gardeners' World' & 'Country Life' summer 2007. Variety of surfaces; gravel, grass, ramps, not suitable for small-wheeled chairs. Electric buggy available FOC for visitors please book in advance 01522 694308. Award-winning sensory tour for blind & visually impaired visitors. Call for details. &

⑧ ◆ EASTON WALLED GARDENS
Easton NG33 5AP. Sir Fred & Lady Cholmeley, 01476 530063, www.eastonwalledgardens.co.uk. *7m S of Grantham. 1m off A1 N of Colsterworth roundabout. Follow village signposts via B6403.* **Adm £4.50, chd 50p. Weds, Fris, Suns & Bank Hol Mons 1 April to 30 Sept (11-4). Snowdrops 10-23 Feb (11-4). For NGS: Wed 6 June (11-4).** 12 acres of forgotten gardens undergoing extensive renovation. Set in parkland with dramatic views. C16 garden with Victorian embellishments. Italianate terraces; yew tunnel; snowdrops and cut flower garden. David Austin roses, iris, daffodil and sweet pea collections. Please wear sensible shoes suitable for country walking. Featured in Saturday 'Telegraph' 2006. Access at all times to toilets, tearoom, shop. Gardens access may depend on weather conditions, upper gardens only. &

Pageant of naturalised spring bulbs and scented shrubs from Feb to May . . .

⑨ [NEW] 15 ELMHIRST ROAD
Horncastle LN9 5AT. Sylvia Ravenhall, 01507 526014, john.ravenhall@btinternet.com. *From A158 Lincoln Rd turn into Accommodation Rd, go to end, turn L into Elmhirst Rd. No 15 approx 80yds on L.* **Adm £2, chd free. Visitors welcome by appt June & July. Individual, groups and/or coaches.** Plantswoman's long and narrow town garden with beds and borders of mainly herbaceous plants combined with climbers, shrubs and small trees. Variety of hostas are grown in containers and in the ground. Winding paths with shallow steps give varied access to all areas.

Scree beds, old sinks with alpines and steps leading down to large pond with cascade . . .

THE ELMS
See Nottinghamshire.

⑩ FISHTOFT DROVE GARDENS
Frithville, Boston PE22 7ES. *3m N of Boston, 1m S of Frithville. Unclassified rd. On W side of the West Fen Drain.* Home-made teas at Holly House. **Combined adm £3, chd free (share to Pilgrim Heart & Lung Fund). Sun 3 June (12-5).**

BARLEY END COTTAGE
Andy & Yvonne Mathieson. *100yds W of Holly House* ⅕-acre traditional cottage garden, very informal. Relaxed mixture of borders, shrubs, vegetables, natural areas, with some quirky features.

HOLLY HOUSE
Sally & David Grant Approx 1-acre informal mixed borders, scree beds, old sinks with alpines and steps leading down to large pond with cascade and stream. Small woodland area. Quiet garden with water feature. New wildlife area. Interviewed on Radio Lincolnshire May 2006. Some gravel paths, steps and slopes. &

POTTERY COTTAGE
Carol & Mike Day Small garden approx ⅕-acre in cottage garden style. Small pond; covered arches with roses and clematis; gravelled area with water feature, full of unusual and interesting herbaceous plants. Formal pond.

SYCAMORE COTTAGE
Roy & Jane Lovett Approx 1-acre with mature trees, recently developed; mixed borders. Woodland area, formal kitchen garden and ponds.

11 GOLTHO HOUSE
Goltho LN8 5NF. Mr & Mrs S Hollingworth,
www.golthogardens.com. *10m E of Lincoln. On A158, 1m before Wragby. Garden on LH-side (not in Goltho Village).* Home-made teas. **Adm £3, chd free. Suns 29 Apr; 8 July (1-5).**
4¹/₂-acre garden started in 1998 but looking established with long grass walk flanked by abundantly planted herbaceous borders forming a focal point. Paths and walkway span out to other features incl nut walk, prairie border, wild flower meadow, rose garden and large pond area.

⚔ ❀ ☕

12 ◆ GRANTHAM HOUSE
Castlegate, Grantham NG31 6SS. Earl of Leitrim & Mr A Kerr, 01476 564705. *In Grantham. Entrance in Castlegate opp St Wulfram's Church.* **Adm £4, chd £2, concessions £3. First Sun of each month Apr to Nov (2-5). For NGS: Suns 17 June; 19 Aug (2-5).**
3-acre series of secret gardens created by the late Lady Wyldbore Smith and now under restoration and renovation. Lawns, a woodland walk, rockery and greenhouse, orchard, walled garden, Lady Molly's garden, vegetable and herb gardens are among its inspirational features. Featured in 'Gardens Illustrated' June 2006. Wheelchair access to most areas but all paths are gravel.

♿ ⚔ ☕

13 ◆ GRIMSTHORPE CASTLE
Bourne PE10 0LY. Grimsthorpe & Drummond Castle Trust, 01778 591205, www.grimsthorpe.co.uk. *3m NW of Bourne. 8m E of A1 on A151 from Colsterworth junction.* **Castle & garden adm £8, concessions £7, chd £3.50, garden only adm £3.50, chd £2, concessions £3. Suns & Thurs Apr & May. Suns to Thurs June to Sept (12-6). For NGS: Sun 22 Apr; Thur 14 June (12-6).**
15 acres of formal and woodland gardens incl bulbs and wild flowers. Formal gardens encompass fine topiary, roses, herbaceous borders and unusual ornamental kitchen garden. Some gravel paths, occasional steps.

♿ ⚔ ☕

14 ◆ GUNBY HALL
Spilsby PE23 5SS. The National Trust, 01790 810039, www.gunbyhall.ic24.net. *2¹/₂m NW of Burgh-le-Marsh. 7m NW of*

Skegness. *On A158. Signed off Gunby roundabout.* **Adm £3, chd £1.50. For NGS: Sun 24 June (2-6).**
7 acres of formal and walled gardens; old roses, herbaceous borders; herb garden; kitchen garden with fruit trees and vegetables. Tennyson's 'Haunt of Ancient Peace'. House built by Sir William Massingberd 1700. No 6 bus leaves Skegness every hour and drops off at gate. Gravel paths but wheelchairs allowed on lawns.

♿ ❀ ☕

15 ◆ HALL FARM
Harpswell, Gainsborough DN21 5UU. Pam & Mark Tatam, 01427 668412, www.hall-farm.co.uk. *7m E of Gainsborough. On A631. 1¹/₂ m W of Caenby Corner.* **Adm £3, chd free. Open daily (8-onwards). Nursery closed weekends. For NGS: Sun 2 Sept (10-5).**
1¹/₂-acre garden with mixed borders of trees, shrubs, old roses and unusual perennials. Sunken garden, pond, courtyard garden, walled gravel garden and orchard. Short walk to old moat and woodland. Free seed collecting in garden Sept 2. Featured in 'Daily Telegraph' weekend gardening supplement July 2006.

♿ ⚔ ❀ ☕

16 ◆ HARRINGTON HALL
Harrington, Spilsby PE23 4NH. Mr & Mrs David Price, www.harringtonhallgardens.co.uk. *6m NW of Spilsby. Turn off A158 (Lincoln-Skegness) at Hagworthingham, 2m to Harrington.* Home-made teas. **Adm £2.50, chd free. Sun 5 Aug (2-5).**
Approx 6-acre Tudor and C18 walled gardens, incl 3 walled gardens; herbaceous borders, croquet lawn leading to viewing terrace, Tennyson's High Hall Garden in 'Maud'. Organic kitchen garden, shrub borders, roses and wildlife pond. Gravel paths, lawns.

♿ ⚔ ❀ ☕

17 HOLLY TREE FARM
Hallgate, Sutton St Edmund PE12 0LN. Mr & Mrs C Pate, 01945 700773. *18m SE of Spalding. 16m from Peterborough, 8m from Wisbech. In village facing S take R into Chapel Rd. Next L onto Hallgate, farm 1st on R.* Cream teas. **Adm £2, chd free. Wed 25, Thur 26 Apr; Wed 30, Thur 31 May; Sun 10 June (2-6), Wed 27, Thur 28 June; Wed 25, Thur 26 July; Wed 29, Thur 30 Aug. Weds & Thurs (11-4). Visitors also welcome by appt, coaches and groups 10+ any day for NGS.**
3-acre family garden, perennial beds full of cultivated and native plants for wildlife. Vegetables, fruit, scree, all in cottage garden-style; white beds, chickens. Spinney with native wild flowers. Organic. Dew pond for wildlife. Featured in 'Garden Answers' 2006.

♿ ⚔ ❀ ☕

HOLMES VILLA
See Nottinghamshire.

18 HOLYWELL HALL
Holywell PE9 4DT. Mr & Mrs R Gillespie, 01780 410665. *8m N of Stamford. From A1 signed Clipsham. Through Clipsham then turn R to Holywell. Entrance to Hall 2m on L.* Home-made teas. **Adm £3, chd 50p. Fri 22 June (2-6). Visitors also welcome by appt, weekdays only.**
The gardens at Holywell are among the most handsome and historically interesting in S Lincolnshire. Nestled in a vale they are laid out on a broad S-facing slope overlooking C18 lake. Numerous water features, walled vegetable garden, stunning herbaceous borders, chapel, fishing temple and orangery.

☕

THE HOMESTEAD
See Leicestershire & Rutland.

The gardens at Holywell are among the most handsome and historically interesting in S Lincolnshire . . .

⑲ KEXBY HOUSE

Gainsborough DN21 5NE. Herbert & Jenny Whitton, 01427 788759. *12m NNW of Lincoln. 6m E of Gainsborough. On B1241, outskirts of Kexby village.* Light refreshments & cream teas. **Adm £3, chd free. Sun 3 June (11-5).** Visitors also welcome by appt, coaches pemitted. Groups no more than 52.

Approx 5 acres of gardens which have evolved over last 100yrs. Long herbaceous borders, unusual plants, wildlife pond and bog garden, scree gardens and all-white border, wild flower area. New perennial prairie-style meadow. Featured in 'The Independent', - 'Ten best gardens to visit' summer 2006. All garden accessible except for scree beds.

Wildlife pond and bog garden, scree gardens and all-white border, wild flower area . . .

⑳ LES ALLÉES

12 Frieston Road, Caythorpe NG32 3BX. Alan & Marylyn Mason. *8m N of Grantham. From Grantham A607 towards Lincoln. L turn to Caythorpe village, immed L again into Frieston Rd. No 12 300yds ahead.* Cream teas. **Adm £3, chd free. Sun 17 June (2-6).**

A plantsman's garden created by Alan Mason, TV gardener and garden designer. Ornamental potager, woodland walk, specimen trees and shrubs, Italian avenue of cypresses. Pond; large mixed borders; tree house; subtropical border. A garden of different styles and atmospheres which link seamlessly. Avenues and allées lead round the garden.

㉑ LITTLE PONTON HALL

Grantham NG33 5BS. Mr & Mrs Alastair McCorquodale. *2m S of Grantham. 1/2m E of A1 at S end of Grantham bypass.* Home-made teas 6

May; Light refreshments 9, 10 Feb 2008. **Adm £3.50, chd free. Sun 6 May (2-5); Sat 9, Sun 10 Feb 2008 (11-4).**

3 to 4-acre garden. Spacious lawns with cedar tree over 200yrs old. Many varieties of old shrub roses and clematis; borders and young trees. Stream, spring blossom and hellebores; bulbs and river walk with massed snowdrops and aconites. Formal walled kitchen garden and listed dovecote. Victorian greenhouses with many plants from exotic locations. Local village church open. Featured in 'The English Garden' Jan 2006. Special car park for disabled visitors. Good access on all hard paths (not suitable on grass). Disabled WC.

MANOR FARM HOUSE
See Nottinghamshire.

㉒ MARIGOLD COTTAGE

Hotchin Road, Sutton-on-Sea LN12 2JA. Stephanie Lee, 01507 442151, www.marigoldcottage.ic24.net. *From High St facing sea, turn R at Corner House Café, along Furlong's Rd past playing fields, round bend, into Hotchin Rd. Garden 2nd on L.* **Adm £2, chd free. Sun 13 May (11-4).** Visitors also welcome by appt May to Sept.

1/2-acre seaside garden containing a large variety of unusual hardy perennials. Paths, pergolas, arches and secret trails make the garden magical. Features incl Japanese bed, slate dry water feature, planting schemes to excite the palette and Oriental courtyard with wheelchair friendly raised beds. Featured in 'Daily Telegraph', GGG 2007; 'Lincolnshire Pride' Feb 2006. Winner Sutton-on-Sea Horticultural Society large garden category.

㉓ MARTIN GARDENS

LN4 3QY. *15m SE of Lincoln. On B1191. 4m W of Woodhall Spa. All gardens on main rd. Parking on roadside. Blankney Barff garden signed off B1189.* Home-made teas at Holmdale House. **Combined adm £3, chd 50p (share to Martin 'Lives'). Sun 3 June (11-5).**

49 HIGH STREET
Helen & Laurie Whittle. *Opp Royal Oak PH*
Wildlife-friendly, organic and

environmentally low impact, with long flowering season of nectar and berry-rich species. 2 ponds, mixed native hedging and established dry garden. Herbaceous perennials, cottage border and drought-tolerant species. All plants for sale are peat free.

HOLMDALE HOUSE
High Street. Ian Warden & Stewart MacKenzie, www.holmdalehouse.co.uk
1-acre plantsman's garden started March 2000, surrounding Victorian farmhouse and barns (not open). Informal mixed borders planted to reflect owners' interest in unusual hardy plants, especially good foliage and variegated leaf forms. Collection of hostas, large pond, courtyard gardens and nursery. Newly acquired 1/2 acre under development. Unfenced pond.

NEW LABOURERS COTTAGE
Blankney Barff. Mrs Linda Brighty. *Signed off B1189 between Metheringham & Martin*
1850s cottage in approx 6 acres. 2 ponds, bog garden, long border of herbaceous perennials, hedged rose garden, various trees, vegetable patch. Over past 10 yrs we have changed a meadow into a wildlife-friendly garden. 2 unfenced ponds. Carr dyke at bottom of slope.

MILL HILL HOUSE
See Nottinghamshire.

㉔ NEW THE MOAT
Newton, Sleaford NG34 0ED. Mr & Mrs Mike Barnes. *Off A52 halfway between Grantham & Sleaford. In Newton village, opp church.* **Adm £2.50, chd free. Thur 17 May (2-6).**
21/2-acre country garden, formerly a farmyard, now 5yrs old. Island mixed beds, natural pond, courtyard garden with topiary and many interesting trees and plants.

㉕ MONMOUTH HOUSE
Monmouth Lane, Long Sutton
PE12 9LH. Mr & Mrs G Hoyles.
*1¹/₂ m N of Long Sutton. On B1359.
Follow signs to Butterfly and Wildlife
Park. Continue ¹/₂ m - Lutton village
sign. Take 1st R down Monmouth
Lane.* **Adm £3, chd free,
concessions £2.50. Sun 13 May
(1.30-5.30).**
2¹/₂ acres of mature gardens with
mature trees set in 12 acres of park
surrounded by ¹/₂ m of woodland walk.
Sunken garden, herbaceous borders,
raised lily pond, Victorian walled
garden with box parterre, cut flower
beds, loggia paved area and wild
flowers.
&♿ ✗ ☕

NEWBRAY HOUSE
See Nottinghamshire.

**㉖ NEW OLD QUARRY
LODGE**
15 Barnetby Lane, Elsham, nr
Brigg DN20 0RB. Mel & Tina
Welton. *6m S of Humber Bridge.
Leave M180 at J5. Drive past 'Little
Chef' into Elsham village. Old
Quarry Lodge is 1st house on R on
entering village. Home-made teas.*
**Adm £2.50, chd free. Suns 8
July; 19 Aug (11-5).**
Approx ¹/₂-acre sloping garden with
formal and informal features.
Abundant borders and island beds
with architectural focal points,
Mediterranean influence in parts.
Highly imaginative garden with
exciting mixture of the flamboyant
and the quintessentially 'English'.
Winner Best Front Garden in
village. Gravel drive to house.
Gentle slope to garden at rear. No
steps.
♿ ☕

㉗ THE OLD RECTORY
East Keal PE23 4AT. Mrs Ruth Ward,
01790 752477. *2m SW of Spilsby. Off
A16. Turn into Church Lane by PO. Tea
22 Apr; Home-made teas, Morning
Coffee, Ploughman's Lunch by WI 27
May.* **Adm £2, chd free. Sun 22 Apr
(2-5); Sun 27 May (11-4.30). Visitors
also welcome by appt for
individuals, small or large groups.**
Beautifully situated, with fine views,
rambling cottage garden on different
levels falling naturally into separate
areas, with changing effects and
atmosphere. Steps, paths and vistas
to lead you on, with seats well placed

for appreciating special views and
plant combinations or relaxing and
enjoying the peace. New dry border.
Partial wheelchair access only.
✗ ❀ ☕

㉘ THE OLD VICARAGE
Low Road, Holbeach Hurn
PE12 8JN. Mrs Liz Dixon-Spain,
01406 424148, lizds@ukonline.co.uk.
*2m NE of Holbeach. Turn off A17 N to
Holbeach Hurn, past post box in
middle of village, 1st turn R into Low
Rd. Old Vicarage on R approx 400yds.*
**Adm Combined with Old White
House adm £4, chd free. Sun 24
June (12-5). Visitors also welcome
by appt.**
2 acres of gardens with mature trees,
old grass tennis court and croquet
lawns surrounded by borders of
shrubs, roses, herbaceous; informal
areas incl pond and bog garden, wild
flowers, grasses and bulbs, shrub
roses and herb garden in old paddock
area. Environmentally maintained and
fun for kids too.
✗ ❀ 🛏

㉙ OLD WHITE HOUSE
Holbeach Hurn PE12 8JP. Mr & Mrs
A Worth. *2m N of Holbeach. Turn off
A17 N to Holbeach Hurn, follow signs
to village, go straight through, turn R
after Rose & Crown at Baileys Lane.
Home-made teas.* **Combined with
The Old Vicarage adm £4, chd
free. Sun 24 June (12-5).**
1¹/₂ acres of mature garden, featuring
herbaceous borders, roses, patterned
garden, herb garden and wild garden
with small pond. Walled kitchen
garden.
♿ ☕

㉚ NEW ORCHARD HOUSE
42 Horncastle Road, Woodhall
Spa LN10 6UZ. Mr & Mrs
Geoffrey Grantham. *On B1191,
1m from centre of Woodhall Spa
on Horncastle Rd. Teas by
Woodhall Spa Country Markets.*
**Adm £2, chd free. Sun 1 July
(2-6).**
New woodland garden designed
with shallow soils over sand. A
natural slope of 1metre was
converted to a terrace where pines
dominate. Gravel leads to unusual
perennials within a crescent of yew.
Beyond is long grass with
ornamental trees, bulbs and wild
flowers. Small greenhouse and
shade bed complete the picture.
✗ ❀ ☕

㉛ 68 PENNYGATE
Spalding PE11 1NN. Mr & Mrs
Carroll, 01775 767554. *1m W of
Spalding. Take A151 towards
Bourne. Turn R onto Park Rd
immediately after rail crossings.
Then 1st L onto Pennygate. No 68 on
L. Home-made teas.* **Adm £2, chd
free. Sat 9, Sun 10 June; Wed 11,
Sat 14, Sun 15 July; Sat 11, Sun 12
Aug (10-4). Visitors also welcome by
appt.**
A plantswoman's garden, island beds
and border planted with a wide range
of flowering perennials and shrubs,
large pond with rocky and bog garden.
♿ ✗ ❀ ☕

㉜ SAXBY VILLAGE GARDENS
LN8 2DQ. *10m N of Lincoln. 4m S of
Caenby Corner; 2¹/₂ m E of A15.
Cream teas at The Garden House.*
**Combined adm £2.50, chd free. Sun
9 Sept (2-5).**
☕

THE GARDEN HOUSE
Chris Neave & Jonathan
Cartwright, www.
thegardenhousesaxby.com
1-acre garden. Pond, water
features, formal hedges,
potager, Mediterranean garden,
Dutch garden, long terrace,
planting for yr-round interest.
Pergola, wonderful views across
open countryside. Adjacent to
C18 classical church. Gravel drive.
♿ ✗ ❀

NEW WEST BARN
Mrs E Neave
Formal walled courtyard garden
with loggia, box hedging, shrub
roses, climbers and herbaceous
planting. Water feature and pots
with seasonal planting.
✗

㉝ ♦ 73 SAXILBY ROAD
Sturton by Stow LN1 2AA. Charles &
Tricia Elliott, 01427 788517. *9m NW
of Lincoln. On B1241. Halfway
between Lincoln & Gainsborough.*
**Adm £1.50, chd free. Visitors always
welcome to nursery and garden
between Mar & Oct but please
phone first. NGS collection box. For
NGS: Sun 8 July (1-5).**
Smallish plot mainly devoted to a wide
selection of perennial flowering plants
and tall grasses. Relatively new shrub
border with some unusual shrubs and
small trees. Also large display of tender

fuchsias. All this and small hardy plant nursery in open and exposed position. Exhibition of paintings by garden owners.

34 2 SCHOOL HOUSE

Stixwould LN10 5HP. Andrew & Sheila Sankey, 01526 352453. *1¹/₂m N of Woodhall Spa. From roundabout in Woodhall Spa, take rd to Bardney past Petwood Hotel. Follow rd for 1¹/₂m and at sharp RH bend turn off L into Stixwould. Garden is on main rd opp red phone box.* **Adm £1.50, chd free. Sun 27, Mon 28 May; Sun 15 July (2-5). Visitors also welcome by appt May to Sept, please ring first.**¹/₄-acre garden, redesigned in Oct 1994 by owners in cottage garden style, to incl front garden with unusual perennials and shrubs, herb garden, and small turf maze. Featured in 'Amateur Gardening' 2006.

35 WALCOT HALL

Barnack PE9 3EU. Mr & Mrs Darby Dennis. *3m S of Stamford. Take Walcot Rd out of Barnack. Entrance & car park 400yds beyond cricket club.* Home-made teas. **Adm £3.50, chd free. Sun 10 June (2-6).** Arboretum of 20 acres with lake, ornamental ponds, stone follies and rose garden surrounding Carolean house, not open. Teas & stalls in cobbled courtyard in aid of Barnack Village School. All wheelchair access across gravel & grass.

Whole new world on entering from street . . .

36 NEW WASHDYKE FARM

Lincoln Road, Fulbeck NG32 3HY. Mrs Anna Greenhalgh, 01400 272880. *10m N of Grantham; 15m S of Lincoln. On A607 in dip opp Washdyke Lane.* Cream teas. **Adm £2.50, chd free. Visitors welcome by appt from 19 May to 30 June. Coach parties & small groups welcome.**
Approx 2 acres with meandering paths leading to interesting features with contrasting moods. Lawns with cottage-style mixed borders; attractive waterside planting alongside stream; wildlife pond and woodland walk with mature trees.

37 68 WATTS LANE

Louth LN11 9DG. Mr & Mrs R Grasham, 01507 601004/07977 318145. *¹/₂m S of Louth town centre. Watts Lane off B1200 Louth to Mablethorpe rd. Turn by Browns Rover Garage and Londis shop. Sun only, extra parking at rear of Browns, 300yds from garden.* Home-made teas. **Adm £1.50, chd free. Wed 11 July (11-6); Sun 12 Aug (1-6). Visitors also welcome by appt July**

& Aug, coaches permitted.
Blank canvas of ¹/₅ acre. Developed over 12yrs into lush, colourful, tropical to traditional plant packed haven. A whole new world on entering from street. Generous borders, raised tropical island, long hot tropical border, ponds, water features, summerhouse, conservatory with grapevine, cutting garden and secluded seating along garden's journey. Featured in 'Garden Answers' & 'Garden News', 2006.

38 WOODLANDS

Peppin Lane, Fotherby, Louth LN11 0UW. Ann & Bob Armstrong, 01507 603586. *2m N of Louth. On A16. Leave bypass (A16) signed Fotherby. Woodlands is situated nr far end of Peppin Lane, a no through rd, running E from village centre. No parking at garden. Please park on RH verge opp allotments and walk (approx 200yds) to garden.* Home-made teas. **Adm £2, chd free. Suns 15 Apr; 27 May; 17 June; 19 Aug (11-5). Visitors also welcome by appt.**
Mature woodland garden being further developed by the present owners. Packed with rare and unusual perennials, shrubs, ferns and climbers. Meandering paths lead to surprises around every corner. In contrast, the planting nearer the house takes advantage of the more open aspect but is equally interesting. Award winning professional artist's studio/gallery open to visitors. Also exhibition by Mary Coe of decorative pieces for the garden in wood, metal and glass. Plant nursery featured in RHS Plantfinder 2006, 2007.

LONDON

Opening Dates

February

SUNDAY 25
Myddelton House Gardens, Enfield

March

SATURDAY 10
The Elms, Kingston-upon-Thames

SUNDAY 11
The Elms, Kingston-upon-Thames

April

SUNDAY 1
Chelsea Physic Garden, SW3

SATURDAY 14
The Elms, Kingston-upon-Thames

SUNDAY 15
Edwardes Square, W8
The Elms, Kingston-upon-Thames
7 The Grove, N6
167 Rosendale Road, SE21

SUNDAY 22
Natural History Museum Wildlife
Garden, SW7

WEDNESDAY 25
7 Sibella Road, SW4 (Evening)
18 Sibella Road, SW4 (Evening)

SATURDAY 28
The Holme, NW1
Royal College of Physicians Garden,
NW1

SUNDAY 29
5 Burbage Road, SE24
The Holme, NW1
Malvern Terrace Gardens, N1
209 Massingberd Way, SW17
Mulberry House, SE21
Myddelton House Gardens, Enfield
3 The Park, N6
Royal College of Physicians Garden,
NW1
5 St Regis Close, N10
7 Sibella Road, SW4
18 Sibella Road, SW4
Stanley Crescent Garden, W11
47 Winn Road, SE12

May

SATURDAY 5
Stone (Zen) Garden, W3

SUNDAY 6
Elm Tree Cottage, South Croydon
14 Frank Dixon Way, SE21
Kew Gardens Group
94 Oakwood Road, NW11
13 Queen Elizabeth's Walk, N16
Southside House, SW19
Stone (Zen) Garden, W3

MONDAY 7
Kew Gardens Group
Waltham Forest Register Office, E17

SATURDAY 12
The Elms, Kingston-upon-Thames

SUNDAY 13
Albion Square Gardens, E8
Eccleston Square, SW1
The Elms, Kingston-upon-Thames
79 Holmdene Avenue, SE24
2 Millfield Place, N6
Southside House, SW19
Southwood Lodge, N6
Summerlawn, Northwood
The Watergardens, Kingston-upon-
Thames
2 Western Lane, SW12

WEDNESDAY 16
12 Lansdowne Road, W11

SATURDAY 19
Lambeth Community Care Centre,
SE11
Stone (Zen) Garden, W3
Tudor Road Gardens, Hampton

SUNDAY 20
18 Cranmer Road, Hampton Hill
De Beauvoir Gardens, N1
15 Dukes Avenue, N10
46 Dukes Avenue, N10
Kew Gardens Station Group
64a Kings Road, Richmond
Lambeth Community Care Centre,
SE11
Little House A, NW3
London Wildlife Trust, SE15
Natural History Museum Wildlife
Garden, SW7
15 Norcott Road, N16
22 Scutari Road, SE22
Stone (Zen) Garden, W3
64 Thornhill Road, E10
Tudor Road Gardens, Hampton
11 Woodlands Road, SW13
33 Wood Vale, N10

SATURDAY 26
Lambeth Palace, SE1
Museum of Garden History, SE1
Penge Gardens, SE20
Tewkesbury Lodge Garden Group,
SE23 (Evening)

SUNDAY 27
Little Lodge, Thames Ditton
Myddelton House Gardens, Enfield
Penge Gardens, SE20
Tewkesbury Lodge Garden Group,
SE23

WEDNESDAY 30
Whitton CRC, Richmond

June

SATURDAY 2
38 Killieser Avenue, SW2 (Evening)
Regents College's Garden, NW1
St Helena Terrace, Richmond
(Evening)
St Michael's Convent, Richmond

SUNDAY 3
180 Adelaide Road, NW3
37 Alwyne Road, N1
97 Arthur Road, SW19
61 Barnwell Road, SW2
13 Cambridge Road, SW20
24 Chestnut Road, SE27
Chiswick Mall, W4
142 Court Lane, SE21
Elm Tree Cottage, South Croydon
71 Fallowcourt Avenue, N12
Islington Gardens Group 1, N1
Highgate Village, N6
Lower Clapton Gardens, E5
263 Nether Street, N3
101 Pitt Crescent, SW19
62 Rattray Road, SW2
167 Rosendale Road, SE21
7 St George's Road, Twickenham
64 Thornhill Road, E10

WEDNESDAY 6
Little Lodge, Thames Ditton (Day &
Evening)

THURSDAY 7
Fenton House, NW3 (Evening)

SATURDAY 9
Royal College of Physicians Garden,
NW1

SUNDAY 10
Barnes Gardens, SW13
Choumert Square, SE15
26 College Gardens, E4
Dulwich Gardens, SE21
66A East Dulwich Road, SE22
Fishponds House, Surbiton
Holly Cottage, Hampton
239a Hook Road, Chessington
1a Hungerford Road, N7
62 Hungerford Road, N7
Old Court, SW20
Kew Green Gardens
46 Lincoln Road, Northwood Hills
263 Nether Street, N3
North House, SE21
174 Peckham Rye, SE22
2a Penn Road, N7
Royal College of Physicians Garden,
NW1
South End Road Gardens, NW3
(Evening)
Springfield Lodge, SW15
78 Tufnell Park Road, N7
208 Walm Lane, Flat 1, NW2
340 Walton Road, West Molesey

WEDNESDAY 13
239a Hook Road, Chessington
(Evening)

THURSDAY 14
The Hurlingham Club, SW6

FRIDAY 15
12 Eliot Vale, SE3 (Evening)
28 Granville Park, SE13 (Evening)
46 Lincoln Road, Northwood Hills
(Evening)
The Pagoda, SE3 (Evening)

SATURDAY 16
35 Camberwell Grove, SE5 (Evening)
Roots and Shoots, SE11

SUNDAY 17
15a Buckland Crescent, NW3
Eatonville Road Gardens, SW17
Frognal Gardens, NW3
5 Hillcrest Avenue, NW11
Holly Cottage, Hampton
79 Holmdene Avenue, SE24
28 Old Devonshire Road, SW12
Ormeley Lodge, Richmond
Pembridge Cottage, Twickenham
Petersham House, Petersham
Roots and Shoots, SE11
27 St James Avenue, W13
South London Botanical Institute,
SE24
68 Wandle Road, SW17

WEDNESDAY 20
5 Burbage Road, SE24 (Evening)
5 Hillcrest Avenue, NW11 (Evening)
2 Millfield Place, N6 (Evening)
28 Old Devonshire Road, SW12
(Evening)

SUNDAY 24
80 Bromfelde Road, SW4
5 Cecil Road, N10
158 Culford Road, N1
36 Downs Hill, Beckenham
Lyndhurst Square Gardens, SE15
19 Montana Road, SW17
Pembridge Cottage, Twickenham
5 St Regis Close, N10
41 Southbrook Road, SE12
60a South Croxted Road, SE21
47 Winn Road, SE12

SATURDAY 30
27 Wood Vale, N10

July

SUNDAY 1
18 Cranmer Road, Hampton Hill
6 Methuen Park, N10 (Day &
Evening)
19 Oakhill Road, Orpington
66 Woodbourne Avenue, SW16
27 Wood Vale, N10
82 Wood Vale, SE23

WEDNESDAY 4
Roots and Shoots, SE11 (Evening)

SUNDAY 8
Elm Tree Cottage, South Croydon
66A East Dulwich Road, SE22
5 Greville Place, NW6
Islington Gardens Group 2, N1
Railway Cottages, N22

MONDAY 9
Ham House & Garden, Richmond

SUNDAY 15
12 Aberdare Gardens, NW6
180 Adelaide Road, NW3
All Seasons, W5
136 Avenue Road, W3
52A Berrylands Road, Surbiton
71 Central Hill, SE19
170 Doyle Gardens, NW10
24 Hills Road, Buckhurst Hill
41 Mill Hill Road, W3
95 North Road, Kew (Day & Evening)
57 St Quintin Avenue, W10
Short Lots Allotments, Kew

SATURDAY 21
14 Radlet Avenue, SE26 (Evening)

SUNDAY 22
157 Hampstead Way, NW11
47 Maynard Road, E17
5 St Regis Close, N10
2 Western Lane, SW12
86 Willifield Way, NW11

WEDNESDAY 25
208 Walm Lane, Flat 1, NW2
(Evening)

SUNDAY 29
29 Addison Avenue, W11
47 Maynard Road, E17
57 St Quintin Avenue, W10

August

SUNDAY 5
13 Queen Elizabeth's Walk, N16
340 Walton Road, West Molesey
(Evening)

SUNDAY 12
66A East Dulwich Road, SE22
Summerlawn, Northwood

SUNDAY 26
19 Montana Road, SW17
28 Multon Road, SW18

September

SATURDAY 1
The Holme, NW1

SUNDAY 2
66A East Dulwich Road, SE22
(Evening)
Golf Course Allotments, N11
The Holme, NW1
27 St James Avenue, W13

SUNDAY 9
7 Byng Road, EN5
54 Ferndown, Northwood Hills
27 St James Avenue, W13

SUNDAY 16
Chiswick House Kitchen Garden, W4
6 Methuen Park, N10

October

SUNDAY 14
The Watergardens, Kingston-upon-
Thames

February 2008

SUNDAY 24
Myddelton House Gardens, Enfield

Gardens open to the public

Chelsea Physic Garden, SW3
Fenton House, NW3
Ham House & Garden, Richmond
Museum of Garden History, SE1
Myddelton House Gardens, Enfield
Natural History Museum Wildlife
Garden, SW7
Roots and Shoots, SE11

By appointment only

51 Cholmeley Crescent, N6
Columcille, Chislehurst
116 Hamilton Terrace, NW8
Hornbeams, Stanmore
5 New Road, N8
13 Redbridge Lane West, E11
4 Stradbroke Grove, Buckhurst Hill

The Gardens

12 ABERDARE GARDENS, NW6

NW6 3PY. Mrs O Bishop. Located ½ m from the West Hampstead, Finchley Rd, Swiss Cottage & Hampstead tube stns. Buses: on West End Lane 139, 328, C11; on Finchley Rd 13, 82, 113, 187, 268, 777. **Adm £2.50, chd free. Sun 15 July (2-6).**
Intimate, densely-planted 40ft x 100ft garden with a strong sense of design that evolves as conditions change. Emphasis on leaf texture and pattern but generally muted, complementary flower colours. Laid out to be seen from the house but concealed elements reveal themselves during a walk around the garden. Designed for all-yr interest. Some unusual plants and a pot patio.
✗ ✿ ☕

The trees and sky are big, you could be in the country . . .

29 ADDISON AVENUE, W11

W11 4QS. David & Shirley Nicholson. No entry for cars from Holland Park Ave, approach via Norland Square & Queensdale Rd. Tube: Holland Park. Buses: 94, 148. **Adm £2, chd free. Sun 29 July (2-6).** Also open **57 St Quintin Ave.**
Garden designed to be at its peak in July and August. Unusual wall shrubs, itea, schizophragma, clerodendrum, surround beds of colourful perennials, phlox, monarda, agastache, eupatorium. A pear tree dominates the central lawn and a giant Euonymus japonicus, 150yrs old, amazes all who see it.
✗

180 ADELAIDE ROAD, NW3

Swiss Cottage NW3 3PA. Simone Rothman. 100yds from Swiss Cottage tube stn. Buses: 13, 46, 82, 113 on Finchley Rd; 31 & C11 on Adelaide Rd. **Adm £2, chd free. Suns 3 June; 15 July (3-5).**
Small 25ft x 30ft S-facing walled garden with profuse and colourful climbers and shrubs. Numerous densely-planted containers on gravel with roses, herbaceous perennials, annuals and box. Front garden with lawn and shrubs.
✗

ALBION SQUARE GARDENS, E8

E8 4ES. 2m N of Liverpool St stn (mainline & tube). 1m S of Dalston/Kingsland stn (mainline). Buses: 67, 149, 242, 243, alight Downham Rd. By car approach from Queenbridge Rd northbound, turning L into Albion Drive leading to Albion Square. Middleton Rd runs parallel to Albion Drive on N side of Square. Home-made teas. **Combined adm £5, chd free. Sun 13 May (2-5.30).**
☕

15 ALBION DRIVE

Izi Glover & Michael Croton
Much-used 100ft family garden with defensive box hedging, trained fruit trees, meadow area, pond, vegetable patch and silver birch glade. Tree house tucked away. Native plants combine with foxglove tree in front garden.
✗ ✿

12 ALBION SQUARE

Michael & Sarah Parry
Surprisingly spacious garden with a Victorian Gothic church backdrop. Trees and shrubs allow unfolding areas of interest incl established borders, sunny herb garden and willow arbour.

24 MIDDLETON ROAD

Ann Jameson
Walled garden. Lawn surrounded by beds with mixed planting; fruit trees incl medlar and mulberry. Actinidia spreading to the rooftop on S and E wall of the house, producing kiwi fruit Dec to Apr.
⚬

NEW ALL SEASONS, W5
97 Grange Road, Ealing W5 3PH. Dr Benjamin & Mrs Maria Royappa. Tube: walking distance Ealing Broadway. Light refreshments & teas. **Adm £2, chd free. Sun 15 July (1-6).**
Garden designed and planted by owners since moving in 2003. Features incl ponds, pergolas, Japanese gardens, tropical house for orchids and exotics, aviaries, recycled features, composting and rain water harvesting, orchard, kiwi, grape vines, architectural and unusual plants, collections incl ferns, bamboos, conifers and cacti.
✗ ☕

37 ALWYNE ROAD, N1

N1 2HW. Mr & Mrs J Lambert. Buses: 38, 56, 73, 341 on Essex Rd; 4, 19, 30, 43 on Upper St, alight at Town Hall; 271 on Canonbury Rd, A1. Tube: Highbury & Islington. Home-made teas. **Adm £2.50, chd free (share to Rose Bowl Youth Club). Sun 3 June (2-6).**
The New River curves around the garden, the trees and sky are big, you could be in the country. Clipped box, holly and yew keep things in order; pots reclaim space for strong colours. Hidden formal garden; old-fashioned roses along the river. Shelter if it rains. Agapanthus, astrantia, clipped box and other carefully chosen plants for sale. Wheelchairs possible only with own assistant for 3 entrance steps.
⚬ ✗ ✿ ☕

97 ARTHUR ROAD, SW19

SW19 7DP. Tony & Bella Covill. Wimbledon Park tube, then 200yds up hill on R. Light refreshments & teas. **Adm £2, chd free. Sun 3 June (2-6).** Also open **13 Cambridge Rd & 101 Pitt Crescent.**
Long garden views over Wimbledon Park, developed over 16yrs. Interesting mix of herbacecus shrubs giving yr-round colour. Lawns, secret areas, small pond and rose arch leading to small box garden with mulberry tree.
⚬ ✗ ☕

136 AVENUE ROAD, W3

Acton W3 8QG. Rexton Bunnett & John Muir. Tube: Acton Town, exit Bollo Bridge Rd, cross rd, bear L up Gunnersbury Lane, Avenue Rd 1st on R. **Adm £2.50, chd free. Sun 15 July (2-6).** Also open **41 Mill Hill Rd.**
150ft x 40ft minimalist garden with terrace and ponds; grasses, tranquil circular seating area with drystone walls, surrounded by bamboos. Featured by Anna Pavord in 'The Independent' & on cover of The Yellow Book 2007.

Tranquil circular seating area with drystone walls . . . on cover of The Yellow Book 2007 . . .

BARNES GARDENS, SW13
SW13 0JB. Teas at 8 Queen's Ride. Adm £2 each garden, chd free, concessions £1. Combined adm ticket £6. Sun 10 June (2-6).

6 CUMBERLAND ROAD
Fred & Pat Tuckman. *Buses: 33, 72, 209, 283, 419 to Red Lion, Barnes. Walk to Ferry Rd and follow to path on L after Westmoreland Rd. In this cul-de-sac continue, taking 1st rd on L (Cumberland Rd)* Developed over the years as an informal country garden. Successive swathes of colour from a combination of trees, shrubs and plants, marking the different seasons. Sunny patio, 'secret' garden surrounded by scented shrubs, wild patch, herb corner, small pond and some fruit. (Share to the Royal Hospital for Neuro-Disability).
&

8 QUEEN'S RIDE
H H Sir Frank & Lady White. *Mainline: Barnes, R down Rocks Lane, then L Queen's Ride. Bus: 22 to Putney Hospital. Disabled parking in drive* Country-style, informal large garden on a tree-lined corner site facing Barnes Common. Croquet lawn surrounded by a variety of mixed borders. Rose beds and History of the Rose garden. Garden quiz.
&

🆕 2 ST MARY'S GROVE
Tim & Hilary Steele. *5 mins walk across Common from Barnes stn. Private rd, free parking* Contemporary walled urban family garden divided into a decked area with raised herb bed and pergola, pool area with lavender border, lawn with border of maples, birches and grasses, and, to the rear of the garden, a children's play area separated by olive trees and bamboo.

12 WESTMORELAND ROAD
Mrs Norman Moore. Raised stone terrace planted with choisya, wisteria, jasmine and decorative herbs. Two lower lawns, densely planted borders and pretty gazebo with solanum, golden hop, roses and clematis. Circular lawn with mulberry tree, hydrangeas, ferns and hostas.

🆕 61 BARNWELL ROAD, SW2
SW2 1PN. Mark & Dorothée Irving. *10 mins walk from Brixton tube/mainline or Herne Hill mainline. Buses: 37 & 196.* Adm £2, chd free, concessions £1.50. Sun 3 June (2-6). Also open 62 Rattray Rd. Small town garden created from a concrete patch. A mixture of architectural planting, bamboos and evergreen climbers, many in pots, grow alongside English roses and shrubs. Small bonsai collection can be viewed from the kitchen.

52A BERRYLANDS ROAD
Surbiton KT5 8PD. Dr Tim & Mrs Julia Leunig. *A3 to Tolworth; A240 (dir Kingston) for approx 1m, then R into Berrylands Rd (after Fire Stn). 52A is on R after Xrds.* Home-made teas. Adm £2, chd free. Sun 15 July (2.30-5.30). Jason Payne designed and planted T-shaped garden. Lawn and patio surrounded by lavender, cistus, albizia, tetrapanex, abutilon, roses and ginger. Natural wooded area under copper beech arranged around pond, stream and waterfall with eucalyptus, bamboo, tree fern, gunnera etc. Featured in 'Easy Gardening'.

Successive swathes of colour from a combination of trees, shrubs and plants, marking the different seasons . . .

80 BROMFELDE ROAD, SW4
SW4 6PR. Susan Collier, 020 7820 3628, susan@colliercampbell.com. *Buses & tube: Clapham North. 2nd turning on R off Gauden Rd.* Home-made teas. Adm £2, chd free. Sun 24 June (2-6). Visitors also welcome by appt June, Aug & Sept for groups of 10+. Cardoons rise from gravel and pebbles, with echeveria and various

aeonium in the front garden. In the back garden, 65ft x 30ft, a paved outdoor 'dining room' looks onto abundant perennials creating a river of colour along a winding path leading to an urban water feature, bamboos, and the studio garden - a family space opening onto the beginnings of a little orchard and vegetable garden. Feature by Anna Pavord in 'The Independent'. GGG.

15A BUCKLAND CRESCENT, NW3
NW3 5DH. Lady Barbirolli. *Tube: Swiss Cottage. Buses: 46, 113 (6 mins) or 268 (request stop nearby).* Adm £2.50, chd free. Sun 17 June (2.30-5.30). $1/3$-acre; well-kept and interesting collection of shrubs and plants, incl a small bamboo bed, in well-designed garden, personally designed and maintained at all times.
&

5 BURBAGE ROAD, SE24
SE24 9HJ. Crawford & Rosemary Lindsay, 020 7274 5610. *Nr junction with Half Moon Lane. Herne Hill mainline stn, 5 mins walk. Buses: 2, 3, 37, 40, 68, 196.* Home-made teas. Adm £2.50, chd free. Sun 29 Apr (2-5). Evening Opening £3, wine, Wed 20 June (6-8.30). Visitors also welcome by appt. Garden of member of The Society of Botanical Artists. 150ft x 40ft with large and varied range of plants. Herb garden, herbaceous borders for sun and shade, climbing plants, pots, terraces, lawns. Newly planted gravel areas to reduce watering.

7 BYNG ROAD, EN5
High Barnet EN5 4NW. Mr & Mrs Julian Bishop, 020 8440 2042. Home-made teas. Adm £2, chd free (share to Barnet Hospital Special Care Baby Unit). Sun 9 Sept (2-5). Visitors also welcome by appt. Plantaholic heaven, packed with unusual flowers, incl many salvias, rudbeckias and crocosmias. Organic garden divided into different sections - bright 'hot' coloured area and more subdued planting through an arch. Tropical border. Experimental Piet Oudolf-inspired front garden with knautias, alliums, lavender and contrasting yellows. Many pots full of pampered treasures.

35 CAMBERWELL GROVE, SE5
SE5 8JA. Lynette Hemmant & Juri Gabriel, 020 7703 6186, jurigabriel@compuserve.com. *From Camberwell Green go down Camberwell Church St. Turn R into Camberwell Grove.* **Adm £3.50, chd free (share to The St Giles Trust, Camberwell). Evening Opening wine, Sat 16 June (5-9). Visitors also welcome by appt, groups of 10+.** 120ft x 20ft garden with backdrop of St Giles Church. Evolved over 21yrs into country-style garden brimming with colour and overflowing with pots. In June spectacular roses swamp the artist's studio and festoon an old iron staircase.

13 CAMBRIDGE ROAD, SW20
SW20 0SQ. Mike & Gail Werkmeister. *1m Wimbledon town centre. Mainline stn: Raynes Park, 5 mins walk. Tube: Wimbledon. Buses: 57, 131, 152, 163, 200. Close to Coombe Lane (A238) junction of A3.* **Adm £2, chd free (share to NCT). Sun 3 June (12-6). Also open 97 Arthur Rd & 101 Pitt Crescent.** Garden designer's secluded garden of approx 1/6 acre. Terrace with formal pond leads to lawn, gravel paths and mixed borders abundantly planted with shrubs and herbaceous plants for yr-round interest. Features incl unusual plants, yew hedges, mulberry and strawberry trees and and a conservatory with prolific grapevine.

Vegetables, herbs, fruit and flowers are emerging from the wilderness . . .

5 CECIL ROAD, N10
Muswell Hill N10 2BU. Ben Loftus. *Just off Alexander Park Rd between Muswell Hill & N Circular Rd, off Roseberry Rd.* **Adm £2.50, chd free. Sun 24 June (2-5.30). Also open 5 St Regis Close.** Garden designer's sloping garden with unusual small trees, shrubs and perennials. Garden office with green roof of bulbs etc. Featured in '25 Beautiful Gardens'.

71 CENTRAL HILL, SE19
SE19 1BS. Sue Williams. *Stns: Gipsy Hill & Crystal Palace. On Central Hill, midway between Harold Road & Rockmount Road, is narrow, unmade road. Proceed to bottom of this and garden is through cast iron gates. No parking in lane.* Home-made teas. **Adm £3, chd free. Sun 15 July (2-4).** Hidden away at end of unmade track lies this 1/2-acre 'secret garden'. Formerly a Victorian nursery, the garden is now an eclectic mix of large traditional herbaceous beds and structural Mediterranean planting. Wildlife pond, 2 formal ponds and numerous objects of C19 architectural salvage provide further interest.

◆ CHELSEA PHYSIC GARDEN, SW3
66 Royal Hospital Road SW3 4HS. Chelsea Physic Garden self-funding charity, 020 7352 5646, www.chelseaphysicgarden.co.uk. *Bus: 239. Tube: Sloane Square (10 mins). Parking Battersea Park (charged). Entrance in Swan Walk (except wheelchairs).* **Adm £7, chd £4, concessions £4. Open Feb & Apr to Oct on certain days, please ring or visit website for details. For NGS: Sun 1 Apr (12-6).** Oldest Botanic Garden in London. 3 3/4 acres; medicinal and herb garden, perfumery border; family order beds; historical walk, glasshouses. Cool fernery and Robert Fortune's tank pond.

NEW 24 CHESTNUT ROAD, SE27
West Norwood SE27 9LF. Paul Brewer & Anne Rogerson. *Stns: W Norwood or Tulse Hill. Buses: 2, 68, 196, 322, 432, 468. Off S end of Norwood Rd, nr W Norwood Cemetery.* Home-made teas. **Adm £1.50, chd 20p, concessions £1 (share to Sound Minds). Sun 3 June (2-5). Also open 167 Rosendale Rd.** Cottage-style front garden. Rear garden with patios, rockery and pond. Decking and pergola. Unusual gazebo inspired by half-remembered Indonesian holiday. Lush planting with bananas, ferns, bamboos, gunnera. Assortment of pots. Penguin.

CHEVENING
See Kent.

CHISWICK HOUSE KITCHEN GARDEN, W4
Burlington Lane W4 2RP, www.kitchengarden.org.uk. *Access via Burlington Lane, Staveley Rd or A4 to Chiswick House and Grounds. Access to Kitchen Garden through the camellia house/conservatory.* Home-made teas. **Adm £1.50, chd free (share to Motor Neurone Disease Society). Sun 16 Sept (1-5).** This 2 1/2-acre walled garden was created by Sir Stephen Fox, financier to Charles II in 1683, but was neglected from the 1980s. The Chiswick House Kitchen Garden Association is now in its 2nd yr of work with local school children who are reviving the garden. Vegetables, herbs, fruit and flowers are emerging from the wilderness, creating an oasis that combines productivity with beauty, heritage varieties with practicality. Featured in 'Sunday Times'. Some uneven ground. Disabled WC.

CHISWICK MALL, W4
W6 9TN. Tube: Stamford Brook. *Buses: 27, 190, 267 & 391 to Young's Corner from Hammersmith through St Peter's Sq under A4 to river. By car A4 westbound turn off at Eyot Gdns S, then R into Chiswick Mall.* Home-made teas. **Individual adm charge. Sun 3 June (2-6).** Riverside community near Chiswick Eyot.

EYOT COTTAGE
Mrs Peter Trumper. **Adm £2, chd free** Two interconnecting gardens, both with beautiful river frontage. One an old walled garden recently replanted with many unusual white plants and shrubs. Other an upper terrace garden laid out by owners with imaginative use of old stones and pavers.

16 EYOT GARDENS, W6
Ms Dianne Farris. **Adm £1.50, chd free, OAP 50p** Small town garden. Front garden planted to complement Victorian house. Back garden shows what can be done with a small space, by using the walls for yr-round interest. Terrace, fountain and garden art.

LINGARD HOUSE
Rachel Austin, 020 8747 1943.
Adm £2, chd free. Visitors also
welcome by appt June only.
Walled garden divided into brick
courtyard and terrace with huge
acacia tree; formal lawn with
miniature pond and water-spout
and unusual herbaceous planting.
Wire-work pergola reveals wild
garden with ancient apple trees,
climbing roses and beehive.

SWAN HOUSE
Mr & Mrs George Nissen. Adm
£2, chd free
Informal walled garden.
Herbaceous border, fruit trees,
small vegetable garden. Tiny
greenhouse. Small wild flower area.
2 ponds and a rill.

51 CHOLMELEY CRESCENT, N6
Highgate N6 5EX. Ernst & Janet
Sondheimer, 020 8340 6607,
ernst@sondheimer.fsnet.co.uk.
*Between Highgate Hill & Archway Rd,
off Cholmeley Park. Tube: Highgate.*
Adm £2, chd free. Visitors welcome
by appt.
Approx 1/6-acre garden with many
alpines in screes, peat beds, tufa,
troughs and greenhouse; shrubs,
rhododendrons, camellias, magnolias,
pieris, ceanothus etc. Clematis, bog
plants, roses, primulas, tree ferns.
Water features. Garden on steep slope
with many steps and narrow paths.

CHOUMERT SQUARE, SE15
SE15 4RE. The Residents. *Via
wrought iron gates off Choumert
Grove. Peckham Rye mainline stn is
visible from the gates, & buses galore
(12, 36, 37, 63, 78, 171, 312, 345)
less than 10 mins walk. Free car park 2
mins.* Light refreshments, teas & wine.
Adm £2.50, chd 50p, concessions
£1.50 (share to St Christopher's
Hospice). Sun 10 June (1-6).
About 46 mini gardens with maxi-
planting in a Shangri-la situation that
the media has described as a 'Floral
Canyon', which leads to small
communal 'secret garden'. Open day
has village fête atmosphere with many
art stalls and delicious refreshments.
Best Residential Garden Southwark in
Bloom (part of London in Bloom).

26 COLLEGE GARDENS, E4
Chingford E4 7LG. Lynnette Parvez.
*2m from Walthamstow. 15 mins walk
Chingford mainline stn. 97 bus from*

*Walthamstow Central tube stn. Alight
at College Gardens then short walk
down hill.* Light refreshments & teas.
Adm £2, chd free. Sun 10 June (2-5).
Large suburban garden, approx
2/3 acre. Sun terrace leads to
established borders and variety of
climbing roses. Beyond this, wildlife
pond and lawn, small woodland walk
with spring plants and orchard. A
further garden area was recently
uncovered and will be restored and
planted over time.

COLUMCILLE
9 Norlands Crescent, Chislehurst
BR7 5RN. Nancy & Jim Pratt, 020
8467 9383,
nancyandjim@btinternet.com. *Off
A222 turn into Cricket Ground Rd, then
1st R into Norlands Cres. approx 1/2 m
from Chislehurst BR stn. Buses: 162 or
269, Bank House stop.* Adm £2, chd
free. Visitors welcome by appt June
to Sept, for groups of 6-24, day &
evening visits.
Small garden featuring Japanese
sanctuary, influenced by Zen tradition,
incl water feature, lanterns, traditional
Japanese plants and garden shed
transformed into a tea house. Also
cottage garden section with colourful
display of roses, lupins, peonies and
delphiniums, especially in June; dahlias
and day lilies Aug and Sept.

COTTAGE FARM
See Kent.

142 COURT LANE, SE21
Dulwich SE21 7EB. Jeremy & Jackie
Prescott. *Nr Court Lane entrance to
Dulwich Park, 1/2 m from Dulwich
Village (N Dulwich mainline stn & P4
bus). Also buses 40, 176, 185.* Light
refreshments & teas. Adm £2, chd
free (share to St Christopher's
Hospice). Sun 3 June (2-6).
1/2-acre garden at former home of
Anne Shelton (the Forces' Favourite),
backing on to Dulwich Park. Urban
garden planted from 1994 featuring
rose garden.

18 CRANMER ROAD
Hampton Hill TW12 1DW. Bernard
Wigginton, 020 8979 4596. *Between
A312 (Uxbridge Rd) & A313 (Park Rd).
Bus: 285 from Kingston stops at end
of rd. Stn: Fulwell 15 mins walk.* Adm
£2, chd free. Suns 20 May; 1 July
(2-5).

Visitors also welcome by appt May
to July only.
Medium-sized garden with herbaceous
and mixed borders. WW2 air raid
shelter transformed as rockery and
water garden with azaleas,
helianthemum and foliage plants.
Dahlia bed, containers with seasonal
planting and small wild flower meadow.
Wheelchair access to main lawn; care
needed on narrow and uneven paths
elsewhere.

About 46 mini gardens with maxi-planting in a Shangri-la situation . . .

158 CULFORD ROAD, N1
N1 4HU. Gillian Blachford, 020 7254
3780. *Tubes: Highbury & Islington
buses 30 or 277 from St Paul's Rd; or
Angel tube then buses 38 or 56, alight
Culford Rd.* Adm £2, chd free. Sun 24
June (2-6). Visitors also welcome by
appt June only.
Small town garden (15ft x 85ft) with
country feel. Winding path and
herbaceous borders, incl shrubs, small
trees and perennials. Many unusual
plants.

DE BEAUVOIR GARDENS, N1
N1 4LH. *Tubes: Highbury & Islington
then buses 30 or 277 from St Paul's
Rd; or Angel tube then 38 or 73 bus,
alight at stop after Essex Rd stn. Cars
via Southgate Rd - park in Northchurch
Rd or via Kingsland & Downham Rd.*
Home-made teas at 51 Lawford Rd.
Combined adm £5 or £2 each
garden. Sun 20 May (2-6).
3 mature gardens in leafy enclave of
period houses.

132 CULFORD ROAD
Mr & Mrs J Ward, 020 7684
0648. *Alight at the Alms Houses
bus stop. Culford Rd is opp.*
Visitors also welcome by appt in
May & June, for groups of 10 +.
100ft x 30ft garden paved and laid
with chippings, shingle and
cobbles. Large shrubs and island
beds divide a 'stone' garden from
the first, part dominated by large

vine, rose and honeysuckle-covered pergola dining area. Many places to sit. Fern beds, tree ferns, plants for shade and for hot and dry areas. Sunken garden close to house with alpine plants in sinks; herbs and bonsai.

51 LAWFORD ROAD
Carol Lee & Andrea McPherson. *Entrance to Lawford Rd (cul-de-sac) from Downham Rd* Small garden 16ft x 45ft at rear of Victorian terraced house. Bricked with different levels, lots of pots and pond with waterfalls. Hostas, ferns and anything that will grow in a pot. Foliage a speciality.

NEW 23 NORTHCHURCH ROAD
John Walsh & Dean Hollowood Tranquil front garden of woodland shrubs, ferns, grasses belies the exuberance of the rear, whose modest space packs subtropical giants: tree ferns, bananas and cannas jostle for space around a pond with bamboos and reeds.

Architectural planting, gravel and ponds, plunge pool, swing raised viewing platforms . . .

36 DOWNS HILL
Beckenham BR3 5HB. Marc & Janet Berlin, 020 8650 9377. *3m W of Bromley. 2 mins from Ravensbourne mainline stn nr top of Foxgrove Rd.* Home-made teas. Adm £2, chd free (share to NSPCC). Sun 24 June (2-5). Visitors also welcome by appt. Long 2/3-acre E-facing, award-winning, garden sloping steeply away from house. Ponds, water courses and sheltered patio area with many tender unusual plants and hundreds of pots. Wooded area, dense planting of trees, shrubs and flowers. New raised beds, paths and patio areas. Art display, music.

NEW 170 DOYLE GARDENS, NW10
NW10 3SU. James Duncan Mattoon, 020 8961 6243. *Tube: Kensal Green, up College Rd, L into Liddell Gdns which becomes Doyle Gdns.* Light refreshments & teas. Adm £2.50, chd free. Sun 15 July (2-7). Visitors also welcome by appt at any time. Professional plantsman's private fantasy garden with an impossibly tropical theme: musa, trachycarpus, yucca, puya, plumbago, grasses. Garden 100% organic and incl many native and introduced wild flowers to help create a natural effect and promote wildlife. Frog and newt pond, log piles and over 350 plant species, living with slugs and snails!

15 DUKES AVENUE, N10
N10 2PS. Vivienne Parry. *Short walk from main Muswell Hill roundabout. Buses: 43, 134, alight Muswell Hill Broadway or 7 from Finsbury Park. Tube: Highgate, then bus 43 or 134.* Home-made teas. Adm £2, chd free. Sun 20 May (2-5). Also open 46 Dukes Ave & 33 Wood Vale. Mediterranean-style gravel front garden in silver, lilacs, pinks and blues. Small lawned back garden with wide variety of plants. Colour in both areas provided by constantly changing containers and pots. Featured in 'Good Housekeeping'.

NEW 46 DUKES AVENUE, N10
Muswell Hill N10 2PU. Judith Glover, www.judithglover.com. *Short walk from main Muswell Hill roundabout. Tube: Highgate then bus 43 or 134 to Muswell Hill Broadway or bus 7 from Finsbury Park.* Adm £2.50, chd free. Sun 20 May (2-5). Also open 15 Dukes Ave & 33 Wood Vale. Designer and botanical illustrator's country-style gardan described as being 'just on the right side of controlled chaos'. Organic, curvy beds with foxgloves, aquilegias, irises and valerian anchored with clipped evergreens. Topiary, grasses and driftwood throne from medal-winning garden designed for Chelsea Flower Show. Featured in 'Evening Standard'. Steep steps not suitable for small children or the infirm.

DULWICH GARDENS, SE21
SE21 7BJ. *Mainline: London Bridge to N Dulwich & from Victoria to W Dulwich then 10-15 mins walk. Tube: Brixton then P4 bus passes both gardens. Street parking.* Home-made teas. Combined adm £4.50, chd free (share to Macmillan, London Branch). Sun 10 June (2-5). Also open North House & 174 Peckham Rye.
2 Georgian houses with large gardens, 2 mins walk from Dulwich Picture Gallery and Dulwich Park.

103 DULWICH VILLAGE
Mr & Mrs N Annesley About 1/2-acre 'country garden in London'. Long herbaceous border, spacious lawn, ornamental pond, roses and many and varied other plants, plus fruit and vegetable garden.

105 DULWICH VILLAGE
Mr & Mrs A Rutherford About 1/2-acre, mostly herbaceous with lawns and lots of old-fashioned roses. Shrubbery, ornamental pond, water garden. Very pretty garden with many unusual plants.

Just on the right side of controlled chaos . . .

66A EAST DULWICH ROAD, SE22
East Dulwich SE22 9AT. Kevin Wilson, 020 8693 3458, kevin-wil@supanet.com. *Basement flat overlooking Goose Green, opp Dulwich swimming baths. Walking distance East Dulwich mainline stn. Buses: 37, 176, 185.* Adm £2.50, chd £1 (share to Goose Green School). Suns 10 June; 8 July; 12 Aug (12-6). Evening Opening £3.50, wine, Sun 2 Sept (4-9). Visitors also welcome by appt, parties of 10+.
Secret tranquil 100ft garden with decking, architectural planting, gravel and ponds, plunge pool, swing raised viewing platforms. Have taken over 1/3 of next door garden and have verandah, 4 person swing and vegetable garden. Featured in RHS 'The Garden', 'The Independent' & on BBC Gardeners' World.

NEW EATONVILLE ROAD GARDENS, SW17
Tooting Bec SW17 7SL. *400 yds from Tooting Bec tube, just off Trinity Rd.* Home-made teas. **Combined adm £5, chd free. Sun 17 June (2-6). Also open 28 Old Devonshire Rd & 68 Wandle Rd.**
Three small S-facing gardens, all same side of the road, similar size and aspect but very different styles. Delicious cakes and excellent plant sale.

NEW 14 EATONVILLE ROAD
Liz Riches & Julie Fleck
Just can't resist plants! An evolving mixture of edible, scented and decorative planting creates a slightly chaotic green framework. Many small patio pots with tender, Mediterranean plants. Front garden is stuffed full of colourful herbs.

20 EATONVILLE ROAD
Pamela & Gethyn Davies
Garden designer's experiment in planting combinations with unusual perennials, shrubs and fragrant climbers next to culinary herbs and salad leaves. Garden on two levels with small water feature and lawn.

NEW 22 EATONVILLE ROAD
Mr & Mrs Allday
Very simple, formal garden with raised beds, lawn and dining terrace all on one level. Bay and myrtle lollipop trees form a strong design statement, softened with hostas and ornamental grasses.

ECCLESTON SQUARE, SW1
SW1V 1NP. Roger Phillips & the Residents. *Off Belgrave Rd nr Victoria stn, parking allowed on Suns.* Home-made teas. **Adm £3, chd £1.50. Sun 13 May (2-5).**
Planned by Cubitt in 1828, the 3-acre square is subdivided into mini-gardens with camellias, iris, ferns and containers. Dramatic collection of tender climbing roses and 20 different forms of tree peonies. National Collection of ceanothus incl more than 70 species and cultivars.

EDWARDES SQUARE, W8
W8 6HL. Edwardes Square Garden Committee. *Tube: Kensington High St & Earls Court. Buses: 9, 10, 27, 28, 31, 49 & 74 - bus stop, Odeon Cinema. Entrance in South Edwardes Square.* Cream teas & Pimms. **Adm £3.50, chd free. Sun 15 Apr (1-5).**
One of London's prettiest secluded garden squares. 3½ acres laid out differently from other squares, with serpentine paths by Agostino Agliothe, Italian artist and decorator who lived at no.15 from 1814-1820, and a beautiful Grecian temple which is traditionally the home of the gardener. Romantic rose tunnel winds through the middle of the garden. Good displays of bulbs and blossom.

12 ELIOT VALE, SE3
Blackheath SE3 0UW. Frances & Graham High. *Mainline stns: Blackheath 7 mins, Lewisham 12 mins walk. Eliot Vale on SW side of Blackheath, short walk from A2.* **Evening Opening £3.50 (share to Ataxia Telangiectasia Soc), wine, Fri 15 June (6-9). Also open 28 Granville Park & The Pagoda.**
Designed for disabled with slopes and space for wheelchairs; high-level pond; shaped beds with a variety of plants incl roses, bamboo, succulents and miniature box hedging. Contemporary sculpture. Surprising L-shaped garden combining open visibility with a few 'hidden' discoveries.

ELM TREE COTTAGE
85 Croham Road, S Croydon CR2 7HJ. Wendy Witherick & Michael Wilkinson. *2m S of Croydon. Off B275 from Croydon, off A2022 from Selsdon, bus 64.* **Adm £2.50, chd free. Suns 6 May; 3 June; 8 July (1-5).**
Cottage garden transformed into an oasis of sharp gardening. Agaves, grasses, yuccas, olives, kniphofia, iris, alliums, phormiums, phlomis, figs. Topiary boxwood, taxus and much more. Designed to be drought-tolerant/low maintenance. Not suitable for those unsteady on their feet and beware agave spikes! Featured in 'Evening Standard'.

THE ELMS
13 Wolverton Avenue, Kingston-upon-Thames KT2 7QF. Prof & Mrs R Rawlings. *1m E of Kingston. On A308. Kingston Hospital & Norbiton mainline stn 100yds. Enter via garage in Manorgate Rd at foot of Kingston Hill. Some parking restrictions on Sats.* Home-made teas. **Adm £2, chd free (share to Terrence Higgins Trust). Sats, Suns 10, 11 Mar; 14, 15 Apr; 12, 13 May (2.30-4.30).**
55ft x 25ft garden owned by 'plantaholic'! Trees, shrubs, climbers, herbaceous and ground cover plants, some rare. Pool, fruit trees and soft fruits. Roof garden not open on NGS days. Featured in 'Amateur Gardening'.

NEW 71 FALLOWCOURT AVENUE, N12
Finchley N12 0BE. Yasuko & John O'Gorman. *7 mins walk from West Finchley stn, between Ballards Lane & Finchley High Rd. Buses: 82, 125, 263 & 460 to Finchley Memorial Hospital.* Home-made teas & light refreshments. **Adm £2, chd free. Sun 3 June (2-5.30). Also open 263 Nether St.**
Well maintained S-facing plot, 120ft x 30ft. Fairly new (5 yrs) but densely planted garden, at its first peak in May/June. Sunlit borders and shaded area with an intimate patio at rear, not immediately visible from the house. Many Japanese varieties: tree peonies, maples, wisteria, magnolias, cherry blossoms, azaleas, bamboo and irises.

◆ FENTON HOUSE, NW3
Hampstead Grove NW3 6RT. The National Trust, 020 7435 3471. *300yds from Hampstead tube. Entrances: top of Holly Hill & Hampstead Grove.* For NGS: **Evening Opening £3.50, chd £1.50, Thur 7 June (6.30-8.30).**
Timeless 1½-acre walled garden, laid out on three levels, containing imaginative plantings concealed by yew hedges. The herbaceous borders

Sunlit borders and shaded area with an intimate patio at rear . . .

give yr-round interest while the brick-paved sunken rose garden provides a sheltered hollow of scent and colour. The formal lawn area contrasts with the rustic charm of the kitchen garden and orchard. Vine house.

54 FERNDOWN
Northwood Hills HA6 1PH. David & Ros Bryson, 020 8866 3792, david@bryson77.freeserve.co.uk. *Tube: Northwood Hills 5 mins walk. R out of stn, R down Briarwood Drive then 1st R.* Home-made teas. **Adm £2.50, chd free (share to RSPCA). Sun 9 Sept (10-5). Visitors also welcome by appt.**
Unusual collection of exotics, cacti and Australasian plants. Palm trees, tree ferns and bananas set in an original design. Elevated deck overlooks the garden underplanted with rare ferns and aroids.

FISHPONDS HOUSE
Fishponds Park, 219 Ewell Road, Surbiton KT6 6BE. Robert & Belinda Eyre-Brook. *1m from Tolworth junction on A3 towards Kingston on A240. House in middle of The Fishponds, a public park bordered by Ewell Rd, Browns Rd, King Charles Rd & Hollyfield Rd. House is behind the main pond. Park in neighbouring rds. No vehicle access to park other than for disabled; disabled access from Ewell Rd.* Home-made teas. **Adm £2, chd free. Sun 10 June (2-5).**
Large garden, part formal, part terrace, with adjoining woodland overlooking a large duck pond. Partly redesigned by Andy Sturgeon and filled with structural plants and grasses. Visitors could visit the park for a picnic before garden opening.

14 FRANK DIXON WAY, SE21
SE21 7ET. Frank & Angie Dunn. *Stn: W Dulwich. From Dulwich Village pass Dulwich Gallery on R, Frank Dixon Way (private rd) 500 metres on L.* Home-made teas. **Adm £2, chd free. Sun 6 May (2-5).**
Large family garden surrounded by mature trees, low maintenance shrub borders and annual plantings. Lawns and a spectacular rowan. Sit-on railway around the garden for children's rides.

FROGNAL GARDENS, NW3
Hampstead NW3 6UY. *Tube; Hampstead. Buses: 46, 268 to Hampstead High St. Frognal Gardens 2nd R off Church Row from Heath St.* Home-made teas. **Combined adm £3, chd 50p. Sun 17 June (2-5).**
Two neighbouring gardens divided by path lined with trellises of cascading roses and clematis, underplanted with carpets of flowers.

5 FROGNAL GARDENS
Ruth & Brian Levy
Long narrow structured garden romantically planted with soft colours and profusion of unusual climbers and cottage perennials.

5A FROGNAL GARDENS
Ian & Barbara Jackson
Small, beautifully landscaped garden with lawn, colourful flower beds and containers. A garden to enjoy and relax in.

NEW GOLF COURSE ALLOTMENTS, N11
Winton Avenue N11 2AR. GCAA/Haringey, www. gcaa.pwp.blueyonder.co.uk. *Tube: Bounds Green approx 1km. Buses: 102, 229 to Sunshine Garden Centre, Durnsford Rd. Then Bidwell Gardens (on foot through park) to Winton Ave. Gate opp junction with Blake Rd.* Light refreshments & teas. **Adm £2.50, chd free (share to GCAA). Sun 2 Sept (1-4).**
Large, long-established allotment with over 200 plots maintained by culturally diverse community growing a wide variety of flowers, fruit and vegetables - some working towards organic cultivation. Picturesque corners and charming sheds. Annual Show day. Prizewinning exhibits incl photography on display. Tour of best plots. Sale of produce, BBQ, raffle & stalls. Limited wheelchair access, some steps and uneven surfaces.

28 GRANVILLE PARK, SE13
SE13 7EA. Joanna Herald. *Parking available on street, Suns & eves. 10 mins walk up hill (N) towards Blackheath from Lewisham mainline & DLR stns.* **Evening Opening £3.50**

(share to Cystic Fibrosis), wine, Fri 15 June (6-9). Also open **12 Eliot Vale & The Pagoda**.
Garden designer's family garden in three sections. Pool garden, mixed herbaceous and shrub planting with bulbs around circular lawns, gravel garden and sunken terrace with pots. 100ft x 35ft.

Large, long-established allotment with over 200 plots maintained by culturally diverse community . . .

NEW 5 GREVILLE PLACE, NW6
NW6 5JP. Dr & Mrs T Laub, 07860 822313, renée@laub.co.uk. *Tube: Kilburn Park.* Home-made teas. **Adm £2.50, chd free. Sun 8 July (2-6). Visitors also welcome by appt, coaches permitted.**
Newly-created garden establishing fast. Large front garden with herbaceous planting. Behind the house a stream links two ponds and meanders through a woodland garden. Good collection of ferns and many unusual plants. Interesting Victorian pots.

7 THE GROVE, N6
Highgate Village N6 6JU. Mr Thomas Lyttelton, 07713 638161. *The Grove is between Highgate West Hill & Hampstead Lane. Tube: Archway or Highgate. Buses: 143, 210, 271 to Highgate Village from Archway, 214 from Camden Town.* Home-made teas. **Adm £2.50, chd free (share to North London Hospice). Sun 15 Apr (2-5.30). Also open with Highgate Village Sun 3 June. Visitors also welcome by appt.**
1/2 acre designed for max all-yr interest with its variety of conifers and other trees, ground cover, water garden, vistas, 19 paths, surprises. Exceptional camellias in April. Many narrow paths, can be slippery.

◆ HAM HOUSE & GARDEN

Ham, Richmond TW10 7RS. **The National Trust**, 020 8439 8230, www.nationaltrust.org.uk. *Mid-way between Richmond & Kingston. W of A307 on Surrey bank of R Thames. Follow National Trust signs.* **House & garden £9, chd £5, family £22. Garden only £3, chd £2, family £7. Opening days & times vary according to season; please phone or visit website for details. For NGS: Mon 9 July (11-6).**
The beautiful C17 gardens incl much-photographed Cherry Garden, featuring lavender parterres flanked by hornbeam arbours; S terrace with clipped yew cones, hibiscus and pomegranate trees; eight grass plats; maze-like wilderness; C17 orangery with working kitchen garden and licensed café and terrace.

116 HAMILTON TERRACE, NW8

NW8 9UT. **Mr & Mrs I B Kathuria, 020 7625 6909.** *Tubes: Maida Vale, 5 mins walk, St John's Wood, 10 mins walk. Buses: 16 & 98 from Marble Arch to Cricklewood.* **Adm £2.50. Visitors welcome by appt.**
Lush front garden full of dramatic foliage with a water feature and tree ferns. Large back garden of different levels with Yorkshire stone paving, many large terracotta pots and containers, water feature and lawn. Wide variety of perennials and flowering shrubs, many unusual, and subtropical plants, succulents, acers, ferns, hebes, climbers, roses, fuchsias and prizewinning hostas. Packed with colour and rich foliage of varied texture.

157 HAMPSTEAD WAY, NW11

Hampstead Garden Suburb NW11 7YA. **Richard & Carol Kemp.** *Tube: Golders Green, then H2 bus to Hampstead Way.* **Adm £2, chd free. Sun 22 July (2-5). Also open 86 Willifield Way.**
Charming, 100ft split-level SW-facing cottage garden containing a wealth of colourful and informally planted hardy perennials and succulents, against a backdrop of interesting shrubs. Designed for all-yr interest. Take care, steps slippery when wet.

HIGHGATE VILLAGE, N6

N6 6JU. *The Grove is between Highgate West Hill & Hampstead Lane. Tube: Archway or Highgate. Buses: 143, 210, 214, 271 to Highgate Village.* Home-made teas. **Combined adm £4, chd free (share to North London Hospice). Sun 3 June (2-5.30).**
The Grove is a famous Georgian terrace with breathtaking views over Hampstead Heath.

THE GROVE

Mr Cob Stenham, 020 7299 5562. Visitors also welcome by appt May to July, no coaches.
Delightful two-tiered garden. Formal upper garden with a mixture of Mediterranean and traditional plants and flowers; Cooper's Burmese rose and wildlife pond with fountain. Woodland area; hidden garden, greenhouse, laburnum tunnel and silver pear arch in bottom garden.

7 THE GROVE

Mr Thomas Lyttelton
(See separate entry).

5 HILLCREST AVENUE, NW11

NW11 0EP. **Mrs R M Rees, 020 8455 0419, ruthmrees@aol.com.** *Hillcrest Ave is off Bridge Lane. Buses: 82, 102, 460 to Temple Fortune. Tube: Golders Green or Finchley Central. Walk down Bridge Lane.* Home-made teas. **Adm £2, chd free (share to Alzheimers Society, Barnet). Sun 17 June (2-6). Evening Opening £3, wine, Wed 20 June (5-9). Visitors also welcome by appt.**
Small labour-saving colourful garden with many interesting features; rockery, fish pond, conservatory, tree ferns, secluded patio. Urban jungle front garden with drought-resistant plants, traditional back garden. Prizewinning front garden, Hampstead Horticultural Society.

24 HILLS ROAD

Buckhurst Hill IG9 5RS. **Sue Hargreaves.** *Situated between Epping and Woodford. 5m from M 25 J26, off*

A104 Epping New Rd. Mainline: Chingford or Buckhurst Hill. Renowned organic and wheat-free cakes. **Adm £1.50, chd 50p. Sun 15 July (2-6).**
Herbalist's organic garden designed by artist. Narrow Victorian garden featuring elements of potager using traditional and contemporary materials and planting. Many unusual features and details. Five distinctive areas linked together: shady sunken terrace, herb garden, raised sleeper herbaceous beds, vegetable and trained fruit trees.

HOLLY COTTAGE

40 Station Road, Hampton TW12 2DA. **Ms M Cartwright.** *3m W of Kingston. Buses: 68 & 267 to Hampton Church. From river end 5 mins walk. Buses: 111 & 216 pass the house. Alight police stn 100yds. Hampton mainline stn 5 mins.* Home-made teas. **Adm £2, chd 50p. Suns 10, 17 June (2-5.30).**
Long front garden planted for winter and spring interest leads on to enchanting paved cottage garden (30ft x 25ft). Densely planted, it contains many hardy geraniums. Pergola, planted in shades of blue and white, links the two gardens. Ferns, pool, home-grown mistletoe on old apple tree.

🆕 79 HOLMDENE AVENUE, SE24

North Dulwich SE24 9DL. **Ros Badger.** *Stns: N Dulwich & Herne Hill, 5 mins walk.* Home-made teas. **Adm £2, chd free. Suns 13 May; 17 June (2-5.30). Also open 17 June South London Botanical Institute.**
Small city garden, 20ft x 30ft, crammed with large perennials, lilac tree in full bloom in May. Designed as an outdoor room to give maximum visual effect from the large glass kitchen doors. Small front garden set behind antique French railings.

THE HOLME, NW1

Inner Circle, Regents Park NW1 4NT. **Lessee of The Crown Commission.** *Opp Open Air Theatre. Tube: Regents Park or Baker St.* **Adm £3, chd £1, family ticket £7. Sats, Suns 28, 29 Apr; 1, 2 Sept (2.30-5.30). Also open 28, 29 Apr Royal College of Physicians Garden.**

Urban jungle front garden with drought-resistant plants, traditional back garden . . .

4-acre garden filled with interesting and unusual plants. Sweeping lakeside lawns intersected by islands of herbaceous beds. Extensive rock garden with waterfall, stream and pool. Formal flower garden with unusual annual and half hardy plants, sunken lawn, fountain pool and arbour. Gravel paths.

& ﾑﾏ

239A HOOK ROAD
Chessington KT9 1EQ. **Mr & Mrs D St Romaine, 020 8397 3761,**
derek@gardenphotolibrary.com. *4m S of Kingston. A3 from London, turn L at Hook underpass onto A243 Hook Rd. Garden approx 300yds on L. Parking opp in park. Buses: K4, 71, 465 from Kingston & Surbiton to North Star PH.* **Adm £2.50, chd £1. Sun 10 June (2-6). Evening Opening £3.50, wine, Wed 13 June (6-9). Visitors also welcome by appt.**
Garden photographer's garden. $^1/_4$-acre garden divided into two. Flower garden contains a good mix of herbaceous plants, shrubs, climbers and topiary. Also gravel garden, rose tunnel and pond. Potager, divided by paths into small beds, has many vegetables, soft fruit, fruit trees and herbs all planted with flowers.

ﾑﾏ

HORNBEAMS
Priory Drive, Stanmore HA7 3HN. **Dr & Mrs R B Stalbow, 020 8954 2218,**
barbara@6stalbow.wanadoo.co.uk. *5m SE of Watford. Tube: Stanmore. Priory Drive private rd off Stanmore Hill (A4140 Stanmore-Bushey Heath Rd).* Home-made teas. **Adm £3, chd free. Visitors welcome by appt.**
Yr-round garden with creative landscaping designed by owner. In winter incl viburnums, witch hazels, snowdrops; spring incl species tulips and spectacular cornus Eddies White Wonder; summer incl colourful containers and ornamental potager; autumn incl Muscat grape shading conservatory, cyclamen and schizostylus. All this and much more.

& ﾑﾏ ⊕ ﾒ

1A HUNGERFORD ROAD, N7
N7 9LA. David Matzdorf. *Tube: Caledonian Rd, 6 mins walk. Buses: 29 & 253 to Hillmartin Rd stop in Camden Rd; 17, 91 & 259 to last stop in Hillmartin Rd; 10 to York Way at Market Rd & 274 to junction of Market Rd & Caledonian Rd.* **Adm £2, chd £1 (share to Terrence Higgins Trust).**

Sun 10 June (10-6). Also open **62 Hungerford Rd & 2A Penn Rd.**
Unique eco-house with walled, lush front garden planted in modern-exotic style. Floriferous 'green roof' resembling scree slope. Front garden densely planted with palms, acacia, ginger lilies, brugmansias, bananas, euphorbias and spiky plants. The 'green roof' is planted with alpines, sedums, mesembryanthemums, bulbs, grasses, agaves, aloes, bromeliads and aromatic herbs - access only to part of roof for safety reasons (can be seen from below). Garden and roof each 50ft x 18ft.

ﾑﾏ ⊛

Unique eco-house with walled, lush front garden planted in modern-exotic style . . .

62 HUNGERFORD ROAD, N7
N7 9LP. John Gilbert & Lynne Berry. *Directions as 1a Hungerford Rd.* **Adm £2, chd £1. Sun 10 June (2-6). Also open 1a Hungerford Rd & 2A Penn Rd.**
Mature town garden at rear of Victorian terrace house which has been designed to maximise space for planting and create several different sitting areas, views and moods. Arranged in a series of paved rooms each 'over-stuffed' with a good range of shrubs and perennials.

ﾑﾏ

THE HURLINGHAM CLUB, SW6
Ranelagh Gardens SW6 3PR, 020 7471 8209,
vanessa.parrott@hurlinghamclub. org.uk. *Main gate at E end of Ranelagh Gardens. Tube: Putney Bridge (110yds).* Light refreshments, teas & wine. **Adm £5, chd free. Thur 14 June (guided tours at 2 & 4pm). Visitors also welcome by appt for groups.**
40-acre 'country-house' garden with lawns mainly laid to bowls, croquet and tennis, surrounded by shrubberies, herbaceous borders and formal bedding. Several mature trees of interest. 2-acre lake with water fowl. River walk.

& ﾑﾏ ﾒ

ISLINGTON GARDENS GROUP 1, N1
N1 1YY. *Tube: Kings Cross or Angel. Buses: 17, 91, 259 to Caledonian Rd.* Home-made teas at Thornhill Square. **Combined adm £6 or £2 each garden, (£1.50 Barnsbury Wood), chd free. Sun 3 June (2-6).**
Contrasting gardens in the Barnsbury Conservation Area.

BARNSBURY WOOD
Islington Council. *Off Crescent Street, N of Thornhill Square*
Colourful borders lead to Islington's hidden secret. A place of peace and relaxation, the borough's only site of mature woodland and one of London's smallest nature reserves. Wildlife gardening advice and information available. Some bumpy, grassy paths.

& ﾑﾏ

13 COLLEGE CROSS
Diana & Stephen Yakeley
Black slate bench and glass balustrade provide contemporary design interest in this peaceful green oasis. Paved areas for dining surrounded by architectural plants chosen for form and texture are enlivened by white flowers incl several different types of lily. Good examples of plants that work in London shade for all-yr interest.

ﾑﾏ

44 HEMINGFORD ROAD
Dr Peter Willis
Surprisingly lush, country-style garden in the city with interesting trees, shrubs, perennials, lawns and pond in a very small space. Matured over 28 yrs in symbiosis with honey fungus.

ﾑﾏ

36 THORNHILL SQUARE
Anna & Christopher McKane
Old roses, hardy geraniums, clematis and alliums give a country garden atmosphere in curved beds in this 120ft long garden. Bonsai collection displayed on the patio. Many unusual plants propagated for sale.

ﾑﾏ ⊛

Matured over 28 years in symbiosis with honey fungus . . .

ngs gardens open for charity

GARDENS
OF **THE** NGS

1. **Edith Terrace**
   Cheshire Rob Taylor
2. **Sherwood**
   Devon Clive Bournsell
3. **Stonehealed Farm**
   Sussex Leigh Clapp

"Up the garden path"

"Perfectly placed pots"

"Purple haze"

"Take a seat"

Photograph Twofour Group

Garden Bramble Hayes, Devon Photograph Twofour Group

TRICKS**OFTHE**TRADE

CAROL KLEIN GETS HER HANDS DIRTY TO HELP AMATEUR GARDENERS

Carol Klein, plantswoman extraordinaire, brought her infectious enthusiasm for plants and their growers to Open Gardens, a new series aired on BBC2 during autumn 2006. She travelled up and down the country visiting every possible type of garden, from small seaside haven to large wild Cumbrian fell, all with one thing in common – they want to be accepted into The National Gardens Scheme and gain a place in its legendary Yellow Book. In the series Carol got her hands dirty in an effort to help 20 amateur gardeners open their private paradises to the paying public for the very first time. Every garden in The National Gardens Scheme must offer its visitors at least 45 minutes of interest – it's not the size of a garden that is important but the interesting range of planting – so Carol's contribution helped enormously as these gardens aimed for horticultural heaven.

Garden Bramble Hayes, Devon Photograph Twofour Group

Each programme featured two gardens: one as it prepared to open its gates to the public for the first time in 2006; the second, a hopeful, as it strived to pass the strict criteria needed to be one of the new gardens opening in 2007.

Garden Consall Hall, Staffordshire Photograph Twofour Group

Carol Klein runs her own, very successful nursery and is well-known to British gardeners as one of Europe's foremost plantswomen, having appeared on countless television and radio gardening shows. Carol considers the problems of each garden, providing down-to-earth, practical advice to help them achieve Yellow Book status.

Gardens featured that opened for the first time in 2006

3 Court Walk, Staffordshire
The Birches, Glamorgan
Bramble Hayes, Devon
Consall Hall, Staffordshire
The Gargoyle, Bristol
Glan-y-cwm, Glamorgan
Kennet House, Devon
Littleham House, Devon
Lyford Grange, Oxfordshire
Meadow House, Cumbria

Gardens featured that are NEW for 2007

The Brodder, Staffordshire
Fern Dene, Staffordshire
Glan-y-llyn, Glamorgan
Lakesland, Devon
Little Winsors, Devon
The Old Bakery, Bristol
Owlsbarn, Devon
Sprint Mill, Cumbria
Wolf House, Glamorgan

Garden 10 Fern Dene, Staffordshire Photograph Martin Clifford-Jones

Garden 10 Fern Dene, Staffordshire Photograph Martin Clifford-Jones

Garden Lyford Grange, Oxfordshire Photograph Amateur Gardening

"For visitors, it's a fantastic opportunity to gain knowledge and swap ideas in a relaxed environment"

Carol Klein

"What lies beyond…"

"Go with the flow"

"Wild at heart"

"Boxing clever"

ISLINGTON GARDENS GROUP 2, N1

N1 2QW. *Tube: Highbury & Islington. Mainline stn: Canonbury. Buses: 30, 277 along St Paul's Rd.* Home-made teas at 5 Northampton Park. **Combined adm £3.50 or £2 each garden, chd free. Sun 8 July (2-6).** Visitors can walk to each garden via the small park known as St Paul's Shrubbery.

5 NORTHAMPTON PARK
N1 2PP. Anne Brogan & Andrew Bernhardt. *Off St Paul's Rd (N side)*
L-shaped, S-facing, walled garden divided by lavender, yew and box hedging. Currently evolving from cool blues and whites, with foliage and leaf shade, to splashes of hot Mediterranean influence.

60 ST PAUL'S ROAD
N1 2QW. John & Pat Wardroper, pwardroper@blueyonder.co.uk. *Buses: 30, 277 stop outside.* **Visitors also welcome by appt.**
70ft x 20ft walled garden designed to form 3 separate rooms: tree-shaded York stone patio with ferns, lawn with shrub border and arch leading to sitting area planted for scent. High hedges give a sense of seclusion and the sound of 3 fountains creates a peaceful atmosphere. Certificate of Excellence in Small Back Garden category London Gardens Society All London Championship 2006.

KEW GARDENS GROUP
TW9 3HA. *2m N of Richmond. Nearest station Kew Gardens, both gardens within 5 mins walk. Buses: 391 to Kew Gardens stn, 65 to Kew Gardens, Victoria Gate.* Teas at 7 Maze Rd. **Adm £2 each garden, chd free. Sun 6, Mon 7 May (2-5).**

38 LEYBORNE PARK
Ann & Alan Sandall
120ft long mature garden; lawn with mixed borders; patio; interesting collection of pots and containers. Bamboos, peonies, pinks, auriculas, hostas.

7 MAZE ROAD
Celia Fisher
Cottage garden divided into 4 triangular beds packed with spring flowers incl irises, primulas and euphorbias, enlivened by pots, sculptures and ceramics. Owner is an art historian who writes and lectures on plants in art.

NEW KEW GARDENS STATION GROUP
Kew TW9 4DA. Home-made teas at 355 Sandycombe Road. **£2 each garden, combined adm £5, chd free. Sun 20 May (2-6).**
Three gardens nr Kew Gardens Stn.

NEW 355 SANDYCOMBE ROAD
Kew. Henry Gentle & Sally Woodward Gentle. *200m S of Kew Gardens Station. Garden entrance between house nos. 351 & 353.* **(share to React).**
Unexpectedly large urban garden on two levels. Terracing with wooden sleepers, bricks and decking provide distinct areas of interest incl lavenders, olives, grasses, euphorbias and other plants for sandy soils and shady areas. A garden for adults and children alike. Featured in '4-homes'.

NEW 31 WEST PARK ROAD
Anna Anderson. *By Kew Gardens Stn, on E side of railway line*
Modern botanical garden with an oriental twist. Emphasis on foliage and an eclectic mix of plants, reflecting pool and rotating willow screens which provide varying views or privacy. Dry bed, shady beds, mature trees and a private paved dining area with dappled light and shade.

42 WEST PARK ROAD
Kew TW9 4DA. Michael Anderson. *3 mins walk from Kew Gardens tube stn*
Small S-facing walled garden in Kew village. On various levels and features incl decking bisected by a rill to reflecting pool. Pebble areas inset with reclaimed rail sleepers and Indian sandstone terrace. Diverse planting evolves through the seasons creating yr-round interest. Featured in 'The English Garden' & 'Evening Standard'.

KEW GREEN GARDENS
TW9 3AH, 020 8940 7014. *NW side of Kew Green. Tube: Kew Gardens. Mainline stn: Kew Bridge. Buses: 65, 391. Entrance via towpath.* Home-made teas. **Combined adm £5, chd free. Sun 10 June (2-6).** Visitors also welcome by appt July only.
Four long gardens behind adjacent C18 houses on the Green; close to Royal Botanic Gardens.

65 KEW GREEN
Mr & Mrs Dixon
Long, narrow garden divided into four separate mini-gardens, with a large summerhouse. Organic.

69 KEW GREEN
Mr & Mrs John Godfrey
Mature English garden, profusely planted. Formal garden and terrace nr house, wilder further down. New nuttery, meadow planting. Interesting shrubs and plants.

71 KEW GREEN
Mr & Mrs Jan Pethick
Large and informal London garden, laid out around tall, old trees; traditional border, irises and shaded borders within woodland. Well-established shrubs in crowded planting.

73 KEW GREEN
Donald & Libby Insall
The garden wanders from the main lawn and border by house, through woodland and surprises by arriving at a modern planting of espaliered miniature fruit trees.

38 KILLIESER AVENUE, SW2
SW2 4NT. Mrs Winkle Haworth, 020 8671 4196, winklehaworth@hotmail.com. *Mainline stn: Streatham Hill, 5 mins walk. Buses: 133, 137, 159 to Telford Ave. Killieser Ave 2nd turning L off Telford Ave.* **Evening Opening £3.50, wine, Sat 2 June (5-8). Visitors also welcome by appt.**
Densely-planted, romantic, 90ft x 28ft garden divided into four distinct areas. Unusual perennial plants and shrubs provide the backbone. Miniature cascade, wall fountain, Gothic seating arbour and new gravel garden with drought-tolerant plants. Rose-filled parterre provides a formal element. Featured in 'House and Garden' (Germany) & 'The English Garden'. Prizewinner London Gardens Society.

64A KINGS ROAD
Richmond TW10 6EP. Jill & Ged Guinness. Tube & mainline: Richmond, 1/2m. Bus: 371 to Kings Rd. 64a is between 58 & 64. Home-made teas. Adm £2, chd free. Sun 20 May (2.30-6).
Cool, green, modern garden surrounds slightly sunken house built 2000. Underground tanks collect rainwater for pumping onto garden in summer. Idiosyncratic planting dictated by position of house. While form and foliage take precedence over flowers, fruit and football are important too. Anna Pavord article in 'The Independent'.

> ## Cool, green, modern garden . . . while form and foliage take precedence over flowers, fruit and football are important too . . .

LAMBETH COMMUNITY CARE CENTRE, SE11
Monkton Street SE11 4TX. Lambeth Community Care Centre. Tube or buses to Elephant & Castle, cut behind Leisure Centre to Brook Drive. Turn into Sullivan Rd, passage to Monkton St. Buses: 3, 109, 159 or drive (ample parking) to Kennington Rd; at Ship PH turn into Bishop's Terrace, 1st R to Monkton St. Light refreshments & teas. Adm £2, chd/concessions 50p. Sat 19, Sun 20 May (2-5).
2/3-acre garden. Mixed shrubs, trees, interesting walkways and mixed borders. Topiary and display pots. Challenge Cup winner, London Gardens Society. Help required with steep slopes; wheelchair handrails everywhere.

LAMBETH PALACE, SE1
SE1 7JU. The Church Commissioners, www.archibishopofcanterbury.org. Mainline stn and tube: Waterloo. Tube: Westminster, Lambeth North &

Vauxhall, all about 10 mins walk. Buses: 3, C10, 76, 77, 77a, 344. Entry to garden on Lambeth Palace Rd (not at gatehouse). Home-made teas. Adm £3, chd £1, concessions £2 (share to Lambeth Palace Garden). Sat 26 May (2-5.30). Also open Museum of Garden History.
Lambeth Palace garden is one of the oldest and largest private gardens in London. Site occupied by Archbishops of Canterbury since end C12. Formal courtyards with historic white fig (originally planted 1555). Parkland-style garden with mature trees, woodland and native planting, pond, hornbeam allée. Also formal rose terrace, summer gravel border, herb garden and beehives. Gravel paths, but level.

12 LANSDOWNE ROAD, W11
W11 3LW. The Lady Amabel Lindsay. Turn N off Holland Park Ave nr Holland Park stn or W off Ladbroke Grove halfway along. Buses: 12, 88, GL 711, 715. Bus stop & tube: Holland Park, 4 mins. Adm £2.50, chd free. Wed 16 May (2-6).
Medium-sized fairly wild garden; borders, climbing roses, shrubs; mulberry tree 200yrs old.

46 LINCOLN ROAD
Northwood Hills HA6 1LD. Philip Simpson & Sharon Foster, 01923 450639. 10 mins walk from Northwood Hills tube stn in Joel St (B472), turn into Norwich Rd, then 3rd turning on R. Light refreshments & teas. Adm £2, chd free. Sun 10 June (1-5.30). Evening Opening £3.50, wine, Fri 15 June (6-9). Visitors also welcome by appt.
95 x 25ft suburban garden containing a diverse range of plants and many features, planted mainly for foliage effect. Herbaceous border, 2 small ponds and other water features. Over 30 acers and 200+ hostas in 2 pergola areas. Woodland area with summerhouse.

LITTLE HOUSE A, NW3
16A Maresfield Gardens, Hampstead NW3 5SU. Linda & Stephen Williams. 5 mins walk Swiss Cottage or Finchley Rd tube. Off Fitzjohn's Ave and 2 doors away from Freud Museum (signed). Light refreshments & teas. Adm £2.50, chd free. Sun 20 May (2-6).
1920s Arts & Crafts house (not open)

built by Danish artist Arild Rosenkrantz. Newly created (2002) award-winning front and rear garden set out formally with water features, stream and sculpture. Unusual shrubs and perennials, many rare, incl Paeonia rockii and Dicksonia fibrosa. Wide collections of hellebores, hostas, toad lilies, acers, clematis and astrantia. Featured in 'Evening Standard'.

LITTLE LODGE
Thames Ditton KT7 0BX. Mr & Mrs P Hickman. 2m SW of Kingston. Mainline stn Thames Ditton 5 mins. A3 from London; after Hook underpass turn L to Esher; at Scilly Isles turn R towards Kingston; after 2nd railway bridge turn L to Thames Ditton village; house opp library after Giggs Hill Green. Adm £2.50, chd free (share to Cancer Research UK). Sun 27 May (11.30-5.30); Wed 6 June (2.30-6) & (6-8.30) Evening Opening £3.50, wine.
Partly walled informal flower garden filled with shrubs and herbaceous plants that create an atmosphere of peace. Small secret garden; terracotta pots; stone troughs and sinks; roses; clematis; topiary; very productive parterre vegetable garden.

NEW LONDON WILDLIFE TRUST, SE15
Centre for Wildlife Gardening, 28 Marsden Road, Peckham SE15 4EE, 020 7252 9186, www.wildlondon.org.uk. Stn: East Dulwich, 10 mins walk. Behind Goose Green, between Ondine & Oglander Rds. Light refreshments & teas. Adm £2, chd free (share to London Wildlife Trust). Open Tues, Weds, Thurs & Suns 10.30-4.30, closed 2 weeks Christmas. For NGS: Sun 20 May (12.30-4.30).
Inspirational community wildlife garden. Hedges, ponds and meadows complement beds brimmimg with herbs, cottage garden plants and wild flowers. Yr-round interest. Organic vegetable beds, wild flower nursery and tree scheme, beehives. Visitor Centre with wildlife gardening displays and advice, workshops and children's craft activities. Picnic and family areas. Environmental games. Raffle. Green Pennant Award.

LOWER CLAPTON GARDENS, E5

E5 0RL. *Tubes: Bethnal Green, then bus 106, 254, or Manor House, then bus 253, 254, alight Lower Clapton Rd.* Teas at 58 Rushmore Rd. **Combined adm £3, chd free. Sun 3 June (2-6).** Lower Clapton is an area of Victorian villas on a river terrace stretching down to the R Lea. A varied group of gardens each reflecting their owner's taste and providing tranquillity in an otherwise hectic area of E London.

8 ALMACK ROAD

Mr Philip Lightowlers
Long walled garden in 2 rooms: the first has a yellow and blue theme, with grass, shrubs and water feature; the second a sunny pink garden with brick paths and secluded seating area.

58 RUSHMORE ROAD

Annie Moloney, 07989 803196, anniemoloney58@yahoo.co.uk. *If driving, entry to Rushmore Rd via Atherdon or Millfields Rd only.* **Visitors also welcome by appt.** Garden on two levels: lower level 2 x 3 metres, lots of pots and wall fountain; upper level 3 x 4 metres reached by spiral staircase. Many subtropical plants, tree fern, oleander and many climbers.

LYNDHURST SQUARE GARDENS, SE15

SE15 5AR. *Stn: Peckham Rye (reduced service on Suns), 5 mins walk NW. Buses: 36 from Oval tube or 171 from Waterloo. Free parking in Lyndhurst Square.* Home-made teas & wine. **Combined adm £4, chd free (share to Terrence Higgins Trust). Sun 24 June (2-5.30).** Two charming and unusual gardens in this early Victorian Gothic garden square in the heart of Southwark.

3 LYNDHURST SQUARE

Mr Stephen Haines
Sophisticated cottage garden approx 80ft x 50ft. Old roses, herbaceous borders, many climbers on house and in garden, sunken garden with fountain and container planting, surrounded by mature trees. Beautiful old-fashioned greenhouse. Steep area to side of house, no guard rails. Please take care, especially wheelchairs.

NEW 5 LYNDHURST SQUARE

Martin Lawlor & Paul Ward
90ft x 50ft secret garden in the heart of London offering a mix of traditional and unusual herbaceous plants and shrubs. The design combines Italianate and Gothic themes and offers a secluded green vista.

MALVERN TERRACE GARDENS, N1

N1 1HR. *Approach from S via Pentonville Rd into Penton St, then into Barnsbury Rd. From N via Thornhill Rd opp Albion PH. Tube: Angel, Highbury & Islington. Buses: 19, 30 to Upper St, Town Hall.* Home-made teas. **Combined adm £2.50, chd free. Sun 29 Apr (2-5.30).** Group of unique 1830s London terrace houses built on the site of Thomas Oldfield's dairy and cricket field. Cottage-style gardens in cobbled cul-de-sac. Music and plant stall.

209 MASSINGBERD WAY, SW17

Elizabeth & Patrick Palmer-Cafferkey. *Tube: Tooting Bec, then buses 249, 319 to Doctor Johnson Ave. Broad brick path diagonally to Church Lane, then 100yds to L. Car park by bus stop, alternatively Birchwood Rd.* Home-made teas. **Adm £2, chd 50p (share to Sightsavers). Sun 29 Apr (2-6).** 21ft x 25ft garden of newly-built house. Planned by owner 4yrs ago around mature listed crab apple. Entirely blue and white for a sense of distance and space. All plants acquired cheaply and small (and already jostling for room!) incl rarities eg from Australia/NZ.

47 MAYNARD ROAD, E17

Walthamstow E17 9JE. Don Mapp, 020 8520 1565, don.mapp@gmail.com. *10 mins walk from Walthamstow (central stn). Bus to Tesco on Lea Bridge Rd then walk through Barclay Path or bus W12 to Addison Rd. Turn R to Beulah Path.* Home-made teas. **Adm £2, chd free. Suns 22, 29 July (11-6). Visitors also welcome by appt July & Aug only.** Plant collector's paradise. An eclectic mix of exotic plants in a 40ft x 16ft space, entered via a densely planted front garden. Display of botanical watercolours by local artist Helen Pettifer.

Flowing curves and unique planting create a magical, peaceful space . . . architectural gate doubles as a swing . . .

NEW 6 METHUEN PARK, N10

Muswell Hill N10 2JS. Yulia Badian, yulia@gardenshrink.com. *Tube: Highgate. Buses: 43, 134 to Muswell Hill Broadway, 3rd on L off Dukes Ave.* Home-made teas. **Adm £2.50, chd free. Sun 1 July (2-5.30) & Evening opening (7-11) £5, incl wine & nibbles. Sun 16 Sept (2-6.30). Visitors also welcome by appt, max 6 visitors.** Contemporary garden designed by Chelsea medal-winning designer for her family. Flowing curves and unique planting mingle a magical, peaceful space. Fruit trees, perennials and grasses mingle happily with large-leaved tropical plants such as *Hedychium gardnerianum, Musa basjoo* and oleander. Architectural gate doubles as a swing; path around raspberry hedge leads to a tree house. Evening lights & sound installation.

41 MILL HILL ROAD, W3

Acton W3 8JE. Marcia Hurst. *Tube: Acton Town, turn R, Mill Hill Rd 3rd on R.* Home-made teas. **Adm £2.50, chd free (share to Microloan Foundation). Sun 15 July (2-6). Also open 136 Avenue Rd.** 120ft x 40ft garden. Hot gravel garden with unusual plants. Lawn with herbaceous border and lavender hedge. Raised terrace with topiary. Owner compulsive plantaholic.

2 MILLFIELD PLACE, N6

N6 6JP, 020 8348 6487, daisydogone@aol.com. *Off Highgate West Hill, E side of Hampstead Heath. Buses: C2, C11 or 214 to Parliament Hill Fields.* Home-made teas (Sun only). **Adm £2.50, family ticket £5. Sun 13 May (2-6). Evening Opening £3.50,** wine & light refreshments Wed 20 June (5.30-9). Also open Sun 13 May **Southwood Lodge.** Visitors also welcome by appt May & June.
1½-acre spring and summer garden with camellias, rhododendrons, many flowering shrubs and unusual plants. Spring bulbs, herbaceous borders, small orchard, spacious lawns.

  ⅙ ⊁ ☕

Subtropical suburban oasis, designed to defy global warming . . .

19 MONTANA ROAD, SW17

SW17 8SN. Nigel Buckie, 020 8682 9300, box@objectarchitecture.co.uk. *Tube: Tooting Bec.* Home-made teas. **Adm £2, chd free. Suns 24 June; 26 Aug (1-5.30).** Also open Sun 26 Aug **28 Multon Rd.** Visitors also welcome by appt.
Architect's exotic garden. Palms, bananas, ferns, agaves, cacti and exotic colour from gingers, cannas and eucomis. There are two seating areas, one with rill water feature, the other among herbs and kitchen garden.

⊁ ☕

MULBERRY HOUSE, SE21

37a Alleyn Park SE21 8AT. Mr & Mrs A Bingham. *1m S of Dulwich Village. Off A205 (S Circular Rd) by Dulwich College playing fields. Continue under railway bridge bearing L. Garden opp Dulwich College Prep School.* **Adm £2, chd free. Sun 29 Apr (2-5).**
Large family garden surrounded by mature trees. New planting scheme by Iris Lynch commenced 2004, development ongoing. Formal terrace with pond and semi-formal planting. Steps to lawn and herbaceous borders. Pond with wildlife. Parterre with mulberry, bay, apple and plum trees, vines and roses. Front garden redesigned in 2006.

⊁ ⊛ ☕

NEW 28 MULTON ROAD, SW18

SW18 3LH. Victoria & Craig Orr. *Mainline: 10mins walk from Earlsfield or Wandsworth Common. Bus: 219 & 319 along Trinity Rd.* **Adm £2, chd free. Sun 26 Aug (2-6).** Also open **19 Montana Rd.**
70ft x 40ft subtropical suburban oasis, designed to defy the depredations of global warming, garden pests and kids without recourse to carbon emissions, chemicals or cranial damage. Contemporary in concept, but not minimalist, planting incl phormium, loquat, fig, cordyline, canna, tree fern, astelia, yucca and grasses. Spectacular golden-stemmed bamboo in front garden. Innovative features incl Arundo donax (Spanish reed) as screen for trampoline. Lots of seating, and goldfish pond. Featured in 'The Independent'.

⊁ ☕

◆ MUSEUM OF GARDEN HISTORY, SE1

Lambeth Palace Road SE1 7LB, 020 7401 8865, www.museumgardenhistory.org. *Bus: 507 Red Arrow from Victoria or Waterloo mainline & tube stns (C10 only on Sundays); alight Lambeth Palace. Tube: Lambeth North, Vauxhall, Waterloo.* **Adm £3, chd free,** concessions £2.50 (share to Museum of Garden History). Daily, not 2 week Christmas period. For NGS: Sat 26 May (10.30-5). Also open **Lambeth Palace.**
Historic tools, information displays, changing exhibitions, shop and café housed in former church of St-Mary-at-Lambeth. Reproduction C17 knot garden with period plants, topiary and box hedging.

  ⅙ ⊁ ⊛ ☕

◆ MYDDELTON HOUSE GARDENS

Bulls Cross, Enfield EN2 9HG. Lee Valley Regional Park Authority, 01992 702200, www.leevalleypark.org.uk. *2m N of Enfield. J25 (A10) off M25 S towards Enfield. 1st T-lights R into Bullsmoor Lane, L at end along Bulls Cross. E slip rds at J25 closed till late 2007, exit at J26 if coming from E.* Light refreshments & teas on NGS days. **Adm £2.50, chd /concessions £1.90 (prices may alter). Mon to Fri, Apr to**

Sept (10-4.30), Oct to Mar (10-3); Suns Easter to end Oct (12-4). For NGS: Suns 25 Feb; 29 Apr; 27 May; 24 Feb 2008.
4 acres of gardens created by E A Bowles. Gardens feature diverse and unusual plants incl National Collection of award-winning bearded irises. Large pond with terrace, conservatory and interesting historical artefacts. A garden for all seasons. Dedicated wheelchair route.

  ⅙ ⊁ ⊛ NCCPG ☕

◆ NATURAL HISTORY MUSEUM WILDLIFE GARDEN, SW7

Cromwell Road SW7 5BD, 020 7942 5011, www.nhm.ac.uk/wildlife-garden. *5 mins walk from S Kensington tube stn.* Light refreshments & teas. **Adm £2, chd free.** For NGS: Suns 22 Apr; 20 May (2-5).
Garden designed and created in 1995 to show examples of typical habitats found in lowland Britain, incl deciduous woodland, meadow, chalk downland, fen and heathland. Areas linked by meandering paths and three ponds provide a central focus. Despite its central London location the garden has already attracted an impressive and varied amount of wildlife, which is being monitored by museum staff and volunteers. Meet the scientists and learn about some of the garden's wildlife. First prize Brighter Kensington & Chelsea Scheme, Wildlife Garden.

  ⅙ ⊁ ⊛ ☕

263 NETHER STREET, N3

N3 1PD. Judy & Malcolm Wiseman. *Turn L from W Finchley tube. House is on the L, 2mins along the rd. Parking in roads off Nether St. House is directly facing Penstemon Close.* Home-made teas. **Adm £2.50, chd £1. Suns 3, 10 June (2.30-5.30).** Also open 3 June **71 Fallowcourt Ave.**
Sculptor's garden, designed as an outdoor gallery. Toes, noses and hands peep out unexpectedly between smaller plants whilst lush, dramatic foliage acts as a backdrop to the sculpture. A garden to delight and stimulate visitors, incorporating art, horticulture and a certain amount of irreverent fun and frivolity. Introduced into this deliberately non floriferous garden are new works incl cement paintings, furniture, sounds and strange airs.

⊁ ☕

Toes, noses and hands peep out unexpectedly . . .

5 NEW ROAD, N8

Crouch End N8 8TA. **The Misses S & M West**, 020 8340 8149. *Bus: W7 Muswell Hill to Finsbury Park or W5. Alight Wolsey Rd. New Rd is cul-de-sac. Some parking rear of Health Centre, better parking Middle Lane or Park Rd.* **Donations welcome.** Visitors welcome by appt.
Traditional country garden 60ft x 24ft in heart of Crouch End, evolved over 50yrs. Small prizewinning front garden adjoins colourful conservatory leading to back garden planted for yr-round interest. Many unusual and borderline tender plants - abutilons, streptocarpus, achimenes, crinum. Fruit trees, ornamental shrubs and trees, small pond, lawn and productive greenhouse create a delightful experience of cherished nostalgia.

15 NORCOTT ROAD, N16

N16 7BJ. **Amanda & John Welch.** *Buses: 67, 73, 76, 149, 243. Clapton & Rectory Rd mainline stns. One way system - by car approach from Brooke Rd which crosses Norcott Rd, garden in S half.* Home-made teas. **Adm £2, chd free (share to SENSE). Sun 20 May (2-6).**
Largish (for Hackney) walled back garden developed by present owners over 27yrs, with pond, long-established fruit trees, abundantly planted with a great variety of herbaceous plants, especially perennial geraniums and campanulas, day lilies, flag and other irises.

NORTH HOUSE, SE21

93 Dulwich Village SE21 7BJ. **Vivian Bazalgette & Katharine St John-Brooks.** *Dulwich Village next to Oddbins, 8 mins straight walk from N Dulwich stn or 10 mins from W Dulwich stn via Belair Park. Bus P4.* Light refreshments & teas. **Adm £2, chd free (share to Dulwich Helpline). Sun 10 June (2-5). Also open Dulwich Gardens & 174 Peckham Rye.**
²/₃-acre mature garden with lawns, trees, climbing roses and flowerbeds, unusual shape, pleasant borrowed landscape. Gravel at front of property.

95 NORTH ROAD

Kew TW9 4HQ. **Michael le Fleming & Colin Chenery.** *50yds S of Kew Gardens stn on its E down-line side. Exit in North Rd.* Home-made teas (2-7). **Adm £2, chd free. Day & Evening Opening** wine, **Sun 15 July (11-7).**
This old-fashioned garden is designed to disguise its basic plot and to conceal nearby buildings. It winds through mixed planting and foliage contrasts with summer hot spots of reds and golds, but has hidden corners of peace and shade. A stone terrace, pond, conservatory, pots and urns complete an eclectic scene. Bric-a-brac stall.

19 OAKHILL ROAD

Orpington BR6 0AE. **Theresa Ansett & John Mangold.** *3m SE of Bromley. J4 M25 take A224 signed Orpington. From Orpington town centre, S on High St to war memorial roundabout, R onto Station Rd, then R on The Approach, L at top, Oakhill Rd 1st on R.* Home-made teas. **Adm £2, chd free (share to Harris HospisCare). Sun 1 July (1-5).**
Dramatic, modern, low maintenance front garden. SW-facing rear plot (110ft x 30ft) divided by trellis, arches and pergola into 4 main areas. Deep borders, densely planted with shrubs and herbaceous for yr-round interest. Secluded deck with water feature and pots leading to pebble-surrounded wildlife pond and fruit garden.

Traditional country garden in the heart of Crouch End . . .

94 OAKWOOD ROAD, NW11

NW11 6RN. **Michael Franklin.** *Hampstead Garden Suburb. Tube: Golders Green. Bus: H2 to Northway.* Home-made teas. **Adm £2.50, chd free. Sun 6 May (2-5.30).**
Large garden divided into 2 rooms by box hedging and an arch. Lawns, woodland with apple and pear blossom, old wisteria, tree peonies, beds filled with colour and foliage.

NEW OLD COURT, SW20

Almer Road, Wimbledon SW20 0EN. **Maggie & Earl Guitar.** *Last house on R in Almer Rd, off Copse Hill. Park in Drax Ave. Mainline: Raynes Park 15-20 mins walk. Buses: 57 & 200 to end of Copse Hill.* Home-made teas. **Adm £2.50, chd free. Sun 10 June (2-5).**
Interesting mature trees and water are major features in this large Lutyens-style garden, designed by Robin Williams. The design compartmentalises the garden to take advantage of the varying changes in ground levels, whilst creating the best possible views along the axes of the more important windows and doors. Wheelchair access to terrace only.

28 OLD DEVONSHIRE ROAD, SW12

SW12 9RB. **Georgina Ivor.** *Tube and mainline: Balham, 5 mins walk.* Cream teas. **Adm £2, chd 50p (share to Trinity Hospice). Sun 17 June (2-5.30). Evening Opening £3,** Pimms, **Wed 20 June (6-8.30). Also open 17 June only Eatonville Road Gardens & 68 Wandle Rd.**
Drought-tolerant plants thrive in the sun-drenched front garden. A pear tree dominates the secluded 45ft x 20ft rear garden, with curving lawn surrounded by planting for yr-round interest. A eucalyptus tree and solanum crispum add height, while a balustraded wooden balcony creates another level for herbs and tender climbers. 2nd place Best Blooming Front Gardens, Wandsworth in Bloom.

ORCHARD COTTAGE

See Kent.

ORMELEY LODGE

Ham Gate Avenue, Richmond TW10 5HB. **Lady Annabel Goldsmith.** *From Richmond Park, exit at Ham Gate into Ham Gate Ave. 1st house on R. From Richmond A307, 1¹/₂m past New Inn on R, 1st turning on L. House is last on L. Bus: 65.* **Adm £3, chd £1. Sun 17 June (3-6). Also open Petersham House.**
Large walled garden in delightful rural setting on Ham Common. Wide herbaceous borders and box hedges. Walk through to orchard with wild flowers. Vegetable garden, knot garden, aviary. Trellised tennis court with roses and climbers.

THE PAGODA, SE3

Pagoda Gardens SE3 0UZ. Caroline & Philip Cooper. *Blackheath mainline. Lewisham mainline/DLR 10 mins walk.* **Evening Opening £3.50** (share to Cystic Fibrosis), wine, Fri 15 June (6-9). Also open **12 Eliot Vale & 28 Granville Park.**

$1/2$-acre historic garden surrounding historic house, Jekyll-Jungle. Variety of gardens - terraced formal with 60ft rill; informal water garden with stream; lush subtropical planting; white garden, orientally-inspired pergola and details.

Three gardens: wildlife, contemporary and cottage garden all within easy walking distance . . .

3 THE PARK, N6

N6 4EU. Mr & Mrs G Schrager, 020 8348 3314, bunty1@blueyonder.co.uk. *3 mins from Highgate tube, up Southwood Lane. The Park is 1st on R. Buses: 43, 134, 143, 263.* Home-made teas. **Adm £2, chd £1** (share to St Mary's Hospital Kidney Patients' Assn). Sun 29 Apr (2-5). Also open **5 St Regis Close.** Visitors also welcome by appt at any time.

Large garden with pond and frogs, fruit trees and eclectic planting. Interesting plants for sale.

174 PECKHAM RYE, SE22

SE22 9QA. Mr & Mrs Ian Bland. *Overlooks Peckham Rye Common from Dulwich side. Reached by alley to side of house.* Home-made teas. **Adm £2, chd free** (share to St Christopher's Hospice). Sun 10 June (2.30-5.30). Also open **Dulwich Gardens & North Road.**

100ft x 30ft rear garden originally designed by Judith Sharpe. Easy-care and child-friendly, the garden is frequently changed but always displays a wide variety of contrasting foliage and yr-round interest. Best in early June when pink and blue flowers predominate, especially in new woodland and semi-shade borders.

PEMBRIDGE COTTAGE

10 Strawberry Hill Road, Twickenham TW1 4PT. Ian & Lydia Sidaway, 020 8287 8993, iansidaway@blueyonder.co.uk. *1m from Twickenham town centre. Close to Strawberry Hill mainline stn.* Light refreshments, teas & wine. **Adm £2, chd free.** Suns 17, 24 June (2-6). Visitors also welcome by appt.

140ft x 20ft constantly evolving artist's garden with studio building. Divided into several brick, gravel and wooden seating areas. Strong evergreen shrub structure providing yr-round interest. Many thin Italian cypress, maples, trimmed and shaped box, lonicera, lavender, santolina, laurels and viburnum. Euphorbias, bamboo, herbs, ferns and gunnera. A packed garden influenced by Mediterranean, Japanese and N European styles.

PENGE GARDENS, SE20

SE20 7QG. *1m from Beckenham or Crystal Palace. 6 mins walk from Penge East, Anerley & Kent House stns, and Ave Road Tramlink stop. Buses 75, 157, 176, 194, 197, 227, 249, 342, 354, 356, and 358.* Home-made teas at Stodart Rd 26 May & Kenilworth Rd 26, 27 May. **Combined adm £4, individual gdns £2 each,** chd free (share to St Christopher's Hospice). Sat 26, Sun 27 May (2-5).

3 gardens: wildlife garden, contemporary garden and cottage garden all within easy walking distance, nr junction A213 & A234.

9 HOWARD ROAD

Marc Carlton & Nigel Lees, 020 8659 5674, www.foxleas.com. Visitors also welcome by appt Apr 1 to July 31.

40ft x 120ft suburban garden. Organic and wildlife friendly, designed to incorporate many native species, but without sacrificing aesthetic standards. Wetland areas, nectar border and wild bee house. Information sheets available about many aspects of gardening for wildlife. Featured in 'Gardens Illustrated'.

26 KENILWORTH ROAD

Mhairi & Simon Clutson, 020 8402 9035, mhairi@grozone.co.uk. *5 mins walk from Kent House mainline stn. Buses: 176, 194, 227, 312, & 358.*

Visitors also welcome by appt May, June & July only.

Small contemporary garden on 2 levels, designed in 1995 to be easily maintained and have a strong Mediterranean theme. Circular paved and gravelled area planted with many rare Mediterranean native shrubs, perennials and bulbs. Bold architectural planting provides all-yr interest.

26 STODART ROAD

Anerley. Les Miller & Elizabeth Queen. Not open 27 May.

Small sloping town garden on different levels. Mature shrubs and trees provide green oasis. Rose arches, clematis, honeysuckle and tiny pond. Shady area with ferns, hellebores and symphytum. A cottage garden in an urban environment. Winner Penge in Bloom, planter display & hanging baskets.

2A PENN ROAD, N7

N7 9RD. Mr & Mrs P Garvey. *Tube: Caledonian Rd. Turn L out of stn and go N up Caledonian Rd for approx 700yds. Penn Rd on LH-side. Buses: 17, 91, 259 along Caledonian Rd; 29, 253 to nearby Nags Head.* Home-made teas. **Adm £2, chd free.** Sun 10 June (2-6). Also open **1a & 62 Hungerford Rd.**

100ft x 30ft walled garden; long, shady, side entrance border; small seaside-themed front garden. Huge variety of plants in well stocked borders. Over 60 containers. Greenhouse and small vegetable plot. Mature trees create secluded feel close to busy urban thoroughfares. Winner Islington in Bloom, Best Front Garden.

PENSHURST PLACE

See Kent.

PETERSHAM HOUSE

Petersham TW10 7AA. Francesco & Gael Boglione. *Stn: Richmond, then 65 bus to Dysart PH. Entry to garden off Petersham Rd, through nursery.* Home-made teas. **Adm £3, chd free.** Sun 17 June (12-4.30). Also open **Ormeley Lodge.**

Broad lawn with large topiary, generously planted double borders. Productive vegetable garden with chickens.

101 PITT CRESCENT, SW19

SW19 8HR. Karen Grosch. *Tube: Wimbledon Park 10 mins walk. Bus: 156 along Durnsford Rd. Limited parking in Pitt Crescent.* Light refreshments & teas. **Adm £2, chd free. Sun 3 June (2-6). Also open 97 Arthur Rd & 13 Cambridge Rd.**
Small terraced town garden of 100ft x 25ft, cleverly planted with shrubs and ornamental trees on different levels. Soft colours of grey, green and variegated plants. Pebbled patio leads up to vine-covered pergola, in turn leading to enclosed fruit and vegetable garden edged with roses and clematis, with apple and plum arbour, greenhouse, formal raised beds. Featured in 'Homes & Gardens' & GGG. Wheelchair access to bottom terrace only.

Transformation from railway cottage backyard to plant lover's richly planted secluded courtyard garden . . .

13 QUEEN ELIZABETH'S WALK, N16

N16 5UZ. Lucy Sommers, 020 8800 3163, lucy.sommers@dsl.pipex.com. *From Manor House tube go S down Green Lanes, then 2nd left off Lordship Park.* Light refreshments. **Adm £2.50, chd free. Suns 6 May; 5 Aug (2-5). Visitors also welcome by appt, groups of 10+.**
Plantsperson's 30m x 7m garden for all seasons with emphasis on foliage, textures and unusual plants from China, Australia and central America in both sunny and shady areas. Interest for children without encroaching on the plants or design, and with fairly minimal maintenance. Overhead rainwater irrigation system. Drought-tolerant plants, succulents, bromeliads, leonotis. Quirky front garden leaf sculpture fence.

---

14 RADLET AVENUE, SE26

SE26 4BZ. Chester Marsh. *Stn: Forest Hill. At end of cul-de-sac off Thorpewood Ave. Easy parking.* Light refreshments, teas & wine. **Evening Opening £3.50, wine, Sat 21 July (6-8).**
Unusual and evolving garden on several levels with many semi-tropical plants and rare trees providing an overhead canopy and a feeling of jungle. Some more open spaces with drought-resistant plants and water features. Steep paths lead to more surprises. An excitingly different garden in this part of London. Some steep and narrow paths. Not suitable for very young children or pushchairs.

RAILWAY COTTAGES, N22

Alexandra Palace N22 7SN. *Tube: Wood Green, 10 mins walk. Stn: Alexandra Palace, 3 mins. Buses: W3, 184, 3 mins. Free parking in Bridge Rd, Buckingham Rd, Palace Gates Rd, Station Rd.* Home-made teas at 2 Dorset Road. **Combined adm £3.50, chd free. Sun 8 July (2-6).**
Front gardens of a row of railway cottages and 2 railway cottage back gardens.

15 BRIDGE ROAD

Sherry Zeffert, 020 8881 9904, www.gardenguru.biz. Visitors also welcome by appt.
Magical transformation from railway cottage backyard to plant lover's richly planted secluded courtyard garden. Circular island bed surrounded by gravel paths and densely planted borders. Profusion of perennials, over 40 climbers and large collection of species clematis. Raised terrace packed with specimen camellias, bamboos, grasses, ferns, evergreen irises and figs. Plant list available. Inspirational use of limited space. Featured in 'Evening Standard'. Steep steps, not suitable for small children or elderly.

2 DORSET ROAD

Jane Stevens
Tranquil country-style back garden full of interest. Topiary and clipped box contrasts with climbing roses, jasmine and honeysuckle. Long mixed hedge and pond. Mulberry,

---

quince, fig and apple trees. Mixed borders with shrubs, herbaceous and annuals chosen for scent and colour. Containers and pots provide all-yr interest and colour.

14 DORSET ROAD

Cathy Brogan
Front garden of railway cottage with mixed planting, herbs, flowers, amelanchier and aromatic hedge. Emphasis on sustainability and organic methods.

22 DORSET ROAD

Mike & Noreen Ainger
Small but interesting front garden incl jasmine, flax, fig, fuchsia, vines and climbing rose.

62 RATTRAY ROAD, SW2

SW2 1BD. Elspeth Thompson. *5-10 mins walk from Brixton tube or mainline.* Home-made teas. **Adm £2, chd free, concessions £1.50. Sun 3 June (2-6). Also open 61 Barnwell Rd.**
Garden writer's small front and back town gardens. Drought-tolerant front garden with silver and mauve plantings. Back garden 20ft x 20ft approx, incl decking and metal grille on several levels, designed to incorporate access from house on ground and basement floors. Bold planting in wide shady bed and custom-built planters, and up trellis on walls. Mirrors, lights, containers. Signed copies of owner's books for sale. Featured in 'Sunday Telegraph'. Wheelchair access to main level of garden.

13 REDBRIDGE LANE WEST, E11

E11 2JX. Kathy Taylor, 020 8989 8310, kathy@kathytaylordesigns.co.uk. *2 mins drive from Redbridge roundabout at N Circular/A12/M11 junction (off M11 link road towards Leytonstone). Tube: Wanstead, 5 mins walk.* **Adm £3, chd free. Visitors welcome by appt spring, early/mid July & autumn best times, for groups of 10+.**
Designed by Chelsea medal winner, 14 x 6.5 metres, 2-roomed garden created 5yrs ago, gardened with a minimum of chemicals. S-facing end comprises decking, gravel, wildlife pond with bog area and mixed planting for a sunny aspect. The N-facing end has raised beds with plants for sun and semi-shade. Featured in 'Ideal Home' & BBC 'Gardeners' World'.

REGENTS COLLEGE'S GARDEN, NW1

Inner Circle, Regents Park
NW1 4NS. *Located at the junction of York Bridge & the Inner Circle. Baker St tube 5 mins walk. Buses: 13, 18, 27, 30, 74, 82, 113, 139, 159, 274. Enter main gate or garden gate adjacent to footbridge at Clarence Gate.* **Adm £2, chd /concessions £1. Sat 2 June (11-5).**
Described as a Secret Garden, this former Botanic Garden has been sympathetically developed so as to retain its intrinsic charm and relaxed, naturalistic atmosphere. Garden areas flow together and host a diverse selection of plants. Also the new subtropical 'folly' garden, tea garden and oriental room are essential viewing.
& ⊕ ☕

Sheltered by groves of bamboo, bananas and palms . . .

◆ **ROOTS AND SHOOTS, SE11**
Walnut Tree Walk SE11 6DN.
Trustees of Roots and Shoots, 020 7587 1131, www.rootsandshoots.org.uk. *Tube: Lambeth North. Buses: 3, 59,159. Just off Kennington Rd, 5 mins from Imperial War Museum. No car parking on site. Pedestrian entrance through small open space on Fitzalan St. Light refreshments & teas.* **Adm £2, concessions £1, chd free. Mon to Fri all yr (9-4), also Sats May & June (10-2). For NGS: Sat 16, Sun 17 June (11-4). Evening Opening** £3, wine, Weds 4 July (6.30-8.30).
$1/2$-acre wildlife garden run by innovative charity providing training and garden advice. Summer meadow, observation beehives, 2 large ponds, hot borders, Mediterranean mound, old roses and echiums. New for this yr: learning centre with photovoltaic roof, solar heating, rainwater catchment, three planted roofs, one brown roof. Study room. Producers' Fair Sun 10 June with exhibitions, local organic produce and crafts. Children's art/drama activities. New shop with Fairtrade and organic goods and London honey.
& ⋊ ⊕ ☕

167 ROSENDALE ROAD, SE21

West Dulwich SE21 8LW. Mr & Mrs A Pizzoferro, 020 8766 7846. *At junction of Rosendale & Lovelace Rds. Stns: Tulse Hill, West Dulwich. Home-made teas.* **Adm £2, chd free (share to London Children's Flower Society). Suns 15 Apr (2-5); 3 June (2-6). Also open 3 June 24 Chestnut Rd.** Visitors also welcome by appt.
Back garden 100ft long with stream (which runs naturally in winter), through small woodland area. Bog garden and wildlife pond bordered by timber deck. Central shingle and cobble circle surrounded by generous mixed borders. Collections of hostas, acers and pittosporums in pots in alleyway. Front garden has a hotter colour theme with range of euphorbias.
⋊ ⊕ ☕

NEW ROYAL COLLEGE OF PHYSICIANS GARDEN, NW1
11 St Andrew's Place, Outer Circle, Regents Park NW1 4LE. *Tube: Great Portland St, turn L along Marylebone Rd for 100yds, R to Outer Circle, 150yds on R.* **Adm £3, chd free. Sats, Suns 28, 29 Apr; 9, 10 June (1-5). Also open 28, 29 Apr The Holme.**
Garden replanted in 2005/06 to display plants used in conventional and herbal medicines around the world and in past centuries, and plants with historical links to physicians associated with the College. The plants are labelled and arranged by continent. Featured in 'The Garden' & 'Camden New Journal'.
&

7 ST GEORGE'S ROAD
St Margaret's, Twickenham
TW1 1QS. Mr & Mrs R Raworth, 020 8892 3713, jenny@jraworth.freeserve.co.uk, www.raworthgarden.com. *$1^1/_2$m SW of Richmond. Off A316 between Twickenham Bridge & St Margaret's roundabout. Home-made teas.* **Adm £3, chd 50p. Sun 3 June (11-5). Visitors also welcome by appt May & June for groups of 12+.**
Exuberant displays of old English roses and vigorous climbers with unusual herbaceous perennials. Massed scented crambe cordifolia. Pond with bridge converted into child-safe lush bog garden. Large N-facing luxuriant conservatory with rare plants and

climbers. Pelargoniums a speciality. Sunken garden and knot garden. Featured on BBC TV Gardeners' World.
⋊ ⊕ ☕

NEW ST HELENA TERRACE
Richmond TW9 1NR. *Tube & mainline stn: Richmond, then 5 mins walk via Richmond Green to Friars Lane towards river, just beyond car park.* **Evening Opening,** wine, Sat 2 June (6-8). **Combined adm £4, chd free.**
Two small secret artists' studio gardens.

NEW 1 ST HELENA TERRACE
Christina Gascoigne, 020 8940 3894, cgascoigne@britishlibrary.net. **Visitors also welcome by appt, not suitable for coaches.**
Walled secret garden with water. Limited wheelchair access.
&

NEW 3 ST HELENA TERRACE
Raphael & Marillyn Maklouf
Profusion of plants, pots and imaginative water design. Roses and climbing plants in abundance. Original use of limited space.
⋊

NEW 27 ST JAMES AVENUE, W13
Ealing W13 9DL. Andrew & Julie Brixey-Williams. *7m from Central London. Uxbridge Rd (A206) to West Ealing; Leeland Terrace leads to St James Ave.* **Adm £3, chd free. Suns 17 June; 2, 9 Sept (2-5.30).**
Designed by leading exotic designer Jason Payne, our garden takes advantage of London's astonishing microclimate to create an evocation of far-away landscapes. Sheltered by groves of bamboo, bananas and palms, and divided by a full-width butterfly-shaped pond, the garden features many Antipodean and Asian rarities, incl a wide variety of grevillea.
☕

ST MICHAEL'S CONVENT
56 Ham Common, Richmond
TW10 7JH. Community of the Sisters of the Church. *2m S of Richmond. From Richmond or Kingston, A307, turn onto the common*

at the Xrds nr New Inn, 100yds on the R adjacent to Martingales Close. Mainline trains to Richmond & Kingston also tube to Richmond, then bus 65 from either to Ham Common. **Adm £3, chd free (share to Church Extension Assn). Sat 2 June (11-4).** 4-acre organic garden comprises walled vegetable garden, orchards, vine house, ancient mulberry tree, extensive borders, meditation and Bible gardens.

57 ST QUINTIN AVENUE, W10
W10 6NZ. Mr H Groffman, 020 8969 8292. 1m from Ladbroke Grove or White City tube. Buses: 7 & 70 from Ladbroke Grove stn; 220 from White City, all to North Pole Rd. Light refreshments & teas. **Adm £2.50, chd £1.50. Suns 15, 29 July (2-7). Also open 29 July 29 Addison Ave. Visitors also welcome by appt July only, groups of any size.** 30ft x 40ft walled garden; wide selection of plant material. Patio; unusual shrubs for foliage effects; hanging baskets; special features and focal points. Special floral display to celebrate HM The Queen's Diamond Wedding anniversary. Exhibition featuring highlights of the garden's history, incl photos, letters, newspaper/magazine articles and awards achieved. Prizewinner Kensington Gardeners' Club & London Gardens Society.

5 ST REGIS CLOSE, N10
Alexandra Park Road N10 2DE. Ms S Bennett & Mr E Hyde, 020 8883 8540. 2nd L in Alexandra Park Rd from Colney Hatch Lane. Tube: Bounds Green or E Finchley then bus 102 or 299. Alight at St Andrew's Church on Windermere Rd. Bus: 43 or 134 to Alexandra Park Rd. Home-made teas. **Adm £2.50, chd free. Suns 29 Apr; 24 June; 22 July (2-7). Also open 29 Apr 3 The Park & 24 June 5 Cecil Rd. Visitors also welcome by appt.** Unique artists' garden renowned for colourful architectural features created on site, incl Baroque temple, pagodas, turquoise raku-tiled mirrored oriental enclosure concealing plant nursery. American Gothic garden shed alongside new compost heap with medieval pretensions. Maureen Lipman's favourite garden - humour and trompe-l'oeil combine with wildlife-friendly carp ponds, waterfalls, lawns, abundant borders and imaginative container planting to create an

inspirational restoring experience. Open ceramics studio. Featured on BBC2 Digging Deep.

Octagonal lawn is surrounded by deep herbaceous beds with lilac and cloud-pruned ceanothus . . .

NEW 22 SCUTARI ROAD, SE22
East Dulwich SE22 0NN. Sue Hillwood-Harris & David Hardy, 020 8693 3710, david.hardy04@btinternet.com. S side of Peckham Rye Park. B238 Peckham Rye/Forest Hill Rd, turn into Colyton Rd (opp Herne Tavern). 3rd on R. Bus: 63. Stn: East Dulwich. Home-made teas. **Adm £2.50, chd free. Sun 20 May (2-6). Visitors also welcome by appt.** Our pretty new garden, created from really boring scratch 3 yrs ago, is still work in progress, but already has cottagey area, water, trees and multitudinous shrubs. Distinct probability of chickens (new-laid eggs for NGS funds). Tea and cakes will be of same memorable standard as at our former Yellow Book address.

SHORT LOTS ALLOTMENTS
Watcombe Cottages, Kew TW9 3HA. Short Lots Users' Group. NE side of Kew Green. Mainline: Kew Bridge. Tube: Kew Gardens. Buses: 65, 391. Entrance from Watcombe Cottages off Kew Green by Kew pond, or from towpath. Home-made teas at St Anne's Church, Kew Green. **Adm £2.50, chd free. Sun 15 July (2-5).** Long-established, tree-fringed allotment site of 50 plots of different shapes and sizes, tucked away between Bushwood Rd and riverbank. Wide variety of fruit, flowers and vegetables. Partial wheelchair access, main path only.

7 SIBELLA ROAD, SW4
SW4 6JA. Mrs Jane Landon. From Clapham High Rd, take Gauden Rd. 2nd R into Bromfelde Rd, Sibella Rd on L. From Wandsworth Rd, take Albion Ave, continue over Larkhill Rise into Sibella Rd. Tube: Clapham North less than 10 mins walk. **Adm £2, chd free. Sun 29 Apr (3-7), Evening Opening £3.50, wine, Wed 25 Apr (6-8). Also open 18 Sibella Rd.** Long NW-facing garden with contrasting areas and country feel. Central specimen maple tree surrounded by lawn and mixed herbaceous borders. Shady areas nr house with woodland planting, tiarellas, pulmonaria, tulips and other spring bulbs. Far beds with new planting designed to overcome some of the problems of heat and drought. Featured in 'The Times'.

18 SIBELLA ROAD, SW4
SW4 6HX. Judith & Michael Strong. Directions, see 7 Sibella Rd. **Adm £2, chd free. Sun 29 Apr (3-6). Evening Opening £3.50, wine, Wed 25 Apr (6-8). Also open 7 Sibella Rd.** Small walled garden where the formal layout is softened by colour-themed planting. Mediterranean-inspired patio and miniature woodland area under old bramley. The tiny octagonal lawn is surrounded by deep herbaceous beds with lilac and cloud-pruned ceanothus adding height. Different varieties of dicentras, hostas, ferns, foxgloves and white alliums frame the terrace, roses and clematis (over 25 varieties) climb the walls and festoon the trees. In spring bulbs and flowering shrubs combine with colourful emerging foliage. Featured in 'The English Garden'.

60A SOUTH CROXTED ROAD, SE21
SE21 8BD. Anthony & Grainne Tuite, 07958 921264, anthonytuite@fsmail.net. Mainline: West Dulwich. No 3 bus alight S Croxted Rd 1st stop after junction with Park Hall Rd. Entry by side gate. Home-made teas. **Adm £2.50, chd free. Sun 24 June (2-6). Visitors also welcome by appt.** 80ft x 28ft garden divided into 5 areas with decked walkway linking both ends of garden. Shaped lawn with mixed herbaceous borders, grasses, specimen trees in variety of large containers; water features, large

mosaic salamander and handmade metalworks. 1st Prize winner London Garden Society competition (large back garden). Featured in 'The Times' & '4 Homes'.

SOUTH END ROAD GARDENS, NW3

NW3 2RJ. *Tube: Hampstead, then walk down Hampstead High St, L into Downshire Hill, South End Rd gardens facing Freemason's Arms PH.* **Evening Opening £4.50, chd free, wine, Sun 10 June (6-8).** Part of historic Hampstead opposite the Heath.

95 SOUTH END ROAD
Ms Deborah Moggach
Profusely planted cottage front garden. Back garden with ponds and hens.

97 SOUTH END ROAD
Dr Edward Brett
Small cottage garden. Small Italianate back garden.

101 SOUTH END ROAD
Mr & Mrs Paul Lindsay, 020 7435 5926. Visitors also welcome by appt April & May, no groups.
Country garden in London. Long cottage borders lead to house. Back garden is romantic, arbours and pergolas covered in roses and clematis; ponds and fountains; fruit trees, shrubs, perennials and mirrors. Camden Gardens Award.

SOUTH LONDON BOTANICAL INSTITUTE, SE24
323 Norwood Road SE24 9AQ, www.slbi.org.uk. *Mainline stn: Tulse Hill. Buses: 68, 196, 322 & 468 stop at junction of Norwood & Romola Rds.* Home-made teas. **Adm £2, chd free** (share to South London Botanical Institute). **Sun 17 June (2-5). Also open 79 Holmdene Ave.**
London's smallest botanic garden, formally laid out with paved paths. Densely planted with over 500 labelled species and many rare and interesting plants of worldwide origin incl medicinal, carnivorous, British plants and ferns. Exhibition of botanical paintings. Featured in 'The English Garden'.

NEW 41 SOUTHBROOK ROAD, SE12
Blackheath SE12 8LJ. Barbara & Marek Polanski. *Off Sth Circular at Burnt Ash Rd. Mainline stns: Lee & Hither Green, both 10 mins walk.* Home-made teas. **Adm £2.50, chd free. Sun 24 June (2-5.30). Also open 47 Winn Rd.**
Large suburban garden in rural setting. Formal paving and pond to the rear divided from the main garden by a parterre with climbing roses and arbours. Large lawn with deep herbaceous borders. Sunny terrace close to house.

SOUTHSIDE HOUSE, SW19
3-4 Woodhayes Road, Wimbledon Common SW19 4RJ. Pennington Mellor Munthe Charity Trust, www.southsidehouse.com. *1m W of Wimbledon Village. House at junction of Cannizaro, Southside and Woodhayes Rds.* **Adm £2.50 (garden only), chd free. Suns 6, 13 May (11-5).**
Romantic country garden extending to almost 2 acres. Mature trees and hedges and a long informal canal form the structure of this unique and amusing garden. 2 grottos, 2 temples, pet cemetery, young orchard and wild flower meadow. Many of the smaller plantings are being gradually renovated. Lovely swathes of bluebells and small fernery. House open for guided tours Sats, Suns, Weds, from Easter Sat to 30 Sept. Closed Wimbledon tennis fortnight.

SOUTHWOOD LODGE, N6
33 Kingsley Place N6 5EA. Mr & Mrs C Whittington, 020 8348 2785. *Tube: Highgate, 4 mins walk Highgate Village. Off Southwood Lane. Buses: 143, 210, 214, 271.* **Adm £2.50, chd free. Sun 13 May (2-5.30). Also open 2 Millfield Place. Visitors also welcome by appt Apr to early July only.**
Secret garden hidden behind C18 house (not open), laid out last century on steeply sloping site, now densely planted with wide variety of shrubs, climbers and perennials. Pond, waterfall, frogs and newts. Some recent and conspicuous deaths have prompted replanting of several areas. Many unusual plants are grown and propagated for sale. Paths & steps may be slippery when wet.

SPRINGFIELD LODGE, SW15
348 Upper Richmond Road SW15 6TL. Mrs J K Lucien-Scholle & Robert Scholle. Home-made teas. **Adm £3, chd free. Sun 10 June (2-5.30).**
One of the houses built for Admiral Nelson's Captains. Mature country garden with herbaceous borders, roses, clematis, hostas and climbers. Specimen mulberry tree over 140yrs old, 80yr-old espaliered fruit trees. Fishponds, tree house with grapevines, conservatory, small vegetable garden. Chickens in coop converted from original garden keeper's house. Large terrace and seating areas with swings for relaxing.

NEW STANLEY CRESCENT GARDEN, W11
Notting Hill W11 2NA. The Trustees. *Tube: Holland Park. Entrance in Kensington Park Gardens, adjacent to 1 Stanley Crescent.* **Adm £2, chd free. Sun 29 Apr (2-5).**
2¹/₂-acre communal garden in Notting Hill, part of the Ladbroke Estate, much of which was designed and built by Thomas Allom in the 1850s. Regarded by many as one of the least altered squares in the area, it has been described as a plantsman's garden.

NEW STONE (ZEN) GARDEN, W3
55 Carbery Avenue, Acton W3 9AB. Three Wheels Buddhist Centre, www.threewheels.org. *Tube: Acton Town 5 mins walk, 200yds off A406.* Japanese green tea & sweets. **Adm £2, chd free. Sats, Suns 5, 6, 19, 20 May (11-4).**
Pure Japanese Zen garden (so no flowers) with twelve large and small rocks of various colours and textures set in islands of moss and surrounded by a sea of grey granite gravel raked in a stylised wave pattern. Garden surrounded by trees and bushes outside a cob wall. Oak-framed wattle and daub shelter with Norfolk reed thatched roof. Learn about the principles and symbolism of the garden and take part in a formal Japanese tea ceremony.

4 STRADBROKE GROVE
Buckhurst Hill IG9 5PD. Mr & Mrs Brighten, 020 8505 2716, carol@cbrighten.fsnet.co.uk. *Between Epping & Woodford, 5m from M25 J26.Tube: Buckhurst Hill, turn R cross rd to Stradbroke Grove.* **Adm £2. Visitors welcome by appt.** Secluded garden, designed to enhance its sloping aspect. Steps wind downwards to thickly planted pergola, leading to rose-screened vegetable and fruit garden. Central gravelled area with an unusual mix of grasses, shells, pots and succulents.

Theatrical and elegant formal town garden gradually dissolves into informal woodland . . .

NEW SUMMERLAWN
29 Astons Road, Moor Park, Northwood HA6 2LB. Frankie & Leslie Lipton. Cream teas & light refreshments. **Adm £3, chd free. Suns 13 May; 12 Aug (2-6).** Approx ³/₄ acre laid out in 3 rooms: herbaceous, formal and orchard, each with water feature. House and garden set within Conservation Area with fine views. Paths leading to 6 terraces with seating areas, gazebo and summerhouse. Wildlife-friendly garden for all seasons. Guide dogs allowed. Unprotected ponds.

TEWKESBURY LODGE GARDEN GROUP, SE23
Forest Hill SE23 3QD. *Off S Circular (A205) behind Horniman Museum & Gardens. Stn: Forest Hill, 10 mins walk. Buses 176, 185, 312, P4.* Home-made teas at 53 Ringmore Rise. **Combined adm £4, chd free (share to Marsha Phoenix Trust & St Christopher's Hospice). Evening Opening £5, wine, Sat 26 May (6-9). Sun 27 May (2-6).** A group of very different gardens with spectacular views. Open studio at The Coach House.

THE COACH HOUSE
3 The Hermitage. Pat Rae Sculptor's mature courtyard and roof garden, crammed full of unusual plants and sculptures. Water features, wildlife interest, vegetables and decorative plants in containers large and small, many of which have been fired in the artist's kiln and are for sale.

27 HORNIMAN DRIVE
Rose Agnew Small, low maintenance, N-facing front garden with shrubs creating tapestry of green. Evolving back garden with emphasis on colour harmony using perennials, roses and shrubs. Vegetable areas, greenhouse, views over S London and N Downs.

53 RINGMORE RISE
Valerie Ward Corner plot with spectacular views over London. Front garden inspired by Beth Chatto's dry garden, with stunning borders in soft mauves, yellows and white. Rear garden on three levels. Themed beds, some shaded, others sunny. Large pond; patio with pergola. Sloping garden with some steps.

30 WESTWOOD PARK
Jackie McLaren Garden designer's sloping creation, herb garden, water features, winding paths with modern elements, unusual plant combinations. Unusual pots and hanging baskets link patio and garden. Steep slopes, regret no pushchairs.

64 THORNHILL ROAD, E10
E10 5LL. Mr P Minter & Mr M Weldon. *Off Oliver Rd, nr Leyton Orient football ground. Leyton tube 10 mins walk.* Home-made teas. **Adm £3, chd free. Suns 20 May; 3 June (2-6).** Theatrical and elegant formal town garden gradually dissolves into informal woodland in this most unexpected 165ft x 30ft plot. With a host of devoted regular visitors this deeply atmospheric and well-designed garden is packed with architectural and botanical interest and would well repay the effort of a longer journey. NEW in 2007: a long-awaited 14ft lily pond replaces one of the lawns.

TUDOR ROAD GARDENS
Hampton TW12 2NG, 020 8941 3315, contact Ms Rita Armfield, 45 Tudor Road, TW12 2NG, email rita-armfield@artistdesign.fsnet.co.uk. *3m W of Kingston. Bus: R70 from Twickenham & Richmond to Tudor Ave, Hampton. Buses: 111, 216 to Hampton mainline stn. Tudor Rd 7 mins walk.* Home-made teas. **Combined adm £5, chd free (share to British Heart Foundation). Tickets available at 45 Tudor Road only. Sat 19, Sun 20 May (2-7). Visitors also welcome by appt 21-26 May only, for groups of 10+.** Three neighbouring gardens in leafy W London suburb.

43 TUDOR ROAD
Annie & Duncan Macpherson Subdivided garden with numerous pots and many established azaleas and rhododendrons. A raised area with gravel path, shrubs and cottage garden plants leads to a sunken lawn, surrounded by ferns. Grasses and woodland setting.

45 TUDOR ROAD
Rita & Colin Armfield Surprising W-facing garden (140ft x 25ft). Chinese side entrance gate - wall mural painted by owner/artist Rita Armfield. Raised terrace with seating and many planted pots, citrus, fig, palms etc. Spring shrubs and trees divide the garden into rooms. York stone path gently curves past pond and waterfall, greenhouse and herbaceous planting through to bamboos, ferns and raised woodland area. Small art exhibition and interesting workshop. Featured in 'Woman's Weekly'.

88 TUDOR ROAD
Alexandra & Barrington Skinner Pretty 130ft x 20ft Edwardian-style garden. Old climbing Noisette rose covered arbour, weeping cherry tree and fish pond. Lawns surrounded by mixed plantings. Small vegetable patch with selected produce. Plenty of seating for those relaxing summer evenings. Natural areas with logs and nettles for wildlife. Hobbies studio.

NEW 78 TUFNELL PARK ROAD, N7

N7 0DT. Chris Cook & Liz de Keller. *Tube: Tufnell Park, approx ³/₄ way down Tufnell Park Rd, opp church.* **Adm £2, chd free. Sun 10 June (2-4.30). Nearby gardens also open. See diary section.**
Charming N-facing town garden designed as a series of small paved terraces dividing peaceful sitting areas. Large climbing roses frame the garden, and strong colours are used sparingly to contrast with a range of softer tones. Small wildlife pond.

NEW 208 WALM LANE, FLAT 1, NW2

NW2 3BP. Miranda Hands & Chris Mason. *Tube: Kilburn. Garden at junction of Exeter Rd & Walm Lane. Buses: 16, 32, 189, 226, 245, 260, 266, 316 to Cricklewood Broadway, then consult A-Z.* Home-made teas. **Adm £2.50, chd free. Sun 10 June (2-6.30). Evening Opening £3.50, wine & light refreshments, Wed 25 July (5-9).**
Large S-facing oasis of green with big sky. Meandering lawn with island beds, fishpond with fountain, curved and deeply planted borders of perennials and flowering shrubs. Shaded mini woodland area of tall trees underplanted with rhododendrons, ferns and hostas with winding path through oriental-inspired summerhouse to secluded circular seating area.

WALTHAM FOREST REGISTER OFFICE, E17

106 Grove Road, Walthamstow E11 2RS. Garden Curator, Teresa Farnham, 020 8530 6729, farnhamz@yahoo.co.uk. *On corner of Grove Rd & Fraser Rd. Bus to Lea Bridge Rd, Bakers Arms & 5 mins walk up Fraser Rd.* Home-made teas. **Adm £1, chd free. Mon 7 May (11-4). Visitors also welcome by appt.**
Front and rear gardens of former Victorian vicarage in Walthamstow, created using cuttings as well as plants from seed to survive drought and shallow soil, and plants that look after themselves until they are pruned! Walkway, planted with roses and passion flowers, leads to honeysuckle and clematis arbour. Mixed borders and recently planted oak. Good to visit for low maintenance ideas for yr-round

cover. Chemical-free. Hedgehogs, frogs and many bird species use the garden as it has matured over the past 10yrs. Quiet area for contemplation. Demonstration of propagation from cuttings, which may be available for visitors.

NEW 340 WALTON ROAD

West Molesey KT8 2JD. Anita Newman & Garry Wilson. *1¹/₂m W of Hampton Court. Mainline stn: Hampton Court. Buses: 216, 411 alight Lord Hotham PH, ¹/₂ min walk.* Home-made teas. **Adm £2, chd free. Sun 10 June (2-6). Evening Opening £3, wine & light refreshments, Sun 5 Aug (6-9.30).**
Long, narrow SW-facing garden, 25metres x 5metres, featuring Mediterranean patio with pergola, water feature, variety of climbers and containers, creating intimate dining areas, leading down onto lawned garden cleverly designed to maximise space. Incl covered seating area, shrubs, trees, climbers, fig tree, lavenders and arum lilies, all forming calm, green oasis.

NEW 68 WANDLE ROAD, SW17

SW17 7DW. Tris & Richard Williams. *Tube: Tooting Bec. Buses: 219 & 319 along Trinity Rd.* Light refreshments, cream teas & wine. **Adm £2, chd free. Sun 17 June (10-6). Also open Eatonville Road Gardens & 28 Old Devonshire Rd.**
Predominantly informal, mature English country garden with subtle infusion of both exotic and Mediterranean designs. Laid to lawn and borders of shrubs, climbers and herbaceous, incl wisterias, choisya, euphorbias, lavenders, delphiniums, agapanthus, roses and garden art. Established pond set in tropical 'den' of exotic planting; bamboos, tree ferns and cannas leading to Mediterranean courtyard. Wildlife friendly. Step from patio to lawn, ramp available.

THE WATERGARDENS

Warren Road, Kingston-upon-Thames KT2 7LF. The Residents' Association. *1m E of Kingston. From Kingston take A308 (Kingston Hill) towards London; after about ¹/₂m turn R into Warren Rd.* **Adm £3, chd £1. Suns 13 May; 14 Oct (2-4.30).**
Japanese landscaped garden originally part of Coombe Wood Nursery, approx 9 acres with water cascade features. Some steep slopes and steps.

2 WESTERN LANE, SW12

SW12 8JS. Mrs Anne Birnhak, annebirnhak@castlebalham.fsnet. co.uk. *Tube: Clapham South or Balham. Wandsworth Common mainline stn. Please park in Nightingale Lane.* **Adm £2. Suns 13 May; 22 July (3-4.30). Visitors also welcome by appt, groups of 10+.**
Enchanting patio garden, 28ft x 22ft, crammed with 2000 different plants. Walkways offer views of the spectacular clematis collection (250 varieties). Stunning wooden pergola, thundering waterfall, metal parasols and containers stacked in tiers. Anne's insatiable appetite for collecting rare plants gives visitors the opportunity to enjoy a constantly changing display. Featured on BBC Gardeners' World. No access for wheelchairs, prams or bicycles.

WHITTON CRC

1 Britannia Lane, off Constance Road, Whitton TW2 7JX. London Borough of Richmond. *3m W of Richmond. Mainline stn: Whitton. Bus: H22 alight at Whitton stn. No parking in Britannia Lane. Free parking in Constance Rd & surrounding streets.* Light refreshments & teas. **Adm £2, chd free. Wed 30 May (11-3).**
Narrow 180ft organic garden maintained by staff and people with learning disabilities whose day centre occupies the remainder of the site. The cottage-style planting has produced a mass of colour and scent with a lavender and fuchsia bed, mixed borders, butterfly garden, wildlife pond and raised bed of shrubs and roses.

English country garden with exotic and Mediterranean designs . . .

86 WILLIFIELD WAY, NW11
Hampstead Garden Suburb
NW11 6YJ. Diane Berger. *Tube: Golders Green, then H2 bus to Willifield Way.* Home-made teas. **Adm £2, chd free. Sun 22 July (2-5). Also open 157 Hampstead Way.**
Award-winning cottage garden with lots of interest and variety. Terrace pond area; pergola with roses & clematis; deck; hot border; herbaceous bed; lots of interesting perennials, trees & shrubs. A plantsman's delight. 1st in Hampstead Horticultral Society Medium Garden Competition.

47 WINN ROAD, SE12
Lee SE12 9EY. Mr & Mrs G Smith. *8m SE Central London. 15 mins walk from Lee or Grove Park stns from Charing Cross. By car A20 Sidcup bypass or A205 S Circular.* Home-made teas. **Adm £2, chd free (share to The Fifth Trust). Suns 29 Apr; 24 June (2-5). Also open 24 June 41 Southbrook Rd.**
1/3-acre plantsman's mature garden maintained by owners. Mixed borders, alpine beds, fruits and vegetables, three greenhouses with displays of pelargoniums, fuchsias, begonias, cacti and succulents.

27 WOOD VALE, N10
N10 3DJ. Mr & Mrs A W Dallman. *Muswell Hill 1m. A1 to Woodman PH; signed Muswell Hill. From Highgate tube, take Muswell Hill Rd, sharp R into Wood Lane leading to Wood Vale.* Home-made teas. **Adm £2, chd under 12 50p, under 5 free (share to**

Cancer Research UK, Sat & Hornsey Royal British Legion, Sun). **Sat 30 June; Sun 1 July (1.30-6).**
3/4-acre garden, 300ft long, abounding with surprises. Herbaceous borders, shrubbery, pond and a new feature every yr. Once inside you would think you were in the countryside. Seating for over 90 people, with shady areas and delicious home-made teas. Every effort is made to make our visitors welcome.

NEW 33 WOOD VALE, N10
N10 3DJ. Mona Abboud, 020 8883 4955. *Tube: Highgate, 10 mins walk. Buses: W3 & W7 to top of Park Rd.* **Adm £2, chd free. Sun 20 May (2-5). Also open 15 & 46 Dukes Ave. Visitors also welcome by appt May & June only.**
Very long garden entered via steep but safe staircase. Unusual Mediterranean shrubs with emphasis on shapes, textures and foliage colour. Garden on two levels, first more formal with a centrepiece fountain, second meandering.

82 WOOD VALE, SE23
SE23 3ED. Nigel & Linda Fisher. *Off S Circular Rd. Mainline stn: Forest Hill. Buses: 176, 185, 363 & P13. Ample street parking.* Home-made teas. **Adm £2.50, chd free (share to Southwark MIND). Sun 1 July (2-5).**
Large 90ft x 180ft contemporary garden designed by Christopher Bradley-Hole. A jigsaw of perennial and

grass bays with a range of views offering yr-round interest for plantsmen, designers and children. Starred garden in GGG.

66 WOODBOURNE AVENUE, SW16
SW16 1UT. Brian Palmer & Keith Simmonds. *Enter from Garrads Rd by Tooting Bec Common (by car only).* Home-made teas. **Adm £2, chd 50p. Sun 1 July (1-6).**
Garden designer's garden, constantly evolving. Cottage-style front garden 40ft x 60ft containing roses and herbaceous plants with a subtropical twist with bananas and palms. Rear garden approx 40ft x 80ft with recently added features, shrubs, trees and gazebo, creating a tranquil oasis in an urban setting. 12th yr of opening in 2007.

11 WOODLANDS ROAD, SW13
SW13 0JZ. Victor & Lesley West. *Take Vine Rd off Upper Richmond Rd to find Woodlands Rd 2nd L.* Cream teas. **Adm £2, chd 50p. Sun 20 May (12-6).**
Higgledy piggledy planting of trees, shrubs and perennials hides a softly structured garden design. Gentle colour schemes planted for low maintenance throughout the seasons with special emphasis on attracting birds, bees and pondlife, all of which makes for a relaxed town space.

THE WORLD GARDEN AT LULLINGSTONE CASTLE
See Kent.

London County Volunteers

NORFOLK

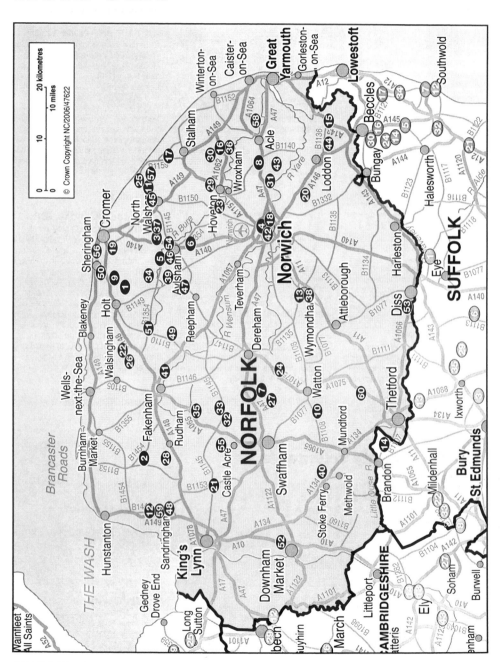

Opening Dates

February

SUNDAY 11
② Bagthorpe Hall
㉜ Lexham Hall

April

SUNDAY 1
⑧ Burlingham Gardens
⑭ Desert World Gardens
㉑ Gayton Hall

SUNDAY 8
(60) Wretham Lodge

MONDAY 9
㊲ The Old Cottage
(60) Wretham Lodge

SATURDAY 21
⑰ East Ruston Old Vicarage

SUNDAY 22
⑦ Bradenham Hall

SUNDAY 29
⑩ Clermont House
⑫ Croft House

May

SUNDAY 6
㉞ Mannington Hall
㊷ The Plantation Garden
(51) Stody Lodge

MONDAY 7
(57) Witton Hall

SUNDAY 13
㊸ Plovers Hill
㊺ Rivermount
(51) Stody Lodge

SUNDAY 20
⑩ Clermont House
㉖ Hindringham Hall
㉚ How Hill Farm
㉜ Lexham Hall
㊿ Sheringham Park
(51) Stody Lodge

SUNDAY 27
㊴ Oulton Hall
(51) Stody Lodge
(58) Woodlands Farm

MONDAY 28
㊲ The Old Cottage
㊹ Raveningham Hall
(51) Stody Lodge

June

SUNDAY 3
⑥ Bolwick Hall
㊱ The Mowle
㊿ Sheringham Park
(51) Stody Lodge

FRIDAY 8
㉙ Hoveton Hall Gardens

SUNDAY 10
① Baconsthorpe Old Rectory
③ Beck House
⑬ 57 Damgate
㊳ Old Sun House

WEDNESDAY 13
㉝ Litcham Hall (Evening)

THURSDAY 14
⑩ Clermont House (Evening)

SUNDAY 17
⑪ The Cottage
⑯ The Dutch House
㉕ Hill Cottage
㉗ Holme Hale Hall
㉟ Manor House Farm
㊵ Oxburgh Hall Garden & Estate
(60) Wretham Lodge

FRIDAY 22
(52) Stow Hall (Evening)

SUNDAY 24
⑲ Felbrigg Hall
㊼ Salle Park

July

SUNDAY 1
⑭ Desert World Gardens
㉓ Heggatt Hall
㉔ High House Gardens
㉘ Houghton Hall Walled Garden
(55) The Wicken

SUNDAY 8
④ Bishop's House
⑤ Blickling Hall

FRIDAY 13
㊶ Pensthorpe Nature Reserve & Gardens (Evening)

SUNDAY 15
③ Beck House
㊲ The Old Cottage
㊵ Oxburgh Hall Garden & Estate
㊻ 10 St Michael's Close
(54) West Lodge

SUNDAY 22
⑦ Bradenham Hall
⑨ Chestnut Farm
㊸ Plovers Hill
(59) Woodwynd

SUNDAY 29
⑳ The Garden in an Orchard

August

SUNDAY 12
⑤ Blickling Hall
㉙ Hoveton Hall Gardens
㊸ Plovers Hill
㊾ Severals Grange

SUNDAY 19
⑱ The Exotic Garden
㉟ Manor House Farm
㊲ The Old Cottage

September

SUNDAY 2
(53) Sundown

SUNDAY 9
⑲ Felbrigg Hall
㊷ The Plantation Garden

SUNDAY 16
㉔ High House Gardens
(58) Woodlands Farm

SATURDAY 22
⑳ The Garden in an Orchard

SUNDAY 23
⑦ Bradenham Hall
⑮ Devils End
⑳ The Garden in an Orchard

SUNDAY 30
㉞ Mannington Hall

October

SATURDAY 6
⑰ East Ruston Old Vicarage

Gardens open to the public

⑤ Blickling Hall
⑦ Bradenham Hall
⑰ East Ruston Old Vicarage
⑱ The Exotic Garden
⑲ Felbrigg Hall
㉘ Houghton Hall Walled Garden
㉙ Hoveton Hall Gardens
㉞ Mannington Hall
㊵ Oxburgh Hall Garden & Estate
㊶ Pensthorpe Nature Reserve & Gardens
㊷ The Plantation Garden
㊹ Raveningham Hall
㊽ Sandringham Gardens
㊾ Severals Grange
㊿ Sheringham Park
(51) Stody Lodge

By appointment only

㉒ Hawthorn House
㉛ Lake House
(56) Withern

The Gardens

① BACONSTHORPE OLD RECTORY
Holt NR25 6LU. Mr & Mrs David McCosh, 01263 577611. *3m SE of Holt. Follow sign to Baconsthorpe from Holt bypass for 3m. Rectory is beside church at far end of village.* Home-made teas. **Adm £3, chd free. Sun 10 June (2-6).** Visitors also welcome by appt and groups, May, June, July & Sept.
Well-established herbaceous borders, interesting shrubs and kitchen garden within framework of old box hedges and walls. Large conservatory and sunken garden. Views of church past mulberry tree and thatched summerhouse. Huge copper beech and ilex dominate S lawn. Decorative outbuildings and yards. Visiting nurseries, plants for sale.
ᄒ ᄒ ⊕ ☕

Collection of mature trees, woodland walks around stream and mill pond . . .

② BAGTHORPE HALL
Bagthorpe PE31 6QY. Mr & Mrs D Morton. *3¹/₂m N of East Rudham, off A148. At King's Lynn take A148 to Fakenham. At East Rudham (approx 12m) turn L by Cat & Fiddle PH. 3¹/₂m into hamlet of Bagthorpe. Farm buildings on L, wood on R, white gates set back at top.* Home-made teas, soup for lunch. **Adm £3, chd free. Sun 11 Feb (11-4).** Snowdrops carpeting woodland walk, snowdrop walk.
ᄒ ⊕ ⊨ ☕

③ BECK HOUSE
Bridge Road, Colby, nr Aylsham NR11 7EA. Hazel & Tony Blackburn, 01263 733167. *14m N of Norwich. Take B1145 from N Walsham to Aylsham, after 3¹/₂m turn R into Bridge Rd opp Banningham Bridge Old Garage, next to school (Colby).* Home-made teas. **Adm £2.50, chd free. Sun 10 June; also open The Old**

Cottage Sun 15 July (11-5). Visitors also welcome by appt.
1¹/₂ acre, packed borders of unusual perennials, shrubs and trees, large natural pond and paths through wild areas with lovely views across the river. S-facing front garden with drought-loving plants; sit and enjoy the tranquil views on the many seats provided. Parents be aware dangers for children: pond and river unfenced, gravel drive.
ᄒ ᄒ ⊕ ☕

④ BISHOP'S HOUSE
Bishopgate, Norwich NR3 1SB. The Bishop of Norwich, www.norwich.anglican.org. *City centre. Entrance opp Law Courts on Bishopgate on N side of Cathedral (not through The Close). Through Archway on R. Public car parking nearby. No parking at Bishop's House.* Home-made teas. **Adm £2.50, chd free. Sun 8 July (2-5).**
4-acre walled garden dating back to C12. Extensive lawns with specimen trees. Borders with many rare and unsual shrubs. Spectacular herbaceous borders flanked by yew hedges. Rose beds, meadow labyrinth, kitchen garden, woodland walk and long border with hostas. New bamboo walk. Popular plant sales area. Some gravel paths.
ᄒ ᄒ ⊕ ☕

⑤ ◆ BLICKLING HALL
Aylsham NR11 6NF. The National Trust, 01263 738030, www.nationaltrust.org.uk/blickling. *15m N of Norwich. 1¹/₂m NW of Aylsham on N side of B1354.* **House and Garden adm £8.50, chd £4.25, Garden only adm £5.50, chd £2.75. Weds to Suns 17 Mar to 28 Oct. For NGS: Suns 8 July; 12 Aug (10.15-5.15).**
Large garden, orangery, crescent lake, azaleas, rhododendrons, herbaceous borders. Historic Jacobean house. 80yds of new double border planted in 2006, in the style of Norah Lindsay. Wheelchairs and batricars available.
ᄒ ᄒ ⊕ ☕

⑥ BOLWICK HALL
Marsham NR10 5PU. Mr & Mrs G C Fisher, 01263 732131, www.bolwick.com. *¹/₂m S of Aylsham. On A140 towards Aylsham, take 1st R past Plough PH at Marsham, then next R onto private rd to front of Hall.* Home-made teas. **Adm £3, chd free. Sun 3 June (1-5).** Visitors also welcome by appt.

Landscaped gardens and park, attributed to Humphry Repton, surrounding late Georgian hall (not open) and stable block. Collection of mature trees, woodland walks around stream and mill pond, as well as more recently planted borders and working vegetable garden. Partial wheelchair access.
ᄒ ᄒ ⊕ ☕

⑦ ◆ BRADENHAM HALL
Bradenham IP25 7QP. Chris & Panda Allhusen, 01362 687243/687279, info@bradenhamhall.co.uk. *6m E of Swaffham. 5m W of East Dereham off A47. Turn S signed Wendling & Longham. 1m turn S signed Bradenham, 2m.* **Garden only adm £4, chd free. 2nd & 4th Suns Apr to Sept. For NGS: Suns 22 Apr; 22 July; 23 Sept (2-5.30).**
A garden for all seasons. Flower gardens, formally designed and richly planted, formal rose gardens, paved garden, unusual climbers, herbaceous and shrub borders, traditional kitchen gardens with 2 glasshouses. Arboretum of over 800 different trees, all labelled. Massed daffodils in spring. A delight and an education.
ᄒ ᄒ ⊕ ☕

⑧ BURLINGHAM GARDENS
31 Main Road, North Burlingham NR13 4TA. Ms Linda Laxton, 01603 716615, linda@wildflowers.co.uk. *7m E of Norwich. Off A47 signed North Burlingham, onto slip rd, near far end on L into grounds of British Wild Flower Plants.* Home-made teas. **Adm £2.50, chd free. Sun 1 Apr (10-3.30).** Visitors also welcome by appt.
The National Collection of Forsythia. 70 species and varieties, the majority in flower, incl dwarf, semi dwarf and larger varieties, over 300 planted in a walk and beds in lovely surroundings. Wild flower nursery (open), incl preview of plants grown for a garden at this years Chelsea Flower Show. Plants for sale, nursery open. Norfolk Wildlife trust holding activities for adults and children, incl environmental awareness walks and childrens competition.
ᄒ ⊕ NCCPG ☕

⑨ CHESTNUT FARM
West Beckham NR25 6NX. Mr & Mrs John McNeil Wilson, 01263 822241. *2¹/₂m S of Sheringham. Mid-way between Holt & Cromer. 1m S off the A148 at the Sheringham Park entrance. Sign post indicates 'By Rd to*

W Beckham'. Chestnut Farm located behind the village sign. Lots of free parking, WC. Light refreshments & teas. **Adm £3, chd free. Sun 22 July (11-5). Visitors also welcome by appt, Apr to Aug, coaches permitted.**
3-acre garden, incl herbaceous border, woodland walk, traditional kitchen garden, pond and small aboretum. Plant collection built up over 40yrs by keen gardener and plant enthusiast, which incl many rare and unusual trees and shrubs surrounding C16 farmhouse (not open). Garden Art by Judith Campbell. Featured on Radio Norfolk. Dogs on leads.

⑩ CLERMONT HOUSE
Little Cressingham IP25 6LY. Mr & Mrs John Davies,
www.clermonthousegarden.com.
3m SW of Watton. From Watton, take B1108 towards Lt Cressingham. Turn L off B1108 at Lt Cressingham. Entrance $^1/_2$ m on L. Home-made teas. **Adm £3, chd free. Sun 29 Apr; Sun 20 May (2-5). Evening Opening Thur 14 June (6.30-8.30) with Tour by Garden Owner (6.45).**
Established since 1984, approx 13 acres lawns, woodland garden, developing arboretum, formal walled garden, lake and turf labyrinth inspired by visit to Chartres in 2003. Several woodland walks, many flowering shrubs, daffodils, narcissus and spring flowering bulbs. Collections of Acer, Malus, Crataegus, Aesculus, Betula, Sorbus, Quercus and many other specimens. Managed to maximise its wildlife. Featured in EDP - Norfolk Magazine. Some gravel paths and steep slope to pond.

⑪ THE COTTAGE
Hennesseys Loke, Edingthorpe Green NR28 9SS. Tim & Mary Richardson. 2$^1/_2$ m NE of North Walsham. Off B1150 halfway between Bacton and North Walsham, turn L at village sign and follow signs to car park and cottage. Home-made teas at Hill Cottage. **Adm £2.50, chd free (share to Diane Fossey Gorilla Fund). Sun 17 June (11-5). Open with Hill Cottage.**
$^1/_2$-acre garden with 4 ponds, bog areas, densely planted with reeds, bamboos and gunneras. Roses, clematis and shrubs all jostle for space giving the garden a lush and relaxed atmosphere. A haven for wildlife and all creatures are respected. No chemicals

for over 30yrs within the garden. 3 summerhouses provide tranquil and restive settings. Featured in EDP Norfolk Magazine. Partial wheelchair access, unfenced ponds.

⑫ CROFT HOUSE
111 Manor Road, Dersingham PE31 6YW. Walter & Jane Blaney.
8m NE of King's Lynn. Take A149 N from King's Lynn then B1440 into Dersingham. At T-lights turn R into Chapel Rd. In $^1/_2$ m bear R into Manor Rd. Croft House opp church car park. Park in adjacent rds & church hall car park. Cream teas in adjacent Church hall with parking. **Adm £3, chd free. Sun 29 Apr (2-5).**
An evolving garden designed with hidden areas of special interest. Paths meander through shrubberies, mature woodlands and around ponds, leading to formal gardens and orchard. Patios around the house incl formal pond, gravel mosaic and statuary. Springtime brings a riot of colour, continuing through to autumn.

⑬ NEW 57 DAMGATE
Wymondham NR18 0BG. Mary Lewis Coe. Passing Wymondham Cross, L into car park. Walk from top of car park bearing R into Chandlers Hill. Balloons will be seen. Home-made teas at Old Sun House. **Combined with Old Sun House adm £4, chd free. Sun 10 June (11-5).**
A path winds through my small garden, but my love of plants is huge! I grow ferns, climbers an herbaceous assortment. There are pots for less hardy souls, grasses and shrubs. Alpine sinks, tiny pond and lovely medlar tree. Some pieces of garden ornaments by owner.

⑭ DESERT WORLD GARDENS
Santon Downham IP27 0TU. Mr & Mrs Barry Gayton, 01842 765861.
4m N of Thetford. On B1107 Brandon 2m. Light refreshments & teas. **Adm £2.50, chd free. Suns 1 Apr; 1 July (1-5). Visitors also welcome by appt.**
1$^1/_4$ acres plantsman's garden, specialising in tropical and arid plants, hardy succulents - sempervivums, hanging gardens of babylon (plectranthus). Main garden - bamboos, herbaceous primula theatre, spring/summer bulbs, particularly lilies. View from roof garden, Radio Norfolk gardener. Garden 26yrs old, mostly grown from seed and cuttings, maintained by Barry, framed by forest. Glasshouses cacti/succulents 12500, viewing by appt only on a different day. Plant identification or any advice given. Can view large garden at place of work - Public Gardens Thetford 3 miles away. In heart of Breckland forest - free.

⑮ NEW DEVILS END
Church Lane, Haddiscoe NR14 6PB. Peter Manthorpe. 7m SW of Gt Yarmouth. Nr junction of A143 & B1136. Park in Haddiscoe Church car park, accessed from B1136. Short walk to garden. Home-made teas in church. **Adm £3.50, chd free. Sun 23 Sept (2-6).**
Romantic, 1-acre enthusiasts garden laid out on S-facing slope with some steep steps. Contains parterre, topiary, woodland walks, pond, potager and colour-themed borders. Many interesting plants incl cyclamen, colchicums, dahlias and asters for autumn colour.

⑯ THE DUTCH HOUSE
Ludham NR29 5NS. Mrs Peter Seymour, 01692 678225. 5m W of Wroxham. B1062 Wroxham to Ludham 7m. Turn R by Ludham village church into Staithe Rd. Gardens $^1/_4$ m

A path winds through my small garden, but my love of plants is huge! I grow ferns, climbers an herbaceous assortment . . .

from village. Home-made teas. **Adm £3, chd free. Sun 17 June (2-5). Visitors also welcome by appt, June only.**
Long, narrow garden of approx 2½ acres leading through marsh and wood to Womack Water. Designed and planted originally by the painter Edward Seago and recently replanted by the present owner. Access to Womack Water limited due to steep bridge and uneven paths. Featured on Radio Norfolk Roy Waller. Wheelchair access possible but difficult, terrace, cobbles and steps.

 点 ᐟ☖ ☕

Long, narrow garden of approx 2½ acres leading through marsh and wood to Womack Water . . .

⑰ ◆ EAST RUSTON OLD VICARAGE
East Ruston NR12 9HN. Alan Gray & Graham Robeson, 01692 650432, www.e-rustonoldvicaragegardens. co.uk. *3m N of Stalham. Turn off A149 onto B1159 signed Bacton, Happisburgh. After 2m turn R 200yds N of East Ruston Church (ignore sign to East Ruston).* **Adm £5, chd £1. Weds, Fris, Sats, Suns & Bank Hol Mons 25 Mar to 27 Oct. For NGS: Sats 21 Apr; 6 Oct (2-5.30).**
20-acre exotic coastal garden incl traditional borders, exotic garden, desert wash, sunk garden, topiary, water features, walled and Mediterranean gardens. Many rare and unusual plants, stunning plant combinations, wild flower meadows, old-fashioned cornfield, vegetable and cutting gardens. Featured in & on many publications & TV.

点 ᐟ☖ ✿ ☕

ELY GARDENS I
See Cambridgeshire.

ELY GARDENS II
See Cambridgeshire.

⑱ ◆ THE EXOTIC GARDEN
126 Thorpe Road, Thorpe, Norwich NR1 1UL. Mr Will Giles, 01603 623167, www.exoticgarden.com. *Off A47. New entrance & car park via side entrance of Alan Boswell Insurance 126 Thorpe Rd next to DEFRA. Approx ½m from Thorpe railway stn.* **Adm £4, chd free. Suns 17 June to 14 Oct. For NGS: Sun 19 Aug (1-5).**
Exotic city garden covering approx 1 acre on a S-facing hillside incl new ½-acre garden. In high summer the garden is a riot of colour among towering architectural plants such as cannas, bananas, aroids, palms etc giving the garden a truly subtropical feel, especially with its use of houseplants as bedding. BBC Radio Norfolk gardener.

ᐟ☖ ✿ ☕

⑲ ◆ FELBRIGG HALL
Cromer NR11 8PR. The National Trust, 01263 837444. *2½m SW of Cromer. S of A148; main entrance from B1436.* Light refreshments & teas. **Adm £3.50, chd £1.50. For NGS: Suns 24 June; 9 Sept (11-5).**
Large pleasure gardens; mainly lawns and shrubs; orangery with camellias; large walled garden restored and restocked as fruit, vegetable, herb and flower garden; vine house; dovecote; dahlias; National Collection of *Colchicum*; wooded parks. 1 electric and 2 manual wheelchairs available.

点 ᐟ☖ NCCPG ☕

⑳ THE GARDEN IN AN ORCHARD
Mill Road, Bergh Apton NR15 1BQ. Mr & Mrs R W Boardman, 01508 480322. *6m SE of Norwich. Off A146 at Hellington Corner signed to Bergh Apton. Down Mill Rd 300yds.* Light refreshments & teas. **Adm £2.50, chd free. Sun 29 July; Sat 22, Sun 23 Sept (11-6). Visitors also welcome by appt.**
3½-acre garden created by the owners set in old orchard. Many rare plants set out in an informal pattern of wandering paths. ½ acre of wild flower meadows, many bamboos, species roses and Michaelmas daisies. 9 species of eucalyptus. A plantsman's garden. Exhibition of Botanical Embroidery. Grass paths may be difficult when wet.

点 ✿ ☕

㉑ GAYTON HALL
Gayton PE32 1PL. The Earl & Countess of Romney, 01553 636259. *6m E of King's Lynn. On B1145; R on*

B1153. R down Back St 1st entrance on L. Home-made teas. **Adm £3, chd free (share to tba). Sun 1 Apr (2-5.30). Visitors also welcome by appt from Apr to Oct, please call.**
20-acre water garden, with over 2m of paths. Lawns, woodland, lakes, streams and bridges. Many unusual trees and shrubs. Spring bulbs and autumn colour. Traditional and waterside borders. Primulas, astilbes, hostas, lysichitums, gunneras and many more. Gravel and grass paths.

点 ☕

㉒ HAWTHORN HOUSE
Hindringham NR21 0PT. Bryony Jacklin, 01328 878441. *18m SW of Cromer. Between Fakenham and Holt, off A148. Take Hindringham Rd at Crawfish PH. Continue 2m to village, past church, 2nd R.* **Adm £2, chd free. Visitors welcome by appt. Teas by arrangement.**
Large 3-acre garden featuring herbaceous borders, island beds, pond and bog, gravel and herb gardens, willow work, traditional kitchen garden, orchard, butterfly garden and wild beds. Gravel paths around house.

点 ᐟ☖ ✿ ☕

㉓ NEW HEGGATT HALL
Horstead. Mr & Mrs Richard Gurney. *6m N of Norwich. Take B1150 North Walsham rd out of Norwich go for N 6m. R at small Xrds signed Heggatt Hall. Turn L at T-junction house 400yds on L.* Home-made teas. **Adm £3.50, chd free. Sun 1 July (2-5).**
Elizabethan house (not open) set in large gardens surrounded by parkland with ancient chestnut trees. Herbaceous border, sunken garden. Walled knot/rose garden leading into kitchen garden with wisteria walk and further flower beds.

☕

㉔ HIGH HOUSE GARDENS
Blackmoor Row, Shipdham IP25 7PU. Mr & Mrs F Nickerson. *6m SW of Dereham. Take the airfield or Cranworth Rd off A1075 in Shipdham. Blackmoor Row is signed.* Home-made teas. **Adm £3, chd free. Suns 1 July (1-5.30); 16 Sept (2-5).**
Large country garden with colour-themed herbaceous borders with extensive range of perennials. Box-edged rose and shrub borders.

Woodland garden, pond and bog area. Small orchard, fruit and vegetable garden. Glasshouse with interesting plants.

25 HILL COTTAGE
School Road, Edingthorpe NR28 9SY. Shirley Gilbert, 01692 403519, shirley@flandershouse.demon.co.uk 3m NE of North Walsham. Off B1150 halfway between North Walsham and Bacton, leave main rd at Edingthorpe Green and continue straight towards Paston for ³/₄m. Cottage on L at top of hill. Parking in adjacent field. Light refreshments & teas. **Adm £2.50, chd free. Sun 17 June (11-5). Open with The Cottage. Visitors also welcome by appt, incl groups.**
Cottage garden, approx ¹/₄ acre, surrounding former farm workers' cottages. Organically cultivated and densely planted with both traditional and unusual varieties of drought resistant climbers, shrubs, perennial and annuals. Fruit, vegetable and herb gardens, greenhouse and pond. A real butterfly and wildlife paradise. Small nursery. Member of Norfolk Cottage Garden Society.

26 NEW HINDRINGHAM HALL
Blacksmiths Lane, Hindringham NR21 0QA. Mrs Tucker. 7m from Holt/Fakenham. Off A148 Thursford, at Crawfish PH signed Hindringham. After village hall L into Holme Lane after the church. Light refreshments & teas at village hall. **Adm £3, chd free, £5 incl tea & scone/coffee & biscuit. Sun 20 May (11-4).**
Moated Tudor house (not open) with water garden alongside stream, large walled working vegetable garden and Victorian nut walk. Formal flower beds within the moat.

27 HOLME HALE HALL
Holme Hale IP25 7ED. Mr & Mrs Simon Broke, 01760 440328, broke@freenet.co.uk. 6m E of Swaffham, 8m W Dereham. Exit A47 King's Lynn/Norwich rd at Necton Garden Centre. Continue through Necton village and Holme Hale village approx 1¹/₂m. At Xrds turn L, Hall

gates on L immed after Low Common Rd. Light refreshments & teas. **Adm £4, chd free. Sun 17 June (2-6). Visitors also welcome by appt, May to Oct.**
Contemporary walled kitchen garden and front garden designed and planted in 2000 by Chelsea award winner Arne Maynard. The garden incorporates herbaceous, trained fruit, vegetables and traditional lean-to greenhouse. The garden is noted for its spring display, incl 3500 late spring tulips and its mid-summer and autumn flowering. Partial wheelchair access.

Moated Tudor house (not open) with water garden alongside stream . . .

28 ◆ HOUGHTON HALL WALLED GARDEN
Houghton PE31 6UE. The Marquess of Cholmondeley, 01485 528569, www.houghtonhall.com. 11m W of Fakenham. Signed from A148 approx halfway between King's Lynn and Fakenham. **House and Garden Adm £8, chd £3, family £20, Garden only Adm £5, chd £2, family £15. Weds, Thurs, Suns & Bank Hol Mons Easter Sun to 30 Sept. For NGS: Sun 1 July (11-5.30).**
5-acre walled garden, divided by clipped yew hedges into 'garden rooms'. Stunning 120yd double herbaceous border, full of colour all summer. Orchid greenhouse, rustic temple. Rose parterre with old and new roses, sunken fountain and statues. Mixed kitchen garden. Wisteria pergola, pleached limes, spring and summer bulbs. Croquet lawn. New contemporary sculpture in the park will be open for Easter. Permanent pieces by Richard Long, James Turrell, (Houghton Skyspace) Stephen Cox and Sol LeWitt.

29 ◆ HOVETON HALL GARDENS
nr Wroxham NR12 8RJ. Mr & Mrs Andrew Buxton, 01603 782798, www.hovetonhallgardens.co.uk. 8m N of Norwich. 1m N of Wroxham Bridge. Off A1151 Stalham Rd - follow brown tourist signs. **Adm £4.50, chd 5-14yrs £2.50 , concessions, wheelchairs & carers £2.50. Easter Sun, Bank Hols Mon, Suns April & Sept; Weds, Thurs, Fris, Suns, Bank Hols Mons May - Aug. For NGS: Fri 8 June; Sun 12 Aug (10.30-5).**
Early C19 house (not open). 15-acre gardens and grounds featuring daffodils, azaleas, rhododendrons and hydrangeas in woodland. Mature, walled herbaceous garden. Water plants, lakeside walk and walled kitchen garden. Woodland and gravel paths.

30 HOW HILL FARM
Ludham NR29 5PG. Mr P D S Boardman. 2m W of Ludham. On A1062; then follow signs to How Hill. Farm garden S of How Hill. **Adm £3, chd free. Sun 20 May (1-5).**
2 pretty gardens around house, 3rd started 1968 leading to 3 acre Broad dug 1978 with views over R Ant and Turf Fen Mill. About 10 acres incl Broad, 4 ponds, site of old Broad with 5ft Tussock sedges, about an acre of indigenous ferns under oak and alder. Paths through rare conifers, rhododendrons, azaleas, ornamental trees, shrubs, bamboos and herbaceous plants. Collection of holly species and varieties. Received prestigious Wolf-Fenton award by Holly Society of America 2005. Some sloping and soft paths.

31 LAKE HOUSE
Postwick Lane, Brundall NR13 5LU. Mr & Mrs Garry Muter, 01603 712933. 5m E of Norwich. On A47; take Brundall turn at roundabout. Turn R into Postwick Lane at T-junction. **Adm £3.50, chd free. Visitors welcome by appt for groups of 10+, coaches permitted.**
2 acres of water gardens set among magnificent trees in steep cleft in river escarpment. Informal flower beds with interesting plants; naturalist's paradise; unsuitable for young children or the infirm. Stout shoes advisable. Beautiful lake - shore restoration. Featured in BBC 'The Flying Gardener'.

32 LEXHAM HALL
nr Litcham PE32 2QJ. Mr & Mrs Neil
Foster. *2m W of Litcham. 6m N of
Swaffham off B1145.* Light
refreshments & teas (Feb), Home-
made teas (May). **Adm £3.50, chd
free. Suns 11 Feb (11-4); 20 May
(2-6).**
Fine C17/18 Hall (not open). Parkland
with lake and river walks. Formal
garden with terraces, yew hedges,
roses and mixed borders. Traditional
kitchen garden with crinkle crankle
wall. 3-acre woodland garden with
azaleas, rhododendrons, spring bulbs,
incl snowdrops and rare trees. Dogs
on leads welcome Feb only. Snowdrop
walk - Feb.
  ৬ ⊁ ⊛ ☕

33 LITCHAM HALL
Litcham PE32 2QQ. Mr & Mrs John
Birkbeck. *From Swaffham take A1065
N for 5m then R to Litcham. House on
L entering village.* Georgian red brick
with stone balls on gateposts. Light
refreshments. **Evening Opening £4,
chd £2, wine, Wed 13 June (5-8).**
Attractive 3-acre garden surrounding
fine C18 listed house (not open).
Italianate formal garden with box
hedges, lavender and antique urns.
Mixed borders, pleasant walks through
wild area with mature trees and
shrubs, small pond and extensive
lawns. Partial wheelchair access.
  ⊨ ☕

34 ♦ MANNINGTON HALL
nr Saxthorpe/Corpusty NR11 7BB.
The Lord & Lady Walpole, 01263
584175,
www.manningtongardens.co.uk.
*18m NW of Norwich. 2m N of
Saxthorpe via B1149 towards Holt. At
Saxthorpe/Corpusty follow sign posts
to Mannington.* **Adm £4, chd free,
concessions £3. Suns May to Sept
(12-5), Weds, Thurs, Fris June to
Aug (11-5). For NGS: Suns 6 May; 30
Sept (2-5).**
20 acres feature shrubs, lake, trees
and roses. History of the Rose display
and period gardens. Borders. Sensory
garden. Extensive countryside walks
and trails. Moated manor house and
Saxon church with C19 follies. Wild
flowers and birds. Featured on BBC TV
'History of the Rose' and 'Gardeners
World'.
  ৬ ⊁ ⊛ ☕

35 MANOR HOUSE FARM
Wellingham PE32 2TH. Robin &
Elisabeth Ellis, 01328 838 227. *7m
from Fakenham, 8m from Swaffham,
¹/₂m off A1065 N of Weasenham.*
Garden is beside the church. Home-
made teas. **Adm £3, chd free. Suns
17 June; 19 Aug (2-6).**
Charming 4-acre garden surrounds an
attractive farmhouse. Many interesting
features. Formal box-edged quadrants
with obelisks. 'Hot Spot' with grasses
and gravel. small arboretum with
specimen trees, pleached lime walk,
vegetable parterre and rose tunnel.
Unusual 'Taj' garden with old-
fashioned roses, tree peonies, lilies and
pond. Small herd of Formosan Sika
deer.
  ⊁ ⊨ ☕

36 THE MOWLE
Staithe Road, Ludham NR29 5NP.
Mrs N N Green, 01692 678213. *5m
W of Wroxham. B1062 Wroxham to
Ludham 7m. Turn R by Ludham village
church into Staithe Rd. Garden ¹/₄m
from village.* Home-made teas. **Adm
£3, chd free. Sun 3 June (1.30-5.30).
Visitors also welcome by appt
anytime, please call first.**
Approx 2¹/₂ acres running down to
marshes. The garden has undergone
major alterations and now incls
Japanese garden and enlarged wildlife
pond with bog garden, other features
to encourage wildlife planned.
  ৬ ⊁ ⊛ ☕

37 THE OLD COTTAGE
Colby Corner, nr Aylsham
NR11 7EB. Judith & Stuart Clarke,
01263 734574,
www.enchantinggardens.co.uk. *14m
N of Norwich. Take B1145 from
Aylsham to N Walsham. After 3¹/₂m
turn L opp Banningham Bridge Inn
Garage onto Bridge Rd. Pass Colby
school on R & continue straight,
following Colby Corner sign. Garden
on the L, parking by the poly tunnel.*
Light refreshments & teas. **Adm £3,
chd free. Mons 9 Apr; 28 May; Suns
15 July; 19 Aug (11-5).** Visitors also
welcome by appt.
Lots of interest throughout the yr, with
plants seen in the garden setting on
sale from 'Enchanting Plants Nursery'
on site. Delicious homemade cakes
and light lunches using Norfolk
produce. Featured in 'The English
Garden' , 'Homes & Gardens' Euro
Edition & 'Amateur Gardening'.
  ৬ ⊁ ⊛ ⊨ ☕

38 NEW OLD SUN HOUSE
Damgate, Wymondham
NR18 0BH. Leonie Woolhouse.
*At T-lights on B1172 at edge of
Wymondham turn to town centre.
Immed turn L, follow main st, 50
metres past market cross, turn L
into car park. From top of car park
down Chandlers Hill turn R then L
into Damgate.* Home-made teas.
**Combined with 57 Damgate
adm £4, chd free. Sun 10 June
(11-5).**
Plantspersons garden, approx
1¹/₃ acre, borders, mature trees,
river frontage, old roses, bog
garden, fruit trees, wild flower
meadow, new mini arboretum.
Hens, shrubs, ferns, interesting
out-buildings. Colour and interest
at all times of yr. Owners artwork
and crafts for sale; % to NGS.
  ৬ ⊁ ☕

39 OULTON HALL
Oulton, Aylsham NR11 6NU. Clare &
Bolton Agnew. *4m W of Aylsham.
From Aylsham take B1354. After 4m
Turn L for Oulton Chapel, Hall is ¹/₂m
on R. From B1149 (Norwich/Holt rd)
take B1354, next R, Hall is ¹/₂m on R.*
Light refreshments & teas. **Adm £3.50,
chd free. Sun 27 May (12-5).** Visitors
also welcome by appt, by written
application.
C18 manor house (not open) and
clocktower set in 6-acre garden with
lake and woodland walks. Chelsea
designer's own garden - herbaceous,
Italian, bog, wild, verdant, sunken and
parterre gardens. All flowing from one
to another but connected by vistas.
Developed over 15yrs with emphasis
on structure, height and texture.
  ৬ ⊁ ⊛ ☕

Unusual
'Taj' garden
with old-
fashioned roses,
tree peonies,
lilies and pond.
Small herd
of Formosan
Sika deer . . .

40 ◆ OXBURGH HALL GARDEN & ESTATE
Oxborough PE33 9PS. The National Trust, 01366 328258. *7m SW of Swaffham. At Oxborough on Stoke Ferry rd.* **Adm £3.50, chd £2. Sats to Weds 25 Mar to 27 Sept 11-5.30; 30 Sept to 29 Oct 11.4.30. For NGS: Suns 17 June; 15 July (11-5).**
Hall and moat surrounded by lawns, fine trees, colourful borders; charming parterre garden of French design. Orchard and vegetable garden. Woodland walks. A garden steward is on duty on open days to lead 4 free tours throughout the day.
 ⅃ ✗ ❀ ☕

quarry. Undergoing restoration by volunteers. Remarkable architectural features incl 60ft Italianate terrace, unique 30ft Gothic fountain, restored rustic bridge and summerhouse. Surrounded by mature trees. Beautifully tranquil atmosphere.
 ⅃ ✗ ❀ ☕

43 PLOVERS HILL
Buckenham Road, Strumpshaw NR13 4NL. Mr & Mrs J E Saunt, 01603 714587, jamessaunt@hotmail.com. *9m E of Norwich. Off A47 at Brundall continuing through to Strumpshaw village. Turn R 300yds past PO, then R at T-junction. Plovers Hill is 1st on R up*

Formal Georgian pleasure gardens with yew topiary, rose gardens, lawns, specimen trees and exotically planted orangery . . .

41 ◆ PENSTHORPE NATURE RESERVE & GARDENS
Fakenham NR21 0LN. Bill & Deb Jordan, 01328 851465, www.pensthorpe.com. *1m E of Fakenham. On A1067 to Norwich.* **Daily Jan-Mar (10-4), Apr-Dec (10-5). For NGS: Evening Opening £3.50, chd £1.75, concessions £2.75, Fri 13 July (4.30-7.30).**
500 acres of unspoilt Wensum Valley, with miles of nature trails winding by 7 beautiful lakes teeming with breeding and migratory waterfowl. 3 magnificent gardens, incl the spectacular Millennium garden by Chelsea double award winner Piet Oudolf, and New Wave garden by renowned English designer Julie Toll.
 ⅃ ✗ ❀

42 ◆ THE PLANTATION GARDEN
4 Earlham Road, Norwich NR4 7NH. Plantation Garden Preservation Trust, 01603 621868, www.plantationgarden.co.uk. *Nr St John's R C Cathedral. Parking available in Black Horse PH Earlham Rd.* Teas Suns mid Apr to end Sept. **Adm £3, chd free. Daily (9-6 or dusk if earlier). For NGS: Suns 6 May; 9 Sept (2-5).**
3-acre Victorian town garden created 1856-97 in former medieval chalk

the hill. Home-made teas. **Adm £3, chd free, concessions £2.50** (share to How Hill Educational Trust). **Suns 13 May; 22 July; 12 Aug (11-5).** Visitors also welcome by appt.
Well-established 1-acre garden divided into several 'rooms'. Main lawn garden flanked by wide herbaceous borders, leads through high yew hedge arch to secret garden featuring; mature mulberry, grasses, sedums, hemerocallis and hostas; spring bulbs in May. To rear, top fruit and soft fruit orchard and vegetable garden. Contemporary award-winning orangery. Garden sculpture.
 ⅃ ☕

44 ◆ RAVENINGHAM HALL
Raveningham NR14 6NS. Sir Nicholas Bacon, www.raveningham.com. *14m SE of Norwich. 4m from Beccles off B1136.* **Adm £4, chd free, concessions £3. Mon-Fri, Easter to end of Aug (11-4 no teas) Bank Hols Suns, Mons (2-5). For NGS: Mon 28 May (2-5).**
Traditional country house garden with an interesting collection of herbaceous plants and shrubs. Restored Victorian conservatory and walled kitchen garden. Newly planted arboretum, lake and herb garden. Contemporary sculpture.
 ⅃ ❀ ☕

45 RIVERMOUNT
Hall Lane, Knapton NR28 9SW. Mrs E Purdy. *2m NE North Walsham. B1150 through North Walsham towards Bacton. 2nd turning on L after Blue Bell PH & pond. Ample parking.* Home-made teas. **Adm £3, chd under 12 free. Sun 13 May (11-5).**
Traditional style garden. Brick terrace, sloping lawn to woodland garden. Herbaceous borders enclosed by climbing rose trellis. Paved kitchen garden with herb garden and old-fashioned rose beds. Many unusual and species plants and bulbs. Orchard and wild flower meadow walk. Not brilliant for wheelchairs but manageable with assistance. Gravel paths and narrow brick paths.
 ⅃ ✗ ❀ ☕

46 10 ST MICHAEL'S CLOSE
Aylsham NR11 6HA. Mr M I Davies, 01263 732174. *8m S of Cromer, 12m N of Norwich. Aylsham NW on B1354 towards Blickling Hall; 500yds from market place, turn R, Rawlinsons Lane, then R again. Park in St Michael's Infants School, in Rawlinsons Lane.* Cream teas. **Adm £2, chd free. Sun 15 July (11-5). Open with West Lodge.** Visitors also welcome by appt.
Front gravelled area with mixed shrub and herbaceous border; small rockery. Back garden with large variety of shrubs, herbaceous plants, bulbs, small lawn, roses, azaleas. Pond, aviary.
 ✗ ❀ ☕

47 NEW SALLE PARK
Salle, Norwich NR10 4SF. Sir John White. *1m N of Reepham. Off B1145, between Cawston & Reepham.* Home-made teas. **Adm £4, chd under 16 free , concessions wheelchairs & carers. Sun 24 June (12-5).**
Very varied estate gardens consisting of delightful, fully productive Victorian kitchen garden with original vine houses, double herbaceous borders, display glasshouse, ice house, orchard and wild flowers. Formal Georgian pleasure gardens with yew topiary, rose gardens, lawns, specimen trees and exotically planted orangery. Gravel and bark paths, gentle slopes.
 ⅃ ✗ ❀ ☕

High walls and cloisters planted with scented and tender climbers . . .

48 ◆ SANDRINGHAM GARDENS
Sandringham PE35 6EN. Her Majesty The Queen, 01553 612908, www.sandringhamestate.co.uk. *6m NW of King's Lynn. By gracious permission, the House, Museum & Gardens at Sandringham will be open.* House and Garden adm £9, concessions £7, chd £5, Garden only adm £6, chd £3.50, concessions £5. Daily 7 Apr to 20 July, reopening daily 31 July to 28 Oct (garden 10.30-5) (house 11-4.45).
60 acres of formal gardens, woodland and lakes, with rare plants and trees. Donations are given from the Estate to various charities.

49 ◆ SEVERALS GRANGE
Holt Road, Wood Norton NR20 5BL. Jane Lister, 01362 684206, www.hoecroft.co.uk. *8m S of Holt, 6m E of Fakenham. 2m N of Guist on LH-side of B1110. Guist is situated 5m NE of Fakenham on A1067 Norwich rd.* Home-made teas. Adm £2, chd free. Thurs to Suns Apr to mid Oct (Donations to NGS) 10-4. For NGS: Sun 12 Aug (2-5).
This 16yr-old garden has evolved from a bare field and is a perfect example of how colour, shape and form can be created by the use of foliage plants, from large shrubs to small alpines. Movement and lightness is achieved by interspersing these plants with a wide range of ornamental grasses, which are at their best in late summer. Gold medal winners at Norfolk & Suffolk County Shows. Featured in 'Garden News'.

50 ◆ SHERINGHAM PARK
Upper Sheringham NR26 8TL. The National Trust, 01263 820550, www.nationaltrust.org.uk. *2m SW of Sheringham. Access for cars off A148 Cromer to Holt Rd, 5m W of Cromer, 6m E of Holt, signs in Sheringham*

town. Light refreshments & teas. Adm Car parking £3.60. Daily (dawn til dusk). For NGS: Suns 20 May; 3 June (dawn til dusk).
50 acres of species rhododendron, azalea and magnolia. Also numerous specimen trees incl handkerchief tree. Viewing towers, waymarked walks, sea and parkland views. Special walkway and WCs for disabled. Electric wheelchairs available. Small shop.

51 ◆ STODY LODGE
Melton Constable NR24 2ER. Mrs Ian MacNicol, 01263 860572 (9-12 noon), www.stodyestate.co.uk. *16m NW of Norwich, 3m S of Holt. Off B1354. Signed from Melton Constable on Holt Rd.* Adm £4.50, chd under 12 free. For NGS: Suns, 6 May to 3 June; Mon 28 May (2-5). Donation to NGS.
Spectacular gardens having one of the largest concentrations of rhododendrons and azaleas in East Anglia with both Japanese water gardens and formal garden. Stunning walks and vistas are enhanced by a large variety of mature trees, magnolias, acers and cedars. Daffodils in early May give way to carpets of bluebells. Parties of 20+ mid week by arrangement.

52 STOW HALL
Stow Bardolph PE34 3HU. Lady Rose Hare. *2m N of Downham Market. Off A10.* Light refreshments & teas. Adm £3.50, chd free. Evening Opening £3, Fri 22 June (5-9).
Large garden with mature trees, small secluded areas with alpines, bulbs, irises and roses. High walls and cloisters planted with scented and tender climbers. Victorian kitchen garden containing a mix of old fruit trees, apples, pears, quince, medlar and mulberry and recently planted old Norfolk varieties of apples. Photographic competition,

demonstrations of local crafts, light music. Featured on Anglia TV 'The Countryside' series, and in 'The English Garden'.

53 SUNDOWN
Hall Lane, Roydon, Diss IP22 5XL. Elizabeth Bloom, 01379 642074. *2m W of Diss. From Diss take A1066 Thetford Rd, ¹/₂m after Roydon White Hart PH, turn R into Hall Lane. Sundown ¹/₄m on L. From Thetford - on A1066, approx 1m after Blooms of Bressingham, turn L into Hall lane.* Home-made teas. Adm £2.50, chd free. Sun 2 Sept (11-5). Visitors also welcome by appt, groups of 20+.
1-acre plantsman's garden established over 35yrs. Densely planted with wide variety of unusual perennials, shrubs and trees for colour and foliage yr-round. Woodland walk featuring rhododendrons and other woodland favourites; formal pond and patio area. Featured in 'Gardens Monthly' Autumn special edition.

54 WEST LODGE
Aylsham NR11 6HB. Mr & Mrs Jonathan Hirst. *¹/₄m NW of Aylsham. Off B1354 Blickling Rd out of Aylsham, turn R down Rawlinsons Lane, garden on L.* Home-made teas. Adm £3, chd free. Sun 15 July (2-5). Open with 10 St Michaels Close.
9-acre garden with lawns, splendid mature trees, rose garden, well stocked herbaceous borders, ornamental pond, magnificent C19 walled kitchen garden (maintained as such). Georgian House (not open) and outbuildings incl a well-stocked toolshed (open) and greenhouses.

55 THE WICKEN
Castle Acre, nr King's Lynn PE32 2BP. Mr & Mrs Alistair Keith. *2m N of Castle Acre. On Gt Massingham Rd, (Peddars Way) at Xrds signed on R to The Wicken.* Cream teas. Adm £3, chd free. Sun 1 July (1.30-5).
Walled garden with formal layout featuring gazebo, greenhouses and a fusion of traditional and new-wave European planting. Further walled areas incl blue and white themed pool garden. Sweeping ha-ha lawn with fine views is flanked with shrub and perennial borders. Formally planted courtyard leads to woodland gardens.

56 WITHERN
Sandy Lane, West Runton
NR27 9NE. Margaret & Clive
Mitchell, 01263 837397. *3m W of
Cromer. From A148 Cromer/Holt rd on
entering Aylmerton from Cromer turn R
at Roman Camp Inn into Sandy Lane.
Continue to junction, turn L, garden
faces you. Disabled parking in gravel
drive, short distance to gate, help
available.* Home-made teas. **Adm
£2.50, chd free. Visitors welcome by
appt, May to Aug only, incl coaches.**
Plantaholic's woodland garden of over
1 acre with winding paths through
plantings of rhododendrons, spring
bulbs, ferns, hellebores, hostas,
fuchsias, grasses, collection of
hydrangeas and much more. Open
lawned area, herbaceous border,
vegetable garden, fruit trees,
greenhouses. Glass sculpture, bottle
bank, lead, slate and other features.
Many alterations taking place 2006/07.
  ♿ ❊ ☕

57 WITTON HALL
nr North Walsham NR28 9UF. Sally
Owles. *3¹/₂ m NW of North Walsham.
Off B1150 halfway between North
Walsham & Bacton. Take R fork to
Bacton Woods picnic area, driveway
200yds on L.* Light refreshments &
teas. **Adm £3, chd free. Mon 7 May
(11-5).**
A natural woodland garden. Walk past
the handkerchief tree and wander
through carpets of English bluebells,
rhododendrons and azaleas. Stunning
views over farmland to the sea.
Wheelchair access difficult through
woodland paths.
  ❊ ☕

58 WOODLANDS FARM
Stokesby, Gt Yarmouth NR29 3DX.
Vivienne Fabb. *2m E of Acle. From
Norwich A47 to Acle, A1064 to Caister,
1st R after bridge over river to
Stokesby. Turn L into Filby Rd just past*

A natural
woodland
garden. Walk
past the
handkerchief
tree and
wander through
carpets of
English
bluebells . . .

*Bungalow Stores, 1st L after the end of
30mph limit. From Gt Yarmouth A1064
via Caister, L to Stokesby & Runham
then as above.* Light refreshments &
teas. **Adm £3, chd free. Suns 27
May; 16 Sept (11-5).**
Large mature garden with trees,
interesting shrubs and herbaceous
plants. Good spring and autumn
colour. Vegetable garden and
woodland walk. Gravel paths.
  ❊ 🏠 ☕

59 WOODWYND
6 Dodds Hill Road, Dersingham
PE31 6LW. Mr & Mrs D H Dingle,
01485 541218. *8m NE of King's Lynn.
³/₄m N of Sandringham House. Take
B1440 from Sandringham & continue
into Dersingham. Turn R into Dodds Hill
Rd just past the Feathers Hotel.* Light
refreshments & teas. **Adm £3, chd
free. Sun 22 July (11.30-5). Visitors
also welcome by appt, July only.**

Our NGS visitors all agree - it is one of
the finest private gardens you are likely
to see. From dry gravel garden to deep
woodland dell - uncommon plants too
numerous to tell. With 1¹/₂ acres there
is so much to see. Delicious home-
made cakes so do stop for tea. Steep
slopes in dell.
  ❊ ♿ ☕

60 WRETHAM LODGE
East Wretham IP24 1RL. Mr Gordon
Alexander. *6m NE of Thetford. A11 E
from Thetford, L up A1075, L by village
sign, R at Xrds then bear L.* Teas in St
Ethelbert's Church. **Adm £2.50, chd
free. Sun 8, Mon 9 Apr (11-5); Sun
17 June (2-5).**
In spring masses of species tulips,
hellebores, fritillaries, daffodils and
narcissi; bluebell walk. In June
hundreds of old roses. Walled garden,
with fruit and interesting vegetable
plots. Mixed borders and fine old trees.
Double herbaceous borders. Wild
flower meadows.
❊ ☕

Our NGS
visitors all
agree - it is
one of the
finest private
gardens you
are likely to
see . . .

Norfolk County Volunteers

County Organisers
Fiona Black, The Old Rectory, Ridlington, North Walsham, NR28 9NZ, 01692 650247, blacks7@email.com
Anthea Foster, Lexham Hall, King's Lynn, PE32 2QJ, 01328 701341, antheafoster@lexhamestate.co.uk

County Treasurer
Neil Foster, Lexham Hall, King's Lynn PE32 2QJ, 01328 701288, neilfoster@lexhamestate.co.uk

Publicity
Annette Bowler, 260 Aylsham Road, Norwich NR3 2RG, 01603 301110, annette.bowler@ntlworld.com

Assistant County Organisers
Stephanie Powell, Creake House, Wells Road, Fakenham NR21 9LG, 01328 730113, stephaniepowell@creake.com
Jim & Jan Saunt, Plovers Hill, Buckenham Road, Strumpshaw NR13 4NL, 01603 714587, jamessaunt@hotmail.com

NORTHAMPTONSHIRE

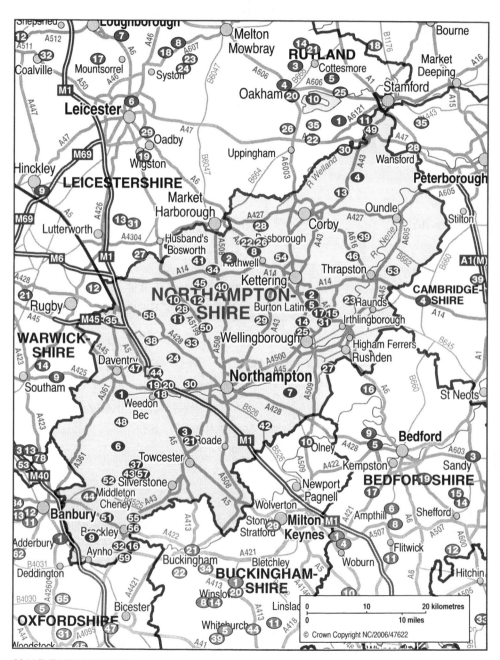

Opening Dates

February

SUNDAY 18
2 Beech House
27 Greywalls

SUNDAY 25
14 Dolphins

March

WEDNESDAY 7
59 Woodchippings

April

SUNDAY 1
40 Maidwell Hall

WEDNESDAY 4
59 Woodchippings

SATURDAY 7
41 The Maltings

SUNDAY 8
16 Evenley Wood Garden
41 The Maltings

MONDAY 9
16 Evenley Wood Garden
23 Great Addington Manor
41 The Maltings

SUNDAY 15
20 Flore Spring Gardens
45 The Old Rectory, Haselbech

SUNDAY 22
34 Kelmarsh Hall

May

SUNDAY 6
16 Evenley Wood Garden
24 Great Brington Gardens
26 Greenway

MONDAY 7
16 Evenley Wood Garden

SATURDAY 12
39 Lyveden New Bield

SUNDAY 13
28 Guilsborough and Hollowell Gardens
33 Holdenby House Gardens

SATURDAY 19
6 Canons Ashby House

SUNDAY 20
51 Steane Park

WEDNESDAY 23
59 Woodchippings

SUNDAY 27
1 Badby and Newnham Gardens
13 Deene Park
16 Evenley Wood Garden

37 Lois Weedon House
43 Old Barn

MONDAY 28
16 Evenley Wood Garden

June

SUNDAY 3
36 Litchborough Gardens
48 Preston Capes Gardens

THURSDAY 7
26 Greenway (Evening)

SATURDAY 9
53 Titchmarsh House

SUNDAY 10
14 Dolphins
17 Finedon Gardens
25 Great Harrowden Lodge
35 Kilsby Gardens
47 Park House
50 Spratton Gardens
52 Sulgrave Gardens
54 Top Lodge

THURSDAY 14
31 67-69 High Street

SATURDAY 16
41 The Maltings

SUNDAY 17
8 Cedar Farm
38 Long Buckby Gardens
41 The Maltings
49 Rosebriar
55 Turweston Gardens

WEDNESDAY 20
59 Woodchippings

THURSDAY 21
31 67-69 High Street (Evening)

SATURDAY 23
19 Flore Gardens
42 The Menagerie

SUNDAY 24
19 Flore Gardens
30 Harpole Gardens

July

SUNDAY 1
4 Bulwick Gardens
9 Charlton Gardens
29 Hannington Gardens
34 Kelmarsh Hall
57 Weedon Lois Gardens
58 West Haddon Gardens

SUNDAY 8
3 Bronte House
21 The Folly

WEDNESDAY 11
59 Woodchippings

THURSDAY 12
26 Greenway (Evening)

SATURDAY 14
5 Burton Latimer Gardens

SUNDAY 15
5 Burton Latimer Gardens
7 Castle Ashby House

THURSDAY 19
15 Driftwood (Evening)

SUNDAY 22
10 Coton Lodge
15 Driftwood

SUNDAY 29
18 Flore Fields
22 Froggery Cottage
44 The Old Rectory, Brockhall

August

SUNDAY 5
12 Cottesbrooke Hall Gardens

September

SATURDAY 1
6 Canons Ashby House

SUNDAY 2
13 Deene Park

SATURDAY 8
39 Lyveden New Bield

SUNDAY 9
11 Coton Manor Garden
26 Greenway
46 The Old Rectory, Sudborough

February 2008

SUNDAY 24
14 Dolphins

Gardens open to the public

6 Canons Ashby House
7 Castle Ashby House
10 Coton Lodge
11 Coton Manor Garden
12 Cottesbrooke Hall Gardens
13 Deene Park
33 Holdenby House Gardens
34 Kelmarsh Hall
39 Lyveden New Bield
42 The Menagerie
46 The Old Rectory, Sudborough

By appointment only

32 Hill Grounds

The Gardens

① BADBY AND NEWNHAM GARDENS

Daventry NN11 3AR. *3m S of Daventry. E side of A361.* Home-made teas at St Mary's Church. **Combined adm £3.50, chd free. Sun 27 May (2-6).**

CHURCH HILL

Dr & Mrs C M Cripps
Medium-sized country garden with internal yew and beech hedges enclosing mixed borders. Some interesting plants, clipped yews, shady border, pond, vegetable garden and conservatory.

HILLTOP

Church Street. David & Mercy Messenger
Constantly evolving 3-acre cottage-style, with mature trees and shrubs to focus, and separate areas. Lovely views, dense planting, spring bulbs. Largely organic. Garden room and newly extended vegetable beds. Copper cascade water feature. Current challenge - a wild flower meadow.

THE MILL

Charles & Susan Rose
Extensive mixed garden with gravel garden and large borders, designed and planted by James Alexander-Sinclair. Woodland walk with a mixture of traditional and contemporary planting.

NEWHAM GRANGE FARM

Mr & Mrs Peter Morton
1½-acre mature country garden with views over farmland. Large mixed borders, interesting trees, shrubs, old fashioned roses, climbers and unusual hardy perennials.

🆕 SHAKESPEARES COTTAGE

Sarah & Jocelyn Hartland-Swan
Small garden surrounding C18 thatched cottage, reclaimed by present owners after some years of neglect. Raised stone beds, sloping lawn to rear, mixed borders. Flagstone, terracotta and gravelled seating areas with colourful pots.

Flagstone, terracotta and gravelled seating areas with colourful pots . . .

THE OLD HOUSE

Dr & Mrs M MacGregor
A medium-sized enclosed garden with fine views over Badby woods. Secluded courtyard, mostly stone-raised beds, densely planted with many traditional herbaceous plants and roses.

② BEECH HOUSE

73 Church Street, Burton Latimer NN15 5LU. Mr & Mrs Nicholas Loake, 01536 723593, gloake@mac.com. *4m S of Kettering. From High St turn into Church St by War Memorial, Beech House is on the L 100yds past the church.* Home-made teas. **Adm £2.50, chd free. Sun 18 Feb (10-4). Visitors also welcome by appt.**
Semi-formal garden with winter/spring interest. Clipped box and yew hedging frame borders containing over 150 cultivars of snowdrops plus hellebores etc.

③ 🆕 BRONTE HOUSE

Eastcote Road, Tiffield NN12 8AF. Susan Bell. *6m SW Northampton. 1m NW Towcester off A43, L past The George, ¾ m on, just past double bend.* Home-made teas. **Adm £3.50, chd free (share to Holy Cross Church). Sun 8 July (12-6). Combined with The Folly.**
Former paddock developed as a garden in 2002. Mixed herbaceous planting, lawns, pergola, bed of bamboo and ferns, wildlife garden and pond. Courtyard with exotic plants.

④ BULWICK GARDENS

Corby NN17 3DZ. *10m SW of Stamford. ½ m off A43.* Home-made teas at Bulwick Hall. **Combined adm £2.50, chd free. Sun 1 July (2-5).**
Unspoilt Northamptonshire stone conservation village. Interesting C14 church and PH.

BULWICK HALL

Mr & Mrs G T G Conant
Formal terraced 8-acre walled garden leading to river and island. Double herbaceous borders, holly walk ending at attractive C17 wrought iron gates. C19 orangery and C17 arcade, large kitchen garden, fine mature trees, topiary, peacocks. (House not open). Short gravel entry.

19 CHURCH LANE

David Haines
Small cottage garden with fruit trees and vegetables, courtyard and water features.

THE SHAMBLES

12 Main Street.
Roger Glithero
Herbaceous plants, many containers, vegetable garden with fruit and original village well, lawns, hedges and stone walls.

⑤ BURTON LATIMER GARDENS

NN15 5NX. *3m S of Kettering. Approached from A14, A509 & A6. Parking by kind permission of Sunseeker Windows 72-84 Station Road.* Home-made teas at 58 Station Road & 14 Bridle Road. **Combined adm £2, chd free. Sat, Sun 14 & 15 July (1.30-5.30).**

14 BRIDLE ROAD

Mr & Mrs John Hollis
Long shrub border to side of bungalow, through arch to wildlife pond, leading to lawn with colourful borders, vegetable plot with fruit trees and bushes to rear.

36 STATION ROAD

John & Pat Freeman, 01536 723693, patricia.freeman1@tesco.net. **Visitors also welcome by appt, afternoons 2-21 July, no coaches.**
Picket fenced cottage style garden with a variety of shrubs and plants, patios, pergolas and water features, benefiting from a

lovely back drop of mature trees beyond old stone wall.

58 STATION ROAD
Bill & Daphne Frum, 01536 722455. Visitors also welcome by appt, afternoons 2-21 Jul, no coaches.
100ft town garden specialising in clematis in more than 75 different situations, many in containers. Areas of special interest with hostas, grasses, ferns, fuchsias, and lilies. Fruit and vegetables in raised beds.

6 ♦ CANONS ASHBY HOUSE
Daventry NN11 3SD. The National Trust, 01327 860044, canonsashby@national trust.org.uk. *12m NE of Banbury, 9m S of Daventry. On unclassified rd between B4525 and A5. Follow NT signs.* House and Garden Adm £6.50, chd £3.50, Garden only Adm £2.50, chd free. For NGS: Sats 19 May; 1 Sept (11-5).
Formal gardens of London and Wise style enclosed by walls. Gate piers from 1710, fine topiary, axial arrangement of paths and terraces, wild flowers, old varieties of fruit trees, herb border, newly planted gardens. Home of the Dryden family since C16, Manor House 1550. Ramp access to garden on request. Gravel paths.

7 ♦ CASTLE ASHBY HOUSE
Northampton NN7 1LQ. Earl Compton, 01604 696187, petercox@castleashby.co.uk. *6m E of Northampton. 1½ m N of A428; turn off between Denton & Yardley Hastings.* Adm £2.80, chd £1.90 10+, concessions £1.90. Apr-Sept (10-5), Oct-Mar (10-4). For NGS: Sun 15 July (11-5).
View to parkland incl avenue planted at suggestion of William III in 1695, lakes by Capability Brown, Italian gardens with orangery, extensive lawns and trees. Elizabethan house (not open). Gravel paths.
&

8 CEDAR FARM
Desborough NN14 2QD. Mr & Mrs R Tuffen, 01536 763992, thetuffenfamily@aol.com. *6m N of Kettering, 5m S of Market Harborough. Signed from centre of Desborough.* Home-made teas. Adm £2.50, chd

free. Sun 17 June (2-6). Visitors also welcome by appt.
2-acre garden with a further 8 acres. Secret garden with roses and clematis. Avenue of 24 mature limes. Large colour planted borders filled with many unusual plants and shrubs. New large mirror pond, wildlife ponds, vegetable garden. Massed snowdrops and spring bulbs, wonderful autumn colour, walks through small arboretum.
& ♣️ ☕

9 CHARLTON GARDENS
Banbury OX17 3DR. *7m SE of Banbury, 5m W of Brackley. From B4100 turn off N at Aynho, or from A422 turn off S at Farthinghoe.* Home-made teas at The Cottage. Combined adm £3.50, chd free. Sun 1 July (2-5.30).
Well preserved stone village, lunch at pub.

THE COTTAGE
Lady Juliet Townsend
Flowering shrubs, raised cottage garden, lawns, woodland walk, stream and lakes.
& ☕

HOLLY HOUSE
Miss Alice Townsend
Walled garden with beautiful views. C18 house, not open. Some shallow steps in garden.
&

NEW HOME FARM HOUSE
Mrs N Grove-White
Paved courtyard with tubs, containers and climbers. Walled garden with roses and clematis, herbaceous border and fruit garden.

10 ♦ COTON LODGE
Guilsborough NN6 8QE. Peter Hicks & Joanne de Nobriga, 01604 740215, www.cotonlodge.co.uk. *10m NW of Northampton, 10m E of Rugby. 1m W of Guilsborough on West Haddon Rd on L.* Adm £3.50, chd free. Thurs to Sun & Bank Holiday Mons May-Sept. For NGS: Sun 22 July (12-5).
Mature 2-acre garden with panoramic views over beautiful unspoilt countryside. Intimate enclosed areas are complemented by an informal woodland stream and pond giving interest throughout the seasons. Massed tulips and wisteria in spring, rose covered arches and scents in summer and hot exotic planting for autumn.

11 ♦ COTON MANOR GARDEN
Guilsborough NN6 8RQ. Mr & Mrs Ian Pasley-Tyler, 01604 740219, www.cotonmanor.co.uk. *10m N of Northampton, 11m SE of Rugby. From A428 & A5199 follow tourist signs.* Adm £5, chd £2, concessions £4.50. Tues to Sats, Apr-Sept. Suns in April & May. Bank Holiday weekends. For NGS: Sun 9 Sept (12-5.30).
10-acre garden set in peaceful countryside with old yew and holly hedges, extensive herbaceous borders containing many unusual plants, rose, water, herb and woodland gardens, famous bluebell wood, wild flower meadow. Adjacent specialist nursery with over 1000 plant varieties propagated from the garden. Garden on a slope with some gravel paths. Limited wheelchair access.

Massed snowdrops and spring bulbs, wonderful autumn colour, walks through small arboretum . . .

⑫ ◆ COTTESBROOKE HALL GARDENS
Creaton NN6 8PF. Mr & Mrs A R Macdonald-Buchanan, 01604 505808, www.cottesbrookehall.co.uk. *10m N of Northampton. Signed from J1 on A14.* House and Garden Adm £7.50, chd £3.50, concessions £6, Garden only Adm £5, chd £2.50 (5-14 yrs), concessions £4. Weds & Thurs, May, June; Thurs, July to Sept. For NGS: Sun 5 Aug (2-5.30).
Notable gardens of great variety incl fine old cedars and specimen trees, herbaceous borders, water and wild gardens. Unusual plants. Route maps for wheelchair users.
&. ⅍ ⊛ ☕

COWPER & NEWTON MUSEUM GARDENS
See Buckinghamshire.

⑬ ◆ DEENE PARK
Corby NN17 3EW. Mr E Brudenell & The Hon Mrs Brudenell, 01780 450278, admin@deenepark.com. *5m N of Corby. On A43 Stamford-Kettering rd.* Adm £4, chd £1.50, concessions £3. Suns & Bank Hols; Jun - Aug. For NGS: Suns 27 May; 2 Sept (2-5).
Interesting garden set in beautiful parkland. Large parterre with topiary designed by David Hicks echoing the C16 decoration on the porch stonework, long mixed borders, old-fashioned roses, Tudor court and white garden. Large lake and waterside walks with rare mature trees in natural garden.
&. ⅍ ☕

⑭ DOLPHINS
Great Harrowden NN9 5AB. Mr & Mrs R C Handley. *2m N of Wellingborough. 5m S of Kettering on A509.* Light refreshments & teas at Dolphins (Feb). Adm £2 Feb, £3 June, chd free. Suns 25 Feb (10-4); 10 June (2-6); 24 Feb 2008 (10-4). Combined with **Great Harrowden Lodge** 10 June.
2-acre country garden surrounding old stone house (not open). Many old roses grown among interesting trees, shrubs and wide range of hardy perennials. Irises and peonies a special favourite. Early opening for snowdrops and hellebores. Gravel paths. See Finedon Gardens for teas in June. BBC Radio Northampton.
&. ⅍ ⊛ ☕

⑮ DRIFTWOOD
11b Thrapston Road, Finedon NN9 5DG. Bill & Elaine Gardiner, 01933 680708. *3m NE of Wellingborough. A14 junction11, W to Finedon. 3rd house on R as you enter. A510 3m E of Wellingborough, cross A6, 1/4 m on L next to shed showroom.* Light refreshments & cream teas. Adm £3.00, chd free. *Evening Opening* wine,Thur 19 July (6-9); Sun 22 July (2-6). Visitors also welcome by appt.
5-yr old 1/2-acre garden featuring small lake with island. Well stocked with fish, various water birds, wildlife and aquatic plants, surrounded by lawns, flower beds, shrubs and pergolas. Craft demonstration - woodturning.
&. ⅍ ⊛ ☕

⑯ EVENLEY WOOD GARDEN
Brackley NN13 5SH. R T Whiteley, 01280 703329, www.evenleywoodgarden.co.uk. *3/4 m S of Brackley. A43, turn L to Evenley straight through village towards Mixbury, 1st turning L.* Home-made teas. Adm £3.50, chd £1. Sun & Mon 8, 9 Apr; 6, 7 May; 27, 28 May (2-6). Visitors also welcome by appt for groups 10+, £4 each.
Woodland garden spread over a 60-acre mature wood. Acid and alkaline soil. Magnolias, rhododendrons, azaleas, malus, quercus, acers, euonymus collection and many other species. Large collection of bulbous plants.
&. ⊛ ☕

⑰ FINEDON GARDENS
NN9 5JN. *2m NE of Wellingborough. 6m SE Kettering, A6/A510 junction.* Home-made teas at 67- 69 High St. Combined adm £2.50, chd free. Sun 10 June (2-6).
☕

67-69 HIGH STREET
Mary & Stuart Hendry. Visitors also welcome by appt.
(See separate entry).
&. ⅍ ⊛

🆕 INDEGARDEN
24 Albert Road. Ray & Honor Parbery
Approx 50ft - walk through pergola with climbers, colourful mixed border of annuals and perennials, pots and containers, miniature house in the garden.
&. ⅍ ⊛

🆕 4 IRTHLINGBOROUGH ROAD
Jenny & Roger Martin
Small front garden with cottage style planting and enclosed rear garden with raised beds, raised fish pond and containers.
⅍

7 WALKERS WAY
Mrs D Humphrey
Small recently-established garden with gravel areas, decking, containers and pond.
⅍ ⊛

⑱ FLORE FIELDS
NN7 4JX. Lady Morton. *2m E of Weedon. On A45 midway between Northampton & Daventry. From Flore take Brockhall Rd 1m. Lodge at end of drive.* Cream teas. Adm £3, chd free. Sun 29 July (2-5.30). combined with **The Old Rectory, Brockhall**.
2 large herbaceous borders, rose beds, shrubs, spacious lawns with mature trees.
&. ⅍ ⊛ ⊟ ☕

⑲ FLORE GARDENS
NN7 4LQ. *7m W of Northampton. 5m E of Daventry. On A45.* Lunches & home-made teas in Church & Chapel School Room. Combined adm £3.50, chd free (share to All Saints Church). Sat, Sun 23, 24 June (11-6).
Part of the established (45th) Village Flower Festival. Maps provided at official car park.

Long mixed borders, old-fashioned roses, Tudor court and white garden . . .

Workshops during day – penstemons from seeds to winter care . . .

24 BLISS LANE
John & Sally Miller
Small cottage garden filled with flowers, fruit, herbs and vegetables. Victorian-style greenhouse and recently re-planted mixed border and dry garden.

BLISS LANE NURSERY
Geoff & Chris Littlewood
Informal garden and nursery opening out to a larger garden with views overlooking the Nene Valley, closely packed perennial plants in wide borders with small trees and shrub roses.
🎔

NEW 17 THE CRESENT
Lindsey Butler
30m long with shrub and perennial borders, patios and seating areas.

THE GARDEN HOUSE
Edward & Penny Aubrey-Fletcher
Former walled kitchen garden replanted when the new house was built in the 90s. Approx 1/2-acre of formal design with informal planting. Gravel paths.
♿

THE MANOR HOUSE
Wendy Amos, 01327 340386.
Visitors also welcome by appt, June & July.
1-acre garden with mature trees, newly planted avenue of 120 hornbeam, yew house. Pond with newts, walled kitchen garden. Partial wheelchair access, some gravel and split level, but enjoyment not impaired!
♿ 🎔

THE OLD BAKERY
John Amos & Karl Jones
5yr-old garden arranged over different levels. Divided into smaller 'rooms' with terraces and a small lawn. Many unusual plants for full sun and shade. Formal and informal planting. C19 pergola

with 'Empresses of India' theme. Small vegetable garden. Presenter, 'The Green Wellie Show', Radio Northamptonshire.
🎔

NEW 31 SPRING LANE
Margaret Clarke
A small garden, still evolving. Front planted for dry conditions, herbaceous beds, shrubs and some vegetables in containers at the back.
🎔

NEW 33 SPRING LANE
Rosemary Boyd
Small garden with herbaceous flower beds, fruit trees and a vegetable and herb area.
🎔

20 FLORE SPRING GARDENS
NN7 4LQ. 7m W of Northampton. 5m E of Daventry on A45. Home-made teas at the Chapel School Room. Combined adm £3, chd free. Sun 15 Apr (2-6).
Map provided at the official car park.
🌼 ☕

BLISS LANE NURSERY
Chris & Geoff Littlewood
Spring colours consisting of acer phoenix, hellebores, anemones and bluebells, with drifts of daffodils and tulips in the borders. Views over Nene valley.
🎔

THE CROFT
John & Dorothy Boast
1/3-acre cottage garden planted for yr-round interest. Deciduous trees and shrubs, perennials and spring flowering bulbs.

3 MEADOW FARM CLOSE
Eric & Jackie Ingram
Newly developed woodland garden with spring planting around the house.

4 MEADOW FARM CLOSE
Bob & Lynne Richards
A small comfortable pretty garden.
🎔

21 NEW THE FOLLY
The Folly, Eastcote Road, Tiffield NN12 8AF. Mrs A R Bowen-Jones. 6m SW Northampton. 1m NW Towcester off A43, L past The George, 1/4 m, L into drive. Adm £3.50, chd free (share to Holy Cross Church). Sun 8 July (12-6). Combined with Bronte House.
1-acre garden with mixed herbaceous beds, duck pond, summerhouse, mature trees. Ornamental pond with waterfall.
🎔

22 FROGGERY COTTAGE
85 Breakleys Road, Desborough NN14 2PT. Mr John Lee, 01536 760002, johnlee@froggerycottage85. fsnet.co.uk. 6m N of Kettering. 5m S of Market Harborough. Signed off A6 & A14. Lunches & home-made teas. Adm £2, chd free. Sun 29 July (11.30-6). Visitors also welcome by appt, Jul & Aug, groups 10+.
3/4-acre plantsman's garden full of rare and unusual plants. National Collection of 425 varieties of penstemons incl dwarfs and species. Artefacts on display incl old ploughs and garden implements. Workshops during day - penstemons from seeds to winter care.
♿ ✿ NCCPG ☕

GILMORTON GARDENS
See Leicestershire & Rutland.

23 GREAT ADDINGTON MANOR
Great Addington NN14 4BH. Mr & Mrs G E Groome. 7m SE of Kettering. Junction 11, A510 exit off A14 signed Finedon & Wellingborough. Turn 2nd L to the Addingtons. Home-made teas in Village Hall. Adm £3, chd 5+ £1. Mon 9 Apr (2-5).
41/2-acre manor gardens with lawns, mature trees, mulberry, yew hedges, pond and spinney. Spring daffodils, new terrace 2005. Gravel paths, steps & slopes.
♿ ☕

24 GREAT BRINGTON GARDENS
NN7 4JJ. 7m NW of Northampton. Off A428 Rugby Rd. 1st L turn past main gates of Althorp. Home-made lunches & teas at Reading Room and Church. Combined adm £3, chd free. Sun 6 May (11-5).
Tickets (maps and programmes provided) at Church, Reading Room & free car park. 7 gardens of great variety signed in village. Small attractive stone

and thatch village with Spencer and Washington connections and C12 church. Village history exhibition.

BEARD'S COTTAGE
Captain Bill Bellamy, 01604 770257, bill.bellamy@talk21.com. Visitors also welcome by appt, not a show garden just a peaceful place to sit. 1/2 acre of lawns, shrubs and herbaceous borders. Large orchard with maturing bluebells and primroses in three small copses.

8 BEDFORD COTTAGES
Anne & Bob Billingsby
Long sloping N-facing garden with outstanding views. Designed, created and maintained by the owners. Many shrubs and herbaceous plants for all-yr interest.

Not a show garden just a peaceful place to sit . . .

BRINGTON LODGE
Mr & Mrs P J Cooch
Old garden on edge of village, approx 3/4 acre, partially walled with a number of spring flowering trees and shrubs.

MEADOW VIEW
Marcel & Molly Van Cleemput
Easy maintenance garden with 2 ponds, water features, and a new garden retreat.

THE OLD RECTORY
Mr & Mrs R Thomas
3-acre garden with mature trees, yew hedging, formal rose garden, vegetable garden, flower borders and 1/3-acre orchard.

RIDGWAY HOUSE
Mr & Mrs R Steedman
11/2 acres with lawns, herbaceous borders and many spring-flowering shrubs and bulbs. Gravel drive.

THE STABLES
Mr & Mrs A George
Small cottage garden containing shrubs, herbaceous plants and climbers. Compact and unusual shape with water feature and summer house.

25 GREAT HARROWDEN LODGE
The Slips NN9 5AE. Mrs J & Mr R M Green. *2m N of Wellingborough. 5m S of Kettering on A509. Situated 3/4 m from Great Harrowden Church on lane to Finedon.* **Adm £3, chd free. Sun 10 June (2-6). Combined with Dolphins.**
11/4-acre garden on a dry exposed site. Wide variety of herbaceous plants in long borders and island beds. Herb garden.

26 GREENWAY
Pipewell Road, Desborough NN14 2SN. Robert Bass. *6m NW of Kettering, 5m SE of Market Harborough. On B576. 150 metres E of Pipewell Rd railway bridge and Travis Perkins builders' yard.* Home-made teas. **Adm £2, chd free. Suns 6 May; 9 Sept (2-6). Evening Openings** wine, **Thurs 7 June; 12 July (6-9).**
Constantly evolving arboretum style garden set in 1/3 acre with over 50 acers (Japanese maple cultivars) in containers and open planting. Many garden structures, water features, statuary and containers to provide year round interest. Covered seating areas for contemplation.

27 GREYWALLS
Farndish NN29 7HJ. Mrs P M Anderson, 01933 353495, patricia@greywalls.tradaweb.net. *21/2 m SE of Wellingborough. A609 from Wellingborough, B570 to Irchester, turn to Farndish by cenotaph. House adjacent to church.* Teas. **Adm £3, chd free. Sun 18 Feb (12-4). Visitors also welcome by appt in Feb.**
2-acre mature garden surrounding old vicarage (not open). Over 50 varieties of snowdrops, drifts of hardy cyclamen and hellebores. Alpine house and raised alpine beds. Water features and natural ponds with views over open countryside. Special Orpington hen's eggs for sale. Radio Northampton. Partial wheelchair access.

Three interconnecting gardens, three acres, with views . . .

28 GUILSBOROUGH AND HOLLOWELL GARDENS
NN6 8PY. *10m NW of Northampton. 10m E of Rugby. Between A5199 & A428. Parking for Guilsborough Gardens in field at Guilsborough House.* Lunches & cream teas. **Combined adm £3.50, chd free. Sun 13 May (11-5).**
Maps provided. Small village mentioned in Domesday Book with shop, coffee shop, pub and interesting church - all open.

DRIPWELL HOUSE
Mr J W Langfield & Dr C Moss, 01604 740755. Visitors also welcome by appt.
3-acre mature garden. Many fine trees and shrubs on partly terraced slope. Rock garden, herbaceous borders, herb, wild flower and vegetable gardens, soft fruit and apple orchard. Unusual shrubs, rhododendrons and azaleas in woodland garden.

FOUR ACRES
The Green. Mark & Gay Webster
Incorporating 2 smaller gardens; Little Four Acres (Mark & Judithe Revitt-Smith) and Walter's Yard (Frances & Richard Scammell). 3 inter-connected gardens approx 3 acres in exposed position with beautiful views. Mature mixed shrub and herbaceous borders, patio gardens with water features, potager, wildlife pond. Long gravel drive.

GOWER HOUSE
Peter & Ann Moss, 01604 740755. Visitors also welcome by appt in May & June.
Small garden evolving since 1991 on part of Dripwell vegetable garden. Plantsman's garden with herbaceous, alpine, climbing plants and shrubs.

GUILSBOROUGH HOUSE
Mr & Mrs John McCall
Country garden, terraces, lawns and hedges, mature trees. Plenty of room and shade for picnic in field - improved access.

NORTOFT GRANGE
Sir John & Lady Lowther
We offer you a warm welcome, lovely views, herbaceous borders and a wild flower meadow. Bring a picnic and feed the fish in our pond.

THE OLD HOUSE
Richard & Libby Seaton Evans
Approx 1 acre of lawns, herbaceous borders, roses, shrubs and walled kitchen garden. Additional woodland with wild flowers, paddocks and a wonderful view, enhanced by llamas.

NEW THE OLD VICARAGE
John & Christine Benbow
1½-acre garden revitalised over the past five years. Colourful herbaceous borders with spring bulbs, especially tulips. Woodland areas, small pond, new walled vegetable garden leading down to orchard in meadow.

ROSEMOUNT
Mr & Mrs J Leatherland, 01604 740354. Visitors also welcome by appt, in Feb for groups 10+.
½-acre plantsman's garden. Unusual plants and shrubs, alpine garden, fish pond, small collections of clematis, camellias and abutilons. Snowdrops, hellebores and spring bulbs. Interviewed by Radio Northamptonshire.

29 HANNINGTON GARDENS
Hannington Village NN6 9HH. *5m S of Kettering. On A43 Hannington is signed at Xrds opposite garage.* Light refreshments & teas at Village Hall, School Lane. **Combined adm £2.50, chd free. Sun 1 July (11-5).**
Small village combining Grade II listed stone dwellings with modern homes. Historically and architecturally interesting C13 church - unique nave with central pillars - associated with the Gilbertine monasteries of Norman

times and with 2 bishops. Plant sale in aid of Hannington Church.

BROOKMEAD
6 Orchard Close. Mr & Mrs A Shardlow. *Orchard Close is 1st R turn on entering village*
Established medium-sized garden featuring lawns, shrubs and herbaceous borders. Climbers, seating areas and small water feature. Open countryside views.

HEATHCOTE
Bridle Way. Paul Briggs. *Entering village from A43 Bridle Way is 1st L at end of Bridle Road*
Mature medium-sized garden comprising lawn, herbaceous borders, trees, incl fruit, and vegetable patch. Features ponds, hidden garden paths and steeply sloping banks providing yr-round interest.

KARMIRA
Bridle Road. Mr & Mrs P Gyselynck. *On entering village from A43 Bridle Rd is 1st L*
Medium-sized garden of lawns, shrubs and herbaceous borders. Mature trees, patio and seating areas. Pot plants, pergola walk, dovecote and fish pond.

RECTORY COTTAGE
Mr & Mrs J Robinson. *Next to church*
Recently professionally redesigned and landscaped garden. Sympathetic use of natural materials around C17 stone cottage (not open). Knot garden, shrubs and herbaceous borders set in beautiful location next to village church.

30 HARPOLE GARDENS
NN7 4BX. *4m W Northampton. On A45 towards Weedon. Turn R at The Turnpike Hotel into Harpole.* Home-made teas at The Close. **Combined adm £3, chd free. Sun 24 June (12-6).**
Village maps given to all visitors.

THE CLOSE
Michael Orton-Jones
Old-fashioned English country garden with large lawns, herbaceous borders and mature trees. Stone house (not open).

New – walled vegetable garden leading down to orchard in a meadow . . .

74 LARKHALL LANE
Mr & Mrs J Leahy
Medium-sized informal garden with a wide variety of plants, shrubs, some mature trees, climbers, alpines, grasses, small pond and a variety of pots.

17 MANOR CLOSE
Mr & Mrs I Wilkinson
Small, well stocked garden with lawns, gravel areas, pond and mixed borders.

19 MANOR CLOSE
Mr & Mrs E Kemshed
40yds x 10yds flower arranger's garden on an estate, cultivated by present owners since 1975.

MILLERS
Mr & Mrs M Still
Old stone farmhouse (not open) with approx 1 acre of lawns and mixed borders, mainly shrubs, some mature trees, good views overlooking the farm and strawberry field.

THORPE HOUSE
Mr & Mrs R Fountain
Secluded largely walled garden, extending to approx ½ acre. Sunken area with pond and ceramic features. Lawns and herbaceous borders with some unusual plants and shrubs. No access to kitchen garden, steps to pond, some gravel.

31 67-69 HIGH STREET
Finedon NN9 5JN. **Mary & Stuart
Hendry,** 01933 680414. *6m SE
Kettering, junction A6 & A510.* **Adm
£2, chd free.** *Evening Openings*
**wine, Thurs 14 & 21 June (5-9).
Visitors also welcome by appt Feb
to Sept, groups 4+.**
Constantly evolving, $1/3$-acre rear
garden of C17 cottage (not open).
Mixed borders, obelisks and
containers, kitchen garden and herb
bed. Spring garden, snow drops and
hellebores, late summer borders. Also
open with Finedon Gardens. Featured
in 'Kitchen Garden' Jan 07.

32 HILL GROUNDS
Evenley NN13 5RZ. **Mr & Mrs C F
Cropley,** 01280 703224,
bob@cropley.co.uk. *1m S of
Brackley. On A43. Turn L into Evenley.
R off Church Lane.* **Adm £4 inc tea or
coffee, chd free. Visitors welcome
by appt all year.**
Plantsman's garden of 2 acres,
surrounded by C19 200yd yew hedge.
Planted for yr-round interest. Bulbs,
terrace, rose pergola, double
herbaceous borders. Many rare and
less hardy plants grown. Millennium
'arborette'.

Historic site with many borders, water features, bog garden and an Old England feel . . .

**33 ◆ HOLDENBY HOUSE
GARDENS**
Northampton NN6 8DJ. **Mr & Mrs
James Lowther,** 01604 770074,
www.holdenby.com. *6m NW of
Northampton. Signed from A5199 &
A428.* **Adm £5, chd £3.50,
concessions £4.50. Suns & Bank
Hol Mons, Apr to Sept 1-5. For NGS:
Sun 13 May (1-5).**

Just 2m across the fields from
Althorp, this impressive house (not
open) and garden were built from the
Elizabethan remains of the largest
house in England. Miniature
Elizabethan garden by Rosemary
Verey. Fragrant border replanted by
Rupert Golby. Silver border and
kitchen garden. Falconry centre.
Partial wheelchair access.

34 ◆ KELMARSH HALL
Northampton NN6 9LT. **The
Kelmarsh Trust,** 01604 686543,
www.kelmarsh.com. *5m S of Market
Harborough. On A508, $1/2$ m N of
junction with A14. Entrance at Xrds in
Kelmarsh Village.* **House and Garden
Adm £5, chd 5-12yr £3, concessions
£4.50, Garden only Adm £4, chd
£2.50, concessions £3.50. See
website or phone for details. For
NGS: Suns 22 Apr; 1 July (2-5).**
1730 Palladian house by James Gibbs.
C18 landscape with lake, woods and
triangular walled garden. C20 garden
by Nancy Lancaster. Spring bulbs, rose
gardens, scented garden, herbaceous
borders planted by Norah Lindsay,
woodland walks and cut flower
borders. Gravel paths.

35 KILSBY GARDENS
CV23 8XP. *5m SE of Rugby. 6m N of
Daventry on A361. On A428 turn R on
B4038 through village.* Teas at Kilsby
Village Hall. **Combined adm £3, chd
free. Sun 10 June (2-6).**
Compact village with interesting mix of
old and new houses, 2 pubs, village
school and historic church. Pleasantly
rural with good ridge and furrow fields
around. Embroidery exhibition in Kilsby
Room.

NEW HUNT HOUSE
Linda Harris
Historic site with many borders,
water features, bog garden and
an Old England feel. Ramp to
main garden, some gravel and
cobbles.

THE MANOR COTTAGE
Mr & Mrs D Ward
Small garden attached to C17
thatched cottage. Fruit trees,
pond, rhododendrons and
azaleas, enc by stone walls on 3
sides. Mature borders. Open
again after 4yr break.

PYTCHLEY HOUSE
Mr & Mrs T F Clay
Garden downsized to $1/2$-acre and
being developed and re-shaped. 2
ponds, one a C19 reservoir
discovered while creating a new
herbaceous bed. Linked lawns
with island beds. Vegetables in
deep beds, fruit trees and soft
fruit.

RAINBOW'S END
7 Middle Street CV23 8XT. **Mr &
Mrs J Madigan**
Ever-changing garden with mirror
features, large pond and pergolas.

NEW 5 THE LAWNS
Mr C Smedley
Small, partially secluded garden
split into 2 distinct areas incl
vegetables and fruit. Shows
what can be done with limited
space on a modern housing
development. Gravel drive.

36 LITCHBOROUGH GARDENS
NN12 8JF. *10m SW of Northampton,
nr Towcester. Please use car park nr
village green. Village maps provided.*
**Combined adm £3, chd free (share
to St Martin's Church). Sun 3 June
(2-6).**
A small attractive ironstone village with
conservation area, listed buildings and
C13 church.

NEW ABBOTS LEA
M Cronin
Lawn with surrounding flower
beds.

BRUYERE COURT
Mr R M Billington
3 acres of landscaped garden.
Lawns, 2 ornamental lakes with
rock streams and fountain,
shrubs, rhododendrons, azaleas
and herbaceous borders, old-
fashioned roses, ornamental trees
and conifers.

THE HALL
Mr & Mrs A R Heygate
Large garden with open views of
parkland, laid to lawns and
borders with clipped hedges.
Extensive woodland garden has
large numbers of specimen trees
and shrubs. Walks wind through
this area and around the lakes.

4 KILN LANE
Mr & Mrs Morling
300yr-old cottage (not open) with modern cottage garden. Developed over 10yrs following levelling, terracing and hard landscaping incl the construction of 2 ponds, retaining existing trees and shrubs.

NEW 2 KILN LANE
Anna Steiner
Flag-like sculptures capturing natural elements of the garden, wind, shadows and movement. A green garden with oak tree and willows.

ORCHARD HOUSE
Mr & Mrs B Smith, 01327 830144, benz@btinternet.com. Visitors also welcome by appt. Landscape architects' country garden surrounding listed building (not open) designed for low maintenance. Orchard, pools, conservatory and working pump.

TIVY FARM
Mr & Mrs Pulford
Lawn sloping down to large wildlife pond surrounded by beautiful trees. Patio with lovely pots and containers.

51 TOWCESTER ROAD
Mr Norman Drinkwater
Small council house garden featuring lawns, shrubs, rockery and productive vegetable garden.

37 LOIS WEEDON HOUSE
NN12 8PJ. Sir John & Lady Greenaway. 7m W of Towcester. On the eastern edge of village. Last entrance on R going E towards Wappenham. Cream teas. Adm £3, chd free. Sun 27 May (2-6). Combined with **The Old Barn.** Large garden with terraces and fine views, lawns, pergola, water garden, mature yew hedges, pond. Some slopes.

Capturing natural elements, wind, shadows and movement . . .

38 LONG BUCKBY GARDENS
NN6 7RE, www.longbuckby.net. 8m NW of Northampton, midway between A428 & A5. 5 gardens in village close to Square, WC and parking. Mill House at junction of A428 and Ravensthorpe Rd, 1m distant. Home-made teas at 45 Brington Road. Combined adm £3, chd free. Sun 17 June (1-6).

NEW 23 BERRYFIELD
Mr & Mrs C M Robins
Lawns, gravel bed with pots, pond, patios, stone feature, flower beds, greenhouse. General ornamental garden.

45 BRINGTON ROAD
Derick & Sandra Cooper, 01327 843762. Visitors also welcome by appt.
1/3-acre organic village garden designed to create haven of peace and harmony, home to unusual wildlife. Features incl rose walk, 4 varied water features, Victorian-style greenhouse and summerhouse surrounded by box-edged raised vegetable plots. All constructed from reclaimed materials.

NEW 36 HIGH STACK
Mike & Jenny Pollard
Patio area, lawn, paths, various flowerbeds and shrubs.

MILL HOUSE
Ken and Gill Pawson, 01604 770103, gill@gpplanning.co.uk. Visitors also welcome by appt in June.
Site of East Haddon windmill. Over 1 acre on Northamptonshire sand, developed over 14 yrs. Large vegetable plot, orchard, pond, pergola and shady areas. Plant combinations and layout are echoes of Home Farm by Dan Pearson.

NEW THE RED HOUSE
Mercedes Ostermann van Essen
Centered around a pond with paths leading to and around it. The emphasis is on landscaping mainly of a traditional nature using Japanese planting in parts to highlight certain areas.

TORESTIN
10 Lime Ave. June Ford
1/3-acre mature garden divided into 3 separate areas incorporating water features, rockeries and pergolas. Interesting perennials, clematis and roses.

LOUGHTON VILLAGE GARDENS
See Buckinghamshire.

39 NEW ♦ LYVEDEN NEW BIELD
Oundle PE8 5AT. The National Trust, 01832 205358, lyveden@nationaltrust.org.uk. 5m SW of Oundle, 3m NE of Brigstock. Signed off A247 & A6116. Adm £4, chd free. Sat, Sun; Feb-Mar; Wed to Sun; Apr-Oct; daily Aug. For NGS: Sats 12 May; 8 Sept (10.30-5).
One of England's oldest garden landscapes, abandoned in 1605 after family involvement in the Gunpowder Plot, Lyveden still retains original terraces, prospect mounts, canals and the impressive garden lodge built to symbolise the Tresham's catholic faith. Recently replanted 5-acre orchard of pre-C17 tree varieties. Garden tour at 2pm.

40 MAIDWELL HALL
Maidwell NN6 9JG. Maidwell Hall School. 6m S of Market Harborough. A508 N from Northampton. Entrance via main drive off A508 on S edge of village. Adm £3, chd £3. Sun 1 Apr (2-5).
45 acres of lawns, playing fields, woodland, daffodils, spring bulbs, mature rose garden, lake and arboretum.

41 THE MALTINGS
Clipston LE16 9RS. Mr & Mrs Hamish Connell, 01858 525336, jconnell@jconnell.demon.co.uk. 4m S of Market Harborough, 9m E of Kettering. From A14 take A508 N. Turn L for Clipston in approx 2m. 2 houses away from Old Red Lion. Cream teas. Adm £3, chd free. Sat 7 Apr (1-6), Sun 8, Mon 9 Apr (11-6); Sat 16 June (1-6), Sun 17 June (11-6). Visitors also welcome by appt, groups of 10+. Meals at village pubs.
3/4-acre sloping plantsman's garden mostly designed by the present owner over the last 7 years. Many unusual

plants, shrubs, old and new trees. Over 50 different clematis, wild garden walk, spring bulb area, over 20 different species roses, 2 ponds connected by a stream, bog garden, many different fruits and vegetables. Home made cake stall. Older people may need a stick and some help.

🕻 ☕

42 ◆ **THE MENAGERIE**
Newport Pagnell Road, Horton NN7 2BX. Mr A Myers, 01604 870957,
www.menageriehorton.co.uk. 6m S of Northampton. 1m S of Horton. On B526, turn E at lay-by, across field. Adm £5, chd £1.50 under 12, concessions £4. Mon, Wed,Thurs, May to Sept & last Sun in month. For NGS: Sat 23 June (2-6).
Newly developed gardens set around C18 folly, with 2 delightful thatched arbours. Recently completed large formal walled garden with fountain, used for vegetables, fruit and cutting flowers. Recently extended exotic bog garden and native wetland area. Also rose garden, shrubberies, herbaceous borders and wild flower areas.

🕻 🕻 ⊛ ☕

MIDDLETON CHENEY GARDENS
See Oxfordshire.

43 **OLD BARN**
Weedon Lois NN12 8PL. Mr & Mrs John Gregory, 01327 860577,
irisgregory@tiscali.co.uk. 7m N of Brackley. In the centre of the village adjacent to the parish church. Adm combined £3, chd free. Sun 27 May (2-6). Combined with **Lois Weedon House**. Visitors also welcome by appt for goups 10+, June & July.
Garden has matured over the last 25yrs and reflects the owner's enthusiasm for hardy plants, inc collections of campanula, euphorbia, geraniums and violas supported by clematis and roses.

🕻 ⊛

Contemporary garden planted for year round interest on an exposed site . . .

44 **NEW** **THE OLD RECTORY, BROCKHALL**
NN7 4JY. Mrs J Quarmby, 01327 340280,
jane.quarmby@tqtraining.co.uk. 2m E of Weedon towards Flore. In village, as you enter from Flore, opp church. Cream teas at Flore Fields. **Adm £3, chd free. Sun 29 July (2-5.30). combined with Flore Fields.** Visitors also welcome by appt for groups 10+, Aug & Sept, share to Brockhall Church.
4½-acres being restored by the owners with advice from Bunnie Guinness and Johnnie Amos. Large sweeping lawns, very colourful flower cutting gardens, newly created shady planting area, ½-acre working kitchen garden, arboretum, pool garden and herbaceous borders. Concert in church in evening. Gravel, bark & mown paths.

🕻 ⊛ ☕

45 **THE OLD RECTORY, HASELBECH**
NN6 9LJ. Mr & Mrs P C Flory, 01604 686432. 12m N of Northampton. L turn off A508 just S of A14 junction, 2m to village. A14 junction 2, take A508 towards Northampton. 1st R to Haselbech. Home-made teas. **Adm £3, chd free (share to St Michael's Church). Sun 15 Apr (2-6).** Visitors also welcome by appt, incl coaches.
1-acre garden set in 9 acres, incl tree plantations, with glorious unspoilt views, surrounding Georgian rectory (not open). Old walled garden, herbaceous borders, rose garden and potager vegetable garden. Very pretty spring garden with a lot of early colour. Dell full of spring bulbs and primroses. Drifts of many varieties of daffodils.

🕻 🕻 ⊛ ☕

46 ◆ **THE OLD RECTORY, SUDBOROUGH**
NN14 3BX. Mr & Mrs A Huntington, 01832 733247,
www.oldrectorygardens.co.uk. 8m NE of Kettering. Exit 12 off A14. Village just off A6116 between Thrapston & Brigstock. **Adm £4, chd free. Tues to end Sept. For NGS: Sun 9 Sept (2-6).**
Classic 3-acre country garden with extensive borders of unusual plants, roses, shrubs, trees, pond and stream surrounding Georgian Rectory (not open). Woodland walk. Potager designed in 1985 by Rosemary Verey, the owners are now assisted by Rupert Golby. Featured in 'The Garden'. Some gravel paths.

🕻 🕻 ☕

47 **PARK HOUSE**
Norton NN11 5ND. Mr & Mrs J H Wareing Russell, 01327 702455. 3½ m N of Weedon. (A5) 2nd Norton/Daventry turn on L off A5. Entrance L before village. Home-made teas. **Adm £3, chd free. Sun 10 June (2-5).** Visitors also welcome by appt.
Approx 5 acres. Lawns leading down to lakes. Large variety of trees and shrubs, herbaceous borders, heather beds, azaleas, roses and ¼ m lakeside walk.

🕻 🕻 ⊛ ☕

48 **PRESTON CAPES GARDENS**
NN11 3TF. 6m SW of Daventry. 13m NE of Banbury. 3m N of Canons Ashby. Between A361 & A5. Light lunches & home-made teas at Old West Farm. **Combined adm £3.50, chd free. Sun 3 June (12-5).**
Unspoilt rural village in the Northamptonshire uplands. Local sandstone houses & cottages, Norman Church. Village maps for all visitors.

CITY COTTAGE
Mr & Mrs Gavin Cowen
Mature garden in the middle of attractive village. Walled herbaceous border, rose beds, flowering shrubs and wisteria.

🕻 🕻 ⊛

NEW **LADYCROFT**
Mervyn & Sophia Maddison
Contemporary garden, planted since 2005 for yr-round interest, on exposed site with fine views. Gravel drive.

🕻 🕻

LANGDALE HOUSE
Michael & Penny Eves
Approx 1-acre country garden with far-reaching views maintained solely by the owners. Sun and shade loving plants, many chosen primarily for foliage. New for 2007, pergola walk, raised Mediterranean gravel bed and wildlife pond.

NORTH FARM
Mr & Mrs Tim Coleridge
Rural farmhouse garden maintained by owners. Outstanding view towards Fawsley and High Wood.

OLD WEST FARM
Mr & Mrs Gerard Hoare. $3/4$ m E of Preston Capes
Rural 2-acre garden. Borders of interesting and unusual plants, roses and shrubs. Woodland area underplanted with shrubs. Exposed site with shelter planting, maintained by the owners without help, so designed for easy upkeep. Small vegetable garden.

NEW VILLAGE FARM
Trevor & Julia Clarke
Large garden on steeply sloping site. Interesting trees and shrubs, 3 large wildlife ponds and wonderful views over unspoilt countryside.

WEST ORCHARD FARM HOUSE
Mr & Mrs Nick Price
1-acre informal garden with outstanding views. Renovated completely by Caroline Price and replanted with shrubs and herbaceous plants.

49 ROSEBRIAR
83 Main Road, Collyweston
PE9 3PQ. Jenny Harrison, 01780 444389. On A43 $3 1/2$ m SW of Stamford. 4 doors from pub. **Adm £3, chd free. Sun 17 June (11-5).**
Visitors also welcome by appt.
The garden, which is on quite a steep slope, contains a variety of areas with alpine and grass beds, water feature with stream and bog garden, surrounded by herbaceous and shrub borders lavishly planted with exciting combinations, linked by gravel paths and patios.

CROFT ACRE
See Leicestershire & Rutland.

50 SPRATTON GARDENS
NN6 8HL. $6 1/2$ m NNW of Northampton. From Northampton on A5199 turn L at Holdenby Rd for Spratton Grange Farm, after $1/2$ m turn L up long drive. For other gardens turn R at Brixworth Rd. Car park signed. Refreshments & teas at St Andrews Church. **Combined adm £3.50, chd free. Sun 10 June (12-5.30).**
Attractive village with many C17 ironstone houses and C12 church. Tickets and maps at car park and gardens.

9 GLEBELANDS
Mr & Mrs R Smith
Garden with shrubs, fish pond extended into a secret garden with wildlife pond.

THE GRANARY
Mr & Mrs R A Shackleton
Semi-formal courtyard garden with circular pond, walled rear garden with circular lawn, mixed shrub and flower borders, archways through to small orchard.

11 HIGH STREET
Philip & Frances Roseblade
Small and compact, making full use of a difficult shape. Neat hedging and topiary.

HOMELEIGH COTTAGE
Mr & Mrs T Evans
Small split-level old-fashioned cottage garden, herbaceous and mixed borders and archway with lower courtyard garden.

MULBERRY COTTAGE
Mr & Mrs M Heaton
$1/2$-acre part cottage-style. Feature mulberry tree, lawns, herbaceous, rose and shrub borders, shady planting and water features.

Sun and shade loving plants, many chosen for foliage . . .

NORTHBANK HOUSE
Mr & Mrs J Knight
$1/3$-acre part walled cottage garden with herbaceous and shrub borders, roses, vegetables and lawns.

SPRATTON GRANGE FARM
Dennis & Christine Yardy
2-acre garden in an elevated position with superb country views, courtyard, parterre and large walled area with mature borders. A naturally fed pond with bog garden leading to a small spinney. Steep slopes in pond area.

THE STABLES
Mr & Mrs A Woods
$3/4$-acre garden planted for all-yr colour with shrubs, herbaceous borders, rockery, scree planting, ponds and pergola. Some gravel paths.

WALTHAM COTTAGE
Norma & Allan Simons
Small cottage garden that has evolved over the years - some interesting features.

51 STEANE PARK
NN13 6DP. Lady Connell. 2m from Brackley towards Banbury. On A422 between Brackley & Farthinghoe, 6m E of Banbury. Cream teas. **Adm £4.50, chd £1. Sun 20 May (11-6).**
Beautiful trees in 80 acres of parkland, old waterway and fishponds, 1620 church in grounds. The gardens are constantly being remade and redesigned in sympathy with old stone house and church. Limited access for wheelchairs.

STOKE ALBANY HOUSE
See Leicestershire & Rutland.

52 SULGRAVE GARDENS
nr Banbury OX17 2RP. 8m NE of Banbury. Just off B4525 Banbury to Northampton rd, 7m from J11 off M40. Home-made teas at The Cottage. **Combined adm £4, chd free. Sun 10 June (2-6).**
Small historic village with lovely stone houses, C14 church and C16 manor house, home of George Washington's ancestors. Award winning community owned and run village shop. Plant sales in aid of Northants Wildlife Trust.

Cream teas. **Adm £2.50, chd free.
Sun 10 June (2-5.30). Visitors also
welcome by appt June & July.**
1½-acre garden surrounding main
house (not open) set in countryside.
Many structural features enhanced by
large collection of climbers,
herbaceous plants and shrubs
separating defined areas, incl water
garden with pond, stream, waterfalls
and woodland area. Mediterranean
and secluded garden.
  ᴴ ⌖ ⊗ ☕

Set around C17 watermill and pond, winding stream, new woodland and pathways . . .

CHURCH COTTAGE
Church Street. **Hywel & Ingram
Lloyd**
½-acre garden with shrubs, trees,
rambling roses and pond. Mixed
planting for colour, form and scent
throughout the yr. Good range of
shade tolerant plants, developing
wild area. Fine view.

FERNS
Helmdon Road. **George & Julia
Metcalfe**
Approx ⅙ acre providing
conditions for a wide range of
plants, incl Mediterranean gravel
garden, mixed borders in sun and
shade, fern collection, damp area
and small alpine house.
  ᴴ ⌖ ⊗

NEW GREENFIELDS
Mrs S Harding
Small newly reclaimed garden with
restoration work still in progress.
Lawns with borders planted with
old varieties of fruit trees amongst
shrubs, roses and herbs. Lovely
landscape view.

MILL HOLLOW BARN
David Thompson
3-acre garden with different levels
and aspects, being developed for
all-yr interest and to house a wide
range of plants. Water gardens,
shrubberies, herbaceous borders
and gravel garden. New 4-acre
extension open 2007.

NEW THE OLD FARMHOUSE
Peter & Moo Mordaunt
Spacious garden with trees,
lawns, borders and a pretty bridge
over a tiny trickle of a stream
overlooking countryside.

SULGRAVE MANOR GARDEN
Sulgrave Manor Board, 01295
760205, enquiries
@sulgravemanor.org.uk. Visitors
also welcome by appt for
groups 10+, all yr.
Formal gardens, created in the

1920s by Sir Reginald Blomfield,
with orchard, parterre, lawns and
herbaceous borders. The Manor
hosts the National Garden of The
Herb Society with themed beds.
  ⌖ ⊗

THREEWAYS
Alison & Digby Lewis
Old cottage garden on 2 levels
enclosed by stone walls. Mainly
herbaceous perennial planting
with old roses, clematis and white
wisteria on walls. Various fruit
trees and bushes, container
grown vegetables.
  ⌖

NEW THE WATERMILL
Mr & Mrs A J Todd
Contemporary garden set around
C17 watermill and pond.
Extensive mixed planting in
borders and gravel, winding
stream, new woodland and
pathways. Designed by James
Alexander Sinclair.

53 TITCHMARSH HOUSE
Chapel Street NN14 3DA. **Sir Ewan
& Lady Harper, 01832 732439.** *2m N
of Thrapston. 6m S of Oundle. Exit A14
at A605 junction, Titchmarsh signed as
turning to E.* **Adm £3, chd free. Sat 9
June (12-5). Visitors also welcome
by appt April, May only.**
4½-acres extended and laid out since
1972. Cherries, magnolias,
herbaceous, irises, shrub roses, range
of unusual shrubs, walled borders and
ornamental vegetable garden. Tea and
refreshments at village fête which is in
aid of village organisations.
  ⌖ ᴴ

54 TOP LODGE
Violet Lane, Glendon NN14 1QL.
Glenn & Anne Burley, 01536 511784.
*3m NW of Kettering. Take A6003 to
Corby, off roundabout W of Kettering
turn L onto Glendon Rd, signed at T-
lights, approx 2m L into Violet Lane.*

55 TURWESTON GARDENS
Brackley NN13 5JY. *A43 from M40
J10. On Brackley bypass turn R on
A422 towards Buckingham, ½ m turn
L sign Turweston.* Cream teas at
Versions Farm. **Combined adm £3,
chd free. Sun 17 June (2-5.30).**

THE OLD SCHOOL HOUSE
Mr & Mrs Hugh Carey
Small cottage garden with clipped
box hedges surrounding
herbaceous borders.

VERSIONS FARM
Turweston. Mrs E T Smyth-
Osbourne
3-acre plantsman's garden,
wide-range of unusual plants,
shrubs and trees. Old stone
walls, terraces, old-fashioned
rose garden, pond. Conservatory.
Mostly wheelchair access.
  ⌖ ᴴ ⊗ ☕

TURWESTON MILL
Mr & Mrs Harry Leventis.
5 acres. Mill stream, formal water
garden and wildlife ponds. Trees,
lawns and herbaceous borders.
  ⌖

WALTON GARDENS
See Leicestershire & Rutland.

57 WEEDON LOIS GARDENS
NN12 8PL. *7m N of Brackley. 8m W of
Towcester. In centre of village, close to
Parish Church.* Home-made teas.
**Combined adm £3, chd free. Sun 1
July (2-6).**
☕

HOME CLOSE
Clyde Burbidge
2-acre garden estabished over
last 8 yrs. Informal cottage garden
surrounding stone barn
conversion. Meadow, ponds and
small spinney, vegetable garden,
new herbaceous borders. Gravel
paths, some steps.
  ⌖ ᴴ

Densely and abundantly planted for colour and scent. Snowdrops, hellebores and woodland garden in spring. Vibrant perennials in hot borders in summer . . . planting especially for insects . . .

WEST COTTAGE & 45 WEST END
Geoff & Rosemary Sage, 01788 510334, geoffsage@aol.com. Visitors also welcome by appt, July to Sept. 1 acre of mixed borders, lawns, ponds, lawn tennis court, kitchen garden and greenhouses with straw bale cultivation. Many containers and baskets. Newly extended developing wildlife and wild flower garden with mushroom cultivation.
&

WILDWOOD
See Oxfordshire.

59 WOODCHIPPINGS
Juniper Hill NN13 5RH. Richard Bashford & Valerie Bexley. *3m S of Brackley. Off A43. 3m N J10 M40, S of Croughton roundabout take L turn, 1/2 m to Juniper Hill.* Adm £2.50, chd free. Weds 7 Mar; 4 Apr; (2-5) Weds 23 May; 20 June; 11 July (2.30-6). 1/3-acre plantsman's garden surrounding stone cottage. Densely and abundantly planted for colour and scent. Snowdrops, hellebores and woodland garden in spring. Vibrant perennials in hot borders in summer. Planting especially for insects. Narrow paths may be unsuitable for infirm or very young. Small nursery.

OLD BARN
Mr & Mrs John Gregory, 01327 860577, irisgregory@tiscali.co.uk
Over the past 25yrs this garden has matured and reflects the owner's enthusiasm for hardy plants, incl collections of campanula, euphorbia, geranium and violas supported by clematis and roses.

58 WEST HADDON GARDENS
NN6 7AY. *10m NW of Northampton. Off A428 between Rugby & Northampton, 4m E of M1 J18. Village now bypassed.* Cream teas at West Cottage. Combined adm £3.50, chd free. Sun 1 July (2-6).

CLOVER COTTAGE
Helen & Stephen Chown
Walled cottage garden with terraces, cobbles, gravel, pots and decking. Very sunny sheltered space with a lovely lemon tree, orange bush & bougainvillea.

NEW THE CROWN COURTYARD
Mark Byrom
Public House courtyard with C16 outbuildings decorated with hanging baskets, containers and cascading flora.

LIME HOUSE
Lesley & David Roberts
1/2-acre walled garden with rockeries, herbaceous borders, walk-through shrubbery, rose beds, croquet lawn. Summerhouse, patio with greenhouse and a variety of garden statues and ornaments.

WESLYAN COTTAGE
Arnie & Gillean Stensones
Small walled garden with walkways and paved sitting areas. Colourful borders, pond and summer house.

Sunny sheltered place with a lovely lemon tree, orange bush and bougainvillea . . .

NORTHUMBERLAND

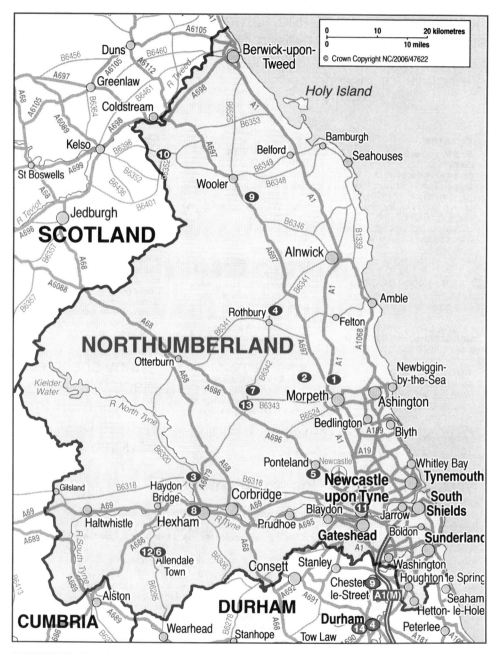

Opening Dates

March

SUNDAY 18
⑪ Moorbank Botanic Garden

April

SATURDAY 21
② Bide-a-Wee Cottage

SUNDAY 29
⑪ Moorbank Botanic Garden
⑬ Wallington

May

SUNDAY 13
③ Chesters Walled Garden

MONDAY 21
⑨ Lilburn Tower

June

SUNDAY 10
① Ashfield

SUNDAY 17
⑥ Greystones
⑩ Mindrum

THURSDAY 21
⑦ Herterton House

July

SUNDAY 1
⑤ 9 Grenville Court
⑫ Thornley House

WEDNESDAY 4
⑪ Moorbank Botanic Garden (Evening)

SUNDAY 8
④ Cragside

THURSDAY 19
⑦ Herterton House

SUNDAY 22
⑧ Hexham Community Walled Garden

August

THURSDAY 2
⑦ Herterton House

SUNDAY 5
⑬ Wallington

October

SUNDAY 28
⑪ Moorbank Botanic Garden

Gardens open to the public

② Bide-a-Wee Cottage
③ Chesters Walled Garden
④ Cragside
⑦ Herterton House
⑫ Thornley House
⑬ Wallington

The Gardens

① ASHFIELD
Hebron NE61 3LA. Barry & Rona McWilliam. *3m N of Morpeth. 1¹/₂ m E of Heighley Gate. 1m off A1 on C130. S side of Hebron. Car park is through field gate.* Cream teas. **Adm £3, chd free, concessions £2. Sun 10 June (12-5).**
Plantsmans garden, largely grown from seed. Set within 5 acres are collections of sorbus, betula and malus, beautiful hedging and remarkable alpines from around the world. Open spaces are bounded by herbaceous and shrub borders which contrast with the tranquil woodland set with meandering grass paths and varied under planting. Woodland walk. Featured in 'Morpeth Herald', various articles & on Radio Newcastle.
 ♿ ⊛ ☕

② ◆ BIDE-A-WEE COTTAGE
Stanton, Morpeth NE65 8PR. Mr M Robson, www.bideawee.co.uk. *7m NNW of Morpeth. Turn L off A192 out of Morpeth at Fairmoor. Stanton is 6m along this rd.* **Adm £2.50, chd free.** Weds & Sats 21 Apr to 29 Aug. For NGS: Sat 21 Apr (1.30-4).
Unique secret garden created over the last 26yrs out of a small sandstone quarry, it features rock and water. Unusual perennials are woven within a matrix of ferns, trees and shrubs. The garden contains the National Collection of centaurea, and many other plants seldom seen. Featured in 'Gardens Illustrated'.
 ♿ ⋇ ⊛ NCCPG

③ ◆ CHESTERS WALLED GARDEN
Chollerford NE46 4BQ. Mrs S White, 01434 681483, www.chesterswalledgarden.co.uk. *6m N of Hexham. Off the B6318. ¹/₂ m W of Chollerford.* **Adm £3, chd under 10 free.** Daily mid Mar to end Oct . For NGS: Sun 13 May (10-5).
Delightful 2-acre walled garden, planted in relaxed style; wild flowers mingle with unusual perennials and extensive collection of herbs. Three National Collections; marjoram, sanguisorba and thyme, grown on famous Thyme Bank. Roman garden; knot garden, ponds and vegetables. Organically run, the walled garden is a haven for wildlife incl red squirrels.
 ♿ ⋇ ⊛ NCCPG

④ ◆ CRAGSIDE
Rothbury NE65 7PX. The National Trust, 01669 621267, www.nationaltrust.org.uk. *13m SW of Alnwick. (B6341); 15m NW of Morpeth (A697).* **Adm £7.70, chd £3,.30.** For NGS: Sun 8 July (10.30-5).
Formal garden in the 'High Victorian' style created by the 1st Lord Armstrong. Fully restored Italian terrace, orchard house, carpet bedding, dahlia walk and fernery. 3¹/₂ acres of rock garden with its restored cascades. Extensive grounds of over 1000 acres famous for rhododendrons and beautiful lakes.
 ⋇ ☕

Organically run, the walled garden is a haven for wildlife including red squirrels . . .

⑤ 9 GRENVILLE COURT
Darras Hall NE20 9HT. Mr & Mrs J C Scott, 01661 825002, kathjohn@talktalk.net. *2m SW of Ponteland. A696, turn L after crossing river travelling N (signed Darras Hall). At the end of Darras Rd turn R (Western Way) 2nd turning on L.* Home-made teas. **Adm £2.50, chd free. Sun 1 July (2-5.30). Visitors also welcome by appt especially in Feb for snowdrops (over 80) and at other times.**
¹/₃ acre of mixed borders; a number of small gardens within the garden. Special interest in hardy geraniums (over 100) and hostas. National Collection of *Brunnera macrophylla*. Featured in 'North East Exclusive'.
 ♿ ⋇ ⊛ NCCPG ☕

6 GREYSTONES
The Dene, Allendale NE47 9PX. Paul Procter. *10m S of Hexham. On N edge of Allendale, turn opp Deneholm Centre, 400yds on R. Disabled parking in drive, otherwise walk from Allendale village (10 mins).* Home-made teas. **Adm £3, chd free (share to Compassion in World Farming). Sun 17 June (2-5).**
Ann Procter's garden is a 1¹/₂-acre S-facing garden with panoramic views. Just 8yrs old, already looking mature. Formed by a series of terraces graded from formal nr house, through species-rich meadows down to pretty woodland stream. Well-planted borders, rock garden and natural ponds, with diverse wildlife. Bird hide in wood. Live music and display of artwork in connection with Shakespeare Now. Featured in 'The Northumbrian'. North Pennines Wild Plant Festival 'Plants on High'. Very limited disabled access.

7 ◆ HERTERTON HOUSE
Hartington NE61 4BN. Mr Frank Lawley, 01670 774278. *12m W of Morpeth. 23m NW of Newcastle. 2m N of Cambo on the B6342 signed to Hartington. Brown signs.* **Adm £3, chd free. Mons, Weds, Fris, Sats & Suns 1 Apr to 30 Sept.** For NGS: Thurs 21 June; 19 July; 2 Aug (1.30-5.30).
1 acre of formal garden in stone walls around C16 farmhouse (not open). Incl small topiary garden, physic garden, flower garden, fancy garden, gazebo and nursery garden.

A feline theme is evident throughout this child friendly garden . . .

8 HEXHAM COMMUNITY WALLED GARDEN
Whetstone Bridge Road NE46 3JB. Queen Elizabeth High School, 07930 969756 (Emma Thompson), 01434 607350 (Keda Norman). *¹/₂ m W of Hexham. From Hexham bus stn drive in a westerly direction. When you reach 3 way T-lights - Fox PH on R, turn L up Allendale Rd, after layby on L, take 2nd R turn up lane. Car park will be signed.* **Adm £2, chd free, concessions £1.50. Sun 22 July (11-4). Visitors also welcome by appt.**
¹/₄-acre walled garden developed by young people and community groups. Cottage garden style incl ponds, vegetables, fruit and herbaceous planting. Victorian greenhouse. Willow tunnels. Partial wheelchair access: Gravel paths wooden decking, grassy areas.

9 LILBURN TOWER
Alnwick NE66 4PQ. Mr & Mrs D Davidson. *3m S of Wooler. On A697.* Home-made teas. **Adm £3, chd free. Mon 21 May (2-6).**
10 acres of walled and formal gardens incl conservatory and large glasshouse. Approx 30 acres of woodland with walks and pond garden. Rhododendrons and azaleas. Also ruins of Pele Tower, and C12 church. Wheelchair access to woodland garden only.

10 MINDRUM
nr Cornhill on Tweed & Yetholm TD12 4QN. Hon P J & Mrs Fairfax. *6m SW of Coldstream, 9m NW of Wooler. 4m N of Yetholm. 5m from Cornhill on Tweed on B6352.* Home-made teas. **Adm £3, chd free. Sun 17 June (2-6).**

Old-fashioned roses; rock and water garden; shrub borders. Wonderful views along Bowmont Valley. Approx 3 acres. Small childrens potting and play corner, and crèche.

⑪ MOORBANK BOTANIC GARDEN
Claremont Road, Newcastle upon Tyne NE1 7RU. University of Newcastle, 01434 602403, richards@hightrees60.fsnet.co.uk. *3/4 m from Newcastle Haymarket. W end of Claremont Rd, just E of Cat & Dog shelter. Shared entrance with Town Moor Superintendents Farm (blue gate). 12 mins walk up Claremont Rd from Exhibition Park entrance roundabout. No parking in garden.* **Adm £2.50, chd free (share to Friends of Moorbank Garden). Suns 18 Mar; 29 Apr; 28 Oct (2-5). Evening Opening** wine, **Wed 4 July (6-9). Visitors also welcome by appt, for groups of 15+, coaches permitted.**
3 acre university botanic garden with collections of rare conifers, rhododendrons, sorbus, pond, perennials, herb garden, meadow. Extensive plantings under glass with tropical plants, succulants, insectivorous plants. Many original collections, originally from Kilbryde Gardens, Corbridge. Outside plantings maintained with volunteer help. Guided tours of garden. Practical demonstrations.

⑫ NEW ◆ THORNLEY HOUSE
Allendale, Northum NE47 9NH. Ms Eileen Finn, 01434 683255, e.finn@ukonline.co.uk. *1m W of Allendale. From Allendale town, down hill from Hare & Hound to 5th rd junction, 1m Thornley House is big house in field in front.* **Adm £3, chd free.** For NGS: **Sun 1 July (2-5).**
Unusual 1-acre garden consisting of woodland, stream, pond, vegetable and fruit garden, rose avenue and mixed planting. A feline theme is evident throughout this child friendly garden. Seek and find quiz is available for family fun. Real cats and ornamental animals enhance this garden. Live classical music. Resident Maine Coons.

⑬ ◆ WALLINGTON
Cambo NE61 4AR. The National Trust, 01670 773600, www.nationaltrust.org.uk. *12m W of Morpeth. From N B6343; from S via A696 from Newcastle, 6m W of Belsay, B6342 to Cambo.* **House and Garden adm £8, chd £4, Garden only adm £5.50, chd £2.75. Garden daily Apr - Sept 10-7, Oct 10-6, Nov - Mar 10-4.** For NGS: **Suns 29 Apr; 5 Aug (10-7).**
Walled, terraced garden with fine herbaceous and mixed borders; Edwardian conservatory; 100 acres woodland and lakes. National Collection of sambucus. House dates from 1688 but altered, interior greatly changed c1740; exceptional rococo plasterwork by Francini brothers. Garden tour 2pm.
NCCPG

Wonderful views along Bowmont Valley . . . small childrens potting and play corner . . .

Northumberland County Volunteers

County Organiser
Shanah Smailes, The Stables, Chapman's Court, Catterick Village DL10 7UE, 01748 812887, shanna@smailes.go-plus.net

County Treasurers
Anne & David John Kinniment, Sike View, Kirkwhelpington NE19 2SA, 01830 540393, anne@kinniment.freeserve.co.uk

Publicity
Susie White, Chesters Walled Garden, Chollerford, Hexham NE46 4BQ, 01434 681483, susie@chesterswalledgarden.fsnet.co.uk

Assistant County Organiser
Patricia Fleming, Wooperton Hall, Alnwick NE66 4XS, 01668 217009

NOTTINGHAMSHIRE

Opening Dates

February

SUNDAY 18
5 The Beeches

SUNDAY 25
5 The Beeches

April

SUNDAY 8
24 Felley Priory

SUNDAY 15
26 Gardeners' Cottage

SUNDAY 22
3 Ashdene
45 The Old Vicarage

SUNDAY 29
3 Ashdene
5 The Beeches

May

SUNDAY 6
18 Darby House
(61) University of Nottingham Gardens

MONDAY 7
13 7 Collygate
28 Gorene

SATURDAY 12
(60) Teversal Manor Gardens

SUNDAY 13
45 The Old Vicarage
(58) Squirrel Lodge

SUNDAY 20
3 Ashdene
7 Bishops Manor
20 Dumbleside
37 61 Lambley Lane

SUNDAY 27
44 Norwell Nurseries
48 Papplewick Hall

MONDAY 28
34 Holmes Villa
41 Mill Hill House

June

SUNDAY 3
16 Cropwell Butler Gardens
35 Home Farm Cottage

WEDNESDAY 6
16 Cropwell Butler Gardens (Evening)

SUNDAY 10
8 Cherry Tree House
36 134 Julian Road
38 Manor Farm House
42 Newbray House
(51) 117 Pierrepont Road
(56) 284 Rutland Road

WEDNESDAY 13
36 134 Julian Road (Evening)
(51) 117 Pierrepont Road (Evening)
(56) 284 Rutland Road (Evening)

FRIDAY 15
4 Baxter Farm (Evening)
9 Chestnut Cottage (Evening)

SATURDAY 16
10 59 Church Lane
31 The Hayloft

SUNDAY 17
2 29 Ash Grove
11 4 Clare Valley
29 Gringley Gardens
50 Penrhyn House
(63) Weston Lodge

WEDNESDAY 20
2 29 Ash Grove (Evening)
6 Bishops Cottage (Evening)
30 Hall Farm Cottage (Evening)

SUNDAY 24
1 30 Albert Road
5 The Beeches
13 7 Collygate
15 Cottage Farm
19 37 Davies Road
21 21 Ella Road
43 Norwell Gardens

WEDNESDAY 27
43 Norwell Gardens (Evening)

July

SUNDAY 1
39 Meadowside
46 Orchard House
(52) Redlands
(64) White House

THURSDAY 5
25 Fuchsia View (Evening)

SATURDAY 7
(60) Teversal Manor Gardens (Day & Evening)

SUNDAY 8
25 Fuchsia View
27 16 Glensford Gardens
49 48 Penarth Gardens

WEDNESDAY 11
14 Cornerstones (Evening)

SATURDAY 14
12 Clumber Park Walled Kitchen Garden

SUNDAY 15
14 Cornerstones
22 Elm House
23 The Elms
40 Melrose

WEDNESDAY 18
(57) 125 Shelford Road (Evening)

THURSDAY 19
25 Fuchsia View (Evening)

SUNDAY 22
28 Gorene
47 20 The Paddocks
(54) Rose Cottage

WEDNESDAY 25
47 20 The Paddocks (Evening)

SUNDAY 29
25 Fuchsia View

August

WEDNESDAY 1
26 Gardeners' Cottage (Evening)

SUNDAY 5
46 Orchard House

SUNDAY 12
14 Cornerstones
(54) Rose Cottage

SUNDAY 19
(61) University of Nottingham Gardens

SUNDAY 26
(58) Squirrel Lodge

September

SUNDAY 9
5 The Beeches (Day & Evening)
(54) Rose Cottage

SUNDAY 16
17 Cropwell Court

SUNDAY 23
45 The Old Vicarage
(57) 125 Shelford Road

SUNDAY 30
33 Holme Pierrepont Hall

October

SATURDAY 6
(60) Teversal Manor Gardens

Gardens open to the public

12 Clumber Park Walled Kitchen Garden
24 Felley Priory
32 Hodsock Priory Gardens
33 Holme Pierrepont Hall
44 Norwell Nurseries
(60) Teversal Manor Gardens

By appointment only

(55) Roselea
(59) 14 Temple Drive

The Gardens

Over 100 varieties of snowdrops, and spring bulbs . . .

① 30 ALBERT ROAD
West Bridgford, Nottingham
NG2 5GS. Jan & Simon Johnson.
*From Trent Bridge take A52
Radcliffe/Grantham Rd. 1/2 m turn R
(Mabel Grove), L into Albert Rd. Car
park on R after park. Garden signed
from car park.* **Combined adm £3.50**
(share to LAM Action). **Sun 24 June**
(1-5). Combined with **21 Ella Road
& 37 Davies Rd.**
This compact well-stocked formal
walled garden, with many
complementary plants, demonstrates
the possibilities of a town garden.
🎋

② 29 ASH GROVE
Keyworth NG12 5DH. Lynn & Gary
Longworth, 0115 937 3200,
lynnmackl@hotmail.co.uk. *8m SE of
Nottingham. Turn off A606 Melton Rd.
Signed Plumtree/Keyworth. Drive
through Plumtree under railway bridge.
Turn L at Keep L sign onto Nicker Hill,
R onto Wolds Dr, 2nd L to Beech Ave.
2nd R into Ash Grove. 29 is at far end
of cul-de-sac.* Home-made teas. **Adm
£2.50, chd free** (share to Oasis
Breast Cancer Trust). **Sun 17 June**
(1-5.30). **Evening Opening** £3.50,
wine, Wed 20 June (6-8.30). Visitors
also welcome by appt mid June/mid
July.
The generous size of this beautifully
crafted garden is totally unexpected in
the top corner of Ash Grove. It has a
plant diversity that would fill a much
larger garden and an intensity of colour
and form that has been composed and
arranged over many years by the
discerning and not easily satisfied eyes
of its proud owners.
🎋 ⊛ ☕

③ ASHDENE
Radley Road, Halam NG22 8AH.
Glenys & David Herbert, 01636
812335, david@herbert.newsurf.net.
*1m W of Southwell. From B6386 in
Halam village 300yds past church.*
Light refreshments & home-made teas.
**Adm £3, chd free. Suns 22, 29 Apr;
20 May** (1-5.30). Visitors also
welcome by appt.
Many mature trees incl magnificent
walnut (200yrs), paulownia (50yrs) and
mulberry. Japanese-style garden incl
mature spiral yew. Species and
scented rose and woodland gardens.
Many clematis, hebes.
�ⁿ ⊛ 🏠 ☕

④ BAXTER FARM
Willoughby on the Wolds LE12 6SY.
Peter & Pru Tatham, 01509 880975,
tatham@onetel.com. *10m S of
Nottingham, 12m N of Leicester.
About 1/4 m off A46 at E end of Main
St.* **Combined adm £3, chd free** (if
accompanied). **Evening Opening**
wine, Fri 15 June (6-9). Combined
with **Chestnut Cottage.** Visitors
also welcome by appt.
Old farmhouse and barns. 1-acre
garden planted last 25yrs.
Conservatory, old cattle drinking pond
now planted, herbaceous borders,
informal plantings of old roses, hardy
geraniums, salvias and many climbers.
Pergola, Chinese garden, beech and
yew hedged walks. Kitchen garden.
⚅ ⊛

⑤ THE BEECHES
The Avenue, Milton, Tuxford
NG22 0PW. Margaret & Jim Swindin,
01777 870828. *12m N of Newark. Exit
A1 at Markham Moor roundabout, take
Walesby sign into village (1m).* Soup &
roll (Feb) Home-made teas Apr & June.
**Adm £2.50 (Feb) £3 (April & June),
chd free. Suns 18, 25 Feb** (11-4);
Suns 29 Apr; 24 June (2-5); **Evening
Opening** £3.50, wine, Sun 9 Sept (4-
7). Visitors also welcome by appt
Feb, Apr, May, Sept.
1-acre all seasons garden well stocked
with colourful, desirable plants incl over
100 varieties of snowdrops, and spring
bulbs. Herbaceous areas incl over 50
different clematis and a wild flower
meadow. Tunnel and raised beds with
organically grown fruit and vegetables,
together with many autumn species
and grasses are at their best in our
Sept opening. Newcastle Mausoleum
open in Apr, June & Sept. Access to
ancient hay meadow in June.
⚅ 🎋 ⊛ ☕

⑥ BISHOPS COTTAGE
89 Main Street, Kinoulton NG12 3EL.
Ann & Steve Hammond. *8m SE of
West Bridgford. Kinoulton is off A46
just N of intersection with A606. Into
village, pass school & village hall.
Garden on R after bend on Main St.*

Evening Opening. Combined adm
£4, wine, Wed 20 June (6.30-8.30).
Combined with **Hall Farm Cottage.**
This large mature cottage garden with
its remnants of the old orchard and
mixed herbaceous beds is the stuff of
dreams. Scented plants to please the
senses and extended colour
throughout the season make this a
very restful garden with views over the
open countryside. Home-made
preserves for sale. Appeared in
'Nottinghamshire Gardens' 2006.
Gravel path at entrance.
⚅ 🎋 ⊛

⑦ BISHOPS MANOR
Bishops Drive, Southwell NG25 0JR.
The Rt Reverend George Cassidy,
Bishop of Southwell. *Centre of
Southwell, end of Bishops Dr on S side
of Minster.* **Adm £3, chd free. Sun 20
May** (1-5).
House built into part of old medieval
palace of the Archbishops of York.
Ruins form delightful enclosed garden,
lawns and 4-seasons tree garden in
unusual setting. Large garden with
Edwardian layout, includes herb knot
garden and other features. Gravel
paths. Steep slope to walled garden.
Teas available at Minster Refectory,
adjacent.
⚅ 🎋 ☕

**⑧ NEW CHERRY TREE
HOUSE**
Church Hill, Plumtree,
Nottingham NG12 5ND. Drs H &
C Lewis. *6m SE of Nottingham.
Enter Plumtree from A606, 100yds
down hill from church.* Cream teas,
cake stall. **Adm £2.50, chd free.
Sun 10 June** (2-5).
On visiting Cherry Tree House
prepare to be enchanted by a
romantic, exuberant and colourful
mix of flowers, bordered by
winding narrow grass paths and
babbling streams. Only 150ft long,
this garden has magical charm.
Some bridges may be slippery if
wet.
🎋 ⊛ ☕

Romantic, exuberant and colourful mix of flowers . . .

9 NEW CHESTNUT COTTAGE

Main Street, Willoughby-on-the-Wolds LE12 6SY. Dr Olivia Williams. *10m S of Nottingham;12m N of Leicester. About ¼m off A46 at W end of Main St.* **Adm £3, chd free. Evening Opening** wine, Fri 15 June (6-9). Combined with **Baxter Farm.**
One of the owner's artistic outlets! This small S-facing garden was re-landscaped by the owner in 1999, with a wildlife pond, decking, summerhouse, water feature and container plants. Many interesting and unusual plants. 10 mins walk from Baxter Farm. Access is flat, but narrow paths.

10 59 CHURCH LANE

Thrumpton, Nottingham NG11 0AW. Valerie & John Collins, 0115 983 0533. *7m SW of Nottingham. Thrumpton is off A453 between Nottingham and J24 of M1. From Nottingham, 1st R signed Thrumpton approx 2m after Crusader PH in Clifton. In ½m R. No 59 is ½m on LH-side. From M1 approx 3m along A453 turn L just after power stn. 1st R, then L in ½m. No 59 is ½m on L.* Car park will be signed. Light refreshments & teas in village hall. **Combined adm £2.50, chd free. Sat 16 June (12-6). Combined with The Hayloft.** Visitors also welcome by appt.
His and hers gardens. No prizes for guessing whose is whose. Front garden is a dry stream with grasses and splashes of colour leading to a natural pond and marginal area. Back garden, with small wild flower patch, and woodland with livestock grazing beyond, is packed full with plants, shrubs and trees, all carefully arranged with an artistic eye.

11 4 CLARE VALLEY

The Park, Nottingham NG7 1BU. Gudrun Sowerby. *Enter the Park either via Castle entrance (pass gate house on L then take 1st R turn into Park Valley. Follow rd round LH-bend and Clare Valley is ahead). Or via Derby Rd entrance (pass through gates and take 2nd rd on L down steep hill to one way system. Turn L to pass bowling and tennis clubs and Clare Valley is next L turn).* Teas at Weston Lodge.

Combined adm £3, chd free. Sun 17 June (2-6). Combined with Penrhyn House and **Weston Lodge.**
This heavily shaded garden demonstrates what will grow, and indeed what can be achieved under a tall tree canopy. Colour and impact of informed planting will delight all those who view it from the high rear terrace, and then descend down the steps into it.

Packed full with plants, shrubs and trees . . .

12 ♦ CLUMBER PARK WALLED KITCHEN GARDEN

Clumber Park, Worksop S80 3AZ. The National Trust, 01909 476592, www.nationaltrust.org.uk. *4m S of Worksop. From main car park follow directions to the Walled Kitchen Garden. Turn L up Cedar Ave to wrought iron gates.* **Adm £2, chd free,** NT members free, £4.50 (per vehicle) entry to Clumber Park; coaches, cyclists, pedestrians free. Park open all yr except Sat 18 Aug (concert day) & 25 Dec. Walled kitchen garden open 31 Mar-30 Sept 10-6 Sat & Sun, 10-5 Mon to Fri. For NGS: Sat 14 July (10-6).
Beautiful 4-acre walled kitchen garden, growing unusual and old varieties of vegetables, fruit trees, herbs and ornamentals, incl the magnificent recently extended 400ft long double herbaceous borders. 450ft long glasshouse (the longest owned by the National Trust), with grape vines, peaches, nectarines and figs. Museum of gardening tools. Featured in 'Nottinghamshire Today' & 'Yorkshire Post' Aug 2006. Gravel paths, some on slope.

13 7 COLLYGATE

Swingate, Kimberley NG16 2PJ. Doreen Fahey & John Arkinstall. *6m W of Nottingham. From M1 J26 take A610 towards Nottingham. L at next island on B600 into Kimberley. At Sainsbury's mini island take L. L at top. Park on this rd in 500yds. Collygate on R.* Home-made teas. **Adm £2, chd free. Mon 7 May; Sun 24 June (1-5).**
Delightful garden created by serious plant addicts tucked away at the end of a short narrow lane in Swingate. It

greets you with an impact of unexpected colour and delights you with the variety and sensitivity of the planting. A peaceful backwater in an urban setting.

14 NEW CORNERSTONES

15 Lamcote Gardens, Radcliffe-on-Trent, Nottingham NG12 2BS. Judith & Jeff Coombes, 0115 845 8055, judith.coombes@ntlworld.com. *4m E of Nottingham. From A52 take Radcliffe exit at the RSPCA junction, then 2nd L just before hairpin bend.* Home-made teas. **Adm £2.50, chd free. Suns 15 July; 12 Aug (2-6). Evening Opening £3.50, wine, Wed 11 July (6-9).** Visitors also welcome by appt June to Aug for groups 10+.
Our garden, approaching ½ an acre, is continually evolving with the aim of achieving a long season of colour and interest from flowing herbaceous borders and an abundance of produce from the newly-created potager vegetable/fruit garden. Many unusual and tender plants, bananas, palms, fish pond, greenhouse and areas for relaxation. Some barked paths.

Delightful garden created by serious plant addicts . . .

THE COTTAGE
See Derbyshire.

15 COTTAGE FARM

Widmerpool Lane, Keyworth NG12 5BA. Malcolm Plant & Brenda Smith, 0115 937 2022. *8m SE of Nottingham. From A606, take sign to Plumtree/Keyworth. In Keyworth, L fork along Nicker Hill, R along Willow Brook, next L towards Widmerpool. 1st house on R among trees.* **Adm £2.50, chd free. Sun 24 June (11-5).** Visitors also welcome by appt June to July, max group 25. No coaches.

Peaceful cottage garden and extensive grounds, in all 12 acres comprising informal planting of herbaceous borders, old apple orchard, wildlife pond, mature woodland and meadow. Take a wild flower walk, stroll under lofty elms, spy varied birdlife. Environmental and nature features.

  ♿ ✕ ✿ ☕

Thoughtful planting has made for easy maintenance . . .

16 NEW CROPWELL BUTLER GARDENS
NG12 3AA. *Cropwell Butler lies to the E of Nottingham close to A52 junction with A46. Car Parking to rear of village hall on Main Street.* Teas at Laurel House 3 June; wine at Mulberry House 6 June. **Combined adm £3.50, chd free. Sun 3 June (2-6). Evening Opening £4.50, wine, Wed 6 June (5-8).**
Cropwell Butler is a small, attractive country village on the edge of the Vale of Belvoir. Blend of traditional cottages and more modern properties, many with fine gardens. There is limited through traffic and various footpaths offering a range of pleasant walks. Refreshments & plant stall.

NEW LAUREL HOUSE
Tythby Road. John & Gaye Fawcett
This generous, well-maintained garden has several attractive features, a summerhouse, stepped terrace and pond among them, but its large old fruit trees and wide sweeps of lawn give it a special, timeless character. Small unfenced pond.
 ♿ ☕

NEW THE MALT HOUSE
Main Street. Vanessa Hope
An old side gate off the street gives access to this cottage garden on four levels with hidden corners, pond and old low pantiled outbuilding. The sympathetic planting allows its busy owner to unwind without being overburdened by its upkeep. Steps to four levels. Unfenced pond.

NEW MULBERRY HOUSE
Back Lane. Mrs Isabel Smith.
Back Lane is off Radcliffe Rd and runs parallel to Main St
This elegant, small modern garden is geometric and angular and belies the belief that straight lines and nature do not work well together.Thoughtful planting has made for easy maintenance and great appeal and surrounds a substantial water feature of contemporary design. Unfenced pond presents some risk to children.
 ♿ ✕

NEW REDLAND HOUSE
Main Street. Shelagh Barnes, 0115 933 3082. Visitors also welcome by appt.
This is a rare chance for the garden visitor to see a larger than average garden under development. Overgrown Leylandii and unwanted shrubs and ivy have been grubbed out, the soil enriched and expert, knowledgeable and enthusiastic planting under a flower arranger's keen eye is underway. This is a garden to watch! In a couple of years it will be stunning, but if you miss it now you will be unable fully to appreciate it then. Gravel paths, paved and grass slopes.
 ♿ ✕

17 NEW CROPWELL COURT
Cropwell Road, Cropwell Butler NG12 2LZ. Mr & Mrs M Rowen. *1m S of A52/A46 junction (Saxondale roundabout). A46/Cropwell Rd junction follow signs to Radcliffe-on-Trent. At Radcliffe-on-Trent A52/Cropwell Rd junction follow signs to Cropwell Butler.* Home-made teas. **Adm £3, chd free (share to Prince's Trust, Notts). Sun 16 Sept (2-6).**

Large garden with mature herbaceous borders and sunken box garden. Walled kitchen and herb garden with greenhouse. New area started in 2006, work still ongoing. Re-furbished Victorian greenhouse. Well-manicured lawns. Parkland with mature trees and small wild flower area. Garden for all seasons with good autumn colour. Some steps, and heavy going for wheelchairs.
 ♿ ✕ ✿ ☕

18 DARBY HOUSE
10 The Grove, Southey Street, Nottingham NG7 4BQ. Jed Brignal, 07960 065042. *3/4m NE of city centre take A610, turn R into Forest Rd, first L into Southey St.* **Adm £2, chd free. Sun 6 May (2-5). Visitors also welcome by appt.**
Unusual city garden designed and developed by artist owner is a tranquil oasis in unlikely location. Victorian walled garden with ponds, waterfall, gazebos and a fairy-tale shady area surrounded by mature trees. House (1849) and garden provide temporary home and sanctuary for actors, writers, dancers and other creative visitors.
 ✿

19 NEW 37 DAVIES ROAD
West Bridgford, Nottingham NG2 5JE. Sandie & Alan Lorenzo. *See 30 Albert Rd for directions.* **Combined adm £3.50, chd free (share to LAM). Sun 24 June (1-5). Combined with 21 Ella Rd & 30 Albert Rd.**
Attractive town garden designed and created in recent years from 1950s urban formality. Its clever low maintenance layout, planting and landscaping features bring a sense of tranquillity to the middle of busy West Bridgford. Steps. Gravel paths.
 ✕

20 DUMBLESIDE
17 Bridle Road, Burton Joyce NG14 5FT. Mr & Mrs P Bates, 0115 931 3725. *5m NE of Nottingham. In Burton Joyce turn off A612, Nottingham to Southwell Rd into Lambley Lane. Bridle Rd is an impassable looking rd to the R off Lambley Lane. Car parking easiest BEYOND garden.*

Combined adm £3.50 for both gardens. **Sun 20 May (2-6). Combined with 61 Lambley Lane.** Visitors also welcome by appt.
2 acres of varied habitat. Natural spring and stream planted with primulas, fritillaries and fine specimen shrubs. A small meadow is being developed with large variety of bulbs and wild flowers planted and seeded into grass. 60yd mixed border. Ferns are an important feature in spring, cyclamen in Aug and Sept and through the winter.
占 ⊕

㉑ 21 ELLA ROAD
West Bridgford, Nottingham NG2 5GX. Jane Needham & Terry Smith. *For directions see 30 Albert Rd.* Combined adm £3.50, chd free (share to LAM Action). **Sun 24 June (1-5). Combined with 37 Davies Road & 30 Albert Road.**
Circular lawns, to divide and create planting opportunities, uplift interest, and form the structure of this plant-intense garden. Tricky steps.
⚼

㉒ NEW ELM HOUSE
5 Mapperley Hall Drive, Nottingham NG3 5EP. Malcolm Bescoby & Michael Blood. *1m N of Nottingham city centre. On R off A60 to Mansfield.* Home-made teas. Combined adm £2.50, chd free. **Sun 15 July (1-5). Combined with Melrose, 3 Mapperley Hall Drive.**
Small town garden on two levels. Intensively planted with tropical and herbaceous specimens to complement the architectural features which include summerhouse, pond and statues. Two gardens are connected by an ornamental cast iron gate. Flights of steps in and out of gardens.
☕

㉓ THE ELMS
Main Street, North Leverton DN22 0AR. Tim & Tracy Ward, 01427 881164, Tracy@wardt2.fsnet.co.uk. *5m E of Retford, 6m SW of Gainsborough. From Retford town centre take the rd to Leverton for 5m, into North Leverton with Habblesthorpe.* Light refreshments & teas. Adm £2.50, chd free. **Sun 15 July (2-6).** Visitors also welcome by appt.
This small garden is very different,

creating an extension to the living space. Inspiration comes from tropical countries, giving a Mediterranean feel. Palms and bananas, along with other exotics, create drama, and yet make a statement true to many gardens, that of peace and calm. North Leverton Windmill (English Heritage) is located just outside village.
占 ⚼ ⊕ ☕

㉔ ♦ FELLEY PRIORY
Underwood NG16 5FJ. The Hon Mrs Chaworth Musters, 01773 810230. *8m SW of Mansfield. Off A608 ½m W M1 J27.* Adm £3, chd free, concessions £2.50. **Tues, Weds & Fris (9-12.30) all yr; every 2nd & 4th Wed Mar to Oct (9-4); every 3rd Sun Mar to Oct (11-4). For NGS: Sun 8 Apr (11-4).**
Garden for all seasons with yew hedges and topiary, snowdrops, hellebores, orchard of daffodils, herbaceous borders and old-fashioned rose garden. There are pergolas, a medieval garden, a small arboretum and borders filled with unusual trees, shrubs, plants and bulbs. The grass-edged pond is planted with primulas, bamboo, iris, roses and eucomis. Refreshments by Marie Curie.
占 ⚼ ⊕ ☕

The abundance of colour in this garden is achieved by the dense planting of roses and fuchsias . . .

㉕ FUCHSIA VIEW
9 Winster Avenue, Carlton NG4 3RW. Mr & Mrs J Thorp, 0115 911 5734. *4m N of Nottingham. Follow the Carlton Rd into Carlton. Turn L at Tesco past police stn. Over the mini island pass the cemetery up Cavendish Rd. R into Cromford Ave. 1st L into Winster Ave.* Home-made & cream teas. Adm £2, chd free. **Suns 8, 29 July (11-5). Evening Opening £2.50, wine, Thurs 5, 19 July (6-9).** Visitors also welcome by appt.

The abundance of colour in this garden is achieved by the dense planting of roses and fuchsias with a supporting cast of mixed perennials inc penstemons. The warmth of the welcome and the teas are outstanding. The variety of places to sit and soak up the vibrance of colour, makes a splendid place to visit and enjoy the long views over Carlton. Featured on ITV 'Britain's Best Back Gardens' 2006.
⚼ ⊕ ☕

㉖ GARDENERS' COTTAGE
Rectory Lane, Kirkby in Ashfield NG17 8PZ. Martin & Chris Brown, 01623 489489. *1m W of Kirkby. From the A38, take the B6018 towards Kirkby in Ashfield. Straight across mini island. Rectory Lane (no parking) is at the side of St Wilfrid's Church, on Church St.* Home-made teas. Adm £2.50, chd free. **Sun 15 Apr (1-5). Evening Opening £3.50, wine, Wed 1 Aug (6-9).** Visitors also welcome by appt.
An exciting garden full of unusual plants and imaginative features which will not disappoint even the most discerning visitor, or one who is looking for inspiration. It is under continual development as the owners seek satisfaction from their labours.
⚼ ⊕ ☕

㉗ 16 GLENSFORD GARDENS
Nottingham NG5 5BG. Don & Vicky Butt, 0115 976 4633, buttdon@hotmail.com. *5m N of Nottingham city centre. From N or city, approach on A611 (Nottingham-Hucknall). Opposite Bulwell golf course turn into Bestwood Park Dr West at T-lights. 1st L Brownlow Dr. Glensford Gardens is 4th R. Park on Brownlow Dr please.* Home-made teas. Adm £2.50, chd free. **Sun 8 July (1-5).** Visitors also welcome by appt in July groups of 10+.
Garden packed with surprises, colourful containers, hanging baskets and fish pond with its own stream and waterfalls. There's something for everyone incl palm trees, cordylines and bananas! Featured in magazines and on BBC TV and described by Tommy Walsh of 'Groundforce' as 'paradise'. Highly praised by John Stirland and Martin Fish BBC TV garden presenters. Featured in 'Woman's Own' July 2006; 'Up the Garden Path' BBC E Mids Today July 2006.
⚼ ⊕ ☕

28 GORENE

20 Kirby Road, Beauvale Estate, Newthorpe NG16 3PZ. Gordon & Irene Middleton, 01773 788407. *5m NE of Nottingham. From M1 J26 take A610 (Eastwood & Kimberley bypass) exit Langley Mill (not Eastwood). At island turn R to Eastwood to 1st set of T-lights. Keep L down Mansfield Rd, turn R at bollards (Greenhills Rd).Turn R at the 7th rd - Kirby Rd.* Adm £2, chd free. Mon 7 May; Sun 22 July (1-5). Visitors also welcome by appt. A warm welcome awaits you at this small, but intensely packed garden where the teas and cakes have become legendary! This garden proves just how much can be achieved in a small space, with water features, secret garden and exotic aviary.

29 NEW GRINGLEY GARDENS

Gringley-on-the-Hill, Doncaster DN10 4QX. *On A631 between Bawtry & Gainsborough. Approach Gringley on A631. From dual carriageway bypass there is clear signage into village. Parking is on streets of village.* Home-made teas. Combined adm £3, chd free (share to St Peter & St Paul Church, Gringley-on-the-Hill). Sun 17 June (1.30-5.30). Tranquil village on the northern tip of Nottinghamshire. Picturesque old cottage properties coupled with tasteful new development.

APPLETON HOUSE FARM

Finkell Street. Mr & Mrs R Round
Peaceful S-facing farmhouse garden in rooms, partly walled with Victorian gazebo. Formal canal pond garden, mixed borders, secret garden. Vegetable plot containing some old HDRA varieties; all gardened organically.

HONEYSUCKLE COTTAGE

Hunters Drive. Miss J Towler
This old garden is tucked away in a corner of the village and has a real cosy feel to it. It has been carefully crafted around old sheds, ancient walls and paving, and has sympathetic planting giving great charm.

NEW THE SUMMER HOUSE

High Street. Helena Bishop
This newly established garden has yet to achieve maturity but already its design and extensive broad landscape are enviable.

NEW VICARAGE COTTAGE

High Street. John & Susan Taylor
Tucked in by The Summer House and opposite the local inn, this small cottage and delightful little garden will make those who dream of retirement think it heaven.

NEW YEW TREE COTTAGE

Middle Bridge Road. Sue Tallents
Peaceful 1¼-acre garden still undergoing restoration. New areas include a pond, vegetable and herbaceous beds, shrub and woodland borders. Areas of old orchard remain and garden is planted and cared for with wildlife in mind. Unfenced pond. Slippery slope if wet.

HALL FARM

See Lincolnshire.

30 NEW HALL FARM COTTAGE

Hall Lane, Kinoulton NG12 3EF. Mrs Bel Grundy. *8m SE of West Bridgford. Kinoulton is off A46 just N of intersection with A606. Into village to T-junction with PH on L. Turn L & immed R on to Hall Lane. Pass PO. Cottage is at very end of lane on L.* Combined adm £4, chd free (share to Macmillan Cancer Support). Evening Opening Wed 20 June (6.30-8.30). Combined with Bishops Cottage.
Plantaholic's small cottage garden. A masterclass in the positioning and management of plants which have to move if they don't behave! Extensive collection of home-grown bonsai demonstrates attention to detail and the quality of 'plants for sale' ensures that Bel has no escape from her addiction.

31 THE HAYLOFT

Wood Farm Court, Thrumpton NG11 0BA. Cate Webster, thecatlady@hotmail.co.uk. *7m SW of Nottingham. A453 from Nottingham. 3rd turn R signed Thrumpton after Crusader roundabout. 1st R Church Lane, 20yds on L is Wood Farm Court. From J24 M1 take A453 towards Nottingham, 3m, 1st turn L signed Thrumpton after power stn, next turning R, L into Church Lane. The Hayloft is 20yds on L. Please park in designated area, not in Church Lane.* Light refreshments & teas in village hall. Combined adm £2.50, chd free. Sat 16 June (12-6). Combined with 59 Church Lane. Visitors also welcome by appt May to Oct.
Walled courtyard garden that cleverly demonstrates what is possible in a small space. Well-stocked, with mostly unusual varieties of shrubs and climbers, many of them in pots, to allow versatility of aspect and soil type. Don't miss the cats' garden room.

Walled courtyard garden that cleverly demonstrates what is possible in a small space . . .

32 ◆ HODSOCK PRIORY GARDENS

Blyth S81 0TY. Sir Andrew & Lady Buchanan & Mr George Buchanan (Hodsock Priory Trust), 01909 591204, gb@hodsockpriory.com. *2m from A1(M) at Blyth. 4m N of Worksop off B6045, Blyth-Worksop rd approx 2m from A1. Well signed.* Adm £4, chd £1 (6-16) under 6 free. Daily Feb to 4 Mar (10-4).
5-acre private garden on historic Domesday site. Sensational winter garden plus snowdrop wood. Many fragrant winter flowering shrubs, trees, hellebores and bulbs. Some gravel. Wood NOT suitable for wheelchairs if wet.

33 ◆ HOLME PIERREPONT HALL
Holme Pierrepont, Nottingham NG12 2LD. Mr & Mrs Robin Brackenbury, 0115 933 2371, www.holmepierreponthall.com. *5m E of Nottingham. From Nottingham A52 E-bound, follow signs for National Watersports Centre. Continue 1m past main entrance. House on LH-side next to church. Park outside church.* **House and garden adm £4.50, chd £1, garden only adm £3, chd £1. Mons, Tues, Weds 5 Feb to 28 Mar; Sun 18 Feb Snowdrop Sunday; Sun 18 Mar Hellebore Sunday; Sun 1 Apr Wild Tulip Sunday. For NGS: Sun 30 Sept (2-5).**
In the courtyard the romantic summer planting gives way to the fiery tones of autumn from dahlias and crocosmias. The sharpness of the newly clipped yews in the East Garden, contrasts with the more relaxed feel of the new autumn border with grasses and late flowering perennials in shades of purple and gold.
  ♿ ☕

34 HOLMES VILLA
Holmes Lane, Walkeringham, nr Gainsborough DN10 4JP. Peter & Sheila Clark, 01427 890233, clarkshaulage@aol.com. *4m NW of Gainsborough. A620 from Retford or A631 from Bawtry/Gainsborough & A161 to Walkeringham then towards Misterton. Follow yellow signs for last mile.* **Cream teas. Adm £2, chd free. Mon 28 May (1-5). Visitors also welcome by appt.**
1¾-acre plantsman's interesting and inspirational garden; surprises around every corner with places to sit and ponder; gazebos; arbours; ponds; hosta garden; unusual perennials and shrubs for flower arranging. Featured in 'Lincoln Pride', 'Yorkshire Post', 2006 and local press and radio.
♿ ♟ ❀ ☕

35 HOME FARM COTTAGE
Blind Lane, Oxton NG25 0SS. Pauline & Brian Hansler. *4m SW of Southwell. From B6386 turn into Oxton village (Blind Lane). Home Farm Cottage is on L opp Green Dragon PH, immed before T-junction.* **Adm £2, chd free (share to Animal Accident Rescue Unit). Sun 3 June (12-5).**
Each corner of this magical cottage garden offers the visitor a new and exciting experience. At every turn, from the hidden alpine garden, through the imaginative stumpery and woodland

grotto to the selection of unusual plants, it reveals a horticultural heaven.
♟ ❀

THE HOMESTEAD
See Leicestershire & Rutland.

36 NEW 134 JULIAN ROAD
West Bridgford, Nottingham NG2 5AN. Trish Briggs. *1m from water sports centre. ½m from Trent Bridge on Radcliffe Rd, A52 L into Trent Boulevard. Julian Rd is 8th on R.* **Tea at Rutland Rd 10 June; wine at Pierrepont Rd 13 June. Combined adm £3.50, chd free. Sun 10 June (2-6). Evening Opening £4.50, wine, Wed 13 June (6-9). Combined with 284 Rutland Rd & 117 Pierrepont Rd.**
This small garden is entered from a high terrace full of pots and tubs. After descending the broad staircase the enclosed planting gives the visitor the feeling of a tranquil, secluded, cool, green cave. Borders of shrubs and perennials lead to several sitting areas. Steep steps to enter garden.
♟

KEXBY HOUSE
See Lincolnshire.

37 61 LAMBLEY LANE
Burton Joyce NG14 5BG. Mr & Mrs R B Powell. *6m N of Nottingham. In Burton Joyce turn off A612 Nottingham to Southwell Rd into Lambley Lane.* **Combined adm £3.50, chd free. Sun 20 May (2-6). Combined with Dumbleside.**
Approx ¾-acre of spring flowering shrubs, plants and bulbs. Mixed borders, greenhouse and terrace, cacti, vegetable garden. Colourful display of azaleas and camellias. Unusual plants for sale. Steep drive to entrance.
❀

38 MANOR FARM HOUSE
Plungar Road, Granby NG13 9PX. Brenda & Philip Straw. *14m E of Nottingham. 2m off A52 signed Granby. Next to church.* **Teas at Newbray House. Combined adm £3.50, chd free (share to Hope & Homes for Children). Sun 10 June (2-6). Combined with Newbray House, Granby.**

⅓-acre garden surrounding grade II listed C18 farmhouse. Cottage garden style planting with climbing roses, hardy geraniums, delphiniums, white garden, yellow corner, daisy steps and mixed borders. Church wall, brick outbuildings and old walnut tree provide perfect backdrop for this plant enthusiasts' garden.
♿ ♟

39 MEADOWSIDE
Main Street, Epperstone NG14 6AD. John & Barbara Phillips. *8m NE of Nottingham, 5m SW of Southwell. Epperstone lies off the A6097 between Lowdham & Oxton. Meadowside is opp Cross Keys PH on Main St.* **Home-made teas. Adm £2.50, chd free. Sun 1 July (12-5).**
Well-established front and larger than average rear garden that enjoys an extensive open outlook over fields, stocked with plant collections, shrubs and trees. It has been meticulously worked over many years to achieve a garden full of colour and impact that without doubt will give pleasure to the visitor. No toilet facilities.
♿ ♟ ❀ ☕

40 NEW MELROSE
3 Mapperley Hall Drive, Nottingham NG3 5EP. Sir Joseph & Lady Pope. *1m N of Nottingham city centre. On R off A60 to Mansfield.* **Home-made teas at Elm House. Combined adm £2.50, chd free. Sun 15 July (1-5). Combined with Elm House.**
This town garden set on two levels has evolved gradually and is complementary to Elm House, which is connected by an ornamental iron gate. Strong Japanese influence with the use of stone lanterns and a stream which gurgles prettily over rocks and shingle. Acers, camellias and hostas add a light touch to this peaceful garden. Flights of steps in and out of gardens.
♟

Colourful display
of azaleas and
camellias . . .

41 MILL HILL HOUSE

Elston Lane, East Stoke NG23 5QJ. Mr & Mrs R J Gregory, 01636 525460, millhill@talk21.com. *5m S of Newark. Elston Lane. On A46 turn to Elston. Garden ½m on R. Entrance via car park (signed).* Adm £2, chd free. Mon 28 May (11-5). Visitors also welcome by appt, coaches/groups. ½-acre country garden close to site of Battle of East Stoke (1487). Closely planted with many unusual hardy/half hardy plants providing yr-round interest and tranquil atmosphere. This established and mature garden is now enjoying some new planting that is revitalising its old-fashioned charm. National Collection of Berberis.
🕸 NCCPG

42 NEWBRAY HOUSE

Church Street, Granby NG13 9PU. Shirley & Stan Taylor, 01949 859090, shirley.oxby@btinternet.com. *14m E of Nottingham. 2m off A52 signed Granby.* Home-made teas. Combined adm £3.50 (share to Hope and Homes for Children). Sun 10 June (2-6). Combined with **Manor Farm House.** Visitors also welcome by appt May to July, groups 10+.
With views towards Belvoir Castle, this 2-acre garden has been developed to complement the attractive Victorian house. Strong structure is overlaid by imaginative planting. Many unusual plants are found in large herbaceous beds full of colour and interest over a long season. Ponds, gravel, herb and vegetable areas. Scented roses and wisteria climb pergolas and walls. Picnics in the orchard.
♿ ✿ 🕸 ☕

> Strong structure is overlaid by imaginative planting. Many unusual plants are found in large herbaceous beds full of colour . . .

43 NORWELL GARDENS

NG23 6JX. *6m N of Newark. Off A1 at Cromwell turning.* Home-made teas in village hall. Combined adm £3, chd free. Sun 24 June (2-5.30). **Evening Opening** £3.50, wine, Wed 27 June (6.30-9).
Also open, parish church of St

Lawrence with its beautiful C15 clerestory. Also history trail and display focusing on the C19 restoration of the church. Enjoy the views across the water meadows.
☕

NEW BLACK HORSE FARM

Main Street. Mr & Mrs Craig Bown
Extensive country garden, with many features and a great variety of planting and landscaping.
♿ ✿

CHERRY TREE HOUSE

5 Foxhall Close Mr & Mrs S Wyatt
New garden with many innovative features. Formal box front garden with decorative mulches. Decking, water features, lush plantings with architectural screens and colourful schemes.
✿

NORTHFIELD FARM

Ossington Road. Mr & Mrs D Adamson. *½m from village hall down Ossington Rd*
Well laid out country and family garden with large vegetable plot, herbaceous border, herb garden and water feature.
✿

NORWELL NURSERIES

Woodhouse Road Andrew & Helen Ward, 01636 636337, wardha@aol.com. Visitors also welcome by appt.
(See separate entry).
♿ ✿ 🕸

SOUTHVIEW COTTAGE

Main Street. Mr & Mrs Les Corbett
Richly planted cottage garden with mature trees, mixed borders. Imaginatively planted gravel garden. Pond and wildlife, natural plantings.
✿

44 ♦ NORWELL NURSERIES

Woodhouse Road, Norwell NG23 6JX. Andrew & Helen Ward, 01636 636337, wardha@aol.com. *6m N of Newark. Turn off A1 at Cromwell turning.* Adm £2, chd free. Daily (10-5) except Sats & Tues from 1 Mar to 20 Oct. Closed Aug. For NGS: Sun 27 May (2-5.30).
A treasure trove of over 2000 different, beautiful, rare and unusual plants set out in ¾-acre plantsman's garden incl woodland with orchids and meconopsis, specimen grasses. Large alpine and scree area, bell garden with penstemons and dierama, and patio plants. Extensive herbaceous borders, hot beds and sumptuous colour-themed beds.
♿ ✿ 🕸 ☕

45 THE OLD VICARAGE

Halam Hill, Halam Village NG22 8AX. Mrs Beverley Perks. *1m W of Southwell. On approach to Halam village down hill on LH-side.* Home-made teas. Adm £2.50, chd free. Suns 22 Apr; 13 May; 23 Sept (1-5).
This 2-acre, rapidly maturing, colourful garden, has much to excite the plant hunter. Its wooded and sloping aspect, and use of texture and design, all contribute towards its peaceful country garden atmosphere. A paradise of nooks and crannies for children and adults alike. Lots of woodland birdsong. Slippery when wet as on hillside. Ask for assistance.
☕

46 ORCHARD HOUSE

High Oakham Road, Mansfield NG18 5AJ. Mr & Mrs Michael Bull, 01623 623884. *S side of Mansfield. High Oakham Rd joins the A60-Nottingham Rd at junction with Forest Rd and Waverley Rd, leading to Atkin Lane at the western end.* Home-made teas. Adm £2.50, chd free. Suns 1 July; 5 Aug (1-5). Visitors also welcome by appt June, July, August only. Groups 5-50.
This mature garden is one of Mansfield's treasures in a quiet and secluded area. Diverse colourful planting of shrubs, herbaceous borders and specimen trees. Clever use of water, statuary and other unique features enhance this garden, providing interest for discerning gardeners throughout the summer.
✿ 🕸 ☕

Mainly organic encouraging a variety of wildlife . . .

47 20 THE PADDOCKS
Nuthall NG16 1DR. Mr & Mrs
Bowness-Saunders, 0115 938 4590.
*5m NW of Nottingham. From M1 J26,
A610 towards Nottingham. At 1st
roundabout take B600 towards
Kimberley. Paddocks is 2nd rd on L
after Three Ponds PH. Parking in cul-
de-sac restricted, please park on main
rd or on L as you enter The Paddocks.*
Home-made teas. **Adm £2.50, chd
free. Sun 22 July (1-5). Evening
Opening £3.50, wine, Wed 25 July
(6-9). Visitors also welcome by appt.**
Fun garden shared with children and
dogs which unlike oil and water do mix
in this unusual combination of
interesting gardens. Many inspirational
ideas incl beach, well, living willow
structures, ponds, mature trees,
herbaceous borders and vegetables.
Mainly organic encouraging a variety of
wildlife. A gardener's playground not to
be missed (200 x 80ft).
&. ✗. ✿ ⊛ ☕

48 PAPPLEWICK HALL
Papplewick NG15 8FE. Mr & Mrs J
R Godwin-Austen,
www.papplewickhall.co.uk. *7m N of
Nottingham. N end of Papplewick
village on B683, off the A60. Parking at
Hall.* **Adm £2.50, chd free (share to
St James' Church). Sun 27 May
(2-5).**
This mature 8-acre established garden,
mostly shaded woodland, abounds
with rhododendrons, hostas, ferns,
and spring bulbs. A programme of replanting ornamental trees and shrubs
is being carried out.
&. ✗. ☕

**49 NEW 48 PENARTH
GARDENS**
Sherwood Vale, Nottingham
NG5 4EG. Josie & Geoff
Goodlud. *Approx 2½m N of
Nottingham city centre off B684
(Woodborough Rd). From city, turn
L into Woodthorpe Rd, after
Millennium Garage, L again
(Penarth Rise). L again to Penarth
Gardens (No 48).* **Adm £2.50, chd
free. Sun 8 July (1-5).**
One of Nottingham city's hidden
gems is to be found in the unlikely
setting of a small back garden in
Sherwood Vale, but it will please
and surprise both by its planting
and bold design. Its setting is
amongst dense housing packed
into the old Nottingham brickworks
quarry, the overgrown face of
which is steadily being transformed
into an extension to a densely
packed garden.
✗. ⊛

Herbaceous borders with an abundance of species and varieties . . .

50 PENRHYN HOUSE
Clumber Road East, The Park,
Nottingham NG7 1BD. Bill & José
Russell. *At junction of Clumber Rd
East and Tunnel Rd. Entry to The Park
Estate from Derby Rd or Castle Gate.*
Teas at Weston Lodge. **Combined
adm £3, chd free. Sun 17 June (2-6).
Combined with 4 Clare Valley &
Weston Lodge.**
The Park private estate boasts many
fine houses and gardens, and some
alas have seen better times. Not so
here, where the elegance and formality
of the garden perfectly complements
the grandeur of a house (not open),
from that long-gone Victorian era.
✗. ⊛

**51 NEW 117 PIERREPONT
ROAD**
West Bridgford, Nottingham
NG2 5DX. Maggie Smith & Jason
Williams. *2m SW of Nottingham
city centre. From Trent Bridge take
A52 (Radcliffe Rd), ½m turn L, turn
R onto Rutland Rd. Pierrepont Rd
1st turn on L.* Tea at Rutland Rd 10
June. **Combined adm £3.50, chd
free. Sun 10 June (2-6). Evening
Opening £4.50, wine, Wed 13
June (6-9). Combined with 134
Julian Rd & 284 Rutland Rd.**
This tiny front garden packed with
plants will tempt the visitor. Small
well-planned back garden
designed with artistry, to be a
magnet to children, as well as a
delightful garden to enjoy and in
which to relax. Display of
contemporary art by local artists.
✗.

52 REDLANDS
136 Papplewick Lane, Hucknall
NG15 8EG. Mr & Mrs J Smith, 0115
963 1936, j-js@lineone.net. *5m N of
Nottingham. From Nottingham on
A611, turn R at Byron cinema. Turn L
at 3rd mini island. Garden approx
400yds on R.* Light refreshments &
teas. **Adm £2, chd free (share to
Neurodegenerative Support Group
at QMC). Sun 1 July (11-5). Visitors
also welcome by appt for garden
clubs and groups.**
¼-acre, long, plantsman's garden.
Herbaceous borders with an
abundance of species and varieties.
Many ornamental trees and shrubs.
Two ponds, incl wildlife pond. Patio
areas with baskets and containers
displaying a wide variety of
interesting and unusual plants. An
established garden with many
interesting features.
✗. ⊛ ☕

54 ROSE COTTAGE
82 Main Road, Underwood
NG16 5GN. Mrs Marie Lowe. *10m N
of Nottingham. 1½m from J27 M1.
Take B608 towards Heanor. Join
B600, after about 200yds turn R into
Main Rd by large sign for Hole in the
Wall Inn.* Cream teas. **Adm £1.50, chd
free. Suns 22 July; 12 Aug; 9 Sept
(2-6).**
Flower arranger's cottage garden with
ponds; shrubs; small secret garden.
Rear garden of approx 1000 sq yds
with surprise features, partly developed
from a field over last few yrs. Goats.
✗. ⊛

Featured in Flora magazine and 'Nottingham Evening Post', 2006. Some uneven paths.

⚐ ❀ ☕

⑤⑤ ROSELEA
40 Newark Road, Coddington NG24 2QF. Bruce & Marian Richmond, 01636 676737, richmonds@roselea47.fsnet.co.uk. 1½m E of Newark. Leave A1 signed Coddington, 100yds from junction S; 300yds from junction N. **Visitors welcome by appt only.** Atmospheric garden full of enchantment, with winding paths through pergolas, many different plants and climbers, interest all yr-round. Continual introduction of new plants keeps the visitor searching for more. Gravel paths in back garden.

♿ ⚐ ❀

Atmospheric garden full of enchantment . . .

⑤⑥ NEW 284 RUTLAND ROAD
West Bridgford NG2 5EB. Cynthia Cordery & Jack Thomson. 1m E of Trent Bridge, Nottingham. ½m from Trent Bridge on A52 turn L over canal at pedestrian crossing. Turn R on Rutland Rd to very end. Garden on R. Wine at Pierrepont Rd. **Combined adm £3.50, chd free. Sun 10 June (2-6). Evening Opening £4.50, Wed 13 June (6-9). Combined with 117 Pierrepont Road and 134 Julian Road.**
284 Rutland Road is beyond where the road seems to finish. It is bordered by the Adbolton Brook, a walk along the Grantham Canal and with a borrowed landscape of arable fields. The garden is a wildlife haven with meadow/orchard area alongside established borders, mature trees and lawns. Limited disabled parking. Very deep water alongside.

♿ ☕

⑤⑦ 125 SHELFORD ROAD
Radcliffe on Trent NG12 1AZ. John & Elaine Walker, 0115 911 9867. 4m E of Nottingham. From A52 follow signs to Radcliffe. In village centre take turning for Shelford (by Co-op). Approx ¾m on LH-side. Home-made teas. **Adm £2.50, chd free. Sun 23 Sept (2-5.30). Evening Opening £3.50, wine, chd free, Wed 18 July (6-9). Visitors also welcome by appt for groups of 10+.**
One third of an acre designed for overall effect of colour, texture and movement, incorporating many unusual varieties especially hardy perennials and grasses. Front garden is formal with packed, overflowing borders incl hot and cool colour-themed beds and prairie-style borders planted for late summer colour. Back is based on flowing curves with informal planting and incl gazebo, pond, bog garden and jungle area with turf dragon. 'A stunning garden', Monty Don. 'Back garden is truly spectacular', Prof David Stevens. Hand-crafted garden mirrors and artwork for sale. Finalist 'Daily Mail National Garden Competition' 2006.

❀ ☕

⑤⑧ SQUIRREL LODGE
2 Goosemoor Lane, Retford DN22 7JA. Peter & Joan Whitehead. 1m S of Retford. Travelling S out of Retford on A638, last R turn before railway bridge. Home-made teas. **Adm £2, chd free. Suns 13 May; 26 Aug (2-5).**
The garden visitor will be well rewarded for journeying a little further north in the county by a garden that has been skilfully crafted into a corner plot. Some is in deep shade, but the colour and vibrance of this garden will both delight and please, just as much as will the welcome and the teas. Local artist will be working in the garden. Examples of work on display. Featured on Lincolnshire Radio and in 'Gardening News', 2006.

❀ ☕

Designed for overall effect of colour, texture and movement . . .

⑤⑨ 14 TEMPLE DRIVE
Nuthall NG16 1BE. Mr & Mrs T Leafe, 0115 927 1118. 4m NW of Nottingham. From M1 leave at J26, A610 towards Nottingham. Circle 1st roundabout in A6002 then Nottm Rd lane, leave on minor rd ahead and follow L and R to Temple Drive. From Nottingham take A610, turning off at Broxtowe Inn, Cinderhill onto Nottingham Rd. Temple Drive 3rd on L. **Adm £2, chd free. Visitors welcome by appt any time.**
Plant lovers' garden. Colourful herbaceous and shrub borders with many unusual plants, specimen trees, alpine troughs, shrub roses, ferns, over 140 hardy geraniums and 40 clematis. Plants from the garden for sale for NGS. Fruit and vegetable garden. Something of interest throughout the year. Groups and individuals welcome.

♿ ❀

⑥⓪ ◆ TEVERSAL MANOR GARDENS
Buttery Lane, Teversal Old Village, Nr Sutton in Ashfield NG17 3JN. Mrs Janet Marples, 01623 554569, www.teversalmanor.co.uk. 4m NW of Mansfield. From M1 J28: take A38 towards Mansfield. After 3m turn L onto A6014 Skegby. After 2m turn R at mini island for Teversal. Turn R at Carnarvon Arms for Teversal Village. R into Buttery Lane. Manor on R after 2 sharp bends. From M1 J29: take A6175 for Clay Cross. Turn off 1st L for Stanley. 1m after Stanley just before Carnarvon Arms turn L for Teversal Village. Then as above. **Adm £4.50, chd £2.50, concesssions £3.50. Phone or see website for public opening times. For NGS: Sats 12 May; 6 Oct (10-6). Evening Opening £4.50, wine, Sat 7 July (10-9).**
Teversal Manor featured as Wragby Hall in D H Lawrence's 'Lady Chatterley's Lover'. It is one of the East Midlands' oldest gardens and was developed on a grand scale. Neglected for many decades, it is now being brought back to life. The terrraced site is now being gardened in a different, but interesting style in its magnificent setting. The exciting redevelopment of the garden is an ongoing project that is being undertaken with great enthusiasm. 7 July music, after teatime and wine. Featured in 'Nottinghamshire Today', 2006. Steep steps and gravel paths.

♿ ⚐ ❀ ☕

During summer the walled garden will be alive with vibrant exotic plantings . . .

61 UNIVERSITY OF NOTTINGHAM GARDENS
University Park, Nottingham NG7 2RD. Ian Cooke, www.nottingham.ac.uk/estate/friends. *1¹/₂ m W of Nottingham city centre. We suggest visitors arrive at the north entrance which is on the A52 adjacent to the QMC roundabout. The event is based at the Millennium Garden which is on University Park and well signed within the campus. No buses within campus on Sunday.* **Adm £2.50, chd free. Suns 6 May; 19 Aug (2-5).** University Park has many beautiful gardens incl the award-winning Millennium Garden with its dazzling flower garden, timed fountains and turf maze. Visitors in late spring will see extensive plantings of bulbs throughout the park incl in our Jekyll Garden. During summer the walled garden will be alive with vibrant exotic plantings. In total 300 acres of landscape and gardens. Green Flag 2006. Some gravel paths and inclines.
&

WARTNABY GARDENS
See Leicestershire & Rutland.

63 NEW WESTON LODGE
Hardwick Road, Nottingham NG7 1EP. Susan & Stephen Whittle. *The Park. 500yds W of Nottingham city centre. Enter The Park from Derby Rd at Walton's Hotel; take 3rd rd on R. Follow to the bottom; last house on L, OR by Castle Gate House entrance. Continue the length of Lenton Rd. House is at junction of Lenton/Hardwick Rd.* Light refreshments & teas. **Combined adm £3, chd free. Sun 17 June (2-6). Combined with Penrhyn House & 4 Clare Valley.** Elegant, Mediterranean-style award-winning city garden that has been exotically planted. Sunny terraces for outdoor family living. Gravel path and some small steps. Unfenced pond.
🌡 ☕

64 NEW WHITE HOUSE
39 Melton Road, Tollerton, Nottingham NG12 4EL. Joan Dean, 0115 937 5031, jimdean@supanet.com. *5m S of Nottingham. From Wheatcroft island take A606 Melton Mowbray. Approx 1¹/₂ m from island, 3 doors from PO.* Light refreshments & teas. **Adm £2.50, chd free. Sun 1 July (1-5). Visitors also welcome by appt.** This garden is entered through a wisteria covered doorway and the garden simply opens out. The separate areas seem to be seamlessly linked together. A generous terrace leads to a colourful well-stocked mixed garden, then to a well-managed wildlife pond, with adjacent superbly fitted out Wendy House.
🌡 ❀ ☕

Nottinghamshire County Volunteers

County Organisers
Martin & Chris Brown, Gardeners' Cottage, Rectory Lane, Kirkby in Ashfield, Nottingham NG17 8PZ, 01623 489489

County Treasurer
Pat Webb, 25 Greenbank Drive, Sutton in Ashfield, Nottingham NG17 2DY, 01623 556447

Assistant County Organisers
Mary Hepburn, 6 Miller Hives Close, Cotgrave, Nottingham NG12 3QY, 0115 989 9012

Leaflet Coordinator
Bernard Theobald, 37 Loughborough Road, Ruddington, Nottingham NG11 6LL, 0115 984 1152

OXFORDSHIRE

Opening Dates

February

SUNDAY 18
72 Waterperry Gardens

March

SUNDAY 18
71 Wadham College

April

SUNDAY 1
3 Ashbrook House
15 Buckland Lakes
23 Epwell Mill
37 Kingston Bagpuize House
41 Magdalen College
43 Merton College Fellows' Garden
48 The Old Rectory
56 St Hilda's College
68 Trinity College

TUESDAY 3
64 Stansfield

MONDAY 9
10 Brook Cottage
36 Kencot Gardens

SATURDAY 14
53 The Queen's College

SUNDAY 15
39 Lime Close

SUNDAY 22
57 St Hugh's College
72 Waterperry Gardens

SUNDAY 29
8 Blewbury Manor
26 Garsington Manor
77 Wick Hall & Nurseries

May

TUESDAY 1
64 Stansfield

WEDNESDAY 2
80 Woolstone Mill House

THURSDAY 3
45 Monks Head

SUNDAY 6
1 Adderbury Gardens
12 Broughton Grange
45 Monks Head
65 Steeple Aston Gardens
78 Wildwood

WEDNESDAY 9
80 Woolstone Mill House

SATURDAY 12
79 Wood Croft

SUNDAY 13
32 Holywell Manor

WEDNESDAY 16
80 Woolstone Mill House

SATURDAY 19
28 Greys Court
30 Hearns House

SUNDAY 20
30 Hearns House

WEDNESDAY 23
80 Woolstone Mill House

SUNDAY 27
5 Barton Abbey
29 Headington Gardens
73 Wayside

MONDAY 28
21 Church Farm Field
23 Epwell Mill
63 Sparsholt Manor

WEDNESDAY 30
80 Woolstone Mill House

June

SATURDAY 2
31 Hill Court
47 The Old Manor House

SUNDAY 3
24 Evelegh's
31 Hill Court
39 Lime Close

MONDAY 4
45 Monks Head (Evening)

TUESDAY 5
64 Stansfield

WEDNESDAY 6
80 Woolstone Mill House

SUNDAY 10
6 Blenheim Palace
14 Broughton Poggs & Filkins Gardens
35 Iffley Gardens
40 Lyford Grange

WEDNESDAY 13
80 Woolstone Mill House

FRIDAY 15
4 Asthall Manor (Evening)

SUNDAY 17
4 Asthall Manor
7 Blewbury Gardens
9 Brize Norton Gardens
40 Lyford Grange
42 Manor Farm
44 Middleton Cheney Gardens
51 Osse Field
54 Radcot House
59 Sibford Gower Gardens
75 Wheatley Gardens

WEDNESDAY 20
80 Woolstone Mill House

SUNDAY 24
8 Blewbury Manor
13 Broughton Grounds Farm
52 The Priory Garden
70 Upper Chalford Farm

WEDNESDAY 27
80 Woolstone Mill House

July

SUNDAY 1
12 Broughton Grange
55 9 Rawlinson Road
60 Somerville College
70 Upper Chalford Farm
73 Wayside
74 Westwell Manor
76 Whitehill Farm

TUESDAY 3
64 Stansfield

WEDNESDAY 4
80 Woolstone Mill House

THURSDAY 5
69 University of Oxford Botanic Garden (Evening)

WEDNESDAY 11
80 Woolstone Mill House

SUNDAY 15
16 Chalkhouse Green Farm
17 Charlbury Gardens
18 Chastleton Gardens
37 Kingston Bagpuize House
71 Wadham College

WEDNESDAY 18
80 Woolstone Mill House

SUNDAY 22
54 Radcot House
81 Worcester College

TUESDAY 24
30 Hearns House (Evening)

WEDNESDAY 25
80 Woolstone Mill House

SATURDAY 28
20 Christ Church Masters', Pocock and Cathedral Gardens
43 Merton College Fellows' Garden

SUNDAY 29
11 Broughton Castle
61 191 South Avenue
68 Trinity College

August

WEDNESDAY 1
80 Woolstone Mill House

SUNDAY 5
- **27** Greenfield Farm
- **61** 191 South Avenue

TUESDAY 7
- **64** Stansfield

WEDNESDAY 8
- **80** Woolstone Mill House

WEDNESDAY 15
- **80** Woolstone Mill House

WEDNESDAY 22
- **80** Woolstone Mill House

SUNDAY 26
- **30** Hearns House
- **58** Salford Gardens

MONDAY 27
- **10** Brook Cottage
- **30** Hearns House

WEDNESDAY 29
- **80** Woolstone Mill House

September

SUNDAY 2
- **3** Ashbrook House
- **21** Church Farm Field
- **23** Epwell Mill

TUESDAY 4
- **64** Stansfield

WEDNESDAY 5
- **80** Woolstone Mill House

SUNDAY 9
- **48** The Old Rectory

WEDNESDAY 12
- **80** Woolstone Mill House

SUNDAY 16
- **37** Kingston Bagpuize House
- **38** Lady Margaret Hall
- **54** Radcot House

WEDNESDAY 19
- **80** Woolstone Mill House

SUNDAY 23
- **26** Garsington Manor
- **72** Waterperry Gardens

WEDNESDAY 26
- **80** Woolstone Mill House

Private gardens opening regularly for the NGS
- **46** Old Church House
- **80** Woolstone Mill House

Gardens open to the public
- **6** Blenheim Palace
- **10** Brook Cottage
- **11** Broughton Castle
- **28** Greys Court

- **37** Kingston Bagpuize House
- **41** Magdalen College
- **69** University of Oxford Botanic Garden
- **72** Waterperry Gardens

By appointment only
- **2** The Arches
- **19** Chivel Farm
- **22** Clock House
- **25** The Filberts
- **33** Home Close
- **34** Home Farm
- **49** The Old Vicarage
- **50** 40 Osler Road
- **62** South Newington House
- **66** Swalcliffe Lea House
- **67** Tadmarton Manor

The Gardens

1 **ADDERBURY GARDENS**
OX17 3LS. *3m S of Banbury. J10 M40, onto A43 signed Northampton, then A4260 to Adderbury, or A4260 S from Banbury.* Home-made teas at Church House. **Combined adm £4, chd free (share to Katharine House Hospice). Sun 6 May (2-6).**
Attractive Hornton stone village with a fine church. Village maps given to all visitors.
☕

BERRY HILL HOUSE
Berry Hill Road. Mr & Mrs J P Pollard. *Off A4260 signed Milton, Bloxham, W Adderbury*
2 acres; mature trees and lawns with countryside views; features separate garden areas linked together informally in a tranquil setting; many unusual plant varieties; kitchen garden and orchard.
🌿 ✿

CROSSHILL HOUSE
Manor Road. Mr & Mrs Gurth Hoyer Millar
Georgian house (not open) surrounded by 4-acre classic Victorian walled gardens.
🌿

NEW **HOLLY BANK**
Berry Hill Road. Malcolm & Erica Brown
Interesting re-development of one third of an acre garden with island beds which include a variety of trees, shrubs, bulbs and herbaceous plants. Limited wheelchair access. Main lower

part of garden is accessible but upper terrace access has quite steep steps.
🌿

HOME FARM HOUSE
Manor Road. Mr & Mrs J V Harper
2 acres; lawns, mature trees and shrubs, landscaped paddock, carp pond and flower borders.
♿

THE OLD VICARAGE
Church Lane. Peter & Christine Job. *Opp church*
Large garden with unusual plants, walled garden, ha ha, ponds and meadow walk to Japanese maple plantation.
♿ ✿

PLACKETTS
High Street. Dr D White. *Nr Church*
Queen Anne cottage (not open); 0.2-acre walled garden, sheltered gravel courtyard. Main garden exposed and sunny with views. Many tulips, euphorbias, primulas, anemones. Numerous clematis, roses and lilies.
🌿

Garden with island beds which include a variety of trees, shrubs, bulbs and herbaceous plants . . .

2 **THE ARCHES**
16 Swalcliffe Road, Tadmarton OX15 5TE. Mr & Mrs J Bolland, 01295 788264. *5m SW of Banbury.* On B4035. **Adm £2, chd free. Visitors welcome by appt Apr to July only.**
1/5-acre garden designed and created by present owners since 1983. Formal front garden with conifers and ornamental grass bed. Rear garden with trees and a series of garden 'rooms' in various themes. Two summerhouses and plenty of seats. Garden for sitting in.
♿ 🌿

3 ASHBROOK HOUSE
Blewbury OX11 9QA. **Mr & Mrs S A Barrett.** *4m SE of Didcot. Turn off A417 in Blewbury into Westbrook St. 1st house on R.* **Adm £2.50, chd free. Suns 1 Apr; 2 Sept (2-6).**
3½-acre chalk garden with small lake, stream, spring bulbs and herbaceous borders. New glasshouse and bog garden. Plant sale 1 April. Gravel drive. One steep slope.
& ✿ ☕

4 ASTHALL MANOR
Asthall, nr Burford OX18 4HW. **Rosanna Taylor, www.onformsculpture.co.uk.** *3m E of Burford. At roundabout between Witney & Burford on A40, take turning to Minster Lovell. Turn immed L (signed to Asthall). At bottom of hill, follow avenue of trees and look for car park signs. Home-made teas in village.* **Adm £4, chd free. Sun 17 June (2-7). Evening Opening £6, wine, Fri 15 June (6-9).**
6 acres of garden surround this C17 manor house (not open) once home to the Mitford family and overlooking the R Windrush. Sloping parterres and formal lawns, woodland lake, wild flower meadows, grass mound, banks of wild roses and borders spilling over gravel paths. C12 village church open (Sunday) adjacent to garden.
☕

Sweeping lawns and picturesque lake . . .

5 BARTON ABBEY
Steeple Barton OX25 4QS. **Mr & Mrs P Fleming.** *8m E of Chipping Norton. On B4030, ½m from junction of A4260 & B4030. Home-made teas.* **Adm £3, chd free. Sun 27 May (2-5).**
15-acre garden with views from house (not open) across sweeping lawns and picturesque lake. Walled garden with colourful herbaceous borders, separated by established yew hedges and espalier fruit, contrasts with more informal woodland garden paths with vistas of specimen trees and meadows. Working glasshouses and fine display of fruit and vegetables.
& ✿ ☕

BARTON HOUSE
See Warwickshire & part of West Midlands.

6 gardens in a charming downland village. . . .

6 ◆ BLENHEIM PALACE
Woodstock OX20 1PX. **His Grace the Duke of Marlborough, 01993 810531, hearter@blenheimpalace.com.** *8m N of Oxford. Bus: 20 Oxford-Chipping Norton, alight Woodstock.* **Adm £4, chd £2, concessions £3. Info listed on www.blenheimpalace.com. For NGS: Sun 10 June (10.30-5.30).**
Blenheim Gardens, originally laid out by Henry Wise, include the formal Water Terraces and Italian Garden by Achille Duchêne, Rose Garden, Arboretum, and Cascade. The Secret Garden, opened in 2004, offers a stunning garden paradise for all seasons. Blenheim Lake, created by 'Capability' Brown and spanned by Vanbrugh's Grand Bridge, is the focal point of over 2,000 acres of landscaped parkland. The Pleasure Gardens complex includes the Herb and Lavender Garden and Butterfly House. Other activities incl the Marlborough Maze, putting greens, adventure play area, giant chess and draughts. Some difficulty with pushing wheelchairs over gravel. Wheelchairs take alternative route to gardens. Mobility scooters for hire.
& ✕

7 BLEWBURY GARDENS
OX11 9QB. *4m SE of Didcot. On A417. Follow yellow signs for car parks. Home-made teas at St Michael's Church.* **Combined adm £4, chd free. Sun 17 June (2-6).**
6 gardens in a charming downland village. Village Festival taking place. Featured on 'Gardeners' World'.
☕

CHAPMANS
Jenny Craig
²/₃-acre garden with listed house (not open) and stream. Informal cottage beds with established and new herbaceous planting featuring some unusual plants. Small wild flower meadow.
& ✕ 🛏

GREEN BUSHES
Phil & Rhon Rogers
A garden for plant lovers created around a C16 cottage (not open). Large range of plants grown in a variety of settings; colour-themed borders, ponds and poolside planting, alpine troughs, ferns, pleached limes and roses.
✕

HALL BARN
Malcolm & Deirdre Cochrane
Garden and paddocks extend to 4 acres with traditional herbaceous borders and a kitchen garden. Special features include a quality croquet lawn, C16 dovecote, a thatched cob wall and clear chalk streams.
& ✕

NEW HALL BARN CLOSE
Lindy & Richard Farrell
Garden around this C16 cottage has evolved over last 25 yrs. It features mature shrubs, unusual herbaceous perennials, cottage garden favourites and the box caterpillar seen on 'BBC Gardeners' World'. Unprotected stream, mainly lined by borders but stream crossing point (grassed) has steep drop on one side (c. 3ft).
& ✿

NEW INN COTTAGE
Mrs L Fergusson
Small garden redesigned in 2002 addressing the problem of a steep narrow garden. Features a shady courtyard with interesting pond leading up through a series of terraces planted with climbers tumbling down the walls.
✕

NEW NOTTINGHAM FEE HOUSE
Mrs Carolyn Anderson
Newly designed garden surrounding timber-framed house (not open). 1/3 acre. Gravel paths, clipped boxes, grasses, perennials and shrubs.
✕

8 BLEWBURY MANOR
Blewbury OX11 9QJ. **Mr & Mrs M R Blythe.** *4m SE of Didcot. Turn off A417 in Blewbury into Westbrook St, after 1/3m bear R at sign to village hall (car parking in school car park & in village hall car park). Continue into Berry Lane & house is 20yds on L.* Home-made

teas. **Adm £4, chd £2 (5-16). Suns 29 Apr; 24 June (2-6).** Part C17 Manor House (not open) with moat set in a garden of about 10 acres. Features incl a parterre; flower garden, herbaceous and mixed borders; pergola; decorative vegetable and herb garden; stream planting and woodland area; lake and newly laid out sunken gravel garden surrounded by hornbeam allées.

Stream planting and woodland area . . .

⑨ BRIZE NORTON GARDENS
OX18 3LY. *3m SW of Witney. Brize Norton village, S of A40, or on Burford Rd.* Teas at Lingermans. **Combined adm £3.50, chd free (share to Brize Norton Church). Sun 17 June (1-6).** Pretty village. Church open with Flower Festival. Teas by WI in Elderbank Hall. Large recreation ground for picnics. Ice creams & plants available for NGS.

BARNSTABLE HOUSE
Manor Road. Mr & Mrs P Butcher
C17 converted Cotswold stone barn (not open) with Mediterranean-style patio and planting. Courtyard garden with lawn surrounded by tightly packed borders against a backdrop of lime trees.

CHURCH FARM HOUSE
Philip & Mary Holmes
A garden designed with seating areas at different levels and viewpoints and including herb garden, rockery, water features, mixed borders, pergola, gazebo, greenhouse and pool enclosure with bougainvillea and oleanders. Gravel entrance drive and uneven path.

16 DAUBIGNY MEAD
Bob & Margaret Watts
Garden is loosely based on room system, divided into various sections. Contains many shrubs. Water feature. Stream runs the

length of garden. Back lawn is home to two guinea pigs.

GRANGE FARM
Burford Road. Mr & Mrs Mark Artus
Family garden in lovely peaceful setting with C17 dovecote in back field as well as new vegetable garden and children's play area.

LINGERMANS
Burford Road. Mrs E Dobson. *Approx 2m from village.* Visitors also welcome by appt in writing, Lingermans, Burford Rd, Brize Norton OX18 3NZ. Small groups, no more than 10. 1 acre. Lawns, mature trees, herbaceous borders for plantsmen. Sunken garden with pergola, centred border with old-fashioned roses, wildlife area with frog pond, secret garden.

PAINSWICK HOUSE
Carterton Road. Mr & Mrs T Gush
Approx 3/4-acre mature garden; old apple trees; herb garden; vegetable garden.

ROSEDALE
Burford Road. Mr & Mrs S Finlayson
Set on the site of former quarry, this third of an acre garden has been re-established over the past 25yrs. Informal herbaceous borders and terrace in a sheltered S-facing location.

SCHOOL GARDEN
Station Road. Brize Norton Primary School
Flowers; vegetables; beautiful pond area; sound garden, willow dome and quiet area. All created and maintained with the help of the school children.

STONE COTTAGE
Station Road. Mr & Mrs K Humphris
Cottage garden with country feel. Patio area, wisteria and pear tree surrounded by pots, pergola, raised beds and perennial borders. One border contains a good selection of hostas and ferns. Another is full of delphiniums. Gravel drive.

⑩ ♦ BROOK COTTAGE
Well Lane, Alkerton OX15 6NL. Mrs David Hodges, 01295 670303 or 670590,
www.brookcottagegarden.co.uk. *6m NW of Banbury. 1/2m off A422. Follow signs in village.* DIY tea, coffee, biscuits daily; other refreshments for groups by appt. **Adm £4, chd free, concessions £3. 9 Apr to 31 Oct, every Mon to Fri incl Bank Hols (9-6). For NGS: Mon 9 Apr; Mon 27 Aug (9-6).**
4-acre hillside garden formed since 1964. Wide variety of trees, shrubs and perennials in areas of differing character. Water gardens; gravel garden; colour coordinated borders. Over 200 shrub and climbing roses. Many clematis; interesting throughout season.

⑪ ♦ BROUGHTON CASTLE
nr Banbury OX15 5EB. The Lord Saye & Sele, 01295 262624. *21/2m SW of Banbury. On Shipston-on-Stour rd (B4035).* **House and garden adm £6.50, concession £5.50, chd £2.50, garden only adm £3, chd £1, concessions £2. Weds & Suns 1 May to 15 Sept; also Thurs in July & Aug; Bank Hol Suns & Mons (2-5). For NGS: Sun 29 July (2-5).** 1 acre; shrubs, herbaceous borders, walled garden, roses, climbers seen against background of C14-C16 castle surrounded by moat in open parkland. House also open, extra charge.

⑫ BROUGHTON GRANGE
Wykham Lane, Broughton OX15 5DS. *1/4m out of village. From Banbury take the B4035 to village of Broughton. At the Seye & Sele Arms PH turn L up Wykham Lane (one way). Follow rd out of village along lane for 1/4m. Entrance on R.* **Adm £5, chd free. Suns 6 May; 1 July (9-5).** An impressive 25 acres of gardens and light woodland in an attractive Oxfordshire setting. The centrepiece is a large terraced walled garden created by Tom Stuart-Smith in 2001. Vision has been used to blend the gardens into the countryside. Good early displays of bulbs followed by outstanding herbaceous planting in summer. Formal and informal areas combine to make this a special site incl newly laid arboretum with many ongoing projects.

⑬ 🆕 BROUGHTON GROUNDS FARM

North Newington OX15 6AW. Mr & Mrs Andrew Taylor. *3m from Banbury. 3m off B4035 through North Newington. Leave Banbury on Shipston Rd, B4035. Turn R to N Newington, follow rd signed Shutford. On L ¾m signed B & B.* Home-made teas. **Adm £2.50, chd free (share to FWAG). Sun 24 June (2-5).**
One of the few farms to achieve recognition under the 'High Level Stewardship Scheme'. You will see rare wild flowers, grasses and wildlife in an area set in an 18 acre meadow. Also includes an old mill race and views of the deserted (1914) village of Hazelford. An area 'species rich'.

🐾 🛏 🍵

⑭ BROUGHTON POGGS & FILKINS GARDENS

GL7 3JH. *3m N of Lechlade. 5m S of Burford.* Home-made teas in village hall. **Combined adm £3.50, chd free. Sun 10 June (2-5.30).**
Two beautiful Cotswold stone villages. Gardens of widely varied scale and character. Village maps will be available. Classic car show. Communally-run village shop (ices etc). Swinford Museum of Cotswold tools and artefacts. Woollen weavers.

🍵

BROUGHTON HALL

Broughton Poggs. Karen & Ian Jobling
Formal walled garden, together with less formal grounds; ha-ha and views out to Thames valley; medieval carp pond; Roman well. Gravel paths.

♿ ✿

You will see rare wild flowers, grasses and wildlife in an area set in an 18 acre meadow . . .

BROUGHTON POGGS MILL

Charles Payne & Avril Inglis. *On B4477 as it crosses Broadwell Brook, between Filkins & Broughton Poggs*
Contemporary garden, with newly-formed linked 'rooms' in a traditional Cotswold watermill setting, dramatically combining local materials with modern planting. Fast-running unfenced water.

🐾

CORNER COTTAGE

Broughton Poggs. Mr E Stephenson
Flowers, shrubs, fish pond, strong character. Gravel paths.

♿

🆕 DOLPHIN HOUSE

Filkins. Mr & Mrs James Moir
Garden of informal character for wildlife, with formal elements. Rose garden.

FILKINS FARMHOUSE

Filkins. Chris & Barbara Bristow
Traditional walled farmhouse garden. Lawns, borders, rose trellis, orchard. Gravel paths.

♿

🆕 FILKINS MOOR

Mr & Mrs A A G Woodford
Mature garden of excellent structure and foliage contrasts with something of interest at every season.

♿

GOODFELLOWS

Filkins. Kate & Clive Morley
House (not open) reconstructed in 1970's in a setting of stream and pools, trees and paddocks. Walled garden and stone terraces (1930's) alongside 'canal'. Steps & uneven levels in walled garden. Unfenced stream & pools.

♿

LITTLE PEACOCKS

Filkins. Colvin & Moggridge, 01367 860225
Garden made by Brenda Colvin 1956 onwards, very strong structure from walls and colours and textures of foliage. Gravel drive.

♿ ✿

🆕 NO 1 COACH HOUSE

Filkins. Mrs Elizabeth Gidman
Small, intensive, semi-formal walled garden of many elements:

terrace, pool, pergola, seats, form and texture of plants, grey plants.

PIP COTTAGE

Filkins. G B Woodin
Village house garden - formal in front; lawn, hedges and a view at the back. Steps to part of back garden.

♿ 🐾

ST PETER'S HOUSE

Filkins. John Cambridge Esq
Large garden of lawns and trees, herbaceous borders, rose garden (2005), sunken paved garden with pool. Gravel drive.

♿

⑮ BUCKLAND LAKES

nr Faringdon SN7 8QR. The Wellesley family. *3m NE of Faringdon. Signed to Buckland off A420, lane between two churches.* Home-made teas. **Adm £3, chd free (share to Richard Wellesley Memorial Transport). Sun 1 Apr (2-6).**
Six acres of parkland surround the lakeside walk, designed by Richard Woods; fine trees; daffodils; shrubs. Norman church adjoins garden. C18 icehouse; thatched boathouse; exedra and temple. Fairly steep slope down to lakes.

♿ 🍵

⑯ CHALKHOUSE GREEN FARM

nr Kidmore End RG4 9AL. Mr & Mrs J Hall, 01189 723631. *2m N of Reading, 5m SW of Henley-on-Thames. Situated between A4074 & B481. From Kidmore End take Chalkhouse Green Rd. Follow yellow signs.* Cream teas. **Adm £3, chd free, wheelchairs & carers free. Sun 15 July (2-6).** Visitors also welcome by appt, Apr to Oct, any number possible.
1-acre garden and open traditional farmstead. Herbaceous borders, herb garden, shrubs, old-fashioned roses, trees incl medlar, quince and mulberries, walled ornamental kitchen garden. Rare breed farm animals incl an ancient breed of British White cattle, sheep, Suffolk punch horse, donkeys, Berkshire pigs, piglets, goats, chickens, ducks and turkeys. Vintage farm machinery displays. Farm trail and donkey rides, vintage tractor trailer rides. Swimming in covered pool, plant stall. Farm Trail - leaflets giving historical background of village and farm.

♿ 🐾 ✿ 🍵

Enter the Forbidden Garden which has inspiration for the 'Alice' stories . . .

⑰ CHARLBURY GARDENS

OX7 3PP. *6m SE of Chipping Norton.* Light refreshments & teas at Charlbury Memorial Hall. **Combined adm £3, chd free. Sun 15 July (2-6).** Large Cotswold village on B4022 Witney-Enstone rd.

GOTHIC HOUSE

Mr & Mrs Andrew Lawson. *In Church St, nr Bell Hotel* 1/3-acre walled garden, designed for sculpture display and colour association. New area of planted squares replaces lawn. False perspective, pleached lime walk, trellis, terracotta containers. Gravel paths, small steps.

HEATHFIELD

Browns Lane. **Helen & Trevor Jones, 01608 810644, trevor.jones@ophiopogon.com.** *In Browns Lane between Spendlove car park & The Bull.* **Visitors welcome by appt.** 1/2-acre walled garden. Mixed borders, with a variety of interesting plants, have been created over the last eight years, by the owners, around newly designed landscape features and existing trees. Some gravel paths.

LYDBROOK

Crawborough. **Aija & Christopher Hastings.** *Close to centre of Charlbury on a road from the Playing Close* A typical long 1930's garden that has been divided into a number of rooms including patios, lawns and a small vegetable patch. Planting includes some exotic species such as tree ferns, bananas and bamboos. Featured in BBC 'Easy Gardening' magazine Sept 2006.

⑱ CHASTLETON GARDENS

GL56 0SZ. *4m NW of Chipping Norton. 3m SE of Moreton-in-Marsh on A44.* Light refreshments & cream teas. **Combined adm £5, chd free. Sun 15 July (2-6).**

3 very different gardens: Prue Leith's 5 acre garden with views, lake, Cotswold terraces (one red), rose tunnel, woods, vegetable and flower parterres; Glebe Cottage (Pearse's) plantsman's gardener's cottage with pond and alpines, baskets and pots; and Chastleton House, Jacobean manor house with topiary and parkland.

CHASTLETON GLEBE

Prue Leith 5 acres, old trees, terraces (one all red); small lake, island; Chinese-style bridge, pagoda; formal vegetable garden; views; rose tunnel. Vegetable and flower parterres. Gravel paths & grass areas dependent on weather.

◆ CHASTLETON HOUSE

The National Trust. *From A436 off A44. Car park 270yds from garden* 3-acre garden with a typical Elizabethan/Jacobean layout, ring of fascinating topiary at its heart. At Chastleton House (not open) the rules of modern croquet were codified in 1866. Croquet lawn survives.

1 GLEBE COTTAGE

Mr & Mrs Ray Pearse Plantsman's garden comprising intensely planted island beds, herbaceous borders, alpine garden, pond, many clematis, baskets and pots. Won Moreton-in-Marsh Show Amateur Garden 2006.

⑲ CHIVEL FARM

Heythrop OX7 5TR. **Mr & Mrs J D Sword, 01608 683227, rosalind.sword@btinternet.com.** *4m E of Chipping Norton. Off A361 or A44.* **Visitors welcome by appt.** Beautifully designed country garden, with extensive views, designed for continuous interest. Colour-schemed borders with many unusual trees, shrubs and herbaceous plants. Small formal white garden. Conservatory.

⑳ CHRIST CHURCH MASTERS', POCOCK AND CATHEDRAL GARDENS

Oxford OX1 1DP, www.chch.ox.ac.uk. *Enter from St Aldate's into War Memorial Gardens, into Christ Church Meadow, then through Masters' Garden main gate.* **Adm £2.50 (share to Oxford & District Mencap). Sat 28 July (2-5). Combined with Merton Adm £3.50.** The Masters' Garden created in 1926 features a newly planted herbaceous and shrub border with a range of seasonal colours. Venture through into the Pocock Garden, pass the oriental plane, planted in 1636, and shade-loving plants, then enter the Forbidden Garden which has inspiration for the 'Alice' stories. Gravel paths through main gardens.

㉑ NEW CHURCH FARM FIELD

Church Lane, Epwell OX15 6LD. **Mr V D & Mrs D V D Castle, 01295 788473.** *7 1/2m W of Banbury on N side of Epwell.* **Adm £2, chd free. Bank Hol Mon 28 May; Sun 2 Sept (2-6). Combined with Epwell Mill adm £3. Visitors also welcome by appt.** Woods; arboretum with wild flowers (planting started 1992); over 150 different trees and shrubs in 4 1/2 acres. Paths cut through trees for access to various parts. Can be slippery at times.

CLIVEDEN

See Buckinghamshire.

㉒ CLOCK HOUSE

Coleshill SN6 7PT. **Denny Wickham & Peter Fox, 01793 762476.** *3 1/2m SW of Faringdon. On B4019.* **Adm £2.50, chd free. Visitors welcome by appt.** Rambling garden on hilltop overlooking NT parkland and Vale of the White Horse. On the site of Coleshill House, burnt down in 1952, the floor plan has been laid out as a garden with lavender and box 'walls' and gravel 'rooms' full of self-sown butterfly-attracting flowers. Exuberant, not too tidy, garden with unusual plants; walled garden; greenhouse; vegetables.

🔟 EPWELL MILL
nr Banbury OX15 6HG. **Mrs William Graham & Mrs David Long.** *7m W of Banbury. Between Shutford & Epwell.* Home-made teas. **Adm £2, chd free. Sun 1 Apr; Bank Hol Mon 28 May; Sun 2 Sept (2-6). Combined with Church Farm, Epwell.**
Medium-sized peaceful garden, interestingly landscaped in open country, based around former watermill with terraced pools. Spring bulbs in April, azaleas in May and early autumn colour in September. White double border.

🟤 EVELEGH'S
High Street, Long Wittenham OX14 4QH. **Dr & Mrs C S Ogg.** *3m NE of Didcot. Take A415 from Abingdon to Clifton Hampden, turn R at T-lights. Cross river to Long Wittenham. Drive into village - Evelegh's is next to The Plough on RH-side.* Home-made teas by WI in village hall. **Adm £3, chd free. Sun 3 June (2-6).**
³/₄-acre garden leading through areas of different characters to River Thames. Well stocked with many unusual shrubs, bulbs and perennials, incl collections of old bush roses, delphiniums, tree and herbaceous peonies, irises and clematis. Art exhibition.

EVENLEY WOOD GARDEN
See Northamptonshire.

🟤 THE FILBERTS
North Moreton OX11 9AT. **Mr & Mrs S Prescott & Mrs Gladys Kirkman,** 01235 815353, janetmprescott@aol.com. *3m SE of Didcot. Off A4130 (Didcot-Wallingford rd).* Home-made teas. **Adm £3, chd free. Visitors welcome by appt in June & July for groups. Coaches permitted.**
1-acre garden featuring island beds planted for shade, architectural foliage and drought tolerance. Colourful mixed borders with many unusual plants, over 120 varieties of clematis and more than 50 of penstemon; lily and fish ponds; vegetable garden; sweet peas; rose beds in parterre form and an orchard. Gravel paths, some narrow.

🟤 GARSINGTON MANOR
28 Southend, nr Oxford OX44 9DH. **Mrs R Ingrams.** *3m SE of Oxford. N of B480. 1¹/₂m S of Wheatley.* Home-made teas. **Adm £4, chd free. Sun 29 Apr; Sun 23 Sept (2-5).**
C17 house of architectural interest (not open). Monastic fish ponds, water garden, dovecote c1700; flower parterre and Italian garden laid out by Philip and Lady Ottoline Morrell; fine trees and yew hedges. Gravel paths, steps.

🟤 **NEW** GREENFIELD FARM
Christmas Common, nr Watlington OX49 5HG. **Andrew & Jane Ingram, 01491 612434.** *4m from J5 of M40, 7m from Henley. J5 M40; A40 towards Oxford for ¹/₂m; turn L signed Christmas Common. ³/₄m past Fox & Hounds. Turn L at 'Tree Barn' sign.* Home-made teas. **Adm £3, chd free** (share to Farming and Wildlife Advisory Group). **Sun 5 Aug (12-5). Visitors also welcome by appt June, Aug or Sept only. Groups of 10-30.**
10-acre wild flower meadow, surrounded by woodland, established 10 yrs ago under the Countryside Stewardship Scheme. Traditional Chiltern chalkland meadow in beautiful peaceful setting with 80 species of perennial wild flowers and grasses (incl Chiltern gentian, pyramidal and greater-spotted orchids). ¹/₂m walk from parking area. Opportunity to return via typical Chiltern beechwood. Wide range of invertebrates, from grasshoppers to butterflies. Dogs on lead or under control only.

🟤 ◆ GREYS COURT
Rotherfield Greys, Henley-on-Thames RG9 4PG. **The National Trust, 01491 628529, www. nationaltrust.org.uk/greyscourt.** *3m W of Henley-on-Thames. Signed from Nettlebed taking B481. Direct route from Henley-on-Thames town centre (unsigned for NT): follow signs to*

Badgemore Golf Club towards Rotherfield Greys, about 3m out of Henley. **Adm £4, chd £2. For NGS: Sat 19 May (12-5).**
8 acres amongst which are the ruined walls and buildings of original fortified manor. Rose, cherry, wisteria and white gardens; lawns; kitchen garden; ice house; Archbishop's maze. Tudor house (not open) with C18 alterations on site of original C13 house fortified by Lord Grey in C14. Donkey wheel and tower. A band plays during the afternoon. Free tours with gardener-in-charge. Separate parking nr mansion. Gardens partly accessible, slopes, loose gravel paths & some cobbles.

🟤 HEADINGTON GARDENS
Old Headington, Oxford OX3 9BT. *2m E from centre of Oxford. After T-lights, centre of Headington, towards Oxford, 2nd turn on R into Osler Rd. Gardens at end of rd in Old Headington.* Teas at Ruskin College. **Combined adm £3, chd free. Sun 27 May (2-6).**
Attractive village of Saxon origin hidden within the bounds of Oxford.

THE COACH HOUSE
The Croft, Headington. **Mr & Mrs David Rowe.** *After T-lights in centre of Headington, 2nd turn on R towards Oxford into Osler Rd. R again off Osler Rd*
Two linked gardens of differing character: one laid to lawn with formal hedges, flower beds and small woodland area; the other a sunny courtyard with ponds on two levels, a gravel garden and sculpture. Limited wheelchair access, some gravel paths.

NEW 35 ST ANDREWS ROAD
Old Headington. **Mrs Alison Soskice.** *Opp end of Osler Rd*
Charming ¹/₄-acre garden with trees, shrubs and herbaceous plants incl magnificent Kiftsgate rose flowering in May. Gravel drive, but wheelchair access nr entrance to reduce travel over gravel.

NEW 37 ST ANDREWS ROAD
Headington. **Judith & David Marquand.** *Driveway to 37 lies between 33 & 35 St Andrew's Rd*
Two small delightful linked

Traditional Chiltern chalkland meadow in beautiful peaceful setting . . .

gardens (against a backdrop of neighbours' mature trees), paved in 2003-4 and re-planted to provide all-yr interest. Gravelled drive and entry area.

  ⅄ ✕

STOKE COTTAGE
Stoke Place. Steve & Jane Cowls. *End of Osler Rd to St Andrew's Rd to Stoke Place* Mature trees and old stone walls provide a framework for a linked series of paths and flower beds containing many contrasting shrubs and plants which give an atmosphere of seclusion.

  ⅄ ✕

③⓪ HEARNS HOUSE
Gallows Tree Common RG4 9DE. John & Joan Pumfrey, 0118 972 2848. *5m N of Reading, 5m W of Henley. From A4074 turn E at The Fox, Cane End.* Home-made teas. **Adm £2.50, chd free. Sat 19, Sun 20 May; Sun 26, Mon 27 Aug (10-12 & 2-5). Evening Opening £7.50, wine, Tue 24 July (6-9).** Visitors also welcome by appt, not suitable for coaches. 2-acre garden in woodland setting provides design and planting ideas for small as well as larger gardens. Good foliage and single colour areas with totally drought-tolerant paved courtyard, water features and shady walks. Black spiral garden. Wide variety of hardy plants incl many new varieties, chosen and propagated for yr-round interest in the garden and in the nursery. Jazz evening Tues 24 July with picnic tables available. Studio open with exhibition of artworks on 20 May.

  ⅄ ✕ ⊛ ☕

③① HILL COURT
Tackley OX5 3AQ. Mr & Mrs Andrew C Peake. *9m N of Oxford. Turn off A4260 at Sturdy's Castle.* Home-made teas. **Adm £2.50, chd free. Sat 2, Sun 3 June (2-6).** Walled garden of 2 acres with yew cones at top of terrace as a design feature by Russell Page in the 1960s. Terraces incl silver, pink and blue plantings, white garden, herbaceous borders, shrubberies, orangery. Many rare and unusual plants. Entry incl History Trail with unique geometric fish ponds (1620), C17 stables, pigeon house, C18 lakes, ice house (not suitable for wheelchairs). Local crafts for sale. Music on Sun. Gravel paths, steep slopes, paving.

  ⅄ ✕ ⊛ ☕

③② HOLYWELL MANOR
Manor Road, Oxford OX1 3 UH. Balliol College Graduate Centre. *1m E of Carfax. In town centre. Corner of Manor Rd & St Cross Rd off Longwall.* **Adm £2, chd free. Sun 13 May (2-5).** Garden of approx 1 acre, not normally open to the public. Imaginatively laid out 50yrs ago around horse chestnut to give formal and informal areas. Mature gingko avenue, spinney with spring flowers and bulbs. Unfenced pond.

  ✕ ⊛

Secluded old village with renowned Norman church ... short footpath from Mill Lane leads to scenic Iffley Lock ...

③③ HOME CLOSE
Southend, Garsington OX44 9DH. Miss M Waud & Dr P Giangrande, 01865 361394. *3m SE of Oxford. Southend. N of B480. Opp Garsington Manor.* **Adm £3, chd free.** Visitors welcome by appt 1 June to 30 Sept. 2-acre garden with listed house (not open) and granary. Trees, shrubs and perennials planted for all-yr interest. Terraces, walls and hedges divide the garden into ten distinct areas.

  ✕

③④ HOME FARM
Balscote OX15 6JP. Mr Godfrey Royle, 01295 738194. *5m W of Banbury. ½m off A422.* Light refreshments & teas. **Adm £3, chd free.** Visitors welcome by appt. C17 house and barn (not open), - ½-acre plant lover's peaceful garden giving yr-round interest with unusual plants, coloured foliage, flowering shrubs, bulbs and perennials created by garden owners over 20yrs in an informal way. Two lawns give a feeling of spaciousness and a small terrace has views of surrounding countryside. Featured in GGG 2006.

  & ☕

③⑤ IFFLEY GARDENS
Iffley Village OX4 4EJ. *2m S of Oxford. Within Oxford's ring rd, off A4158 from Magdalen Bridge to Littlemore roundabout.* Map provided at each garden. Home-made teas in church hall. **Combined adm £3.50, chd free, concessions £2. Sun 10 June (2-6).** Secluded old village with renowned Norman church, featured on cover of Pevsner's Oxon guide. Short footpath from Mill Lane leads to scenic Iffley Lock and Sandford to Oxford towpath.

  ☕

6 ABBERBURY AVENUE
Philippa Scoones
Established 1-acre family garden with mature borders, shrubs, terrace, formal vegetable garden, water garden and wild flower area. Many features of the original 1930s layout remain. Unusual and interesting plants throughout.

  &

15 ABBERBURY ROAD
Allen & Boglarka Hill
Variety of beds planted over the last 10yrs in different styles featuring many shrubs, climbers, and perennials.

  ✕

65 CHURCH WAY
Mrs J Woodfill
Small English cottage garden with a few Californian plants.

  ✕ ⊛

71 CHURCH WAY
Mr & Mrs Harrison, 01865 718224. Visitors also welcome by appt. Small garden, professionally designed. Mixed planting of small trees, shrubs, herbaceous plants. View of river valley across to Boars Hill.

122 CHURCH WAY
Sir John & Lady Elliott
Small secluded cottage style garden with trees, shrubs, roses and herbaceous plants behind listed house (not open) with view of church tower.

  & ✕

THE THATCHED COTTAGE
2 Mill Lane. Mr & Mrs Bones, 01865 711453, chrisbones01@yahoo.co.uk. *Mill Lane.* Visitors also welcome by appt. Delightful ¾-acre garden tucked

behind C16 village house (not open). Range of specimen trees and plants in terracing; water features, formal gardens and water meadow with Thames frontage.

36 KENCOT GARDENS
nr Lechlade GL7 3QT. *5m NE of Lechlade. E of A361 between Burford & Lechlade. Teas in village hall.* **Combined adm £3, chd free. Mon 9 Apr (2-6).** Charming Cotswold village with interesting Norman church. Possibility of organist playing in church in afternoon.

THE ALLOTMENTS
Amelia Carter Trust
Six plots containing vegetables, fruit and flowers, with emphasis on organic gardening.

DE ROUGEMONT
Mr & Mrs D Portergill
1/2-acre garden with very varied planting: over 350 named plants; beds for perennials, conifers, fuchsias, herbs and roses; spring bulbs; vegetables and fruit trees; soft fruit cage; greenhouse with vine; well. Sloping gravel drive, help available.

&

THE GARDENS
Lt Colonel & Mrs John Barstow
1/4-acre garden featuring shrubs, spring bulbs, dahlias, roses, herbaceous, rock plants, old apple trees and well.

IVY NOOK
Mr W Gasson
Cottage garden; rockeries, lawns, mixed borders with yr-round colour.

Naturalised daffodils, fritillaries, wood anemones in mature orchards . . .

KENCOT HOUSE
Mr & Mrs Andrew Patrick
2-acre garden with lawns, trees, borders; quantities of daffodils and other spring bulbs; roses and over 50 different clematis; notable ginkgo tree. Interesting carved C13 archway.

MANOR FARM
Mr & Mrs J R Fyson
2-acre garden. Naturalised daffodils, fritillaries, wood anemones in mature orchards, incl quince, medlar and mulberry; pleached limewalk, pergola with rambling gallica roses. Pair of resident geese and small flock of bantams patrol the paddock. C17 listed house, not open.

& ⋈ ⊛

PINNOCKS
Mr & Mrs J Coxeter
Two gardens are divided by house. Both have mixed shrub and herbaceous borders and front garden has magnificent magnolia.

37 ◆ KINGSTON BAGPUIZE HOUSE
nr Abingdon OX13 5AX. Mrs Francis Grant, 01865 820259, www.kingstonbagpuizehouse.org.uk. *5m W of Abingdon. In Kingston Bagpuize just off A415, 1/4m S of A415/A420.* **House and garden adm: adult £5, concessions £4.50, chd £2.50, garden only adm £3, chd free. Open many days throughout the year. Please phone or visit website for details. For NGS: Suns 1 Apr; 15 July; 16 Sept (2-5).** Notable collection of unusual trees, incl magnolias, shrubs, perennials and bulbs, incl snowdrops, providing yr-round interest and colour. Large mixed borders, interesting summer flowering trees and shrubs. Some gravel paths. Disabled WC. Steps into tearoom, but also outside area with tables & chairs.

& ⋈ ⊛ ☕

38 LADY MARGARET HALL
Norham Gardens, Oxford OX2 6QA. Principal & Fellows of Lady Margaret Hall. *1m N of Carfax. From Banbury Rd, R at T-lights into Norham Gdns.* Home-made teas. **Adm £2.50, chd free. Sun 16 Sept (2-5.30).** Colourful late borders enhance the beautiful buildings of this college set in a large and well-stocked garden. Unique sunken garden, charming river

walk and mature trees are just some of the features of this wonderful garden. Exhibition of prints by Head Gardener, Ben Pritchard. Unfenced river boundary.

& ⋈ ⊛ ☕

39 LIME CLOSE
35 Henleys Lane, Drayton OX14 4HU. M C de Laubarede, mail@mclgardendesign.com. *2m S of Abingdon. Henleys Lane is off main rd through Drayton.* Light refreshments & teas. **Adm £3, chd free (share to CLIC Sargent). Suns 15 Apr; 3 June (2-5.30). Visitors also welcome by appt in writing or email for groups 10+ until end June.** 3-acre mature plantsman's garden with rare trees, shrubs, perennials and bulbs. Mixed borders, raised beds, pergola, unusual topiary and shade borders. Herb garden designed by Rosemary Verey. Listed C16 house (not open). New cottage garden focusing on colour combinations and an iris garden with over 100 varieties of tall bearded irises.

& ⊛ ☕

40 LYFORD GRANGE
Lyford OX12 0EQ. Mrs Charles Dingwall, 01235 868227, sdingwall@hotmail.co.uk. *5m N of Wantage. Just E of Lyford village approx 1m from Charney Bassett, W Hanney & Southmoor.* Home-made teas. **Adm £2.50, chd free (share to Juvenile Diabetes Foundation). Sun 10, 17 June (2-6). Visitors also welcome by appt in June. Coach parties welcome.** 1 1/2 acres formal and informal gardens, incl mixed borders and large newly planted pond, surround C15 house (not open) where St Edmund Campion was captured in 1581. Rural setting in the Vale of the White Horse. Featured on BBC2 'Open Gardens' with Carol Klein 2006, 'Amateur Gardening', June 2006.

& ⋈ ⊛ ☕

41 ◆ MAGDALEN COLLEGE
Oxford OX1 4AU. Magdalen College, 01865 276050, mark.blandford-baker@magd.ox.ac.uk, www.magd.ox.ac.uk. *Entrance in High St.* **Adm £3, chd £2, concessions £2. See website for other opening dates. For NGS: Sun 1 Apr (1-6).** 60 acres incl deer park, college lawns, numerous trees 150-200yrs old, notable herbaceous and shrub

plantings; Magdalen meadow, where purple and white snake's-head fritillaries can be found, is surrounded by Addison's Walk, a tree-lined circuit by the R Cherwell developed since the late C18. An ancient herd of 60 deer is located in the grounds.

⑫ **MANOR FARM**
Minster Lovell OX29 0RR. Lady Parker, 01993 775728. *1½m W of Witney. Off B4047 rd between Witney/Burford. Follow sign opp White Hart down to R Windrush, 100yds over bridge turn R at Old Swan & up village street. Manor Farm is last house on R before continuing to Crawley. Parking: enter at end of 1st field towards Crawley if approaching from village. Drive back across field to enter close to garden. No parking in village.* Home-made teas. **Adm £2.50, chd free. Sun 17 June (2-5). Visitors also welcome by appt May, June, July, weekends only.**
6-acre garden of C15 farmhouse (not open) with open access to adjoining Minster Lovell Hall ruins. Old shrub and climbing roses, fish ponds, herbaceous and lawns. Old barns within garden area. Grasses area.

Ancient mulberry said to have associations with James I . . .

⑬ **MERTON COLLEGE FELLOWS' GARDEN**
Oxford OX1 4JD. Warden & Fellows. *Merton St, parallel to High St.* **Adm £2.50, chd free. Sun 1 Apr; Sat 28 July (2-5). Combined adm £3.50 with Magdalen Sun 1 Apr; with Christ Church Sat 28 July.**
Ancient mulberry said to have associations with James I; specimen trees incl Sorbus and Malus vars; long mixed border; recently established herbaceous bed; view of Christ Church meadow.

⑭ **MIDDLETON CHENEY GARDENS**
OX17 2NP. *3m E of Banbury. From M40 J11 follow A422, signed Middleton Cheney. Map available at all gardens.* Home-made teas at Peartree House. **Combined adm £3, chd free. Sun 17 June (1-6).**
Large village with a diversity of gardens. Late C13 church with Pre-Raphaelite stained glass and William Morris ceiling open 1-6 with gardens.

NEW CHURCH COTTAGE
12 Church Lane. David Thompson. *Back garden off High Street*
Entry to private back garden through rear garden of 8 Church Lane. Typical English cottage garden-style with 'Mediterranean' influences. Public front garden by church path, yellow and white themed borders.

NEW 8 CHURCH LANE
Mr & Mrs Style. *Gate entrance next to 37 High Street*
Cottage garden in the process of being renovated since 2005. Mixed borders, vegetable and fruit area, pergola.

15 CHURCH LANE
Dr Jill Meara. *Entrance in narrow lane to L of church spire*
A series of open spaces incl cottage garden, vegetable patch, orchard area and field ending in a stream.

NEW 5 LONGBURGES
Mr & Mrs D Vale. *Access is via a good footpath at rear of garden*
Small SW-facing garden on three levels with patios, ponds, lawn and planting. Collection of acers predominate with herbaceous, mixed and spring borders. Small container grown fruit and herb patio.

38 MIDWAY
Margaret & David Finch. *Take High St. First R into Bull Baulk. L into Midway*
Small front garden. Back garden with mixed borders and shrubs. Water feature with pond and waterfall and other interesting features.

PEARTREE HOUSE
Roger & Barbara Charlesworth. *Glovers Lane is 200yds N of All Saints Church*
Approx ⅓-acre cottage garden with extensive water feature.

2 QUEEN STREET
Lynn Baldwin. *At roundabout take 1st exit. Queen St is 1st L after 30 mph sign*
Small front and back garden. Informal and densely planted.

14 QUEEN STREET
Brian & Kathy Goodey
Mature cottage garden that has evolved through family use. Rooms in a rectangle where there is always room for an extra plant.

27 STANWELL LEA
Frank & Jane Duty. *B4525 Northampton. Xrds R into village. Take L Stanwell Drive, L Stanwell Lea*
Cottage garden with surprises, Water feature and penstemon collection.

⑮ **MONKS HEAD**
Weston Road, Bletchingdon OX5 3DH. Sue Bedwell, 01869 350155. *Approx 4m N of Kidlington. From A34 take B4027 to Bletchingdon, turn R at Xrds into Weston Rd.* Home-made teas at church 6 May. **Adm £2.50, chd free. Thur 3, Sun 6 May (2-5). Evening Opening** light refreshments & wine, Mon 4 June (6-8). **Visitors also welcome by appt all yr. £2 groups 10+; £3 groups of under 10.**
Plantaholics' garden for all-yr interest. Bulb frame and alpine area, greenhouse.

⑯ **OLD CHURCH HOUSE**
Priory Road, Wantage OX12 9DD. Dr & Mrs Dick Squires, 01235 762785. *Situated near to Parish Church nr Wantage market square.* Light refreshments & teas at museum in Church St. **Adm £2, chd free (share to Vale & Downland Museum, Wantage). Daily Apr to Oct (10.30-4.30). Visitors also welcome by appt.**
Unusual town garden running down to the Letcombe Brook. Much interest

with different levels, follies, water, mature trees and many special plants. A charming host.

 ♿ ➗ ☕

47 THE OLD MANOR HOUSE
Manor Farm Lane, Chesterton OX26 1UD. **Sylvia & Geoffrey Strivens**. *2m SW of Bicester. From M40 J9 take A41 Bicester. In 1¹/₂m turn to Chesterton. At Red Cow PH turn R. In 100yds turn R by church into Manor Farm Lane (no parking, cul-de-sac). Cars can be left in village. Disabled parking in church car park.* Cream teas. **Adm £3, chd free. Sat 2 June (2-6).**
2¹/₂-acre dry stone walled garden. Extensive herbaceous and mixed borders. Rose and herb gardens. Double lime avenue planted 1986 enclosed by shrub borders. Large lawned area planted 1988 with oak and hornbeam circles and specimen trees. Mill pond and stream. Listed Norman undercroft dated 1140 with small explanatory exhibition, listed C17 house (not open) incorporating remains of medieval manor house.

♿ ➗ ⚦ ☕

48 THE OLD RECTORY
Coleshill SN6 7PR. **Sir George & Lady Martin**. *3m SW of Faringdon. Coleshill (NT village) is on B4019.* Home-made teas. **Adm £2, chd free. Suns 1 Apr; 9 Sept (2-5).**
Medium-sized garden; lawns and informal shrub beds; wide variety shrubs, incl old-fashioned roses, 50yr-old standard wisteria. Distant views of Berkshire and Wiltshire Downs. House (not open) dates from late C14.

♿ ☕

THE OLD RECTORY FARNBOROUGH
See Berkshire.

OLD THATCH
See Buckinghamshire.

49 NEW THE OLD VICARAGE
Main Street, Bledington, Chipping Norton OX7 6UX. **Sue & Tony Windsor**, 01608 658525, tony.windsor@tiscali.co.uk. *6m SW of Chipping Norton. 4m SE of Stow-on-the-Wold. On the main st, B4450, through Bledington. NOT next to church.* **Adm £3, chd free. Visitors welcome by appt all year. Teas by arrangement.**
1¹/₂-acre garden attached to late

Mediterranean fantasy in a cold climate . . .

Georgian (1843) vicarage (not open). Rose garden with over 350 David Austin roses, borders of hardy perennials, small pond and paddock with shrubs and beds. Garden situated on sloping ground, all accessible but quite hard work. Small pond not fenced.

♿ ⚦

50 40 OSLER ROAD
Oxford OX3 9BJ. **Mr & Mrs N Coote**, 01865 767680, nicholas@coote100.freeserve.co.uk. *2m E from centre of Oxford. Off London Rd, ³/₄m inside ring rd. After T-lights in centre of Headington towards Oxford, 2nd turn on R, Osler Rd.* **Adm £3. Visitors welcome by appt.**
Spacious 31yr-old town garden ²/₃ acre with mature specimens of exotics. Passion for design and planting, use of decorative pots, mosaic paths, whitewashed walls, shutters; Mediterranean fantasy in a cold climate.

♿ ➗

51 OSSE FIELD
Appleton OX13 5JZ. **Mrs J Blackwell**. *6m W of Oxford. ¹/₂m N of A420.* Cream teas. **Adm £3, chd free. Sun 17 June (2-6).**
7 acres of mature and newly planned garden. Superb borders. Walled and white gardens recently designed by Martin Lane Fox. Rose garden. Meadow walk to water garden. Large ornamental kitchen garden.

♿ ➗ ⚦ ☕ ☕

52 THE PRIORY GARDEN
Church Lane, Charlbury OX7 3PX. **Dr D El Kabir & Colleagues**. *White gate off St Mary's church yard.* **Adm £3, chd free (share to Wytham Hall Ltd). Sun 24 June (2-6).**
1 acre of formal terraced topiary gardens with Italianate features. Foliage colour schemes, shrubs, parterres with fragrant plants, old roses, water features, sculpture and inscriptions aim to produce a poetic, wistful atmosphere. Arboretum of over 3 acres borders the R Evenlode and incl wildlife garden and pond. Gravel paths.

♿ ➗ ⚦

53 THE QUEEN'S COLLEGE
High Street, Oxford OX1 4AW. **The Queen's College**. *Between Carfax and Magdalen Bridge.* **Adm £2.50, chd free, concessions £2. Sat 14 Apr (2-6).**
Front and back quadrangles are formally arranged. To the left are the Provost's and the Fellows' Gardens. The former, situated beside the Library, has many interesting plants. The latter, renovated a few years ago, is developing into an interesting garden. The Nuns' Garden has also been replanted following restoration of the intervening walls.

➗

54 RADCOT HOUSE
Clanfield OX18 2SX. **Robin & Jeanne Stainer**, 01367 810231, rstainer@radcothouse.co.uk. *1¹/₄m S of Clanfield. On A4095 bet Witney & Faringdon, 200yds N of Radcot bridge.* Cream teas. **Adm £3, chd free. Suns 17 June; 22 July; 16 Sept (2-6). Visitors also welcome by appt.**
Country house garden in several sections. Started 7yrs ago, garden comprises walled area containing mostly contemporary planting, hot coloured beds, several shady areas, formal pond, wood and fruit trees, water feature reflecting the flood plain location and vegetable cages/glasshouse. Convenient seating at key points enables relaxed observation and reflection. Featured on BBC Oxford 2006. Unfenced ponds.

♿ ☕

55 9 RAWLINSON ROAD
Oxford OX2 6UE. **Rani Lall**, 01865 559614. *³/₄m N of Oxford Centre. Rawlinson Rd runs between Banbury & Woodstock Rds midway between Oxford City Centre & Summertown shops.* **Adm £2.50, chd free. Sun 1 July (2-6). Also open Somerville College. Visitors also welcome by appt.**
Small town garden with structured disarray of roses. Terrace of stone inlaid with brick and enclosed by Chinese fretwork balustrade, chunky brick and oak pergola covered with

roses, wisteria and clematis; potted topiary. Until autumn, garden delightfully replete with aconites, lobelias, phloxes, daisies and meandering clematis. Featured in 'Times' online 1 Sept 2006.

&. ✕

56 ST HILDA'S COLLEGE
Cowley Place, Oxford OX4 1DY. St Hilda's College. ½m E of Oxford/Carfax centre. Approx 15mins walk E of city centre. Cross Magdalen Bridge & turn R at roundabout into Cowley Place. College lodge at end on R, or park in public car park at St Clements. **Adm £2.50, chd free. Sun 1 Apr (2-5).**
Approx 5 acres laid to lawns with mature trees and flower beds with flood plain meadow containing interesting wild flowers; walk by River Cherwell. Some gravel paths. No access to flood plain meadow for wheelchairs.

&. ✕

57 ST HUGH'S COLLEGE
St Margaret's Road, Oxford OX2 6LE. 1m N of city centre. Corner of St Margaret's Rd & Banbury Rd. **Adm £2.50, chd free, concessions £1.50. Sun 22 Apr (2-5.30).**
Springtime garden, well planted with a variety of flowering bulbs, fine trees, shrub borders and herbaceous plantings in a 14 acre site.

&. ☕

Tumbling rambling roses, softly coloured herbaceous borders . . .

58 SALFORD GARDENS
nr Chipping Norton OX7 5YL. 2m NW of Chipping Norton. Off A44 Oxford-Worcester rd. Home-made teas at The Old Rectory. **Combined adm £3, chd free. Sun 26 Aug (2-6).**
Small village on the edge of the Cotswolds, with an attractive church.
☕

MANOR FARM
Mrs P G Caldin
Small mature well-stocked garden.
&. ✕

OLD RECTORY
Mr & Mrs N M Chambers, 01608 643969. Visitors also welcome by appt May, June, July.
1½ acres mainly enclosed by walls. Yr-round interest, with some unusual plants in mixed borders, many old roses, orchard and vegetable garden.
&. ✕ ⊛

WILLOW TREE COTTAGE
Mr & Mrs J Shapley
Small walled twin gardens with shrub and herbaceous borders, many clematis; one garden created from old farmyard with large alpine garden. Small grass beds.
&. ✕ ⊛

59 SIBFORD GOWER GARDENS
OX15 5RX. 7m W of Banbury. Nr the Warwickshire border, S of B4035, in centre of village nr Wykham Arms PH. Home-made teas at Temple Mill (garden not open for NGS). **Combined adm £3, chd free. Sun 17 June (2-6).**
Small village with charming thatched houses and cottage gardens.
☕

BUTTSLADE HOUSE
Temple Mill Road (also known as Colony Road).
Mrs Diana Thompson
7-yr-old garden designed by previous owner. Areas of formal and informal planting. ⅓ of an acre packed with plants. Roses a speciality.
⌂

NEW CARTER'S YARD
Sue & Malcolm Bannister. Use entrance up steps next to Wykham Arms
Work is in progress on this S-facing cottage garden. Since Sept 2005 the new owners have cleared leylandii hedges and over mature trees and are in the process of re-planting. 8 steps up into garden. Possibility of building work. Use entrance next to Wykham Arms.

GOWERS CLOSE
Judith Hitching & John Marshall
Garden writer's cottage garden, tucked behind a wisteria clad thatched house (not open). Box parterre, herb garden, clipped yew hedges, rose smothered pergola and bosky borders in purples and pinks.
✕ ⌂

THE MANOR HOUSE
Temple Mill Road. Mr & Mrs Martyn Booth
Combination of well established garden and charming extensive patio area provides romantic setting for rambling thatched Manor House (not open).

60 SOMERVILLE COLLEGE
Woodstock Road, Oxford OX2 6HD. Somerville College. ½m E of Carfax Tower. Enter from the Woodstock Rd, S of the Radcliffe Infirmary. **Adm £2, chd free (share to Friends of Oxford Botanic Garden). Sun 1 July (2-6).**
Approx 2 acres, robust college garden planted for yr-round interest. Formal bedding, colour-themed and old-fashioned mixed herbaceous borders.
&. ✕ ☕

61 191 SOUTH AVENUE
Abingdon OX14 1QX. Susan Hammersley, 01235 524957. On outskirts of N Abingdon. Leaving Abingdon on Oxford Rd turn L at T-lights opp Boundry House PH into Northcourt Rd, 2nd R into Sellwood Rd & follow signs via Holland Rd into South Ave. **Adm £2, chd free (share to Multiple Sclerosis). Suns 29 July; 5 Aug (2-6).**
Long narrow back garden designed to create an illusion of width. Divided into three areas - formal patio and pond; perennial borders with interesting and unusual plants, mirror feature and gravel planting; potager and small jungle area with variety of palms. Soft landscape continually changing and being added to. Live music by Abbey Brass on first Sun. Gravel path may restrict hand pushed wheelchairs, but motorised ones can be used.
&. ✕ ☕

62 SOUTH NEWINGTON HOUSE
Barford Road, South Newington OX15 4JW. Mr & Mrs John Ainley, 01295 721207, rojoainley@btinternet.com, www.southnewingtonhouse.co.uk. 6m SW of Banbury. South Newington is between Banbury and Chipping Norton, on A361; take lane signed The Barfords, 200yds on L. Light refreshments & teas. **Adm £3, chd free. Visitors welcome by appt no group too small. Please phone.**
C17 yeomans hall house (not open) set in 5 acres paddocks and garden. A charming garden, created for yr-round interest. Tumbling rambling roses,

softly coloured herbaceous borders. Ponds, organic fruit and vegetables. Walled garden has been re-designed to place more emphasis on the parterre and box topiary.

63 SPARSHOLT MANOR
nr Wantage OX12 9PT. Sir Adrian & Lady Judith Swire. *3¹/₂m W of Wantage. Off B4507 Ashbury Rd.* Home-made teas in village hall. **Adm £2, chd free. Mon 28 May (2-6).** Lakes and wildfowl; ancient boxwood, wilderness and summer borders. Wheelchair access around house and its immediate surroundings.

64 STANSFIELD
49 High Street, Stanford-in-the-Vale SN7 8NQ. Mr & Mrs David Keeble, 01367 710340. *3¹/₂m SE of Faringdon. Park in street.* Home-made teas. **Adm £2, chd free. Tues 3 Apr; 1 May; 5 June; 3 July; 7 Aug; 4 Sept (10-4). Visitors also welcome by appt.** 1¹/₄-acre plantsman's garden on alkaline soil. Wide variety of unusual trees, shrubs and hardy plants. Scree, damp and kitchen gardens, copse underplanted with woodlanders as well as flower arrangers' and drought resistant plants. Guided tours if wished.

65 STEEPLE ASTON GARDENS
OX25 4SQ. *14m N of Oxford, 9m S of Banbury. ¹/₂m off A4260.* Light refreshments & teas in village hall. **Combined adm £3.50, chd free. Sun 6 May (1-6).** Beautiful stone village bordering Cherwell valley; interesting church and winding lanes with a variety of charming stone houses and cottages. Map available at all gardens.

THE LONGBYRE
Mr Vaughan Billings
Hornton stone house (not open) in ¹/₄ acre. Garden constructed out of old orchard. Water feature, mixed perennials, shrubs, tubs on different levels. Limited wheelchair access.

PAYNE'S HILL HOUSE
Paines Hill. Tim & Caroline Edwards
Old-established walled garden with newly planted rose garden

opens out to views across the middle of the village. Borders are mixed and colour-themed.

PRIMROSE COTTAGE
Richard & Daphne Preston
Former walled kitchen garden, until the early 1950s, of about 1-acre. For the following 45 yrs it became a commercial vegetable garden. Now a garden in three parts, comprising lawns, herbaceous borders, glasshouses, large vegetable plot, ponds and much more.

KRALINGEN
North Side. Mr & Mrs Roderick Nicholson. *Possible to park on North Side, with care. Large car park at Steeple Aston Village Hall* 2-acre informal garden created gradually over many yrs by present owners. Many varieties of interesting trees and shrubs and mixed borders lead down to the tranquil woodland/water/bog garden, with fritillaries, wood anemones and candelabra primulas.

66 SWALCLIFFE LEA HOUSE
Swalcliffe Lea OX15 6ET. Jeffrey & Christine Demmar, 01295 788278. *6m W of Banbury. Off the B4035. At Lower Tadmarton, turn (as posted) to Swalcliffe Lea & Shutford. Turn L, single track road. Bear R at fork, 250yds to entrance, take 1st drive on L.* **Adm £2, chd free. Visitors welcome by appt.** Mature terraced garden with densely planted mixed borders; pergola, herb garden, vegetable garden and orchard. Two informal ponds. Stream and small woodland. Range of specimen trees, many varieties of clematis and other herbaceous plants. Some slopes and uneven steps. 2 unfenced ponds.

67 TADMARTON MANOR
Tadmarton OX15 5TD. Mr & Mrs R K Asser, 01295 780212. *5m SW of Banbury. On B4035.* **Adm £2.50, chd free. Visitors welcome by appt.** Old-established 2¹/₂-acre garden; beautiful views of unspoilt countryside; fine trees, great variety of perennial plants and shrubs; tunnel arbour; C15 barn and C18 dovecote. Agapanthus bed (Aug); bank of autumn cyclamen; stilted hornbeam hedge. Wildlife pond.

68 TRINITY COLLEGE
Oxford OX1 3BH. Dr C R Prior, Garden Master. *Central Oxford. Entrance in Broad St.* Cream teas 1 Apr; Home-made teas 29 July. **Adm £2, chd free, concessions £1.50. Suns 1 Apr; 29 July (2-5).** Historic main College Gardens with specimen trees incl aged forked catalpa, spring bulbs, fine long herbaceous border and handsome garden quad originally designed by Wren. President's Garden surrounded by high old stone walls, mixed borders of herbaceous, shrubs and statuary. Fellows' Garden: small walled terrace, herbaceous borders; water feature formed by Jacobean stone heraldic beasts. New award-winning lavender garden and walk-through rose arbour.

New award-winning lavender garden . . .

VERSIONS FARM
See Northamptonshire.

TURWESTON MILL
See Northamptonshire.

TYTHROP PARK
See Buckinghamshire.

69 ◆ UNIVERSITY OF OXFORD BOTANIC GARDEN
Rose Lane, Oxford OX1 4AZ. University of Oxford, 01865 286690, www.botanic-garden.ox.ac.uk. *Situated at E end of High Street in central Oxford, on the banks of the R Cherwell by Magdalen Bridge & opp Magdalen College Tower.* **Phone or see website for other opening times.** For NGS: **Evening Opening** Thur 5 July (6-8). **Adm £3, chd free, concessions £2.20.** The Botanic Garden contains more species of plants per acre than anywhere else on earth. These plants are grown in 9 glasshouses, water and rock gardens, large herbaceous border, walled garden and every available space. In total there are 6,700 different plants to see. National Collection of Euphorbia. Gravel paths.

70 UPPER CHALFORD FARM
between Sydenham & Postcombe
OX39 4NH. Mr & Mrs Paul Rooksby.
4¹/₂m SE of Thame. M40 J6, then
A40. At Postcombe turn R signed
Chalford (turn L if on A40 from Oxford
direction). In 0.9m drive on LH-side at
1st telegraph pole. (House is ¹/₂ -way
Sydenham to Postcombe). Cream
teas. **Adm £3, chd free. Suns 24
June; Sun 1 July (2-6).**
Rambling 1 acre garden surrounding
C17 farmhouse (not open). Unusual
trees, shrubs, perennials, abundant old
roses and topiary. Stream fed ponds
with fish. Native woodland under
restoration with dogwood, guelder
rose, spindles and native plants.
Peaceful seating. Gravel drive.
& ⚘ ☕

71 WADHAM COLLEGE
Oxford OX1 3PN. The Warden &
Fellows. Central Oxford. Parks Road.
**Adm £2.50, chd free (share to Sobell
House Hospice). Suns 18 Mar; 15
July (2-6).**
5 acres, best known for trees, spring
bulbs and mixed borders. In Fellows'
main garden, fine ginkgo and Magnolia
acuminata; bamboo plantation; in
Back Quadrangle very large Tilia
tomentosa 'Petiolaris'; in Mallam Court
white scented garden est 1994; in
Warden's garden an ancient tulip tree;
in Fellows' private garden, Civil War
embankment with period fruit tree
cultivars, recently established
shrubbery with unusual trees and
ground cover amongst older plantings.
& ⚘

**WARMINGTON VILLAGE
GARDENS**
See Warwickshire & part of West
Midlands

72 ◆ WATERPERRY GARDENS
Wheatley OX33 1JZ. Mrs P Maxwell,
Secretary, 01844 339226,
www.waterperrygardens.co.uk. 9m
E of Oxford. M40 J8 from London (turn
off Oxford-Wheatley, first L to
Wheatley, follow brown rose symbol).
J8a from Birmingham (turn R Oxford-
Wheatley over A40, first R Wheatley,
follow brown rose symbol. We are
2¹/₂m N of Wheatley. **Adm Feb £3;
other dates £4.50, chd (10-16) £3,
under 10 free, concessions Feb £3;
other dates £3.75. Jan-Mar (10-5);
Apr-Oct (10-5.30); Nov-Dec (10-5).
For NGS: Suns 18 Feb (10-5); 22
Apr; 23 Sept (10-5.30).**
8-acre garden featuring rock and

alpine gardens, waterlily canal, formal
and rose gardens, shrub and
herbaceous borders incl our famous
200ft long border. Riverside walks and
meadow pastures, nursery beds and
trained fruit orchards. Other facilities
incl plant centre, craft gallery, museum
and Saxon church. National Collection
of Saxifraga. Featured in national press
& regional TV & radio, both BBC & ITV,
2006. Access good to most parts of
garden, some areas may be difficult
when wet.
& ⚘ ❀ [NCCPG] ☕

73 WAYSIDE
82 Banbury Road, Kidlington
OX5 2BX. Margaret & Alistair
Urquhart, 01865 460180,
alistair@urquhart82.wanadoo.co.uk.
5m N of Oxford. On the RH-side of
A4260 travelling N through Kidlington.
**Adm £2.50, chd free. Suns 27 May
(2-6); 1 July (4-7). Visitors also
welcome by appt May to July only.**
¹/₄-acre garden with wide variety of
plants and mature trees; mixed
borders with hardy geraniums, clematis
and bulbs. Conservatory, greenhouse
and fern house with tender plants.
Woodland garden with unusual
species of tree ferns and extensive
collection of hardy ferns; drought
resistant planting in gravel garden.
⚘ ❀ ☕

74 WESTWELL MANOR
nr Burford OX18 4JT. Mr & Mrs T H
Gibson. 2m SW of Burford. From A40
Burford-Cheltenham, turn L ¹/₂m after
Burford roundabout on narrow rd
signed Westwell. Unspoilt hamlet with
delightful church. **Adm £4, chd free
(share to St Mary's Church,
Westwell). Sun 1 July (2-6.30).**
6 acres surrounding old Cotswold
manor house (not open), knot garden,
potager, shrub roses, herbaceous
borders, topiary, earth works,
moonlight garden, rills and water
garden. Some unprotected water.
Some surfaces slippery in wet weather,
stone and wood.
⚘ ❀

**75 NEW WHEATLEY
GARDENS**
Wheatley OX33 1XX. 5m E of
Oxford. Leave A40 at Wheatley,
turn into High St. Gardens at W
end of High St. Cream teas at The
Manor House. **Combined adm £3,
chd free. Sun 17 June (2-6).**
Three adjoining gardens in the
historic coaching village of

Wheatley. Access from the High St,
the original Oxford to London Rd,
before it climbs onto the Shotover
plain.
☕

**NEW BREACH HOUSE
GARDEN**
Liz Parry. Entrance via The Manor
House
1-acre garden with coppiced
hazelwood. Main established area
with extensive shrubs and
perennials, also a more
contemporay reflective space with
a wild pond.
❀

THE MANOR HOUSE
High Street, Wheatley. Mr & Mrs
Edward Hess, 01865 875022.
Visitors also welcome by appt.
1¹/₂-acre garden of Elizabethan
manor house (not open). Formal
box walk; herb garden, cottage
garden with rose arches and a
shrubbery with old roses. A
romantic oasis in this busy village.
Limited wheelchair access. Two
shallow steps, some gravel.
Disabled parking can be arranged
in advance.
& ❀

NEW THE STUDIO
S & A Buckingham. Access via
The Manor house
Cottage-style walled garden
developed from previous farm
yard. Herbaceous borders,
climbing roses and clematis,
shrubs, vegetable plot and fruit
trees. Gravel drive & shallow step
between Manor House & Studio.

**WHICHFORD & ASCOTT
GARDENS**
See Warwickshire & part of West
Midlands.

76 WHITEHILL FARM
Widford nr Burford OX18 4DT. Mr &
Mrs Paul Youngson, 01993 823218.
1m E of Burford. From A40 take turn
signed Widford. Follow signs to
Whitehill Farm Nursery. Home-made
teas. **Adm £2.50, chd free. Sun 1
July (2-6). Visitors also welcome by
appt June, July & Aug only.**
2 acres of hillside gardens and
woodland with spectacular views
overlooking Burford and Windrush
valley. Informal plantsman's garden
being continuously developed in
various areas. Herbaceous and shrub
borders, pond and bog area, old-

fashioned roses, ground cover, ornamental grasses, bamboos and hardy geraniums.

WHITEWALLS
See Buckinghamshire.

77 WICK HALL & NURSERIES
Audlett Drive, Radley OX14 3NF. Mr & Mrs P Drysdale. *2m NE of Abingdon. Between Abingdon & Radley on Audlett Drive.* Home-made teas & cream teas. **Adm £2, chd 50p. Sun 29 Apr (2-5).**
Approx 10 acres lawns and wild garden; topiary; pond garden; rockeries; walled garden enclosing knot garden; young arboretum. Early C18 house (not open), barn and greenhouses, large display of old horticultural and agricultural tools.

78 WILDWOOD
Farnborough OX17 1EL. Mr & Mrs M Hart. *5m N of Banbury, 8m S of Southam. On A423 at Oxon/Warwicks border. Next to Farnborough Garden Centre.* Home-made teas. **Adm £2, chd free. Sun 6 May (2-5).**
Delightful 1/2-acre garden in the country set amongst mature trees and shrubs

providing a haven for wildlife. Garden is stocked with many unusual plants and shrubs and also contains interesting rustic garden features, many of which are made by the owner.

79 WOOD CROFT
Boars Hill OX1 5DH. St Cross College. *2m S of Oxford. From ring rd follow signs to Wootton & Boars Hill. From junction at top Hinksey Hill, house 1st on L.* **Adm £2, chd free (share to Royal Marsden Hospital Charity). Sat 12 May (2-5).**
1 1/2 acres designed and planted by the late Prof G E Blackman FRS. Rhododendrons, camellias, azaleas, many varieties primula in woodland and surrounding natural pond; fine trees. Featured in 'Oxford Times' 2006. Woodlands paths & large ponds.

WOODCHIPPINGS
See Northamptonshire.

80 WOOLSTONE MILL HOUSE
Woolstone, nr Faringdon SN7 7QL. Mr & Mrs Anthony Spink, 01367 820219. *7m W of Wantage. 7m S of Faringdon. Woolstone is a small village off B4507 below Uffington White Horse*

Hill. **Adm £3, chd free (share to Woolstone All Saints Church). Weds, 2 May to 26 Sept (2-5). Visitors also welcome by appt.**
1 1/2-acre garden in pretty hidden village. Stream runs through garden. Large mixed herbaceous and shrub circular border bounded by yew hedges. Topiary. Medlars and old-fashioned roses. Kitchen garden. C18 mill house and barn, not open. Partial wheelchair access. Bridge over stream not suitable for wheelchairs.

81 WORCESTER COLLEGE
Worcester Street, Oxford OX1 2HB. The Provost & Fellows. *Central Oxford, entrance in Beaumont St.* Home-made teas Teas only available 2-4pm. **Adm £2.50, chd free. Sun 22 July (2-5).**
26 acres. Woodland walks and lake created in the early C19 in the picturesque style; over 800 trees and shrubs, many unusual. Tropical bed and two large herbaceous borders; many unusual and rare plants. Tree fern grove. Winner 2006 'Oxford in Bloom' Gold, Best Display by Oxford University Colleges. Gravel paths.

Oxfordshire County Volunteers

County Organisers
John Ainley, South Newington House, South Newington, Nr Banbury OX15 4JW, 01295 721207, rojoainley@btinternet.com
Angela Baker, Hartford Greys, Sandy Lane, Boars Hill, Oxford OX1 5HN, 01865 739360

County Treasurer
David White, Placketts, High Street, Adderbury, Banbury OX17 3LS, 01295 812679, david.white@doctors.org.uk

Leaflets
Catherine Pinney, Pond House, Pyrton, Watlington OX49 5AP, 01491 612638,

Assistant County Organisers
North Roberta Ainley, South Newington House, South Newington, Nr Banbury OX15 4JW, 01295 721207 rojoainley@btinternet.com
North Lynn Baldwin, 2 Queen Street, Middleton Cheney, Banbury OX17 2NP, 01295 711205, baldwinlynn@aol.com
West Michael & Susan Drew, Middle Farm, Hailey, Witney OX29 9UB, 01993 702624, michael.drew@totalise.co.uk
North West Priscilla Frost, 27 Ditchley Road, Charlbury, Chipping Norton OX7 3QS, 01608 810578, info@oxconf.co.uk
South Diana Gordon, Bishop Oak, Jarn Way, Old Boars Hill, Oxford OX1 5JF, 01865 735107
East Charles & Lyn Sanders, Uplands, Old Boars Hill, Oxford OX1 5JF, 01865 739486, sandersc4@hotmail.com
South West Victoria Whitworth, Abbey Farm, Goosey, Faringdon SN7 8PA, 01367 710252, v.whitworth@yahoo.co.uk

SHROPSHIRE

Opening Dates

February

SUNDAY 11
2 Attingham Park

April

SUNDAY 1
19 Knowbury Cattery

SUNDAY 8
30 Preen Manor

TUESDAY 10
32 Radnor Cottage

SUNDAY 15
26 Moortown

SUNDAY 22
4 Brownhill House

May

FRIDAY 4
42 Wollerton Old Hall

SUNDAY 6
19 Knowbury Cattery
36 Swallow Hayes

MONDAY 7
25 Millichope Park
29 Oteley

TUESDAY 8
4 Brownhill House

SUNDAY 13
15 Hodnet Hall Gardens
41 Windy Ridge

SATURDAY 19
10 Dudmaston Hall Gardens

SUNDAY 20
5 Chyknell
13 Gate Cottage

TUESDAY 22
4 Brownhill House

FRIDAY 25
42 Wollerton Old Hall

SUNDAY 27
1 Adcote School
6 The Citadel
23 The Manor House
28 The Old Vicarage
33 Ruthall Manor
38 Walcot Hall

MONDAY 28
4 Brownhill House (Evening)
24 Marehay Farm
38 Walcot Hall

TUESDAY 29
32 Radnor Cottage

THURSDAY 31
30 Preen Manor

June

SUNDAY 3
3 Bluebell Cottage
19 Knowbury Cattery
21 Longner Hall
35 Stanley Hall
36 Swallow Hayes
41 Windy Ridge

TUESDAY 5
4 Brownhill House

FRIDAY 8
8 Cruckfield House

SUNDAY 10
1 Adcote School
16 Holly Grove
24 Marehay Farm
27 Morville Hall Gardens

SATURDAY 16
40 Whittington Village Gardens

SUNDAY 17
40 Whittington Village Gardens

TUESDAY 19
4 Brownhill House

SUNDAY 24
9 David Austin Roses
17 Holmcroft
20 Little Heldre

THURSDAY 28
30 Preen Manor

July

SUNDAY 1
7 The Cottage
12 Field House
19 Knowbury Cattery
31 Preston Hall

TUESDAY 3
4 Brownhill House
32 Radnor Cottage

WEDNESDAY 4
39 Weston Park

THURSDAY 5
24 Marehay Farm

SUNDAY 15
18 Jessamine Cottage

TUESDAY 17
4 Brownhill House

THURSDAY 19
30 Preen Manor

SUNDAY 29
37 Valducci Flower & Vegetable Gardens

August

WEDNESDAY 1
24 Marehay Farm

SUNDAY 5
11 Edge Villa
19 Knowbury Cattery

SUNDAY 19
20 Little Heldre
41 Windy Ridge

SUNDAY 26
18 Jessamine Cottage

September

SUNDAY 2
4 Brownhill House
19 Knowbury Cattery
41 Windy Ridge

SUNDAY 9
34 Shoothill House

SATURDAY 15
14 Harnage Farm

October

SUNDAY 7
19 Knowbury Cattery
30 Preen Manor

SUNDAY 21
25 Millichope Park

Gardens open to the public

2 Attingham Park
9 David Austin Roses
10 Dudmaston Hall Gardens
18 Jessamine Cottage
39 Weston Park
42 Wollerton Old Hall

By appointment only

22 Lower Hall

Newly created stream with oriental theme. Small bluebell wood and kitchen garden . . .

The Gardens

ABERNANT
See Powys.

① ADCOTE SCHOOL
Little Ness SY4 2JY. Adcote School Educational Trust Ltd. *8m NW of Shrewsbury. Via A5, turn off NE follow signs to Little Ness.* Home-made teas. **Adm £3, chd free. Suns 27 May; 10 June (2-5).**
26 acres; fine trees incl beeches, tulip trees, oaks (American and evergreen), atlas cedars, wellingtonia etc. Rhododendrons, azaleas; landscaped garden. House (part shown) designed by Norman Shaw RA; Grade I listed building; William Morris wallpapers; de Morgan tiles.
&. ⋈ ⊛ ☕

② ◆ ATTINGHAM PARK
Shrewsbury SY4 4TP. The National Trust, 01743 708162, www.nationaltrust.org.uk. *4m SE of Shrewsbury. From M54 follow A5 to Shrewsbury then B4380 to Atcham.* **Garden only adm £3.30, chd £1.65. For times & dates of opening, please see website or tel. For NGS: Sun 11 Feb (10-4).**
Attingham Park (house not open) is a landscape park designed by Humphry Repton. There are attractive walks through the grounds and along the river which is lined with swathes of snowdrops from late January. There are also extensive walks through the woodland and deer park. Mobility buggys and wheelchairs available to loan free of charge.
&. ⊛ ☕

BIRCH TREES
See Staffordshire & part of West Midlands.

③ NEW BLUEBELL COTTAGE
Aston SY11 4JH. Rob & Deborah Lewis. *1m E of Oswestry. Off A5. Signed Mile End Golf course.* Home-made teas. **Adm £3, chd free. Sun 3 June (2-5.30).**
1½ acres of lawns, specimen trees, ponds and various water features. Elevated gazebo with views of Breidden Hills. Newly created stream with oriental theme. Small bluebell wood and kitchen garden. Several seating areas. Some gravel paths.
&. ⊛ ☕

BODYNFOEL HALL
See Powys.

1 THE BRODDER
See Staffordshire & part of West Midlands.

④ BROWNHILL HOUSE
Ruyton XI Towns SY4 1LR. Roger & Yoland Brown, 01939 261121, www.eleventowns.co.uk. *10m NW of Shrewsbury. On B4397. Park at Bridge Inn.* Home-made teas. **Adm £3, chd free. Sun 22 Apr; Tues 8, 22 May; 5, 19 June; 3, 17 July; Sun 2 Sept (1.30-5). Evening Opening** Mon 28 May (6.30-8.30). Visitors also welcome by appt May to Aug.
Unusual and distinctive hillside garden (over 600 steps) bordering R Perry. Great variety of plants and styles from laburnum walk and formal terraces to woodland paths, plus large kitchen garden. Approx 100 varieties of plants for sale, proceeds to NGS.
⋈ ⊛ ⋈ ☕

3 CHURCH TERRACE
See Powys.

⑤ CHYKNELL
Bridgnorth WV15 5PP. Mr & Mrs W S R Kenyon-Slaney. *5m E of Bridgnorth. Between Claverley & Worfield. Signed off A454 Wolverhampton to Bridgnorth & A458 Stourbridge to Bridgnorth.* **Adm £3, chd free. Sun 20 May (2-6).**
5 acres of magnolias, rhododendrons, azaleas, roses and herbaceous plants; interesting shrubs and fine trees in tranquil park setting. Formal structure of hedged compartments designed by Russell Page in 1951. Hungry light soil susceptible to drought.
⋈ ⊛ ☕

CIL Y WENNOL
See Powys.

⑥ THE CITADEL
Weston-under-Redcastle SY4 5JY. Mr Beverley & Mrs Sylvia Griffiths, www.thecitadelweston.co.uk. *12m N of Shrewsbury. On A49. At Xrds turn R for Hawkstone Park, through village of Weston-under-Redcastle, ¼m on R beyond village.* Home-made teas. **Adm £3, chd free. Sun 27 May (2-5.30).**
Imposing castellated house (not open) stands in 4 acres. Mature garden, with fine trees, rhododendrons, azaleas, acers and heathers. Herbaceous borders; walled potager and Victorian thatched summerhouse provide added interest. Paths meander around and over sandstone outcrop at centre.
&. ⋈ ☕

⑦ NEW THE COTTAGE
2 Farley Dingle, Much Wenlock TF13 6NX. Mr & Mrs P D Wight. *2m E of Much Wenlock. On A4169 Much Wenlock to Telford rd. At the end of the dead end lane, signed Wyke. Parking is limited.* Light refreshments & teas. **Adm £3. Sun 1 July (11-6).**
Cottage garden, set at end of small valley, enclosed by woodland. A natural stream surrounded by hosta's, ferns and shrubs meanders through the garden. The sides of the valley have been terraced to create a natural amphitheatre of shrubs. Steps, bridges and paths abound. Children under 16yrs must be supervised.
⋈ ⊛ ☕

Natural stream surrounded
by hosta's, ferns and shrubs
meanders through the
garden . . .

8 CRUCKFIELD HOUSE
Ford SY5 9NR. Mr & Mrs G M Cobley, 01743 850222. *5m W of Shrewsbury. A458, turn L towards Shoothill.* Home-made teas. **Adm £4, chd £1. Fri 8 June (2-6). Visitors also welcome by appt June & July only, groups of 25 +.**
4-acre romantic S-facing garden, formally designed, informally and intensively planted with substantial variety of unusual herbaceous plants. Nick's garden, with many species trees and shrubs, surrounds a large pond with bog and moisture-loving plants. Ornamental kitchen garden with pretty outbuildings. Rose and peony walk. New courtyard fountain garden and an extensive shrubbery. Organically managed for a number of years.

Extensive views over beautiful Severn Valley . . .

CWM-WEEG
See Powys.

9 ◆ DAVID AUSTIN ROSES
Bowling Green Lane, Albrighton WV7 3HB. Mr & Mrs David Austin. *8m NW of Wolverhampton. 4m from Shifnal (A464) L into Bowling Green Lane; or J3, M54 to Albrighton, follow brown signs.* **Adm £3, chd free.** For NGS: **Sun 24 June (10-6).**
Breeders of the famous English roses. 900 varieties old roses, shrub, species and climbing roses. Semi-wild private garden, trees and water garden with many plants. House garden has not been sprayed so is therefore not a tidy garden. Sculpture by Pat Austin. Dogs on leads.

DINGLE NURSERIES & GARDEN
See Powys.

10 ◆ DUDMASTON HALL GARDENS
Quatt, nr Bridgnorth WV15 6QW. The National Trust, 01746 780866, dudmaston@nationaltrust.org.uk. *4m SE of Bridgnorth. On A442.* **Adm £4.60, chd £2.50. Sun to Mon 1 Apr to 30 Sept.** For NGS: **Sat 19 May (12-6).**
9 acres with a good mixture of herbaceous borders incl large border in front of the brew house with a beautiful back drop of 2 mature wisterias. The Lady Labouchere rose border looks and smells fantastic, rockery with lavender, erigeron and caryopteris. Wide range of large and small trees incl *Cornus kousa*.

11 EDGE VILLA
Edge, nr Yockleton SY5 9PY. Mr & Mrs W F Neil. *6m from Shrewsbury. From A5 take either A488 signed to Bishops Castle or B4386 to Montgomery for approx 6m then follow NGS signs.* Home-made teas. **Adm £3, chd free. Sun 5 Aug (2-6).**
2 acres of newly planted garden with outstanding views of S Shropshire hills. Herbaceous borders, self-sufficent organic vegetable plot. New orchard with chickens, foxes permitting. Featured in 'Shropshire Star'. Gravel paths and grass slopes.

12 FIELD HOUSE
Clee St Margaret SY7 9DT. Dr & Mrs John Bell. *8m NE of Ludlow. Turning to Stoke St Milborough & Clee St Margaret, 5m from Ludlow, 10m from Bridgnorth along B4364. Through Stoke St Milborough to Clee St Margaret. Ignore R turn to Clee Village. Field House on L.* Home-made teas. **Adm £3, chd free. Sun 1 July (2-6).**
1-acre garden created since 1982 for yr-round interest. Mixed borders; rose walk; pool garden; herbaceous borders. Donkeys, sheep and ducks.

FIELD HOUSE FARM
See Staffordshire & part of West Midlands.

13 GATE COTTAGE
Cockshutt SY12 0JU. G W Nicholson & Kevin Gunnell. *10m N of Shrewsbury. On A528. At Cockshutt take rd signed English Frankton. Garden 1m on R. Parking in adjacent field.* **Adm £2.50, chd 50p. Sun 20 May (1-5).**

Garden at present about 2 acres. Informal mixed plantings of trees, shrubs, herbaceous plants of interest to flower arrangers and plantsmen. Pool, rock garden and informal pools. Large collection of hostas; old orchard with roses. Constant alterations being made to incl items of unusual growth or colour.

GLANSEVERN HALL GARDENS
See Powys.

14 HARNAGE FARM
Cound SY5 6EJ. Mr & Mrs Ken Cooke. *8m SE of Shrewsbury. On A458. Turn to Cound 1m S of Cross Houses. Harnage Farm 1m, bearing L past church.* Home-made teas. **Adm £3, chd free. Sat 15 Sept (12-5).**
1/2-acre farmhouse garden; stocked with herbaceous plants, shrubs and climbers. Extensive views over beautiful Severn Valley. 15 min woodland walk through fields to conservation wood and Ian's wildlife pool.

HEATH HOUSE
See Staffordshire & part of West Midlands.

15 HODNET HALL GARDENS
nr Market Drayton TF9 3NN. Mr & The Hon Mrs Heber-Percy, 01630 685786 (Secretary), www.hodnethallgardens.co.uk. *51/2m SW of Market Drayton. 12m NE Shrewsbury. At junction of A53 & A442.* Light refreshments & teas. **Adm £4, chd £2. Sun 13 May (12-5).**
60-acre landscaped garden with series of lakes and pools; magnificent forest trees, great variety of flowers, shrubs providing colour throughout season. Unique collection of big-game trophies in C17 tearooms. Kitchen garden. Partial wheelchair access, gravel and grass paths.

16 HOLLY GROVE
Church Pulverbatch SY5 8DD. Peter & Angela Unsworth, 01743 718221. *6m S of Shrewsbury. Midway between Stapleton & Church Pulverbatch. From A49 follow signs to Stapleton & Pulverbatch.* Home-made teas. **Adm £3, chd free. Sun 10 June (2-6). Visitors also welcome by appt.**
3-acre garden set in S Shropshire countryside. Yew and beech hedges enclosing 'rooms', box parterres,

pleached limes, vegetable garden, rose and herbaceous borders containing many rare plants. New arboretum, lake and wild flower meadows. Opportunity to see rare White Park cattle and Soay sheep.

 ⟁ ⚹ ⊛ ☕

17 NEW HOLMCROFT
Wyson Lane, Ludlow SY8 4NW.
Mrs C Dowding. *4m S of Ludlow. 6m N of Leominster. From Ludlow or Leominster leave A49 at Brimfield sign. From Tenbury Wells turn L when A456 meets A49, then 1st L into Brimfield.* Home-made teas. **Adm £2.50, chd free. Sun 24 June (2-5.30).**
¾ acre set around C17 cottage. Sunken water garden and series of terraced gardens. Long borders with mixed planting, camomile bank and herb 'partier'. Over 20 species of trees and over 80 herbaceous plant varieties. Woodland garden, kitchen garden and orchard with spectacular views of Clee Hill. C12 church with timber framed tower (open to the public). Garden on slope but paths allow wheelchair access to most areas.

 ⟁ ⚹ ⊛ ☕

18 ◆ JESSAMINE COTTAGE
Kenley SY5 6NS. Lee & Pamela Wheeler, 01694 771279, www.stmem.com/jessamine-cottage. *6m W of Much Wenlock. Signed from B4371 Much Wenlock to Church Stretton rd and from A458 Shrewsbury to Much Wenlock rd at Harley.* **Adm £3, chd £1. Weds to Suns & Bank Hols, 28 Apr - 2 Sept. For NGS: Suns 15 July; 26 Aug (2-6).**
3-acre garden. Mature wildlife pond; large wild flower meadow; mixed island beds; lime avenue; large kitchen garden; parterre; stream and woodland. Rose garden and ornamental trees, large range of attractive perennials and shrubs provide all season colour.

 ⟁ ⚹ ⊛ ☕

'Nearest the Pin' golf challenge for childrens play area . . .

19 NEW KNOWBURY CATTERY
Knowbury SY8 3LR. Mr & Mrs Procter, 01584 890895. *7m E of Ludlow. From Ludlow A4117, 2nd turn signed Knowbury, pass village hall on R. Then 1st L.* Light refreshments & teas. **Adm £3, chd free. Suns 1 Apr; 6 May; 3 June; 1 July; 5 Aug; 2 Sept; 7 Oct (1-6). Visitors also welcome by appt, no access for coaches.**
S-facing hillside garden (100ft), with panoramic views started in 1994. Main garden; lawn with shrubs and herbaceous borders. Features incl: 3 pools, stream, wildlife area's, fruit/vegetable and herb area's, shrub walk, orchard, courtyard aviary and apiary. Different levels with some steep slopes, uneven ground and gravelled area's. Children's treasure hunt.

 ⊛ ☕

20 LITTLE HELDRE
Buttington SY21 8TF. Peter & Gillian Stedman, 01938 570457, peter.stedman@tesco.net. *12m W of Shrewsbury. Off A458. From Welshpool take A458 Shrewsbury rd for 3m, turn R into Heldre Lane. From Shrewsbury turn L past Little Chef at Trewern into Sale Lane, follow signs.* Home-made teas. **Adm £2.50, chd free. Suns 24 June; 19 Aug (2-5.30). Visitors also welcome by appt, 1 May to end Aug, no coaches.**
1¾-acre garden on steep N-facing slope. Terracing; lawns; shrubs; herbaceous borders; pond; gunnera; wooded dingle circular walk. Moon gate giving extensive views to Berwyn Mountains.

 ⚹ ☕

21 LONGNER HALL
Atcham, Shrewsbury SY4 4TG. Mr & Mrs R L Burton. *4m SE of Shrewsbury. From M54 follow A5 to Shrewsbury, then B4380 to Atcham. From Atcham take Uffington rd, entrance ¼m on L.* Light refreshments & teas. **Adm £3, chd 50p. Sun 3 June (2-5).**
A long drive approach through parkland designed by Humphry Repton. Walks lined with golden yew through extensive lawns, with views over Severn Valley. Borders containing roses, herbaceous and shrubs, also ancient yew wood. Enclosed walled garden containing mixed planting,

Woodland garden, kitchen garden and orchard with spectacular views of Clee Hill . . .

garden buildings, tower and game larder. Some gravel paths, woodland walk not suitable for wheelchairs.

 ⟁ ⚹ ☕

22 LOWER HALL
Worfield WV15 5LH. Mr & Mrs C F Dumbell, 01746 716607. *3½m E of Bridgnorth. ½m N of A454 in village centre.* **Adm £3.50, chd free. Visitors welcome by appt, mid May to mid July.**
4 acres on R Worfe. Garden developed by present owners. Courtyard with fountain, walled garden with old-fashioned roses, clematis and mixed borders. Water garden with pool, primula island and rock garden. Woodland garden with rare trees incl magnolias, paper bark and Japanese maples. Courtyard garden with gravel, bridges to woodland garden have slight slopes.

 ⟁

23 NEW THE MANOR HOUSE
Richards Castle SY8 4EG. Chris Cooke. *3m S of Ludlow. Take lane adjacent to All Saints Church, Richards Castle off B4361. Garden on R after ½m.* Cream teas. **Adm £3, chd free. Sun 27 May (1-6).**
Elevated, S-facing, 5½ acre contoured site with extensive views over the Teme valley. The garden comprises formal lawns, flower beds and herbaceous borders corporating a fully integrated but discrete 6 hole golf course with mature feature planting. Ponds, dells, herb garden and tennis lawn provide further points of interest. 'Nearest the Pin' golf challenge for childrens play area.

 ⚹ ☕

24 MAREHAY FARM
Gatten, Ratlinghope SY5 0SJ. Stuart
& Carol Buxton, 01588 650289.
6¹/₂m W of Church Stretton. 6m S of
Pontesbury, 9m NNE of Bishops
Castle. 1¹/₂m from 'The Bridges' Xrds
& the intersection of the Longden,
Pulverbatch & Bishops Castle rd and
the minor rd from Church Stretton to
the Stiperstones. Home-made teas.
Adm £2.50, chd free. Mon 28 May;
Sun 10 June; Thur 5 July; Wed 1
Aug (11-5). Visitors also welcome by
appt, mid May to mid July.
In 1982 a building society surveyor
reported 'there is no garden and at this
height (1100ft). elevation and aspect
there never will be!' Since 1990.

25 MILLICHOPE PARK
Munslow SY7 9HA. Mr & Mrs L Bury.
8m NE of Craven Arms. From Ludlow
(11m) turn L off B4368, ³/₄m out of
Munslow. Home-made teas. Adm £4,
chd free. Mon 7 May; Sun 21 Oct
(2-6).
13-acre garden with lakes, woodland
walks, fine specimen trees, wild flowers
and herbaceous borders, good
autumn colour.

26 MOORTOWN
nr Wellington TF6 6JE. Mr David
Bromley. 8m N of Telford. 5m N of
Wellington. Take B5062 signed
Moortown 1m between High Ercall &
Crudgington. Adm £4, chd £1. Sun
15 Apr (2-5.30).
Approx 1-acre plantsman-acres
garden. Here may be found the old-
fashioned, the unusual and even the
oddities of plant life, in mixed borders
of 'controlled-acre confusion.

27 MORVILLE HALL GARDENS
nr Bridgnorth WV16 5NB. 3m W of
Bridgnorth. On A458 at junction with
B4368. Home-made teas. **Combined
adm £4.50, chd £1 (share to Morville
Church). Sun 10 June (2-5).**
A varied and interesting group of
gardens that immediately surround a
beautiful Grade 1 listed mansion
(house not open), also Poplar Cottage
Farm (1m away).

THE COTTAGE
Mr & Mrs Begg
Informal walled garden, partly
lawned with many interesting
features incl small fish pond, a
haven for birds and wildlife.

'There is no garden and at this height (1100ft), elevation and aspect there never will be!' . . .

THE DOWER HOUSE
Dr Katherine Swift
1¹/₂-acre sequence of gardens in
various historical styles designed
to tell the history of British
gardening from medieval times to
the present, incl turf maze, cloister
garden, Elizabethan knot garden,
Edwardian fruit and vegetable
garden, C18 canal garden, wild
garden.

1 THE GATEHOUSE
Mr & Mrs Rowe
1/2-acre walled garden with
combining, formal and woodland
areas with colour-filled
herbaceous borders.

2 THE GATEHOUSE
Mrs G Medland
Small cottage garden with
colourful borders.

MORVILLE HALL
Dr & Mrs J C Douglas & The
National Trust
4-acre garden in fine setting, incl
box parterre, mature shrub
borders, pond garden, medieval
stewpond and a small award-
winning vineyard.

SOUTH PAVILION
Mr & Mrs B Jenkinson
Walled courtyard garden with a
collection of hebes and cistus.

POPLAR COTTAGE FARM
Elizabeth & Barry Bacon. 1m
NW of Morville on A458
1/3-acre flower arranger-acres
garden; yr-round interest, many
unusual plants.

28 THE OLD VICARAGE
Vicarage Road, Clun SY7 8JG. Mr &
Mrs Peter Upton. 16m NW of Ludlow.
From Ludlow take A49 N to Craven
Arms. At 1st roundabout, turn L on
B4368 to Clun. L beyond The Sun PH,
cross bridge and go straight ahead to
church. Turn L by lych gate into
Vicarage Rd, garden on R (car park
just beyond garden). Home-made

teas. **Adm £3, chd free. Sun 27 May
(2-6).**
A garden since 1680s extending to 2
acres. Lower lawn has wall border and
oval garden around a Gothic fountain
and cloisters which lead into the Lion
Court. Upper garden has plat with
clipped yews and double border
leading to beech rotunda and
woodland walk. Archway leading to
wisteria allée, fruit and herb gardens.
Featured in 'Shropshire Star'.

29 OTELEY
Ellesmere SY12 0PB. Mr & Mrs R K
Mainwaring, 01691 622514. 1m SE of
Ellesmere. Entrance out of Ellesmere
past Mere, opp Convent nr to
A528/495 junction. Home-made teas.
Adm £3, chd free. Mon 7 May (2-6).
Visitors also welcome by appt,
groups of 10+, coaches permitted.
10 acres running down to Mere, incl
walled kitchen garden; architectural
features; many interesting trees,
rhododendrons and azaleas; views
across Mere to Ellesmere Church.
Wheelchairs only if dry. Some steep
slopes and some gravel which can be
avoided.
&. ⊗ ♨

POWIS CASTLE GARDEN
See Powys.

30 PREEN MANOR
Church Preen SY6 7LQ. Mrs Ann
Trevor-Jones, 01694 771207. 6m W
of Much Wenlock. Signed from B4371.
Home-made teas. Adm £3.50, chd
50p 5-16yrs. Suns 8 Apr; 7 Oct (2-5);
Thurs 31 May; 28 June; 19 July (2-6).
Visitors also welcome by appt, June
& July only, groups of 10+.
6-acre garden on site of Cluniac
monastery and Norman Shaw
mansion. Kitchen, chess, water and
wild gardens. Fine trees in park;
woodland walks.
⅍ ⊗ ♨

31 PRESTON HALL
Preston Brockhurst SY4 5QA. C C &
L Corbet. 8m N of Shrewsbury. On
A49. Cream teas. Adm £3, chd free.
Sun 1 July (2.30-6).
Garden around stone Cromwellian
house (not open). Interesting
perennials, trees and shrubs. Good
walk around meadow, woodland walk,
cutting garden and courtyard garden.
Tennis court available. Grass paths,
ramp into courtyard garden.

32 RADNOR COTTAGE
Clun SY7 0JA. Pam & David
Pittwood, 01588 640451. *7m W of
Craven Arms. 1m E of Clun on B4368.*
Home-made teas. **Adm £2.50, chd
50p (share to The Joliba Trust). Tues
10 Apr; 29 May; 3 July (2-6).** Visitors
also welcome by appt April - June.
2 acres on S-facing slope, overlooking
Clun Valley. Wide variety of garden
habitats all densely planted. Incl sunny
terracing with paving and dry-stone
walling; alpine troughs; cottage garden
borders; damp shade for white flowers
and gold foliage; pond, stream and
bog garden; orchard; rough grass with
naturalised bulbs and wild flowers.
⚫ ⚫ ⚫

33 RUTHALL MANOR
Ditton Priors WV16 6TN. Mr & Mrs G
T Clarke, 01746 712608. *7m SW of
Bridgnorth. Ruthall Rd signed nr
garage.* Teas in Shropshire County
Council tea room. **Adm £3, chd free.
Sun 27 May (1-5).** Visitors also
welcome by appt, spring and
summer.
1-acre garden with ha-ha and old
horse pond planted with water and
bog plants. Rare specimen trees.
Designed for easy maintenance with
lots of ground cover and unusual
plants. New gravel art garden and
dryer climate adaptions. Dogs on
leads. Featured in Shropshire Gardens
Revisited.
⚫ ⚫ ⚫

34 SHOOTHILL HOUSE
Ford, Shrewsbury SY5 9NR. Colin &
Jane Lloyd. *5m W of Shrewsbury.
A458 turn L towards Shoothill.* Home-
made teas. **Adm £2.50. Sun 9 Sept
(2-5.30).**
6-acre garden, newly developed,
incorporating woodland, wild flower
meadows, childrens' garden and
several lawned areas surrounded by
mixed borders. Large well maintained
Victorian greenhouse in newly
renovated walled kitchen garden.
Mature wildlife pond surrounded by
species trees and shrubs with
extensive views over Welsh hills.
⚫ ⚫ ⚫

SMITHY COTTAGE
See Staffordshire & part of West
Midlands.

35 STANLEY HALL
Bridgnorth WV16 4SP. Mr & Mrs M J
Thompson. *1/2 m N of Bridgnorth.
Leave by N gate; B4373; turn R at*
Stanley Lane. Home-made teas. **Adm
£3, chd 50p. Sun 3 June (2-6).**
Drive 1/2 m with rhododendrons,
azaleas, fine trees and chain of pools.
⚫ ⚫

36 SWALLOW HAYES
Rectory Road, Albrighton WV7 3EP.
Mrs P Edwards, 01902 372624,
patedwards570@hotmail.com. *7m
NW of Wolverhampton. M54 exit 3.
Rectory Rd to R, 1m towards
Wolverhampton off A41 just past
Wyevale Garden Centre.* Home-made
teas. **Adm £3, chd free. Suns 6 May;
3 June (2-6).** Visitors also welcome
by appt, anytime.
2 acres planted since 1968 with
emphasis on all-yr interest and ease of
maintenance. National Collections of
Hamamelis and Russell lupins. Nearly
3000 different plants, most labelled.
Children's trail; hardy geraniums, trees,
shrubs, herbaceous ferns,
groundcover and bulbs. Featured in
'Shropshire Star' & 'Express & Star'.
Shropshire Radio. Gravel paths
suitable for wheelchairs.
⚫ ⚫ NCCPG ⚫

TAN-Y-LLYN
See Powys.

**37 VALDUCCI FLOWER &
VEGETABLE GARDENS**
Vicarage Road Site, Meole Brace
SY3 0NR. Luigi Valducci, 07921
368968, valbros@btconnect.com.
*2m W of Shrewsbury. Meole Brace
Garden & Allotment Club. On A5 exit at
Dobbies roundabout, direction
Shrewsbury. Follow sign for Nuffield
Hospital, opp hospital Stanley Lane,
follow Stanley Lane until you reach
Vicarage Rd. Car park on R, garden on
L.* Light refreshments & teas. **Adm £3,
chd free. Sun 29 July (12-5).** Visitors
also welcome by appt July - Aug.
1200 sq yds of gardens and allotments
containing 4 greenhouses, orchard and
site of Valducci National Collection of
Brugmansias (Angel's Trumpets) with
over 63 varieties. An Italian style of
gardening focusing on vegetables and
flowers with a European feel.
⚫ ⚫ ⚫ NCCPG ⚫

38 WALCOT HALL
Lydbury North SY7 8AZ. Mr & Mrs C
R W Parish, 01588 680570,
www.walcothall.co.uk. *4m SE of
Bishop's Castle. B4385 Craven Arms
to Bishop's Castle, turn L by Powis
Arms, in Lydbury North.* Light
refreshments & teas. **Adm £3.50, chd
free, concessions £2.50. Sun 27,
Mon 28 May (1.30-5.30).** Visitors
also welcome by appt for groups of
10+ throughout the year.
Arboretum planted by Lord Clive of
India's son. Cascades of
rhododendrons, azaleas amongst
specimen trees and pools. Fine views
of Sir William Chambers's Clock
Towers, with lake and hills beyond.
Walled kitchen garden; dovecote; meat
safe; ice house and mile-long lakes.
Outstanding ballroom where excellent
teas are served. Russian wooden
church, grotto and fountain under
construction; tin chapel. Beautiful
borders and rare shrubs.
⚫ ⚫

THE WERN
See Powys.

WESTLAKE FISHERIES
See Powys.

Mature wildlife pond surrounded by species trees and shrubs with extensive views over Welsh hills . . .

39 ◆ WESTON PARK
Weston-under-Lizard, Shifnal
TF11 8LE. The Weston Park
Foundation, 01952 852100,
www.weston-park.com. *6m E of
Telford. Situated on A5 at Weston-
under-Lizard. J12 M6 & J3 M54.*
House and Garden **Adm £7, chd £5,
concessions £6, Garden only Adm
£4, chd £2.50, concessions £3.50.
See website for opening dates &
times. For NGS: Wed 4 July (11-5).**
Capability Brown landscaped gardens
and parkland. Formal gardens restored
to original C19 design, rose garden
and long border together with colourful
adjacent Broderie garden. New yew
hedge maze and orchard in the walled
garden. Head Gardener Finalist of
Horticultral Week award, Professional
Gardener of the Year.
⚫ ⚫

Highly praised by Roy Lancaster for the quality of both design and planting. Full of ideas that could be adapted for both smaller and larger sites . . .

40 WHITTINGTON VILLAGE GARDENS

nr Oswestry SY11 4EA. *2¹/₂ m NE of Oswestry. Daisy Lane & Top St, Whittington. Turn off B5009 150yds NW of church into Top St. Car parking at Whittington Castle (charge) & Top St.* Home-made teas at Greystones, Daisy Lane. **Adm £3, chd free. Sat 16, Sun 17 June (1-5).** Group of adjacent gardens full of 'take-home' ideas. Tiny courtyard packed with vibrant colour, designer plot featuring collection of pots set in a framework of clipped box. Old cottage garden, re-vamped for easier maintenance. Delightful family garden, crammed with a profusion of roses and flowering plants. Extensive, well-established garden incorporating island beds and wild meadow. Productive vegetable garden, with wonderful countryside views.
☕

41 NEW WINDY RIDGE

Church Lane, Little Wenlock, Telford TF6 5BB. George & Fiona Chancellor, 01952 507675, fionachancellor@btinternet.com. *2m S of Wellington. Follow signs for Little Wenlock from the north (junction7, M54) or east (off A5223 at Horsehay). Park at 'The Huntsman' PH in centre of village.* **Adm £3, chd free. Suns 13 May; 3 June; 19 Aug (2-6); 2 Sept (2-3).** Visitors also welcome by appt anytime, groups of 10+, coaches permitted. Award-winning ²/₃ acre village garden highly praised by Roy Lancaster for the quality of both design and planting. Full of ideas that could be adapted for both smaller and larger sites. For plan, plant list and pictures see garden website www.gardenschool.co.uk. Gravel and grass paths.
♿ ⚹ ⊛ ☕

42 ◆ WOLLERTON OLD HALL

Wollerton TF9 3NA. Mr & Mrs J D Jenkins, 01630 685760, www.wollertonoldhallgarden.com. *4m SW of Market Drayton. On A53 between Hodnet & A53-A41 junction. Follow brown signs.* **Adm £4.50, chd £1. Fris, Suns, Bank Hol Mons, 6 Apr - Sept. For NGS: Fris 4, 25 May (12-5).** 4-acre garden created around C16 house (not open). Formal structure creates variety of gardens each with own colour theme and character. Planting is mainly of perennials, the large range of which results in significant collections of salvias, clematis, crocosmias and roses. Featured on BBC Gardeners Question Time - recommended garden to visit; BBC2 Digging Deep.
♿ ⚹ ⊛ ☕

WOODHILL

See Powys.

Shropshire County Volunteers

County Organiser
Chris Neil, Edge Villa, Edge, Yockleton, Shrewsbury SY5 9PY, 01743 821651, bill@billfneil.fsnet.co.uk

County Treasurer
Melinda Laws, 50 Sheinton Street, Much Wenlock TF13 6HU, 01952 727237, melinda@mlaws.freeserve.co.uk

Publicity
James Goodall, Rectory Cottage, Chetton, Bridgnorth WV16 6UF, 01746 789221

Assistant County Organisers
Christine Brown, Pelham Grove, Cound, Shrewsbury SY5 6AL, pelham-grove@breathemail.net
Fiona Chancellor, Windy Ridge, Little Wenlock TF6 5BB, 01952 507675
Jonathan Elcock, Riversmead, Waterloo Street, Ironbridge TF8 7AA, silurist@aol.com

SOMERSET & BRISTOL AREA

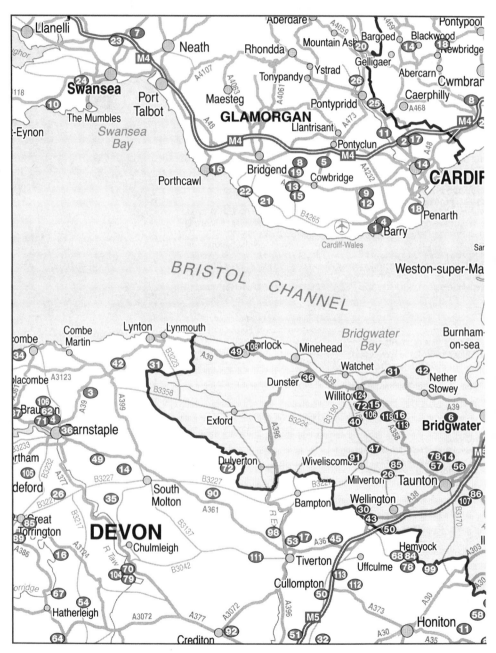

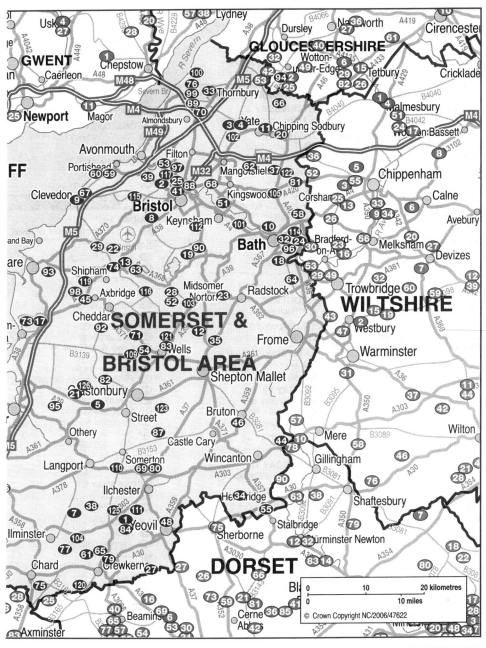

© Crown Copyright NC/2006/47622

Opening Dates

February

SUNDAY 4
99 Rock House

SATURDAY 10
103 Sherborne Garden

SUNDAY 11
103 Sherborne Garden

MONDAY 12
103 Sherborne Garden

TUESDAY 13
103 Sherborne Garden

WEDNESDAY 14
103 Sherborne Garden

March

TUESDAY 6
56 Hestercombe Gardens

SUNDAY 11
74 Langford Court

SATURDAY 17
45 Frankie Howerd's Garden

SUNDAY 18
45 Frankie Howerd's Garden

THURSDAY 29
36 Dunster Castle Gardens

SATURDAY 31
45 Frankie Howerd's Garden
101 Saltford Farm Barn
73 Stowleys

April

SUNDAY 1
40 Elworthy Cottage
42 Fairfield
45 Frankie Howerd's Garden
120 Wayford Manor

SUNDAY 8
45 Frankie Howerd's Garden

MONDAY 9
40 Elworthy Cottage

THURSDAY 12
40 Elworthy Cottage

SUNDAY 15
21 Catcott Gardens
28 Coley Court
32 Crowe Hall
99 Rock House

WEDNESDAY 18
85 Moss Cottage

SUNDAY 22
7 Barrington Court
50 Hangeridge Farm
60 25 Hillcrest Road
69 Kingsdon Nursery

120 Wayford Manor

TUESDAY 24
115 Tyntesfield

THURSDAY 26
10 Bath Priory Hotel

SUNDAY 29
63 Holt Farm
79 Lower Severalls
80 Lytes Cary Manor
123 Westbrook House

May

WEDNESDAY 2
86 The Mount Somerset Hotel

THURSDAY 3
44 Forest Lodge
67 Jasmine Cottage

SUNDAY 6
20 Camers
21 Catcott Gardens
45 Frankie Howerd's Garden
69 Kingsdon Nursery
71 Kites Croft
79 Lower Severalls
120 Wayford Manor

MONDAY 7
45 Frankie Howerd's Garden
120 Wayford Manor

WEDNESDAY 9
98 Rackley House

THURSDAY 10
67 Jasmine Cottage

SATURDAY 12
65 Hooper's Holding
79 Lower Severalls

SUNDAY 13
31 Court House
65 Hooper's Holding
97 18 Queens Gate

WEDNESDAY 16
98 Rackley House

THURSDAY 17
67 Jasmine Cottage

SUNDAY 20
50 Hangeridge Farm
60 25 Hillcrest Road
75 Lift The Latch
83 Milton Lodge

WEDNESDAY 23
85 Moss Cottage
98 Rackley House

THURSDAY 24
40 Elworthy Cottage
44 Forest Lodge
67 Jasmine Cottage

SATURDAY 26
45 Frankie Howerd's Garden
49 Greencombe

SUNDAY 27
16 4 Brendon View
45 Frankie Howerd's Garden
52 Harptree Court
107 Stoke St Mary Gardens
118 Vellacott
119 Watcombe
120 Wayford Manor

MONDAY 28
40 Elworthy Cottage
45 Frankie Howerd's Garden

WEDNESDAY 30
86 The Mount Somerset Hotel
121 Wellfield Barn

THURSDAY 31
9 Barum
67 Jasmine Cottage

June

FRIDAY 1
38 East Lambrook Manor Gardens

SATURDAY 2
40 Elworthy Cottage
61 Hinton St George Gardens
81 Marshfield Gardens

SUNDAY 3
5 Ashcott Gardens
8 Barrow Court
16 4 Brendon View
21 Catcott Gardens
27 Coker Wood Cottage
32 Crowe Hall
41 Emmaus House
61 Hinton St George Gardens
81 Marshfield Gardens
82 Meare Gardens
103 Sherborne Garden
113 Triscombe Nurseries
118 Vellacott
124 Wyndham Estate Gardens

TUESDAY 5
56 Hestercombe Gardens

WEDNESDAY 6
118 Vellacott
119 Watcombe

THURSDAY 7
9 Barum
67 Jasmine Cottage
77 Little Garth
92 Overbrook Cottage

FRIDAY 8
104 South Meade

SATURDAY 9
37 Dyrham Park
45 Frankie Howerd's Garden

48 190 Goldcroft
55 Henstridge Gardens
98 Rackley House
104 South Meade

SUNDAY 10
2 Abbots Leigh House
25 Clifton Gardens
35 Darkey Pang Tso Gang
37 Dyrham Park
45 Frankie Howerd's Garden
48 190 Goldcroft
55 Henstridge Gardens
58 Hill Lodge
63 Holt Farm
68 28 Kensington Road
83 Milton Lodge
96 Prior Park Landscape Garden
98 Rackley House
104 South Meade
120 Wayford Manor

MONDAY 11
48 190 Goldcroft (Evening)

WEDNESDAY 13
47 Gaulden Manor

THURSDAY 14
9 Barum
47 Gaulden Manor
67 Jasmine Cottage
77 Little Garth
92 Overbrook Cottage

FRIDAY 15
57 Higher Yarde Farm (Evening)

SATURDAY 16
34 The Dairy House
45 Frankie Howerd's Garden
51 Hanham Court
55 Henstridge Gardens
57 Higher Yarde Farm
88 26 Northumberland Road
73 Stowleys

SUNDAY 17
34 The Dairy House
45 Frankie Howerd's Garden
55 Henstridge Gardens
57 Higher Yarde Farm
70 Kingston
76 The Lintels
79 Lower Severalls
87 Northfield House
88 26 Northumberland Road
89 The Old Bakery
91 Olive Cottage
95 Penwood Farm

MONDAY 18
95 Penwood Farm

WEDNESDAY 20
35 Darkey Pang Tso Gang (Evening)
85 Moss Cottage
122 West Littleton Gardens (Evening)

THURSDAY 21
19 1 Bromley Villas (Evening)

67 Jasmine Cottage
77 Little Garth
92 Overbrook Cottage
105 Special Plants

FRIDAY 22
24 Claverton Manor

SATURDAY 23
29 Congresbury Gardens
95 Penwood Farm
101 Saltford Farm Barn (Evening)

SUNDAY 24
6 Barford Park
12 Binegar Village Gardens
22 Cedar House
26 Cobbleside
68 28 Kensington Road
84 Montacute House
95 Penwood Farm
101 Saltford Farm Barn
106 Stogumber Gardens

THURSDAY 28
40 Elworthy Cottage
67 Jasmine Cottage
77 Little Garth
92 Overbrook Cottage

SATURDAY 30
34 The Dairy House
45 Frankie Howerd's Garden

July

SUNDAY 1
1 Abbey Farm
18 Brewery House
34 The Dairy House
43 Fernhill
45 Frankie Howerd's Garden
50 Hangeridge Farm
93 3 Palmer's Way

MONDAY 2
1 Abbey Farm

TUESDAY 3
1 Abbey Farm

WEDNESDAY 4
43 Fernhill

THURSDAY 5
40 Elworthy Cottage
67 Jasmine Cottage
77 Little Garth

SATURDAY 7
23 The Chalet

SUNDAY 8
33 Daggs Allotments
73 Laburnum Cottage
112 Tranby House

WEDNESDAY 11
86 The Mount Somerset Hotel

THURSDAY 12
67 Jasmine Cottage
77 Little Garth

SUNDAY 15
17 Brent Knoll Gardens
19 1 Bromley Villas
45 Frankie Howerd's Garden
59 Hillcrest Gardens
68 28 Kensington Road
83 Milton Lodge
111 Tintinhull

TUESDAY 17
39 Easton-in-Gordano Gardens

THURSDAY 19
67 Jasmine Cottage
77 Little Garth
105 Special Plants

SUNDAY 22
41 Emmaus House
93 3 Palmer's Way
110 Sutton Hosey Manor

TUESDAY 24
39 Easton-in-Gordano Gardens

THURSDAY 26
67 Jasmine Cottage
77 Little Garth

SATURDAY 28
20 Camers

SUNDAY 29
7 Barrington Court
20 Camers
30 Cothay Manor Gardens
50 Hangeridge Farm
68 28 Kensington Road

TUESDAY 31
39 Easton-in-Gordano Gardens

August

THURSDAY 2
36 Dunster Castle Gardens
77 Little Garth

FRIDAY 3
62 10 Holly Close (Evening)

SATURDAY 4
45 Frankie Howerd's Garden

SUNDAY 5
43 Fernhill
45 Frankie Howerd's Garden
100 Rook Farm
126 Zool House

TUESDAY 7
115 Tyntesfield

WEDNESDAY 8
43 Fernhill

THURSDAY 9
10 Bath Priory Hotel
59 Hillcrest Gardens
77 Little Garth

FRIDAY 10
62 10 Holly Close (Evening)
78 Little Yarford Farmhouse (Evening)

SATURDAY 11
78 Little Yarford Farmhouse

SUNDAY 12
78 Little Yarford Farmhouse
112 Tranby House

MONDAY 13
78 Little Yarford Farmhouse

TUESDAY 14
86 The Mount Somerset Hotel

WEDNESDAY 15
86 The Mount Somerset Hotel

THURSDAY 16
77 Little Garth
105 Special Plants

SATURDAY 18
11 Beechwell House (Evening)

SUNDAY 19
16 4 Brendon View
91 Olive Cottage
126 Zool House

THURSDAY 23
77 Little Garth

SATURDAY 25
45 Frankie Howerd's Garden

SUNDAY 26
45 Frankie Howerd's Garden
71 Kites Croft

MONDAY 27
15 Braglands Barn
45 Frankie Howerd's Garden
46 Gants Mill & Garden

THURSDAY 30
77 Little Garth

September

SUNDAY 2
41 Emmaus House
68 28 Kensington Road (Evening)
94 Park Farm

THURSDAY 6
67 Jasmine Cottage

SATURDAY 8
79 Lower Severalls

SUNDAY 9
11 Beechwell House
68 28 Kensington Road (Evening)
72 Knoll Cottage
117 University of Bristol Botanic Garden

WEDNESDAY 12
85 Moss Cottage

THURSDAY 13
67 Jasmine Cottage

THURSDAY 20
105 Special Plants

SATURDAY 22
45 Frankie Howerd's Garden

SUNDAY 23
45 Frankie Howerd's Garden
63 Holt Farm

October

SUNDAY 7
80 Lytes Cary Manor
97 18 Queens Gate

SUNDAY 14
66 Ingle Cottage

SUNDAY 21
75 Lift The Latch

SUNDAY 28
113 Triscombe Nurseries

Private gardens opening regularly for the NGS

64 Homewood Park Hotel
77 Little Garth

Gardens open to the public

7 Barrington Court
24 Claverton Manor
30 Cothay Manor Gardens
32 Crowe Hall
36 Dunster Castle Gardens
37 Dyrham Park
38 East Lambrook Manor Gardens
40 Elworthy Cottage
41 Emmaus House
44 Forest Lodge
46 Gants Mill & Garden
47 Gaulden Manor
49 Greencombe
56 Hestercombe Gardens
79 Lower Severalls
80 Lytes Cary Manor
83 Milton Lodge
84 Montacute House
96 Prior Park Landscape Garden
103 Sherborne Garden
105 Special Plants
111 Tintinhull
115 Tyntesfield
117 University of Bristol Botanic Garden

By appointment only

3 Algars Manor
4 Algars Mill
13 Bourne House
14 Boweys and Rose Cottage
53 4 Haytor Park
54 Henley Mill
90 2 Old Tarnwell
102 Serridge House
109 Sunnyside
114 8 Trossachs Drive
116 Ubley Hill Farm House
125 Yews Farm

The Gardens

1 ABBEY FARM
Montacute TA156UA. Mr & Mrs G
Jenkins, 01935 823572,
gnjrj@dial.pipex.com. *4m from Yeovil.
Follow A3088, take slip rd to
Montacute, turn L at T-junction into
village. Turn R between Church &
King's Arms (no through rd).* Home-
made teas Sun only. Adm £3.50, chd
free. Sun 1, Mon 2, Tues 3 July (2-
5.30). Visitors also welcome by appt.
2¹/₂ acres of mainly walled gardens on
sloping site, provide the setting for
Cluniac medieval Priory gatehouse.
Interesting plants incl roses, shrubs,
grasses, clematis. Herbaceous
borders, white garden, gravel garden.
Small arboretum. Pond for wildlife -
frogs, newts, dragonflies. Fine
mulberry, walnut and monkey puzzle
trees. Seats for resting. One gravel
path, one steep slope.
🚻 ✖ 🐕 ☕

**2 NEW ABBOTS LEIGH
HOUSE**
34 Church Road, Abbots Leigh
BS8 3QP. Tim & Beckie Brettell.
*From Bristol, take A369 towards
M5. R turn in Abbots Leigh opp
George Inn. Garden on R just
before village green.* Cream teas.
Adm £2.50, chd free. Sun 10
June (12-5).
Large country garden with
imposing cedar of Lebanon which
oversees many different features
incl pergola walkway, rose garden,
canal, lily pond with bridge,
woodland area, fruit and vegetable
garden, cutting garden, meadow
and lawns. Very peaceful, relaxing
garden.
🐕 ☕

3 ALGARS MANOR
Station Road, Iron Acton BS37 9TB.
Dr & Mrs J M Naish, 01454
228372/3, johnnaish@msn.com. *9m
N of Bristol. 3m W of Yate/Chipping
Sodbury. Turn S off Iron Acton bypass
B4059, past village green, 200yds,
then over level Xing (Station Rd).*
Visitors welcome by appt for
entrance to both Algars Manor &
Algars Mill gardens, groups &
garden clubs particularly welcome.
Combined adm £3, chd free.
2 acres of woodland garden beside R
Frome, mill stream, native plants mixed
with collections of 60 magnolias and

70 camellias, eucalyptus and other unusual trees and shrubs. Mar/Apr camellias, magnolias; Apr/May/June rhododendrons, azaleas; Oct autumn colours. Limited wheelchair access, some uneven ground and steep slopes.

&

④ ALGARS MILL
Station Road, Iron Acton BS37 9TD. Mr & Mrs John Wright, 01454 228373/2. *9m N of Bristol. 3m W of Yate/Chipping Sodbury. (For directions see Algars Manor).* **Visitors welcome by appt for entrance to both Algars Manor & Algars Mill gardens. Combined adm £3, chd free.**
2-acre woodland garden bisected by R Frome; spring bulbs, shrubs; very early spring feature (Feb-Mar) of wild Newent daffodils. 300-400yr-old mill house (not open) through which millrace still runs.

⑤ ASHCOTT GARDENS
TA7 9QB. *3m W of Street on A39. Turn opp Ashcott Inn into Middle St. At T-junction turn R to car park at village hall.* Home-made teas at village hall. **Combined adm £4, chd free. Sun 3 June (2-5.30).**
A pleasant and friendly village situated in the Polden Hills.

☕

NEW CHERRY ORCHARD
17 Chapel Hill. Geoff & Sue Wilton
Wildlife-friendly garden, various perennials/shrubs. Archway with stone and gravel paths. Lawns, patio area, tubs incl geraniums, fuchsias. Lily/fish pond, waterfall, vegetable plot, several fruits. Majestic Bramley tree sheltering rear of property.

✖

NEW CHURCH FARM
High Street. Judith Bond
Mature cottage garden on 3 terraces of 3/4 acre. House dates back to C13 and is surrounded by trees, shrubs and herbaceous plants. Features brick potting shed and Somerset Linhay.

✖

NEW HOLLY TREE COTTAGE
Chapel Hill. Robin & Denise Wale
Quiet garden, set in middle of village, with peaceful combination of new and mature planting. Minimal slope to garden.

&

MANOR HOUSE
11 Middle Street. Peter & Daphne Willis
1/4-acre garden with mixed herbaceous planting, small pond and bog area with some hardy exotics. Water feature and gravel garden planted with alpines and grasses. Pergola dividing ornamental garden from vegetables grown in raised beds.

& ✖

22 MIDDLE STREET
Mary & David Adkins
1/2-acre garden developed over the past 6yrs. Herbaceous border, pond, small shady area, vegetables, wild area planted with trees and shrubs. Gravel drive.

& ✖ ⊛

TREMERRYN
Middle Street. Mr & Mrs Hemmings
Small but colourful garden. One steep slope.

& ✖

⑥ BARFORD PARK
Spaxton TA5 1AG. Mr & Mrs Michael Stancomb. *4 1/2 m W of Bridgwater. Midway between Enmore & Spaxton.* Cream teas. **Adm £2.50, chd free. Sun 24 June (2-5.30).**
10 acres incl woodland walk. Formal garden, wild garden and water garden, surrounding a Queen Anne house (not open) with park and ha-ha. Partial wheelchair access.

& ⊛ ☕

⑦ ◆ BARRINGTON COURT
Ilminster TA19 0NQ. The National Trust, 01460 241938, www.nationaltrust.org.uk. *5m NE of Ilminster. In Barrington village on B3168.* **Adm £7, chd £3. Mar to Oct daily (not Weds).** For NGS: **Suns 22 Apr; 29 July (11-5).**
Well known garden constructed in

1920 by Col Arthur Lyle from derelict farmland (the C19 cattle stalls still exist). Gertrude Jekyll suggested planting schemes for the layout. Paved paths with walled rose and iris, white and lily gardens, large kitchen garden.

& ✖ ⊛ ☕

⑧ BARROW COURT
Barrow Court Lane, Barrow Gurney BS48 3RP. Mrs Jo Collins, Organiser. *16m NE of Weston-super-Mare & 8m SW of Bristol. On A370. Turn off onto A3130 to Barrow Gurney. Turn immed R into Barrow Court Lane. 1/2 m up lane turn R into Barrow Court.* Home-made teas. **Adm £2, chd £1. Sun 3 June (2-6).**
Early C20 listed Italianate garden, designed by Inigo Thomas. Formal areas are set on 3 levels and incl parterres, fish pond, balustrades and gazebos. Also a small arboretum and wild spinney. Wheelchair access to lower garden only.

⊛ ☕

⑨ BARUM
50 Edward Road, Clevedon BS21 7DT. Marian & Roger Peacock, www.50-barum.freeserve.co.uk. *12m W of Bristol. M5 J20, follow signs to pier, continue N, past Walton Park Hotel, turn R at St Mary's Church. Up Channel Rd, over Xrds, turn L into Edward Rd at top.* **Adm £2, chd free. Thurs 31 May; 7, 14 June (2-5).**
Informal 1/3-acre plantsman's garden, reclaimed by the owners since 1991 from years of neglect. Now crammed with shrubs and perennials from around the world, incl tender and exotic species using the clement coastal climate and well-drained soil. The vegetable patch uses a no-tread bedding system growing several tender crops.

✖ ⊛

⑩ BATH PRIORY HOTEL
Weston Road, Bath BA1 2XT. Jane Moore, Head Gardener, 01225 331922, www.thebathpriory.co.uk. *Close to centre of Bath. From Bath centre take Upper Bristol Rd, turn R at end of Victoria Park & L into Weston Rd.* Home-made teas. **Adm £2.50, chd free (share to Dorothy House Hospice). Thurs 26 Apr; 9 Aug (2-5). Visitors also welcome by appt.**
3-acre walled garden. Main garden has croquet lawn, herbaceous borders and dell with snowdrops and spring bulbs. Adjoining garden has summer meadow and woodland borders with specimen trees. Formal pool

Features brick potting shed and Somerset Linhay . . .

surrounded by roses leads to stone gazebo overlooking the vegetable garden which supplies the restaurant. Some gravel paths. Award winner Bath in Bloom.

 ⛿ ♨

3 magical playhouses (Ruth's Cottage, Tom's Lodge and Charlotte's Post Office) . . .

⑪ BEECHWELL HOUSE
51 Goose Green, Yate BS37 5BL. Tim Wilmot, 01454 318350, www.beechwell.com. *10m NE of Bristol. From centre of Yate (Shopping & Leisure Centre) or Station Rd B4060, turn N onto Church Rd. After ¹/₂ m turn L onto Greenways Rd then immed R onto continuation of Church Rd. Goose Green starts after 200yds. After 100yds take R-fork, garden 100yds on L.* Cream teas. **Adm £3, chd free. Sun 9 Sept (1-6). Evening Opening £4, wine, Sat 18 Aug (6-9).** Visitors also welcome by appt June-Sept for groups of 10+.
Enclosed, level, subtropical garden created over last 17yrs and filled with exotic planting, incl palms (over 12 varieties), tree ferns, yuccas, agaves and succulent bed, phormiums, bamboos, bananas, aroids and other 'architectural planting'. Wildlife pond and koi pond. C16 40ft deep well. Rare plant raffle every hour. Runner up in 'The Times' Back Garden of the Year Competition & featured in 'The Times' ('The Eden Complex').

♨

⑫ NEW BINEGAR VILLAGE GARDENS
BA3 4UE. *On A37 Binegar (Gurney Slade), at George Inn, follow sign to Binegar 1m past PH and church to Xrds at Binegar Green. From Wells B3139, 4m turn R signed Binegar, 1m to Xrds at Binegar Green.* Cream teas in aid of RDA. **Adm £3, chd free. Sun 24 June (2-5.30).**
One of the highest villages on the Mendips with C13 church.

♨

NEW CHURCH FARM HOUSE
Turners Court Lane. Susan & Tony Griffin, 01749 841628. *From Xrds, 300yds E (signed to Old Down), R to garden. Limited parking.* **Visitors also welcome by appt May, June, July.**
3 connected areas of garden, 2 walled, approx 1 acre. Views to church and hills beyond. New landscaping has created borders which are being developed, featuring English roses, flowering shrubs, herbaceous perennials, iris and allium planted in colour themes. Gravel forecourt.

⛿

NEW THE COACH HOUSE
Bennetts Lane. James Shanahan & Richard Higgins, 01749 840973. *From Green, 100yds along Bennetts Lane on R.* **Visitors also welcome by appt June, July, Aug.**
3 acres. Gardens under development but beech hedges define overall plan. Collections of fuchsia and old French roses. Formal flower gardens contrast with walks and lawns with long Mendip vistas under a big sky. Gravel and grass paths.

NEW SPINDLE COTTAGE
Angela & Alban Bunting. *Binegar Green, parking on the Green*
The garden has always been a place for children to romp about. Low maintenance with 3 magical playhouses (Ruth's Cottage, Tom's Lodge and Charlotte's Post Office), built for our grand-children by Alban and all the visiting children that come on holiday. Cottage garden flower beds, productive vegetable plot, hedgehog house. Wildlife pond on Green. Featured in 'Country Living'.

🛏

⑬ BOURNE HOUSE
Bourne Lane, Burrington BS40 7AF. Mr & Mrs C Thomas, 01761 462494. *12m S of Bristol. N of Burrington. Turn off A38 signed Blagdon-Burrington; 2nd turning L.* **Visitors welcome by appt, max 30, no coaches.**
5 acres, 2 paddocks. Stream with waterfalls and lily pond; pergola; mature trees and shrubs. Mixed borders; large area hardy cyclamen and rose bed. Spring bulbs.

⑭ BOWEYS AND ROSE COTTAGE
Church Lane, Kingston-St-Mary TA2 8HR. Mr N Palfrey, Mrs G Campbell, Mrs J M Palfrey & Miss D Palfrey, 01823 451868, www.country-matters.co.uk. *2¹/₂ m N of Taunton. Close to church in village. No parking at house, please use church car park. Disabled parking at Boweys.* **Visitors welcome by appt June/July only.**
Two interconnecting gardens. Mature cottage-style and garden in-the-making. Interesting stone walling and buildings, stone summerhouses, gazebo and pergola, stone steps and cobbles. Small pond and rill. Topiary, shrubs and climbers. Partial wheelchair access via gravel paths, paved slopes.

⑮ BRAGLANDS BARN
Stogumber TA4 3TP. Simon & Sue Youell, www.braglandsbarn.com. *4m SE of Williton. From Taunton follow A358 for 11m. Turn L at 1st sign to Stogumber. 200metres after Stogumber stn.* Home-made teas pm only. **Adm £2.50, chd free. Mon 27 Aug (11-5.30).**
1-acre garden created since 1995 on site that contains areas of waterlogged clay and well-drained sand. Herbaceous borders, shrubs and trees with many rare and unusual plants. Pond and bog garden. Planted to provide colour and interest over a long period, especially late summer. Aim of garden is to grow interesting plants in an informal setting.

⛿ ♨

BRAMBLE HAYES
See Devon.

⑯ 4 BRENDON VIEW
Crowcombe TA4 4AG. Chris Hayes. *9m NW of Taunton. Off A358 signed Crowcombe. Garden opp turning for Hagleys Green.* **Adm £2, chd free. Suns 27 May; 3 June; 19 Aug (2-5.30).**
Modest-sized, plantsman's garden, S-facing with views of the Quantock Hills. Subtropical planting, mixed herbaceous borders. Vegetables. Over 400 species of cacti in 2 greenhouses, many in flower in May & June.

⛿

⑰ BRENT KNOLL GARDENS
TA9 4DF. *2m N of Highbridge. Off A38 & M5 J22.* Cream teas at Copse Hall. **Combined adm £4.50, chd free. Sun 15 July (2-6).**
Beautiful Church. The Knoll is an iron-age hill fort, National Trust.

NEW ANVIL COTTAGE
Jean Owen
Ideas for a small garden.

COPSE HALL
Mrs S Boss & Mr A J Hill, 01278 760301, susan.boss@gmail.com. **Visitors also welcome by appt.**
Several acres incl terraced gardens, crinkle crankle kitchen garden wall, ponds, New Zealand plants, shrubs, beech wood and Soay sheep. Dogs on leads. Partial wheelchair access.

NEW CROFT COTTAGE
Malcolm & Sheila Holness
Approx ³/₄ acre under present ownership since 2002. Consists of original, previously-neglected garden and main garden taken from adjoining field in 2000. Much new planting, young and mature trees, vegetable patch, pergola and novel new centrepiece.

⑱ BREWERY HOUSE
Southstoke, Bath BA2 7DL. John & Ursula Brooke, 01225 833153.
2¹/₂m S of Bath. A367 Radstock Rd from Bath. At top of dual carriageway turn L onto B3110. Straight on at double roundabout. Next R into Southstoke. Cream teas. **Adm £2.50, chd 50p. Sun 1 July (2-5.30). Visitors also welcome by appt July only.**
Established garden on 2 levels with fine views to the S. Herbaceous perennials, grasses, bamboos, euphorbias, hydrangeas, clematis. All organic. Upper garden surrounded by 10ft stone wall. Trees incl walnut, davidia, medlar, apple, mulberry etc. Large pool/water garden. A number of unusual plants. Featured in 'The Guardian'.

⑲ 1 BROMLEY VILLAS
Bromley Road, Stanton Drew BS39 4DE. Mr & Mrs S Whittle. *7m S of Bristol. From A37 Chelwood roundabout take A368 towards Chew Valley Lake. 2nd turning on R. Follow car park signs. Park only in designated car park. Strictly no parking on*

Bromley Rd. Home-made teas Sun only. **Adm £3, chd free. Sun 15 July (12-6). Evening Opening £4.50,** wine, Thur 21 June (6-9).
A lawnmower's nightmare! Rose arches, rills, raised beds, fire pit, sculptured mounds, circular vegetable beds and luxuriously planted perennial beds, not to mention menagerie and fruit trees. Are my husband's whinges justified? You decide. We look forward to seeing you. Art for sale. Indian runner ducks and rare breed hens.

BURROW FARM GARDENS
See Devon.

⑳ CAMERS
Old Sodbury BS37 6RG. Mr & Mrs A G Denman, 01454 322430, dorothydenman@camers.org. *2m E of Chipping Sodbury. Entrance in Chapel Lane off A432 at Dog Inn.* Home-made teas. **Adm £3, chd free. Sun 6 May; Sun 29 July (2-5.30). Visitors also welcome by appt for groups of 15+.**
Elizabethan farmhouse (not open) set in 4 acres of garden and young woodland with spectacular views over Severn Vale. Garden is divided into range of formal and informal areas planted with very wide range of species to provide yr-round interest. Parterre, topiary, Japanese garden, bog shade and prairie areas, waterfalls, white and hot gardens, woodland walks. Some steep slopes.

Natural, buzzing, 'greeny-yallery' garden . . .

㉑ CATCOTT GARDENS
TA7 9HF. *8m NE of Bridgwater. Off A39 between Bridgwater and Street to Catcott. Continue straight to Xrds. At King William PH straight downhill to T-junction. Turn L, passing Barton Farm on R. No parking at house. Please follow signs to school car park. 1st entry and map at Barton Farm.* Home-made teas at Barton Farm. **Combined adm £4, chd free. Suns 15 Apr; 6 May; 3 June (2-6).**
Nestling on N slope of Polden Hills, with extensive views over Somerset levels, Catcott is an old village still retaining much of its original character. The 2 gardens are in the ancient core

of the village where old blue lias limestone-built properties predominate. Exhibition by Somerset Wildlife Trust.

BARTON FARM
18 Manor Road. Mr & Mrs P H S Mackay
Natural, buzzing, 'greeny-yallery' garden using foliage and grasses as textural elements. Wide variety of native and cultivated plants has been used to create habitats and food sources for wildlife. Large pond. Sloping Dorset binding stone paths.

ZOOL HOUSE
Les Durston
(See separate entry).

㉒ CEDAR HOUSE
High Street, Wrington BS40 5QD. Jenny Denny, 01934 863375. *12m S of Bristol on A38. Follow sign for Wrington after airport & on reaching village, garage on L. T-junction turn R up hill. House on L. Parking in village (or at house by special arrangement).* Home-made teas. **Adm £3, chd free. Sun 24 June (11-5). Visitors also welcome by appt June/July.**
Mature formal garden with specimen trees; lawns; walled herbaceous borders, rose beds, mixed borders, hostas and hydrangea bed, leading to orchard, sculpture park and pond fed by warm springs.

㉓ THE CHALET
52 Charlton Road, Midsomer Norton BA3 4AH. Sheila & Chris Jones. *1/2m from centre of Midsomer Norton. Just off A367. Past the White Post Inn towards Radstock, turn L immed after next mini roundabout into Charlton Rd.* Disabled parking only at house. Home-made teas. **Adm £2, chd free. Sat 7 July (2-5.30).**
Covering 1 acre, garden contains lots of interest with plenty of lawns, mixed borders, vegetable garden and 80yr-old rotating cedar shingle summerhouse. Topiary is slowly becoming a feature. A quiet, relaxing garden next to a busy rd, shared by Orchard Lodge (52a), the next generation of the family. Live music in the garden.

CHIDEOCK MANOR
See Dorset.

CHIFFCHAFFS
See Dorset.

24 ♦ CLAVERTON MANOR
Claverton, Bath BA2 7BD. American Museum in Britain, 01225 460503, www.americanmuseum.org. *2m E of Bath. The American Museum is signed from Bath city centre and from A36 Warminster rd. Coaches must only approach via city centre up Bathwick Hill.* Adm £5, chd £3, concessions £4. Tue to Sun, 18 Mar to 28 Oct; Mons Bank Hols & Aug. For NGS: Fri 22 June (12-5).
Located in AONB with stunning views across the Avon Valley, garden incl replica of George Washington's Mount Vernon garden, a Colonial Herb garden and American Arboretum. Explore a unique mixture of American botanical discoveries made 200yrs ago by Lewis and Clark or walk the Backwoods Trail through manor's upper woodland. Wheelchair access very limited.

25 CLIFTON GARDENS
Bristol BS8 3LH. *Close to Clifton Suspension Bridge between the Mansion House & Christ Church.* Teas at 43 Canynge Road. **Combined adm £2.50, chd free. Sun 10 June (2-5).**

BELL COTTAGE
2 Camp Road. Jeff & Margaret Palmer
Yr-round town garden of exotic character; rockeries, pond, pergolas.
&⊁ ✿

43 CANYNGE ROAD
Martin Appleby
Happy garden for children and birds: organic vegetables; lovely summerhouse. Each separate lawn area has a different mood. Featured in 'The Bristol Magazine'.
& ⊁

NEW 3 NORLAND ROAD
Mrs J C Torrens
Charming town garden filled with relaxed and varied planting, full of yr-round interest. Shrubs, small trees, bulbs and perennials.

11 PERCIVAL ROAD
Mr & Mrs R L Bland
Small, enclosed urban garden, most plants in containers. Large variety of individual, interesting plants. 70 tree species.
⊁ ✿

Tropical garden packed with unusual plants . . .

26 COBBLESIDE
North Street, Milverton TA4 1LG. Mr & Mrs C Pine, 01823 400404, ampgardendesign@aol.com. *7m W of Taunton. On B3227. L at Milverton roundabout.* Adm £3, chd free. Sun 24 June (2-5.30). Visitors also welcome by appt for groups.
³/₄-acre walled garden incl herb garden, potager and wildlife pond, new raised bed. Wheelchair access to most parts.
& ⊁ ✿

27 NEW COKER WOOD COTTAGE
Pendomer, Yeovil BA22 9PD. David & Anthea Lovelock. *3m S of Yeovil. On rd between Pendomer and Halstock. Park at railway and walk ¹/₄m up.* Cream teas. Adm £3, chd free (share to St Margarets Hospice). Sun 3 June (2-6).
Sloping 1-acre garden terraced with dry stone walls in wooded rural setting. Knot garden, formal and informal plantings. Vegetable garden, pond. 5th yr of development. Croquet and children's treasure hunt. Fair organ. Craft displays.
 ✿ ☕

28 COLEY COURT
Coley BS40 6AN. Mrs M J Hill. *1m E of East Harptree. From A39 take Chewton Mendip take B3114 for 2m. Well before E Harptree turn R at sign Coley and Hinton Blewett.* Cream teas at New Manor Farm Shop, N Widecombe. **Adm £2.50, chd free. Sun 15 Apr (2-5).**
Early Jacobean house (not open). 1-acre garden, stone walls, spring bulbs; 1-acre old mixed orchard.
⊁ ✿ ☕

29 CONGRESBURY GARDENS
BS49 5EX. *8m N of Weston-super-Mare. 13m S of Bristol on A370. At T-lights in Congresbury head E signed Churchill - Cheddar. From A38, take B3133 to Congresbury.* Teas at Oakside & 3 Silver Mead. **Combined adm £3, chd free. Sat 23 June (10.30-5).**

FERNBANK
High Street. Simon & Julia Thyer. *100yds along High St from Ship & Castle*
Informal ¹/₃ acre, narrow uneven paths. Jungle-like conservatory. Hundreds of potted plants. 2 ponds, arbour, well pump, kitchen garden, raised beds. Picturesque potting shed and greenhouse and free range rare bantams.
⊁

MIDDLECOMBE NURSERY
Nigel J North, www.middlecombenursery.co.uk. *On the edge of Congresbury, on the Bristol side, turn to Wrington along the Wrington rd off the A370 Weston to Bristol rd. Garden 200yds on L*
Series of gardens covering 1 acre, many different styles and features. Excellent shrub borders. Patio gardens, pond and water features, lawns, deck areas etc. Dogs on leads. Gravel drive, large lawn, no disabled toilet facilities.
& ✿

NEW OAKSIDE
Paul Laws, 01934 832052, laws.family4@tiscali.co.uk. *200yds along High St from Ship & Castle.* Visitors also welcome by appt all yr.
28metres x 48metres. Tropical garden packed with unusual plants. Bananas, elephant ears, dutaras, cannas, bamboo, agaves, konjac acers. Various sitting areas, decking, pergolas, water features, doves. Best Back Garden and Water Feature, Weston Mercury.
& ⊁

3 SILVER MEAD
Terry & Geraldine Holden. *500yds along High St from Ship & Castle, R into Silver St, 1st L into Silver Mead*
¹/₃ acre of shrub borders and trees developed over the past 20yrs from farmland. Two 'hot' Mediterranean-type patios, water features, wisteria-covered pergola. Many pots, lavender walk. Organic vegetable plot. Meadow area, wooden arbour. Short, steep slope to main part of garden but can be viewed from top.
& ⊁ ✿

30 ◆ COTHAY MANOR GARDENS

Greenham, nr Wellington TA21 0JR. Mr & Mrs Alastair Robb, 01823 672283. *5m SW of Wellington. At M5 J26 or 27 take direction Exeter or Wellington respectively. Approx 4m take direction Greenham. After 1m follow tourist signs. In lane keep always L. Car park 1m.* **Adm £4.50, chd under 12 £2.50. Weds, Thurs, Suns & Bank Hols, Apr to Aug. For NGS: Sun 29 July (2-6).** Few gardens are as evocatively romantic as Cothay. Laid out in 1920s and replanted in 1990s within the original framework, Cothay encompasses a rare blend of old and new. Plantsman's paradise set in 12 acres of magical gardens. Gravel paths. Featured in 'Telegraph' magazine.

⚘ ⅍ ⊛

31 COURT HOUSE

East Quantoxhead TA5 1EJ. Sir Walter & Lady Luttrell. *12m W of Bridgwater. Off A39; house at end of village past duck pond.* Home-made teas in village hall. **Adm £3, chd free. Sun 13 May (2-5.30).** Lovely 5-acre garden; trees, shrubs, many rare and tender; herbaceous and 3-acre woodland garden. Views to sea and Quantocks.

⚘ ⊛ ☕

32 ◆ CROWE HALL

Bath BA2 6AR. Mr John Barratt, 01225 310322. *1m SE of Bath. L up Widcombe Hill, off A36, leaving White Hart on R.* Limited parking. **Adm £3, chd £1. For NGS: Suns 15 Apr; 3 June (2-6).** Large varied garden; fine trees, lawns, spring bulbs, series of enclosed gardens cascading down steep hillside. Italianate terracing and Gothic Victorian grotto contrast with park-like upper garden. Dramatic setting, with spectacular views of Bath. Lovely walks through the fields along mown grass paths.

33 NEW DAGGS ALLOTMENTS

High Street BS35 2AW. *Thornbury. Park in free car park off Chapel Str.* **Adm £2, chd free. Sun 8 July (2-5).** Situated in historic town on edge of Severn Vale. 105 plots, all in cultivation, many organic, incl vegetables, soft fruit, herbs and flowers for cutting. Primary school plot, past winner of RHS Gold Cup. Narrow, steep, grass paths between plots.

⚘ ⅍ ⊛ ☕

34 NEW THE DAIRY HOUSE

Stowell, Sherborne DT9 4PD. Paul & Penelope Burns, 01963 370754, paul.burns@totalise.co.uk. *5m NE of Sherborne, 5m SW of Wincanton. From N & E: A357 S from A303, R to Stowell after 3m. From S & W: A30 to Milborne Port, L North St, R past railway bridge.* **Adm £2.50, chd free, concessions £2. Sat 16, Sun 17, Sat 30 June; Sun 1 July (11-6). Also open Henstridge Gardens 16, 17 June. Visitors also welcome by appt mid-Mar to end July, no coaches.** Close-planted borders, trellis, pergola and paths divide garden into rooms, leading to maturing small wood. All our own work, incorporating materials from Salisbury Workhouse and other sources. Pulmonarias, geraniums, euphorbias, symphytums, plus spectacular rambling roses. 'A fascinating and artistic place to wander and ponder' (Saunday). Owners' paintings on view and needlepoint tapestry kits for sale. Unfenced pond.

⚘ ⊛ 🛏 ☕

35 ◆ DARKEY PANG TSO GANG

High Street, Oakhill BA3 5BT. Chrissy & Graham Price, 01749 840795, www.darkeypang.org.uk. *3m N of Shepton Mallet. Off A367 in Oakhill High St opp converted chapel.* **Adm £3, chd 50p (share to The Mendip Society). Sun 10 June (2-6). Evening Opening, wine, Wed 20 June (6.30-9.30). Visitors also welcome by appt.** ³/₄-acre garden creatively designed and landscaped by owners since 1981. Crammed with trees, shrubs, herbaceous and climbers, the garden is an adventure along winding paths with a lushness of greens and leaf combinations linking wild and cultivated areas with grotto, terraces, pergola, wildlife pond and bog garden with the recently-discovered cave being a major feature.

⅍ ⊛ ☕

All our own work, incorporating materials from Salisbury Workhouse and other sources . . .

DICOT
See Devon.

36 ◆ DUNSTER CASTLE GARDENS

Dunster TA24 6SL. The National Trust, 01643 821314, www.nationaltrust.org.uk. *3m SE of Minehead. NT car park approached direct from A39 Minehead to Bridgwater rd, nr to A396 turning.* Car park charge to non-NT members. **Adm grounds only £4.60, chd £2.10, family £11. Opening days & times vary according to season; please phone or visit website for details. For NGS: Thurs 29 Mar; 2 Aug (10-5).** Hillside woodland garden surrounding fortified mansion, previously home to the Luttrell family for 600yrs. Terraced areas, interlinked by old carriage drives and paths, feature tender plants. National Collection of Arbutus (Strawberry Tree). Fine views over polo lawns and landscape with C18 features. Self-drive battery-operated vehicle available. Meet the gardeners, who will demonstrate equipment and techniques. Map to show wheelchair-friendly route. Powered buggy available on request.

⚘ ⅍ NCCPG ☕

DURCOMBE WATER
See Devon.

37 ◆ DYRHAM PARK

Bath SN14 8ER. The National Trust, 01179 372501, www.nationaltrust.org.uk. *12m E of Bristol. 8m N of Bath. Approached from Bath to Stroud rd (A46), 2m S of Tormarton interchange with M4 exit 18.* **House and garden adm £9, garden only adm £3.80, chd £2, family £8.50. Fri to Tues. For NGS: Sat 9, Sun 10 June (11-5).** Situated on W side of late C17 house. Herbaceous borders, yews clipped as

buttresses, ponds and cascade, parish church set on terrace. Niches and carved urns. Long lawn to old West entrance. Restored orangery. Deer park with designated walks giving magnificent views. Steep slopes in park, cobbles in courtyard.

& ᚷ ⊕ ☕

38 ◆ **EAST LAMBROOK MANOR GARDENS**
East Lambrook TA13 5HH. Robert & Marianne Williams, 01460 240328, marianne@eastlambrook.com. *2m N of South Petherton. Off A303 at South Petherton. Follow brown flower signs.* **Adm £3.95, chd free, concessions £3.50. Daily. For NGS: Fri 1 June (10-5).**
One of England's best loved privately owned gardens created by the late Margery Fish and made famous through her many books and lectures. Intriguing cottage-style garden with important collection of plants, many of which she saved from virtual extinction. Ongoing restoration programme which will help improve many historically important areas. Restored display of the collection of geraniums. Featured on BBC Gardeners' World. Partial wheelchair access, gravel paths and steps.

ᚷ ⊕ ☕

39 **EASTON-IN-GORDANO GARDENS**
BS20 0NB. *5m W of Bristol. M5 J19 Gordano Services, exit Bristol. Turn L for Easton-in-Gordano, past King's Arms PH. Park in church hall car park by football field & follow directions in car park.* Home-made teas at 36 Church Road. **Combined adm £3, chd free. Tues 17, 24, 31 July (2-5).**
☕

36 CHURCH ROAD
Mr & Mrs I Crichton
$1/4$-acre garden developed around ancient dewpond. Unusual secret garden incl large pond with fish, waterfall, and bridge built by local school. Herbaceous borders contain many flower arrangers' plants. Limited wheelchair access.

& ᚷ ⊕

16 GORDANO GARDENS
Mr & Mrs Milsom
Cottage-style garden 80ft long with many pretty and unusual features incl decked area, natural pond with waterfall, grasses and herbaceous plants.
ᚷ

40 ◆ **ELWORTHY COTTAGE**
Elworthy TA4 3PX. Mike & Jenny Spiller, 01984 656427, www.elworthy-cottage.co.uk. *12m NW of Taunton. On B3188 between Wiveliscombe & Watchet.* **Adm £2, chd free. Thurs only 22 Mar to 26 July (10-4). Please phone for other times. For NGS: Sun 1, Mon 9, Thur 12 Apr; Thur 24, Mon 28 May; Sat 2, Thur 28 June; Thur 5 July (10-4).**
1-acre plantsman's garden & nursery in tranquil setting. Island beds, scented plants, clematis, unusual perennials and shrubs to provide yr-round interest. Planted to encourage birds, bees and butterflies, lots of birdsong. Wild flower areas, decorative vegetable garden, living willow screen. Stone ex privy and pigsty feature. Featured in 'Somerset Country Gardener' and 'Gardens Monthly'.
ᚷ ⊕

41 ◆ **EMMAUS HOUSE**
Clifton Hill, Bristol BS8 1BN. Sisters of La Retraite, 0117 907 9950, www.emmaushouse.org.uk. *From Clifton Downs down to Clifton Village to bottom of Regent St on R. Opp Saville Place.* **Adm £2.50, chd free. For NGS: Suns 3 June; 22 July; 2 Sept (11-4).**
$1^1/2$ acres with Victorian walled kitchen garden, also fruit, formal herb and Zen gardens. Rose and herbaceous borders, lawns, secret garden with summerhouse. Courtyard garden with original stone watercourse. Ponds with fountains and fine views towards Dundry. Recently excavated remains of old coach house in wild garden. Partial wheelchair access only. Bristol in Bloom Gold Cerificate, Commercial Business category. Terraced gardens with steps.

& ᚷ ⊕ ⌂ ☕

Alpine and bog garden with waterfalls and pools . . .

42 **FAIRFIELD**
nr Stogursey TA5 1PU. Lady Gass. *7m E of Williton. 11m NW of Bridgwater. From A39 Bridgwater to Minehead rd turn N; garden $1^1/2$ m W of Stogursey. No coaches.* **Adm £3, chd free. Sun 1 Apr (2-5.30).**
Woodland garden with bulbs, shrubs and fine trees; paved maze. Views of Quantocks and sea. Partial wheelchair access.

& ᚷ ⊕ ☕

43 **FERNHILL**
nr Wellington TA21 0LU. Peter & Audrey Bowler, 01823 672423, www.sampfordarundel.org.uk/fernhi ll. *1m W of Wellington. On A38, White Ball Hill. Past Beam Bridge Hotel stay on A38 at top of hill, follow signs on L into garden & car park.* Home-made teas. **Adm £2.50, chd free. Suns, Weds 1, 4 July; 5, 8 Aug (2-5). Visitors also welcome by appt June/July/Aug only for groups of 10+.**
Mature wooded garden in approx 2 acres with rose, herbaceous, shrub and mixed borders, all unique in colour and content. Interesting octagonal pergola; alpine and bog garden with waterfalls and pools leading to shady arbour. Fine views over ha-ha to Blackdowns and Mendips.

ᚷ ⊕ ☕

FORDE ABBEY GARDENS
See Dorset.

44 **NEW** ◆ **FOREST LODGE**
Penselwood BA9 8LL. Mr & Mrs James Nelson, 01747 841283 (eve). *$1^1/2$ m N of A303, 3m E of Wincanton. Leave A303 at B3081 (Wincanton to Gillingham rd), up hill to Pen Selwood, L towards church. $1/2$ m, garden on L.* **Adm £2.50, chd free. For NGS: Thurs 3, 24 May (2-5). Also open in Dorset (within 1m) Snape Cottage and Chiffchaffs, Chaffeymoor.**
3-acre mature garden with many camellias and rhododendrons. Lovely views towards Blackmore Vale. Part formal with pleached hornbeam allée and rill, part water garden with lake.
ᚷ ⊕ ☕

FRANKHAM FARM
See Dorset.

45 NEW FRANKIE HOWERD'S GARDEN
Webbington Road, Cross, Axbridge BS26 2EF. Christopher Byrne, 01934 732013. *3m from Cheddar Gorge. From M5 J22, past Sanders Garden World, A38 towards Bristol Airport 4m. After The Lamb PH, L to Cross and L at T-junction. Garden immed on R. A38 S, down Shute Shelve, R for ¹/₂ m. Garden on R.* Cream teas. **Adm £5, chd £3 (share to local charities - see website for details). Sats, Suns 17, 18, 31 Mar; 1, 8 Apr; Sun 6, Mon 7, Sat 26, Sun 27, Mon 28 May; Sats, Suns 9, 10, 16, 17, 30 June; Suns 1, 15 July; Sats, Suns 4, 5, 25, 26, Mon 27 Aug; Sat 22, Sun 23 Sept (10.30-6.30).**
Unique garden dating back to 1907 perhaps more interesting for its associations and history than for its planting. Located in an area of outstanding natural beauty, the house has welcomed distinguished visitors including Liz Taylor, Richard Burton, June Whitfield and Princess Margaret. Former home of Frankie Howerd. Art exhibitions. Display of Egyptian and Roman antiquities. 4000 items of memorabilia belonging to Frankie Howerd. Local wildlife centre. Ideal base for walkers on Mendip Hills. Lovely old inns within walking distance. Featured in National Press and on BBC and local TV/Radio 4.
&⬛ ⊕ ☕

Lovingly-designed, content and design belie its 1-acre size . . .

46 ◆ GANTS MILL & GARDEN
Bruton BA10 0DB. Alison & Brian Shingler, 01749 812393, www.gantsmill.co.uk. *¹/₂ m SW of Bruton. From Bruton centre on Yeovil rd, A359, under railway bridge, 100yds uphill, fork R down Gants Mill Lane.* **Garden adm £3, chd £1. Mill & garden £5, chd £1. Suns, Thurs & Bank Hols 15 May to end Sept. For NGS: Mon 27 Aug (2-5).**
³/₄-acre garden. Clematis, rose arches and pergolas; streams, ponds, bog garden; brick circle, grasses in gravel; garden sculpture exhibition; riverside walk to the top weir; colour-themed planting with many iris, oriental poppies, delphiniums, day lilies, dahlias; also vegetable, soft fruit and cutting flower garden. The garden is overlooked by the historic watermill, also open on NGS day. Partial wheelchair access. Featured in 'Woman's Weekly'.
& ⬛ ☕

47 ◆ GAULDEN MANOR
Tolland TA4 3PN. Mr & Mrs J Le G Starkie, 01984 667213. *9m NW of Taunton. Nr Lydeard St Lawrence, off A358 & B3224.* **Adm £3.25, chd £1. Suns, Thurs & Bank Hols June to Aug (2-5). For NGS: Wed 13, Thur 14 June (2-5).**
Medium-sized garden made by owners. Herb, bog, scent and butterfly gardens. Bog plants, primulas and scented geraniums. Large stew pond with island. Secret garden beyond. House not open. Gentle slopes.
& ⊁ ⊕

48 190 GOLDCROFT
Yeovil BA21 4DB. Eric & Katrina Crate, 01935 475535. *Take A359 from roundabout by Yeovil College, then 1st R.* Home-made teas. **Adm £2, chd 50p. Sat 9, Sun 10 June (2-5). Evening Opening £2, wine, Mon 11 June (4-8). Visitors also welcome by appt for large or small groups, coaches permitted.**
¹/₄ acre. Colour-themed shrub and herbaceous borders and island beds, rose garden, raised pond, seaside deck, fernery, hosta walk, arbour surrounded by silver bed, vegetable garden designed for the visually impaired and greenhouse. Many mature shrubs and trees and sensory features.
⊁ ⊕ ☕

GREAT CHALFIELD MANOR
See Wiltshire.

49 ◆ GREENCOMBE
Porlock TA24 8NU. Miss Joan Loraine, 01643 862363. *¹/₂ m W of Porlock. L off rd to Porlock Weir.* **Adm £5, chd £1. Sat to Wed, Apr to July. For NGS: Sat 26 May (2-6).**
60yr-old garden on edge of ancient woodland, overlooking Porlock Bay. Choice rhododendrons, azaleas, camellias, maples, roses, hydrangeas, ferns, and many other plants. National Collections of *Polystichum, Erythronium, Vaccinium* and *Gaultheria.* Completely organic, with compost heaps on show.
& ⊁ ⊕ **NCCPG**

GUYERS HOUSE
See Wiltshire.

50 HANGERIDGE FARM
Wrangway TA21 9QG. Mrs J M Chave, 01823 662339. *2m S of Wellington. 1m off A38 bypass signed Wrangway. 1st L towards Wellington Monument over mway bridge 1st R.* Home-made teas. **Adm £2, chd free. Suns 22 Apr; 20 May; 1, 29 July (11-5). Visitors also welcome by appt.**
Informal, relaxing, 30 yr-old family garden set under Blackdown Hills. Seats to enjoy views across Somerset landscape. Atmospheric mix of herbaceous borders, mixed rockeries and newly-created oriental garden, this lovingly-designed and still-evolving garden contains wonderful flowering shrubs, heathers, mature trees, rambling climbers and bulbs in season. Content and design belie its 1-acre size.
& ⊁ ⊕ ⬛ ☕

51 NEW HANHAM COURT
Julian & Isabel Bannerman. *5m E of Bristol centre. Old Bristol Rd A431 from Bath, through Wilsbridge, L down Court Farm Rd for 1m, L down Ferry Rd at St Stephens Green, before Chequers PH.* **Adm £5, chd free. Sat 16 June (2-6).**
A remarkable cluster of mediaeval/Georgian buildings in a surprisingly rural setting right on E edge of Bristol. Last decade has seen creation of romantic scented garden, formal in parts, with woodland dell, orchard and monastic pond. Huge number of scented roses and peonies.
⊁

52 HARPTREE COURT
East Harptree BS40 6AA. Mr & Mrs
Richard Hill & Mr & Mrs Charles Hill.
*8m N of Wells. A39 Bristol rd to
Chewton Mendip, then B3114 to E
Harptree, gates on L. From Bath, A368
Weston-super-Mare rd to W Harptree.*
Cream teas. **Adm £3, chd free. Sun
27 May (2-6).**
Spacious garden designed when the
house was built in 1797. Two ponds
linked by a romantic waterfall and a
stream, flanked by large trees.
Herbaceous borders, lily pond and
formal garden are among other
features.
♿ ❀ 🛏 ☕

Secret spaces and plant-packed beds in this plantaholics' hideaway . . .

53 4 HAYTOR PARK
Bristol BS9 2LR. Mr & Mrs C J Prior,
0117 985 6582,
pat_prior@blueyonder.co.uk. *3m NW
of Bristol city centre. Edge of Coombe
Dingle. From A4162 Inner Ring Rd
between A4 Portway & A4108
Falcondale Rd, take turning into
Coombe Bridge Ave, Haytor Park is
1st turning L. No parking in Haytor
Park.* **Adm £3.50 incl tea and cake,
chd free. Visitors welcome by appt
for individuals/groups.**
Secret spaces, with lots to see on
every level, are linked by arches and
winding paths around curvaceous
plant-packed beds in this plantaholics'
hideaway. Always changing, discover
something for every season of the year,
different plants, a pond or two, wildlife,
sculpture and pots-a-plenty. Featured
in BBC 'Easy Gardening' magazine.
❀ ⊕ ☕

HAZELBURY MANOR GARDENS
See Wiltshire.

HEDDON HALL
See Devon.

54 HENLEY MILL
Wookey BA5 1AW. Peter & Sally
Gregson, 01749 676966,
www.millcottageplants.co.uk. *2m W
of Wells. Off A371. Turn L into Henley
Lane, driveway 50yds on L.* Home-
made teas. **Adm £3, chd free.
Visitors welcome by appt Apr to
Sept, incl coaches and groups.**
2½ acres beside R Axe. Traditional and
unusual cottage plants informally
planted in formal beds with roses,
oriental poppy borders, shady 'folly
garden' and late summer borders with
grasses and perennials. Ornamental
kitchen garden. Rare Japanese
hydrangeas. Featured on BBC Escape
to the Country.
♿ ❀ ⊕ ☕

55 HENSTRIDGE GARDENS
BA8 0QE. 01963 364321,
marysmclean@btinternet.com. *6m E
of Sherborne. 9m W of Shaftesbury on
A30.* Home-made teas at Cherry
Bolberry Farm. **Combined adm £5,
chd free. Sats, Suns 9, 10, 16, 17
June (2-6). Visitors also welcome by
appt end May/June for groups of
10+.**
Village map given to all visitors.
☕

CHERRY BOLBERRY FARM
Furge Lane. Jenny Raymond. *In
centre of Henstridge, turn R at
small Xrds signed Furge Lane.
Continue straight on to farm*
1-acre owner-designed garden
planted for yr-round interest with
wildlife in mind. Colour-themed
island beds, shrub and
herbaceous borders, unusual
perennials, vegetable and flower
cutting gardens, greenhouses,
large pond and nature pond.
Extensive views.
♿ ❀ ⊕ 🛏

35 OLD STATION GARDENS
Mary McLean. *2nd turning R on
Shaftesbury Rd, A30. Follow
yellow signs*
Small owner-designed
plantaholic's garden. Many exotics
mixed with roses, clematis and
herbaceous. Raised beds,
pergolas, patio and pond.
Floriferous and abundant planting
with added spring underplanting
of bulbs to give extra interest.
♿ ❀ ⊕

ROSE COTTAGE
Church Street. Carol Perrett. *At
T-lights turn into Henstridge, take*

2nd R into Church St
¼-acre plantswoman's cottage
garden on site of former village
pond, exuberantly planted with
impressive effect to suit damp
conditions. Emphasis on scent,
colour, form and texture to create
a wildlife haven.
♿ ❀ ⊕

56 ◆ HESTERCOMBE GARDENS
Cheddon Fitzpaine TA2 8LG. Mr P
White, Hestercombe Gardens Trust,
01823 413923,
www.hestercombegardens.com. *4m
N of Taunton. Follow tourist signs.*
**Adm £6.95, chd free, concessions
£6.25, groups of 20+ £5.50, all
prices incl 10% donation. Daily all yr
(closed Xmas Day). For NGS: Tues 6
Mar; 5 June (10-5).**
Georgian landscape garden designed
by Coplestone Warre Bampfylde,
Victorian terrace/shrubbery and
stunning Edwardian Lutyens/Jekyll
formal gardens together make up 40
acres of woodland walks, temples,
terraces, pergolas, lakes and
cascades.
⊕ ☕

57 HIGHER YARDE FARM
Staplegrove, Taunton TA2 6SW.
Anita & Tom Harris. *3m NW of
Taunton. Off A358; at Staplegrove
village, L turn past church. ¾m at
T-junction turn R. 100yds L turn.
600yds entrance on L.* Home-made
teas. **Adm £2.50, chd free. Sat 16,
Sun 17 June (2-6). Evening
Opening £5, wine, Fri 15 June (6-9).**
3-acre informal country cottage garden
with herbaceous and shrub borders.
Stream divides more formal area from
wild flower meadow, wildlife pond and
developing woodlands. Our 20-yr
gardening practice is for the benefit
and encouragement of all forms of
wildlife. Some gravel paths, steep
banks by pond and deep water.
♿ ⊕ ☕

58 HILL LODGE
Northend, Batheaston BA1 8EN.
Susan & Sydney Fremantle, 01225
852847. *4m NE of Bath. Turn N in
Batheaston village up steep, small rd
signed Northend & St Catherine. Hill
Lodge ¾m on L. Parking in courtyard
for disabled, frail & elderly.* Home-
made teas. **Adm £3, chd free.
Sun 10 June (2-5). Visitors also
welcome by appt mid-May for
alpines, throughout summer until
Autumn (asters).**

Individuals or groups, no coaches. 3-acre country garden used for work experience by horticultural students because of variety of features incl stream, small wildlife lake, 2 ponds, bog garden, herbaceous borders, alpine bed, rose/clematis pergola, small cottage garden room, vegetable garden, orchard, coppice and hill with trees and view. Small lake with nesting waterfowl. Plants for sale in aid of Off The Record Young Carers' Service. Some slopes.

59 HILLCREST GARDENS
Redcliffe Bay BS20 8HN. 2¹/₂m from Portishead. Take Nore Rd S out of Portishead centre for 2¹/₂m. Past Feddon Village (old Nautical School), Hillcrest Rd is 1st L. Home-made/cream teas. **Combined adm £3, chd free. Sun 15 July (10.30-5); Thur 9 Aug (2-6).**
Coastal village with stunning views of Wales and the Bristol Channel. Weather permitting spectacular sunsets.

25 HILLCREST ROAD
Colin & Molly Lewis. (see separate entry).

LITTLE GABLE
2 Hillcrest Road. Bill & Maureen Lloyd
Garden built virtually from scratch over 11 yrs. Lawned area with pond and herbaceous border, gravel garden and small Japanese garden, all with panoramic views over the Channel. Enclosed patio area with rhododendrons & azaleas. A particular feature is the hydrangea hedge.

60 25 HILLCREST ROAD
Redcliffe Bay BS20 8HN. Colin & Molly Lewis. 2¹/₂m from Portishead. Take Nore Rd S out of Portishead centre for 2¹/₂m. Past Feddon Village (old Nautical School). Hillcrest Rd is 1st L. Home-made/cream teas. **Adm £2, chd free. Suns 22 Apr; 20 May (10.30-5).**
Sloping garden with 3 terraces; bottom - a lawn, middle - a formal garden with central fountain and extensively planted, top - a large patio with wisteria-covered pergola and spectacular water feature. Front garden is a riot of colour.

HILLESLEY HOUSE
See Gloucestershire North & Central.

HILLTOP
See Dorset.

Alocasias, bamboos, tree ferns, phormiums, bananas, palms and aquatics . . .

61 HINTON ST GEORGE GARDENS
TA17 8SA. 3m N of Crewkerne. N of A30 Crewkerne-Chard; S of A303 Ilminster Town Rd, at roundabout signed Lopen & Merriott, then R to Hinton St George. Home-made teas. **Combined adm £3, chd free. Sat 2, Sun 3 June (2-5.30).**
Pretty village with thatched Hamstone houses and C15 church. Wood turning and mosaic in progress at Hooper's Holding.

HOOPER'S HOLDING
45 High Street. Ken & Lyn Spencer-Mills
(See separate entry).

THE OLD MALT HOUSE
High Street TA17 8SE. Lord & Lady Peyton
1¹/₂-acre plantsman's garden with views to Mendips. Wide variety of interesting trees, shrubs and perennials. Formal pool, sculptures.

HODGES BARN
See Gloucestershire North & Central.

HOLBROOK GARDEN
See Devon.

62 10 HOLLY CLOSE
Pucklechurch BS16 9TD. Eamonn & Jackie Mooney. 10m NE of Bristol. Pucklechurch is on B4465. From centre of village, take Abson Rd past community centre on L, 1st R into Oaktree Ave, then 1st L. Parking in Oaktree Ave or Abson Rd. **Adm £3, chd free. Evening Openings** wine, **Fris 3, 10 Aug (6-8.30).**
Extensive range of hardy and tender exotic plants packed into small suburban garden. Incl colocasias, alocasias, bamboos, tree ferns, phormiums, bananas, palms and aquatics.

63 HOLT FARM
Blagdon BS40 7SQ. Mr & Mrs Tim Mead. 12m S of Bristol. Off A368 Weston-super-Mare to Bath rd, between Blagdon & Ubley. Entrance to Holt Farm approx ¹/₂ m outside Blagdon, on LH-side. Home-made teas. **Adm £2.50, chd free. Suns 29 Apr; 10 June; 23 Sept (2-5).**
Contemporary planting. Quirky sculptures. Bountiful bulbs. Autumnal 'fireworks'. 'Posh' vegetable patch. Great views. Sinful teas. Unfenced ponds.

64 HOMEWOOD PARK HOTEL
Abbey Lane, Hinton Charterhouse BA2 7TB. Homewood Park Hotel, www.homewoodpark.co.uk. 6m S of Bath. Just off A36 Warminster rd, before village of Hinton Charterhouse. Cream teas. **Adm £3, chd £1.50. Sun to Thur, Apr to Sept (2-5).**
Set in 10 acres of formal and informal gardens, incl circular rose garden and large herbaceous borders, rolling lawns and cut flower garden. Also large parkland with mature trees. Gold Award 'Bath in Bloom'. Gravel paths.

65 HOOPER'S HOLDING
45 High Street, Hinton St George TA17 8SE. Ken & Lyn Spencer-Mills, 01460 76389, kenlyn@devonrex.demon.co.uk. (see directions for Hinton St George Gardens). Home-made teas. **Adm £2.50, chd free. Sat 12, Sun 13 May (2-6). Also opening with Hinton St George Gardens** Sat, Sun, 2, 3 June. Visitors also welcome by appt.
¹/₃-acre garden in colour compartments; lily pool; azaleas, rare herbaceous and shrubby plants, many

exotics. Pedigree cats. Garden mosaics developing. New jungle conservatory.

  🌳 ☕

HORTUS
See Devon.

IFORD MANOR
See Wiltshire.

66 NEW INGLE COTTAGE
Inglestone Common, Hawkesbury GL9 1BS. Mrs Ann Fisher. 2^1/$_2$ m S of Wotton-under-Edge. Between Wickwar (on B4060) and Hawkesbury (W side A46). Home-made teas. **Adm £2, chd free. Sun 14 Oct (2-5).** Approx 2 acres of shrubs and trees. Some unusual varieties. Good autumn colours. Good views of Cotswold escarpment. Nearby nature reserve and woodland walks. Gravel entrance, grass.

  🌳 ✕ ☕

INWOODS
See Wiltshire.

67 JASMINE COTTAGE
26 Channel Road, Clevedon BS21 7BY. Mr & Mrs M Redgrave, 01275 871850, www.bologrew.pwp.blueyonder.co. uk. 12m W of Bristol. M5 J20. Follow signs to seafront & pier, continue N on B3124, past Walton Park Hotel, turn R at St Mary's Church. Wheelchair access at rear entrance in The Avenue. **Adm £2, chd free. Every Thur, 3 May to 26 July; Thurs 6, 13 Sept (11-4). Visitors also welcome by appt May to 13 Sept.**
Mature garden with specimen trees and shrubs. Pergola walk beside colourful herbaceous border leading to extensive bed of salvias and tender perennials. Unusual climbers grown for summer display. Adjacent nursery open May to Sept. Featured in 'Bristol Evening Post'. RHS Recommended Garden 2007.

  🌳 ✕ ❀

Wander down winding paths to rockery where cypress-like columnars and yuccas lend a Mediterranean air . . .

68 28 KENSINGTON ROAD
St George, Bristol BS5 7NB. Mr Grenville Johnson & Mr Alan Elms, 0117 949 6788, victorianhouse@blueyonder.co.uk. 2^1/$_2$ m E of Bristol City centre. Take A420 in direction of St George towards Kingswood & Chippenham Rd. At Bell Hill St George, turn into Kensington Rd. Entrance to garden in Cromwell Rd at side of house. **Adm £2. By appt only Suns 10, 24 June; 15, 29 July (2-5) and for Evening Openings £3.50, wine, Suns 2, 9 Sept (7-9).**
Award-winning, small courtyard town house garden on 2 decked levels incorporating classical features and statuary. Garden is packed with luscious exotic planting, palms, ferns, topiary and grasses with an accent on pattern, colour, texture and form. Imposing rocky outcrop, dry riverbed path, pond and temple ruin folly all add to the intrigue. Max 5 adults can be accommodated. Finalist Daily Mail National Garden Competition; featured on BBC Gardeners' World and BBC Radio.

  ✕

KIA-ORA FARM & GARDENS
See Devon.

69 KINGSDON NURSERY
Somerton TA11 7LE. Patricia Marrow, 01935 840232. 2m SE of Somerton. Off B3151 Ilchester rd. From Ilchester roundabout on A303 follow NT signs to Lytes Cary; L opp gates, ^{1}/$_2$ m to Kingsdon. Drive through village, nursery signs on L, gate. **Adm £2.50, chd free. Suns 22 Apr; 6 May (2-7).**
2-acre plantsman's garden with lovely plants to see. Large nursery. Selection of trees, shrubs and herbaceous and rock plants for sale. Knowledgeable gardener to help with new or established gardens.

  🌳 ❀

70 NEW KINGSTON
Tockington Green BS32 4LG. John & Carol Phillpott. 2m N of Almondsbury. Off A38. **Adm £1.50, chd free. Sun 17 June (2-6). Also open The Old Bakery (1m).**
Compact courtyard garden with fishpool, village well, trees, shrubs, perennials and bedding.

  ✕

71 KITES CROFT
Westbury-sub-Mendip BA5 1HU. Dr & Mrs W I Stanton, 01749 870328. 5m NW of Wells. On A371 Wells to Cheddar rd, follow signs from Westbury Cross. Home-made teas. **Adm £2.50, chd free. Suns 6 May; 26 Aug (2-5). Visitors also welcome by appt.**
2-acre sloping garden planted for colour throughout season with fine views to Glastonbury Tor. Wander down winding paths to rockery where cypress-like columnars and yuccas lend a Mediterranean air, pass ponds and lawn to densely-planted mixed borders, shrubs and perennials. Fruit trees incl figs, walnut and mulberry. In the wood primroses, bluebells and cyclamen thrive.

  ❀ ☕

72 KNOLL COTTAGE
Stogumber TA4 3TN. Elaine & John Leech, 01984 656689, john@knoll-cottage.co.uk. 3m SE of Williton. From Taunton take A358 towards Minehead. After 11m turn L to Stogumber. In centre of Stogumber, R towards Williton. After ^{1}/$_3$ m, R up narrow lane, follow signs for parking. Home-made teas. **Adm £2.50, chd free. Sun 9 Sept (2-5.30). Visitors also welcome by appt.**
2-acre garden started from fields in 1998. Extensive mixed beds with shrubs, perennials and annuals. Over 80 different roses. Woodland area incl many different rowans, hawthorns and birches. Pond, vegetable and fruit area.

  ❀ 🛏 ☕

73 LABURNUM COTTAGE
Middle Street, Brent Knoll TA9 4BT. Catherine Weber, 01278 760594. 2m N of Highbridge. Off M5 at J22. Follow A38 in Bristol direction for ^{1}/$_2$ m, turn L into Brent Knoll. 1m then R at junction, 1st L into Middle Str. Cream teas. **Adm £2.50, chd free. Sun 8 July (2-5.30). Visitors also welcome by appt July, groups only.**

$1/2$-acre garden, recently developed, to display collection of over 400 varieties of hemerocallis (day lilies) incl many unusual forms and spider types, some for sale. Large, sweeping borders with mixed plantings of shrubs, perennials and many grasses. Registered hemerocallis display garden. Gravel paths.
  & ✗ ⊗ ☕

74 LANGFORD COURT
Langford BS40 5DA. Sir David & Lady Wills. *11$1/2$m S of Bristol. 150yds S of A38 Bristol to Bridgwater rd. 1$1/2$m N of Churchill T-lights. Signed Upper Langford.* Home-made teas. **Adm £3, chd free. Sun 11 Mar (2-5).** 3$1/2$ acres. Lawns and trees, good display of daffodil and crocus. Topiary with Thyme Walk. Pleasant setting and outlook. Water garden and woodland walk.
✗ ⊗ ☕

75 NEW LIFT THE LATCH
Blacklands Lane, Forton, Chard TA20 2NF. Pauline & David Wright. *1$1/2$m S of Chard. Signed in Forton village. Blacklands Lane is off B3162 at E end of Forton. Parking at Alpine Grove Touring Park.* Home-made teas at Forton Football Club. **Adm £2.50, chd free. Suns 20 May; 21 Oct (2-6).** Many different types of colourful shrubs set around pond, alongside pretty stream.
 & ✗ ☕

76 THE LINTELS
Littleton-on-Severn BS35 1NS. Mr & Mrs Ernest Baker. *10m N of Bristol, 3$1/2$m SW of Thornbury. From old Severn Bridge on M48 take B4461 to Alveston. In Elberton, take 1st L to Littleton-on-Severn. 4th house 100yds past Field Lane.* **Adm £2, chd free. Sun 17 June (2-5).** Small cottage-type garden in front of house with good variety of herbaceous plants. Main attraction Japanese garden at rear with waterfall, koi carp, stream, teahouse.

77 LITTLE GARTH
Dowlish Wake TA19 0NX. Roger & Marion Pollard, 01460 52594. *2m S of Ilminster. Turn R off Ilminster to Crewkerne rd at Kingstone Cross, then L, follow Dowlish Wake sign. Turn L at Glebe Cottage (white cottage) before reaching church. Turn R following signs. Speke Hall car park in front of*

nearby church may be used. **Adm £2.50, chd free. Every Thur, 7 June to 30 Aug (10-5.30). Visitors also welcome by appt June, July, Aug, incl coaches and groups.** $1/2$-acre plantsman's garden for all seasons with many interesting and unusual perennials. Although essentially cottage style, emphasis is placed on the artistic arrangement of plants, using foliage, grasses and colour themes.
 & ✗

78 LITTLE YARFORD FARMHOUSE
Yarwood, Kingston St Mary TA2 8AN. Brian Bradley, 01823 451350. *3$1/2$m N of Taunton. On Kingston St Mary rd. At 30mph sign turn L at Parsonage Lane. Continue 1$1/4$m W, to Yarford sign. Continue 400yds. Turn R up concrete rd. Park on L.* Cream teas (except eve). **Adm £3, chd free. Sat, Sun 11, 12 Aug (2-6), Mon 13 Aug (11-6). Evening Opening £7.50, wine, Fri 10 Aug (6-8.30). Visitors also welcome by appt, no large coaches.** Creative landscaping around C17 farmhouse (not open). Interesting specimen trees including pendulous and variegated cultivars, especially beech. 3 adults' ponds, shrubs, climbers, herbaceous and grasses. Music 10 Aug. Some slopes.
 & ✗ ⊗ ☕

LITTLETON DREW GARDENS
See Wiltshire.

79 ♦ LOWER SEVERALLS
Crewkerne TA18 7NX. Mary Pring, 01460 73234, www.lowerseveralls.co.uk. *1$1/2$m NE of Crewkerne. Signed off A30 Crewkerne to Yeovil rd or A356 Crewkerne to A303.* Home-made teas. **Adm £3, chd free. Tues, Weds, Fris, Sats Mar to July & Sept (10-5). For NGS: Sun 29 Apr; Sun 6 May, Sat 12 May; Sun 17 June; Sat 8 Sept. Suns (2-5), Sats (10-5).** 3-acre plantsman's garden beside early Hamstone farmhouse. Herbaceous borders and island beds with collections of unusual plants, shrubs and interesting features incl dogwood basket, wadi, herb garden. Green roofed building. Nursery specialises in herbs, geraniums and salvias. Partial wheelchair access. Featured in RHS handbook.
 & ✗ ⊗ ☕

Japanese garden with waterfall, koi carp, stream and teahouse . . .

80 ♦ LYTES CARY MANOR
Kingsdon TA11 7HU. National Trust, 01458 224471, www.nationaltrust.org.uk. *3m SE of Somerton. Signed from Podimore roundabout at junction of A303, A37, take A372.* **Please phone or visit website for details of dates, times and prices. For NGS: Suns 29 Apr; 7 Oct.** Garden laid out in series of rooms with many contrasts, topiary, mixed borders and herbal border based on famous C16 Lytes Herbal, which can be seen in house.
 & ✗ ⊗ ☕

81 MARSHFIELD GARDENS
Marshfield SN14 8LR. *7m NE of Bath. From Bath A46 to Cold Ashton Roundabout, turn R onto A420. Marshfield 2m. From M4 J18, turn R onto A46 and L at Cold Ashton Roundabout.* Home-made teas at 111 High Street. **Combined adm £3.50, chd free. Sat 2, Sun 3 June (2-6).** 4 gardens in large, interesting village.
☕

43 HIGH STREET
Linda & Denis Beazer. *Entrance from Weir Lane*
Walled garden with terraced potager and companion planting (created 2002) leading to lawned area with shrubs and herbaceous borders and pond.
✗

111 HIGH STREET
Joy & Mervyn Pierce. *Bristol end of village*
Large garden and paddock, split into many areas. Pond, summerhouse, many seating places, vegetable garden, walnut tree planted by owner 47 yrs ago. Quiet, relaxing garden.
 &

NEW MONTAGUE HOUSE
Old School Court. Mr & Mrs
David Dodd. *Opp Weir Cottage*
New garden started in April 2006.
Grass, gravel, flower borders, box
trees, espaliered apple trees and
little lavender walk. Old dry stone
walls form 2 sides. Wonderful view
across fields. Approx 100 sq yds.
🐾

WEIR COTTAGE
Weir Lane. Ian & Margaret
Jones. *Off east end of High St.
Turn R before Old School into
Weir Lane*
Approx 1/4-acre garden divided
into terraces. S-facing, open
aspect. Lawn, borders and
vegetable garden.

THE MEAD NURSERY
See Wiltshire.

Rest in cool summerhouse before returning via damp border and shady bank of ferns, hostas and hellebores . . .

82 MEARE GARDENS
Meare BA6 9TY. *3m W of
Glastonbury. B3151 from Glastonbury
to Wedmore into Meare. New House
on L, parking along St Marys
Rd/Oxenpill. Home-made teas.
Combined adm £3, chd free. Sun 3
June (2-6).*
Meare village has a long history of
farming and drainage with several C14
ecclesiastical buildings.
☕

NEW KNIGHTS COTTAGE
Oxenpill. Mr & Mrs Turner-
Welch. *Continue through village
after leaving The New House.
At L on leaving village*
Cottage garden, mixed plantings.
Water features and courtyard

area. Partial wheelchair access,
some uneven paths.
♿ 🐾

MEAREWAY FARM
3 Meareway. Lee & Emma
Butler. *Continue past The New
House, next R into Meareway. 1st
house on L past new houses.
Minimal parking in Meareway Lane*
Interesting S-facing garden. Mixed
ornamental cottage plantings with
some formality. Unusual plants
and integrated vegetable growing
within ornamental planting
schemes. New children's play area
and willow house.
🐾 ⊛

THE NEW HOUSE
St Mary's Road. Joan & Ashley
Middleton. *Parking in St Mary's
Rd, opp Great House Court Lane*
Cottage garden of approx 1/2 acre.
Attractive landscaping with
interesting plants and shrubs.
Ornamental koi carp pond and
marginal plants.
🐾 ⊛

MELPLASH COURT
See Dorset.

83 ◆ MILTON LODGE
Wells BA5 3AQ. D C Tudway Quilter,
01749 672168,
www.miltonlodgegardens.co.uk.
*1/2 m N of Wells. From A39 Bristol-
Wells, turn N up Old Bristol Rd; car
park first gate on L.* Adm £4, chd
under 14 free. Tues, Weds, Suns &
Bank Hols Easter to 31 Oct (2-5).
For NGS: Suns 20 May; 10 June; 15
July (2-6).
Mature Grade II listed terraced garden
with outstanding views of Wells
Cathedral and Vale of Avalon. Mixed
borders, roses, fine trees. Separate
7-acre arboretum.
🐾 ⊛ ☕

84 ◆ MONTACUTE HOUSE
Montacute TA15 6XP. The National
Trust, 01935 823956,
www.nationaltrust.org.uk. *4m W of
Yeovil. NT signs off A3088 & A303.*
House and Garden Adm £8.80, chd
£4.40, Garden only Adm £5, chd
£2.20. Daily, not Tues, 17 Mar to 28
Oct. For NGS: Sun 24 June (11-5).
Magnificent Elizabethan house with
contemporary garden layout. Fine
stonework provides setting for
informally planted mixed borders and
old roses; range of garden features
illustrates its long history.
♿ 🐾 ⊛

85 NEW MOSS COTTAGE
Halse TA4 3AF. Mr & Mrs D K
Caine, 01823 430909. *6m NW of
Taunton. Off A358 Minehead. Turn
at Bishops Lydeard signed Ash
Priors and Halse (W Somerset
railway). After Ash Priors Common,
keep L into Halse Village (approx
2m from A358).* Cream teas and
light refreshments. Adm £2, chd
free. Weds 18 Apr; 23 May; 20
June; 12 Sept (11-4). Visitors
also welcome by appt Apr/May/
June & Sept only.
1/2-acre rural garden started in
2001. From semi-formal cottage
garden, pass through vine-covered
pergola to herbaceous borders
and vegetable beds. Find the
secret garden with raised fishpond
and white planting. Follow
espaliered apple trees to
shrubbery, geranium bank and
wildlife ponds surrounded by
palms and grasses and rest in cool
summerhouse before returning via
damp border and shady bank of
ferns, hostas and hellebores.
🐾 ⊛ 🛏 ☕

**86 NEW THE MOUNT
SOMERSET HOTEL**
TA3 5NB. *4m SE Taunton. Follow
A358 from Taunton, brown sign
turn R into Stoke Rd, follow to T-
junction, L. Hotel on R.* Cream
teas. Adm £2.50, chd free. Weds
2, 30 May; 11 July; Tue 14, Wed
15 Aug (2-4).
Approx 4 acres. Currently
undergoing restoration and new
planting programme. Country
house, Victorian gardens. Home-
produced preserves available to
purchase.
♿ ☕

NEWTON FARM
See Devon.

87 NORTHFIELD HOUSE
Barton Rd, Barton St David
TA11 6BJ. Mr & Mrs D R Clarke. *4m
E of Somerton. From A37 Lydford
traffic lights take B3153 Somerton rd.
In Keinton Mandeville, turn R into
Barton Rd, 100yds before derestriction
sign. From Somerton take B3153
Castle Cary rd. In Keinton Mandeville,
turn L into Barton Rd, 100yds after
30mph sign. House 250yds on L
immed beyond Barton St David sign.*
Teas. Adm £3, chd free. Sun 17 June
(2-5).

2 acres of semi-formal gardens, orchard and ponds with splendid views over Somerset levels to Glastonbury Tor and Mendips. Main features are rose arbour, nepeta beds and Shona sculptures. Large pond, children should be supervised.
  👩‍🦽 ☕

88 26 NORTHUMBERLAND ROAD
Redland BS6 7BB. Gwendoline Todd. *Bristol. 5 mins walk from Redland stn, close to & parallel with Cranbrook Rd.* Home-made teas at nearby garden. **Adm £2, chd free. Sat 16, Sun 17 June (11-5).**
Fragrant country cottage garden in middle of city with emphasis on scent and yr-round interest. This delightful small garden is packed with a wide range of plants and climbers. Patio is taken over by unusual plants and herbs in pots to provide constantly changing display. Front garden has been planted to give a completely different feel and has a jungle effect.
🎋 ☕

89 NEW THE OLD BAKERY
The Street, Olveston BS35 4DR. Christine Healey. *3m N of Almondsbury, off A38.* Home-made teas. **Adm £1.50, chd free. Sun 17 June (2-6). Also open Kingston (1m).**
Small walled S-facing cottage garden. Good selection of herbaceous plants, small pond for frogs, rose and wisteria arbour. Recently added in 2006 a gravel garden, designed by Carol Klein, containing many new and interesting plants. Featured on BBC2's Open Gardens.
👩‍🦽 🎋 ✿ ☕

THE OLD MALTHOUSE
See Wiltshire.

THE OLD RECTORY, NETHERBURY
See Dorset.

90 2 OLD TARNWELL
Stanton Drew BS39 4EA. Mrs Mary Payne, 01275 333146, maryjpayne@yahoo.co.uk. *6m S of Bristol. Between B3130 & A368 just W of Pensford. Detailed directions will be given when appt is made.* **Adm £3, chd free. Visitors welcome by appt June/July only, max 10 people.**

A quart of good plants poured into a quarter-pint sized plot. Front garden planted in contemporary 'steppe' style in shades of yellow and orange. Back garden more traditional in style with cool shades and abundant clematis. Interesting design details offer plenty of ideas for small gardeners! Regret not suitable for children. Featured in RHS 'The Garden'.
🎋

THE OLD VICARAGE
See Devon.

91 OLIVE COTTAGE
Langley Marsh, Wiveliscombe TA4 2UJ. Mrs Frankie Constantine, 01984 624210. *1m NW of Wiveliscombe. From Taunton take B3227 to Wiveliscombe. Turn R at T-lights. At Square turn R past White Hart & continue 1m. Olive Cottage on R before Three Horseshoes PH.* Home-made teas. **Adm £2, chd free (share to St Margaret's Hospice). Suns 17 June; 19 Aug (2-6). Visitors also welcome by appt.**
An informal cottage garden of about ²/₃ acre created by the owner over 29yrs. Small pond, rockery and bog garden, together with shrubs, perennials, climbers and trees create colour and interest throughout the yr. Productive kitchen garden and 2 greenhouses where many of the plants are raised. Some gravel paths, 2 short slopes.
👩‍🦽 🎋 ✿ ☕

92 OVERBROOK COTTAGE
Lower Cocklake, nr Wedmore BS28 4HF. Margaret & Stanley Castle, 01934 712420, mcastle@cocklake.demon.co.uk. *1m E of Wedmore. Take B3151 from Wedmore towards Cheddar for 1m. Turn R following sign to Draycott & Nyland. Cottage after 3 bungalows on R.* **Adm £2.50, chd free. Every Thur in June (2-5). Visitors also welcome by appt June only for groups of 10-20.**
¹/₁₀-acre cottage garden redesigned in 1997. New features are seating area under the birch and small summerhouse with verandah against east wall. Planting continues to evolve to create an interesting space to explore. Tearooms and inns at Wedmore for refreshment. Plant sales in aid of Greyhound Rescue. Gravel paths. Featured in 'Amateur Gardening'.
👩‍🦽 🎋 ✿

Enjoy your home-made tea among bougainvilleas and other tropical plants in conservatory . . .

OZLEWORTH PARK
See Gloucestershire North & Central.

93 3 PALMER'S WAY
Hutton BS24 9QT. Mary & Peter Beckett, 01934 815110, macbeckett@clara.co.uk. *3m S of Weston-super-Mare. From A370 (N or S) follow signs to Hutton. In village turn L at PO, then 1st L into St Mary's Rd. Car park at St Mary's field, signed, 2 mins walk. From A371 turn R at PO. 1st L off St Mary's Rd and 1st L into Palmer's Way. Very limited disabled parking at garden.* Home-made teas. **Adm £2.50, chd free. Suns 1, 22 July (2-6). Visitors also welcome by appt, Weds in July only.**
Informal tapestry of densely-packed mixed planting with sculptures and found objects from 4 continents. Cottage plants, unusual perennials incl hardy geraniums, euphorbias, ferns, grasses, climbers, fruit and herbs. Knot garden surrounds Minarette fruit trees. Gravel beds. Wildlife ponds. Enjoy your home-made tea among bougainvilleas and other tropical plants in conservatory. Some steps.
👩‍🦽 🎋 ✿ ☕

94 PARK FARM
Alderley GL12 7QT. Mr & Mrs A J V Shepherd, 01453 842123, diana.shepherd@btconnect.com. *1¹/₂m S of Wotton-under-Edge. Just before village.* Home-made teas. **Adm £3, chd free. Sun 2 Sept (2-5). Visitors also welcome by appt.**
The walk with its waterside plants and large koi carp is the pivotal attraction in a scenically designed 2¹/₂-acre garden. Maturing herbaceous borders, young trees and rose garden. Sunken garden.
👩‍🦽 🎋 ✿ ☕

Over 400 different varieties of rose – old, 'new' English and modern . . .

PEMBERLEY LODGE
See Gloucestershire North & Central.

95 PENWOOD FARM
Parchey, Chedzoy TA7 8RW. Mr & Mrs E F W Clapp, 01278 451631. *3¹/₂ m E of Bridgwater. Take A39 from Bridgwater. Bridge over M5, turn sharp R into Chedzoy Lane. At T-junction in village turn L. Pass church approx ³/₄ m. Penwood Farm facing sharp LH-bend. From Stawell off Glastonbury rd, cross bridge over King's Sedgemoor Drain (Parchey River).* 1st house on L. Adm £2.50, chd free (share to Chedzoy Playing Field Association). Sun 17, Mon 18, Sat 23, Sun 24 June (2-5). Visitors also welcome by appt June & July only, coaches permitted.
Plant lover's garden of approx ³/₄ acre. Terrace, patio, pergola, gravel, rock, water and kitchen gardens. Over 400 different varieties of rose - old, 'new' English and modern; collections of clematis, hosta, penstemon, shrubs and herbaceous perennials, many unusual plants and trees. Koi carp pond with Japanese-style bridge.

PIKES COTTAGE
See Devon.

96 ◆ PRIOR PARK LANDSCAPE GARDEN
Ralph Allen Drive, Bath BA2 5AH. The National Trust, 01225 833922, www.nationaltrust.org.uk. *4m S of Bath. Visitors are advised to use public transport as there is no parking at Prior Park or nearby, except for disabled visitors. Telephone 01225 833422 for 'How to get there' leaflet.* Adm £4.80, chd £2.70. Daily, not Tues, 3 Mar to 28 Oct (11-5.30). Sats, Suns 3 Nov to 24 Feb 2008 (11-dusk). For NGS: Sun 10 June (11-5.30).
Beautiful and intimate C18 landscape garden created by Bath entrepreneur Ralph Allen (1693-1764) with advice from the poet Alexander Pope and Capability Brown. Sweeping valley with magnificent views of the city, Palladian bridge and lakes. The Wilderness Project, supported by the Heritage Lottery Fund, is in the final stage of restoration.

97 18 QUEENS GATE
Stoke Bishop BS9 1TZ. Sheila & Eric White, 0117 962 6066. *3m NW of Bristol. From M5 J17, follow A4018 (Bristol West) to Westbury-on-Trym. At village centre join Stoke Lane, go over T-lights, past shops to T-junction. Turn R for 500yds then L at mini-roundabout & immed R into Druid Stoke Ave. Access lane on R between 20 & 22. No parking/access via Queens Gate.* Home-made teas. Adm £2.50, chd free. Suns 13 May (2-6); 7 Oct (2-5). Visitors also welcome by appt all yr, groups welcome, teas by prior arrangement.
All-yr garden with adjoining woodland garden. Various design features and numerous unusual plants, grasses and containers. The borders are colour themed and there is a pergola and a small Japanese garden. Gravel area and alterations to other areas for ease of maintenance. Opening for autumn colour and grasses.

98 RACKLEY HOUSE
Rackley Lane, Compton Bishop BS26 2HJ. R & J Matthews, 01934 732311. *2m W of Axbridge. SE Weston-super-Mare. Leave A38 at Cross & take rd to Loxton, Bleadon. Rackley Lane approx 1¹/₂ m from Cross; Rackley House is only house on RH-side at end of lane.* Teas May, cream teas June only. Adm £2.50, chd free. Weds 9, 16, 23 May; Sat 9, Sun 10 June (2-6). Visitors also welcome by appt.
¹/₂-acre garden on S-facing slope with light alkaline soil. Features incl iris garden, rockery and scree, small knot garden, pond and terrace. Some unusual plants and variety of cyclamen, old-fashioned roses and penstemons. Fairly steep slopes, ramps provided for some steps. Help available if required.

REGENCY HOUSE
See Devon.

RIDLEYS CHEER
See Wiltshire.

THE RIVER HOUSE
See Wiltshire.

99 ROCK HOUSE
Elberton BS35 4AQ. Mr & Mrs John Gunnery, 01454 413225. *10m N of Bristol. 3¹/₂ m SW Thornbury. From Old Severn Bridge on M48 take B4461 to Alveston. In Elberton, take 1st turning L to Littleton-on-Severn & turn immed R.* Adm £2, chd free (share to St John's Church). Suns 4 Feb (11-4) for snowdrops; 15 Apr (2-6). Visitors also welcome by appt.
1-acre walled garden undergoing improvement. Pond and old yew tree, mixed borders, cottage garden plants and developing woodland.

100 ROOK FARM
Chapel Road, Oldbury-on-Severn BS35 1PL. Eileen Mantell & Richard Bennett. *3m W of Thornbury. From A38 and B4061 follow Oldbury Power Stn signs into Butt Lane. Oldbury Village signs to Chapel Rd.* Home-made teas. Adm £3, chd free. Sun 5 Aug (1-5).
Country garden with unusual trees. 2 well-stocked wildlife ponds. Productive vegetable and fruit garden. Gravel garden and perennial borders. Developing woodland area with stumpery.

101 SALTFORD FARM BARN
565a Bath Road, Saltford BS31 3JS. Eve Hessey, 01225 873380, eve.hessey@blueyonder.co.uk. *6m W of Bath. On A4 between Bath & Bristol, Saltford Farm Barn is 1st house on R as you enter village from Bath or last house on L as you leave village from Bristol. Parking arrangements will be signed - busy A4 not suitable for parking.* Home-made teas. Adm £3, chd free. Sat 31 Mar (2-5); Sun 24 June (11-5). Evening Opening £3.50, wine, Sat 23 June (6-8.30). Visitors also welcome by appt.
1-acre garden with 5 main separate gardens. Ornamental vegetable garden with trained fruit trees contained within scented hedges of lavender, rosemary and box. Woodland garden with seasonal shrubs and trees underplanted with spring bulbs, hellebores, ferns, foxgloves and alpine strawberries. Garden of reflection depicting owner's life in New Zealand and England, labyrinth, meadow and orchard. Handmade crafts for sale.

102 NEW SERRIDGE HOUSE
Henfield Road, Coalpit Heath
BS36 2UY. Mrs J Manning,
01454 773188. *9m N of Bristol.
On A432 at Coalpit Heath T-lights
(opp church), turn into Henfield Rd.
R at PH, 1/2 m small Xrds, house
with iron gates on corner.* **Adm £4
incl tea and cake, chd free.
Visitors welcome by appt
July/Aug only, groups of 10+.**
21/2-acre garden with mature trees,
heather and conifer beds, island
beds mostly of perennials,
woodland area with pond.

Garden of reflection depicting owner's life in New Zealand and England . . .

103 ◆ SHERBORNE GARDEN
Litton BA3 4PP. Mr & Mrs John
Southwell, 01761 241220. *15m S of
Bristol. 15m W of Bath, 7m N of Wells.
On B3114 Litton to Harptree rd, 1/2 m
past The Kings Arms. Car park in field.*
**Adm £3, chd free. Suns/Mons June-
Sept, other days by appt.** For NGS:
Daily Sat 10 Feb to Wed 14 Feb
(10.30-3.30) for snowdrops and
hellebores; Sun 3 June (11-5).
41/2-acre gently sloping garden of
considerable horticultural interest.
Small pinetum, giant grasses area,
woodland garden and 3 linked ponds
with bridges. Collections of hollies
(100), ferns (250), Asian wild roses with
hybrids and climbing species, all well
labelled, hemerocallis, water lilies and
unusual trees and shrubs. Picnic area.
&

**SNAPE COTTAGE PLANTSMAN'S
GARDEN**
See Dorset.

104 SOUTH MEADE
Meade Lane, Seavington St Mary
TA19 0QL. Charo & Robin Ritchie.
*3m E of Ilminster. Via old 303 to
Seavington St Michael, down Water
Str to Seavington Millennium Village
Hall and follow signs after parking as
indicated.* **Home-made teas 9/10 June
(2-6). Adm £2.50, chd free. Fri to Sun
8, 9, 10 June (11-7).**
Garden was started a few yrs ago.
Large variation of plants and shrubs
incl over 60 clematis mixed through the
English, Mediterranean and Japanese
areas. Water feature. Local watercolour
artist exhibiting.

105 ◆ SPECIAL PLANTS
Nr Cold Ashton SN14 8LA. Derry
Watkins, 01225 891686,
www.specialplants.net. *6m N of Bath
on A46. From Bath on A46, turn L into
Greenways Lane just before
roundabout with A420.* **Adm £3, chd
free. Weds July & Aug (11-5).** For
NGS: Thurs 21 June; 19 July; 16
Aug; 20 Sept (11-5).
Architect-designed 3/4-acre hillside
garden with stunning views. Started
autumn 1996. Exotic plants, many
collected in S Africa. Gravel gardens
for borderline hardy plants. Black and
white (purple and silver) garden.
Vegetable garden and orchard. Hot
border. Lemon and lime bank. Annual,
biennial and tender plants for late
summer colour. Spring-fed pond. Bog
garden. Woodland walk. New allium
alley. Adjoining nursery, open Mar
through Oct. Featured on Radio 4
Woman's Hour, Black & White
Gardening.

106 STOGUMBER GARDENS
TA4 3TH. *11m NW of Taunton. On
A358. Sign to Stogumber, W of
Crowcombe. Cream teas at village hall.*
**Combined adm £3, chd free. Sun 24
June (2-6).**
Six delightful gardens of interest to
plantsmen in lovely village at edge of
Quantocks.
☕

BROOK HOUSE
Brook Street. Dr & Mrs J
Secker-Walker
Enclosed partially-walled garden,
redesigned over last 3 yrs.
Terraced patio area, lawn, mixed
borders leading to small bog
garden by brook and meadow with
recently-restored wildlife pond.

BUTTS COTTAGE
Mr & Mrs J A Morrison
Cottage garden with old roses, old-
fashioned perennials, alpines,
pond, small vine house and
organic fruit and vegetable garden.

CRIDLANDS STEEP
Mrs A M Leitch
Large and interesting garden with
collection of trees and wildlife
pond.
⊛

KNOLL COTTAGE
Elaine & John Leech
(See separate entry).
⊨

**NEW MEADOWSWEET
COTTAGE**
4 Hill Street. Mr & Mrs D Illman
Partly walled garden of just under
1/2 acre developed over last 4 yrs.
Mixed perennial and shrub garden
divided into areas by rose and
clematis trellising, with fruit and
vegetable garden at bottom.

POUND HOUSE
Mr & Mrs B Hibbert. *Opp car park*
Old orchard on terraced sloping
site, garden started 2000. Young
trees, shrub borders, herbaceous
plants, rockery, organic vegetable
garden and courtyard with climbing
plants and herbs.

107 STOKE ST MARY GARDENS
TA3 5BY. *21/2 m SE of Taunton. From
M5 J25 take A358 S towards Ilminster.
Turn 1st R after 11/2 m. 1st R in
Henlade then 1st L signed Stoke St
Mary. Car parking in field on S side of
village, no parking at either garden.*
Home-made teas at Tuckers
Farmhouse. **Combined adm £3, chd
free. Sun 27 May (2-5).**
Village nestles below beautiful
backdrop of Stoke Hill. The 2 gardens
lie between C13 church (with stained
glass windows by the renowned
Patrick Reyntiens) and popular Half
Moon Inn. Playground at nearby Village
Hall for parents with young children.
Both gardens incl wildlife areas and
Somerset Wildlife Trust will have a stall
at Tuckers Farmhouse. Village events
will be held incl craft stalls at Village
Hall and art exhibition at Fyrse
Cottage. Featured in 'Gardeners'
World', 'Somerset Life' and local press.
☕

FYRSE COTTAGE
Miss S Crockett
1/2-acre cottage garden with oriental flavour started in 2003. Pond and stream, pergola, informal planting and birch avenue leading to 1/2-acre field with mixed native trees.

TUCKERS FARMHOUSE
Rebecca Pow & Charles Clark, 01823 443816, rebecca@powproductions.tv. **Visitors also welcome by appt.** Family garden in lovely rural location. Formal/cottage-style extending to natural with wildlife. Jekyll-style border and 'busy persons' gravel/grass border. Topiary, exotic planting in courtyard and pear tree avenue. Camassias/alliums in May. Kids cricket pitch. Fruit garden and raised bed vegetable garden developed for TV Roots and Shoots series. Gravel & Jekyll borders devised for BBC 'Gardeners' World' magazine and vegetable garden for 'Kitchen Garden' magazine.

&. ⊕

STOURHEAD GARDEN
See Wiltshire.

108 STOWLEYS
Bossington Lane, Porlock TA24 8HD. Rev R L Hancock. *NE of Porlock. Off A39. 6m W of Minehead.* Cream teas. **Adm £2, chd free. Sats 31 Mar; 16 June (2-6).** Medium-sized garden, approx 2 acres with magnificent views across Porlock Bay and Bristol Channel. Daffodils, roses, unusual tender plants incl leptospermum, drimys and embothrium. Watchet Town Band & plant sale 16 June. Gravel paths.

&. ⊕ ☕

109 SUNNYSIDE
Yarley Hill, Yarley BA5 1PA. Nigel Cox & Patsy Koeb, 01749 674905, nigel.cox16@btinternet.com. *3m W of Wells. 2m along B3139 Wedmore Rd. After Pheasant Inn at Wookey reach village sign for Yarley. 100yds beyond, turn L up Yarley Hill, house 200yds on L.* **Visitors welcome by appt May to July only.** 1/2-acre cottage garden with large variety of plants, some rare. Collection of subtropical plants, incl bananas, cannas, hedychium, summer-flowering bulbs and many varieties of salvia. Featured in 'Amateur Gardening'.

※ ⊕

110 SUTTON HOSEY MANOR
Long Sutton TA10 9NA. Roger Bramble. *2m E of Langport, on A372. Gates N of A372 at E end of Long Sutton.* Home-made teas. **Adm £3, chd £2. Sun 22 July (2.30-6).** 3 acres, of which 2 walled. Lily canal through pleached limes leading to amelanchier walk past duck pond; rose and juniper walk from Italian terrace; Judas tree avenue; *Ptelea* walk. Ornamental potager. Drive-side shrubbery. Music by players from Sinfonia of Westminster.

&. ※ ⊕ ☕

111 ◆ TINTINHULL
nr Yeovil BA22 8PZ. The National Trust, 01935 823956, www.nationaltrust.org.uk. *5m NW of Yeovil. Tintinhull village. Signs on A303, W of Ilchester.* **Adm (please phone or visit website for details). Weds to Suns, 17 Mar to 28 Oct.** For NGS: **Sun 15 July (11-5).** C17 and C18 house (not open). Famous 2-acre garden in compartments, developed 1900 to present day, influenced by Hidcote; many good and uncommon plants.

&. ※ ⊕ ☕

Village events including craft stalls and art exhibition . . .

112 TRANBY HOUSE
Norton Lane, Whitchurch BS14 0BT. Jan Barkworth. *5m S of Bristol. 1/2 m S of Whitchurch. Leave Bristol on A37 Wells Rd, through Whitchurch village, 1st turning on R signed Norton Malreward.* Home-made teas. **Adm £2.50, chd free. Suns 8 July; 12 Aug (2-5).** 1 1/4-acre informal garden, designed and planted to encourage wildlife. Wide variety of trees, shrubs and flowers; ponds and wild flower meadow.

※ ⊕ ☕

113 NEW TRISCOMBE NURSERIES
West Bagborough TA4 3HG. Stuart Parkman. *8m Taunton, 15m Minehead. On A358, signed between villages of W Bagborough and Crowcombe.* Teas at Triscombe Stables. **Adm £2.50, chd free. Suns 3 June; 28 Oct (2-5.30).** Private arboretum planted since 1986 in lovely location overlooking fields up to the Quantocks (SSSI). Acers, Japanese azaleas, oak, coccinea splendens, conifers. Parrotia, cornus chinensis and more, underplanted incl cowslips. Featured in 'Wiltshire Guardian'.

※ ⊕ ☕

114 8 TROSSACHS DRIVE
Bathampton BA2 6RP. Sheila Batterbury, 01225 447864, http://bathampton.net/home/sheilabatterburysgarden.htm. *1m E of Bath. On A36. From Bath, 2nd R up Warminster Rd (A36) into Trossachs Drive. From Warminster, 3rd L on entering Bathampton.* **Visitors welcome by appt (except winter) for individuals and groups of 10+.** Terraced garden with views over Bath. Winding paths, ponds and waterfalls. Unusual plants and shrubs, rockeries, bog garden, herbaceous perennials, old roses, sitting areas with fine views over the countryside. An interesting garden with the benefit of National Trust woods as backdrop. A haven for wildlife. A plantswoman's garden. Featured in 6 national newspapers and on BBC4, HTV and Belfast radio. Slopes through terraces.

&. ※ ⊕

115 NEW ◆ TYNTESFIELD
Wraxall BS48 1NT. The National Trust, 01275 461900, www.nationaltrust.org.uk. *7m SW of Bristol. Nr Nailsea, entrance off B3128. Follow AA signs.* **House and garden adm £9.90, chd £5, garden only adm £5, chd £2.50. Sats to Weds, 17 Mar to 4 Nov (10.30-5, last adm 4).** For NGS: **Tues 24 Apr; 7 Aug (10.30-4).** Acquired by National Trust in 2002. Currently undergoing a conservation project, the estate is open with temporary facilities. Formal terraces frame the house, then walk along the Holly Walk to the arboretum, known as 'Paradise'. The walled working kitchen garden produces vegetables, fruit and flowers for the estate. Guided walks by gardeners, call 01275 461900 for details. Gravel paths. 1km walk from car park to house.

&. ※ ⊕ ☕

Elizabethan manor mentioned in C17 for its 'fair and pleasant garden' . . .

116 UBLEY HILL FARM HOUSE
Ubley Drove, Blagdon BS40 7XN.
Peter Gilraine, 01761 462663. *2m SE of Blagdon. From A38 (20m S of Bristol) at Churchill traffic lights, turn L onto A368 to Blagdon, 2m turn R onto B3134 (Burrington Combe), proceed to top of hill, 3m. Ubley Drove on L. ¹/₂m down this no-through-rd, garden at end on R.* Home-made teas. **Adm £3, chd free. Visitors welcome by appt May to Sept incl.**
1-acre garden set in secluded spot on top of Mendips with far-reaching views over Severn Estuary and Chew Valley. Sheltered S-facing lawn with herbaceous borders, raised flower beds and bog garden. Sit awhile in our courtyard garden and take in the almost subtropical splendour before climbing terraced rockeries to view wildlife pond and waterfall. Wild flower meadows and mass blooming of orchids in June. A plantsman's delight. Resident artist's studio, fine art, photography and illustration.

117 ◆ UNIVERSITY OF BRISTOL BOTANIC GARDEN
BS9 1JB. 01173 314912, botanic-garden@bristol.ac.uk. *¹/₂m W of Durdham Down. By car from city centre, proceed across Downs towards Stoke Bishop, crossing T-lights at edge of Downs. Stoke Park Rd, 1st turning R off Stoke Hill. Parking opp in Churchill Hall Car Park.* **Adm £4.50, chd free. For NGS: Sun 9 Sept (2-5).**
New Botanic Garden being developed with organic flowing network of paths which lead visitors through collections of Mediterranean flora, rare natives, useful plants (incl European and Chinese herbs) and those that illustrate plant evolution. New Angiosperm Phyllogeny display illustrates latest understanding of flowering plant relationships. First new University Botanic Garden to be developed in the UK for 30 yrs. Tours of garden at 2.15 and 2.45. Plant auction at 4pm. Winner of SW Britain in Bloom 'Best New Initiative Project for 2006'.

118 VELLACOTT
Lawford, Crowcombe TA4 4AL.
Kevin & Pat Chittenden, 01984 618249. *9m NW of Taunton. Off A358, signed Lawford.* Home-made teas. **Adm £2.50, chd free. Sun 27 May; Sun 3, Wed 6 June (12-5). Visitors also welcome by appt incl coaches.**
1-acre cottage garden with splendid views. Mixed herbaceous and shrub borders, grasses, alpines and ponds. A collection of trees, mainly betula and sorbus grown for bark and berries. Ornamental vegetable garden and other interesting features.

119 WATCOMBE
92 Church Road, Winscombe BS25 1BP. Peter & Ann Owen, 01934 842666. *2m NW of Axbridge. From Axbridge, A371 to A38 N. Turn R up hill then next L into Winscombe Hill. After 1m reach The Square. Pink house on L after further 150yds down hill.* Cream teas May, home-made teas June. **Adm £2.50, chd free. Sun 27 May; Wed 6 June (2-6). Visitors also welcome by appt.**
³/₄-acre mature Italianate garden with colour-themed, informally planted mixed borders. Topiary, box hedging, lime walk, pleached hornbeams, orchard, vegetable plot, 2 small formal ponds, many unusual trees and shrubs.
   🚾 🎔 ☕

WATERDALE HOUSE
See Wiltshire.

120 WAYFORD MANOR
Crewkerne TA18 8QG. Mr & Mrs Robin Goffe, 01460 73253, robingoffe@btinternet.com. *3m SW of Crewkerne. Turning N off B3165 at Clapton; or S off A30 Chard to Crewkerne rd.* Cream teas. **Adm £3, chd £1. Suns 1, 22 Apr; Sun 6, Mon 7, Sun 27 May; Sun 10 June (2-5). Visitors also welcome by appt.**
The mainly Elizabethan manor (not open) mentioned in C17 for its 'fair and pleasant' garden was redesigned by Harold Peto in 1902. Formal terraces

with yew hedges and topiary have fine views over W Dorset. Steps down between spring-fed ponds pass mature and new plantings of magnolia, rhododendron, maples, cornus and, in season, spring bulbs, cyclamen, giant echium. Primula candelaria, arum lily, gunnera around lower ponds. Featured in RHS 'The Garden' calendar.
   🎔 ☕

121 WELLFIELD BARN
Wells BA5 3AG. David & Virginia Nasmyth, 01749 675129. *¹/₂m N of Wells. From A39 Bristol to Wells rd turn R at 30mph sign into Walcombe Lane. Entrance at 1st cottage on R, parking signed.* **Adm £2.50, chd free. Wed 30 May (11-6). Visitors also welcome by appt, coaches permitted (max 29 seater).**
1¹/₂-acre gardens, made by owners over the past 10yrs from concrete farmyard. Ha-ha, wonderful views, pond, lawn, mixed borders, grass walks and interesting young trees. Structured design integrates house with landscape. New areas under development. Moderate slopes.

122 NEW WEST LITTLETON GARDENS
SN14 8JE. *8m N of Bath. M4 J18, take A46 S to Bath. Sign to West Littleton 1m after J18. From Bath take turning after Dyrham Park. 1m to village. Parking signed. Alternative parking for Cadwell Hill Barn 600yds on far side of village.* **Combined adm £3, chd free. Evening Opening, wine, Wed 20 June (4-8).**
Attractive Cotswold stone village surrounded by farmland. 2 dozen houses and 2 working farms on by-road just within Badminton Estate. Tiny church with one of only two bell towers of the kind in England.

NEW CADWELL HILL BARN
Mr & Mrs J Edwards. *¹/₃m beyond village on Marshfield side* Created from barren fields with a need for windbreaks. Imaginative use of architectural trees and shrubs forms a series of intricate small enclosures and walkways incl pleached lime walk. Some gravel paths.
   🚾 🎔

LITTLETON HOUSE
Mr Christopher Bell
Structured herbaceous borders and less formal beds. Roses a speciality incl climbers on arches. Old farm buildings and dry stone walls provide architectural backdrop.
&

NEW ST JAMES'S GRANGE
Mr & Mrs David Adams, www.stjamesgrange.com. *On R just past red phone box at top of village green*
In delightful setting overlooking unusual C13 church spire. Dry stone walls support pleached lime terracing and courtyard's raised mixed borders and enclose kitchen garden. Trees, shrubs, lavender beds, rose pergola, parterre, box hedging and water. A garden with French overtones. Gravel paths.
&

123 NEW WESTBROOK HOUSE
West Bradley BA6 8LS. Keith Anderson. *4m E of Glastonbury. From A361 at W Pennard follow signs to W Bradley (2m).* **Adm £3, chd free. Sun 29 Apr (11-5).**
1½ acres formal gardens with mixed borders planted in last 3 yrs; newly-planted orchard with spring bulbs and wild flowers.
&

WESTON HOUSE
See Dorset.

A garden with French overtones . . .

124 NEW WYNDHAM ESTATE GARDENS
Williton TA4 4HH. *7m SE of Minehead, 1½m S of Williton, opp agricultural machines showroom (signed St Peter's & Bakelite Museum). Follow narrow lane, past tiny St Peter's Church to lodge (Estate Office) & through white iron gates. No coaches.* Home-made teas at Aller Farmhouse.
Combined adm £4, chd free. Sun 3 June (2-6).

NEW ALLER FARMHOUSE
Mr Richard Chandler, 01984 633702. Visitors also welcome by appt May/June only for groups of 10-25. No coaches.
2-3 acres. Hot, dry, sunny, S-facing, surrounded by pink stone walls and sub-divided into separate compartments by same. 'Cliff Garden' is old 3-sided quarry. Old magnolias, figs, Judas, etc; newer acacias; many unusual and/or tender

plants. Garden now 14yrs old in present form. Take care, slippery paths if wet, some steep slopes.

ORCHARD WYNDHAM
William Wyndham & The Trustees
Garden of historic house (not open) in parkland setting: woods, interesting old trees, borders, bulbs, rose walk, small lake, wild garden.

125 YEWS FARM
East Street, Martock TA12 6NF. Louise & Fergus Dowding, 01935 822202. *Turn off main str through village at Market House, onto East St, past PO, garden 150yds on R.* **Adm £3.50, chd free. Visitors welcome by appt late June/July for groups of 15+.**
1 acre of theatrical planting in walled gardens. Sculptural combinations of shape, leaf and texture. Tall plants and strange seedheads. 12ft high echium in

jungle garden. Working organic vegetable garden feeds growing family. Pigs and hens in our farmyard are our living compost heap. Featured in 'Country Homes and Interiors'.

126 ZOOL HOUSE
8 Steel Lane, Catcott TA7 9HP. Les Durston, 01278 722267, leslie@ldurston.wanadoo.co.uk. *8m NE of Bridgwater. For parking, see Catcott Gardens details. For parking at other times, please contact direct.* Home-made teas. **Adm £4, chd free. Suns 5 Aug, 19 Aug (2-6). Open with Catcott Gardens 15 Apr, 6 May, 3 June. Visitors also welcome by appt 1 May to 19 Aug.**
³/₄-acre garden, established from an old orchard (previously quarried) containing shrubs, bulbs and herbaceous planting, together with summer bedding. This garden is continually evolving with new plantings and other mature items being removed.

Sculptural combinations of shape, leaf and texture. Tall plants and strange seedheads . . .

Bristol Area County Volunteers

Somerset County Volunteers

STAFFORDSHIRE

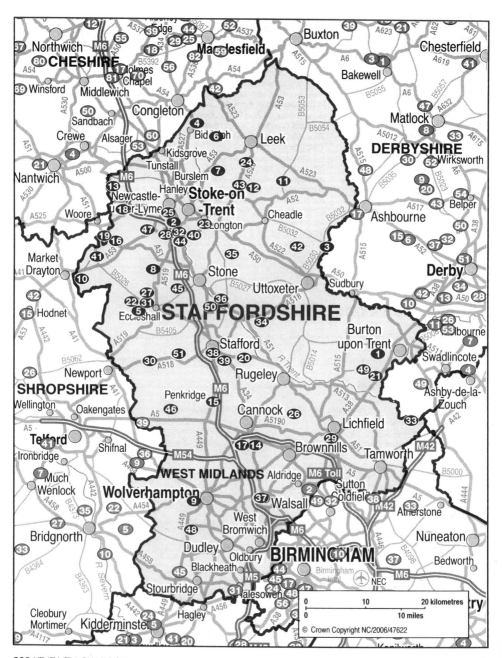

Opening Dates

February

MONDAY 19
42 Stonehill Quarry Garden

MONDAY 26
42 Stonehill Quarry Garden

March

MONDAY 5
42 Stonehill Quarry Garden

MONDAY 12
42 Stonehill Quarry Garden

SUNDAY 18
42 Stonehill Quarry Garden

MONDAY 19
42 Stonehill Quarry Garden

SUNDAY 25
38 23 St Johns Road

April

SUNDAY 1
19 Field House Farm

SUNDAY 8
41 Smithy Cottage

SATURDAY 14
29 Millennium Garden

MONDAY 16
42 Stonehill Quarry Garden

MONDAY 23
42 Stonehill Quarry Garden

FRIDAY 27
50 Yarlet House

MONDAY 30
42 Stonehill Quarry Garden

May

THURSDAY 3
41 Smithy Cottage

FRIDAY 4
38 23 St Johns Road

SUNDAY 6
18 10 Fern Dene
51 Yew Tree Cottage

THURSDAY 10
41 Smithy Cottage

SUNDAY 13
22 Heath House

WEDNESDAY 16
1 Bankcroft Farm

THURSDAY 17
41 Smithy Cottage

FRIDAY 18
23 High Trees

SUNDAY 20
2 Barn House
3 The Beeches
17 Dorset House

WEDNESDAY 23
1 Bankcroft Farm

THURSDAY 24
41 Smithy Cottage

SATURDAY 26
32 The Old Dairy House

SUNDAY 27
32 The Old Dairy House
36 Romer Farm
40 Silverwood
51 Yew Tree Cottage

MONDAY 28
23 High Trees
36 Romer Farm

TUESDAY 29
12 Consall Hall Landscape Garden

WEDNESDAY 30
1 Bankcroft Farm

THURSDAY 31
41 Smithy Cottage
48 The Wombourne Wodehouse

June

SATURDAY 2
18 10 Fern Dene
43 Tanglewood Cottage

SUNDAY 3
5 Birch Trees
13 Courtwood House
20 The Garth
43 Tanglewood Cottage

THURSDAY 7
41 Smithy Cottage

FRIDAY 8
38 23 St Johns Road

SATURDAY 9
45 Victoria Cottage

SUNDAY 10
45 Victoria Cottage

WEDNESDAY 13
1 Bankcroft Farm

THURSDAY 14
41 Smithy Cottage

FRIDAY 15
36 Romer Farm (Day & Evening)

SATURDAY 16
27 Lower House

SUNDAY 17
4 Biddulph Grange Garden
19 Field House Farm

22 Heath House
23 High Trees
27 Lower House
39 Shepherds Fold Gardens

MONDAY 18
37 15 St Johns Road (Evening)

WEDNESDAY 20
1 Bankcroft Farm

THURSDAY 21
41 Smithy Cottage

SATURDAY 23
10 1 The Brodder
11 37 Brookfields Road
29 Millennium Garden

SUNDAY 24
3 The Beeches
8 The Bowers
9 43 Broad Lane
11 37 Brookfields Road
20 The Garth
21 Grafton Cottage
29 Millennium Garden
47 Wilkins Pleck
49 Woodside House

WEDNESDAY 27
1 Bankcroft Farm

THURSDAY 28
41 Smithy Cottage

FRIDAY 29
50 Yarlet House

SATURDAY 30
24 The Hollies

July

SUNDAY 1
6 Blackwood House Farm
21 Grafton Cottage
24 The Hollies
26 Lilac Cottage
30 The Mount

THURSDAY 5
41 Smithy Cottage

SUNDAY 8
7 Bleak House
23 High Trees
46 The Wickets

THURSDAY 12
41 Smithy Cottage

SATURDAY 14
5 Birch Trees
9 43 Broad Lane
34 The Old School House

SUNDAY 15
15 4 Dene Close
17 Dorset House
34 The Old School House

49 Woodside House

THURSDAY 19
41 Smithy Cottage

SATURDAY 21
36 Romer Farm

SUNDAY 22
7 Bleak House (Evening)
8 The Bowers
22 Heath House
36 Romer Farm

THURSDAY 26
41 Smithy Cottage

SUNDAY 29
2 Barn House (Evening)
3 The Beeches
25 6 Kendal Place
26 Lilac Cottage
47 Wilkins Pleck

August
THURSDAY 2
41 Smithy Cottage

SATURDAY 4
9 43 Broad Lane (Evening)
35 The Old Vicarage

SUNDAY 5
21 Grafton Cottage
23 High Trees
28 Manor Cottage Garden
35 The Old Vicarage
37 15 St Johns Road
49 Woodside House

THURSDAY 9
41 Smithy Cottage

TUESDAY 14
16 Dorothy Clive Garden

THURSDAY 16
41 Smithy Cottage

SATURDAY 18
9 43 Broad Lane (Evening)
14 12 Darges Lane (Evening)

TUESDAY 21
16 Dorothy Clive Garden

THURSDAY 23
41 Smithy Cottage

SUNDAY 26
5 Birch Trees
31 Muirfield
51 Yew Tree Cottage

MONDAY 27
5 Birch Trees
31 Muirfield

THURSDAY 30
41 Smithy Cottage

September
SATURDAY 1
24 The Hollies

SUNDAY 2
6 Blackwood House Farm
24 The Hollies
33 The Old Rectory, Clifton
Campville

THURSDAY 6
41 Smithy Cottage

SUNDAY 9
10 1 The Brodder

THURSDAY 13
41 Smithy Cottage

FRIDAY 14
38 23 St Johns Road

SUNDAY 16
4 Biddulph Grange Garden

THURSDAY 20
41 Smithy Cottage

THURSDAY 27
41 Smithy Cottage

October
MONDAY 22
42 Stonehill Quarry Garden

MONDAY 29
42 Stonehill Quarry Garden

November
MONDAY 5
42 Stonehill Quarry Garden

Private gardens opening regularly for the NGS
41 Smithy Cottage

Gardens open to the public
4 Biddulph Grange Garden
12 Consall Hall Landscape Garden
16 Dorothy Clive Garden
44 Trentham

The Gardens

1 **BANKCROFT FARM**
Tatenhill DE13 9SA. Mrs Penelope
Adkins. *2m SW of Burton-on-Trent.
Branston Rd. Take Tatenhill Rd off A38
Burton-Branston flyover. 1m, 1st house
on L approaching village. Parking on
farm.* **Adm £2, chd free. Weds, 16,
23, 30 May; 13, 20, 27 June (2-5).**
Lose yourself for an afternoon in our
1½ acre organic country garden.
Arbour, gazebo and many other
seating areas to view ponds and
herbaceous borders, backed with
shrubs and trees with emphasis on
structure, foliage and colour.

Productive fruit and vegetable gardens,
wildlife areas and adjoining 12 acre
native woodland walk. Picnics
welcome. Gold Medal for vegetable &
rear garden. Winner Best Wildlife Pond
- Brighter Borough competition.
🏃 ⊗ ☕

2 **BARN HOUSE**
Clayton Road, Newcastle-u-Lyme
ST5 4AB. Mike & Catherine French,
01782 636650,
frenchmike@talk21.com. *1m S of
Newcastle. ½m from exit 15 M6. L to
A519 Clayton Rd to Newcastle.
Straight over next roundabout. Barn
House is on L after 80yds before
pedestrian crossing lights. 1¼m from
Newcastle town centre S towards M6,
pass the Nuffield Hospital, Barn House
is 80yds on the R after pedestrian
crossing lights up drive. Parking
available on Sundays at the Nuffield
Hospital. Teas.* **Adm £2.50, chd free.
Sun 20 May (2-5); Evening
Opening £3.50, wine & light
refreshments, Sun 29 July (5-9).
Visitors also welcome by appt for
groups of 10+.**
Beautiful landscaped ¾-acre garden
created by a surgeon whilst on call for
kidney transplantation. 3 ponds linked
by waterfalls and camellia walk make
this an oasis of peace in suburbia.
'Secret' garden with rockeries and
mature specimen trees and shrubs
with a potager/market garden to boot.
Easy maintenance garden.
🏃 ⊗ ☕

3 **THE BEECHES**
Mill Street, Rocester ST14 5JX. Mr &
Mrs K Sutton, 01889 590631,
joy@joy50.orangehome.co.uk. *5m N
of Uttoxeter. On B5030, turn R into
village by JCB factory. By Red Lion PH
take rd for Marston Montgomery.
Garden 250yds on R. Home-made
teas.* **Adm £2.50, chd free. Suns 20
May; 24 June; 29 July (1.30-5).
Visitors also welcome by appt May
to July, groups of 10+.**
Stunning plant lover's garden of approx
⅔ acre, enjoying views of surrounding
countryside. Formal box garden,
vibrant colour-themed herbaceous
borders, containing many unusual
varieties, shrubs incl rhododendrons,
azaleas (looking good in May), pools,
roses, fruit trees, clematis and climbing
plants yr-round garden. Cottage
garden planting with a secret round
every corner. Gold Prize winner - East
Staffordshire Brighter Borough.
♿ 🏃 ⊗ ☕

4 ♦ **BIDDULPH GRANGE GARDEN**

Grange Road, Biddulph ST8 7SD. The National Trust, 01782 517999, www.nationaltrust.org.uk. *3¹/₂m SE of Congleton. 7m N of Stoke-on-Trent off the A527. Congleton to Biddulph rd.* **Adm £5.40, chd £2.70. Wed to Sun 17 Mar to 28 Oct, incl Bank Hol Mon.** For NGS: Suns 17 June; 16 Sept (11.30-5.30).

Exciting and rare survival of high Victorian garden extensively restored since 1988. Conceived by James Bateman, the 15 acres are divided into a number of smaller gardens designed to house specimens from his extensive plant collection. An Egyptian Court, Chinese Temple and Willow Pattern bridge, pinetum and arboretum combine to make the garden a miniature tour of the world.

⚰ ✿ ☕

5 **BIRCH TREES**

Copmere End, Eccleshall ST21 6HH. Susan & John Weston, 01785 850448. *1¹/₂m W of Eccleshall. On B5026, turn at junction signed Copmere End. After ¹/₂m straight across Xrds by Star Inn.* Home-made teas. **Adm £2.50, chd free. Sun 3 June; Sat 14 July; Sun 26, Mon 27 Aug (1.30-5.30). Visitors also welcome by appt.**

Peaceful ¹/₂-acre country garden with views over surrounding countryside. Plant enthusiasts' garden with many rare and unusual varieties, designed with wildlife in mind. Herbaceous borders, peat bed, water features and vegetable plot.

& ⚰ ✿ ☕

6 🆕 **BLACKWOOD HOUSE FARM**

Horton ST13 8QA. Anne & Adam James. *4m W of Leek. 6m N of Stoke on Trent. A53 Stoke to Leek turn off at Black Horse PH in Endon, go to T-junction, turn R into Gratton Lane. Take 4th L (approx 2¹/₂m) signed Lask Edge, over ford up bank, farm on L.* Home-made teas. **Adm £3, chd free. Suns 1 July; 2 Sept (2-5).**

1¹/₂ acre country cottage garden with spectacular views. Large mixed borders, rockery, natural stream and koi carp pond. Grass and gravel paths through shrubs and trees. Lovely colourful wildlife garden packed with plants.

⚰ ✿ ☕

Paths through shrubs and trees. Lovely colourful wildlife garden packed with plants . . .

7 **BLEAK HOUSE**

Bagnall ST9 9JT. Mr & Mrs J H Beynon, 01782 534713. *4m NE of Stoke-on-Trent. A5009 to Milton Xrds, turn for Bagnall. 2m up hill past golf course to corner opp Bagnall Heights.* Home-made teas. **Adm £2.50, chd free. Sun 8 July (1-5). Evening Opening £3.50, wine, Sun 22 July (5-9). Visitors also welcome by appt June & July only, groups of 10+, coaches permitted.**

1 acre on many levels. Natural stone quarry with jungle planting, pool and waterfall. Italianate terraces with canal, rose garden, white garden planted in Edwardian style around Edwardian house (not open), many unusual plants. N Staffs bee keepers with display hive and local honey, candles etc. Reputedly the best cakes in Staffs. Featured in 'Gardeners World' & 'Gardens Illustrated'.

⚰ ✿ ☕

8 **THE BOWERS**

Church Lane, Standon, nr Eccleshall ST21 6RW. Maurice Thacker & Sheila Marriott, 01782 791244, metbowers@aol.com. *5m N of Eccleshall. Take A519 & at Cotes Heath turn L signed Standon. After 1m turn R at Xrds by church, into Church Lane ¹/₂m on L.* Home-made teas. **Adm £2.50, chd free. Suns 24 June; 22 July (1-5). Visitors also welcome by appt June & July only.**

Romantic multi-roomed cottage garden set in ³/₄-acre quiet rural location. Strong colour-themed borders planted with rare and unusual perennials. Over 130 clematis, height and blossom in abundance. Water feature, collections of hardy geraniums and hostas. Winner Large Garden - Stone in Bloom.

⚰ ✿ ☕

9 **43 BROAD LANE**

Bradmore, Wolverhampton WV3 9BW. Bob Parker & Greg Kowalczuk, 01902 332228, roboparker@blueyonder.co.uk. *2m SW of Wolverhampton. 2m from town centre on SW side. Follow signs for*

Bantock House, adjacent to Bantock Park. Broad Lane is part of B4161. 200yds from Bradmore Arms T-light. Home-made teas. **Adm £2.50, chd free. Sun 24 June; Sat 14 July (1.30-5.30). Evening Openings £3.50, wine, Sats 4, 18 Aug (7.30-10.30). Visitors also welcome by appt June & July.**

Escape the hustle and bustle of busy urban surroundings and enter the secure solitude of the high walled secret garden. Fantasy of one's childhood: a magical Aladdin's cave, full of the unexpected. Over 1000 candles flicker and lanterns glow in the evening, evoking mysterious moods in this small well-planted garden. Daylight is no less enchanting, the background is green, juxtaposed with restrained colour. A plantsman's garden, but different. Classical music throughout the garden. Featured in 'Express & Star' & 'Amateur Gardening'; Wolf FM (radio), Daily Mail Finalist Garden of the Year.

✿ ☕

10 🆕 **1 THE BRODDER**

Old Springs TF9 2PQ. Jackie Burwood. *2m E of Market Drayton. On A53 Market Drayton to Newcastle under Lyme. Turn R to Alminton. Through village, cottage on RH-side. Parking in signed field. Uneven sufaces.* Home-made teas. **Adm £2.50, chd free. Sat 23 June; Sun 9 Sept (2-5).**

Pretty, plant lovers country garden trying to survive and stay sane against rabbits and moles. Experimental planting against these hungry pests. Lovely views across rolling countryside. Featured on BBC2 Open Gardens.

⚰ ✿ ☕

11 **37 BROOKFIELDS ROAD**

Ipstones ST10 2LY. Pat & Pam Murray. *7m SE of Leek. From N on A523 turn on to B5053 southwards at Green Man Pub, Bottomhouse. From*

S on A52 turn N on to B5053 at Froghall. In the centre of Ipstone Village tight turn opp Trading Post shop into Brookfields Rd. Home-made teas. **Adm £2.50, chd free. Sat 23, Sun 24 June (2-6).**
Organic, exciting country garden with secluded white garden, herbaceous borders and glorious views. Sloping ground encompasses raised vegetable beds, greenhouse terrace and cutting border. Winding willow tunnel leads to wild flower meadow, woodland area and stream with bridge and stepping stones crossing. Dry stone wall, hedge laying and vernacular buildings created by owners. Sensible shoes essential. (Children delight in the unexpected).

⑫ ◆ CONSALL HALL LANDSCAPE GARDEN
Wetley Rocks ST9 OAG. William Podmore, 01782 551947, www.consallgardens.co.uk. 7m from Stoke-on-Trent, Leek & Cheadle. A52 after Cellarhead Xrds. Turn L on to A522, after ¼m turn R to Consall & straight on through village. Garden entrance ¾m on R. Ample free car park. **Adm £4, chd £1. Every Wed, Sun & Bank Hol Mon 1 Apr to 30 Sept.** For NGS: Tue 29 May (10-5).
Beautiful secluded 70-acre landscape garden. Easy access to many exceptional vistas enhanced by lakes and trees with bridges, grottoes and follies. Covered seats enabling the garden to be enjoyed in all weathers. Featured in Local Life & on BBC Open Gardens. WC.
🚻 ➤ ✿ ☕

⑬ COURTWOOD HOUSE
Court Walk, Betley CW3 9DP. Mike & Edith Reeves, 01270 820715, thereeve@homecall.co.uk. 6m S of Crewe. On A531 going toward Keele & Newcastle-u-Lyme or from J16 of the M6 pick up the A531 off the A500 on the Nantwich rd. In Betley Village into courtyard by sign 'Betley Court'. Home-made teas (£1.25 incl cake). **Adm £2.50, chd 50p. Sun 3 June (2-5). Visitors also welcome by appt, no coaches, no restrictions on group size.**
Small L-shaped (under ¼ acre) 200yr-old, walled ex-kitchen garden. Created and owned by an artist, the garden is designed as a huge walk-through sculpture, with different paths and directions. Many creations, structures and water features, with hidden spaces and seating areas. Laid to bushes and shrubs with strong shapes

and effects, rather than just flowers and colour. At night the garden is illuminated by coloured spot-lights and transformed into a fairy grotto atmosphere. Small art gallery, display of paintings in the summerhouse/studio. Winner Crew Chronicle 'Best Kept Garden' award. Featured in 'Sunday Sentinel' & on BBC Open Gardens.
➤ ☕

At night the garden is illuminated by coloured spot-lights and transformed into a fairy grotto . . .

⑭ 12 DARGES LANE
Great Wyrley WS6 6LE. Mrs A Hackett, 01922 415064, annhackett@fsmail.net. 2m SE of Cannock. From A5 take A34 towards Walsall. Darges Lane is 1st turning on R (over brow of hill). House on R on corner of Cherrington Drive. **Adm £2.50, chd 50p. Evening Opening Sat 18 Aug (7-9). Visitors also welcome by appt.**
¼-acre well-stocked plantsman's and flower arranger's garden on two levels. Foliage plants a special feature. Mixed borders incl trees, shrubs and rare plants giving yr-round interest. Features constantly changing. National Collection of lamiums. Collection of 93 clematis. The overall effect is attractive and enticing to the plant lover.
➤ ✿ **NCCPG**

⑮ 4 DENE CLOSE
Penkridge ST19 5HL. David & Anne Smith, 01785 712580. 6m S of Stafford. On A449 from Stafford. At far end of Penkridge turn L into Boscomoor Lane, 2nd L into Filance Lane, 3rd R Dene Close. Please park with consideration in Filance Lane. Disabled only in Dene Close. Home-made teas. **Adm £2.50, chd free. Sun 15 July (11-5). Visitors also welcome by appt.**
Medium-sized plant lovers' garden has been created over 35 yrs. Wide variety of herbaceous perennials, foliage plants; over 60 varieties of grasses, incl miscanthus, pennisetums and

bamboos. Gravelled areas and mixed borders, some colour themed, small water feature. 'Rainbow border' 54ft long with many perennials incl achilleas, hemerocallis and heleniums. Featured in 'Express & Star. Highly Commended - Stafford in Bloom,.
➤ ✿ ☕

⑯ NEW ◆ DOROTHY CLIVE GARDEN
Willoughbridge, Market Drayton TF9 4EU. Willoughbridge Garden Trust, 01630 647237, www.dorothyclivegarden.co.uk. £m SE of Bridgemere Garden World. From M6 J15 take A53, then A51 midway between Nantwich & Stone, 2m from village of Woore. **Adm £4.50, chd free, 11-16 £1, concessions £3.80. Open daily 31 Mar to 28 Oct.** For NGS: Tues 14, 21 Aug (10-5.30).
12 informal acres, incl superb woodland garden, alpine scree, gravel garden, fine collection of trees and spectacular flower borders. Re-known in May when woodland quarry is brilliant with rhododendrons. Creative planting over last 4yrs has produced stunning summer borders. Much to see, whatever the season.
🚻 ✿ ☕

⑰ DORSET HOUSE
68 Station Street, Cheslyn Hay WS6 7EE. Mary & David Blundell, 01922 419437, mary.marshall@homecall.co.uk. 2m SE of Cannock. J11 M6. A462 towards Willenhall, L at island, follow rd to next island. R into one-way system (Low St), at T-junction L into Station St. A5 Bridgetown L over M6 toll rd to island, L into Coppice Rd. At T-junction R into Station St. Home-made teas. **Adm £2.50, chd free. Suns 20 May; 15 July (12-5). Visitors also welcome by appt May & June, groups of 10+, coaches permitted.**
Inspirational ½-acre plantaholic's country garden giving all-yr interest. Many unique features, wealth of unusual rhododendrons, acers, shrubs and perennials, planted in mixed borders. Clematis-covered arches, intimate seating areas, hidden corners, water features, stream, all creating a haven of peace and tranquillity. Featured in 'Express & Star & 'Staffordshire Life'.
🚻 ➤ ✿ ☕

18 NEW 10 FERN DENE
Madeley, Crewe CW3 9ER.
Martin & Stella Clifford-Jones.
*10m W of Newcastle under Lyme.
Madeley is on A525 between
Keele/ Woore. Enter Moss Lane
next to Madeley Pool. 2nd R,
Charles Cotton Drive. At end turn R
then L into the bridle path, 1st R to
Fern Dene.* Home-made teas.
**Adm £3, chd free (share to
Haemochromatosis Society).
Sun 6 May; Sat 2 June (2-5).**
Garden occupies 1 acre on sloping
site with natural springs. Designed
to encourage wildlife with several
ponds, native plants and woodland
walk. Planting incls many trees and
shrubs especially acers, cornus
and salix. Unusual features incl
grass spiral and oriental garden.
Featured on BBC2 Open Gardens.

19 FIELD HOUSE FARM
Pipe Gate TF9 4HD. Vicki & Brian
Walker, 01630 647522. *10m SW of
Newcastle-under-Lyme. 12m E of
Nantwich. 8m SE of Market Drayton.
On A51 at Pipe Gate. Turn at
Chetwode Arms towards Norton in
Hales. 100yds turn L, 50yds turn L -
equal distance between Bridgemere
Garden World & Dorothy Clive Garden.*
Home-made teas. **Adm £3, chd free.
Suns 1 Apr; 17 June (2-5).** Visitors
also welcome by appt 1 Apr to 10
June & Aug, groups of 10+.
Coaches permitted.
Lovely country-house garden with long
vistas and sweeping lawns down to a
natural brook. Cottage garden planting
and seating to enjoy small feature
gardens. Spring bulbs on the wild
flower walk (350 metres) were
described as 'spiritual' by a visitor.
New features: opening date in June to
appreciate roses. Small orchard
planted in 2006. Featured in 'Sentinel
& 'Shropshire Star. Car parking for
disabled at house. Lawns not suitable
for wheelchairs if wet.

20 THE GARTH
2 Broc Hill Way, Milford ST17 0UB.
Mr & Mrs David Wright, 01785
661182. *4¹/₂m SE of Stafford. A513
Stafford to Rugeley rd; at Barley Mow
turn R (S) to Brocton; L after ¹/₂m.*
Cream teas. **Adm £2.50, chd free.
Suns 3, 24 June (2-6).** Visitors also
welcome by appt.
¹/₂ acre garden of many levels on
Channock Chase AONB. Acid soil

loving plants. Series of small gardens,
water features, raised beds. Rare trees,
island beds of unusual shrubs and
perennials, many varieties of hosta and
ferns. Ancient sandstone caves.
Winner of Stafford in Bloom.

21 GRAFTON COTTAGE
Barton-under-Needwood DE13 8AL.
Margaret & Peter Hargreaves, 01283
713639, marpeter@onetel.com. *6m
N of Lichfield. Leave A38 for Catholme
S of Barton, follow sign to Barton
Green, ¹/₄m on L.* Cream teas. **Adm
£2.50, chd free (share to Alzheimer's
Research Trust). Suns 24 June; 1
July; 5 Aug (1.30-5.30).** Visitors also
welcome by appt for groups.
Coaches permitted.
Step into an English cottage garden
and roam around the winding paths
clothed with highly scented flowers, old
fashioned roses, dianthus, sweet peas,
phlox, lilies. Stately delphiniums form a
backdrop to the herbaceous borders.
Over 100 clematis ,incl 30 from the
viticella collection wander, through
trellises and amongst campanula,
achillea, viola and many more unusual
perennials. Textured plants, artemisia,
atrepex, heuchera form the basis of
colour-themed borders, use of cottage
garden annuals add to the tranquillity.
Small vegetable plot. Featured in Staffs
County Magazine, BBC Gardeners'
World.

22 HEATH HOUSE
**Offley Brook, nr Eccleshall
ST21 6HA.** Dr D W Eyre-Walker,
01785 280318. *3m W of Eccleshall.
Take B5026 towards Woore. At
Sugnall turn L, after 1¹/₂m turn R
immed by stone garden wall. After 1m
straight across Xrds.* **Adm £3, chd
free (share to Adbaston Church).
Suns 13 May; 17 June; 22 July (2-5).**
Visitors also welcome by appt.
1¹/₂-acre country garden of C18 miller's
house in lovely valley setting,

overlooking mill pool. Plantsman's
garden containing many rare and
unusual plants in borders, bog garden,
woodland, alpine house, raised bed
and shrubberies.

23 HIGH TREES
**18 Drubbery Lane, nr Longton Park
ST3 4BA.** Peter & Pat Teggin, 01782
318453. *5m S of Stoke-on-Trent. Off
A5035, midway between Trentham
Gardens & Longton. Opp Longton
Park.* Cream teas. **Adm £2.50, chd
free. Fri 18, Mon 28 May; Suns 17
June; 8 July; 5 Aug (2-5).** Visitors
also welcome by appt June & July,
groups of 10+.
Restful plantsperson's secluded
suburban garden. Many unusual plants
flow easily from the gravel driveway,
through arches and trellis of clematis
and roses, to lush herbaceous
planting. Vibrant, hot, dry areas
contrast with the subdued tones of
ferns and hostas. Featured in ''Sentinel
on Sunday', & on Satellite TV.

24 NEW THE HOLLIES
**Leek Road, Cheddleton
ST13 7HG.** Tim & Amanda
Bosson, 01538 361079, tim-
bosson@hotmail.com. *2m S of
Leek. On A520. Large arrow to
direct.* Cream teas. **Adm £2.50,
chd free. Sats, Suns 30 June; 1
July; 1, 2 Sept (2-6).** Visitors also
welcome by appt.
On edge of village a private walled
garden and a delight to see.
Amanda and Tim invite you to
wander around their secret oasis
whilst watching their amazing
water feature. Impressive formal
garden which features an array of
colour surrounded by shrubs and
trees. Devon Cream Teas are a
speciality for this couple from
Devonshire and the cream is
specially sent up.

Devon Cream Teas are a speciality for this couple from Devonshire and the cream is specially sent up . . .

㉕ NEW 6 KENDAL PLACE
Newcastle-under-Lyme ST5 3QT.
Joanne Barnes. *1m S of
Newcastle-under-Lyme. Leave
Newcastle on A519 Clayton Rd.
1st R Abbots Way, 1st L Earls Dr,
175yds, 2nd R Kendal Place. 2m
from M6 J15 L onto A519 over 2
roundabouts, 1st L into Abbots
Way then as above. Please park
with consideration (cul-de-sac).*
Adm £2.50, chd free. Sun 29 July
(2-5).
Passionate about pots. In small
well-designed Gold Medal winning
garden a jewel box of beautiful
plant treasures giving inspiration
and ideas. Well tended clusters of
phormiums, grasses, ferns, ricinus,
agapanthus, colourful containers
and hanging baskets. Featured in
'Sunday Sentinel', Gold Medal -
Newcastle-under-Lyme - Britain in
Bloom Residential Gardens 2
Silver, 1 Bronze.
✖ ⊛

㉖ LILAC COTTAGE
Chapel Lane, Gentleshaw, nr
Rugeley WS15 4ND. Mrs Sylvia
Nunn,
www.lilaccottagegarden.co.uk. *5m
NW of Lichfield. Approx midway
between Lichfield & Rugeley on A51 at
Longdon, turn W into Borough Lane
signed Cannock Wood & Gentleshaw.
Continue 1m to T-junction. L for 1¹/₂m
to Gentleshaw. From Burntwood,
A5190 head N on Rugeley Rd at
Burntwood Swan island; turn L at Xrds
approx ¹/₂m past Nags Head PH, over
Xrds to Gentleshaw. Parking only at
Cannock Wood and Gentleshaw village
hall. Roadside disabled & elderly
parking only at Lilac Cottage. Teas.*
Adm £2.50, chd free. Suns 1, 29 July
(1.30-5).
Plant enthusiast's 1-acre country
garden with emphasis on colour-
themed borders and plant
associations. Wealth of unusual
perennials, especially geraniums,
hostas, penstemons and achilleas,
interspersed with English roses,
interesting trees and shrubs. Small

wildlife pool, bog garden, vibrant hot
border, shady walks, tranquil sunken
garden, sweeping vistas. All-yr interest.
Unusual plants for sale. Pleasant walks
nearby on Gentleshaw Common and
'Castle Ring' Cannock Chase.
Featured in 'Gardening Which',
'Amateur Gardening', 'Express' & Star'
& local press & radio. Some gravel
paths.
⬥ ✖ ⊛ ☕

㉗ LOWER HOUSE
Eccleshall ST21 6NF. John & Anthea
Treanor. *2m W of Eccleshall. On
B5026 Loggerheads Rd turn R at
sharp double bend. House ¹/₂m on L.*
Home-made teas. Adm £3, chd free
(share to St Chads & Holy Trinity
Churches, Eccleshall). Sat 16, Sun
17 June (2-6).
1-acre country garden with spectacular
views, has evolved over last 20yrs.
Recent project work incls sunken
garden, terraces and sea-worn shingle
bed. large vegetable garden, ponds
and many unusual plants. Featured in
'Staffordshire Life'.
⬥ ⊛ ☕

㉘ MANOR COTTAGE GARDEN
2 Manor Cottage, Hanchurch,
Stoke-on-Trent ST4 8SD. Dr & Mrs
Clement, 01782 644112,
darren@lushgardendesign.co.uk. *4m
S of Newcastle-under-Lyme. From J15
M6 follow A519 S towards Eccleshall.
Straight on at T-lights, past Hanchurch
village, under M6, 2nd R onto private
rd.* Home-made teas. Adm £2, chd
free. Sun 5 Aug (11-5). Visitors also
welcome by appt Aug only, for small
groups max 12.
Welcome to 'the jungle'. This small
semi-tropical garden comprises a small
courtyard garden with phormiums and
other architectural foliage plants. Off
the courtyard the main garden, 'the
jungle', incl bananas, bamboos, ferns,
foxglove trees, cannas and day lilies in
abundance. Small informal pond.
Good end-of-season interest. Featured
in 'Sentinel on Sunday'.
✖ ⊛ ☕

**㉙ NEW MILLENNIUM
GARDEN**
Knowle Lane, Lichfield
WS14 9RB. Carol Cooper, 01543
262544. *1m S of Lichfield. Off A38
along A5192 towards Lichfield fork
¹/₄m before Shoulder of Mutton
PH. Park in field on L.* Home-made
teas. Adm £3.50, chd free.
Sat 14 Apr; Sat 23, Sun 24 June
(2-6). Visitors also welcome by
appt.
Formal white gardens inspired by
Sissinghurst. Millennium bridge
over landscaped water garden,
leading to attractive walks along
rough mown paths, through
maturing woodland and seasonal
wild flowers. Paintings by local
artist with international reputation.
Uneven surfaces & gravel paths.
⬥ ✖ ⊛ ☕

MILLPOOL
See Cheshire & Wirral.

㉚ THE MOUNT
Coton, Gnosall ST20 0EQ. Andrew &
Celia Payne, 01785 822253. *8m W of
Stafford. 4m E of Newport. From
Stafford take A518 W towards
Newport/Telford. Go through Gnosall,
over canal. Garden on edge of Gnosall
Village, on LH-side of A518. Parking
approx 200yds signed up lane.* Home-
made teas. Adm £2.50, chd free. Sun
1 July (2-5.30). Visitors also
welcome by appt, July & Aug only.
Approx ³/₄-acre colourful plantsman's
garden incl bog area with small wildlife
pool, cottage-style front garden and
herbaceous borders. Large variety of
plants incl hardy geraniums, hostas,
euphorbias, ferns, bamboos, plus
numerous tender perennials.
✖ ⊛ ☕

㉛ MUIRFIELD
Pershall ST21 6NE. Nigel & Lindsay
Von-Elbing. *1m W of Eccleshall. Take
B5026 out of Eccleshall towards
Loggerheads. Muirfield is 1st house on
R after the sign for the R Sow.* Home-
made teas. Adm £2.50, chd free. Sun
26, Mon 27 Aug (12.30-5).
Transformed by the present owner
who twice won local gardening
competitions when at the High St. This
dwelling was originally part of the
Cadbury's dairy (c1920). Low
maintenance has become high
maintenance with themed herbaceous
borders; 3 ponds; tropical hideaway;
bog and gravel gardens; woodland
area; mini orchard; fruit cage and

Millennium bridge over landscaped water garden, leading to attractive walks along rough mown paths . . .

vegetable garden. Emphasis on wildlife and relaxation. Featured in local press for flowering & fruity banana. Some steps and gravel paths.

🚻 ⊛ ☕

32 THE OLD DAIRY HOUSE
Trentham Park, Stoke-on-Trent ST4 8AE. Philip & Michelle Moore. *S edge of Stoke-on-Trent. Behind Trentham Gardens on rd to Trentham Church and Trentham Park Golf Club. From A34 turn into Whitmore Rd B5038. 1st L and follow NGS signs.* Adm £2.50, chd free. Sat 26, Sun 27 May (1-5.30).
Grade 2 listed house (not open) designed by Sir Charles Barry forms backdrop to this 2-acre garden in peaceful parkland setting.

💢 ⊛

33 THE OLD RECTORY, CLIFTON CAMPVILLE
B79 0AP. Martin & Margaret Browne, 01827 373533, mbrowne526@aol.com. *6m N of Tamworth. 2m W of M42 J11, in centre of Clifton Campville. Village signed off B5493 from Statfold or No Man's Heath. Entrance to garden on S side of Main St at top of hill, between bus shelter and school.* Home-made teas. Adm £2.50, chd free. Sun 2 Sept (1-5). Visitors also welcome by appt for groups.
Tranquil 2-acre garden around historic former Rectory developed over 25yrs by the present owners. Enjoy a garden on an ancient site with established trees and diverse range of flora with interest all season. Explore its differing textures and colour palette at the beginning of autumn. Paths give easy access to lawns, borders, fruit and vegetables. Small walled garden and gravel areas.

🚻 💢 ⊛ ☕

34 THE OLD SCHOOL HOUSE
Stowe-by-Chartley, Stafford ST18 0LG. Keith & Wendy Jones. *5m S of Stone. Adjacent to village hall, 7m from Stafford A51 at Weston. A518 E towards Uttoxeter. Approx 1½m past Amerton Farm. After approx ½m turn R signed Stowe (Bridge Lane). L at T-junction past church & Cock Inn. 100yds on R.* Lunches (Sun only), Home-made teas. Adm £2.50, chd free. Sat 14 (2-6), Sun 15 July (11-5).
Informal cottage-style garden of ½ acre; developed from former school yard. Mixed herbaceous borders; lawn and recycled paved sitting areas;

rockery, small pond, containers. Unexpected garden hidden from the road creating a tranquil setting within a small country village. Stowe-by-Chartley - Best Kept Small Village.

⊛ ☕

35 THE OLD VICARAGE
Fulford, nr Stone ST11 9QS. Mike & Cherry Dodson. *4m N of Stone. From Stone A520 (Leek). 1m R turn to Spot Acre and Fulford, turn L down Post Office Terrace, past village green/pub, take 2nd L. Good parking.* Home-made teas. Adm £3, chd free. Sat 4, Sun 5 Aug (12-5).
2 acres rescued from dereliction, around Victorian House (not open), in lovely rural valley. Established shrubs and conifers form framework to sloping site. Island beds stuffed with interesting herbaceous plants, wildlife friendly pond, terraced rose beds. Separate area with wide range organically grown vegetables in raised beds; fruit cage; greenhouse. Summerhouse and seating areas for teas. Featured in 'Stone Gazette' & 'Sunday Sentinel'.

🚻 💢 ⊛ ☕

Mixed herbaceous borders; lawn and recycled paved sitting areas . . .

ORCHARD HOUSE
See Cheshire & Wirral.

36 ROMER FARM
Burston ST18 0DT. John & Marie Lowe, www.romerfarm.co.uk. *3m SE of Stone. 5m NE of Stafford on A51. Approx ¾m from Sandon village in the direction of Stone on A51, R into farm track and continue to end. Map on website.* Teas. Adm £3, chd free. Sun 27, Mon 28 May; Sat 21, Sun 22 July (1-5). **Day & Evening Opening** Fri 15 June (2-8). Visitors also welcome by appt June, July only.
Relaxed 1-acre country garden with lovely views over surrounding countryside. Large pond; wild flower area; herbaceous borders; ivy knot garden; fernery; secret gardens within

yew hedges and unique deep-bed kitchen garden. Childrens treasure hunt. Winner Stone in Bloom.

💢 ⊛ 🍴 ☕

37 15 ST JOHNS ROAD
Pleck, Walsall WS2 9TJ. Maureen & Sid Allen, 01922 442348. *2m W of Walsall. Off J10 M6. Head for Walsall on A454 Wolverhampton Rd. Turn R into Pleck Rd A4148 then 4th R into St Johns Rd.* Adm £2, chd free. Sun 5 Aug (12-5). **Evening Opening** Mon 18 June (6-9). Visitors also welcome by appt July only. Coaches permitted.
Long narrow garden. Plant lovers paradise, some unusual, tropical planting. Pool with carp, surrounded with lush foliage, small trees, shrub border and lots of perennials and grasses. The lawn leads to Japanese style area with bridge and stream, shady walk then into the gravel garden, very pretty planted for wildlife, pool.

💢 ⊛ ☕

38 23 ST JOHNS ROAD
Stafford ST17 9AS. Colin & Fiona Horwath, 01785 258923, fiona_horwath@yahoo.co.uk. *½m S of Stafford Town Centre. On A449. Through entrance into private park, therefore please park considerately.* Home-made teas. Adm £2.50, chd free. Sun 25 Mar; Fris 4 May; 8 June; 14 Sept (2-5). Visitors also welcome by appt.
Town garden with a country feel packed with interesting plants and run organically. Many bulbs, shady walk, herbaceous borders, wildlife pond and bog garden. Climbers ramble over pergolas and arches; herb garden; rockery and raised vegetable beds. Victorian-style greenhouse. New water features for 2007. Featured in 'Sentinel on Sunday'.

💢 ⊛ ☕

39 SHEPHERDS FOLD GARDENS
Stafford ST17 4SF. *3m S of Stafford. Follow A34 out of Stafford towards Cannock, 2nd R onto the Wildwood Estate. Follow ring rd around, Shepherds Fold is 5th turning on L. Limited parking in cul de sac. Please use as drop off & park on ring rd.* Home-made teas at no. 8. **Combined adm £3, chd free. Sun 17 June (11.30-5).**
Deceptive gardens with views over open countryside.

⊛ ☕

7 SHEPHERDS FOLD
Avril & David Tooth
W-facing plant lovers' garden with many interesting features incl variety of unusual pots and water feature. Themed area with sun house. Some areas only accessible via steps.

8 SHEPHERDS FOLD
David & Janet Horsnall
Maturing S-facing garden on heavy clay. Variety of different areas and terraces. Plantsman's garden with magnificent roses, quiet areas with architectural plants and wide range of perennials. Parts of the garden can only be accessed by steps.

9 SHEPHERDS FOLD
Peter & Alison Jordan
S-facing garden on heavy clay soil. Informal cottage planting, interesting terraces and features, yr-round interest, unusual perennials. Some areas only accessible by steep steps.

Rockery and large stone and slate feature . . .

40 SILVERWOOD
16 Beechfield Road, Trentham
ST4 8HG. Dr M & Mrs S Akhtar,
01782 643313,
sarah.akhtar4@btinternet.com. *3m S of Stoke on Trent. From A34 Trentham Gardens roundabout take A5035 Longton Rd. After Nat West Bank take R turn into Oaktree Rd. From Longton (A50) follow A5035 into Trentham. After PH take L turn into Oaktree Rd, which becomes Beechfield Rd. Parking limited.* Home-made teas. **Adm £2.50, chd free (share to Breast Cancer Campaign). Sun 27 May (2-6). Visitors also welcome by appt June only.**
An eclectic garden that showcases plants and artefacts from all over the world. Small town garden presented as an Eastern bazaar containing a wealth of unusual plants and trees. Woodland area, herbaceous beds and a gravel area with tropical planting. Opening in May for late spring colour. Featured in 'The Sunday Times', BBC Midlands Today.
  ⛓ ✂ ✿ ☕

41 SMITHY COTTAGE
Mucklestone TF9 4DN. Diana
Standeven, 01630 672677. *8m SW of Newcastle-under-Lyme. On B5026 between Woore A51 & Loggerheads A53 opposite Mucklestone Church.* Teas. **Adm £2.50, chd free. Sun 8 Apr; Every Thurs, 3 May to 27 Sept (2-5). Visitors also welcome by appt at weekends.**
An eclectic mix of rarities satisfying the most picky plantsperson in a conservation rural village. Featured in 'Amateur Gardening', BBC2 Open Garden & ITV Central.
✂ ✿ ☕

42 STONEHILL QUARRY GARDEN
Great Gate, Croxden, nr Uttoxeter
ST10 4HF. Mrs Caroline Raymont.
6m NW of Uttoxeter. A50 to Uttoxeter. Take B5030 to JCB Rocester, L to Hollington & Croxden Abbey. Third R into Keelings Lane & Croxden Abbey. At Great Gate, T-junction L to Stonehill. **Adm £2.50. Mons 19, 26 Feb; 5, 12 Mar, Sun 18, Mon 19 Mar. Mons 16, 23, 30 Apr; 22, 29 Oct; 5 Nov (2-5).**
6-acre quarry garden incorporating numerous ornamental trees and shrubs (magnolias, acers, catalpa, Davidia, paeonias, azaleas) underplanted with unusual Asiatic and American woodlanders (lilies, trillium, erythroniums, paris, podophyllum, arisaemas, hellebores), bamboo 'jungle', rock garden, mixed borders. Spring bulbs and hellebores. Autumn colour of particular interest with new winter bark feature to give a 'zing' to dreary days. C13 Cistercian Abbey ruins (1km) adm free, Churnet Valley (2½ km). Unsuitable for children.
⛓ ✂ ✿ ☕

43 TANGLEWOOD COTTAGE
Consall Lane, Wetley Rocks
ST9 0AA. Paul & Deirdre Nicholls,
01782 551456,
deepinthewood@tiscali.co.uk. *5m NE of Stoke-on-Trent. A52 to Cellarhead, A520 to Wetley Rocks, sharp R to A522 at Powys Arms. ¼m first L into Consall Lane, garden 50yds on R. Parking on lane, wheelchair users on drive. Diasabled drop off outside gate. No parking at house.* Cream teas. **Adm £2.50, chd free (share to Hope Hospital, Salford, Premature Baby Unit). Sat 2, Sun 3 June (1.30-5). Visitors also welcome by appt June (rhododendrons), late Aug/Sept (dahlias), small groups (mini bus) welcome.**

Restored relaxing country garden of 2 acres. Many rhododendrons and woodland walks. Open borders and ponds, many shade-loving plants, protected trees and wildlife. Lovely spring clematis and wisteria. Features incl fernery under woodland shade, potager with vegetables, alpines and candelabra primula in profusion. Featured in 'Leek Local Life & Sunday Sentinal. Stone steps in some areas. Wheelchair access around orchard and patio, some access to woodland in dry weather - easy access for teas.
⛓ ✂ ✿

44 NEW ◆ TRENTHAM
Stone Road, Stoke-on-Trent
ST4 8AX. Michael Walker, 01782
657341, www.trentham.co.uk.
Well signed on roundabout, A34 with A5035. **Adm £6.50, chd £5, concessions £6. Open daily 10-6.**
One of the largest garden regeneration projects in Britain, using award winning designers Tom Stuart-Smith and Piet Oudolf, who have introduced vast contemporay plantings, using over 300,000 choice perennials and bulbs. Collection of show gardens and new 7 acre garden by Piet Oudolf. Featured in 'Gardens Illustrated' & 'The Garden'.
⛓ ✂ ✿ ☕

45 VICTORIA COTTAGE
Moss Lane, off Yarnfield Lane,
Yarnfield ST15 0PW. John &
Maureen Hammersley, 01785
761159, jkh@talktalk.net. *2m W of Stone. Approx 5m from Stafford town centre and 8m from Stoke-on-Trent off A34. Turn into Yarnfield Lane alongside Wayfarer Inn. Approx 1m along Yarnfield Lane after motorway bridge turn R into Moss Lane & immed R into large driveway for parking. Light refreshments & teas.* **Adm £2.50, chd free. Sat 9, Sun 10 June (11-5). Visitors also welcome by appt.**
Ever maturing garden approx 1 acre. Large well-stocked koi and fish pond reached via gravelled pergola walks with walk over bridge to decking area. Small bog garden, rockery and large stone and slate feature; seated area around water feature with raised beds. Good overall selection of trees, pines and shrubs with well stocked borders. Plants for Sale. Main access by gravel paths.
⛓ ✂ ✿ ☕

Putting course and garden chess board . . .

46 THE WICKETS
47 Long Street, Wheaton Aston
ST19 9NF. Tony & Kate Bennett,
01785 840233,
ajtonyb@tiscali.co.uk. *8m W of
Cannock. From M6 J12 turn W
towards Telford on A5; across A449
Gailey roundabout; A5 for 1¹/₂m; turn
R signed Stretton, 150yds turn L
signed Wheaton Aston; 2¹/₂m turn L;
¹/₂m over canal bridge; garden on R.
Or Bradford Arms Wheaton Aston 2m.*
**Adm £2.50, chd free. Sun 8 July
(1-5.30). Visitors also welcome by
appt.**
¹/₃-acre garden of many features, full of
ideas for smaller gardens. A more
open front garden is contrasted by
many themed areas behind the house.
Pond, dry stream, clock golf, gravel
beds and many hanging baskets and
containers. Popular and pleasant walks
along Shropshire Union Canal just
25yds away.
  🚶 ✕ ☕

47 NEW WILKINS PLECK
Whitworth, nr Newcastle-under-
Lyme ST5 5HN. Sheila & Chris
Bissell, 01782 680351. *5m SW
from Newcastle-under-Lyme. Take
A53 SW from Newcastle-under-
Lyme. At Whitmore turn R at
Mainwaring Arms PH. Signed RH-
side at Cudmore Fisheries. Please
NO Dogs in car, park in field at
landowners instruction.* **Adm
£4.50, chd free. Suns 24 June;
29 July (2-5). Visitors also
welcome by appt.**
5¹/₂ acres of paradise in North
Staffordshire.
✕ ⊛ ☕

**48 THE WOMBOURNE
WODEHOUSE**
Wolverhampton WV5 9BW. Mr &
Mrs J Phillips, 01902 892202. *4m S
of Wolverhampton. Just off A449 on
A463 to Sedgley.* Home-made teas.
**Adm £3.50, chd free. Thur 31 May
(2-5.30). Visitors also welcome by
appt May, June & July.**
18-acre garden laid out in 1750. Mainly
rhododendrons, herbaceous border,
woodland walk, water garden and
irises in walled kitchen garden. Partial
wheelchair access.
✕ ⊛ ☕

49 WOODSIDE HOUSE
Barton Gate, Barton-under-
Needwood DE13 8AP. Mrs Selvam
Webster, 01283 716046,
www.selvamsgarden.com. *5m SW of
Burton upon Trent. Take B5016 out of
Barton-under-Needwood. Turn R at
Little India Restaurant, entrance
300yds on RH-side. Please park on
grass verge and walk to garden
(approx 100yds along drive).* Cream
teas. **Adm £3.50, chd free (share to
St Giles Hospice). Suns 24 June; 15
July; 5 Aug (1-5). Visitors also
welcome by appt.**
Waterlogged 1¹/₂ acre field set in rolling
countryside transformed by energetic
and passionate Sri-Lankan woman into
a unique garden with an emphasis on
colour, scent, texture and form. Many
exotic and unusual plants. Oriental
garden with stream, waterfalls and
pond, rose walk, cottage garden, large
koi pond with rockery and waterfall.
Small arboretum and woodland.
✕ ⊛ ☕

50 NEW YARLET HOUSE
Stafford ST18 9SU. Mr & Mrs
Nikolas Tarling. *2m S of Stone.
Take A34 from Stone towards
Stafford, turn L into Yarlet School
and L again into car park.* Home-
made teas. **Adm £3, chd free
(share to Staffordshire Wildlife
Trust). Fris 27 Apr; 29 June (2-5).**
4 acre garden with extensive
lawns, walks and herbaceous
borders. Water garden with rare
lilies, putting course and garden
chess board. Sweeping views
across Trent Valley to Sandon.
Gravel paths.
 🚶 ☕

51 YEW TREE COTTAGE
Podmores Corner, Long Lane, White
Cross, Haughton ST18 9JR. Clive &
Ruth Plant, 01785 282516,
pottyplantsz@aol.com. *4m W of
Stafford. Take A518 W Haughton, turn
R Station Rd (signed Ranton) 1m, then
turn R at Xrds ¹/₄m on R.* Home-made
teas. **Adm £2.50, chd free. Suns 6,
27 May; 26 Aug (2-5). Visitors also
welcome by appt anytime, please
ring and we will advise if worth your
trip.**
Cottage garden of ¹/₃ acre designed by
plantaholics to complement Victorian
cottage. Many unusual perennials incl
shade lovers such as meconopsis and
arisaema. Gardeners are passionate
about salvia and lathyrus. Gravel and
vegetable gardens, courtyard. Come
and sit in our new oak timbered
orangery and take tea. Featured in
''Staffordshire Life' magazine.
 🚶 ✕ ⊛ ☕

Staffordshire County Volunteers

County Organiser
Diana Standeven, Smithy Cottage, Mucklestone, Market Drayton, Salop TF9 4DN, 01630 672677

County Treasurer
Sue Jones, Church Farm Cottage, Mucklestone, Market Drayton TF9 4DN, suejones@rockcottagecrafts.com

Publicity
Bert Foden, The Cottage, Tongue Lane, Brown Edge, Stoke on Trent ST6 8UQ, 01782 513033, jeanandbert@Btinternet.com

Assistant County Organisers
John & Susan Weston, Birch Trees, Copmere End, Stafford ST21 6HH, 01785 850448, sueweston@copmere.fsnet.co.uk;

Secretary
Sarah Akhtar, Silverwood, 16 Beechfield Road, Stoke-on-Trent ST4 8HG, sarah.akhtar4@btinternet.com

SUFFOLK

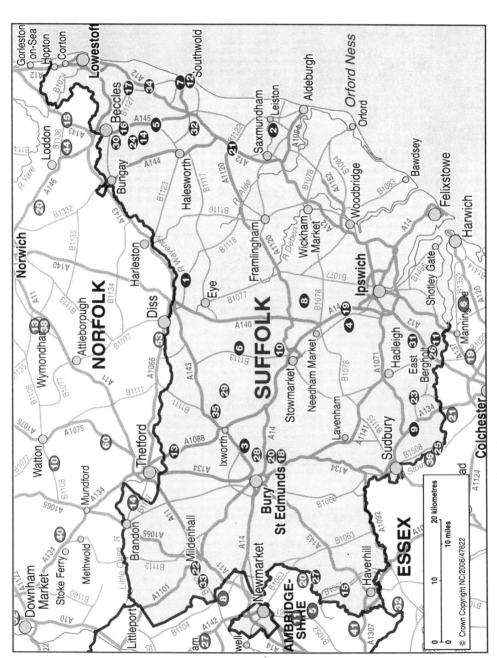

Opening Dates

February

SUNDAY 18
14 Gable House

March

SUNDAY 25
11 East Bergholt Place

April

SUNDAY 1
15 Great Thurlow Hall
28 The Wallow
29 Walsham Gardens

SUNDAY 8
26 Rosemary

TUESDAY 10
32 Woottens

WEDNESDAY 11
32 Woottens

THURSDAY 12
32 Woottens

SUNDAY 15
11 East Bergholt Place

TUESDAY 17
32 Woottens

WEDNESDAY 18
32 Woottens

THURSDAY 19
32 Woottens

SATURDAY 21
4 Blakenham Woodland Garden

SUNDAY 22
4 Blakenham Woodland Garden

TUESDAY 24
32 Woottens

WEDNESDAY 25
32 Woottens

THURSDAY 26
32 Woottens

SATURDAY 28
33 Worlington House

SUNDAY 29
33 Worlington House

May

TUESDAY 1
32 Woottens

WEDNESDAY 2
32 Woottens

THURSDAY 3
32 Woottens

SUNDAY 6
25 Rosedale

TUESDAY 8
32 Woottens

WEDNESDAY 9
32 Woottens

THURSDAY 10
32 Woottens

SATURDAY 12
35 Wyken Hall

SUNDAY 13
35 Wyken Hall

TUESDAY 15
32 Woottens

WEDNESDAY 16
32 Woottens

THURSDAY 17
32 Woottens

SUNDAY 20
5 Brampton Willows Gardens
23 The Priory

TUESDAY 22
32 Woottens

WEDNESDAY 23
32 Woottens

THURSDAY 24
32 Woottens

SUNDAY 27
8 Brook Hall
17 Henstead Exotic Garden

MONDAY 28
8 Brook Hall
26 Rosemary

TUESDAY 29
32 Woottens

WEDNESDAY 30
32 Woottens

THURSDAY 31
32 Woottens

June

SATURDAY 2
22 Mildenhall Gardens

SUNDAY 3
3 Barton Mere
14 Gable House
16 Hall Farm
22 Mildenhall Gardens
31 Windmill Cottage

TUESDAY 5
32 Woottens

WEDNESDAY 6
32 Woottens

THURSDAY 7
32 Woottens

SATURDAY 9
30 White House Farm

SUNDAY 10
5 Brampton Willows Gardens
34 Wrentham Gardens

TUESDAY 12
32 Woottens

WEDNESDAY 13
32 Woottens

THURSDAY 14
32 Woottens

SUNDAY 17
2 Ashlie
9 The Coach House
19 Lime Kiln House
21 Magnolia House

TUESDAY 19
32 Woottens

WEDNESDAY 20
32 Woottens

THURSDAY 21
32 Woottens

SATURDAY 23
1 Abbey Farm (Evening)
7 Bridge Foot Farm
12 The Elms

SUNDAY 24
7 Bridge Foot Farm
8 Brook Hall
10 Columbine Hall
12 The Elms

TUESDAY 26
32 Woottens

WEDNESDAY 27
32 Woottens

THURSDAY 28
32 Woottens

July

TUESDAY 3
32 Woottens

WEDNESDAY 4
32 Woottens

THURSDAY 5
32 Woottens

SUNDAY 8
24 Redisham Hall
25 Rosedale

TUESDAY 10
32 Woottens

WEDNESDAY 11
32 Woottens

THURSDAY 12
32 Woottens

TUESDAY 17
32 Woottens

WEDNESDAY 18
32 Woottens

THURSDAY 19
32 Woottens

SUNDAY 22
2 Ashlie
6 Bresworth House

TUESDAY 24
32 Woottens

WEDNESDAY 25
32 Woottens

THURSDAY 26
32 Woottens

TUESDAY 31
32 Woottens

August

WEDNESDAY 1
32 Woottens

THURSDAY 2
32 Woottens

TUESDAY 7
32 Woottens

WEDNESDAY 8
32 Woottens

THURSDAY 9
32 Woottens

TUESDAY 14
32 Woottens

WEDNESDAY 15
32 Woottens

THURSDAY 16
32 Woottens

TUESDAY 21
32 Woottens

WEDNESDAY 22
32 Woottens

THURSDAY 23
32 Woottens

SUNDAY 26
2 Ashlie

TUESDAY 28
32 Woottens

WEDNESDAY 29
32 Woottens

THURSDAY 30
32 Woottens

September

SUNDAY 2
16 Hall Farm

TUESDAY 4
32 Woottens

WEDNESDAY 5
32 Woottens

THURSDAY 6
32 Woottens

TUESDAY 11
32 Woottens

WEDNESDAY 12
32 Woottens

THURSDAY 13
32 Woottens

SUNDAY 16
18 Home Farm House
20 The Lucy Redman School of Garden Design

TUESDAY 18
32 Woottens

WEDNESDAY 19
32 Woottens

THURSDAY 20
32 Woottens

TUESDAY 25
32 Woottens

WEDNESDAY 26
32 Woottens

THURSDAY 27
32 Woottens

October

SUNDAY 14
11 East Bergholt Place

Gardens open to the public

4 Blakenham Woodland Garden
9 The Coach House
13 Euston Hall
19 Lime Kiln House
32 Woottens
35 Wyken Hall

By appointment only

27 Thrift Farmhouse

The Gardens

1 ABBEY FARM
Abbey Hill, Hoxne IP21 5AL. Mr & Mrs John Ball, 01379 668222, cball@uea.ac.uk. *5m E of Diss. In Hoxne village at N end of Cross St. Entrance on Abbey Hill*. Home-made teas. Adm £2.50, chd free. **Evening Opening** wine, Sat 23 June (5-7.30). Visitors also welcome by appt May - July only, groups of 10+, coaches permitted.
3 acres of mature garden surrounding attractive C16 house (not open). Herbaceous planted courtyard, lawns with species roses and shrub beds. Walled kitchen garden with paved potager. All surrounded by grasses, informal areas with trees, ponds and mown walks. Some parts of the garden not suitable for wheelchairs.
    ♿ ✗ ☕

2 ASHLIE
St Andrews Road, Knodishall, Saxmundham IP17 1UR. Mr & Mrs H Williams, 01728 831054. *1m SW of Leiston. From A12 take A1094 signed to Aldeburgh. Turn L at sign for Leiston onto B1069, garden opp Butchers Arms PH*. Some parking at garden, further parking on common land on Mill Rd at side of PH. Adm £2.50, chd free. Suns 17 June; 22 July; 26 Aug (11-5). Visitors also welcome by appt.
Peaceful 1/2-acre garden with gloriously colourful planting. Lavender walks, tumbling roses, honeysuckle and clematis with pretty seating areas. Lovely vistas and decorative focal points, tranquil pond area, vibrant hot border, hidden walk, young woodland area, many grasses, subtropical area with cannas, bananas and exotic plants. Hot border vibrant in July. Some gravel paths.
    ♿ ✗ ☕

Unique water feature and recycled iron sculptures . . .

3 BARTON MERE
Thurston Road, Gt Barton IP31 2PR.
Mr & Mrs C O Stenderup. *4m NE of Bury St Edmunds. From Bury St Edmunds take A143 towards Ixworth. After Gt Barton turn R at Bunbury Arms PH. Continue past turnings to Pakenham & Barton Hamlet. Entrance to drive on L 100yds after Barton Hamlet tourist sign.* **Adm £3, chd free. Sun 3 June (2-5.30).**
C16 house (not open) with later Georgian façade, set in parkland overlooking lake (The Mere). Mainly walled gardens with roses, herbaceous borders, shrubs, large vegetable garden and conservatory.

4 ◆ BLAKENHAM WOODLAND GARDEN
Little Blakenham IP8 4LZ. Lord Blakenham, 07760 342131, blakenham@btinternet.com. *4m NW of Ipswich. Follow signs at Little Blakenham, 1m off B1113.* **Adm £3, chd £1.50. For NGS: Sat 21, Sun 22 Apr (10-5).**
Beautiful 6-acre woodland garden with variety of rare trees and shrubs. Chinese rocks and a landscape sculpture. Especially lovely in spring with daffodils, camellias, magnolias and bluebells followed by roses in early summer. Featured in 'Sunday Times Magazine'.

5 BRAMPTON WILLOWS GARDENS
Town Fen, London Road, Brampton NR34 8EB. Mr & Mrs Robert Yates, www.bramptonwillows.co.uk. *7m S of Beccles on A145. Brampton Willows sign at roadside, garden 200yds down track.* Light refreshments & teas. **Adm £3.50, chd free. Suns 20 May; 10 June (12-5).**
Flower and vegetable gardens created in 2000 and still evolving. Designed to show the extensive use of woven willow. Large woven willow features, pond and 15 acres of commercial willow beds, particularly attractive in the spring. Featured in 'English Garden Magazine' and 'Country Homes & Interiors'. Gravel paths.

6 BRESWORTH HOUSE
Cotton IP14 4RG. Keith & Ann Bullock, 01449 780102. *6m N of Stowmarket. Between B1113 & A140 close to Cotton Church.* Home-made teas. **Adm £2.50, chd free. Sun 22 July (2-5).** Visitors also welcome by

appt April to July, clubs welcome, conducted tours available.
Quiet 1-acre garden sheltered by mature indigenous trees. Unique water feature and recycled iron sculptures. Interesting collection of plants, ornamental trees and shrubs, vegetable plot, cows grazing next door.

7 NEW BRIDGE FOOT FARM
Reydon, Southwold IP18 6PS. David & Susan Evan Jones, 01502 725293. *A1095 on main rd into Southwold. Follow signs to Southwold. Honey coloured house on LH-side opp new development before Bridge Rd and bridge.* Cream teas. **Adm £2.50, chd free. Sat 23, Sun 24 June (2-5).** Open with **The Elms**. Visitors also welcome by appt, June, July, Aug.
Totally redesigned garden 2002, comprising 3 mainly gravelled areas. Front garden with geraniums and clematis, hidden garden with arbour and new planting for 2007 behind old outbuildings, shaded 'L' shaped garden with raised bed of perennials, climbers and shrubs.

8 BROOK HALL
Church Road, Crowfield IP6 9TG. Mr & Mrs D S Pumfrey, 01449 711575. *3m N of Coddenham. 1m S of Stonham Aspal, Pettaugh A1120, 1/4m from Crowfield Church. Brook Hall is reached down a farm drive.* Home-made teas. **Adm £3, chd free. Sun 27, Mon 28 May; Sun 24 June (Mon 10-3), (Sun 11-5).** Visitors also welcome by appt, June only; groups of 10+, coaches permitted.
Tranquil 1 1/2 acres surround a classic Suffolk farmhouse (not open). Relaxing country garden with informal mixed borders. Clematis, rambling roses, shrubs, trees and containers. Kitchen garden with polytunnel and greenhouse. Large natural pond, small wilderness, a place for wildlife.

9 ◆ THE COACH HOUSE
Assington CO10 5LQ. Mrs Justine Ferrari, 01787 211364, ferrarifrs@aol.com. *5m S of Sudbury. On A134. Turn R into Assington village. On sharp LH-bend turn R into The Coach House.* **Adm £3, chd free. For**

Particularly beautiful in autumn with newly cut topiary and autumn colours . . .

NGS: Sun 17 June (2-6).
Semi-formal 2-acre plantswoman's garden generously planted with herbaceous borders incl colour-themed beds. Pond garden, potager, woodland beds and wild flower areas. Many different shrubs, roses and climbers. Free range pure-bred hens.

10 COLUMBINE HALL
Stowupland IP14 4AT. Hew & Leslie Stevenson, www.columbinehall.co.uk. *1 1/2 m NE of Stowmarket. Turn N off A1120 opp Shell garage across village green, then R at T-junction into Gipping Rd. Garden on L just beyond derestriction sign.* Home-made teas. **Adm £3, chd free. Sun 24 June (2-6).**
Formal gardens, designed by George Carter, surround moated medieval manor house (not open). Also, outside the moat, bog garden, Mediterranean garden, colour-themed vegetable garden, orchards and parkland. Gardens developed since 1994 with constant work-in-progress, incl transformed farm buildings, wilderness and eyecatchers. Some gravel paths.

11 EAST BERGHOLT PLACE
East Bergholt CO7 6UP. Mr & Mrs Rupert Eley. *On B1070 towards Manningtree, 2m E of A12. Situated on the edge of East Bergholt.* Home-made teas. **Adm £3, chd free. Suns 25 Mar; 15 Apr; 14 Oct (2-5).**
15-acre garden originally laid out at the beginning of the century by the present owner's great grandfather. Full of many fine trees and shrubs some of which are rarely seen in East Anglia. Particularly beautiful in spring when the rhododendrons, magnolias and camellias are in full flower, and in autumn with newly cut topiary and autumn colours. National Collection of deciduous euonymus.

12 NEW THE ELMS
Lorne Road, Southwold
IP18 6EP. Mr & Mrs I P
Drummond, 01502 723744,
ipdrummond@aol.com. *10m from
Lowestoft. At end of A1095, 4m
from A12 at Blythburgh. Through
High St to Market Sq bear R into
Queen St, 2nd R in to Lorne Road.
Garden 100yds on RH-side.*
Cream teas at **Bridge Foot
Farm**. Adm £2.50, chd free. Sat
23, Sun 24 June (2-5). Open with
Bridge Foot Farm. Visitors also
welcome by appt, May, June,
July, no large parties.
Walled garden 1/3-acre in centre of
seaside town. Unusual plants and
herbaceous borders.

☀ ⊕ ☕

Pots brimming with tender plants are grouped on the vine shaded terrace . . .

13 ◆ EUSTON HALL
Thetford IP242QP. His Grace The
Duke of Grafton, 01842 766366,
www.eustonhall.co.uk. *12m N of
Bury St Edmunds. 3m S of Thetford on
A1088.* House and Garden adm £6,
chd £3, OAPs £5, Garden only adm
£4, chd £3. Thurs 14 June to 13
Sept; Suns 24 June; 15 July; 2 Sept
(2.30-5).
Terraced lawns, herbaceous borders,
rose garden, C17 pleasure grounds,
lake and watermill. C18 house open;
famous collection of paintings. C17
church; temple by William Kent. Craft
shop.

&. ☀ ☕

14 GABLE HOUSE
Halesworth Road, Redisham
NR34 8NE. Mr & Mrs John Foster,
01502 575298. *5m S of Beccles.
Between Beccles & Halesworth on
Ringsfield/Ilketshall St Lawrence rd.
Car parking nearby.* Home-made teas.
Adm £2.50, chd free (share to St
Peter's Church, Redisham). Sun 18
Feb (snowdrop day 11-4.30); Sun 3

June (11-5). Visitors also welcome
by appt.
1-acre garden contains a wide range of
interesting plants. In Feb visitors can
see over 200 varieties of snowdrops
together with cyclamen, hellebore and
early flowering bulbs. Wide range of
summer flowering plants. 3 greenhouses each contain plants from
alpines to tender species, many for
sale.

☀ ⊕ ☕

15 GREAT THURLOW HALL
Haverhill CB9 7LF. Mr & Mrs George
Vestey. *12m S of Bury St Edmunds,
4m N of Haverhill. Great Thurlow village
on B1061 from Newmarket; 3 1/2 m N of
junction with A143 Haverhill/Bury St
Edmunds rd.* Teas. Adm £2.50, chd
free. Sun 1 Apr (2-5).
River walk and trout lake with extensive
and impressive display of daffodils and
blossom. Spacious lawns, shrubberies
and roses. Walled kitchen garden.
Some gravel.

&. ☕

16 HALL FARM
Weston, Beccles NR34 8TT. Mr &
Mrs Peter Seppings, 01502 715065,
peterstebbings@pennylane.entadsl.
com. *1 1/2 m S of Beccles. On A145.
The entrance is the same as for Winter
Flora, continue 300yds along the drive
to the private house.* Home-made
lunches, wine and teas. Adm £2.50
(incl tea), chd free. Suns 3 June; 2
Sept (11.30-5). Visitors also
welcome by appt, May to Sept,
coaches permitted.
The large photogenic pond set in 1 1/2
acres is surrounded by primulas, iris
and rushes with several seats incl
colourful frog. Pots brimming with
tender plants are grouped on the vine
shaded terrace whilst clemetis and
roses smother the pergola. Down
sizing the closely planted parterre has
been our priority during the autumn.
Additional paving and complete
replanting with global warming in mind,
has brought a little more order to this
pretty garden. Ferns and hellebores are
shaded by the walnut tree.
Conservatory with ample seating if the
weather is bad.

&. ⊕ ☕

**17 HENSTEAD EXOTIC
GARDEN**
Yew Cottage, Henstead NR34 7LD.
Andrew Brogan, 01502 743006.
*Equal distance between Beccles,
Southwold & Lowestoft approx 5m.*

*1m from A12 turning after Wrentham
(signed Henstead) very close to
B1127.* Home-made teas in
summerhouse. Adm £2.50, chd free.
Sun 27 May (1-6). Visitors also
welcome by appt.
Unusual 1-acre garden featuring large
palms, bananas and exotic plants, 2
streams, 20ft tiered walkway leading to
Thai style wooden covered pavilion.
Mediterranean and jungle plants
around 3 large ponds with fish and.
'Suffolk's most exotic garden.
Mediterranean meets North Africa' -
Suffolk magazine.

☀ ⊕ ☕

18 HOME FARM HOUSE
Rushbrooke IP30 0EP. Anita Wigan,
07768 045300,
stephenfrankland@btinternet.com.
*3m SE of Bury St Edmunds. A14 J44,
proceed towards town centre, after
50yds 1st exit from roundabout then
immed R. Proceed 3/4 m to T-junction,
turn L, follow rd for 2m Rushbrooke
Church on L, turn R into drive opp
church.* Home-made teas. Adm £3,
chd free. Sun 16 Sept (2-5). Also
open **The Lucy Redman School of
Garden Design**. Visitors also
welcome by appt, max 10 visitors.
3 acres walled garden with mixed
shrubs and herbaceous borders, roses
and formal lawns. 1-acre organic
kitchen garden plus glasshouses with
peaches, apricots, nectarines, grapes
and figs etc. 5-acre parkland with moat
garden, specimen trees and orchard.
Small cottage garden alongside moat.

&. ☀ ⊕ ☕

19 ◆ LIME KILN HOUSE
Old Ipswich Road, Claydon
IP6 0AD. Kathy Kalafat & Tim Young,
01473 833332,
www.limekilnroses.co.uk. *3m N of
Ipswich. Off A14 J52 signed B1113
Bramford, Blakenham & Claydon, take
Claydon exit from roundabout, then 1st
R into Old Ipswich Rd. Garden 100
metres on L, behind large beech trees.*
Adm £3, chd £1. For garden open
days, dates & time please see
website or tel. For NGS: Sun 17
June (11-6).
Currently under renovation. Wild
romantic garden of approx 2 acres.
Originally an old Suffolk farmhouse with
working lime kiln. Gardens established
in 1920's following the removal of old
farm buildings. In the1970/80's a
famous Rosarium established by
Humphrey Brooke for the preservation
and conservation of old roses.
Neglected in parts since his death in

1988 the roses are still magnificent in the summer months. Old roses grow in wild profusion, over pergolas, arches, walls and summerhouses, up trees and over each other. Very old beech and lime trees, Irish yews and mulberry.

㉔ THE LUCY REDMAN SCHOOL OF GARDEN DESIGN
6 The Village, Rushbrooke IP30 0ER. Lucy Redman & Dominic Watts, 01284 386250, www.lucyredman.co.uk. *3m E of Bury St Edmunds. From A14 Bury St Edmunds, E Sudbury exit, proceed towards town centre. After 50yds, 1st L exit from roundabout and immed R. 3/4m to T-junction, turn L, follow rd for 2m. Before church turn R between white houses, past brick well, thatched house on L.* Home-made teas at Home Farm House. **Adm £2, chd free. Sun 16 Sept (2-5). Also open Home Farm House. Visitors also welcome by appt.**
Thatched cottage surrounded by 1/2-acre quirky plantsman's family garden divided into compartments with impressive colour-coordinated borders containing many interesting combinations of unusual shrubs, roses, grasses and perennials. Grass parterre, turf tree seat, sculptures, wildlife pond, sedum roofed pavilion. Unusual bulb and rhizome garden, willow igloo and tunnel. Featured in 'Suffolk Magazine', 'East Magazine' & 'County Homes & Interiors'.

㉑ MAGNOLIA HOUSE
Yoxford IP17 3EP. Mr Mark Rumary, 01728 668321. *4m N of Saxmundham. Centre of Yoxford on A1120.* **Adm £2.50, chd free. Sun 17 June (2-5.30). Visitors also welcome by appt.**
Small, completely walled, romantic garden, tucked behind a pretty C18 village house (not open). Ingeniously designed to appear larger and planted to provide yr-round colour, scent and horticultural interest. Contains ancient mulberry, raised Moorish-style pool and attractive pots and urns.

㉒ MILDENHALL GARDENS
IP28 7ED. *15m W of Bury St Edmunds. 5 mins from Mildenhall centre. From Fiveways roundabout at Barton Mills on A11 follow signs to Mildenhall. Gardens all within 5 mins walk of town centre car parks.* Home-made teas at 28 Kingsway. **Combined adm £3, chd free. Sat 2, Sun 3 June (2-5).**
Historic market town with famous Suffolk church.

6A CHURCH WALK
Mr & Mrs D G Reeve, 01638 715289, j.reeve05@tiscali.co.uk. **Visitors also welcome by appt.**
Walled garden surrounding modern bungalow. Sunken paved area, raised bed with pond and waterfall. Patio with water feature, established rockery, many herbaceous plants and shrubs incl collection of hemerocallis. Featured in 'Amateur Gardening' 2005.

CROSSBILLS
David & Yvonne Leonard. *Please park on industrial estate opp house*
1/4-acre partially walled garden on edge of town the light, sandy Breckland soil has been developed into 2 separate areas of gravel gardens. Many varieties of cistus, lavender and drought tolerant plants.

28 KINGSWAY
Nick & Anne Berry, 01638 714180, nickberry@onetel.net. **Visitors also welcome by appt.**
Varied garden containing 2 modern sculptures surrounded by bamboos, grasses and herbaceous borders. Ingenious irrigation system. Established grapevines in greenhouse. Conservatory contains collections of carnivorous plants and orchids. Garden recently redesigned with dry gravel area. Featured in 'Amateur Gardening'.

TIGGYWINKLE COTTAGE
18 Wamil Way. Mrs Marion Turner
Small cottage garden designed around a central courtyard containing a variety of unusual plants for both hot and shady areas. Climbing roses and clematis give height and seclusion to areas for relaxation. Featured in 'Gardeners Monthly'.

㉓ THE PRIORY
Stoke-by-Nayland CO6 4RL. Mr & Mrs H F A Engleheart. *5m SW of Hadleigh. Entrance on B1068 to Sudbury (NW of Stoke-by-Nayland).* Home-made teas. **Adm £3, chd free. Sun 20 May (2-5).**
Interesting 9-acre garden with fine views over Constable countryside; lawns sloping down to small lakes and water garden; fine trees, rhododendrons and azaleas; walled garden; mixed borders and ornamental greenhouse. Wide variety of plants; peafowl. Some gravel paths, slight slope.

㉔ REDISHAM HALL
Beccles NR34 8LZ. The Palgrave Brown Family. *5m S of Beccles. From A145, turn W on to Ringsfield-Bungay rd. Beccles, Halesworth or Bungay, all within 5m.* Home-made teas. **Adm £3, chd free. Sun 8 July (2-6).**
C18 Georgian house (not open). 5-acre garden set in 400 acres parkland and woods. Incl 2-acre walled kitchen garden (in full production) with peach house, vinery and glasshouses. Lawns, herbaceous borders, shrubberies, ponds and mature trees.

㉕ ROSEDALE
40 Colchester Road, Bures CO8 5AE. Mr & Mrs Colin Lorking. *6m SE of Sudbury. 9m NW of Colchester on B1508. As you enter the village of Bures, garden on L. From Sudbury follow signs through village towards Colchester, garden on R as you leave village.* Home-made teas. **Adm £2, chd free. Suns 6 May; 8 July (12-5.30).**
Approx 1/3-acre plantsman's garden; many unusual plants, herbaceous borders, pond, woodland area.

Small, completely walled, romantic garden, tucked behind a pretty C18 village house (not open) . . .

26 ROSEMARY

Rectory Hill, East Bergholt CO7 6TH. Mrs N E M Finch, 01206 298241. *9m NE of Colchester. Turn off A12 onto B1070 to East Bergholt, 1st R Hadleigh Rd, bear L at end of rd. At junction with Village St turn R, pass Red Lion PH, post office & church. Garden 100yds down from church on L.* Home-made teas. **Adm £2.50, chd free. Sun 8 Apr; Mon 28 May (2-5). Visitors also welcome by appt.** This romantic garden, which appeals particularly to artists, has been developed over 34yrs. Planted to reveal paths and vistas. Over 100 old-fashioned roses. 2 bog beds, unusual trees, good bulbs and many unusual plants. Planted for all seasons.

    ➡ ⊕ ⊨ ☕

SHRUBS FARM

See Essex.

27 THRIFT FARMHOUSE

Kirtling Cowlinge CB8 9JA. Mrs Jan Oddy, 01440 783274, janoddy@yahoo.co.uk. *7m N of Newmarket. Great Bradley Rd from Kirtling - Great Bradley Rd from Cowlinge. Turn R at Xrds to Kirtling. Car parking in adjacent meadow.* **Visitors welcome by appt, Apr to Oct, groups up to 20.** Forever changing, 6 acres, attractive country cottage garden, set around thatched house (not open). Island beds, full of mixed trees, shrubs and perennials, shady woodland areas. Natural pond, orchard of mixed fruits and meadows of sheep and wild flowers. Gravel, lawns and inclines.

    ➡ ✕ ⊕ ⊨

28 THE WALLOW

Mount Road, Bury St Edmunds IP31 2QU. Linda & Mike Draper, 01284 788055, info@thewallow.co.uk. *2m E of Bury St Edmunds. Leave A14 J45 at Rougham Industrial Site, 1/2m along Sow Lane to T-junction at Battlies Corner. Take L towards BSE for*

1/2m along Mount Rd. Home-made teas. **Adm £2.50, chd free. Sun 1 Apr (2-5). Visitors also welcome by appt Jun - Aug for groups of 10+ (max 30).** 2 1/4 acres of garden with wild pond, flower meadows, orchard, potager, silver birch planting with snakeshead fritillaries and herbaceous borders. Yr-round interest. Owner keen propagator, small nursery, new woodland planting. Partial wheelchair access: sloping grass, ok for pushed chairs, easy access to grassy area.

    ➡ ✕ ⊕ ⊨ ☕

29 WALSHAM GARDENS

Walsham-le-Willows IP31 3AD. *11m E of Bury St Edmunds. From A143 to Diss take turning for Walsham-le-Willows to Xrds.* Home-made teas in Priory Room. **Combined adm £3, chd free under 16 (share to St Marys Church, Walsham-le-Willows). Sun 1 Apr (1-5).**

THE BEECHES

Grove Road. Dr A J Russell 150yr-old, 3-acre garden, which incl specimen trees, pond, potager, memorial garden, lawns and variety of beds. Improvements to stream area.

    ➡

NEW BRIDGE HOUSE

David & Ann Daniels Approx 1 acre, divided into manageable areas by use of hedges, pathways and mature trees.

THE GRANGE

Colin & Maureen Brown Large farmhouse garden. Beds of heathers, conifers and shrubs surround the lawn behind the house. Waterfall flowing into 2 ponds, summerhouse, statues and topiary. New rose beds have been created.

    ➡ ✕

NEW MALTINGS HOUSE

The Street. Mrs P D Blyth Spring garden. Hostas, bluebells, primroses, aconites, daffodils, shrubs, laburnham, snowdrops and crocuses. Walled garden with partial wild patch under hazel trees. Croquet lawn and large vegetable area with fruit cage. Gravel drive.

    ➡

NEW NUNN'S YARD

The Street. Steve Colby 3 acres, long term landscaping, tree and hedge planting. Areas completed are split into planting themes, statues, archways, shrubs, herbaceous, perennials and specimen trees.

NEW THE OLD BAKERY

The Street. Mr & Mrs R Barber. *400yds E of church in Main St* Long irregular shaped garden with herbaceous borders, seating areas and lawns, tapering alongside the village stream before turning and opening into a kitchen garden. Mature trees offer areas of dappled shade. Gravel paths.

    ➡ ✕

30 NEW WHITE HOUSE FARM

Ringsfield NR34 8JU. James & Jan Barlow, 0777 0395398 Head gardener. *2m SW of Beccles. From Beccles take B1062 towards Bungay, after 1 1/2m turn L, signed Ringsfield. Continue for 1m passing Ringsfield Church. Garden 300yds on L over small white railed bridge.* Home-made teas. **Adm £3, chd £1. Sat 9 June (11-5). Visitors also welcome by appt, all year min 4, max 20 visitors.** Fine garden of approx 30 acres with superb views over the Waveney Valley. Formal gardens and parkland with specimen trees, copses and lawns, good deal of mixed hedging. NB Beck and 2 ponds are not fenced.

    ⊕ ☕

Mature trees offer areas of dappled shade . . .

31 WINDMILL COTTAGE

Mill Hill, Capel St Mary IP9 2JE. Mr & Mrs G A Cox, 01473 311121. *3m SW of Ipswich. Turn off A12 at Capel St Mary. At far end of village on R after 1 1/4m.* Home-made teas. **Adm £2.50, chd free. Sun 3 June (2-6). Visitors**

Bird, bee and butterfly garden in a Versailles design with pond, herbs, box and lavender planting . . .

also welcome by appt.
¹/₂-acre plantsman's cottage-style garden. Island beds, pergolas with clematis and other climbers. Many trees and shrubs, wildlife ponds and vegetable area.

🌺 ❀ ☕

32 ◆ WOOTTENS
Blackheath Road, Wenhaston
IP19 9HD. Mr M Loftus, 01502 478258, www.woottensplants.co.uk. *18m S of Lowestoft. On A12 & B1123, follow signs to Wenhaston.* **Adm £1, chd/concessions 50p.** For NGS: Tues, Weds, Thurs, 10 Apr to 27 Sept. Bearded iris field 24 May to 10 June; Iris sibirica field Sats, Suns 9, 10, 16, 17 June; Hemerocallis field Sats, Suns 7, 8, 14, 15, 21, 22 July (9.30-5).
Small romantic garden, redesigned in 2003. Scented-leafed pelargoniums, violas, cranesbills, lilies, salvias, penstemons, primulas, etc. 2 acres of bearded iris, ¹/₄ acre of iris sibiricas, 1 acre of hemerocallis. Featured in 'Gardeners World Magazine'. Wheelchair users will need assitance with access to fields.

♿ 🌺 ❀

33 WORLINGTON HOUSE
Mildenhall Road, Worlington
IP28 8RX. Rupert & Linz Osborn. *2m S of Mildenhall. Take A1102 from Mildenhall towards Fordham. Garden on RH-side 3 down from Worlington Hall Hotel. From Newmarket A11 take 3rd exit signed Worlington, at Walnut*

Tree junction turn R, garden 2nd on L. Tea & cake. **Adm £2.50, chd free. Sat 28, Sun 29 Apr (10-3).**
Mature garden comprising 3 areas of interest. Serpentine walled garden with herbaceous borders, grasses, roses and box hedging with pond, water feature and sandstone terracing. Bird, bee and butterfly garden in a Versailles design with pond, herbs, box and lavender planting. 1-acre mature woodland with specimen trees and woodland walk and magnolia grove. Wonderful dragon carving (featured in local press). Gravel paths.

♿ 🌺 ▨ ☕

34 WRENTHAM GARDENS
NR34 7JF. *4m N of Southwold. 5m S of Lowestoft. From A12 in centre of Wrentham take B1127 Southwold Rd. Small car park at junction followed by 3 laybys on L. Some parking available at no 70.* Light refreshments & teas. **Combined adm £2.50, chd free. Sun 10 June (11-6).**
All gardens within 600yds of junction. Spread out village along A12. Some interesting buildings - C15 church and Georgian Meeting House.

☕

LILBOURNE
70 Southwold Road. Mr & Mrs Richard Wood
Attractive country garden that slopes away from the house towards a meadow. Divided into 3 sections with interesting mixed borders of herbaceous and cottage plants. Shallow steps

have to be negotiated to reach garden.

MILL COTTAGE
34 Southwood Road. Gillian Innes, 01502 675281. *Visitors also welcome by appt, June & July only.*
Picturesque ¹/₃-acre plantsman's garden. Mixed herbaceous, shrubs, roses, vegetables and fruit for a difficult site. Hidden yard garden.

🌺 ❀

68 SOUTHWOLD ROAD
Mrs C Reeve
Open aspect sloping down to meadow, broken by islands of trees, shrubs and ornamental plants together with old favourite cottage garden perennials. Tree-house, accessed at own risk. Gentle grass slopes.

♿ 🌺 ▨

35 ◆ WYKEN HALL
Stanton IP31 2DW. Sir Kenneth & Lady Carlisle, 01359 253420, www.wykenvineyards.com. *9m NE of Bury St Edmunds. Along A143. Follow signs to Wyken Vineyards on A143 between Ixworth & Stanton.* **Adm £3, chd free, concessions £2.50.** For NGS: Sat 12, Sun 13 May (2-6).
4-acre garden much developed recently; knot and herb garden; old-fashioned rose garden, wild garden, nuttery, pond, gazebo and maze; herbaceous borders and old orchard. Woodland walk, vineyard.

♿ 🌺 ❀ ☕

Open aspect sloping down to meadow . . .

Suffolk County Volunteers

County Organiser
Patricia Short, Ruggs Hall, Raydon, Ipswich IP7 5LW, 01473 310416

County Treasurers
East Geoffrey Cox, Windmill Cottage, Mill Hill, Capel St. Mary, Ipswich IP9 2JE, 01473 311121, gaandemcox@lineone.net
West David Reeve, 6a Church Walk, Mildenhall IP28 7ED, 01638 715289

Assistant County Organisers
Joan Brightwell, Bucklesham Hall, Bucklesham IP10 0AY, 01473 659263
Jenny Reeve, 6a Church Walk, Mildenhall IP28 7ED, 01638 715289, j.reeve05@tiscali.co.uk
Hans Seiffer, Garden House Farm, Rattlesden Road, Drinkstone, Bury St Edmunds IP30 9TN, 01449 736434, hans.seiffer@dial.pipex.com,
Joby West, The Millstone, Friars Road, Hadleigh, IP7 6DF, 01473 823154

SURREY

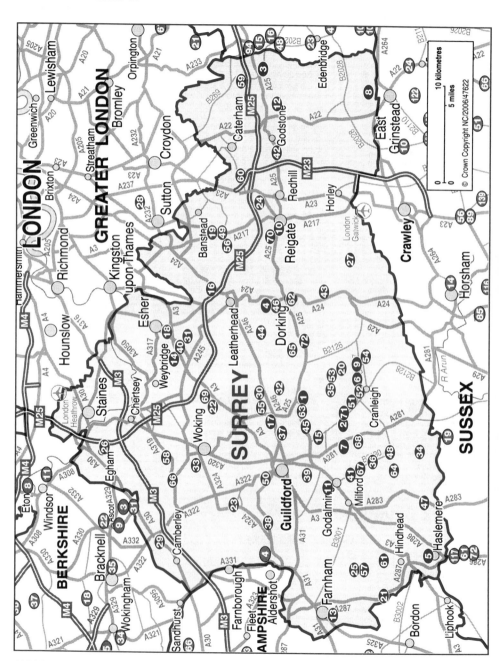

Opening Dates

February

SUNDAY 11
24 Gatton Park

WEDNESDAY 14
24 Gatton Park

March

SUNDAY 11
1 Albury Park

April

SUNDAY 1
17 Clandon Park

WEDNESDAY 11
10 Caxton House

SATURDAY 14
68 Wintershall Manor

SUNDAY 15
20 Coverwood Lakes
36 Lodkin
58 Timber Hill

WEDNESDAY 18
49 41 Shelvers Way

SATURDAY 21
22 Dunsborough Park

SUNDAY 22
20 Coverwood Lakes
41 Munstead Wood
49 41 Shelvers Way
67 Winkworth Arboretum

SUNDAY 29
20 Coverwood Lakes
30 Hatchlands Park
52 Spring Cottage

May

SUNDAY 6
13 Chestnut Cottage
20 Coverwood Lakes
39 Loseley Park
43 The Old Croft
52 Spring Cottage
66 Westways Farm

MONDAY 7
43 The Old Croft
64 Vann
65 Walton Poor House

TUESDAY 8
64 Vann

WEDNESDAY 9
64 Vann

THURSDAY 10
64 Vann

FRIDAY 11
64 Vann

SATURDAY 12
21 Crosswater Farm
64 Vann

SUNDAY 13
14 Chestnut Lodge
20 Coverwood Lakes
21 Crosswater Farm
40 Moleshill House
64 Vann
68 Wintershall Manor

THURSDAY 17
40 Moleshill House

FRIDAY 18
53 Spurfold (Evening)

SATURDAY 19
8 Braekenas

SUNDAY 20
7 Birtley House
8 Braekenas
29 Hall Grove School
35 Knowle Grange
38 Longer End Cottage
45 Postford House
46 Quinneys

MONDAY 21
12 Chauffeur's Flat

TUESDAY 22
12 Chauffeur's Flat

WEDNESDAY 23
12 Chauffeur's Flat

THURSDAY 24
12 Chauffeur's Flat

FRIDAY 25
12 Chauffeur's Flat

SATURDAY 26
12 Chauffeur's Flat

SUNDAY 27
12 Chauffeur's Flat
41 Munstead Wood
43 The Old Croft
51 Smithwood House

MONDAY 28
43 The Old Croft
51 Smithwood House
62 6 Upper Rose Hill

June

SUNDAY 3
18 Claremont Landscape Garden
36 Lodkin
62 6 Upper Rose Hill
64 Vann
65 Walton Poor House

MONDAY 4
26 Great Fosters
64 Vann

TUESDAY 5
26 Great Fosters
64 Vann

WEDNESDAY 6
26 Great Fosters
64 Vann

THURSDAY 7
26 Great Fosters
64 Vann

FRIDAY 8
34 Howicks (Evening)
64 Vann

SATURDAY 9
22 Dunsborough Park
34 Howicks
64 Vann

SUNDAY 10
6 Barhatch Farm
9 Burstowe's Croft
44 Polesden Lacey
54 Square Leg Cottage
64 Vann

WEDNESDAY 13
9 Burstowe's Croft
50 67 & 69 Shepherds Lane
54 Square Leg Cottage

FRIDAY 15
53 Spurfold (Evening)

SATURDAY 16
63 Vale End (Evening)

SUNDAY 17
11 Charterhouse
23 Four Aces
31 Heathside
38 Longer End Cottage
60 Tollsworth Manor
63 Vale End

MONDAY 18
12 Chauffeur's Flat

TUESDAY 19
12 Chauffeur's Flat

WEDNESDAY 20
12 Chauffeur's Flat

THURSDAY 21
12 Chauffeur's Flat
57 Tilford Cottage (Evening)

FRIDAY 22
4 Ashleigh Grange (Evening)
12 Chauffeur's Flat
48 The Round House (Evening)

SATURDAY 23
12 Chauffeur's Flat
56 35 Tadorne Road
57 Tilford Cottage
59 Titsey Place Gardens

SUNDAY 24
- ④ Ashleigh Grange
- ⑤ Bardsey
- ⑫ Chauffeur's Flat
- ⑮ Chinthurst Lodge
- ⑯ Chipchase
- ㊶ Munstead Wood
- ㊽ The Round House
- ㊻ 35 Tadorne Road
- ㊼ Tilford Cottage
- ㊹ Upper Ridgeway Farm

WEDNESDAY 27
- ⑮ Chinthurst Lodge

FRIDAY 29
- ㊺ Stuart Cottage (Evening)

July

SUNDAY 1
- ㉓ Four Aces (Day & Evening)
- ㉝ Horsell Allotments & Birch Cottage Garden

FRIDAY 6
- ㉑ Woodbury Cottage (Evening)

SATURDAY 7
- ② Appletrees (Evening)
- ㉑ Woodbury Cottage

SUNDAY 8
- ② Appletrees
- ㉑ Woodbury Cottage
- ㉒ Wotton House

WEDNESDAY 11
- ⑲ The Copse Lodge (Evening)
- ㊿ 67 & 69 Shepherds Lane (Evening)
- ㊳ Vale End

SATURDAY 14
- ㊸ The Old Croft

SUNDAY 15
- ⑯ Chipchase
- ⑲ The Copse Lodge
- ㉕ Gorse Cottage
- ㊸ The Old Croft
- ㉒ Wotton House

WEDNESDAY 18
- ⑯ Chipchase
- ⑲ The Copse Lodge (Evening)

SATURDAY 21
- ㊾ Titsey Place Gardens

SUNDAY 22
- ㊾ 41 Shelvers Way
- ㊺ Stuart Cottage
- ㉒ Wotton House

SUNDAY 29
- ㉘ 72 Green Wrythe Lane
- ㉕ Walton Poor House
- ㉒ Wotton House

August

SUNDAY 5
- ㊷ Odstock

FRIDAY 10
- ㊼ Spurfold (Evening)

SATURDAY 11
- ㊸ The Old Croft
- ㊾ Titsey Place Gardens

SUNDAY 12
- ㊲ Long Barton
- ㊸ The Old Croft

SUNDAY 19
- ㉓ Four Aces
- ㊳ Longer End Cottage

TUESDAY 21
- ㊹ Wisley RHS Garden (Evening)

MONDAY 27
- ㊺ Stuart Cottage (Evening)

September

SATURDAY 1
- ㉑ Woodbury Cottage

SUNDAY 2
- ⑱ Claremont Landscape Garden
- ㊴ Loseley Park
- ㉑ Woodbury Cottage

WEDNESDAY 5
- ㉑ Woodbury Cottage

SATURDAY 8
- ㉒ Dunsborough Park

SUNDAY 9
- ⑭ Chestnut Lodge
- ㊳ Longer End Cottage

SUNDAY 16
- ㉟ Knowle Grange

October

SUNDAY 7
- ① Albury Park
- ㊸ Winkworth Arboretum

SUNDAY 14
- ㉚ Hatchlands Park
- ㊿ Walton Poor House

SUNDAY 21
- ⑳ Coverwood Lakes

February 2008

SUNDAY 17
- ㉔ Gatton Park

WEDNESDAY 20
- ㉔ Gatton Park

Gardens open to the public

- ⑰ Clandon Park
- ⑱ Claremont Landscape Garden
- ⑳ Coverwood Lakes
- ㉑ Crosswater Farm
- ㉔ Gatton Park
- ㉚ Hatchlands Park
- ㊴ Loseley Park

- ㊹ Polesden Lacey
- ㊼ Ramster
- ㊾ Titsey Place Gardens
- ㊸ Winkworth Arboretum
- ㊹ Wisley RHS Garden

By appointment only

- ③ Arden Lodge
- ㉗ Green Lane Farm
- ㉜ Hookwood Farmhouse
- ㉑ Woodhill Manor

The Gardens

① ALBURY PARK

Albury GU5 9BH. Trustees of Albury Estate. *5m SE of Guildford. From A25 take A248 towards Albury for ¼m, then up New Rd, entrance to Albury Park immed on L.* Home-made teas. **Adm £3, chd free. Suns 11 Mar; 7 Oct (2-5).**

14-acre pleasure grounds laid out in 1670s by John Evelyn for Henry Howard, later 6th Duke of Norfolk. ¼m terraces, fine collection of trees, lake and river. Albury Park Mansion gardens also open (by kind permission of Historic House Retirement Homes Ltd. House not open). Gravel path and slight slope.

ANGLESEY ROAD

See Hampshire.

② APPLETREES

Stonards Brow, Shamley Green GU5 0UY. Mr & Mrs A Hodgson, 01483 898779, tonyhodgson@waitrose.com. *5m SE of Guildford. A281 Guildford to Horsham rd, turn L at Shalford on B2128 via Wonersh to Shamley Green. Turn R before Red Lion PH, then R into Sweetwater Lane. At top of lane turn R into Stonards Brow or follow signs to car park at Xrds when entering village. From Ewhurst/Cranleigh turn L at village stores, proceed down Hullbrook Lane following signs into Lordshill and car park.* Cream teas. **Adm £2.50, chd free. Sun 8 July (2-6). Evening Opening £4, wine & cheese, Sat 7 July (5-8).** Visitors also welcome by appt in July, for groups of 15+ for morning coffee, afternoon teas or evening visits.

¼-acre garden with many interesting features. Several small water features incl koi pond. Summerhouse, greenhouses, raised railway sleeper beds, pergolas. Shrub and perennial borders. Patio and gravel area with

several colourful containers. Raised vegetable beds; jungle beds with bananas and an elevated walkway; new secret garden and white water garden. Obelisks and clematis, all on a sandy loam soil. An ideas garden. Most areas wheelchair accessible, assistance available.

  ♿ ⊛ ☕

③ ARDEN LODGE
Pastens Road, Limpsfield RH8 0RE. Mr & Mrs C Bruce-Jones, 01883 722171, chris.bruce-jones@virgin.net. *1m E of Oxted. From A25 take B269 Edenbridge Rd for 200yds. R down Brick Kiln Lane. Pastens Rd 2nd turning L, house at end of rd.* Refreshments by arrangement. **Adm £3, chd free. Visitors welcome by appt Easter to July for groups & individuals.**
2-acre garden on greensand with extensive views. Sunken garden with formal fishpond and arbour; pergola; herbaceous border; rhododendrons, azaleas and much formal and informal mixed planting with interesting trees, shrubs, roses and containers. Some gravel paths.

  ♿ ✗ ☕

Plenty of seats to relax and enjoy your tea . . .

④ ASHLEIGH GRANGE
off Chapel Lane, Westhumble RH5 6AY. Clive & Angela Gilchrist, 01306 884613, clive.gilchrist@btinternet.com. *2m N of Dorking. From A24 at Boxhill/Burford Bridge follow signs to Westhumble. Through village & L up drive by ruined chapel (1m from A24).* Home-made teas. **Adm £2.50, chd free. Sun 24 June (2-5.30). Evening Opening £3.50, wine, Fri 22 June (6-8). Visitors also welcome by appt in May & June.**
3½-acre sloping chalk garden in charming rural setting. Many areas of interest incl rockery and water feature; raised ericaceous bed; prairie-style bank; mixed herbaceous and shrub borders; foliage plants; woodland walk and fernery. Newly-planted slope with outstanding views. Featured in 'Surrey Life'.

  ♿ ⊛ ☕

⑤ NEW BARDSEY
11 Derby Road, Haslemere GU27 1BS. Maggie & David Boyd. *¼m N of Haslemere stn. Turn off B2131 (which links A287 to A286 through town) 400yds W of stn into Weydown Rd, 3rd R into Derby Rd, garden 400yds on R.* Home-made teas. **Adm £3, chd free. Sun 24 June (11-5).**
Two-acre garden on greensand and clay, separated into 4 distinct areas. Fragrant herb and rose parterre bordered by lavender and box; pink, purple and white herbaceous borders; raised vegetable beds and caged fruit garden. In lower garden several natural and temperamental ponds, planting and area of young fruit trees. Wheelchair users will need help for slopes and gravel paths.

  ♿ ✗ ⊛ ☕

⑥ BARHATCH FARM
Barhatch Lane, Cranleigh GU6 7NG. Mr & Mrs P M Grol. *2m N of Cranleigh. A281 from Guildford, L at B2128 to Cranleigh through village, take Ewhurst Rd for 1m, turn L into Barhatch Rd which becomes Barhatch Lane. Garden 1st on R after Cranleigh Golf & Leisure Club.* Home-made teas. **Adm £3, chd free. Sun 10 June (11-5).**
6-acre garden, created by present owners, surrounding listed Tudor farmhouse (not open). Herbaceous borders and abundance of old roses, incl romantic rose tunnel. Walled pond, ornamental pond, interesting sunken Zen garden. Wild flower and allium meadow leading to yew tree walk. Gravel drive, partial wheelchair access.

  ♿ ✗ ⊛ ☕

BENTLEY VILLAGE GARDENS
See Hampshire.

⑦ NEW BIRTLEY HOUSE
Bramley GU5 0LB. Mr & Mrs Simon Whalley. *5m S of Guildford. From Guildford S on A281. Through Bramley look out for Birtley Courtyard on L on S-bend. Immed after, on R, entrance to Birtley House.* Home-made teas. **Adm £4, chd free. Sun 20 May (2-5).**
48 acres of restored parkland, woods and gardens. Herbaceous and shrub borders, lake, pond, secret garden, rose garden,

kitchen garden, orchard. Wide variety of trees and shrubs. Bulbs, wisteria, bluebell wood and rhododendrons in spring. Nature trail/bluebell walk approx 30mins. Some gravel paths, main features accessible; regret nature trail unsuitable for wheelchairs.

  ♿ ⊛ ☕

BOXWOOD HOUSE
See Berkshire.

⑧ BRAEKENAS
West Hill Road, Dormans Park RH19 2ND. Ann & Ray Lindfield. *3m N of East Grinstead. From London on A22 turn L at T-lights in Blindley Heath - Ray Lane. In Lingfield turn R at 2nd roundabout - East Grinstead Rd. Fork L into Blackberry Lane, keep racecourse on L, turn L at bottom of hill, R into Dormans Park. Then 1st L, 2nd R.* Home-made teas. **Adm £2, chd free. Sat 19, Sun 20 May (2-6).**
Created 46 yrs ago by present owners, a garden for all seasons with lovely specimen shrubs and trees, incl azaleas and camellias. Immaculate vegetable plot.

  ♿ ✗ ⊛ ☕

BROADHATCH HOUSE
See Hampshire.

⑨ BURSTOWE'S CROFT
The Green, Ewhurst GU6 7RT. Wendy & Richard Worby. *3m E of Cranleigh. Take B2127 from obelisk at E end of Cranleigh. 2m to Ewhurst village. Take 2nd R signed Horsham & Ellens Green, garden 200yds on R. Parking further 200yds at cricket green or Plough Lane.* Home-made teas. **Adm £2.50, chd free. Sun 10, Wed 13 June (11-5).**
Gently-sloping 1-acre country garden divided by mixed planting of scented shrubs, herbaceous plants, ornamental and fruit trees. Informal rose garden with rose-covered gazebo, many old-fashioned varieties. Vegetable garden with raised beds and greenhouse. Gravel garden with fishpond. Plenty of seats to relax and enjoy your tea. Short walk to Square Leg Cottage, also open.

  ♿ ✗ ⊛ ☕

⑩ CAXTON HOUSE
67 West Street, Reigate RH2 9DA RH2 9DA. Bob & Marj Bushby. *On A25 towards Dorking, approx ¼m W of Reigate on L. Parking on rd.* Home-

Touching the senses, all sure-footed visitors may explore the many surprises on this exuberant escape from reality . . .

made teas. **Adm £3, chd free (share to Heart Foundation). Wed 11 Apr (2-5).**
Large garden with wildlife wood, 3 ponds, lots of spring planting - primroses, bulbs and large collection of hellebores.

    ⑪ **CHARTERHOUSE**
Hurtmore Road, Godalming
GU7 2DF. *1/2 m N of Godalming town centre at top of Charterhouse Hill. Follow signs for Charterhouse from A3 & Godalming town centre.* Light refreshments & teas. **Adm £3, chd free. Sun 17 June (2.30-5).**
Extensive grounds with mature trees and mixed borders around beautiful old buildings. Two historical borders planted with species available prior to 1872, based on the writings of William Robinson; several enclosed individual gardens. Headmaster's garden, originally designed by Gertrude Jekyll, with long herbaceous border, pergola, mixed borders, Lutyens summerhouse and double dry stone wall.

CHARTS EDGE
See Kent.

⑫ **CHAUFFEUR'S FLAT**
Tandridge Lane, Tandridge
RH8 9NJ. Mr & Mrs Richins. *2m E of Godstone. Turn off A25 for Tandridge. Take drive on L past church. Follow arrows to circular courtyard.* Home-made teas Sats, Suns only. **Adm £2.50, chd free (share to Sutton & Croydon MS Therapy Centre). 21 to 27 May incl; 18 to 24 June incl (10-5).**
Enter 1-acre tapestry of magical secret gardens with magnificent views. Touching the senses, all sure-footed visitors may explore the many surprises on this exuberant escape from reality. Imaginative use of recycled materials creates an inspired variety of ideas, while wild and specimen plants reveal an ecological haven.

⑬ **NEW CHESTNUT COTTAGE**
15 Jubilee Lane, Boundstone,
Farnham GU10 4SZ. Mr & Mrs David Wingent. *2 1/2 m SW of Farnham. From A31 roundabout take A325 to Petersfield, 1/2 m bear L. 1/2 m over staggered Xrds, 4th turning on R after Sandrock PH.* Home-made teas. **Adm £2.50, chd free. Sun 6 May (2-5.30).**
1/2-acre garden created by owners on different levels. Rhododendrons, azaleas, acers and conifers. Long pergola with wisteria and roses, attractive gazebo copied from the original at NT Hunting Lodge in Odiham. Peaceful setting.

⑭ **CHESTNUT LODGE**
Old Common Road, Cobham
KT11 1BU. Mr & Mrs R Sawyer. *From A3 take A245 towards Cobham bearing L at 2nd roundabout onto A307. Just after Dagenham Motors turn L into Old Common Rd, Chestnut Lodge at very end.* Home-made teas. **Adm £4. Regret children not admitted. Suns 13 May; 9 Sept (12-6) with music from 'The Weyward Singers' both afternoons.**
Very interesting 5-acre garden offering unrivalled opportunity to enjoy fine specimen trees, wonderful wisteria, shrubs and rare and exotic plants at close quarters. Areas near house formally planted, while opposite is large naturalised pond, home to many waterfowl incl flamingos. Formal areas planted round rectangular pools are complemented by bonsai and topiary which lead to an aviary walk with many fine tropical birds. Some gravel paths.

⑮ **CHINTHURST LODGE**
Wonersh Common Road, Wonersh
GU5 0PR. Mr & Mrs M R Goodridge. *4m S of Guildford. From A281 at Shalford turn E onto B2128 towards Wonersh. Just after Wonersh rd sign, before village, garden on R.* Home-made teas. **Adm £3, chd free. Sun**

24, Wed 27 June (12-5.30).
1-acre yr-round garden, herbaceous borders, white garden, specimen trees and shrubs, gravel garden with water feature, small kitchen garden, fruit cage, 2 wells, ornamental ponds, millennium parterre garden, herb area.

⑯ **CHIPCHASE**
Park Road, Ashtead KT21 2QP.
Peter & Valerie Gray, 01372 275106.
2m NE of Leatherhead. From A24 just S of Ashtead Village turn into Greville Park Rd (park here). Park Rd (for disabled parking) is approx 100yds on L by post box. Home-made teas. **Adm £2.50, chd free. Sun 24 June; Sun 15, Wed 18 July (11-5). Visitors also welcome by appt in June & July only, for groups of 10+.**
Garden designed and constructed by owners, with emphasis on low maintenance and minimal digging and watering by using membrane and mulch. Herbaceous border, trees, shrubs, pergola, rose rope, hanging baskets, troughs, water feature and large shingle area with grasses and drought-tolerant planting. Extensive alterations to the front garden completed in 2006.

⑰ ◆ **CLANDON PARK**
West Clandon GU4 7RQ. The National Trust, www.nationaltrust.org.uk. *3m E of Guildford on A247. From A3 follow signs to Ripley to join A247 via B2215.* House & garden £7.20, chd £3.60. Garden only £3.60, chd £1.80. Tues to Thurs & Suns 18 Mar to 28 Oct. For NGS: **Sun 1 Apr (11-5).**
Garden around the house laid out informally, apart from parterre beneath S front. To the S a mid C18 grotto. Principal front faces parkland, laid out in the style of Capability Brown around 1770. Created in 1901, Dutch garden modelled on the pond garden at Hampton Court Palace. Large bulb field looks stunning in spring.

⑱ ◆ **CLAREMONT LANDSCAPE GARDEN**
Portsmouth Road, Esher KT10 9JG.
The National Trust, 01372 467806, www.nationaltrust.org.uk. *1m SW of Esher. On E side of A307 (no access from A3 bypass).* **Adm £5.60, chd £2.80. Apr to Oct daily 10-6. Nov to Mar Tues to Suns 10-5 or dusk. For NGS: Suns 3 June; 2 Sept (10-6).**

One of the earliest surviving English landscape gardens, begun by Vanbrugh and Bridgeman before 1720 and extended and naturalized by Kent and Capability Brown. Lake, island with pavilion; grotto and turf amphitheatre; viewpoints and avenues.

⑲ THE COPSE LODGE
Brighton Road, Burgh Heath
KT20 6BL. Marian & Edward
Wallbank, 01737 361084. *6m S of Sutton. On A217. 200yds past T-lights at junction with Reigate Rd. Turn L into Heathside Hotel, park in hotel car park courtesy of hotel. Proceed on foot 80yds to garden. Disabled parking at garden.* Home-made teas. **Adm £3, chd free. Sun 15 July (1.30-6). Evening Openings £3.50, wine, Weds 11, 18 July (6-9). Visitors also welcome by appt in July & Aug, for groups of 10+.**
Very unusual 1 acre garden with architectural features and exciting planting. Large Japanese garden abounds with acers, bamboo, wisteria and bonsai. Wander through the tea house and emerge refreshed to enjoy the contrast of exotic planting and beautiful tender specimens. New potager kitchen garden. Featured in 'Surrey Life' & '25 Beautiful Gardens'.

⑳ ♦ COVERWOOD LAKES
Peaslake Road, Ewhurst GU6 7NT.
The Metson Family. *7m SW of Dorking. From A25 follow signs for Peaslake; garden 1/2m beyond Peaslake.* **Adm £4, chd £2. For NGS: Suns 15, 22, 29 Apr; 6, 13 May (2-6); 21 Oct (11-4.30).**
14-acre landscaped garden in stunning position in the Surrey Hills with 4 lakes and bog garden. Extensive rhododendrons, azaleas, primulas and fine trees. 3 1/2-acre lakeside arboretum. Marked trail through the working farm with cows and calves, sheep and horses, extensive views of the surrounding hills.

㉑ ♦ CROSSWATER FARM
Crosswater Lane, Churt GU10 2JN.
Mrs E G Millais & Family, 01252 792698, www.rhododendrons.co.uk. *6m S of Farnham, 6m NW of Haslemere. From A287 turn E into Jumps Rd 1/2m N of Churt village centre. After 1/4m turn acute L into Crosswater Lane & follow signs for Millais Nurseries.* Home-made teas

NGS days only. **Adm £3, chd free. Daily 16 Apr to 8 June (10-5). For NGS: Sat 12, Sun 13 May (2-5).**
Idyllic 6-acre woodland garden. Plantsman's collection of rhododendrons and azaleas, incl rare species collected in the Himalayas, hybrids raised by the owners. Everything from alpine dwarfs to architectural large-leaved trees. Ponds, stream and companion plantings incl sorbus, magnolias and Japanese acers. Trial gardens of new varieties. Featured on BBC TV Gardeners' World; Silver Gilt medal at RHS Chelsea, Rothschild Challenge Cup for best exhibit of rhododendrons. Grass paths soft after rain.

㉒ DUNSBOROUGH PARK
Ripley GU23 6AL. A J H Baron
Sweerts de Landas Wyborgh. *6m NE of Guildford. Entrance across Ripley Green via The Milkway opp Wylie & Mar.* Home-made teas. **Adm £3.50, chd free. Sats 21 Apr (12-5); 9 June with music (11-4) ; Sat 8 Sept (11-5) .**
Extensive walled gardens of 6 acres redesigned by Penelope Hobhouse and Rupert Golby. Good structure with much box hedging creating many different garden rooms. Exciting long herbaceous borders with beautiful standard wisterias. Unusual 70ft ginkgo hedge and ancient mulberry tree. Atmospheric water garden recently redesigned and restored. Fabulous display of tulips in Apr with 7000 bulbs and large cut flower garden. Music on Sat 9 June. Gravel paths & steep areas in water garden.

THE ELMS
See London.

ETON COLLEGE GARDENS
See Berkshire.

FAIRACRE
See Berkshire.

㉓ FOUR ACES
Chapel Lane, Pirbright GU24 0JY.
Mr & Mrs R V St John Wright, 01483 476226, janesjw@yahoo.com. *5 NW of Guildford. On A322 Bagshot rd, just before Brookwood arch, opp West Hill Golf Club, L into Cemetery Pales. After village sign sharp L into Chapel Lane. House 100yds on R. Overflow parking in village green car park 250yds.* Home-made teas. **Adm £3, chd free. Suns 17 June; 19 Aug (2-5). Day & Evening Opening teas & wine, Sun 1 July (2.30-7.30). Visitors also welcome by appt May to Aug for groups of 10+, max 40.**
2/3-acre plantsman's garden with herb garden, walled garden, ponds, terraces with pergolas and pots. Mixed borders

Wander through the tea house and emerge refreshed to enjoy the contrast of exotic planting and beautiful tender specimens . . .

overflowing with shrubs, old-fashioned and other roses, perennials, all planted in informal cottage garden style.

FROGMORE HOUSE GARDEN
See Berkshire.

FROYLE GARDENS
See Hampshire.

㉔ ♦ GATTON PARK
Merstham RH2 0TW. Royal
Alexandra & Albert School, 01737 649068, www.gattonpark.com. *3m NE of Reigate. 5 mins from M25 J8 (A217) or from top of Reigate Hill, over M25 then follow sign to Merstham. Entrance is off Rocky Lane accessible from Gatton Bottom or A23 Merstham.* Teas NGS days only. **Adm £3.50, chd free. 1st Sun of each month Feb to Oct (1-5). For NGS: Sun 11 Feb (10-4), Wed 14 Feb (12-4); Sun 17, Wed 20 Feb 2008.**
Formerly home to the Colman family (of mustard fame), now the grounds of the Royal Alexandra and Albert School. Hidden gardens within historic Capability Brown parkland. 1910 Edwardian Japanese garden restored for Channel 4's 'Lost Gardens'.

Dramatic 1912 Pulham rock garden, walled gardens, lakeside trail. Restoration of gardens ongoing and maintained by volunteers. Ivan Hick's children's trail behind main lake. Massed snowdrops in Feb/Mar. Featured in 'Surrey Life'. Limited wheelchair access.

&. ⚘ ☕

25 GORSE COTTAGE
Tilford GU10 2EA. A M How. *5m SE of Farnham. Midway between Farnham & Hindhead. Garden is opp The Grange, approx 1½m from Tilford Green at Rushmoor end of village. Rushmoor sign outside garden fence.* **Adm £2.50, chd free. Sun 15 July (2-5.30).**
Approx ¾-acre plantsman's informal garden in tranquil rural setting with lawns, mature trees, herbaceous borders and shrubs. Pond and stream with moisture loving plants.

&. ⋈ ☕

A plantaholic's delight, worked organically – an oasis in suburbia . . .

26 GREAT FOSTERS
Stroude Road, Egham TW20 9UR, www.greatfosters.co.uk. *1m S of Egham. On A30 at T-lights opp Virginia Water, turn down Christchurch Rd B389. Continue over roundabout and after railway bridge turn L at T-lights into Stroude Rd. Great Fosters approx ¾m on R. Light refreshments & teas.* **Adm by donation, suggested donation £4 per person. Mon 4 June to Thur 7 June incl (10-5).**
Within the 50-acre estate, this wonderful and inspiring garden has been beautifully restored over the last 11yrs. Framed on 3 sides by a Saxon moat, the knot garden of intricate design has fragrant beds of flowers and herbs and is bordered by clipped hedges and topiary. Beyond, find the grass amphitheatre, large lake, wisteria-draped Japanese bridge, sunken rose garden and tranquil lily pond. Partial wheelchair access.

&. ⋈ ⊨ ☕

27 GREEN LANE FARM
Cudworth Lane, Newdigate RH5 5BH. Mr & Mrs P Hall, 01306 631214. *8m S of Dorking. On A24 turn L at Beare Green roundabout signed Newdigate. R at T-junction in Newdigate, L at Church, R into Cudworth Lane. Farm ¼m on R.* Home-made teas. **Adm £2.50, chd free. Visitors welcome by appt late June to early Aug only, for groups of 15+. Coaches permitted.**
1½-acre garden created from cow paddock in 2000. Emphasis on colour in mixed borders, containers, gravel area with many lovely grasses, unique oak summerhouse, beautiful restored gypsy vardo (caravan). Farm walk circling 3 lakes.

&. ⚘ ☕

28 72 GREEN WRYTHE LANE
Carshalton SM5 2DP. Mrs G Cooling. *1m E of Sutton. From Carshalton Ponds turn N across ponds into North St. Continue to Wrythe Green, then 1st R into Green Wrythe Lane.* Home-made teas. **Adm £2.50, chd free (share to Royal Marsden Hospital). Sun 29 July (10.30-4.30).**
170ft x 50ft colourful cottage style garden of various habitats, incl herbaceous borders, woodland area, wildlife pond. A plantaholic's delight, worked organically - an oasis in suburbia. Cover from the elements. Painted pot stall.

⋈ ⚘ ☕

29 HALL GROVE SCHOOL
Bagshot GU19 5HZ. Mr & Mrs A R Graham & Mr & Mrs P D Smithson, www.hallgrove.co.uk. *6m SW of Egham. M3 to J3, follow A322 1m until sign for Sunningdale A30, 1m E of Bagshot, opp Long Acres garden centre, entrance at footbridge. Ample car park.* Home-made teas. **Adm £4, chd free. Sun 20 May (2-5.30).**
Formerly small Georgian country estate, now co-educational preparatory school. Grade II listed house (not open). Mature parkland with specimen trees. Tour comprises three contrasting private gardens within the old estate. Historical features incl ice house, old walled garden, heated peach wall. Much recent development. Lots of ideas for keen gardeners. Live music at 4pm.

&. ⋈ ⚘ ☕

30 ◆ HATCHLANDS PARK
East Clandon GU4 7RT. The National Trust, 01483 222482, www.nationaltrust.org.uk. *4m E of Guildford. In East Clandon, off A246. A3 from London, follow signs to Ripley to join A247 & via West Clandon to A246. From Guildford take A25 then A246 towards Leatherhead at West Clandon.* **House & garden £6.60, chd £3.30. Garden only £3.30, chd £1.70. 1 Apr to 28 Oct: Parkland daily (11-6); House (2-5.30) Tues, Weds, Thurs & Suns (also BH Mons, Fris in Aug). For NGS: Suns 29 Apr; 14 Oct (11-6).**
Garden and park designed by Repton in 1800. Follow one of the park walks to the stunning bluebell wood in spring. In autumn enjoy the changing colours on the long walk. S of the house a small parterre designed by Gertrude Jekyll in 1913 to flower in early June. House open.

&. ☕

31 HEATHSIDE
10 Links Green Way, Cobham KT11 2QH. Miss Margaret Arnott & Mr Terry Bartholomew, 01372 842459. *1½m E of Cobham. Off A245 Cobham to Leatherhead rd. From Cobham take 4th turning L after Esso Garage into Fairmile Lane. Straight on at mini-roundabout into Water Lane for ½m. Links Green Way 3rd on L.* Home-made teas. **Adm £2.50, chd free. Sun 17 June (11-5). Visitors also welcome by appt.**
Terraced ⅓-acre garden with many unusual plants. Many roses and clematis over hand-made obelisks and pergola. Numerous varieties of hostas displayed in terracotta pots. Parterre with sundial, two formal ponds, alpine wall and colourful urns.

⋈ ⚘ ☕

HECKFIELD PLACE
See Hampshire.

239A HOOK ROAD
See London.

32 HOOKWOOD FARMHOUSE
Fullers Farm Road, off Shere Road, West Horsley KT24 6ET. Sarah & Eric Mason, 01483 284760. *6m E of Guildford. From A246 turn R into Staple Lane (signed Shere) at end of dual carriageway. At top of Staple Lane turn L then 1st L into Shere Rd (signed W Horsley) & first L into Fullers Farm Rd. From Leatherhead L into Greendene (signed Shere), 1st R into*

Shere Rd, L into Fullers Farm Rd. **Adm £3, chd free. Visitors welcome by appt in May & June, no coaches.** Approx 2 acres gently sloping garden on N Downs. Wide variety of mature trees and shrubs, many unusual. Herbaceous borders, alpines and many bulbs, wildlife pond and small vegetable garden. Courtyard garden in old farmyard, large gravelled area with borders surrounding laburnum tunnel to main garden.

Bog garden – assuming we have water!

33 HORSELL ALLOTMENTS & BIRCH COTTAGE GARDEN
GU21 4PN. 1½m W of Woking. From Woking follow signs to Horsell, along High St, Bullbeggars Lane at Chobham end of Village. Nearest parking by Cricketers PH, Horsell Birch. Limited parking in village. Home-made teas at Birch Cottage. **Combined adm £3, chd free. Sun 1 July (11-4).** 'War of the Worlds' village. Church with Norman keep and a number of period properties.

BIRCH COTTAGE GARDEN
5 High Street. Celia & Mel Keenan. Entrance on High St opp Bullbeggars Lane
Created since 1999, smallish garden designed to reflect the 400yr-old Grade II listed cottage. Active dovecote, gravel garden, shrubs and perennials, archway with climbers through to potager, developing knot garden, courtyard with containers and hanging baskets.

HORSELL ALLOTMENTS
Bullbeggars Lane. Horsell Allotment Assn, www.windowonwoking.org.uk/ sites/haa. Disabled parking only on site
Large site with over 100 individual plots growing a variety of flowers, fruit and vegetables. Mixture of modern, well known, heritage and unusual vegetables, many not seen in supermarkets.

34 NEW HOWICKS
Hurlands Lane, Dunsfold GU8 4NT. Revd & Mrs Roger ter Haar, 01483 200654, sarahterhaarhowicks@hotmail. com. 6m S of Godalming. Through Dunsfold village, cricket pitch on L, then next L marked Knightons Lane, Howicks and Hurlands. Howicks ¾m on L. Cream teas. **Adm £3, chd free. Sat 9 June (2-5). Evening Opening,** wine, £4, Fri 8 June (5-9). **Visitors also welcome by appt in early March for bulbs, early May for cowslips, June for roses and borders.**
4½-acre garden around medieval/Stuart beamed cottage (not open) with hedged rose garden leading to secluded walled Italian courtyard with interesting water feature. Extensive lawns and long herbaceous borders. An ancient orchard underplanted with wonderful mixed wild flowers incl spring bulbs followed by masses of orchids.

KIMPTON HOUSE
See Hampshire.

35 NEW KNOWLE GRANGE
Hound House Road, Shere GU5 9JH. Mr P R & Mrs M E Wood, 01483 202108, prmewood@hotmail.com. 8m S of Guildford. From Shere (off A25), through village for ¾m. After railway bridge, continue 1½m past Hound House on R (stone dogs on gatepost). After 100yds turn R at Knowle Grange sign, go to end of lane. Home-made teas. **Adm £5, chd free. Suns 20 May; 16 Sept (11-5). Visitors also welcome by appt in May, June & Sept only, for groups of 15+.**
80-acre idyllic hilltop position. Extraordinary and exciting new 7-acre gardens, created from scratch since 1990 by Marie-Elizabeth Wood, blend the free romantic style with the strong architectural frame of the classical tradition. Walk the rural one-mile Bluebell Valley Unicursal Path of Life and discover its secret allegory. Deep unfenced pools, high unfenced drops.

LITTLE COOPERS
See Hampshire.

LITTLE LODGE
See London.

36 LODKIN
Lodkin Hill, Hascombe GU8 4JP. Mr & Mrs W N Bolt, 01483 208323, willibolt2@aol.com. 3m S of Godalming. Just off B2130 Godalming to Cranleigh rd, on outskirts of Hascombe; take narrow lane signed to garden. Home-made teas. **Adm £3.50, chd free. Suns 15 Apr; 3 June (2-5). Visitors also welcome by appt at any time.**
Country garden of approx 4½ acres developed over the last 30yrs. Woodland, pond, stream, restored Victorian greenhouses. Kitchen garden and flower borders. Spring bulbs in profusion. New shrub rose border; large azaleas, rhododendrons and flowering trees. Wide variety of fruit trees, bushes and bog garden - assuming we have water! Partial wheelchair access, garden very steep in parts.

37 LONG BARTON
12 Longdown Road, Guildford GU4 8PP. Harry & Rose-Marie Stokes, 01483 504514. 1m E of Guildford. A246 (Epsom Rd) from Guildford, after ½m turn R into Tangier Rd. At top turn L into Warren Rd, becoming One Tree Hill. At Xrds turn sharp R into Longdown Rd, last house on R in rd. Home-made teas. **Adm £3, chd free. Sun 12 Aug (10-5). Visitors also welcome by appt, groups of 12+.**
Interesting 2-acre garden attempts to enhance the glory of its setting in the beautiful Surrey Hills. Hundreds of Japanese maples, knot garden, cyclamen lawns, pagan love temple, specimen trees, topiary and large formal fish pond. Wrought iron, stonework and 3 water features. Many alpines. Mobile/steel sculpture. New second 1000sq metre knot garden.

38 LONGER END COTTAGE
Normandy Common Lane, Normandy GU3 2AP. Ann & John McIlwham, 01483 811858, jmcilwham@hotmail.com. 4m W of Guildford on A323. At War Memorial Xrds in Normandy turn R into Hunts Hill Rd then 1st R into Normandy Common Lane. Home-made teas. **Adm £3, chd free (share to St Mark's**

Short woodland path with shade-loving plants leads from dovecote to beehives . . .

Church, Wyke 19 Aug only). Suns 20 May; 17 June; 19 Aug; 9 Sept (1-6). Visitors also welcome by appt, groups of 10+, coaches permitted. 1½-acre garden divided into rooms with wide variety of plants, shrubs and trees incl roses, delphiniums, tree ferns, gunnera, grasses etc. Knot garden, laburnum walk, wild flower meadow and folly add to the attraction of the garden. 2007 brings more interest with the introduction of new beds in the front garden. Uneven drive.
  👤 🐕 ☕

③⑨ ◆ LOSELEY PARK
Guildford GU3 1HS. Mr & Mrs M G More-Molyneux, 01483 304440, www.loseley-park.com. *4m SW of Guildford. Leave A3 at Compton S of Guildford, on B3000 for 2m. Signed. Guildford stn 2m, Godalming stn 3m.* House & gardens £7, chd £3.50, concessions £6.50. Garden only £4, chd £2, concessions £3.50. Garden Tues to Suns May to Sept (11-5); House May to Aug, Tues to Thurs & Suns (1-5). Also Bank Hol Mons May & Aug. For NGS: Sun 6 May; 2 Sept (11-5).
Delightful 2½-acre walled garden based on design by Gertrude Jekyll. Award-winning rose garden (over 1,000 bushes, mainly old-fashioned varieties), extensive herb garden, fruit/flower garden, white garden with fountains, and spectacular organic vegetable garden. Magnificent vine walk, herbaceous borders, moat walk, ancient wisteria and mulberry trees. Wild flower meadow.
  👤 🐕 ☸ ☕

LOWDER MILL
See Sussex.

④⓪ MOLESHILL HOUSE
The Fairmile, Cobham KT11 1BG. Penny & Maurice Snell, 01932 864532, www.pennysnellflowers.co.uk. *2m NE of Cobham. On A307 Esher to Cobham Rd next to free car park by A3 bridge, at entrance to Waterford Close.* Home-made teas. Adm £3, chd free. Sun 13, Thur 17 May (2-5). Visitors also welcome by appt, parties of 10+.
To meet the challenges of climate

change, significant replanning and replanting has taken place in this romantic garden surrounding Victorian house. Short woodland path with shade-loving plants leads from dovecote to beehives. Informally planted colour-coordinated borders contrast with the strict formality of topiary box and garlanded cisterns. Mediterranean courtyard with bright colours and tender plants, conservatory, fountains, bog garden, pleached avenue of 38 Sorbus *lutescens*, pots and many unusual features. Garden 5 mins from Claremont Landscape Garden, Painshill Park & Wisley, also adjacent excellent dog-walking woods. Featured on Japanese TV, in GGG & Leigh Clapp's 'Garden Details'.
  🐕 ☸ ☕

④① MUNSTEAD WOOD
Heath Lane, Godalming GU7 1UN. Sir Robert & Lady Clark. *2m SE of Godalming. Take B2130 Brighton Rd towards Horsham. After 1m church on R, Heath Lane just after on L. Entrance to Munstead Wood 400yds on R. Parking on L of Heath Lane. Limited parking on road.* Home-made teas. Adm £3, chd free (share to GUTS). Suns 22 Apr; 27 May; 24 June (2-5). This former home of Gertrude Jekyll (designed by Edwin Lutyens) is surrounded by a 10-acre restored garden incl woodland, rivers of daffodils, paths through azaleas and rhododendrons, sunken rockery, lawns, shrubbery, rose-covered pergola, tank garden, topiary box, clematis garland, borders. Doorway in bargate wall to spring and summer gardens. Primula garden behind yew hedge. Some gravel paths.
  👤 ☸ ☕

④② ODSTOCK
Castle Square, Bletchingley RH1 4LB. Averil & John Trott, 01883 743100. *3m W of Godstone. Just off A25 in Bletchingley. At top of village nr Red Lion PH. Parking in village, no parking in Castle Square.* Home-made teas. Adm £2.50, chd free. Sun 5 Aug (11-5). Visitors also welcome by appt.
⅔-acre plantsman's garden maintained by owners and developed for all-yr

interest. Special interest in grasses and climbers, 76 at last count. Japanese features; dahlias. No-dig, low-maintenance vegetable garden. Children's quiz. Disabled parking by gate, short gravel path.
  👤 🐕 ☸ ☕

④③ THE OLD CROFT
South Holmwood RH5 4NT. David & Virginia Lardner-Burke, www.lardner-burke.org.uk. *3m S of Dorking. From Dorking take A24 S for 3m. Turn L at sign to Leigh-Brockham into Mill Road. ½m on L, 2 free car parks in NT Holmwood Common. Follow signs for 500yds along woodland walk. Disabled and elderly: for direct access tel 01306 888224.* Cream teas. Adm £3, chd free. Suns, Bank Hol Mons 6, 7, 27, 28 May; Sats, Suns 14, 15 July; 11, 12 Aug (2-6).
'5-acre paradise garden' (Surrey Life) encompasses many gardens of exquisite natural beauty. Stunning and imaginative vistas; many unusual specimen trees and shrubs, lake, colourful bog gardens, woodland, roses, tropical bamboo maze. Through wisteria-clad pergola experience the first magnificent view of curving lawns bordered by flowering cherries underplanted with herbaceous perennials. Glorious colour in all seasons. Take time to explore this serene garden's magic ambience. Visitors return again and again.
  👤 ☸ ☕

④④ ◆ POLESDEN LACEY
Bookham RH5 6BD. The National Trust, 01372 452048, www.nationaltrust.org.uk. *1½m S of Great Bookham. Nr Dorking, off A246 Leatherhead to Guildford rd.* House & garden £10.50, chd £5.20, family £26.20. Garden only £6.50, chd £3.20, family £16.20. Opening dates and times vary according to season. Please phone or visit website for details. For NGS: Sun 10 June (11-5).
30 acres formal gardens in an exceptional setting on the North Downs; walled rose garden, winter garden, lawns; magnificent views. Regency villa dating from early 1820s, remodelled after 1906 by the Hon Mrs Ronald Greville. King George VI and Queen Elizabeth the Queen Mother spent part of their honeymoon here. No dogs in formal gardens.
  👤 ☸ ☕

45 POSTFORD HOUSE
172 Dorking Road, Chilworth
GU4 8RN. Mrs M R Litler-Jones. *4m
SE of Guildford. A248 Guildford to
Dorking rd, garden between boundary
of Chilworth and Albury.* Home-made
teas. **Adm £3, chd free. Sun 20 May
(11-5).**
25 acres of woodland and formal
gardens, incl rose and vegetable
garden. Lovely walk along stream with
rhododendrons, azaleas and
established trees. Care to be taken
along streams and bridges.

Interesting at all seasons, starting with a mass of spring bulbs with over 100 varieties of daffodils . . .

46 QUINNEYS
Camilla Drive, Westhumble
RH5 6BU. Peter & Jane Miller. *1m N
of Dorking. Turn L off A24 (going N)
into Westhumble St, just before Boxhill
roundabout. After ¼m, pass Boxhill
and Westhumble stn & go through
archway into Camilla Dr. House 3rd on
L. Limited parking at garden. Parking
available at Boxhill stn (3 mins walk).
Coming from Leatherhead (going S) on
A24 turn R just after Boxhill
roundabout signed Westhumble stn.
Then as above.* Home-made teas.
Adm £3, chd free. Sun 20 May (2-6).
3 acres created at the breakup of the
neighbouring great estate of Camilla
Lacey. The garden incorporates some
of the original cedar trees; the present
owners have planted a mini arboretum,
and have used the concept of
'tapestry' hedges to good effect. Also
incl some rare trees and shrubs, an
ancient glorious wisteria,
rhododendrons and azaleas in full
flower. Interesting water garden. Efforts
now focussed on the establishment of
a 'Jekyll' herbaceous border. New
interesting shrubs and rhododendrons.

47 ◆ RAMSTER
Chiddingfold GU8 4SN. Mr & Mrs
Paul Gunn, 01428 654167,
www.ramsterevents.com. *1½m S of
Chiddingfold. On A283; large iron
gates on R.* **Adm £5, chd free,
concessions £4.50. Daily 6 Apr to 24
June (10-5).**
Mature woodland garden of
exceptional interest with lakes, ponds
and woodland walk. Outstanding
collection of fine rhododendrons and
azaleas in bloom in early spring with
stunning varieties of camellias,
magnolias and carpets of bluebells.
Many rare trees and shrubs, wild flower
areas, bog garden. A truly beautiful
and peaceful garden. Embroidery
exhibition 20 Apr to 1 May.

48 THE ROUND HOUSE
Dunsfold Road, Loxhill GU8 4BL.
Mrs Sue Lawson, 01483 200375,
suelaw.law@btinternet.com. *4m S of
Bramley. Off A281. At Smithbrook
Kilns turn R to Dunsfold. Follow to T-
junction. Go R (B2130). After 1.2m
Park Hatch on R, enter park, follow
drive to garden.* Home-made teas.
**Adm £3, chd free. Sun 24 June (1-6).
Evening Opening £4.50, wine, Fri
22 June (5-dusk).** Visitors also
welcome by appt in May & June for
groups of 10+, no coaches.
2½-acre walled Victorian garden on
sloping site. Extensive restoration
project started in 2002 still in progress.
Orchard with apple and plum trees.
Herbaceous beds with varieties of
annuals and perennials, roses and
mixed planting. Former greenhouse
beds with peonies and dahlias.
Serpentine walks, ornamental
fishpond, 75 metre lavender walk. Far
reaching views from top of garden.
Gravel paths, steep slopes.

SHALFORD HOUSE
See Sussex.

49 41 SHELVERS WAY
Tadworth KT20 5QJ. Keith &
Elizabeth Lewis, 01737 210707. *6m
S of Sutton off A217. 1st turning on R
after Burgh Heath T-lights heading S.
400yds down Shelvers Way on L.*
Home-made teas. **Adm £2.50, chd
free. Wed 18, Suns 22 Apr; 22 July
(1.30-5).** Visitors also welcome by
appt May to July for groups of 10+.
½-acre back garden of dense and
detailed planting, interesting at all
seasons, starting with a mass of spring
bulbs with over 100 varieties of

daffodils. In one part, beds of choice
perennials are interlaced by paths and
backed by unusual shrubs and mature
trees; in the other, cobbles and shingle
support grasses and special plants for
dry conditions. Featured in 'Womans
Weekly' & 'Surrey Life'.

50 67 & 69 SHEPHERDS LANE
Guildford GU2 9SN. Charles & Gwen
Graham & Mrs J Hall, 01483 566445,
charlesadgraham@btopenworld.
com. *1m NW of Guildford. From A3
take A322 Worplesdon Rd. Turn L at T-
lights at Emmanuel Church into
Shepherds Lane. Gardens on L on
brow of hill. Alternatively, via A323
Aldershot Rd and Rydes Hill Rd,
Shepherds Lane 2nd on R.* Home-
made teas. **Adm £2, chd free. Wed
13 June (1.30-5). Evening Opening
with music £3, wine, Wed 11 July
(6-9).** Visitors also welcome by appt.
Enter No. 67 via fuchsia-lined alley
onto patio, passing pond and gravel
beds towards fern walk and white
garden. Enjoy colour-themed shrub
and herbaceous borders, architectural
grass garden and fruit garden. Enter
garden of No. 69 via rose arch to find
peaceful enclosure with silver, pink and
purple beds and stunning specimen
trees. Handbell music by Pilgrim
Players (playing 7.30-8.30) at Evening
Opening 11 July.

**51 NEW SMITHWOOD
HOUSE**
Smithwood Common Road,
Cranleigh GU6 8QY. Barbara
Rubenstein. *2m N of Cranleigh.
From Cranleigh turn R at cricket
ground passing Cranleigh School.
1½m N of school and 1st house
on R past Winterfold turn. From
Guildford A281, 1m S of Bramley
turn L onto B2128. At roundabout
R then immed L into Smithwood
Common Rd, 2nd house on R.*
Home-made teas. **Adm £3, chd
free. Sun 27, Mon 28 May (2-6).**
3-acre park-like garden
surrounding listed Georgian
farmhouse (not open) with formal
and informal areas. Many mature
specimen trees and shrub borders.
Sculpture walk with musical theme
and water features. Formal yew
walk with topiary and garden
temple. Natural pond with waterfall
and ornamental planting, and
secluded seating areas.

52 SPRING COTTAGE
Smithwood Common Road,
Cranleigh GU6 8QN. Mr & Mrs D E
Norman, 01483 272620. *1m N of
Cranleigh. From Cranleigh cricket
ground take rd signed Cranleigh
School. Garden is ¼m N of Cranleigh
School entrance. From Guildford
A281, follow signs to Cranleigh. Turn L
immed after roundabout into
Smithwood Common Road. Garden
1¼m on R.* Home-made teas. **Adm
£3, chd free. Suns 29 Apr; 6 May
(11-5).** Visitors also welcome by
appt in May only.
Come and see our 1¼-acre garden at
tulip time. Spring bulbs in woodland
area and small meadow. Lovely views.
Enjoy a mix of flowers and foliage,
colours and shapes. Plenty of seating
to enjoy your tea and relax by pond.
  ⅗ ✗ ⊕ ⊫ ☕

Unusual herbaceous plants vie for attention among cottage garden favourites . . .

53 SPURFOLD
Peaslake GU5 9SZ. Mr & Mrs A
Barnes, 01306 730196,
spurfold@btinternet.com. *8m SE of
Guildford. A25 to Shere. Turn R
through Shere village & up hill. Over
railway bridge 1st L to Peaslake. In
Peaslake turn L after village stores
Radnor Rd. Approx 500yds up single
track lane to car park.* **Evening
Openings** £4.50, wine, Fris 18 May;
15 June; 10 Aug (5-8). Visitors also
welcome by appt May to Aug.
Wonderful garden set in area of
outstanding natural beauty. Approx 4
acres, large herbaceous and shrub
borders, formal pond with Buddha
head from Cambodia, sunken gravel
garden with topiary box and water
feature, four terraces, beautiful lawns,
mature rhododendrons and azaleas,
woodland path, and gazebos. Garden
contains unique collection of Indian
elephants and other objets d'art.
Featured in 'Surrey Life' & on BBC TV
Digging Deep.
✗ ⊕ ☕

54 SQUARE LEG COTTAGE
The Green, Ewhurst GU6 7RR.
Monica & Anthony Rosenberg. *3m E
of Cranleigh. Directions as Burstowe's
Croft, garden opp cricket green.*
Home-made teas. **Adm £2.50, chd
free. Sun 10, Wed 13 June (11-5).**
Approx 1-acre garden overlooking the
cricket green at the front. Cottage-style
planting with informal pond, rose
arbour and small fernery. Raised
vegetable and herb beds. Paddock
with mulberry, cherry and plum trees.
Short walk to **Burstowe's Croft**, also
open.
⅗ ✗ ☕

SQUERRYES COURT
See Kent.

55 STUART COTTAGE
Ripley Road, East Clandon
GU4 7SF. Mr & Mrs J M Leader,
01483 222689. *4m E of Guildford. Off
A246 or from A3 through Ripley until
roundabout, turn L and continue
through West Clandon until T-lights,
then L onto A246. East Clandon 1st L.*
Home-made teas. **Adm £3, chd free.
Sun 22 July (12-5). Evening
Openings** £4, wine, Fri 29 June,
Mon 27 Aug (5.30-8.30) **with music
27 Aug only. Visitors also welcome
by appt, groups of 15+.**
½-acre partly walled garden using
some traditional box shapes and
hedging to offer formality in the
otherwise informal garden of this C16
cottage. Wisteria and rose/clematis
walks give shade to the S/W aspect
while rosemary and lavender edge the
brick paths. Unusual herbaceous
plants vie for attention among cottage
garden favourites. From decorative
organic kitchen garden walk to small
chequerboard orchard. Featured in
GGG.
⅗ ⊕ ☕

SUNNINGDALE PARK
See Berkshire.

56 35 TADORNE ROAD
Tadworth KT20 5TF. Dr & Mrs J R
Lay. *6m S of Sutton. On A217 to large
roundabout, 3m N of M25 J8. Take
B2220 signed Tadworth. Tadorne Rd
2nd on R.* Home-made teas. **Adm
£2.50, chd free. Sat 23, Sun 24 June
(2-6).**
⅓-acre hedged garden with a colourful
herbaceous border, shrubby island
beds, rose and clematis-covered
pergola leading to secluded seating
area, potager-style vegetable plot, soft

fruit, woodland corner, varied patio
display and plant-filled conservatory.
✗ ☕

57 TILFORD COTTAGE
Tilford Road, Tilford GU10 2BX. Mr
& Mrs R Burn, 01252 795423,
tilfordcottagegarden.co.uk. *3m SE of
Farnham. From Farnham stn along
Tilford Rd. Tilford Cottage opp Tilford
House. Parking on village green.*
Home-made teas. **Adm £5, chd free.
Evening Opening,** wine, Thur 21
June (6-9). Sat 23, Sun 24 June (10-
4). Visitors also welcome by appt at
most times for groups of 10+.
Artist's garden with a surprise at every
turn. Herb garden within yew hedging,
knot garden with box and topiary, with
flower and Japanese garden with slate
river. Victorian glasshouse, hosta beds,
rose, apple and willow arches,
herbaceous borders and children's fairy
grotto. Monet-style bridge, river walk,
bog gardens and Mediterranean
terrace. Many quiet areas for
contemplation. Holistic healing centre
situated within grounds open for view.
Steep slopes, easy access to main
lawn.
⅗ ⊕ ☕

58 TIMBER HILL
Chertsey Road, Chobham
GU24 8JF. Mr & Mrs N Sealy. *4m N
of Woking. 2½m E of Chobham and
⅓m E of Fairoaks aerodrome on A319
(N side). 1¼m W of Ottershaw, J11
M25.* Light refreshments & teas in old
Surrey barn. **Adm £3, chd under 12
free. Sun 15 Apr (11.30-4.30).**
15 acres of field, parkland and garden
incl woodland garden with
rhododendrons, camellias, magnolias
and spring bulbs. Fine oaks,
liquidambar, tulip tree. Shrub and
groundcover borders surround house.
Some slopes and rough ground in
wood.
⅗ ✗ ☕

59 ◆ TITSEY PLACE GARDENS
Titsey Hill, Oxted RH8 0SD. The
Trustees of the Titsey Foundation,
01273 715361, www.titsey.org. *3m N
of Oxted. A25 between Oxted &
Westerham, turn L into Limpsfield
Village down High St, turn L (on sharp
bend) into Bluehouse Lane & R into
Water Lane. Follow rd under M25
through park to walled garden car
park. Brown signs from A25 at
Limpsfield.* **Adm £3.50, chd £1. Weds
& Suns 9 May to 30 Sept, & summer
Bank Hols.**

For NGS: Sats 23 June; 21 July; 11 Aug (1-5). Garden only on these days. Car park & picnic area open from 12.
One of the largest surviving estates in Surrey. Magnificent ancestral home and gardens of the Gresham family since 1534. Walled kitchen garden restored early 1990s. Golden Jubilee rose garden. Etruscan summer house adjoining picturesque lakes and fountains. 15 acres of formal and informal gardens in idyllic setting within the M25.

⑥⓪ TOLLSWORTH MANOR

Rook Lane, Chaldon CR3 5BQ. Carol & Gordon Gillett. *2m W of Caterham. From Caterham-on-the-Hill, take B2031 through Chaldon. 300yds out of Chaldon take concrete farm track on L. Parking in farmyard beyond house.* Home-made teas. **Adm £3, chd free. Sun 17 June (11-5).**
Old-fashioned country garden, created from derelict site over 23yrs by present owners. Well-stocked herbaceous borders with old-fashioned roses, peonies, delphiniums. Wildlife pond and duck pond with ducks. Lovely views over surrounding farmland. New raised peat bed. Shetland pony. Gravel drive & uneven paths.

TREETOPS
See Hampshire.

⑥① UPPER RIDGEWAY FARM
Hyde Lane, Thursley GU8 6QR. Mr & Mrs Pat Coles. *5m SW of Godalming. From A3 enter Thursley, go through village to T-junction, approx 1m. Turn L to Churt, and approx ³/₄ m L into Sailors Lane, ¹/₂ m R into Hyde Lane, then follow farm sign. House opp duck pond.* Home-made teas. **Adm £3, chd free. Sun 24 June (11-5).**
Attractive early C15 farmhouse, from 1960 to 2004 home of Coles strawberries. Approx 1-acre garden, well stocked with shrubs, trees and large variety of unusual perennial plants in double herbaceous border. Vegetable garden, pond and well-maintained lawns. Wide doorway WC.
⎣ ⋈ ❀ ☕

⑥② 6 UPPER ROSE HILL
Dorking RH4 2EB. Peter & Julia Williams, 01306 881315. *Town centre. From roundabout at A24/A25 junction follow signs to town centre. Turn L (under cedar tree) after Cricketers PH by flint wall. Parking*

available in rd & behind Sainsbury's (5 mins walk). Home-made teas. **Adm £2.50, chd free. Mon 28 May; Sun 3 June (11-5.30). Visitors also welcome by appt.**
¹/₂-acre plantsman's informal terraced garden on dry sand. Surprising secluded setting with striking outlook onto St Paul's Church. Planted for yr-round interest of foliage and form; fruit and vegetables, gravel bed and alpine troughs, borders and rockeries. Range of drought-tolerant plants. Autumn colour, grasses attractive into Oct. Unusual, interesting home-propagated hardy plants for sale. Featured in 'Surrey Life'.

Deeply tranquil, almost secretive garden in North Downs . . .

⑥③ VALE END
Chilworth Road, Albury GU5 9BE. Mr & Mrs John Foulsham, 01483 202296. *4m SE of Guildford. From Albury take A248 W for ¹/₄ m.* Home-made teas. **Adm £3, chd free. Sun 17 June; Wed 11 July (2-5). Evening Opening with music £4, wine, Sat 16 June (6-8.30). Visitors also welcome by appt.**
1-acre walled garden on many levels in beautiful setting overlooking mill pond. Richly diverse planting of roses, shrubs, annuals and perennials on light sandy soil. Clipped yew walk with festooned rope swag, tiny courtyard, fruit, vegetable and herb garden. Pantiled water cascade.
❀ ☕

⑥④ VANN
Hambledon GU8 4EF. Mrs M Caroe, 01428 683413, www.vanngarden.co.uk. *6m S of Godalming. A283 to Wormley. Turn L at Hambledon. Follow yellow Vann signs for 2m. Please do not park in rd, park in field.* Home-made teas 7 May only. **Adm £4, chd free. Mon 7 May (2-6), Tues 8 May to Sun 13 May incl (10-6); Sun 3 June to Sun 10 June incl (10-6). Visitors also welcome by appt.**
English Heritage registered garden of 4¹/₂ acres surrounding Tudor and William and Mary house (not open) with later additions and alterations by W D Caröe. Old cottage garden,

pergola, ¹/₄-acre pond, Gertrude Jekyll water garden 1911, azaleas, spring bulbs and woodland, mixed borders. Fritillaria *meleagris* in Mar/Apr. Island beds, crinkle crankle wall. Maintained by owner with 3 days' help per week. Garden used for filming Agatha Christie's *After the Funeral*. Water garden paths not suitable for wheelchairs, but many others are.
⎣ ⋈ ❀ ☕

WALBURY
See Hampshire.

⑥⑤ WALTON POOR HOUSE
Ranmore RH5 6SX. Nicholas & Prue Calvert. *6m NW of Dorking. From Dorking take rd to Ranmore, continue for approx 4m, after Xrds in dip 1m on L. From A246 at East Horsley go S into Greendene, 1st L Crocknorth Rd, 1m on R.* Home-made teas. **Adm £3, chd free. Mon 7 May; Suns 3 June; 29 July (11.30-5.30); Sun 14 Oct (2-5).**
Deeply tranquil, almost secretive garden in N Downs. Area of Outstanding Natural Beauty. Paths wind between 4 acres of fine mature trees and colourful shrubs. Pond fringed with bold-foliaged plants; hideaway dell; formal herb garden linked with the well-known herb nursery. Relaxtion therapy! Herb talk 3pm.
⎣ ⋈ ❀ ☕

WAYSTRODE MANOR
See Kent.

⑥⑥ WESTWAYS FARM
Gracious Pond Road, Chobham GU24 8HH. Paul & Nicky Biddle, 01276 856163. *4m N of Woking. From Chobham Church proceed over roundabout towards Sunningdale, 1st Xrds R into Red Lion Rd to junction with Mincing Lane.* Home-made teas. **Adm £2.50, chd free (share to Chobham Floral Club). Sun 6 May (10-5). Visitors also welcome by appt.**
Open 8-acre garden surrounded by woodlands planted in 1930s with mature and some rare rhododendrons, azaleas, camellias and magnolias, underplanted with bluebells, erythroniums, lilies and dogwood; extensive lawns and sunken pond garden. Working stables and sandschool. Lovely Queen Anne House (not open) covered with listed *Magnolia grandiflora*. Victorian design glasshouse. Limited wheelchair access to woodland.
⎣ ❀ ☕

WHEATLEY HOUSE
See Hampshire.

67 ◆ WINKWORTH ARBORETUM
Hascombe Road, nr Godalming GU8 4AD. The National Trust, 01483 208477, www.nationaltrust.org.uk. *2m S of Godalming on B2130. Coaches by written arrangement. Stn: Godalming 3m.* Adm £5, chd £3, family ticket £11. Daily all yr, dawn to dusk. For NGS: Suns 22 Apr; 7 Oct (10-5).
110 acres of rolling Surrey hillside set in a valley leading down to a reservoir and wetland area. Planted with rare trees and shrubs leading to impressive displays in spring with magnolias, azaleas and bluebells matched by the dramatic reds, golds and browns of maples, cherries etc during autumn. Limited wheelchair access.

68 WINTERSHALL MANOR
Bramley GU5 0LR. Mr & Mrs Peter Hutley, 01483 892167, www.wintershall-estate.com. *3m S of Bramley Village. On A281 turn R, then next R. Wintershall Drive next on L. Bus: AV33 Guildford-Horsham, alight Palmers Cross, 1m.* Light refreshments & teas. Adm £3, chd free, disabled £1.50. Sat 14 Apr; Sun 13 May (2-5). Visitors also welcome by appt all yr.
2-acre garden and 200 acres of park and woodland. Bluebell walks in spring, wild daffodils, rhododendrons, specimen trees. Lakes and flight ponds; superb views. Chapel of St Mary, stations of Cross, Rosary Walk and St Francis Chapel. Some gravel paths and steep slopes.

69 ◆ WISLEY RHS GARDEN
GU23 6QB. Royal Horticultural Society, www.rhs.org.uk. *1m NE of Ripley. SW of London on A3 & M25 (J10). Follow signs.* All yr, not Christmas Day. Mon to Fri 10-6, Sat & Sun 9-6 (Nov-Feb 4.30). For NGS: Special Evening Opening with music Tue 21 Aug (6-9) Adm (incl RHS members) £7, chd under 15 free (share to RHS Wisley Garden). Reserve table for dinner 01483 211773.
Primary garden of the RHS and centre of its scientific and educational activities. Arboretum, alpine and wild garden, rock garden, mixed borders, model gardens, model fruit and vegetable garden, rose garden, orchard and trial grounds. Picnics not allowed in the garden.

70 WOODBURY COTTAGE
Colley Lane, Reigate RH2 9JJ. Shirley & Bob Stoneley, 01737 244235. *1m W of Reigate. M25 J8, A217 (direction Reigate). Immed before level Xing turn R into Somers Rd, cont as Manor Rd. At very end turn R into Coppice Lane & follow signs to car park. Garden is 300yds walk from car park.* Home-made teas. Adm £3, chd free. Sats, Suns 7, 8 July; 1, 2 Sept, Wed 5 Sept (Sats, Weds 2-5, Suns 11-5). Evening Opening £4, wine, Fri 6 July (5-8). Visitors also welcome by appt July & Sept only for groups of 10+.
Cottage garden of just under ¼-acre, made and maintained by owners. Garden is stepped on slope with mixed planting, enhanced by its setting under Colley Hill. A rich diversity of plants, colour-themed, still vibrant in Sept.
🅺 ❁ ☕

71 NEW WOODHILL MANOR
Woodhill Lane, Shamley Green GU5 0SP. Kate Halls/Stephanie Gallo, 01483 891004, stephanie@smithkingdom.com. *5m S of Guildford. Directions on application when booking visit.* Adm £4. Visitors welcome by appt mid Apr to mid Aug for groups of 10+, max 30. Regret no children, coaches or professional photographers.
Imaginative, colourful private gardens, parkland and ponds in 20 acres. Stunning views. Spring bulbs and bluebells, established formal and herbaceous beds, creative parterres, wisteria, vines, lavenders and roses. Fine mature trees (tulip tree, cedar, mulberry and monkey puzzles). Organic fruit and vegetable beds. Wild flower meadow in 2nd yr. Partial wheelchair access.
🅺 ❁

72 WOTTON HOUSE
Guildford Road, Dorking RH5 6HS. Hayley Conference Centres Ltd. *3m W of Dorking. On A25 towards Guildford. Gravel driveway (signed), adjacent to Wotton Hatch PH.* Home-made teas. Adm £2.50, chd free. Suns 8, 15, 22, 29 July (11-4).
20 acres of parkland featuring Italian garden created in 1640 by George Evelyn and designed by his brother John, the eminent designer and diarist. Terraced mount, classical garden temple, statuary, tortoise house (uninhabited), and grottoes. Recently restored and widely held to be the first example of an Italian-style garden in England.
🅺 ⊨ ☕

Surrey County Volunteers

County Organiser
Mrs Gayle Leader, Stuart Cottage, East Clandon GU4 7SF, 01483 222689

County Treasurer
Mr Roger Nickolds, Old Post House, East Clandon GU4 7SE, 01483 224027, rogernickolds@hotmail.com

Publicity
Mrs Pauline Elliott, Finches, Meadow Way, West Horsley KT24 6LL, 01483 284554, pauline.elliott@tiscali.co.uk

Assistant County Organisers
Mrs Anne Barnes, Spurfold, Radnor Road, Peaslake GU5 9SZ, 01306 730196
Mr Keith Lewis, 41 Shelvers Way, Tadworth KT20 5QJ, 01737 210707
Mrs Jane St John Wright, Four Aces, Chapel Lane, Pirbright GU24 0JY, 01483 476226
Mrs Shirley Stoneley, Woodbury Cottage, Colley Lane, Reigate RH2 9JJ, 01737 244235
Mrs Averil Trott, Odstock, Castle Square, Bletchingley RH1 4LB, 01883 743100

ng*s* gardens open
for charity

Music
in the garden

The wonderful garden at WISLEY will be open for a special
charity evening for the National Gardens Scheme by kind
permission of the Royal Horticultural Society

Tuesday 21st August 2007 6–9 pm

Musical entertainment around the garden for your pleasure

The Wisley Flower Show marquee will be open from 7– 8.30 pm
The Wisley Shop and Plant Centre will close at 9pm

Admission £7 - children 15 & under free
– also applies to RHS members

The Terrace Restaurant and Conservatory Café will be open. If you
wish to reserve a table for dinner in the Terrace Restaurant, please
phone 01483 211773
Advance bookings for groups only
Please phone Anne Barnes 01306 730196 between 10–5 pm

Also a Barbecue (weather permitting)
We suggest you bring a torch – it may be dark when you leave

ADEQUATE PARKING
SORRY NO PICNICS INSIDE THE GARDEN

SUSSEX

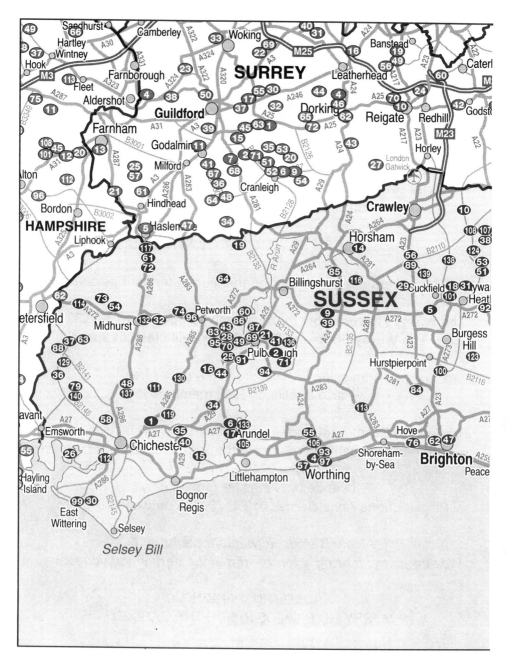

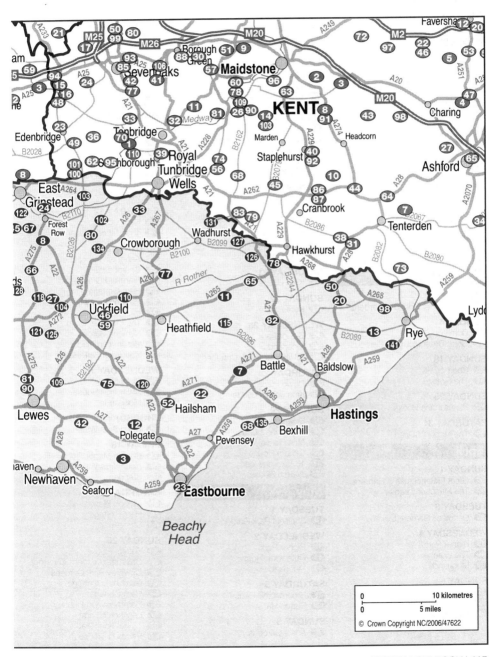

Opening Dates

February

SUNDAY 11
79 Mitchmere Farm

TUESDAY 13
100 Pembury House

WEDNESDAY 14
100 Pembury House

THURSDAY 15
79 Mitchmere Farm
100 Pembury House

SUNDAY 18
79 Mitchmere Farm

TUESDAY 20
100 Pembury House

WEDNESDAY 21
100 Pembury House

THURSDAY 22
100 Pembury House

SATURDAY 24
50 Great Dixter House & Gardens

SUNDAY 25
36 Dormers
50 Great Dixter House & Gardens

March

SATURDAY 3
50 Great Dixter House & Gardens

SUNDAY 4
36 Dormers
50 Great Dixter House & Gardens

SUNDAY 18
25 Champs Hill
49 The Grange

SUNDAY 25
102 Penns in the Rocks

SATURDAY 31
74 The Manor of Dean

April

SUNDAY 1
50 Great Dixter House & Gardens
74 The Manor of Dean

TUESDAY 3
35 Denmans Garden (Evening)

WEDNESDAY 4
16 Bignor Park
49 The Grange
80 Moorlands

SUNDAY 8
12 Bates Green
19 Bradstow Lodge
60 Horsebridge House

WEDNESDAY 11
16 Bignor Park
19 Bradstow Lodge
64 Kiln Copse Farm
80 Moorlands

SATURDAY 14
106 6 Plantation Rise
112 Rymans
114 Sandhill Farm House

SUNDAY 15
15 Berri Court
26 Chidmere Gardens
42 Firle Place
64 Kiln Copse Farm
84 Newtimber Place
87 Northwood Farmhouse
106 6 Plantation Rise
112 Rymans
117 Shalford House

MONDAY 16
15 Berri Court
26 Chidmere Gardens
87 Northwood Farmhouse

WEDNESDAY 18
16 Bignor Park
80 Moorlands

SATURDAY 21
63 Kent House

SUNDAY 22
63 Kent House

WEDNESDAY 25
16 Bignor Park
80 Moorlands
138 46 Westup Farm Cottages

SATURDAY 28
37 Down Place
65 King John's Lodge

SUNDAY 29
37 Down Place
65 King John's Lodge
73 Malt House
90 Offham House
97 18 Pavilion Road
134 Warren House

May

TUESDAY 1
118 Sheffield Park Garden

WEDNESDAY 2
16 Bignor Park
43 Fittleworth House
80 Moorlands

SATURDAY 5
21 Broomershill House
125 Sutton Hall

SUNDAY 6
5 Ansty Gardens

17 4 Birch Close
21 Broomershill House
27 Clinton Lodge
73 Malt House
82 Mountfield Court
97 18 Pavilion Road
125 Sutton Hall
130 Upwaltham Barns

MONDAY 7
17 4 Birch Close
73 Malt House
123 Stonehealed Farm
130 Upwaltham Barns
134 Warren House

WEDNESDAY 9
7 Ashburnham Place
11 Bateman's
16 Bignor Park
43 Fittleworth House
49 The Grange
80 Moorlands

SATURDAY 12
53 Ham Cottage
74 The Manor of Dean

SUNDAY 13
8 Ashdown Park Hotel
25 Champs Hill
46 Framfield Grange
53 Ham Cottage
54 Hammerwood House
57 Highdown
74 The Manor of Dean
89 Nymans Garden
98 Peasmarsh Place
116 Sedgwick Park House

WEDNESDAY 16
16 Bignor Park
43 Fittleworth House
80 Moorlands

THURSDAY 17
61 Houndless Water

FRIDAY 18
24 Caxton Manor
61 Houndless Water
122 Standen

SATURDAY 19
24 Caxton Manor
53 Ham Cottage
124 Stonehurst

SUNDAY 20
9 Bakers House
26 Chidmere Gardens (Evening)
32 Cowdray Park Gardens
48 Gardeners Cottage
53 Ham Cottage
54 Hammerwood House
67 Legsheath Farm
97 18 Pavilion Road
100 Pembury House

- (117) Shalford House
- (134) Warren House

WEDNESDAY 23
- (16) Bignor Park
- (43) Fittleworth House
- (49) The Grange
- (80) Moorlands
- (121) Sparrow Hatch
- (138) 46 Westup Farm Cottages

THURSDAY 24
- (31) Copyhold Hollow
- (121) Sparrow Hatch

SATURDAY 26
- (38) Duckyls Holt
- (65) King John's Lodge
- (107) The Priest House

SUNDAY 27
- (20) Brickwall
- (30) Cookscroft
- (38) Duckyls Holt
- (56) High Beeches
- (65) King John's Lodge
- (103) Perryhill Farmhouse
- (110) Rose Cottage
- (111) Roundhill Cottage

MONDAY 28
- (30) Cookscroft
- (38) Duckyls Holt
- (111) Roundhill Cottage
- (134) Warren House

WEDNESDAY 30
- (16) Bignor Park
- (43) Fittleworth House
- (80) Moorlands

June

FRIDAY 1
- (51) Great Lywood Farmhouse
- (66) Latchetts

SATURDAY 2
- (23) 51 Carlisle Road
- (51) Great Lywood Farmhouse
- (59) Hobbs Barton
- (66) Latchetts
- (70) Little Poynes
- (72) Lowder Mill
- (76) The Martlets Hospice
- (85) The Nook

SUNDAY 3
- (13) Beauchamps
- (23) 51 Carlisle Road
- (52) Hailsham Grange
- (55) The Healing Garden
- (57) Highdown
- (59) Hobbs Barton
- (70) Little Poynes
- (72) Lowder Mill
- (76) The Martlets Hospice
- (85) The Nook
- (90) Offham House
- (97) 18 Pavilion Road
- (103) Perryhill Farmhouse

- (127) Tinkers Bridge Cottage

MONDAY 4
- (59) Hobbs Barton
- (137) West Dean Gardens

WEDNESDAY 6
- (43) Fittleworth House
- (80) Moorlands
- (83) New Barn

THURSDAY 7
- (101) Penland Farmhouse
- (105) Pindars
- (129) Uppark
- (133) Warningcamp House

SATURDAY 9
- (63) Kent House
- (81) Mount Harry House & Mount Harry Lodge
- (86) North Springs
- (88) Nyewood House
- (95) Park Lodge
- (101) Penland Farmhouse
- (112) Rymans
- (114) Sandhill Farm House

SUNDAY 10
- (12) Bates Green
- (27) Clinton Lodge
- (62) Hove Clematis Gardens
- (63) Kent House
- (75) Marchants Hardy Plants
- (77) Mayfield Gardens
- (86) North Springs
- (88) Nyewood House
- (93) Palatine Gardens
- (96) 6 Park Terrace (Day & Evening)
- (112) Rymans
- (114) Sandhill Farm House

MONDAY 11
- (27) Clinton Lodge

WEDNESDAY 13
- (43) Fittleworth House
- (80) Moorlands

THURSDAY 14
- (128) Town Place
- (132) The Walled Garden at Cowdray (Evening)

FRIDAY 15
- (37) Down Place
- (51) Great Lywood Farmhouse (Evening)
- (69) Little Hill (Evening)

SATURDAY 16
- (10) Bankton Cottage
- (23) 51 Carlisle Road (Evening)
- (37) Down Place
- (47) The Garden House
- (74) The Manor of Dean
- (92) Old Scaynes Hill House
- (128) Town Place
- (141) Winchelsea's Secret Gardens

SUNDAY 17
- (4) Ambrose Place Back Gardens

- (9) Bakers House
- (34) Dale Park House
- (37) Down Place
- (74) The Manor of Dean
- (92) Old Scaynes Hill House
- (97) 18 Pavilion Road
- (109) Ringmer Park
- (135) West Bexhill Gardens

MONDAY 18
- (27) Clinton Lodge

WEDNESDAY 20
- (3) Alfriston Clergy House
- (43) Fittleworth House
- (49) The Grange
- (80) Moorlands
- (105) Pindars
- (121) Sparrow Hatch

THURSDAY 21
- (121) Sparrow Hatch

FRIDAY 22
- (66) Latchetts (Evening)

SATURDAY 23
- (14) 4 Ben's Acre
- (38) Duckyls Holt
- (45) Fountain Cottage
- (68) Little Common Gardens
- (107) The Priest House
- (73) Ridge House

SUNDAY 24
- (5) Ansty Gardens
- (38) Duckyls Holt
- (80) Moorlands
- (99) 33 Peerley Road
- (104) Pheasants Hatch
- (73) Ridge House
- (109) Ringmer Park
- (110) Rose Cottage
- (120) Siggle Wriggle
- (128) Town Place

MONDAY 25
- (27) Clinton Lodge
- (104) Pheasants Hatch

WEDNESDAY 27
- (43) Fittleworth House
- (65) King John's Lodge (Evening)
- (80) Moorlands

THURSDAY 28
- (133) Warningcamp House
- (140) Wildham

FRIDAY 29
- (110) Rose Cottage (Evening)

SATURDAY 30
- (138) 46 Westup Farm Cottages

July

SUNDAY 1
- (52) Hailsham Grange
- (55) The Healing Garden
- (89) Nymans Garden
- (128) Town Place

136 West Chiltington Village Gardens
140 Wildham

MONDAY 2
27 Clinton Lodge

WEDNESDAY 4
43 Fittleworth House
80 Moorlands

THURSDAY 5
129 Uppark

FRIDAY 6
10 Bankton Cottage (Evening)
110 Rose Cottage (Evening)
116 Sedgwick Park House (Evening)

SATURDAY 7
10 Bankton Cottage
63 Kent House
71 Little Wantley

SUNDAY 8
63 Kent House
71 Little Wantley
78 Merriments Gardens
116 Sedgwick Park House
128 Town Place
136 West Chiltington Village Gardens

MONDAY 9
27 Clinton Lodge

WEDNESDAY 11
43 Fittleworth House
80 Moorlands
130 Upwaltham Barns

THURSDAY 12
15 Berri Court (Evening)
128 Town Place

FRIDAY 13
66 Latchetts
113 St Mary's House & Gardens

SATURDAY 14
33 Crown House
66 Latchetts
74 The Manor of Dean
113 St Mary's House & Gardens
126 Swiftsden Farm Oast

SUNDAY 15
33 Crown House
74 The Manor of Dean
93 Palatine Gardens
117 Shalford House
126 Swiftsden Farm Oast
131 Villa Elisabetta

MONDAY 16
69 Little Hill

WEDNESDAY 18
43 Fittleworth House
49 The Grange
80 Moorlands

SATURDAY 21
125 Sutton Hall

SUNDAY 22
125 Sutton Hall

WEDNESDAY 25
43 Fittleworth House
80 Moorlands

THURSDAY 26
41 Ebbsworth

FRIDAY 27
41 Ebbsworth

SUNDAY 29
58 4 Hillside Cottages

MONDAY 30
27 Clinton Lodge

August

WEDNESDAY 1
80 Moorlands

FRIDAY 3
53 Ham Cottage (Evening)

SATURDAY 4
16 Bignor Park

SUNDAY 5
16 Bignor Park
99 33 Peerley Road

MONDAY 6
27 Clinton Lodge

WEDNESDAY 8
80 Moorlands

FRIDAY 10
66 Latchetts

SATURDAY 11
66 Latchetts

SUNDAY 12
25 Champs Hill
102 Penns in the Rocks

WEDNESDAY 15
80 Moorlands

SATURDAY 18
22 Butlers Farmhouse
74 The Manor of Dean

SUNDAY 19
22 Butlers Farmhouse
26 Chidmere Gardens
74 The Manor of Dean
103 Perryhill Farmhouse

MONDAY 20
26 Chidmere Gardens

WEDNESDAY 22
29 Colwood House
80 Moorlands

THURSDAY 23
39 Durrance Manor (Evening)

SATURDAY 25
14 4 Ben's Acre

SUNDAY 26
29 Colwood House

39 Durrance Manor
103 Perryhill Farmhouse

MONDAY 27
83 New Barn

WEDNESDAY 29
80 Moorlands

September

SATURDAY 1
112 Rymans

SUNDAY 2
112 Rymans

WEDNESDAY 5
11 Bateman's
80 Moorlands
130 Upwaltham Barns

SATURDAY 8
65 King John's Lodge

SUNDAY 9
65 King John's Lodge
91 The Old Post Office
123 Stonehealed Farm

WEDNESDAY 12
43 Fittleworth House
80 Moorlands

THURSDAY 13
132 The Walled Garden at Cowdray (Evening)

SATURDAY 15
70 Little Poynes

SUNDAY 16
12 Bates Green
70 Little Poynes
75 Marchants Hardy Plants

WEDNESDAY 19
80 Moorlands

THURSDAY 20
18 Borde Hill Garden, Park & Woodland
133 Warningcamp House

SATURDAY 22
74 The Manor of Dean
114 Sandhill Farm House

SUNDAY 23
42 Firle Place
74 The Manor of Dean
78 Merriments Gardens
105 Pindars
114 Sandhill Farm House
115 Sarah Raven's Cutting Garden

WEDNESDAY 26
80 Moorlands

SATURDAY 29
56 High Beeches

SUNDAY 30
109 Ringmer Park
117 Shalford House

October

TUESDAY 2
(118) Sheffield Park Garden

WEDNESDAY 3
⑯ Bignor Park

WEDNESDAY 10
⑯ Bignor Park

TUESDAY 16
㉟ Denmans Garden (Evening)

WEDNESDAY 17
⑯ Bignor Park

THURSDAY 18
(61) Houndless Water

FRIDAY 19
(61) Houndless Water

SUNDAY 21
㉘ Coates Manor
(98) Peasmarsh Place

WEDNESDAY 24
⑯ Bignor Park

SUNDAY 28
㊿ Great Dixter House & Gardens

WEDNESDAY 31
⑯ Bignor Park

February 2008

SUNDAY 10
(79) Mitchmere Farm

THURSDAY 14
(79) Mitchmere Farm

SUNDAY 17
(79) Mitchmere Farm

TUESDAY 26
(100) Pembury House

WEDNESDAY 27
(100) Pembury House

THURSDAY 28
(100) Pembury House

March 2008

TUESDAY 4
(100) Pembury House

WEDNESDAY 5
(100) Pembury House

THURSDAY 6
(100) Pembury House

Private gardens opening regularly for the NGS

⑯ Bignor Park
㊸ Fittleworth House
(80) Moorlands
(139) Whitehouse Cottage

Gardens open to the public

③ Alfriston Clergy House
⑥ Arundel Castle
⑪ Bateman's
⑱ Borde Hill Garden, Park & Woodland
㉗ Clinton Lodge
㉟ Denmans Garden
㊷ Firle Place
㊿ Great Dixter House & Gardens
(52) Hailsham Grange
(56) High Beeches
(57) Highdown
(65) King John's Lodge
(78) Merriments Gardens
(89) Nymans Garden
(94) Parham Gardens
(107) The Priest House
(113) St Mary's House & Gardens
(115) Sarah Raven's Cutting Garden
(118) Sheffield Park Garden
(122) Standen
(129) Uppark
(132) The Walled Garden at Cowdray
(137) West Dean Gardens

By appointment only

① 2 Adelaide Cottages
② Alcheringa
㊵ Eastergate House
㊹ Five Oaks Cottage
(119) Sherburne House

The Gardens

① 2 ADELAIDE COTTAGES

Halnaker PO18 0NG. Mrs Joan Mezulis, 01243 773685. *3½ m NE of Chichester. On A285. 200yds on L after Anglesey Arms PH.* **Adm £2.50, chd free. Visitors welcome by appt Feb to Oct.**
Unexpected, hidden garden of ½ acre at end of path. Blaze of summer colour in herbaceous borders; vegetables from unusual seeds brought from Latvia. Wide variety of trees and shrubs, set in a tranquil paddock. Small pond with goldfish, frogs, water snails etc. Owner-maintained. Featured in 'Sussex Life'.

② ALCHERINGA

Silverwood, West Chiltington RH20 2NG. Trevor & Ksenia Watts, 01798 812549, trevwatts@btinternet.com. *3m N of Storrington, 2m E of Pulborough. From Pulborough turn off A283 into West Chiltington Rd then R into Monkmead Lane, L into Nyetimber Lane. B2139 from Storrington L into Fryern Rd, L into Monkmead Lane, then R into Nyetimber Lane. Silverwood at Monkmead Lane end.* **Adm £2.50, chd free. Visitors welcome by appt.**
Mature woodland garden within ¾-acre site with framework of unusual trees and shrubs, providing sheltered environment for many tender species. Some outstanding specimen plants, plant list exceeds 1000. Herb, vegetable, and fruit gardens, pond and fernery, new 10m x 2m shrub and herbaceous bed.

③ ◆ ALFRISTON CLERGY HOUSE

Alfriston BN26 5TL. The National Trust, 01323 870001, www.nationaltrust.org.uk. *4m NE of Seaford. Just E of B2108, in Alfriston village, adjoining The Tye & St Andrew's Church. Bus: RDH 125 from Lewes, Autopoint 126 from Eastbourne & Seaford.* **Adm £3.60, chd £1.80. Opening dates and times vary according to season. Please phone or visit website for details. For NGS: Wed 20 June (10-5).**
Enjoy the scent of roses and pinks in a tranquil setting with views across the meandering R Cuckmere. Visit this C14 thatched Wealden hall house, the first building to be acquired by the National Trust in 1896. Our gardener will be available to talk to you and welcome you to this peaceful cottage garden.

Blaze of summer colour in herbaceous borders; vegetables from unusual seeds brought from Latvia . . .

④ AMBROSE PLACE BACK GARDENS
Richmond Road, Worthing BN11 1PZ. *'... a horticultural phenomenon'* D. Telegraph. *Take Broadwater Rd into town centre, turn R at Town Hall T-lights into Richmond Rd. Garden entrances on L opp Library. Parking in rds.* Afternoon teas/cakes at 'Way-In Café', Worthing Tabernacle Church by £1.50 prepaid ticket only from 10 Ambrose Place. **Gardens adm £3.50, chd under 14 free. Sun 17 June (11-1, 2-5).** Start Tour at Ambrose Villa in Portland Rd or 1 Ambrose Place next to St Paul's Community Centre. Limited access to some gardens.

1 AMBROSE PLACE
Mrs M M Rosenberg
Traditional walled garden; shrubs, pond, climbing plants.

3 AMBROSE PLACE
Tim & Fiona Reynoldson
Delightful English cottage garden.

4 AMBROSE PLACE
Mark & Caroline Robson
Paved garden, raised herbaceous borders, lawn and flowering summer plants.

5 AMBROSE PLACE
Pat & Sue Owen
Paved town garden with raised borders, variety of flowering shrubs and herbaceous plants.

6 AMBROSE PLACE
Mr & Mrs P Morgan
Lawned garden with charming colourful borders and summerhouse.

7 AMBROSE PLACE
Mark & Susan Frost
Moorish-style small courtyard garden, with conservatory.

8 AMBROSE PLACE
Claire & Steve Hughes
Children's wonderland garden with colourful borders.

9 AMBROSE PLACE
Anna & Derek Irvine
Small courtyard with trough fountain leads through greenhouse to paved town garden with three further fountains and a brick rill.

10 AMBROSE PLACE
Alan & Marie Pringle
Mediterranean garden with Alhambra-inspired pond, cypress trees and lush borders.

11 AMBROSE PLACE
Mrs M Stewart
Mature garden with roses, summerhouse, flowering plants.

12 AMBROSE PLACE
Peter & Nina May
Rediscovered designer garden being brought back to life.

13 AMBROSE PLACE
Linda Gamble
Charming courtyard garden with colourful seasonal flowers.

14 AMBROSE PLACE
Andy & Lucy Marks
Paved town garden, roses, flowering shrubs, summer perennials and fig tree.

AMBROSE VILLA
Mark & Christine Potter
Victorian-style secret garden with pond, mature trees and shrubs. Flower and vegetable borders and long-established fruit-bearing vine and fig. Delightful shady areas and summerhouse.

⑤ ANSTY GARDENS
Haywards Heath RH17 5AW. *3m W of Haywards Heath on A272. 1m E of A23. Start in car park signed in Ansty village.* Ploughmans at Whydown Cottage in May. Home-made teas at Apple Tree Cottage in May & The Barn House in June. **Combined adm £4, chd free. Suns 6 May (1-6); Sun 24 June (1.30-6).**

APPLE TREE COTTAGE
Deaks Lane. Mr & Mrs G J Longfield
2-acre garden surrounds C16 cottage (not open) with mature trees, herbaceous and raised beds, rockery, fernery and vegetable garden with fruit cage. Usual and unusual plants in cottage style. Views over farmland and woodland.

THE BARN HOUSE
Cuckfield Road. Mr & Mrs M Dykes
Pretty walled garden of formal design with box hedging and informal cottage planting. Pond surrounded by azaleas. Delightful views.

BRENFIELD
Bolney Road. Dr & Mrs A Mace
Major private collection of cacti and succulents.

LEAFIELD
Bolney Road. Mr & Mrs Paul Dupée
$2^{1}/_{2}$ acres. Rockery and herbaceous borders, incl many hardy geraniums, acers, eucalyptus and young olive and fig trees. Meadow and woodland areas. Exhibition of owner's contemporary watercolours of flowers. Garden game for children.

NETHERBY
Bolney Road. Mr & Mrs R Gilbert
$^{1}/_{2}$-acre cottage garden, with 3 ponds and Japanese bridge. Laburnum arch. Home preserves for sale.

WHYDOWN COTTAGE
Bolney Road. Mrs M Gibson & Lance Gibson
1-acre woodland garden, with water features. Many unusual trees, incl an embothrium. Fresh planting annually. Ideas for the smaller garden.

Mediterranean garden with Alhambra-inspired pond, cypress trees and lush borders . . .

6 ◆ ARUNDEL CASTLE
Arundel BN18 9AB. Arundel Castle Trustees Ltd, 01903 882173, www.arundelcastle.org. *In the centre of Arundel, N of A27.* Castle & gardens £12, concessions £9.50, chd £7.50, family £32. Gardens only adult/chd £6.50. 31 Mar to 28 Oct (10-5), not Mons (but open Bank Hol Mons). Castle Rooms 12-5, last entry 4.
Home of the Duke and Duchess of Norfolk. 40 acres of grounds and gardens surround the historic castle (open to the public). 2 restored Victorian glasshouses with exotic fruit and vegetables. Walled flower and kitchen gardens, with architectural plants and wrought iron features. Specialising in unusual tender perennials and plants for mild climates. C14 Fitzalan Chapel white garden. Featured in 'The English Garden', 'Garden News' and 'Gardening Which' and on BBC TV Antiques Roadshow and Meridian TV.
&. ⋔ 🍵

7 ASHBURNHAM PLACE
Battle TN33 9NF. Mr Rhod Jones - Ashburnham Christian Trust, www.ashburnham.org.uk. *5m W of Battle on A271.* Home-made teas. Adm £3, chd free. Wed 9 May (1-5).
220 acres of landscaped grounds and gardens originally designed by Capability Brown. Glorious views over 3 lakes, with bridge and terraces designed by George Dance. Features incl scented prayer garden, working kitchen gardens within 4-acre walled garden and C19 winter garden. Lakeside and woodland walks.
&. ⋔ ⊛ 🍵

8 ASHDOWN PARK HOTEL
Wych Cross RH18 5JR. Mr Kevin Sweet. *6m S of E Grinstead. Take A22, 3m S of Forest Row turn L at Wych Cross by garage, 1m on R. From M25 take M23 S, exit J10 on A264 to E Grinstead. Approach from S on A22, turn R at Wych Cross.* Adm £3.50, chd free. Sun 13 May (2-5).
186 acres of parkland, grounds and gardens surrounding Ashdown Park Hotel. Restoration work started in 2005 on the walled garden with the planting of herbaceous perennials, roses, lime trees, box hedging and wall-trained fruit trees. A peaceful oasis in the heart of Ashdown Forest. Woodland walks. Gravel paths, slopes, some uneven paths.
&. ⋔ 🍵

9 BAKERS HOUSE
Bakers Lane, Shipley RH13 8GJ. Mr & Mrs Mark Burrell, 01403 741215. *5m S of Horsham. Take A24 to Worthing, then A272 W, 2nd turn to Dragon's Green, L at George & Dragon PH, Bakers Lane then 300yds on L.* Home-made teas. Adm £3, chd free (share to St Mary the Virgin, Shipley). Suns 20 May; 17 June (2-6). Visitors also welcome by appt.
Large Wealden garden, lake, laburnum tunnel, shrubs, trees, rose walks of old-fashioned roses; scented knot garden, bog gardens, lemon and olive walk. Gravel paths, partial wheelchair access.
&. ⋔ ⊛ 🍵

10 BANKTON COTTAGE
Turners Hill Road, Crawley Down RH10 4EY. Robin & Rosie Lloyd, 01342 718907, rosie.lloyd@dsl.pipex.com. *4m W of East Grinstead. 2½m E of M23 J10. On B2028 1m N of Turners Hill Xrds. Parking only on rd.* Home-made teas. Adm £3.50, chd free. Sats 16 June; 7 July (2-5.30). Evening Opening £4.50, wine, Fri 6 July (6-8.30). Visitors also welcome by appt late May to early Aug, for groups of 20+.
Almost unanimously described as a 'romantic' garden by visitors, the old walled kitchen garden has beds of herbaceous perennials, roses and clematis, box-edged lavender parterre and serpentine yew hedging. Beyond, lake, swans, bog garden and woodland. Many terracotta pots planted up. Featured in 'Sussex Life'.
&. ⋔ ⊛ 🍵

September peaks with cyclamen, colchicum, asters, heleniums, miscanthus, verbenas, sedums and butterflies . . .

11 ◆ BATEMAN'S
Burwash TN19 7DS. The National Trust, 01435 882302, www.nationaltrust.org.uk. *6m E of Heathfield. ½m S of A265 on rd leading S at W end of Burwash, or N from Woods Corner (B2096).* Adm £6.80, chd £3.40. Sats to Weds Mar to Oct. For NGS: Weds 9 May; 5 Sept (11-5).
Home of Rudyard Kipling from 1902-1936. Kipling planted yew hedges and rose garden, as well as constructing the pear alley and pond. The mill, within the grounds, grinds local wheat into flour.
&. ⋔ 🍵

12 BATES GREEN
Arlington, nr Hailsham BN26 6SH. Carolyn & John McCutchan, 01323 485152, www.batesgreen.co.uk. *3½m SW of Hailsham and of A22. 2m S of Michelham Priory. 2½m N from Wilmington on A27. Bates Green on small back rd (Tyehill Road) running from Yew Tree Inn in the centre of Arlington village to Caneheath nr Old Oak Inn.* Light refreshments & teas. Adm £4, chd free. Suns 8 Apr; 10 June; 16 Sept (11-5). Also open 10 June & 16 Sept Marchants Hardy Plants. Visitors also welcome by appt.
Plantsman's 2-acre tranquil garden with pond and organic raised bed vegetable garden. April: woodland behind meadow carpeted in anemones; shaded areas incl narcissi, primroses, violets and pulmonaria; tulips in herbaceous borders. June: alliums, hardy geraniums, kniphofias, hemerocallis, grasses, salvias and poppies. September: peaks with cyclamen, colchicum, asters, heleniums, miscanthus, verbenas, sedums and butterflies.
&. ⋔ ⊛ 🍵

13 BEAUCHAMPS
Float Lane, Udimore, Rye TN31 6BY. Matty & Richard Holmes. *3m W of Rye. 3m E of Broad Oak Xrds. Turn S off B2089 down Float Lane ½m.* Home-made teas. Adm £4, chd free. Sun 3 June (2-6).
Informal country garden, with wide range of unusual herbaceous plants, shrubs and trees incl fine specimens of Cornus controversa 'Variegata' and Crinodendron hookerianum. Small orchard, kitchen garden and copse. Garden maintained and plants for sale propagated by owners. Good views of beautiful Brede Valley.
&. ⋔ ⊛ 🍵

14 4 BEN'S ACRE
Horsham RH13 6LW. Pauline Clark.
Approach Horsham on A281 via Henfield/Cowfold. R into St Leonards Rd at PH, 4th R into Brambling Rd and follow signs. From Dorking Rd A24, L at A264 roundabout (Crawley/Gatwick), over 1st roundabout, 2nd L at next roundabout, Horsham B2195. Over T-lights into Harwood Rd, L at roundabout, Comptons Lane. Over mini roundabout, L into Heron Way and follow signs. Extra parking in Grebe Cres if necessary. Home-made teas. **Adm £2.50, chd free (share to Born Free). Sats 23 June; 25 Aug (11.30-5.30).**
On the edge of St Leonards Forest, a terraced sloping 100ft x 45ft plant-lover's garden. See the roses and perennials in June with our gold and cream borders, designed and planted by owner, with water features, ornaments, pots and seats for viewing. Our new scree bed looks good in August with grasses and late-season flowers, and new features for 2007. Featured in 'Amateur Gardening', 'County Times' & on Sky TV Secret Gardens.
⚲ ✿ ☕

15 BERRI COURT
Main Road, Yapton BN18 0EB. Mr & Mrs J C Turner. 5m SW of Arundel. A2024 Littlehampton to Chichester rd. In centre of village between Shoulder of Mutton & The Olive Branch PHs. Car park is opp T-junction next to the Free Church chapel. **Adm £3, chd free. Sun 15, Mon 16 Apr (11-5). Evening Opening, wine, Thur 12 July (6-9).**
Intensely planted 2-acre garden of wide interest; trees, flowering shrubs, heathers, eucalyptus, daffodils, shrub roses, hydrangeas and lily pond.
⚲ ✿ ☕

16 BIGNOR PARK
Pulborough RH20 1HG. The Mersey Family, www.bignorpark.co.uk. 5m S of Petworth and Pulborough. Well signed from B2138. Nearest village Sutton. Home-made teas 4, 5 Aug only. **Adm £3, chd free. Weds 4 Apr to 30 May (2-5); Sat 4, Sun 5 Aug (12-5); Weds 3 to 31 Oct (2-5).**
11 acres of garden to explore, with magnificent views of S Downs. Interesting trees, shrubs, wild flower areas with swathes of daffodils in spring. Old walled flower and vegetable gardens. Plenty of seats for

contemplation, and shelter if it rains. Temple, Greek pavilion and unusual sculptures. Surprises for children. Rare-breed Suffolk punches in the stable. Dogs on leads welcome. Plant sale 4, 5 Aug only.
⚲ ✿ ☕

Experimental planting to cope with increasing dry conditions . . .

17 4 BIRCH CLOSE
Arundel BN18 9HN. Elizabeth & Mike Gammon, 01903 882722. 1m S of Arundel. From A27/A284 roundabout at W end of Arundel take Ford Rd. After 1/2m turn R into Maxwell Rd. Follow signs for 1/2m. Home-made teas. **Adm £2.50, chd free. Sun 6, Mon 7 May (2-5). Visitors also welcome by appt in May only for groups.**
1/3 acre of woodland garden on edge of Arundel with woods on three sides. Wide range of mature trees and shrubs (incl silver birch, chestnut, stewartia, acer, rhododendron, viburnum and cornus alternifolia) and many hardy perennials. Particular emphasis on spring flowers (bluebells, narcissi, tulips, alliums, camassia and forget-me-nots) and clematis (over 100 incl 8 different montana). All set in a tranquil setting with secluded corners, meandering paths and plenty of seating.
✕ ✿ ☕

18 ◆ BORDE HILL GARDEN, PARK & WOODLAND
Balcombe Road, Haywards Heath RH16 1XP. Borde Hill Garden Ltd, 01444 450326, www.bordehill.co.uk. 1 1/2 m N of Haywards Heath. **Adm £6.50, chd £3.50, concessions £5.50. 1 Apr to 31 Oct (10-6 or dusk if earlier). For NGS: Thu 20 Sept (10-6).**
Glorious garden set in a stunning 200-acre landscape. Created over the last 100yrs to be a series of garden rooms, incl rose, Italian and subtropical dells. 'Champion' trees complement rare shrubs from rhododendrons to magnolias. Woodland gardens and lakeside walks.
⚲ ✿ ☕

19 BRADSTOW LODGE
The Drive, Ifold RH14 0TE. Ian & Elizabeth Gregory. 1m S of Loxwood. From A272/A281 take B2133 (Loxwood). 1/2m S of Loxwood take the Plaistow rd, after 800yds turn R into The Drive (by village shop). Follow signs. Parking in The Drive only, please park considerately. Home-made teas. **Adm £3, chd free. Sun 8, Wed 11 Apr (2-5).**
Plantsman's garden on Wealden clay created and developed over the past 6yrs by owners. Triangular garden with different areas giving wide-ranging and varied plantings from wild to formal. Ponds, bog garden, knot garden, greenhouse and vegetable areas. Many pots and containers and raised beds. Some new experimental planting to cope with increasing dry conditions.
⚲ ✕ ☕

BRAEKENAS
See Surrey.

20 BRICKWALL
Rye Road, Northiam TN31 6NL. The Frewen Educational Trust Ltd, www.frewencollege.co.uk. 8m NW of Rye. S end of Northiam High St at A28/B2088 junction. Rail and bus: Rye, Northiam to Hastings service. Home-made teas. **House & garden £5. Garden only £3, chd under 16 free. Sun 27 May (2-5).**
Listed garden surrounding a Grade I listed Jacobean Mansion (also open) and currently housing school for dyslexic children. Gardens incl chess garden with topiary yew pieces and number of Stuart characteristics: brick walls, clipped yew and beech are particular features, also small arboretum. Uneven paths.
⚲ ✿ ☕

21 BROOMERSHILL HOUSE
Broomershill Lane, Pulborough RH20 2HZ. 1m N of Pulborough. From A283 turn up Broomershill Lane at White Horse PH, signed Murrells Nursery; garden on R after nursery. From A29 turn up Broomershill Lane, continue up hill, garden on L before nursery. Home-made teas. **Adm £3, chd free. Sat 5, Sun 6 May (2-6).**
2-acre garden originally created by award-winning designer Fiona Lawrenson for all-yr interest. Herbaceous walk with espaliered fruit on old brick walls; pleached hornbeams, reflective pool, summerhouse, grasses border and decorative vegetable garden. Glorious

views to S Downs across meadows. Zen garden planned for 2007. Cobbled courtyard and some gravel.

  ᵹ 📷 ☕

22 BUTLERS FARMHOUSE
Butlers Lane, Herstmonceux BN27 1QH. Irene Eltringham-Willson, www. irenethegardener.zoomshare.com. *3m E of Hailsham. Take A271 from Hailsham, go through the village of Herstmonceux, turn R signed Church Rd then approx 1m turn R.* Home-made teas. **Adm £3.50, chd free. Sat 18, Sun 19 Aug (2-5).**
Lovely rural setting for ½-acre garden surrounding C16 farmhouse (not open) with views of S Downs. Mainly herbaceous with rainbow border, small pond with dribbling frogs and Cornish-inspired beach corner. Still being restored to former glory, as shown in old photographs, but with a few quirky twists. Relax and listen to live jazz in the garden.

  ᵹ 📷 ✿ ☕

23 51 CARLISLE ROAD
Eastbourne BN21 4JR. Mr & Mrs N Fraser-Gausden, 01323 722545, fgausden@ic24.net. *200yds inland from seafront (Wish Tower), close to Congress Theatre.* **Adm £3, chd £1. Sat, Sun 2, 3 June (2-5.30). Evening Opening** £4 wine, Sat 16 June (6-8). Visitors also welcome by appt.
Walled, S-facing garden (82ft sq) with mixed beds intersected by stone paths and incl small pool. Profuse and diverse planting. Wide selection of shrubs, old roses, herbaceous plants and perennials mingle with specimen trees and climbers.

  📷 ✿ ☕

24 🆕 CAXTON MANOR
Wall Hill, Forest Row RH18 5EG. Adele & Jules Speelman. *1m N of Forest Row, 2m S of E Grinstead. From A22 take turning to Ashurstwood, entrance on L after ⅓m, or 1m on R from N.* Home-made teas. **Adm £3.50, chd free. Fri 18, Sat 19 May (2-5).**
Delightful Japanese-inspired gardens planted with mature rhododendrons, azaleas and acers, surrounding large pond with massive rockery and waterfall, beneath the home of the late Sir Archibald McIndoe (house not open). Elizabethan-style parterre at rear of house.

  ᵹ 📷 ✿ ☕

25 CHAMPS HILL
Waltham Park Road, Coldwaltham RH20 1LY. Mr & Mrs David Bowerman, 01798 831868. *3m S of Pulborough. On A29, turn R to Fittleworth into Waltham Park Rd; garden 400yds.* Home-made teas. **Adm £4, chd free. Suns 18 Mar; 13 May; 12 Aug (2-5). Visitors also welcome by appt, groups of 10+, coaches permitted.**
27 acres of acid-loving plants around sand pits and woodland. Superb views. Sculptures.

  ᵹ 📷 ✿ ☕

Small pond with dribbling frogs and Cornish-inspired beach corner . . . with a few quirky twists. Relax and listen to live jazz in the garden . . .

26 CHIDMERE GARDENS
Chidham Lane, Chidham PO18 8TD. Jackie & David Russell, 01243 572287, www.chidmeregardens.com. *6m W of Chichester at SE end of Chidham Lane by pond in village.* Home-made teas. **Adm £3.50, chd free. Sun 15, Mon 16 Apr (2-6); Evening Opening,** wine, **Sun 20 May (5-8); Sun 19, Mon 20 Aug (2-6). Visitors also welcome by appt.**
First open in 1935, the garden is reopening after 5yrs refurbishment. C15 house (not open) is excitingly situated next to Chidmere Pond, so much so that the well-filled greenhouse which borders the mere feels almost like a houseboat. Divided by tall yew and hornbeam hedges, the garden has fine flowering treees, roses and well-stocked herbaceous borders. Recent projects incl wild flower meadow, alpine greenhouse, fruit and vegetable garden and orchards with over 150 varieties of apples used to produce Chidmere Farm apple juice. Featured in 'Chichester Observer'. Gravel paths, assistance may be needed.

  ᵹ ☕

27 ♦ CLINTON LODGE
Fletching TN22 3ST. Lady Collum, 01825 722952, garden@clintonlodge.com. *4m NW of Uckfield. From A272 turn N at Piltdown for Fletching, 1½m.* **Adm £4, chd free. For NGS: Suns 6 May, 10 June. Mons 11, 18, 25 June; 2, 9, 30 July; 6 Aug (2-5.30).**
6-acre formal and romantic garden, overlooking parkland, with old roses, double herbaceous borders, yew hedges, pleached lime walks, copy of C17 scented herb garden, medieval-style potager, vine and rose allée, wild flower garden. Canal garden, small knot garden and shady glade. Caroline and Georgian house, not open. Group visits by arrangement.

  📷 ✿ ☕

28 COATES MANOR
Fittleworth RH20 1ES. Mrs G H Thorp, 01798 865356. *3½m SW of Pulborough. Turn off B2138 signed Coates.* Home-made teas. **Adm £3, chd free. Sun 21 Oct (11-5). Visitors also welcome by appt.**
1 acre, mainly shrubs and foliage of special interest, surrounding Elizabethan house (not open). Flowing design punctuated by clipped shrubs and specimen trees. Paved walled garden with interesting perennials, clematis, scented climbers and smaller treasures. Cyclamen, nerines, amaryllis, berries and coloured foliage give late season interest.

  📷 ✿ ☕

29 COLWOOD HOUSE
Cuckfield Lane, Warninglid RH17 5SP. Mr & Mrs Patrick Brenan. *6m W of Haywards Heath. From W, 6m SE of Horsham, entrance on B2115 (Cuckfield Lane). From E, N & S, turn from A23, proceed W towards Warninglid for ¾m.* Light refreshments & teas. **Adm £3, chd free (share to Warninglid Village Hall). Wed 22, Sun 26 Aug (2-6).**
9 acres newly-extended gardens, with mature and specimen trees from the last century. Lawns and woodland paths, formal and informal flower beds; 100ft terrace and herbaceous border overlooking flower-rimmed croquet lawn, parterre garden, herb and rose gardens. Cut turf labyrinth and forsythia tunnel. Water features and fountains; ornaments; gazebos and pavilions. Pets' cemetery. Gravel paths.

  ᵹ ✿ ☕

5-acre garden started from fields in 1988 . . . what two fully-employed couples have achieved at the weekends . . . !

30 COOKSCROFT
Bookers Lane, Earnley PO20 7JG.
Mr & Mrs J Williams, 01243 513671,
www.cookscroft.com. *6m S of
Chichester. At end of Birdham Straight
take L fork to E Wittering. 1m on,
before sharp bend, turn L into Bookers
Lane. 2nd house on L.* Home-made
teas. **Adm £3, chd free. Sun 27, Mon
28 May (2-6). Visitors also welcome
by appt Mar to Nov, coaches
permitted.**
5-acre garden started from fields in
1988. Many trees grown from
provenance seeds or liners. Collections
of eucalyptus, birch, snake bark
maples and unusual shrubs. 3 ponds
with waterfalls. Cottage garden and
Japanese garden. Interesting and
developing garden, incl woodland area:
what two fully-employed couples have
achieved at the weekends! Featured in
'Chichester Observer'.

31 COPYHOLD HOLLOW
Copyhold Lane, Borde Hill,
Haywards Heath RH16 1XU.
Frances Druce,
www.copyholdhollow.co.uk. *2m N of
Haywards Heath. Follow signs for
Borde Hill Gardens. With BHG on L,
over brow of hill and take 1st R signed
Ardingly. Garden 1/2m.* Home-made
teas. **Adm £3, chd free. Thur 24 May
(2-4.30).**
Enchanting N-facing 1 1/2-acre cottage
and woodland garden, in a hollow
surrounding C16 listed house (not
open) behind 1000yr-old box hedge.
Mixed borders, pond and bog garden.
Ongoing planting of shrubs with native
trees, wild bulbs and flowers to
encourage wildlife. Rough hewn oak
steps up 'Himalayan Glade'.

32 COWDRAY PARK GARDENS
Midhurst GU29 0AY. The Viscount &
Viscountess Cowdray. *1m E of
Midhurst on A272. Follow A272
towards Petworth and Haywards
Heath, entrance on R 200yds past
Cowdray Park Golf Club. From
Petworth follow A272 towards*

*Midhurst, entrance on L after entering
park through wrought iron gates.* Light
refreshments & cream teas. **Adm £3,
chd free (share to RHS). Sun 20 May
(2-5).**
Avenue of wellingtonias, woodland
walk; grass garden, rhododendrons,
azaleas; lakes; large variety of trees
and shrubs, herb parterre. Lebanon
cedar 300yrs old; pleasure garden
surrounded by ha-ha, themed
herbaceous border; laburnum tunnel,
cherry avenue and valley garden. Deep
unfenced water.

33 CROWN HOUSE
Sham Farm Lane, Eridge TN3 9JU.
Major L Cave (Retd), 01892 864389.
*3m SW of Tunbridge Wells. Signed
from A26 Tunbridge Wells to
Crowborough rd, approx 400yds.
Buses: 29 (1/2 hourly service), also 225,
228 & 229. In Eridge take Rotherfield
turn S (Sham Farm Lane), 1st R, house
1st on L, short walk from bus stop.*
Home-made teas. **Adm £3, chd free.
Sat 14, Sun 15 July (2-6). Visitors
also welcome by appt May to Sept
(not Weds) for small groups at short
notice & larger groups at one week's
notice.**
1 1/2 acres with pools, rose garden and
rose walk, herbaceous borders and
heather border, herb garden. Full size
croquet lawn. Laid out as a series of
garden rooms in the style of Gertrude
Jekyll. Panoramic views of the High
Weald and Eridge Park. Aerial
photographs showing development of
garden since 1969. Rose walk not
suitable for wheelchairs.

34 DALE PARK HOUSE
Madehurst BN18 0NP. Robert &
Jane Green, 01243 814260,
robertgreen@farming.co.uk. *4m W of
Arundel. Take A27 E from Chichester or
W from Arundel, then A29 (London) for
2m, turn L to Madehurst & follow red
arrows.* Home-made teas. **Adm £3,
chd free. Sun 17 June (2-5). Visitors
also welcome by appt.**
Set in parkland on S Downs with
magnificent views to sea. Large walled

garden with 200ft herbaceous border,
mixed borders and rose garden. Rose
and clematis arches, interesting
collection of hostas, foliage plants and
shrubs, orchard and kitchen garden.

35 ◆ DENMANS GARDEN
Denmans Lane, Fontwell BN18 0SU.
Michael Neve & John Brookes,
01243 542808, www.denmans-
garden.co.uk. *5m from Chichester &
Arundel. Off A27, 1/2m W of Fontwell
roundabout.* **Adm £4.25, chd £2.50,
senior citizen £3.80, family £12.50.
Open daily (9-5, or dusk if earlier),
not 25, 26 Dec & 1 Jan. For NGS:
Evening Openings, wine, Tues 3
Apr; 16 Oct (5-7).**
Nearly 4-acre garden designed for yr-
round interest through use of form,
colour and texture. Home of John
Brookes, renowned garden designer
and writer, it is a garden full of ideas to
be interpreted within smaller home
spaces. Award-winning café.

36 DORMERS
West Marden PO18 9ES. Mr & Mrs
John Cairns. *10m NW of Chichester.
On B2146. In centre of village turn up
hill towards Rowlands Castle.* **Adm £2,
chd free. Suns 25 Feb; 4 Mar (12-4).**
Village garden on chalk, started from
scratch in 1997. Cottage-style
planting, mainly herbaceous and bulbs,
hellebores in early spring. Each area
with a different colour scheme, small
but productive vegetable patch.

37 DOWN PLACE
South Harting GU31 5PN. Mr & Mrs
D M Thistleton-Smith, 01730
825374. *1m SE of South Harting.
B2141 to Chichester, turn L down
unmarked lane below top of hill.* Cream
teas. **Adm £3, chd free (share to
Friends of Harting Church). Sat 28,
Sun 29 Apr; Fri 15 to Sun 17 June
incl (2-6). Visitors also welcome by
appt Apr to July.**
7-acre hillside, chalk garden on the N
side of S Downs with fine views of
surrounding countryside. Extensive
herbaceous, shrubs and rose borders
on different levels merge into natural
wild flower meadow renowned for its
collection of native orchids. Fully
stocked vegetable garden and
greenhouses. Spring flowers and
blossom. Featured in 'Kitchen Garden'
magazine.

38 DUCKYLS HOLT

Selsfield Road, West Hoathly
RH19 4QN. Mrs Diana Hill & Miss
Sophie Hill, 01342 810282,
sophie@duckylsholt.fsnet.co.uk. *4m
SW of East Grinstead, 6m E of
Crawley. At Turners Hill take B2028.
After 1m S fork L to West Hoathly.*
Home-made teas. **Adm £3, chd free.
Sat 26, Sun 27, Mon 28 May; Sat 23,
Sun 24 June (11-6). Opening with
The Priest House 26 May,
combined adm £4. Also with The
Priest House & Fountain Cottage
23 June, combined adm £5. Visitors
also welcome by appt.**
Delightful cottage garden of approx 2
acres on many different levels. Small
herb garden, colourful formal and
informal plantings, herbaceous
borders, rose border and newly-
restored formal rose garden, chickens
and runner ducks (mink and fox
permitting). Mature azaleas and
rhododendrons in season.

🌼 ☕

Artistic and quirky mix of unusual
cultivars and self-seeding English
natives. Designed to attract insects
and birds . . . a wildlife garden . . .

39 DURRANCE MANOR

Smithers Hill Lane, Shipley
RH13 8PE. Gordon & Joan Lindsay.
*7m SW of Horsham. Take A24 to
A272 (S from Horsham, N from
Worthing), then turn W towards
Billingshurst. Go 1.7m to 2nd turning
on L signed to Countryman PH.
Durrance 2nd on L.* Home-made teas.
**Adm £3, chd free. Evening
Opening, wine, Thur 23 Aug (6-9).
Sun 26 Aug (2-6).**
2 acres of Wealden clay, surrounding
C15 hall house (not open). Ha-ha
overlooking Chanctonbury Ring. Long
and colourful high summer border,
Mediterranean-style garden with
grasses, espaliered fruit trees behind
mixed border, gravelled courtyard with
exotic planting, large pond with pond-
side planting, orchard with wild
flowering meadow, other shrub
borders, vegetable garden. Featured
on Life TV Secret Gardens. Gravel
paths.

♿ 🍴 ☕

40 EASTERGATE HOUSE

Church Lane, Eastergate PO20 3UT.
Michael & Jacintha Hutton, 01243
544195,
eastergate@freenetname.co.uk. *7m
E of Chichester. On A27 turn R at
Fontwell roundabout onto A29. At War
Memorial turn immed into Church Lane
for approx 250yds.* **Adm £3, chd free.
Visitors welcome by appt.**
1-acre walled and hedged garden has
herbaceous borders interplanted with
shrubs and roses, water garden and
paved potager. In spring superb
magnolia and wisteria.

41 EBBSWORTH

Nutbourne RH20 2HE. Mrs F
Lambert. *2¹⁄₂m E of Pulborough. Take
A283 E from junction with A29 (Swan
Corner) 2m with 2 L forks signed
Nutbourne. Pass Rising Sun & follow
signs to garden.* Home-made teas.
**Adm £3, chd free. Thur 26, Fri 27
July (2-5).**
Charming, well-planted, owner-
maintained cottage garden,
surrounding old cottage (not open).
Roses and lilies, together with
herbaceous borders. Man-made
stream and ponds planted with water
plants.

🍴 ☕

42 ♦ FIRLE PLACE

Lewes BN8 6LP. 8th Viscount Gage,
01273 858567. *3m E of Lewes. On
A27 turn R from Lewes & L from
Eastbourne. Follow tourist signs.*
**House & garden £7, chd £5. Garden
only £3, chd /concessions £2.
House only May to Sept, Wed, Thur
& Sun 2-4.30. For NGS: Suns 15 Apr;
23 Sept (12-5).**
'The Pleasure Grounds'. Wild
woodland garden dating back to C16
currently undergoing renovation,
situated above Firle Place (also open)
giving far-reaching views over Firle Park
towards the Sussex Weald. Woodland
paths and avenues leading to hidden
glades, each with themed plantings.
Garden only open NGS days. Garden

Fair with local crafts & garden stalls.
House open from 1pm, discount for
garden visitors.

🌼 ☕

43 FITTLEWORTH HOUSE

Bedham Road, Fittleworth
RH20 1JH. Edward & Isabel
Braham, 01798 865074 Mark
Saunders. *3m SE of Petworth. Just off
A283, midway between Petworth and
Pulborough, 200yds along lane signed
Bedham.* **Adm £2.50, chd free. Weds
2 May to 25 July incl; Wed 12 Sept
(all dates 2-5). Visitors also welcome
by appt Apr to Sept for groups of
4+.**
Mature 3-acre garden encompassing
wisteria-covered Georgian House (not
open). Working walled kitchen garden
features wide range of vegetables. Fruit
cages, cut flowers, apple tunnel and
150ft cutting border. Magnificent cedar,
rose garden, formal fountain garden,
rhododendrons, lawns and mixed
borders. Smaller walled garden
features greenhouses and old potting
shed. Head Gardener on hand to
answer questions. Vegetable display
on 12 Sept. Featured in 'Kitchen
Garden' magazine.

♿ 🌼

44 FIVE OAKS COTTAGE

West Burton RH20 1HD. Jean &
Steve Jackman, 07939 272443,
jestjsck@tiscali.co.uk. *5m S of
Pulborough. From A29 4m S of
Pulborough, take B2138 signed to
Fittleworth & Petworth. Turn immed L &
L again at T-junction. 1m on the L.
Please follow these directions to avoid
coming through the village.* **Adm
£2.50. Visitors welcome by appt all
year, only by prior phone call please.
Regret not suitable for children.**
Artistic and quirky mix of unusual
cultivars and self-seeding English
natives. Designed to attract insects
and birds. Comments in the visitors'
book incl: 'so different', 'refreshing and
magical' and 'full of things to make you
smile'. A wildlife garden. Small nursery.
Hand-made metal plant supports,
paintings and greetings cards available.

🍴 🌼

45 FOUNTAIN COTTAGE

North Lane, West Hoathly
RH19 4QG. Clem & Rosemary
Watson. *4m SW of East Grinstead.
Turn E to West Hoathly 1m S of
Turners Hill at Selsfield Common
junction on B2028. 2m SE, turn R into
North Lane. Garden nr The Priest*

House. Home-made teas at Duckyls Holt. **Adm £2, chd free. Combined adm £5 with The Priest House & Duckyls Holt. Sat 23 June (11-5.30).** Delightful small cottage garden of approx 1/4 acre with roses and mixed flower beds and a profusion of seasonally planted tubs and pots.
🎔 ☕

46 FRAMFIELD GRANGE
Framfield TN22 5PN. Mr & Mrs Jack Gore. *3m E of Uckfield. From Uckfield take B2102 to Framfield 2 1/2 m. Continue through Framfield on B2102. The Grange is approx 1/4 E on R.* Home-made teas. **Adm £4, chd free. Sun 13 May (2-5).** 10 acres of garden with shrub borders, wild flower meadow and lakes. Woodland walks, bluebell glades. Many hybrids and species of rhododendrons and azaleas. Beautifully kept walled kitchen garden.
♿ ❀ ☕

47 NEW THE GARDEN HOUSE
5 Warleigh Road, Brighton BN1 4NT. Bridgette Saunders & Graham Lee, 01273 702840, the_garden_house@hotmail.com *1 1/2 m N of sea front. 1st turning L off Ditchling Rd, heading N from sea front.* Home-made teas. **Adm £3, chd free (share to The Martlets Hospice). Sat 16 June (2-5). Visitors also welcome by appt at any time.** Tucked away in the heart of the city, this 'secret' walled garden is full of trees, shrubs, organic vegetables and herbaceous perennials, with a pond and many quirky and fun features. In Victorian times it was a market garden supplying cut flowers to Brighton's shops...now it's a delightful surprise.
🎔 ❀ ☕

48 GARDENERS COTTAGE
West Dean PO18 0RX. Jim Buckland & Sarah Wain. *6m N of Chichester. Follow signs to West Dean Gardens and park in Gardens car park. Follow signs to cottage.* Home-made teas. **Adm £2.50, chd free. Sun 20 May (11-5).** Small serene and secluded theatrical retreat with strong emphasis on texture, foliage and good structure created by trees. Topiary, labyrinthine

paths, interesting spaces. Separate courtyard, garden with pond. Featured in 'Country Homes & Interiors'.
🎔 ☕

49 THE GRANGE
Fittleworth RH20 1EW. Mr & Mrs W Caldwell. *3m W of Pulborough. A283 midway Petworth-Pulborough; in Fittleworth turn S onto B2138 then turn W at Swan PH.* Home-made teas. **Adm £3, chd free. Sun 18 Mar; Weds 4 Apr; 9, 23 May; 20 June; 18 July (2-5.30).** 3-acre garden sloping to the R Rother. Walled and formal garden enclosed by yew hedges nr house with old roses and thyme lawn. Spring flowering shrubs, specimen trees and herbaceous borders, hot garden, small potager and orchard. Plant sale 18 Mar only. Gravel paths.
♿ ❀ ☕

In Victorian times it was a market garden supplying cut flowers to Brighton's shops . . .

50 ◆ GREAT DIXTER HOUSE & GARDENS
Northiam TN31 6PH. Olivia Eller/Great Dixter Charitable Trust, 01797 252878, www.greatdixter.co.uk. *8m N of Rye. 1/2 m NW of Northiam off A28.* **House & garden £7.50, chd £3. Garden only £6, chd £2.50. Tues to Suns Apr to Oct (2-5), May to Sept gardens open at 11. For NGS: Sats, Suns 24, 25 Feb; 3, 4 Mar (10-4); Suns 1 Apr; 28 Oct (2-5).** Designed by Lutyens and Nathaniel Lloyd whose son, Christopher, officiated over these gardens for 55yrs, creating one of the most experimental and constantly changing gardens of our time. Wide variety of interest from clipped topiary, wild meadow flowers, natural ponds, formal pool and the famous long border and exotic garden. A long and varied season is aimed for. New special NGS openings for snowdrops and crocuses in Feb/Mar. Study days and events available all-yr.
♿ 🎔 ❀ ☕

51 GREAT LYWOOD FARMHOUSE
Lindfield Road, Ardingly RH17 6SW. Richard & Susan Laing. *2 1/2 m N of Haywards Heath. Take B2028 for Ardingly. 2m from centre of Lindfield, turn L down single track.* Home-made teas. **Adm £3.50, chd free. Fri 1, Sat 2 June (2-6). Evening Opening £5, wine, Fri 15 June (6-8).** Approx 1 1/2-acre terraced garden surrounding C17 Sussex farmhouse (not open). Landscaped and planted since 1997, with views to S Downs. Featuring lawns and grass walks, mixed borders, rose garden, kitchen garden and orchard, walled garden with dovecote.
🎔 ❀ ☕

52 ◆ HAILSHAM GRANGE
Vicarage Road, Hailsham BN27 1BL. Noel Thompson Esq, 01323 844248, noel-hgrange@amserve.com. *Adjacent to church in centre of Hailsham. Turn L off Hailsham High St into Vicarage Rd, park in public car park.* **Adm £3.50, chd free. For NGS: Suns 3 June; 1 July (2-5.30).** Formal garden designed and planted in grounds of former early C18 Vicarage (not open). Series of garden areas representing modern interpretation of C18 formality; Gothic summerhouse; pleached hedges; herbaceous borders, colour-themed romantic planting in separate garden compartments. Group visits by arrangement. Some gravel paths.
♿ 🎔 ❀ 🛏 ☕

53 HAM COTTAGE
Hammingden Lane, Highbrook, Ardingly RH17 6SR. Peter & Andrea Browne. *5m N of Haywards Heath. On B2028 1m S of Ardingly turn into Hammingden Lane. Signed to Highbrook, then follow NGS signs.* Home-made teas. **Adm £3, chd free. Sats, Suns, 12, 13, 19, 20 May (2-6). Evening Opening £4, wine, Fri 3 Aug (5-9).** 8 acres of undulating garden mostly created from agricultural land. Interesting variety of trees and shrubs, rhododendrons, azaleas and camellias round the pond. 2 areas of woodland, one with a drift of bluebells, the other with a sandstone outcrop, part of which forms a small amphitheatre. Stream-fed bog garden, formal garden with theme planting and vegetable garden, all created by present owners. Energy-saving devices on display: solar powered system for night-time

greenhouse heating system & house water heating; photovoltaic modules and wind turbine for lighting. Hilly paths, wheelchair users need fit accomplice.

♿ ⊕ ⊨ ☕

54 HAMMERWOOD HOUSE
Iping GU29 0PF. Mr & Mrs M Lakin. *3m W of Midhurst. 1m N of A272 Midhurst to Petersfield rd. Well signed.* Home-made teas. **Adm £3, chd free (share to St Mary's Church). Suns 13, 20 May (1-6).**
Large garden with some herbaceous planting although much admired for its rhododendrons, azaleas, acers, cornus and arboretum. 1/4 m walk to wild water garden.

♿ ⊕ ☕

55 THE HEALING GARDEN
35 Hayling Rise, High Salvington, Worthing BN13 3AL. Ivan & Janice Mitchell, 01903 263183. *2m NW of Worthing. From Brighton/Worthing follow A27 towards Arundel past Warren Rd roundabout and Offington Corner roundabout, up Crockhurst Hill into Arundel Rd. Hayling Rise on R marked by bus shelter, no 35 on L past church. From A24 head W to Arundel at Offington Corner roundabout.* Home-made teas. **Adm £2.50, chd free. Suns 3 June; 1 July (10-5). Visitors also welcome by appt May to July for small groups, guided walk with herbalist.**
Medicinal herb garden containing over 700 different types of trees, shrubs and plants from all over the world. Many of the plants will not be found anywhere else in Sussex. Although still a young garden, there is plenty to please the senses. It looks good, it smells good, and by golly it does you good! Herbalist (owner) will be delighted to help and advise visitors about medicinal plants. Featured in 'Amateur Gardening' & on Life TV Secret Gardens.

♿ ✗ ⊕ ☕

56 ◆ HIGH BEECHES
Handcross RH17 6HQ. High Beeches Gardens Conservation Trust, 01444 400589, www.highbeeches.com. *5m NW of Cuckfield. On B2110, 1m E of A23 at Handcross.* **Adm £5.50, chd under 14 free. 17 Mar to 31 Oct daily (not Weds). For NGS: Sun 27 May; Sat 29 Sept (1-5).**
25 acres of enchanting landscaped woodland and water gardens with

spring daffodils, bluebells and azalea walks, many rare and beautiful plants, wild flower meadows and glorious autumn colours. Picnic area. National Collection of Stewartia.

✗ NCCPG ☕

57 ◆ HIGHDOWN
Littlehampton Road, Goring-by-Sea BN12 6PW. Worthing Borough Council, 01903 2239999 ext 1112, www.worthing.gov.uk. *3m W of Worthing. Off A259. Stn: Goring-by-Sea, 1m.* **Collection box. Open daily 12 Mar to 30 Sept, Mons to Fris Oct to Feb, not Christmas period. Visit website for hours. For NGS: Suns 13 May; 3 June (10-6).**
Famous garden created by Sir Frederick Stern situated in chalk pit and downland area containing a wide collection of plants. Spring bulbs, peonies, shrubs and trees. Many plants were raised from seed brought from China by great collectors like Wilson, Farrer and Kingdon-Ward. Green Flag award. Woodchip paths and slopes, not suitable for less able.

✗ NCCPG

It looks good, it smells good, and by golly it does you good! Herbalist (owner) will be delighted to help and advise visitors . . .

---

58 4 HILLSIDE COTTAGES
Downs Road, West Stoke PO18 9BL. Heather & Chris Lock, 01243 574802. *3m NW of Chichester. From A286 at Lavant, head W for 1 1/2 m, nr Kingley Vale.* **Adm £2.50, chd free. Sun 29 July (2-5). Visitors also welcome by appt June, July & Aug.**
Garden 120ft x 27ft in established rural setting, created from scratch in 1996. Densely planted with mixed borders and shrubs, large collection of roses, clematis and fuchsias. Profusion of colour and scent in an immaculately maintained small garden.

✗ ☕

59 HOBBS BARTON
Streele Lane, Framfield, nr Uckfield TN22 5RY. Mr & Mrs Jeremy Clark. *3m E of Uckfield. From Uckfield take B2102 E to Framfield, or approaching from S leave A22 at Pear Tree junction S end of Uckfield bypass. Garden signed from centres of Framfield & Buxted.* Home-made teas. **Adm £4, chd free. Sat 2, Sun 3, Mon 4 June (2-5.30).**
In a peaceful pastoral setting, typical of rural Sussex and well removed from the noise of traffic, this is a mature garden of 2 3/4 acres developed by the present owners over the past 34yrs. Wide sweeping lawns lead to areas planted with many types of rose, shrubberies and herbaceous borders; numerous specimen trees incl *Metasequoia glyptostroboides*, liriodendron, giant prostrate junipers; pretty water features; part-walled vegetable and fruit garden. Developing woodland garden.

♿ ✗ ⊕ ☕

60 HORSEBRIDGE HOUSE
Fittleworth Road, Wisborough Green RH14 0HD. J R & K D Watson. *2 1/2 m SW of Wisborough Green. From Wisborough Green take A272 towards Petworth. Turn L into Fittleworth Rd, signed Coldharbour, proceed 2m. At sign 'Beware low flying owls' turn R into Horsebridge House. From Fittleworth take Bedham Lane, 2 1/2 m NE.* Home-made teas. **Adm £3.50, chd free. Sun 8 Apr (10-4.30).**
Formal garden divided into rooms centred on 1920s croquet lawn. Unusual hedging and shrub planting, spring cherry, apple and pear blossom with underplanted daffodils. Formal vegetable garden with box hedging; asparagus bed. Large play area for children under 5 with parental supervision. Featured in 'Sussex Life'.

✗ ☕

61 HOUNDLESS WATER
Bell Vale Lane, Fernhurst GU27 3DJ. Mark & Rebecca Smith, 01428 641438. *1 1/2 m S of Haslemere, 6m N of Midhurst. Take A286 N from Midhurst towards Haslemere, through Fernhurst. Take 2nd R after Kingsley Green into Bell Vale Lane, garden 1st on L.* Home-made teas. **Adm £3, chd free. Thur 17, Fri 18 May; Thur 18, Fri 19 Oct (11-4). Visitors also welcome by appt.**
5-acre Victorian garden, gardened by current owners since 2002. Mature plantings of azaleas, rhododendrons

and acid-loving trees, underplanted with bluebells. Restored listed greenhouse. Small kitchen garden and orchard. Formal borders nr house lead to stone steps to wild flower meadow.

Once known as God's acre, now God's half acre!

62 HOVE CLEMATIS GARDENS
Home-made teas at 64 Old Shoreham Road. **Individual adm. Sun 10 June (2-5.30).**

64 OLD SHOREHAM ROAD
Hove. Brian & Muriel Bailey, 01273 889247, baileybm@ntlworld.com. *A270. On S side between Shirley Drive & Upper Drive.* **Adm £2, chd free. Visitors also welcome by appt.** 12.6m by 33.6m designed and built by owners. Automatic watering. Lots of features and many hostas and clematis.

& ⚘

27 THIRD AVENUE
Hove. Mrs Michael Fisher, 01273 736302, jayfish@macdream.net. *Third Ave runs from Hove Town Hall in Church Rd to seafront. Pay parking in st.* **Adm £3, chd free. Visitors also welcome by appt June only.**
Small hidden town garden sheltered by high walls, with an interesting collection of climbers and shrubs. Pots used extensively to provide changing colour and interest all yr.

63 KENT HOUSE
East Harting GU31 5LS. Mr & Mrs David Gault, 01730 825206. *4m SE of Petersfield. On B2146 at South Harting take Elstead to Midhurst rd E for ½m. Just W of Turkey Island, turn N up no through road for 400yds.* Home-made teas (not Apr). **Adm £3, chd free (share to Friends of Harting Church). Sats, Suns 21, 22 Apr (2-5); 9, 10 June; 7, 8 July (2-6). Also open 9, 10 June Nyewood House & Sandhill Farm House. Visitors also welcome by appt at any time.**
1½-acre garden with fine trees, ha-ha, shade-loving plants for Apr and May,

walled garden, exceptional views of the Downs from pretty Georgian house (not open). Mixed borders of unusual shrubs and herbaceous plants. Short slope up driveway.

& ⚘ ☕

64 KILN COPSE FARM
Kirdford RH14 0JJ. Bill & Pat Shere. *4m NE of Petworth. Take A283 from Petworth then fork R signed Kirdford & Balls Cross. Through Balls Cross, over narrow bridge then 400yds on L.* Home-made teas. **Adm £3, chd free. Wed 11, Sun 15 Apr (12-5.30).**
1½-acre garden with yr-round interest. Beautiful wild flowers in spring in a natural setting of woodland, ponds, bridges and stepping stones! A real adventure for children. Partial wheelchair access.

& ⚘ ☕

KIMPTON HOUSE
See Hampshire.

65 ◆ KING JOHN'S LODGE
Sheepstreet Lane, Etchingham TN19 7AZ. Jill & Richard Cunningham, 01580 819232, www.kingjohnslodge.co.uk. *2m W of Hurst Green. A265 Burwash to Etchingham. Turn L before Etchingham Church into Church Lane which leads into Sheepstreet Lane after ½m. L after 1m.* **Adm £3, chd free. Nursery & garden open all yr.** For NGS: Sats (2-6), Suns (11-5) 28, 29 Apr; 26, 27 May; 8, 9 Sept. **Evening Opening**, wine, Wed 27 June (6-9).
4-acre romantic garden for all seasons surrounding an historic listed house (not open). Formal garden with water features, rose walk and wild garden and pond. Rustic bridge to shaded ivy garden, large herbaceous borders, old shrub roses and secret garden. Further 4 acres of meadows, fine trees and grazing sheep. Newly-opened nursery.

& ⚘ 🛏 ☕

66 LATCHETTS
Freshfield Lane, Danehill RH17 7HQ. Mr & Mrs Laurence Hardy, 01825 790237, laurence@flb.uk.com. *5m NE of Haywards Heath. SW off A275. In Danehill turn into Freshfield Lane at War Memorial. 1m on R for Latchetts Farmhouse).* Cream teas. **Adm £4, chd free. Fris, Sats 1, 2 June; 13, 14 July; 10, 11 Aug (1.30-5.30). Evening Opening**, wine, Fri 22 June (5.30-8.30). **Visitors also welcome by appt, coaches welcome.**
6 acres, some traditional, some modern, incl the Christian walled

garden, fine lawns, colourful planting, vegetables in raised beds, fascinating water features plus a Mound. Circle, Sunken and Sundial Gardens and woodland fern stumpery. Humour, variety and lots to see contribute to the immense popularity of this idiosyncratic garden. 'Safari Hunt' for children. Featured in GGG.

& ⚘ ☕

67 LEGSHEATH FARM
nr Forest Row RH19 4JN. Mr & Mrs M Neal, 01342 810230, legsheath@btinternet.com. *4m S of E Grinstead. 2m W of Forest Row, 1m S of Weirwood Reservoir.* Home-made teas. **Adm £4, chd free. Sun 20 May (2-5). Visitors also welcome by appt.**
Panoramic views over Weirwood reservoir. Exciting 10-acre garden with woodland walks, water gardens and formal borders. Of particular interest, clumps of wild orchids, fine davidia, acers, eucryphia and rhododendrons. Mass planting of different species of meconopsis on the way to ponds.

⚘ ☕

68 LITTLE COMMON GARDENS
Bexhill TN39 4SR. *2m W of Bexhill. To Little Common roundabout, then follow directions for each garden.* Cream teas & Ploughmans. **Combined adm £3, chd free (share to St Michael's Hospice). Sat 23 June (10-5).**
Active village with strong horticulture and flower arranging societies.

☕

41A BARNHORN ROAD
Pat & Dave Crouch. *At roundabout continue on A259 (Barnhorn Rd) approx 400 yds. Garden on L, park in adjacent rds* Plantaholic's garden incl many geraniums, grasses, cornus, penstemons and over 60 varieties of clematis. Stile and folly are two quirky features to be seen. Award for front garden, Bexhill in Bloom.

FRIARS CHARM
Maple Walk. Mr & Mrs George Rogers. *S at roundabout, R at Coop Store, down Meads Ave to Maple Walk. Park in st*
Once known as God's acre, now God's half acre! Plantswoman's adapted garden after building a new house. Conservation pond with great crested newts. Herbaceous borders and terraced gardens. Unfenced ponds.

 ⚘

1¹/₂-acre lake excavated in 1997 with unusual cantilevered jetty and impressive marginal planting . . . new stumpery . . .

⑥⑨ LITTLE HILL
Hill Farm Lane, Codmore Hill, Pulborough RH20 1BW. Barbara & Derek James. *1m N of Pulborough. Hill Farm Lane off A29 by The Rose PH, garden 10th on L. Overflow parking in field before garden entrance, follow signs.* Light refreshments & teas. **Adm £3, chd free. Evening Opening**, wine & cheese, Fri 15 June (7-9). Mon 16 July (2-5).
4 acres of formal gardens with sunken rose garden and pond, tiered rock garden with waterfall and pond, rose and grape arbour in middle of box-hedged beds, hidden rhododendron dell. Some annuals, perennials, shrubs, trees and small orchard, vegetable plot and fruit cage. Wild flowers. Some gravel and stone paths, mostly lawn.
   ⅏ ⸎ ☕

⑦⓪ LITTLE POYNES
Lower Street, Fittleworth RH20 1JE. Wade & Beth Houlden. *3m W of Pulborough. Off A283, between Pulborough and Petworth. Lower St B2138. Parking on School Lane, village hall car park and in lane by St Mary's Church.* Home-made teas. **Adm £2.50, chd free. Sats, Suns 2, 3 June; 15, 16 Sept (2-6).**
Informal village garden of approx ¹/₂ acre in the process of being redesigned by the owners. Sunny and shady areas providing the opportunity for varied planting and places to sit. Vegetable area and cut flower beds.
⸎ ⊛ ☕

⑦① LITTLE WANTLEY
Fryern Road, Storrington RH20 4BJ. Hilary Barnes. *1m W of Storrington. Follow signs to West Chiltington. Entrance approx 1m on R in Fryern Rd. Parking in field.* Home-made teas. **Adm £3.50, chd free. Sat 7, Sun 8 July (2-5.30).**
Naturalistic garden of approx 3¹/₂ acres. Wide range of plants grown in neutral/acid soil with deep mixed herbaceous borders. Secret garden reached by pergola walk. 1¹/₂-acre lake excavated in 1997 with unusual

cantilevered jetty and impressive marginal planting. New stumpery. Music by The Wheelwrights Brass Quintet. Winner Daily Mail National Garden Competition 2006. Deep water: children must be strictly supervised.
   ⅏ ⸎ ⊛ ☕

⑦② LOWDER MILL
Bell Vale Lane, Fernhurst, nr Haslemere GU27 3DJ. Anne & John Denning, 01428 644822. *1¹/₂m S of Haslemere. 6m N of Midhurst. Follow A286 out of Midhurst towards Haslemere, through Fernhurst and take 2nd R after Kingsley Green into Bell Vale Lane. Lowder Mill approx ¹/₂m on R.* Home-made teas. **Adm £3, chd £1.50. Sat 2, Sun 3 June (11-5). Visitors also welcome by appt.**
Mill House and former water mill on Sussex/Surrey/Hampshire border. Set in 3 acres of gardens, courtyard, lake, ponds, orchard and kitchen garden. The gardens had been neglected, but, redesigned by Bunny Guinness in 2002, they are being restored by the present owners, with work still ongoing. Unusual chickens, ducks and resident kingfishers.
⸎ ⊛ ☕

⑦③ MALT HOUSE
Chithurst Lane, Rogate GU31 5EZ. Mr & Mrs G Ferguson, 01730 821433. *3m W of Midhurst. From A272, 3¹/₂m W of Midhurst turn N signed Chithurst then 1¹/₂m, very narrow lane; or at Liphook turn off A3 onto old A3 (B2070) for 2m before turning L to Milland, then follow signs to Chithurst for 1¹/₂m.* **Adm £3, chd free** (share to Chithurst Church roof restoration fund & Borden Wood Village Hall). **Sun 29 Apr; Sun 6, Mon 7 May (2-6). Visitors also welcome by appt.**
6 acres; flowering shrubs incl exceptional rhododendrons and azaleas, leading to 50 acres of arboretum and lovely woodland walks plus many rare plants and trees.
☕

⑦④ THE MANOR OF DEAN
Pitshill, Tillington GU28 9AP. Mr & Mrs James Mitford, 07887 992349, emma.mitford@uk.pwc.com. *3m W of Petworth. On A272 from Petworth to Midhurst. Pass through Tillington village. A272 then opens up to short section of dual carriageway. Turn R at end of this section and proceed N, entrance to garden approx ¹/₂m.* Light refreshments & teas. **Adm £2.50, chd free. Sats, Suns 31 Mar, 1 Apr; 12, 13 May; 16, 17 June; 14, 15 July; 18, 19 Aug; 22, 23 Sept (2-5). Visitors also welcome by appt, not Tues or Weds. No parking for coaches.**
Approx 3 acres. Traditional English garden, herbaceous borders, spring bulbs, grass walks, walled kitchen garden with vegetables and fruit. Asparagus bed. Lawns, rose garden and informal areas. Some house renovation in progress; may affect parts of the garden.
⸎ ☕

⑦⑤ MARCHANTS HARDY PLANTS
2 Marchants Cottages, Mill Lane, Laughton BN8 6AJ. Graham Gough & Lucy Goffin. *From Laughton Xrds on B2124 (at Roebuck Inn), proceed E for ¹/₂m, at Xrds turn S signed Ripe down Mill Lane; on R.* **Adm £3, chd free. Suns 10 June; 16 Sept (2-5). Also open Bates Green.**
Young atmospheric 2-acre garden and nursery with remarkable backdrop of Firle Beacon and S Downs. Imaginatively designed and sensitively planted with rich tapestry of unusual plants, incl many graceful and noble grasses. Featured in 'Daily Telegraph' & RHS 'The Garden'.
   ⅏ ⸎ ⊛

⑦⑥ THE MARTLETS HOSPICE
Wayfield Avenue, Hove BN3 7LW, www.themartlets.org. *From Old Shoreham Rd (A270), 600yds W of A2023 junction, turn N into Holmes Ave. ¹/₄m L into Wayfield Ave. From A27T Hove exit, take King George VI Ave. Turn L at 1st T-lights immed R into Holmes Ave, ¹/₂m turn R into Wayfield Ave.* **Adm £3, chd free. Sat 2, Sun 3 June (2-5).**
1-acre garden with courtyard. Mainly informal plantings. Rose bower, water feature and wild flower bank. Peaceful garden with private secluded areas which are enjoyed by patients and their families. Maintained by volunteer gardeners who will greet visitors.
   ⅏ ⸎ ⊛ ☕

77 MAYFIELD GARDENS
N20 6TE. *10m S of Tunbridge Wells.
Exit A267 into Mayfield. At N end of
village turn R at Costcutter, signed car
park.* 2 new gardens on R of car park.
*From there take South St E to
Fletching St for further gardens, then
East St for house in Warren.* Home-
made teas at Warren House.
**Combined adm £3.50, chd free. Sun
10 June (2-5.30).**
Attractive old Wealden village in
conservation area dating back to
Saxon times.

NEW LAUREL COTTAGE
South Street. Barrie Martin
Cottage garden with variety of
plants and shrubs and attractive
view.

MAY COTTAGE
Fletching Street. Kathleen & Ian
Lyle
Cottage garden. Wide variety of
interesting plants, shrubs and
trees, raised beds, small pond.

SUNNYBANK COTTAGE
Fletching Street. Eve & Paul
Amans
S-facing informal garden with
views and well-stocked feature
bank with numerous specimen
shrubs.

NEW UPPERCROSS HOUSE
South Street. Mrs Rosemary
Owen
Cottage garden with good views.
Plenty of shrubs and plants and
water feature.

WARREN HOUSE
The Warren. C Lyle
2-acre family garden with good
range of shrubs, meadow and
stream. Sculptures.

78 ◆ MERRIMENTS GARDENS
Hurst Green TN19 7RA. Mr D Weeks
& Mrs P Weeks, 01580 860666,
info@merriments.co.uk. *1m N of
Hurst Green. Between Hawkhurst &
Hurst Green.* **Adm £4, chd £2.** Good
Fri to end Sept, Mon to Sat. For NGS:
Suns 8 July; 23 Sept (10.30-5.30).
4-acre garden of richly and
imaginatively planted deep curved
borders, colour themed using a rich
mix of trees, shrubs, perennials,
grasses and many unusual annuals

which ensure an arresting display of
colour, freshness and vitality from
spring to autumn.

79 MITCHMERE FARM
Stoughton PO18 9JW. Neil & Sue
Edden, 02392 631456,
sue@mitchmere.ndo.co.uk.
*5¹/₂m NW of Chichester. Turn off the
B2146 at Walderton towards
Stoughton. Farm is ³/₄m on L,
¹/₄m beyond the turning to Upmarden.*
**Adm £3, chd free. Sun 11, Thur 15,
Sun 18 Feb (11-4); Sun 10, Thur 14,
Sun 17 Feb 2008.** Visitors also
welcome by appt mid Jan to mid
Mar, £5 a head incl tea.
1¹/₂-acre garden started in 1991 in
lovely downland position. Unusual
trees and shrubs, many coloured
stems or catkins growing in dry gravel,
briefly wet most years when the
Winterbourne rises and flows through
the garden. Drifts of snowdrops and
crocuses. Small collection of special
snowdrops. Small formal kitchen
garden, free-range bantams. Wellies
advisable. Local craftspeople selling
garden-related products; Snowdrop
Trust stall. Featured in 'Country Living',
'Sussex Life' & W Sussex Gazette'.
Gravel and shallow steps but
alternative grass paths.

80 MOORLANDS
Friar's Gate, nr Crowborough
TN6 1XF. Dr & Mrs Steven Smith &
Dr Lucy & Mr Mark Love, 01892
652474. *2m N of Crowborough. St
Johns Rd to Friar's Gate. Or turn L off
B2188 at Friar's Gate signed Horder
Hospital.* Cream teas (Teas by request
on Weds). **Adm £4, chd free. Every
Wed 4 Apr to 26 Sept (11-5). Sun 24
June (2-6).** Visitors also welcome by
appt.
4 acres set in lush valley deep in
Ashdown Forest; water garden with
ponds, streams and river; primulas,
rhododendrons, azaleas. River walk
with grasses and bamboos. Rockery
restored to original 1929 design. The
many special trees planted 27yrs ago
make this garden an arboretum.

**81 MOUNT HARRY HOUSE &
MOUNT HARRY LODGE**
Ditchling Road, Offham BN7 3QW.
Lord & Lady Renton, Mr & Mrs
Stewart-Roberts. *2m N of Lewes. On
S side of Ditchling Rd B2116, ¹/₂m W
of A275.* Home-made teas. **Adm £4,
chd free. Sat 9 June (2-5).**

2 adjoining 7-acre and 1-acre terraced
gardens on chalk. Herbaceous and
shrubbery borders, wild flower walk,
specimen trees, laburnum walks,
walled garden, dell garden,
conservatory, ornamental tree nursery.
In beautiful downland setting.

Coloured stems or catkins growing in dry gravel . . .

82 MOUNTFIELD COURT
nr Robertsbridge TN32 5JP. Mr &
Mrs Simon Fraser. *3m N of Battle. On
A21 London-Hastings; ¹/₂m from
Johns Cross.* Home-made teas. **Adm
£3, chd free. Sun 6 May (2-5).**
3-acre wild woodland garden;
walkways through exceptional
rhododendrons, azaleas, camellias and
other flowering shrubs; fine trees and
outstanding views. Small paved herb
garden.

83 NEW BARN
Egdean, nr Petworth RH20 1JX. Mr
& Mrs Adrian Tuck, 01798 865502.
*2m SE of Petworth. ¹/₂m S of Petworth
turn off A285 to Pulborough, at 2nd
Xrds turn R into lane. Or 1m W of
Fittleworth take L fork to Midhurst off
A283.* 150yds turn L. Light
refreshments & teas, coffee from 10.30
(not June). **Adm £3, chd free. Wed 6
June; Mon 27 Aug (10.30-5.30).**
Visitors also welcome by appt.
Converted C18 barn (not open) with
2-acre garden in beautiful peaceful
farmland setting. Large natural pond
and stream. Owner-maintained and
planned for yr-round interest from
snowdrops, camellias, spring flowers,
masses of bluebells, azaleas, water-
irises, roses, shrubs and herbaceous
through to autumn colour. Trees
planted for flower, bark and leaf. Seats
and 2 swings.

84 NEWTIMBER PLACE
Newtimber BN6 9BU. Mr & Mrs
Andrew Clay, www.newtimber.co.uk.
*7m N of Brighton. A23, take A281
towards Henfield, turning between
Poynings & Pyecombe, signed NGS.*
Home-made teas. **Adm £3.50, chd
free. Sun 15 Apr (2-5.30).**

Beautiful C17 moated house (not open). Gardens and woods full of bulbs and wild flowers in spring. In summer, roses, herbaceous border and lawns. Moat flanked by water plants. Mature trees. Wild garden, ducks, chickens and fish.

85 NEW THE NOOK
New Road, Southwater RH13 9AU. Les White, 01403 730401, leswhite500@btinternet.com. *2m N of Horsham at N end of Southwater. At Hop Oast roundabout on A24 S of Horsham, take rd to Southwater. Next roundabout, 2nd exit. New Rd is on R towards end of stretch of straight rd.* Light refreshments & teas. **Adm £3, chd free (share to St Catherine's Hospice). Sat 2, Sun 3 June (10-5). Visitors also welcome by appt.**
Primarily a wildlife garden. Stone, bark and decking pathways lead you around natural streams, ponds, rocks and woodpiles. Ferns, grasses, bamboos and mature trees dominate the scene, although there are contrasting areas such as Mediterranean, patio, planted walls and traditional borders. Exhibition and sale of original pictures, pottery and woodcrafts by local art club. Interesting ponds, but deep in places. Children must be supervised.

86 NEW NORTH SPRINGS
Bedham, nr Fittleworth RH20 1JP. Mr & Mrs R Haythornthwaite. *Between Fittleworth and Wisborough Green. From Wisborough Green take A272 towards Petworth. Turn L into Fittleworth Rd signed Coldharbour. Proceed 1½m. From Fittleworth take Bedham Lane off A283 and proceed for approx 3m NE. Limited parking.* **Adm £3, chd free. Sat 9, Sun 10 June (12-5).**
Hillside garden with good views surrounded by mixed woodland. Focus on structure with a wide range of trees and shrubs. Stream, pond and bog area. Well-grown plants incl roses, clematis, hostas, rhododendrons and azaleas.

87 NORTHWOOD FARMHOUSE
Blackgate Lane, Pulborough RH20 1DF. Mrs Pat Hill, 01403 700740. *1m N of Pulborough. On A29, turn NW into Blackgate Lane & follow lane for 2m then follow signs.* Home-made teas. **Adm £2, chd free. Sun 15, Mon 16 Apr (2-5). Visitors also welcome by appt.**
Cottage garden with bulbs, roses, pasture with wild flowers and pond. All on Wealden clay, surrounding Sussex farmhouse (not open) dating from 1520.

88 NYEWOOD HOUSE
Nyewood, nr Rogate GU31 5JL. Mr & Mrs C J Wright, 01730 821563. *4m E of Petersfield. From A272 at Rogate take South Harting rd for 1½m. Turn L at pylon towards South Downs Hotel. Nyewood House 2nd on R over cattle grid.* Cream teas Sat at Nyewood House, Sun at The Malthouse, The Street, South Harting (1½m). **Adm £3, chd free. Sat 9, Sun 10 June (2-6). Also open Kent House & Sandhill Farm House. Visitors also welcome by appt in June only, for groups of 12+, no coaches.**
Victorian country house garden with stunning views of S Downs. 3 acres comprising formal gardens with rose walk and arbours, pleached hornbeam, colour-themed herbaceous borders, shrub borders, lily pond and kitchen garden. Wooded area featuring wild orchids as well as new plantings of shrubs and trees. Gravel driveway.

Bog garden, loggery . . .

89 ◆ NYMANS GARDEN
Handcross RH17 6EB. The National Trust, 01444 405250, www.nationaltrust.org.uk. *4m NW of Cuckfield. On B2114 at Handcross signed off M23/A23 London-Brighton rd, SE of Handcross. Bus: 73 from Hove or Crawley & 271 from Haywards Heath.* **Adm £7.70, chd £3.80. Opening days & times vary according to season. Please phone or visit website for details. For NGS: Suns 13 May; 1 July (11-6).**
One of the great gardens of the Sussex Weald. Walled garden with fountain, hidden sunken garden, rose garden, romantic ruins and woodland walks. A few rooms in Nymans House are open.

90 OFFHAM HOUSE
Offham BN7 3QE. Mr S Goodman & Mr & Mrs P Carminger. *2m N of Lewes on A275. Cooksbridge stn ½m.* Home-made teas. **Adm £3.50, chd free (share to Cooksbridge Recreation Ground). Suns 29 Apr; 3 June (1-5).**
Fountains, flowering trees, double herbaceous border, long peony bed. 1676 Queen Anne house (not open) with well-knapped flint facade. Herb garden. Walled kitchen garden with glasshouses.

91 THE OLD POST OFFICE
London Road, Coldwaltham RH20 1LG. Patrick & Stephanie Fane. *2m S of Pulborough. On A29. 300yds S of St Giles' Church. Parking in Sandham Hall car park next door.* **Adm £2.50, chd free. Sun 9 Sept (2-5).**
Enthusiastic plantaholic's garden, meandering through L-shaped plot. Designed to reveal itself in stages with planting for yr-round colour, form and texture. Plants for sandy soil or special areas (bog garden, loggery) incl trees, shrubs, roses, climbers, perennials and bulbs. 2 ponds, potager, hillock with summerhouse. Unfenced ponds, small children must be supervised.

92 OLD SCAYNES HILL HOUSE
Clearwater Lane, Scaynes Hill RH17 7NF. Sue & Andy Spooner, 01444 831602, a-spooner@btopenworld.com. *2m E of Haywards Heath. On A272, 50yds down Sussex border path beside Shell Garage shop, & opp Farmers Inn. No parking at garden (drop off only), please park considerately in village.* Home-made teas. **Adm £3, chd free (share to Court Meadow Assn). Sat 16, Sun 17 June (2-5.30). Visitors also welcome by appt June & July only for groups of 10+.**
In memory of Sarah Robinson. Entrance archway with steps leading to 1-acre natural garden on S-facing slope of predominantly heavy clay. Mature trees and shrubs with some unusual specimens. Several colourful herbaceous borders and island beds with ornamental grasses. Many roses, small wild flower meadow with orchids, woodland walk, small orchard, fruit and vegetable area, bog garden and natural-looking pond.

93 PALATINE GARDENS
Palatine Road, Worthing BN12 6JP.
Mrs Jennie Rollings, 01903 242431,
www.goring-by-sea.com/palatine.
*1m W of Worthing. Turn S off A259 at
roundabout onto The Boulevard,
signed Goring. Take R turn at next
roundabout into Palatine Rd. School
approx 100yds on R.* **Adm £2.50, chd
free. Suns 10 June; 15 July (11-5).
Visitors also welcome by appt.**
Award-winning school garden created
by teachers, volunteers and pupils with
special needs: large and small ponds,
bog garden, wildlife area, rockeries,
sea garden, mosaics, oriental garden,
Thinking garden, labyrinth, dry garden
and interesting tree collection. Pupils
who helped make the gardens act as
guides. Gold Award & Best in County,
SE in Bloom Schools Competition.

Using every inch
of space to
create unusual
places for adults
and children to
play . . .

94 ♦ PARHAM GARDENS
Parham Park, Storrington, nr
Pulborough RH20 4HS. Home of
Lady Emma & Mr James Barnard,
01903 742021,
www.parhaminsussex.co.uk. *4m SE
of Pulborough. On A283 Pulborough-
Storrington rd.* **House & garden £7,
chd £3.50, concessions £6. Garden
only £5, chd £2.50, concessions £4.
Weds, Thurs, Suns, Bank Hol Mons
Easter Sun to end Sept; also Tues,
Fris in Aug. Gardens & restaurant
from 12, House 2-5.**
Famous for its long tradition of
beautiful arrangements within the
house, all the flowers at Parham are
grown in its romantic walled garden.
Regimented rows contrast dramatically
with enormous herbaceous borders
overflowing with 'Edwardian opulence'!
Weird vegetables, bride maze, lake
and arguably the most sensual
greenhouse in Sussex.

95 PARK LODGE
Bedham Lane, Fittleworth
RH20 1JH. Mark & Louise Saunders.
*3m SE of Petworth. On A283 midway
between Petworth and Pulborough on*
lane signed to Bedham and
Wisborough Green, 150yds on L. **Adm
£2.50, chd free. Sat 9 June (1-5).**
1/2-acre head gardener's cottage
garden with borders planted for yr-
round colour. Small vegetable garden,
pergola and summerhouse, spring
garden and wildlife pond. Also open
the adjacent working walled kitchen
garden and greenhouses of Fittleworth
House (see separate entry), featuring a
wide range of vegetables, flowers and
fruit.

96 6 PARK TERRACE
Tillington, Petworth GU28 9AE. Mr &
Mrs H Bowden, 01798 344114,
isabellebowden@aol.com. *On A272,
between Midhurst & Petworth. 1m W
of Petworth, turn uphill at sign to
Tillington Village, past Horseguards PH
and church, no 6 is past village hall.
Please do not park in residents'
spaces but further up the lane.* Light
refreshments, teas & wine. **Adm £2.50,
chd free. Day & Evening Opening
Sun 10 June (11-9). Visitors also
welcome by appt 1 to 19 May & 11
June onwards (not Hampton Court
Show week). Groups of 10+,
coaches permitted. Refreshments
for groups on request.**
Garden designed for entertaining or
quiet retreats in complete privacy.
Terrace under the vine, 2 ponds, aviary,
archways of roses, wisteria, box
hedges, dry beds surrounded by
herbaceous and shrubs. Another leafy
tunnel leads to the large dome covered
by fruit trees and climbers. Terrace,
pigsty, greenhouse, fern walk, more
beds. Sunset terrace with S Downs
views. The garden resounds with the
water from all the fountains made by
Humphrey.

97 18 PAVILION ROAD
Worthing BN14 7EF. Andrew
Muggeridge & Ya-Hui Lee, 01903
821338. *Nr Worthing main stn.* **Adm
£2. Suns 29 Apr; 6, 20 May; 3, 17
June (1-4). Visitors also welcome by
appt.**
Town garden. This is a plantsman's
garden, many unusual perennials, lots
of grasses, alliums, many infill plants
used throughout the season.
Sunflowers, leonotis, seasonal pots,
the design and planting is always
changing, described as organised
chaos, plenty to see. Not suitable for
children.

98 PEASMARSH PLACE
Church Lane, Peasmarsh TN31 6XE.
Viscount Devonport. *31/2m NW of
Rye. From A268 in Peasmarsh take
Church Lane (signed Norman Church),
garden 1m on R after church.* Home-
made teas. **Adm £3.50, chd free.
Suns 13 May; 21 Oct (2-5).**
7-acre garden surrounding Peasmarsh
Place (not open). Yew-enclosed rose
garden and various features with an
Alice in Wonderland connection. Fine
display of spring flowers and autumn
colour. Contains National Collections of
limes and sweet chestnuts. Large and
varied arboretum mostly planted since
1976 with fine walks and outdoor
sculpture.

99 33 PEERLEY ROAD
East Wittering PO20 8PD. Paul &
Trudi Harrison, 01243 673215,
stixandme@aol.com. *7m S of
Chichester. From A286 take B2198 to
Bracklesham. Turn R into Stocks Lane
then L at Royal British Legion into
Legion Way & follow rd round to
Peerley Rd halfway along.* **Adm £2,
chd free. Suns 24 June; 5 Aug (12-
4). Visitors also welcome by appt at
any time.**
Small garden 65ft x 32ft, 110yds from
sea. Packed full of ideas and unusual
plants using every inch of space to
create unusual rooms and places for
adults and children to play. Specialising
in unusual plants that grow well in
seaside conditions. A must for any
suburban gardener. Great winter
interest. Featured in 'The Guardian'.

100 PEMBURY HOUSE
Ditchling Road (New Road), Clayton,
nr Hassocks BN6 9PH. Nick & Jane
Baker,
http://uk.geocities.com/pembury.gar
den@btinternet.com. *6m N of
Brighton. On B2112, 110 metres from
A273. Feb & Mar openings: some
parking at the house, otherwise
parking at village green. May opening:
parking at village green, disabled
parking only at the garden.* Light
refreshments & teas: May opening at
Church Hall, otherwise at garden. **Adm
£3, chd free. Tues, Weds, Thurs, 13
Feb to 22 Feb (11-4) £2.50, chd free;
Sun 20 May (11-5.30) £3, chd free;
Tues, Weds, Thurs, 26 Feb to 6 Mar
2008.**
All-yr interest is a feature of our owner-
maintained 3-acre garden. In Feb the
flowering shrubs, hellebores and drifts

of snowdrops are at their best, with each individual hellebore flower asking to be turned up and admired. Winding paths through borders, paved areas and woodland, with views to the S Downs and surrounding countryside. Limited wheelchair access in winter.

  ♿ ✿ ☕

101 PENLAND FARMHOUSE
Hanlye Lane, Haywards Heath
RH17 5HR. Chris & Anne French, 01444 453799, annefrench@hotmail.co.uk. *½m NW of Haywards Heath. From B2036 Cuckfield follow signs to Borde Hill Gardens. Penland Farm is 100yds from exit of Hanlye Lane onto Balcombe Rd.* Cream teas. **Adm £3, chd free. Thur 7 June (2-5.30), Sat 9 June (2-6). Visitors also welcome by appt in June only for groups of 10+, £4 per person.**
Redeveloped since 1999, 8 connected garden areas set in 1 acre around converted farmhouse and cottage (not open). Stocked with trees, shrubs and herbaceous plants for yr-round interest. Walled garden with parterre, wisteria pergola with walkway and colourful theme borders. Featured in 'Real Homes'.

♿ ☕

102 PENNS IN THE ROCKS
Groombridge TN3 9PA. Lady Gibson. *7m SW of Tunbridge Wells. On B2188 Groombridge to Crowborough rd just S of Plumeyfeather corner.* Home-made teas. **Adm £4, chd £1. Suns 25 Mar; 12 Aug (2.30-5.30).**
Large wild garden with rocks, lake, C18 temple and old walled garden with herbaceous, roses and shrubs. House (not open) part C18. Dogs under control in park only (no shade in car park). Group visits by arrangement.

✖ ✿ ☕

103 PERRYHILL FARMHOUSE
Hartfield TN7 4JP. John & Diana Whitmore. *7m E of East Grinstead. Midway between E Grinstead & Tunbridge Wells. 1m N of Hartfield on B2026. Turn into unmade lane adjacent to Perryhill Nurseries.* Home-made teas. **Adm £4, chd free. Suns 27 May; 3 June; 19, 26 Aug (2-5).**
1½ acres, set below beautiful C15 hall house (not open), with stunning views of Ashdown Forest. Herbaceous and mixed borders, formal rose garden and climbing rose species, water garden, parterre, pergola. Many varieties of unusual shrubs and trees. Croquet

lawn (open for play). Top and soft fruit. Productive Victorian greenhouse. Dahlia mania corner. Group visits by arrangement. Featured in GGG.

♿ ✖ ✿ ☕

Each individual hellebore flower asking to be turned up and admired . . .

104 PHEASANTS HATCH
Piltdown TN22 3XR. Mrs G E Thubron, 01825 722960. *3m NW of Uckfield on A272.* Home-made teas. **Adm £3, chd free. Sun 24, Mon 25 June (2-6). Visitors also welcome by appt.**
Old romantic garden, spreading like intimate green rooms and passageways over 2 acres. Rose gardens with ponds and fountains; beautiful herbaceous borders; foliage, white and secret gardens. Peacocks. Open to the public for over 50yrs.

♿ ✿ ☕

105 PINDARS
Lyminster BN17 7QF. Mr & Mrs Clive Newman. *2m S of Arundel. Lyminster on A284 between A27 & A259. 1m S of A27 Pindars on L. Park beyond house in designated field.* Home-made teas. **Adm £2.50, chd free. Thur 7, Wed 20 June; Sun 23 Sept (2-5).**
A garden that, like Topsy, 'just growed'! A weed-filled field 40 or so yrs ago, the owner/gardeners have tried to create a garden with interesting nooks and corners and broad flowing curves. There is a wide diversity of planting with special emphasis on unusual plants and varied foliage. Mediterranean-style gravel and grasses area around swimming pool. Rugosa hedge; vegetable garden; mature trees.

♿ ✖ ✿ 🛏 ☕

106 6 PLANTATION RISE
Worthing BN13 2AH. Mr & Mrs N Hall, 01903 262206. *2m from sea front on outskirts of Worthing. A24 meets A27 at Offington roundabout. Proceed into Offington Lane. Take 1st R into The Plantation, 1st R again - Plantation Rise. Please park in The Plantation, short walk to Plantation Rise.* Light refreshments & teas. **Adm £2.50, chd free. Sat 14, Sun 15 Apr**

(10-4) Visitors also welcome by appt.
Award-winning garden 70ft x 80ft lovingly landscaped by owners. Featuring pond, summerhouse, pergolas, various trees and shrubs. Perennial plants, all-yr colour. Spring bulbs and heathers. Past winner Daily Mail National Garden of the Year. Featured in 'Chichester Observer' & 'Sussex Life'.

♿ ✖ ✿ ☕

107 ♦ THE PRIEST HOUSE
North Lane, West Hoathly RH19 4PP. Sussex Archaeological Society, 01342 810479, priest@sussexpast.co.uk. *4m SW of East Grinstead. Turn E to West Hoathly 1m S of Turners Hill at the Selsfield Common junction on B2028. 2m S turn R into North Lane. Garden ¼m further on.* **Garden only £1, chd free. Within walking distance of Duckyls Holt. Combined adm £4, chd free. Tues to Suns Mar to Oct (10.30-5.30).** For NGS: Sats 26 May; 23 June. Opening with **Duckyls Holt** 26 May, combined adm £4. Also with **Duckyls Holt** & **Fountain Cottage** 23 June, combined adm £5.
C15 timber-framed house with cottage garden. Large selection of culinary and medicinal herbs in small formal garden with mixed herbaceous borders, plus long-established yew topiary, box hedges and espalier apple trees. Small woodland garden with fernery. Adm to Priest House Museum £1 for NGS visitors.

✿

108 RIDGE HOUSE
East Street, Turners Hill RH10 4PU. Mr & Mrs Nicholas Daniels, 01342 715344. *4m SW of East Grinstead. 3m E of Crawley. On B2110, 5m SE of J10 M23. Via A264 & B2028. 30yds E of Crown PH on Turners Hill Xrds. Parking at recreation ground E of Ridge House.* Home-made teas. **Adm £3, chd free. Sat 23, Sun 24 June (2-6). Visitors also welcome by appt June only, coaches permitted.**
1-acre garden with mixed borders, Victorian greenhouse, pond, dell and productive vegetable garden. Nigel's garden gives all-yr interest and offers a quiet corner to absorb the beautiful view of the High Weald of Sussex. The garden offers interest, calm and unexpected vistas. Steep slope, wheelchair possible but care needed.

♿ ☕

109 RINGMER PARK
Ringmer, Lewes BN8 5RW. Deborah & Michael Bedford. *On A26 Lewes to Uckfield rd. 1¹/₂m NE of Lewes, 5m S of Uckfield.* Home-made teas. **Adm £4, chd free. Suns 17, 24 June; 30 Sept (2-5).**
Intensively planted 6-acre garden. 600 roses, some within formal rose garden and shrub rose border, others along clematis pergola and the many mixed beds. Brilliant hot garden, double herbaceous borders, white pool garden. Foxtail lilies in June, colchicums in Sept. Beautiful views of the Downs.

110 ROSE COTTAGE
Hadlow Down TN22 4HJ. Ken & Heather Mines, 01825 830314, kenmines@hotmail.com. *6m NE of Uckfield. After entering village on A272, turn L (100yds) by phone box just after New Inn, follow signs.* Home-made teas. **Adm £3, chd free. Suns 27 May; 24 June (2-5.30). Evening Openings £5, wine, Fris 29 June; 6 July (6-8). Visitors also welcome by appt.**
Plantsman's ²/₃-acre garden incorporating modern sculpture, reclaimed materials and mouldering church carvings. Old-fashioned roses, exuberant planting and luxuriance within a strong design results in a garden that visitors find harmonious and tranquil and evokes childhood memories. Self-seeding is encouraged, so a constantly-changing garden. Home-grown plants for sale, incl HDRA 'Heritage' vegetables. Bug hunt and fact sheets for adults and children.

111 ROUNDHILL COTTAGE
East Dean PO18 0JF. Mr Jeremy Adams, 01243 811447. *7m NE of Chichester. Take A286 towards Midhurst. At Singleton follow signs to Charlton/East Dean. In East Dean turn R at Star & Garter Inn, Roundhill is approx 100yds.* Home-made teas. **Adm £3, chd free. Sun 27, Mon 28 May (2-6). Visitors also welcome by appt.**
1-acre country garden set in tranquil fold of the S Downs, designed in 1980 by Judith Adams whose inspiration came from French Impressionists and continued by her daughter Louise, whose love of secret gardens, wild flower meadows and crumbly gothic ruins all show to delightful effect in a garden full of surprises. Come and enjoy.

112 RYMANS
Apuldram PO20 7EG. Mrs Michael Gayford, 01243 783147. *1m S of Chichester. Take Witterings rd, at 1¹/₂m SW turn R signed Apuldram; garden down rd on L.* Home-made teas. **Adm £3.50, chd free. Sats, Suns 14, 15 Apr; 9, 10 June; 1, 2 Sept (2-5). Visitors also welcome by appt.**
Walled and other gardens surrounding lovely C15 stone house (not open); bulbs, flowering shrubs, roses, ponds, potager. Many unusual and rare trees and shrubs. Exhibition and sale of work by Fine Cell Work, charity teaching and marketing prison inmates' fine needlework. Featured in 'The English Garden'.

113 ◆ ST MARY'S HOUSE & GARDENS
Bramber BN44 3WE. Mr Peter Thorogood, 01903 816205, www.stmarysbramber.co.uk. *1m E of Steyning. 10m NW of Brighton in Bramber Village off A283.* **Adm £3.50, chd £1. House & garden open Suns, Thurs & Bank Hol Mons May to end Sept (2-6 last entry 5). For NGS: Fri 13, Sat 14 July (2-5.30).**
Over 5 acres of gardens, incl charming formal topiary beds, pools and fountains, the ancient ivy-clad 'Monk's walk', large example of the prehistoric *Ginkgo biloba*, and magnificent *Magnolia grandiflora*; all around Grade I listed C15 timber framed medieval house, once a pilgrim inn. The Victorian 'Secret' gardens also incl splendid 140ft fruit wall, rural museum, terracotta garden, the delightful Jubilee rose garden and heated pineapple pits and former circular orchard under restoration. Featured in Brighton 'Evening Argus'.

114 SANDHILL FARM HOUSE
Nyewood Road, Rogate GU31 5HU. Rosemary Alexander, 01730 818373, www.englishgardeningschool.co.uk. *4m SE of Petersfield. From A272 Xrds in Rogate, take rd S signed Nyewood/Harting. Follow rd for approx 1m over small bridge. Sandhill Farm House on R, over cattle grid.* Teas (Suns only) at The Malthouse, South Harting. **Adm £3.50, chd free. Sat 14 Apr; Sats, Suns 9, 10 June; 22, 23 Sept (2-5). Also open 9, 10 June Kent House & Nyewood House. Visitors also welcome by appt.**

Front and rear gardens are broken up into garden rooms. Front garden incl small woodland area planted with early spring flowering shrubs and bulbs, white garden and hot dry terraced area. Rear garden has mirror borders, small decorative vegetable garden and 'red' border. New grit garden. Home of author and Principal of The English Gardening School.

Old-fashioned roses, exuberant planting . . .

115 ◆ SARAH RAVEN'S CUTTING GARDEN
Perch Hill Farm, Willingford Lane, Brightling TN32 5HP. Sarah Raven, 01424 838013, www.thecuttinggarden.com. *7m SW of Hurst Green. From A21 Hurst Green take A265 Heathfield Rd for 6m. In Burwash turn L by church, go 3m to Xrds at top of hill. At large green triangle, R down Willingford Lane, garden ¹/₂m on R.* **Adm £4, chd under 14 free, concessions £2.50. 28 Apr; 16 June; 25 Aug (9.30-5). For NGS: Sun 23 Sept (11-5).**
Inspirational, intensive and productive 2-acre garden with rooms full of annuals and biennials for picking. New vegetable and fruit garden. Extravagant mix of colour and structure: salvias, cardoons, artichokes, brilliantly-coloured dahlias, zinnias, gladioli, cannas, jungly corn and banana foliage.

116 SEDGWICK PARK HOUSE
Horsham RH13 6QQ. John & Clare Davison, 01403 734930, www.sedgwickpark.co.uk. *1m S of Horsham off A281. Take A281 towards Cowfold/Brighton. Hillier Garden Centre on R, then 1st R into Sedgwick Lane. After Sedgwick sign post, enter N gates of Sedgwick Park. Enter also by W gates via Broadwater Lane, from Copsale or Southwater A24.* Home-made teas. **Adm £4, chd free. Suns 13 May; 8 July (12-6). Evening Opening, wine & light refreshments, Fri 6 July (6.30-9.30). Visitors also welcome by appt in summer months, also to ground floor of house & castle site.**
Extensive parkland, meadows and woodland of approx 120 acres. Formal

gardens originally landscaped by Harold Peto featuring 20 interlinking pools, cascades and impressive water garden known as 'The White Sea'. Large Horsham stone terraces and lawns look out onto clipped yew hedging and mature trees incl rare, 'Champion' specimen trees. Beautiful secluded rosewalk and colourful herbaceous borders. Azaleas, rhododendrons and colourful walkways form superb setting for the house. Beyond finest views to S Downs, Chanctonbury Ring and Lancing College Chapel. Uneven stone paving, steps and unfenced ponds. Small children must be supervised.

  ♿ ✿ ☕

⑰ SHALFORD HOUSE
Square Drive, Kingsley Green GU27 3LW. Vernon & Hazel Ellis. *2m S of Haslemere. Just S of border with Surrey on A286. Square Drive is at brow of hill, to the E. Turn L after 0.2m and follow rd to R at bottom of hill.* Home-made teas. **Adm £3.50, chd free. Suns 15 Apr; 20 May; 15 July; 30 Sept (2-6).**
Garden created from scratch over last decade with designer Sally Court. Terraces, streams, ponds, waterfall, sunken and walled gardens, herbaceous borders, meadow with wild orchids. Wonderful hilly setting. 10-acre garden merging into 7 acres woodland with further 30 acres of woods with beeches, rhododendrons, ponds and clearing with new trees. Woodland walk for children. Featured in 'Chichester Observer'.

  ✖ ☕

⑱ ◆ SHEFFIELD PARK GARDEN
Sheffield Park TN22 3QX. The National Trust, 01825 790231, www.nationaltrust.org.uk. *10m S of E Grinstead. 5m NW of Uckfield; E of A275.* **Adm £7, chd £3.50, family £17.50. Opening days & times vary according to season; please phone or visit website for details. For NGS: Tues 1 May; 2 Oct (10.30-5.30).**
Magnificent 120 acres (40 hectares) landscaped garden laid out in C18 by Capability Brown and Humphry Repton. Further development in early yrs of this century by its owner Arthur G Soames. Centrepiece is original lakes, with many rare trees and shrubs. Beautiful at all times of the year, but noted for its spring and autumn colours. National Collection of Ghent azaleas.

  ♿ ✖ ✿ NCCPG ☕

⑲ SHERBURNE HOUSE
Eartham, nr Chichester PO18 0LP. Mr & Mrs Angus Hewat, phone/fax 01243 814261. *6m NE of Chichester. Approach from A27 Chichester-Arundel rd or A285 Chichester-Petworth rd, nr centre of village, 200yds S of church.* **Adm £3, chd free. Visitors welcome by appt, also groups, June & July best. Refreshments by arrangement.**
Chalk garden of approx 2 acres. Shrub and climbing roses, lime-tolerant shrubs, herbaceous, grey-leaved and foliage plants, pots, water feature, small herb garden, kitchen garden potager with octagonal pergola, fruit cage, wild flower meadow and conservatory.

  ♿ ✖ ✿ ☕

⑳ SIGGLE WRIGGLE
Nash Street, Chiddingly/Hailsham BN27 4AA. Mr Paul Hastie, 01825 873134, siggle1@aol.com. *3m NW of Hailsham. From A22 Eastbourne to Uckfield. 1m NW of Boship roundabout turn R into Nash St, signed Gun Hill. 400yds on L opp Marigolds Farm. Please park in Nash St.* **Adm £3.50, chd free. Sun 24 June (12-5). Visitors also welcome by appt, May to July & Sept, Oct.**
Garden of shadows and light. Developing 2-acre garden planted and maintained by present owner since 1996. Garden fans out from C16 cottage (not open) bedecked with old roses. Hornbeam walk, pond, rose garden, 300ft mixed border, woodland garden, small fruit and vegetable garden, beech ave, yew roundel and rough meadow. Extensive bamboo collection. Gravel paths and some steep steps.

  ♿ ✖ ✿ ☕

㉑ SPARROW HATCH
Cornwell's Bank, nr Newick BN8 4RD. Tony & Jane Welfare, 01825 723057. *5m E of Haywards Heath. From A272 turn R into Oxbottom Lane (signed Barcombe), ½m fork L into Narrow Rd, continue to T-junction & park in Chailey Lane (no parking at house).* **Adm £2.50, chd free. Weds, Thurs 23, 24 May; 20, 21 June (2-5). Visitors also**

Potager with octagonal pergola . . .

welcome by appt.
⅓ acre plantsman's cottage garden. Developed by owners into various different areas allowing maximum space for plantaholic's diverse collection of plants, many unusual.

  ✖ ✿

㉒ ◆ STANDEN
West Hoathly Road, East Grinstead RH19 4NE. The National Trust, 01342 323029, www.nationaltrust.org.uk. *1½m S of E Grinstead. Signed from B2110 & A22 at Felbridge.* **House & garden £7.50, chd £3.75. Garden only £4.40, chd £2.20. Weds to Suns & Bank Hols 17 Mar to 28 Oct (11-5.30). House also open Mons 16 July to 2 Sept. For NGS: Fri 18 May (11-5.30).**
Approx 12 acres of hillside garden, packed with surprises. Features incl quarry, bamboo gardens and 3 summerhouses. Lovely views over the Medway and Ashdown Forest.

  ♿ ✖ ✿ ☕

㉓ STONEHEALED FARM
Streat Lane, Streat BN6 8SA. Lance & Fiona Smith, 01273 891145, afionasmith@hotmail.com. *2m SE of Burgess Hill. From Ditchling B2116, 1m E of Westmeston, turn L (N) signed Streat, 2m on R immed after railway bridge.* Home-made teas. **Adm £3.50, chd free. Mon 7 May; Sun 9 Sept (2-5.30). Visitors also welcome by appt in May & Sept for groups of 10+.**
Developing garden begun in 1996 surrounding C17 house (not open). Approx 1½ acres overlooking S Downs. Formal front garden, brick terrace with pool and seasonal pots, shady pond area with tree platform. Hot and cool borders, raised vegetable beds. Planted for all seasons balancing structure with informality. Newly-planted lime walk and walnut grove. Featured in 'Sussex Life'.

  ♿ ✖ ✿ ☕

㉔ STONEHURST
Selsfield Road, Ardingly RH17 6TN. Mr & Mrs M Holman. *1¼m N of Ardingly. On B2028 opp Wakehurst place.* **Adm £4, chd free. Sat 19 May (12-5).**
Gardens of approx 12 acres laid out early in the last century with a wealth of architectural brick and stone work. Fine views across the Cob Valley and to S Downs. Amongst established planting is large collection of camellias.

  ✖ ☕

125 NEW SUTTON HALL
Spithurst Road, Barcombe, nr
Lewes BN8 5EB. Mr & Mrs J R
Sclater. *4m N of Lewes, 6m S of
Uckfield. From Lewes take A26,
then L to Barcombe. 2m from
centre of Barcombe on Newick Rd.
2m from A272 in Newick.* Home-
made teas. **Adm £4, chd free
(share to Newick Reading
Room). Sats, Suns 5, 6 May; 21,
22 July (2-5.30).**
Mixture of classical Victorian and
modern semi-formal garden, incl
an arboretum and plantings of
Japanese azaleas and
rhododendron hybrids. Vegetables
etc are still grown in the walled
garden. Ornamental cherries and
pears, flowering shrubs, lakes, fine
parkland, rare trees and bluebell
woods make this a place to stroll
and linger in. Mainly gravel paths,
some slopes.
  占 ⊛ ☕

126 SWIFTSDEN FARM OAST
Ticehurst Road, Hurst Green
TN19 7QT. John & Julie Gilbert. *2m
NW of Hurst Green. On S side of
B2099 approx 2m E of Ticehurst
village & ½m W of A21. Short way
along bridle path (unmade, single-track
with passing places). Parking at the
Oast.* Home-made teas. **Adm £3, chd
free (share to Robertsbridge United
Reformed Church). Sat 14, Sun 15
July (2-6).**
8-acre steep countryside site. Oast
House (not open) surrounded by small,
intimate gardens and informal terraces.
Extensive range of herbaceous plants,
shrubs and trees. Vegetable garden
and fruit trees. Cactus collection.
Chickens, bees, rare-breed sheep.
Native woodland. Conservation areas
left for wildlife. Good views.
  苗 ⊛ ☕

127 TINKERS BRIDGE COTTAGE
Tinkers Lane, Ticehurst TN5 7LU.
Mrs M A Landsberg, 01580 200272.
*11m SE of Tunbridge Wells. From
B2099 ½m W Ticehurst, turn N to
Three Leg Cross for 1m, R after Bull
Inn. House at bottom of hill.* **Adm £4
incl tea, chd free. Sun 3 June (2.30-
5.30). Visitors also welcome by appt
Mar to Sept.**
12 acres landscaped; stream garden
nr house (not open) leading to
herbaceous borders, wildlife meadow
with ponds and woodland walks.
  占 ⊛ ☕

128 TOWN PLACE
Ketches Lane, Freshfield, nr
Sheffield Park RH17 7NR. Mr & Mrs
A C O McGrath, 01825 790221,
www.townplacegarden.org.uk. *3m E
of Haywards Heath. From A275 turn W
at Sheffield Green into Ketches Lane
for Lindfield. 1¾m on L.* Cream teas.
**Adm £4, chd free. Thur 14, Sat 16,
Sun 24 June; Suns 1, 8, Thur 12 July
(2-6). Visitors also welcome by appt
in June & July for groups of 20+, £6
per person.**
3 acres with over 600 roses, 150ft
herbaceous border, walled herb
garden, shrubbery, ancient hollow oak,
orchard and potager. 'Green' Priory
Church and Cloisters. C17 Sussex
farmhouse (not open). Garden Award
by Sussex Heritage Trust. Featured in
'The Independent' as one of The 10
Best Gardens, 'Sussex Life' &
international press.
  占 苗 ⊛ ☕

Developed from an old orchard and wild areas of bracken, nettles and brambles . . .

129 ◆ UPPARK
South Harting GU31 5QR. The
National Trust, 01730 825415,
www.nationaltrust.org.uk. *1½m S of
S Harting. 5m SE of Petersfield on
B2146.* **House & garden £7.50, chd
£3.75. Garden only £3, chd £1.50.
Suns to Thurs Apr to end Oct. For
NGS: Thurs 7 June; 5 July (11.30-5).**
Intimate restored picturesque garden
nestles behind Uppark House, in
contrast to the sweeping panoramic
views to the S. Gardener leads tours at
12 and 2.30 to tell the history and
development of the site. Fine restored
mansion. Fire and restoration
exhibition.
  占 苗 ⊛ ☕

130 UPWALTHAM BARNS
Upwaltham GU28 0LX. Roger & Sue
Kearsey. *6m S of Petworth. 6m N of
Chichester on A285.* Light
refreshments & teas. **Adm £3, chd
free (share to St Mary the Virgin).**

**Sun 6, Mon 7 May; Weds 11 July; 5
Sept (11-5).**
Unique farm setting has been
transformed into a garden of many
rooms. Entrance is a tapestry of
perennial planting to set off C17 flint
barns. At the rear, walled terraced
garden redeveloped and planted in an
abundance of unusual plants.
Extensive vegetable garden. New ideas
for 2007. Roam at leisure, relax and
enjoy at every season, with lovely
views of S Downs and C12 Shepherds
Church (open to visitors). Tulip
spectacular 6, 7 May.
  占 苗 ⊛ ☕

131 VILLA ELISABETTA
Cousley Wood, Wadhurst TN5 6HA.
Jim & Kathy Cooper, 07803 134720.
*6m S of Tunbridge Wells. Off B2100
halfway between Wadhurst and
Lamberhurst.* Light refreshments &
teas. **Adm £3, chd free. Sun 15 July
(2-5). Visitors also welcome by
appt, small groups only, parking
limited.**
1½ acre garden behind small semi-
detached house (not open). Developed
from an old orchard and wild areas of
bracken, nettles and brambles. Quiet
location. Herbaceous beds, shrub
borders, specimen trees, formal and
woodland gardens.
  占 苗 ⊛ ☕

**132 ◆ THE WALLED GARDEN AT
COWDRAY**
Cowdray Park, Midhurst GU29 9AL.
Jan Howard, 01730 816881,
www.walledgardencowdray.co.uk.
*¼m from centre of Midhurst. Entrance
off mini roundabout on A272 going
towards Petworth.* **Adm £4.50, chd
free, concessions £3.50. Open all yr.
Please phone in advance to check
opening times. For NGS: Evening
Openings, wine, Thurs 14 June; 13
Sept (5.30-8.30).**
In a unique location next to the
Cowdray ruins on the edge of
Midhurst, surrounded by the world-
renowned polo grounds and Capability
Brown parkland. The 1-acre Tudor
pleasure style Walled Garden, with
exuberantly planted rose walks,
herbaceous borders, knot and herb
garden and raised vegetable beds, has
been restored by Jan Howard of
'Room in the Garden'. Fruit is trained
on the ancient walls and a beautiful
new glasshouse houses exotic tender
plants.
  占 苗 ⊛ ☕

133 WARNINGCAMP HOUSE
Warningcamp, Arundel BN18 9QY.
David & Sarah Houghton King. *2m NE of Arundel off A27. Leaving Arundel towards Worthing cross railway bridge, take 1st L signed Burpham. Follow rd for approx 1m, take 1st turn at junction and gate faces you.* Home-made teas. **Adm £3, chd free (share to Friends of Burpham Church). Thurs 7, 28 June; 20 Sept (10-5).**
Formal garden laid out in 1920s to reflect the Victorian house first built in 1820. Incl kitchen garden and cutting flowers, lovingly restored with working Victorian glasshouse. Formal garden to front of house features scented 'peony and pinks' walk, rose garden, long borders and parterre. Gravel paths, some uneven surfaces.

134 WARREN HOUSE
Warren Road, Crowborough TN6 1TX. Mr & Mrs M J Hands, 01892 663502, michaelhands@fsmail.net. *1¹/₂m SW of Crowborough Cross. Towards Uckfield, 4th turning on R. 1m down Warren Rd. From South 2nd L after Blue Anchor.* Home-made teas. **Adm £3, chd free. Sun 29 Apr; Bank Hol Mon 7, Sun 20, Bank Hol Mon 28 May (2-5).**
Beautiful house (not open) steeped in history with 9-acre garden and views over Ashdown Forest. Series of gardens old and new, displaying wealth of azaleas, rhododendrons, impressive variety of trees and shrubs. Sweeping lawns framed by delightful walls and terraces, woodlands, ponds.

135 WEST BEXHILL GARDENS
Bexhill-on-Sea TN39 3UJ. *¹/₂m W of centre of Bexhill. Proceed to Little Common roundabout on A259.* Home-made teas at 64 Cranston Ave. **Combined adm £4, chd free. Sun 17 June (11-5).**

1 ASHCOMBE DRIVE
Richard & Liz Chown. *Exit roundabout S into Cooden Sea Rd, 3rd L into Kewhurst Ave, 1st L into Ashcombe Dr, 400yds on R*
Be surprised at what can be achieved in a modest space. Cleverly landscaped, this secret garden delights its visitors. Curvaceous beds and extravagant planting combine to make this a truly romantic garden.

64 CRANSTON AVENUE
G & M Stokes. *From roundabout, take A259 E (towards Hastings), after approx 1m turn R into Sutherland Ave, 3rd turning on R into Cranston Ave*
Established town garden owned by avid plant collectors with an eye for the unusual.

66 CRANSTON AVENUE
Karen Hewgill. *Directions as No 64*
Surprising large town garden - definitely not formal but interesting - with themed areas to amuse. Potter around this quirky garden to discover hidden surprises.

136 WEST CHILTINGTON VILLAGE GARDENS
RH20 2LA. *2m E of Pulborough. 3m N of Storrington. At Xrds in centre of West Chiltington opp Queens Head.* Home-made teas. **Combined adm £3.50, chd free. Suns 1, 8 July (1.30-5.30).**
2 adjoining ¹/₂-acre plantsman's gardens with contrasting designs and features.

HUNTERS BARN
The Hollow. Ann & Derek Frost. Converted barn (not open). Garden completely reshaped and replanted in 3 different areas by present owners. Formal area for sitting and wild area still being developed. Water feature.

PALMER'S LODGE
Broadford Bridge Road. Richard Hodgson, 01798 812751. *Visitors also welcome by appt, July only.*
Charming ¹/₂-acre plantsman's garden with herbaceous and shrub borders. Fruit and vegetable garden, small greenhouse.

137 ◆ WEST DEAN GARDENS
West Dean PO18 0QZ. Edward James Foundation, 01243 818210, www.westdean.org.uk. *5m N of Chichester. On A286.* **Adm £6, chd £3, concessions £5.50. Daily Mar to Oct (10.30-5); Weds to Suns Nov to Feb (10.30-4). Closed Christmas & New Year. For NGS: Mon 4 June (10.30-5).**
35-acre historic garden in tranquil

downland setting. 300ft long Harold Peto pergola, mixed and herbaceous borders, rustic summerhouses, redeveloped water and spring garden, specimen trees. Restored 2¹/₂-acre walled garden contains fruit collection, 13 Victorian glasshouses, apple store, large working kitchen garden, extensive plant collection. Circuit walk (2¹/₄ m) climbs through parkland to 45-acre St Roche's Arboretum. National Collections of Aesculus and liriodendron.

138 46 WESTUP FARM COTTAGES
Balcombe RH17 6JJ. Chris & Sarah Cornwell, 01444 811891. *3m N of Cuckfield. ¹/₄m N Balcombe stn, turn L off B2036 immed before Balcombe Primary School (signed). ³/₄m.* **Adm £2, chd free. Weds 25 Apr; 23 May; Sat 30 June (12-5). Visitors also welcome by appt, groups of 5+, coaches welcome.**
Hidden in the Sussex countryside, this cottage garden combines the functionality of its origins with unique and unusual features, linked by intimate paths through lush and subtle planting. Brilliant use of small space.

139 WHITEHOUSE COTTAGE
Staplefield Lane, Staplefield RH17 6AU. Mr Barry Gray. *5m NW of Haywards Heath. E of A23 & 2m S of Handcross. In Staplefield at Xrds by cricket pavilion take marked Staplefield Lane for 1m.* **Adm £2, chd free. Open daily throughout the year during daylight hours, no appointment necessary.**
4 acres of woodland with mixed shrubs, paths beside stream linked by ponds. Best in April, May and June.

140 WILDHAM
East Marden/Stoughton PO18 9JG. Consie & Mark Dunn, 01243 535202, consiedunn@waitrose.com. *4m SE of South Harting. B2141 to Chichester, turn R to East Marden, in East Marden follow signs to Stoughton, garden up track on R 1m from wishing well.* Home-made teas. **Adm £2.50, chd free. Thur 28 June; Sun 1 July (11-6). Visitors also welcome by appt May to July incl.**
Very informal chalk garden on steep hill. Dripping with roses and clematis, unusual shrubs. Glorious position. God's garden with minor interference from an idle amateur. Exciting new developments, plus more hard work

and help, promise an even better garden next season.

141 WINCHELSEA'S SECRET GARDENS
TN36 4AB. *2m W of Rye.* Home-made teas (not NGS) in New Hall, adjoining A259 & cricket pitch. **Combined adm £5, chd free. Sat 16 June (2-6).** Winchelsea is a beautiful medieval town, founded in 1288 by Edward I. Notable buildings incl the splendid C14 church and Court Hall. It is one of the few surviving C13 English towns where the streets are laid out in a grid system. Because of this, the gardens are hidden behind old walls. Many of the gardens open this year have lovely water features and wonderful views of the sea or across the beautiful Brede Valley. Town maps given to all visitors.

THE ARMOURY
Castle Street. Mr & Mrs Jasper Laid out as several different garden rooms. Shallow steps and gravel area.

&

CLEVELAND HOUSE
Rookery Lane. Mr & Mrs J Jempson
1½-acre mature walled garden with large potager, lawn with water feature. Long covered walk, rose garden, 2 formal ponds, large old indoor vine. Featured in 'The English Garden'. Gravel paths.

&

3 HIHAM GREEN
Susi Nicholson
Very small Mediterranean garden with fan-trained peach, olive and fig in containers and lots of pots.

THE OAST HOUSE
Rectory Lane. Major & Mrs J Le B Freeman
Garden with shrubs and mixed planting. Courtyard 'container garden'. Small kitchen garden with 'wooden boxed' deep beds and strawberry table.

OLD CASTLE HOUSE
Castle Street. Mrs F Packard
Walled garden with varied trees, shrubs and pond.

THE RETREAT
Barrack Square. Mo & Paul Anderson
Small garden, created 3yrs ago, wrapped around 3 sides of the house, each section with a different theme.

SOUTH MARITEAU
Monks Walk. Mr & Mrs Robert Holland
⅓-acre garden consisting of 3 themed rooms: seaside, romantic and orchard. Ponds.

Sussex County Volunteers
East Sussex
County Organiser
Rosie Lloyd, Bankton Cottage, Turners Hill Road, Crawley Down RH10 4EY, 01342 718907, rosie.lloyd@dsl.pipex.com
County Treasurer
Robin Lloyd, Bankton Cottage, Turners Hill Road, Crawley Down RH10 4EY, 01342 718907, robin.lloyd@dsl.pipex.com
Publicity
Sara Turner, 9 Terminus Avenue, Bexhill-on-Sea TN39 3LS, 01424 210716, sara.kidd@btconnect.com
West Sussex
County Organiser
Carrie McArdle, Message Cottage, Kirdford RH14 0JR, 01403 820272, carrie.mcardle@btinternet.com
County Treasurer
Peter Edwards, Quince Cottage, The Street, Pulborough RH20 1PA, 01798 831900, peteredwards425@btinternet.com

ngs
gardens open for charity

Delightful informal gardens of over 3 acres surrounding Manor House. The long-neglected water garden has been fully restored. Charming walled garden for tea. Eccentric head gardener . . .

Thorley Manor, Isle of Wight

WARWICKSHIRE
Birmingham & part of the West Midlands

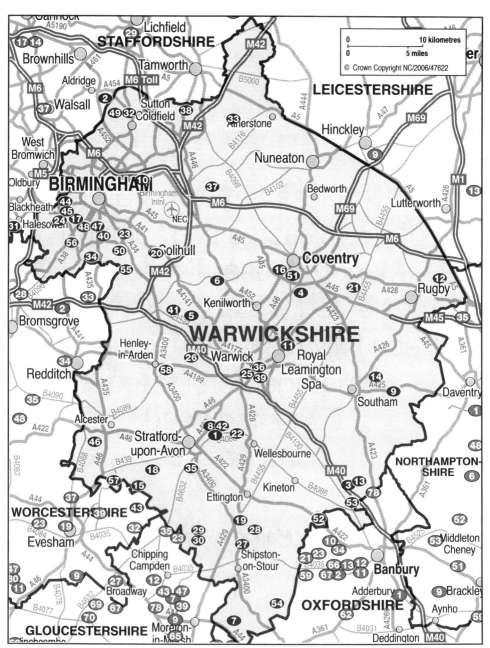

Opening Dates

February

SUNDAY 11
46 Ragley Hall Gardens

SATURDAY 24
18 Elm Close

SUNDAY 25
18 Elm Close

April

SUNDAY 15
1 Alveston Gardens
11 19 Church Lane
47 56 Salisbury Road

WEDNESDAY 18
24 89 Harts Green Road

SUNDAY 22
29 Ilmington Gardens

SUNDAY 29
22 Greenlands
44 50 Pereira Road

May

MONDAY 7
16 Earlsdon Gardens

TUESDAY 8
19 The Folly Lodge

SATURDAY 12
25 Hill Close Gardens

WEDNESDAY 16
24 89 Harts Green Road

SUNDAY 20
2 Ashover
17 Edgbaston Garden Sculpture Trail
55 Wits End

SUNDAY 27
7 Barton House
43 Pebworth & Broad Marston Gardens

MONDAY 28
6 Balsall Common Gardens
43 Pebworth & Broad Marston Gardens

June

SUNDAY 3
31 Inglenook
38 Middleton Hall
49 Stoneleigh House

WEDNESDAY 6
23 Hall Green Gardens

SUNDAY 10
11 19 Church Lane
15 Dorsington Gardens

22 Greenlands
32 18 Ladywood Road

TUESDAY 12
19 The Folly Lodge

SUNDAY 17
26 Holywell Gardens
30 Ilmington Manor
37 Maxstoke Castle
51 Styvechale Gardens
54 Whichford & Ascott Gardens
56 Woodbrooke Quaker Study Centre

WEDNESDAY 20
24 89 Harts Green Road

THURSDAY 21
21 Garden Organic Ryton
41 Packwood House

SATURDAY 23
33 Latimers Rest

SUNDAY 24
12 Clifton-upon-Dunsmore Village Gardens
27 Honington Village Gardens
33 Latimers Rest
40 Moseley Gardens South
45 Pereira Road Gardens
53 Warmington Village Gardens

SATURDAY 30
3 Avon Dassett Gardens

July

SUNDAY 1
3 Avon Dassett Gardens
23 Hall Green Gardens
28 Idlicote Gardens
55 Wits End

SUNDAY 8
10 Castle Bromwich Hall Gardens
48 Secret Garden
50 Stonor Road Gardens

TUESDAY 10
19 The Folly Lodge

SATURDAY 14
20 Garden of Tranquillity & Festival Garden

SUNDAY 15
31 Inglenook
35 Manor Cottage

WEDNESDAY 18
24 89 Harts Green Road

SATURDAY 28
33 Latimers Rest

SUNDAY 29
33 Latimers Rest
34 Little Indonesia

August

SUNDAY 5
2 Ashover
55 Wits End

TUESDAY 14
19 The Folly Lodge

September

WEDNESDAY 5
24 89 Harts Green Road

TUESDAY 11
19 The Folly Lodge

THURSDAY 13
5 Baddesley Clinton Hall

SATURDAY 15
25 Hill Close Gardens

SUNDAY 16
4 Avondale Nursery
22 Greenlands

WEDNESDAY 26
52 Upton House

October

SUNDAY 7
46 Ragley Hall Gardens

February 2008

SUNDAY 10
46 Ragley Hall Gardens

Gardens open to the public

4 Avondale Nursery
5 Baddesley Clinton Hall
9 Bridge Nursery
10 Castle Bromwich Hall Gardens
21 Garden Organic Ryton
24 89 Harts Green Road
25 Hill Close Gardens
36 The Master's Garden
38 Middleton Hall
39 The Mill Garden
41 Packwood House
46 Ragley Hall Gardens
52 Upton House

By appointment only

14 The Cutting Gallery
57 Woodpeckers
58 Wootton Grange

The Gardens

1 ALVESTON GARDENS
CV37 7QN. *2m E of Stratford-upon-Avon. Off B4086, Stratford to Wellesbourne rd.* Home-made teas. Combined adm £3, chd free. Sun 15 Apr (1-5).
Small village with Festival of Flowers at recently renovated old church.

THE BOWER HOUSE
Mr & Mrs P Hart
(See separate entry).

LONG ACRE
Dr & Mrs N A Woodward
1-acre owner designed mature garden progressively developed since 1976. A large variety of trees and shrubs. Pergola, patios, pond, rockery, spinney walk and new fern garden.

PARHAM LODGE
Mr & Mrs Edwards
(See separate entry).

2 ASHOVER
25 Burnett Road, Streetly B74 3EL. Jackie & Martin Harvey, 0121 353 0547. *8m N of Birmingham. Off B4138.* Cream teas. Adm £2.50, chd free. Suns 20 May; 5 Aug (1.30-5.30). Visitors also welcome by appt May-Aug, incl coaches.
Secluded 1/3-acre, romantic country-style garden, profusion of mixed planting. Vibrant in May with tapestry of azaleas, tulips and complementary plants. In summer packed, colour-themed herbaceous borders, artistically planted with flowers and foliage to give maximum effect of colour, form and texture. Extended hot border a special feature. Established pond and waterfalls, grasses and ferns. Featured in 'Garden News' 2006, to be featured in 'Gardener's World' 2007.

3 AVON DASSETT GARDENS
Southam CV47 2AE. *7m N of Banbury. From Banbury turn L at M40 J12 onto B4100. 2nd L into village.* Park in village & at top of hill. Home-made teas at The Coach House 30 Jun & Old Mill Cottage 1 July. Combined adm £4, chd free (share to Myton Hamlet Hospice). Sat 30 June; Sun 1 July (2-6).
Small, pretty Hornton stone village. 2 churches open for visitors.

AVON COTTAGE
Mrs M J Edginton
Interesting contrasts between cottage garden, courtyard and vegetable garden.
&

AVON HOUSE
Mrs L Dunkley
Mature garden, principally shrubs, featuring hostas.
&

THE COACH HOUSE
Mr & Mrs G J Rice
(See separate entry).

HILL TOP FARM
Mrs N & Mr D Hicks
1 acre. Display of bedding plants, perennials, shrubs, conifers and heathers. Extensive kitchen garden. Greenhouses.

THE LIMES
Mr & Mrs B Anderson
Large ecological garden. Wide variety of roses, shrubs and trees.
&

OLD MILL COTTAGE
Mr & Mrs M J Lewis
Conservation garden of 3/4 acre with shrubs, perennial borders and rockeries. Collection of alpines and herbs. Pond and tropical garden. Mediterranean gravel garden.
&

THE OLD NEW HOUSE
Mr & Mrs W Allen
1-acre, formal rose garden, herbaceous borders and specimen trees.
&

THE OLD RECTORY
Lily Hope-Frost
2-acre mature garden with colourful terrace and wide stone steps leading to fountain and small wood, surrounding listed house (not open) mentioned in Domesday Book. Many places to sit. Entrance to church through walled garden.

NEW ORCHARD END
Jill Burgess
1-acre garden with fruit trees, old yew and box hedging, large pond and herbaceous borders.
&

POPPY COTTAGE
Mr & Mrs R Butler
Newly established pretty cottage garden. Water feature and kitchen garden.
&

4 ◆ AVONDALE NURSERY
at Russells Nursery, Mill Hill, Baginton CV8 3AG. Mr Brian Ellis, 024 7667 3662, www.avondalenursery.co.uk. *3m S Coventry. At junction of A45/A46 take rd to Baginton, 1st L to Mill Hill.* Park in Russell's Nursery. Adm £2, chd free. Tues to Sun, Mar to Sept, 10-12.30, 2-5. For NGS: Sun 16 Sept (11-4). Also open with Styvechale Gardens.
Plantaholic nurseryman's garden. Formal layout for easy access, ever increasing collection of rare and unusual well labelled cottage garden plants. All yr interest, incl many geums, geraniums, shasta daisies, crocosmia, michaelmas daisies and ornamental grasses.
&

5 ◆ BADDESLEY CLINTON HALL
Knowle B93 0DQ. The National Trust, 01564 783294, www.nationaltrust.org.uk. *7 1/2 m NW of Warwick. 3/4 m W of A4141 Warwick to Birmingham rd nr Chadwick End.* House and Garden Adm £8, chd £4, Garden only Adm £4, chd £2. Telephone or see website for opening times & days. For NGS: Thur 13 Sept (12-5.30).
Medieval moated manor house little

Vibrant in May with a tapestry of azaleas, tulips and complementary plants . . .

Vegetables, fruit, herbs and an apiary . . .

changed since1634. Walled garden and herbaceous borders, natural areas, lakeside walk, nature trail. Gravel paths, some steep slopes around lake area.

BALSALL COMMON GARDENS
CV7 7AR. *5m W of Coventry, 10m N of Warwick. 5m S of M42/M6 intersection. From T-lights at junction of A452/B4101, go E on B4101 towards Coventry for 1m. L into Hodgetts Lane. Teas at the Scout Room, Holly Lane & Elmcroft.* **Combined adm £4, chd free. Mon 28 May (11-6).**
A variety of gardens to suit most interests. Map available at each garden. Please note that a car or cycle is necessary in order to get round to all these gardens.

THE BUNGALOW
Mr & Mrs G Johnson
2 acres with mixed borders, pond and lawns.
&

THE COTTAGE
Enid & John Hinton
Developing garden with mixed borders, mature trees and wildlife pond with waterlilies.
&

NEW ELMCROFT
Mr & Mrs E Owen
Cottage garden with mixed shrub and herbaceous borders and containers. Small wildlife pond, ornamental raised koi tank and pagoda.

FIRS FARM
Mr & Mrs C Ellis
1-acre garden, courtyard with tubs, walled garden, formal garden with mixed borders and pergola supporting varieties of honeysuckle. Open grassed area with fruit and ornamental trees.

MERIGLEN
Mr & Mrs J Webb
Mixed borders of shrubs and perennials, conservatory and greenhouse.
&

THE PINES
Mr & Mrs C Davis
1¹/₂-acre formal garden divided into series of ornamental areas, vegetables, fruit, herbs and apiary.
&

WHITE COTTAGE FARM
Mr & Mrs J Edwards. *Off Holly Lane. Drive up the feeder lane to garden with ample parking*
1¹/₂-acre cottage garden, mixed borders, pond, sunken garden.

32 WOOTTON GREEN LANE
Dr & Mrs Leeming
Lawns, water features, ornamental water fowl.

BARTON HOUSE
Barton-on-the-Heath GL56 0PJ. **Mr & Mrs I H B Cathie.** *2m W of Long Compton. 2m off A3400 Stratford-upon-Avon to Oxford rd. 1¹/₄m off A44 Chipping Norton to Moreton-in-Marsh rd.* Cream teas. **Adm £4, chd £2. Sun 27 May (2-6).**
6 acres with mature trees, azaleas, species and hybrid rhododendrons, magnolias, moutan tree peonies. Collection of arbutus. Japanese garden, catalpa walk, rose garden, secret garden and many rare and exotic plants. Victorian kitchen garden. Exotic garden with palms, cypresses and olive trees established 2002. Vineyard planted 2000 - wine tasting. Manor house by Inigo Jones (not open). Other visits 01608 674303 for groups 25+. Disabled WC.

THE BOWER HOUSE
CV37 7QN. **Mr & Mrs P Hart.** Visitors also welcome by appt, combined with **Parham Lodge** (01789 26955),

---

all yr, for groups. Also open with Alveston Gardens.
1-acre owner-designed mature garden. Trees, shrubs & hostas. Water garden, rill, pergolas, rockery & alpine sinks.

BRIDGE NURSERY
Tomlow Road, Napton CV47 8HX.
Christine Dakin, 01926 812737, www.bridge-nursery.co.uk. *3m E of Southam. Brown tourist sign at Napton Xrds on the A425 Southam to Daventry rd.* **Adm £2, chd free. Apr-Oct (10-4).**
This challenging 1-acre garden (clay soil, exposed position) is home to an exciting range of rare and unusual plants. Grass paths meander round well-stocked informal borders. A haven for wildlife. Features incl a large pond, bamboo grove (with panda sculptures) and willow dome.
&

CASTLE BROMWICH HALL GARDENS
B36 9BT. **Castle Bromwich Hall Gardens Trust, 0121 749 4100,** www.cbhgt.org.uk. *4m E of Birmingham. 1m J5 M6 (exit N only).* **Adm £3.50, chd 50p, concessions £3. Phone or check web for details of opening days & times. For NGS: Sun 8 July (1.30-5.30).**
Restored C18 formal walled gardens provide visitors with the opportunity to see a unique collection of historic plants, shrubs, medicinal and culinary herbs and fascinating vegetable collection. Intriguing holly maze. Several fruits within the orchards and along the paths incl apple, pear, apricot, quince, medlar, fig and cherry. Guided tours.

⑪ 19 CHURCH LANE
Lillington, Leamington Spa CV32 7RG. **David & Judy Hirst, 01926 422591.** *1¹/₂m NE Leamington Spa. Take A445 towards Rugby. Church Lane is on RH-side just beyond roundabout junction with B4453. Garden on corner of Hill Close. Enter via driveway in Church Lane.* **Adm £2, chd free. Suns 15 Apr; 10 June (2-5.30). Visitors also welcome by appt,Tues in Mar (for hellebores), Mons in July.**
Plantpersons' cottage style suburban garden with several aspects and areas. A rich variety of planting for yr-round interest. Narrow paths. Not suitable for the very young or infirm.

⑫ CLIFTON-UPON-DUNSMORE VILLAGE GARDENS

nr Rugby CV23 0DF. 2½m E of Rugby. From M6 J1(S) take A426 towards Rugby. Take 1st L signed Clifton-upon-Dunsmore. From M1 J18 take A5 N for 3m. L turn signed Clifton-upon-Dunsmore. Park in village. Home-made teas at Townsend Memorial Hall, opp church. **Combined adm £3, chd free (share to St Marys Church). Sun 24 June (2-6).** Maps at all gardens. Church flower festival.

41 SOUTH ROAD
Janice & Alan Duffin
Medium-sized garden. Arbour with pots, trellis and pergola with many named rambler roses and climbing plants. Colourful herbaceous borders.

CLIFTON HALL FARM
Mr & Mrs R G Spencer
Plantsman's garden, yr round borders with shrubs and perennials. Jungle and novel alpine areas.

CLIFTON MANOR
Andrew Kypri
Large garden surrounding manor house. Edwardian sunken rose garden, herbaceous borders recently designed and replanted. Series of pools, shade garden, mature trees.

CLIFTON MILL
Denise & John Davies
Large farmhouse-style garden with mill pool and a series of interconnecting areas. Paved area, gravel garden. Orchard, wide herbaceous mixed borders, many clematis and mature trees. Park in farmyard.

NEW DUNSMORE LODGE
Vincent & Mary Davies
Cottage garden with a large collection of honeysuckle and clematis.
⊛

NEW THE GABLES
Mrs M Starkie
Surrounded by open farmland, herbaceous borders and a cottage style front garden. Continuing to improve, rabbits permitting. Slope at end of garden.

JARDIN DE SOL
Mr & Mrs Murrell
Developing medium-sized garden, newly planted and designed by owners. Paved area, lawn and large greenhouse. Many interesting plants.

NEW MAGPIE LODGE FARM
Mrs Spencer
Panoramic views, perennial and shrub borders, bridge over dry pond.

⑬ THE COACH HOUSE
Bitham Hall, Avon Dassett CV47 2AH. **Mr & Mrs Rice, 01295 690255.** 7m N of Banbury. From J12 M40 S on B4100. Signed in village. Home-made teas. **Adm £2.50, chd free. Visitors also welcome by appt all yr, inc groups & coaches. Also open with Avon Dasset Gardens.** Sloping 2-acres, part of former Victorian garden overlooking Edge Hill. Walls give shelter and support to many climbers and more tender perennials and shrubs. Planted to give all yr interest. Woodland area, alpines, fruit and vegetable plots.
⊛

Continuing to improve . . . rabbits permitting!

⑭ THE CUTTING GALLERY
Station Road, Stockton CV47 8HA. **Julia & Tony Prior, 01926 817572, www.cuttinggallery.co.uk.** 2m N of Southam. From Southam take A426 towards Rugby. 1st R into Stockton, through village, L after sports ground (Station Rd). ¾m turn L in front of Countrywide Stores. Garden is opp at Red Brick House. **Adm £3, chd free (share to Multiple Sclerosis Soc). Visitors welcome by appt all yr, inc groups.** Wooded wildlife garden of about 1 acre. Part SSSI on the edge of old cement quarry, incl organic kitchen garden, informal planting, ponds and sculpture trail with viewpoints overlooking lovely countryside.

Seasonal highlights start with snowdrops in Feb, violets and cowslips in May then orchids in June. Artists studios also open. Art activities. BBC Radio Coventry & Warwickshire July 2006.

⑮ DORSINGTON GARDENS
CV37 8AR. 6m SW of Stratford-upon-Avon. On B439 from Stratford turn L to Welford-on-Avon, then R to Dorsington. Light refreshments & teas in marquees at The Old Manor and The Old Rectory. **Combined adm £5, chd free (share to St Peters Church). Sun 10 June (12-5).** Pretty conservation area village. Maps given to all visitors. For information 01789 720581.

THE BARN
Mr & Mrs P Reeve
2 tier country garden with shrubs, herbaceous borders and vegetable patch.

NEW CEDAR BARN
Mr & Mrs N Simpson-Stern
Cottage style with some unusual trees and shrubs, vegetable garden.

COLLETTS FARM
Mr & Mrs D Bliss
Trees and shrubs, container flowers. Highly productive kitchen garden with fan-trained fruit.

DORSINGTON ARBORETUM
Mr F Dennis
12 acres with collection of several hundred trees from around the world leading to Udde Well Pond (ancient well) and willow walk.

2 DORSINGTON MANOR
Mr & Mrs C James
¾-acre garden, relaxed & peaceful in style, full of perennials, shrubs & trees.

GLEBE COTTAGE
Mr & Mrs A Brough
Over ¾ acre of land reclaimed into an uncomplicated garden which, over several yrs, has developed into interesting and varied garden rooms. A surprise at each turn.

KNOWLE THATCH
Mr & Mrs P Turner
Large garden with mature trees, shrubs and herbaceous borders.

WHITE GATES
Mr & Mrs A Carus
Cottage garden with shrubs, mature trees and shrub roses.

herbaceous borders, vegetable plot, yr-round interest and colour.

87 ROCHESTER ROAD
Edith Lewin
Peaceful, mature cottage garden.

54 SALISBURY AVENUE
Peter & Pam Moffit
Plantaholic's garden with a large variety of plants, clematis and small trees, some unusual.

A feeling of space and simplicity touched with a hint of grandeur . . .

MILFIELD
Mrs H Dumas
Small but beautifully planted cottage garden with a feeling of space and simplicity touched with a hint of grandeur in the form of the statuesque urns.

THE MOAT HOUSE
Mr & Mrs R Vaudry
6-acre moated garden incl orchard with wild flower meadow. Walled garden, herbaceous borders, rose and lavender beds, walled vegetable garden.

THE OLD MANOR
Mr F Dennis
3 acres with fairy walk, herb garden, ornamental fish pond, sunken water garden leading to Highfield, (Mr F Dennis) with its Mediterranean garden, container plants and bonsai collection.

THE OLD RECTORY
Mr & Mrs N Phillips
2-acre Victorian garden with mature trees incl old espalier fruit trees. Box hedges, herbaceous borders, many old roses, large pool, small wood.

SAPPHIRE HOUSE
Mrs D Sawyer
Orchard, vegetable garden, shrub beds, lawns and large walnut trees.

THE WELSHMAN'S BARN
Mr F Dennis
5 acres with Japanese garden, Oz maze, bronze sculpture garden of heroes, wild flower garden & stream.

WINDRUSH
Mrs M B Mills
Country garden with shrubs, cottage plants and roses.

⑯ EARLSDON GARDENS
CV5 6FS. *Coventry. Turn towards Coventry at A45/A429 T-lights. Take 3rd L turn into Beechwood Ave, Earlsdon Gardens.* **Combined adm £2.50, chd free. Mon 7 May (11-3).** Maps available at all gardens.

3 BATES ROAD
Victor & Judith Keene
Large established garden, with lots of spring interest incl rhododendrons, azaleas and mature trees, plus a kitchen garden.

155 BEECHWOOD AVENUE
Nigel & Jan Young
Garden with open traditional character, constantly being enhanced with interesting planting. Water feature.

59 THE CHESILS
John Marron & Richard Bantock
Herbaceous plants jostle for attention in a richly planted garden on several levels. Also open with **Styvechale Gardens.**

40 HARTINGTON CRESCENT
Viv & George Buss
Surprisingly large garden with interest for all ages, water feature and fern garden.

114 HARTINGTON CRESCENT
Liz Campbell & Denis Crowley
Large, mature, pretty garden on several levels with hidden aspects.

36 PROVIDENCE STREET
Rachel Culley & Steve Shiner
Large peaceful cottage garden. Water features, packed

NEW SMITHY COTTAGE
Jane & Peter Woodward
New garden constructed on different levels around early C17 cottage. Inc sunken garden, kitchen garden, summer house terrace, pond and perennial borders. Also open with **Styvechale Gardens.**

⑰ EDGBASTON GARDEN SCULPTURE TRAIL
5 Farquhar Road East B15 3RD. **John Alexander-Williams, 0121 454 1279, johnaw@blueyonder.co.uk.** *4m SW of Birmingham. Under 1m from Birmingham Botanical Gardens. Farquhar Rd East is a triangle off Farquhar Rd, between Somerset & Richmond Hill Rds in Edgbaston.* **Adm £2.50, chd £1. Sun 20 May (2-5.30). Visitors also welcome by appt any day, any time.**
Town garden of ⅓-acre. Evolved over 21 yrs to provide interlinking areas of interest with hidden walks and arches designed, to create sculpture trail. Some 80 sculptures by owner provide surprise and amusement and set off very personal collection of shrubs, trees and plants.

⑱ ELM CLOSE
Binton Road, Welford-on-Avon CV37 8PT. **Eric & Glenis Dyer, 01789 750793, dyerg@btclick.com.** *5m SW of Stratford. Off B4390. Elm Close is between Welford Garage & The Bell Inn.* Home-made teas. **Adm £3, chd free. Sat 24, Sun 25 Feb (2-5). Visitors also welcome by appt for groups of 10+ or £30 for small groups.**
⅔-acre packed with super plants and stocked for yr-round colour and interest. Clematis, daphnes, peonies and hellebores a particular speciality. Featured in 'The English Garden' Nov 2006. Gravel front drive.

EPWELL MILL
See Oxfordshire.

⑲ THE FOLLY LODGE
Halford CV36 5DG. Mike & Susan
Solomon, 01789 740183. *3m NE
Shipston-on-Stour. On A429 (Fosse
Way). In Halford take turning to Idlicote.
Garden on R past Feldon Edge.*
Home-made teas. **Adm £2.50, chd
free. Tues 8 May; 12 June; 10 July;
14 Aug; 11 Sept (2-5).** Visitors also
welcome by appt for groups 6+.
Winding paths lead through colour-
themed borders to hidden and
surprising spaces. The informal
planting scheme is enhanced by
ceramics, sculptures and mosaics
made by the owner. An artist's and
plant-lover's garden described by
visitors as 'a unique garden that we will
remember for a long time'. Gravel
paths.
  👥 ✕ ⊕ ☕

Winding paths through colour themed borders to hidden and surprising spaces . . .

**⑳ GARDEN OF TRANQUILLITY
& FESTIVAL GARDEN**
911-913 Warwick Road B91 3ER.
Marie Curie Hospice. *¼m SE of
Solihull. Car park kindly provided by
Solihull School on B4025 between
town & hospice. Disabled badge
holders park at hospice.* Home-made
teas. **Adm £2, chd free. Sat 14 July
(1.30-5).**
The hospice garden of tranquillity
invites you to stroll down a garden path
which has secluded seating areas,
water features, mixed planting and
climbers. The festival garden is a family
garden with playhouse, seating area
and water feature.
👥 ✕ ⊕ ☕

㉑ ◆ GARDEN ORGANIC RYTON
Wolston Village CV8 3LG. Garden
Organic, 024 7630 3517,
www.gardenorganic.org.uk. *5m SE
of Coventry. On rd to Wolston, off A45.*
**Adm £5, chd £2.50, concessions
£4.50.** Daily except Christmas week

(9-5). For NGS: Thu 21 June (9-5).
The UK's national centre for organic
gardening offers visitors 10 acres of
beautiful gardens from 'Vegetable
Inspirations' to 'Diversity in
Landscape'. Enjoy the Vegetable
Kingdom exhibition for all the family.
See how beautiful the organic
approach can be.
👥 ✕ ⊕

㉒ GREENLANDS
Stratford Road, Wellesbourne
CV35 9ES. Elizabeth Street. *4m E of
Stratford-upon-Avon. Situated at the
Loxley/Charlecote crossroads on the
B4086, next to airfield.* Home-made
teas. **Adm £2.50, chd free. Suns 29
Apr; 10 June; 16 Sept (11-5).**
1-acre with mature trees, shrubs,
herbaceous borders and semi-wild
areas. Winding paths and secluded
garden rooms. 2 gravel gardens and
tree lined vistas. Art - paintings on view
in studio. Some bark chip paths.
👥 ⊕ ☕

㉓ HALL GREEN GARDENS
Birmingham B28 8SQ. *Off A34, 3m
city centre, 6m from M42 J4. Nr
station.* Home-made teas at 16
Burnaston Rd & 36 Ferndale Rd.
**Combined adm £3, chd free. Wed 6
June; Sun 1 July (2-6).**

16 BURNASTON ROAD
Howard Hemmings & Sandra
Hateley, 0121 624 1488. Visitors
also welcome by appt June &
July, for groups.
S-facing formal lawn and border
garden with interesting features
incl an unusual log display, multi-
coloured gravel, and bark covered
shrub border, manicured conifers,
water feature and arch way
leading to tranquil seating area.
✕ ☕

37 BURNASTON ROAD
Mrs C M Wynne-Jones, 0121
608 2397. Visitors also welcome
by appt June & July, for groups.
Approx ⅛ acre, well-planted
suburban garden. Interesting array
of plants by experienced
propagator. Patio, lawn, mixed
borders and shade area.
Vegetables and soft fruit.
👥 ✕ ⊕

36 FERNDALE ROAD
Mrs A A Appelbe & Mrs E A
Nicholson, 0121 777 4921.
Visitors also welcome by appt
June & July, for groups.
Large suburban florist's garden.

Well planted with many unusual
plants. Garden divided into three
distinct areas; large ornamental
garden, small formal garden, small
kitchen garden. Pool with small
waterfall.
👥 ✕ ⊕ ☕

120 RUSSELL ROAD
Mr D Worthington. Not open 6
June.
Plantsman's sub-divided garden
designed by owner. Features
formal raised pool, shrubs,
climbers, old roses, herbaceous
and container planting.
✕ ⊕

㉔ ◆ 89 HARTS GREEN ROAD
Harborne B17 9TZ. Mrs Barbara
Richardson, 0121 427 5200. *3m SE
of Birmingham. Off Fellows Lane-War
Lane.* **Adm £2, chd free. For NGS:
Weds 18 Apr; 16 May; 20 June; 18
July; 5 Sept (2-5).**
Wildlife-friendly split-level garden
protected by mature trees. Extensively
planted with unusual herbaceous
perennials, shrubs and climbers incl
over 80 varieties of clematis. Herbs
and edible flowers border a path
through the rockery. Large display of
plants in containers featuring
vegetables, half hardy perennials and
shade plants. Pond. Nursery listed in
Plant Finder.
✕ ⊕

㉕ ◆ HILL CLOSE GARDENS
Warwick CV34 6HF. Hill Close
Gardens Trust, 01926 493216, www.
hillclosegardens.warwick.uk.com.
*Town Centre. Entry from Friars St. by
Bread & Meat Close. Car park by
entrance.* **Adm £3, chd free. Fri &
Sun (2-5), Sat (11-5), 1 Apr-9 Oct.
For NGS: Sats 12 May; 15 Sept (11-
5).**
Re-opened after Heritage Lottery
funded restoration in 2006. These
gardens were once refuge and
recreation for the town centre
residents. High hedges, enclosed
secret gardens containing pretty brick
summer houses and gnarled old fruit
trees. Collection of unusual plants.
New visitor centre. Sloping garden with
rolled ash paths. Disabled WC.
👥 ⊕ ☕

㉖ HOLYWELL GARDENS
Claverdon, Warwick CV35 7BH,
01926 842331. *5m W of Warwick.
Take A4189 towards Henley-in-Arden,
turn R in Claverdon for Shrewley, take
2nd L for Holywell.* Home-made teas

at Manor Farm. **Combined adm £4, chd free. Sun 17 June (11-6). Visitors also welcome by appt for groups 10+ in June.** A secluded, quiet hamlet.

HOLYWELL FARM
Ian and Ann Harper
2¹/₂ acre mature garden with open views.

MANOR FARM
Don & Margaret Hanson, 01926 842331
Romantic garden surrounding Elizabethan farmhouse (not open) with natural duck pond. Yew and box hedges divide white border and cottage garden. Barn walls clothed with climbing roses.

27 HONINGTON VILLAGE GARDENS
Shipston CV36 5AA. *1¹/₂m N of Shipston-on-Stour. Take A3400 towards Stratford then turn R signed Honington.* Home-made teas. **Combined adm £4, chd free. Sun 24 June (2.15-5.30).**
C17 village, recorded in Domesday, entered by old toll gate. Ornamental stone bridge over the Stour and interesting church with C13 tower and late C17 nave after Wren.

HOLTS COTTAGE
Mr & Mrs R G Bentley
Cottage garden being restored to original layout and opening onto parkland. Interesting trees incl fruit trees and shrubs with herbaceous borders and ponds.

HONINGTON GLEBE
Mr & Mrs J C Orchard
2-acre plantsman's garden consisting of rooms planted informally with yr-round interest in contrasting foliage and texture. Old walled garden laid out with large raised lily pool and parterre filled with violas and perennials.

HONINGTON HALL
B H E Wiggin
Extensive lawns and fine mature trees with river and garden monuments. Carolean house (not open). Parish church adjoins house.

NEW MALT HOUSE RISE
Mr & Mrs M Underhill
Small garden, well stocked with interesting established shrubs and many container plants.

THE OLD HOUSE
Mr & Mrs I F Beaumont
Small structured cottage garden formally laid out with box hedging and small fountain. Informally planted, giving an almost billowing, frothy appearance.

ORCHARD HOUSE
Mr & Mrs Monnington
Small developing garden created in recent yrs by owners with informal mixed beds and borders.

Romantic garden, duck pond, barn walls clothed with climbing roses . . .

28 IDLICOTE GARDENS
CV36 5DT. *3m NE of Shipston-on-Stour.* Home-made teas at Idilcote House. **Combined adm £4, chd free (share to St James the Great Church). Sun 1 July (2-6).**
Delightful hamlet with stunning views, large village pond and Norman church.

BADGERS FARM
Sir Derek & Lady Hornby
Lawns with panoramic views and herbaceous borders lead to encl rose garden, vegetable garden, pond and orchard walk.

NEW 1 BICKERSTAFF COTTAGES
Mr & Mrs C Balchin
Medium-sized cottage garden with a mix of flowers and vegetables and an ornamental pond.

2 BICKERSTAFF COTTAGES
Mr D Amos
Delightful small enclosed cottage garden with ornamental pond. Considerably updated in the last 1¹/₂ yrs.

3 BICKERSTAFF COTTAGES
Miss A Cummins
Small cottage garden.

BICKERSTAFF FARM
Sir John & Lady Owen
Recently planted garden. Mainly shrub borders and roses.

IDLICOTE HOUSE
Mrs R P G Dill
Extensive gardens with mature trees and shrubs, formal area and spectacular views. Enclosed vegetable garden with flower borders. Norman Church and C18 dovecote in grounds. Grade II listed C18 house (not open).

THE OLD FORGE
Mr & Mrs J Terry
Planted in 2003 for easy maintenance.

THE OLD RECTORY
Mr & Mrs G Thomson
Conventional old rectory garden with views of Idlicote Hill. Small fruit cage, one-third wilderness, conservatory.

STONE COTTAGE
Mr & Mrs C Rosser
Traditional cottage garden with some interesting shrubs and trees.

WOODLANDS
Captain & Mrs P R Doyne
Shrubs and herbaceous plants. Spectacular views beyond walled garden.

㉙ ILMINGTON GARDENS
Shipston-on-Stour CV36 4LA. *8m S of Stratford-upon-Avon. 4m NW of Shipston-on-Stour off A3400. 3m NE of Chipping Campden.* Home-made teas in Village Hall. **Combined adm £4, chd free (share to Warwickshire & Northamptonshire Air Ambulance). Sun 22 Apr (2-6).**
Most attractive Cotswold village with 2 inns and Norman church. Ilmington traditional Morris dancers.
🏺

CRAB MILL
Mr & Mrs L Hodgkin
Terraced garden with dry stone walls and sunken courtyard round C18 house (not open). Daffodils, clematis and camellias. Paths through orchard with bluebells, cherry blossom and fritillaries. Steps to rose garden.
&

FOXCOTE HILL
Mr & Mrs M Dingley
Garden developed on sloping site on edge of village retaining most of old orchard with naturalised bulbs. Paths through orchard give views over countryside towards Edge Hill. Paved courtyard with fountain.

FOXCOTE HILL COTTAGE
Miss A Terry
Hillside garden with dry stone walls enclosing banks planted with alpines and spring bulbs.
🐾

FROG ORCHARD
M Naish
Open garden surrounding an interesting modern house (not open), with trees and flowers beds, bordered on one side by a pretty little stream.
&

THE GREY HOUSE
Mr & Mrs B Blackie
Formal lawns and beds with orchard on elevated site surrounding Georgian farmhouse, overlooking village and distant views.
🐾

Fuchsia bushes
light courtyards
with water
gardens . . .

㉚ ILMINGTON MANOR
Front Street CV36 4LA. **Mr & Mr Taylor, 01608 682230, mtilmington@btinternet.com.** *8m S of Stratford-upon-Avon. Nr Shipston-on-Stour.* **Adm £3, chd free. Sun 17 June (2-6). Also open with Ilmington Gardens. Visitors also welcome by appt.**
Daffodils in April. Hundreds of old and new roses, ornamental trees, shrubs and herbaceous borders, pond, gardens, topiary. House (not open) dates from 1600.
&

㉛ INGLENOOK
20 Waxland Road, Halesowen B63 3DW. **Ron & Anne Kerr.** *1/4m from Halesowen town centre. M5 J3 take A456 to Kidderminster, R at 1st island, 1st L into Dogkennel Lane. Waxland Rd 2nd L.* 2 car parks in town centre, limited roadside parking. Home-made teas. **Adm £2.50, chd free. Suns 3 June; 15 July (1-5).**
Charming garden featuring waterfalls which cascade over rocks down to ponds set within a woodland area. A path meandering through the trees brings you back to the lawn and patio. Hidden area hosts greenhouses, vegetable plots, asparagus beds and mixed borders. Enjoy panoramic views from the raised decked area with its semi-tropical planting overlooking terraces which display a wide variety of low-growing conifers.
🐾 ✿ ☕

㉜ 18 LADYWOOD ROAD
Four Oaks, Sutton Coldfield B74 2SW. **Ann & Ron Forrest.** *2m N of Sutton Coldfield. Off A454, Four Oaks Road, nr stn.* Home-made teas. **Adm £2.50, chd free. Sun 10 June (1-5).**
Spacious informal garden on Four Oaks Estate. Approx 1 1/4 acres, secluded and densely planted with roses, peonies, irises and lupins in herbaceous beds. Pond with fountain. Feature cedar tree, azaleas and rhododendrons.
& ✿ ☕

㉝ NEW LATIMERS REST
CV9 2HS. **Gerald & Christine Leedham, 01827 875526.** *3m S of Atherstone on B4116. From A5 Atherstone, at island, take Merevale Lane to Baxterley. From M42 J9 take A4097 for Kingsbury. At island follow signs to Hurley & Baxterley, garden nr church.*

Home-made teas. **Adm £3, chd free. Sat & Sun 23, 24 June; 28, 29 July (1-6). Visitors also welcome by appt, June-Aug.**
Debut opening for garden of contrasts in beautiful Baxterley. Brilliant Austin roses star in 2 acres of lush lawns. Floral borders below stately trees. Fuchsia baskets light courtyards with water gardens, herbs and dahlias leading to Good Life veggies with melons and tomatoes and a young arboretum beyond.
& 🐾 ☕

㉞ LITTLE INDONESIA
20 Poston Croft, Kings Heath, Birmingham B14 5AB. **Dave & Pat McKenna, 0121 628 1397, pat_mckenna66@hotmail.com.** *1 1/2m from Kings Heath High St. Poston Croft is 6th L off Broad Lane, which is off A435 Alcester Rd.* Home-made teas. **Adm £2.50, chd free. Sun 29 July (11-4). Visitors also welcome by appt in July OR Sept, groups 10+.**
A garden that is the realisation of my dreams. An amazing plant paradise with the feel of entering a jungle, even though we are in the heart of Birmingham. Planted so that it seems to go on for ever. Plants of unusual leaf shapes and textures. Bananas, cannas and grasses jostle with one another for space. A plantaholic's paradise. Steps down to garden.
🐾 ☕

㉟ NEW MANOR COTTAGE
CV37 8HU. **Andrew & Judith Slater.** *2m SW of Stratford-on-Avon. On B4632 towards Broadway, turn into village, cottage at end of village on L.* Home-made teas. **Adm £3, chd free (share to Mary Mare School for the Deaf). Sun 15 July (2-6).**
15C thatched cottage with garden frontage to R Stour tributary. Developing cottage garden featuring GII listed Victorian greenhouse, mixed borders, water birds and wildlife. Country walk past Old Mill House to R Stour.
& 🐾 ✿ ☕

㊱ ♦ THE MASTER'S GARDEN
Lord Leycester Hospital CV34 4BH. **The Governors.** *W end of Warwick High St, behind hospital.* **Adm £2, chd free. Apr-Sept (10-4.30).**

Restored historic walled garden hidden behind the medieval buildings of this home for retired ex-servicemen, also open to the public. Mixed shrub and herbaceous planting with climbing roses and clematis, Norman arch, ancient Egyptian Nilometer, thatched summerhouse, gazebo, knot garden and C18 pineapple pit.

③⑦ MAXSTOKE CASTLE
Coleshill B46 2RD. Mr & Mrs M C Fetherston-Dilke. *2¹/₂ m E of Coleshill. E of Birmingham, on B4114. Take R turn down Castle Lane, Castle drive 1¹/₄ m on R.* Cream teas. **Adm £5, chd £3 (under 5 free), concessions £3 (share to church). Sun 17 June (11-5).** Approx 5 acres of garden and grounds with herbaceous, shrubs and trees in the immed surroundings of this C14 moated castle. Price includes Castle opening which is this day only. Gravel paths. Castle has no disabled access.

③⑧ NEW ◆ MIDDLETON HALL
Tamworth B78 2AE. Middleton Hall Trust, 01827 283095, middletonhalltrust@btconnect. com. *4m S of Tamworth, 2m N J9 M42. On A4091 between The Belfry & Drayton Manor.* **Adm £3, chd £1, concessions £2.50. Suns & Bank Hol Mons, 9 Apr-30 Sept, except 6 & 27 May, 26 Aug. For NGS: Sun 3 June (1-5).** Two walled gardens set in 40 acres of grounds surrounding GII Middleton Hall, the C17 home of naturalists Sir Francis Willughby and John Ray. Large colour themed herbaceous borders radiating from a central pond, restored gazebo, pergola planted with roses and wisteria. Courtyard garden with raised beds. SSSI Nature Trail, craft centre, music in Hall.

③⑨ ◆ THE MILL GARDEN
55 Mill Street, Warwick CV34 4HB. Open in memory of Arthur Measures, 01926 492877. *Off A425 beside castle gate at the bottom of Mill St. Use St Nicholas car park.* **Adm £1.50, chd free with adult. 1 Apr to 31 Oct (9-6).** ¹/₂-acre garden with abundance of

plants, shrubs and trees beneath the walls of Warwick Castle beside the R Avon. Place of peace and beauty.

5 acres of garden and grounds and the castle is open for this day only!

④⓪ MOSELEY GARDENS SOUTH
Birmingham B13 9TF. *3m city centre. Halfway between Kings Heath and Moseley village. From A435 turn at the main Moseley T-lights on to St Mary's Row/Wake Green Rd. Grove Ave is 2nd on R. From here take 1st R, Oxford Rd, then 1st L, School Rd. Prospect Rd is 3rd on L, Ashfield Rd is 4th on R.* Home-made teas at 10 &18 Grove Avenue. **Combined adm £3.50, chd under 12 free. Sun 24 June (2-6).**

33 SCHOOL ROAD
Ms J Warr-Arnold
Mixed garden containing many plants with interesting histories and traditional uses. Come and spot the dragons!.

7 ASHFIELD ROAD
Hilary Bartlett & John Dring
Small garden with secluded, cottage feel. Attractive pond with rockery, waterfall and shingle bank.

10 GROVE AVENUE
Steve & Anita Harding
Suburban garden with herbaceous borders, pond area and summer house.

18 GROVE AVENUE
Richard & Judy Green, 0121 449 2477. Visitors also welcome by appt.
Small peaceful urban garden stocked with wide variety of unusual trees, shrubs and perennials, planted for colour and foliage.

19 PROSPECT ROAD
Mr A J White, 0121 449 1234. Visitors also welcome by appt.
Well planted suburban garden with plenty of colour.

65 SCHOOL ROAD
Wendy Weston
Small shady garden with patio, pergola and pond. Designed for easy maintenance.

④① ◆ PACKWOOD HOUSE
Hockley Heath B94 6AT. The National Trust, 01564 783294, www.nationaltrust.org.uk. *11m SE of Birmingham. 2m E of Hockley Heath.* **House and Garden Adm £7, chd £3.50, Garden only Adm £4, chd £2. Telephone or see website for opening times & days. For NGS: Thu 21 June (11-5.30).** Carolean yew garden representing the Sermon on the Mount. Tudor house with tapestries, needlework and furniture of the period. Gravel paths, steps to raised terrace.

④② PARHAM LODGE
CV37 7QN. Mr & Mrs K C Edwards, 01789 268955. Visitors also welcome by appt, combined with **Bower House**, all yr for groups. Also open with **Alveston Gardens**.
29-yr-old garden with a small wood, large old cedars, copper beech, hornbeams and a large pond. Sunny and shady seating areas, terraces, pots and topiary. Variety of unusual shrubs for all seasons, roses. Large island bed incl a variety of grasses, herbaceous bed and small orchard with daffodils. Birds and wildlife encouraged.

④③ PEBWORTH & BROAD MARSTON GARDENS
Stratford-upon-Avon CV37 8XZ. *9m SW of Stratford-upon-Avon. On B439 at Bidford turn L towards Honeybourne, after 3m turn L at Xrds signed Pebworth.* Home-made teas at Nolan Cottage & Pebworth Village Hall. **Combined adm £4, chd free. Sun & Mon 27, 28 May (2-6).** Peaceful village with beautiful church. Some parts are very old - Shakespeare referred to 'Piping Pebworth'. ¹/₂ m down the road is the hamlet of Broad Marston with some thatched cottages, an ancient priory and manor.

Designed for relaxation and pottering, yet still full of interest . . .

1 ELM CLOSE
Mr & Mrs G Keyte
Small cottage garden, very well stocked and with many features of interest.
 ♿ 🚷 ⊛

ICKNIELD BARN
Sheila Davies
Very small walled cottage garden which almost becomes a part of the living room! Designed for relaxation and pottering, yet still full of interest.
♿ 🚷

IVYBANK
Mr & Mrs R Davis
1/3-acre garden with ferns, ivies, roses and shrubs. Nursery holds National Collection of Pelargoniums and Hederas.
♿ 🚷 ⊛ NCCPG

THE KNOLL
Mr K Wood
Cottage-style walled garden.
🚷

MARTINS
Tim & Linda Collins
3/4-acre informal gardens with ponds, vegetable patch and unusual plants.
♿ 🚷 ⊛

NOLAN COTTAGE
Mr & Mrs R Thomas
Cottage garden of 3/4 acre with ponds, vegetable garden, ferns, mixed borders and wild garden area with many places to sit and contemplate.
♿ 🚷 ⊛

PEBWORTH MANOR
Mr & Mrs J Lloyd
Open lawns with extensive views across the Vale of Evesham towards the Malvern Hills. Herbaceous borders, mature trees. Large vegetable garden.
♿ 🚷

PETTIFER HOUSE
Mr & Mrs M Veal
Traditional cottage garden, herbaceous beds, shrubberies, rock garden, lavender hedges and vegetable garden.
♿ 🚷 ⊛

THE ROWANS
Mr & Mrs D Fox
Gardens in a garden, looked after by two amateurs.
♿ 🚷

44 50 PEREIRA ROAD
Harborne B17 9JN. Peg Peil, 0121 427 7573. *Between Gillhurst Rd & Margaret Grove, 1/4 m from Hagley Rd or 1/2 m from Harborne High St.* **Adm** £2, chd free. Sun 29 Apr (2-5). Also open with **Pereira Road Gardens.** Visitors also welcome by appt. Plantaholic's garden with over 1000 varieties, many unusual. Large bed of plants with African connections. Many fruits, vegetables, herbs, grasses. Plant sales in aid of CAFOD.
🚷 ⊛

45 PEREIRA ROAD GARDENS
Harborne B17 9JN. *Between Gillhurst Rd & Margaret Grove, 1/4 m from Hagley Rd or 1/2 m from Harborne High St.* Home-made teas at 10 Pereira Rd. **Combined adm** £3, chd free. Sun 24 June (2-5).
☕

NEW 10 PEREIRA ROAD
Muriel May
S aspect sloping garden with steps, shaded, mature silver birch and acid-loving shrubs, some landscaping.
🚷

NEW 14 PEREIRA ROAD
Mike Foster
Well established suburban garden with mixed herbaceous and shrub borders, small fruit and vegetable area. Wildlife friendly with 2 ponds and natural area.
🚷

27 PEREIRA ROAD
Dr & Mrs John Hurdley
N-facing garden on 2 levels, with 2 ponds and a wide variety of plants and fruit. Interesting landscaping.

50 PEREIRA ROAD
Peg Peil
(See separate entry).
🚷 ⊛

55 PEREIRA ROAD
Emma Davies & Martin Commander
Sloping gravelled garden with mixed planting, grasses and small pond. Featured in 'Pond & Gardening' Jun 2006.

46 ◆ RAGLEY HALL GARDENS
Alcester B49 5NJ. Marquess & Marchioness of Hertford, 07917 425664, rossbarbour@ragleyhall.com. *2m SW of Alcester. Off A435/A46 8m from Stratford-upon-Avon.* **House and Garden Adm** £8, chd £4.50, concess £6.50, family £25, Garden only Adm £3, chd free. 17 Mar-30 Sept. For NGS: Suns 11 Feb (11-3); 7 Oct (10-4.30); 10 Feb 2008 (11-3). 24 acres of gardens, predominantly mature broadleaved trees, within which a variety of cultivated and non-cultivated areas have been blended to achieve a garden rich in both horticulture and bio-diversity. The winter garden, spring meadows and bulbs make way for summer meadows, herbaceous borders, annual bedding and rose beds to provide a rich tapestry of form, colour and contrast all yr. Feb for large snowdrop displays and new winter garden planted 2005.
🚷 ☕

47 56 SALISBURY ROAD
Moseley B13 8JT. Peter & Wendy Binham, 0121 449 7482. *2 1/2 m S of Birmingham. From A435 Alcester Rd, R into B4217 (Salisbury Road). House 300yds on R. Park in Amesbury Rd.* Light refreshments & teas. **Adm** £2.50, chd free. Sun 15 Apr (2-6). Visitors also welcome by appt, groups 10 max, 2 weeks notice. Approx 1/3-acre N-facing town garden, overlooking lake in private park. Terraced garden, mixed planting, mainly shrubs. Patio, gazebo, rose trellis, gravel walk, raised beds, small and larger pond, water feature.
🚷 ⊛ ☕

48 NEW SECRET GARDEN
73 Sir Johns Road, Selly Oak
B29 7EP. Mrs Carol Dockery. *S of Birmingham, off A441.* **Adm £2.50, chd free. Sun 8 July (1.30-5.30).**
18ft x 99ft, unexpected in suburbia, full of tropical plants. Tree ferns, cordylines, bananas, alocasias, rare yucca. Eighty pots scattered around. Different levels leading to sun house, places to sit & contemplate, come and enjoy. No parking in Sir Johns Rd, use Oakfield Rd.
&

49 NEW STONELEIGH HOUSE
17a Wentworth Road, Four Oaks B74 2SD. Richard & Gillian Mason. *1½m N Sutton Coldfield on A5127. L at Four Oaks Station, 100yds on L.* Cream teas. **Adm £2.50, chd free. Sun 3 June (1-5).**
½-acre, mixed beds and borders with mature trees and rhododendrons. Ornamental and wildlife pond, raised beds vegetable plot, various pots and planters. Front garden wild flower meadow.
& & &

50 STONOR ROAD GARDENS
Hall Green B28 0QJ. *3m W of Solihull. From Robin Hood island on A34 take Baldwins Lane exit. Stonor Rd is 2nd L.* Home-made teas at 172 Stonor Road. **Combined adm £3, chd free. Sun 8 July (2-5).**
4 very different gardens demonstrating the variety of design and planting that can be achieved in a modest space. Home-made preserves.

152 STONOR ROAD
Mrs Hull & Mr Dale
Designed for modern living with outdoor dining area, pergola, well planted borders with interesting collection of grasses. Hanging baskets, hostas & clematis.
&

154 STONOR ROAD
Mrs J Seager
Small suburban garden with choice plants both in borders and containers. Large pool, with waterfalls and koi carp, bordered by alpine bed. Interesting collection of bonsai.
&

A wildlife garden bursting and brimming with unusual plants . . .

166 STONOR ROAD
Mrs & Mrs R Healey
Very colourful garden with well planted borders, immaculate lawn and a wealth of hanging baskets and containers. Very attractive seating areas at the bottom of the garden.
& & &

172 STONOR ROAD
Mrs O Walters, 0121 745 2894, gwenowalt@yahoo.co.uk.
Visitors also welcome by appt, Mar to Sept, individuals or small groups.
Plantswoman's garden (approx 65ft x 24ft) with wide variety of plants, some not considered hardy in this area. Scree, containers, shade beds, ferns, climbers, conservatory, gravel stream and small wildlife pond. Always something new.
& &

51 NEW STYVECHALE GARDENS
Stivichall CV3 5BE. *From A45 take B4113, Leamington Road, towards Coventry. 2nd R into Baginton Road. The Chesils is 1st L.* Cream teas at 59 The Chesils, Smithy Cottage & Avondale Nursery. **Combined adm £2.50, chd free (share to Myton Hospice). Sun 17 June (11-6) Avondale Nursery (10-4).**
Maps at all gardens. For information 02476 411176.
&

AVONDALE NURSERY
Mr Brian Ellis
(See separate entry).
& & &

59 THE CHESILS
John Marron & Richard Bantock
See entry under Earlsdon Gardens.
&

NEW 91 THE CHESILS
Graham & Pat White
A series of rooms incl water, gravel and a wildlife garden bursting and brimming with unusual plants.
& &

NEW 16 DELAWARE ROAD
Val & Roy Howells
A garden of interest with architectural plants such as phormiums, palms and bamboos. Peaceful seating areas with water features.
&

NEW SMITHY COTTAGE
Jane & Peter Woodward
See entry under Earlsdon Gardens.
& &

NEW 6 TOWNSEND CROFT
Jean & John Garrison
To the front an herbaceous border and heathers surround decoratively paved and planted area. To the back are deep colourful herbaceous borders with gazebo, water features, hidden garden and mature trees. Interesting and varied planting.
&

52 ◆ UPTON HOUSE
Banbury OX15 6HT. The National Trust, 01295 670266, www.nationaltrust.org.uk. *7m NW of Banbury. On A422, 1m S of Edgehill.* **House and Garden Adm £8, chd £4, Garden only Adm £4.80, chd £2.40.** Phone or use website for opening times & days. For NGS: **Wed 26 Sept (12-5).**
Large terraced garden, S-facing valley with herbaceous borders, roses, water garden, kitchen garden, lawns growing from seed to seed. National Collection of Asters, which should be at their best in the autumn. House contains an internationally important collection of paintings, porcelain and tapestries.
& & **NCCPG**

53 WARMINGTON VILLAGE GARDENS
OX17 1BX. *5m NW of Banbury. Off B4100.* Home-made teas. **Combined adm £4, chd free (share to Warmington PCC Restoration Fund). Sun 24 June (2-6).**
Village map given to all visitors.

Undulating, softly planted gardens spilling down through mature trees and shrubs . . .

THE GLEBE HOUSE
Mrs J Thornton
Village garden of 1/4 acre with lawns, mature trees, roses, shrubs and perennials. Interesting conifer border established 1976. Flagstone terrace with distant views over countryside.
  🏵 ✗ 🛏

GROVE FARM HOUSE
Richard & Kate Lister
This large garden is now taking shape after 5yrs of development. A field, which originally ran to the back door, has new paths, hedges, trees and beds - herbaceous and edible - and a knot garden.
✗

THE MANOR HOUSE
Mr & Mrs G Lewis
Large garden, fruit and vegetable plot, flower beds, knot garden.
🏵 ✗

SPRINGFIELD HOUSE
Jenny & Roger Handscombe
Interesting house (1539) set in 1/2-acre, very informal country garden.
✗ 🛏

UNDEREDGE
Mr & Mrs J Dixon
Small colourful garden with pond and roses.
✗

WESTERING
Mr & Mrs R Neale
Attractive medium-sized garden with vegetable plot, flower beds, patio area and chickens.
🏵 ✗

54 WHICHFORD & ASCOTT GARDENS
CV36 5PQ. *6m SE of Shipston on Stour. Turn E off A3400 at Long Compton for Whichford.* Teas in the Reading Room adjacent to Church. **Combined adm £3.50, chd free. Sun 17 June (2-6).**
Enjoy a stroll around two peaceful stone villages on the edge of the Cotswolds with C13 church, pottery and inn.
☕

ASCOTT LODGE
Charlotte Copley
Beautiful views, lawns sloping down to pond, well stocked shrub borders, courtyard garden. Many interesting plants. Gravel paths.
🏵 ✗

BROOK HOLLOW
Mr & Mrs J A Round
Terraced hillside garden with large variety of trees, shrubs and plants, stream and water features. Competition for children. Wheelchair access to lower garden only.
🏵 ⊕

THE OLD HOUSE
Whichford. Mr & Mrs T A Maher
Undulating, softly planted gardens spilling down through mature trees and shrubs to wildlife ponds. Gravel paths.
🏵 ✗

THE OLD RECTORY
Whichford. Mr & Mrs P O'Kane
Informal garden structured around ponds and streams with interesting borders.
🏵 ✗

SEPTEMBER HOUSE
Mrs J Clayton
Secluded peaceful garden, in full colour in June, with roses and other interesting plants.
🏵

THE WHICHFORD POTTERY
Mr & Mrs J B M Keeling,
www.whichfordpottery.com
Secret walled garden, unusual plants, large vegetable garden and rambling cottage garden. Featured in 'Warwickshire Life' May 2006.
🏵 ✗

WILDWOOD
See Oxfordshire.

55 WITS END
59 Tanworth Lane, Shirley B90 4DQ.
Sue Mansell, 0121 744 4337. *2m SW of Solihull. Take B4102 from Solihull, 2m. R at island onto A34. After next island (Sainsbury's) Tanworth Lane is 1st L off A34.* Home-made teas. **Adm £2, chd free. Suns 20 May; 1 July; 1 Aug (2-5). Visitors also welcome by appt, groups of 10+.**
Peaceful and interesting all-yr-round plantaholic's cottage-style garden. Hundreds of perennials, alpines and shrubs, many new rare and unusual in various shaped beds (some colour co-ordinated) and borders. Gravel area, alpine sinks, rockery, extensive shade and small waterfall, river and bog. Millenium Wheel of sleepers and crazypaving in woodland setting. Plants in aid of Alzheimers Society. Assistance available for shallow steps.
  ⊕ ☕

56 WOODBROOKE QUAKER STUDY CENTRE
1046 Bristol Road, Selly Oak B29 6LJ, www.woodbrooke.org.uk. *4m SW of Birmingham. On A38 Bristol Rd, S of Selly Oak, opp Witherford Way.* Light refreshments & teas. **Adm £3, chd £1.50. Sun 17 June (2.30-5.30).**
10 acres of organically-managed garden and grounds. Grade II listed former home of George Cadbury (not open). Herbaceous and shrub borders, walled garden with herb garden, potager and cutting beds, Chinese garden, orchard, arboretum, lake and extensive woodland walks. Very fine variety of trees. Craft stalls. Limited wheelchair access to woodland & lake.
  ✗ ⊕ ☕

57 WOODPECKERS
The Bank, Marlcliff, nr Bidford-on-Avon B50 4NT. Drs Andy & Lallie Cox, 01789 773416, andrewcox@doctors.org.uk. *7m SW of Stratford-upon-Avon. Off B4085 between Bidford-on-Avon & Cleeve Prior.* Teas. **Adm £4, chd free. Visitors welcome by appt.**
Peaceful 2 1/2-acre plantsman's country garden designed and maintained by garden-mad owners since 1965. A garden for all seasons. Unusual plants, hidden surprises, interesting trees, colour-themed borders, potager and knot garden. Wooden sculptures of St Fiacre and The Green Man carved by the owner. Lovely garden buildings of framed green oak. Featured in 'The English Garden' Feb 2006.
  ✗ ⊕ ☕

58 WOOTTON GRANGE
Pettiford Lane, Henley-in-Arden B95
6AH. Mrs Jean Tarmey, 01564
792592. *1m E of Henley-in-Arden.
Take 1st R off A4189 Warwick Rd on
to Pettiford Lane, garden is 300yds on
R. From A3400 in Wootton Wawen
turn by craft centre on to Pettiford
Lane, garden 1m on L.* Home-made
teas. **Adm £2, chd free. Visitors
welcome by appt, inc groups from
February.**
1-acre farm garden with yr-round
interest surrounding early Victorian
farmhouse (not open). Wide variety of
unusual plants incl bulbs, hellebores,
clematis, roses and alpines. Bog
garden, grass feature, kitchen garden.
&. ⊕ ☕

Did you find
the wine
tasting from
their own
vineyard?

Warwickshire County Volunteers

County Organiser
Warwickshire Julia Sewell, Dinsdale House, Baldwins Lane, Upper Tysoe, Warwick CV35 0TX, 01295 680234
    sewelljulia@btinternet.com
West Midlands Jackie Harvey, Ashover, 25 Burnett Road, Streetly, Sutton Coldfield B74 3EL, 0121 353 0547

County Treasurer
Warwickshire John Wilson, Victoria House, Farm Street, Harbury, Leamington Spa CV33 9LR, 01926 612572
West Midlands Martin Harvey, Ashover, 25 Burnett Road , Streetly, Sutton Coldfield B74 3EL, 0121 353 0547

Assistant County Organiser
Warwickshire Mary Lesinski, The Master's House, Lord Leycester Hospital, High Street, Warwick CV34 4BH, 01926 499918
    lordlycester@btinternet.com
Warwickshire Peter Pashley, Millstones, Mayfield Avenue, Stratford-upon-Avon CV37 6XB, 01789 294932

WILTSHIRE

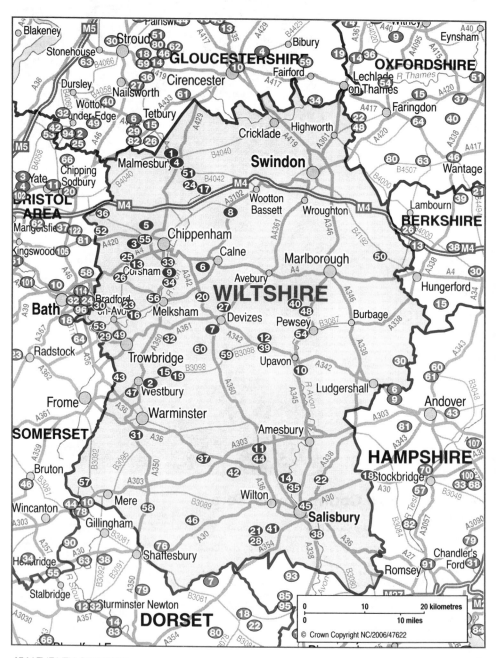

Opening Dates

February

SUNDAY 4
23 Great Chalfield Manor

SATURDAY 10
34 Lacock Abbey Gardens

SUNDAY 11
34 Lacock Abbey Gardens

SATURDAY 17
34 Lacock Abbey Gardens

SUNDAY 18
34 Lacock Abbey Gardens

March

SUNDAY 18
1 Abbey House Gardens

SUNDAY 25
13 Corsham Court

April

SUNDAY 1
42 Manor House Farm
44 The Mill House
54 Sharcott Manor

WEDNESDAY 4
54 Sharcott Manor

SUNDAY 8
7 Broadleas Gardens Charitable Trust
36 Littleton Drew Gardens

MONDAY 9
36 Littleton Drew Gardens

SUNDAY 15
13 Corsham Court
52 Ridleys Cheer

SUNDAY 22
35 Little Durnford Manor
48 Oare House

SUNDAY 29
29 Iford Manor
30 Inwoods

May

WEDNESDAY 2
20 Enfield
54 Sharcott Manor

THURSDAY 3
20 Enfield

SUNDAY 6
58 Waterdale House

WEDNESDAY 9
20 Enfield

THURSDAY 10
20 Enfield

FRIDAY 11
39 Mallards

SUNDAY 13
49 The Old Malthouse
52 Ridleys Cheer

WEDNESDAY 16
16 The Courts
20 Enfield
47 Oak Tree Cottage
50 The Old Mill

THURSDAY 17
20 Enfield

FRIDAY 18
41 Manor House
45 Mompesson House

SUNDAY 20
12 Conock Manor
18 Downs View
26 Hazelbury Manor Gardens
40 Manor Farm
55 Sheldon Manor
56 32 Shurnhold

WEDNESDAY 23
20 Enfield

THURSDAY 24
20 Enfield
55 Sheldon Manor

SUNDAY 27
22 The Grange
28 Hyde's House
36 Littleton Drew Gardens
37 Long Hall

MONDAY 28
36 Littleton Drew Gardens

WEDNESDAY 30
20 Enfield
59 Windmill Cottage

THURSDAY 31
20 Enfield
55 Sheldon Manor

June

SUNDAY 3
6 Bowood Rhododendron Walks
8 33 Calne Road
46 North Cottage & Woodview Cottage

WEDNESDAY 6
8 33 Calne Road
20 Enfield
54 Sharcott Manor

THURSDAY 7
20 Enfield
55 Sheldon Manor

FRIDAY 8
9 Cantax House (Evening)

39 Mallards
59 Windmill Cottage

SUNDAY 10
9 Cantax House
15 Court Lane Farm
21 Faulstone House
40 Manor Farm
51 The Pound House
52 Ridleys Cheer

MONDAY 11
15 Court Lane Farm

WEDNESDAY 13
20 Enfield
50 The Old Mill

THURSDAY 14
15 Court Lane Farm
20 Enfield
53 The River House
55 Sheldon Manor

FRIDAY 15
41 Manor House

SUNDAY 17
5 Bolehyde Manor
10 Chisenbury Priory
14 The Court House
17 Dauntsey Gardens
19 Edington Gardens
32 Keevil Gardens
33 Lackham Gardens
35 Little Durnford Manor
56 32 Shurnhold

WEDNESDAY 20
20 Enfield

THURSDAY 21
20 Enfield
53 The River House
55 Sheldon Manor

FRIDAY 22
39 Mallards
59 Windmill Cottage

SATURDAY 23
11 Cockspur Thorns
24 Great Somerford Gardens
44 The Mill House
57 Stourhead Garden

SUNDAY 24
3 Biddestone Manor
11 Cockspur Thorns
24 Great Somerford Gardens
25 Guyers House
31 Job's Mill
38 Longford Castle
44 The Mill House
49 The Old Malthouse
55 Sheldon Manor

WEDNESDAY 27
20 Enfield
50 The Old Mill

THURSDAY 28
🔟 Enfield
🟡 Sheldon Manor

July

SUNDAY 1
🟤 North Cottage & Woodview Cottage (Evening)

WEDNESDAY 4
🟤 Sharcott Manor

FRIDAY 6
🟤 Mallards
🟤 Windmill Cottage

SATURDAY 7
🟤 Beggars Knoll

SUNDAY 8
🟤 Beggars Knoll
🟤 Blicks Hill House
🟤 Downs View
🟤 Worton Gardens

SUNDAY 15
🟤 32 Shurnhold

FRIDAY 20
🟤 Windmill Cottage

SUNDAY 22
🟤 Lackham Gardens
🟤 Oare House

August

WEDNESDAY 1
🟤 Sharcott Manor

SUNDAY 19
🟤 Broadleas Gardens Charitable Trust
🟤 The Mead Nursery

September

WEDNESDAY 5
🟤 Sharcott Manor

FRIDAY 7
🟤 Manor House

SUNDAY 9
🟤 Oak Tree Cottage
🟤 Sharcott Manor

WEDNESDAY 12
🟤 The Old Mill

SUNDAY 16
🟤 The Courts

February 2008

SUNDAY 3
🟤 Great Chalfield Manor

SATURDAY 9
🟤 Lacock Abbey Gardens

SUNDAY 10
🟤 Lacock Abbey Gardens

SATURDAY 16
🟤 Lacock Abbey Gardens

SUNDAY 17
🟤 Lacock Abbey Gardens

Private gardens opening regularly for the NGS

🔟 Enfield
🟤 Sharcott Manor

Gardens open to the public

🟤 Abbey House Gardens
🟤 Bowood Rhododendron Walks
🟤 Broadleas Gardens Charitable Trust
🟤 Corsham Court
🟤 The Courts
🟤 Great Chalfield Manor
🟤 Iford Manor
🟤 Lackham Gardens
🟤 Lacock Abbey Gardens
🟤 The Mead Nursery
🟤 Mompesson House
🟤 Sheldon Manor
🟤 Stourhead Garden

By appointment only

🟤 Home Covert Gardens & Arboretum

The Gardens

🟤 ◆ **ABBEY HOUSE GARDENS**
Malmesbury Town Centre
SN16 9AS. Barbara & Ian Pollard,
01666 827650,
www.abbeyhousegardens.co.uk. *5m
N of J17 M4. Beside C12 Abbey.
Parking in town centre (short stay) or
follow brown signs to long stay (via
steps to gardens).* Adm £5.50, chd
£2, concessions £5. Daily 21 Mar to
21 Oct. For NGS: Sun 18 Mar (11-
5.30).
5 beautiful acres planted by present
owner. Over 130,000 spring bulbs
especially tulips; 'medieval' herb
garden; topiary; knot garden;
herbaceous borders; laburnum walk;
UK's largest private collection of roses
(over 2000); unique auricula theatre;
ornamental trees; rare plants; wooded
walk to river, 'monastic' fish ponds,

waterfall and fernery. Colour, peace
and contrast. Featured in 'Garden
News' and on BBC Radio Wiltshire.
Steep slope to river garden.
&. ℵ ❀ ⊛ ☕

BATH PRIORY HOTEL
See Somerset & Bristol Area.

🟤 **BEGGARS KNOLL**
Newtown, Westbury BA13 3ED.
Colin Little & Penny Stirling, 01373
823383,
silkendalliance@onetel.com. *1m SE
of Westbury. Turn off B3098 at White
Horse Pottery, up hill towards the
White Horse for 1km. Limited parking
at end of drive.* Adm £3, chd free
(share to Wiltshire Wildlife Trust). Sat
7, Sun 8 July (2-6). Visitors also
welcome by appt.
1-acre garden on chalky hillside with
woodland backdrop. Strong Chinese
influence throughout incl pavilions,
ponds, gateways and rare Chinese
plants. Each garden room is named, in
the Chinese fashion, including a newly-
developing bamboo grove and
pavilion. Also large vegetable patch,
mixed border, podocarp collection and
outstanding views.
ℵ ❀ ☕

BEVERSTON CASTLE
See Gloucestershire North &
Central.

🟤 **BIDDESTONE MANOR**
Biddestone SN14 7DJ. Mr H Astrup,
01249 713211. *5m W of Chippenham.
On A4 between Chippenham &
Corsham turn N. From A420, 5m W of
Chippenham, turn S. Car park, please
do not park on rd.* Home-made teas.
Adm £3.50, chd free. Sun 24 June
(2-5). Visitors also welcome by appt,
for gardening groups of 10+, Thurs
pm & evenings.
Peaceful 8-acre garden with sweeping
lawns, small lake and streams, topiary,
arboretum with species roses. Walled
kitchen garden, orchard with wild
flowers, cutting garden, herbaceous,
shrub and rose borders. Beautiful C17
manor house (not open) with ancient
dovecote and outbuildings.
&. ℵ ❀ ☕

Each garden room is named, in the
Chinese fashion, including a newly-
developing bamboo grove . . .

4 NEW BLICKS HILL HOUSE
Blicks Hill, Malmesbury SN16 9HZ. Alan & Valerie Trotman. *½ m E of Malmesbury. W of bypass, between roundabouts.* Home-made teas. **Adm £3.50, chd free. Sun 8 July (12-5.30).**
1-acre garden on sloping site with mature trees. Colourful plantsman's garden created over the past 3yrs and still being developed, with many unusual plants. Unique pergola leading into woodland glade. Herbaceous border, shrub beds and small rockery.
✗ ☕

5 BOLEHYDE MANOR
Allington SN14 6LW. The Earl & Countess Cairns, 01249 652105. *1½ m W of Chippenham. On Bristol Rd (A420). Turn N at Allington Xrds. ½ m on R. Parking in field.* Home-made teas. **Adm £3.50, chd 50p (share to Kington St Michael Church). Sun 17 June (2.30-6). Visitors also welcome by appt.**
Series of gardens around C16 manor house (not open), enclosed by walls and topiary, densely planted with many interesting shrubs and climbers, mixed rose and herbaceous beds; inner courtyard with troughs full of tender plants; wild flower orchard, vegetable, fruit garden and greenhouse yard. Collection of tender pelargoniums; adventure tree house for children. Featured in 'Wiltshire Life' & 'Evening News'. Some steps.
& ❀ ☕

6 ◆ BOWOOD RHODODENDRON WALKS
nr Chippenham SN11 9PG. The Marquis of Lansdowne, 01249 812102, www.bowood.org. *3½ m SE of Chippenham. Entrance off A342 between Sandy Lane & Derry Hill villages.* **Adm £4.95, chd free, concessions £4.45. Late Apr to early June.** For NGS: **Sun 3 June (11-6).**
This 60-acre woodland garden of azaleas and rhododendrons is one of the most exciting of its type in the country. From the individual flowers to the breathtaking sweep of colour formed by hundreds of shrubs, surrounded by carpets of bluebells, this is a garden not to be missed. Planting first began in 1850 and some of the earliest known hybrids feature among the collection. Bowood House and Gardens a separate attraction, 2m from Rhododendron Walks. Featured in 'Country Life', 'Telegraph' & 'Guardian'.
✗

BREWERY HOUSE
See Somerset & Bristol Area.

7 ◆ BROADLEAS GARDENS CHARITABLE TRUST
Devizes SN10 5JQ. Lady Anne Cowdray, 01380 722035. *1m S of Devizes. On A360 or follow tourist signs from Long Street.* **Adm £5, chd £1.50 (under 10), groups of 10+ £4.50. Apr to Oct Suns, Weds & Thurs (2-6).** For NGS: **Suns 8 Apr; 19 Aug (2-6).**
9-acre garden; sheltered dell planted with many unusual trees and shrubs. Azaleas, rhododendrons and magnolias with underplantings of trilliums, erythroniums and many others. Herbaceous borders and perennial garden full of interesting plants. Partial wheelchair access.
& ❀

Moisture-loving plants along mill leat; carp pond, orchard and wild garden . . .

8 33 CALNE ROAD
Lyneham SN15 4PT. Sue & Sam Wright. *7m N of Calne. Next to RAF Lyneham entrance.* Home-made teas. **Adm £2, chd 50p, concessions £1.50. Sun 3, Wed 6 June (1-5).**
Approx ¾-acre informal garden comprising modest collection of hostas, clematis and roses. Small kitchen garden, pond and mature orchard with bantams, chickens, geese, doves and dovecote. Green oasis surrounded by activity.
& ✗ ❀ ☕

9 CANTAX HOUSE
Lacock SN15 2JZ. Andrew & Deborah van der Beek. *3m S of Chippenham. Off A350 between Chippenham & Melksham. Entrance to garden in Cantax Hill.* Home-made teas 10 June. **Adm £3, chd free**

(share to Amnesty International). **Sun 10 June (2-6). Evening Opening** wine, **Fri 8 June (5-9).**
Queen Anne former vicarage (not open). Medium-sized garden of colour, pattern and scent; designed and maintained by artist owner; interesting and unusual plants; hornbeam spire and other topiary projects in yew; old orchard wild garden; sculpture by owner and friends; brook with stepping stones; good views of village. Last opening before we move. Sculpture workshop Fri. Gravel paths.
& ✗ ❀ ☕

CHALK COTTAGE
See Dorset.

10 CHISENBURY PRIORY
East Chisenbury SN9 6AQ. Mr & Mrs John Manser, 07810 483984, john.manser@shaftesbury.co.uk. *3m SW of Pewsey. Turn E from A345 at Enford then N to E Chisenbury, main gates 1m on R.* Cream teas. **Adm £3, chd free. Sun 17 June (2-6). Visitors also welcome by appt.**
Medieval Priory with Queen Anne face and early C17 rear (not open) in middle of 5-acre garden on chalk; mature garden with fine trees within clump and flint walls, herbaceous borders, shrubs, roses. Moisture-loving plants along mill leat; carp pond, orchard and wild garden, many unusual plants.
& ✗ ❀ ☕

CLAVERTON MANOR
See Somerset & Bristol Area.

11 NEW COCKSPUR THORNS
Berwick St James, Salisbury SP3 4TS. Stephen & Ailsa Bush, 01722 790445, stephenjdbush@ukonline.co.uk. *8m NW of Salisbury. S of A303, on B3083 at S end of village.* Home-made teas. **Sat 23, Sun 24 June (2-6). Opening with The Mill House, combined adm £4, chd free. Visitors also welcome by appt at any time.**
1¾-acre garden, redesigned 5yrs ago, featuring roses (which should be particularly colourful in June), herbaceous border, shrubbery, kitchen garden, mature and new trees. Beech, yew and thuja hedgings planted to divide the garden. Special parking for wheelchairs.
& ☕

Herbaceous borders, waterside planting, yew hedges, rambler roses and wild flowers . . .

CONHOLT PARK
See Hampshire.

⑫ CONOCK MANOR
Chirton SN10 3QQ. Mrs Bonar Sykes, 01380 840227. *5m SE of Devizes. Off A342.* Cream teas. **Adm £3, chd free (share to St John's Church, Chirton). Sun 20 May (2-5).** Visitors also welcome by appt June, July & Aug only, for groups of up to 10, no coaches.
Mixed borders, flowering shrubs; extensive replanting incl new arboretum; interesting decorative brickwork with tiled water runnels to replace old borders. C18 house in Bath stone (not open). Trees of interest incl Liriodendron tulipifera, Zelkova, Catalpa and many different magnolias. Some gravel paths.
&. ✕ ⊛ ☕

⑬ ◆ CORSHAM COURT
nr Chippenham SN13 0BZ. Mr James Methuen-Campbell, 01249 701610, www.corsham-court.co.uk. *4m W of Chippenham. S of A4.* House & garden £6.50, chd £3, concessions £5. Garden only £2.50, chd £1.50, concessions £2. Opening days & times vary according to season. Please phone or visit website for details. For NGS: Suns 25 Mar; 15 Apr (2-5.30).
Park and gardens laid out by Capability Brown and Repton. Large lawns with fine specimens of ornamental trees; lily pond with Indian bean trees; spring bulbs; young arboretum; C18 bath house; Elizabethan mansion with alterations.
&. ⊛

⑭ THE COURT HOUSE
Lower Woodford SP4 6NQ. Mr & Mrs J G Studholme. *3m N of Salisbury. On Woodford Valley rd, parallel to A360 & A345.* Home-made teas. **Adm £3, chd free. Sun 17 June (2-6).**
3½-acre garden on the banks of the Avon. Herbaceous borders, waterside planting, yew hedges, rambler roses and wild flowers. Ancient site of Bishop's Palace in the time of Old Sarum.
&. ⊛ ☕

⑮ COURT LANE FARM
Bratton BA13 4RE. Lt Col & Mrs Anthony Hyde. *2m E of Westbury. Off B3098.* Home-made teas. **Adm £2.50, chd free. Sun 10, Mon 11, Thur 14 June (2-6).**
1-acre garden of C17/C18 thatched cottage (not open). On varied levels with mostly informal planting developed over past 33yrs. Lawns and paths lead to hidden areas, features and unusual vistas. Pots, perennials, herbs and shrubs mingle with rambling roses, fruit and vegetables. 70 varieties of hardy geraniums. Numerous trees and wildlife areas. New pond and other recent changes.
✕ ⊛ ☕

⑯ ◆ THE COURTS
Holt BA14 6RR. The National Trust, 01225 782875, www.nationaltrust.org.uk. *2m E of Bradford-on-Avon. S of B3107 to Melksham. In Holt follow NTsigns, park at Village Hall.* **Adm £5, chd £2.50. 17 Mar to 28 Oct (not Weds). For NGS: Wed 16 May; Sun 16 Sept (11-5.30).**
3½ acres of formal gardens divided by yew hedges and raised terraces. Features incl conservatory, lily pond, colour-themed herbaceous borders, pleached limes, Venetian gates and stone ornaments. 3½ acres wild flower and arboretum; many fine trees. C15 house (not open). Small kitchen garden. Some uneven paths; access map available.
&. ✕ ⊛ ☕

CROWE HALL
See Somerset & Bristol Area.

⑰ DAUNTSEY GARDENS
SN15 4HW. *5m SE of Malmesbury. Approach via Dauntsey Rd from Gt Somerford, 1¼m from Volunteer Inn.* Home-made teas at Idover House. **Combined adm £5, chd free. Sun 17 June (2-5).**
☕

THE COACH HOUSE
Col & Mrs J Seddon-Brown
Small walled garden. Herbaceous borders and well-established climbing roses, clematis and other trees and shrubs.
&. ✕

DAUNTSEY PARK WALLED GARDEN
Miss Ann Sturgis
5-acre garden, incl 2-acre walled garden with yew topiary and box-edged gravel paths. Espaliered fruit trees and wide range of organically-grown vegetables. Rebuilt range of greenhouses. Orchard and woodland walk.
&. ✕

IDOVER HOUSE
Mr & Mrs Christopher Jerram
Medium-sized mature garden in established setting with many mature trees incl two large wellingtonias. Spacious lawns, herbaceous borders, formal rose garden; swimming pool garden, duck pond; yew hedge walk to kitchen garden and woodland garden.
&. ✕ ☕

THE OLD POND HOUSE
Mr & Mrs Stephen Love
Informal 1½-acre garden, currently being developed (does it ever stop?); large lily pond, lawns, wild flowers, orchard with path leading to Dauntsey Park Walled Garden. Steep-sided lily pond, unfenced pool.
✕

Informal 1½-acre garden, currently being developed (does it ever stop?) . . .

⑱ NEW DOWNS VIEW
Stockbridge Road, Lopcombe Corner SP5 1BW. Chris & Ross Walker. *7m E of Salisbury. At junction of A30 & A343. Parking 200 metres from junction, on A343.* **Adm £2.50, chd free. Suns 20 May; 8 July (2-6).**
Approx 40m x 30m garden designed, built and planted over the last 4 yrs into a grassed area. Vegetable garden and new fruit trees, decked seating spot and terrace with formal planting, sloping down to more informal part around wildlife pond.
✕ ☕

DYRHAM PARK
See Somerset & Bristol Area.

 EDINGTON GARDENS
BA13 4QF. *4m NE of Westbury. On B3098 between Westbury & West Lavington. Park off B3098 in church car park or in Monastery Rd opp Monastery Garden House.* Home-made teas in Parish Hall. **Combined adm £5, chd free. Sun 17 June (2-6).** Village map marking gardens given to all visitors.

BONSHOMMES COTTAGE
Mr Michael Jones. *Through Old Vicarage garden*
1/4-acre hillside garden with mixed herbaceous, roses, shrubs. Some long-established Japanese knotweed has been retained as a practical feature.

EDINGTON PRIORY
Mr & Mrs R Cooper
4-acre gardens with medieval well, walls and carp lake. Herbaceous borders, kitchen garden and extensive lawns with shrubs and roses.

THE MONASTERY GARDEN
Mr & Mrs Allanson-Bailey
2½-acre garden with many varieties of spring bulbs and shrub roses; 3-acre additional walled garden; medieval walls of national importance. Featured in 'The English Garden'.

THE OLD VICARAGE
Mr J N d'Arcy
2-acre garden on greensand on hillside with fine views. Intensively planted with herbaceous borders, wall borders, gravel garden, small waterfall and shrubs. Arboretum with growing range of unusual trees. Woodland plants, bulbs and lilies, with recently introduced species from abroad. National Collection of evening primroses, with over 20 species.
NCCPG

 ENFIELD
62 Yard Lane, Netherstreet, Bromham SN15 2DT. Graham & Elizabeth Veals, 01380 859303, graham@vealsgd.freeserve.co.uk. *4m NW of Devizes. E off A342 into Yard Lane, garden 1/4m on R. Limited parking.* **Adm £2, chd free. Every Wed & Thur from 2 May to 28 June (10.30-6).** Visitors also welcome by appt.

1/2-acre garden in a quiet location, intensively planted in 4 sections with alpines, shrubs, mini-woodland and herbaceous borders which incl many old favourites as well as several more unusual species.

FAULSTONE HOUSE
Bishopstone SP5 4BQ. Miss Freya Watkinson. *6m SW of Salisbury. Take minor rd W off A354 at Coombe Bissett, after 3m turn S into Harvest Lane 300yds E of White Hart Inn.* **Adm £2.50, chd free. Sun 10 June (2-6).** Separate smaller gardens in large garden surrounding Old Manor House (not open). C14 Defence Tower converted to pigeon loft in C18. Many old-fashioned roses, herbaceous plants (some unusual), vegetable garden. Meadow with river frontage set in rural surroundings, including the Faulstone herd of Belted Galloways.

GANTS MILL & GARDEN
See Somerset & Bristol Area.

Long-established Japanese knotweed has been retained as a practical feature . . .

THE GRANGE
Winterbourne Dauntsey SP4 6ER. Mr & Mrs Rebdi. *4m NE of Salisbury on A338.* Cream teas. **Adm £3, chd free. Sun 27 May (2-6).** Spacious 6-acre garden with R Bourne running through. Clipped box, borders. Laburnum, rose and clematis arched walk, lily pond, vegetable and herb garden. Wild natural area. Restored C17 thatched barn, open. Gravel paths.

♦ GREAT CHALFIELD MANOR
nr Melksham SN12 8NH. Mr & Mrs R Floyd & The National Trust, 01225 782239, patsy@greatchalfield.co.uk. *3m W of Melksham. Take B3107 from Melksham then 1st R to Broughton Gifford. Follow sign for Atworth, turn L for 1m to Manor. Park on grass*

outside. **House & garden £6, garden only £4. Suns Apr to Oct (2-5). Tues to Thurs guided House tours (11-5).** For NGS: Sun 4 Feb (2-4.30) £3.50, chd free; Sun 3 Feb 2008. Garden and grounds of 7 acres laid out 1905-12 by Robert Fuller and his wife to designs by Alfred Parsons, Capt Partridge and Sir Harold Brakspear. Incl roses, daffodils, spring flowers, topiary houses, borders, terraces, gazebo, orchard, autumn border. C15 moated manor (not open) and adjoining Parish Church. Snowdrops and aconites enhance moat walk in early spring.

GREAT SOMERFORD GARDENS
SN15 5JB. *4m SE of Malmesbury. 4m N of M4 between J16 & J17; 2m S of B4042 Malmesbury to Wootton Bassett rd; 3m E of A429 Cirencester to Chippenham rd.* Light refreshments & teas at The Mount House. **Combined adm £4, chd free (share to MIND). Sat 23, Sun 24 June (1.30-5.30).** Medium-sized village, bordered by R Avon, with thriving community, school, pub, post office and general stores. Also has possibly the oldest allotments in the country which are well used. River walk.

CLEMATIS
Dauntsey Road. Mr & Mrs Arthur Scott
Small but active charming village garden created about 18yrs ago. Very well stocked herbaceous borders, shrubs, fruit trees and a pond, with small collection of approx 20 clematis.

1 HOLLOW STREET
Bridget Smith
1/4-acre, next door to Old Maltings. Lilies, penstemon and other assorted perennials.

THE MOUNT HOUSE
Park Lane. Mr & Mrs McGrath
Mostly re-landscaped manor house garden; 3 acres of lawns, herbaceous beds, shrubs, large trees and fruit and vegetable garden. The Mount area leading down to R Avon has been sympathetically replanted. Ancient barn also open.

THE OLD MALTINGS
Hollow Street. Dr & Mrs S Jevons
Front garden with extensive and interesting herbaceous and shrub borders. Behind house is walk down to and across R Avon into conservation area with plantations of native trees and shrubs.

SOMERFORD HOUSE
Mr & Mrs Martin Jones
3-acre garden developed over the last 27yrs which incorporates the original orchard and features roses, shrubs, old wisteria, perennials, rockery and pool, vegetables and soft fruit. Bridge over ha-ha slippery when wet.

Impressive yew topiary and clipped beeches around large lawn; herbaceous and mixed borders ablaze in summer . . .

25 GUYERS HOUSE
Pickwick, Corsham SN13 0PS. Mr & Mrs Guy Hungerford. *4m SW of Chippenham. Guyers Lane signed directly off A4 opp B3109 Bradford-on-Avon turning.* Adm £3, chd free. Sun 24 June (2-5.30).
6-acre garden. Herbaceous borders, yew walks, pleached hornbeam walk. Extensive lawns, ponds, walled garden, rose hoops, climbing and shrub roses; walled kitchen garden, orchard, herbs.

26 HAZELBURY MANOR GARDENS
Wadswick, nr Box SN13 8HX. *5m SW of Chippenham. 5m NE of Bath. From A4 at Box, A365 to Melksham, at Five Ways junction L onto B3109; 1st L, drive immed on R.* Home-made teas. Adm £4.50, chd free. Sun 20 May (2-6).

8 acres Grade II landscaped organic gardens around C15 fortified manor (not open). Impressive yew topiary and clipped beeches around large lawn; herbaceous and mixed borders ablaze in summer; laburnum and lime walkways; rose garden, stone circle and rockery. Walled kitchen garden.

HILL LODGE
See Somerset & Bristol Area.

HILLTOP
See Dorset.

27 HOME COVERT GARDENS & ARBORETUM
Roundway SN10 2JA. Mr & Mrs John Phillips, 01380 723407. *1m N of Devizes. On minor rd signed Roundway linking A361 to A342, 1m from each main rd.* Adm £4, chd free. Visitors welcome by appt.
Extensive garden on greensand created out of ancient woodland since 1960. Situated below the Downs with distant views. Formal borders around the house contrast with water gardens in the valley below. Wide range of trees, shrubs and plants grown for yr-round interest. Mar/Apr camellias, magnolias, erythroniums. May/June rhododendrons, malus, davidia, many flowering trees. July/Aug hydrangeas, eucryphias.

HOMEWOOD PARK HOTEL
See Somerset & Bristol Area.

28 HYDE'S HOUSE
Dinton SP3 5HH. Mr George Cruddas. *9m W of Salisbury. Off B3089 nr Dinton Church.* Adm £3.50, chd free. Sun 27 May (2-5).
3 acres of wild and formal garden in beautiful situation with series of hedged garden rooms. Numerous roses and borders. Large walled kitchen garden, herb garden and C13 dovecote (open). Charming C16/18 Grade I listed house (not open), with lovely courtyard. NT walks around park and lake.

29 ◆ IFORD MANOR
nr Bradford-on-Avon BA15 2BA. Mr & Mrs Hignett, 01225 863146. *7m S of Bath. Off A36, brown tourist sign to Iford 1m. Or from Bradford-on-Avon or Trowbridge via Lower Westwood village (brown signs).* Adm £4.50, chd under 10 free, concessions £4. Easter Mon & Suns Apr & Oct; May to Sept: Tues, Weds, Thurs, Sats,

Suns & Bank Hol Mons (2-5). For NGS: Sun 29 Apr (2-5).
Very romantic award-winning Italian-style terraced garden, listed Grade I, home of Harold Peto 1899-1933; house not open.

30 INWOODS
Farleigh Wick BA15 2PU. Mr & Mrs D S Whitehead. *3m NW of Bradford-on-Avon. From Bath via A363 towards Bradford-on-Avon; at Farleigh Wick, 100yds past Fox & Hounds, R into drive.* Adm £3, chd 50p. Sun 29 Apr (2-6).
5 acres with lawns, borders, flowering shrubs, wild garden, wild flower wood.

31 JOB'S MILL
Crockerton BA12 8BB. The Lady Silvy McQuiston. *1½m S of Warminster. Down lane E of A350, S of A36 roundabout.* Home-made teas. Adm £2.50, chd free (share to Butterfly Conservation). Sun 24 June (2-6).
Delightful medium-sized terraced garden through which R Wylye flows. Herbaceous border and water garden.

32 KEEVIL GARDENS
BA14 6NA. *6m E of Trowbridge, S of A361. All gardens within walking distance, nr W end of Main St. Car park at Fieldhead House.* Combined adm £3.50, chd free. Sun 17 June (2-6).
Quiet village with unspoiled largely C14-C18 main street and C13/14 church.

NEW EDGECOMBE COTTAGE
Madeline & Brian Webb
Thatched cottage with approx ¼ acre of garden lovingly established over the last 15 yrs. Herbaceous borders, varieties of perennials, roses, pergolas and water feature.

FIELDHEAD HOUSE
Peter & Janie Dixon
Recently extended garden of former vicarage set in approx 2 acres. Contains roses, clematis etc with kitchen garden, pond, small orchard, fine hedging and Italianate swimming pool area (viewable but not open).

LONGLEAZE HOUSE
John & Olga Gower Isaac
C18 village farmhouse (not open).
1-acre garden developed over last
8yrs with shrubs, climbers,
species roses, herbaceous
perennials, bulbs etc. Children's
pirate ship.
&. ⚡

1-acre hidden garden sloping down to the upper River Avon and tucked into woodland . . .

33 ♦ **LACKHAM GARDENS**
Lacock SN15 2NY. Wiltshire College
Lackham, 01249 466800,
www.lackhamcountrypark.co.uk. *4m
S of Chippenham. On A350, 7m S of
M4 J17, between Chippenham and
National Trust village of Lacock.* Home-
made teas NGS days. **Adm £2, chd
free, concessions £1.50. Aug (not
Sats) & themed days Mar to Oct
(other adm rates may apply). For
NGS: Suns 17 June; 22 July (10-5
last adm 4).**
Large walled garden, greenhouses,
lawn paths separating plots with variety
of interesting shrubs, vegetables, cut
flowers, bedding and fruit plants.
Pleasure gardens: sensory garden,
ornamental pond, mixed borders,
lawns; woodland walks, laurel maze,
various plant collections. Museum of
Agriculture and Rural Life incl
horticultural equipment. Tractor trailer
and miniature train rides. Special
'Woodcraft in Action' day 22 July.
Students won 2 Gold Medals for show
gardens, Large Gold Medal & Best in
Show for vegetable garden exhibit at
Bath & West Show & at National
Amateur Gardening Show.
&. ⚡ ⊗ NCCPG 🍵

34 ♦ **LACOCK ABBEY
GARDENS**
Chippenham SN15 2LG. The
National Trust, 01249 730459,
www.nationaltrust.org.uk. *3m S of
Chippenham. Off A350.* Follow NT

signs. Use public car park just outside
Abbey. Teas in village. **Adm £2.50,
chd free. Daily 23 Feb to 31 Oct (11-
5.30).** For NGS: Sats, Suns 10, 11,
17, 18 Feb 2007 (11-4); Sats, Suns 9,
10, 16, 17 Feb 2008.
Victorian woodland garden with pond,
botanic garden and exotic tree
specimens. Display of early spring
flowers with carpets of aconites,
snowdrops, crocuses and daffodils.
C13 Abbey with C18 Gothic additions.
&. ⚡ ⊗

35 **LITTLE DURNFORD MANOR**
nr Salisbury SP4 6AH. The Earl &
Countess of Chichester. *3m N of
Salisbury. Just beyond Stratford-sub-
Castle.* Home-made teas. **Adm £3,
chd £1. Suns 22 Apr; 17 June (2-6).**
Extensive lawns with cedars, walled
gardens, fruit trees, large vegetable
garden, small knot and herb gardens.
Terraces, borders, sunken garden,
water garden, lake with islands, river
walks, labyrinth walk.
&. ⊗ 🍵

36 **LITTLETON DREW GARDENS**
SN14 7LL. *6m W of Chippenham. Nr
The Gibb PH on B4039. Car parking
on rd to Littleton Drew and walk down
to Goulters Mill, or drive or walk up to
Barton Cottage.* Home-made teas.
**Combined adm £3.50, chd under 12
free. Easter Sun & Mon 8, 9 Apr; Sun
27 May, Bank Hol Mon 28 May (2-5).**
🍵

BARTON COTTAGE
Littleton Drew. Beryl Willis. *Turn
N off B3095, 2nd cottage on L.
Park opp.*
Small garden surrounding
Elizabethan Cotswold cottage.
Densely planted with many
unusual perennials, topiary, pond
with ferns and small potager incl
espalier apples, standard
redcurrant and gooseberries. Over
70 different clematis.

GOULTERS MILL FARM
The Gibb. Mr & Mrs Michael
Harvey, 01249 782555. *Parking
at top of 300yd drive;
elderly/disabled at the Mill.*
**Visitors also welcome by appt,
for groups of 10+.**
Approx 3/4-acre cottage garden;
mixed perennials, salvias,
eremurus, old-fashioned roses;
water garden, walk through
woodland and wild flower
meadow. Topiary privet and box.
Anemone nemorosa, hellebores,

prunus blossom and some
heathers. Featured in 'Amateur
Gardening'. Gravel paths. Rockery
garden not suitable for disabled.
&. ⚡ ⊗ 🛏

37 **LONG HALL**
Stockton BA12 0SE. Mr & Mrs N H
Yeatman-Biggs. *7m SE of
Warminster. S of A36, W of A303
Wylye interchange.* Cream teas. **Adm
£3, chd free. Sun 27 May (2-5).**
4-acre mainly formal garden. Series of
gardens within a garden with clipped
yews, flowering shrubs, fine old trees,
masses of spring bulbs and fine
hellebore walk. C13 Hall (not open).
&. 🍵

38 **LONGFORD CASTLE**
nr Bodenham, Salisbury SP5 4EF.
The Earl of Radnor. *3m SE of
Salisbury. Turning off A338, entry in
village of Bodenham.* Home-made
teas. **Adm £3, chd free. Sun 24 June
(2-5).**
Woodland wild garden, parterre now
converted to perennial garden, walled
kitchen garden and shady garden.
Gardens backed by Longford Castle
(1592) and encompass stretches of
Hampshire Avon and R Ebble.
&. 🍵

39 **MALLARDS**
Chirton SN10 3QX. Tim & Jenny
Papé, 01380 840593,
jennypape@tiscali.co.uk. *41/2 m SE of
Devizes. Just N of A342. Through
village, garden on R.* **Adm £2.50, chd
free. Fris 11 May; 8, 22 June; 6 July
(2-5). Visitors also welcome by appt
May, June & July for individuals &
groups. No coach access.**
1-acre hidden garden sloping down to
the upper R Avon and tucked into
woodland. Waterside and miniature
dell, woodland glade and walk, rose
garden, herbaceous borders and
gravel bed, all informally planted with
many unusual plants and with careful
use of colour.
&. ⚡ ⊗

40 **MANOR FARM**
Huish SN8 4JN. Mr & Mrs J Roberts.
*3m NW of Pewsey. Huish is signed
from A345 by White Hart PH in Oare.
Follow lane for 1m into Huish, turn R
by dead-end sign.* Home-made teas.
**Adm £3, chd free. Suns 20 May; 10
June (2-5).**
Evolving garden in fine downland
setting. Featuring woodland pond,
gravel garden, standing stones and

grotto. Good variety of clematis, herbaceous beds, shrubs, wisteria, clipped hedging and pleached lime walk. Interesting collection of trees planted in the last 13yrs. Landscaped farmyard with stocked duck pond and thatched granary. Some narrow paths; pond walk not suitable for wheelchairs.

  ⚧ 🐈 🍵

41 MANOR HOUSE
Stratford Tony SP5 4AT. Mr & Mrs H Cookson, 01722 718496, lucindacookson@care4free.net. *4m SW of Salisbury. Take minor rd W off A354 at Coombe Bissett. Garden on S after 1m.* Home-made teas. **Adm £3, chd free. Fris 18 May; 15 June; 7 Sept (2-5).** Visitors also welcome by appt.
Varied 4-acre garden. Formal and informal areas, small lake fed from R Ebble, herbaceous beds with spring to autumn colour, pergola-covered vegetable garden, parterre garden, orchards, shrubberies, interesting mature and newly-planted trees, many contemporary features (gazebo, fountain, gates, sculptures). Sitting areas to enjoy both external and internal views. Featured in 'Wiltshire Life'.

  ⚧ 🐈 ⚙ 🍵

42 MANOR HOUSE FARM
Hanging Langford SP3 4NW. Miss Anne Dixon. *9m NW of Salisbury. S of A36 Salisbury to Warminster rd. 3m SE of A303 Wylye interchange. Follow signs from Steeple Langford. Ample parking.* Home-made teas in village hall. **Adm £3, chd free. Sun 1 Apr (2-6).**
C14/C16 Wiltshire manor house (not open). Series of gardens within traditional Wiltshire 'hats and boots' walls, containing herbaceous plants, clematis, wisteria and ponds. 250yr-old Bramley apple tree. Secret garden in walls of shearing barn. Orchard with shrubs incl tree peonies. Unusual daffodil and tulip species. Lovely riverside walk to teas. Some gravel paths.

  ⚧ ⚙ 🍵

43 ◆ THE MEAD NURSERY
Brokerswood, nr Rudge BA13 4EG. Mr & Mrs S Lewis-Dale, 01373 859990, www.themeadnursery.co.uk. *3m W of Westbury. E of Rudge. Follow signs for Country Park at Brokerswood. Halfway between Rudge & Country Park.* Adm £2.50, incl home-made

teas, NGS day only. **Weds to Sats & Bank Hol Mons Feb to mid Oct (9-5); Suns (12-5); closed Easter Sun & 15 Aug.** For NGS: **Sun 19 Aug (12-5).** 1¼-acre nursery and garden giving ideas on colour and design with herbaceous borders, raised alpine beds, sink garden and bog bed. Well-drained Mediterranean-style raised bed and small wildlife pond. Nursery with extensive range of herbaceous perennials, alpines, pot-grown bulbs and grasses. Featured in 'Wiltshire Life'.

  ⚧ 🐈 ⚙ 🍵

6 years ago our garden did not exist . . . imagination, hard work and good soil have provided what you see today . . .

44 THE MILL HOUSE
Berwick St James SP3 4TS. Diana Gifford Mead. *8m NW of Salisbury. S of A303 on B3083, S end of village.* Home-made teas (not NGS, 1 Apr in Hanging Langford Village Hall). **Adm £2.50, chd free. Sun 1 Apr; Sat 23, Sun 24 June (2-6). Opening with Cockspur Thorns 23, 24 June, combined adm £4, chd free.**
Come and see R Till (SSSI) and old unspoilt water meadow (under countryside stewardship). Over 100 species of old-fashioned roses and amazing climbers in trees. May be water vole and dragonflies in pond. Variety of spring flowers and daffodils.

  ⚧ 🚶 🍵

45 ◆ MOMPESSON HOUSE
The Close, Salisbury SP1 2EL. The National Trust, 01722 335659, www.nationaltrust.org.uk. *Enter Cathedral Close via High St Gate, Mompesson House on R.* **Garden adm £1.50, chd free. Sat to Wed, 24 Mar to 28 Oct, 11-5 (last entry 4.30).** For NGS: **Fri 18 May (11-4).**
The appeal of this comparatively small but attractive garden is the lovely setting in Salisbury Cathedral Close,

with a well-known Queen Anne house. Planting as for an old English garden with raised rose and herbaceous beds around the lawn. Climbers on pergola and walls; shrubs and small lavender walk. Cake stall.

  ⚧ 🐈 ⚙ 🍵

46 NORTH COTTAGE & WOODVIEW COTTAGE
Tisbury Row, nr Tisbury SP3 6RZ. Jacqueline & Robert Baker, Diane McBride. *12m W of Salisbury. From A30 turn N through Ansty, L at T-junction, towards Tisbury. From Tisbury take Ansty rd. Entrance nr junction signed Tisbury Row.* Home-made teas. **Adm £2.50, chd free. Sun 3 June (2-6). Evening Opening, wine, teas & light refreshments Sun 1 July (5-9).**
Two cottage gardens divided into rooms, designed and developed over many yrs to incl fruit and vegetable areas, greenhouses and allotment. 4-acre smallholding containing orchard, ponds and coppice wood. Attractive perennial and annual planting provides season-long colour and variety. Various water features. Craft stall with pottery, jewellery & lace-making demonstration. Smoke-fired pottery demonstration (July only).

  🐈 ⚙ 🍵

47 NEW OAK TREE COTTAGE
Hisomley, Dilton Marsh BA13 4DB. Chris & Pam Good. *2m SW of Westbury. Signs from A36, A350 & A3098. Single track roads, parking on grass.* Home-made teas. **Adm £2.50, chd free. Wed 16 May; Sun 9 Sept (2-5).**
6 yrs ago our garden, vegetable garden and orchard did not exist. Imagination, hard work and good soil have provided what you see today. The garden around the house leads to over 50 old apple varieties in the orchard; then enjoy the view as you walk to the fledgling vineyard.

  ⚧ 🐈 ⚙ 🍵

48 OARE HOUSE
Rudge Lane, nr Pewsey SN8 4JQ. Mr Henry Keswick. *2m N of Pewsey. On Marlborough Rd (A345).* Home-made teas. **Adm £3, chd free (share to Order of St John). Suns 22 Apr; 22 July (2-6).**
Fine house (not open) in large garden

with fine trees, hedges, spring flowers, woodlands; extensive lawns and kitchen garden. Partial wheelchair access, some steps and gravel paths.

49 THE OLD MALTHOUSE
Lower Westwood BA15 2AG. Simon & Amanda Relph, 01225 864905. *2m SW of Bradford-on-Avon. Take B3109 S, R to Westwood at 1st Xrds after leaving Bradford-on-Avon; 300yds past The New Inn on R.* Home-made teas 24 June only. **Adm £2.50, concessions £2, chd 50p (share to Tulsi Trust). Suns 13 May (2-6); 24 June (2-5.30). Visitors also welcome by appt.**
1 acre. At front, small garden with unusual water feature. To the side, long border against N-facing wall with mainly white flowering shrubs and herbaceous plants. Through the wall to 3 garden rooms: lawn surrounded by shrubs; another small lawn with semi-circular flame border facing splendid magnolia across pond; gravel courtyard with 6 island beds, 2 lily ponds and sculptured water feature enclosed by rose-covered pergola on two sides. Featured on Radio Wilts.

50 THE OLD MILL
Ramsbury SN8 2PN. Mr & Mrs James Dallas. *5m NE of Marlborough. From W go down High St, bear R at The Bell, signed Hungerford. Garden behind yew hedge on R 100yds beyond The Bell.* **Adm £3.50, chd free. Weds 16 May; 13, 27 June; 12 Sept (2-5).**
Garden in grounds of disused mill house on R Kennet. Mill stream, millrace and pool take up nearly 1/2 acre of 5 acres. Side streams, criss-crossed by bridges, meander through mixture of wild and cultivated area. Nr house, colour-themed borders, gravelled areas full of unusual plants; an exciting blend of traditional and contemporary features, in keeping with peaceful and pretty setting. New features for 2007. Featured in 'The English Garden'.

51 THE POUND HOUSE
Little Somerford SN15 5JW. Mr & Mrs Michael Baines, 01666 823212. *2m E of Malmesbury on B4024. In village turn S, leave church on R. Car park on R before railway bridge.* Home-made teas & wine. **Adm £2.50, chd free. Sun 10 June (3-7). Visitors**

also welcome by appt May to Sept, for any number.
Large garden surrounding former rectory. Mature trees, hedges and spacious lawns. Well-stocked herbaceous borders, roses, shrubs, pergola, parterre, swimming pool garden, water, ducks, chickens and alpacas.

PRIOR PARK LANDSCAPE GARDEN
See Somerset & Bristol Area.

52 RIDLEYS CHEER
Mountain Bower SN14 7AJ. Mr & Mrs A J Young, 01225 891204, antonyoung@ridleyscheer.co.uk. *9m WNW of Chippenham. At The Shoe, on A420 8m W of Chippenham, turn N then take 2nd L & 1st R.* Home-made teas. **Adm £3.50, chd under 14 free. Suns 15 Apr; 13 May; 10 June (2-6). Visitors also welcome by appt.**
1 1/2-acre informal garden with unusual trees and shrubs, incl acers, liriodendrons, magnolias, daphnes, hellebores, hostas and euphorbias. Over 125 different rose varieties incl hybrid musks, albas, tree ramblers and species roses, planted progressively over past 36yrs; also potager, miniature box garden, 2-acre arboretum planted 1989, and 3-acre wild flower meadow. Starred garden in GGG. Alternative wheelchair exit to avoid grass slope.

53 THE RIVER HOUSE
Avoncliff, nr Bradford-on-Avon BA15 2HB. Marian McNeir, 01225 865066. *2m W of Bradford-on-Avon. By car: from B-on-A up Jones Hill, turn R at Avoncliff sign, down to canal and park by tearoom. By train: 10 mins from Bath Spa and 2 mins from B-on-A, Avoncliff is a request stop. By bicycle and on foot: along canal towpath. Limited parking in Avoncliff so alternative methods recommended.* Home-made teas. **Adm £3, chd free. Thurs 14, 21 June (2-6). Visitors also welcome by appt June to Aug, for individuals & small groups. No coaches.**
Former mill (not open) with creatively planted, well established gardens on sloping site between canal and river. The river garden has lovely views of the Avon and the weir, and the hillside garden has lush planting and interesting vistas. Lily pond, bantams and, with luck, kingfishers. Small old-fashioned vegetable and soft fruit

garden. Prizewinner W Wilts garden award, featured in 'Bath Life'. Easy access to river garden, steep slopes & bridge to hillside garden. Not suitable for small children because of river.

Lush planting and interesting vistas. Lily pond, bantams and, with luck, kingfishers . . .

54 SHARCOTT MANOR
nr Pewsey SN9 5PA. Captain & Mrs D Armytage, 01672 563485. *1m SW of Pewsey. Via A345 from Pewsey towards Salisbury. Turn R signed Sharcott at grass triangle. 400yds up lane, garden on L over cattle-grid.* Home-made teas. **Adm £3, chd under 14 free. Sun 1 Apr (2-6); Weds (11-5) 4 Apr; 2 May; 6 June; 4 July; 1 Aug; 5 Sept. Sun 9 Sept (2-6). Visitors also welcome by appt at any time for small groups & coaches.**
6-acre plantsman's garden on greensand with water, planted for yr-round interest. Mature trees, many climbers and tree roses. Densely-planted mixed borders of shrubs, roses and perennials with unusual plants. Woodland walk round 1/3-acre lake. Carpeted with narcissi in spring. Raised kitchen garden. Small collection of ornamental waterfowl. Wheelchair access to tea area and part of garden. Some gravel paths and grass slopes.

55 ◆ SHELDON MANOR
nr Chippenham SN14 0RG. Kenneth & Caroline Hawkins, 01249 653120, www.sheldonmanor.co.uk. *1 1/2m W of Chippenham. Take A420 W. 1st L signed Chippenham RFC, entrance approx 1/2m on R.* Light refreshments & teas Suns 20 May, 24 June only. **House (only open Suns) & garden £8, garden only £4.50, chd under 12 free. Thurs & Suns Easter to 1 Oct (2-4). For NGS: Suns 20 May; 24 June & every Thurs 24 May to 28 June (2-4).**
Wiltshire's oldest inhabited manor

house with C13 porch and C15 chapel. Gardens with ancient yews, mulberry tree and profusion of old-fashioned roses blooming in May and June. BBC TV location for Jane Austen's *Persuasion*. Featured in 'Lifestyle', 'The English Home' & 'Brides'.

56 NEW 32 SHURNHOLD
Melksham SN12 8DG. Alvin & Judith Howard, 01225 704839, bolingbroke.design@tinyworld. co. uk. *1/4m W of Melksham. On A365 nr George Ward School.* Adm £2.50, chd free. Suns 20 May; 17 June; 15 July (2-6). Visitors also welcome by appt all-yr, for up to 20 visitors.
Eccentric 1/3-acre garden featuring Japanese, Roman and French styles. Incl Chinese pavilion, Gothic summerhouse, Tudor tree house, permanent tent, fernery, rose garden, ponds, fountains and water features. Short steep drive, gravel paths.

SHUTE FARM
See Dorset.

SNAPE COTTAGE PLANTSMAN'S GARDEN
See Dorset.

SPECIAL PLANTS
See Somerset & Bristol Area.

57 ◆ STOURHEAD GARDEN
Stourton BA12 6QD. The National Trust, 01747 841152, www.nationaltrust.org.uk. *3m NW of Mere on B3092.* Follow NT signs. Garden only £6.60, chd £3.60, family £15.80. House & garden £11, chd £5.50, family £26.20. Garden daily all yr. House 17 Mar to 28 Oct 11.30-4.30, closed Weds & Thurs. For NGS: Sat 23 June (9-7).
One of the earliest and greatest landscape gardens in the world,

creation of banker Henry Hoare in 1740s on his return from the Grand Tour, inspired by paintings of Claude and Poussin. Planted with rare trees, rhododendrons and azaleas over last 250yrs. Buggy and shuttle available.

TROSSACHS DRIVE
See Somerset & Bristol Area.

Chinese pavilion, Gothic summerhouse, Tudor tree house, permanent tent . . .

58 WATERDALE HOUSE
East Knoyle SP3 6BL. Mr & Mrs Julian Seymour, 01747 830262. *8m S of Warminster. N of East Knoyle, garden signed from A350.* Home-made teas. Adm £3, chd free. Sun 6 May (12-6). Visitors also welcome by appt.
4-acre mature woodland garden with rhododendrons, azaleas, camellias, maples, magnolias, ornamental water, bog garden, herbaceous borders. Bluebell walk.

WESTON HOUSE
See Dorset.

59 WINDMILL COTTAGE
Kings Road, Market Lavington SN10 4QB. Rupert & Gill Wade, 01380 813527. *5m S of Devizes.* Turn E off A360 1m N of West Lavington, 2m S of Potterne. At top of hill turn L into Kings Rd, L into Windmill Lane after 200yds. Limited parking. Adm £2.50, chd free. Wed 30 May; Fris 8, 22 June; 6, 20 July (1.30-5.30). Visitors also welcome by appt late May to July only.

1-acre cottage-style garden on greensand. Mixed beds and borders with long season of interest, roses on pagoda, large vegetable patch for kitchen and exhibition at local shows, polytunnel and greenhouse. Whole garden virtually pesticide free for last 11yrs.

60 WORTON GARDENS
SN10 5SE. *3m SW of Devizes. A360 Devizes to Salisbury, turn W in Potterne or just N of West Lavington. From Seend turn S at Bell Inn, follow signs to Worton. Access to car park on High St, opp school.* Home-made teas. Combined adm £4, chd free. Sun 8 July (2-6).

ASHTON HOUSE
Mrs Colin Shand
1/2-acre garden in 3 sections with herbaceous borders, many shrubs and birch grove; walled courtyard, small gravel garden and raised vegetable garden. House burnt down before 2006 opening but garden being fully maintained while house is rebuilt. Featured in 'Garden News'. Short flight of steps into garden.

BROOKFIELD HOUSE
Mr & Mrs Graham Cannon
1-acre part-walled garden with mixed borders and separate fruit and vegetable garden, rose garden and fine views.

THE GRANGE
Mr & Mrs Simon Jacobs
11/2-acre garden in 5 sections. Box hedging, pond garden, herbaceous borders, unusual trees and walled kitchen garden. Rose garden, lawns and fine views around early C17 timber-framed house (not open). Some gravel paths.

Wiltshire County Volunteers
County Organisers
Mr & Mrs Sean Magee, Byams House, Willesley, Tetbury, Glos GL8 8QU, 01666 880009, sean@magees.demon.co.uk
Assistant County Organisers
Mrs David Armytage, Sharcott Manor, Pewsey SN9 5PA, 01672 563485
Mrs Robert Coate, Colts Corner, Upper Woodford, Salisbury SP4 6PA, 01722 782365
Mrs Anthony Heywood, Monkton House, Monkton Deverill BA12 7EX, 01985 844486
Mrs Colin Shand, Ashton House, Worton, Devizes SN10 5RU, 01380 828866

ngs gardens open
for charity

Talking about garden
descriptions my son says
'Our garden has really
lovely flowers, but I don't
get my dinner for hours
hours and hours . . . !'

Bridge Farm House, Yorkshire

WORCESTERSHIRE

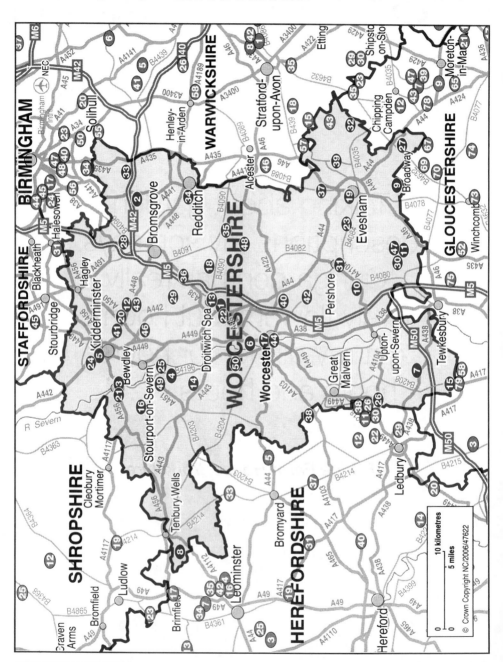

Opening Dates

February

SATURDAY 3
17 The Greyfriars

WEDNESDAY 14
12 Dial Park

THURSDAY 15
12 Dial Park

March

SUNDAY 25
26 Little Malvern Court

SATURDAY 31
48 White Cottage

April

SUNDAY 1
12 Dial Park
23 Holland House
48 White Cottage

FRIDAY 6
40 Spetchley Park Gardens

SUNDAY 8
32 4 Poden Cottages
46 Whit Lenge Gardens

MONDAY 9
15 Gadfield Elm House
32 4 Poden Cottages
46 Whit Lenge Gardens

TUESDAY 10
49 The White House

SUNDAY 15
48 White Cottage

MONDAY 16
48 White Cottage

SUNDAY 22
1 24 Alexander Avenue
10 1 Church Cottages
25 Little Larford

SATURDAY 28
16 Gladderbrook Farm
44 The Walled Garden

SUNDAY 29
3 The Antiquary
25 Little Larford
38 Shuttifield Cottage
48 White Cottage

May

SATURDAY 5
48 White Cottage

SUNDAY 6
46 Whit Lenge Gardens
48 White Cottage

MONDAY 7
26 Little Malvern Court
46 Whit Lenge Gardens
48 White Cottage

SATURDAY 12
13 Dorset House
38 Shuttifield Cottage
44 The Walled Garden

SATURDAY 19
48 White Cottage

SUNDAY 20
16 Gladderbrook Farm
28 Marlbrook Gardens
37 St Egwins Cottage
48 White Cottage
99 24 Braces Lane
99 Saranacris

WEDNESDAY 23
37 St Egwins Cottage

THURSDAY 24
35 Red House Farm

SATURDAY 26
38 Shuttifield Cottage
44 The Walled Garden
48 White Cottage

SUNDAY 27
3 The Antiquary
4 Astley Towne House
10 1 Church Cottages
21 High Bank
27 Luggers Hall
32 4 Poden Cottages
39 South Littleton Gardens
46 Whit Lenge Gardens
47 Whitcombe House
48 White Cottage

MONDAY 28
15 Gadfield Elm House
32 4 Poden Cottages
39 South Littleton Gardens
46 Whit Lenge Gardens
48 White Cottage

June

SATURDAY 2
34 88 Rectory Road
48 White Cottage

SUNDAY 3
22 Hiraeth
34 88 Rectory Road
48 White Cottage

WEDNESDAY 6
19 Harrells Hardy Plants Nursery
Garden

SATURDAY 9
5 27 Avill Grove
13 Dorset House
38 Shuttifield Cottage

44 The Walled Garden
50 Worlds End Nurseries

SUNDAY 10
1 24 Alexander Avenue
2 Alvechurch Gardens
5 27 Avill Grove
7 Birtsmorton Court
23 Holland House
31 Pershore Gardens
32 4 Poden Cottages
50 Worlds End Nurseries

WEDNESDAY 13
37 St Egwins Cottage

SATURDAY 16
48 White Cottage

SUNDAY 17
10 1 Church Cottages
14 Eastgrove Cottage Garden
Nursery
16 Gladderbrook Farm
19 Harrells Hardy Plants Nursery
Garden
43 Tythe Barn House
47 Whitcombe House

WEDNESDAY 20
22 Hiraeth

SATURDAY 23
33 Pump Cottage
38 Shuttifield Cottage
44 The Walled Garden

SUNDAY 24
4 Astley Towne House
21 High Bank
24 Honeybrook House Cottage
27 Luggers Hall
32 4 Poden Cottages
37 St Egwins Cottage

TUESDAY 26
33 Pump Cottage

WEDNESDAY 27
18 Hanbury Hall
37 St Egwins Cottage

FRIDAY 29
22 Hiraeth (Evening)

SATURDAY 30
3 The Antiquary
45 Westacres

July

SUNDAY 1
2 Alvechurch Gardens
15 Gadfield Elm House
45 Westacres
48 White Cottage

TUESDAY 3
33 Pump Cottage

SATURDAY 7
5 27 Avill Grove

SUNDAY 8
5 27 Avill Grove
6 Beckett Drive Gardens
20 Harvington Hall
28 Marlbrook Gardens
40 Spetchley Park Gardens
(99) 24 Braces Lane
(99) Saranacris

WEDNESDAY 11
22 Hiraeth
37 St Egwins Cottage

THURSDAY 12
1 24 Alexander Avenue (Evening)

SATURDAY 14
34 88 Rectory Road
38 Shuttifield Cottage
42 The Tynings (Evening)
44 The Walled Garden

SUNDAY 15
16 Gladderbrook Farm
19 Harrells Hardy Plants Nursery Garden
34 88 Rectory Road
50 Worlds End Nurseries

SUNDAY 22
24 Honeybrook House Cottage
37 St Egwins Cottage

WEDNESDAY 25
37 St Egwins Cottage

SUNDAY 29
1 24 Alexander Avenue
3 The Antiquary
4 Astley Towne House
22 Hiraeth
42 The Tynings

August

WEDNESDAY 1
37 St Egwins Cottage

SUNDAY 5
19 Harrells Hardy Plants Nursery Garden
21 High Bank

WEDNESDAY 8
8 Burford House Gardens
37 St Egwins Cottage

SUNDAY 12
22 Hiraeth
28 Marlbrook Gardens
(99) 24 Braces Lane
(99) Saranacris

SATURDAY 18
38 Shuttifield Cottage

SUNDAY 19
16 Gladderbrook Farm
24 Honeybrook House Cottage

SATURDAY 25
48 White Cottage

SUNDAY 26
4 Astley Towne House
46 Whit Lenge Gardens
48 White Cottage

MONDAY 27
9 The Chase
15 Gadfield Elm House
46 Whit Lenge Gardens
48 White Cottage

September

SUNDAY 2
19 Harrells Hardy Plants Nursery Garden

SATURDAY 8
28 Marlbrook Gardens (Evening)
48 White Cottage
(99) 24 Braces Lane
(99) Saranacris

SUNDAY 9
16 Gladderbrook Farm
48 White Cottage

SATURDAY 22
48 White Cottage

SUNDAY 23
48 White Cottage

Gardens open to the public

8 Burford House Gardens
14 Eastgrove Cottage Garden Nursery
17 The Greyfriars
18 Hanbury Hall
19 Harrells Hardy Plants Nursery Garden
20 Harvington Hall
26 Little Malvern Court
36 Riverside Gardens at Webbs of Wychbold
40 Spetchley Park Gardens
41 Stone House Cottage Gardens
46 Whit Lenge Gardens
48 White Cottage
50 Worlds End Nurseries

By appointment only

11 Conderton Manor
29 New House Farm
30 Overbury Court

Free-range rare breed hens add charm to this tranquil oasis . . .

The Gardens

1 24 ALEXANDER AVENUE

Droitwich Spa WR9 8NH. Malley & David Terry, 01905 774907, terrydroit@aol.com. *1m S of Droitwich. Droitwich Spa towards Worcester A38.Or from M5 J6 to Droitwich Town centre.* **Adm £3, chd free. Suns 22 Apr; 10 June; 29 July (2-6). Evening Opening £4, wine, Thur 12 July (6-9). Visitors also welcome by appt.**
40 x 10metres garden is a lesson in what can be done in a small space. Turning a barren patch of grass into a paradise. High hedges, clad with clematis from the 100+ varieties grown, obscure views of neighbouring houses. Borders filled with dazzling array of interesting plants, many rare. Fine collection of ferns. Alpines grow in stone troughs and gravel garden. 'A garden of immaculate artistry'. Viticella clematis (July). Featured in 'Amateur Gardening' & GGG.

2 ALVECHURCH GARDENS

B48 7LP, 0121 445 4335. *3m N of Redditch, 3m NE of Bromsgrove. From Bromsgrove M42 J2 (Hopwood) L on A441 to next island L B4120 signed Alvechurch. From Redditch A441 to Bordesley Island on B4120 signed Alvechurch. From Birmingham, Kings Norton A441 to island at bottom of Hopwood Hill. 2nd exit signed B4120 Alvechurch.* Light refreshments & teas. **Combined adm £5, chd free. Suns 10 June; 1 July (2-6pm).**
Large village - much new development but interesting core - buildings spanning medieval to Edwardian - church on hill. Approx 15 gardens of diverse character and size. Maps.

THE BARN
John & Jill Alexander
3/4-acre open aspect garden with borders and island beds, variety of shrubs. Large natural pool with summerhouse and jetty.

We had a mallard sitting on eggs in our hanging basket. Many visitors were concerned about how the ducklings would get out . . .

NEW 38 BEAR HILL
Mark & Kathy Collinson
Professionally landscaped terraced garden comprising several themed areas with wide variety of colours and styles, which incl a series of arches, patios and water features.

1A BLYTHESWAY
John & Lorna Sage
Large front garden, bordering 2 sides of bungalow. Mixture of varieties of shrubs and herbaceous perennials, with overall effect of being a cottage garden. Small enclosed courtyard with container plants.

NEW 40 BRANDEN ROAD
Ann Griffiths
Corner front garden, lawned with mainly roses, conifers, perennials and annuals.
&

28 CALLOW HILL ROAD
Martin & Janet Wright
Flat rear garden designed to appear larger than it is, with curving paths, views through archways, shrub borders, herbaceous border, pond, waterfall and rockery. Front garden mix of shrubs, perennials and rockery with similar aim.
⊕

NEW THE COACH HOUSE
School Lane. Lynne Clark
Small partially walled, L-shaped garden on 2 levels overlooking church, with a feature non-varital vine across the house. Partially raised beds with cottage plants.
⊕

HILL COTTAGE
Scarfield Hill. Philip & Elisabeth Aubury
1/2-acre informal garden surrounding Victorian house (not open). Planted for yr-round interest, colour, scent and to encourage wildlife. Small pool and water feature, shrub and

herbaceous borders. Fruit and vegetable gardens, field meadow.
& ✕ ⊕

NEW THE OLD SWAN
9 Swan Street. Ray Yarnell. *Opp The Swan PH*
Cottage garden divided between blue brick yard with lots of colour in pots. Rear garden with winding path between deep mixed borders and interesting modern features.
✕

RECTORY COTTAGE
Celia & Steve Hitch
Riverside garden with established trees and borders, secret garden, ducks and moorhens, bog garden to be constructed. Courtyard garden with many climbers and colourful containers. Kitchen garden with 2 greenhouses, fruit and vegetables. We had a mallard sitting on eggs in our hanging basket. Many visitors were concerned about how the ducklings would get out - they managed it successfully. Steep garden in areas by river.
& ✕ ▐▀▌

NEW SUNNYMEAD
Station Road. Anne & Andy Humphries
Wrap around informal garden with shrubs, herbaceous borders and fruit trees. Beautiful views.
&

19 RED LION STREET
Mrs E A Waters. *Access down alleyway/right of way behind Georgian terrace cottages*
Long garden. New owner 8yrs ago, cleared own and next door's site in order to re-landscape. New features added each yr incl herbaceous borders, pool and summerhouse.
✕ ⊕

30 RED LION STREET
Val James
Cottage garden, small water feature.

NEW 29 TANYARD LANE
Kate & Peter Glover
Cottage style garden incl clematis, roses, raised vegetable beds, espalier fruit trees, sundeck, patio, swing and sunsail together with seasonal pots in a walled setting.
& ✕

NEW 31 TANYARD LANE
Peter & Eileen McHugh
Small partly walled garden, with shrubs, perennials, conifers and roses. Pots with annual colour and topiary are a feature of this fairly new garden.
&

③ NEW THE ANTIQUARY
48 High Street, Bewdley DY12 2DJ. Karen Raine. *3m W of Kidderminster. (B4194) Bewdly Centre. Follow signs to garden parking in Gardener's Meadow car park by the river.* Light refreshments & teas. **Adm £2.50, chd free (share to Brambles Trust). Suns 29 Apr; 27 May; Sat 30 June; Sun 29 July (12-4).**
Hidden away behind unassuming High St. Frontage 200ft SW facing walled town house garden with 4 distinct rooms separated by wisteria pergola and jasmine arch. Herbaceous garden, pond, herb garden, developing meadow, orchard area and vegetable plot. Free-range rare breed hens add charm to this tranquil oasis. 2nd place Bewdley in Bloom.
✕ ☕

④ ASTLEY TOWNE HOUSE
Astley DY13 0RH. Tim & Lesley Smith, 01299 822299. *3m W of Stourport-on-Severn. On B4196 Worcester to Bewdley Road.* Home-made teas. **Adm £3, chd free. Suns 27 May; 24 June; 29 July; 26 Aug (1-5). Visitors also welcome by appt.**
2 1/2 acres incl sub-tropical planting. Winding paths through jungle garden incorporating bananas, palms and many other rare and exotic plants. Stumpery garden with many tree ferns and woodland temple. Tree top high safari lodge, revolving classical summerhouse and stone columns with statuary. Featured in Historic Gardens of Worcestershire by Timothy Mowl.
⊕ ☕

5 **27 AVILL GROVE**
Kidderminster DY11 5DJ. Chris & Carol Cox. *1m N of Kidderminster town centre. Off A442, R into Marlpool Lane beside Jacksons PH & 2nd R approx 250yds. Limited parking in cul de sac.* Home-made teas. **Adm £2, chd free. Sats 9, Suns 10 June; 7, 8 July (11-5).**
Compact urban garden, front garden, rich mixture of herbaceous planting and small trees. Cool shady courtyard with lush foliage under canopy of golden *Robinia*. Creative use of steep rear garden, consisting of enclosed room, with seating arches, container plants and trees. Terraced vegetable plot, small greenhouse with Hydroponic units and propagation house.
🌿 😳 ☕

6 **BECKETT DRIVE GARDENS**
Northwick WR3 7BZ. *1½m N of Worcester city centre. Cul-de-sac off A449 Ombersley Rd directly opp Granthams garage, 1m S of Claines roundabout on A449.* Home-made teas at 6 Beckett Drive. **Combined adm £2.50, chd free. Sun 8 July (10-5).**
Two individual but contrasting gardens both with an abundance of plants and interesting design ideas.
☕

5 BECKETT DRIVE
Jacki & Pete Ager
Intriguing design ideas and something of interest around every corner. Flowerbeds are stocked with shrubs, perennials and alpines in a landscaped setting. The garden incls some unexpected and surprising features. Featured in 'Amateur Gardening'.
🌿 😳

6 BECKETT DRIVE
Guy Lymer
Eclectic mix of planting, modern sculpture and water features with lighting for each. Established shrubs for yr-round interest are complemented by exotic plants, ornamental grasses and a natural arbour.
🌿

7 **BIRTSMORTON COURT**
nr Malvern WR13 6JS. Mr & Mrs N G K Dawes. *7m E of Ledbury. On A438.* Home-made teas. **Adm £4, chd free. Sun 10 June (2-6).**
Fortified manor house (not open) dating from C12; moat; Westminster pool, laid down in Henry VII's reign at time of consecration of Westminster Abbey; large tree under which Cardinal Wolsey reputedly slept in shadow of ragged stone; white garden. Newly planted potager; topiary.
&. 🌿 ☕

8 ◆ **BURFORD HOUSE GARDENS**
Tenbury Wells OX18 4PA. Burford Garden Company, 01584 810777, www.burford.co.uk. *1m W of Tenbury Wells. 8m from Ludlow on A456.* **Adm £3.50, chd £1. Daily Mons to Suns Jan to Dec. For NGS: Wed 8 Aug (9-6).**
The 7 acres of Burford House gardens sweep along the banks of the picturesque R Teme. Originally designed by the late John Treasure in 1952 around early Georgian house (now containing an Interior furnishings shop), the gardens contain National Collection of clematis. Giant *Wisteria macrobotrys* 'Burford' and around 2000 other kind of plants.
🌿 😳 NCCPG ☕

CAVES FOLLY NURSERY
See Herefordshire.

9 **THE CHASE**
Old Hall Close, School Road, Aston Somerville WR12 7JN. Karen & Mike Fesemeyer, 01386 853442, fesey@aol.com. *2m W of Broadway. Entering Aston Somerville Village from A46 Evesham to Cheltenham Rd there is a 90° RH-bend past village hall. Continue straight for approx 200yds passing Broadway Rd at Old Hall Close. Entrance to garden from School Rd. Garden on LH-side. Parking on site.* Home-made teas. **Adm £2.50, chd free. Mon 27 Aug (2-5pm). Visitors also welcome by appt, for groups of 20+, coaches permitted, refreshments by arrangement.**
Superb 6-acre parkland garden with 2-acre lake stocked with specimen carp, and natural wildlife haven. Formal

lawns, knot garden, fernery, bamboo, gunnera and exotic plants, wooded wild area, yew maze and bluebell wood. Stunning 6ft copper chinese dragon and lifesize male lion. Undergoing continual planting and enhancement by current owners. Featured in 'Gloucestershire Echo' and on BBC Gloucestershire Radio.
🌿 😳 ☕

10 **1 CHURCH COTTAGES**
Church Road, Defford WR8 9BJ. John Taylor. *3m SW of Pershore. A4104 Pershore to Upton rd. Turn into Defford. Black & white cottage at side of church. Parking in village hall car park.* Home-made teas. **Adm £3, chd free. Suns 22 Apr; 27 May; 17 June (11-5).**
True countryman's ⅓-acre garden, interesting layout. Specimen trees; water features; vegetable garden; aviary, poultry; cider making. Featured in 'Amateur Gardening'.
🌿 ☕

11 **CONDERTON MANOR**
nr Tewkesbury GL20 7PR. Mr & Mrs W Carr, 01386 725389, carrs@conderton.wanadoo.co.uk. *5½m NE of Tewkesbury. On Bredon - Beckford rd or from A46 take Overbury sign at Beckford turn.* **Adm £4. Visitors welcome by appt.**
7-acre garden with magnificent views of Cotswolds. Flowering cherries and bulbs in spring. Formal terrace with clipped box parterre; huge rose and clematis arches mixed borders of roses and herbaceous plants, bog bank and quarry garden. Many unusual trees and shrubs make this a garden to visit at all seasons.
&. 🌿

12 **DIAL PARK**
Chaddesley Corbett DY10 4QB. David & Olive Mason, 01562 777451, olivemason@btinternet.com. *4½m from Kidderminster, 4½m from Bromsgrove. On A448 midway between Kidderminster & Bromsgrove. Limited parking at garden, or park in village or at village hall.* Home-made teas. **Adm £2.50, chd free. Wed 14, Thur 15 Feb (11-4); Sun 1 Apr (2-5). Visitors also welcome by appt, all yr-round for groups & individuals, coaches permitted.**
Approx ¾-acre garden in rural setting in conservation area on edge of attractive village. Large collections of snowdrops, antique daffodil varieties and hardy ferns. Very wide range of

Stunning 6ft copper chinese dragon and lifesize male lion . . .

plants planted for yr-round interest. Small collection of country tools and bygones. Featured in 'Garden News' & 'Garden Style'.

🏃 ⊛ ☕

⑬ DORSET HOUSE
Blackfriars Avenue, Droitwich Spa WR9 8DR. AgeCare, 01905 772710, www.agecare.org.uk. *S side of Droitwich Spa town centre off The Saltway. From M5 J6 to Droitwich Spa on A38. Residential Care Home. Elderly & Frail.* Teas. **Adm £2.50, chd free. Sats 12 May; 9 June (2.30-430).** Colourful 3-acre garden situated in the grounds of a care home. Numerous flower beds and borders, containing many unusual perennials and shrubs. Interesting combination of vegetables and fruit in borders. Sensory garden with water feature. Prize winner Droitwich in Bloom. Gravel paths.

& 🏃 ☕

Small collection of country tools and bygones . . .

⑭ ◆ EASTGROVE COTTAGE GARDEN NURSERY
Sankyns Green, Shrawley WR6 6LQ. Malcolm & Carol Skinner, 01299 896389, www.eastgrove.co.uk. *8m NW of Worcester. On rd between Shrawley (B4196) & Great Witley (A443). Follow brown tourist signs to Sankyns Green.* Teas (NGS day only). **Adm £4, chd free. Thurs to Sats 26 Apr to 14 July, 6 Sept to 6 Oct, Bank Hols incl Mons (May). For NGS: Sun 17 June (2-5).**
32nd year of opening for unpretentious garden surrounded by ancient cloud hedge and comprising many intimate areas, winding brick paths, great (alpine) wall of china, red hot lloydian area, long blue, white and yellow border. Inspired planting invites quiet sitting. 2 acre arboretum with wide ride. Winding paths and grass labyrinth. Excellent nursery. Wild flowers in glade.

& 🏃 ⊛ ☕

⑮ GADFIELD ELM HOUSE
Malvern Road, Staunton GL19 3PA. Canon & Mrs John Evans, 01452 840302. *7m W of Tewkesbury. 12m S of Malvern. 1m from Staunton Cross on the Malvern Rd (B4208). 2m SE J2 M50.* Home-made teas. **Adm £2, chd free. Mons 9 Apr; 28 May; 27 Aug; Sun 1 July (2-6). Visitors also welcome by appt.**
Garden created over 25yrs from scratch. Vistas, temples, statues, herbaceous borders. Field walk with view of Malverns, Bredon Hill and the Cotswolds. Rare breed poultry. Gravel paths.

& ☕

⑯ GLADDERBROOK FARM
High Oak, Heightington DY12 2YR. Mike & Sue Butler, 01299 879923, sue.butler4@btinternet.com. *3m W of Stourport-on-Severn. Take A451 from Stourport. At Dunley turn R signed Heightington. After 2m turn R signed High Oak follow rd for 3/4 m. Park at High Oak Farm by kind permission of Mr & Mrs T Sprague.* Garden 100yds down lane. Teas. **Adm £3, chd free. Sat 28 Apr; Suns 20 May; 17 June; 15 July; 19 Aug; 9 Sept (12-5pm). Visitors also welcome by appt also groups.**
Plantsman's 1-acre graden on heavy clay with stunning views, developed from a field since 2001. Unusual trees, shrubs, perennials and grasses. 2-acre spring wild flower meadow, developing arboretum, small orchard, vegetable plot, water feature and nursery with unusual plants for sale. Stout shoes advisable.

🏃 ⊛ ☕

⑰ ◆ THE GREYFRIARS
Friar Street, Worcester WR1 2LZ. The National Trust, 01905 23571, greyfriars@nationaltrust.org.uk. *In Friar Street within the centre of Worcester. Please use city car parks.* **Adm £1.50 (incl NT members), chd free. For NGS: Sat 3 Feb (12-4).**
Delightful city garden created from the clearance of back to back housing. An archway leads through to the walled garden containing a beautiful display of spring bulbs incl snowdrops and daffodils.

🏃 ⊛ ☕

⑱ ◆ HANBURY HALL
School Road, Droitwich WR9 7EA. The National Trust, 01527 821214 Neil Cook. *3m NE of Droitwich. 6m S of Bromsgrove. Signed off B4090 and*

B4091. **Adm £4.50, chd £2.25. For NGS: Wed 27 June (11-4).**
Re-creation of C18 formal garden by George London. Parterre, fruit garden and wilderness. Mushroom house, orangery and Ice house, William and Mary style house dating from 1701. Opportunity to meet the gardeners and to see behind the scenes in the walled garden.

& 🏃 ⊛ ☕

⑲ ◆ HARRELLS HARDY PLANTS NURSERY GARDEN
Rudge Road, Evesham WR11 4JR. Liz Nicklin & Kate Phillips, 01386 443077, www.harrellshardyplants.co.uk. *1/4 m from centre of Evesham. From High St turn into Queens Rd opp Catholic church. Turn R at end of Queens Rd, then L into Rudge Rd. Approx 150yds on R is a small lane to nursery gardens.* **Adm £2.50, chd free. Open Suns 10-12noon, & private visits. For NGS: Wed 6 June (10-12); Suns 17 June; 15 July; 5 Aug; 2 Sept (2-5).**
Informal 1 acre garden on W-facing slope overlooking cricket ground and R Avon. Large collections of hemerocallis, grasses and hardy perennials, many unusual. Jewel bed, bog garden, prairie border, sunshine bed and new for 2007 'cottage garden corner'. Featured in 'Gloucestershire Echo', 'Worcestershire Life' & on UK Style Gardens 'Nations Favourite Blooms'.

🏃 ⊛ ☕

⑳ ◆ HARVINGTON HALL
Harvington DY10 4LR. The Roman Catholic Archdiocese of Birmingham, 01562 777846, www.harvingtonhall.com. *3m SE of Kidderminster. 1/2 m E of A450 Birmingham to Worcester Rd & about 1/2 m N of A448 from Kidderminster to Bromsgrove.* **House and Garden adm £5, chd £3.50, concessions £4.30, Garden only £2, chd 50p. Weds to Suns Apr to Sept; w/ends Mar & Oct, Bank Hols. For NGS: Sun 8 July (11.30-4.30).**
Romantic Elizabethan moated manor house with island gardens. Small Elizabethan-style herb garden, tended by volunteers from the Hereford and Worcs Gardens Trust. The main Hall gardens are looked after by volunteers who 'adopt' a bed. Tours of the Hall, which contains secret hiding places and rare wall paintings, are also available.

& 🏃 ⊛ ☕

21 HIGH BANK
Cleobury Road, Bewdley DY12 2PG.
Stuart & Ann McKie. *3¹/₂ m W of*
Kidderminster. A456. ¹/₂ m W of
Bewdley town centre on B4190
(signed Tenbury). Parking available opp
garden entrance. Home-made teas.
Adm £2.50, chd free. Suns 27 May;
24 June; 5 Aug (11-5).
Beautiful garden approx ¹/₃-acre with
many old and protected trees.
Restored in keeping with Edwardian
house (not open). Featuring original
summerhouse, rhododendrons and
azaleas (May). Large collection of
roses, herbaceous borders, courtyard
garden, pergola walk and water
features. Garden is still being
developed. Winner large private garden
category of Bewdly in Bloom.
🖈 ❀ ☕

22 HIRAETH
30 Showell Road, Droitwich
WR9 8UY. Sue & John Fletcher,
07752 717243 / 01905 778390,
jfletcher@inductotherm.co.uk. *1m S*
of Droitwich. On The Ridings estate.
Turn off A38 roundabout into Addyes
Way, 2nd R into Showell Rd, 500yds
on R. Home-made teas. **Adm £2.50,**
chd free. Suns, Weds 3, 20 June; 11,
29 July; 12 Aug (Sun 2-6), (Wed 12-
5). Evening Opening £4.50, wine,
Fri 29 June (6.30-9). Visitors also
welcome by appt.

Woodland walk with numerous bird boxes and viewpoint overlooking cottage towards Severn valley . . .

Traditional cottage garden at rear
incorporating pool, waterfall feature,
200yr-old wooden stile and oak
sculptures. Time is needed to inspect
the collection of herbaceous plants,
hostas, ferns and other new and
unusual varieties. Front garden
contains numerous trees, shrubs and
ornamental barrels, rose arch.
🖈 ❀ ☕

23 HOLLAND HOUSE
Main Street, Cropthorne WR10 3NB.
Mr Peter Middlemiss. *5m W of*
Evesham. Equidistant between
Evesham and Pershore. Travel on
B4084 (old A44) & take turning signed
Cropthorne village centre (on R from
Evesham, on L from Pershore). Follow
road round to R & then Holland House
car park signed to the L. Please park in
the car park & not on the rd. **Adm £3,**

chd free. Suns 1 Apr; 10 June (2-5).
Formal gardens laid out by Lutyens in
1904 with rose garden; thatched
house dating back to C16 (not open).
Lovely riverside setting with banks of
early daffodils in March and roses in
June.
🖈 ☕

24 NEW HONEYBROOK
HOUSE COTTAGE
Honeybrook Lane,
Kidderminster DY11 5QS. Gerald
Majumdar, 01562 67939,
www.cottagegarden.org.uk.
1¹/₂ m N of Kidderminster. On A442
leaving Kidderminster towards
Bridgnorth, 300yds from the island
at the Three Crowns & Sugar Loaf
PH turn R into Honeybrook Lane.
Cream teas. **Adm £3, chd free.**
Suns 24 June; 22 July; 19 Aug
(11-5). Visitors also welcome by
appt.
Large country garden developed
since 2003, approx 2-acres incl N-
facing slope. Paths connect the
cottage garden, woodland, prairie
garden, shade borders, wildlife
pond and borders, brook and long
tree lined walk. Many seating
areas, pergola, gazebos, viewing
deck and beautiful views.
🖈 ❀ ☕

KILIMA LODGE
See Herefordshire.

25 LITTLE LARFORD
Scots Lane, Astley Burf DY13 0SB.
Lin & Derek Walker, 01299 823270.
3m W of Stourport-on-Severn. Take
A451 from Stourport, turn L onto
B4196 for Worcester. After 1m turn L
signed Larford Lakes. Garden approx
1¹/₂ m further on. Access via Larford
Lane or Seedgreen Lane. Home-made
teas. **Adm £2.50, chd free. Suns 22,**
29 Apr (12-5). Visitors also welcome
by appt.
Hillside ¹/₂-acre garden surrounding
picturesque thatched cottage (not
open) in woodland setting. 'Tulip and
Daffodil Time' - many thousands of
tulips and daffodils in ambitious
bedding displays amongst shrub and
herbaceous borders. Colourful

containers and hanging baskets, cut
flower and vegetable garden,
glasshouse and frames. Woodland
walk with numerous bird boxes and
viewpoint overlooking cottage towards
Severn valley. Featured in 'Garden
News'.
🖈 ❀ ☕

26 ◆ LITTLE MALVERN COURT
Little Malvern WR14 4JN. Mrs T M
Berington, 01684 892988. *3m S of*
Malvern. On A4104 S of junction with
A449. **Adm £4, chd 50p. Weds &**
Thurs 18 Apr to 19 July (2.15-5). For
NGS: Sun 25 Mar; Mon 7 May (2-5).
10 acres attached to former
Benedictine Priory, magnificent views
over Severn valley. Intriguing layout of
garden rooms and terrace round
house designed and planted in early
1980's; water garden below feeding
into chain of lakes; wide variety of
spring bulbs, flowering trees and
shrubs. Notable collection of old-
fashioned roses. Topiary hedge and
fine trees.
🖈 ❀ ☕

THE LONG BARN
See Herefordshire.

LONGACRE
See Herefordshire.

27 LUGGERS HALL
Springfield Lane, Broadway
WR12 7BT. Kay & Red Haslam. *5m S*
of Evesham. Turn off Broadway High
St by Swan Hotel, bear L into
Springfield Lane. Luggers Hall is on the
L approx 300yds along. Some parking
but limited - if possible use car parks
which are close by. Cream teas. **Adm**
£3, chd free. Suns 27 May; 24 June
(2-6).
2¹/₂-acre formal garden originally
designed by the famous Victorian
garden artist Alfred Parsons. Features
incl rose garden; parterre; walled
garden; potager; white garden; koi
pool and herbaceous borders, all
connected by gravel paths with seating
areas. An abundance of clipped box
and yew hedging; plus Victorian hazel
walk. Children with caution due to
deep water feature. Gravel paths.
♿ ❀ 🛏 ☕

28 MARLBROOK GARDENS
Bromsgrove B60 1DY,
www.marlbrookgardens.com. *2m N*
of Bromsgrove. 1m N of M42 J1,
follow B4096 signed Rednal, turn L at
Xrds into Braces Lane. 1m S of M5 J4,

Louise Adams, Garden Owner, Photographer

LABOUR OF LOVE

WHY LOUISE ADAMS WANTS TO SHARE THE MAGIC OF HER GARDEN WITH OTHERS

As a child, our family garden in Chichester was a beautiful place to play in. Giant Crack Willows with their trunks rotting away creating secret hideaways, usually used for escaping from older brothers. Rocky outcrops and boggy areas were the perfect places to search for those illusive fairies.

But it was the summer of 1979 that changed my view of gardening. Moving to East Dean with the family, I was immediately struck by the beauty of the surrounding countryside. Evening sunlight cast long shadows on the hill, a beautiful backdrop to our new garden at Roundhill Cottage which, at the time, consisted of a few old apple trees, shrubs, and mainly laid to lawn. But it had a magic. My parents spent months digging up flint and builders' rubble.

My mother was a passionate gardener. We went to many Yellow Book gardens, enthused by Sissinghurst, Hidcote, Beth Chatto's garden and West Dean, where Ivan Hicks would chat about planting ideas. The garden was taking shape (it had taken 11 years to design) when my mother died in her prime at 51. I was 27 and living down the lane so was able to help with the gardening. Working as a photographer on a newspaper I was able to gain knowledge while photographing Sussex gardens.

All my spare time was spent reading about and visiting gardens and specialist nurseries, watching gardening programmes and making annual trips to Chelsea and Hampton Court flower shows.

I have definitely inherited my mother's passion for gardening. I feel so privileged to have a profession which allows me to expand my hobby. Press work is so eclectic; photographing Pierce Brosnan or ballooning are exciting highlights, but walking through a farmer's field of roses for a feature was like entering a Monet painting, just intoxicating and magical.

By opening the garden under the NGS I hope people will be inspired, as I am when visiting other gardens. It gives me the incentive to create new structures and design schemes so visitors who come year after year can see new ideas.

Garden Roundhill Cottage, Sussex
Photographs Louise Adams

Neil Lucas, Garden Owner, Nurseryman and Chelsea Gold Medal Winner

EVERYTHING
IN THE GARDEN

INDIVIDUAL CHARACTER IS WHAT MAKES A
GOOD GARDEN STAND OUT

I have always loved plants. Right from my earliest memories of
going with my mother to buy yet another individual pansy from the
local shop, subsequently taking it proudly back to the collection in
my own part of the family garden, I have been captivated by their
incredible beauty and adaptability.

As a teenager, my summers were spent with my grandfather
in his garden helping tend his collection of over 2,000
hybrid delphiniums, which would literally stop traffic in
the nearby road when in full bloom. To see the annual
miracle of, in this case, a delphinium go from a clump
of rather un-pretty dormant roots to a towering spike of
fabulous flower in only a few months gave me a thrill that
has to this day never paled.

Now that I have grown up (well, a bit anyway), my interest
has widened to include the use of plants in a garden
setting. No longer am I content just to collect plants; I want
to know where and how to use them to best effect. One plant
is still very beautiful to me, but several of them growing together
happily with neighbours that together make a contribution to the
garden scene is even more satisfying.

As a garden opener I am frequently asked what makes a garden,
what are the most important elements that must be included?

To me a garden is essentially a community; a combination
of different elements that have to grow together to make
the whole thing work. So what do all the most memorable
communities (human or plant), have in common?
They have a make-up or character that makes them distinct.
That almost indefinable 'something', that is recognisably
different from everyone else.

Garden Knoll Gardens, Dorset
Photography Dianna Jazwinski www.fizzphotos.com

Neil Lucas Knoll Gardens

The gardens I like and remember most are those that have a distinct character of their own. In my view the one essential criteria for success is simply that a garden should have a feel, a character, that defines it as an individual space worth visiting.

Exhibiting at Chelsea is very much like creating a garden. Certainly the effect is comparatively short-term, but essentially we are aiming for the same thing; that 'something' that defines our stand as our individual character. As the exhibit has only to last a very short time we also aim for a high level of the 'wow factor' timed, hopefully, to coincide with the arrival of the judges.

The highs and lows of Chelsea are rather like running a garden for a season, though telescoped into only a few days. There is optimism, occasional despair, and delightful elation when something goes well.

One thing is for certain, as long as I am around I shall continue to get a 'buzz' from what I do; nothing else even begins to come close.

"No longer am I content just to collect plants"

Liz Auld, Garden Owner

ON THEIR DOORSTEP

RESIDENTS RALLY ROUND TO SHOW VISITORS
A **HOME AWAY FROM HOME**

August 2005. "Let's open our gardens for the National Gardens Scheme," she said. "Are you mad?" we said. "No one would want to pay to see our gardens; they aren't good enough."

Little did we know that in July 2006 we would host around 400 visitors and have our gardens photographed for Lancashire Magazine.

The months of planning paid off and we opened as a group of six gardens, which was very much a community event (helped by the glorious sunshine)! The local church opened its doors for people to look around and the Girl Guides made refreshments. Neighbours and friends who were not opening their gardens organised ticket and plant sales. There were activities for children including quizzes, pot-making, catching tadpoles and making crêpes.

There were obvious worries of "will it be in flower?" and "what if I don't know the name of the plant they ask me about?". But, the reality was that people just wanted to admire our gardens – if we didn't know the name of a plant it showed we were human!

The grand finale was a well deserved BBQ, where we reflected on our day and the coming together of our neighbourhood… different ages, different backgrounds, different levels of gardening expertise and six very different gardens!

Garden Wroxham Gardens, Lancashire
Photographs Michael Edwards

Jenny Wood-Hill, Group Co-ordinator

MOVING WITH THE TIMES

YEAR BY YEAR, A SLEEPY VILLAGE WELCOMES RISING NUMBERS OF VISITORS

Each year on a Sunday in June rows of parked cars replace the grazing sheep and horses in two of our local fields as our small, sleepy village between Stratford-on-Avon and the Cotswolds is transformed with over 1,000 visitors. Dorsington has been opening its gardens for the NGS since 1976, when two gardens opened. This has steadily grown to 13 gardens plus an arboretum. Visitors have between 12-5pm to visit, enjoy lunchtime snacks or cakes and tea in one of our two marquees, buy plants from our plant stall, and take provided transport to the out-of-village gardens. Entertainment for the children is also laid on.

Although this is a big enterprise for such a small village, it means that everyone gets roped in to help and so there is a good community spirit on the day! As co-ordinator I don't open my garden, and try to take some administrative pressure off the garden openers. Villagers help with serving the teas, making cakes/sandwiches, selling plants, car parking, manning the church etc. Making so much money for the NGS' charities is a good motivation, in addition to which we keep a proportion for our church which is always in need of more funds.

> "Everyone gets roped in to help and there is a good community spirit"

Garden Dorsington Gardens, Warwickshire

A FLOWER ARRANGER'S TALE

THE UNEXPECTED PATH THAT LED **BRIDGET MARSHALL** TO HER ROLE AS A **COUNTY ORGANISER FOR YORKSHIRE**

Having initially planted our garden in a rather haphazard way to provide foliage for flower arranging, in 1985 I enrolled at Askham Bryan to improve my horticultural knowledge and basic skills. My course leader Miss Galloway described our lawns as "mown herbage" and I knew that there was much to be done and plenty to learn!

Through friendship with the owners of gardens here in Yorkshire, especially York Gate, Ling Beeches and The Manor House and a much loved copy of the Well Tempered Garden by Christopher Lloyd we have created and now open the garden here at The Old Vicarage.

In 1987 I took over from Lady Veale as County Organiser for the old West Riding of Yorkshire and its 20 NGS gardens. Last year, 74 opened for the NGS in my area and over 100 in Yorkshire as a whole.

The NGS provides immense pleasure, not only for the owners who enjoy sharing their gardens and raising money for charity, but also for the thousands of visitors. They can learn so much about the practicality of gardening under difficult conditions, look at plant associations and get ideas for hard landscape and design.

During my years as County Organiser I have been involved with the NGS as a Trustee (liaising with our charities), and as Regional Chairman. As County Organisers we are the link between the garden owners and the NGS management at Head Office and receive invaluable help from our county teams and beneficiary volunteers.

We are always delighted when a new garden is offered to the NGS. Usually the garden is far more impressive than the owner will admit and it is those unexpected moments discovering unknown achievements that are so exciting and make the role of County Organiser a thoroughly enjoyable experience.

Garden The Old Vicarage, Yorkshire
Photographs Bridget Marshall

GROWING SUPPORT

GET OUT AND ABOUT WITH MEMBERS AND VOLUNTEERS OF THE NGS

Every year the NGS pops up all around England and Wales at the garden and flower shows enjoyed by garden owners and garden visitors alike. It's a great time to meet up with old friends and a wonderful opportunity to make new ones. Chelsea wouldn't be Chelsea without the NGS – and even Alan Titchmarsh found time to stop by and say hello. At several Royal Horticultural Society shows – Cardiff, London, Malvern and Tatton Park – our hardworking volunteers could be found selling The Yellow Book, handing out county leaflets and generally spreading their enthusiasm for the NGS. For the first time in 2006 the famous yellow arrows could be seen at the BBC Gardeners' World Live show at the NEC.

With a few sleepless nights behind them, the Devon county team again produced an award-winning display at the Devon County Show. Across England and Wales, the NGS banner went up time after time – at the Harrogate Flower Show, The Royal Norfolk Show, in Hertfordshire, Cornwall, Hampshire and Llangollen, and at events and shows too numerous to mention.

Photograph Wendy Morton

In addition, throughout the year, NGS county team members can be found at local horticultural societies, Women's Institutes, the University of the Third Age and at many other clubs and societies giving slide show talks with wonderful pictures of the gardens.

Of course, you are most likely to come across the NGS and its volunteers at garden openings – there's always something that needs to be done! And we never forget the countless number of volunteers who work to support the NGS behind-the-scenes – treasurers, leaflet co-ordinators and distributors, garden finders and the cake bakers!

Come and meet the NGS – we are always looking for more volunteers. Just contact any of the county team members listed after the garden entries or visit www.ngs.org.uk

"Chelsea wouldn't be Chelsea without the NGS"

Kathy Brown, Garden Owner, Landscape Gardener

THE **HEAT** IS **ON**

THE PERFECT **PLANT CHOICES** FOR A GARDEN WITH LOTS OF **SUN AND LOW RAINFALL**

Certain ornamental grasses seem to cope exceedingly well in our recent hot, dry summers. For early interest, low *Stipa tenuissima* and taller *Stipa gigantea*, are both top choices for a soft fountain effect with *Stipa calamagrostis* 'Karl Foerster' and 'Overdam' offering great contrast for their bolt upright habit. For late summer, I love to plant soft *Pennisetums* and towering *Miscanthus*. Both provide a surge of flowers in September. For edgers, evergreen *Festuca glauca* and *Sesleria caerulea* are excellent. Foliage interest is wonderful right through to March whilst those with seed heads, now old gold, are piercingly beautiful in the low winter sunlight.

Colourful perennials, annuals and bulbs also seem to thrive in our dry summers including *Echinops, Eryngium, Echinacea* (new 'Fatal Attraction' is super), *Perovskia* 'Blue Spire' (also striking for its white winter stems), bronze fennel and *Sedum spectabile* and Californian poppies *Eschscholzia* which self-seed gloriously. *Alliums* such as 'Purple Sensation, 'Karatviense', and 'Unifolium' mix well with the perennials and lower grasses.

For low water requirements with containers, I use tender succulents. I especially enjoy *Echeveria secunda glauca, E. elegans*, or larger *E. gigantea* all with coral pink flowers. Small-leaved *Lampranthus* with peachy pink or burnt orange daisy-like flowers makes a brilliant underplanting to *Agave, Dasylirion* or tall bronze *Aeonium arboreum purpureum*. *Erigeron karvinskianus* can be used to similar effect. Hardy *Sempervivums* are also a good choice and associate well with hardy *Sedums*. Hot sun suits them all. With little need to repot, they just get bigger and better.

Container Recipe: Rosettes & Feathers
Painted terracotta pot 20cm (8") across, 10cm (4") deep
Gritty compost
Plants include:
1 Echeveria elegans
1 Echeveria gigantea
1 Aloe variegata

This is a planting scheme which will mature gracefully over many years in dry sunny conditions having all year round foliage interest, with the bonus of coral pink flowers in late spring and early summer. Enjoy outside in the summer months and on a conservatory window sill (or heated greenhouse) in the winter months.

Garden The Manor House, Stevington, Bedfordshire
Photography Kathy Bown

follow A38 signed Bromsgove, turn L at T-lights into Braces Lane. Car park available. Home-made teas. **Combined adm £4.50, chd free (share to County Air Ambulance). Suns 20 May; 8 July; 12 Aug (1.30-6). Evening Opening £5, wine, Sat 8 Sept (6-9.30).** 'Experience the Difference' in 2007 with another new and contrasting garden added to those open 2006. 4 gardens, from gentle to steeply sloping, with a wide range of plants, gardening styles and features. Sept 8 - why not re-visit us and see gardens under lights.

24 BRACES LANE
Lynn & Alan Nokes, 0121 445 5520, alyn.nokes@virgin.net. **Visitors also welcome by appt, groups of 15+.** Gentle sloping garden (175ft x 38ft) landscaped by owners. Features Mediterranean patio with exotic planting, pond, stream and rockery. Lawned area with borders stocked with shrubs and herbaceous plants. Vegetable garden with raised beds, greenhouses, wildlife pond and views from summerhouse.

OAK TREE HOUSE
504 Birmingham Road. Di & Dave Morgan, 0121 445 3595, davidmorgan@ukonline.co.uk. **Visitors also welcome by appt, groups of 15+.** Well stocked mature plantsman's cottage garden with winding grass paths, water features, secluded patio, garden seating and open vista. For 2007 we've added an alpine area and widened the garden. Also hidden front garden.

🆕 185 OLD BIRMINGHAM ROAD
Bruce Heideman & Sue James Developing organic garden with a mix of traditional and modern planting. Winding path on a gentle slope leads you from the upper garden with its raised koi pond to the large fruit and vegetable garden.

SARANACRIS
28A Braces Lane. John & Janet Morgan, 0121 445 5823, saranacris@btinternet.com. **Visitors also welcome by appt,**

groups of 15+.
Unusual and challenging terraced garden created by owners. 'Jungle Style' planting with dense foliage and profusion of colour. Mature trees, unusual plants, ponds, stream and many other features. Roof garden and conservatory. New for 2007 100sq ft glasshouse planted with exotics.

29 NEW HOUSE FARM
Elmbridge Lane, Elmbridge WR9 0DA. Charles & Carlo Caddick, 01562 851249, carlocaddick@hotmail.com. *2½m N of Droitwich Spa. From Droitwich take A442 to Cutnall Green. Take lane opp The Chequers PH and proceed 1m to T-junction, turning L towards Elmbridge Green & Elmbridge. Continue along lane passing church and church hall. At T-junction turn into Elmbridge Lane, garden on L.* Home-made teas. **Adm £2.50, chd free. Visitors welcome by appt.** Georgian farmhouse garden created around barns and attractive outbuildings. Mature shrub borders, unusual wild pond area with hostas, zantedeschia and many unusual spring bulbs. Recently created raised bed vegetable garden with gravel paths and focal point of an old stone perry wheel. English hand-thrown terracota garden pots.

Winding path on a gentle slope . . .

THE ORCHARDS
See Herefordshire.

30 OVERBURY COURT
nr Tewkesbury GL20 7NP. Mr & Mrs Bruce Bossom, 01386 725111, suzie@overburyestate.co.uk. *5m NE of Tewkesbury. Village signed off A46.* **Visitors welcome by appt adm £2.50, minimum charge for groups of 8+ £20.** Georgian house 1740 (not open); landscape garden of same date with stream and pools; daffodil bank and grotto. Plane trees, yew hedges; shrubs; cut flowers; coloured foliage; gold and silver, shrub rose borders. Norman church adjoins garden.

PEBWORTH & BROAD MARSTON GARDENS
See Warwickshire & part of West Midlands.

31 PERSHORE GARDENS
WR10 1JF. Janet Stott, 01386 555349, janetstott@aol.com. *Centre of Pershore. On the B4084 bet Worcester and Evesham. Gardens located nr to centre of Pershore, in Bridge St, Broad St, High St and a few gardens nr to Abbey Park.* Teas at 8 High Street. **Adm £5, chd free, concessions £4. Sun 10 June (2-6).** A variety of gardens tucked away behind the town houses of Pershore, elegant facades hiding horticultural treasures - tiny courtyards, walled gardens, formal gardens, some sweeping down to the river, and much in between. Tickets and maps can be obtained from Number 8 (8 High St) where teas will be served from 2-4.30pm (last orders).

THE PICTON GARDEN
See Herefordshire.

32 4 PODEN COTTAGES
Honeybourne WR11 7PS. Patrick & Dorothy Bellew, 01386 438996, pots@poden.freeserve.co.uk. *6m E of Evesham. At the Gate Inn take the Pebworth, Long Marston rd, turn R at end of the Village for Mickleton. 1m on Mickleton Rd.* Home-made teas. **Adm £3, chd free. Suns 8, Mons 9 Apr; 27, 28 May (11-6); Suns 10, 24 June (2-6). Visitors also welcome by appt, 8 April until July, groups welcome.** ⅓-acre cottage and rose garden which has been planted by the owners. Grass paths wind through mixed herbaceous borders. 100 different roses old and modern, shrubs, small terrace and pond. Fine views over the Cotswold Hills. All-yr colour. Filmed for Japanese TV.

33 🆕 PUMP COTTAGE
Hill Lane, Weatheroak B48 7EQ. Mr Barry Knee. *3m E of Alvechurch. 1½m from J3 M42 off N-bound c'way of A435 (signed Alvechurch). Parking in adjacent field.* Home-made teas. **Adm £2.50, chd free. Sat 23, Tues 26 June; 3 July (11-5).** C19 cottage, charming plantsman's garden, approx 1 acre, adjoining open fields. Extensively

planted, cottage garden, paths meandering through rockery and water features, romantic area with trees, shrubs and roses. Large natural pool, water lilies, boardwalk, wildlife area. Planted 15yrs ago, being redeveloped. Restricted wheelchair access to some areas, some slopes, steps and uneven ground, access to wc via steps.

🕭 🏃 👄

34 88 RECTORY ROAD
Headless Cross, Redditch B97 4LL. Richard & Carole Poolton. *1m S of Redditch. From A448 take the exit signed Headless Cross, Walkwood etc, turn L at island. Turn opp Archers PH. Rectory Rd on RH-side.* Home-made teas. **Adm £2, chd free. Sats 2, Suns 3 June; 14, 15 July (11-5).**
130ft by 25ft garden at rear of Victorian end terraced property divided into 4 separate, intimate 'rooms'. Created by present owners since 1994. Aromatic courtyard, formal pond in evergreen setting. Tranquil oriental-style garden leading to an area with rockery, grasses and ferns, shrubbery, log garden. Featured in 'Garden Answers'. Winners, Redditch Best Garden 2006.

🏃 👄

THE RED HOUSE
See Gloucestershire North & Central.

35 RED HOUSE FARM
Flying Horse Lane, Bradley Green B96 6QT. Mrs M M Weaver, 01527 821269. *7m W of Redditch. On B4090 Alcester to Droitwich Spa. Ignore sign to Bradley Green. Turn opp The Red Lion PH.* **Adm £2, chd free. Thu 24 May (11-5). Visitors also welcome by appt, all yr.**
1/2-acre plantsman's cottage garden in C18 farmhouse setting. Mixed planting with mature trees, shrubs, roses, herbaceous perennials giving all-yr-round colour and interest. Adjacent nursery open daily.

🏃 ⊛

36 ♦ RIVERSIDE GARDENS AT WEBBS OF WYCHBOLD
Wychbold, nr Droitwich WR9 0DG. Webbs of Wychbold, 01527 860000, www.webbsofwychbold.co.uk. *2m N of Droitwich Spa. 1m N of M5 J5 on A38. Follow tourism signs from motorway.* **Adm free for NGS all yr. Open daily all yr except Christmas &**

Boxing Day & Easter Sun. For opening times please tel or see website.
Riverside gardens occupy 2 1/2-acres of themed gardens incl National Collection of *Potentilla fruticosa*, colour spectrum garden, white garden, dry garden, David Austin roses, grass garden and many others under continual development. The New Wave section opened in 2004; designed by Noel Kingsbury, this area features a series of plantings of naturalised perennials for differing situations. These are both eye catching and wildlife friendly. Once established they will require minimum maintenance.

🕭 🏃 ⊛ **NCCPG** 👄

37 ST EGWINS COTTAGE
1 Church Lane, Norton, Evesham WR11 4TL. Anne & Brian Dudley, 01386 870486. *2m N of Evesham. On B4088. Park in St Egwins Church car park only (not in Church Lane).* Home-made teas at St Egwins Church (Sun only). **Adm £2.50, chd free. Suns 20, Weds 23 May; 13, 24, 27 June; 11, 22, 25 July; Weds 1, 8 Aug (2-5). Visitors also welcome by appt.**
C16 1/2-timbered thatched cottage (not open) in open countryside within conservation area, next to C12 church (open). Mature cottage garden packed with many unusual and traditional plants incl ferns, hardy geraniums, phlox and shrubs for yr-round interest. Small vegetable garden and chickens.

🏃 ⊛ 👄

38 SHUTTIFIELD COTTAGE
Birchwood, Storridge WR13 5HA. Mr & Mrs David Judge, 01886 884243. *8m W of Worcester. Turn R off A4103 opp Storridge Church to Birchwood. After 1 1/4m L down steep tarmac drive. Please park on roadside but drive down if walking is difficult.* Home-made teas. **Adm £3.50, chd free. Sun 29 Apr; Sats 12, 26 May; 9, 23 June; 14 July; 18 Aug (1-5.30). Visitors also welcome by appt.**
Superb position and views. 3-acre garden with extensive herbaceous borders, primula and stump bed, many unusual trees, shrubs and perennials, colour-themed for interest throughout the year. Walks in the 20-acre wood

with ponds and natural wild areas where anemones, bluebells, rhododendrons and azaleas are a particular feature in spring. Large old rose garden with many spectacular mature climbers. Small deer park and vegetable garden.

🏃 ⊛ 👄

39 SOUTH LITTLETON GARDENS
nr Evesham WR11 8TJ. Lady Harford, 01386 830478, carolynharford@aol.com. *4m NE of Evesham. On B4085. Car parking and toilets on recreation ground. Transport provided to outlying gardens.* Light refreshments & teas. **Combined adm £4.50, chd free. Sun 27, Mon 28 May (12-6).**
Group of gardens around South Littleton, in the heart of the beautiful Vale of Evesham - and again by popular request, the allotments, with 15-20 plots under cultivation. Gardens vary in size and character from the traditional to the unusual - a great way to spend the Bank Hol. Coaches welcome. Map of gardens provided in programme.

🏃 ⊛ 👄

40 ♦ SPETCHLEY PARK GARDENS
nr Worcester WR5 1RS. Mr R J Berkeley, 01453 810303, www.spetchleygardens.co.uk. *2m E of Worcester. On A44.* **Adm £6, chd free, concessions £5.50. Weds to Suns & Bank Hols Mons Mar to end Sept 11-6 last entry 5; Sats, Suns Oct 11-4. For NGS: Fri 6 Apr; Sun 8 July (11-6 last entry 5).**
30-acre garden containing large collection of trees; shrubs and plants, many rare and unusual. Red and fallow deer in nearby park. A wonderful display of spring bulbs, but masses of colour throughout spring and summer. Every corner of this beautiful garden reveals some new vista, some new treasure of the plant world.

🕭 🏃 👄

STANTON GARDENS
See Gloucestershire North & Central.

Paths meandering through rockery and water features, romantic area with trees, shrubs and roses . . .

41 ◆ **STONE HOUSE COTTAGE GARDENS**
Stone DY10 4BG. James & Louisa Arbuthnott, 01562 69902, www.shcn.co.uk. *2m SE of Kidderminster. Via A448 towards Bromsgrove, next to church, turn up drive.* **Adm £3, chd free. Weds to Sats mid Mar to mid Sept (10-5).**
A beautiful and romantic walled garden adorned with unusual brick follies, exuberantly and richly planted. Holds one of the largest collections of rare plants in the country. Adjacent nursery, climbers a speciality.

42 **THE TYNINGS**
Church Lane, Stoulton, nr Worcester WR7 4RE. John & Leslie Bryant, 01905 840189, johnlesbryant@onetel.com. *5m S of Worcester; 3m N of Pershore. On the B4084 (formerly A44) between M5 J7 & Pershore. The Tynings lies beyond the church at the extreme end of Church Lane. Ample parking.* Home-made teas. **Adm £3, chd free. Sun 29 July (2-5). Evening Opening £4,** wine, Sat 14 July (6-8.30). Visitors also welcome by appt, also groups mid May to mid Aug.
Plantsman's 1/2-acre garden in a rural setting with views of Stoulton Church, generously planted with unusual shrubs and trees. Island beds, herbaceous borders and water features contain a large collection of species and hybrid lilies (member of RHS Lily Group), euphorbias and ferns. Tree ferns, bamboos and a bog garden add to the surprises round every corner. Planting list available. WC.

43 **TYTHE BARN HOUSE**
Chaddesley Corbett DY10 4QB. Judy & John Berrow, 01562 777014, j.berrow@virgin.net. *41/2m from Bromsgrove; 41/2m from Kidderminster. On A448. 150yds towards Kidderminster from the turn into Chaddesley Corbett village. Parking in village (The Talbot & Swan PH) or at village hall (200 yds). Walking difficulties park in private lane.* Home-made teas. **Adm £2.50, chd free. Sun 17 June (2-5.30pm).** Visitors also welcome by appt, June & July only, groups of 10+. Parking space for coach.
3/4-acre romantic garden created in old farm rickyard, within old farm building complex in conservation area. Incl old and modern roses; herbs and

herbaceous borders. Small terrace garden. Shrubs and trees together with a small vegetable plot. Lovely view of the church and surrounding countryside.

Romantic garden created in old farm rickyard, within old farm building complex in conservation area . . .

44 **THE WALLED GARDEN**
6 Rose Terrace, off Fort Royal Hill, Worcester WR5 1BU. Julia & William Scott, 01905 354629, herbgarden@onetel.com. *1/2m from cathedral. Via Fort Royal Hill, off London Rd (A44). Park on first section of Rose Terrace & walk the last 20yds down track.* **Adm £2, chd free. Sats 28 Apr; 12, 26 May; 9, 23 June; 14 July (1-5).** Visitors also welcome by appt.
A hidden peaceful oasis in the city. C19 walled kitchen garden restored to life in 1995. It is undergoing continuing restoration and change. Herbs, flowers, fruit and vegetables, organically grown, provide a tapestry of colour and scent.

45 **WESTACRES**
Wolverhampton Road, Prestwood DY7 5AN. Mrs Joyce Williams. *3m W of Stourbridge. A449 in between Wall Heath (2m) & Kidderminster (6m). Parking Beechwood Bonsai (next door).* Light refreshments & teas. **Adm £2.50, chd free. Sat 30 June; Sun 1 July (11-5).**
Semi rural 3/4-acre formal garden with raised koi pool, leading to areas with collections of hostas, ferns, acers and newly planted woodland. Conifer and ornamental grass beds. Plenty of places to sit, relax and have a cup of tea and cake.

46 ◆ **WHIT LENGE GARDENS**
Hartlebury DY10 4HD. Mr & Mrs K J Southall, 01299 250720, www.whit-lenge.co.uk. *5m S of Kidderminster. Take A449 from Kidderminster towards Worcester, then A442 (signed Droitwich) over small island, 1/4m, 1st R into Whitlenge Lane. Follow signs.* **Adm £2, chd free. Open all yr except Christmas, Mon to Sat (9-5), Sun (10-5). For NGS: Suns 8, Mons 9 Apr; 6, 7, 27, 28 May; 26, 27 Aug (Sun 10-5 - Mon 9-5).**
3 acre show garden of professional designer with over 800 varieties of trees, shrubs etc. Twisted pillar pergola, camomile lawn, waterfalls and pools. Mystic features of the Green Man, 'Sword in the Stone' and cave fernery. Walk the labyrinth and take refreshments in 'The Old Potting Shed' tearoom.

47 **WHITCOMBE HOUSE**
Overbury, nr Tewkesbury GL20 7NZ. Faith & Anthony Hallett, 01386 725206. *9m S of Evesham. 9m N of Cheltenham, 5m E of Tewkesbury. Signed Overbury take A46 at Beckford Inn or at roundabout junction of A46, A435 & B4077 take small lane signed Overbury or take Bredon rd out of Tewkesbury. In village turn up hill, garden 1st on L before village hall.* Home-made teas. **Adm £3, chd free, concessions £2.50. Suns 27 May; 17 June (2-5).** Visitors also welcome by appt Apr to Sept, coaches welcome, groups up to 50.
Garden set in 1-acre of walled garden. Large herbaceous borders, set among old fruit trees, weeping beech and magnificent Indian Bean tree, give shape and height. Shrubberies, countless roses and more raised beds beside gravel paths and high walls complement the air of informality and colour. A stream runs swiftly over waterfalls through the garden under the Captain's Bridge and is surrounded on all sides with primulas, arums and marginals. Allow plenty of time to relax and enjoy the tranquillity and variety, lots of plants available too and delicious teas. 27 May Art & Craft Fair being held at village hall.

48 ◆ **WHITE COTTAGE**
Stock Green, nr Inkberrow B96 6SZ. Mr & Mrs S M Bates, 01386 792414, cranesbilluk@aol.com. *2m W of Inkberrow, 2m E of Upton Snodsbury. A422 Worcester to Alcester, turn at*

brown sign for Cottage Garden also Stock Green, 1½m to T- junction, turn L. **Adm £2, chd free, concessions £1.50. Fris to Tues 18 Mar to 30 Sept (10-5). By appt in Aug. For NGS: Sats, Suns, Mons 31 Mar; 1, 15, 16, 29 Apr; 5, 6, 7, 19, 20, 26, 27, 28 May; 2, 3, 16 June; 1 July; 25, 26, 27 Aug; 8, 9, 22, 23 Sept (10-5pm).** 2 acres, herbaceous and shrub beds, stream and spring wild flower area, rose garden, raised woodland bed, large specialist collection of hardy geraniums. Adjacent nursery.

♿ ❒ ⟢ ☕

⑳ THE WHITE HOUSE
Dunley, nr Stourport-on-Severn DY13 0UF. Tony & Linda Tidmarsh. *2m W of Stourport. Take A451 from Stourport-on-Severn towards Great Witley. Dunley 1st village, follow signs to car park.* **Adm £2, chd free. Tue 10 Apr (1-5).** Classical-style garden divided by yew hedges, shrub borders and brick walls into separate gardens around a central lawn. Various features celebrate events in the owners' family. Italian garden contains cascade made of copper. 4 pools, one incorporating the girls' entrance to Tipton Board School. Pretty spring flowers. Featured in Historic Gardens of Worcestershire by Timothy Mowl.

♿

Italian garden contains cascade made of copper . . .

㊿ 🆕 ♦ WORLDS END NURSERIES
Moseley Road, Hallow WR2 6NJ. Kristina & Robin Pearce, 01905 640977, www.worldsendgarden.co.uk. *4m NW of Worcester. At Hallow PO follow lane to Sinton Green. Ignore L turn to Wichenford, garden next on R.* **Adm £2.50, chd free. Tues to Sats June, July, Sept 11-4. For NGS: Sat 9, Suns 10 June; 15 July (11-5).** ³/₄-acre garden developed over last 3yrs, reflects the passions of its owners. An extensive range of herbaceous plants, grasses, ferns especially hostas with over 200 varieties. Garden laid out to mixed borders, with clearly labelled plants. New rill garden planted last year is still in progress.

♿ ❎ ☕

Worcestershire County Volunteers

County Organiser
Judy Berrow, Tythe Barn House, Chaddesley Corbett DY10 4QB, 01562 777014, j.berrow@virgin.net

County Treasurer
Cliff Woodward, 11 Trehernes Drive, Pedmore, Stourbridge DY9 0YX, 01562 886349

Publicity
Richard Armitage, 11 Myatts Field, Harvington, Evesham WR11 8NG, 01386 871211

Leaflet Coordinator
Alan Nokes, 24 Braces Lane, Marlbrook, Bromsgrove B60 1DY, 0121 445 5520, alyn.nokes@virgin.net

Assistant County Organisers
Mike George, 55 Hawkwood Crescent, Worcester WR2 6BP, 01905 427567
Jeanie Neil, Viewlands, Blakeshall, Wolverley, Kidderminster DY11 5XL, 01562 850360, theviewlands@aol.com

Tucked away in the heart of the city, this 'secret' walled garden is full of trees, shrubs, organic vegetables and herbaceous perennials, with a pond and many quirky and fun features. In Victorian times it was a market garden supplying cut flowers to Brighton's shops . . . now it's a delightful surprise . . .

The Garden House, Sussex

YORKSHIRE

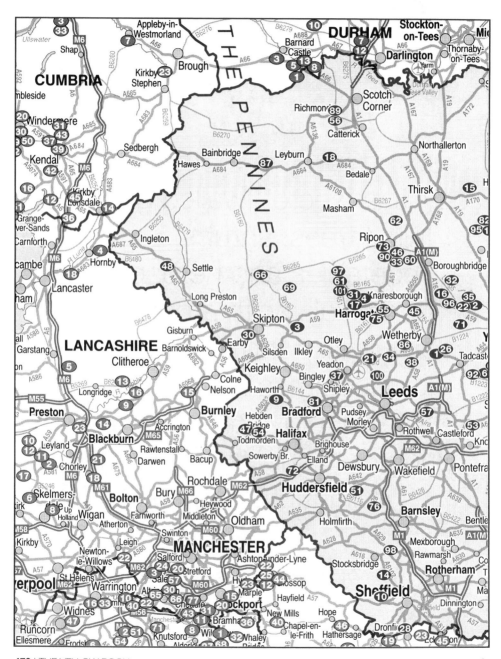

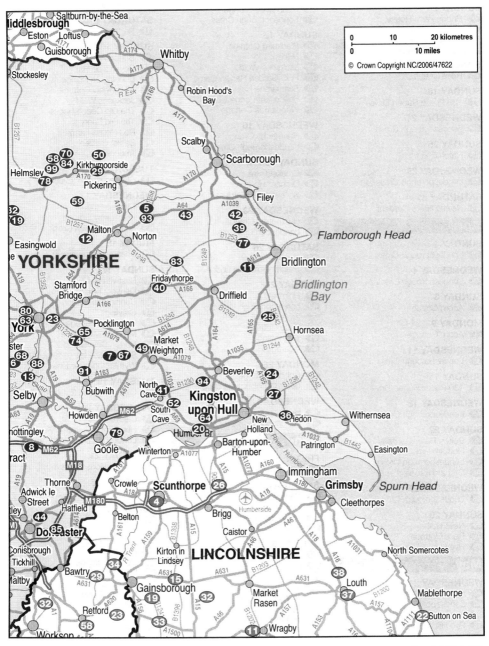

Opening Dates

February

SUNDAY 18
76 Rose Cottage

SUNDAY 25
8 Bridge Farm House
76 Rose Cottage

March

SUNDAY 4
76 Rose Cottage

SUNDAY 18
71 130 Prince Rupert Drive

WEDNESDAY 21
49 Londesborough Cross

SUNDAY 25
35 Hatch End

WEDNESDAY 28
49 Londesborough Cross

SATURDAY 31
60 Newby Hall & Gardens

April

SUNDAY 1
49 Londesborough Cross

WEDNESDAY 4
49 Londesborough Cross

SUNDAY 8
1 Acorn Cottage

MONDAY 9
1 Acorn Cottage

WEDNESDAY 11
49 Londesborough Cross

SUNDAY 15
71 130 Prince Rupert Drive

WEDNESDAY 18
49 Londesborough Cross

SUNDAY 22
6 Bolton Percy Gardens
41 Hotham Hall
49 Londesborough Cross
68 Orchard House

WEDNESDAY 25
49 Londesborough Cross

SUNDAY 29
59 Ness Hall
76 Rose Cottage
78 Rye Hill

May

WEDNESDAY 2
42 Hunmanby Grange
49 Londesborough Cross
59 Ness Hall
78 Rye Hill

SUNDAY 6
80 Secret Garden

WEDNESDAY 9
3 Beacon Hill House
42 Hunmanby Grange
49 Londesborough Cross

SUNDAY 13
5 Blackbird Cottage
38 Hillbark
43 Jacksons Wold
75 RHS Garden Harlow Carr
79 Saltmarshe Hall
88 Stillingfleet Lodge
97 Woodlands Cottage

WEDNESDAY 16
42 Hunmanby Grange
49 Londesborough Cross

SUNDAY 20
21 Creskeld Hall
68 Orchard House
99 Wytherstone Gardens

WEDNESDAY 23
42 Hunmanby Grange
49 Londesborough Cross

SATURDAY 26
70 Pennyholme
84 Sleightholmedale Lodge

SUNDAY 27
40 Holmfield
49 Londesborough Cross
73 24 Red Bank Road
76 Rose Cottage
91 Tregonning
92 Vicarage House

MONDAY 28
16 Cobble Cottage
32 Great Ouseburn Gardens

WEDNESDAY 30
42 Hunmanby Grange
49 Londesborough Cross

June

FRIDAY 1
82 Shandy Hall (Evening)

SATURDAY 2
58 Nawton Tower Garden
70 Pennyholme
71 130 Prince Rupert Drive
84 Sleightholmedale Lodge

SUNDAY 3
20 The Court
42 Hunmanby Grange
44 Jasmine House
57 Millrace Nursery
58 Nawton Tower Garden
78 Rye Hill
94 26 West End

WEDNESDAY 6
42 Hunmanby Grange
49 Londesborough Cross
66 The Old Croft
69 Parcevall Hall Gardens

SATURDAY 9
11 Burton Agnes Hall

SUNDAY 10
11 Burton Agnes Hall
24 Dowthorpe Hall
25 Dunnington Manor
37 4 Highview Cottage
43 Jacksons Wold
65 The Old Coach House
67 The Old Priory
74 Red House Farm
80 Secret Garden
91 Tregonning

TUESDAY 12
15 Cleaves House (Evening)

WEDNESDAY 13
15 Cleaves House
42 Hunmanby Grange
49 Londesborough Cross

FRIDAY 15
82 Shandy Hall (Evening)

SUNDAY 17
4 Birstwith Hall
23 Derwent House
25 Dunnington Manor
31 Graylings
39 Holly Tree Cottage
54 Mayroyd Mill House
62 Norton Conyers
79 Saltmarshe Hall
99 Wytherstone Gardens

TUESDAY 19
15 Cleaves House (Evening)

WEDNESDAY 20
15 Cleaves House
42 Hunmanby Grange
49 Londesborough Cross

THURSDAY 21
53 Maspin House (Evening)

SATURDAY 23
28 Fernleigh

SUNDAY 24
9 Brookfield
16 Cobble Cottage
22 Croft Cottage
28 Fernleigh
36 Hedon Gardens
38 Hillbark
40 Holmfield
53 Maspin House
56 Millgate House (Evening)
64 Oakwood House
76 Rose Cottage

88 Stillingfleet Lodge
89 Swale Cottage
96 Whixley Gardens
98 Wortley Hall
101 Yorke House

WEDNESDAY 27
9 Brookfield
30 The Grange
42 Hunmanby Grange
49 Londesborough Cross

July

SUNDAY 1
14 72 Church Street
33 Greencroft
46 Kirkella
48 Lawkland Hall
51 Lower Crawshaw

WEDNESDAY 4
49 Londesborough Cross
50 Low Askew
93 The Walled Garden at Scampston

SUNDAY 8
38 Hillbark
43 Jacksons Wold
49 Londesborough Cross
61 Nidderdale Gardens
72 2 Prospect Place
80 Secret Garden

WEDNESDAY 11
30 The Grange
49 Londesborough Cross
66 The Old Croft
78 Rye Hill

SATURDAY 14
71 130 Prince Rupert Drive
84 Sleightholmedale Lodge

SUNDAY 15
10 Brookside Cottage
13 Cawood Gardens
39 Holly Tree Cottage
77 Rudston House
84 Sleightholmedale Lodge

SUNDAY 22
26 East Wing, Thorp Arch Hall
63 The Nursery

WEDNESDAY 25
30 The Grange

SUNDAY 29
52 39 Market Place
81 4 Shaftesbury Court
87 Stainsacre
90 Thorpe Lodge

August

SUNDAY 5
31 Graylings

SUNDAY 12
2 Barley Mow
75 RHS Garden Harlow Carr

85 Southways

SUNDAY 19
99 Wytherstone Gardens

WEDNESDAY 22
49 Londesborough Cross

SUNDAY 26
8 Bridge Farm House
49 Londesborough Cross

WEDNESDAY 29
49 Londesborough Cross

September

SUNDAY 2
17 Cold Cotes
57 Millrace Nursery
76 Rose Cottage

WEDNESDAY 5
49 Londesborough Cross

SUNDAY 9
7 Boundary Cottage
71 130 Prince Rupert Drive

SUNDAY 16
88 Stillingfleet Lodge

SUNDAY 30
60 Newby Hall & Gardens

Private gardens opening regularly for the NGS

42 Hunmanby Grange
49 Londesborough Cross

Gardens open to the public

11 Burton Agnes Hall
12 Castle Howard
18 Constable Burton Hall Gardens
34 Harewood House
47 Land Farm
60 Newby Hall & Gardens
62 Norton Conyers
69 Parcevall Hall Gardens
75 RHS Garden Harlow Carr
82 Shandy Hall
83 Sledmere House
88 Stillingfleet Lodge
93 The Walled Garden at Scampston
99 Wytherstone Gardens
100 York Gate

By appointment only

19 The Cottage
27 Evergreens
29 Friars Hill
45 Kelberdale
55 The Mews Cottage
86 Spring Close Farm
95 The White House

The Gardens

1 ACORN COTTAGE
50 Church Street, Boston Spa
LS23 6DN. Mrs C M Froggatt, 01937
842519. *1m SE of Wetherby. Off A1
on A659 Church St opp Central
Garage.* Home-made teas. **Adm £3
incl teas, chd free. Sun 8, Mon 9 Apr
(11-5). Visitors also welcome by
appt mid Mar to mid May,
individuals, groups & coaches
permitted.**
You are invited to come and spend
peaceful time in this small well
established alpine garden full of spring
delights. Three generations of the
family have collected the plants and
bulbs, and these have recently been
rearranged and the garden significantly
altered for ease of maintenance and
access without losing the character
and uniqueness of this fine collection.
Small single steps.
    ♿ ⋔ ☕

Wide range of interesting plants both ornamental and edible . . .

2 BARLEY MOW
Moor Monkton YO26 8JA. Dr & Mrs
Mike Ashford. *5m NW of York. Off
A59.* Home-made teas. **Adm £2.50,
chd free. Sun 12 Aug (11-6).**
This plant enthusiast's ³/₄-acre garden
has wide range of interesting plants
both ornamental and edible. Garden
peaks in late summer with vivid
herbaceous borders and bold
subtropical planting. Other features incl
trellis draped with colourful climbers;
formally trained apples and pears;
pond, greenhouses, vegetable garden
and wide range of less usual fruit.
Featured in Autumn Gardening edition
'Womans Weekly'. Gravel path.
♿ ⋔ ✿ ☕

3 BEACON HILL HOUSE
Langbar, nr Ilkley LS29 0EU. Mr & Mrs D H Boyle, 01943 607544. *4m NW of Ilkley. 1¼m SE of A59 at Bolton Bridge.* Home-made teas. **Adm £3, chd free, concessions £2.50** (share to Riding for the Disabled). Wed 9 May (1.30-6). Visitors also welcome by appt late Feb to July, please call to arrange.
Fairly large garden, facing S and sheltered by woodland, on the slopes of Beamsley Beacon at 900ft above sea-level. An old fernery and big windbreak survive from original Victorian garden. Today, features of particular interest are snowdrops, early flowering rhododendrons in spring, and enormous climbing and rambling roses in July. Some unusual flowering trees and shrubs, several mixed borders, 2 ponds, which attract wildlife, small kitchen garden and cool greenhouse.
🅺 ⊛ 🍵

Quiz for children 'Round & Round the garden' . . .

4 BIRSTWITH HALL
High Birstwith, nr Harrogate HG3 2JW. Sir James & Lady Aykroyd. *5m NW of Harrogate. Between Hampsthwaite & Birstwith villages, close to A59 Harrogate/Skipton rd.* Teas. **Adm £3, chd free.** Sun 17 June (2-5). Visitors also welcome by appt, coaches permitted. Please write.
Large 8-acre garden nestling in secluded Yorkshire dale with newly (2004) planted formal garden and ornamental orchard, extensive lawns, picturesque stream, large pond and Victorian greenhouse.
& ⊛ 🍵

5 BLACKBIRD COTTAGE
Scampston YO17 8NG. Mrs Hazel Hoad. *5m E of Malton. Off A64 to Scarborough through Rillington, turn L signed Scampston only. Follow signs.* Home-made teas. **Adm £2.50, chd free.** Sun 13 May (10-5).
⅓-acre plantswoman's garden made from scratch since 1986. Great wealth of interesting plants, with shrub and herbaceous border. Alpines a

speciality. Please visit throughout the day to ease pressure on small but inspirational garden.
🅺 ⊛ 🍵

6 BOLTON PERCY GARDENS
YO23 7BA. *5m E of Tadcaster. 10m SW of York. Off A64 (Leeds - York).* Light lunches & teas at Bolton Percy Parish Room from 12.30. **Combined adm £3.50, chd free.** Sun 22 Apr (12.30-5).
🍵

BOLTON PERCY CEMETERY
Bolton Percy All Saints
An opportunity to meet Roger Brook who gardens an acre of old village churchyard where garden plants are naturalised. Beautiful C15 church with acclaimed millennium window. Plants sale incl dicentras from National Collection.
🅺 ⊛ NCCPG

WINDY RIDGE
Mr & Mrs J S Giles. *Marsh Lane* Natural cottage-style garden sloping down to the Ings, greatly influenced by Margery Fish. Wide collection of Elizabethan and Barnhaven primroses. Paths meander through natural plantings of unusual hardy plants.
🅺 ⊛

7 NEW BOUNDARY COTTAGE
Seaton Ross, York YO42 4NF. Roger Brook, 01759 319156, twinponds@talktalk.net. *5m SW of Pocklington. From A64 York, take Hull exit & immed B1228, approx 8m, then follow signs Seaton Ross. From M62 Howden north on B1228 approx 11m, R turn to Seaton Ross. Both routes usually signed to Drag Racing! ½m further before Seaton Ross.* Cream teas. **Adm £2.50, chd free.** Sun 9 Sept (12-5).
First opening of horticulturist Roger Brook's new ¾-acre plantsmans garden, after 6yrs not yet mature, incl twin ponds, gravel borders, cactus and succulent planting, mixed and herbaceous borders, boggy plantings, acid border, rock garden, young specimen trees, unorthodox vegetables, fruit and seasonal container displays. National Collection of Dicentre.
& 🅺 ⊛ NCCPG 🍵

8 BRIDGE FARM HOUSE
Long Lane, Great Heck DN14 0BE. Barbara & Richard Ferrari, 01977 661277. *6m S of Selby. 3m N of M62 (J34) A19 turn E at roundabout to Snaith onto A645, straight on at T-lights then 1st R to Great Heck. House 1st on L, park in adjacent field.* Home-made teas. **Adm £2.50, chd free.** Suns 25 Feb; 26 Aug (12-3). Visitors also welcome by appt.
Large all-yr round organic garden designed and created by owners over just 4yrs. Creatively planted with many unusual and interesting plants incl; long double borders, ponds, bog, gravel, pots, poultry, wildlife areas, vegetables, working compost heaps, trees, woodland, spring interest borders and named varieties of snowdrops and hellebores. WC not accessible to wheelchairs.
& 🅺 ⊛ 🍵

Talking about garden descriptions my son says 'Our garden has really lovely flowers, but I don't get my dinner for hours and hours . . . !'

9 BROOKFIELD
Jew Lane, Oxenhope BD22 9HS. Mrs R L Belsey, 01535 643070. *5m SW of Keighley. Take A629 towards Halifax. Fork R onto A6033 towards Haworth. Follow signs to Oxenhope. Turn L at Xrds in village. 200yds after PO fork R, Jew Lane.* Light refreshments & teas. **Adm £2.50, chd free.** Sun 24, Wed 27 June (1-5). Visitors also welcome by appt June & July, coaches permitted.
1-acre, intimate garden, incl large pond with island and mallards. Many varieties of candelabra primulas and florindaes, azaleas, rhododendrons. Unusual trees and shrubs, screes, greenhouse and conservatory. New series of island beds. Quiz for children 'Round & Round the garden'.
🅺 ⊛ 🍵

❿ NEW BROOKSIDE COTTAGE
**Brookside Bank Road,
Stannington S6 6GU. Shirley
Samworth.** 2½ m from Sheffield
city centre. M1 J36, A61 (Sheffield)
to Hillsborough. Follow signs for
Stannington/Dungworth. Cream
teas. **Adm £2, chd free. Sun 15
July (2-5).**
Long triangular shaped garden
sloping steeply away behind old
cottages, overlooking fields and
woodland. Steps between 3 levels
lead to areas of differing interest,
giving senses of both secrecy and
surprise planted and arranged with
artistic flair in the cottage style.
Finalist in BBC Gardeners World,
Gardener of the Year.

⓫ ◆ BURTON AGNES HALL
**Driffield YO25 4ND. Mrs S Cunliffe-
Lister, 01262 490324, www.burton-
agnes.com.** Between Driffield &
Bridlington. Burton Agnes is on A614.
**House and Garden adm £6, chd £3,
concessions £5.50, Garden only
adm £3.50, chd £1.50, concessions
£3.25 (donation to NGS). For dates
& times see website or tel. For NGS:
Sat 9, Sun 10 June (11-5).**
8 acres. Lawns with clipped yew and
fountains; woodland gardens and
walled garden containing potager;
herbaceous and mixed borders; maze
with thyme garden; jungle garden;
campanula collection garden and
coloured gardens containing giant
games boards. Collections of hardy
geraniums, clematis, penstemons and
many unusual perennials. February
(Snowdrops). Gardeners' Fair £3.50; 9,
10 June. HHA/Christie 'Garden of the
Year Award' & featured in various
newspapers & magazines.

⓬ ◆ CASTLE HOWARD
**nr York YO60 7DA. Castle Howard
Estate Ltd, 01653 648333,
www.castlehoward.co.uk.** 15m NE of
York, 6m W of Malton. Off the A64.
**House & Garden £10, chd £6.50,
concession £9. Garden & grounds
£7.50, chd £5 , concession £6.50.
Daily 1 Mar to 4 Nov 10-4.**
Formal grounds laid out from C18 to
present, incl fountains, lakes, cascades
and waterfalls. Woodland garden, Ray
Wood, has collection of rhododendron
species and hybrids amounting to 800
varieties. Notable collection of acers,

nothofagus, arbutus, styrax, magnolia
and conifers. Formal rose gardens incl
old, China and Bourbon roses, hybrid
teas and floribunda. Ornamental
vegetable garden planted in 2006.

⓭ CAWOOD GARDENS
YO8 3UG. 5m N of Selby. On B1223
5m NW of Selby & 7m SE of Tadcaster.
Between York & A1 on B1222. Home-
made teas. **Combined adm £4, chd
free. Sun 15 July (12-5).**
An attractive, historic, riverside village.
Village maps given at all gardens.
☕

9 ANSON GROVE
**Tony & Brenda Finnigan, 01757
268888. Visitors also welcome
by appt, groups of 10+.**
Enjoy tranquillity in this small
orientally-influenced garden with
winding paths and raised areas.
Although compact, imaginative
design has created a garden of
interest with 4 pools, water
features, Zen garden, pagoda and
over 30 grasses. Crafts and plants
for sale.

ASH LEA
Michael & Josephine Welbourn
Shrubs and fernery lead to
colourful formal borders, in
contrast to a relaxed atmosphere
by a clear pool, leading to dining
area and traditional vegetable
garden edged in clipped box.
🦮

21 GREAT CLOSE
**David & Judy Jones, 01751
268571. Visitors also welcome
by appt, groups of 10+.**
All-yr interest, with mixed planting
in ever-changing borders, incl
vegetables, herbs, grasses and
many unusual and some exotic
perennials. Ponds, stream and
new rose walk make a colourful
but relaxing garden.
🦮 ❀

⓮ 72 CHURCH STREET
**Oughtibridge S35 0FW. Linda &
Peter Stewart, 0114 286 3847,
lindastewart@talktalk.net.** 6m N of
Sheffield. M1 (J36) A61 (Sheffield).
Turn R at Norfolk Arms PH. In
Oughtibridge follow one-way system
turning L immed after zebra crossing.
**Adm £2.50, chd free. Sun 1 July (2-
5). Visitors also welcome by appt.**
Wildlife-friendly ⅓-acre garden on N-
facing slope. Informal beds providing

yr-long interest have mixed plantings of
trees, shrubs, phormiums, bamboos,
grasses, ferns, bulbs and perennials
which lead to a natural stream with a
backdrop of native woodland.
Featured on BBC 'Gardeners' World'.
🦮 ❀

⓯ CLEAVES HOUSE
**Thirlby YO7 2DQ. Margaret & Tony
May, 01845 597606.** 3m NE of Thirsk.
From A170 in Sutton under Whitestone
Cliff take turning signed Felixkirk.
Almost immed take rd R signed Thirlby.
Light refreshments & teas. **Adm £3,
chd free. Weds 13, 20 June (11-5).
Evening Openings** wine, **Tues 12,
19 June (6-9). Visitors also welcome
by appt 1 to 21 June. Not suitable
for anything larger than 16 seater
mini-bus.**
Informal 2-acre garden on sloping site
with beautiful views. Bold, interesting
planting with many unusual trees,
shrubs, roses, pond and bog area,
small wood. Enthusiastically gardened
and planted by the owners since 1991.
Parts of garden not accessible by
wheelchair, particularly if wet.
🦮 🦮 ❀ ☕

Areas of differing interest, giving senses of both secrecy and surprise . . .

⓰ COBBLE COTTAGE
**Rudgate, Whixley YO26 8AL. John
Hawkridge & Barry Atkinson, 01423
331419.** 3m E of A1 off A59 York -
Harrogate. Combined with **Great
Ouseburn Gardens** £3.50, Mon 28
May (11-5) also **Whixley Gardens**
£5, Sun 24 June (12-5). Visitors also
welcome by appt, June & July,
groups of 10+.
Imaginatively designed, constantly
changing, small cottage garden full of
decorative architectural plants and old
family favourites. Interesting water
garden, containers and use of natural
materials. Secret courtyard garden and
new Japanese garden.
🦮 ❀

17 COLD COTES
Cold Cotes Road, nr Kettlesing, Harrogate HG3 2LW. Penny Jones, Ed Loft, Doreen & Joanna Russell, 01423 770937, www.coldcotes.com. *7m W of Harrogate. Off A59. After Black Bull PH turn R to Menwith Hill/Darley.* Light refreshments & teas. **Adm £2.50, chd free. Sun 2 Sept (11-5). Visitors also welcome by appt, May to end Oct, groups 10+, coaches permitted.**
Large peaceful garden with expansive views is at ease in its rural setting. Series of discreet gardens incl formal areas around house, streamside walk and sweeping herbaceous borders inspired by the designer Piet Oudolf which are at their height in late summer, lead to a newly developed wooden garden with wonderful autumn colour. Curiosity Strong Art Group and range of art activities.

❀ ⊛ ⊨ ☕

18 ◆ CONSTABLE BURTON HALL GARDENS
nr Leyburn DL8 5LJ. Mr Charles Wyvill, 01677 450361, www.constableburtongardens.co.uk. *3m E of Leyburn. Constable Burton Village. On A684, 6m W of A1.* **Adm £3, chd 50p, concessions £2.50. Daily Sat 17 Mar to Sun 14 Oct (9-6).**
Large romantic garden with terraced woodland walks. Garden trails, shrubs, roses and water garden. Display of daffodils and over 5000 tulips planted annually amongst extensive borders. Fine John Carr house (not open) set in splendour of Wensleydale countryside.

♿ ⊛

Many interesting features, courtyards and a 'pretty potty patio' . . .

19 THE COTTAGE
Oulston, nr Coxwold YO61 3RA. Tony & Jane Cowan, 01347 868113. *9m SE of Thirsk. 16m N of York, E of A19. Oulston is between Easingwold (4m) & Coxwold (2m). Garden opp telephone box.* **Visitors welcome by appt, May to Sept.**
2/3-acre garden designed, planted and developed by present owners since

1999. Formal beds with informal plantings of herbaceous and shrubby plants, roses and herbs, opening to grassy area with naturalised flowers and trees. Late summer borders, vegetables and soft fruits. Beautiful open country views.

❀

20 THE COURT
Humber Road, North Ferriby HU14 3DW. Guy & Liz Slater, 01482 633609. *7m W of Hull. Travelling E on A63 towards Hull, follow sign for N Ferriby. Through village to Xrds with war memorial, turn R & follow rd to T-junction with Humber Rd. Turn L & immed R into unmarked cul-de-sac, last house on LH-side.* Home-made TEAS. **Adm £2, chd free. Sun 3 June (1-5). Visitors also welcome by appt.**
Restful and secluded, informal garden with yr-round interest. Hidden seating areas and summerhouses, small pond and waterfall. 2/3-acre garden surrounded by trees contains laburnum and wisteria tunnel which leads to well-planted shady woodland area, around tennis court. Many interesting features, courtyards and a 'pretty potty patio'. Local hand-made pottery for sale.

♿ ⊛ ☕

21 CRESKELD HALL
Arthington, nr Leeds LS21 1NT. J & C Stoddart-Scott. *5m E of Otley. On A659 between Pool & Harewood.* Home-made teas. **Adm £3, chd free. Sun 20 May (12-5).**
Historic picturesque 3 1/2-acre Wharfedale garden with beech avenue, mature rhododendrons and azaleas. Gravel path from terrace leads to attractive water garden with canals set amongst woodland plantings. Walled kitchen garden and flower garden. Specialist nurseries.

♿ ❀ ⊛ ☕

22 CROFT COTTAGE
Green Hammerton YO26 8AE. Alistair & Angela Taylor, 01423 330330, alistair@alistairtaylor1.wanadoo.co.uk. *6m E of Knaresborough. 3m E of A1M adjacent to A59. Entrance through orchard off old Harrogate rd.* Home-made teas. **Adm £2.50, chd free. Combined with Whixley Gardens £5, chd free. Sun 24 June (12-5). Visitors also welcome by appt.**
Secluded 1/2-acre cottage garden divided into a number of garden

rooms. Conservatory, clipped yew, old brick, cobbles and pavers used for formal areas leading to water feature, mixed borders and orchard with wild flowers.

❀ ☕

23 DERWENT HOUSE
59 Osbaldwick Village, Osbaldwick YO10 3NP. Dr & Mrs D G Lethem, 01904 410847, davidlethem@tiscali.co.uk. *2m E of York. On village green at Osbaldwick off A1079. Parking in old school yard opp church.* Home-made teas. **Adm £2.50, chd free. Sun 17 June (1.30-5). Visitors also welcome by appt in June.**
3/4-acre, attractive village garden extended in 1984 to provide new walled garden, summer house, conservatories and terraces designed by Martin Stancliffe, surveyor to the fabric of St Paul's Cathedral. Rose garden, box parterres, pelargoniums, hardy geraniums and ornamental allée of apple and pears. Double herbaceous border leads to meadow with species roses and eucalyptus.

❀ ⊛ ☕

24 DOWTHORPE HALL
Skirlaugh HU11 5AE. Mr & Mrs J Holtby, 01964 562235, john.holtby@farming.co.uk. *6m N of Hull, 8m E of Beverley. On the A165 Hull to Bridlington Rd halfway between Coniston & Skirlaugh on the RH-side travelling N. Signed at the bottom of drive which has white railings.* **Adm £3, chd free. Sun 10 June (11-5). Visitors also welcome by appt.**
3 1/2 acres owned by professional garden designer. Kitchen garden, orchard, Mediterranean-style planting, small gravel garden and main lawn area surrounded by shrubs, beautiful mature trees and sumptuous herbaceous borders. Pond with island.

♿ ⊨

25 DUNNINGTON MANOR
Dunnington, nr Driffield YO25 8EG. Marygold & Eric Baines. *12m N of Beverley. Take the Dunnington turn on the A165 between Brandsburton & Beeford. The house is 1st after the village sign. Parking directions willl be given.* Cream teas. **Adm £3.00, chd free. Suns 10, 17 June (2-5).**
Areas of different interest open up in 2 acres of traditional borders, lawns, hedges and orchard, surrounded by superb mature trees.

♿ ❀ ☕

26 EAST WING, THORP ARCH HALL
Thorp Arch LS23 7AW. Fiona & Chris
Royffe, 01937 843513,
plantsbydesign@btinternet.com. *1m
S of Wetherby. Take A659 into Boston
Spa centre. Turn at HSBC over bridge
to Thorp Arch, at end of Main St turn L
into Thorp Arch Park & R over cattle
grid.* Home-made teas. **Adm £3, chd
free. Sun 22 July (12-5). Visitors also
welcome by appt, May to Sept,
groups of 15+, incl coaches.**
³/₄-acre surrounding East Wing of C18
John Carr house (not open). Inspiring,
imaginatively developed contemporary
garden in parkland setting. Striking
views, dramatic combinations of plants
framed by yew hedges and trained
trees. Courtyards, ponds, potager,
earth sculpture and dry garden, newly
designed features for 2007.
Photographic exhibition. Featured in
'Homes & Antiques' Magazine and
'Modern Family Gardens'.

Auricula
theatre and
paved area
for drought
resistant plants
in pots . . .

THE ELMS
See Nottinghamshire.

27 EVERGREENS
119 Main Road, Bilton HU11 4AB.
Phil & Brenda Brock, 01482 811365.
*5m E of Hull. Leave city by A165. Exit
B1238. Bungalow ¹/₂ m on L opp Asda
car park entrance.* **Visitors welcome
by appt.**
1 acre with mosaics and sundials,
tower, raised beds, rockeries and
landscaped pond. Japanese garden,
seaside garden, summerhouse.
Collection of dwarf conifers. 'Fun'
items. Photographs showing
development of garden, front garden
redesigned 2005.

28 NEW FERNLEIGH
9 Meadowhead Avenue,
Meadowhead S8 7RT. Mr & Mrs
S Littlewood, 01142 747234. *4m
S of Sheffield city centre. A61,
A6102, B6054 roundabout, exit
B6054 towards Dronfield
Woodhouse. Meadowhead Ave
2nd R.* Light refreshments & teas.
**Adm £2.50, chd free. Sat 23, Sun
24 June (1-5.30). Visitors also
welcome by appt, June & July,
groups of 12+.**
Plantswomans ¹/₃-acre cottage
style garden with large variety of
unusual plants set in differently
planted sections to provide all-yr
interest. Auricula theatre and paved
area for drought resistant plants in
pots.

29 FRIARS HILL
Sinnington YO62 6SL. Mr & Mrs C J
Baldwin, 01751 432179,
friars.hill@abelgratis.co.uk. *4m W of
Pickering. On A170.* **Adm £2.50, chd
free. Visitors welcome by appt, Apr
to July, up to 40 visitors, coaches
permitted.**
1³/₄-acre plantswoman's garden
containing over 2500 varieties of
perennials and bulbs, with yr-round
colour. Early interest with hellebores,
bulbs and woodland plants.
Herbaceous beds. Hostas,
delphiniums, old roses and alpine
troughs.

30 THE GRANGE
Carla Beck Lane, Carleton
BD23 3BU. Mr & Mrs R N Wooler,
01756 709342. *1¹/₂ m SW of Skipton.
Turn off A56 (Skipton-Clitheroe) into
Carleton. Keep L at Swan PH,
continue through to end of village &
turn R into Carla Beck Lane. From
Skipton town centre follow A6131.
Turn R to Carleton.* Cream teas. **Adm
£3, chd free (share to Sue Ryder
Care Manorlands Hospice). Weds 27
June; 11, 25 July (1-5). Visitors also
welcome by appt in July & Aug,
groups 10+.**
Now reaching maturity, a plantsman's
garden of over 4 acres of different
features restored by the owners during
the last 12 years. Large herbaceous
border with ha-ha, walled garden, rose
and clematis walk, ornamental grass
beds, water features and vegetable
beds, some unusual mature tree
specimens. Some steps and gravel
paths.

31 GRAYLINGS
Niddside HG3 2PW. Phil & Paddy
Mayes, 01423 781531,
paddymayes@btinternet.com. *6m W
of Harrogate. Off A59, take B6451 to
Pateley Bridge. R at Wellington Inn to
Darley. Park in adjacent field.* Home-
made teas. **Adm £3, chd free. Suns
17 June; 5 Aug (12-5). Visitors also
welcome by appt, groups of 10+.**
1-acre tranquil garden bordered by
farmland on banks of R Nidd set in an
Area of Outstanding Natural Beauty.
Designed and maintained by owners
since 1995. Immaculate lawns
meander through borders planted for
yr-round interest. Forest and
ornamental trees, shrubs, roses, 'hot'
borders and many containers planted
with tender perennials. Feature border
with ornamental grasses. Many seating
areas, canal and small courtyard, both
with fountains.

**32 GREAT OUSEBURN
GARDENS**
YO26 9RG. *13m NW of York. Off
B6265. 4m E of A1(M) J47 (A59).
Before Green Hammerton take B6265
towards Boroughbridge. Follow signs
to Great Ouseburn. Car parking at
Tinkers Hollow.* Home-made teas at
Cedar Croft. **Combined adm £3.50,
chd free. Mon 28 May (11-5).**
The source of the R Ouse at the Old
Workhouse is at the entrance to this
picturesque village. Gardens nr church.

CEDAR CROFT
Main Street YO26 9RG. Jane &
Nick Butler
¹/₂-acre garden created by owners
over last 30yrs on S side of listed
Georgian house (not open) with
mature trees and lovely views over
Ousebeck towards Whixley Moor.
3 large herbaceous, mixed shrub
and rose borders provide foliage
interest and colour throughout the
yr. Summerhouse, terrace with
pots and small parterre to N side.
Gravel drive.

COBBLE COTTAGE
Whixley. John Hawkridge &
Barry Atkinson
(See separate entry).

TINKERS HOLLOW
Church Field Lane YO26 9SG.
Heather & Eric Sugden
Just over 1 acre, with wide range
of features. 4 very different ponds,
waterfall and stream play a key

role in extending the diverse range of plants grown. Attractive pergola walk-ways provide link to bog, perennial and shrub borders. Folly adds intrigue to wild area of the garden.

 ♿ ❀

33 GREENCROFT
Pottery Lane, Littlethorpe, nr Ripon HG4 3LS. Mr & Mrs David Walden, 01765 602487. *1m SE of Ripon. Off A61 Ripon bypass, follow signs to Littlethorpe. Turn R at church (Pottery Lane) to Bishop Monkton for 1½m. On RH-side after Littlethorpe Pottery (open). Car parking in field opp and at Pottery.* Home-made teas. **Combined with Kirkella adm £3, chd free. Sun 1 July (12-5). Visitors also welcome by appt.**
½-acre informal garden made and built by owners. Special ornamental features incl gazebo, temple, pavilion, stone wall with mullions, pergola and formal pool. Long herbaceous borders lead to circular enclosed garden planted with late flowering perennials, annuals and exotics. Log cabin with shingle roof built alongside large pond.

✕ ☕

GRINGLEY GARDENS
See Nottinghamshire.

34 ♦ HAREWOOD HOUSE
nr Leeds LS17 9LG. Harewood House Trust, 01132 181010, www.harewood.org. *7m N of Leeds. On A61.* **House and Garden adm £11.30, chd £6.50, concessions £10. Daily 15 Mar to 16 Dec (10-4), see website or tel for details.**
160 acres of gardens within 1000 acres of 'Capability' Brown landscaped parkland. Elaborate Victorian terrace comprising box scrolls filled with seasonal bedding, enhanced by Italianate fountains and statues, all framed by extensive flower borders. Charming informal walks through woodland gardens around 32-acre lake to walled vegetable garden. Cascade and picturesque Himalayan garden with an array of exotic plants.

 ☕

35 HATCH END
Nun Monkton YO26 8EW. Tim & Julie Beaumont, 01423 330573, tim.beaumont@btinternet.com. *7m W of York ringroad, 6m E of A1M. Take A59, follow sign to Nun Monkton at Kirk Hammerton. 2m at end of lane.* Teas. **Adm £3, chd free. Sun 25 Mar (12-5). Visitors also welcome by appt, groups of 10+.**
Atmospheric ⅔-acre garden surrounding C17 cottage (not open) on 18 acre village green with tallest maypole in UK. Evolving since 1996, planting and design melded with circa 80yr-old trees. Serpentine yew hedge, lime walk, copper beech hedges and old brick walls create vistas. Mound, labyrinth, parterre, croquet lawn, potager and raised formal herb garden. Small courtyard with water feature. Gravel paths and drive.

♿ ✕ ☕

36 NEW HEDON GARDENS
HU12 8JN. *Follow A1033 from Hull, towards Hedon..* Light refreshments & teas. **Combined adm £5, chd free. Sun 24 June (11-5).**
Historic market town, with royal charters dating back to C12. Present mayor is its 660th. Wonderful collection of ancient and civic silver incl England's oldest civic mace. St Augustines Church (open). 'The King of Holderness' also dates back to then. Map will be provided at 1st garden visited to show others and indicating car parking. Museum & church open.

NEW 32 BAXTERGATE
John & Barbara Oldham, 01482 898382. **Visitors also welcome by appt, min 6 visitors.**
Superb, well designed garden made in 5yrs by former owners of The White Cottage, Halsham. Gravel and raised beds with many unusual plants, minute vegetable garden and fish pond.

✕ ❀

NEW CALEGARTH
Ivy Lane. John & Jennifer Dennis. *Ivy Lane runs W from the Market Hill area (the green next to the church), turn into cul-de-sac 300yds down lane on L* This ⅓ acre 1986 garden has many specimen coniferous and flowering shrubs, enclosed terrace and dell. Following the original concept of a new visita round every corner and all-yr interest. Wheelchair access if dry.

♿ ✕

NEW 56 ROSLYN CRESCENT
Ernie & Monica Kendall
Small town garden for plant enthusiasts, with yr-round interest, featuring hostas, mini hostas, ferns and other shade loving plants.

✕

NEW WESTFIELD
13 Ketwell Lane. Graham & Wendy Stephenson, 01482 896581, g@stephenson.karoo.co.uk. **Visitors also welcome by appt, groups of 10+.**
Informal garden consisting of mixed herbaceous and shrub borders surrounding 2 lawns. Garden features incl ornamental pond, patio area, raised planters, water feature, pergola, gazebo and greenhouse to back drop of mature trees.

✕

37 4 HIGHVIEW COTTAGE
High End, off Station Road, Esholt BD17 7QT. Howard & Julia Shaw, 01274 588510. *1½m from Guiseley. Off A6038. Turn to Esholt opp Marriott Hollins Hall Hotel. Under viaduct, take 1st L.* Light refreshments & teas. **Adm £2, chd free. Sun 10 June (11-5). Visitors also welcome by appt.**
Small garden in woodland setting developed to make best use of a sloping S-facing site. Steep steps lead to, and narrow gravel paths link, well structured terraced areas densely planted with conifers, shrubs and flowers, creating lovely views both into and out of the garden.

✕ ❀ ☕

38 HILLBARK
Church Lane, Bardsey LS17 9DH. Tim Gittins & Malcolm Simm, www.hillbark.co.uk. *4m SW of Wetherby. Turn W off A58 into Church Lane, garden on L before church..*

Historic market town, with royal charters dating back to C12. Present mayor is its 660th . . .

Home-made teas. **Adm £3, chd free. Suns 13 May; 24 June; 8 July (11-5). Visitors also welcome by appt.** 1-acre country garden, on open S-facing slope, started in 1987. Shrubs and perennials with interesting foliage, and some annuals, provide yr-round colour. Hidden arbours and surprising views amongst lively plantings. Descent to a number of interconnecting ponds and large natural pond with ducks and marginal planting. Woodland area, approached by bridges across stream. Unusual garden ceramics. Regional Winner - Country Homes & Interiors Country Garden. Featured in 'The English Garden'. .

39 NEW HOLLY TREE COTTAGE
Back Street, Burton Fleming YO25 3PD. Susan & Philip Cross. *11m NE of Driffield. 11m SW of Scarborough, 7m NW of Bridlington. From Driffield B1249 before Foxholes turn R to Burton Fleming. From Scarborough A165 R to Burton Fleming.* Home-made teas. **Adm £2.50, chd free. Suns 17 June; 15 July (1-5).** The owners' 3rd NGS garden, but different in size and shape. Superbly designed small garden planted with over 100 clematis and 50 roses, hardy geraniums, unusual plants and shrubs in colour-themed mixed borders. Attractive seating areas, pergolas, water features and wildlife areas.

HOLMES VILLA
See Nottinghamshire.

40 HOLMFIELD
Fridaythorpe YO25 9RZ. Susan & Robert Nichols, 01377 236627, susan.nichols@which.net. *9m W of Driffield. From York A166 through Fridaythorpe. 1m turn R signed Holmfield. 1st house on lane.* Home-made teas. **Adm £2.50, chd free. Suns 27 May; 24 June (11-5). Visitors also welcome by appt.** Informal 2-acre country garden on gentle S-facing slope. Developed from a field over last 19yrs. Large mixed borders, octagonal gazebo. Vegetable and fruit areas. Collection of phlomis. Adjacent nursery. Featured in 'The Journal'. Some gravel areas.

41 HOTHAM HALL
Hotham YO43 4UA. Stephen & Carolyn Martin, 01430 422054. *15m W of Hull. Nr North Cave, J38 of M62 turn towards North Cave, follow signs for Hotham.* **Adm £3, chd free. Sun 22 Apr (2-5). Visitors also welcome by appt.** C18 Grade II house (not open), stable block and clock tower in mature parkland setting with established gardens. Lake with bridge over to newly planted island (arboretum). Garden with Victorian pond and mixed borders. Selection of spring flowering bulbs. Childrens nature trail.

42 HUNMANBY GRANGE
Wold Newton YO25 3HS. Tom & Gill Mellor, 01723 891636, www.hunmanbygrange.co.uk. *12½m SE of Scarborough. Hunmanby Grange is a farm between Wold Newton & Hunmanby on the rd from Burton Fleming to Fordon.* Tea (Weds), Home-made teas (Sun). **Adm £2.50, chd free. Weds 2 May to 27 June (1-5); Sun 3 June (11-5). Visitors also welcome by appt May to Sept, coaches welcome.** 3-acre garden created from exposed open field, on top of Yorkshire Wolds nr coast. Hedges and fences now provide shelter from wind, making series of gardens with yr-round interest and seasonal highlights. Adjacent nursery.

43 JACKSONS WOLD
Sherburn YO17 8QJ. Mr & Mrs Richard Cundall. *11m E of Malton, 10m SW of Scarborough. A64 in Sherburn. T-lights take Weatherthorpe Rd. R fork to Hesterton Wold.* Cream teas. **Adm £2.50, chd free. Suns 13 May; 10 June; 8 July (1-5).** 2-acre garden with stunning views of the Vale of Pickering. Walled garden with mixed borders, numerous old shrub roses underplanted with unusual

perennials. Woodland paths lead to further shrub and perennial borders. Lime avenue with wild flower meadow. Traditional vegetable garden with roses, flowers and box edging framed by Victorian greenhouse. Adjoining nursery. Featured in 'Daily Express', 'Malton Gazette & Herald', 'Prestige Magazine'.

44 JASMINE HOUSE
145 The Grove, Wheatley Hills, Doncaster DN2 5SN. Ray & Anne Breame, 01302 361470. *2m E of Doncaster. 1m E of Doncaster Royal Infirmary off A18. Turn R into Chestnut Ave (Motor Save on corner).* Home-made teas. **Adm £2, chd free (share to The Richard Foundation). Sun 3 June (1-5). Visitors also welcome by appt.** Small enchanting garden for all seasons with distinctive design features, skilled planting and wide range of unusual plants in borders and pots. Climbers festoon archways that lead to enclosed gardens displaying grasses, ferns, alpines, bonsai and tender perennials.

45 KELBERDALE
Wetherby Road, Knaresborough HG5 8LN. Stan & Chris Abbott, 01423 862140, chris@kelberdale.fsnet.co.uk. *1m S of Knaresborough. On B6164 Wetherby rd. House on L immed after new ring rd (A658) roundabout.* **Visitors welcome by appt, spring & summer to mid-July for groups 10+, coaches welcome.** Owner-made and maintained, inspirational medium-sized plantsman's garden with river views. Full of yr-round interest with large herbaceous border, conifer and colour beds. Alpines and pond. Vegetable and wild garden with wildlife pond.

Attractive seating areas, pergolas, water features and wildlife areas . . .

46 NEW KIRKELLA
Pottery Lane, Littlethorpe
HG4 3LW. Mrs Jacky Barber. *1m
SE of Ripon. From A61 Ripon
bypass follow signs to Littlethorpe.
Turn R at church Pottery Lane.
Park in field not in rd please.*
Home-made teas at Greencroft.
**Combined with Greencroft adm
£3, chd free. Sun 1 July (12-5).**
Plantswoman and flower arrangers
small bungalow garden created
recently by owner to give constant
interest. Gravel garden with
Mediterranean feel instead of
previous driveway, paved rear
garden full of unusual and half-
hardy perennials with decorative
summerhouse, collections of
planted containers, small water
feature and living willow hedge
concealing small productive
vegetable plot.

✼ ✿

Interesting
stonework
and lots of
nooks and
crannies . . .

47 ◆ LAND FARM
Colden, Hebden Bridge HX7 7PJ.
Mr J Williams, 01422 842260. *8m W
of Halifax. From Halifax at Hebden
Bridge go through 2 sets T-lights. Take
turning circle to Heptonstall. Follow
signs to Colden. After 2¼m turn R at
'no through' rd, follow signs to garden.*
**Adm £3, chd free. Weekends &
Bank Hols May to end Aug (10-5).
Groups welcome evenings by prior
arrangement £6 incl tour &
refreshments.**
6 acres incl alpine, herbaceous, formal
and newly developing woodland
garden, meconopsis varieties in June,
cardiocrinum *giganteum* in July.
Elevation 1000ft N-facing. C17 house
(not open). Art Gallery.

✿ ☕

48 LAWKLAND HALL
Austwick LA2 8AT. Mr & Mrs G
Bowring. *3m N of Settle. Turn S off
A65 at Austwick/Lawkland Xrd or
Giggleswick stn.* Home-made teas.
**Adm £3, chd free. Sun 1 July (12.30-
5.30).**
Developing 3-acre garden surrounding
charming Grade 1 Elizabethan hall (not
open). Old stone walls, listed potting
shed, beech, yew and box hedges.
Heather-thatched gazebo in rose
garden, clipped yew cones in lawn
leading to small lake created in 2004,
mixed borders incl old fashioned roses,
formal kitchen garden.

✼ ✿ ⊨ ☕

49 LONDESBOROUGH CROSS
Shiptonthorpe YO43 3PA. Mr & Mrs
J W Medd. *2m From Market
Weighton, 5m from Pocklington.
A1079 Hull to York rd . Turn off in
Shiptonthorpe down the side of
church. Londesborough Cross is at
bottom of Town St.* Cream teas (Suns),
Home-made teas (Weds). **Adm £3,
chd free. Weds, 21 Mar to 11 July;
Suns 1, 22 Apr; 27 May; 8 July; 26
Aug; Weds, 22 Aug to 5 Sept;
(Weds1-4) (Suns 1-5).**
In 21yrs railway goods yard
transformed by owners into delightful
garden with ponds, bog area, large
herbaceous borders, screes and rock
garden. Pergola and arches planted
with clematis and good hosta
collection. Woodland garden planted
with large collection of hardy ferns,
many rare, and plants for shade incl
trilliums and meconopsis. New
thatched log cabin. Some
woodchipped paths, slopes.

♿ ✼ ✿ ☕

50 LOW ASKEW
Cropton YO18 8ER. Mr & Mrs Martin
Dawson-Brown. *5m W of Pickering.
Signed to Cropton from A170.
Between the villages of Cropton &
Lastingham.* Home-made teas. **Adm
£2.50, chd free, concessions £2.
Wed 4 July (1-5).**
Designed by present owners to
harmonize with the ancient and
beautiful valley of the R Seven in which
garden is situated. Now in its 3rd
decade new plantings and ideas
underway. Plants stall incl rare
pelargoniums. Enchanting riverside
walk.

✿ ☕

51 LOWER CRAWSHAW
Emley HD8 9SU. Mr & Mrs Neil
Hudson, 01924 840980,
janehudson42@btinternet.com. *8m
E of Huddersfield. From Huddersfield
turn R to Emley off A642 (Paul Lane).
M1 J39 (A636) direction Denby Dale,
1m after Bretton roundabout turn R to
Emley, ½m beyond Emley village turn
R (Stringer House Lane) continue for
¾m. Car park in adjacent field.* Home-
made teas. **Adm £3, chd free. Sun 1
July (12-5).** Visitors also welcome by
appt in May, June & July.
3-acre garden in open country on
eastern slopes of the Pennines,
surrounding 1690's farmhouse (not
open) with extensive range of old farm
buildings. Garden created by owners
since 1996. Natural stream runs
through the garden, dammed on
several levels and opening into 2 large
ponds. Walled potager created from
old barn, enclosed rose garden,
orchard, and courtyard. Naturalistic
planting of many unusual shrubs, trees
and perennials.

✼ ✿ ☕

52 NEW 39 MARKET PLACE
South Cave HU15 2BS. Lin &
Paul Holland. *12m W of Hull.
From A63 turn N to South Cave on
A1034. House on LH-side opp PO,
before Xrds.* Home-made teas.
**Adm £2, chd free. Sun 29 July
(2-5).**
Small walled garden with eclectic
planting. Established trees, cottage
garden plants and evergreen
shrubs. Rockeries, gravel fernery
with grasses and water feature.
Interesting stonework and lots of
nooks and crannies. A few shallow
steps and gravel paths.

✿ ☕

53 MASPIN HOUSE
Hillam Common Lane, Hillam
LS25 5HU. Howard & Susan
Ferguson, 01977 684922,
ferguson@maspin-house.co.uk. *7m
W of Selby. 4m E of A1 on A63. Turn R
after leaving Monk Fryston signed
Birkin, Beale, Kellington. L at T-
junction. House 1m on L.* Home-made
teas. **Adm £3, chd free. Sun 24 June
(2-6). Evening Opening Thur 21
June (4-8).** Visitors also welcome by
appt anytime.
3-acre country garden planted for yr-
round colour with interesting layout.
Designed, planted and maintained by

owners. Paths, pergolas, terraces and stonework complemented by wide variety of plants, many unusual, used in imaginative combinations. Ponds and formal canal. Woodland with creative underplanting. Orchard, with shrubs, climbing roses and new summerhouse. Gravel drive.

 ♿ ☰ ☕

54 MAYROYD MILL HOUSE
Mayroyd Lane, Hebden Bridge HX7 8NS. Richard Easton & Steve Mackay, 01422 845818. *At Hebden Bridge (A646) follow signs to Railway Stn. Car parking at stn.* Home-made teas. Adm £2.50, chd free. Sun 17 June (1-5.30). Visitors also welcome by appt, June & Aug only, groups of 10+.
Steep steps lead down to approx 1/3-acre S-facing designers' garden with bold herbaceous and ornamental grass plantings created for naturalistic effect. Many rare and unusual plants; woodland shade; bog areas and riverbank walk. National Collection of astrantias in full flower at time of opening. Featured in 'English Garden' & 'Country Homes & Interiors'.

☰ Ⓢ NCCPG ☕

55 THE MEWS COTTAGE
1 Brunswick Drive, Harrogate HG1 2PZ. Mrs Pat Clarke, 01423 566292, patriciamclarke@hotmail.com. *W of Harrogate town centre. From Cornwall Rd, N side of Valley Gardens, 1st R (Clarence Dr), 1st L (York Rd), 1st L (Brunswick Dr).* Home-made teas. Adm £2.50, chd free. Visitors welcome by appt, coaches welcome, unrestricted numbers from Mar to Nov.
Small tranquil garden on sloping site featuring a terracotta tiled courtyard with trompe-l'oeil. A garden of special interest to hardy planters over a long season; recommended for an August visit when a large collection of phlox paniculata is in flower. Featured in 'Garden Answers'.

☰ ☕

56 MILLGATE HOUSE
Millgate, Richmond DL10 4JN. Tim Culkin & Austin Lynch, 01748 823571, www.millgatehouse.com. *Centre of Richmond. House is located at bottom of Market Place opp Barclays Bank. Next to Halifax Building Soc.* Adm £2.50, chd £1.50. Day & Evening Opening Sun 24 June (8-8). Visitors also welcome by appt.

SE walled town garden overlooking R Swale. Although small, the garden is full of character, enchantingly secluded with plants and shrubs. Foliage plants incl ferns and hostas. Old roses, interesting selection of clematis, small trees and shrubs. RHS associate garden. Immensely stylish, national award-winning garden. Featured in 'Guardian Weekend' & on BBC TV. Dogs on leads.

☰ ⌁

Although small, the garden is full of character, enchantingly secluded . . . immensely stylish . . .

57 NEW MILLRACE NURSERY
84 Selby Road, Garforth LS25 1LP. Mr & Mrs Carthy, 0113 2869233. *5m E of Leeds. On A63 in Garforth. 1m from M1 J46, 3m from A1.* Home-made teas. Adm £2, chd free. Suns 3 June; 2 Sept (1-5).
Over looking a secluded valley. Garden developed over last 7yrs to incl large herbaceous borders containing many unusual perennials, shrubs and trees. The immediate garden also incl an ornamental pond, vegetable garden and small woodland. The outer garden leads through a wild flower meadow to large bog garden and fishing ponds. Specialist nursery.

♿ Ⓢ ☕

58 NAWTON TOWER GARDEN
Nawton YO62 7TU. Douglas Ward Trust, 01439 771218. *5m NE of Helmsley. From A170, between Helmsley & Nawton village, at Beadlam turn N 2 1/2 m to Nawton Tower.* Adm £1.50, chd free. Sat 2, Sun 3 June (2-6). Visitors also welcome by appt, May & June, coaches permitted, groups min £15.
Large garden; heathers, rhododendrons, azaleas, shrubs, bluebells, bulbs and trees. Partial wheelchair access, grass walks only - some steps and slopes.

Ⓢ

59 NESS HALL
Nunnington YO62 5XD. Mr & Mrs D Murray Wells. *6m E of Helmsley, 22m N of York. From B1257 Helmsley-Malton rd turn L at Slingsby signed Kirkbymoorside, 3m to Ness.* Home-made teas. Adm £3.50, chd free. Sun 29 Apr; Wed 2 May (2-5).
Large walled garden, mixed and herbaceous borders, undergoing reconstruction; orchard with shrubs and climbing roses. Featured in 'Country Life'.

♿ ☕

60 ◆ NEWBY HALL & GARDENS
Ripon HG4 5AE. Mr R C Compton, 0845 4504068, www.newbyhall.com. *2m E of Ripon. Signed from A1 & Ripon town centre.* House and Garden £9.50, chd/disabled £6.80, concessions £8.50, Garden only £7, chd/disabled £5.50, concessions £6. Tues to Sun & Bank Hol Mons 31 Mar to 30 Sept; Mons July & Aug . For NGS: Sat 31 Mar; Sun 30 Sept (11-5.30).
40 acres extensive gardens laid out in 1920s. Full of rare and beautiful plants. Formal seasonal gardens, stunning double herbaceous borders to R Ure and National Collection holder *Cornus*. Miniature railway and adventure gardens for children. Sculpture Park (June to Sept). Gold Award - Yorkshire in Bloom.

♿ ☰ Ⓢ NCCPG ☕

61 NEW NIDDERDALE GARDENS
HG3 4EW. *4m SE of Pateley Bridge, 10m NW of Harrogate. On B6451 & B6165. Limited wheelchair access. Parking at each garden.* Home-made teas. Combined adm £6, chd free. Sun 8 July (11-5).
Picnic area at Yorke House. Map provided.

☕

NEW THE OLD TWINE MILL
Low Laithe HG3 4BU. Jenny & Chris Robinson. *In Low Laithe turn L 50 metres after PH* Romantic garden setting around C19 watermill (not open) on banks of R Nidd. Walled garden

with old English roses leads to large naturalistic sunken pool planted in the Japanese style with rock escarpment and summerhouse. Grass riverside terraces with architectural features, bridges, arches and obelisk overlook the weir and millrace. Short walk along the river to folly, water meadow and plantation. Partial wheelchair access.

&

ORCHARD HOUSE
Dacre Banks. Mr & Mrs J T Spain, 01423 780502. Visitors also welcome by appt.
2 acres of simple natural uncontrived garden blending into beautiful surrounding countryside and providing a haven for wildlife. Shrub and perennial plantings from shade to full sun together with productive fruit and vegetables.

✗ ✿

WOODLANDS COTTAGE
Mr & Mrs Stark
(See separate entry).
& ✗ ✿

YORKE HOUSE
Mr Anthony & Mrs Pat Hutchinson
(See separate entry).
& ✿

Short walk along the river to folly, water meadow and plantation . . .

62 ◆ NORTON CONYERS
Wath, nr Ripon HG4 5EQ. Sir James & Lady Graham, 01765 640333, norton.conyers@bronco.co.uk. *4 m N of Ripon. Take Melmerby & Wath sign off A61 Ripon-Thirsk. Go through villages, boundary wall on R. Signed entry 300metres. Teas 17 June only.* **Adm £3, chd free. Easter & Bank Hol Suns, Mons Apr, May & Aug; Suns, Mons 3 June to 30 July. Daily 4 to 7 July (2-5, last adm 4.40). For NGS: Sun 17 June (2-5).**
Large C18 walled garden of interest to garden historians. Interesting iron entrance gate; borders, yew hedges and orangery with an attractive little pond in front. House, which was visited

by Charlotte Brontë, and is an original of Thornfield Hall in 'Jane Eyre'. House closed for repairs (tel for reopening date).
& ✗ ✿ ☕

63 NEW THE NURSERY
15 Knapton Lane, Acomb YO26 5PX. Tony Chalcraft & Jane Thurlow. *2½m W of York. Follow B1224 towards Acomb & York city centre, from A1237 York ringroad. Turn L at first mini roundabout into Beckfield Lane. Knapton Lane 2nd L after 150 metres.* Home-made teas. **Adm £2, chd free. Sun 22 July (1-6).**
Attractive 1-acre organic fruit and vegetable garden behind suburban house created from previous nursery. Bush and trained fruit trees (incl 40+ varieties apples and pears), large and small greenhouses, productive vegetables grown in bed and row systems interspersed with informal ornamental plantings providing colour and habitat for wildlife. Winner - West Riding Organic Shield of Organic Excellence.
✗ ☕

64 NEW OAKWOOD HOUSE
Todds Close, Tranby Lane, Swanland HU14 3NT. Judy & Mike Sketch. *8m W of Hull. M62, A63 towards Humber Bridge - Beverley A164 - L at 2nd roundabout into Swanland. Take 2nd R into Todds Close, house 1st on R.* Home-made teas. **Adm £2.50, chd free. Sun 24 June (11-5).**
Plant lovers garden. Good backbone of plants - under-planted with herbaceous plants, all-yr round colour and interest, sun baked border and shady areas. Several seating areas with different views of the garden.
✗ ☕

65 THE OLD COACH HOUSE
Church Lane, Elvington YO41 4AD. Simon & Toni Richardson. *8m SE of York. From A1079, immed after leaving York outer ring road turn onto B1228 for Elvington. No parking except for disabled in Church Lane. Please park in village.* Light refreshments & teas at village hall. **Combined with Red House Farm adm £3, chd free. Sun 10 June (12-5).**

Delightful atmospheric owner-made 2-acre garden. Grass paths meander through trees and sunlit borders past summerhouse and round large pond to pergola, vegetables and meadow beyond. Enclosed flower garden with ornamental pool adjacent to house.
& ✗ ✿ ☕

66 THE OLD CROFT
Linton Falls, BD23 6BG. Janet & Martin Wood, 01756 752317. *1m SE of Grassington, 8m N of Skipton. Off B6265, turn to Linton, through village, over Xrds, follow signs to Linton Falls. Use this or Grassington car park, no parking at garden. Access across water meadow.* **Adm £2, chd free. Weds 6 June; 11 July (2-5). Visitors also welcome by appt June & July only.**
Small cottage garden with profuse planting. Waterfall effect of cascading colour, created by a series of predominately perennial colour-themed island beds, descends from a gazebo with beautiful views of the R Wharfe and leads to a pool, patio and curved pergola walk. Featured in 'Yorkshire Life'.
☕

67 THE OLD PRIORY
Everingham YO42 4JD. Dr J D & Mrs H J Marsden, 01430 860222, marsd13@aol.com. *15m SE of York, 5½m from Pocklington. 2m S of the A1079 York-Hull Rd. Everingham has 3 access rds, the Old Priory is to the east of the Village. Car parking at the Village Hall opp, disabled people may be dropped off/park at the Old Priory.* Home-made teas, wine & beer in village hall. **Adm £3, chd free. Sun 10 June (1-5). Visitors also welcome by appt, best mid May to late June.**
Country garden of about 2 acres of dry sandy loam and wet peat land. Conservatory, polytunnel, walled vegetable garden and various nooks and crannies. Mixed herbaceous borders drop down to bog garden where paths bridge the stream into less formal garden which leads to lake. Short woodland walk.
& ✗ ✿ ☕

68 ORCHARD HOUSE
Appleton Roebuck YO23 7DD. David & Sylvia Watson, 01904 744460. *8m SW of York. 3m from A64 Bilborough Top flyover on Main St in Appleton Roebuck.* Home-made teas. **Adm £2.50, chd free. Suns 22 Apr; 20 May (11-5). Visitors also welcome**

by appt, Apr & May, groups of 10+, coaches permitted. Fascinating 1-acre garden created and maintained by owners in harmony with surrounding countryside. Brimming with unusual features and ideas. Paths of brick, cobble and grass wind through extensive colourful plants to old oak revolving summerhouse, exposed tree roots with sunken garden and grotto. Parasol bed, 'torr' with chapel of rest, lily pond, rill, stream, wildlife pond.

Narrow paths lead from cottage herbaceous borders and pond to shade areas and secret garden with camomile lawn . . .

69 ◆ **PARCEVALL HALL GARDENS**
Skyreholme BD23 6DE. Walsingham College, 01756 720311, www.parcevallhallgardens.co.uk. *9m N of Skipton. Signs from B6160 Bolton Abbey-Burnsall rd or off B6265 Grassington-Pateley Bridge.* **Adm £5, chd 75p. Daily 1 April to 31 Oct (10-5). For NGS: Wed 6 June (10-5).** 16 acres in Wharfedale sheltered by mixed woodland; terrace garden, rose garden, rock garden, fish ponds. Mixed borders, tender shrubs (desfontainea, crinodendron, camellias); autumn colour. Birdwatching, old apple orchard for picnics.

70 **PENNYHOLME**
Fadmoor YO62 7JG. Mr & Mrs P R Wilkinson. *7m NE of Helmsley. From A170 between Kirkbymoorside & Nawton, turn L. From Fadmoor turn L, signed 'Sleightholmedale only' continue N up dale, across 3 cattle grids, to garden. No buses.* Home-made teas. Also open **Sleightholmedale Lodge Sats 26 May; 2 June (1-5).** Enchanting 10-acre country garden. Unique river and dale setting. Extensive collection of magnificent rhododendrons and azaleas in mature oak wood circular walk. Currently developing traditional rose/mixed borders, water features, wildlife garden and tree garden.

71 **130 PRINCE RUPERT DRIVE**
Tockwith, York YO26 7PU. Mr & Mrs B Wright. *7m E of Wetherby. From B1224 Wetherby/York rd turn N to Cattal, after 1m turn R at Xrds to Tockwith. 1st turning on R in village. Please do not park in the cul-de-sac.* Home-made teas. **Adm £2.50, chd free. Suns 18 Mar; 15 Apr; Sats 2 June; 14 July; Sun 9 Sept (1-5).** 1/2-acre enthusiast's garden planted for yr-round interest from early hellebores, cyclamen and bulbs to late perennials and grasses mixed with our large fern collection, in beds connected by gravel paths. Many plants grown from seed, incl wild-collected seed. Rock and bog gardens, pond and pergola, glasshouses, shade house, kitchen garden with vegetables and trained fruit, small nursery. Featured in 'Garden News'.

72 **2 PROSPECT PLACE**
Outlane HD3 3FL. Carol & Andy Puszkiewicz, 01422 376408, carol-puszkiewicz@talktalk.net. *5m N of Huddersfield. 1m N of M62. J24 (W) take A643 to J23 (E) follow A640 to Rochdale. At derestriction sign leaving Outlane turn R (Gosport Lane). Parking in adjacent field.* Home-made teas. **Adm £2.50, chd free. Sun 8 July (12-5).** Visitors welcome by appt June & July for groups of 6+. Long intimate garden high in the Pennines (900ft). Narrow paths lead from cottage herbaceous borders and pond to shade areas and secret garden with camomile lawn, chocolate and silver borders surrounding circular bed and productive kitchen garden with trained fruit and flowers. Evolving wild area with native trees, large pond with indigenous planting, narrow stream and meadow.

73 **24 RED BANK ROAD**
off Whitcliffe Lane, Ripon HG4 2LE. Margaret & David Rivers. *3/4m from Ripon town centre. Follow Harrogate Rd (old A61 not bypass) turn off at Nissan showroom (Whitcliffe Lane),* Red Bank Rd is 3rd on R (about 1m). Home-made teas. **Adm £2, chd free. Sun 27 May (2-5).** Plant enthusiasts' small garden recently remodelled, now planted for yr-round interest. Raised beds, rockeries and gravel contain wide variety of perennials incl species peonies (some grown from seed), alpines and shrubs chosen to be able to cope with the difficult conditions of dry sun and dry shade.

74 **RED HOUSE FARM**
Church Lane, Elvington YO41 4HD. Professor & Mrs E Macphail. *From A1079 immediately after leaving Yorks outer ring road, turn S onto B1228 for Elvington. No parking, except for diasabled in Church Lane. Please park in village.* Light refreshments & teas in village hall. **Combined with The Old Coach House adm £3, chd free. Sun 10 June (12-5).** Large country garden developed over 24yrs. Extensive mixed borders with fine collection of hardy perennials, shrubs and roses. Maturing hedges partially divide the garden, long rose pergola leads to wildlife pond and wild flower meadow. Attractive courtyard with interesting plantings and 1/2-acre young wood.

75 ◆ **RHS GARDEN HARLOW CARR**
Harrogate HG3 1QB. Royal Horticultural Society, 01423 565418, www.rhs.org.uk/harlowcarr. *11/2m W of Harrogate town centre. On B6162 (Harrogate - Otley).* Refreshments at new Bettys Café tearooms. **Adm £6, chd £2. Open all yr except Christmas Day, for times see website or tel. For NGS: Suns 13 May; 12 Aug (9.30-6).** One of Yorkshire's most relaxing yet inspiring locations! Highlights incl spectacular herbaceous borders, streamside garden, alpines, scented and kitchen gardens. 'Gardens Through Time', woodland and wild flower meadow. Events all yr.

76 **ROSE COTTAGE**
High Hoyland, nr Barnsley S75 4BQ. Mrs M & Dr A Owen Griffiths. *4m NE of Denby Dale. Nr Cannon Hall Country Park, Barnsley. M1 J38 (A637-Huddersfield). Turn L after 75yds (Jebb Lane). After 2m L at T-junction. L in High Hoyland (Upperfield Lane).* Teas.

Adm £2.50, chd free. Suns 18, 25 Feb; 4 Mar (1-4); Suns 29 Apr; 27 May; 24 June; 2 Sept (2-5). Garden for all seasons; romantic in summer and interesting throughout the winter. New borders with collection of hamamelis, cornus, cyclamen, hellebores, and some of the 200+ collection of special snowdrops replace laurels. Rose gardens, topiary, sun and shade borders, walks with clematis, ivies, meconopsis, perennials, bulbs and trilliums lead to wild flower meadow with species roses and small copse. Featured in 'Garden Style'.

⚔ ⊛ ☕

Garden for all seasons; romantic in summer and interesting throughout the winter . . .

77 RUDSTON HOUSE
Rudston, nr Driffield YO25 4UH. Mr & Mrs Simon Dawson, 01262 420400. *5m W of Bridlington. On B1253. S at Bosville Arms for approx 300yds.* Cream teas. **Adm £3, chd free. Sun 15 July (11-5). Visitors also welcome by appt, in July for groups of 10+.**
Birthplace of authoress Winifred Holtby. Victorian farmhouse (not open) and 3 acres of exuberant garden with fine old trees, lawns, paths with clipped box hedges, conifers, shrubs, greenhouses, roses, interesting potager with named vegetable varieties, hosta beds with lilies, and short woodland walk, with pond. Plenty of seats and interesting corners and features; children love to explore. Partial wheelchair access.

♿ ⊛ ☕

78 RYE HILL
15 Station Road, Helmsley YO62 5BZ. Dr & Mrs C Briske. *Centre of Helmsley. Signed at Helmsley bridge on A170 (Thirsk-Scarborough).* Home-made teas. **Adm £2.50, chd free (share to St Catherine's Hospice, Private Visits only). Suns, Weds 29 Apr; 2 May; 3 June; 11 July (2-5). Visitors also welcome by appt, May, June & July. please write.**
Plantswoman's garden designed, constructed and maintained by owners. Divided into interlinking compartments, each planted in different style: formal, woodland and cottage. Intense planting using unusual plants for yr-round colour and interest. Conservatory, well stocked with tender species, ponds and many architectural features. New projects each yr.

♿ ⚔ ⊛ ☕

79 SALTMARSHE HALL
Saltmarshe DN14 7RX. Mr & Mrs Philip Bean, 01430 430199, pmegabean.aol.com. *6m E of Goole. From Howden (M62, J37) follow signs to Howdendyke & Saltmarshe. House in park W of Saltmarshe village.* Home-made teas. **Adm £3, chd free. Suns 13 May; Sun 17 June (12-5). Visitors also welcome by appt in May & June.**
Large lawns, fine old trees, R Ouse and a Regency house (not open) with courtyards provide setting for shrubs, climbers, herbaceous plants and roses. Of special interest to plantsmen and garden designers are pond garden, walled garden and large herbaceous border. Approx 10 acres.

♿ ⚔ ⊛ ☕

80 SECRET GARDEN
10 Sherwood Grove, Acomb, York YO26 5RD. Mr & Mrs A C Downes, 01904 796360, chrisdownes15@hotmail.com. *2m W of York centre. From York on A59, turn L into Beckfield Lane opp Manor School at mini roundabout, 1/4 m before Western ring rd. Take 1st R, 2nd L, or leave A1237 at junction with A 59 towards York, 1/4 m turn R at Manor School.* **Adm £2, chd free. Suns 6 May; 10 June; 8 July (11-5). Visitors also welcome by appt, no coaches.**
3/4-acre hidden garden developed and extended over 30yrs and largely remodelled in last 7yrs. Dry riverbed garden, rockery, large pond with stream and waterfall, perennial garden, small woodland area. Mixed plantings incl many unusual plants, 5 greenhouses with vine and tender plant collections, euphorbia and grass beds plus over 100 hosta varieties. Small nursery. Featured in 'The Journal'.

⚔ ⊛

81 4 SHAFTESBURY COURT
Shaftesbury Avenue, Bradford West BD9 6BQ. Mrs Pam Greenwood, 01274 495307. *Between Bradford Royal Infirmary & Allerton. Follow Duckworth Lane W into Pearson Lane. Shaftesbury Avenue 3rd turn on R off Pearson Lane. Please park in Shaftesbury Avenue but not on grass verges, access to Shaftesbury Court by foot.* Home-made teas. **Adm £2.50, chd free. Sun 29 July (11-5). Visitors also welcome by appt.**
1/4-acre plant lover's garden for all seasons especially concentrating on late summer colour, woodland plants and bulbs in spring. Narrow paths divide borders full of many rare and unusual perennials, small shrubs and bulbs for both sun and shade, the boundary walls are festooned with climbers. Featured in 'Yorkshire Today'.

⚔ ⊛ ☕

82 ◆ SHANDY HALL
Coxwold YO61 4AD. The Laurence Sterne Trust, 01347 868465, www.asterisk.org.uk. *N of York. From A19, 7m from both Easingwold & Thirsk, turn E signed Coxwold.* **Adm £2.50, chd £1. Garden Suns to Fris May to Sept (11-4.30); for House see website for details or tel. For NGS: Evening Openings Fris 1, 15 June (5.30-9).**
Home of C18 author Laurence Sterne. 2 walled gardens, 1 acre of unusual perennials interplanted with tulips and old roses in low walled beds. In old quarry, another acre of trees, shrubs, bulbs, climbers and wild flowers encouraging wildlife, incl over 130 recorded species of moths. Moth trap evenings on NGS openings. Featured on South Bank Show, Radio York & in BBC 'Gardens Illustrated' & 'Yorkshire Post'. Wheelchairs with help.

♿ ⚔ ⊛

83 ◆ **SLEDMERE HOUSE**
Driffield YO25 3XG. Sir Tatton
Sykes, 01377 236637,
www.sledmerehouse.com. *7m W of
Driffield. 17m from city of York, 10m
from Beverley. Sledmere House is
35min drive from M62.* **House and
Garden adm £6, chd £2,
concessions £5.50, Garden only
adm £4, chd £1, (RHS) concessions
£3. For details of openings & times
see website or tel.**
Award winning garden incl, octagonal
walled garden, herbaceous borders,
roses, perennials, bulbs and parterre.
'Capability ' Brown inspired
landscaped park with mature beech
trees and 'eyecatchers'. Sledmere
Garden Show Sat 19 May . Yorkshire
in Bloom - Silver Gilt Award.

  ♿ ⊕ ☕

84 **SLEIGHTHOLMEDALE
LODGE**
Fadmoor YO62 6JG. Dr & Mrs O
James, 01751 431942. *6m NE of
Helmsley. Parking can be limited in wet
weather.* **Teas 14, 15, July only. Adm
£3, chd free. Sats 26 May; 2 June
(1-5); Sat 14, Sun 15 July (2-6). Also
opening with Pennyholme Sats 26
May; 2 June. Visitors also welcome
by appt for any number at any time,
no coaches.**
Hillside garden, walled rose garden
and herbaceous borders. Not suitable
for wheelchairs.

🛏 ☕

85 **NEW** **SOUTHWAYS**
Doncaster Road, Branton
DN3 3LT. Susan & Michael
Stevens. *3m SE of Doncaster.
M18 J4 to Armthorpe. L at
roundabout through Cantley Old
Village. L at roundabout B1396 to
Branton.* Light refreshments & teas

Extensive
colour-themed
flower borders,
walled rose
garden, canals
and fruit
trees . . .

& Mediterranean delicacies. **Adm
£2, chd free. Sun 12 Aug (12-5).
Visitors also welcome by appt,
May to Aug.**
Enclosed Mediterranean themed
garden with unusual tropical, half
hardy and drought tolerant plants
in 1/4 acre. From the entrance a
large paved area leads to fruit and
flower garden with greenhouses,
organic vegetables and herbs in
raised beds. The garden behind is
designed for late summer colour
with hanging baskets, tropical
plants, annuals, grasses and
dahlias with ornamental pool and
arbour. Doncaster in Bloom - Gold
Award.

♿ ✖ ⊕ ☕

86 **SPRING CLOSE FARM**
Gill Lane, Kearby LS22 4BS. John &
Rosemary Proctor, 0113 2886310.
*3m W of Wetherby. A661 from
Wetherby town centre, turn L at
bottom of Spofforth Hill to Sicklinghall.
1m after village turn L at Clap Gate
towards Kearby.* **Visitors welcome by
appt, June only, groups of 20+,
coaches permitted.**
Large mature yet evolving quiet
country garden, originally an exposed
site, now divided into garden rooms
sheltered by clipped yew and beech
hedging, with allées and tranquil water
garden leading to new orchard with ha-
ha and stunning views over Wharfe
Valley. Underplanted roses, mulberry
trees and herbaceous borders with
archways to walled garden with small
greenhouse, and enclosed cottage
garden.

♿ ✖

SQUIRREL LODGE
See Nottinghamshire.

87 **NEW** **STAINSACRE**
Carperby DL8 4DD. Colin & Pat
Jackson. *7m W of Leyburn. From
A684 1m N of Aysgarth Falls.*
Home-made teas in village hall.
**Adm £2.50, chd free. Sun 29 July
(1-5).**
1-acre site on S-sloping hillside
created by owners since 1996.
Deep mixed borders and island
beds with wide variety of hardy and
unusual perennials. 2 small wildlife
ponds and artificial stream. Open
grassed area with native trees and
gravel area with specimen hostas.

♿ ✖ ⊕ ☕

88 ◆ **STILLINGFLEET LODGE**
Stewart Lane, Stillingfleet, Nr York
YO19 6HP. Mr & Mrs J Cook,
01904 728506, www.
stillingfleetlodgenurseries.co.uk. *6m
S of York. From A19 York-Selby take
B1222 towards Sherburn in Elmet.*
**Adm £3, chd under 5 free, 5-16yrs
50p. Weds, Fris, Sats May to July &
Sept; Weds, Fris Aug (1-4). For NGS:
Suns 13 May; 24 June; 16 Sept
(1.30-5).**
Plantsman's garden subdivided into
smaller gardens, each based on
colour theme with emphasis on use
of foliage plants. Wild flower meadow
and natural pond. 55yds double
herbaceous borders. Organic garden.
Adjacent nursery. Featured in
'Independent' , 'Country Living' and
'Yorkshire Life'. WC not suitable for
disabled.

♿ ✖ ⊕ ☕

89 **SWALE COTTAGE**
Station Road, Richmond DL10 4LU.
Julie Martin & Dave Dalton.
*Richmond town centre. On foot,
facing bottom of Market Place, turn
L onto Frenchgate, then R onto
Station Rd. House 1st on R.* Home-
made teas. **Adm £2, chd free. Sun
24 June (2-6).**
1/2-acre urban oasis on steep site, with
sweeping views and hidden corners.
Several enclosed garden rooms on
different levels. Mature herbaceous,
rose and shrub garden with some
areas of recent improvement.
Magnificent yew and cedar. Organic
vegetables and soft fruit, pond,
orchard, adjacent paddock with sheep
and hens. Some steep slopes and
rough paths.

♿ ✖ ⊕ ☕

90 **THORPE LODGE**
Knaresborough Road, Ripon
HG4 3LU. Mr & Mrs T Jowitt,
www.thorpelodge.co.uk. *1m S of
Ripon. On Ripon-Bishop Monkton-
Knaresborough rd 3/4m from Ripon
bypass.* Home-made teas. **Adm £4,
chd free. Sun 29 July (1-6).**
Beautiful, large country garden of
12 acres with extensive colour-themed
flower borders, walled rose garden,
canals and fruit trees. Pleached
hornbeam walk and allées leads to
walks through mature woodland with
vistas and ponds. Courtyard with
exotic shrubs and tender plants in
pots. Area for picnics.

♿ ⊕ 🛏 ☕

91 TREGONNING
Ellerton YO42 4NZ. Deirdre Falcon & John Barwick, 01757 288578, deirdrefalcon@hotmail.com. *12m S of York. On B1228 to Elvington & Howden. 10m N of M62 J37. Next to village pond.* Home-made teas. **Adm £2.50, chd free. Suns 27 May; Sun 10 June (2-5). Visitors also welcome by appt May & June, groups of 10+, coaches welcome.**
1½-acres created over 30yrs, organic garden with fruit, vegetables and wild flower meadow. Annual and perennial wild flower borders. Over 60 species of old roses, climbers and dovecote. Large herbaceous border. Pergola walk, wild-life ponds, bog gardens, Victorian wells, rockeries and terrace. Large collection of seed-grown bonsai. Partial wheelchair access.

92 VICARAGE HOUSE
Kirkby Wharfe LS24 9DE. Mr & Mrs R S A Hall. *1m S of Tadcaster. (A162) turn L (B1223) after 1m turn L to Kirkby Wharfe. Park in adjacent field.* Home-made teas. **Adm £2.50, chd free. Sun 27 May (1-5).**
Secluded 1-acre country garden surrounded by mature trees, colour-themed border, extensive herbaceous borders, raised beds. Species primulae and aquilegias. Gravel paths.

93 ♦ THE WALLED GARDEN AT SCAMPSTON
Rillington YO17 8NG. Sir Charles & Lady Legard, 01944 759111, www.scampston.co.uk. *5m E of Malton. ½m N of A64, signed Scampston only.* **House and Garden adm £9.50, chd £5, Garden only adm £5, chd £3, concessions £4.50. For details of openings & dates see website or tel. For NGS: Wed 4 July (10-5).**
An exciting modern garden designed by Piet Oudolf who has filled the 4½-acre walled garden with a series of hedged enclosures. In early July the extravagantly planted perennial meadow will be looking at its best. The garden contains many rare species, all carefully labelled, and is a must for any keen plantsman. Featured in 'Hull Journal', 'Gardens Illustrated' & on TV. Hidden Treasure Houses, BBC Radio 4 Woman's Hour.

94 26 WEST END
Walkington HU17 8SX. Miss Jennifer Hall, 01482 861705. *2m SW of Beverley. On the B1230, 100yds beyond Xrds in centre of village on the R.* Teas at 18 West End (nearly next door). **Adm £3, chd free. Sun 3 June (1.30-5). Visitors also welcome by appt, in June for groups 6+.**
Charming and interesting 1-acre cottage garden opening into old wooded gravel pit still being developed by owner. Many rare plants collected over 20yrs.

95 THE WHITE HOUSE
Husthwaite YO61 4QA. Mrs A Raper, 01347 868688. *5m S of Thirsk. Turn R off A19 signed Husthwaite. 1½m to centre of village opp parish church.* **Visitors welcome by appt.**
Come and meet the gardener, an enthusiastic plantswoman. Exchange ideas and visit a 1-acre country garden with herb garden, conservatory and gardens within the garden. Herbaceous, particularly a hot summer border and shrubs and many fascinating unusual plants. Landscaping and planting in the old orchard.

96 WHIXLEY GARDENS
YO26 8AR. *Between York & Harrogate. 3m E of A1(M) off A59 York-Harrogate. Signed Whixley.* Light refreshments & teas at The Old Vicarage. **Combined adm £5, chd free. Sun 24 June (12-5). Also open Croft Cottage.**

ASH TREE HOUSE
High Street. Mr & Mrs E P Moffitt
Well designed unusual garden of approx ¼-acre with extensive rockeries making full use of sloping site. Established herbaceous plants, shrubs and climbers achieve a cottage garden effect. Access only by steps.

THE BAY HOUSE
Stonegate. Mr & Mrs Jon Beckett
Densely planted courtyard garden on differing levels.

COBBLE COTTAGE
John Hawkridge & Barry Atkinson
(See separate entry).

THE OLD VICARAGE
Mr & Mrs Roger Marshall
Delightful ¾-acre walled flower garden with mixed borders, unusual shrubs, climbers, roses, hardy and half-hardy perennials, bulbs and hellebores. Paths and garden structures lead to new vistas and hidden areas using the garden's natural contours.

97 WOODLANDS COTTAGE
Summerbridge, nr Harrogate HG3 4BT. Mr & Mrs Stark, 01423 780765, www. woodlandscottagegarden.co.uk. *4m E of Pateley Bridge, 10m NW of Harrogate. On the B6165 (Ripley-Pateley Bridge) ½m W of Summerbridge.* Home-made teas. **Adm £2.50, chd free. Sun 13 May (1.30-5). Combined with Nidderdale Gardens adm £6, Sun 8 July. Visitors also welcome by appt May - Aug, groups 10+ welcome and coaches.**
1-acre plantswomen's garden in Nidderdale. Garden is designed to harmonise with the surrounding countryside and has several differing areas of planting with many unusual plants, natural rock outcrops, wild flower meadow and vegetable garden. Gravel paths, some slopes.

Come and meet the gardener, an enthusiastic plantswoman. Exchange ideas and visit a 1-acre country garden . . .

98 NEW **WORTLEY HALL**
Wortley Village S35 7DB, 0114
2882100, www.wortleyhall.com.
*9m NW of Sheffield & 5m SW of
Barnsley. On A629 Huddersfield -
Sheffield rd in Wortley village,
signed Wortley Hall & Gardens.*
Light refreshments & teas. **Adm
£3, chd free. Sun 24 June (10-4).**
Visitors also welcome by appt,
May to Sept, groups 15+, can
incl guided tour.
26 acres of elegant Italianate
gardens set within landscaped
parkland. Formal gardens with
sunken garden, arbour and clipped
yew balls all framed with seasonal
bedding and perennial borders
leading to walled organic kitchen
garden. Informal walks through
pleasure grounds reveal C18/19
plantings incl 500yr old hollow oak,
lake and ice house. Guided tours
with Gardeners throughout the day.
Featured on Radio Sheffield. Silver
award - Yorkshire in Bloom. Partial
wheelchair access.
&. ✗ ⊛ ⊨ ☕

99 ◆ **WYTHERSTONE GARDENS**
Pockley YO62 7TE. Lady Clarissa
Collin, 01439 770012,
www.wytherstonegardens.com. *2m
NE of Helmsley. Signed from A170.*
**Adm £3.50, chd £1 under 6 free.
Suns 3 June; 22 July, 9 Sept; Weds
6 June to 9 Sept. For NGS: Suns 20
May; 17 June; 19 Aug (1-5).**
A true plantsman's garden set in 8
acres of rolling countryside on edge of
the North York Moors. The garden is
divided by beech hedges, creating
interlinked specialised 'feature'

Informal walks through pleasure grounds reveal C18/19 plantings incl 500 year old hollow oak, lake and ice house . . .

gardens, incl Mediterranean,
ericaceous, terraced, good small
arboretum (incl, the most northerly
Wollemia nobilis planted outside), fern
garden and paeonia garden. Plants not
thought hardy in the north of England
grow happily on Wytherstone's free
draining soil. Delightful on-site nursery
where all the plants are propagated
from the garden. New for 2007 foliage
and bamboo garden.
&. ✗ ⊛ ☕

100 ◆ **YORK GATE**
Back Church Lane, Adel LS16 8DW.
Perennial, 0113 267 8240,
www.perennial.org.uk. *5m N of
Leeds centre. 2¼m SE of Bramhope,
signed from A660. Park in Church*

Lane nr church and take public
footpath through churchyard & straight
on to garden gate. Tea & biscuits only.
**Adm £3.50, chd free. Thurs, Suns &
Bank Hol Mons, 8 Apr to 30 Sept (2-
5), for evening opening times please
see website or tel.**
1-acre masterpiece and outstanding
example of C20 English garden design.
Within a series of inner gardens are
shrubs and herbaceous borders,
ponds, pinetum, dell, fern border, nut
walk, white and silver borders, kitchen
garden and famous herb garden with
topiary. Each area has its own unique
architectural features and evergreens
are used to great effect throughout.
Featured in 'The Guardian' & 'The Daily
Telegraph'.
✗ ⊛ ☕

101 **YORKE HOUSE**
Dacre Banks, Nidderdale HG3 4EW.
Anthony & Pat Hutchinson, 01423
780456, www.yorkehouse.co.uk. *4m
SE of Pateley Bridge, 10m NW of
Harrogate. On B6451. Car park.*
Home-made teas. **Adm £3, chd free.
Sun 24 June (11-5). Open with
Nidderdale Gardens Sun 8 July.**
Visitors also welcome by appt June
to Aug, incl coaches.
Flower arranger's 2-acre garden with
colour-themed borders full of flowering
and foliage plants and shrubs.
Extensive water feature incl large
ornamental ponds and stream. Other
features incl nut walk, rose pergola,
patios, gazebo, Millennium garden and
wildlife area. The garden enjoys
beautiful views across Nidderdale.
Picnic area. Gentle slopes.
&. ⊛ ☕

Yorkshire County Volunteers

County Organiser
North Yorks Jane Baldwin, Riverside Farm, Sinnington, York YO62 6RY, 01751 431764, wnbaldwin@yahoo.co.uk
East Yorks Sally Bean, Saltmarshe Hall, Saltmarshe, Howden, Goole DN14 7RX, 01430 430199, pmegabean@aol.com
West & South Yorks Bridget Marshall, The Old Vicarage, Whixley, York YO26 8AR, 01423 330474,
    biddymarshall@btopenworld.com

County Treasurer
Angela Pugh, Savage Garth, Nun Monkton, York YO26 8ER, 01423 330456, angie.pugh@btinternet.com

Publicity
Felicity Bowring, Lawkland Hall, Austwick, Lancaster LA2 8AT, 01729 823551, diss@austwick.org

County Booklet & Advertising
Tim Gittins, Hillbark, Church Lane, Bardsey, Leeds LS17 9DH, 01937 574968, timgittins@aol.com

Assistant County Organisers
Deborah Bigley, The Old Rectory, Great Langton, Northallerton DL7 0TA, 01609 748915
Annabel Fife, Langton farm, Great Langton, Northallerton DL7 0TA, 01609 748446
Jane, Hudson Lower Crawshaw, Emley, Huddersfield HD8 9SU, 01924 840980, janehudson42@btinternet.com

ngs gardens open for charity

Come and visit the NGS stand at the Shows

13th & 14th March
RHS London Flower Show,
Vincent Square, London

20th–22nd April
Cardiff Flower Show

26th–29th April
Harrogate Flower Show

10th–13th May
Malvern Flower Show, Three Counties
Showground, Malvern

22nd–26th May
Chelsea Flower Show, London

13th–17th June
BBC Gardeners World Live, NEC Birmingham

28th–29th July
The Gardening Show, Llangollen

WALES

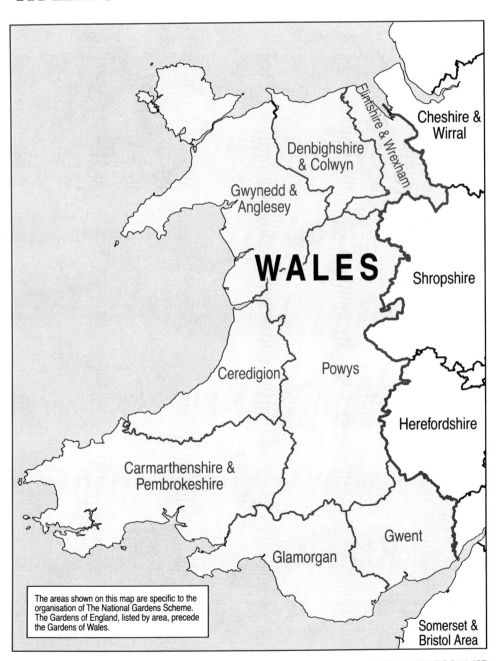

Cheshire & Wirral

Flintshire & Wrexham

Denbighshire & Colwyn

Gwynedd & Anglesey

WALES

Shropshire

Ceredigion

Powys

Herefordshire

Carmarthenshire & Pembrokeshire

Gwent

Glamorgan

The areas shown on this map are specific to the organisation of The National Gardens Scheme. The Gardens of England, listed by area, precede the Gardens of Wales.

Somerset & Bristol Area

CARMARTHENSHIRE & PEMBROKESHIRE

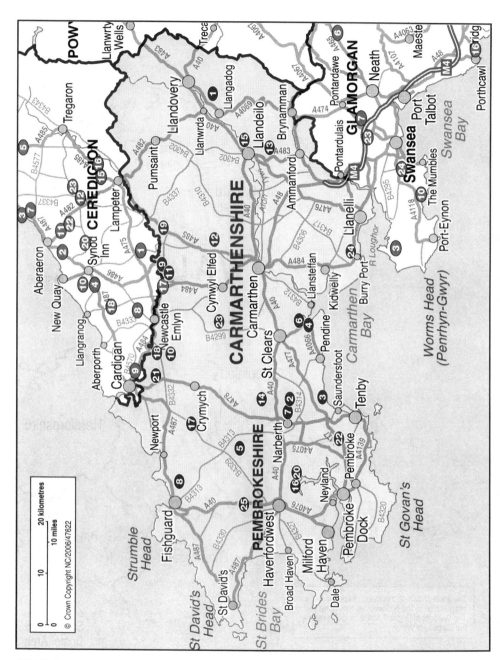

Opening Dates

March

SUNDAY 11
- ⑱ Nant-yr-Eryd

SUNDAY 18
- ⑨ Farmyard Nursery Woodland Garden

April

SUNDAY 8
- ⑨ Farmyard Nursery Woodland Garden

SATURDAY 14
- ㉕ Weir Castle

SUNDAY 15
- ⑲ Norwood Gardens
- ㉕ Weir Castle

SUNDAY 29
- ㉒ Rosewood

May

SUNDAY 6
- ⑳ Picton Castle & Woodland Gardens

SUNDAY 13
- ③ Colby Woodland Garden
- ⑭ Llwyngarreg
- ⑮ Maesquarre

MONDAY 14
- ⑮ Maesquarre

TUESDAY 15
- ⑮ Maesquarre

WEDNESDAY 16
- ⑮ Maesquarre (Evening)

THURSDAY 17
- ⑮ Maesquarre

FRIDAY 18
- ⑮ Maesquarre

SATURDAY 19
- ⑮ Maesquarre
- ㉕ Weir Castle

SUNDAY 20
- ⑩ Ffynone
- ㉕ Weir Castle

SUNDAY 27
- ⑦ Dyffryn Farm

June

SATURDAY 9
- ㉔ Tradewinds

SUNDAY 10
- ㉔ Tradewinds

SUNDAY 17
- ② Coed-y-Ffynnon
- ⑱ Nant-yr-Eryd

SATURDAY 23
- ② Coed-y-Ffynnon
- ㉕ Weir Castle

SUNDAY 24
- ⑭ Llwyngarreg
- ㉕ Weir Castle

FRIDAY 29
- ⑬ Llwyn Cyll (Evening)

July

SUNDAY 1
- ⑲ Norwood Gardens

SATURDAY 7
- ⑪ Glandwr

SUNDAY 8
- ⑪ Glandwr
- ⑫ Glangwili Lodges

WEDNESDAY 11
- ⑫ Glangwili Lodges

SATURDAY 14
- ㉒ Rosewood
- ㉕ Weir Castle

SUNDAY 15
- ① Cilgwyn Lodge
- ⑥ Delacorse
- ⑳ Picton Castle & Woodland Gardens
- ㉕ Weir Castle

SUNDAY 22
- ㉓ The Cors

SATURDAY 28
- ㉕ Weir Castle

SUNDAY 29
- ㉑ Rhosygilwen Mansion
- ㉕ Weir Castle

August

SUNDAY 5
- ⑧ Dyffryn Fernant
- ㉓ The Cors (Evening)

WEDNESDAY 8
- ⑦ Dyffryn Farm

MONDAY 13
- ㉕ Weir Castle

TUESDAY 14
- ㉕ Weir Castle

WEDNESDAY 15
- ㉕ Weir Castle

THURSDAY 16
- ㉕ Weir Castle

FRIDAY 17
- ㉕ Weir Castle

SATURDAY 18
- ㉕ Weir Castle

SUNDAY 19
- ㉕ Weir Castle

September

SATURDAY 1
- ㉕ Weir Castle

SUNDAY 2
- ⑲ Norwood Gardens
- ㉕ Weir Castle

SUNDAY 16
- ㉔ Tradewinds

Gardens open to the public

- ③ Colby Woodland Garden
- ⑧ Dyffryn Fernant
- ⑨ Farmyard Nursery Woodland Garden
- ⑰ Moorland Cottage Plants
- ⑲ Norwood Gardens
- ⑳ Picton Castle & Woodland Gardens
- ㉓ Tradewinds

By appointment only

- ㉔ 2 Tyfri
- ⑤ Cwm Pibau
- ⑯ Millinford

The Gardens

ALLTYRODYN MANSION
See Ceredigion/Cardiganshire.

① **CILGWYN LODGE**
Llangadog SA19 9LH. Keith Brown & Moira Thomas, 01550 777452, keith@cilgwynlodge.co.uk. *3m NE of Llangadog village. 4m SW of Llandovery. Turn off A40 into centre of Llangadog. Bear L in front of village shop then 1st R towards Myddfai. After 2½m pass Cilgwyn Manor on L then 1st L. Garden ¼m on L.* Home-made teas. **Adm £2.50, chd free. Sun 15 July (1-5).** Visitors also welcome by appt, coaches and parties welcome.
Fascinating 1-acre garden set in glorious countryside comprising 2 separate gardens incl fruit and vegetables, shrubs and a wide variety

Jungly courtyard, fernery, large pond . . .

of herbaceous plants with over 200 varieties of hostas, displayed in extensive colour-themed borders. Large waterlily and wildlife pond and formal koi pond. Plenty of seating to enjoy the garden. Featured in 'Carmarthen Journal'. One garden wheelchair-accessible, other has slopes and gravel paths.

 ♿ ✕ ⊛ ☕

❷ COED-Y-FFYNNON
Lampeter Velfrey SA67 8UJ. Col R H Gilbertson, 01834 831396, rh.gilbertson@virgin.net. *2½m SE of Narberth. From Penblewin roundabout on A40 follow signs to Narberth & then to crematorium. Straight on through Llanmill & Lampeter Velfrey. Garden ½m on L. Home-made teas.* **Adm £2.50, chd free. Sun 17, Sat 23 June (2-6). Visitors also welcome by appt in June & July.**
Enthusiast's 1-acre garden with over 140 varieties of old fashioned roses. Informal planting and naturalistic garden style with ample provision for wildlife. Roses at their best mid-June to mid-July. Relaxed rural setting. Talks and guided tour available.

 ♿ ⊛ ☕

❸ ◆ COLBY WOODLAND GARDEN
Amroth SA67 8PP. The National Trust, 01834 811885. *6m N of Tenby. 5m SE of Narberth. Signed by brown tourist signs on coast rd & A477.* **Adm £4, chd £2. Open daily Apr to Oct. House not open. For NGS: Sun 13 May (10-5).**
8-acre woodland garden in a secluded and tranquil valley with fine collection of rhododendrons and azaleas. Walled garden open by kind permission of Mr and Mrs A Scourfield Lewis. Some steep areas.

 ♿ ✕ ⊛ ☕

❹ THE CORS
Newbridge Road, Laugharne SA33 4SH. Nick Priestland, 01994 427219, www.the-cors.co.uk. *12m SW of Carmarthen. From Carmarthen, turn R in centre of Laugharne at The Mariners PH. At bottom of Newbridge Rd on R. Use public car parks, 5 mins walk.* Home-made teas. **Adm £3, chd free. Sun 22 July (2-6). Evening Opening, wine, Sun 5 Aug (6-9). Visitors also welcome by appt.**
Approx 2½ acres set in beautiful wooded valley bordering river. Large bog garden with ponds, gunnera, bamboos and tree ferns. Well-

designed plantsman's garden with unusual architectural and exotic planting and sculptures. Best Chef and Gardener in BMW Best Food Ride.

 ♿ ✕ ⊛ ☕ ☕

Up-river from Dylan Thomas Boathouse Museum . . . 3-acre garden beside Tâf Estuary, in beautiful landscape . . .

❺ CWM PIBAU
New Moat SA63 4RE. Mrs Duncan Drew, 01437 532454. *10m NE of Haverfordwest. 3m SW of Maenclochog.* **Adm £3, chd free. Visitors welcome by appt.**
5-acre woodland garden surrounded by old deciduous woodland and streams. Created in 1978, contains many mature, unusual shrubs and trees from Chile, New Zealand and Europe, set on S-facing sloping hill. More conventional planting nearer house.

❻ DELACORSE
Laugharne SA33 4QP. Annie Hart. *13m SW of Carmarthen. On A4066 from St Clears, after Cross Inn turn L signed to Ant's Hill Caravan Park, continue ½m. Access to garden further ½m on bumpy track with traffic controls. Parking in field. Alternatively, on foot from Laugharne, 20 mins walk along footpath up-river from Dylan Thomas Boathouse Museum.* Home-made teas. **Adm £2.50, chd free. Sun 15 July (11-5).**
3-acre garden beside Tâf Estuary, in peaceful, beautiful landscape with fine views. Scented walled garden, with chamomile lawn; sheltered courtyard with exotics; mixed borders providing all-yr interest; lawns and informal pond areas, with living willow work, merging into woodland, reed beds and salt marsh. Extensive organic kitchen garden. Donkey rides, willow weaving workshop, organic soft fruit for sale.

 ♿ ⊛ ☕ ☕

❼ DYFFRYN FARM
Lampeter Velfrey, Narberth SA67 8UN. Dr & Mrs M J R Polson, Mr & Mrs D Bradley, 01834 861684, sally.polson@virgin.net. *3m E of Narberth. From junction of A40 & A478 follow signs for crematorium, continue down into Llanmill. Then uphill, at brow turn L at Bryn Sion Chapel Xrds (before Lampeter Velfrey). After ½m rd turns R under railway bridge. Dyffryn Farm straight ahead, parking under bridge and immed on R.* Home-made teas. **Adm £2.50, chd free. Sun 27 May; Wed 8 Aug (12-5). Visitors also welcome by appt, coaches permitted.**
Large relaxed garden developed into several areas on different levels in a 'naturalised' way (not landscaped or contrived) using our mature, rural, secluded valley backcloth to full benefit. Highlights incl 60+ bamboos, grasses, herbaceous plants, unusual shrubs; stream, pond with island; small woodland; tropical and tender succulents in pots. Wheelchair access in dry weather.

 ♿ ✕ ⊛ ☕

❽ ◆ DYFFRYN FERNANT
Llanychaer, Fishguard SA65 9SP. Christina Shand & David Allum, 01348 811282, www.genuslocus.net. *3m E of Fishguard, then ½m inland. A487 Fishguard to Cardigan. After approx 3m, at end of long straight hill, turn R signed Llanychaer with blue rd signs 'unsuitable for long vehicles'. After exactly ½m is Dyffryn track, on L behind LH bend, with wooden sign.* **Adm £3, chd free. Suns fortnightly Easter to end Sept & Bank Hol Mons. For NGS: Sun 5 Aug (10-5).**
Adventurous 6-acre garden making the most of the dramatic landscape. Profusion of choice perennials, shrubs and young trees, designed to be appreciated in contrasted areas. Lush bog garden; intriguing sculptures, incl obelisk; jungly courtyard, fernery, large pond, new grasses garden - and much more. Runner-up Garden of the Year S4C Club Garddio, featured in GGG & on Radio Pembrokeshire.

 ✕ ⊛ 🛏

❾ ◆ FARMYARD NURSERY WOODLAND GARDEN
Llandysul SA44 4RL. Mr Richard Bramley, 01559 363389, www.farmyardnurseries.co.uk. *½m S of Llandysul. Off Carmarthen rd B4336, 2nd L opp Valley Services garage. Approx 1m following signs.*

Adm £2, chd free. For NGS: Suns 18 Mar; 8 Apr (8.30-5). Established 1-acre shaded woodland and herbaceous garden incl new woodland plantings. Peaceful walks with magnificent views, natural wildlife-friendly water features, sunken walled garden. Extensive hosta, fern and bulb planting providing all-yr-interest. Adjoining plantsman's nursery. National Collection of Tricyrtis and biggest collection of hand-pollinated hellebores in the country. Gold Medal & Best in Show at RHS Hampton Court & Tatton Park.

Biggest collection of hand-pollinated hellebores in the country . . .

⑩ FFYNONE
Boncath SA37 0HQ. Earl & Countess Lloyd George of Dwyfor, 01239 841610. *9m SE of Cardigan. 7m W of Newcastle Emlyn. From Newcastle Emlyn take A484 to Cenarth, turn L on B4332, turn L again at Xrds just before Newchapel.* Home-made teas. **Adm £3, chd free. Sun 20 May (1-5). Visitors also welcome by appt.**
Large woodland garden designated Grade I on Cadw register of historic gardens in Wales. Lovely views, fine specimen trees, rhododendrons, azaleas, woodland walks. House (also Grade I) by John Nash (1793), not open. Later additions and garden terraces by F Inigo Thomas c1904. Steep paths, limited wheelchair access.

⑪ GLANDWR
Pentrecwrt SA44 5DA. Mrs Jo Hicks, 01559 363729. *15m N of Carmarthen, 2m S of Llandysul, 7m E of Newcastle Emlyn. On A486. At Pentrecwrt village, take minor rd opp Black Horse PH. After bridge keep L for 1/4 m. Glandwr is on R.* Cream teas. **Adm £2, chd free. Sat 7, Sun 8 July (11-5). Visitors also welcome by appt.**
Delightful 1-acre cottage garden, bordered by a natural stream, with colour-themed areas and rockery. Mature natural woodland provides an intriguing walk with various shade plants, ground covers, shrubs and many surprises.

⑫ GLANGWILI LODGES
Llanllawddog SA32 7JE. Chris & Christine Blower. *7m NE of Carmarthen. Take A485 from Carmarthen. After Stag & Pheasant PH in Pontarsais turn R for Llanllawddog and Brechfa. 1/2 m after Llanllawddog Chapel, rd bears sharply R, Glangwili Lodges 100yds on R.* Light refreshments & teas. **Adm £2, chd free. Sun 8 July (11-4), Wed 11 July (1-5).**
16 acres incl 1-acre walled garden, former nursery to Glangwili Mansion. Restoration initiated 5 yrs ago. Borders with colourful perennials and cottage-style beds. Rockery, alpines, water features; collections of maples and unusual trees; wild flower meadow. Woodland stream walks. Valley setting with superb views of Gwili Valley and Brechfa Forest.

⑬ LLWYN CYLL
Trap SA19 6TR. Liz & John Smith, 01558 822398, liz-johntrap @amserve.com. *3m SE of Llandeilo. In Trap turn towards Glanaman & Llandybie (at The Cenan Arms). Llwyn Cyll is 1/2 m on L adjoining Llwyn Onn. Parking limited.* Teas & wine. **Adm £2, chd £1. Evening Opening, wine, Fri 29 June (4.30-7.30). Visitors also welcome by appt almost daily Apr to Sept. If possible please ring to avoid disappointment.**
31/2-acre country garden of yr-round interest. Abundant and colourful terraced and walled borders, small arboretum, orchard and vegetable garden. Sun and shade areas with sympathetic planting. A plantsman's garden with many rarities, especially magnolias and specimen trees.

⑭ LLWYNGARREG
Llanfallteg SA34 0XH. Paul & Liz O'Neill, 01994 240717, lizpaulfarm@yahoo.co.uk. *19m W of Carmarthen. A40 W from Carmarthen, turn R at Llandewi Velfrey to Llanfallteg. Garden 1/2 m further on, 2nd farm on R.* **Adm £2, chd free. Suns 13 May; 24 June (12-5).**
Plantsman's garden of 3 acres with many trees both young and mature.

Bog garden, woodland gardens, long borders, peat beds, gravel garden, vegetable plot and several ponds. Rhododendrons, magnolias, primulas and grasses among many unusual plantings. Several deep water features, young children must be closely supervised. Wheelchair aide needed for short slope.

⑮ MAESQUARRE
Bethlehem Road, Llandeilo SA19 6YA. Mr & Mrs Geoffrey Williams, 01558 822960. *11/2 m E of Llandeilo. From Llandeilo take A483 across R Towy. At Ffairfach mini roundabout turn L along unclassified Bethlehem Rd, garden on R after 2m. Parking nearby.* **Adm £2, chd free. Sun 13 May to Tue 15 May & Thur 17 May to Sat 19 May (2-6). Evening Opening Wed 16 May (5-8). Visitors also welcome by appt.**
Spacious and peaceful garden attempting to combine the owners' interest in unusual shrubs and trees and local flora and fauna. Large closely-planted pond area, slopes of developing and maturing shrubs and trees, natural woodland, with an attractive stream flowing throughout, form the main features of the garden.

⑯ MILLINFORD
Millin Cross SA62 4AL. Drs B & A Barton, 01437 762394. *3m E of Haverfordwest. From Haverfordwest on A40 to Carmarthen, turn R signed The Rhos, take turning to Millin. Turn R at Millin Chapel then immed L over river bridge.* **Adm £3, chd free, concessions £2.50. Visitors welcome by appt.**
Spacious, undulating and peaceful garden of 4 acres on bank of Millin Creek. Varied collection of over 125 different trees, many unusual, plus shrubs, herbaceous plants and bulbs in beautiful riverside setting. Impressive terracing and water features. Visit in spring, summer and early autumn. Two ponds, children must be supervised.

⑰ ◆ MOORLAND COTTAGE PLANTS
Rhyd-y-Groes, Brynberian SA41 3TT. Jennifer & Kevin Matthews, 01239 891363, www.moorlandcottageplants.co.uk. *12m SW of Cardigan. 16m NE of Haverfordwest, on B4329, 3/4 m downhill from cattlegrid (from*

Haverfordwest) and *1m uphill from signpost to Brynberian (from Cardigan).* **Adm £1.80, chd 50p. Daily, not Weds, 19 May to 2 Sept (10.30-5.30).** Country garden located at 720ft on the wild Preseli hillside. 1/2-acre of diverse, mollusc-proof plantings linked by meandering paths. Cottage garden borders, grasses and bamboos, shady areas with ferns. Some rarities. Gardening without pesticides or fungicides encourages abundant wildlife. Nursery specialising in hardy perennials, ornamental grasses & ferns. ⚥ ⊛

18 NEW NANT-YR-ERYD
Abercych, Boncath SA37 0EU. Alan Hall. *5m SE of Cardigan, 5m W of Newcastle Emlyn. Off B4332 Cenarth to Abercych, at N end of Abercych, half way between Newchapel and Cenarth.* **Adm £2, chd free. Sun 11 Mar (11-4); Sun 17 June (11-5).**
Early spring garden featuring approx 50 varieties of daffodils. Established and new topiary gardens. Summer garden featuring old roses. Fernery and topiary, with wild garden. ⚥

19 ◆ NORWOOD GARDENS
Llanllwni SA39 9DU. The Norwood Gardens Partnership, 01559 395386, www.norwoodgardens.co.uk. *8m SW of Lampeter. On A485 Carmarthen to Lampeter rd in village of Llanllwni between Talardd Arms and Belle Vue PH. Tourist signs on approaches.* **Adm £4, chd free, concessions £3. Daily (not Tues) 21 Mar to 28 Oct. For NGS: Suns 15 Apr; 1 July; 2 Sept (10-6).**
Developing 3-acre garden consisting of individual gardens, each with its own character, linked by paths and borders, plus sculpture. Over 80 varieties of daffodil flood the garden with spring colour. Shrubs and herbaceous plants continue to provide colour throughout the yr. Collection of hemerocallis and alliums. ♿ ⊛ ☕

THE OLD VICARAGE
See Ceredigion/Cardiganshire.

20 ◆ PICTON CASTLE & WOODLAND GARDENS
The Rhos SA62 4AS. Picton Castle Trust, 01437 751326, www.pictoncastle.co.uk. *3m E of Haverfordwest. On A40 to Carmarthen, signed off main rd.* **Garden £4.95, chd £2.50, concessions £4.75. House adm additional £1, chd 50p. Daily 1 Apr to 30 Sept, not Mons (but open Bank Hol Mons). For NGS: Suns 6 May; 15 July (10.30-5).**
Mature 40-acre woodland garden with unique collection of rhododendrons and azaleas, many bred over 40yrs, producing hybrids of great merit and beauty; rare and tender shrubs and trees incl magnolia, myrtle, embothrium and eucryphia. Wild flowers abound. Walled garden with roses; fernery; herbaceous and climbing plants and large clearly-labelled collection of herbs. ♿ ⊛

Located at 720ft on the wild Preseli hillside, 1/2-acre of diverse, mollusc-proof plantings . . .

21 RHOSYGILWEN MANSION
Cilgerran, Cardigan SA43 2TW. Glen Peters & Brenda Squires, 01239 841387, www.retreat.co.uk. *5m S of Cardigan. From Cardigan follow A478 signed Tenby. After 6m turn L at Rhoshill towards Cilgerran. After 1/4m turn R signed Rhosygilwen. Mansion gates 1/2m.* **Light refreshments & teas. Adm £3, chd free. Sun 29 July (11-5).** Visitors also welcome by appt Apr to Aug.
20 acres of garden in 55 acre estate. Pretty 1/2m drive through woodland planting. Spacious lightly wooded grounds for leisurely rambling, 1-acre walled garden fully productive of fruit, vegetables and flowers; authentically restored Edwardian greenhouses, many old and new trees, small formal garden. Gravel paths. ♿ ⚥ 🛏 ☕

22 NEW ROSEWOOD
Redberth, nr Tenby SA70 8SA. Mr & Mrs K Treadaway. *3m SW of Kilgetty. On old A477, now bypassed, 80yds from centre of village, on W side. Ample parking on roadside.* **Adm £2, chd free. Sun 29 Apr; Sat 14 July (1-5).**
1/4-acre garden, split into different areas, with mixed plantings and incl National Collection of Clematis (subgenus Viorna) plus many other clematis. Some steps. ⚥ ⊛ **NCCPG**

23 ◆ TRADEWINDS
Ffynnonwen, Penybont, Carmarthen SA33 6PX. Stuart Kemp-Gee & Eve Etheridge, 01994 484744. *10m NW of Carmarthen. A40 W from Carmarthen approx 4m, then turn R onto B4298 to Meidrim. In Meidrim R onto B4299 to Trelech. After approx 51/2m turn R at Tradewinds sign, then approx 1/2m, next to 2nd farm.* **Adm £2.50, chd free. Please telephone for opening times and to arrange group visits. For NGS: Sat 9, Sun 10 June; Sun 16 Sept (11-5).**
11/2-acre plantsman's garden with abundance of herbaceous perennials, shrubs and trees giving yr-round interest for the discerning gardener. Incl liquidambars, Aralia elata variegata and trochodendron. Mixed borders, natural streams and natural pond. Picturesque garden in tranquil setting. Developing garden with ongoing changes and additions. Working artist's gallery open. Children must be supervised. ⚥ ⊛ ☕

1-acre walled garden fully productive of fruit, vegetables and flowers; authentically restored Edwardian greenhouses . . .

24 2 TYFRI
Dandorlan Road, Burry Port
SA16 0DS. Mary Atkin, 01554
835194. *Please phone for directions,
parking limited.* **Adm £2, chd free.**
Visitors welcome by appt June to
Aug.
1-acre mild sheltered garden, steeply
sloping down to small stream via
steps, seats and banks. Mediterranean
bank, herbaceous beds, bog and 2
pond areas. Foliage and form as
important as flowers.

25 WEIR CASTLE
Treffgarne, Wolfscastle SA62 5LR.
D J & D C Morris, 01437 741252. *On
A40 between Haverfordwest and
Fishguard. Approx 5m from
Haverfordwest (before Wolfscastle).
Just past signs for Treffgarne and
Angling Centre, turn L up drive.* **Adm
£2, chd free. Sat, Suns 14, 15 Apr;
19, 20 May; 23, 24 June; 14, 15, 28,
29 July; Mon 13 to Sun 19 Aug incl;
Sat, Sun 1, 2 Sept (11-6).** Visitors
also welcome by appt.
Fairly steep hillside, richly planted with
well-chosen shrubs and perennials,
with attractive features and lovely
views. The result of flair and
imagination and brilliant use of a
difficult site.

1-acre mild
sheltered garden,
steeply sloping
down to small
stream via steps,
seats and banks.
Mediterranean
bank . . .

Carmarthenshire & Pembrokeshire County Volunteers

Joint County Organisers
Mrs Jill Foster, Heron Cottage, Picton Ferry, The Rhos, Haverfordwest, Pembrokeshire SA62 4AR, 01437 751241
Mrs Jane Stokes, Llyshendy, Llandeilo, Carmarthenshire SA19 6YA, 01558 823233, ivor.t.stokes@btopenworld.com

County Treasurer
Mrs Susan Allen, Pen y coed Isaf, Whitland, Carmarthenshire, SA34 0LR, 01994 241269

Publicity
Mrs Jo Hammond, Ashdale, Llanmill, Narberth, Pembrokeshire SA67 8UE, 01834 869140
Mrs Nicky Rogers, Hayston, Merrion, Pembroke, Pembrokeshire SA71 5EA, 01646 661462

CEREDIGION

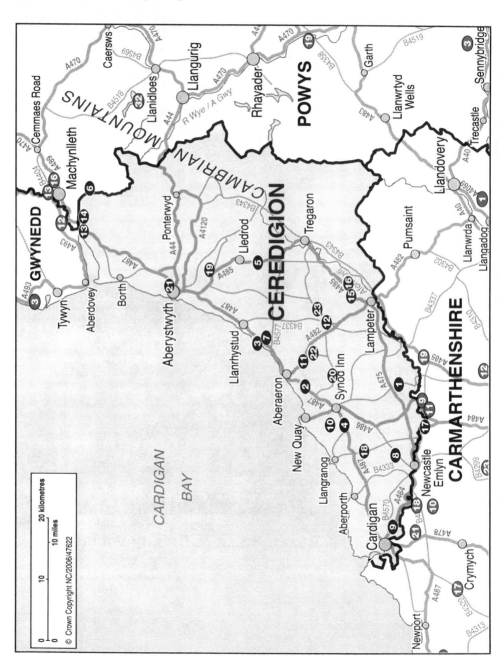

Opening Dates

May

SUNDAY 6
13 Llwyncelyn
14 The Mill House
18 Pant-yr-Holiad

SUNDAY 13
20 Perth Yr Eglwys
21 Plas Penglais, University of Wales Aberystwyth

SUNDAY 20
3 Bron-y-Graig
7 Dyffryn

SUNDAY 27
1 Alltyrodyn Mansion
2 Arnant House
6 Cwmrhaiadr Garden & Nursery

June

SUNDAY 3
8 Garth

SATURDAY 9
23 Winllan Wildlife Garden

SUNDAY 10
5 Bwlch y Geuffordd
10 Heddfan
23 Winllan Wildlife Garden

MONDAY 11
23 Winllan Wildlife Garden

TUESDAY 12
23 Winllan Wildlife Garden

WEDNESDAY 13
23 Winllan Wildlife Garden

THURSDAY 14
23 Winllan Wildlife Garden

FRIDAY 15
23 Winllan Wildlife Garden

SATURDAY 16
4 The Bungalow
23 Winllan Wildlife Garden

SUNDAY 17
12 Llanllyr
23 Winllan Wildlife Garden

MONDAY 18
23 Winllan Wildlife Garden

TUESDAY 19
23 Winllan Wildlife Garden

WEDNESDAY 20
23 Winllan Wildlife Garden

THURSDAY 21
11 Llanerchaeron (Evening)
23 Winllan Wildlife Garden

FRIDAY 22
23 Winllan Wildlife Garden

SATURDAY 23
23 Winllan Wildlife Garden

SUNDAY 24
15 New Hall
16 Oak Meadows at Maesyderi
19 Penbanc
23 Winllan Wildlife Garden

SATURDAY 30
17 The Old Vicarage

July

SUNDAY 1
17 The Old Vicarage

SUNDAY 8
18 Pant-yr-Holiad

SUNDAY 29
22 Ty Glyn Walled Garden

September

SUNDAY 2
9 Glanhelyg

SUNDAY 9
6 Cwmrhaiadr Garden & Nursery

Gardens open to the public

11 Llanerchaeron
22 Ty Glyn Walled Garden

The Gardens

1 **ALLTYRODYN MANSION**
Capel Dewi SA44 4PS. Mr & Mrs Donald Usher. *8m W of Lampeter, off A475. Take B4459 at Rhydowen to Capel Dewi. Entrance on R by South Lodge.* Home-made teas. **Adm £2.50, chd free (share to Capel Dewi Church). Sun 27 May (11-5).** Early C19 garden. Approx 8 acres, mostly mature woodland with many fine trees. Old walled garden. Rare stone-built gothic cold bathhouse. Early C20 lake, Dutch garden and rhododendron plantings. Garden is best viewed in spring when rhododendrons and azaleas are in bloom. Partial wheelchair access.
 ♿ ✹ ★ ☕

2 **ARNANT HOUSE**
Llwyncelyn SA46 0HF. Pam & Ron Maddox, 01545 580083. *On A 487, 2m S of Aberaeron. Next to Llwyncelyn Village Hall. Parking in lay-by opp house.* Light refreshments & teas. **Adm £2.50, chd free. Sun 27 May (1-6). Visitors also welcome by appt.**

Garden created in 5yrs from derelict patch of ground untended for 20yrs. 1-acre, in Victorian style and divided into rooms and themes. Laburnum arch, wildlife ponds, rotunda and tea house. Rhododendrons in May.
♿ ✹ ☕

3 **NEW** **BRON-Y-GRAIG**
4 Bont Estate, Llanon SY23 5LT.
Dr David & Mrs Gill Shepherd. *11m S of Aberystwyth on A487. Through Llanon, L at Old Bakery, immed L again. Last house on R. Park at Bakery.* Light refreshments & teas at Dyffryn. **Adm combined with Dyffryn £3, chd under 12 free. Sun 20 May (11-5).** 1/4-acre plantsman's garden sheltered by 30ft rockfaces of old quarry. Upper patio with views over Cardigan Bay. Newly planted, colour themed gravel garden where grasses and bamboos complement the unusual perennials and bulbs. Raised fruit and unusual vegetable garden. Cake stall in aid of Lymphoedema Support.
✹ ★ ☕

Sheltered by 30ft rockfaces of an old quarry . . . bay views . . .

4 **THE BUNGALOW**
Plwmp SA44 6HJ. Mr & Mrs Barry Crutchley, 01239 654281. *14m N of Cardigan. Take the lane to Post Bach opposite Plwmp PO. Entrance 100yds on L.* **Adm £2.50, chd free. Sat 16 June (11-5). Visitors also welcome by appt.**
1/2-acre garden comprises a wide variety of trees, shrubs and herbaceous perennials and, being positioned high on a ridge overlooking Cardigan Bay, groomed hedges play an important part in giving wind protection. These feature hedges divide the garden into 4 rooms which are entered through clipped arches providing the visitor with many surprises.
♿ ✹ ★ ☕

⑤ BWLCH Y GEUFFORDD

Bronant SY23 4JD. Mr & Mrs J Acres, 01974 251 559, gayacres@aol.com. *6m NW of Tregaron. 12m SE of Aberystwyth off A485. Take turning opp Bronant school for 1¹/₂m then turn L up a ¹/₂m track.* Home-made teas. **Adm £3, chd 50p. Sun 10 June (11-6).** Visitors also welcome by appt, June to Sept incl. 1000ft high, 2-acre wildlife garden featuring lake with water lilies and a series of pools linked by waterfalls, a number of theme gardens, from Mediterranean to woodland and from oriental to exotic jungle with hut. Plenty of sympathetic seating and large sculptures. Exhibiton of sculptures. Pond dipping for children by appointment but not on open day. Gravel paths but specialised wheelchair available to borrow for visitors weighing less than 10stone.

&. ✿ ☕

⑥ CWMRHAIADR GARDEN & NURSERY

Glaspwll SY20 8UB. Mr & Mrs Glynne Jones, 01654 702223, glynne.jones@btinternet.com. *5¹/₂m S of Machynlleth. From Machynlleth head S on A487, after 2m turn L signed Glaspwll. Continue for 3¹/₂m, narrow in parts with few passing places. Turn L at 2nd junction, R at next junction, L at next, continue & turn R at junction signed To the Falls, continue uphill to nursery. Park in farmyard.* Home-made teas. **Adm £2.50, chd free. Suns 27 May; 9 Sept (1-5).** Visitors also welcome by appt, June & Sept.
1-acre garden planted for yr-round effect with many species of evergreen trees and shrubs, incl rhododendron, eucryphia, hoheria, with rarities such as Leptospermum scoparium, Myrtus chequen, Acacia dealbata var subalpina. The garden is situated in a spectacular and peaceful setting. Autumn berries and hydrangeas in Sept.

✿ ☕

Garden has matured into a west Wales rainforest with mature trees and shrubs . . .

⑦ DYFFRYN

Pennant, Llanon SY23 5PB. Mrs Jo Richards. *1m S of Aberystwyth on A487. Through Llanon L at Old Bakery, then 2nd L, follow signs.* Light refreshments & teas. **Adm combined with Bron-y-Graig £3, chd free. Sun 20 May (11-5).** ²/₃-acre garden now 27yrs old has matured into a W Wales rainforest with many mature trees and shrubs. Rooms with paving, seats, water features and oriental touches - bamboos and grasses. Abundant birdlife. Last open 2000. Partial wheelchair access. Guide dogs permitted.

&. ✗ ✿ ☕

ESCGAIRWEDDAN
See Gwynedd

FARMYARD NURSERY WOODLAND GARDEN
See Carmarthenshire & Pembrokeshire.

FELIN Y FFRIDD
See Gwynedd

⑧ **NEW** GARTH

Brongest SA38 9ER. Colin & Jackie Sanders. *From Newcastle Emlyn take B4571 towards Ffostrasol. 2¹/₂m after bridge turn L signed Brongest 1¹/₄. Garth ¹/₂m on R.* Teas. **Adm £2, chd free (share to Parkinson's Disease Soc). Sun 3 June (11-5).** 1¹/₂-acre garden situated above Teifi Valley created by owners 14-yrs ago to blend the natural with the cultivated. Trees & shrubs with some informal beds. Formal hedge divides the garden and surrounds the small knot garden. Culpepper's Herbal inspired herb garden and some alpine troughs behind the house. Plants self seed in the drive. Stoneware & hand-thrown pottery by owner for sale.

✗ ✿ ☕

⑨ **NEW** GLANHELYG

Lon Helyg, Llechryd SA43 2NJ. Mike & Ann Williamson, 01239 682482/682119, www.glanhelyg.co.uk. *3m SE of*

Cardigan. From A484 Cardigan-Newcastle Emlyn, L into Lon Helyg 50yds after Llechryd sign, house at end. Teas. **Adm £2.50, chd under 12 free. Sun 2 Sept (11-4).** Visitors also welcome by appt, Fri & Sat, May-Oct incl coaches. 3¹/₂-acre woodland, meadow and walled garden. Recently re-designed Victorian walled garden contains a large variety of plants, many semi-tender in prairie style planting. Art gallery selling original oil paintings, cards & photos. Partial wheelchair access. Gravel paths.

&. ✿ ☕

GRANDMA'S GARDEN
See Powys.

⑩ HEDDFAN

Pendderw, Llwyndafydd SA44 6BZ. Mrs S Makepeace. *Off A487, 5m S of New Quay, 12m N of Cardigan. At Plwmp PO take Llwyndafydd rd. Turn L at T junction. Take 2nd L (on a bend), at next T-junction turn L. After 20 yds take 'No Through Rd' on R. Heddfan 1m on R.* Home-made teas. **Adm £2.50, chd free. Sun 10 June (10-5).** Beautiful recently created garden of keen plantswoman, which forms the backdrop to an interestingly designed house, lying in the remnants of an old estate surrounded by mature trees. Water features incl large pond whilst shelter and S-facing aspects allow the introduction of Mediterranean plants.

✗ ✿ ☕

⑪ ♦ LLANERCHAERON

SA48 8DG. The National Trust, 01545 570200, www.nationaltrust.org.uk. *2¹/₂m E of Aberaeron. On the A482 Lampeter to Aberaeron.* **House and Garden Adm £6.40, Garden only £5.40. Weds to Suns & Bank Hol Mons, Easter to Oct (11-5). For NGS:** *Evening Opening* **£2.50, child 50p, under 12 free, Thur 21 June (6-9).** Llanerchaeron is a small C18 Welsh gentry estate set in the beautiful Dyffryn Aeron. The estate survived virtually unaltered into the C20. 2 extensive

South facing aspects allow the introduction of Mediterranean plants . . .

restored walled gardens produce home-grown vegetables, fruit and herbs for sale. The kitchen garden sits at the core of the estate with a John Nash villa built in 1795 and home farm, all virtually unaltered since its construction. Midsummer evening opening in The Walled Garden with music, refreshments & plant sales.

   ♿ 🎪 ✿ ☕

12 LLANLLYR
Talsarn SA48 8QB. Mr & Mrs Robert Gee, 01570 470900. *6m NW of Lampeter. On B4337 to Llanrhystud.* Home-made teas. **Adm £3, chd under 12 free. Sun 17 June (2-6). Visitors also welcome by appt, Apr to Oct.**
Large early C19 garden on site of medieval nunnery, renovated & replanted since 1989. Large pool, bog garden, formal water garden, rose & shrub borders, gravel gardens, laburnum arbour, allegorical labyrinth and mount, all exhibiting fine plantsmanship. Yr-round appeal, interesting & unusual plants. Gravel paths.

♿ 🎪 ✿ ☕

13 LLWYNCELYN
Glandyfi SY20 8SS. Mr & Mrs Stewart Neal, 01654 781203, joyneal@btinternet.com. *12m N of Aberystwyth. On A487 Machynlleth (5¹/₂m). From Aberystwyth, turn R just before Glandyfi sign.* Home-made teas. **Adm combined with The Mill House £3, chd under 12 free. Sun 6 May (11-6). Visitors also welcome by appt, incl coaches. All-yr interest.**
8-acre woodland hillside garden/arboretum alongside Dyfi tributary. Collections of hybrid/species rhododendrons flowering Christmas-Aug. Mollis azaleas in many shades, bluebells in ancient oak wood. Rare species and hybrid hydrangeas. Large fernery, many overseas taxa added to natives. Formal garden contains terrace, parterre and potager. Large plant sale. Level formal garden, gravel paths & some steep slopes.

♿ 🎪 ✿ ☕

14 THE MILL HOUSE
Glandyfi SY20 8SS. Professor & Mrs J M Pollock, 01654 781342, jpol781342@aol.com. *12m N of Aberystwyth. On A487 Machynlleth 5¹/₂m. From Aberystwyth, turn R up lane almost directly opp sign for Glandyfi (on L). 2nd house up lane, approx 150yds.* **Adm combined with**

Formal water garden, laburnum arbour, allegorical labyrinth and mount, year round appeal . . .

Llwyncelyn £3, chd under 12 free. Sun 6 May (11-6). Visitors also welcome by appt during May, incl coaches.
Picturesque garden of a former water mill with millstream, millpond, and several waterfalls in woodland setting, about 1¹/₂ acres. Azaleas, rhododendrons and spring colour enhance waterside vistas, which have a Japanese theme. Featured in 'Gardens Monthly' June 2006.

🎪

15 NEW NEW HALL
Bettws Bledrws SA48 8NX. Maureen & Dave Allen. *100yds from church.* **Adm combined with Oak Meadows at Maesyderi £3, chd free. Sun 24 June (11-6).**
Cottage garden established in 2000 from derelict ground by keen plantswoman and her husband. Well stocked herbaceous borders incl interesting trees & shrubs, water garden and koi ponds.

🎪

16 NEW OAK MEADOWS AT MAESYDERI
SA48 8LY. Glenda Johnson. *3m N of Lampeter, 6m S of Tregaron. On A485 midway betweeen Llangybi and Bettws Bledrws, opp layby.* Home-made teas. **Adm combined with New Hall £3, chd free. Sun 24 June (11-6).**
Created over the last 4yrs from rough pasture and maturing well. Designed and maintained by an enthusiastic plantswoman, containing many interesting trees, an eclectic mix of shrubs, cottage garden perennials, water & bog garden. Gravel areas with raised beds, a small woodland with shade-loving plants. Ongoing project and small nursery started 2005.

🎪 ✿ ☕

17 THE OLD VICARAGE
Llangeler SA44 5EU. Mr & Mrs J C Harcourt, 01559 371168. *4m E of Newcastle Emlyn. 15m N of Carmarthen on A484. From N Emlyn turn down lane on L in Llangeler before church.* Cream teas. **Adm £2.50, chd free. Sat 30 June; Sun 1 July (11-6). Visitors also welcome by appt, late June & July.**
A garden gem created since 1993. Less than 1 acre divided into 3 areas of roses, shrubs and a semi-formal pool with an interesting collection of unusual herbaceous plants. Plants in aid of Osteoporosis Soc.

🎪 ✿ ☕

18 PANT-YR-HOLIAD
Rhydlewis SA44 5ST. Mr & Mrs G H Taylor. *10m NE of Cardigan. From A487 take B4334 at Brynhoffnant S towards Rhydlewis, after 1m turn L, driveway 2nd L.* Teas. **Adm £3, chd £1. Suns 6 May; 8 July (2-5).**
5 acres embracing walled garden housing tender plants, alpine beds, water features, rare trees and shrubs, with further 15 acres of woodland setting. Extensive collection rhododendron species. Home of Holiad rhododendron hybrids.

🎪 ✿ ☕

19 NEW PENBANC
Llanilar SY23 4NY. Enfys & David Rennie. *Off A487, 6m SE of Aberystwyth. From Llanfarian take A485 signed Tregaron for 2¹/₂m. Turn L into lane immed after Cwmaur Estate. Penbanc in ¹/₂m, overlooking river bridge. Park in field next to river.* Home-made teas. **Adm £2.50, chd free. Sun 24 June (2-6).**
¹/₂-acre, S-facing sloping cottage garden alongside R Ystwyth with views over valley. Vegetables, orchard and densely planted herbaceous borders created in 2005 with roses, clematis and shrubs. Planted for seasonal colour and scent. Garden of the Year 2006, Merch y Wawr Wales.

🎪 ✿ ☕

20 NEW **PERTH YR EGLWYS**
Mydroilyn, Lampeter SA48 7QX.
Elizabeth Gould & Christopher
May. *Off A 487, 4m S of
Aberaeron. Turn L at Llanarth,
signed Mydroilyn. Through village
to chapel, R to school, R again at
school, 300yds.* Home-made teas.
**Adm £2.50, chd free. Sun 13
May (11-6).**
3-acre well-established arboretum
and garden with many unusual
trees and shrubs. Streamside
walks, extensive bog gardens with
large areas of candelabra primulas,
pulmonarias, irises, various ferns,
bluebell banks. Rhododendrons,
azaleas, extensive perennial
borders, vegetable garden. Large
plant sale.

21 **PLAS PENGLAIS,
UNIVERSITY OF WALES
ABERYSTWYTH**
SY23 3DF. *NE of Aberystwyth on
A487. Entrance alongside Penglais
Lodge, opp side of rd to University
Campus. Park on campus.* Home-
made teas. **Adm £2.50, chd free. Sun
13 May (2-5).**
Sheltered garden of Georgian Mansion
surrounded by native trees and
carpeted with bluebells. Rockery,
walled terrace, pond, extensive lawns,
rhododendrons and many unusual
specimen shrubs and trees. Remains
of old Botany Dept 'order beds'. Large
tropical glasshouse filled with beautiful
and interesting exotic species. Partial
wheelchair access.

22 ◆ **TY GLYN WALLED
GARDEN**
Ciliau Aeron SA48 8DE. Ty Glyn
Davis Trust, 01970 832268,
historicgardenswales@hotmail.com.
*3m SW of Aberaeron. Turn off A482
Aberaeron to Lampeter at Ciliau Aeron
signed to Pennant. Entrance
700metres on L.* **Adm £2.50, chd
free. Daily 11-5. For NGS: Sun 29
July (11-5).**
Secluded L-shaped walled garden in
beautiful woodland setting alongside R
Aeron, developed specifically for
special needs children. S-facing
productive terraced kitchen garden
overlooks herbaceous borders,
orchard and ponds with child
orientated features and surprises
amidst unusual shrubs and perennials.
Newly planted fruit trees selected from
former gardener's notebook of C19.

23 **WINLLAN WILDLIFE
GARDEN**
Talsarn SA48 8QE. Mr & Mrs Ian
Callan, 01570 470612. *8m NNW of
Lampeter. On B4342, Talsarn-
Llangeitho rd.* **Adm £2.50, chd free.
Daily Sat 9 to Sun 24 June (2-5).**
6-acre wildlife garden owned by
botanists happy to share their
knowledge with visitors. Garden incl
large pond, herb-rich meadow, small
woodland and 600yds of river bank
walk. Over 200 species of wild flowers
incl many orchids with attendant
butterflies, dragonflies and birds

Newly planted fruit trees selected from former gardener's notebook of C19 . . .

Ceredigion County Volunteers

ngs gardens open
for charity

Spontaneous readings
of poems, quotes etc on
'gardens' will take place
throughout the afternoon.
Quizzes for children,
treasure hunt . . .

Old Hall, Flintshire & Wrexham

DENBIGHSHIRE & COLWYN

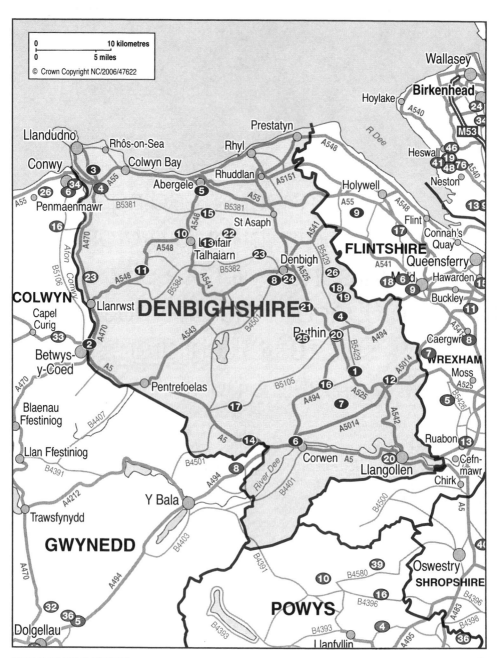

0 | 10 kilometres
0 | 5 miles
© Crown Copyright NC/2006/47622

Opening Dates

March

SUNDAY 18
17 The Old Rectory, Llangynhafal

April

SUNDAY 22
18 The Old Rectory, Llanfihangel Glyn Myfyr

May

SATURDAY 5
7 Dibleys Nurseries

SUNDAY 6
6 Caereuni
7 Dibleys Nurseries

MONDAY 7
6 Caereuni
7 Dibleys Nurseries

SUNDAY 13
2 Beaver Grove House
15 Merlyn

SUNDAY 20
18 The Old Rectory, Llanfihangel Glyn Myfyr
26 The White House

SUNDAY 27
6 Caereuni
14 Maesmor Hall

MONDAY 28
6 Caereuni

June

FRIDAY 1
4 Bryn Celyn (Evening)

SUNDAY 3
4 Bryn Celyn
6 Caereuni

FRIDAY 8
5 33 Bryn Twr & Lynton (Evening)

SATURDAY 9
5 33 Bryn Twr & Lynton

SUNDAY 10
5 33 Bryn Twr & Lynton
16 Nantclwyd Hall
24 Trosyffordd

FRIDAY 22
19 Plas-yn-Llan (Evening)

SUNDAY 24
18 The Old Rectory, Llanfihangel Glyn Myfyr
19 Plas-yn-Llan
22 Tal-y-Bryn Farm

July

SUNDAY 1
6 Caereuni
8 Dolhyfryd (Day & Evening)

MONDAY 2
3 Bodysgallen Hall & Spa

SUNDAY 15
12 Llandegla Village Gardens

SUNDAY 22
20 Ruthin Town Gardens

August

SUNDAY 5
6 Caereuni

SUNDAY 26
6 Caereuni

MONDAY 27
6 Caereuni

By appointment only

1 Arfryn
9 Donadea Lodge
10 Garthewin
11 Glog Ddu
13 Llys-y-Wiwer
21 Stella Maris
22 Tal-y-Bryn Farm
23 Tan y Graig
25 Tyddyn Bach

The Gardens

1 ARFRYN
Pentrecelyn, nr Ruthin LL15 2HR. Mr & Mrs A O Davies, 01978 790475, arfryn@pentrecelyn.fsnet.co.uk. *4m S of Ruthin. On A525 Wrexham rd. At Llanfair Dyffryn Clwyd take B5429 to Graigfechan. Mold-Ruthin A494 to Llanbedr Dyffryn Clwyd turn L after village B5429 to Graigfechan.* **Adm £2.50, chd free. Visitors welcome by appt June, July only, groups 10+.** Situated on hillside 800ft above sea level. 2-acre garden designed for yr-round interest, overlooking wonderful views. Divided into separate rooms - secret garden filled with old roses and hardy geraniums, cottage garden, wild flower bank and lawned gardens with herbaceous and shrub beds. New polytunnel garden featuring half hardy plants, trachycarpus, musa, cannas, etc. Featured in 'YR Herald Cymraeg'.

✗ ✿

2 BEAVER GROVE HOUSE
Betws-y-Coed LL24 0HA. Mr J Heminsley, 01690 710226. *½m S of Betws-y-Coed. Opp side of R Conwy from Betws-y-Coed, one entrance drive on A470, 200yds N of Waterloo Bridge; other entrance 800yds N of bridge on same rd.* Light refreshments & home-made teas. **Adm £2.50, chd 50p, OAP £1 (share to Colwyn Bay Leukaemia Research). Sun 13 May (11.30-5). Visitors also welcome by appt May only, groups 10+.** Magic of a lost, old, unrestored garden; grass paths winding between wonderful old magnolias, azaleas and rhododendrons, leading to small arboretum. Approx 5 acres.

✿ ☕

3 BODYSGALLEN HALL & SPA
nr Llandudno LL30 1RS. Historic House Hotels Ltd, www.bodysgallen.com. *2m from Llandudno. Take A55 to its intersection with A470 towards Llandudno. Proceed 1m, hotel is 1m on R.* **Adm £2.50, chd free. Mon 2 July (2-5).** Garden is well known for C17 box-hedged parterre. Stone walls surround lower gardens with rose gardens and herbaceous borders. Outside walled garden is cascade over rocks. Enclosed working fruit and vegetable garden with espalier-trained fruit trees, hedging area for cut flowers with walls covered in wineberry and Chinese gooseberry. Restored Victorian woodland, walks with stunning views of Conwy and Snowdonia. Runner up 'Wales in Bloom' 2006, Visit Wales. Featured on 'Welsh Herbal' BBC2. The Garden History Society; North Wales Living, 2006. Gravel paths and steep slopes.

♿ ✗ ✿ 🛏 ☕

Magic of a lost, old, unrestored garden; paths winding between wonderful old magnolias, azaleas and rhododendrons

4 BRYN CELYN
Llanbedr LL15 1TT. Mrs S Rathbone, 01824 702077, skrathbone@toucansurf.com. *2m N of Ruthin. From Ruthin take A494 towards Mold. After 1½m, turn L at Griffin PH onto B5429. Proceed 1½m; garden on R.* Home-made & cream teas. Adm £3, chd free (share to St Kentigern Hospice). Sun 3 June (2-6). **Evening Opening** wine & light refreshments, Fri 1 June (6-8). Visitors also welcome by appt.
2-acre garden with lawns surrounded by mixed borders. Walled garden with old-fashioned roses, cistus, lavender, honeysuckle, box balls and fruit trees. Gazebo and pergola leading to Mediterranean garden and woodland.
  👤 ⌖ ❀ ☕

Paths through wild flower meadows and woodland of magnificent trees . . .

5 33 BRYN TWR & LYNTON
Abergele LL22 8DD. Mr & Mrs Colin Knowlson & Mr & Mrs K A Knowlson, 01745 828201, crk@slaters.com. *From A55 heading W, take slip rd to Abergele. Turn L at roundabout then over T-lights; 1st L signed Llanfair T H. 3rd rd on L, No 33 is on L.* Home-made teas. Adm £2.50, chd free, concessions £2 (share to St Kentigern Hospice, St Asaph). Sat 9, Sun 10 June (2-5). **Evening Opening** £2.50, wine, Fri 8 June (6-8). Visitors also welcome by appt, any time, by phone.
2 connected gardens of totally differing styles, one cottage style of planting, the other quite formal. Approx ¾ acre in total, containing patio and pond areas; mixed herbaceous and shrub borders, many unusual plants. New features for 2007.
⌖ ❀ ☕

CAERAU UCHAF
See Gwynedd.

6 CAEREUNI
Godreír Gaer, nr Corwen LL21 9YA. Mr & Mrs Steve Williams. *1m N of Corwen. Take A5 to Bala. Turn R at T-lights onto A494 to Chester. 1st R after lay-by; house ¼m on L.* Adm £2.50, chd free. Sun 6, Mon 7, Sun 27, Mon 28 May; Suns 3 June; 1 July; 5, 26, Aug, Mon 27 Aug (2-5).
⅓-acre uniquely themed, fascinating garden, tropical plants, amazing features. New for 2007 modern metal structure.
👤 ⌖ ☕

7 DIBLEYS NURSERIES
Cefn Rhydd, Llanelidan LL15 2LG. Mr & Mrs R Dibley, www.dibleys.com. *7m S of Ruthin. Take A525 to Xrds by Llysfasi Agricultural College. Turn onto B5429 towards Llanelidan. After 1½m turn L, 1m up lane on L. Brown tourist signs from A525.* Home-made teas. Adm £2.50, chd free. Sat 5, Sun 6, Mon 7 May (10-5).
Large arboretum with wide selection of rare and unusual trees. There will be a lovely display of rhododendrons, magnolias, cherries and camellias. Ride through the garden on a miniature railway. ¾-acre glasshouses are open to show streptocarpus and other pot plants. National Collection of *Streptocarpus.*
⌖ ❀ NCCPG ☕

8 DOLHYFRYD
yn Lawnt, Denbigh LL16 4SU. Captain & Mrs Michael Cunningham, 01745 814805, www.dolhyfryd.com. *1m SW of Denbigh. On B4501 to Nantglyn, from Denbigh - 1m from town centre.* Light refreshments & cream teas; wine in evening. Adm £2.50, chd £1.50. Sun 1 July (2.30-7.30). Visitors also welcome by appt Feb-Sept. Coaches permitted. Groups any size.
Established garden set in small valley of R Ystrad. Acres of crocuses in late Feb/early Mar. Paths through wild flower meadows and woodland of magnificent trees, shade-loving plants and azaleas; mixed borders; walled kitchen garden - recently re-designed. Harpist. Many woodland & riverside birds, incl dippers, kingfishers, grey wagtails. Many species of butterfly encouraged by new planting. Gravel paths.
👤 ⌖ ❀ ☕

9 DONADEA LODGE
Babell CH8 8QD. Mr P Beaumont, 01352 720204. *7m NE of Denbigh. Turn off A541 Mold to Denbigh at Afonwen, signed Babell; T-junction turn L. A55 Chester to Conway take B5122 to Caerwys, 3rd turn on L.* Visitors welcome by appt May, June & July.
1-acre shady garden showing 25yrs of imaginative planting to enhance the magic of dappled shade, moving through different colour schemes, with each plant complementing its neighbour. Over 100 clematis, also a medlar tree over 100yrs old.
👤 ⌖

10 GARTHEWIN
Llanfair T.H. LL22 8YR. Mr Michael Grime, 01745 720288. *6m S of Abergele & A55. From Abergele take A548 to Llanfair TH & Llanrwst. Entrance to Garthewin 250yds W of Llanfair TH on A548 to Llanrwst.* Adm £3, chd free. Visitors welcome by appt in April, May & June.
Valley garden with ponds and woodland areas. Much of the 8 acres have been reclaimed and redesigned providing a younger garden with a great variety of azaleas, rhododendrons and young trees, all within a framework of mature shrubs and trees. Small chapel open.

11 NEW GLOG DDU
Llangernyw, Abergele LL22 8PS. Pamela & Anthony Harris, 01745 860611, www.glogddu.blogspot.com. *1m S of Llangernyw. Through Llangernyw going S on A548. R into Uwch Afon. L after 1m at grass triangle. Follow rd, past new houses, down narrow lane. Glog Ddu is 1st house on R.* Adm £2.50, chd free. Visitors welcome by appt beg June to end Sept, no groups of more than 12.
Recently re-developed garden of approx 2 acres planted for yr-round interest. Rhododendrons, woodland area, herbaceous borders, vegetable garden. Fledgling arboretum featuring rare trees and shrubs, with an emphasis on autumn colour, many of which have been grown from seed, showing what can be achieved on a limited budget.
⌖ ❀

12 LLANDEGLA VILLAGE GARDENS

LL11 3AP. *10m W of Wrexham. Off A525 at Llandegla Memorial Hall.* Cream teas at Llandegla Memorial Hall. **Combined adm £5, chd free. Sun 15 July (2-6).**
Small picturesque village surrounded by moorland. Church with interesting features. Communal garden area by river. Plant stall. Picnic area by river. Wales in Bloom & Neighbourhood Awards; Silver awards 2006.

ERRW LLAN
3 Maes Teg. Mr & Mrs Keith Jackson
$^1/_4$-acre garden made to attract wildlife. Plants grown for birds and butterflies. Trees for a variety of nesting sites. Pond to encourage frogs, toads, newts and damsel flies.

GLAN-YR-AFON
Mr & Mrs D C Ion. *Mini bus from Memorial Hall*
1-acre informal country garden surrounding this 200yr old farmhouse on 3 sides with a wide variety of features incl stream, 2 ponds, herbaceous borders, rockery and several ancient trees.

NEW OLD TY HIR FARM
Chester Road. Mr & Mrs D M Holder. *Mini bus from Memorial Hall*
Open plan garden with wide variety of trees, shrubs and many secret areas to explore.

SWN Y GWYNT
Phil Clark. *Situated in Llandegla Village*
$^1/_4$-acre plantsman's garden, shrubs and associated plants for shade.

NEW VILLAGE COTTAGE
Pat & Walt Standring
Very small country garden with a bit of everything.

Plants grown for birds and butterflies . . .

13 LLYS-Y-WIWER
Llanfair Talhaiarn, Abergele
LL22 8BJ. Irene & Arthur Ames, 01745 540272. *From Abergele after 4m on A548 sharp L turn signed Llannefydd. R at Church House, R at first farm, R over river, 1m along narrow lane. From Henllan B5382 to Brynrhydyrarian. Sharp R signed Llannefydd, L at small Xrds, $^1/_2$m on L.* Home-made teas. **Adm £2.50. Visitors welcome by appt May & June.**
$^1/_2$-acre real cottage garden on steep S-facing hillside in the Aled valley, terraced with dry stone walls. Wide selection of shrubs, perennials and bulbs, some unusual, closely planted for all-yr interest. Limited parking.

14 MAESMOR HALL
Maerdy, Corwen LL21 0NS. Mr & Mrs G M Jackson, 01490 460411, maesmorhall@aol.com. *5m W of Corwen. Take A5 from Corwen, through 2 sets of T-lights. In Maerdy take 1st L after church and opp The Goat PH.* Light refreshments & teas. **Adm £2.50, chd £1, concessions £1.50 (share to Diabetic Assoc). Sun 27 May (12-5). Visitors also welcome by appt.**
Well-established garden with riverside and estate walks featuring a new water garden and white plant garden. The rhododendrons are extensive and provide a fitting backdrop to the parkland. Large azalea beds are a mixture of colour. Wooded walks around the hall together with an arboretum are also an attraction. Latest addition is the largest rose carousel in Wales featuring over 80 roses from David Austin. Patios and front of hall displays. Enormous stone table has been brought down from the surrounding mountain - could have been King Arthur's.

15 NEW MERLYN
Moelfre, Abergele LL22 9RH.
Harry & Gail Roberts. *2$^1/_2$m from Bodelwyddan. Leave A55 to Conwy at Bodelwyddan Castle. Proceed uphill by castle wall to Xrds. Bear R on B5381 towards Betws yn Rhos for 2m. Fork L towards Llanfair T H. Garden 0.4m on R.* Home-made teas. **Adm £2.50, chd free, concessions £2 (share to St Kentigern Hospice, St Asaph). Sun 13 May (2-5).**

2-acre spring garden 800ft above sea level, with unusual rhododendrons and azaleas. Beautiful views. Mixed borders. Damp garden. Courtyard garden.

Largest rose carousel in Wales featuring over 80 roses . . .

16 NANTCLWYD HALL
Ruthin LL15 2PR. Sir Philip & Lady Isabella Naylor-Leyland. *4m S of Ruthin. Take A494 from Ruthin to Corwen. Garden is 1$^1/_2$m from Pwllglas on L, through stone gateway in beech hedge.* **Adm £3, chd 50p. Sun 10 June (2-6).**
Approx 3 acres of formal gardens incl Italian garden, parkland with lake and further grounds. Temples and follies by Sir Clough Williams-Ellis. Grotto by Belinda Eade. Rustic bridge over R Clwyd.

17 THE OLD RECTORY, LLANGYNHAFAL
LL16 4LN. Mr & Mrs Henry Dixon. *3$^1/_2$m N of Ruthin. From Ruthin take A494; Llanbedr take B5429. After $^1/_2$m turn R signed 2$^1/_2$m Llangynhafal. Entrance on R at Xrds.* Light refreshments & home-made teas. **Adm £2.50, chd free (share to Llangynhafal Parish Church). Sun 18 Mar (2-5.30).**
Extensive grounds centred on traditional walled gardens, with bulbs, unusual plants, orchards, blossom and vegetables. Installations, sculptures and water features link the C18 and C21. Tea & cakes.

18 THE OLD RECTORY, LLANFIHANGEL GLYN MYFYR
LL21 9UN. Mr & Mrs E T Hughes, 01490 420568. 2$1/2$m E of Cerrigydrudion. From Ruthin take B5105 SW for 12m to Llanfihangel Glyn Myfyr. Turn R just after Crown PH (follow signs). Proceed for $1/3$m, garden on L. Home-made teas. **Adm £2.50, chd free (share to Cancer Research UK, Mens Cancers). Suns 22 Apr (2-5); 20 May; 24 June (2-6). Visitors also welcome by appt.**
16yr-old garden of approx 1 acre set in beautiful, tranquil, sheltered valley. A garden for all seasons; hellebores; abundance of spring flowers; mixed borders; water, bog, and gravel gardens; walled garden with old roses, pergola, bower and garden of meditation. Also incl garden created 11yrs ago by son (now aged 18) which features hardy orchids and gentians.

  ♿ ✕ ✿ ⊨ ☕

PEN-Y-BRYN
See Flintshire & Wrexham.

19 NEW PLAS-YN-LLAN
Llangynhafal LL16 4LN. Prof & Mrs D Walker. 5m NE of Ruthin. A494 from Ruthin towards Mold. After 1.5m turn L at Griffin Inn onto B5429. After 0.5m R to Llangynhafal. After 2.5m R at postbox. Garden on L immed after St Gynhafal's Church. Home-made & cream teas. **Adm £2.50, chd free (share to Hope House Children's Hospice & CLIC). Sun 24 June (2-6). Evening Opening £2.50, wine & light refreshments, Fri 22 June (6-8).**
Approx 2 acres of garden incl pond area with waterfall, rill and fountain area with old yew tree. Knot garden with topiary and lavender, rose pathway and organic vegetable garden. Many exotic and beautiful plants and shrubs incl a variety of peonies. Book stall. Wildlife: carp, frogs, newts, dragonflies, butterflies. Pond & rill unfenced.

  ✕ ✿ ☕

20 NEW RUTHIN TOWN GARDENS
Centre of Ruthin. From St Peter's Sq. **Combined adm £5. Sun 22 July (11-5).**
Medieval town, many historic buildings set in beautiful Vale of Clwyd. Ruthin Castle. Very old house, St John Trevor. Renowned home-made teas & light refreshments at Annie's & Ruthin Castle. Annie's won 2006 Town Garden Award.

  ☕

NEW ANNIES
5 Upper Clwyd Street. Mr & Mrs J P R & A Holmes. From Ruthin Sq, go down side of Dodds Estate Agent, past bookshop to Annie's teashop.
Garden through double gates by steps
Small town garden with many begonias. Lots of pots, very colourful. 1st prize Ruthin Show 2006 & Town Council 1st prize 2006. Approach via steep hill; gravel in garden area.

  ♿ ✿

NEW BERWYN
Upper Clwyd Street. Susan Evans. 100yds off St Peter's Sq
Tiny walled town garden, all pots.

  ✕

NEW RUTHIN CASTLE
Castle Street. Ruthin Castle Ltd, 01824 702664, www.ruthincastlehotel.com.
Turn L at Natwest Bank. On roundabout in centre of Ruthin. **Visitors also welcome by appt.**
Wonderfully exciting restoration project, progressing fast, of Victorian and formal gardens. Walkways, courtyards, rose garden, dry moats and dungeons in C13 castle ruins. Lawns with rare and beautiful trees. The hotel was frequented by Edward, Prince of Wales.

  ✕ ✿ ⊨

NEW SIR JOHN TREVOR GARDEN
Castle Street. Stuart & Jackie Jones. From St Peter's Sq take Corwen Rd (towards Ruthin Castle). House on L 200yds
Small town garden. Selection of plants and shrubs and patio containers.

  ✕

21 STELLA MARIS
Llanrhaeadr LL16 4PW. Mrs J E Moore, 01745 890475, mumjem@aol.com. 3m SE of Denbigh. Take A525 Denbigh to Ruthin rd. After 3m from Denbigh or 4m from Ruthin turn W to Mynydd Llech. Garden $1/2$m on L. **Adm £2.50. Visitors welcome by appt on third Sun of the months of May, June, July, Aug & Sept. Also groups.**
1-acre garden created to enjoy the wonderful, ever changing views over the Vale of Clwyd. Good collection of specimen trees, interesting shrubs, herbaceous borders with all-yr round interest, gravel garden and ponds. All complement the outstanding scenery.

  ✿ ☕

22 TAL-Y-BRYN FARM
Llannefydd LL16 5DR. Mr & Mrs Gareth Roberts, 01745 540256, llaeth@villagedairy.co.uk. 3m W of Henllan. From Henllan take rd signed Llannefydd. After 2$1/2$m turn R signed Bont Newydd. Garden $1/2$m on L. Home-made teas. **Adm £2.50, chd free. Sun 24 June (2-6). Visitors welcome by appt, May to July, coaches and groups permitted.**
Medium-sized working farmhouse cottage garden. Ancient farm machinery. Incorporating ancient privy festooned with honeysuckle, clematis and roses. Terraced arches, sunken garden pool and bog garden, fountains and old water pumps. Herb wheels, shrubs and other interesting features. Lovely views of the Clwydian range. New water feature. Plant stall, Craft stall and Cake stall.

  ♿ ✿ ⊨ ☕

23 TAN Y GRAIG
Mill Lane, Llannefydd Road, Henllan LL16 5BD. Jim & Barbara Buchanan, 01745 816161. On B5382 Denbigh to Henllan rd. Mill Lane is 100yds below Church Tower off the Llannefydd rd. Garden is top bungalow in Mill Lane. **Visitors welcome by**

Knot garden with topiary and lavender, rose pathway and organic vegetable garden . . .

Unusual trees grown from seed . . .

appt, coaches welcome.
Elevated 1/2-acre garden with panoramic views over surrounding countryside, dissected by terraced walks and backed by a high limestone cliff abundant with wildlife. Large rockery, shrub and perennial beds containing over 500 varieties of plants - many unusual. Small adjacent nursery with all plants propagated from the garden.
✗ ⊗

㉔ TROSYFFORDD
Ystrad LL16 4RL. Miss Marion MacNicoll, 01745 812247. *11/2m W of Denbigh. From A525 Denbigh to Ruthin rd, turn R in outskirts of Denbigh by swimming pool, on Ystrad rd signed Prion & Saron. Follow for 11/2m, Trosyfforrdd is 2nd drive on R after 1st hill.* Adm £3 (tea incl), chd free. Sun 10 June (1-5). Visitors also welcome by appt May to October, any number welcome.
Medium-sized plantsman's garden created from a field since 1940. Unusual trees grown from seed. Mixed borders with roses, herbaceous, shrubs and grasses. New: small arboretum started in 2005. Teas for groups by arrangement or bring a picnic. Lucky dip.
♿ ⊗ ☕

㉕ NEW TYDDYN BACH
Bontuchel, Ruthin LL15 2DG. Mr & Mrs L G Starling, 01824 710248. *4m W of Ruthin. B5105 from Ruthin, turn R at Cross Keys towards Bontuchel/Cyffylliog. Through Bontuchel, river is now on R. Turn L up narrow rd, steep hill just before bridge. House 1st on L.* Adm £2. Visitors welcome by appt July & Aug. Not suitable for coaches, steep hill, narrow rd & limited parking.
Completely organic, very pretty cottage garden with prolific vegetable garden. Wildlife friendly with hedges and wood pile. Greenhouse packed with plants for both pots and the garden.
✗

㉖ THE WHITE HOUSE
Llandyrnog LL16 4LT. Bill & Cherry Palin. *4m E of Denbigh. From Denbigh take rd due E to Llandyrnog. Approx 3m cross roundabout, past Kinmel Arms PH. At X-roads turn L towards Llangwyfan. Garden 1/2m on L.* Home-made teas. Adm £2.50, chd free (share to Hope House Children's Hospice). Sun 20 May (2-5.30).
Approx 2 acres of garden with stream running through feeding large natural ponds with island and bog planting. Spring is our season - small meadow area with bulbs and many varieties of azaleas and rhododendrons. Beautiful views of surrounding hills and countryside.
✗ ⊗ ☕

Completely organic, very pretty cottage garden with prolific vegetable garden . . .

Denbighshire & Colwyn County Volunteers

County Organiser; Leaflet Coordinator
Sue Rathbone, Bryn Celyn, Llanbedr, Ruthin, Denbighshire LL15 1TT, 01824 702077, skrathbone@toucansurf.com

County Treasurer
Elizabeth Sasse, Hendy, Afonwen, Flintshire CH7 5UP, 01352 720220

Assistant County Organisers
Rhian Davey, Fynnon-y-milgy, Llanelidan, Ruthin, Denbighshire LL15 2TD, 01824 750507, rmdavey@f-y-m.net
Marion MacNicoll, Trosyfforrdd, Ystrad Road, Denbighshire LL16 4RL, 01745 812247

FLINTSHIRE & WREXHAM

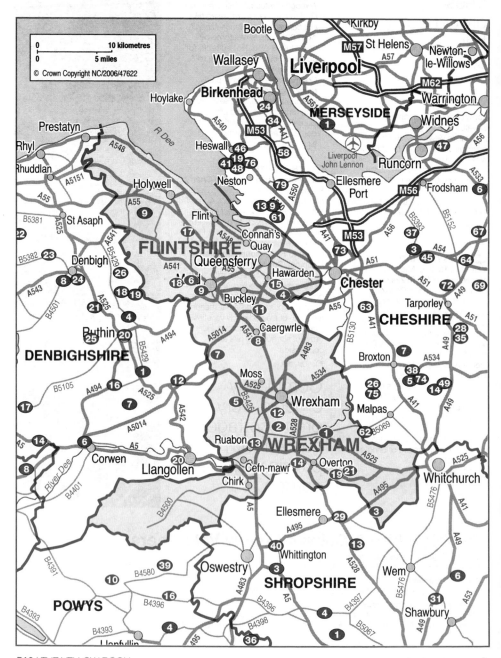

Opening Dates

March

SUNDAY 18
⑫ Erddig Hall

April

SUNDAY 15
⑮ Hawarden Castle
⑲ Park Cottage

May

SUNDAY 13
⑥ Bryn Bellan

SUNDAY 20
⑤ Bryn Amma Cottage

SUNDAY 27
⑩ Dolwen
⑭ The Garden House

June

SUNDAY 3
⑬ Gardden Lodge

SUNDAY 10
② Berthen-Gron-Farm
③ Bettisfield Hall
⑭ The Garden House

THURSDAY 14
⑦ Bryn Hafod

SATURDAY 16
⑦ Bryn Hafod

SUNDAY 17
⑯ Llangedwyn Hall

SUNDAY 24
⑩ Dolwen

July

SUNDAY 1
⑱ Pantymwyn Village Gardens

SUNDAY 8
⑧ Bryn Yorkin Manor
⑨ The Cottage Nursing Home

SUNDAY 15
⑰ The Old Hall

SUNDAY 22
④ Broughton & Bretton Allotments
(Day & Evening)

SUNDAY 29
㉑ Penley Village Gardens

August

SUNDAY 5
⑪ Dove Cottage

SUNDAY 12
① Bangor-on-Dee Village Gardens

September

SUNDAY 2
⑥ Bryn Bellan
⑭ The Garden House

SUNDAY 16
⑲ Park Cottage

SUNDAY 23
③ Bettisfield Hall

Gardens open to the public

⑫ Erddig Hall
⑭ The Garden House

By appointment only

⑳ Pen-y-Bryn

The Gardens

① BANGOR-ON-DEE VILLAGE GARDENS
LL13 0AT. *6m S of Wrexham. On A525 Wrexham to Whitchurch rd. Turn L signed Bangor-on-Dee. Take 1st R turn into Laurels Ave for 'Sunbank'. Go down to T-junction turn R then 1st L into Abbott's Way, leading to Friar's Court. Keep L for no 17, a corner plot.* Home-made teas. **Combined adm £3.50, chd free. Sun 12 Aug (2-5.30).** Picturesque village on the R Dee, beautiful church, well known basket shop and race course.

Picturesque village on the River Dee, beautiful church, well known basket shop and race course . . .

17 FRIARS COURT
Mr & Mrs G P Fitton
Plantswoman's corner plot garden, contains a series of rooms with water features, arches, arbours and well stocked herbaceous borders.
  ⌖

SUNBANK
Norman & Sylvia Jones
Approx 3/4-acre well cared for garden set on 3 lawned levels with wide variety of shrubs and perennials. Surrounded by mature trees and farmland with interesting water features and magnificent views over village and surrounding countryside.

② BERTHEN-GRON-FARM
Sontley, Wrexham. LL13 0UY. Mr & Mrs G N Morris. *2m S of Wrexham. From A483 S of Wrexham take the B5426 signed Bangor-on-Dee, 1st L to Sontley. Alternatively, A525 from Wrexham towards Marchwiel, then R for Sontley.* Home-made teas. **Adm £2.50, chd free. Sun 10 June (1.30-5pm).**
Attractive 1-acre garden on a working farm. Lawns and island beds with a wide variety of shrubs and perennials. Arbour, pergola and interesting water feature. Tulip tree, Indian bean tree (catalpa). Flautist.

③ BETTISFIELD HALL
Bettisfield SY13 2LB. Rev & Mrs David Butterworth. *9m SW of Whitchurch. 7m E of Ellesmere (Shropshire). 18m SE of Wrexham. Off A495 take Bettisfield/Wem rd. Garden opp historic church, St John the Baptist.* Home-made teas. **Adm £2.50, chd free, wheelchairs/guide dogs free. Suns 10 June; 23 Sept (2-5.30).**
On site of historic garden surrounding fortified manor house (not open). Panoramic view. Natural form gardens, sunken garden, herbs, newly established Heritage Welsh orchard. Green oak garden and furniture workshop. Blueberry and other specialist berries being grown under organic principles. Apple day (Sept). Visit Blueberry plantation. Next to Bettisfield/Whixell Moss Nature Reserve (English Nature). Gravel driveway, disabled parking by house.

④ NEW BROUGHTON & BRETTON ALLOTMENTS

Main Road, Broughton CH4 9PD. Broughton & Bretton Area Allotments Association. *5m W of Chester. On A5104 (signed Penyffordd) in village of Broughton.* Home-made teas at War Memorial Institute, Main Rd. **Adm £3, chd free (share to B.I.R.D. Centre). Day & Evening Opening Sun 22 July (2-8).**
Small collection of full and half sized allotment plots used by the local community to grow a mix of vegetables, flowers and soft fruit.
✕ ☕

⑤ BRYN AMMA COTTAGE

Frondeg, Wrexham LL14 4NB. Gillian & Roger Nock. *3m W of Wrexham. From A483 turn onto A525 towards Ruthin, after Coedpoeth Village turn L in Minera on B5426 (Minera Hall Rd), 2m turn R into unnamed lane with passing places, follow signs to field parking.* Home-made teas. **Adm £3, chd free (share to Muscular Dystrophy). Sun 20 May (1-5).**
Approx ½-acre garden on hillside at over 900ft, nr moorland with views over Wrexham. Planted for yr-round interest, woodland slopes to stream with cataracts, flag iris, naturalised ferns and moisture-loving plants. Lawned areas with informal borders, bluebells, perennials, rhododendrons, azaleas, ornamental trees and shrubs. Gravel paths with steep slope at one point.
♿ ✕ ❀ ☕

⑥ NEW BRYN BELLAN

Bryn Road, Gwernaffield CH7 5DE. Gabrielle Armstrong & Trevor Ruddle. *2m W of Mold. Leave A541 atMold on Gwernaffield rd (Dreflan), ½m after Mold derestriction signs turn R to Rhydymwyn & Llynypandy. After 200yds park in field on R.* Home-made teas. **Adm £3, chd free. Suns 13 May; 2 Sept (2-5.30).**
Tranquil elegant garden

transformed from wilderness in just 3yrs. On 2 levels, walled upper garden containing mostly shrubs and bulbs with a Sequoiadendron Wellingtonia. Lower garden, mainly lawn, featuring ornamental cutting garden and potting shed. Some gravel paths.
♿ ✕ ❀ ☕

⑦ BRYN HAFOD

Ffordd-y-Blaenau, Treuddyn, Nr Mold CH7 4NS. Mr & Mrs Ffoulkes Jones. *1m W of Treuddyn. Turn south into Ffordd-y-Blaenau (signed), continue for 1½m.* Home-made teas. **Adm £2.50, chd £1. Thur 14, Sat 16 June (2-5).**
1-acre garden in elevated position amidst farmland and enjoying exstensive views. Wide variety of shrubs and perennials are grown in this plant lovers' garden.
✕ ❀ ☕

⑧ NEW BRYN YORKIN MANOR

Bryn Yorkin Lane, nr Caergwrle LL12 9HT. Laura & Peter Carstensen, **laura@carstensen.co.uk.** *5m NW of Wrexham. Leave A541, at Abermorddu, follow signs for Cymau. Along Cymau Lane, sharp R at Ye Olde Talbot Inn into Bryn Yorkin Lane for ¾m. Narrow lane (passing places). L into Bryn Yorkin Manor through large stone gates. Parking signed.* Teas & wine. **Adm £2.50, chd free. Sun 8 July (2-6).**
Walled gardens of historic manor house (not open) on Hope mountain within small country estate. Kitchen and herb gardens, orchard, formal and informal flower gardens presenting a series of contrasting and beautiful rooms. Ponds, ancient woodland, tower dovecote, panoramic views. Gardens and land are cultivated organically and with wildlife in mind. Sculpture exhibition. Gravel paths.
♿ ❀ ☕

⑨ THE COTTAGE NURSING HOME

54 Hendy Road, Mold CH7 1QS. Mr & Mrs A G & L I Lanini. *10m W of Chester. From Mold town centre take A494 towards Ruthin. 2nd R into Hafod Park. Straight on to T-junction. Turn R onto Hendy Rd. Garden at junction of Hendy Rd & Clayton Rd.* Home-made teas. **Adm £1.50, chd 50p (share to British Heart Foundation). Sun 8 July (2-5).**
Beautiful garden set in approx 1 acre. Well-established shrubs, herbaceous plants and abundance of colourful window boxes and tubs. Heart-shaped patio, incl water feature and pergola, with natural reclaimed stone walling.
♿ ❀ ☕

⑩ DOLWEN

Cefn Coch, Llanrhaeadr-ym-Mochnant SY10 0BU. Bob Yarwood & Jeny Marriott. *14m W of Oswestry. Take B4396 (or B4580 - narrow) W to Llanrhaeadr-ym-Mochnant. Turn R at W end of village opp The Plough Inn & up narrow lane for approx 1km.* Garden on R. Teas. **Adm £3, chd free. Suns 27 May; 24 June (1-6).**
2 acres of hillside garden with pools, stream, small wood and many different types of unusual plants all backed by a stupendous mountain view.
❀ ☕

DONADEA LODGE

See Denbighshire & Colwyn.

⑪ DOVE COTTAGE

Rhos Road, Penyffordd, Nr Chester CH4 0JR. Chris & Denise Wallis. *6m SW of Chester. From Chester A55 S exit A550 follow signs for Corwen. Turn L immed opp Penyffordd railway stn. From Wrexham A541 for Mold, R at Pontblyddyn for Chester, turn R immed opp Penyffordd railway stn.* Home-made teas. **Adm £2, chd free. Sun 5 Aug (2-5).**
Approx 1½-acre garden, many shrubs and herbaceous plants set informally around lawns. Small kitchen garden, 2 ponds (1 wildlife), summerhouse, pergola and woodland planted area. Gravel paths, slight incline.
♿ ✕ ❀ ⌂ ☕

⑫ ◆ ERDDIG HALL

nr Wrexham LL13 0YT. The National Trust, 01978 355314, www.nationaltrust.org.uk. *2m S of Wrexham. Signed from A483/A5125 Oswestry rd; also from A525 Whitchurch rd.* **Adm £2.50, chd free.**

Allotment plots used by the local community to grow a mix of vegetables, flowers and soft fruit . . .

Sat to Wed 24 Mar to 28 Oct (11-5) last entry to house 4. For NGS: Sun 18 Mar (12-4).
Important, listed Grade 1 historic garden. Formal C18 and later Victorian design elements incl pleached lime tree avenues, trained fruit trees, wall plants and climbers, herbaceous borders, roses, herb garden, annual bedding, restored glasshouse and vine house. National Collection of Ivy. Wheelchair access to all relevant parts of the garden.
♿ ✂ **NCCPG** ☕

15 HAWARDEN CASTLE
Hawarden CH5 3B. Sir William & Lady Gladstone. *6m W of Chester. On B5125 just E of Hawarden village. Entrance via farm shop.* **Adm £3, chd £2. Sun 15 Apr (2-6pm).**
Large garden and picturesque ruined castle. Take care and supervise children. Dogs on short leads only.
♿

16 LLANGEDWYN HALL
Llangedwyn SY10 9JW. Mr & Mrs T M Bell. *8m W of Oswestry. On B4396 to Llanrhaeadr-ym-Mochnant about*

18 PANTYMWYN VILLAGE GARDENS
Mold CH7 5EN. *3m W of Mold. From Mold A541 to Denbigh turn L at first mini roundabout, signed Pantymwyn approx 3m from Ruthin A494. Turn L at Cadole approx 1½m to Pantymwyn.* Home-made teas at Wych Elm (not open). **Combined adm £4, chd free. Sun 1 July (2-6).**
Small scenic village with wonderful views of the Clwydian Range and Moel Famau. Live music at Bryn Mor.
☕

NEW BRYN MOR
Cefn Bychan Road. Pam & Andy Worthington
Garden is compact and colourful incl an organic ornamental kitchen garden, shrubs and herbaceous borders.

COEDLE
Pant y Buarth. Richard & Shirley Hughes
Limestone hillside, developing garden, cottage style of approx ½ acre containing rockery, mixed shrub and herbaceous borders, small pond and woodland area.
✂

GREENHEYS
Cefn Bychan Road. Roy & Carol Hambleton
Relaxed style planting of shrubs, perennials and climbers especially clematis. Occasional formal touches.
✂

NEW LONG SHADOWS
Cefn Bychan Road. Dave & Agnes Christmas
Rocky garden filled with a mixture of flowering plants, mature trees, shrubs and hedges. Spectacular views of Moel Famau.
✂

ROWANOKE
Pant y Buarth. Ron & Clare Exley
Limestone hillside garden with different levels. Variety of shrubs, trees, plants, and wildlife pond.
✂

SOUTHERNWOOD
Cefn Bychan Road. Bill & Joan Chadwick
Small garden. Variety of colourful shrubs, flowers and pots.
✂

Spontaneous readings of poems, quotes etc on 'gardens' will take place throughout the afternoon . . .

13 GARDDEN LODGE
Gardden, Ruabon LL14 6RD. Richard & Angela Coles. *5m SW of Wrexham. Heading S on B5605 from Wrexham, through Johnstown. Turn R into Tatham Rd, past Gardden Ind. Est. Turn R after 100yds. Parking in Gardden Ind Est and Tatham Road. Short walk up lane to garden. Disabled visitors limited access.* Home-made teas. **Adm £2.50, chd free. Sun 3 June (12-4.30).**
Within woodland, a secluded and sheltered garden. Specimen tulip tree in the centre surrounded by lawns and rhododendrons, with mixed herbaceous borders and small kitchen garden, terraced garden to rear.
❉ ☕

14 ◆ THE GARDEN HOUSE
Erbistock LL13 0DL. Mr & Mrs S Wingett, 01978 781149. *5m S of Wrexham. On A528 Wrexham to Shrewsbury rd. Follow signs at Overton Bridge to Erbistock Church.* **Adm £3, chd free. Apr to Oct, Wed to Fri (11-5); Sun (2-5). For NGS: Suns 27 May; 10 June; 2 Sept (2-5).**
Shrub and herbaceous plantings in monochromatic, analogous and complementary colour schemes. Rose pergolas, National Collection of hydrangea (over 300 species and cultivars). Sculpture Garden. Large lily pond, Victorian dovecote.
♿ ❉ **NCCPG** ☕

5m W of Llynclys Xrds. Light refreshments & teas. **Adm £3.00, chd free. Sun 17 June (12-5).**
Approx 4-acre formal terraced garden on 3 levels, designed and laid out in late C17 and early C18. Unusual herbaceous plants, sunken rose garden, small water garden, walled kitchen garden and woodland walk.
♿ ✂ ❉ ☕

17 THE OLD HALL
Pentre Road, Halkyn CH8 8BS. Mrs G M Bourchier. *10m NW of Mold. From A55 travelling W take turning L signed Halkyn & Rhosesmor (approx 3m W of Northop). Bear R at Britannia Inn, straight on at give-way sign. Entrance on L. Travelling E leave A55 signed B5123 Halkyn & Rhosesmor, pass under A55 and past Springfield Hotel. Bear L at top of hill, entrance ½m on R.* Home-made teas. **Adm £2.50, chd free. Sun 15 July (2-5.30).**
Approx 2-acre garden around The Old Hall (not open). Wide variety of shrubs, herbaceous and mixed borders, informally planted, with even more surprise features. Garden slopes gently up, with magnificent views over the Dee estuary from the top. Children very welcome. Spontaneous readings of poems, quotes etc on 'gardens' will take place throughout the afternoon. Quizzes for children, treasure hunt etc. Leaflets and cards of the garden available.
✂ ❉ ☕

Attractive village surrounded by farmland with thatched primary school and C16 village pub . . .

⑲ PARK COTTAGE
Penley LL13 0LS. Dr & Mrs S J Sime. *3m E of Overton on Dee. 12m SE Wrexham. Signed from A539. Roadside parking in village involves 250yd walk to garden. Please no parking at house.* Home-made teas. **Adm £2.50, chd £1. Suns 15 Apr; 16 Sept (2-5).**
Relaxed garden emerging on a site of 5 acres. 3½ acres developed so far. Large plant collection specialising in the hydrangea family. Ponds, grass garden, maze and many other features. New areas to see each year. Wide variety of plants from the garden for sale.

⑳ PEN-Y-BRYN
Llangollen LL20 8AA. Mr & Mrs R B Attenburrow, 01978 860223. *14m SW of Wrexham. Located above centre of Llangollen. Groups by appt should apply for directions.* **Visitors welcome by appt.**
3-acre garden on wooded plateau overlooking town with panoramic view. On site of old hall with established trees, shrubs and rhododendrons; walled garden; water features; new folly; extensive lawns and herbaceous borders. Featured in 'English Garden'. Some gravel paths.

㉑ NEW PENLEY VILLAGE GARDENS
LL13 0LU. *12m SE of Wrexham. On A539. In village turn L opp Maelor School if approaching from Wrexham. Follow signs to gardens.* Home-made teas at Penley Hall Stables. **Combined adm £3.50, chd free. Sun 29 July.**
Attractive village surrounded by farmland with thatched primary school and C16 village pub.

NEW 26 OAKWOOD PARK
Eva & Phil Bassett
Young garden started in 2000. Mixed borders with trees, shrubs, perennials and annuals. Roses, clematis and other climbers on trellises. Small pond, bog area and raised borders with fruit trees, berries and vegetables.

PENLEY HALL STABLES
Andrew & Angela Wilson
Approx 1-acre walled garden with shrubs and herbaceous plants, pools and bog garden. Created within old stable yard and surrounding land. Croquet (free tuition).

Flintshire County Volunteers

County Organiser
Angela Wilson, Penley Hall Stables, Penley, Wrexham LL13 0LU, 01948 830439, Wilsons.penley@virgin.net

County Treasurer
Peter Manuel, Tir y Fron,Ruabon, Wrexham LL14 6RW, 01978 821633,

Publicity
Ann Rathbone, Woodfield House, Station Road, Hawarden, CH5 3EG, 01244 532948, ann@rathbone69.fslife.co.uk

Assistant County Organiser
Rosemary Ffoulkes Jones, Bryn Hafod, Ffordd y Blaenau, Treuddyn, Mold CH7 4NS, 01352 771620, randdffoulkesjones@hotmail.com

 gardens open
for charity

Frogmore House Garden

Windsor Home Park

By gracious permission of Her Majesty The Queen Frogmore House Garden will be open to the public on Tuesday 15 May 2007

Visitors to the gardens may also visit the Royal Mausoleum without charge

Opening times:
From 10am to 5.30pm (last admission 4pm)

Admission: £4.00
(accompanied children 16 and under – free)

For more details or to book a ticket please telephone The National Gardens Scheme on 01483 211535 or e-mail: orders@ngs.org.uk. Alternatively write to The National Gardens Scheme, Hatchlands Park, East Clandon, Guildford, Surrey GU4 7RT, stating the number of tickets required and enclosing a sterling cheque made payable to: The National Gardens Scheme

All major credit/debit cards accepted

GLAMORGAN

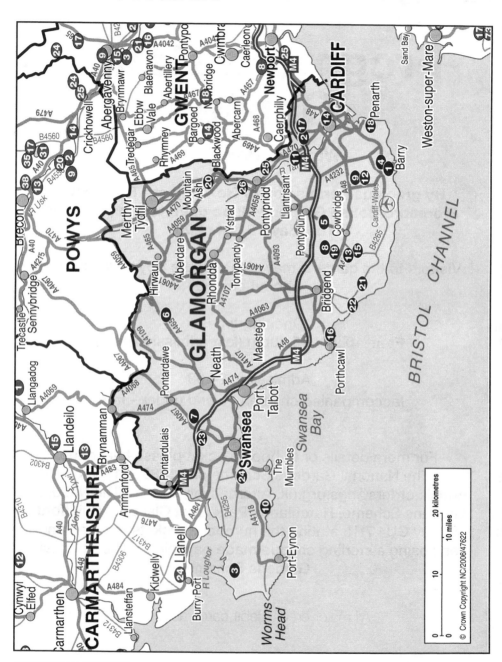

Opening Dates

April

SUNDAY 1
㉒ Slade

WEDNESDAY 11
㉖ 19 Westfield Road

SUNDAY 29
⑲ Penllyn Court

May

SUNDAY 6
⑭ Marlborough Road Gardens

SUNDAY 13
⑮ Nash Manor
㉓ Springfield

WEDNESDAY 16
㉖ 19 Westfield Road

THURSDAY 17
㉔ Touchwood (Day & Evening)

SATURDAY 19
㉕ Ty Nant Corrwg

THURSDAY 24
㉔ Touchwood

SUNDAY 27
⑯ Newton Cottage

June

SATURDAY 2
⑰ North Cardiff Gardens

SUNDAY 3
⑤ Bordervale Plants
⑭ Marlborough Road Gardens

TUESDAY 5
⑭ Marlborough Road Gardens (Evening)

SUNDAY 10
⑬ Llysworney Gardens
㉑ School & College Gardens

THURSDAY 14
⑱ Penarth Gardens

SUNDAY 17
⑦ Brynyrenfys
⑧ Contrasting Terraced Gardens

WEDNESDAY 20
㉖ 19 Westfield Road

SATURDAY 23
㉕ Ty Nant Corrwg (Evening)

SUNDAY 24
⑫ Hen Felin
⑳ Pontygwaith Farm

July

SUNDAY 1
① Barry Gardens
⑤ Bordervale Plants

SATURDAY 7
④ The Birches

SUNDAY 8
③ Big House Farm
④ The Birches

WEDNESDAY 11
㉖ 19 Westfield Road

THURSDAY 12
② The Beachouse (Evening)

FRIDAY 13
② The Beachouse (Evening)

SATURDAY 14
⑥ Brynheulog
⑪ Glan-y-Llyn
㉕ Ty Nant Corrwg

SUNDAY 15
⑥ Brynheulog

SUNDAY 29
⑪ Glan-y-Llyn

Gardens open to the public

⑤ Bordervale Plants
⑨ Dyffryn Gardens

By appointment only

⑩ 11 Eastcliff

The Gardens

① BARRY GARDENS
Barry CF63 2AS. *6m SW of Cardiff.* Home-made teas at 46 Brookfield Ave. **Combined adm £4, chd free. Sun 1 July (2-6).**
Four gardens in Barry, limited parking at each garden.

NEW 47 ANEURIN ROAD
Dave Bryant, 01446 406667, davebryant@uk2.net. *On A4050 Cardiff to Barry, take roundabout marked Barry Docks & Sully. At 2nd roundabout turn R towards Barry town centre, under railway bridge and up hill towards centre. Opp YMCA turn L, then 1st R.* **Visitors also welcome by appt all yr, weekends & after 6 weekdays.**
Small front garden with wide range of plants, sweet peas, dahlias, fuchsias, roses and lilies, all planted in over 300 various types of pots, containers and hanging baskets, all changed over the seasons.
✕ ✿

11 ARNO ROAD
Little Coldbrook. Debbie Palmer. *On A4050 Cardiff to Barry, take roundabout marked Barry Docks & Sully. 2nd R into Coldbrook Rd, 2nd L into Langlands Rd, then 6th R into Norwood Cres, 1st L into Arno Rd*
Plantaholic's small paradise garden. Herbaceous borders, slate scree planted with dwarf hardy geraniums. Alpine bed, ponds and fernery. Formal front garden, informally planted with perennials. Developing winter garden.
✕ ✿

NEW 46 BROOKFIELD AVENUE
Norah Bawn. *On A4050 Cardiff to Barry, take roundabout marked Barry Docks & Sully. 2nd R into Coldbrook Rd E, 2nd R into Meadow Vale, leading to Brookfield Ave. 4th cul de sac on R. No parking in cul de sac, vehicle turning point only*
Unusually shaped large front garden, packed with colourful trees, shrubs, perennials and annuals, with many interesting planting features. Relaxing smaller back garden with summerhouse, raised terrace, water feature and many varied plants. For 3yrs winner Barry in Bloom & Vale of Glamorgan in Bloom. Wheelchair access to front garden only.
♿ ✕ ✿

1 NORTH WALK
Sue Hyett. *From A4050 at roundabout marked Barry & Barry College, turn L. Continue past Barry Hospital, garden by road sign for Barry College, before pedestrian crossing*
Plantsman's garden of three parts: cottage garden, hot gravel garden and difficult, unusually shaped back garden with pond designed for wildlife and mixed raised beds with oriental influences.
✕ ✿

❷ THE BEACHOUSE

10 Clos y Bryn, Rhiwbina, Cardiff CF14 6TR. Annie Jones, 029 2065 5272, anne.c.jones@ntlworld.com. *2m N of Cardiff. From M4 J32 go S on A470. 1st L, before lights R at mini-roundabout at Deri Stores following signs for Wenallt Reservoir and Woodland (3rd L Wenallt Rd). Then 2nd L, 1st R. Disabled parking available, otherwise please use Wenallt Rd.* Light refreshments, teas & wine. **Evening Openings £5, chd free, Thur 12, Fri 13 July (6-10). Visitors also welcome by appt all yr.** Designed in 1999 as lakeland beach with several wooden outbuildings, decks and boardwalks with views. Planted with specimen plants. Designed for all-yr interest and weather, for horticultural excitement and soothing peace. Designed by gardener/owner with MS; unusual solutions to problems encountered by the disabled. Ideal for wheelchair users.

    ⛓ ⚘ ☕

Unusual trees, shrubs and perennials vie for attention with the panoramic view. Wildlife and weed friendly with no bedding!

❸ BIG HOUSE FARM

Llanmadoc SA3 1DE. Mr & Mrs M Mead. *15m W of Swansea. M4 J47. Take A483 signed Swansea. Next roundabout R A484 signed Llanelli. 2nd roundabout L B4296 signed Gowerton. R at 1st T-lights onto B4295. 10m after Bury Green, R to Llanmadoc. Pass Britannia Inn, L at T-junction uphill past red tel box. 100 yds turn R. Honesty car park on R.* Home-made teas. **Adm £2.50, chd free. Sun 8 July (12-6).** Mainly walled coastal garden, just under 1 acre, with stunning views. A variety of interesting plants and shrubs in mixed borders. Small Mediterranean garden and walled kitchen garden.

    ☕

❹ THE BIRCHES

Dingle Close, Barry CF62 6QR. Paul & Peta Goodwin. *6m W of Cardiff. Into Barry from Cardiff on A4050. At 1st roundabout straight on (signed to airport), next roundabout L to Pontypridd Rd, next roundabout 2nd exit to Park Cres, next roundabout 4th exit to Park Rd. After approx 1/2m bear L onto Porth Y Castell; 2nd L to Min Y Mor, 1st L Marine Drive and park. Walk 70yds down field, garden entrance through stone archway.* **Adm £2.50. Sat 7, Sun 8 July (2-6).** Large coastal garden with terraces and different rooms combining hard and soft landscaping. Mediterranean retreat, palm tree area, pergola, water features. Good design, beautiful plants and easy maintenance are equally important. Described as 'stunning' by many visitors at first opening in 2006. Still developing. Not suitable for small children. Featured in 'Garden News' & on BBC TV Open Gardens with Carol Klein.

    ⚒

❺ ◆ BORDERVALE PLANTS

Ystradowen, Cowbridge CF71 7SX. Mrs Claire Jenkins, 01446 774036, www.bordervale.co.uk. *8m W of Cardiff. 10 mins from M4. Take A4222 from Cowbridge. Turn R at Ystradowen postbox, then 3rd L & proceed 1/2m, following brown signs. Garden on R. Parking in rd past corner.* Teas on NGS days only. **Adm £2, chd free. Fris, Sats, Suns, Bank Hols Mar to early Oct. For NGS: Suns 3 June; 1 July (10-5).** Within mature woodland valley (semi-tamed), with stream and bog garden, extensive mixed borders; wild flower meadow, providing diverse wildlife habitats. Children must be supervised. The nursery specialises in unusual perennials and cottage garden plants. 10% of plant sales to NGS on NGS days. Disabled access to nursery, steep slopes in garden.

    ⛓ ⚒ ⚘ ☕

❻ NEW BRYNHEULOG

45 Heol y Graig, Cwmgwrach, Neath SA11 5TW. Lorraine Rudd, 01639 722593, lorraine.rudd@lycos.co.uk. *8m W of Neath. From M4 J43 take A465 to Glyneath, then rd signed Cwmgwrach. Entering village pass Dunraven PH, turn L at school sign, approx 100yds fork L into Glannant Place. Up hill, bear sharp R, approx 200yds turn L up steep*

track. 2nd house on L. Home-made teas. **Adm £3, chd free. Sat 14, Sun 15 July (11.30-5). Visitors also welcome by appt.** Set amid dramatic scenery, this hillside garden reflects the natural beauty of its surroundings. Too many features to mention, but look out for cornflowers, pergola and prairie planting. Keen plantswoman, natural health therapist, growing everything from trees to alpines, orchids to tropical waterlilies. Achieved in less than a yr. Natural Health Centre on site. Hillside walking area.

    ⚒ ⚘ ☕

❼ NEW BRYNYRENFYS

30 Cefn Road, Glais, Swansea SA7 9EZ. Edith & Roy Morgan. *5m W of Neath. M4 J45, take A4067 R at 1st roundabout, then 1st R and follow yellow signs.* Home-made teas. **Adm £2.50, chd free. Sun 17 June (12-6).** If you love plants you'll be at home here. A small surprising garden full of interest. Unusual trees, shrubs and perennials vie for attention with the panoramic view. Wildlife and weed friendly with no bedding! Seating on different levels, so stay a while, unwind and be welcome. Croeso!.

    ⚘ ☕

❽ CONTRASTING TERRACED GARDENS

Graig Penllyn, nr Cowbridge CF71 7RS. *3m NW of Cowbridge. W along A48 passing Cowbridge. Turn R at 1st junction signed 'Task Force Paintball'. Pass through Penllyn village into Graig Penllyn. Parking signed on L in Barley Mow car park, overflow parking next L.* Home-made teas at Glan Y Cwm. **Combined adm £3, chd free. Sun 17 June (2-6).** Small picturesque village nestling in steep-sided valley with pub and children's recreation area. Popular walking area - on circular route from Cowbridge. Parish Field well-known for its flora and fauna.

    ☕

GLAN Y CWM

Jackie & Malcolm Houston, 01446 775014
Formal terraced gardens on steep site. Numerous landscape features with mature and young trees, box topiary and structured

planting. Blend of contemporary design with traditional features. Featured on BBC TV Open Gardens with Carol Klein.

⛯

HIGH LANTERNS
The Rhiw. Mr Fred Furby
Mature terraced woodland 1/2-acre garden. Individual areas linked by paths and steps. Distinct features incl ponds, wild areas, flower beds, steeply-terraced kitchen garden, lawns and patios with seating. Views of village and countryside.

⛯ ⚈

Decked area with palms, enclosed fernery, cactus garden, raised walkway over small pond, bamboos, exotic planting and large collection of hemerocallis . . .

⑨ ♦ DYFFRYN GARDENS
nr Cardiff CF5 6SU. Vale of Glamorgan Council, 02920 593328, www.dyffryngardens.org.uk. *5m N of Cardiff. Exit J33 from the M4, on the A4232 signed Barry; 1st interchange 4th exit A48 signed Cowbridge. In St Nicholas village turn L, Dyffryn is signed.* **Open from 1 Mar. For dates, times and adm charges please phone or visit website.**
Outstanding Grade I listed Edwardian garden. Formal lawns; fountains and pools; seasonal beds; trees and shrubs. Garden rooms, incl Pompeian, Paved Court and Theatre garden. Arboretum contains trees from all over the world incl 3 champion trees - one the original *Acer griseum* collected by 'Chinese' Wilson. The gardens have recently been restored to Thomas

Mawson's original 1904 design with help from Heritage Lottery Fund.

♿ ⚈

⑩ 11 EASTCLIFF
Southgate SA3 2AS. Mrs Gill James, 01792 233310. *7m SW of Swansea. Take the Swansea to Gower rd & travel 6m to Pennard. Through village of Southgate & take 2nd exit off roundabout. Garden 200yds on L.* **Adm £2.50, chd free. Visitors welcome by appt.**
Seaside garden, approx 1/3 acre, and developed in a series of island and bordered beds for all-yr interest. Large number of white, blue-green and unusual plants such as artemesia, melianthus, euphorbia, allium and Mediterranean plants. Woodland area and gravel bed.

♿ ⛯ ⚈

⑪ NEW GLAN-Y-LLYN
50 Cardiff Road, Taffs Well, Cardiff CF15 7QE. John Langford. *2m N of Cardiff, off A470. Exit M4 J32. Go N approx 2m. Castle Coch on R, garden at end of village just after Fagins PH. Parking available at Taffs Well Rugby Club.* Home-made teas. **Adm £2, chd free. Sat 14, Sun 29 July (11-5).**
140ft x 22ft narrow plot leading down to R Taff with views over fields to Garth Mountain. 5yr-old garden divided into rooms. Decked area with palms, enclosed fernery, cactus garden, raised walkway over small pond, bamboos, exotic planting and large collection of hemerocallis. Small cascade of waterfalls going down to river. Featured on BBC TV Open Gardens with Carol Klein. Steep slope to river.

⚈ ☕

⑫ NEW HEN FELIN
Dyffryn, nr St Nicholas, Cardiff CF5 6SU. Rozanne Lord. *5m W of Cardiff. A48 at St Nicholas T-lights turn down Dyffryn Lane, past Dyffryn House. R at T-junction, house at end of village on R before humpback bridge.* Cream teas & wine. **Adm £3, chd free. Sun 24 June (12-7).**
Two-acre garden with stream and vegetable garden. Traditional cottage garden with lovely atmosphere. 200yr-old oak tree.

Wishing well. Music. Plant and gift stalls. Unprotected river access, children must be supervised.

♿ ⚈ ☕

HILLCREST BUNGALOW
See Gwent.

⑬ NEW LLYSWORNEY GARDENS
CF71 7NQ. *2m SW of Cowbridge. W along A48 pasing Cowbridge. Turn L at Pentre Meyrick on B4268 signed Llysworney & Llantwit Major.* Home-made teas in village. **Combined adm £5, chd free. Sun 10 June (2-6).**
Charming small rural village with pub, church, duck pond and friendly people!.

☕

NEW BLACK BARN HOUSE
Linda & Bryn Miles
Newly established garden on site of old barn yard, designed on circular linking themes.

⛯

NEW BROCTON HOUSE
Peter & Colette Evans
Recently extended and renovated garden arranged in terraces overlooking open farmland.

⛯

NEW LITTLE PADDOCK
Mervyn & Hilary Sheldon
Small sheltered garden making maximum use of limited space. Low maintenance. Inter-connecting garden rooms varying from sun terrace, water garden, arbour area, fruit patio and compact kitchen garden.

⛯

NEW PANTILES
Marion & Stewart Murton
Exposed sloping garden making maximum use of horticultural opportunities, with raised vegetables beds and an abundance of pots. A challenging garden.

⛯

NEW WOLF HOUSE
Martyn & Melanie Hurst
Old cottage-style walled garden on different levels with new beds and delightful summerhouse. Featured on BBC TV Open Gardens with Carol Klein.

⛯ ⚈

⑭ NEW MARLBOROUGH ROAD GARDENS

Penylan, Cardiff CF23 5BD.
1¹/₂m NE of Cardiff city centre. M4 J29, Cardiff E A48, then Llanedeyrn/Dock exit, towards Cyncoed and L down Penylan Hill. Marlborough Rd is L at T-lights at bottom of hill. Look out for NGS signs. Light refreshments & teas at 102 Marlborough Rd. **Combined adm £4, chd free, concessions £2. Suns 6 May; 3 June (2-6). Evening Opening,** wine, **Tues 5 June (5-9).**
Victorian suburb of terraced houses with small gardens and many parks. Original artwork of gardens by award-winning artist for sale.
☕

6 ALMA ROAD

Melvyn Rees, 029 2048 2200, mel@tymel.demon.co.uk. Visitors also welcome by appt.
S-facing terraced house garden 30ft x 15ft with many species from the S and E hemispheres, incl *Dicksonia antarctica, D. squarosa* and *Sophora* in a riot of exotic foliage. Slate used as paving material with gravel infill. Decking provides a raised seating area. Featured in 'Gardening News'.
✗ ⊛

NEW 7 CRESSY ROAD

Victoria Thornton
Terraced house garden, 30ft x 15ft, started from scratch in 2000. A secluded haven with a delightful exotic mix of tropical, agaves, bamboos, grasses, bonsai and containerised specimen trees. Conservatory, barrel pond and fern walkway.
✗ ⊛

NEW 102 MARLBOROUGH ROAD

Mrs Judith Griffiths, 02920 492790. Visitors also welcome by appt May, June & July, weekends only.
Come and discover a secret stone-walled garden behind a busy street. A garden of contrasts: Mediterranean-style sunny patio/shady areas. Wander through an informal mix of cottage garden plants, established shrubs and fruit trees.
✗

⑮ NEW NASH MANOR

Cowbridge CF71 7NS. Jennifer, Eric & Guy Williams. 2m SW of Cowbridge. W along A48 passing Cowbridge. Turn L at Pentre Meyrick on B4268 signed Llysworney/Llantwit Major. Through Llysworney, Nash Manor straight ahead. Home-made teas. **Adm £3, chd free. Sun 13 May (10-4).**
Large garden of C16 Grade I listed manor house, gradually being reclaimed. Courtyard with hanging baskets, wisteria and tulips. Walled garden with lily pond and spring bulbs. Many mature trees incl wonderful copper beech. Gravel path.
♿ ✗ ⊛ ☕

Come and discover a secret stone-walled garden behind a busy street. A garden of contrasts . . .

⑯ NEW NEWTON COTTAGE

Newton, Porthcawl CF36 5NT. Mr & Mrs J David. 1m E of Porthcawl. M4 J37, A4229 to Porthcawl. Approx 3m A4106 to Bridgend. 1st roundabout 2nd L on top of hill, on L. Home-made teas. **Adm £2.50, chd free. Sun 27 May (2-6).**
Small informal cottage garden. Mixed borders, good variety of shrubs, climbers and herbaceous plants. Newly-planted box garden. Kitchen garden.
⊛ ☕

⑰ NEW NORTH CARDIFF GARDENS

Thornhill & Llanishen. 4m N of Cardiff. M4 J32 onto A470. Ist L before T-lights. R at mini roundabout, past Deri Inn, 1st L Heol Llanishen Fach, L onto Thornhill Rd. R at roundabout onto Excalibur Drive, past Sainsbury's, 2nd L into Oakridge, then 1st L. Park here, Everest Ave short walk away. Teas at 79 Everest Ave. **Combined adm £3, chd free** (share to Motor Neurone Disease). **Sat 2 June (11-4).**
A vibrant, modern community. Purpose-built shopping area and attractive eateries. Home-made cards for sale.
☕

NEW 79 EVEREST AVENUE

Llanishan. Lisbeth Johns
Mature garden with magnificent views over Cardiff. Herb area with widlife-friendly hedgerow and pond.
✗

NEW 97 OAKRIDGE

Thornhill. Chris Bennett, 02920 763334, christopher@bennett1532. freeserve.co.uk. Visitors also welcome by appt.
Small, interesting, terraced garden with steps leading through a honeysuckle archway. Flowers, fruit and vegetables and a surprise round every corner. A miniature paradise and haven for wildlife.
✗

⑱ NEW PENARTH GARDENS

CF64 3HY. 3m SW of Cardiff. M4 J33, A4232 to Cardiff Bay then B4160 (B4055) for Penarth & Barry. At T-lights, straight across to next lights. Keep L, take 1st exit L to Lower Penarth into Redlands Rd, then 4th L into Cornerswell Rd. 1st L into Coleridge Ave. For Victoria Rd, continue along Redlands Rd to T-lights, straight across then 1st L into Victoria Rd. Home-made teas & wine at 31 Victoria Rd. **Combined adm £3, chd free. Thur 14 June (11-4).**
Old Victorian/Edwardian seaside town. Exhibition of watercolour flower paintings at 77 Coleridge Ave.
☕

NEW 77 COLERIDGE AVENUE
Diana Mead,
www.dianamead.net
Artist's well-stocked garden in three distinct linked areas: cottage-style front with curved 'river bed' gravel and paving path; small side vegetable garden with restricted apple trees; warm sheltered rear garden with tender plants and restricted pear trees. Exhibition of watercolour flower paintings.

NEW 31 VICTORIA ROAD
Maggie Cobley
Slightly larger than average town garden blending modern with traditional. Geometric lawn shapes softened by extensive soft planting. Water features complement the design. Trees and architectural plants afford all-yr shape and form. Newly-planted front garden of similar type.

19 NEW PENLLYN COURT
nr Cowbridge CF71 7RQ. Mr & Mrs John Homfray. *17m W of Cardiff. A48 W of Cardiff towards Bridgend. Bypass Cowbridge, turn R at Pentre Meyrick, then 2nd R, Penllyn Court on L.* **Adm £3, chd free. Sun 29 Apr (2-6).**
Large family garden with semi-formal walled garden, orchard with fruit trees and bulbs, stumpery, mixed plantings of shrubs and spring flowers. Vegetable garden. Gravel paths.

A surprise round every corner. A miniature paradise and haven for wildlife . . .

20 PONTYGWAITH FARM
Edwardsville, nr Treharris CF46 5PD. Mr & Mrs R J G Pearce, 01443 411137. *2m NW of Treharris. N from Cardiff on A470. At roundabout take A4054 (old Ponytpridd to Merthyr rd), travel N towards Aberfan for approx 3m through Quakers Yard and Edwardsville. 1m after Edwardsville turn very sharp L by old black bus shelter, garden at bottom of hill.* Light refreshments & teas. **Adm £2.50, chd free. Sun 24 June (10-6). Visitors also welcome by appt weekends May to Aug. No coaches.**
Large garden surrounding C17 farmhouse adjacent to Trevithick's Tramway. Situated in picturesque wooded valley. Fish pond, lawns, perennial borders, lakeside walk and rose garden. Grade II listed humpback packhorse bridge in garden, spanning R Taff. Gravel path, steep slope down to river.

21 NEW SCHOOL & COLLEGE GARDENS
St Brides Major & Llantwit Major. *See individual entries for directions.* Home-made teas at Atlantic College. **Combined adm £5, £3.50 each garden, chd free. Sun 10 June (11-4).**
School and College approx 3m drive apart, both situated in an Area of Outstanding Natural Beauty, close to Heritage Coast.

ST BRIDES C/W PRIMARY SCHOOL
Heol Yr Ysgol, St Brides Major CF32 0TB. *4m SW of Bridgend. From M4 J35 1st exit to A473. At 3rd roundabout take 2nd exit to A48, over mini roundabout. At next roundabout 1st L to Ewenny Rd, signed Llantwit Major B4265. Continue to St Brides Major, R at Fox & Hounds, 1st L to Heol Yr Ysgol.* Light refreshments & teas. **Adm £2.50, chd free**
This school garden has been developed and maintained by the school's Gardening Club which meets weekly after school and has approx 40 members. Individual gardens within the school grounds incl: Warm Welcome Garden, Woodland, Organic Fruit and Vegetable Garden, Easter Garden, Jewish Garden, Sensory Garden,

School and College gardens approximately 3 miles apart, both situated in an area of outstanding natural beauty, close to Heritage Coast . . .

Patchwork Garden, Butterfly Garden, Flower Diary Garden, Woven Willow Playground, Maze, Nature Reserve and Wild flower Meadow, craft willow bed. Music and willow weaving. Winners school section Biodiversity Competition; Best Kept School Vale of Glamorgan; National winners Wales in Bloom.

ST DONATS CASTLE (ATLANTIC COLLEGE)
St Donats, Llantwit Major CF61 1WF, www.atlanticcollege.org. *6m SW of Cowbridge, 2¼m W of Llantwit Major. From Barry follow B4265 to Llantwit Major. Castle signed at 2nd roundabout. Continue 1m on B4265 turning L at staggered junction. At next T-junction L into St Donats village and enter grounds 2nd gate on R. From Bridgend follow B4265 to Wick and further 1m to staggered junction*
Rare surviving large-scale Tudor terraced garden attached to a predominantly medieval castle, partly restored and added to in the early C20. The 5 terraces of garden cascade down the the SW slope of ground leading from the castle to the shores of the Bristol Channel.

22 SLADE
Southerndown CF32 0RP.
Rosamund & Peter Davies, 01656
880048,
ros@sladewoodgarden.plus.com.
*5m S of Bridgend. M4 J35. Follow
A473 to Bridgend. Take B4265 to St
Brides Major. Turn R in St Brides Major
for Southerndown. At Southerndown
turn L opp 3 Golden Cups PH onto
Beach Rd. Follow rd into Dunraven
Park. Turn 1st L over cattle grid on to
Slade drive.* Home-made teas. **Adm
£3, chd free. Sun 1 Apr (2-6). Visitors
also welcome by appt, groups
welcome, coaches permitted.**
Woodland garden and walk. Display of
early spring flowers: snowdrops,
daffodils, crocus, cyclamen, bluebells.
Mature specimen trees. New
herbaceous borders, terraced lawns,
orchard, hens. Extensive views over
Bristol Channel. Heritage Coast
wardens will give guided tours of
adjacent Dunraven Gardens with slide
shows every 1/2 hr from 3pm.

23 SPRINGFIELD
176 Clasemont Road, Morriston
SA6 6AJ. Carole & Stuart Jones,
01792 773827. *4m N of Swansea.
From M4 J46 follow A48 E for 1m.
From Morriston Cross take A48 W for
1m, garden on A48 50yds from
entrance to Morriston Golf Club.*
Home-made teas & wine. **Adm £2,
chd free. Sun 13 May (2-6). Visitors
also welcome by appt in May &
June.**
Small informal suburban garden with
interesting mix of trees, shrubs, bulbs
and perennials to give yr-round
interest. Incl small pond and pebble
pond and many containerised plants.
Several seating areas give the garden a
relaxed feel. Featured in 'Garden
News'; Swansea in Bloom award.

24 TOUCHWOOD
4 Clyne Valley Cottages, Killay,
Swansea SA2 7DU. Carrie Thomas,
01792 522443,
carrie.thomas@ntlworld.com. *5m W
of Swansea. Take A4118 (Gower rd)
past Killay shops and over mini-
roundabout towards Gower. 2nd L
(halfway down hill) into Clyne Valley
Road, which leads to Clyne Valley
Cottages.* **Adm £2, chd free. Thur 17
May, Day (2-4) & Evening Opening
(6-9). Thur 24 May (2-6). Visitors also
welcome by appt.**
Plantsman's intimate garden, most
items grown from seed. Annuals,
biennials, perennials, bulbs, shrubs,
grasses, climbers, herbs, vegetables
and alpines. National Collection of
Aquilegia vulgaris, hybrids and cultivars
are flowering May and beginning of
June. Set in historical country park, nr
Clyne and Singleton gardens. Featured
in 'The English Garden'.

🐾 ✲ NCCPG

Plantsman's
intimate garden,
most items
grown from
seed. Annuals,
biennials,
perennials, bulbs,
shrubs, grasses,
climbers, herbs,
vegetables and
alpines . . .

25 TY NANT CORRWG
7 Heol-y-Bryn, Rhydyfelin,
Pontypridd CF37 5EH. Sue & Les
Budd, 01443 407628,
susieabudd@aol.com. *3m S of
Pontypridd. From Pontypridd take
A470 S for 2m. Exit Upper Boat
junction, signed Gellihirion Estate.
From roundabout take A4054
Hawthorn Rd. 3rd R into Dynea Rd, up
hill, turn 5th R (still Dynea Rd), continue
up hill along Dynea Lane, R into Heol-
y-Bryn. Signed from A470 Upper Boat
junction.* Light refreshments & teas.
**Adm £2.50, chd free. Sat 19 May (2-
6); Evening Opening, wine, Sat 23
June (5-9). Sat 14 July (2-6). Visitors
also welcome by appt at any time.**
Cleverly designed S-facing hillside
garden connected via paths, steps,
terraces and numerous resting places.
Featuring many unusual plants, a
natural watercourse, wild bird feeding
station, herbs and Mediterranean area
incl fruits and vines. The overall garden
reflects the changes in seasons as it
merges with its natural habitat. Runner-
up Gardening for Wildlife Rhondda
Cynontaf in Bloom.

26 19 WESTFIELD ROAD
Glyncoch, Pontypridd CF37 3AG. Mr
& Mrs Brian Dockerill, 01443
402999,
brian.dockerill@tiscali.co.uk. *10m
NW of Cardiff. From Pontypridd travel
11/2m N along B4273. Take L turn by
school. At top of hill follow rd to L. Take
1st R & R again into Westfield Rd.*
Home-made teas. **Adm £2.50, chd
free. Weds 11 Apr; 16 May; 20 June;
11 July (10-7). Visitors also welcome
by appt.**
Garden of approx 3/4 acre designed as
series of interlinked enclosures each of
different character. Varying habitats in
sun and shade permit wide range of
plants to be grown extending the
interest through the yr.

🐾 ☕

Glamorgan County Volunteers

County Organiser
Rosamund Davies, Slade, Southerndown, Glamorgan CF32 0RP, 01656 880048, ros@sladewoodgarden.plus.com

County Treasurer
Peter Davies, Slade, Southerndown, Glamorgan CF32 0RP, 01656 880048, peter@daviesslade.plus.com

Publicity
Faith Thomas, 13 Plassey Street, Cardiff CF64 1EJ, 02920 402853, faith.thomas@ntlworld.com

Assistant County Organiser
Melanie Hurst, Wolf House, Llysworney, Cowbridge, Vale of Glamorgan CF71 7NQ, 01446 773659, melanie@b-theatre.com

ngs gardens open for charity

Historical garden,
belonging to
George Bernard Shaw
from 1906 until his death
in 1950. Hidden among
the trees is the revolving
summerhouse where
Shaw retreated
to write . . .

Shaw's Corner, Hertfordshire

GWENT

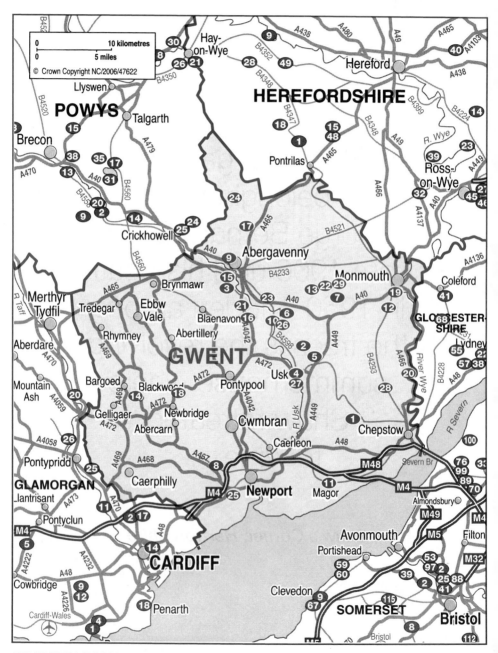

Opening Dates

April

SUNDAY 1
16 Llanover

SUNDAY 8
18 Llwyn-y-Wen Farm

SUNDAY 22
18 Llwyn-y-Wen Farm

SATURDAY 28
10 Glebe House

SUNDAY 29
10 Glebe House

May

SUNDAY 6
14 Hillcrest Bungalow
21 Ochran Mill

MONDAY 7
14 Hillcrest Bungalow

FRIDAY 11
18 Llwyn-y-Wen Farm

SATURDAY 12
12 High Glanau Manor
20 The Nurtons

SUNDAY 13
18 Llwyn-y-Wen Farm
20 The Nurtons
22 The Old Vicarage, Penrhos

FRIDAY 18
18 Llwyn-y-Wen Farm

SUNDAY 20
18 Llwyn-y-Wen Farm

SUNDAY 27
1 Barn Farm

June

SUNDAY 3
13 High House
21 Ochran Mill
29 Woodlands Farm

SATURDAY 9
14 Hillcrest Bungalow
26 Trostrey Lodge

SUNDAY 10
14 Hillcrest Bungalow
15 Llanfoist Village Gardens
26 Trostrey Lodge

THURSDAY 14
21 Ochran Mill (Evening)

SATURDAY 16
5 Cefntilla

SUNDAY 17
1 Barn Farm
5 Cefntilla
17 Llanthony and District Gardens

25 Tredegar House & Park

FRIDAY 22
28 Veddw House (Evening)

SATURDAY 23
4 Castle House
27 Usk Gardens

SUNDAY 24
4 Castle House
7 Coed Cefn
27 Usk Gardens

July

SUNDAY 1
2 Brynderi
9 Gardd-y-Bryn
18 Llwyn-y-Wen Farm
19 Monmouth Allotments and Millennium Field

SATURDAY 7
11 The Hawthorns

SUNDAY 8
11 The Hawthorns
21 Ochran Mill

SUNDAY 15
6 Clytha Park

SUNDAY 29
24 Three Wells

August

SUNDAY 5
21 Ochran Mill

SATURDAY 18
14 Hillcrest Bungalow

SUNDAY 19
14 Hillcrest Bungalow

SUNDAY 26
5 Cefntilla

MONDAY 27
5 Cefntilla

September

SATURDAY 8
20 The Nurtons

SUNDAY 9
20 The Nurtons
21 Ochran Mill

SUNDAY 30
3 Castell Cwrt

Gardens open to the public

20 The Nurtons
23 Penpergwm Lodge
25 Tredegar House & Park
28 Veddw House

By appointment only

8 Croesllanfro Farm

The Gardens

1 BARN FARM
Earlswood, Chepstow NP16 6AT.
Stephen & Felicity Hunt,
01291 650604,
steve.hunt@forestry.gsi.gov.uk. *6m SE of Usk, 7m NW of Chepstow. Off B4235 Chepstow to Usk rd. Turn off at Gaerllwyd Xrds. 1m from main rd.* Home-made teas. **Adm £3, chd free. Suns 27 May; 17 June (2-6). Visitors also welcome by appt Jun & Jul only, groups of 10+.**
Described by many as one of the best gardens they have visited for colour. A real kaleidoscope throughout the summer, with many unusual plants, this garden is a jewel in the heart of the Monmouthshire countryside. Areas for vegetables and fruit and a number of water features, creating a garden to suit all interests.
❌ ✿ ☕

A jewel in the heart of the Monmouthshire countryside . . .

 2 BRYNDERI
Wainfield Lane, Gwehelog, Usk NP15 1RG. Ann & Alwyne Benson, 01291 672976, www.brynderi.co.uk. *2m N of Usk towards Raglan. Follow Monmouth rd signed Gwehelog, L at Hall Inn PH onto Wainfield Lane. Parking in field 100metres from house.* Home-made teas. **Adm £2.50, chd free. Sun 1 July (2-6). Visitors also welcome by appt Mar-Oct, coaches permitted, groups up to 100.**
2 acres incl Kew fountain and pool surrounded by lawn and yews; round lawn with colour-themed borders and vine-covered arbour. Wisteria-clad pergola, knot garden, specimen tree collection in elevated area with stunning views, trained fruit trees and raised beds. New areas being developed. Featured in 'Glorious Gardens of Monmouthshire'.
♿ ❌ ✿ ⛺ ☕

Large sweeping borders of mass-planted perennials fill this 1½-acre garden . . .

❸ CASTELL CWRT
Llanelen NP7 9LE. Lorna & John McGlynn. *1m S of Abergavenny. From Abergavenny/Llanfoist take B4269 signed Llanelen. After passing Grove Farm turn R up single track rd. Rd climbs up steeply over canal. Approx 500yds entrance to Castell Cwrt on L. Separate disabled parking available.* Home-made teas. **Adm £2.50, chd free. Sun 30 Sept for autumn colour and harvest (12-4).**
Large informal family garden in rural surroundings with fine views overlooking Abergavenny. Lawns, established trees, shrubs and herbaceous borders. Organic kitchen and vegetable gardens. Hay meadow, family pets and livestock in fields. Some gravel and grass paths.
& ✗ ⌘ ☕

❹ CASTLE HOUSE
Monmouth Road, Usk NP15 1SD. Mr & Mrs J H L Humphreys, 01291 672563, www.uskcastle.com. *200yds NE from Usk centre. Turn up lane opp fire stn off Monmouth Rd.* **Combined adm £5, weekend ticket £7.50, chd free. Sat 23, Sun 24 June (10-5). Open with Usk Gardens. Visitors also welcome by appt.**
Enjoy views of the Usk valley from the enchanting, romantic ruins of Usk Castle which overlook the early C19 gardens of the Castle House below. Long, herbaceous border backed by castellated, clipped yew hedge; pond, fountain, topiary animals and 'medieval' herb garden, all awaiting discovery by the curious visitor. Fine trees.
& ⌘

❺ CEFNTILLA
Usk NP15 1DG. Lord Raglan. *3m NE of Usk. From S, take B4235 Usk to Chepstow rd to Gwernesney & follow signs N to Cefntilla, about 1m. From N, take Chepstow rd S from Raglan & follow signs through Llandenny.* Home-

made teas. **Adm £3, chd free. Sat 16, Sun 17 June; Sun 26, Mon 27 Aug (12-5).**
Rectangular former Jacobean garden area at rear much extended in 1850s with circumambulatory. 200ft rosebed, shrubs, colourful herbaceous borders, topiary walk with golden and Irish yews, handsome large lily pond, lawns and good trees, set in about 6 acres.
& ⌘ ☕

❻ CLYTHA PARK
Abergavenny NP7 9BW. Sir Richard Hanbury-Tenison, 01873 840300. *Half-way between Abergavenny (4m) and Raglan (4m). On B4598 (not A40).* Home-made teas. **Adm £2.50, chd free. Sun 15 July (2-6). Visitors also welcome by appt June-Sept.**
Large C18 garden around a 1½-acre lake with wide lawns and good trees. Visit the 1790 walled garden or walk around the lake on a serpentine path laid out over 250 yrs ago; a 'secret' garden at the furthest point. The more unusual trees and plants now labelled.
& ⌘ ☕

❼ NEW COED CEFN
Tregaer NP25 4DT. Brian & Alison Willott. *2m N of Raglan. A40/A449 to Raglan junction. Take A40 to Abergavenny, follow sign to Dingestow, immed L to Tregaer. Well-signed along 1½m lane to Coed Cefn.* Home-made teas. **Adm £3, chd free. Sun 24 June (2-6).**
Garden undergoing renovation and development, round C16 house (not open), with many climbing shrubs. Planned for low maintenance and wildlife habitats. Walled kitchen garden with potager, large fruit cage, peaches, figs. Terraces with raised bed and red garden. Shrubbery and laburnum tunnel. 2 large ponds. Old orchard with rambler roses and new fruit trees.
✗ ⌘ ☕

❽ CROESLLANFRO FARM
Rogerstone NP10 9GP. Barry & Liz Davies, 01633 894057, lizplants@aol.com. *3m W of Newport. From M4 J27 take B4591 to Risca. Take 2nd R, Cefn Walk (also signed 14 Locks Canal Centre). Proceed over canal bridge, continue approx ½m to island in middle of lane. White farm gate opp. Limited parking.* **Adm £3,**

chd free. Visitors welcome by appt June-Aug.
Large sweeping borders of mass-planted perennials fill this 1½-acre garden, created over 28 yrs by Liz Davies, garden designer. Wide variety of plants, many unusual, concentrate on form and texture, which fill the late summer borders. Architectural features include folly, grotto and terracing. Featured in 'Period Living'.
& ✗

❾ GARDD-Y-BRYN
The Hill Education & Conference Centre, Abergavenny NP7 7RP. Coleg Gwent. *¼m N of town centre. From A40 in Abergavenny, follow signs to Hill College.* Cream teas. **Adm £3, chd free. Sun 1 July (2-6).**
Recently-restored Victorian walled garden on S-facing slope overlooking Abergavenny and surrounded by mature woodland. Divided into various themed gardens incl fruit, vegetables, flowers for cutting, wild garden. Unusual, interesting, trees and shrubs. Atmospheric Mediterranean garden now complete with intriguing human sundial. Gardening courses run here. Harpist performing in garden.
✗ ⌘ ☕

Atmospheric Mediterranean garden now complete with intriguing human sundial . . .

❿ GLEBE HOUSE
Llanvair Kilgeddin NP7 9BE. Mr & Mrs Murray Kerr. *Midway between Abergavenny (5m) and Usk (5m). On B4598.* Home-made teas. **Adm £3, chd free. Sat 28, Sun 29 Apr (2-6).**
1½ acres with small ornamental vegetable garden and summerhouse. Colourful herbaceous borders filled with tulips, orchard, S-facing terrace and climbers. Set in picturesque Usk Valley with wonderful all-round views.
& ✗ ⌘ ☕

GLIFFAES COUNTRY HOUSE HOTEL
See Powys.

Visit around 15 exciting and contrasting village gardens . . .

11 THE HAWTHORNS

Magor NP26 3BZ. **John & Rosemary Skinner.** *9m W of Chepstow. M4 J23A onto B4245 to Magor, 150yds from roundabout. W side of Magor, well signed. No parking at The Hawthorns, please park in Queen's Gardens (signed).* **Adm £2.50, chd free. Sat 7, Sun 8 July (1-6).**
Formal bedding scheme with standard fuchsias, summer bedding and conifers shaped into domes and archways, perennial garden with covered walkway, water-feature and garden seat with passion flower canopy 'known as The Secret Garden' with dovecote. Partial wheelchair access.

12 HIGH GLANAU MANOR

Lydart NP25 4AD. **Mr & Mrs Hilary Gerrish.** *4m SW of Monmouth. Situated on B4293 between Monmouth & Chepstow. Turn into 'Private Road' opp Five Trees Carp Fishery.* Home-made teas. **Adm £3, chd free. Sat 12 May (2-6).**
Listed Arts and Crafts garden laid out by H Avray Tipping in 1922. Original features incl impressive stone terraces with far-reaching views over the vale of Usk, pergola, herbaceous borders, Edwardian glasshouse, rhododendrons and azaleas.

13 HIGH HOUSE

Penrhos NP15 2DJ. **Mr & Mrs R Cleeve.** *4m N of Raglan. From roundabout on A40 at Raglan take exit to Clytha. After 50 yds turn R to Llantilio Crossenny and follow garden open signs to High House - 10mins through lanes.* Home-made teas. **Combined adm £5, chd free. Sun 3 June (2-6). Open with Woodlands Farm.**
Spacious garden surrounding C17 house (not open). Natural water, new grove of walnuts and plantings of box, elegant terrace, roses and mature espaliered fruit. Set within wonderful rural landscape in hidden part of Monmouthshire.

14 HILLCREST BUNGALOW

Waunborfa Road, Cefn Fforest, Blackwood NP12 3LB. **Mr M O'Leary and Mr B Price, 01443 837029.** *3m W of Newbridge. Follow A4048 to Blackwood town centre or A469 to Pengam T-lights, then NGS signs.* Light refreshments & cream teas. **Adm £2.50, chd free. Sun 6, Mon 7 May; Sat 9, Sun 10 June; Sat 18, Sun 19 Aug (12-6). Visitors also welcome by appt Apr-Sept, incl groups of any size.**
Welcoming 1¹⁄₃-acre garden with fine view over valley. Profusely planted with bulbs, perennials and trees for yr-round colour and interest. Box parterre, gazebo, herb wheel. Elevated viewing terrace; places to sit and enjoy. New May opening for extensive tulip displays.

15 LLANFOIST VILLAGE GARDENS

Brian Barnes, www.llanfoist-open-gardens.co.uk. *1m SW of Abergavenny on B4246. Map provided with ticket. Most gardens within easy walking distance of the village centre. Free minibus to others. Limited wheelchair access to some gardens.* Teas in some gardens, lunch in Village Hall. **Adm £5, chd free (share to Llanfoist Villagers Association). Sun 10 June (10.30-5.30).**
Make this a great day out. Visit around 15 exciting and contrasting village gardens, both large and small, set just below the Blorenge Mountain on the edge of the Black Mountains. This is our 5th annual event and some of the gardens are open for the 1st time, others are back by popular demand. We will be serving cooked lunches and afternoon teas to keep you fortified.

Traditional Welsh dancing and music . . .

16 LLANOVER

nr Abergavenny NP7 9EF. **Mr & Mrs M R Murray, 01873 880232, www.llanover.com.** *4m S of Abergavenny, 15m N of Newport. On A4042.* Home-made teas. **Adm £3, chd free. Sun 1 Apr (2-5). Visitors also welcome by appt March & May only, groups of 10+.**
15-acre garden and arboretum with lakes, streams, cascades and a dovecote. Champion trees present incl *Quercus alba, Aesculus californica, Sorbus wardii, Betula costata* and *Abies concolor.* Many magnolias, camellias and avenue of spring bulbs should be in full bloom. Traditional Welsh dancing and music. No professional photography. Gravel and grass paths, narrow stone bridges.

17 NEW LLANTHONY AND DISTRICT GARDENS

Mrs Sue Torkington. *5m N of Abergavenny. From Abergavenny roundabout take A465 N towards Hereford. 4.8m turn L onto Old Hereford Rd signed Pantygelli 2m. Mynddd Ardrem ¹⁄₂m on R, Mione on L. Dirns to other gardens provided.* Cream teas at Perthi Crwn. **Combined adm £4, chd free (share to Llanthony and District Garden Club). Sun 17 June (10.30-4.30).**
Located in an area of outstanding beauty within the Black Mountains rural communities of Fforest Coal Pit, Cwmyoy and the village of Llanvihangel Crucorney. The garden settings reflect the diversity of the local landscape with views across valleys, mountains and forests.

NEW MIONE

Llanvihangel Crucorney. **Yvonne & John O'Neil**
Established garden with wide variety of plants. Pergola with 6 varieties of climbing roses, wildlife pond, containers with diverse range of planting. Several seating areas, each with a different atmosphere.

NEW MYNYDD ARDREM

Llanvihangel Crucorney. **Linda & Geoff Walsh**
This lovely garden was re-started 6 yrs ago within established mature boundaries, in order to

create a romantic setting for the Victorian house. Beautiful roses, clematis, herbaceous borders, shrubs, trees and a wisteria-clad pergola. Gravel paths.

  ⅋ ✕ ⊛

NEW NANT-Y-BEDD
Fforest Coal Pit. Sue & Ian Mabberley
2 acres at 1200 ft, providing a varied mix of organically-grown vegetables, fruit and flowers. Focal points utilising home-grown willow and hazel. Stream and pond.

✕

NEW PERTH-Y-CRWN
Cwmyoy. Jim Keates
Restored farmhouse garden with stunning views, SW aspect facing valley and mountainside beyond. Sunny, walled garden with fruit, vegetables and flowers, formal rose garden and newly-created wild flower bank.

⊛

Plantswoman's paradise, of great interest to those in search of the unusual . . .

18 LLWYN-Y-WEN FARM
Hafodyrynys Road, Crumlin NP11 5AX. Mrs Helen Lewy, 01495 244797. *11m NW of Newport, 6m W of Pontypool. M4 J28, take A467 to Risca. 11m to Crumlin T-lights, turn R on A472 to Pontypool. Entrance ¼ m on R. Limited parking; lay-bys on main road.* Cream teas. **Adm £3, chd free. Suns 8, 22 Apr; Fris, Suns 11, 13, 18, 20 May; Sun 1 July (2-5).** Visitors also welcome by appt Apr - July.
2 acres of Welsh hillside with spring creating trout pond and bog garden, at best in May, June, July. A plantswoman's paradise, of great interest to those in search of the unusual. Auriculas, primulas, hellebores and shade and damp-loving plants a speciality. Informal mass of flowers in orchard setting. 12metre-long rockery. Additional fields with bluebell walks in May. Featured in 'The Lady' and 'Country Quest' and on S4C Gardening Club.

✕ ⊛ ⊨ ☕

19 MONMOUTH ALLOTMENTS AND MILLENNIUM FIELD
Monmouth Town NP25 3EQ. Mrs Sue Carter. *Southern edge of Monmouth. Follow Garden Open signs from public toilets at bottom of Monnow St (main street in Monmouth) along river bank and under the dual carriageway. Parking at allotments.* Home-made teas. **Adm £2.50, chd free (share to Monmouth Allotments Association). Sun 1 July (2-6).**
Many allotments on site since 1940 gardened by people of all ages with a very wide variety of vegetables, fruit, flowers and sheds.

✕ ⊛ ☕

MOOR PARK
See Powys.

20 ◆ THE NURTONS
Tintern NP6 7NX. Adrian & Elsa Wood, 01291 689253, info@thenurtons.co.uk. *7m N of Chepstow. On A466 opp Old Station.* **Adm £3, chd free. Wed-Sun, Easter-end Sept (11-5). For NGS: Sats, Suns 12, 13 May; 8, 9 Sept (12-5).**
Exciting 2½ acre garden on a secluded historical site with stunning views of the Wye Valley. Very colourful with a large collection of choice plants in hot mediteranean, cool woodland and water feature settings. 1-acre wood is currently being developed as woodland garden. Partial wheelchair access along gravel paths.

✕ ⊨

21 OCHRAN MILL
Llanover NP7 9HU. Elaine & David Rolfe, 01873 737809, www.ochranmill.org.uk. *3m S of Abergavenny. On A4042 midway between Llanover & Llanelen.* Cream teas. **Adm £3, chd free. Suns 6 May; 3 June; 8 July; 5 Aug; 9 Sept (1-5). Evening Opening,** wine, **Thur 14 June (6-9).** Visitors also welcome by appt evenings incl garden clubs and groups, coaches permitted.
Grade II listed water mill (not working) approx 1½-acres. A 'garden in the making' taking shape over last 5 yrs from fields. Large colour-themed herbaceous borders, bog garden, shrub borders, gravel and grasses, woodland borders incl large collection of hellebores. New large water feature and rose/clematis pergola. Large field for picnics, stream for children to dam, pinball and arcade collection (very popular with children and non-gardeners); outdoor art exhibition by

local artist. Runner-up 'Times' Garden of the Year. Gravel paths, gentle slopes.

  ⅋ ✕ ⊛ ☕

22 THE OLD VICARAGE, PENRHOS
Raglan NP15 2LE. Professor & Mrs Luke Herrmann. *3m N of Raglan. At Raglan turn off A40 for Mitcheltroy. Almost immediately turn L for Tregaer. Follow signs for Tregaer, then Penrhos.* Home-made teas. **Adm £2.50, chd free. Sun 13 May (2-5.30).**
Traditional Vicarage garden of 1½ acres in rural surroundings with fine views. Informal mixture of shrubs, spring flowers, roses, perennials and annuals in varied settings; traditional vegetable garden, wooded pond area, mature and newly planted trees; ornamental pots.

✕ ⊛ ☕

23 ◆ PENPERGWM LODGE
nr Abergavenny NP7 9AS. Mr & Mrs Simon Boyle, 01873 840208, www.penplants.com. *3m SE of Abergavenny, 5m W of Raglan. On B4598. Turn opp King of Prussia Inn. Entrance 150-yds on L.* **Adm £3.50, chd free. Thurs to Suns 29 Mar to 30 Sept (2-6),** group visits welcome by appt.
3-acre garden with lawns, mature trees, Italianate parterre and brick-pillared vine walk. Jubilee tower overlooks newly-terraced ornamental garden with cascading water. S-facing terraces planted with rich profusion. Special plant nursery. Some gravel paths.

  ⅋ ⊛ ⊨

24 NEW THREE WELLS
Llanvihangel Crucorney, Abergavenny NP7 7NR. Anthony & Verity Woodward. *8m N of Abergavenny. Off A465 Abergavenny-Hereford rd. At Llanvihangel Crucorney turn downhill at Skirrid PH and 1st R over hump-back bridge. After ⅔ m, L by grass triangle and follow yellow signs. 1-way system in place as very steep, narrow single track lanes. If wet, car park may be 15-minute walk.* Home-made teas. **Adm £3.50, chd free. Sun 29 July (11-6).**
Highest property opening in Monmouthshire. 6-acre smallholding in mountain setting (reaching nearly 1600ft) on Offa's

Dyke footpath in Brecon Beacons National Park. For anyone fit and intrepid who sees beauty in wild places - in upland hay meadows, dry-stone walls and mountain springs, forgotten farm machinery in field corners and gateways framing 70-mile views.

25 ♦ TREDEGAR HOUSE & PARK
Newport NP10 8YW. Newport City Council, 01633 815880, www.newport.gov.uk. *2m SW of Newport town centre. Signed from A48 (Cardiff rd) & M4 J28.* **Adm £2.50, chd 50p. For NGS: Sun 17 June (11-5).**
Series of C18 walled formal gardens surrounding magnificent late C17 house (also open). Early C18 orangery garden with coloured mineral parterres. Open on NGS day Growing Space gardens maintained to a high standard by staff and clients with mental illnesses. Six separate areas incl bog garden, ornamental pond and secret cottage garden. Also open by appt tel 01633 810718.
&. ⚡ ⊛

A pretty cottage garden-cum-orchard packed with interest and a friendly atmosphere . . .

26 TROSTREY LODGE
Bettws Newydd NP15 1JT. Roger & Frances Pemberton. *4m W of Raglan. 7m E of Abergavenny. Off the old A40 (unnumbered). 1m S of Clytha Gates and 1½m N of Bettws Newydd.* Home-made teas Sun only. **Adm £3, chd free. Sat 9, Sun 10 June (12-6).**
Enjoy one of the most glorious views in

the Usk Valley as well as a pretty cottage garden-cum-orchard packed with interest and a friendly atmosphere for a walkabout round this listed Regency house (not open). Visitors welcome to picnic in field. Some gravel paths.
&. ⊛ ☕

27 USK GARDENS
Usk Town NP15 1AF. Mrs M Evans, 01291 672466, www.usktc.fg.co.uk. *From M4 J24 take A449, proceed 8m to Usk exit. Good free parking in town. Map of gardens provided with ticket.* Light refreshments & cream teas. **Combined adm £5, weekend ticket £7.50, chd free (share to local Usk charities). Sat 23, Sun 24 June (10-5). Open with Castle House.**
20+ gardens from small cottage packed with colourful and unusual plants to large gardens with wonderful herbaceous borders. Gardeners' market with wide selection of interesting plants. Featured on HTV News and Grass Roots. Limited wheelchair access to some gardens.
&. ⚡ ⊛ ☕

28 ♦ VEDDW HOUSE
Devauden NP16 6PH. Anne Wareham & Charles Hawes, 01291 650836, www.veddw.co.uk. *5m NW of Chepstow. Off B4293. Signed from PH on the green at Devauden.* **Adm £5.50, chd £1.50. Suns & Bank Hol Mon 3 Jun to 27 Aug (2-5). For NGS: Evening Opening £5.50, wine, Fri 22 June (6-8.30).**
A modern romantic garden: 'One of the 10 best gardens to visit this summer' Katherine Lambert, editor of Good Gardens Guide in 'The Independent'. Featured in 'Gardens Illustrated'.
⚡

29 WOODLANDS FARM
Penrhos NP15 2LE. Craig Loane. *3m N of Raglan. At Raglan, turn off A40 towards Mitcheltroy. Almost immed, turn L for Tregaer, then Penrhos and follow NGS signs.* Home-made teas. **Combined adm £5, chd free. Sun 3 June (2-6). Open with High House.**
An evolving garden with a mixture of

formal modern design and wild informality, incorporating the surrounding countryside by vistas that have been built into the structure of the garden. New hard landscaping, water features and ornamental mound make a return visit this year worthwhile. Featured on Classic FM.
⚡ ⊛ ☕

An evolving garden with a mixture of formal modern design and wild informality . . .

Gwent County Volunteers

County Organiser
Joanna Kerr, Glebe House, Llanvair Kilgeddin, Abergavenny NP7 9BE, 01873 840422, murray@amknet.com
Assistant County Organiser
Sue Carter, St Pega's, 47 Hereford Road, Monmouth NP25 3HQ, 01600 772074, susancarter@gardeneing47.freeserve.co.uk

GWYNEDD

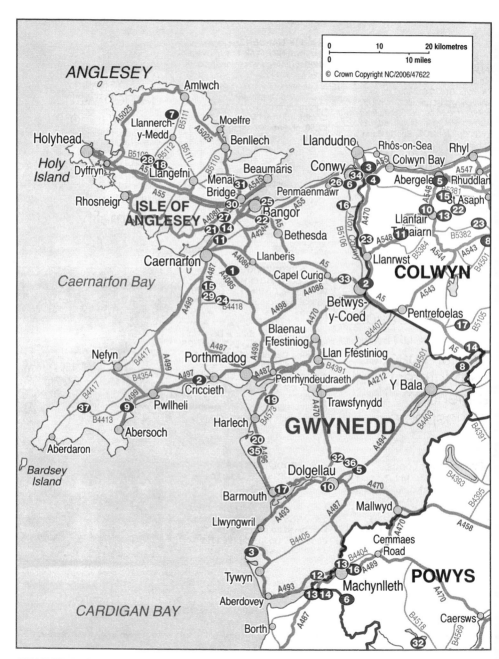

Opening Dates

February

SATURDAY 3
25 Penrhyn Castle

April

FRIDAY 6
27 Plas Newydd

SUNDAY 8
2 Bont Fechan Farm

MONDAY 9
2 Bont Fechan Farm

SUNDAY 15
7 Cae Newydd

SUNDAY 29
23 Maenan Hall

May

SUNDAY 6
16 Gilfach
20 Llanbedr Spring Festival Gardens - Gwyl Wanwyn Llanbedr

SUNDAY 13
2 Bont Fechan Farm
5 Bryn Gwern
10 Craig y Ffynnon

SATURDAY 19
24 Megans Wood Gwernoer Farm

SUNDAY 20
9 Coron
13 Felin y Ffridd
22 Llys-y-Gwynt
24 Megans Wood Gwernoer Farm
30 Tan Dinas
32 Ty Capel Ffrwd

WEDNESDAY 23
14 Foxbrush

SUNDAY 27
4 Bryn Eisteddfod
11 Crug Farm
17 Glandwr Gardens
28 Rhyd

MONDAY 28
37 Y Felin

June

SUNDAY 3
8 Caerau Uchaf
35 Ty Newydd

SUNDAY 10
26 Pensychnant

WEDNESDAY 13
14 Foxbrush

SATURDAY 16
1 Antur Waunfawr
19 Hotel Maes-y-Neuadd

SUNDAY 17
12 Esgairweddan

SATURDAY 23
21 Llanidan Hall

SUNDAY 24
3 Bronclydwr
7 Cae Newydd
16 Gilfach
22 Llys-y-Gwynt
31 Treffos School

July

SUNDAY 1
32 Ty Capel Ffrwd

SATURDAY 7
21 Llanidan Hall

SUNDAY 15
15 Gardd y Coleg
33 Ty Hyll - The Ugly House
34 Ty Mawr
36 Tyn-Twll
37 Y Felin

SUNDAY 22
28 Rhyd
34 Ty Mawr

WEDNESDAY 25
29 St John the Baptist & St George

SUNDAY 29
5 Bryn Gwern

August

SUNDAY 12
16 Gilfach

SATURDAY 18
6 Bunclody

SUNDAY 19
6 Bunclody

TUESDAY 21
19 Hotel Maes-y-Neuadd

Gardens open to the public

1 Antur Waunfawr
11 Crug Farm
15 Gardd y Coleg
19 Hotel Maes-y-Neuadd
25 Penrhyn Castle
26 Pensychnant
27 Plas Newydd
33 Ty Hyll - The Ugly House

By appointment only

18 Gwyndy Bach

The Gardens

1 ◆ **ANTUR WAUNFAWR**
Bryn Pistyll, Waunfawr, Caernarfon LL55 4BJ. Menna Jones, 01286 650721, heulwen@anturwaunfawr.org.uk. 4¹/₂m SE of Caernarfon. On A4085. Waunfawr village, turn L following signs, bear L for approx ¹/₂m. **Donations. Open all yr.** For NGS: Sat 16 June (11-3).
Gardens and 7-acre Nature Park developed by Antur Waunfawr, a community venture providing employment opportunities for people with learning disabilities. Meadows, woodland walks, wildlife and ornamental ponds, soft fruit garden, herbaceous perennial beds. Well stocked wildlife plant nursery, greenhouses.

Interesting trees, shrubs, bamboos; bog garden and wild wooded area . . .

ARFRYN
See Denbighshire & Colwyn.

BEAVER GROVE HOUSE
See Denbighshire & Colwyn.

BODYSGALLEN HALL & SPA
See Denbighshire & Colwyn.

2 **BONT FECHAN FARM**
Llanystumdwy LL52 0LS. Mr & Mrs J D Bean, 01766 522604. 2m W of Criccieth. On the A497 to Pwllheli on L of main rd. Home-made teas. **Adm £2, chd free. Sun 8, Mon 9 Apr; Sun 13 May (11-5). Visitors also welcome by appt.**
Cottage garden with rockery, fish pond, herbaceous border, steps to river. Large variety of plants. Nicely planted tubs; good vegetable garden and poultry. Rhododendron and azaleas.

❸ BRONCLYDWR
Rhoslefain LL36 9LT. Mr & Mrs Michael Bishton. *5m N of Tywyn. Take A493 Dolgellau to Tywyn rd. At Rhoslefain take Tonfanau rd for about ½m. Fork L along private rd to end of tarmac rd then take unmade rd to large house on edge of wood.* Cream teas. **Adm £2.50, chd free. Sun 24 June (1-5).**
1-acre unique plantsman's garden of peaceful historic farmhouse overlooking Cardigan Bay. Many unusual and tender plants are grown incl protea, puya, amicia, echiums, watsonias, arums, *Beschorneria yuccoides*, euryops, restios. Interesting trees, shrubs, bamboos; bog garden and wild wooded area. Gravel paths.
✗ ✿ ☕

❹ BRYN EISTEDDFOD
Glan Conwy LL28 5LF. Dr Michael Senior, 01492 581175. *3½m SE of Llandudno. 3m W Colwyn Bay. Up hill (Bryn-y-Maen direction) from Glan Conwy Corner where A470 joins A55.* Home-made teas. **Adm £2.50, chd 50p. Sun 27 May (2-5). Visitors also welcome by appt.**
8 acres of landscaped grounds incl mature shrubbery, arboretum, old walled 'Dutch' garden, large lawn with ha-ha. Extensive views over Conwy Valley, Snowdonia National Park, Conwy Castle, town and estuary.
♿ ✿ ☕

❺ BRYN GWERN
Llanfachreth LL40 2DH. H O & P D Nurse, 01341 450255. *3m NE of Dolgellau. Do not go to village of Llanfachreth, stay on A494 Bala-Dolgellau rd: 13m from Bala. Take 1st Llanfachreth turn R. From Dolgellau 4th Llanfachreth turn L, follow signs. No coach parking.* Cream teas. **Adm £3, chd free. Suns 13 May; 29 July (10-5). Visitors also welcome by appt.**
Take in the breathtaking views of Cader Idris whilst sitting, walking or eating your cream teas amongst 2 acres of trees, shrubs (azaleas, rhododendrons and pieris in spring, embothriums, hydrangeas etc in summer) and flower beds in a semi-wild cultivated garden providing something for all ages. Home to cats, dogs, guinea fowl, ducks and chickens, not to mention the wild birds that live, nest and visit the garden.
✗ ✿ ☕

❻ NEW BUNCLODY
Henryd Road, Conwy LL32 8TN. Dawn Humphreys, 01492 580930. *1½m S Conwy. Cross Conwy Bridge, L through arch onto B5106 to Gyffin (¼m). Henryn Rd opp corner shop. 1m, passing R turn. Garden 2nd house on R.* Cream teas. **Adm £2.50, chd free. Sat 18 Aug (11-4), Sun 19 Aug (12-4). Visitors also welcome by appt June & Aug for small groups.**
Garden only 4yrs old. ¾ acre. Distinct areas linked by curving paths and beds. Circular lawn surrounded by roses and shrubs. Gazebo with natural stream, pond and bridges. Walled garden, bog garden with boardwalk. Hot house with lotus, giant taro and bougainvillia. Packed with interest. Amazing what has been achieved in a short time.
✗ ✿

Packed with interest. Amazing what has been achieved in a short time . . .

❼ CAE NEWYDD
Rhosgoch, Anglesey LL66 0BG. Hazel & Nigel Bond, 01407 831354. *3m SW of Amlwch. L immed after Amlwch Town sign on A5025 from Benllech, follow signs for leisure centre & Lastra Farm. After L turn for Lastra Farm, follow rd for approx 3m, pass through Rhosgoch, keep to main rd, follow signs for Llyn Alaw. Garden/car park on L.* Home-made teas. **Adm £2.50, chd free. Suns 15 Apr; 24 June (11-4). Visitors also welcome by appt May to Sept.**
Started 2002 from exposed 2½-acre S-facing field, overlooking Llyn Alaw with panoramic views of Snowdonia. Spring borders, mixed beds of interesting shrubs, grasses and perennials; large wildlife pond,

meadow area with cut paths and buddleias, vegetable garden with polytunnel and chicken run. Paved area near house with raised beds and formal pond. Sheltered mature paddock garden with pond/bog area, formal herb bed and walled former pigsty providing additional shelter. Joint 2nd prize-winner Snowdonia Wildlife Garden Competition.
♿ ✗ ✿ ☕

❽ CAERAU UCHAF
Sarnau LL23 7LG. Mr & Mrs Toby Hickish, summersgardens@tiscali.co.uk. *3m NE of Bala. From A5 N of Corwen turn L A494 to Bala. Approx 5m turn R into Sarnau, keep R up hill approx 3m. From Bala take A494 NE. After approx 3m turn L into Sarnau, keep R up hill approx 1m. Coaches park in village.* **Adm £3, chd free, concessions £1. Sun 3 June (2-5). Visitors also welcome by appt.**
Herbaceous borders, lawns, ornamental vegetable garden, woodland walks - some paths rather steep. New developments every yr. Wonderful views. Gravel paths, steep slopes.
♿ ✗ ✿ ☕

❾ CORON
Llanbedrog LL53 7NN. Mr & Mrs B M Jones, 01758 740296. *3m SW of Pwllheli. Turn R off A499 opp Llanbedrog Village sign, before garage, up private drive.* Cream teas. **Adm £2.50, chd free. Sun 20 May (11-5.30). Visitors also welcome by appt.**
6-acre mature garden featuring Davidia involucrata, overlooking Cardigan Bay. Pathways leading through extensively planted areas with rhododendrons, embothriom, azaleas, camellias, bluebell walks, wooded slopes and rock outcrops providing shelter for tender plants, lakes and bog gardens; orchards, walled vegetable and formal garden.
♿ ✗ ✿ ☕

❿ CRAIG Y FFYNNON
Ffordd y Gader, Dolgellau LL40 1RU. Jon & Sh,n Lea. *Take Tywyn rd from Dolgellau main sq. Park on rd by Penbryn Garage. Walk up rd signed Cader Idris. Garden entrance on L 50yds from junction.* Home-made teas. **Adm £3, chd free (share to Tyn Sarn Riding School for the Disabled). Sun 13 May (11-5).**
N-facing 2-acre Victorian garden set

out in 1870s. Majority of garden planted with mature specimen trees, rhododendrons and azaleas predominate. More formal herbaceous borders and greenhouse enclosed by box hedges. Wildlife pond; unusual shade-loving plants and ferns. Wine tasting (12-2). Featured on S4C Clwb Garddio.

11 ◆ CRUG FARM
Griffiths Crossing LL55 1TU. Mr & Mrs B Wynn-Jones, 01248 670232, www.crug-farm.co.uk. *2m NE of Caernarfon. 1/4 m off main A487 Caernarfon to Bangor rd. Follow signs from roundabout.* Adm £2.50, chd free. Nursery Thurs to Suns and Bank Hols 24 Feb to 30 Jun; Thurs to Sats July/Aug/Sept (10-5). For NGS: Sun 27 May (10-6).
3 acres; grounds to old country house (not open). Gardens filled with choice, unusual collections of climbers and herbaceous plants; over 300 species of hardy geraniums. Gold Medal winner at Garden Heaven Show Dublin. Partial wheelchair access.

CWMRHAIADR GARDEN & NURSERY
See Ceredigion/Cardiganshire.

12 ESGAIRWEDDAN
Pennal SY20 9JZ. Mr & Mrs John & Annie Parry. *4m W of Machynlleth. From Machynlleth take A493 towards Aberdovey. Esgairweddan is on R between Pennal & Cwrt.* Home-made teas. Adm £2, chd free. Sun 17 June (2-5).
Small garden with 400yr-old farmhouse (not open), 3/4 m drive from rd entrance leading through oak woodland with wonderful view of Dovey estuary.

13 FELIN Y FFRIDD
Ffriddgate SY20 8QG. Mr & Mrs J W Osselton, 01654 702548. *1m N of Machynlleth. From S, take A487 from Machynlleth to Dolgellau. After approx 1m turn R at B4404 to Llanwrin. Garden short distance on L before bridge. From N, take A487, turn L on B4404.* Cream teas. Adm £2.50, chd free. Sun 20 May (2-5.30). Visitors also welcome by appt.
Approx 1 acre, bordered by R Dulas. Lower garden has pond, gravel paths and old mill where woodland edge is being developed. Upper garden has grass paths, mixed borders and island

beds, where conifers and viburnums contrast with colourful, scented azaleas and rhododendrons. Wide choice of home-grown plants for sale.

14 FOXBRUSH
Felinheli LL56 4JZ. Mr & Mrs B S Osborne, 01248 670463. *3m SW of Bangor. On Bangor to Caernarfon rd, entering village opp Felinheli signpost.* Cream teas. Adm £2, chd free. Weds 23 May; 13 June (3-8). Visitors also welcome by appt March to end June, coaches permitted.
Fascinating 3-acre country garden created around winding river; ponds and small wooded area. Rare and interesting plant collections incl rhododendrons, ferns, clematis and roses; 45ft long pergola; fan-shaped knot garden. Truly a wildlife garden, planted in a very natural style following horrendous devastation caused by floods of 2004. Dogs on leads.

15 ◆ GARDD Y COLEG
Carmel LL54 7RL. Pwyllgor Pentref Carmel Village Committee. *Garden at Carmel village centre. Parking on site.* Adm £2, chd free. For NGS: Sun 15 July (1.30-5).
Approx 1/2 acre featuring raised beds planted with ornamental and native plants mulched with local slate. Benches and picnic area, wide pathways suitable for wheelchairs. Spectacular views. Garden created by volunteers. Featured on HTV Wales News 'Peoples Millions'. Civic Trust Green Pennant Award.

16 GILFACH
Rowen LL32 8TS. James & Isoline Greenhalgh, 01492 650216. *4m S of Conwy. At Xrds 100yds E of Rowen S towards Llanrwst, past Rowen School on L; turn up 2nd drive on L.* Home-made teas. Adm £2, chd free. Suns 6 May; 24 June; 12 Aug (2-5.30). Visitors also welcome by appt.
1-acre country garden on S-facing slope with magnificent views of the R Conwy and mountains; set in 35 acres of farm and woodland. Collection of mature shrubs is added to yearly; woodland garden, herbaceous border, small scree bed and pool. Some slopes and steps but wheelchair access available to main features and viewpoints.

Fascinating 3-acre country garden . . . truly a wildlife garden, planted in a very natural style . . .

17 GLANDWR GARDENS
Glandwr LL42 1TG. *2m E of Barmouth. On A496 7m W of Dolgellau, situated on N side of Mawddach Estuary. Park in or nr layby and proceed L to bridge for gardens.* Home-made teas. Adm £2.50 per garden (share to Wales Air Ambulance). Sun 27 May (11-5).
2 gardens in Glandwr hamlet overlooking the magnificent Cader Idris range and the Mawddach Estuary.

BRONDDWYNANT
Cristina Posner
A garden with stunning views. Many trees and shrubs together with a pond, small lake, ornamental kitchen garden and steep tract of land with drifts of prairie grasses, bulbs and hardy perennials.

PEN Y BRYN
Phil & Jenny Martin
Hidden hillside garden on different levels with range of acid-loving shrubs and enhanced natural rockeries set against breathtaking panoramic views of Cader Idris and the Mawddach Estuary. S-facing with woodland walks and rock cannon.

Drifts of prairie grasses, bulbs and hardy perennials . . .

18 GWYNDY BACH
Llandrygarn LL65 3AJ. Keith & Rosa Andrew, 01407 720651, www.kannonchiku.co.uk. *5m W of Llangefni. From Llangefni take B5109 towards Bodedern, cottage exactly 5m out on the L.* **Visitors welcome by appt.**
3/4-acre artist's garden, set amidst rugged Anglesey landscape. Romantically planted in intimate rooms with interesting rare plants and shrubs, box and yew topiary, old roses and Japanese garden with large koi pond. National Collection of Rhapis miniature Japanese palms. Studio attached. View new paintings and prints by Keith Andrew RCA.
NCCPG

19 ◆ HOTEL MAES-Y-NEUADD
Talsarnau, nr Harlech LL47 6YA. Mr & Mrs P Jackson & Mr & Mrs P Payne, 01766 780200, maes@neuadd.com. *3m NE of Harlech. Take B4573 old Harlech rd at T-junction with A496. Hotel signed 1/4m on L. Take small lane on L immed after sign, just before small bridge on bend. Hotel entrance & car park 1/2 m up hill, through small hamlet (tel box on L). Follow brown signs.* **Adm £2.50, chd under 13 free, concessions £2. Open daily except Christmas and New Year (10-5). For NGS: Sat 16 June; Tue 21 Aug.**
Gardens and grounds of country house hotel, parts of which C14. Views towards Snowdon, Cardigan Bay and Lleyn Peninsula. 80 acres, meadows, woodland walks, 2 working walled gardens, unusual cultivars, cut flower borders; innovative, intensive, organic gardening methods with aesthetic appeal. Fruit & vegetables for sale. Suitable for assisted wheelchair users only. Slate & gravel paths to all vegetable gardens, gravel drive.

20 LLANBEDR SPRING FESTIVAL GARDENS - GWYL WANWYN LLANBEDR
LL45 2PA. *7m N of Barmouth. On A496. Signs in village. Maps in village shops.* Home-made teas at Aber Artro Hall. **Combined adm £10, chd free. Sun 6 May (11-5).**
Glorious, stylish, varied spring gardens in coastal micro-climate. Festival of gardens, music and walking. Sat to Mon, 5 to 7 May (2-5 Sat, 11-5 Sun & Mon). Gate money to NGS Sun only.

Artist's garden, romantically planted in intimate rooms . . .

ABER ARTRO HALL
Paul & Carolyn Morgan. *Turn R off A496 in front of Victoria Inn in Llanbedr (L if coming from Harlech). After 1m turn R at sign Cwm Nantcol & follow arrows*
Arts and Crafts 1910, 5-acre garden by architect Charles Edward Bateman. Terraced borders; riverside walk; fine trees, ponds. Hillside rock and wild garden leads to ancient woodland. Kitchen garden incl fruit pergola; secret Tuscan garden; William Morris 'wallpaper' garden. Partial wheelchair access - ask for reserved parking.

LLWYN
Mr & Mrs Rodney Payne. *Park on A496. Short walk uphill or shuttle service 11-4 on the hour*
Mature 2-acre sloping garden, terrace leading down to formal lawn and pond. Herbaceous borders; wildlife pond, sunken garden, parterre, kitchen garden; woodland. Interesting variety of flowering trees, shrubs and plants, especially beautiful in spring.

PLAS GWYNFRYN
J D S Evans
Spectacular 7-acre landscaped glacial rock garden. Sweeping lawns surrounded by rhododendrons, azaleas, magnolias, fine specimen trees incl taxodium, ginkgo, palms; fish pond, bamboo jungle; herbaceous borders, kitchen garden; woodland paths. Coastal and mountain scenery.

21 LLANIDAN HALL
Brynsiencyn LL61 6HJ. Mr J W Beverley, 07759 305085, beverley.family@btinternet.com. *5m E of Llanfair Pwll. From Llanfair PG (Anglesey) follow A4080 towards*

Brynsiencyn for 4m. Turn at/opp Groeslon PH. Continue for 1m, garden entrance on R. **Adm £2.50, chd £1 (share to CAFOD). Sats 23 June; 7 July (10-4). Visitors also welcome by appt June/July only.**
Walled garden of 1 3/4 acres. Physic and herb gardens, ornamental vegetable garden, herbaceous borders, water features and many varieties of old roses. Sheep, rabbits and hens to see. Children must be kept under supervision. Llanidan Church will be open for viewing. Gravel paths, unfenced water features.

LLWYNCELYN
See Ceredigion/Cardiganshire.

22 LLYS-Y-GWYNT
Pentir Road, Llandygai LL57 4BG. Jennifer Rickards & John Evans, 01248 353863. *3m S of Bangor. 300yds from Llandygai roundabout at J11 of A5 & A55, just off A422. From A5 & A55 follow signs for services (Gwasanaethau) and find 'No Through Road' sign 50yds beyond. Turn R then L.* Home-made teas. **Adm £2.50, chd free. Suns 20 May; 24 June (11-4). Visitors also welcome by appt, incl coaches.**
Rambling 2-acre garden in harmony with and incl magnificent views of Snowdonia. Incorporating large Bronze Age cairn. Designed to wander, with paths to provide shelter and interest. The exposed site planted for wind tolerance, yr-round colour and wildlife. Pond, waterfall and N-facing rockery.

Hillside rock and wild garden . . . secret Tuscan garden . . .

23 MAENAN HALL
Maenan, Llanrwst LL26 0UL. The Hon Mr & Mrs Christopher Mclaren, 0207 602 1983, cmmclaren@gmail.com. *2m N of Llanrwst. On E side of A470, 1/4m S of Maenan Abbey Hotel.* Home-made teas & light refreshments. **Adm £3, chd £2, concessions £2. Sun 29 Apr (10.30-1). Visitors also welcome by appt for groups of 10+ incl coaches.**
About 4 hectares of ground, some

---

steeply sloping, with mature hardwoods; upper part has many ornamental trees, shrubs and roses, walled garden, borders and lawns, all with lovely views over Conway valley and Snowdonia foothills. Rhododendrons, camellias, magnolias, pieris and hydrangeas predominate in woodland dell. Many of the original plants are from Bodnant. Partial wheelchair access. Gravel paths and lawns.

24 MEGANS WOOD GWERNOER FARM
Nantlle LL54 6BB. Mr & Mrs R Black, 01286 880913. *2m E of Penygroes. On B4418 Penygroes to Rhyd-Ddu rd, past big house on L, 1st house on R over cattle grid. Halfway between Talysarn & Nantlle.* Home-made cakes & tea. **Adm £2.50, chd free. Sat 19, Sun 20 May (11-4). Visitors also welcome by appt in May incl groups and coaches.**
3-acre woodland garden set on steep hillside. Panoramic views of the Nantlle valley and Snowdon. Woodland underplanted with over 1000 rhododendrons, azaleas and camellias. Ornamental pond and waterfall on site of mines.

THE MILL HOUSE
See Ceredigion/Cardiganshire.

25 ◆ PENRHYN CASTLE
Bangor LL57 4HN. The National Trust, 01248 353084, www.nationaltrust.org.uk. *3m E of Bangor. On A5122. Buses from Llandudno, Caernarfon, Betws-y-Coed; alight: Grand Lodge Gate. J11 A55, signed from thereon.* **Adm £1, chd free. Opening times and prices vary according to season, please see website for details. For NGS: Sat 3 Feb (11-3).**
Large grounds incl Victorian walled garden; fine trees, shrubs, wild garden, good views. Partial wheelchair access.

26 ◆ PENSYCHNANT
Sychnant Pass, nr Conwy LL32 8BJ. Pensychnant Foundation Wardens Julian Thompson & Anne Mynott, 01492 592595, julian.pensychnant@btinternet.com. *2¹/₂m W of Conwy. At top of Sychnant Pass between Conwy & Penmaenmawr. From Conwy turn L into Upper Gate St by Heddlu/Police; after 2¹/₂m Pensychnant's drive signed on R. From Penmaenmawr, fork R by Mountain View PH; summit of Sychnant Pass after walls, Pensychnant's drive on L.* **Adm £2, chd 50p. Open Wed to Sun, Apr to Sept (11-5). For NGS: Sun 10 June.**
Diverse herbaceous borders surrounded by mature shrubs, banks of rhododendrons, ancient and Victorian woodlands. 12 acre woodland walks with views of Conwy Mountain and Sychnant. Woodland birds. Picnic tables, archaelogical trail on mountain. A peaceful little gem. Large Victorian gothic house (open) with art exhibition. Partial wheelchair access, please phone for advice.

27 ◆ PLAS NEWYDD
Anglesey LL61 6DQ. The National Trust, 01248 714795, www.nationaltrust.org.uk. *2m S of Llanfairpwll. A55 junctions 7 & 8 on A4080.* **House and Garden Adm £6, chd £3, family £15, Garden only Adm £4, chd £2. Sats to Weds 31 Mar to 31 Oct (11-5.30, house 12-4.30). For NGS: Fri 6 Apr.**
Gardens with massed shrubs, fine trees, lawns sloping down to Menai Strait. Magnificent views to Snowdonia. Woodland walk leading to Marine Walk. Australasian arboretum and wild flowers. Terrace garden with summer display and water features. Very good area for bird-watching and fungi in autumn. Rhododendron garden 1 Apr to early June only. C18 house by James Wyatt contains Rex Whistler's largest painting; also Military Museum.

28 RHYD
Trefor, Anglesey LL65 4TA. Ann & Jeff Hubble, 01407 720320, jeffh43@btinternet.com. *7m W of Llangefni. Nr Holyhead. From Bodedern 2¹/₄m along B5109 towards Llangefni, turn L.* Teas. **Adm £2.50, chd free. Suns 27 May; 22 July (11-5). Visitors also welcome by appt Apr to Sept, coaches permitted.**
5 acres of gardens, arboretum, meadows and nature reserve. Herbaceous beds, pergolas, ponds, stream, rockery, garden room and (new 2005) decking and fernery. Many species of roses, climbing and standard. Clematis and rhododendron. Wide variety of herbaceous plants especially hosta and primula. Many places to sit and ponder or watch the wildlife. Winner of Snowdonia Wildlife Garden Competition, Private Garden Section.

29 ◆ ST JOHN THE BAPTIST & ST GEORGE
Lon Batus, Carmel LL54 7AR. Bishop Abbot Demetrius. *7m SE of Caernarfon. On A487 Porthmadog Rd, at Dinas roundabout exit 1st L to Groeslon, turn L at PO for 1¹/₂m. At village centre turn L & L again at Xrds.* **Adm £1, chd free. Wed 25 July (2-5).**
Holy community in the making under the authority of The Orthodox Catholic and Holy Synod of Malan. This is not a garden in the traditional sense but a spiritual retreat from the stresses and strains of modern life, surrounded on all sides by space and rural tranquillity. We are privileged to share a glimpse of a more contemplative life. Monastery open to view.

30 TAN DINAS
Llanfairpwll, Anglesey LL61 5YL. Charles Ellis, 01248 714373, charles.ellis@tesco.net. *2m W of Menai Bridge. On main rd between Llanfairpwll & Britannia Bridge, 250yds from the Marquess of Anglesey's column. Parking in Column car park, access via path through Column woods. Visitors, cars can unload but not park at garden.* Light refreshments & teas. **Adm £2, chd free. Sun 20 May (11-5). Visitors also welcome by appt.**
An interesting 1¹/₂-acre cottage garden. Overlooked by the Marquess of Anglesey's column, 200yds from the Menai Straits. Carefully designed and

A peaceful little gem . . . art exhibition . . .

planted on 3 levels; shrubbery, large pond garden, vegetable and fruit areas, heather garden. Careful planting ensures all-yr colour. Many interesting trees and shrubs are now reaching maturity.

🏕 ☕

③ TREFFOS SCHOOL

Llansadwrn, Anglesey LL59 5SL. Dr & Mrs Humphreys. *2¹/₂ m N of Menai Bridge. A5025 Amlwch/Benllech exit from the Britannia Bridge onto Anglesey. Approx 3m turn R towards Llansadwrn. Entrance to Treffos School is 200yds on LH-side.* Cream teas. **Adm £2.50, chd free. Sun 24 June (12-4).**
7 acres, child-friendly garden, in rural location, surrounding C17 house now run as school. Garden consists of mature woodland, underplanted with spring flowering bulbs and rhododendrons, ancient beech avenue leading down to rockery, herbaceous borders and courtyards. Garden trails and arts & craft activities for children.

♿ 🏕 ❀ ☕

② TY CAPEL FFRWD

Llanfachreth LL40 2NR. Revs Mary & George Bolt, 01341 422006. *4m NE of Dolgellau, 18m SW of Bala. From A470 nr Dolgellau take A497 towards Bala. Turn L after 200yds signed Dolgellau. 1st R signed Llanfachreth, 4m. Uphill to village, L at T-junction, past war memorial on L, ¹/₂ m. Park nr chapel, walk 30yds downhill to garden. No parking beside cottage. From S via Trawsfynydd, go*

through Ganllwyd, 1st L after signpost Llanfachreth. Follow NGS signs. Cream teas. **Adm £2.50, chd free. Suns 20 May; 1 July (11-5). Visitors also welcome by appt May to July incl.**
1-acre cottage garden, started from nothing, still being created. A stream, the ffrwd, runs through garden and flowers and azaleas fill the bank with colour in spring. Wide collection of plants, many unusual. Trees blend into surrounding countryside. Mature roses incl climbers. Hostas, lilies and meconopsis blend together in small bluebell wood. Fuchsias and lilies fill large pots on patio where home-made teas can be enjoyed beside stream. Featured in 'In Britain' as one of the 6 Hidden Gardens of N Wales. Some steep paths.

❀ ☕

③ ♦ TY HYLL - THE UGLY HOUSE

Betws-y-Coed LL24 0DS. Snowdonia Society, 01690 720287, www.snowdonia-society.org.uk. *2¹/₂ m W of Betws-y-Coed. 2¹/₂ m E of Capel Curig on A5.* **Adm £1, chd free. Daily Easter to Oct (9.30-5). For NGS: Sun 15 July (10-4).**
S-facing cottage gardens in grounds of famous grade II listed Ugly House, surrounded by 5 acres of woodland. Attractive gardens managed organically for the benefit of wildlife by volunteers. Terraced herbaceous beds with unusual plantings, wildlife ponds, alpine bed and attractive woodland walk.

❀ ☕

> Home-made teas can be enjoyed beside stream . . . flowers and azaleas fill the bank with colour . . .

③ TY MAWR

Henryd Road, Gyffin LL32 8HN. Mrs M P Davies. *¹/₂ m S of Conwy. Gyffin Village S of Conwy on B5106 (¹/₂ m). Garden in Henryd Rd next to Gyffin church.* **Adm £2, chd free (share to Hope House Hospice). Suns 15, 22 July (1-6).**
Imaginative and densely-planted medium-sized garden with good use of colour. Many interesting and unusual plants, incl wide range of shrubs, grasses and perennials. A cottage garden with a difference, divided into several areas: flowering borders, birch copse, shade house, 2 ponds and lots of places to sit and enjoy it all.

🏕 ❀ ☕

35 NEW TY NEWYDD
Dyffryn Ardudwy LL44 2DB. Guy
& Margaret Lloyd, 01341 247357.
5¹/₂ m N of Barmouth, 4¹/₂ m S of
Harlech. A496 Barmouth to
Harlech rd, ¹/₂ m N of Dyffryn
Ardudwy, area sometimes referred
to as Coed Ystumgwern. At bus
shelter and phone box turn down
lane towards sea, driveway 30yds
on L. Home-made teas. **Adm £2,
chd free. Sun 3 June (10-5).**
Visitors also welcome by appt all
yr. **Access for coaches difficult.**
3¹/₂ acres of maritime garden and
pasture, diversely planted with
trees and shrubs for yr-round
interest. Some areas still being
developed. Extensive vegetable
and fruit areas. Greenhouse and
polytunnel for overwintering tender
subjects, propagation,
spring/summer bedding and
summer salads. Interesting plant
sales.

36 NEW TYN-TWLL
LL40 2DP. Sue & Pete Nicholls.
1¹/₂ m NE of Llanfachreth. From
Dolgellau on Bala rd (A494), 1st L
to Llanfachreth opp Brithdir sign.
Continue up hill, 1st R then 1st L
and follow signs to Tyn Twll. Cream
teas and light refreshments. **Adm
£2.50, chd free. Sun 15 July
(10-5).**
Created by 2 artists, Tyn Twll is set
in 2¹/₂ acres of ancient woodland
with imaginative architectural
features using local materials.
Traditional planting, rockeries,
walled fruit and vegetable garden,
short woodland walk and pond
area in sheltered setting, providing
a haven for wildlife. Illustrated
wildlife and local scenic cards for
sale plus handmade wooden
planters, bird boxes and craft
products made by the owners. All
profits to NGS. Some uneven
ground and sloping slate paths.

37 Y FELIN
Sarn Meyllteyrn, Llyn Peninsula
LL53 8HF. Betty & Ian Wood, 01758
730794, d.i.wood@btinternet.com.
10m W of Pwllheli. On B4413 close to
seaside villages of Abersoch, Nefyn
and Aberdaron on Llyn Peninsula.
Travelling W towards Aberdaron,
50yds from centre of Sarn, The Mill
House Restaurant is on R. Gates to
garden at far end of restaurant car
park. Limited parking here after 2pm,
otherwise park in village. **Adm £2, chd
free (share to Rotary Club of Pwllheli
Trust Fund). Mon 28 May; Sun 15
July (11-5). Visitors also welcome by
appt.**
2-acre garden bounded by upper
reaches of R Soch. Interesting range of
habitats incl bluebell wood, ponds,
streamside, herbaceous borders,
shrubs and vegetables. Haven for
wildlife. Old millpond and working
water wheel are reminders of Y Felin's
past role (since around 1541) as a
water mill. Children need careful
supervision in view of water features.
Featured on S4C Clwb Garddio. Partial
wheelchair access.

Interesting range of habitats incl bluebell wood, ponds, streamside, herbaceous borders, shrubs and vegetables. Haven for wildlife. Old millpond and working water wheel . . .

Gwynedd County Volunteers
County Organiser
North Grace Meirion-Jones, Parc Newydd, Rhosgadfan, Caernarfon LL54 7LF, 01286 831195
South Marian, Osselton, Felin y Ffridd, Friddgate, Machynlleth SY20 8QG, 01654 702548
County Treasurer
North Grace Meirion-Jones, (contact details as above)
South Michael Bishton, Bronclydwr, Rhoslefain, Tywyn LL36 9LT, 01654 710882, m.bishton@btopenworld.com
Assistant County Organisers
Hilary Nurse, Bryn Gwern, Llanfachreth, Dolgellau LL40 2DH, 01341 450255
Mary Bolt, Ty Capel Ffrwd, Llanfachreth, Dolgellau LL40 2NR, 01341 422006

POWYS

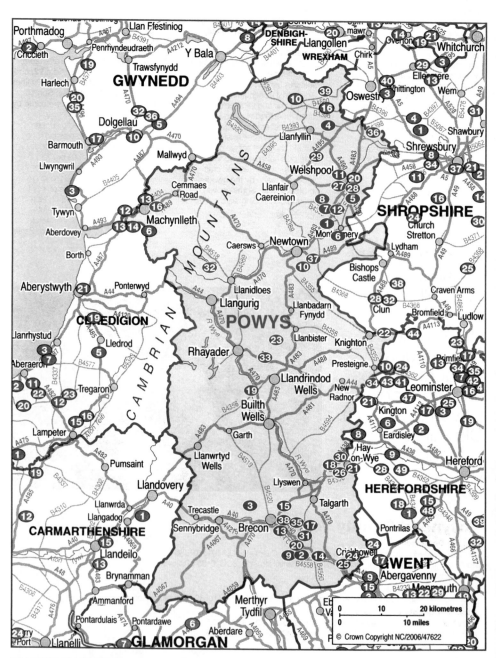

Opening Dates

April

SUNDAY 22
28 Rowan

SUNDAY 29
1 Abernant

May

SATURDAY 5
23 Mill Cottage
29 Tan-y-Llyn

SUNDAY 6
23 Mill Cottage
29 Tan-y-Llyn
30 Tawryn

MONDAY 7
23 Mill Cottage
30 Tawryn

SATURDAY 12
11 Dingle Nurseries & Garden

SUNDAY 13
11 Dingle Nurseries & Garden

SATURDAY 19
7 3 Church Terrace
12 Glansevern Hall Gardens
33 Vale House

SUNDAY 20
14 Gliffaes Country House Hotel
33 Vale House

SUNDAY 27
4 Bodynfoel Hall

MONDAY 28
19 Llysdinam

June

FRIDAY 1
23 Mill Cottage

SATURDAY 2
23 Mill Cottage
29 Tan-y-Llyn
35 The Wern

SUNDAY 3
23 Mill Cottage
28 Rowan
29 Tan-y-Llyn
38 The White House

SUNDAY 10
26 Pen-y-Maes
34 The Walled Garden

SATURDAY 16
5 Brooks Lodge

SUNDAY 17
5 Brooks Lodge
25 The Neuadd, Llanbedr

SUNDAY 24
1 Abernant
17 Llangorse Gardens

SATURDAY 30
31 Treberfydd

July

SUNDAY 1
13 Glanusk
32 Ty Capel Deildre

SATURDAY 7
29 Tan-y-Llyn

SUNDAY 8
15 Glyn Celyn House
20 Lonicera
29 Tan-y-Llyn

MONDAY 9
27 Powis Castle Garden

SATURDAY 14
7 3 Church Terrace
12 Glansevern Hall Gardens

SUNDAY 22
3 Battle House

August

SUNDAY 5
8 Cil y Wennol
24 Moor Park

SUNDAY 12
19 Llysdinam

WEDNESDAY 15
16 Grandma's Garden

September

SATURDAY 15
7 3 Church Terrace
12 Glansevern Hall Gardens

October

SUNDAY 7
18 Llowes Court

SATURDAY 20
11 Dingle Nurseries & Garden

SUNDAY 21
11 Dingle Nurseries & Garden

Gardens open to the public

2 Ashford House
11 Dingle Nurseries & Garden
12 Glansevern Hall Gardens
16 Grandma's Garden
22 Milebrook House Hotel
27 Powis Castle Garden

By appointment only

6 Castell y Gwynt
9 Coity Mawr
10 Cwm-Weeg
21 Lower House
36 Westlake Fisheries
37 Westwinds
39 Woodhill

The Gardens

1 ABERNANT
Garthmyl SY15 6RZ. J A & B M Gleave, 01686 640494. *Mid-way between Welshpool (9m) & Newtown (9m) on A483. 1½ S of Garthmyl. Approached over steep humpback bridge, then straight ahead through gate. No parking for coaches.* Home-made teas. **Adm £2.50, chd free, concessions £2. Suns 29 Apr; 24 June (1-5.30). Visitors also welcome by appt Apr to July.**
Approx 2½ acres incl cherry orchard, lawns, knot garden, roses, lavender, rockery, containers, ornamental shrubs and trees, specimen fern garden, ornamental pond, potager; additional woodland area with natural pond and stream with walks and views of R Severn. Come and picnic in the cherry orchard.

Stream with walks and views of River Severn . . .

2 ◆ ASHFORD HOUSE
Talybont-on-Usk LD3 7YR. Mr & Mrs D A Anderson, 01874 676271. *6½ m SE of Brecon. Off A40 on B4558. 1m SE of Talybont-on-Usk.* **Adm £2.50, chd free. Tues, Apr to Sept (2-6).**
1-acre walled garden surrounded by woodland and wild garden approx 4 acres altogether; restored and developed since 1979. Mixed shrub and herbaceous borders; meadow garden and pond; alpine house and beds; vegetables. A relaxed plantsman's garden. Weekly openings mean visitors may enjoy a peaceful garden in its everyday state.

❸ BATTLE HOUSE
Battle LD3 9RW. Roger & Anne Jones. *3m NW of Brecon. On Craddoc Rd. In Craddoc follow sign to Battle. Battle House is ¼m after the village on L.* Home-made teas. **Adm £3, chd free. Sun 22 July (2-5).**
Large terraced garden, surrounding C18 house (not open), developed over 14yrs but much done recently. Herbaceous and mixed borders, lawns, pond and bog garden, young arboretum and pleached limes, lakes, dovecote and fine walling. Spectacular views of the Brecon Beacons.
& ❀ ☕

❹ BODYNFOEL HALL
Llanfechain SY22 6XD. Mr E Bonnor-Maurice. *10m N of Welshpool via A490 towards Llanfyllin. Take B4393, follow signs.* Home-made teas. **Adm £3, chd 50p, concessions £2. Sun 27 May (2-6).**
Approx 5 acres of garden and woodland, with ponds. Young and mature trees, woodland walks; formal and wild, rhododendrons, azaleas, lovely views, garden sculptures.
& ❀ ☕

❺ NEW BROOKS LODGE
Leighton Park, Welshpool SY21 8LW. Geoff & Valerie Vine. *2m E of Welshpool. SE off A483 onto A490. Just after river/railway bridge, turn L signed Cilcewydd (Leighton). R onto B4388 for 100yds. L at Lodge House, continue up lane to car park.* **Adm £3, chd 50p. Sat 16, Sun 17 June (12-5.30).**
¾-acre garden that has several distinct areas arising from natural topography of site. Incl small walled garden, herbaceous border, shrubberies, woodland garden and courtyard garden. Divided by natural pond and stream, all richly planted. Pond and stream unfenced, children must be supervised. Royal Forestry Society's Charles Ackers Redwood Grove and Pinetum few hundred yds from car park. Oldest and tallest Redwoods in Britain, enjoyable for family groups. Guided tours, by arrangement with warden David Williams, throughout the day.
✗ ❀ ☕

BRYAN'S GROUND
See Herefordshire.

❻ NEW CASTELL Y GWYNT
Montgomery SY15 6HR. Angela & Roger Hughes, 01686 688317, r.dhughes@btinternet.com. *2m S of Montgomery. Please tel for directions.* Home-made teas. **Adm £3. Visitors welcome by appt for groups mid-May to Sept.**
1½-acre garden at 900ft, set within 6 acres of land managed for wildlife. Native woodland corridors with mown rides surround hayfield and pool with turf-roofed summerhouse. Enclosed kitchen garden with boxed beds of vegetables, fruit and cutting flowers, greenhouse, orchard. Shrubberies, deep mixed borders and more formal areas close to house. Outstanding views of Welsh mountains.
❀ ☕

Native woodland corridors with mown rides surround hayfield and pool with turf-roofed summerhouse . . .

❼ 3 CHURCH TERRACE
Berriew, Welshpool SY21 8PF. Mr Jimmy Hancock, 01686 640774. *5m S of Welshpool. In village centre, behind the Church.* **Adm £2, chd free. Sats 19 May; 14 July; 15 Sept (2-6). Visitors also welcome by appt.**
¼-acre garden with river below. Plantsman's garden with trees, shrubs, climbers and diverse range of rare and unusual plants to create interest throughout yr; keen gardeners who feel they need something different to stimulate their garden will see what can be achieved in a small garden. 30ft x 12ft greenhouse with good range of tender, interesting plants. Visitor numbers limited due to size of garden, personal tour incl with owner, Head Gardener, Powis Castle 1972-96.
✗ ❀

❽ CIL Y WENNOL
Berriew SY21 8AZ. Willie & Sue Jack, 01686 640757, williejack@btinternet.com. *5m SW of Welshpool. Berriew is off the A483 Welshpool to Newtown rd. By Berriew School take B4385 towards Castle Caereinion. Cil y Wennol is ¾m along the B4385.* **Adm £3, chd free. Sun 5 Aug (2-5.30). Visitors also welcome by appt, groups welcome.**
3½-acre established garden set around Tudor cottage (not open). Long curving drive, wild grasses and trees lead to oval lawn surrounded with sorbus. Front garden: traditional, formal cottage design with more recent influences. Rear gardens: sweeping array of new-style perennial prairie planting, spectacular views, enclosed vegetable garden and croquet lawn. Entire site combines wildness with smooth line and features crescent-shaped hedges, walks, slate walls and congruent sculptures. Steep steps to main part of garden.
✗ ❀ ☕

❾ COITY MAWR
Talybont-on-Usk LD3 7YN. Mr & Mrs William Forwood, 01874 676664. *6m SE of Brecon. Leave Talybont village on B4558 towards Brecon. Approx ½m at pink cottages take L signed Talybont reservoir, then 1st R up to rd junction; turn L to Coity Mawr at top on R.* **Adm £3, chd free. Visitors welcome by appt.**
4½ acres at 850ft created over 13yrs; work still in progress. Terraced with spectacular view of Black Mountains across Usk valley. Mature trees, unusual plants and shrubs; rose and water gardens; parterre; willow arbour.
& ✗ ❀

CWMRHAIADR GARDEN & NURSERY
See Ceredigion/Cardiganshire.

❿ CWM-WEEG
Dolfor, Newtown SY16 4AT. Dr W Shaefer & Mr K D George, 01686 628992, wolfgang.schaefer@virgin.net. *4½m SE of Newtown. Take A489 E from Newtown for 1½m, turn R towards Dolfor. After 2m turn L down farm track.* Teas. **Adm £3, chd free. Visitors welcome by appt from 15 May to 15 Sept, inaccessible for coaches.**
2½-acre garden set within 12 acres of wild flower meadows and bluebell woodland with stream centred around

C15 farmhouse (not open). Formal garden commenced in 1990s in English landscape tradition with vistas, grottos, lawns and extensive borders terraced with stone walls, translates older garden vocabulary into an innovative C21 concept. Steep paths in wood.

⑪ ◆ DINGLE NURSERIES & GARDEN

Welshpool SY21 9JD. Mr & Mrs D. Hamer, 01938 555145, kerry@dinglenurseries.co.uk. *2m NW of Welshpool. Take A490 towards Llanfyllin and Guilsfield. After 1m turn L at sign for Dingle Nurseries & Garden.* **Adm £2.50, chd free. Open all yr (9-5), closed Xmas wk. For NGS: Sats, Suns 12, 13 May; 20, 21 Oct (9-5).**
4-acre garden on S-facing site, sloping down to lake. Beds mostly colour themed with a huge variety of rare and unusual trees and shrubs. Set in hills of mid Wales this beautiful and well known garden attracts visitors from Britain and abroad.

Pretty kitchen garden with raised beds and rose and sweet pea covered arches. Glorious views over the Black Mountains . . .

FELIN Y FFRIDD
See Gwynedd.

⑫ ◆ GLANSEVERN HALL GARDENS

Berriew SY21 8AH. G & M Thomas, 01686 640644, www.glansevern.co.uk. *5m SW of Welshpool. On A483 at Berriew. Signposted.* **Adm £4, chd free, concessions £3.50. Thurs, Fris, Sats & Bank Hol Mons May to Sept (12-5). For NGS: Sats 19 May; 14 July; 15 Sept (12-5).**
20-acre mature garden situated nr banks of R Severn. Centred on

Glansevern Hall, a Greek Revival house dated 1801 (not open). Noted for variety of unusual tree species; much new planting; lake with island; woodland walk; large rock garden and grotto. Roses and herbaceous beds. Water garden and large walled garden, with fruit, vegetable and ornamental planting. Interesting shelters and follies. Walk down to R Severn through Folly Garden. Commended by Country Life magazine.

&♿ ⊛ ☕

⑬ GLANUSK

Llanfrynach LD3 7UY. Lorraine & Mike Lewis. *1½m SE of Brecon. Leave A40 signed Llanfrynach, Pencelli. Cross narrow bridge, 50metres on R.* Home-made teas. **Adm £3, chd free. Sun 1 July (2-5).**
2-acre garden, 1 acre planted with specimen trees and grass paths. Formal front garden with box balls, beech hedges, lawn, borders, specimen trees and shrubs. Rear garden very steep to R Usk. Crisscross paths, exotic grasses, interesting perennials, shrubs and old yew. Garden developed from scratch over 5 yrs.

⑭ GLIFFAES COUNTRY HOUSE HOTEL

Crickhowell NP8 1RH. Mr & Mrs N Brabner & Mr & Mrs J C Suter. *2½m NW of Crickhowell. 1m off A40.* Home-made teas. **Adm £2.50, chd free. Sun 20 May (2-5).**
Large garden; spring bulbs, azaleas and rhododendrons; ornamental pond; heathers, shrubs and ornamental trees; fine maples; superb position high above R Usk.

♿ ⊛ ☕

⑮ GLYN CELYN HOUSE

Felinfach, nr Brecon LD3 0TY. Mr & Mrs N Paravicini. *4m NE of Brecon. On A470 east of Brecon on hill above Felinfach.* Home-made teas. **Adm £3, chd free. Sun 8 July (2-5).**
12-yr-old 7-acre sloping garden still in the making. 2 streams supply water to fountains and lake. Mixed planting within yew and hornbeam hedges. Woodland walks lead to lake and unusual grotto. Well-established trees among newly-planted shrubs and trees. Pretty kitchen garden with raised beds and rose and sweet pea covered arches. Glorious views over the Black Mountains.

♿ ⊛ ☕

⑯ ◆ GRANDMA'S GARDEN

Plas Dolguog Estates, Machynlleth SY20 8UJ. Diana & Richard Rhodes, 01654 702244, www.smoothhound.co.uk/hotels/plasdolg.html. *1½m E of Machynlleth. Turn L off A489 Machynlleth to Newtown rd. Follow brown tourist signs to Plas Dolguog Hotel.* **Adm £3.50, chd £1.50. Weds & Suns all yr. For NGS: Wed 15 Aug (10-6).**
9 acres. Inspirational jewel. Views of Snowdonia National Park and Dyfi Valley. Peace garden, arboretum, sculptures link cultural/spiritual beliefs, a place to find inner peace. Seven sensory gardens, riverside walk, stone circle, wildlife pond, willow arbour, strategic seating, planting old and new. Great for children and access. Featured on ITV News and in local press. Access statement available. Owner wheelchair user with Assistance dog.

♿ ⊛ 🛏 ☕

THE GRIGGS
See Herefordshire.

HERGEST CROFT GARDENS
See Herefordshire.

IVY COTTAGE
See Herefordshire.

LITTLE HELDRE
See Shropshire.

⑰ LLANGORSE GARDENS

nr Brecon LD3 7TS. *6½m E of Brecon on B4560 4m off A40 at Bwlch.* Home-made teas in Village Hall. **Combined adm £6, chd free. Sun 24 June (2-6).**
3 diverse gardens full of interesting plants, shrubs, trees and vegetables.

⊛ ☕

THE NEUADD, LLANGORSE
LD3 7TS. Mr & Mrs Paul Johnson, 01874 658670. *On N side of village on B4560.* **Visitors also welcome by appt.**
1-acre informal garden; mixed borders, trees and shrubs incl species and old roses; herbaceous plants with emphasis on good foliage and unusual forms of cottage garden and native plants; woodland garden under development. Maintained by owners on organic lines.

♿ ⊛

OAK COTTAGE

Llangorse LD3 7UE. Jill & Mike Jones. *Turn L by grass triangle with tree & bench towards Mynydd Troed. Oak Cottage is last in a terrace of 3 on L opp Ty Mawr* Developed from 2 cottage gardens, it has evolved rather than been planned as new trees, shrubs and plants arrived. An eclectic collection of plants, many grown from seeds gathered from friends, on holidays and from cuttings. Fine views of surrounding hills.

ℵ ⊕

THE OLD VICARAGE

Llangorse LD3 7UB. Major & Mrs J B Anderson, 01874 658639. *Park in Llangorse village and approach through churchyard.* **Visitors also welcome by appt.** Small family garden maintained by owners; interesting herbaceous and shrub borders; lawns, trees and vegetables.

& ℵ ⊕

18 LLOWES COURT

Llowes HR3 5JA. Mr & Mrs Briggs. *3½m W of Hay-on-Wye. On A438 between Clyro & Glasbury-on-Wye on L of rd coming from Hay-on-Wye.* Home-made teas. **Adm £3, chd free. Sun 7 Oct (2-5).** Low-lying garden with walled courtyards surrounding striking C16 house (not open). Summer strolls through lavender, roses and high meadow grasses now change to a brisker pace along the strong lines of the garden landscape - dyke, ditch, grove. 'Willows whiten, aspens quiver'. High bridges, dark grotto (shellwork), deep pools and ducks and hens invite children to run ahead; please keep them with you safely at all times.

& ℵ ⊕ ☕

LLWYNCELYN

See Ceredigion/Cardiganshire.

19 LLYSDINAM

Newbridge-on-Wye LD1 6NB. Sir John & Lady Venables-Llewelyn & Llysdinam Charitable Trust, 01597 860190/860200. *5m SW of Llandrindod Wells. Turn W off A470 at Newbridge-on-Wye; turn R immed after crossing R Wye; entrance up hill.* Home-made teas. **Adm £2.50, chd free. Mon 28 May; Sun 12 Aug (2-6). Visitors also welcome by appt, garden clubs & groups.** Large garden. Azaleas, rhododendrons, water garden and

herbaceous borders, shrubs, woodland garden, Victorian kitchen garden and greenhouses. Fine view of Wye Valley. Gravel paths.

& ⊕ ☕

20 LONICERA

Station Road, Talybont-on-Usk LD3 7JE. Mr & Mrs G Davies. *6m SE of Brecon. ¼m off A40, signed Talybont-on-Usk. 1st bungalow on L.* Teas in the village. **Adm £2.50, chd free (share to Arthritis & Rheumatism Council). Sun 8 July (2-6).** RHS lecturer's ¼-acre garden of varied interest incorporating several small feature gardens. Large collection of modern and shrub roses; heather garden with conifers; herbaceous and woody perennials; colourful summer bedding displays; window boxes, hanging baskets and patio tubs forming extensive house frontage display; greenhouses.

& ℵ ⊕ ☕

> ## An eclectic collection of plants, many grown from seeds gathered from friends . . .

21 LOWER HOUSE

Cusop, Hay-on-Wye HR3 5RQ. Nicky & Pete Daw, 01497 820773, www.lowerhousegardenhay.co.uk. *1m SE of Hay-on-Wye. Leave Hay-on-Wye on B4348. Turn R signed Cusop Dingle. (No through road). After ¾m driveway on R.* **Adm £3, chd free, £2.50 groups of 12+. Visitors welcome by appt Apr-Sept incl garden clubs & groups.** Sheltered valley garden, designed and maintained by owners since 1986 around C18 farmhouse (not open). Luxuriant planting and formal pools, shady courtyard with tree fern and bamboos. Cedar conservatory, terrace with exotic planting. Ornamental vegetable garden with topiary, stream and evolving wild garden, woodland walk, wildlife pond. Long season of interest, best in May/June and Sept. To be featured in 'Gardens Illustrated'.

ℵ ⊕ ⊨

22 NEW ♦ MILEBROOK HOUSE HOTEL

Ludlow Road, Knighton LD7 1LT. Rodney & Beryl Marsden, 01547 528632, hotel@milebrook.kc3ltd.co.uk. *2m E of Knighton. A4113 Knighton to Ludlow, 2m on R, signposted.* **Adm £3, chd free. Thurs only mid-May to mid-Sept and groups by appt.** 3-acre garden. To W, formal lawns, ha-ha and lovely views; to E, sloping terrace with garden rooms of herbaceous borders, kitchen gardens and gazebo. Paddock planted with 600 native trees, wildlife pond and bog garden leading down to R Teme.

ℵ ⊕ ⊨ ☕

23 MILL COTTAGE

Abbeycwmhir LD1 6PH. Mr & Mrs B D Parfitt, 01597 851935, www.abbeycwmhir.co.uk. *8m N of Llandrindod Wells. Turn L off A483 1m N of Crossgates roundabout, then 3½m on L, signed Abbeycwmhir.* Limited parking. **Adm £2, chd free. Sat 5, Sun 6, Mon 7 May; Fri 1, Sat 2, Sun 3 June (dawn to dusk). Visitors also welcome by appt Aug/Sept, max 12, no coaches.** ⅓-acre garden crammed with unusual and rare shrubs, small trees and climbers. Numerous ericaceous plants. Streamed side garden with water feature. Narrow paths and steps.

ℵ ⊕ ⊨

THE MILL HOUSE

See Ceredigion/Cardiganshire.

24 MOOR PARK

Llanbedr NP8 1SS. Leolin Price. *2m NE of Crickhowell. Turn off A40 at fire stn in Crickhowell; continue 2m, signed Llanbedr.* Home-made teas. **Adm £3, chd free. Sun 5 Aug (2-5.30).** 5 acres. Organic kitchen garden with figs, apricots, pears and apples. Lawns, borders, roses. Lake with swans, water garden, tree house and island theatre. Great trees and woodland walk.

& ☕

25 THE NEUADD, LLANBEDR

NP8 1SP. Robin & Philippa Herbert. *1m NE of Crickhowell. Leave Crickhowell by Llanbedr rd. At junction with Great Oak Rd bear L and continue up hill for 0.9m, garden on L. Ample parking.* Home-made teas. **Adm £3,**

chd free. Sun 17 June (2-6).
Garden under restoration and
development. At 750ft in Brecon
Beacons National Park. Walled garden,
sunken garden, winter garden, rock
garden with pool and springs.
Woodland walk and paths. Unusual
plants and trees. Owner is wheelchair
bound but uses an electric buggy as
some paths are steep.

26 PEN-Y-MAES
Hay-on-Wye HR3 5PP. Shân
Egerton. *1m SW of Hay-on-Wye. On
B4350 towards Brecon.* Home-made
teas. **Adm £3, chd free. Sun 10 June
(2-5).**
2-acre garden. Mixed borders; young
topiary; walled formal kitchen garden;
roses, irises, peony border, espaliered
pears. Fine mulberry. Beautiful dry
stone walling.

27 ◆ POWIS CASTLE GARDEN
Welshpool SY21 8RF. The National
Trust, 01938 551929,
www.nationaltrust.org.uk. *1m S of
Welshpool. Turn off A483 3/4 m out of
Welshpool, up Red Lane for 1/4 m.*
Castle and garden adm £9.90; chd
£4.95; group visit £8.90; family
£24.75. Garden only adm £6.90, chd
£3.45, group £5.90; family £17.25.
Opening days and times vary
according to season, please phone
or visit website for details. For NGS:
Mon 9 July (11-6).
Laid out in early C18 with finest
remaining examples of Italian terraces
in Britain. Richly planted herbaceous
borders; enormous yew hedges; lead
statuary, large wild flower areas. One of
the National Trust's finest gardens.
National Collections of *Aralia,
Laburnum.* Guided walks in garden at
11am and 2pm with NGS careership
student gardeners on Mon 9 July.
Manual wheelchairs only, some steep
gradients. Step-free access route map
to garden available.

28 NEW ROWAN
Leighton, Welshpool SY21 8HJ.
Tinty Griffith, 01938 552197. *2m
E of Welshpool. From Welshpool
take B4388 (Buttington to
Montgomery). At Leighton turn L
after school then at church straight
ahead between stone pillars. 1st
on R, parking in churchyard.*
Home-made teas. **Adm £2.50,
chd free. Suns 22 Apr; 3 June (2-
5). Visitors also welcome by
appt Apr to Sept, groups
welcome.**
1 acre of traditional plantsman's
country garden with village church
as backdrop. Discrete paths
meander around island beds and
mixed borders with irises, roses,
unusual and rare plants, trees
dripping with climbers and a series
of planted pools and marshy areas.
Views over Montgomeryshire
countryside. Slopes slippery if wet,
gravel paths.

STAUNTON PARK
See Herefordshire.

29 TAN-Y-LLYN
Meifod SY22 6YB. Callum Johnston
& Brenda Moor, 01938 500370,
www.tanyllyn.the-nursery.co.uk. *1m
SE of Meifod. From Oswestry on A495
turn L in village, cross R Vyrnwy &
climb hill for 1/2 m bearing R at
Y-junction.* Home-made teas. **Adm
£2.50, chd free (share to The 999
Club Trust). Sats, Suns 5, 6 May; 2, 3
June; 7, 8 July (2-5). Visitors also
welcome by appt.**
S-facing sheltered 3-acre garden,
surrounded by small hills, fields and
forest. Steeply sloping, the paths, beds
and hedges have been laid out to
complement the contours of the hill.
Extensive collection of plants in
containers, herb garden, thorn grove,
pond, orchard and wilderness.
Exhibitions, events and entertainments.

30 TAWRYN
6 Baskerville Court, Clyro HR3 5SS.
Chris & Clive Young, 01497 821939.
*1m NW of Hay-on-Wye. Leave A438
Hereford to Brecon rd at Clyro.
Baskerville Court is behind church and
Baskerville Arms Hotel. Please park in
village.* Cream teas & light
refreshments. **Adm £2.50, chd free.
Sun 6, Mon 7 May (11-5).** Visitors
also welcome by appt incl slide-
illustrated talks on the NGS and its
charities to WI, garden clubs etc.
1-acre garden on an oriental theme.
Come and see the Ghost Dragon. Lots
of new crooked paths and planting.
Stunning views of the Black Mountains
and Kilvert's Church. Delicious home-
made cakes. Featured in 'Amateur
Gardening'. Steep with lots of steps
and sitting areas.

31 TREBERFYDD
Bwlch LD3 7PX. David Raikes,
www.treberfydd.net. *61/2 m E of
Brecon. From Crickhowell leave A40 at
Bwlch and take B4560 then L for
Penorth. From Brecon leave A40 at
Llanhamlach. 21/2 m sign for Llangasty
Church, entrance over cattle grid.*
Home-made teas. **Adm £3, chd free.
Sat 30 June (2-5).**
Large garden surrounding impressive
Victorian house (not open); lawns,
roses, herbaceous borders, trees, rock
garden.

32 TY CAPEL DEILDRE
Llanidloes SY18 6NX. Dr Beverley
Evans-Britt, 01686 412602. *41/2 m N
of Llanidloes. Go N from Llanidloes on
B4518. 2m turn L on Clywedog rd,
signed scenic route, 21/2 m on R by
nature walk lay-by.* Home-made teas.
Adm £3, chd £1. Sun 1 July (2-5.30).
Visitors also welcome by appt.
2-acre garden of almost 100% organic
plants has been personally created on
a former waste site over 30 years. A
1350ft windy location with stunning
views of Llyn Clywedog. It consists of
ponds surrounded by walks and
marginal gardens, herbaceous borders
containing many rare perennials, rose
and tuberous begonia gardens and
lawns. Tree house & games for
children. A few steep slopes.

UPPER TAN HOUSE
See Herefordshire.

Discrete paths meander around
island beds and mixed borders with
irises, roses, unusual and rare plants,
trees dripping with climbers . . .

33 NEW **VALE HOUSE**
Nantmel, Rhayader LD1 6EL. Mrs Christine Loran. *6m N of Llandrindod Wells. At Crossgates take A44 to Rhayader. 3m, R at Nantmel village sign. Garden directly behind school.* Home-made teas. **Adm £3, chd free. Sat 19, Sun 20 May (2-5).**
Steeply-sloped garden is dominated by Victorian stone aqueduct and mature trees. Mainly alpines, heathers, climbing shrubs, conifers and large rockeried areas. Four ponds are linked by large steep wooden zig-zagged path. Seating areas. Art exhibition. Not suitable for non-powered wheelchairs.

&. ✕ ⊛ ☕

34 **THE WALLED GARDEN**
Knill LD8 2PR. Dame Margaret Anstee, 01544 267411. *3m SW of Presteigne. On B4362 Walton-Presteigne rd. In Knill village turn R over cattle grid, keep R down drive.* **Adm £3, chd free. Sun 10 June (2-6). Visitors also welcome by appt preferably Mar to Oct.**
4 acres: walled garden; river, bog garden and small grotto; primulas; over 100 varieties of roses, shrub, modern and climbing; peonies; mixed and herbaceous borders; many varieties of shrubs and mature trees; lovely spring garden. Nr C13 church in beautiful valley. Some narrow paths and uneven ground.

&.

35 **THE WERN**
Llanfihangel Talyllyn LD3 7TE. Neil & Lucienne Bennett. *4m E of Brecon. From Brecon, leave A40 (S) at 1st exit onto B4558 to Groesffordd. Follow rd to Llanfihangel Talyllyn. Take 2nd R (no through rd) in front of converted barns to end. From Crickhowell leave A40 (N) at Bwlch. R onto B4560. At Llangorse turn L to Llanfihangel Talyllyn. Take 'no through rd' (2nd L), follow to end.* Home-made teas. **Adm £3, chd free. Sat 2 June (2-6).**

1-acre garden of unusual trees, shrubs and plants. Many young acers, rhododendrons and azaleas. Hot border with banana, cannas and tender plants. Secluded herb garden. Ornamental grass and bamboo garden leading to woodland walk crossing stream. Charming, productive fruit and vegetable garden and polytunnel surrounded by damsons and plums. No disabled access to woodland walk.

&. ✕ ⊛ ⨿ ☕

36 **WESTLAKE FISHERIES**
Domgay Road, Four Crosses SY22 6SJ. Lynn Mainwaring, 01691 831475. *9m N of Welshpool. Turn off A483 in Four Crosses, signed Pysgodfa Fishery. Follow brown tourist signs. Domgay Rd approx 1m.* **Adm £2.50, chd 50p. Visitors welcome by appt all yr.**
A quiet scenic environment of 38 acres, managed organically on the R Vyrnwy with lakes and pools. 2-acre garden containing mixed borders, fish lawn, orchard, potager, herb and cutting garden, large vegetable garden (many unusual varieties grown), greenhouses and fruit cage. Birch walk and purple hazel walk lead to lake walks and wildlife area. NB Deep water, children must be accompanied by adults.

&. ⊛

WESTONBURY MILL WATER GARDEN
See Herefordshire.

37 **WESTWINDS**
Common Road, Kerry SY16 4NY. Ray & Margaret Watson, 01686 670605. *3m E of Newtown. Newtown to Churchstoke Rd (A489), turn R in village onto Common Rd, 400yds on L.* **Adm £3.50 incl cup of tea. Visitors welcome by appt May to Sept, small groups welcome.**
1/3-acre informal garden on several levels with mixed borders, shrubs and pools. Meandering paths and steps lead through the various levels.

✕ ☕

38 **THE WHITE HOUSE**
Groesffordd LD3 7SN. P H Barker & E Dowman. *2½m E of Brecon. On A40 turn L on B4558, at T-junction turn R, go through village, last house on L (opp sign to Llechfaen).* Home-made teas. **Adm £3, chd free. Sun 3 June (2-6).**
2½-acre garden in process of continuous refurbishment. Spring bulbs, azaleas, camellias, rhododendrons, acers and magnolia. Pond, stream, bog garden, unusual trees and lightly wooded area, views to Brecon Beacons. Wheelchair access limited to top lawn.

&. ✕ ⊛ ☕

Four ponds are linked by large steep wooden zig-zagged path . . .

39 **WOODHILL**
Moelfre, Oswestry SY10 7QX. Janet Randell, 01691 791486, www.pco.powys.org.uk/woodhill. *9m W of Oswestry.* **Adm £2.50, chd 50p, disabled free (share to Woods, Hills & Tracks). Visitors welcome by appt, open all yr, short notice OK.**
6 acres. Informal garden designed with wheelchair users in mind set amidst wonderful views of the surrounding hills and mountains on the foothills of The Berwyns nr Snowdonia. Footpaths for disabled access totalling 3/4 m, young arboretum, picnic spot overlooking stream, ponds and wetlands. Sheltered arbour in more formal setting. All-yr interest: bluebell wood in spring; roses in summer; trees, shrubs and berries in autumn; scented winter shrubs. 1000 trees and shrubs planted informally. Abundant wildlife sightings. Electric/push wheelchairs may be available on request.

&.

Powys County Volunteers

County Organiser
North Angela Hughes, Castell y Gwynt, Montgomery SY15 6HR, 01686 668317, r.dhughes@btinternet.com
South Shân Egerton, Pen-y-Maes, Hay-on-Wye, Hereford HR3 5PP, 01497 820423, sre@waitrose.com

County Treasurer
Elizabeth Spear, The Glyn, Berriew, Welshpool SY21 8AY, 01686 640455, eds@glj.co.uk

Publicity
North Elizabeth Spear (contact details as above)

Early Openings 2008

Don't forget early planning for 2008

Gardens across the country open from late January onwards – before the new Yellow Book is published – with glorious displays of colour including hellebores, aconites, snowdrops and carpets of spring bulbs.

Derbyshire

16 FEBRUARY 2008
Cherry Tree Cottage
17 FEBRUARY 2008
Cherry Tree Cottage

Devon

6 JANUARY 2008
Sherwood
13 JANUARY 2008
Sherwood
20 JANUARY 2008
Sherwood
27 JANUARY 2008
Sherwood
3 FEBRUARY 2008
Cherubeer Gardens
Little Cumbre
Sherwood
10 FEBRUARY 2008
Cherubeer Gardens
Little Cumbre
Sherwood
17 FEBRUARY 2008
Little Cumbre
Sherwood
24 FEBRUARY 2008
Little Cumbre
Sherwood

Essex

17 FEBRUARY 2008
Green Island

Gloucestershire North & Central

10 FEBRUARY 2008
Trench Hill
17 FEBRUARY 2008
Trench Hill

Hampshire

17 FEBRUARY 2008
Bramdean House
Little Court
19 FEBRUARY 2008
Little Court
24 FEBRUARY 2008
Little Court
26 FEBRUARY 2008
Little Court

Herefordshire

7 FEBRUARY 2008
Ivy Croft
14 FEBRUARY 2008
Ivy Croft
21 FEBRUARY 2008
Ivy Croft
28 FEBRUARY 2008
Ivy Croft

Lincolnshire

9 FEBRUARY 2008
Little Ponton Hall
10 FEBRUARY 2008
Little Ponton Hall
23 FEBRUARY 2008
21 Chapel Street
24 FEBRUARY 2008
21 Chapel Street

In February the flowering shrubs, hellebores and drifts of snowdrops are at their best, with each individual hellebore flower asking to be turned up and admired . . .

London

24 FEBRUARY 2008
Myddelton House Gardens

Northamptonshire

24 FEBRUARY 2008
Dolphins

Surrey

17 FEBRUARY 2008
Gatton Park
20 FEBRUARY 2008
Gatton Park

Sussex

10 FEBRUARY 2008
Mitchmere Farm
14 FEBRUARY 2008
Mitchmere Farm
17 FEBRUARY 2008
Mitchmere Farm
26 FEBRUARY 2008
Pembury House
27 FEBRUARY 2008
Pembury House
28 FEBRUARY 2008
Pembury House
4 MARCH 2008
Pembury House
5 MARCH 2008
Pembury House
6 MARCH 2008
Pembury House

Warwickshire & part of West Midlands

10 FEBRUARY 2008
Ragley Hall Gardens

Wiltshire

3 FEBRUARY 2008
Great Chalfield Manor
9 FEBRUARY 2008
Lacock Abbey Gardens
10 FEBRUARY 2008
Lacock Abbey Gardens
16 FEBRUARY 2008
Lacock Abbey Gardens
17 FEBRUARY 2008
Lacock Abbey Gardens

Garden Visiting Around the World

Heading off on holiday? Whether you're planning a short trip north of the border or across the channel or a longer visit down under or to our see our North American cousins, why not visit a few of the wonderful gardens open for charity elsewhere in the world?

America

THE GARDEN CONSERVANCY
Publication Open Days Directory
W www.gardenconservancy.org
Visit America's very best, rarely seen private gardens. The Open Days Program is a project of The Garden Conservancy, a non-profit organisation dedicated to preserving America's gardening heritage.

Australia

AUSTRALIA'S OPEN GARDEN SCHEME
Contact Neil Robertson
E national@opengarden.org.au
W www.opengarden.org.au
More than 700 inspiring gardens drawn from every Australian state and territory including tropical gardens, arid-zone gardens as well as featuring Australia's unique flora.

Belgium

JARDINS OUVERTS DE BELGIQUE – OPEN TUINEN VAN BELGÏE
Publication Catalogue of Belgian Open Gardens, published annually in March
Contact Christine de Groote

E info@jardinsouverts.be
W www.jardinsouverts.be
A non-profit organisation founded in 1994. Most of the proceeds from entry fees support charities chosen by garden owners.

France

JARDINS ET SANTÉ
E jardinsetsante@wanadoo.fr
W www.jardins-sante.org
Jardins et Santé is an association with humanitarian aims, created in 2004 by a team of volunteers. The funds raised through the opening of gardens are used to finance scientific research in the field of neurology. Contributions are also made to the development of the therapeutic role of the garden, particularly in hospitals and retirement homes.

Japan

THE N.G.S. JAPAN
Contact Tamie Taniguchi
E tamieta@syd.odn.ne.jp
W www.ngs-jp.org
The N.G.S. Japan was founded in 2001. Most of the proceeds from entry fees support children's and welfare charities as nominated by owners.

Netherlands

THE NEDERLANDSE TUINENSTICHTING (DUTCH GARDEN SOCIETY, NTS)
Publication Open Tuinengids, published annually in March
E nederl.tuinenst@hetnet.nl
W www.tuinenstichting.nl
The Dutch Garden Society was founded in 1980 to protect and restore gardens, public parks and cemeteries.

Scotland

SCOTLAND'S GARDENS SCHEME
Publication Gardens of Scotland
Contact Paddy Scott
T 0131 226 3714
E info@sgsgardens.co.uk
W www.gardensofscotland.org
Founded in 1931, Scotland's Gardens Scheme provides visitors with the opportunity to explore some of Scotland's finest gardens. The funds raised by the owners are donated to The Queen's Nursing Institute of Scotland, The National Trust for Scotland, The Royal Fund for Gardeners' Children and Perennial – The Gardeners' Royal Benevolent Society.

National Plant Collections in the NGS

Over 100 of the gardens that open for The National Gardens Scheme are custodians of National Plant Collections®, the National Council for the Conservation of Plants and Gardens (NCCPG), although this may not always be noted in the garden descriptions.

The NCCPG can be contacted at The Stable Courtyard, Wisley Gardens, Woking, Surrey, GU23 6QP. Tel: 01483 211465. Fax: 01483 212404. Website: www.nccpg.com

A

AESCULUS, LIRIODENDRON
West Dean Gardens
Sussex

AGAPANTHUS
Pine Cottage
Devon

AGAPANTHUS AND PITTOSPORUM
Bicton College
Devon

ANEMONE (JAPANESE)
Heathlands
Hampshire

ANEMONE JAPONICA AND HELLEBORES
Broadview Gardens
Kent

ANEMONE NEMOROSA
Kingston Lacy
Dorset

AQUILEGIA VULGARIS
Touchwood
Glamorgan

ARALIA, LABURNUM
Powis Castle Garden
Powys

ARBUTUS
Dunster Castle Gardens
Somerset & Bristol Area

ARUNCUS AND FILIPENDULA
Windy Hall
Cumbria

ASPLENIUM
Sizergh Castle
Cumbria

ASTER
The Picton Garden
Herefordshire

ASTERS
Upton House
Warwickshire & part of West Midlands

ASTILBE, HYDRANGEA AND POLYSTICHUM (FERNS)
Holehird Gardens
Cumbria

ASTILBE, IRIS ENSATA, TULBAGHIA
Marwood Hill
Devon

ASTRANTIA
Warren Hills Cottage
Leicestershire & Rutland

ASTRANTIA
Mayroyd Mill House
Yorkshire

AUBRIETA, LAWSON CYPRESS, HARDY FUCHSIA AND SKIMMIA
University of Leicester 'Harold Martin' Botanic Garden
Leicestershire & Rutland

B

BEARDED IRIS
Myddelton House Gardens
London

BERBERIS
Mill Hill House
Nottinghamshire

BRUGMANSIA
Valducci Flower & Vegetable Gardens
Shropshire

BRUNNERA MACROPHYLLA
9 Grenville Court
Northumberland & Tyne and Wear

BUDDLEIA, CLEMATIS VITICELLA AND PENSTEMON
Longstock Park Water Garden
Hampshire

C

CEANOTHUS
Eccleston Square, SW1
London

CENTAUREA
Bide-a-Wee Cottage
Northumberland & Tyne and Wear

CLEMATIS
Burford House Gardens
Worcestershire

CLEMATIS (SUBGENUS VIORNA)
Rosewood
Carmarthenshire & Pembrokeshire

CLEMATIS VITICELLA
Hawthornes Nursery Garden
Lancashire, Merseyside & Greater Manchester

CLEMATIS VITICELLA CVS
Roseland House
Cornwall

COLCHICUM
Felbrigg Hall
Norfolk

CORNUS
Newby Hall & Gardens
Yorkshire

CORYLUS, MALUS, PRUNUS, PYRUS, RIBES, VITIS
Brogdale Horticultural Trust
Kent

CYSTOPTERIS
Sizergh Castle
Cumbria

D

DIANTHUS
Dippers
Devon

Kingstone Cottages
Herefordshire

Accommodation available at NGS Gardens

We feature here a list of NGS garden owners or county volunteers who offer accommodation. We have listed them by county and indicated whether they offer Bed & Breakfast (**B&B**), Self-Catering (**SC**), or Hotel (**H**) accommodation. You will also find a reference to accommodation in the main directory with their garden entry, unless the property owner is a member of the county team or does not open their garden.

Bedfordshire

TOFTE MANOR
Souldrop Road, Sharnbrook
MK44 1HH
Mrs S Castleman
T 01234 781425
W www.toftelabyrinth.co.uk
Accommodation 17th century manor house with double and single accommodation of a very high standard. Full use of study (TV), drawing room, library, labyrinth, tennis court and swimming pool. Holistic therapies available. See website for further details.
B&B

Buckinghamshire

BEECH COTTAGE
3 School Lane, Loughton
Milton Keynes
MK5 8AT
Carolyn Rose
T 01908 666271
E carolyn@beechcottage-bandb.co.uk
W www.beechcottage-bandb.co.uk
Accommodation Beech Cottage is a delightful C18 Grade II listed property, situated in this pretty conservation area of Loughton, and set in an attractive, partly walled award winning garden which has been featured in several gardening publications.
See Loughton Village Gardens for details of garden.
B&B

HILL HOUSE
Castle Street, Buckingham
MK18 1BS
Mr & Mrs Thorogood
T 07860 714758
E llt@pjt.powernet.co.uk
Accommodation Two very comfortable double rooms in a lovely Georgian house by the church. Close to Stowe. Evening meal and visits to other private gardens possible by arrangement.
B&B

THE OLD VICARAGE
Padbury, Buckingham
MK18 2AH
Mr & Mrs H Morley-Fletcher
T 01280 813045
E belindamf@freenet.co.uk
Accommodation Twin bedroom with private bathroom in a Victorian house, surrounded by 2½ acres of garden. Breakfast comes from our organic garden, or from local sources wherever possible. Convenient for Silverstone, Stowe and Addington Manor Equestrian Centre.
B&B

Cambridgeshire

SOUTH FARM
Shingay-cum-Wendy, Royston
SG8 0HR
Philip Paxman
T 01223 207581
E philip@south-farm.co.uk
W www.south-farm.co.uk
Accommodation 2 self-contained apartments for 2 or 4 each. They can be self catering. Also 3 double ensuite. Dinner and lunch available. Prices from £80 per night or £70 single. Not usually available Saturdays.
B&B SC

Carmarthenshire

DELACORSE
Laugharne
SA33 4QP
Annie Hart
T 01994 427728
Accommodation C18 farmhouse nestling beside the Taf estuary in peaceful, beautiful surroundings near Dylan Thomas's Boathouse Museum. Also Aberglasney Garden, National Botanic Garden of Wales, Colby Garden (NT). Twin bedroom with private bathroom. Breakfast with home-grown organic produce. B&B £25pppn.
B&B

Cheshire

MANOR FARM
Egerton, Cholmodeley, nr Malpas
SY14 8AW
Tim & Jan Dilworth
T 01829 720261
E manorfarm@btconnnnect.com
W ergertonmanorfarm.co.uk
Accommodation 3 double rooms – all ensuite + 1 twin with private bathroom. Self catering – 2 cottages, each with 1 double and 1 twin bedded room. Prices from £50 per night. Single occ £40 per night.
B&B SC

WESTAGE FARM
Westage Lane, Great Budworth, nr Northwich
CW9 6HJ
Peter & Jean Davies
E pj@budworth94.fsnet.co.uk
Accommodation Beautiful black & white thatched cottage with detached converted small stable with double bed. Situated in 4 acres, near Arley Hall, Tatton Park & Dunham Massey. Breakfast in our garden room with fresh eggs and garden produce. B&B from £60 per room.
B&B

Cornwall

BONYTHON MANOR
Cury Cross Lanes, nr Helston
TR12 7BA
Richard & Sue Nathan
T 01326 240234
E sue@bonythonmanor.co.uk
W www.bonythonmanor.co.uk
Accommodation 4 properties sleeping 10, 6, 4 and 2. All 5* accommodation with ensuite facilities and private gardens. Bookings through 'Rural Retreats' – 01386 701177. www.ruralretreats.co.uk. Cottage refs: Bonython Farmhouse – CW042, Mews Cottage – CW047, St Corantyn Cottage CW048, Spring Water Barn – CW058.
SC

CARWINION
Carwinion, Mawnan Smith, Falmouth
TR11 5JA
A & J Rogers
T 01326 250258
E jane@carwinion.freeserve.co.uk
W www.carwinion.co.uk
Accommodation 1 double, 2 twin/double ensuite rooms in quiet country house set in 14 acres of valley garden. Children & dogs welcome. Rooms £80 per night. Single occ. £45. SC flat sleeps 2. Cottage sleeps 6.
B&B SC

CREED HOUSE
Creed, Grampound, Truro
TR2 4SL
Mr & Mrs William Croggon
T 01872 530372
Accommodation Georgian Rectory, 2 bedrooms with super king beds, 1 with twin beds, all with private or ensuite bathrooms. Prices £90 per night. Single occ. £60.
B&B

EDNOVEAN FARM
Peranuthnoe, Penzance
TR20 9LZ
Christine & Charles Taylor
T 01736 711883
E info@ednoveanfarm.co.uk
W www.ednoveanfarm.co.uk/gardens
Accommodation Granite barn above Mount's bay, stunning views; formal parterre giving way to open terraces; Italian & gravel gardens. Four poster beds, roll top baths, and patchwork quilts. 3 ensuite rooms with private terrace. 5 diamonds.
B&B

HALLOWARREN
Carne, Manaccan, Helston
TR12 6HD
Amanda Osman
T 01326 231224
W www.stanthony.co.uk
Accommodation Victorian cottage – sleeps 2, part of period Cornish farmhouse. All seasons. Traditional barn – sleeps 5. Full central heating. Both equipped to very high standard with all linen supplied. Atmospheric setting in woodland garden bordering stream.
SC

HIDDEN VALLEY GARDENS
Treesmill, nr Par
PL24 2TU
Patricia Howard
T 01208 873225
E hiddenvalleygardens@yahoo.co.uk
W www.hiddenvalleygardens.co.uk
Accommodation Comfortable B&B accommodation in a stone barn conversion set in a 'hidden' valley with a 4 acre display garden. 2 double, 1 twin all en-suite, TV and

tea making facilities. Price £23-£26 per person per night. Single occ. £31-£34.
B&B

TREGOOSE
Grampound, Truro
Anthony & Alison O'Connor
T 01726 882460
W www.tregoose.co.uk
Accommodation 1 double room (four poster), ensuite. 1 twin, ensuite bath with shower over. 1 double with private bath/shower. Prices from £43 per person.
B&B

TREGREHAN GARDEN COTTAGES
Tregrehan House, Par
PL24 2SJ
Tom & Jo Hudson
T 01726 812438
E info@tregrehan.org
W www.tregrehan.org
Accommodation Self catering cottage accommodation on Cornwall's historic Tregrehan Estate, situated between Fowey & Charlestown. Cottages sleep 1-8, short or week breaks, thoughtful hospitality within one of Cornwallis great gardens of outstanding botanical merit. Prices from £162.
SC

TREWOOFE ORCHARD
Lamorna, Penzance
TR19 6BW
Dick & Barbara Waterson
T 01736 810214
E dickwaterson@onetel.com
W www.lamorna-valley.co.uk
Accommodation 1 double ensuite, 1 twin with private bathroom (both with baths). From £70 per night per room. Reduced single rate from Oct – April inc. Three night minimum July – Sept inc. Secluded and tranquil. Non smoking. Special diets catered for.
B&B

Cumbria

BRACKENRIGG LODGE
Windy Hall Road,
Bowness-on-Windermere
LA23 3YH
Lynne Bush
T 015394 47770
E lynne@brackenriggs.co.uk
W www.brackenriggs.co.uk
Accommodation Ideally located, tranquil, rural 3 acre setting, home of roe deer & red squirrels. Close to the village and lake. Resident owner guarantees comfortable, clean accommodation. A real home from home. (SC – one apartment & one cottage).
SC

LAKESIDE HOTEL
Lake Windermere, Newby Bridge
LA12 8AT
Mr N R Talbot
T 015395 30001
E sales@LakesideHotel.co.uk
W www.LakesideHotel.co.uk
Accommodation The best 4* hotel in the Lake District, with a spectacular location on the southern shores of Lake Windermere. Guests enjoy exclusive use of our luxury Health and Leisure Spa. Bedrooms with private gardens available. (78 rooms).
H

LANGHOLME MILL
Woodgate, Lowick Green, Ulverston
LA12 8ES
Mr & Mrs G Sanderson
T 01229 885215
E info@langholmemill.co.uk
W www.langholmemill.co.uk
Accommodation Ten minutes from Lake Coniston with stunning views, this C17 corn mill comprises 4 double bedrooms & large garden designed around the mill race featuring rhododendrons, hostas & acers. Ideal for walkers & families.
SC

LINDETH FELL COUNTRY HOUSE HOTEL
Bowness-on-Windermere
LA23 3JP
Air Cdr & Mrs P A Kennedy
T 01539 443286
E kennedy@lindethfell.co.uk
W www.lindethfell.co.uk
Accommodation on a tree lined drive above Lake Windermere, standing in magnificent private gardens. 14 bedrooms, singles, doubles and family rooms. Price from £45 B&B. Five course dinner available. Many awards including AA Top 200 hotel and Gold Award.
H

SWINSIDE END FARM
Scales, High Lorton, Cockermouth
CA13 9UA
Karen Nicholson
T 01900 85410
E swinside@supanet.com
Accommodation Farmhouse: 2 double ensuite bedrooms and 1 twin with private bathroom. Guest sitting room. Prices from: double £21–£25.50, single £23–£27 depending on length of stay.
B&B

WHITBYSTEADS
Askham, Penrith
CA10 2PG
Thomas and Victoria Lowther
T 01931 712284
E info@gnap.fsnet.co.uk
W www.whitbysteads.org
Accommodation Working hill farm

in the Lake District National Park with beautiful views. 1 double bedroom, ensuite, 1 double & 1 twin bedroom with separate bathroom. Children, dogs & horses welcome. Full English breakfast. £40 – £50 pppn.
B&B

Denbighshire

BODYSGALLEN HALL
Bodysgallen Hall, Llandudno
North Wales
LL30 1RS
Historic House Hotels Ltd.
T 01492 584466
E info@bodysgallen.com
W www.bodysgallen.com
Accommodation Standing in 200 acres of gardens and parkland, Bodysgallen Hall provides all that is best in country house hospitality. 33 rooms and suites, an award winning restaurant and a health and fitness spa are here to indulge in.
H

THE OLD RECTORY
Llanfihangel Glyn Myfyr,
Cerrigydrudion
LL21 9UN
Mr & Mrs E T Hughes
T 01490 420568
E elwynthomashughes@hotmail.com
Accommodation Luxury rural retreat set in idyllic garden and countryside. 1 family room, ensuite, 1 family room with private bathroom. Guest lounge. Price from £30 pppn.
B&B

RUTHIN CASTLE
Castle Street, Ruthin
LL15 2NU
Ruthin Castle Ltd
T 01824 702664
E reception@ruthincastle.co.uk
W www.ruthincastle.co.uk
Accommodation A magical 62 bedroom hotel in a parkland setting, rich in history and character, 23 miles from Chester. The mediaeval castle, built by Edward 1, & owned by the monarchy for extended periods, was rebuilt in 1826. B&B from £45 pppn.
H

TAL-Y-BRYN FARM GUEST HOUSE
Tal-y- Bryn Farm, Llannefydd,
Denbigh
LL16 5DR
Gareth & Falmai Roberts
T 01745 540208
E llaeth@villagedairy.co.uk
W www.villagedairy.co.uk
Accommodation C16 farmhouse, lovely views and garden with lovely historical walks. 3 Double guest rooms with ensuite facilities. TV and internet connections. Tea & coffee facilities. No dogs please.
B&B

Derbyshire

CASCADES
Clatterway, Bonsall, Matlock
DE4 2AH
Mr & Mrs A Clements
T 01629 822464
E enquiries@cascadesgardens.com
W www.cascadesgardens.com
Accommodation Set in the beautiful 4 acre garden on many levels with mature trees and high cliffs, Cascades offers a range of elegant B&B accommodation within the Peak District National Park. ETB 5 Diamonds.
B&B

PARK HALL
Walton Back Lane, Chesterfield
S42 7LT
Kim & Margaret Staniforth
T 01246 567412
E kim.staniforth@virgin.net
Accommodation Well appointed self-contained studio in Park Hall's magnificent gardens. Sleeps 3 (1 double, 1 single). Chatsworth, Haddon Hall, Hardwick Hall, Bolsover Castle and Peak District all within 30 mins. Daily or weekly terms.
SC

THE RIDDINGS FARM
Kirk Ireton, Ashbourne
DE6 3LB
Mr & Mrs P R Spencer
T 01335 370331
W www.members.lycos.co.uk/ivycottage
Accommodation ETC 3*. Delightful, peacefully situated barn conversion looking over Carsington Water. Spacious 2 bedroomed, accommodation, sleeps 3-4. Sorry no pets, no smoking. Towels, linen and electricity included. £200- £320 per week.
Member of NGS County Team
SC

SHATTON HALL FARM COTTAGES
Bamford, Hope Valley
S33 0BG
Angela Kellie
T 01433 620635
E ahk@peakfarmholidays.co.uk
W www.peakfarmholidays.co.uk
Accommodation Three comfortable stone cottages, each with two double bedrooms, open plan living area. 4 star accommodation, around listed Elizabethan farmhouse. Secluded location with good access and within easy reach of Chatsworth House and Haddon Hall.
SC

Devon

ASHWELL
East Street, Bovey Tracey
TQ13 9EJ
Bill & Diane Riddell
T 01626 830031
E bill.riddell@ukgateway.net
W www.ashwell-bb.com
Accommodation Elegant Georgian house set in an acre of walled garden – with its own vineyard. 1 king-sized double & 1 twin room – both ensuite. Tariff £27.50 –£32 pppn. Non smoking. Children welcome. Sorry, no pets.
See Bovey Tracey Gardens for details of garden
B&B

THE CIDER HOUSE
Buckland Abbey, Yelverton,
nr Tavistock
PL20 6EZ
Mrs Sarah Stone
T 01822 853285
E sarah.stone@cider-house.co.uk
W www.cider-house.co.uk
Accommodation House formerly part of Cistercian monastery of Buckland; 1 double & 1 twin room each with private bathroom, plus extra twin room if required. Minimum stay 2 nights. Price £35 per person per night, single occ. £45. Cottage sleeps 5 in 3 bedrooms; sitting room with log fire, dining room, kitchen. Walled garden, use of tennis court.
B&B SC

DARTINGTON HALL
Dartington, Totnes
TQ9 6EL
Dartington Hall Trust
T 01803 847100
E bookings@dartingtonhall.com
W www.dartingtonhall.com
Accommodation There are 51 bedrooms within the C14 medieval Courtyard, most retaining their original character. From beamed ceilings to an etching of a C15 Spanish galleon carved onto a wall, history can be discovered all over the Courtyard and Gardens.
H

KINGSTON HOUSE
Staverton, Totnes
TQ9 6AR
Michael & Elizabeth Corfield
T 01803 762235
E info@kingston-estate.co.uk
W www.kingston-estate.co.uk
Kingston House, 5 Diamonds – Gold award, has 3 beautiful suites and 9 Five Star cottages. The house is set in the gardens, offering delicious food using garden produce whenever possible, excellent wine list. Price on application.
B&B SC

LITTLE ASH FARM
Fenny Bridges
EX14 3BL
Sadie & Robert Reid
T 01404 850271
Accommodation En-suite family room sleeps 4. Family suite, twin and double with bathroom. Single, en-suite. All rooms have TV and tea tray. Full breakfast in large conservatory overlooking garden. From £23. Non smoking.
B&B

NORTH BORESTON FARM
Halwell, Totnes
TQ9 7LD
Rob & Jan Wagstaff
T 01548 821320
E boreston@tiscali.co.uk
Accommodation Converted old granary. Comfortably furnished living room and well equipped kitchen upstairs; bedroom (sleeps 2) with en-suite shower room downstairs. French windows onto own terrace. Covered parking. Ideally located for best of coast, Dartmoor and great gardens.
SC

THE OLD RECTORY
Ashford, Barnstaple
EX31 4BY
Ann Burnham
T 01271 377408
E annburnham@btinternet.com
Accommodation You will enjoy your stay at the recently renovated Old Rectory. Attractive bedrooms with full ensuite. Delicious breakfasts; dinner or supper on request. The view is superb. Log fires in winter.
B&B

REGENCY HOUSE
Hemyock, Cullompton
EX15 3RQ
Mrs Jenny Parsons
T 01823 680238
E jenny.parsons@btinternet.com
Accommodation Regency House is the most beautiful, spacious, Georgian rectory. Accommodation: double room, ensuite, 1 twin with private bathroom. Price £40 per person per night.
B&B

SOUTH BANK
Southleigh, Colyton
EX24 6JB
J Connor
T 01404 871251
Accommodation 2 double rooms (not ensuite) in sunny house with lovely views. Large garden, 3 acre field. Good walking and bird watching in quiet valleys. Near Dartmoor. Exmoor Jurassic coast 3 miles. £18 pppn or £119 per week.

See Southleigh Gardens for details of garden.
B&B

SOUTH HEATHERCOMBE
Manaton, Newton Abbot
TQ13 9XE
Mrs Julia Holden & C & M Pike Woodlands Trust
T 01647 221350
E bandb@heathercombe.com
W www.heathercombe.com
Accommodation Comfortable, well equipped accommodation in C15 Dartmoor longhouse. Twin/double ensuite bedroom & twin/double family room; whirlpool bath, TV/DVD, tea & coffee making, guest's lounge with log fire. Delicious breakfasts. Dogs welcome (kennels). From £28 pn.
See Heathercombe for details of garden.
B&B

ST MERRYN
Higher Park Road, Braunton
EX33 2LG
Ros Bradford
T 01271 813805
E ros@st-merryn.co.uk
W www.st-merryn.co.uk
Lovely house set in peaceful garden. 1 single/twin with private bathroom. 1 double (king-size bed) with private bathroom. 1 double (king-size bed), ensuite shower room. Minimum stay 2 nights. Strictly no smoking. Prices from £25pp.
B&B

WESTCOTT BARTON
Middle Marwood, Barnstaple
EX31 4EF
Howard Frank
T 01271 812842
E westcott_barton@yahoo.co.uk
W www.westcottbarton.co.uk
Accommodation Pretty bedrooms (4 double, 1 twin), all ensuite, all with colour TV and tea/coffee making facilities. Breakfast is a movable feast and evening meals are available on request. No smoking or pets. Not suitable for children under 12 yrs. £45 per person.
B&B

WHITSTONE FARM
Whitstone Lane, Bovey Tracey
TQ13 9NA
Katie & Alan Bunn
T 01626 832258
E katie@whitstonefarm.co.uk
W www.whitstonefarm.co.uk
Accommodation Country house with stunning views over Dartmoor. 1 super king-sized (or twin) room, 1 king-sized room, 1 double sized room – all ensuite. Prices from £65 per night. Single occ. from £45. Guest lounge. Delicious breakfasts

and evening meals (by arrangement) using local organic produce wherever possible. Come and be pampered.
B&B

WINSFORD WALLED GARDEN
Winsford Lane, Halwill Junction
EX21 5XT
Aileen Birks & Michael Gilmore
T 01409 221477
E muddywellies
@winsfordwalledgarden.com
W www.winsfordwalledgarden.com
Accommodation Top quality double ensuite accommodation, located within Victorian walled garden containing 3000 varieties of plants and restored Victorian greenhouses built of teak.
B&B

Dorset

THE DAIRY HOUSE
Stowell, Sherborne
DT9 4PD
Paul & Penny Burns
T 01963 370754
E paul.burns@totalise.co.uk
Accommodation One twin with ensuite shower. One double/family room with private shower, plus further twin to make family suite. Adults £25 pppn, family rate by arrangement. Pretty C18 house; lovely garden. Evening meal available.
See Somerset & Bristol Area for details of garden
B&B

DOMINEYS COTTAGES
Domineys Yard, Buckland Newton, Dorchester
DT2 7BS
Mrs W Gueterbock
T 01300 345295
E cottages@domineys.com
W www.domineys.com
Accommodation 3 delightful highly commended 2 bdrm cottages. Maintained to exceptional standards – TB4*. Enchanting gardens peacefully located in Dorset's beautiful heartland. Flower decked patios and heated summer pool. Babies & children over 5 years welcome. Regret no pets. Many NGS gardens nearby.
See Domineys Yard for details of garden.
SC

KNOWLE FARM
Uploders, Bridport
DT6 4NS
Alison & John Halliday
T 01308 485492
E alison@knowle-farm.fsnet.co.uk
W www.knowlefarmbandb.com
Accommodation Welcoming, relaxing village base for the delights of West Dorset and beyond. Top

quality accommodation in C18 longhouse. Every attention to detail. Super breakfasts. Double, ensuite; twin with private bathroom. Sorry no pets, smoking or children under 12. From £35 pppn.
B&B

THE OLD RECTORY
West Compton, Dorchester
DT2 0EY
Susan Wreford
T 01300 320007
E sue@wreford.f9.co.uk
Accommodation 2 large (double & twin) rooms, ensuite, in hamstone house (1865) in rolling hills near Eggardon Hill iron-age fort. 9 miles from coast, equidistant Dorchester and Bridport. Continental breakfast. Dogs welcome. £25 single, £45 double.
Member of NGS County Team
B&B

Durham

THE COACH HOUSE
The Square, Greta Bridge,
Barnard Castle
DL12 9SD
Peter & Mary Gilbertson
T 01833 627201
E info@coachhousegreta.co.uk
W www.coachhousegreta.co.uk
Accommodation C18 coaching inn, Dickens stayed here! The bridge & house were painted by J. S. Cotman. 2 bedrooms, 1 ensuite,1 private bath. Peaceful setting, river and woodland walks. A good stop off on way to Scotland or the south.
See Gardens in the Square for details of garden.
B&B

Essex

ROSEMARY
Rectory Hill, East Bergholt, Colchester
CO7 6TH
Mrs Natalie Finch
T 01206 298241
Accommodation Situated in the heart of Constable country within easy reach of Harwich and Flatford. Garden featured on Gardener's World. 3 twin rooms – with hand basins, 1 single room. Shared bathroom. Price £28 single, £56 twin.
See Suffolk for details of garden
B&B

Flintshire & Wrexham

DOVE COTTAGE
Rhos Road, Penyffordd, nr Chester
CH4 0JR
Mr & Mrs C Wallis
T 01244 547539
E dovecottage@supanet.com
www.visitwales.com
Accommodation Delightful C17

farmhouse. Luxurious accommodation. 1 double room, ensuite, 1 double room , private shower rm. Single occ. £35-£45, double £50-£60 per night. Convenient for Chester & N Wales.
B&B

Gloucestershire North & Central

BANK VIEW
Victoria Road, Quenington, Cirencester
GL7 5BP
Mr & Mrs J Moulden
T 01285 750573
E jackie.moulden@lineone.net
W www.bankviewbandb.co.uk
Accommodation 4 diamond accommodation, with 1 twin, 2 double ensuite rooms. Non smoking. Relax and unwind in the tranquil Cotswolds. Comfortable rooms look out onto beautiful scenery. Ideally based to visit Cheltenham, Oxford and Cirencester. Lovely local pubs.
See Quenington Gardens for details of garden
B&B

BEECHCROFT
Beech Lane, Brownshill, Stroud
GL6 8AG
Jenny Salt
T 01453 883422
E jenny@beechcroftbb.fsnet.co.uk
W www.undiscovered-cotswold-accommodation.co.uk
Accommodation Quietly situated Edwardian house set in 1/2 acre of garden. Homemade bread & preserves. No smoking. Beautiful countryside and good walking area. Near to Gloucester, Cheltenham & Bath.
See Eastcombe, Bussage and Brownshill Gardens for details of garden
B&B

COOPERS COTTAGE
Wells Cottage, Bisley, nr Stroud
GL6 7AG
Mr & Mrs Michael Flint
T 01452 770289
E flint_bisley@talktalk.net
Accommodation Attractive old beamed cottage, non-smoking, sleeps 2-4. Stands apart in owners' large, beautiful garden with lovely views. Furnished & equipped to high standard. Very quiet, good walking. Village shop & 2 pubs nearby.
See Wells Cottage for details of garden
SC

GRANGE COTTAGE
Mill Lane, Blockley
GL56 9HT
Guy & Alison Heitmann
T 01386 700251
E info@garden-designer.biz

Accommodation 1 twin, 1 double, both ensuite. on a peaceful lane in the centre of the old part of the village. A great area for walking.
See Blockley Gardens for details of garden
B&B

KEMPSFORD MANOR
High Street, Kempsford, Fairford
GL7 4EQ
Mrs Z Williamson
T 01285 810131
E ipek.williamson@tiscali.co.uk
W www.kempsfordmanor.co.uk
Accommodation C17-18 manor house set in peaceful gardens. Fine reception rooms. 3-4 double bedrooms. Price from £30 single occ. Ideal retreat. Home grown organic vegetables. Suitable for small conferences and marquee receptions. 1 mile from Wiltshire border.
B&B

MILL DENE GARDEN
Mill Dene, School Lane, Blockley
Moreton-in-Marsh
GL56 9HU
Mrs Wendy Dare
T 01386 700457
E info@milldene.co.uk
W www.milldenegarden.co.uk
Accommodation 2007 Year of Cotswold Gardens. Small groups of keen gardeners can be accommodated for tours of the many nearby Cotswold gardens & itineraries arranged. www.gardenvisit-cotswolds.co.uk
B&B

Gwent

BRYNDERI
Wainfield Lane, Gwehelog, Usk
NP15 1RG
Ann & Alwyne Benson
T 01291 672976
E brynderi@btopenworld.com
W www.brynderi.co.uk
Accommodation Beautifully furnished single storey self-contained apartment in wing of country home. Self catering or with breakfast provided. Large lounge with French doors to private patio, double bedroom; well equipped kitchen; bathroom with towels; bathrobes and toiletries. WTB 5 star.
B&B SC

LLWYN-Y-WEN FARM
Hafodyrynys Road, Crumlin
NP11 5AX
Mrs H Lewy
T 01495 244797
E robert@lefray.eclipse.co.uk
W www.lefray.eclipse.co.uk
Accommodation Rooms in SC wing of large farmhouse from £30 single and £45 double. Set in 20 acres bordering Forestry Commission

land. Bluebells in May and a haven for wildlife and hundreds of birds. Picturesque walks.
B&B

THE NURTONS
Tintern
NP16 7NX
Elsa Wood
T 01291 689253
E info@thenurtons.co.uk
W www.thenurtons.co.uk
Accommodation 2 B&B suites –
1 twin with double sofa bed & 1 double, each with own private bathroom, sitting room & patio. Scenic, secluded and historical site. Organic produce. £25 – £30 pppn.
B&B

PENPERGWM LODGE
Abergavenny
NP7 9AS
Mr & Mrs S Boyle
T 01873 840208
E boyle@penpergwm.co.uk
W www.penplants.com
Accommodation A large rambling Edwardian house in the lovely Usk valley. Pretty bedrooms have garden views, bathrooms share a corridor, breakfast and relax in the spacious and comfortable sitting room. Great walking in nearby Brecon Beacons National Park.
B&B

Gwynedd

HOTEL MAES-Y-NEUADD
Talsarnau, nr Harlech
LL47 6YA
Peter & Lynn Jackson & Peter Payne
T 01766 780200
E maes@neuadd.com
W www.neuadd.com
Accommodation 15 individually designed ensuite double/twin rooms. C14 manor house with bar, terrace, lounge, conservatory and highly acclaimed restaurant serving fresh, local produce and home grown fruit & vegetables. From £158 per room.
H

Hampshire

APPLE COURT
Hordle Lane, Hordle
SO41 0HU
Charles & Angela Meads
T 01590 642130
E applecourt@btinternet.com
W www.applecourt.com
Accommodation Cottage annexe next to Apple Court. 2 bedrooms, sleeps 4. Kitchen, dining room, conservatory/lounge. Non-smoking. Regret no dogs. Beautiful location near New Forest, Lymington. From £400 per week.
SC

FOREST EDGE
Andover Down, Andover
SP11 6LJ
Annette & David Beeson
T 01264 364526
E david@forest-edge.co.uk
W www.forest-edge.co.uk
Accommodation 2 double and 2 twin rooms (1 converts to super king sized bed), all ensuite. Garden room for breakfast and relaxation. Extensive menu including vegetarian options. Quiet, abuts ancient forest. Car park. Rated 4 diamonds.
B&B

WADES HOUSE
Barton Stacey, Winchester
SO21 3RJ
Tony & Jenny Briscoe
T 01962 760516
E jenny.roo@btinternet.com
Accommodation Luxuriously comfortable family home. 2 double, 2 twin rooms with private facilities & lovely views over 2 acre garden. A garden lover's delight. Sitting room with TV/DVD/video and large open fire. Delicious homemade food. Dinner by arrangement. £50 pppn.
B&B

Herefordshire

ARROW COTTAGE
Ledgemoor, nr Weobley
HR4 8RN
David and Janet Martin
T 01544 318468
E info@arrowcottage.co.uk
W www.arrowcottagegarden.co.uk
Accommodation Lovely self catering detached cottage with 3 double bedrooms, 2 reception rooms and 2 bathrooms. The cottage is available on a weekly basis (rental £300 – £500 pw). Please ring or look at our website for further details.
SC

BROBURY HOUSE
Brobury
HR3 6BS
Mr & Mrs Cartwright
T 01981 500229
E enquiries@broburyhouse.co.uk
W www.broburyhouse.co.uk
Accommodation House – B&B: Large double room, ensuite. 2 large twin rooms each with private bathroom, all with beautiful garden views. Prices from £35 pppn. Cottages – 2 spacious, recently refurbished, self catering cottages. Peak period price £420.00.
B&B SC

THE GREAT HOUSE
Dilwyn, Hereford
HR4 8HX
Tom & Jane Hawksley
T 01544 318007
W www.thegreathouse-dilwyn.co.uk

Accommodation 3 double/twin ensuite bathrooms. Private sunny sitting room with door to garden. Beams, panelling, flag stone floors and enormous log fires. Price £90, single occ. £50. Dinner by arrangement from £20. Licensed. Wolsey Lodge. 4* Visit Britain.
B&B

HOPE END HOUSE
Hope End, Ledbury
HR8 1JQ
Mr & Mrs PJ Maiden
T 01531 635890
E sharonmaiden@btinternet.com
W www.hopeendhouse.com
Accommodation Hope End House, surrounded by 100 acres of historic parkland, where once Elizabeth Barrett roamed. This romantic house has peace at its heart. Our accommodation has been awarded 5*. Our gardens tranquil and peaceful.
B&B

LOWER HOUSE
Cusop Dingle, Hay-on-Wye
HR3 5RQ
Nicky & Pete Daw
T 01497 820773
E nicky.daw@btinternet.com
W www.lowerhousegardenhay.co.uk
Accommodation 1 double + shower; 1 double + private bathroom. From £70 per room. Beautifully furnished old house, lost in 7 acres, by Offa's Dyke Footpath on Welsh Border on edge of Hay-on-Wye.
See Powys for details of garden
B&B SC

Hertfordshire

106 ORCHARD ROAD
Tewin, Welwyn
AL6 0LZ
Linda Adams
T 01438 798147
E alannio@btinternet.com
W www.tewinvillage.co.uk
1 large double room with private bathroom, 1 large twin room, if required, in listed C20th house. Prices from £30pppn.
B&B

SUMMERLAWN
29 Astons Road, Moor Park, Northwood
HA6 2LB
Leslie & Frankie Lipton
T 07768 448897
E leslie@leslielipton.co.uk
Accommodation New, self-contained, luxury suite forming annexe to the main house. Bedroom with queen sized bed, hall, bathroom and kitchen/living room. Close to Moor Park Golf Course. 30 mins central London. Parking,

beautiful views. £65/£75 pn single. £85/90 pn double.
See London for details of garden.
B&B

WEST LODGE PARK
Beales Hotels, Andrew Beale MD
Cockfosters Road, Hadley Wood
EN4 0PY
Beales Hotels
T 0208 216 3900
E westlodgepark@bealeshotels.co.uk
W www.bealeshotels.co.uk
Accommodation 59 bedrooms including Superior, Executive rooms with views over our arboretum. If you are looking for something more modern, try our chestnut lodge rooms which can be found in a separate lodge in our gardens.
H

Isle of Wight

NORTHCOURT
Shorwell
PO30 3JG
Mr & Mrs J Harrison
T 01983 740415
E christine@northcourt.info
W www.northcourt.info
Accommodation B&B in large C17 manor house in 15 acres of exotic gardens, on edge of the downs. 6 double/twin rooms, all ensuite. Price from £60 per room. Also wing of house for up to 14 self-catering.
See Northcourt Gardens for details of garden
B&B SC

WESTBROOK & NORTHBROOK
Brook House, Brook
PO30 4EJ
Mr & Mrs G Walters
T 01983 740535
E belindawalters@hotmail.co.uk
Accommodation Two self-catering properties, one sleeping 6 & the other 4, in the courtyard adjacent to Brook House. Very comfortably furnished and equipped in a pretty and quiet location.
See Brook House for details pf garden.
SC

Kent

3 CHAINHURST COTTAGES
Dairy Lane, Marden, Tonbridge
TN12 9SU
Heather Scott
T 01622 820483 / 07729 378489
E member@heatherscott0.wanadoo.co.uk
Accommodation Comfortable, modern accommodation with private entrance and ensuite bathroom. Quiet rural location, good local pubs. Ideal touring base for historic properties and gardens including

Leeds & Sissinghurst Castle. Visit Britain 4 Diamonds – Silver award. £70 per night.
See Chainhurst Cottage Gardens for details of garden
B&B

BOYTON COURT
Sutton Valence
ME17 3BY
Richard & Patricia Stileman
T 01622 844065
E richstileman@aol.com
Accommodation 2 double rooms (1 king-size, 1 twin) with ensuite bathrooms. Both with spectacular south facing garden and Wealden views. £90 per night. Single occ. £55
B&B

COTTAGE FARM
Cackets Lane, Cudham,
nr Sevenoaks
TN14 7QG
Phil & Karen Baxter
T 01959 534048/532506
E karen@cottagefarmturkeys.co.uk
Accommodation Delightful country cottage: 1 double and 1 twin room, living room, kitchen and bathroom. Full central heating. From £350 per week self catering. B&B £35 pppn based on 2 sharing double/twin room. £45 single occ.
B&B SC

FLINT COTTAGE
Bourne Park, Bishopsbourne,
Canterbury
CT4 5BJ
Mr & Mrs P J Sinnock
T 01227 830691
E lesley@stew-pot.fsnet.co.uk
Accommodation Kentish flint cottage in lovely rural setting. Double, ensuite £60, single occ. £40. Use of garden and summer houses. Garden best time April – June.
B&B

HOATH HOUSE
Chiddingstone Hoath, Edenbridge
TN8 7DB
Mervyn & Jane Streatfeild
T 01342 850362
E janestreatfeild@hoath-T house.freeserve.co.uk
W www.hoathhouse.co.uk
Accommodation Rambling medieval and Tudor house in extensive gardens (most picturesque in daffodil and rhododendron season) with fine views. Convenient for Penshurst, Chartwell and Hever and recommendations for NGS openings across Kent. 2 twin rooms sharing 'Art deco' bathroom. Good access to London and Gatwick.
Member of NGS County Team
B&B

ROCK FARM
Gibbs Hill, Nettlestead, Maidstone
ME18 5HT
Mrs S E Corfe
T 01622 812244
W www.rockfarmhousebandb.co.uk
Accommodation Delightful C18 Kentish farmhouse in quiet, idyllic position on a farm with extensive views. 4 diamond B&B with 1 double and 1 twin room, both ensuite. Price £60, single occ £35.
B&B

STOWTING HILL HOUSE
Stowting, Ashford
TN25 6BE
Richard and Virginia Latham
T 01303 862881
E vjlatham@hotmail.com
Accommodation 2 twins, both with bath. 1 double. A Georgian Manor house set in beautiful North Downs, with walks from our door in quiet rolling valleys and plenty of gardens to visit. Prices from £75, double & from £45, single. Member of NGS County Team
B&B

Lancashire

MILL BARN
Goosefoot Close, Samlesbury,
Preston
PR5 0SS
Chris Mortimer
T 01245 853300
E chris@millbarn.net
Accommodation Mill Barn is a converted barn. 1 double & 1 twin room, neither ensuite. Guests are accommodated as house guests & have full access to all shared rooms – lounge, conservatory, studio etc. as well as the garden.
B&B

THE OLD ZOO
Brockhall Village, Old Langho,
Nr Blackburn
BB6 8DX
Linda & Gerald Hitman
T 01254 244811
E bookingenquiries@ theavenuehotel.co.uk
W www.theavenuehotel.co.uk
Accommodation A modern three star hotel and restaurant offering full service accommodation and guided tours of the gardens for interested groups. Two & three night packages, including visits to other gardens, can be arranged.
H

THE RIDGES
Weavers Brow, Limbrick, Chorley
PR6 9EB
John & Barbara Barlow
T 01257 279981
E barlow.ridges@virgin.net
W www.bedbreakfast-

gardenvisits.com
Accommodation 3 double/twin bedrooms. 1 ensuite, 2 sharing a private bathroom. Second toilet in hallway. Dining room. Prices from £60 per night. Single occ. £35.
B&B

Lincolnshire

THE OLD VICARAGE
Low Road, Holbeach Hurn, Spalding
PE12 8JN
Liz Dixon-Spain
T 01406 424148
E lizds@ukonline.co.uk
W www.specialplacestostay.com
Accommodation Victorian vicarage set in 1½ acres of mature gardens. All local/home produce for breakfasts. Closed mid December – mid March. Children welcome. 2 rooms available, 1 twin/1 double.
B&B

London

38 KILLIESER AVENUE
SW2 4NT
Winkle Haworth
T 020 8671 4196
E winklehaworth@hotmail.com
W www.specialplacestostay.com
Accommodation Luxurious and stylish accommodation, 1 twin bedded room, 1 single – both with private bathroom. Price from £90. Single occ. £50. English breakfast incl.
B&B

Norfolk

BAGTHORPE HALL
Bagthorpe, Kings Lynn
PE31 6QY
Mrs Gina Morton
T 01485 578528
E enquiries@bagthorpehall.co.uk
W www.bagthorpehall.co.uk
Accommodation 2-3 large double bedrooms ensuite, big comfortable beds, organic and homemade breakfast. From £65 for double incl breakfast. £40 single.
B&B

BAY COTTAGE
The Old Cottage, Colby Corner, nr Aylsham
NR11 7EB
Judith & Stuart Clarke
T 01263 734574
E enchanting@btinternet.com
W www.enchantingcottages.co.uk
Accommodation Four star ETB graded country cottage with large garden. Sleeps 7 in 3 bedrooms, plus a self contained garden, oak framed annexe with wheelchair access, which sleeps 2.
See Old Cottage for details of garden
SC

LITCHAM HALL
Litcham, King's Lynn
PE32 2QQ
Mr & Mrs John Birkbeck
T 01328 701389
E h.birkbeck67@amserve.com
Accommodation Lovely rooms in Georgian house. 1 double, 1 twin – both with ensuite bathroom. 1 twin with separate bath. Sitting room available.
B&B

MANOR HOUSE FARM
Wellingham, King's Lynn
PE32 2TH
Robin & Elisabeth Ellis
T 01328 838227
Accommodation Award winning conversion in garden. 2 large airy double bedrooms with ensuite baths & showers and comfortable, spacious sitting room with wood burning stove, TV and books etc plus small kitchen. Breakfast in dining room of main house.
B&B

THE OLD RECTORY
Ridlington, North Walsham
NR28 9NZ
Peter & Fiona Black
T 01692 650247
E blacks7@email.com
W www.oldrectory.northnorfolk.co.uk
Accommodation House: 1 double bedroom, ensuite; 1 double with wash basin and private bathroom. Garden room: large studio, double/twin beds, plus sofa bed, kitchen and bathroom. Prices from £50 per night. 1½ miles from East Ruston Old Vicarage Gardens. Member of NGS County Team
B&B SC

WOODLANDS FARM
Private Road, Stokesby
NR29 3DX
Vivienne Fabb
T 01493 369341
W v.fabb@btinternet.com
Accommodation Convenient for Broads, coast & Norwich. Attractive ensuite rooms with lovely garden views. Outdoor pool & croquet in summer. Year round woodland walks. Evening meals by arrangement using home grown produce when possible. Price £50 double, single occ. £30.
B&B

Northamptonshire

COTON LODGE
West Haddon Road, Guilsborough, Northampton
NN6 8QE
Peter Hicks and Joanne de Nobriga
T 01604 740215
E peter@cotonlodge.co.uk
W www.cotonlodge.co.uk

Accommodation House: 1 king sized double room & 1 twin room both with ensuite bathrooms. Prices from £70 per room per night.
B&B

FLORE FIELDS
Flore, Northampton
NN7 4JX
Lady Morton
T 01327 340226
Accommodation Victorian house in large gardens and park, 1 mile from village. Ample parking. Dinner not provided but several good country pubs serving food close by.
B&B

HUNT HOUSE QUARTERS
Hunt House, Main Road, Kilsby, Rugby
CV23 8XR
Linda Harris
T 01788 823282 / 0775 3679308
E luluharris@
hunthouse.fsbusiness.co.uk
W www.hunthousekilsby.com
Accommodation The Hunt House Quarters is set in a beautiful thatched hunting lodge and covered stables. 4 courtyard rooms are finished to luxury standard 7 awarded 4 AA Diamonds 2006. Tranquil setting.
See Kilsby Gardens for details of garden
B&B

Northumberland

THORNLEY HOUSE
Allendale, Hexham
NE47 9NH
Eileen Finn
T 01434 683255
E e.finn@ukonline.co.uk
W web.ukonline.co.uk/e.finn
Accommodation Beautiful country house, 1 mile west of Allendale, near Hadrian's Wall. 3 bedrooms with facilities, TV & tea makers. 2 lounges with Steinway grand piano and plasma TV. Resident Maine Coon cats. B&B from £26p.n. – £165p.w.
B&B

Nottinghamshire

ASHDENE
Radley Road, Halam, Southwell
NG22 8AH
David C Herbert
T 01636 812335
E david@herbert.newsurf.net
Accommodation Double, ensuite; twin with private bathroom; 4 poster double with shared bathroom. C15 farmhouse with resident's private sitting room. Open fires.
B&B

Oxfordshire

BROUGHTON GROUNDS FARM
North Newington, Banbury
OX15 6AW
Andrew and Margaret Taylor
T 01295 730315
E broughtongrounds@hotmail.com
Accommodation One double, one twin and one single room in 17th Century farmhouse, on working mixed farm, located on the Broughton Castle Estate. Beautiful views and peaceful location. Prices: £27 pppn.
B&B

BUTTSLADE HOUSE
Colony Road, Sibford Gower
OX15 5RX
Mrs Diana Thompson
T 01295 788818
E janthompson50@hotmail.com
W www.buttsladehouse.co.uk
Accommodation Garden annexe: B&B: King size bed/sitting room, ensuite bathroom – from £65 (single £40) pn. SC: Double & twin bedroom, shower & WC, sitting room with kitchen facilities. From £350 per week (B&B may be available – please enquire).
See Sibford Gower Gardens for details of garden
B&B

CHAPMANS BARN
Chapmans, Nottingham Fee, Blewbury
OX11 9PG
Jenny Craig
T 01235 851055
E bnb@chapmansbarn.com
W www.chapmansbarn.com
Accommodation A private annexe to a C17 thatched cottage with 1 bedroom (single, double, twin) ensuite bathroom, sitting room, nestled at the foot of the Berkshire downs. Sun – Thurs £60, Fri/Sat £75.
See Blewbury Gardens for details of garden
B&B

THE GLEBE HOUSE
Village Road, Warmington, Banbury
OX17 1BT
Mrs J Thornton
T 01295 690642
Accommodation Welcoming comfortable ensuite accommodation serving traditional breakfasts. Stone residence set in a beautiful village beneath the Edgehills in the heart of the English countryside. Close for visiting Warwick, Cotswolds and Stratford-on-Avon.
See Warwickshire & part of West Midlands, Warmington Village Gardens for details of garden
B&B

GOWERS CLOSE
Main Street, Sibford Gower, nr Banbury
OX15 5RW
Judith Hitching and John Marshall
T 01295 780348
E j.hitching@virgin.net
Accommodation C17 thatched cottage has 1 double and 1 twin, both ensuite, with low beams and log fires, enchanting garden and friendliest dog for pampered guests to enjoy. Close to Hidcote, Kiftsgate and many Cotswold gardens. Price from £35 pppn.
See Sibford Gardens for details of garden
B&B

SOUTH NEWINGTON HOUSE
South Newington, Banbury
OX15 4JW
Roberta & John Ainley
T 01295 721207
E rojoainley@btinternet.com
W www.southnewingtonhouse.co.uk
Accommodation Cottage annexe: 1 king-size bedroom, sitting room, shower room & kitchen. House: 2 king-size bedrooms & 1 twin all with private bathrooms. Prices £75 – £100 per room per night. Single occ. £50 – £60.
B&B SC

Pembrokeshire

DYFFRYN FERNANT
Dyffryn Fernant, Llanychaer, Fishguard
SA65 9SP
Christina Shand
T 01348 811282
E christina.shand@virgin.net
W www.genuslocus.net
Accommodation Cosy one roomed converted barn in the heart of the garden with wood burning stove. Sleeps 4. Secluded, romantic and peaceful. Self catering.
See Carmarthenshire & Pembrokeshire for details of garden
SC

RHOSYGILWEN MANSION
Rhosygilwen Mansion, Rhoshill
Cardigan
SA34 2JG
Dr Glen Peters
T 01239 841387
E enquiries@retreat.co.uk
W www.retreat.co.uk
Accommodation Country mansion with 9 double/twin bedrooms, 7 en-suite, 1 also a family room. Bed and breakfast per room (for 2 people) from £65, single occupancy from £35. Evening meals available by prior arrangement.
See Carmarthenshire & Pembrokeshire for details of garden
B&B

Powys

MILEBROOK HOUSE HOTEL
Knighton
LD7 1LT
Mr & Mrs R T Marsden
T 01547 528632
E hotel@milebrook.kc3ltd.co.uk
W www.milebrookhouse.co.uk
Accommodation There are 10 comfortable bedrooms with ensuite bathrooms, and an attractive, award winning restaurant serving excellent food and wine. Dinner & lunch available everyday except Monday lunch. Roaring log fires in winter.
H

MILL COTTAGE
Abbeycwmhir, Llandrindod Wells
LD1 6PH
Mr & Mrs B D Parfitt
T 01597 851935
E nkmillcottage@yahoo.co.uk
W www.Abbeycwmhir.co.uk
Accommodation C18 cottage in a peaceful village in the beautiful Cambrian mountains. 1 double/twin with private bathroom. 2 singles (one with dressing room and basin). Private bathroom. Evening meals by arrangement. Ideal for walkers and cyclists.
B&B

PLAS DOLGUOG HOTEL
Felingerrig, Machynlleth
SY20 8UJ
Mr Anthony & Mrs Tina Rhodes
T 01654 702244
E res@plasdolguog.demon.co.uk
W www.plasdolguog.co.uk
Accommodation Family run hotel, David Bellamy Conservation Award, 9 acres including Grandma's Garden. Family & ground floor rooms – all individual with ensuite facilities. Cu Og's restaurant offers panoramic views over the Dyfi Valley & Snowdonia National Park.
See Grandma's Garden for details of garden
H

THE WERN
Llanfihangel Talyllyn, Brecon
LD3 7TE
Lucienne and Neil Bennett
T 01874 658401
E lucienne_bennett@hotmail.com
W www.bennettthewern.vispa.com
Accommodation The Wern B&B for Horse and Rider is situated in the Brecon Beacons National Park. Evening meals available. The food provided is from produce from our gardens. Our guests have full use of our gardens and terraces.
B&B

Shropshire

BROWNHILL HOUSE
Ruyton XI Towns, Nr. Shrewsbury
SY4 1LR
Yoland & Roger Brown
T 01939 261121
E brownhill@eleventowns.co.uk
W www.eleventowns.co.uk
Accommodation Old world
standards, modern facilities & relaxed
atmosphere. Unique 2 acre garden –
must be seen to be believed. Easy
access – Chester to Ludlow,
Snowdonia to Ironbridge and loads of
wonderful gardens. Find out all about
us on our website.
B&B

WALFORD HOUSE
Walford, nr Leintwardine,
Craven Arms
SY7 0JT
Val & Jean Richards
T 01547 540487
Accommodation Late C18 former
farmhouse with lovely garden.
Comfortable B&B. Two double rooms
ensuite, one double with private
bathroom. A warm welcome awaits
you.
See Herefordshire, Walford gardens
for details of garden
B&B

Somerset & Bristol Area

CHERRY BOLBERRY FARM
Furge Lane, Henstridge,
Templecombe
BA8 0RN
Mrs Jennifer Raymond
T 01963 362177
Accommodation Farmhouse B&B
on working organic dairy farm with
Jersey cattle, Oxford sheep & sandy
& black pigs. 1 double and 1 twin,
£22 pppn. Very peaceful setting in no
through lane with far reaching
views.TV, tea & coffee facilities. Full
English breakfast – mainly home
produced produce – served in
conservatory overlooking garden.
Use of swimming pool.
See Henstridge Gardens for details of
garden
B&B

**EMMAUS HOUSE RETREAT &
CONFERENCE CENTRE**
Clifton Hill, Clifton, Bristol
BS8 1BN
Sisters of La Retraite
T 0117 907 9950
E administration@emmaushouse.
org.uk
W www.emmaushouse.org.uk
Accommodation C18 listed
building in the heart of Clifton. 21
single rooms (6 converting to twin

occupancy), 7 ensuite. Prices pppn
from £40 standard to £45 ensuite.
Continental breakfast. Award winning
gardens with extensive views. *Nightly
'curfew' 10.30 pm.* Latest check-in
9.00 pm.
B&B

GANTS MILL & GARDEN
Gants Mill Lane, Bruton
BA10 0DB
Alison & Brian Shingler
T 01749 812393
E shingler@gantsmill.co.uk
W www.gantsmill.co.uk
Accommodation C18 farmhouse
in rural valley, by historic watermill
now generating electricity. Large
comfortable pretty bedrooms with
four-posters. Wide choice of familiar
and unusual breakfasts with best
local ingredients. £35 pppn. Also self
catering Miller's Cottage – sleeping 6.
Vacancies on website.
B&B SC

HANGERIDGE FARM
Wrangway, Wellington
TA21 9QT
Mrs J M Chave
T 01823 662339
E hangeridge@hotmail.co.uk
W www.etribes.com/hangeridge
Accommodation Situated at the
foot of the Blackdown Hills within 5
mins drive from M5 (jn 25 or 26). 1
twin and 1 double room with private
bathroom. B& B £20 pp per night,
B&B and evening meal £28 pp per
night.
B&B

HARPTREE COURT
East Harptree, Bristol
BS40 6AA
Mr & Mrs Charles Hill
T 01761 221729
E location.harptree@tiscali.co.uk
W www.harptreecourt.co.uk
Accommodation 2 double rooms
ensuite and 1 twin room, all well
equipped in elegant period house
surrounded by beautiful landscaped
grounds. £100 B&B with afternoon
tea per room per night. £65 single
occ. Evening meal by arrangement.
B&B

HOMEWOOD PARK HOTEL
Hinton Charterhouse, Bath
BA2 7TB
von Essen Hotels
T 01225 723731
E info@homewoodpark.co.uk
W www.homewoodpark.co.uk
Accommodation Gracious country
house hotel near Bath and one of the
loveliest in the West Country. 19
beautiful bedrooms, individually
furnished to a high standard. Bed
and Breakfast prices from £165.00
per room. See website for special
offers.
H

KNOLL COTTAGE
Stogumber, Taunton
TA4 3TN
Elaine & John Leech
T 01984 656689
E mail@knoll-cottage.co.uk
W www.knoll-cottage.co.uk
Accommodation Visit Britain 4*.
Secluded rural location between the
Quantocks and Exmoor. Beautiful 2
acre garden. Two ensuite bedrooms
with king-sized beds in recently
converted stables. Double from £50.
Single from £30. Dogs welcome.
B&B

MOSS COTTAGE
Halse, Taunton
TA4 3AF
Dennis & June Caine
T 01823 430909
E june@denniscaine.co.uk
Accommodation 1 king size
double room & 1 twin room. Travel
cot available. Private bathroom. £20
pppn inclusive of full English
breakfast. Evening meal by
arrangement. Cash or cheques with
card only please.
B&B

SPINDLE COTTAGE
Binegar Green, Binegar, nr Bath
BA3 4UE
Angela Bunting
T 01749 840497
E angela@spindlecottagelets.co.uk
W www.spindlecottagelets.co.uk
Accommodation Fairytale
picturesque C17 cottage. Set in a
peaceful garden with summer-house,
gazebo, conservatory and three
magical playhouses. Within the
cottage, carvings of mushrooms,
spiders' webs, birds and mice. Quite
magical.
See Binegar Village Gardens for
details of garden
SC

WOODLAND COTTAGE
Chapel Road, Oldbury-on-Severn,
Bristol
BS35 1PL
Jane Perkins
T 01454 414570
Accommodation 1 double room
1 twin room with shared bathroom.
Price £20 pppn.
Member of NGS County Team
B&B

Staffordshire

ROMER FARM
Burston
ST18 0DT
John & Marie Lowe
T 01889 508540
E romer@lowe563.freeserve.co.uk
W www.romerfarm.co.uk
Accommodation A traditional
farmhouse set in the beautiful rolling

countryside of the Trent Valley. Near Stone and close to Trentham Gardens and Shugborough. Convenient for Dorothy Clive Garden, Biddulph Grange, Bridgemere and Stapeley Water Gardens.
B&B

Suffolk

THE COACH HOUSE
Assington
CO10 5LQ
Mrs Justine Ferrari
T 01787 211364
E ferrarifrs@aol.com
W www.englishgardenbandb.co.uk
Accommodation A warm welcome awaits you in our Georgian country house. Pretty rooms, delicious local breakfast. Spend time in our 3 acre, beautiful and peaceful garden in the heart of Constable country. Price £70. Single occ. £40.
B&B

GARDEN FLAT, 68 SOUTHWOLD RD
Wrentham, nr Southwold
NR34 7JF
Mrs Reeve
T 01502 675692
E lillylady@hotmail.co.uk
Accommodation Separately accessed self-contained flat within owner's garden. Open plan kitchen/sitting room, bathroom/power shower, spiral staircase to twin bedroom. Private patio with seating. See Wrentham Gardens, 68 Southwold Rd for details of garden.
B&B SC

THRIFT FARMOUSE
Cowlinge, nr Newmarket
CB8 9JA
Mrs Jan Oddy
T 01440 783274
E janoddy@yahoo.co.uk
Accommodation A delightful thatched farmhouse, in tranquil 6 acres of gardens & meadows. Good local walks & bird watching. Relax in the informal atmosphere of this family home. 1 twin, 1 double in the house, 1 double ensuite in the 'piggery'. Prices from £24-30.
B&B

THE WALLOW
Mount Road, Bury St Edmunds
IP31 2QU
Linda & Mike Draper
T 01248 788055
E info@thewallow.co.uk
W www.thewallow.co.uk
Accommodation 2 suites comprising double bedroom, lounge and bathroom in ranch style bungalow. Surrounded by countryside yet close to the town centre. Easy access to

pub/restaurant via footpath/cycle track 51.
B&B

WORLINGTON HOUSE
Worlington, Bury St Edmunds
IP28 8RX
Linz Osborn
T 01638 711993
Accommodation Splendid C16 listed house with 2 acres of mature gardens – formal and wild. Ideal for Newmarket, Bury St Edmunds & Cambridge. Within walking distance Royal Worlington Golf Course.
B&B

Surrey

GREAT FOSTERS
Stroude Road, Egham
TW20 9UR
The Sutcliffe Family
T 01784 433822
E enquiries@greatfosters.co.uk
W www.greatfosters.co.uk
Accommodation More than 4 centuries of celebrated history have enriched Great Fosters with remarkable heritage. Countless original features remain, with bedrooms varying from historic grandeur to more contemporary in style. Double/twin rooms start from £150 per night.
H

SPRING COTTAGE
Mannings Hill, Smithwood Common, Cranleigh
GU6 8QN
Mr & Mrs David Norman
T 01483 272620
E cjn@springcottage67.freeserve.co.uk
Accommodation 1st floor accommodation in newly built barn. 1 double bedroom, bathroom, large sitting room with TV. Lovely views towards N and S downs. Good walking and cycling. Enjoy garden in all seasons. Prices from £60 per night. Single occ. £40.
B&B SC

WOTTON HOUSE
Guildford Road, Dorking
RH5 6HS
Hayley Conference Centres
T 01306 730000
E wotton@hayleycc.co.uk.
W www.hayley-conf.co.uk
Accommodation Wotton House has 111 ensuite facilities. 91 double rooms, 20 twins and 5 adapted for disabled use. Each room has: Wi-Fi, TV, Safe, tea & coffee making facilities, hairdryers, trouser press & iron. Dry cleaning service.
H

Sussex

COPYHOLD HOLLOW
Copyhold Lane, Borde Hill, Haywards Heath
RH16 1XU
Frances B G Druce
T 01444 413265
E yb@copyholdhollow.co.uk
W www.copyholdhollow.co.uk
Accommodation Guests' sitting room with inglenook fireplace, oak beams, cotton sheets, ensuite bedrooms, C16 home surrounded by countryside. Double/twin £35/£45 pppn, single £45/£55 pn. 4 Stars/Gold Award. Short break gardening holidays.
B&B

HAILSHAM GRANGE
Vicarage Road, Hailsham
BN27 1BL
Noel Thompson
T 01323 844248
E noel-hgrange@amserve.com
W www.hailshamgrange.co.uk
Accommodation Accommodation is available in the main house (a former vicarage circa 1700) & adjoining Coach House. Hailsham Grange exemplifies the classic English style which is synonymous with relaxed comfortable living & old fashioned hospitality. Rates range from £75 – £110 per room per night.
B&B

HAM COTTAGE
Highbrook, Ardingly
RH17 6SR
Mr & Mrs P Browne
T 01444 892746
E aegbrowne@btinternet.com
Accommodation C18 cottage set in 8 acres of landscaped gardens within the heart of Sussex, providing 2 double & 1 twin room each with its own bathroom.
B&B

KING JOHN'S LODGE
Sheepstreet Lane, Etchingham
TN19 7AZ
Jill & Richard Cunningham
T 01580 819232
E kingjohnslodge@aol.com
W www.kingjohnslodge.co.uk
Accommodation B&B in this historic listed house surrounded by 8 acres of gardens, meadows and newly opened propogation nursery. All rooms ensuite. Now awarded 5 diamonds by SE tourist board for its high quality.
B&B SC

NETHERBY
Bolney Road, Ansty, Cuckfield, Haywards Heath
RH17 5AW
Mr & Mrs Russell Gilbert

T 01444 455888
E susan@gilbert58.freeserve.co.uk
W www.visitsussex.org
Accommodation A warm welcome awaits you in this cosy Victorian cottage set in ½ acre garden. Firm beds (2 doubles, 1 twin), excellent breakfasts and sinks in all rooms. Rates £30 pppn. Pets by arrangement.
See Ansty Gardens for details of garden
B&B

PINDARS
Lyminster, Arundel
BN17 7QF
Jocelyne & Clive Newman
T 01903 882628
E pindars@btinternet.com
W www.pindars.co.uk
Accommodation Comfortable, friendly country house with special emphasis on hospitality and good food. Delicious and varied breakfasts, imaginatively cooked. Evening meals (usually available) with vegetables from the prolific garden! Prices from £60 per night.
B&B

73 SHEEPDOWN DRIVE
Petworth
GU28 0BX
Mrs Angela Azis
T 01798 342269
Accommodation 2 twin with shared bathroom. Prices from £55 per room. Single occ. £35. A short walk from the centre of the historic town, no. 73 lies in a quiet 70s cul-de-sac and has glorious garden views.
NGS Vice-President
B&B

TURF LODGE
Sheep Plain, Crowborough
TN6 3ST
Julia Ball
T 01892 655505
E iball20@aol.com
Accommodation Off the beaten track on scenic golf course. 1 double room, en-suite. 1 double room and 1 single room with shared bathroom; tennis court and swimming pool. Garden with stunning views 5 minutes walk across fields.
Member of NGS County Team
B&B

Warwickshire & part of West Midlands

SPRINGFIELD HOUSE
School Lane, Warmington
OX17 1DD
Roger & Jenny Handscombe
T 01295 690286
Accommodation XVIth Century house with log fires and flagstone

floors. 2 well appointed rooms with king or super-king beds and private bathroom. Handy for Cotswolds, Compton Verney and Shakespeare. No Smoking. From £20pppn.
See Warmington Village Gardens for details of garden
B&B

Wiltshire

GOULTERS MILL FARM
The Gibb, Burton, Chippenham
SN14 7LL
Alison Harvey
T 01249 782555
E alison@harvey3512.freeserve.co.uk
Accommodation Delightful rooms in old mill house, all ensuite and equipped with king-sized beds. Convenient for Bristol, Bath or Cotswolds. The house is set in cottage gardens in a steep sided valley.
See Littleton Drew Gardens for details of garden
B&B

THE MILL HOUSE
Berwick St James, Salisbury
SP3 4TS
Diana Gifford Mead/Michael Mertens
T 01722 790331
W www.millhouse.org.uk
Accommodation 4 ensuite, 2 single rooms from £40 pp. High quality accommodation. Very quiet, beautiful garden. Highly sourced and organic food. Part of old farm.
B&B

RIDLEYS CHEER
Mountain Bower, Chippenham
SN14 7AJ
Sue & Antony Young
T 01225 891204
E sueyoung@ridleyscheer.co.uk
Accommodation 1 double with private bathroom. 1 double and 1 twin bedded room with shared bathroom. Prices from £80 per night. Single occ from £40. Dinner £30 per head.
B&B

ST JAMES'S GRANGE
West Littleton, Chippenham
SN14 8JE
David & Carolyn Adams
T 01225 891100
E stay@stjamesgrange.com
W www.stjamesgrange.com
Accommodation A barn conversion which looks like an old farmhouse offering 3 light and airy bedrooms with garden views. Cosy guestis sitting room. One double/twin with ensuite bathroom; one twin, one double sharing adjacent bath/shower. £55-£65.
See Somerset & Bristol Area, West Littleton gardens for details of garden
B&B

Worcestershire

LUGGERS HALL
Springfield Lane, Broadway
WR12 7BT
Kay & Red Haslam
T 01386 852040
E luggershall@hotmail.com
W www.luggershall.com
Accommodation 2 king-size double rooms with beautiful views of gardens and 1 double room all with private en-suite bathrooms. Also self-contained apartment plus separare cottage in adjacent Cotswold village of Broadway. Prices from £65 per night.
B&B SC

RECTORY COTTAGE
Old Rectory Lane, Alvechurch
B48 7SU
Steve & Celia Hitch
T 0121 445 4824
E celiaandsteve@reccott.freeserve.co.uk
W www.rectorycottage-alvechurch.co.uk
Accommodation Rectory Cottage is a large family home in a lovely riverside setting offering spacious and elegant bedrooms, all ensuite and overlooking the gardens. Family room, double room, twin bedded room. Easy access from Jn 2 of M42. Prices from £35 pppn.
See Alvechurch Gardens for details of garden
B&B

Yorkshire

COLD COTES
Cold Cotes Road, Felliscliffe, Harrogate
HG3 2LW
Ed Loft
T 01423 770937
E info@coldcotes.com
W www.coldcotes.com
Accommodation Cold Cotes' guests say this is a special place to stay, tranquil setting, beautiful and comfortable rooms,excellent breakfast, an inspiring garden, with service second to none. We have 5 ensuite guest rooms and have newly introduced light bites and suppers by arrangement. Price from: double £65, single occupancy (when available) £55.
B&B

DOWTHORPE HALL
Hull Road, Skirlaugh, Hull
HU11 5AE
Caroline Holtby
T 01964 562235
E john.holtby@farming.co.uk
Accommodation Dowthorpe Hall provides a twin room, ensuite, a double room with own bathroom & a

single room, all offering the ultimate in luxury. Caroline, a cordon bleu cook, is happy to offer evening meals with home grown ingredients.
B&B

LAWKLAND HALL
Austwick, via Lancaster
LA2 8AT
Mr & Mrs Giles Bowring
T 01729 823551
E diss@austwick.org
Accommodation Relaxed, spacious country house. Choose from 4 double bedrooms (2 twins, 2 doubles) each with private bathroom. Large, comfortable drawing room overlooking the garden and countryside. £40 pp bed & breakfast, served in oak panelled dining room.
B&B

MILLGATE HOUSE
Millgate, Richmond
DL10 4JN
Tim Culkin & Austin Lynch
T 01748 823571
E oztim@millgatehouse.demon.co.uk
W www.millgatehouse.com
Accommodation Prepare to be amazed … something very special … exceptional taste, furnishings from all over the world, stunning position, celebrated garden …. breakfasts are superb. National award winning garden.
B&B SC

RIVERSIDE FARM
Sinnington, nr Pickering, York
YO62 6RY
William and Jane Baldwin
T 01751 431764
E wnbaldwin@yahoo.co.uk
Accommodation Situated in stunning, quiet village, Georgian farmhouse offers high class accommodation, private sitting room, wonderful atmosphere. 1 king-sized double, ensuite. 1 twin with private bathroom. 1 single room. Price: £30 pppn. £40 for single occ. Member of NGS County Team
B&B

SLEIGHTHOLMEDALE LODGE
Fadmoor, Kirbymoorside, York
YO62 7JG
Mrs R James
T 01751 431942
E info@shdcottages.co.uk
W www.shdcottages.co.uk
Accommodation Peaceful, warm cottages round a stone courtyard, adjoining a working farm and garden. Max price – high season – £450 per cottage per week.
SC

THORPE LODGE
Knaresborough Road, Ripon
HG4 3LU
Mr & Mrs T Jowitt
T 01765 602088
E jowitt@btinternet.com
W www.thorpelodge.co.uk
Accommodation Listed Georgian house with 2 large double/twin rooms, both ensuite with bath and shower, television and tea/coffee making facilities. Own sitting room and entrance. Dogs kept and welcome. £90 per night including full English breakfast, £60 single occ. Excellent pubs nearby.
B&B

WORTLEY HALL
Wortley, Sheffield
S35 7DB
Johnathan da Rosa
T 0114 2882100
E nfo@wortleyhall.org.uk
W www.wortleyhall.org.uk
Accommodation The hall has 49 ensuite bedrooms. There is also a lift to the first floor. All bedrooms have a direct telephone line and internet connection, colour television, tea making facilities and shower. Some rooms have a bath.
B&B

Garden Index

This index lists all gardens alphabetically and gives the county in which they are to be found

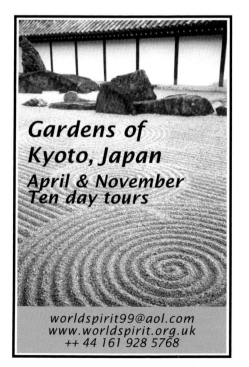

Scotland's Gardens Scheme
Gardens open for charity

Scotland's Gardens Scheme, founded in 1931, raises funds for charity by organising the opening of gardens to the public.

The privately owned gardens that open for us on a certain day or days are our backbone and very few are accessible to the public at other times. Most gardens provide home baked teas and have a plant stall. Children are always welcome.

40% of funds raised goes to charities of the garden owners' choice whilst 60% net is shared between The Queens Nursing Institute Scotland, The Gardens Fund of The National Trust for Scotland, Perennial (The Gardeners' Royal Benevolent Fund) and The Royal Fund for Gardeners' Children.

Our annual handbook, "Gardens of Scotland", containing full details of all our openings, is available in leading bookshops and other appropriate retail and tourist outlets from 1st February.

E-mail: info@sgsgardens.co.uk   Web: gardensofscotland.org

Advertisers Index

Belvoir Fruit Farms 100% good

Cordials by Belvoir Fruit Farms - with the simple good taste of real fruits and flowers... nothing added except a bit of good old-fashioned know-how that comes from making them for 20 years! www.belvoirfruitfarms.co.uk